SOURCEBOOK ON CRIMINAL LAW

Michael Molan, BA, LLM, Barrister
Senior Academic and Head of Law Division
South Bank University

Cavendish
Publishing
Limited

London • Sydney

Second edition first published in Great Britain 2001 by Cavendish Publishing Limited, The Glass House, Wharton Street, London WC1X 9PX, United Kingdom
Telephone: + 44 (0)20 7278 8000   Facsimile: + 44 (0)20 7278 8080

Email: info@cavendishpublishing.com
Website: www.cavendishpublishing.com

© Molan, Mike T   2001
   First edition © Taylor, Alan and Hungerford-Welch, Peter   1997
   Second edition   2001

British Library Cataloguing in Publication Data

Molan, Michael T
Sourcebook on criminal law – 2nd ed – (Sourcebook series)
1 Criminal law – England 2 Criminal law – Wales
I Title II Hungerford Welch, Peter III Taylor, Alan
IV Criminal law
345.4'2

ISBN 1 85941 680 2

Printed and bound in Great Britain

PREFACE

This *Sourcebook* seeks to provide a handy set of reference materials for students studying criminal law on undergraduate or CPE programmes. As such it offers coverage of the mainstream criminal offences through statutory and case law materials.

Since the first edition of this book appeared in 1997 there have been many significant developments in the field of substantive criminal law, primarily through the endeavours of the judiciary. Included in this second edition are comprehensive extracts from key House of Lords decisions such as *B v DPP* (mistake of fact/strict liability); *R v Hinks* (theft); *R v Smith* (provocation); and *R v Powell and Daniels; R v English* (accessorial liability), and the Court of Appeal decision in *R v A (Children) (Conjoined Twins)*. New statutory material includes the Sexual Offences (Amendment) Act 2000; the provisions of the Crime and Disorder Act 1998 relating to racially aggravated offences; and the Criminal Justice (Terrorism and Conspiracy) Act 1998.

An introductory chapter has been added providing 'scene setting' materials on the criminal process and some background information on the likely impact of the Human Rights Act 1998 on the substantive criminal law. Also new for this edition are the substantial extracts from Law Commission Reports and Home Office papers on issues surrounding the reform of the substantive law. These provide a valuable source of information for students seeking to explore an area of substantive law in more depth and help to put the preceding case law and statutory material in context.

I would like to extend my thanks to Alan Taylor and Peter Hungerford-Welch for the foundations they provided in the first edition of this text, and to Cara Annett and Sonny Leong at Cavendish Publishing for their continued support and encouragement.

Producing this second edition would not have been possible without total life support provided by Alison, and the patience of three people who played quietly for so long: thanks Grace, Joy and Miles for being so good.

I have endeavoured to state the law as of 1 August 2001. Any errors and omissions remain my own.

Mike Molan
South Bank University
London
August 2001

CONTENTS

Contents

Contents

TABLE OF CASES

TABLE OF STATUTES

TABLE OF STATUTORY INSTRUMENTS

TABLE OF INTERNATIONAL LEGISLATION

CHAPTER 1

INTRODUCTION TO CRIMINAL LAW: FRAMEWORK AND PROCEDURES

Although the purpose of this text is to provide a range of essential statutory, case law and law reform materials related to the mainstream aspects of substantive criminal law, it is helpful, if not vital, that the reader has some knowledge of how criminal law is created and the procedures to be followed in determining whether a case comes to trial, and how alleged miscarriages of justice might be dealt with. This Chapter aims not only to provide materials that provide such back ground information, but also to consider the likely impact of the Human Rights Act 1998 on the future development of the domestic substantive criminal law.

SOURCES OF CRIMINAL LAW

The criminal law of England and Wales is made up of a patchwork of common law and statutory offences. Offences such as theft, burglary, robbery and deception are based on comparatively recent statutory enactments; see the Theft Act 1968 and Theft Act 1978. Criminal damage offers another example – see the Criminal Damage Act 1971. Other offences, whilst statute based, are somewhat venerable – see for example the Offences Against the Person Act 1861. Problems inevitably arise when trying to apply such legislation to situations that the Victorian draftsman cannot possibly have contemplated; see further Chapter 16. Perhaps surprisingly some very serious offences are not creatures of statute at all, the most notable example being murder. It would be foolish to assume that there is any particular rhyme or reason as to whether or not an offence has the common law or statute as its source. The plain fact is that legislation to create or amend criminal offences has to wait its turn in the queue for parliamentary time. Most governments in recent years have failed to find the time to act upon proposals for fundamental reform put forward by the Law Commission; see below. All too often space is made, on the basis of expediency, for legislation dealing with a narrow matter that happens to be exciting the general public at that particular time. Hence there has been legislation to deal with 'stalking' – see the Protection from Harassment Act 1997 (Chapter 16) – but no thoroughgoing reform of the Offences Against the Person Act 1861. We have had the Theft (Amendment) Act 1996 by way of response to the problem of 'mortgage fraud' but no thorough reappraisal of the operation of the Theft Acts (see Chapter 18).

There is a significant constitutional issue at stake here in terms of who should be creating the criminal law. In a parliamentary democracy there is a very cogent argument that new criminal offences should only be created by Parliament; similarly significant changes in substantive criminal law should only be sanctioned by Parliament. For judges to effect such changes is an apparent breach of the separation of powers. The reality, however, is that there are occasions where the judges feel that, given the failure of Parliament to take the initiative, they have little choice but to act. A good example is provided by the House of Lords' ruling in *R v R* [1991] 3 WLR 767 to the effect that a husband could be guilty of raping his wife. Faced with the choice of either being pilloried for upholding the husband's immunity or usurping the function of Parliament and altering the law, their Lordships opted for the latter. When accused of such judicial activism judges will, of course, insist that, under the theory of the common law, they are 'discovering' the law rather than making it. Where the issue is the correct interpretation of a statute, judges will claim that they are simply giving effect to the intention of Parliament. These answers mask the fact that, parliamentary sovereignty notwithstanding, judges in the higher courts have considerable discretion as to whether or not they will intervene and develop the law in new and bold directions. As Lord Reid observed in *Black-Clawson International Ltd v Papierwerke Waldhoff-Anschaffenburg AG* [1975] AC 591 (at 613):

> We often say that we are looking for the intention of Parliament, but that is not quite accurate. We are seeking the meaning of the words which Parliament used. We are seeking not what Parliament meant but the true meaning of what they said.

In *Shaw v DPP* [1962] AC 220, the defendant was charged, *inter alia*, with conspiracy to corrupt public morals. The House of Lords held, by a majority, that such an offence existed, notwithstanding that there was no clear precedent to that effect. Endorsing the view of the majority that the courts could 'discover' new offences at common law if necessary, Viscount Simonds observed:

> Need I say my Lords, that I am no advocate of the right of judges to create new criminal offences ... But ... in the sphere of criminal law, I entertain no doubt that there remains in the courts of law a residual power to enforce the supreme and fundamental purpose of the law, to conserve not only the safety and order but also the moral welfare of the state, and that it is their duty to guard it against attacks which may be the more insidious because they are novel and unprepared for.

Against this, Lord Reid (dissenting) issued this clear warning

> I think, or at least I hope, that it is now established that the courts cannot create new offences by individuals ... when there is sufficient support from public opinion, Parliament does not hesitate to intervene. Where Parliament fears to tread it is not for the courts to rush in ...

In the course of his speech in *C v DPP* [1996] AC 1, Lord Lowry reviewed the principles upon which judges ought to reflect before engaging in judicial activism. In particular he expressed the view that judges:

- should not be quick to impose their own remedies where the solution was doubtful;

- should be reluctant to act where Parliament had clearly declined to do so, or had legislated in the area without dealing with the difficulty presented by the case in hand;

- should not lightly overturn fundamental legal doctrines;

- should bear in mind that issues of social policy should be left for determination by the legislature;
- should not venture dynamic solutions unless finality was likely to result.

INTERPRETING CRIMINAL STATUTES

B v DPP [2000] 1 All ER 833

For the facts see Chapter 5.

> **Lord Hutton**: ... in a criminal statute intended to protect children the courts should not focus solely on the rights of the accused but should also take into account the right of children to be protected. In ['Interpreting criminal statutes: a crisis of legality?' (1991) 107 LQR 419] ... Professor Ashworth states ... that most English writers on criminal law
>
>> have laid emphasis on liberal ideals such as the principle of legality (in terms of non-retroactivity, maximum certainty and restrictive construction), the presumption of innocence, the principle of autonomy and subjective principles of liability, the doctrine of fair opportunity and so forth.
>
> In the next paragraph Professor Ashworth says:
>
>> It is not sought to deny that the liberal ideals mentioned in the last paragraph have a central place in criminal law doctrine, but they should not be presented as if they stand alone as absolutes. It was suggested above that some judges derive their motivation directly from a conception of the aim of criminal law as penalising those who cause major harms. One of the policies derived from this perspective is the 'thin ice' principle, discussed above; whilst there is a tendency to use a broad phrase such as 'public policy' or 'social defence' to encompass these policies, it is necessary to look more closely at distinct policies and the ends they are claimed to serve. It would not stretch the truth too far to suggest that the typical academic approach has been to emphasise liberal values and the traditional judicial approach to emphasise what they regard as social values in these matters. The first step is to recognise that values of both kinds do and should form part of criminal law doctrine. The next step is to recognise that they will frequently conflict and that, whilst careful discussion of the principles and policies will give some indication as to how conflicts should be resolved, situations will occur in which the courts must make that choice. This makes it crucial that the policies and principles are openly discussed, rather than concealed behind high-sounding phrases about 'legislative intent', 'public policy' or 'the principle of legality'.

CLASSIFICATION OF OFFENCES

Classification by reference to procedure

Criminal offences in England and Wales can be classified by reference to the procedure used at trial. According to this taxonomy there are three types of offence:

- Indictable offences – such as rape, robbery and murder;
- Summary offences – such as insulting behaviour, common assault and indecent exposure;
- Offences triable either way – such as theft, criminal damage (depending on the value of the property damaged), assault occasioning bodily harm contrary to s 47 of the Offences Against the Person Act 1861, and indecent assault.

Indictable offences are triable only in the Crown Court before a judge and jury. Summary offences are triable only in the magistrates' court. Offences triable either way may be tried before either court, depending on the circumstances, in particular the seriousness of the offence and the preferences expressed by the prosecution and defendant; see further s 14 of the Criminal Law Act 1977, as re-enacted by ss 17–25 of the Magistrates' Courts Act 1980.

Classification by reference to police powers

For the purposes of the powers given to police officers and citizens to effect the arrest of suspects, the Police and Criminal Evidence Act 1984 distinguishes between those offences where a power to arrest is provided without an arrest warrant having been issued (arrestable offences – see s 24), and those offences that are 'non-arrestable', that is, where a warrant would normally be required. Section 25 of the Police and Criminal Evidence Act 1984 goes on, however, to specify circumstances where a police officer can exercise a power of arrest in respect of a non-arrestable offence, notwithstanding the absence of a warrant.

Police and Criminal Evidence Act 1984, s 24

(4) Any person may arrest without a warrant

  (a) anyone who is in the act of committing an arrestable offence

  (b) anyone whom he has reasonable grounds for suspecting to be committing such an offence.

(5) Where an arrestable offence has been committed, any person may arrest without a warrant

  (a) anyone who is guilty of the offence

  (b) anyone whom he has reasonable grounds for suspecting to be guilty of it.

(6) Where a constable has reasonable grounds for suspecting that an arrestable offence has been committed, he may arrest without a warrant anyone whom he has reasonable grounds for suspecting to be guilty of the offence.

(7) A constable may arrest without a warrant

  (a) anyone who is about to commit an arrestable offence

  (b) anyone whom he has reasonable grounds for suspecting to be about to commit an arrestable offence.

For these purposes an arrestable offence is one:

- in relation to which the sentence is fixed by law (for example, murder);
- in relation to which a person of 21 years of age or over (not previously convicted) may be sentenced to imprisonment for a term of five years (such as theft and robbery);
- otherwise specifically cited as coming within the scope of the s 24 powers, for example indecent assault, going equipped for stealing, s 60(8)(b) of the Criminal Justice and Public Order Act 1994 – failing to comply with requirement to remove a mask, etc.

Under s 25 a police constable may arrest a suspect on suspicion of having committed a non-arrestable offence if satisfied that any of the general arrest conditions specified in that section are satisfied. These largely relate to circumstances that make the issuing of a summons to attend court impracticable, such as the suspect having no fixed abode, or failing to supply plausible personal details.

THE DECISION TO PROSECUTE

Since the enactment of the Prosecution of Offences Act 1985 the decision to institute criminal proceedings, and the decision as to the offence to be charged has rested with the Crown Prosecution Service (CPS). The criteria borne in mind by the CPS in determining whether or not to prosecute have been published in the form of the Code for Crown Prosecutors.

The Code for Crown Prosecutors

1 Introduction

1.1 The decision to prosecute an individual is a serious step. Fair and effective prosecution is essential to the maintenance of law and order. Even in a small case a prosecution has serious implications for all involved – victims, witnesses and defendants. The Crown Prosecution Service applies the Code for Crown Prosecutors so that it can make fair and consistent decisions about prosecutions.

1.2 The Code helps the Crown Prosecution Service to play its part in making sure that justice is done. It contains information that is important to police officers and others who work in the criminal justice system and to the general public. Police officers should take account of the Code when they are deciding whether to charge a person with an offence.

1.3 The Code is also designed to make sure that everyone knows the principles that the Crown Prosecution Service applies when carrying out its work. By applying the same principles, everyone involved in the system is helping to treat victims fairly and to prosecute fairly but effectively.

2 General Principles

2.1 Each case is unique and must be considered on its own facts and merits. However, there are general principles that apply to the way in which Crown Prosecutors must approach every case.

2.2 Crown Prosecutors must be fair, independent and objective. They must not let any personal views about ethnic or national origin, sex, religious beliefs, political views or the sexual orientation of the suspect, victim or witness influence their decisions. They must not be affected by improper or undue pressure from any source.

2.3 It is the duty of Crown Prosecutors to make sure that the right person is prosecuted for the right offence. In doing so, Crown Prosecutors must always act in the interests of justice and not solely for the purpose of obtaining a conviction.

2.4 It is the duty of Crown Prosecutors to review, advise on and prosecute cases, ensuring that the law is properly applied, that all relevant evidence is put before the court and that obligations of disclosure are complied with, in accordance with the principles set out in this Code.

2.5 The CPS is a public authority for the purposes of the Human Rights Act 1998. Crown Prosecutors must apply the principles of the European Convention on Human Rights in accordance with the Act.

3 Review

3.1 Proceedings are usually started by the police. Sometimes they may consult the Crown Prosecution Service before starting a prosecution. Each case that the Crown Prosecution Service receives from the police is reviewed to make sure it meets the evidential and public interest tests set out in this Code. Crown Prosecutors may decide to continue with the original charges, to change the charges, or sometimes to stop the case.

3.2 Review is a continuing process and Crown Prosecutors must take account of any change in circumstances. Wherever possible, they talk to the police first if they are thinking about changing the charges or stopping the case. This gives the police the chance to provide more information that may affect the decision. The Crown Prosecution Service and the police work closely together to reach the right decision, but the final responsibility for the decision rests with the Crown Prosecution Service.

4 Code Tests

4.1 There are two stages in the decision to prosecute. The first stage is the evidential test. If the case does not pass the evidential test, it must not go ahead, no matter how important or serious it may be. If the case does meet the evidential test, Crown Prosecutors must decide if a prosecution is needed in the public interest.

4.2 This second stage is the public interest test. The Crown Prosecution Service will only start or continue with a prosecution when the case has passed both tests. The evidential test is explained in section 5 and the public interest test is explained in section 6.

5 The Evidential Test

5.1 Crown Prosecutors must be satisfied that there is enough evidence to provide a 'realistic prospect of conviction' against each defendant on each charge. They must consider what the defence case may be, and how that is likely to affect the prosecution case.

5.2 A realistic prospect of conviction is an objective test. It means that a jury or bench of magistrates, properly directed in accordance with the law, is more likely than not to convict the defendant of the charge alleged. This is a separate test from the one that the criminal courts themselves must apply. A jury or magistrates' court should only convict if satisfied so that it is sure of a defendant's guilt.

5.3 When deciding whether there is enough evidence to prosecute, Crown Prosecutors must consider whether the evidence can be used and is reliable. There will be many cases in which the evidence does not give any cause for concern. But there will also be cases in which the evidence may not be as strong as it first appears. Crown Prosecutors must ask themselves the following questions:

Can the evidence be used in court?

(a) Is it likely that the evidence will be excluded by the court? There are certain legal rules which might mean that evidence which seems relevant cannot be given at a trial. For example, is it likely that the evidence will be excluded because of the way in which it was gathered or because of the rule against using hearsay as evidence? If so, is there enough other evidence for a realistic prospect of conviction?

Is the evidence reliable?

(b) Is there evidence which might support or detract from the reliability of a confession? Is the reliability affected by factors such as the defendant's age, intelligence or level of understanding?

(c) What explanation has the defendant given? Is a court likely to find it credible in the light of the evidence as a whole? Does it support an innocent explanation?

(d) If the identity of the defendant is likely to be questioned, is the evidence about this strong enough?

(e) Is the witness's background likely to weaken the prosecution case? For example, does the witness have any motive that may affect his or her attitude to the case, or a relevant previous conviction?

(f) Are there concerns over the accuracy or credibility of a witness? Are these concerns based on evidence or simply information with nothing to support it? Is there further evidence which the police should be asked to seek out which may support or detract from the account of the witness?

5.4 Crown Prosecutors should not ignore evidence because they are not sure that it can be used or is reliable. But they should look closely at it when deciding if there is a realistic prospect of conviction.

6 The Public Interest Test

6.1 In 1951, Lord Shawcross, who was Attorney General, made the classic statement on public interest, which has been supported by Attorneys General ever since: 'It has never been the rule in this country – I hope it never will be – that suspected criminal offences must automatically be the subject of prosecution'. (House of Commons Debates, volume 483, column 681, 29 January 1951.)

6.2 The public interest must be considered in each case where there is enough evidence to provide a realistic prospect of conviction. A prosecution will usually take place unless there are public interest factors tending against prosecution which clearly outweigh those tending in favour. Although there may be public interest factors against prosecution in a particular case, often the prosecution should go ahead and those factors should be put to the court for consideration when sentence is being passed.

6.3 Crown Prosecutors must balance factors for and against prosecution carefully and fairly. Public interest factors that can affect the decision to prosecute usually depend on the seriousness of the offence or the circumstances of the suspect. Some factors may increase the need to prosecute but others may suggest that another course of action would be better.

The following lists of some common public interest factors, both for and against prosecution, are not exhaustive. The factors that apply will depend on the facts in each case.

Some common public interest factors in favour of prosecution

6.4 The more serious the offence, the more likely it is that a prosecution will be needed in the public interest. A prosecution is likely to be needed if:

(a) a conviction is likely to result in a significant sentence;

(b) a weapon was used or violence was threatened during the commission of the offence;

(c) the offence was committed against a person serving the public (for example, a police or prison officer, or a nurse);

(d) the defendant was in a position of authority or trust;

(e) the evidence shows that the defendant was a ringleader or an organiser of the offence;

(f) there is evidence that the offence was premeditated;

(g) there is evidence that the offence was carried out by a group;

(h) the victim of the offence was vulnerable, has been put in considerable fear, or suffered personal attack, damage or disturbance;

(i) the offence was motivated by any form of discrimination against the victim's ethnic or national origin, sex, religious beliefs, political views or sexual orientation, or the suspect demonstrated hostility towards the victim based on any of those characteristics;

(j) there is a marked difference between the actual or mental ages of the defendant and the victim, or if there is any element of corruption;

(k) the defendant's previous convictions or cautions are relevant to the present offence;

(l) the defendant is alleged to have committed the offence whilst under an order of the court;

(m) there are grounds for believing that the offence is likely to be continued or repeated, for example, by a history of recurring conduct; or

(n) the offence, although not serious in itself, is widespread in the area where it was committed.

Some common public interest factors against prosecution

6.5 A prosecution is less likely to be needed if:

(a) the court is likely to impose a nominal penalty;

(b) the defendant has already been made the subject of a sentence and any further conviction would be unlikely to result in the imposition of an additional sentence or order, unless the nature of the particular offence requires a prosecution;

(c) the offence was committed as a result of a genuine mistake or misunderstanding (these factors must be balanced against the seriousness of the offence);

(d) the loss or harm can be described as minor and was the result of a single incident, particularly if it was caused by a misjudgment;

(e) there has been a long delay between the offence taking place and the date of the trial, unless:

- the offence is serious;

- the delay has been caused in part by the defendant;

- the offence has only recently come to light; or

- the complexity of the offence has meant that there has been a long investigation;

(f) a prosecution is likely to have a bad effect on the victim's physical or mental health, always bearing in mind the seriousness of the offence;

(g) the defendant is elderly or is, or was at the time of the offence, suffering from significant mental or physical ill health, unless the offence is serious or there is a real possibility that it may be repeated. The Crown Prosecution Service, where necessary, applies Home Office guidelines about how to deal with mentally disordered offenders. Crown Prosecutors must balance the desirability of diverting a defendant who is suffering from significant mental or physical ill health with the need to safeguard the general public;

(h) the defendant has put right the loss or harm that was caused (but defendants must not avoid prosecution solely because they pay compensation); or

(i) details may be made public that could harm sources of information, international relations or national security;

6.6 Deciding on the public interest is not simply a matter of adding up the number of factors on each side. Crown Prosecutors must decide how important each factor is in the circumstances of each case and go on to make an overall assessment.

The relationship between the victim and the public interest

6.7 The Crown Prosecution Service prosecutes cases on behalf of the public at large and not just in the interests of any particular individual. However, when considering the public interest test Crown Prosecutors should always take into account the consequences for the victim of the decision whether or not to prosecute, and any views expressed by the victim or the victim's family.

6.8 It is important that a victim is told about a decision which makes a significant difference to the case in which he or she is involved. Crown Prosecutors should ensure that they follow any agreed procedures.

Youths

6.9 Crown Prosecutors must consider the interests of a youth when deciding whether it is in the public interest to prosecute. However Crown Prosecutors should not avoid prosecuting simply because of the defendant's age. The seriousness of the offence or the youth's past behaviour is very important.

6.10 Cases involving youths are usually only referred to the Crown Prosecution Service for prosecution if the youth has already received a reprimand and final warning, unless the offence is so serious that neither of these were appropriate. Reprimands and final warnings are intended to prevent re-offending and the fact that a further offence has occurred indicates that attempts to divert the youth from the court system have not been effective. So the public interest will usually require a prosecution in such cases, unless there are clear public interest factors against prosecution.

Police cautions

6.11 These are only for adults. The police make the decision to caution an offender in accordance with Home Office guidelines.

6.12 When deciding whether a case should be prosecuted in the courts, Crown Prosecutors should consider the alternatives to prosecution. This will include a police caution. Again the Home Office guidelines should be applied. Where it is felt that a caution is appropriate, Crown Prosecutors must inform the police so that they can caution the suspect. If the caution is not administered because the suspect refuses to accept it or the police do not wish to offer it, then the Crown Prosecutor may review the case again.

7 Charges

7.1 Crown Prosecutors should select charges which:

(a) reflect the seriousness of the offending;

(b) give the court adequate sentencing powers; and

(c) enable the case to be presented in a clear and simple way.

This means that Crown Prosecutors may not always continue with the most serious charge where there is a choice. Further, Crown Prosecutors should not continue with more charges than are necessary.

7.2 Crown Prosecutors should never go ahead with more charges than are necessary just to encourage a defendant to plead guilty to a few. In the same way, they should never go ahead with a more serious charge just to encourage a defendant to plead guilty to a less serious one.

7.3 Crown Prosecutors should not change the charge simply because of the decision made by the court or the defendant about where the case will be heard.

8 Mode of Trial

8.1 The Crown Prosecution Service applies the current guidelines for magistrates who have to decide whether cases should be tried in the Crown Court when the offence gives the option and the defendant does not indicate a guilty plea.

(See the 'National Mode of Trial Guidelines' issued by the Lord Chief Justice.) Crown Prosecutors should recommend Crown Court trial when they are satisfied that the guidelines require them to do so.

8.2 Speed must never be the only reason for asking for a case to stay in the magistrates' courts. But Crown Prosecutors should consider the effect of any likely delay if they send a case to the Crown Court, and any possible stress on victims and witnesses if the case is delayed.

9 Accepting Guilty Pleas

9.1 Defendants may want to plead guilty to some, but not all, of the charges. Alternatively, they may want to plead guilty to a different, possibly less serious, charge because they are admitting only part of the crime. Crown Prosecutors should only accept the defendant's plea if they think the court is able to pass a sentence that matches the seriousness of the offending, particularly where there are aggravating features. Crown Prosecutors must never accept a guilty plea just because it is convenient.

9.2 Particular care must be taken when considering pleas which would enable the defendant to avoid the imposition of a mandatory minimum sentence. When pleas are offered, Crown Prosecutors must bear in mind the fact that ancillary orders can be made with some offences but not with others.

9.3 In cases where a defendant pleads guilty to the charges but on the basis of facts that are different from the prosecution case, and where this may significantly affect sentence, the court should be invited to hear evidence to determine what happened, and then sentence on that basis.

10 Re-starting a Prosecution

10.1 People should be able to rely on decisions taken by the Crown Prosecution Service. Normally, if the Crown Prosecution Service tells a suspect or defendant that there will not be a prosecution, or that the prosecution has been stopped, that is the end of the matter and the case will not start again. But occasionally there are special reasons why the Crown Prosecution Service will re-start the prosecution, particularly if the case is serious.

10.2 These reasons include:

(a) rare cases where a new look at the original decision shows that it was clearly wrong and should not be allowed to stand;

(b) cases which are stopped so that more evidence which is likely to become available in the fairly near future can be collected and prepared. In these cases, the Crown Prosecutor will tell the defendant that the prosecution may well start again; and

(c) cases which are stopped because of a lack of evidence but where more significant evidence is discovered later.

ESTABLISHING CRIMINAL LIABILITY – THE STANDARD AND BURDEN OF PROOF

The burden of proof in a criminal prosecution normally rests upon the prosecution. Where this is the case the standard of proof is beyond all reasonable doubt. In those exceptional cases where the defendant bears the legal burden of proof, the standard of proof is balance of probabilities.

Woolmington v DPP [1935] AC 462

Lord Sankey LC: Throughout the web of the English criminal law one golden thread is always to be seen ... that it is the duty of the prosecution to prove the prisoner's guilt ... If, at the end of and on the whole of the case, there is a reasonable doubt, created by the evidence given by either the prosecution or the prisoner, as to whether the [elements of the offence have been made out] the prosecution has not made out the case and the prisoner is entitled to an acquittal. No matter what the charge or where the trial, the principle that the prosecution must prove the guilt of the prisoner is part of the common law of England and no attempt to whittle it down can be entertained.

Reversing the burden of proof

R v Lambert; R v Ali; R v Jordan [2001] 1 All ER 1014

The Court of Appeal heard three conjoined appeals, each of which raised a challenge under the Human Rights Act 1998 to statutory provisions in placing the defendant in a criminal trial under a legal burden of proof. In Lambert's case the provision being challenged was the Misuse of Drugs Act 1971, specifically s 5(4) and s 28 which require a defendant charged with possession of a controlled drug, to prove, on the balance of probabilities certain exculpatory facts. The appeals brought by Ali and Jordan, challenged s 2(2) of the Homicide Act 1957, which requires that a defendant raising the defence of diminished responsibility should prove the defence on the balance of probabilities. The appeals were dismissed.

Regarding the effect of the Human Rights Act 1998 on statutory provisions reversing the burden of proof **Lord Woolf CJ** observed:

The 1998 Act can have a significant effect on statutory provisions which purport to depart from the general rule that the onus should be on the prosecution. This is because of art 6 which the 1998 Act makes part of domestic law. Article 6(1) provides: 'In the determination of any criminal charge against him, everyone is entitled to a fair and public hearing ...' and art 6(2) provides: 'Everyone charged with a criminal offence shall be presumed innocent until proved guilty according to law.'

Whether a statutory provision became law before or after the 1998 Act it must be 'read and given effect in a way which is compatible with Convention rights' (including art 6) and if this is not possible the court can make a declaration of incompatibility (ss 3 and 4).

The obligation under s 3 is relied on by the appellants. They contend that art 6 and s 3 now require the courts to depart from the interpretation adopted hitherto of s 2 of the 1957 Act and ss 5 and 28 of the 1971 Act. The sections instead of being interpreted as placing a persuasive burden on the appellants (to establish their case on the balance of probabilities) should be interpreted as placing an evidential burden only on the defendant so that the general burden remains on the prosecution. If that contention is correct, the appellants' appeals will have to be allowed.

There is, however, a prior question to be answered before it is necessary to consider s 3. That is whether s 2 of the 1957 Act and ss 5 and 28 of the 1971 Act as applied hitherto under English law are in conflict with art 6? In answering this question it is necessary to take into account the jurisprudence of the European Court of Human Rights as required by s 2 of the 1998 Act. In doing so it is necessary to have in mind the nature of the convention as an instrument for the protection of fundamental rights. This justifies the adoption of the approach vividly described by Lord Wilberforce in relation to the provisions of a written constitution in *Minister of Home Affairs v Fisher* [1980] AC 319 at 329. It involves giving a broad and purposive approach, not a rigid approach, to the language of the convention, an approach which will make the convention a valuable protection of the fundamental rights of individual members of the public as well as society as a whole.

Mr Owen QC, on behalf of Mr Lambert, submits that there cannot be different standards of fairness. This we are prepared to accept as long as it is also appreciated that what fairness requires can differ depending on the circumstances of the case. Thus, taking an obvious situation, where the defendants are children. Here what would be fair in the case of adults may not be fair in the case of children. Again, take the requirement of a public hearing. As in the case of the common law, art 6 does not require a public hearing if a public hearing would defeat the interests of justice. The convention is not intended to be an instrument of injustice. Mr Owen also submits correctly that the convention is to be distinguished from the Canadian Charter and the South African Constitution in that it does not contain any general savings or limitations clause. However, in practice the distinctions will probably not be significant because, as the European Court of Human Rights jurisprudence makes clear, the court does not have to ignore the wider interests of the public in applying those provisions of the convention which have no express limitation (see *Murray v UK* (1994) 19 EHRR 193). The position is well illustrated by the judgment of the European Court of Human Rights in the case of *Salabiaku v France* (1988) 13 EHRR 379 at 388 (para 28), when the court said:

> Presumptions of fact or of law operate in every legal system. Clearly, the Convention does not prohibit such presumptions in principle. It does, however, require the Contracting States to remain within certain limits in this respect as regards criminal law. If, as the Commission would appear to consider [para 64 of the report], paragraph 2 of Article 6 merely laid down a guarantee to be respected by the courts in the conduct of legal proceedings, its requirements would in practice overlap with the duty of impartiality imposed in paragraph 1. Above all, the national legislature would be free to strip the trial court of any genuine power of assessment and deprive the presumption of innocence of its substance, if the words 'according to law' were construed exclusively with reference of domestic law. Such a situation could not be reconciled with the object and purpose of Article 6, which, by protecting the right to a fair trial and in particular the right to be presumed innocent, is intended to enshrine the fundamental principle of the rule of law [see, *inter alia*, *Sunday Times v UK* (1979) 2 EHRR 245 (para 55)]. Article 6(2) does not therefore

regard presumptions of fact or of law provided for in the criminal law with indifference. It requires States to confine them within reasonable limits which take into account the importance of what is at stake and maintain the rights of the defence.

Salabiaku's case was considered by Lord Hope of Craighead in *R v DPP, ex p Kebilene* [1999] 3 WLR 972 at 997 where he pointed out that account may be legitimately taken, in striking the right balance, of the problem the legislation was designed to address. He added that:

> As a matter of general principle therefore a fair balance must be struck between the demands of the general interest of the community and the protection of the fundamental rights of the individual ...

We agree. In doing this it is important to start with the structure of the offences. If the defendant is being required to prove an essential element of the offence this will be more difficult to justify. If, however, what the defendant is required to do is establish a special defence or exception this will be less objectionable. The extent of the inroad on the general principle is also important. Here it is important to have in mind that art 6(2) is specifically directed to the application of the presumption of innocence of the 'criminal offences' charged. It is also important to have in mind that legislation is passed by a democratically elected Parliament and therefore the courts under the convention are entitled to and should, as a matter of constitutional principle, pay a degree of deference to the view of Parliament as to what is in the interest of the public generally when upholding the rights of the individual under the convention. The courts are required to balance the competing interests involved.

... The change in the law brought about by s 2 was of benefit to defendants who were in a position to take advantage of it. It does not matter whether it is treated as creating a defence to a charge of murder or an exception or as dealing with the capacity to commit the offence of murder. Section 2 still does not contravene art 6. We find ample support for our view in the judgments of the Supreme Court of Canada in *R v Chaulk* [1989] 1 SCR 369 and in the decisions of the European Commission of Human Rights which decide that arguments of this nature are manifestly ill-founded ...

... When applying the convention attention is to be paid to the substance as well as the form of the statutory language creating the offence (*AG of Hong Kong v Lee Kwong-Kut* [1993] AC 951 at 972–73). Prior to the 1971 Act the increasing international concern over the supply of drugs had been reflected in treaties to which this country was a party. When the statutory history of the sections is taken into account (as to which see the speeches in *Warner v Metropolitan Police Comr* [1969] 2 AC 256) it is clear that Parliament had deliberately chosen to produce the result set out already. We regard the substance of the offence as being reflected in the language of the sections. Sections 5(4) and 28 do not impose additional ingredients which have to be proved to complete the offence but a way of avoiding liability for what would otherwise be an offence.

We can well understand why Parliament wanted to restrict the extent of the knowledge required for the commission of the offence and then established a special defence, on which a defendant could rely if he could establish that he had no suspicion as to the nature of the contents of the box. It is commonplace for a defendant to seek to avoid his guilt by saying that he thought he had pornography or gold and not drugs in the box. Such a defence is difficult to rebut. What the offence does is to make the defendant responsible for ensuring that he does not take into his possession containers which in fact contain drugs.

The offence applies to the possession of all controlled drugs. It applies to cannabis as well as cocaine and heroin. The sentence, however, will vary on conviction, depending on the seriousness of the offence. But there is a clear social objective in discouraging trading both in hard drugs and the softer drugs. In addition the level of sentence will reflect the extent to which the defendant was responsible for the drugs being in his possession. He may not be able to prove the statutory defence because he had reason to suspect the contents were controlled drugs, but if he was duped into being in possession this is something which the court can take into account in determining the sentence.

As is stated baldly in Lester and Oliver *Constitutional Law and Human Rights* (1997) p 153, para 142: 'The burden of proof must fall upon the prosecutor, but it may be transferred to the accused when he is seeking to establish a defence.' The criticism, which is made here, is based not so much on the fact that the burden of proof has been transferred, but on the standard of proof which is required. That standard of proof is the normal standard of proof, namely on the balance of probabilities, in this situation under English law in the case of statutory defences. It has been imposed by the legislature deliberately for policy reasons it considered justified. Since 1971 that justification has increased. The method selected had been roundly criticised by Professor Glanville Williams (see for example *Proof of Guilt* (3rd edn, 1963)) but we do not consider that the chosen course of the legislator contravenes art 6. There is an objective justification in the case of drugs for the choice and it is not disproportionate. It is important in considering the validity of the offences that the defendant will only be punished for the offence he has been proved to have committed if he fails in his attempt to rely on the statutory defences. We do not consider the offences contravene art 6.

See further *R v K* (2000) *The Times*, 7 November, extracted in Chapter 17.

Codification and law reform proposals

Clause 13 of the Draft Criminal Code Bill (Law Com 177 Vol I – see below) sought to codify the law relating to burden and standard of proof in criminal trials thus:

13   (1) Unless otherwise provided –

      (a) the burden of proving every element of an offence and any other fact alleged or relied on by the prosecution is on the prosecution;

      (b) where evidence is given (whether by the defendant or by the prosecution) of a defence or any other fact alleged or relied on by the defendant the burden is on the prosecution to prove that an element of the defence or such other fact did not exist.

  (2) Evidence is given of a defence or any other fact alleged or relied on by the defendant when there is such evidence as might lead a court or jury to conclude that there is a reasonable possibility that the elements of the defence or such other fact existed.

(3) The burden is on the defendant to prove any fact necessary to establish –

    (a) any plea made by him in bar to an indictment or any corresponding plea on summary trial;

    (b) the competence of any witness called by him; or

    (c) the admissibility of any evidence tendered by him.

(4) Unless otherwise provided –

    (a) where the burden of proof is on the prosecution the standard of proof required is proof beyond reasonable doubt;

    (b) where the burden of proof is on the defendant the standard of proof required is proof on the balance of probabilities, except where subsection (5) applies.

(5) Where an element of a defence is the fact that another person is guilty and liable to conviction of the offence in the same proceedings, the standard required for proof of that element is proof beyond reasonable doubt.

    ...

The commentary on these clauses observed (Law Com 177 Vol II)

6.1 Burden of proof: the general rule. Subsection (1) states the general rule in *Woolmington v DPP* ... When the evidential burden is satisfied, the burden is on the prosecution to disprove the fact in question. The nature of the evidential burden is described in subsection (2). Unless such evidence is already before the court, the defendant must adduce evidence which might lead a court or jury to conclude that there is a reasonable possibility that the fact alleged existed.

6.2 Exceptions to the general rule. The general rule applies 'unless otherwise provided', whether expressly or by necessary implication, and subject to subsections (3) and (6). Subsection (3) provides for three cases where, under the present law, the burden of proof is, or probably is and, in our opinion, ought to be, on the defendant: to establish any fact necessary to prove (a) a plea in bar, (b) the competence of a witness called by him (c) the admissibility of evidence tendered by him. The House of Lords in *Hunt* ... has confirmed that section 101 of the Magistrates' Courts Act 1980 imposes the burden of proving certain defences on the defendant at a summary trial and that there is a corresponding common law rule of interpretation which achieves the same effect at a trial on indictment. Subsection (6) preserves these rules.

6.3 Standard of proof: Subsection (4) states the general rule for standard of proof – for the prosecution, proof beyond reasonable doubt and, for the defendant, proof on the balance of probabilities. The general rule applies 'unless otherwise provided', whether expressly or by necessary implication, and subject to subsection (5). This is concerned with the rare case of a special defence of the kind found in the Food Act 1984, section 100. An element of the defence is that a third person is guilty and liable to conviction in the same proceedings. The third person ought not to be convicted of the offence unless his guilt is proved beyond reasonable doubt and it is therefore necessary that that should be the standard of proof for this element of the defence.

CRIMINAL APPEALS

A defendant convicted before a magistrates court may appeal to the Crown Court – a procedure that involves a complete re-hearing of the case. Whatever the outcome of the case, it does not have any value in terms of precedent, thus does not contribute to the development of the substantive criminal law. Alternatively a defendant convicted in the magistrates' court can appeal to the Divisional Court on a point of law – known as proceeding by way of case stated. This would be appropriate where the facts are not in dispute. This avenue of appeal is also available to the prosecution if a magistrates' court dismisses the case against a defendant. Rulings of the Divisional Court do create precedents binding on trial courts. Where a defendant has exercised his right to appeal from the magistrates' court to the Crown Court, he still has the option of proceeding by way of case stated in relation to a point of law, before the Divisional Court. Appeal from the Divisional Court in case stated proceedings lies directly to the House of Lords.

Defendant appealing against conviction (following trial on indictment) from the Crown Court to the Court of Appeal

Most of the important appeal cases that give rise to developments in substantive criminal law arise where a defendant who has been convicted in the Crown Court, following trial on indictment, appeals against that conviction (as opposed to appealing against the sentence) to the Court of Appeal (Criminal Division). The statutes that govern this process are the Criminal Appeal Act 1968, and the Criminal Appeal Act 1995.

Under the 1968 Act an accused can appeal as of right against conviction if the trial judge grants a certificate to the effect that the case is fit for appeal. In all other cases the accused will have to obtain leave to appeal from the Court of Appeal. Applications for leave are normally determined by a single judge of the Court of Appeal on the basis of written submissions. Appeal against a refusal of leave will be considered by a full court sitting of the Court of Appeal. Essentially leave should be granted if the appeal indicates that the accused has an arguable case.

Section 2(1) of the 1968 Act, as amended by the 1995 Act, provides that the Court of Appeal 'shall allow an appeal against conviction if they think that the conviction is unsafe ... and shall dismiss such an appeal in any other case'. The use of the criterion 'unsafe' replaces the more detailed approach under the 1968 Act as originally enacted, although it is doubtful that Parliament intended to change the scope of the grounds for allowing an appeal. To this end it is instructive to note that, prior to the 1995 Act, an appeal could be allowed because of a wrong ruling on the law, material irregularity, or because (taking into account all the circumstances) the conviction was unsafe or unsatisfactory

The extent to which a conviction can be regarded as 'safe', notwithstanding unfairness in the trial process, has had to be re-considered following the enactment of the Human Rights Act 1998, and the decision of the European Court of Human Rights in *R v Condron* [2000] Crim LR 679. The result is that the Court of Appeal should not disengage the issue of the fairness of the trial from the issue of whether or not the conviction is safe. In essence *significant* violations of the right to a fair trial provided by Art 6 of the European Convention on Human Rights are, of themselves, likely to render a conviction unsafe; see further *R v Francom* (2000) *The Times*, 24 October.

In *R v Togher and Others* (2000) *The Times*, 21 November, Lord Woolf CJ went so far as observe that the approach of the Court of Appeal should be in step with that of the European Court of Human Rights with the result that the denial of a fair trial contrary to Art 6 would now inevitably lead to a finding that the resulting conviction was unsafe. Such a conclusion is a direct result of the obligation created by s 3(1) of the Human Rights Act 1998 to the effect that domestic legislation, such as the Criminal Appeal Act 1995, should be read, so far as possible, in a manner that gave effect to Convention rights. *R v Davis* (2000) *The Times*, 25 July, whilst not departing from this broad proposition, emphasises that it may still be necessary to look at the circumstances of a particular case before concluding that a violation of Art 6 has rendered a conviction unsafe – it will be a matter of fact and degree.

Even if an appeal against conviction succeeds the accused may still face a retrial. The Court of Appeal has the discretion to order a retrial under s 7 of the 1968 Act if it appears to the court that the interests of justice so require. If there has been a total mistrial the Court of Appeal can issue a writ of *venire de novo* – setting events back to where they were before the irregularity that rendered the trial a mistrial occurred.

Some appeals against conviction will be partially successful in that the Court of Appeal can allow the appeal but substitute a conviction for a lesser-included offence – an obvious example being the quashing of a murder conviction and the substitution of a conviction for manslaughter.

Appeal by the prosecution: against over lenient sentences

By virtue of ss 35 and 36 of the Criminal Justice Act 1988 the prosecution may, following the conviction of the defendant in the Crown Court, appeal to the Court of Appeal (Criminal Division) in respect of the sentence passed, if it is of the view that the sentence is unduly lenient.

Section 36 of the Criminal Justice Act 1988 provides:

(1) If it appears to the Attorney-General

    (a) that the sentencing of a person in a proceeding in the Crown Court has been unduly lenient and

    (b) that the case is one to which this part of this Act applies, he may, with the leave of the Court of Appeal, refer the case to them for them to review the sentencing of that person and on such a reference the Court of Appeal may

(i) quash any sentence passed on him in the proceeding and

(ii) in place of it pass such sentence as they think appropriate for the case and as the court below had power to pass when dealing with him.

...

(6) A reference under subsection (5) above shall be made only with the leave of the Court of Appeal or the House of Lords and leave shall not be granted unless it is certified by the Court of Appeal that the point of law is of general public importance and it appears to the Court of Appeal or the House of Lords (as the case may be) that the point is one which ought to be considered by that House.

Appeal by the prosecution: on a point of law

Where a defendant is acquitted following trial on indictment, the *autre fois acquit* rule (the rule against double jeopardy) prevents the defendant being tried again for the same offence. If the acquittal appears to have arisen because of a misapplication of the law by the trial judge, or because of an apparent loophole in the law, the Crown can test the matter further by proceeding under s 36(1) of the Criminal Justice Act 1972. This provision allows the Attorney General to refer the relevant point of law to the Court of Appeal for a ruling. Although the outcome of the proceedings cannot affect the liability of the acquitted defendant, it does have the same status, in terms of precedent, as any other Court of Appeal decision. The nature and purpose of such a reference was considered by the House of Lords in the following case:

AG's Ref (No 3 of 1994) [1997] 3 All ER 936

For the facts see Chapter 4.

Lord Mustill: The courts have always firmly resisted attempts to obtain the answer to academic questions, however useful this might appear to be. Normally, where an appeal is brought in the context of an issue between parties, the identification of questions which the court should answer can be performed by considering whether a particular answer to the question of law might affect the outcome of the dispute. The peculiarity of a reference under the Act of 1972 is that it is not a step in a dispute, so that in one sense the questions referred are invariably academic. This peculiarity might, unless limits are observed, enable the Attorney General, for the best of motives, to use an acquittal on a point of law to set in train a judicial roving commission on a particular branch of the law, with the aim of providing clear, practical and systematic solutions for problems of current interest. This is not the function of the court ...

Criminal Cases Review Commission

Prior to the enactment of the Criminal Appeal Act 1995 the Home Secretary ʰ the power to refer cases to the Court of Appeal if there was evidence to sʋ that a miscarriage of justice had occurred. The significance of this discretion lay in the fact that it could be exercised notwithstanding that the time limits for lodging an appeal to had expired long ago. Following criticisms of the involvement of politicians in this aspect of the criminal justice process the 1995 Act withdrew the Home Secretary's powers of referral and instead vested them in an independent body, the Criminal Cases Review Commission.

Under s 5 of the 1995 Act (amending s 23 of the Criminal Appeal Act 1968) the Court of Appeal can ask the Criminal Cases Review Commission to investigate a particular case on its behalf:

Criminal Appeal Act 1995

5(1) After section 23 of the 1968 Act insert –

Power to order investigations. 23A(1) On an appeal against conviction the Court of Appeal may direct the Criminal Cases Review Commission to investigate and report to the Court on any matter if it appears to the Court that –

(a) the matter is relevant to the determination of the case and ought, if possible, to be resolved before the case is determined;

(b) an investigation of the matter by the Commission is likely to result in the Court being able to resolve it; and

(c) the matter cannot be resolved by the Court without an investigation by the Commission.

(4) Where the Commission have reported to the Court of Appeal on any matter which they have been directed under subsection (1) above to investigate, the Court –

(a) shall notify the appellant and the respondent that the Commission have reported; and

(b) may make available to the appellant and the respondent the report of the Commission and any statements, opinions and reports which accompanied it.

The powers of the Commission to refer possible miscarriages of justice to the Court of Appeal of its own volition (as regards criminal proceedings in England and Wales) are provided by ss 9 (referral following trial on indictment), 11 (referral following summary trial), 13 (basis for making a referral) and 14 (further issues relating to referral) of the 1995 Act.

Criminal Appeal Act 1995

9(1) Where a person has been convicted of an offence on indictment in England and Wales, the Commission –

(a) may at any time refer the conviction to the Court of Appeal, and (b) (whether or not they refer the conviction) may at any time refer to the Court of Appeal any sentence (not being a sentence fixed by law) imposed on, or in subsequent proceedings relating to, the conviction.

(2) A reference under subsection (1) of a person's conviction shall be treated for all purposes as an appeal by the person under section 1 of the 1968 Act against the conviction.

(3) A reference under subsection (1) of a sentence imposed on, or in subsequent proceedings relating to, a person's conviction on an indictment shall be treated for all purposes as an appeal by the person under section 9 of the 1968 Act against –

(a) the sentence, and

(b) any other sentence (not being a sentence fixed by law) imposed on, or in subsequent proceedings relating to, the conviction or any other conviction on the indictment.

(4) On a reference under subsection (1) of a person's conviction on an indictment the Commission may give notice to the Court of Appeal that any other conviction on the indictment which is specified in the notice is to be treated as referred to the Court of Appeal under subsection (1).

(5) Where a verdict of not guilty by reason of insanity has been returned in England and Wales in the case of a person, the Commission may at any time refer the verdict to the Court of Appeal; and a reference under this subsection shall be treated for all purposes as an appeal by the person under section 12 of the 1968 Act against the verdict.

(6) Where a jury in England and Wales has returned findings that a person is under a disability and that he did the act or made the omission charged against him, the Commission may at any time refer either or both of those findings to the Court of Appeal; and a reference under this subsection shall be treated for all purposes as an appeal by the person under section 15 of the 1968 Act against the finding or findings referred.

...

11(1) Where a person has been convicted of an offence by a magistrates' court in England and Wales, the Commission –

(a) may at any time refer the conviction to the Crown Court, and

(b) (whether or not they refer the conviction) may at any time refer to the Crown Court any sentence imposed on, or in subsequent proceedings relating to, the conviction.

(2) A reference under subsection (1) of a person's conviction shall be treated for all purposes as an appeal by the person under section 108(1) of the [1980 c 43.] Magistrates' Courts Act 1980 against the conviction (whether or not he pleaded guilty).

(3) A reference under subsection (1) of a sentence imposed on, or in subsequent proceedings relating to, a person's conviction shall be treated for all purposes as an appeal by the person under section 108(1) of the Magistrates' Courts Act 1980 against –

(a) the sentence, and

(b) any other sentence imposed on, or in subsequent proceedings relating to, the conviction or any related conviction.

(4) On a reference under subsection (1) of a person's conviction the Commission may give notice to the Crown Court that any related conviction which is specified in the notice is to be treated as referred to the Crown Court under subsection (1).

(5) For the purposes of this section convictions are related if they are convictions of the same person by the same court on the same day.

(6) On a reference under this section the Crown Court may not award any punishment more severe than that awarded by the court whose decision is referred.

(7) The Crown Court may grant bail to a person whose conviction or sentence has been referred under this section; and any time during which he is released on bail shall not count as part of any term of imprisonment or detention under his sentence.

...

13(1) A reference of a conviction, verdict, finding or sentence shall not be made under [ss 9 or 11] unless –

(a) the Commission consider that there is a real possibility that the conviction, verdict, finding or sentence would not be upheld were the reference to be made,

(b) the Commission so consider –

(i) in the case of a conviction, verdict or finding, because of an argument, or evidence, not raised in the proceedings which led to it or on any appeal or application for leave to appeal against it, or

(ii) in the case of a sentence, because of an argument on a point of law, or information, not so raised, and

(c) an appeal against the conviction, verdict, finding or sentence has been determined or leave to appeal against it has been refused.

(2) Nothing in subsection (1)(b)(i) or (c) shall prevent the making of a reference if it appears to the Commission that there are exceptional circumstances which justify making it.

14(1) A reference of a conviction, verdict, finding or sentence may be made under [ss 9 or 11] either after an application has been made by or on behalf of the person to whom it relates or without an application having been so made.

(2) In considering whether to make a reference of a conviction, verdict, finding or sentence under [ss 9 or 11] the Commission shall have regard to –

(a) any application or representations made to the Commission by or on behalf of the person to whom it relates,

(b) any other representations made to the Commission in relation to it, and

(c) any other matters which appear to the Commission to be relevant.

(3) In considering whether to make a reference under [ss 9] the Commission may at any time refer any point on which they desire the assistance of the Court of Appeal to that Court for the Court's opinion on it; and on a reference under this subsection the Court of Appeal shall consider the point referred and furnish the Commission with the Court's opinion on the point.

(4) Where the Commission make a reference under [ss 9 or 11] the Commission shall –

(a) give to the court to which the reference is made a statement of the Commission's reasons for making the reference, and

(b) send a copy of the statement to every person who appears to the Commission to be likely to be a party to any proceedings on the appeal arising from the reference.

(5) Where a reference under [ss 9 or 11] is treated as an appeal against any conviction, verdict, finding or sentence, the appeal may be on any ground relating to the conviction, verdict, finding or sentence (whether or not the ground is related to any reason given by the Commission for making the reference).

(6) In every case in which –

(a) an application has been made to the Commission by or on behalf of any person for the reference under [ss 9 or 11] of any conviction, verdict, finding or sentence, but

(b) the Commission decide not to make a reference of the conviction, verdict, finding or sentence,

the Commission shall give a statement of the reasons for their decision to the person who made the application.

It may be the case that the Commission refers a case to the Court of Appeal many years after the initial conviction. In the intervening years there may be changes in both statute and common law that have a bearing on the law as applied at the original trial. The way in which such factors should be dealt with by the Court of Appeal was considered in *R v Bentley* [1999] Crim LR 330. The effect of changes in statute law in the period of time between the conviction and the review will be ignored. Where there have been changes in the common law, any directions given by the trial judge at the original trial will be considered in the light of the law as it now stands.

Appeal from the Court of Appeal to the House of Lords

The option of appealing against a ruling of the Court of Appeal (Criminal Division) is open to both the prosecution and the defence. The procedure is governed by ss 33 and 34 of the Criminal Appeal Act 1968, which provide as follows:

33(1) An appeal lies to the House of Lords, at the instance of the defendant or the prosecutor, from any decision of the Court of Appeal on an appeal to that court under part I of this act or section 9 (preparatory hearings) of the Criminal Justice Act 1987.

(2) The appeal lies only with the leave of the Court of Appeal or the House of Lords and leave shall not be granted unless it is certified by the Court of Appeal that a point of law of general public importance is involved in the decision and it appears to the Court of Appeal or the House of Lords (as the case may be) that the point is one which ought to be considered by that House.

...

34(1) An application to the Court of Appeal for leave to appeal to the House of Lords shall be made within the period of 14 days beginning with the date of the decision of the court and an application to the House of Lords for leave shall be made within the period of 14 days beginning with the date on which the application for leave is refused by the Court of Appeal.

CODIFICATION OF THE CRIMINAL LAW

As noted above, English criminal law is drawn from a variety of common law and statutory sources. Many of the difficulties, uncertainties and absurdities encountered in an examination of English criminal law stem from the fact there has never been a systematic reappraisal of the criminal law by Parliament. Unlike other jurisdictions, there is no penal code for England and Wales. Building upon earlier work undertaken by the Criminal Law Revision Committee the Law Commission has, since 1981, been engaged in a large scale project to codify, and in certain aspects, reform the substantive criminal law of England and Wales. Volumes I and II of the Law Commission's Report (No 177) *A Criminal Code for England and Wales* attempted to lay the foundations for such a code. Subsequent Law Commission Reports have attempted to take the project further by tackling specific aspects of the substantive law such as manslaughter, non-fatal assaults and intoxication.

The work that has been done to date can be summarised thus:

Law Commission Consultation Paper	Law Commission Report	Home Office Publication
Legislating the Criminal Code: Offences Against the Person and General Principles (LCCP 122)	Legislating the Criminal Code: Offences Against the Person and General Principles (Law Com 218)	Violence: Reforming the Offences Against the Person Act 1861; Offences Against the Person Bill
Legislating the Criminal Code: Intoxication and Criminal Liability (LCCP 127)	Legislating the Criminal Code: Intoxication and Criminal Liability (Law Com 229)	Clause 19 of the Offences Against the Person Bill
Assisting and Encouraging Crime (LCCP 131)		
Law Commission Working Paper No 50, Inchoate Offences	Criminal Law: Conspiracy to Defraud (Law Com 228)	
Legislating the Criminal Code: Involuntary Manslaughter (LCCP 135)	Legislating the Criminal Code: Involuntary Manslaughter (Law Com 237)	Reforming the Law on Involuntary Manslaughter: The Government's Proposals
Criminal Law: Consent (LCCP 134)		
Criminal Law: Consent (LCCP 139)	Consent in Sex Offences: A Report to the Home Office Sex Offences Review (LC Special-1)	Setting the Boundaries: Reforming the Law on Sex Offences
Criminal Law: Misuse of Trade Secrets (LCCP 150)		
Legislating the Criminal Code: Fraud and Deception (LCCP 155)		

Extracts from these various reports have been included, as appropriate, in the Chapters that follow. The case for codification generally was made in Volume I of Law Com 177 as follows:

Law Com 177 Vol I

1.3 English criminal law is derived from a mixture of common law and statute. Most of the general principles of liability are still to be found in the common law, though some for example, the law relating to conspiracy and attempts to commit crime have recently been defined in Acts of Parliament. The great majority of crimes are now defined by statute but there are important exceptions. Murder, manslaughter and assault are still offences at common law, though affected in various ways by statute. There is no system in the relative roles of common law and legislation. Thus, incitement to commit crime – though closely related to conspiracy and attempts – is still a common law offence. Whether an offence is defined by statute has almost always been a matter of historical accident rather than systematic organisation. For example, rape is defined in the Sexual Offences (Amendment) Act 1976 because of the outcry which followed the decision in *Morgan* ... and led to the subsequent Heilbron Report. The legislation in force extends over a very long period of time. It is true that only a very small amount of significant legislation is earlier than the mid-nineteenth century, but that is quite long enough for the language of the criminal law and the style of drafting to have undergone substantial changes.

1.4 There has been a steady flow of reform of the criminal law in recent years but it has been accomplished in somewhat piecemeal fashion. Some of it is derived from our own reports, where in recent years we have been pursuing a policy of putting common law offences into statutory form, and some from reports of the Criminal Law Revision Committee and committees, like the Heilbron Committee, appointed to deal with particular problems. Other reforms have resulted from the initiative of Ministers or private Members of Parliament in introducing Bills. As there is no authoritative statement of general principles of liability or of terminology to which we or these other bodies, or their draftsmen, can turn it would be surprising if there were not some inconsistencies and incongruities in the substance and language of the measures which are proposed and which become law. Some examples are pointed out below. This Report addresses the question whether it is desirable to replace the existing fluctuating mix of legislation and common law by one codifying statute ...

Why codify the criminal law? – The aims of codification

2.1 The Code team identified the aims of codification at the present time as being to make the criminal law more accessible, comprehensible, consistent and certain. These aspirations have a number of theoretical and practical aspects which we examine in more detail below. We believe, however, that there are also fundamental constitutional arguments of principle in favour of codification which we consider first ...

The constitutional arguments for codification

2.2 The constitutional arguments relating to codification were not stressed in the Code team's Report but were mentioned by some commentators on consultation as important arguments in favour of codifying the criminal law. These arguments were developed, in particular, by Professor ATH Smith and were conveniently summarised (as well as being endorsed) by the Society of Public Teachers of Law in their submission to us as follows:

> The virtues and advantages of a Code that [the Code team's Report] identifies (accessibility, comprehensibility, consistency and certainty) relate to essentially lawyerly concerns: what needs to be stressed is that they serve the more profound aspirations of due notice and fair warning characteristic of a system that seeks to adhere to the principle of legality. In the first place, a Code is the mechanism that will best synthesise the criminal law's conflicting aims of social protection and crime prevention with concern for legality and due process. As Professor Wechsler, principal draftsman of the Model Penal Code, has put it, a Code demonstrates that, when so much is at stake for the community and the individual, care has

been taken to make law as rational and just as law can be. A Code will, secondly, provide what the mix of common law and legislation never can, one fixed starting point for ascertaining what the law is. Thirdly, because a Criminal Code makes a symbolic statement about the constitutional relationship of Parliament and the courts, it requires a judicial deference to the legislative will greater than that which the courts have often shown to isolated and sporadic pieces of legislation. Far from it being 'a possible disadvantage of codification' that it places 'limitations upon the ability of the courts to develop the law in directions which might be considered desirable', we believe that for the criminal law this is one of its greatest merits. Then, fourthly, codification will make it possible to effect many much needed and long-overdue reforms in both the General and the Special Parts of the criminal law, that have already been adumbrated in the reports of official bodies ...

With much of this we agree. 'Due notice' or 'fair warning' – by which is meant the idea that the law should be known in advance to those accused of violating it – should clearly be regarded as a principle of major importance in our criminal justice system. While there is room for argument as to how much or how little of the content of the criminal law should be left to be developed by the common law, codification provides the opportunity for ensuring that this principle is followed over a substantial part of the criminal law. Moreover, since the criminal law is arguably the most direct expression of the relationship between a State and its citizens, it is right as a matter of constitutional principle that the relationship should he clearly stated in a criminal code the terms of which have been deliberated upon by a democratically elected legislature.

2.3 We shall return to consider some of the arguments in the passage above in more detail later, for example, the third and fourth arguments concerning codification and the role of the court and the relationship between restatement and reform. Suffice it to note here that we endorse them, subject to the considerations mentioned later. The second argument (that a code will provide a fixed starting point for ascertaining what the law is) relates to accessibility which is considered next. ...

Accessibility and comprehensibility

2.4 If the terms of the criminal law are set out in one well-drafted enactment in place of the present fluctuating mix of statute and case-law, the law must necessarily become more accessible and comprehensible to everyone concerned with the interests of criminal justice. Accessibility and comprehensibility are important values for a number of reasons.

2.5 A large and growing number of people are now involved in administering and advising upon the criminal law. One reason for this is that the volume of work in the criminal courts has hugely increased in recent years. To meet this rise, there has been a substantial increase in the numbers of Crown Court judges, recorders and assistant recorders appointed. Many of these judges are recruited from outside the ranks of specialist criminal practitioners. In the magistrates' courts, magistrates depend upon their clerks for advice on the law: in this area too the number of court clerks has risen to try to meet the increased workload. The position of the common law in criminal matters, and in particular the interface between common law and statutory provisions, undoubtedly contributes to making the law obscure and difficult to understand for everyone concerned in the administration of justice, whether a newly-appointed assistant recorder or magistrates' clerk. Obscurity and mystification may in turn lead to inefficiency: the cost and length of trials may be increased because the law has to be extracted and clarified, and there is greater scope for appeals on misdirections on points of law. Moreover, if the law is not perceived by triers of fact to be clear and fair, there is a risk that they will return incorrect or perverse verdicts through misunderstanding or a deliberate disregard of what they are advised the law is. Finally, the criminal law is a particularly public and visible part of the law. It is important that its authority and legitimacy should not be undermined by perceptions that it is intelligible only to experts.

2.6 Codification would help to meet all these dangers. One of its main aims would be to provide a single clear agreed text, published under the authority of Parliament. The law would immediately become more accessible; all users would have an agreed text as a common starting-point and the scope for dispute about its terms and application should be reduced. The source of the general principles of criminal liability would be found in little more than fifty sections of an Act of Parliament instead of many statutes, thousands of cases and the extensive commentaries on them to be found in the textbooks. While much criminal law would remain outside the Criminal Code Act, the law relating to most of the gravest crimes could be brought within it so that the reader would find it within one volume. Of course, no code or statute on a single subject can ever be truly comprehensive. The interpretive role of the judiciary will continue to be important; indeed, during the early years of legislation on a subject the judges' interpretive role is more crucial than at any time thereafter. Nor do we pretend that codification will make the law accessible to Everyman in the sense that he can pick up one volume and in it find the answer to whatever his problem is.

2.7 It is impossible to quantify the potential savings in time and costs which could be brought about by codification, but they could be substantial. The impact of presenting the criminal law in clear, modern and intelligible terms should be felt at all stages of the criminal process, from operational decisions by police officers to appeals to the higher courts. Practitioners should be assisted in advising clients and preparing for trial, trial judges should find the task of directing juries on the law easier and quicker and the length of time spent arguing points of law on appeal should be reduced.

Consistency

2.8 The Code team commented in their Report that:

> The haphazard development of the law through the cases, and a multiplicity of statutes inevitably leads to inconsistencies, not merely in terminology but also in substance. Codification must seek to remove these. If two rules actually contradict one another they cannot both be the law. The codifier cannot rationally restate both. He must restate one and abolish the other or propose some third rule to replace both. More frequently, the inconsistency is one of principle and policy rather than of mutual contradiction ...

Inconsistency both in terminology and substance is a serious problem in English criminal law. A notable example is the use of the word 'reckless'.

Recklessness is a central element of fault requirements but it has four different meanings depending on whether it is used in the context of non-fatal offences against the person, criminal damage and manslaughter, rape or driving offences. This is impossible to defend. It makes the law unnecessarily complex and less intelligible, and it results in difficulty and embarrassment in directing juries and advising magistrates. Two such offences may well be involved in the same trial when it is clearly undesirable that the law should be seen to be laying down inconsistent tests of liability without any clear policy justification. Another example concerns combinations of preliminary offences (attempt to incite, incitement to conspire, conspiracy to attempt and so on). Some combinations constitute offences known to the law, others do not. No policy can be found to support these distinctions, and the scrutiny group examining the provisions of the draft Code Bill dealing with preliminary offences agreed that in this topic the present law is an irrational mess.

2.9 This kind of inconsistency across a range of offences is not in practice remediable by use of the common law. It is most unlikely, for example, that cases will arise which raise the issue of recklessness in all the relevant offences in an appropriate form. In relation to the preliminary offences it would be impossible for the courts to reintroduce forms of liability which have been expressly abolished by statute. Codification alone, pursuing a conscious policy of the elimination of inconsistency, can deal adequately with this kind of problem. Elimination of inconsistency will also help to ensure that the offence of one accused is dealt with fairly in relation to other offences by other accused. Unjustifiable disparity of treatment can thus be avoided ...

Certainty

2.10 In some areas of the criminal law there is substantial uncertainty as to its scope. Uncertainty can arise where the accidents of litigation and piecemeal legislation leave gaps, so that there is no law at all on a particular point. Alternatively, a statute or case may state the law obscurely, so that it is impossible to be certain as to the law to be applied to a particular problem. Uncertainty is an impediment to the proper administration of criminal justice since it may discourage the bringing of prosecutions where there is a colourable case to answer, and tend to increase the number of unmeritorious but successful submissions of 'no case to answer' if charges are brought. In either event respect for the law may he diminished. Certainty is very important to prevent unwarranted prosecutions being brought at all or prosecutions collapsing or convictions being quashed on appeal. Lack of certainty may also cause difficulties for defence lawyers advising their clients and for judges directing juries.

2.11 The common law method of resolving uncertainty by 'retrospective' declaration of the law is objectionable in principle. It may lead to the conviction of a defendant on the basis of criminal liability not known to exist in that form before he acted. Much criticism was directed at the decision of the House of Lords in *DPP v Shaw* where this was generally perceived to have happened. On the other hand, the effect of an appeal may be to narrow the law retrospectively, either by acknowledging the existence of a defence to criminal liability which was not previously recognised or by altering the definition of a criminal offence. In the ... cases of *Moloney* ... and *Hancock* the House of Lords restated the meaning of 'intention' as the mental element for murder [see further Chapters 4 and 15]. In doing so, the House disapproved the terms of a direction to a jury given ten years earlier in the leading case of *Hyam*. Such a change may give rise to a suggestion not only that the conviction in the earlier case was unsafe but also cast doubt on the validity of the convictions in other cases during the intervening ten year period which had been based on the terms of the direction approved in the earlier case. Such suggestions, which are inherent in the development of the law on a case by case basis, must undermine confidence in this important branch of the law. Statutory changes, on the other hand, do not have retrospective effect. They come into force only after full Parliamentary debate with the commencement of the provisions of the statute. Earlier cases are unaffected.

THE IMPACT OF THE HUMAN RIGHTS ACT 1998 ON SUBSTANTIVE CRIMINAL LAW

The key rights provided by the European Convention on Human Rights (in terms of their impact on substantive criminal law), as incorporated by the Human Rights Act 1998 are as follows:

European Convention on Human Rights

Article 2 – Right to Life

1   Everyone's right to life shall be protected by law. No one shall be deprived of his life intentionally save in the execution of a sentence of a court following his conviction of a crime for which this penalty is provided by law.

2   Deprivation of life shall not be regarded as inflicted in contravention of this Article when it results from the use of force which is no more than absolutely necessary:

    (a) in defence of any person from unlawful violence;

    (b) in order to effect a lawful arrest or to prevent the escape of a person lawfully detained;

    (c) in action lawfully taken for the purpose of quelling a riot or insurrection.

Article 3 – Prohibition of Torture

No one shall be subjected to torture or to inhuman or degrading treatment or punishment.

Article 4 – Prohibition of Slavery and Forced Labour

1   No one shall be held in slavery or servitude.

2   No one shall be required to perform forced or compulsory labour.

3   For the purpose of this Article the term 'forced or compulsory labour' shall not include:

    (a) any work required to be done in the ordinary course of detention imposed according to the provisions of Article 5 of this Convention or during conditional release from such detention;

(b) any service of a military character or, in case of conscientious objectors in countries where they are recognised, service exacted instead of compulsory military service;

(c) any service exacted in case of an emergency or calamity threatening the life or well-being of the community;

(d) any work or service which forms part of normal civic obligations.

Article 5 – Right to Liberty and Security

1 Everyone has the right to liberty and security of person. No one shall be deprived of his liberty save in the following cases and in accordance with a procedure prescribed by law:

(a) the lawful detention of a person after conviction by a competent court;

(b) the lawful arrest or detention of a person for non-compliance with the lawful order of a court or in order to secure the fulfilment of any obligation prescribed by law;

(c) the lawful arrest or detention of a person effected for the purpose of bringing him before the competent legal authority on reasonable suspicion of having committed an offence or when it is reasonably considered necessary to prevent his committing an offence or fleeing after having done so;

(d) the detention of a minor by lawful order for the purpose of educational supervision or his lawful detention for the purpose of bringing him before the competent legal authority;

(e) the lawful detention of persons for the prevention of the spreading of infectious diseases, of persons of unsound mind, alcoholics or drug addicts or vagrants;

(f) the lawful arrest or detention of a person to prevent his effecting an unauthorised entry into the country or of a person against whom action is being taken with a view to deportation or extradition.

2 Everyone who is arrested shall be informed promptly, in a language which he understands, of the reasons for his arrest and of any charge against him.

3 Everyone arrested or detained in accordance with the provisions of paragraph 1(c) of this Article shall be brought promptly before a judge or other officer authorised by law to exercise judicial power and shall be entitled to trial within a reasonable time or to release pending trial. Release may be conditioned by guarantees to appear for trial.

4 Everyone who is deprived of his liberty by arrest or detention shall be entitled to take proceedings by which the lawfulness of his detention shall be decided speedily by a court and his release ordered if the detention is not lawful.

5 Everyone who has been the victim of arrest or detention in contravention of the provisions of this Article shall have an enforceable right to compensation.

Article 6 – Right to a Fair Trial

1 In the determination of his civil rights and obligations or of any criminal charge against him, everyone is entitled to a fair and public hearing within a reasonable time by an independent and impartial tribunal established by law. Judgment shall be pronounced publicly but the press and public may be

excluded from all or part of the trial in the interest of morals, public order or national security in a democratic society, where the interests of juveniles or the protection of the private life of the parties so require, or to the extent strictly necessary in the opinion of the court in special circumstances where publicity would prejudice the interests of justice.

2   Everyone charged with a criminal offence shall be presumed innocent until proved guilty according to law.

3   Everyone charged with a criminal offence has the following minimum rights:

   (a) to be informed promptly, in a language which he understands and in detail, of the nature and cause of the accusation against him;

   (b) to have adequate time and facilities for the preparation of his defence;

   (c) to defend himself in person or through legal assistance of his own choosing or, if he has not sufficient means to pay for legal assistance, to be given it free when the interests of justice so require;

   (d) to examine or have examined witnesses against him and to obtain the attendance and examination of witnesses on his behalf under the same conditions as witnesses against him;

   (e) to have the free assistance of an interpreter if he cannot understand or speak the language used in court.

Article 7 – No Punishment Without Law

1   No one shall be held guilty of any criminal offence on account of any act or omission which did not constitute a criminal offence under national or international law at the time when it was committed. Nor shall a heavier penalty be imposed than the one that was applicable at the time the criminal offence was committed.

2   This Article shall not prejudice the trial and punishment of any person for any act or omission which, at the time when it was committed, was criminal according to the general principles of law recognised by civilised nations.

Article 8 – Right to Respect for Private and Family Life

1   Everyone has the right to respect for his private and family life, his home and his correspondence.

2   There shall be no interference by a public authority with the exercise of this right except such as is in accordance with the law and is necessary in a democratic society in the interests of national security, public safety or the economic well-being of the country, for the prevention of disorder or crime, for the protection of health or morals, or for the protection of the rights and freedoms of others.

Article 9 – Freedom of Thought, Conscience and Religion

1   Everyone has the right to freedom of thought, conscience and religion; this right includes freedom to change his religion or belief and freedom, either alone or in community with others and in public or private, to manifest his religion or belief, in worship, teaching, practice and observance.

2   Freedom to manifest one's religion or beliefs shall be subject only to such limitations as are prescribed by law and are necessary in a democratic society in the interests of public safety, for the protection of public order, health or morals, or for the protection of the rights and freedoms of others.

Article 10 – Freedom of Expression

1 Everyone has the right to freedom of expression. This right shall include freedom to hold opinions and to receive and impart information and ideas without interference by public authority and regardless of frontiers. This Article shall not prevent States from requiring the licensing of broadcasting, television or cinema enterprises.

2 The exercise of these freedoms, since it carries with it duties and responsibilities, may be subject to such formalities, conditions, restrictions or penalties as are prescribed by law and are necessary in a democratic society, in the interests of national security, territorial integrity or public safety, for the prevention of disorder or crime, for the protection of health or morals, for the protection of the reputation or rights of others, for preventing the disclosure of information received in confidence, or for maintaining the authority and impartiality of the judiciary.

Article 11 – Freedom of Assembly and Association

1 Everyone has the right to freedom of peaceful assembly and to freedom of association with others, including the right to form and to join trade unions for the protection of his interests.

2 No restrictions shall be placed on the exercise of these rights other than such as are prescribed by law and are necessary in a democratic society in the interests of national security or public safety, for the prevention of disorder or crime, for the protection of health or morals or for the protection of the rights and freedoms of others. This Article shall not prevent the imposition of lawful restrictions on the exercise of these rights by members of the armed forces, of the police or of the administration of the State.

What is required of domestic courts?

The conventional wisdom prevalent at the time the Human Rights Act 1998 was enacted was to the effect that it would have a very considerable impact on the criminal justice system. The full effects of incorporating the European Convention on Human Rights are yet to become apparent, the Act only fully coming into force in October 2001, but it is clear that its influence is being felt as regards matters of criminal process and the operation of the rules of evidence. More difficult to ascertain is the impact of incorporation on the substantive criminal law of England and Wales.

Section 2(1) of the Human Rights Act 1998 provides that:

A court or tribunal determining a question which has arisen in connection with a Convention right must take into account any (a) judgment, decision, declaration or advisory opinion of the European Court of Human Rights, (b) opinion of the Commission given in a report adopted under Article 31 of the Convention, (c) decision of the Commission in connection with Article 26 or 27(2) of the Convention, or (d) decision of the Committee of Ministers taken under Article 46 of the Convention ...

When interpreting domestic legislation courts must, so far as it is possible, read and give effect to such legislation in a way which is compatible with the Convention rights; see s 3(1).

Hence domestic courts are given a degree of latitude – reference to the jurisprudence of Strasbourg is mandatory – but it need only be taken into account. Legislation must be construed in a manner compatible with the Convention but only so far as is possible.

Three points are particularly worth noting:

• When applying the European Convention on Human Rights a domestic court should be prepared to take a generous view as to whether an activity falls within the protection afforded by the Convention's articles.

• The Convention is to be regarded as a 'living' or 'dynamic' instrument to be interpreted in the light of current conditions. More recent decisions of the European Court of Human Rights will be regarded as carrying more weight than earlier decisions.

• Where an Article of the Convention permits some state interference with the enjoyment of a right, a court assessing the extent to which that interference is compatible with the Convention should consider (i) whether the interference is provided for by law; (ii) whether it serves a legitimate purpose; (iii) whether the interference is proportionate to the end to be achieved; (iv) whether it is necessary in a democratic society; (v) whether it is discriminatory in operation; and (vi) whether the state should be allowed a margin of appreciation in its compliance with the Convention – that is, be allowed to apply the Convention to suit national standards.

The 'quality of law test'

Articles 6 and 7 of the European Convention on Human Rights make reference to concepts such as 'criminal charge' and 'criminal offence'; Arts 9–11 refer to rights being limited as 'prescribed by law'. These expression presuppose a degree of certainty as to whether given conduct is criminal or not, and as to whether the law prescribes certain conduct or not. This in turn raises the possibility of certain aspects of domestic criminal law failing the 'quality of law' test on the basis that the scope of certain offences cannot be clearly identified – the jurisprudence of the European Convention on Human Rights requires that a 'norm' cannot be described as a law unless it can be formulated with sufficient precision so as to enable a citizen to regulate his conduct to avoid incurring liability.

For example in *Hashman and Harrup v UK* [2000] Crim LR 185, anti-hunt protestors who were found not to have breached the peace, were nevertheless ordered by the court to be bound over because they had acted *contra bono mores* (in a way that was wrong in the eyes of the majority of citizens). The European Court of Human Rights held that this was a violation of Art 10 – the expression *contra bono mores* was too vague to satisfy the 'prescribed by law' test, and could not be relied upon to justify detention under Art 5.

In *R v Hinks* [2000] 4 All ER 835 (considered in Chapter 18) Lord Hobhouse (dissenting) was concerned that the effect of the majority view in that case was to create an offence where liability hinged entirely on the issue of whether or not the accused had acted dishonestly. He was particularly concerned at the prospect of a criminal conviction based upon conduct:

> ... which involves no inherent illegality and may only be capable of being criticised on grounds of lack of morality [that is, it is dishonest] ... [t]his approach itself raises fundamental questions. An essential function of the criminal law is to define the boundary between what conduct is criminal and what merely immoral. Both are the subject of the disapprobation of ordinary right-thinking citizens and the distinction is liable to be arbitrary or at least strongly influenced by considerations subjective to the individual members of the tribunal. To treat otherwise lawful conduct as criminal merely because it is open to such disapprobation would be contrary to principle and open to the objection that it fails to achieve the objective and transparent certainty required of the criminal law by the principles basic to human rights.

See further the arguments raised in *R v Smethurst* (2001) *The Times*, 13 April, where the Court of Appeal rejected the contention that s 1 of the Protection of Children Act 1978 (offence of possession child pornography) was in conflict with Art 10 (freedom of expression). The court accepted that the concept of indecency might lack certainty, but was persuaded by the overriding public interest in protecting morality.

Article 2: the right to life

Article 2(2) provides that the right to life is not violated where death results from the use of force by the state that was no more than was *absolutely necessary* to prevent another suffering unlawful violence; in effecting arrest or preventing escape; in quelling a riot or insurrection. The current domestic law allows the use of lethal force by way of self-defence, including the defence of others, where it is *reasonable* in the circumstances. As *Andronicou v Cyprus* [1998] Crim LR 823, illustrates there is the potential for conflict between domestic law on self-defence and the Convention. Further, *McCann v United Kingdom* (1996) 21 EHRR 97 provides that agents of the state can use lethal force under Art 2(2) where they honestly believe, with good reason, that such force is justified. This too is at odds with domestic law which permits D to rely on an honest, albeit mistaken, belief that the use of reasonable force is justified.

Article 3: inhuman and degrading treatment

In *A v UK* (1999) 27 EHRR 611, the European Court of Human Rights heard an application brought by a child who had been beaten with a stick by his stepfather. The applicant's father had been acquitted of charges of causing actual bodily harm contrary to s 47 of the Offences Against the Persons Act 1861, having relied on reasonable chastisement in the circumstances. The court concluded that there had been a violation of Art 3 on the basis that existing domestic law on the defence of lawful chastisement had failed to provide the applicant with adequate protection. Whilst the question of whether, in any given case, the treatment suffered by an applicant reached the minimum level of severity necessary to trigger the operation of Art 3 would depend on the circumstances, where the victim was a child the minimum threshold would be more easily attained. It should be noted that, whilst the court accepted that the United Kingdom could not be held responsible for the actions of a private individual, such as the applicant's stepfather, it was responsible for a system of criminal law that allowed a person inflicting serious harm upon a child to be acquitted on the grounds that the harm was justifiable chastisement. There has been no legislative response to this decision, but the courts have attempted to alleviate the shortcomings of the domestic law by offering guidelines on the availability of the defence; see *R v H (Reasonable Chastisement)* (2001) *The Times*, 18 May. Where a parent raises the defence of lawful chastisement the jury ought to be directed to consider: (i) the nature and context of the defendant's behaviour; (ii) the duration of that behaviour; (iii) the physical and mental consequences in respect of the child; (iv) the age and personal characteristics of the child; (v) the reasons given by the defendant for administering the punishment.

Article 7: Non-retrospectivity

Whilst Art 7 appears to prohibit retrospective criminal legislation, it has proved to be of rather limited scope as regards the retrospective nature of the common law. The applicant in *SW v United Kingdom* (1996) 21 EHRR 363, had been convicted of raping his wife following the House of Lords' decision in *R v R* [1992] AC 599 to the effect that the marital exemption for rape should be abolished. He was unsuccessful in his claim that the common law operated retrospectively, in the sense that his actions, at the time they had been committed, had not constituted a criminal offence. The court ruled that Art 7 did not prohibit 'the gradual clarification of rules of criminal liability through judicial interpretation from case to case, provided that the resultant development is consistent with the essence of the offence and could be reasonably foreseen'.

As Richard Buxton observed in 'The Human Rights Act and the substantive criminal law' [2000] Crim LR 331:

> This is, however, foresight of a somewhat special sort. The accretion of exceptions to the marital rape exemption might on one view be described as an evolution [that] had reached a stage where judicial recognition of the absence of immunity had become a reasonably foreseeable development of the law; but might equally have been thought to indicate that the basic exemption, on which the complainant in *SW v United Kingdom* relied, remained intact and could only be altered by legislation. That was certainly the view of the Law Commission, which published a working paper on rape within marriage shortly before the matter came to a head

in the courts, and of a number of first instance judges who, however reluctantly, had seen themselves as bound by the rule. While hesitating to appeal here to Lord Simonds' famous comparison of foresight and hindsight, if one posits an (admittedly unlikely) visit to his solicitor by Mr R to ask for advice about trying to have intercourse with his wife, it is far from clear that he would have been told with any confidence that (whatever else might be said about his conduct) he was facing a criminal conviction and a sentence of three years' imprisonment.

It would therefore seem that a 'criminal offence' under Article 7 can be an offence merely *in gremio*, provided that its appearance can he said to be foreseeable on the basis of a not very demanding standard of foresight. That adds nothing to the protection of the individual that is provided by English domestic principle, and indeed falls short of what English principle has always been thought to require.

Article 8: the right to privacy

In *ADT v United Kingdom* [2000] Crim LR 1009, the applicant successfully argued that the domestic law prohibiting acts of gross indecency between men in private was incompatible with the right to privacy under Art 8. The police had raided the home of the applicant, a male homosexual. Items seized included video tape recordings of the applicant engaging in consensual group sex acts with up to four other adult men. In agreeing that the proceedings for gross indecency involved a violation of Art 8, the court noted that all the activities had all taken place in the applicant's home and had not been visible to anyone other than those involved. Hence it could not agree that the interference with the applicant's privacy, resulting from the state's reliance on the gross indecency offences, was necessary in a democratic society. The applicant's activities were non-violent, raised no general public health concerns and were restricted to a small number of consenting adults.

Further reading

G Williams, 'The definition of crime' [1955] Current Legal Problems 107

I Dennis, 'The critical condition of criminal law' [1997] Current Legal Problems 213

M Arden, 'Criminal law at the crossroads: the impact on human rights from the Law Commission's perspective and the need for a Code' [1999] Crim LR 439

G Phillipson, 'The Human Rights Act, "horizontal effect" and the common law: a bang or a whimper' (1999) 62 MLR 824

A Ashworth, 'Interpreting criminal statutes: a crisis of legality?' (1991) 107 LQR 419

A Ashworth and M Blake, 'The presumption of innocence in English criminal law' [1996] Crim LR 306

C Wells, 'Codification of the criminal law: restatement or reform?' [1986] Crim LR 314

ATH Smith, 'The Human Rights Act 1998 – (1) The Human Rights Act and the criminal lawyer: the constitutional context' [1999] Crim LR 251

R Buxton, 'The Human Rights Act and the substantive criminal law' [2000] Crim LR 331

CHAPTER 2

ACTUS REUS: THE EXTERNAL ELEMENTS OF AN OFFENCE

Criminal liability generally rests upon proof of two things – *actus reus* and *mens rea*. *Actus reus* literally means 'guilty act', but this is clearly something of a misnomer as the defendant might not bear in any guilt, as in fault, for what has occurred, and, as will be seen, there are many instances where no positive act, as such, has to be established. It is probably more sensible to think of *actus reus* as a term referring to the external elements of an offence, that is, those elements of the offence that have to be established by the prosecution, other than those that relate to the defendant's state of mind.

The type of *actus reus* that has to be established will vary according to the definition of the offence in question. Some obviously require proof of conduct on the part of the defendant, such as is the case with an offence like rape (see further Chapter 17). Other offences require proof that the defendant's actions caused a prohibited consequence. The topic of causation is dealt with in Chapter 3. In some cases it will be sufficient for the prosecution to establish that a particular state of affairs existed. This might be the case with an offence such as being found in the United Kingdom without having permission to remain; see *R v Larsonneur* considered below. Where a defendant is under a legal duty to act his mere failure to act might give rise to the commission of an *actus reus*.

The imposition of criminal liability is based on an assumption that a defendant's acts or omissions at the time of the alleged offence were voluntary, in the sense that he was able to exercise some control over his actions or failure to act. Involuntariness can arise from a number of causes, some of which will found a defence in criminal law, some of which will not. See further intoxication (Chapter 8); duress and necessity (Chapter 13); and insanity and non-insane automatism (Chapter 7).

A STATE OF AFFAIRS AMOUNTING TO AN *ACTUS REUS*

R v Larsonneur (1933) 24 Cr App R 74 (CA)

Lord Hewart CJ: ... The fact is, as the evidence shows, that the appellant is an alien. She has a French passport, which bears this statement under the date 14 March 1933, 'Leave to land granted at Folkestone this day on condition that the holder does not enter any employment, paid or unpaid, while in the United Kingdom', but on 22 March that condition was varied and one finds these words: 'The condition attached to the grant of leave to land is hereby varied so as to require departure from the United Kingdom not later than 22 March 1933'. Then follows the signature of an Under-Secretary of State. In fact, the appellant went to the Irish Free State and afterwards, in circumstances which are perfectly immaterial, so far as this appeal is concerned, came back to Holyhead. She was at Holyhead on 21 April 1933, a date after the day limited by the condition on her passport ...

The appellant was, therefore, on 21 April 1933, in the position in which she would have been if she had been prohibited from landing by the Secretary of State and, that being so, there is no reason to interfere with the finding of the jury. She was found here and was, therefore, deemed to be in the class of persons whose landing had been prohibited by the Secretary of State, by reason of the fact that she had violated the condition on her passport. The appeal, therefore, is dismissed and the recommendation for deportation remains.

Notes and queries

1 Given that Larsonneur was deported against her will to the United Kingdom is there an argument as to the 'voluntariness' of her actions that brought about the *actus reus*? Lanham argues in *'Larsonneur* revisited' [1976] Crim LR 276 that she was the author of her own misfortunes in going to Ireland in order to enter into an arranged marriage that would have enabled here to remain in the United Kingdom. In effect there was prior fault on her part in putting herself in a position where she risked deportation to the United Kingdom against her will.

2 In *Winzar v Chief Constable of Kent* (1983) *The Times*, 28 March (DC), the appellant was convicted of being drunk on the highway (contrary to s 12 of the Licensing Act 1872). He had been taken to a hospital, the doctors there deciding that he was merely drunk asked him to leave. The appellant remained in the hospital and the police were called. They placed the appellant in a police car parked in the road outside the hospital. The appellant was then charged with being drunk on the highway. It was held that the fact that his presence on the highway was not of his own volition and was momentary did not amount to a defence. The *actus reus* merely required proof of a state of affairs – drunkenness in a public place. Again an element of prior fault arises here. Winzar of his own volition became intoxicated and thereby put himself in a position whereby he might be found drunk and disorderly in a public place.

Codification and law reform proposals

Clause 15 of the draft code seeks to codify the meaning to be given to the term 'act' in the following way:

> A reference in this Act to an 'act' as an element of an offence refers also, where the context permits, to any result of the act, and any circumstance in which the act is done or the result occurs, that is an element of the offence, and references to a person acting or doing an act shall be construed accordingly.

As the commentary on the code observes:

> ... Clause 15 is an interpretation clause. It does not define 'act'. It simply explains that where the Code refers to 'an act' or to a person's 'acting' or 'doing an act', the reference embraces whatever relevant results and circumstances the context permits. This clarification of the use of the word 'act' is not in fact essential; for we

believe that no provision of the Code is on a fair reading truly ambiguous in its use of the term. But the clause may prove useful for the avoidance of doubt in those inexperienced in the reading of criminal statutes and as a protection against perverse reading or hopeless argument [Vol II, para 7.6].

An omission to act as an *actus reus*

The basic principle here is that a failure to act can only give rise to the *actus reus* of an offence if the defendant was, at the time of the omission, under a legal duty to act. Legal duties can arise from statute, contract, the holding of a particular public office, or from the common law.

Liability for omission based on statute

The most obvious source of a positive legal duty to act is primary legislation. There are numerous Acts of Parliament that place individuals or companies under a legal duty to act in a a particular way, whether it be the reporting of road accidents involving injury (see s 170(4) of the Road Traffic Act 1988), the duty to provide a safe working environment (see Health and Safety at Work Act 1974) or the statutory duty owed by parents and guardians towards children (see the Children and Young Persons Act 1933). See further *R v Lowe* [1973] QB 702 (CA), considered in Chapter 15.

Liability for omission based on employment

A positive duty to act can be found in the express or implied terms of a contract of employment. An obvious example would be the contractual obligation placed upon a lifeguard at a swimming pool to go to the aid of a swimmer in distress. The fact that the beneficiary of this duty is not a party to the contract is not relevant when assessing the employee's criminal liability

R v Pittwood (1902) 19 TLR 37 (Taunton Assizes)

The defendant was employed as a gatekeeper responsible for closing the gates of a level crossing when a train was due. On this occasion he failed to shut the gate and a hay cart crossing the line was involved in a collision with a train. A man was killed as a result. The defendant was convicted of manslaughter.

> **Wright J:** was clearly of opinion that in this case there was gross and criminal negligence, as the man was paid to keep the gate shut and protect the public. In his opinion there were three grounds on which the verdict could be supported: (1) There might be cases of misfeasance and cases of mere nonfeasance. Here it was quite clear there was evidence of misfeasance as the prisoner directly contributed to the accident. (2) A man might incur criminal liability from a duty arising out of contract. The learned judge quoted in support of this *R v Nicholls* (1875) 13 Cox 75; *R v Elliott* (1889) 16 Cox 710; *R v Benge* (1865) 4 F & F 594; *R v Hughes* (1857) Dears & B 248. The strongest case of all was, perhaps, *R v Instan* ... and that case clearly governed the present charge. (3) With regard to the point that this was only an

occupation road, he clearly held that it was not, as the company had assumed the liability of protecting the public whenever they crossed the road ...

Liability for omission based on relationship and/or reliance

R v Gibbins and Proctor (1918) 13 Cr App R 134 (CA)

Darling J: The two appellants were indicted and tried together for the wilful murder of Nelly Gibbins, the daughter of Gibbins. The facts were that Gibbins's wife had left him, and he was living in adultery with Proctor. There were several children, one of whom was the child of Proctor, in the house. He earned good wages, which he brought home and gave to Proctor to maintain the house and those in it. There is no evidence that there was not enough to keep them all in health. And all were looked after except one, namely Nelly, who was starved to death. Her organs were healthy, and there was no reason why she should have died if she had been supplied with food. She was kept upstairs apart from the others, and there was evidence that Proctor hated her and cursed her, from which the jury could infer that she had a very strong interest in her death ...

It has been said that there ought not to have been a finding of guilty of murder against Gibbins. The court agrees that the evidence was less against Gibbins than Proctor, Gibbins gave her money, and as far as we can see it was sufficient to provide for the wants of themselves and all the children. But he lived in the house and the child was his own, a little girl of seven, and he grossly neglected the child. He must have known what her condition was if he saw her, for she was little more than a skeleton. He is in this dilemma; if he did not see her the jury might well infer that he did not care if she died; if he did he must have known what was going on. The question is whether there was evidence that he so conducted himself as to show that he desired that grievous bodily injury should be done to the child. He cannot pretend that he showed any solicitude for her. He knew that Proctor hated her, knew that she was ill and that no doctor had been called in, and the jury may have come to the conclusion that he was so infatuated with Proctor, and so afraid of offending her, that he preferred that the child should starve to death rather than that he should be exposed to any injury or unpleasantness from Proctor. It is unnecessary to say more than that there was evidence that Gibbins did desire that grievous bodily harm should be done to the child; he did not interfere in what was being done, and he comes within the definition which I have read, and is therefore guilty of murder.

The case of Proctor is plainer. She had charge of the child. She was under no obligation to do so or to live with Gibbins, but she did so, and receiving money, as it is admitted she did, for the purpose of supplying food, her duty was to see that the child was properly fed and looked after, and to see that she had medical attention if necessary. We agree with what Lord Coleridge CJ said in *R v Instan* [1893] 1 QB 450: 'There is no case directly in point, but it would be a slur upon, and a discredit to the administration of, justice in this country if there were any doubt as to the legal principle, or as to the present case being within it. The prisoner was under a moral obligation to the deceased from which arose a legal duty towards her; that legal duty the prisoner has wilfully and deliberately left unperformed, with the consequence that there has been and acceleration of the death of the deceased owing to the non-performance of that legal duty.' Here Proctor took upon herself the moral obligation of looking after the children; she was *de facto*, though not de jure, the wife of Gibbins and had excluded the child's own mother. She neglected the child undoubtedly, and the evidence shows that as a result the child died. So a verdict of manslaughter at least was inevitable.

But it is necessary to go further and see whether it was murder. The evidence is that she had plenty of money; that she kept the child upstairs insufficiently supplied with food; that she hated the child and hit her. There is also evidence that when the child died of starvation both appellants took part in hiding the body and preventing the death from being known. They concocted a story that she had been sent away and was still alive. There is evidence that Proctor told Gibbins to bury the child out of sight, and that he did so in the brickyard where he worked. The jury came to the conclusion that she had done more than wickedly neglect the child; she had deliberately withheld food from it, and therefore we come to the conclusion that there was evidence which justified the jury in returning a verdict against her, not merely of manslaughter, but of murder. The appeals are therefore dismissed.

R v Stone and Dobinson [1977] QB 354 (CA)

Geoffrey Lane LJ: ... In 1972, at 75 Broadwater, Bolton-on-Dearne in Yorkshire, there lived three people. Stone, an ex-miner now aged 67, widowed for 10 years, who is partially deaf, almost totally blind and has no appreciable sense of smell; Gwendoline Dobinson, now aged 43, who had been his housekeeper and mistress for some eight years, and Stone's son called Cyril, aged 34, who is mentally subnormal. Stone is of low average intelligence, Dobinson is described as ineffectual and somewhat inadequate.

There was an addition to that household in 1972. Stone had a younger sister called Fanny, about 61 at the date of her death. She had been living with another sister called Rosy. For some reason, probably because Rosy could not tolerate her any longer, she had decided to leave. She came to live at No 75, where she occupied a small front room. She was in receipt of a pension of £11.60 per week and gave her brother £1.50 towards the rent. She was eccentric in many ways. She was morbidly and unnecessarily anxious about putting on weight and so denied herself proper meals. She would take to her room for days. She would often stay in her room all day until the two appellants went to the public house in the evening, when she would creep down and make herself a meal.

In early spring 1975 the police called at the house. Fanny had been found wandering about in the street by herself without apparently knowing where she was. This caused the appellants to try and find Fanny's doctor. They tried to trace him through Rosy, but having walked a very considerable distance in their search they failed. It transpired that they had walked to the wrong village. Fanny herself refused to tell them the doctor's name. She thought she would be 'put away' if she did. Nothing more was done to enlist outside professional aid.

In the light of what happened subsequently there can be no doubt that Fanny's condition over the succeeding weeks and months must have deteriorated rapidly. By July 1975 she was, it seems, unable or unwilling to leave her bed and, on 19 July, the next-door neighbour, Mrs Wilson, gallantly volunteered to help the female appellant to wash Fanny. She states:

On 19 July Mrs Dobinson and I went to Fanny's room in order to clean her up. When I went into the room there was not a strong smell until I moved her. Her nightdress was wet and messed with her own excreta and the dress had to be cut off. I saw her back was sore; I hadn't seen anything like that before. I took the bedclothes off the bed. They were all wet through and messed. And so was the mattress. I was there for about two hours and Mrs Dobinson helped. She was raw, her back, shoulders, bottom and down below between her legs. Mrs Dobinson appeared to me to be upset because Fanny had never let her attend to her before. I advised Mrs Dobinson to go to the Social Services.

Emily West, the licensee of the local public house, the Crossed Daggers, gave evidence to the effect that during the whole of the period, from 19 July onwards, the appellants came to the public house every night at about 7.00 pm. The appellant Dobinson was worried and told Emily West that Fanny would not wash, go to the toilet or eat or drink. As a result Emily West immediately advised Dobinson to get a doctor and when told that Fanny's doctor lived at Doncaster, Emily West suggested getting a local one. It seems that some efforts were made to get a local doctor, but the neighbour who volunteered to do the telephoning (the appellants being incapable of managing the instrument themselves) was unsuccessful.

On 2 August 1975 Fanny was found by Dobinson to be dead in her bed. The police were called. On arrival they found there was no ventilation in the bedroom, the window had to be hammered open and the bed was so sited that it was impossible to get the door fully open.

At one side of the bed on a chair was an empty mineral bottle and on the other chair a cup. Under the bed was an empty polythene bucket. Otherwise there was no food, washing or toilet facilities in the room. There was excrement on the bed and floor. It was a scene of dreadful degradation.

The pathologist, Dr Usher, gave evidence that the deceased was naked, emaciated, weighing five stone and five pounds, her body ingrained with dirt, lying in a pool of excrement. On the bed on which she was lying were various filthy and crumpled bed-clothes, some of which were soaked in urine. There was excrement on the floor and wrapped in newspapers alongside the bed. There was a tidemark of excreta corresponding with the position in which her body was lying.

At the mortuary Dr Usher found the deceased's body to be ulcerated over the right hip joint and on the underside of the left knee; in each case the ulceration went down to the bone. There were maggots in the ulcers. He found pressure sores over the back of her right shoulder, the outside of the left kneecap to the underside of the left knee, over the right hip joint, to the inner aspect of the left shin and on the left instep where the body had been lying. Such ulcers could not have been produced in less than two to three weeks. The ulcers were due to the general poor condition of the skin and the protruding bones which would have had a greater effect on her than a normal person. She was soaked in urine and excreta.

Her stomach contained no food products but a lot of bile-stained fluid. She had not eaten recently. He found no natural disease. The disinclination to eat was a condition of anorexia nervosa which was not a physical condition but a condition of the brain or mind.

She had been requiring urgent medical attention for some days or even weeks. He said:

If two weeks prior to my seeing the body she had gone into hospital there is a distinct possibility that they may have saved her; and three weeks earlier the chances would have been good. If her condition on 19 July was no worse than that described by Mrs Wilson, then her survival would have been probable.

He said that the cause of death was (1) toxaemia spreading from the infected pressure areas (this could have been alleviated by keeping her clean) and (2) prolonged immobilisation. There was no physical reason for her being immobile. Death was due to immobilisation, which caused the pressure sores, and lack of food. Depression might have caused the lack of mobility. The sores on the left knee he thought did not develop in two weeks. Lack of ventilation would have aggravated the other matters. With regard to the condition of the mattress, he thought it would take weeks to get into that condition.

The Crown alleged that in the circumstances the appellants had undertaken the duty of caring for Fanny who was incapable of looking after herself, that they had, with gross negligence, failed in that duty, that such failure had caused her death and that they were guilty of manslaughter ...

There is no dispute, broadly speaking, as to the matters on which the jury must be satisfied before they can convict of manslaughter in circumstances such as the present. They are: (1) that the defendant undertook the care of a person who by reason of age or infirmity was unable to care for herself; (2) that the defendant was grossly negligent in regard to his duty of care; (3) that by reason of such negligence the person died. It is submitted on behalf of the appellants that the judge's direction to the jury with regard to the first two items was incorrect.

At the close of the Crown's case submissions were made to the judge that there was no, or no sufficient, evidence that the appellants, or either of them, had chosen to undertake the care of Fanny.

That contention was advanced by counsel for the appellant before this court as his first ground of appeal. He amplified the ground somewhat by submitting that the evidence which the judge had suggested to the jury might support the assumption of a duty by the appellants did not, when examined, succeed in doing so. He suggested that the situation here was unlike any reported case. Fanny came to this house as a lodger. Largely, if not entirely due to her own eccentricity and failure to look after herself or feed herself properly, she became increasingly infirm and immobile and eventually unable to look after herself. Is it to be said, asks counsel for the appellants rhetorically, that by the mere fact of becoming infirm and helpless in these circumstances, she casts a duty on her brother and Mrs Dobinson to take steps to have her looked after or taken to hospital? The suggestion is that, heartless though it may seem, this is one of those situations where the appellants were entitled to do nothing; where no duty was cast on them to help, any more than it is cast on a man to rescue a stranger from drowning, however easy such a rescue might be.

This court rejects that proposition. Whether Fanny was a lodger or not she was a blood relation of the appellant Stone; she was occupying a room in his house; Mrs Dobinson had undertaken the duty of trying to wash her, of taking such food to her as she required. There was ample evidence that each appellant was aware of the poor condition she was in by mid-July. It was not disputed that no effort was made to summon an ambulance or the social services or the police despite the entreaties of Mrs Wilson and Mrs West. A social worker used to visit Cyril. No word was spoken to him. All these were matters which the jury were entitled to take into account when considering whether the necessary assumption of a duty to care for Fanny had been proved.

This was *not* a situation analogous to the drowning stranger. They *did* make efforts to care. They tried to get a doctor; they tried to discover the previous doctor. Mrs Dobinson helped with the washing and the provision of food. All these matters were put before the jury in terms which we find it impossible to fault. The jury were entitled to find that the duty had been assumed. They were entitled to conclude that once Fanny became helplessly infirm, as she had by 19 July, the appellants were, in the circumstances, obliged either to summon help or else to care for Fanny themselves.

Re A (Children) (Conjoined Twins: Surgical Separation) [2000] 4 All ER 961

For the facts see Chapter 13 – the court was asked to rule on the legality of an operation to separate conjoined twins. The operation would enable the stronger twin (Jodie) to survive, but would inevitably result in the death of the weaker twin (Mary). Without an operation to separate both twins would die within months. Ward LJ considered the extent to which a failure to permit medical intervention, or a refusal by the doctors to operate might amount to a culpable omission.

Ward LJ: I seem to be the lone voice raising the unpalatable possibility that the doctors and even – though given the horror of their predicament it is anathema to contemplate it – the parents might kill Jodie if they fail to save her life by carrying out the operation to separate her from Mary. Although I recoil at the very notion that these good people could ever be guilty of murder, I am bound to ask why the law will not hold that the doctors and the parents have come under a duty to Jodie. If the operation is in her interests the parents must consent for their duty is to act consistent with her best interests: see Lord Scarman in *Gillick* in the passages I have already set out. I know there is a huge chasm in turpitude between these stricken parents and the wretched parents in *R v Gibbins and Proctor* (1918) 13 Cr App R 134 who starved their child to death. Nevertheless I am bound to wonder whether there is strictly any difference in the application of the principle. They know they can save her. They appreciate she will die if not separated from her twin. Is there any defence to a charge of cruelty under section 1 of the Children and Young Persons Act 1933 in the light of the clarification of the law given by *R v Sheppard* [1981] AC 395 which in turn throws doubt on the correctness of *Oakey v Jackson* [1914] 1 KB 216? Would it not be manslaughter if Jodie died though that neglect? I ask these insensitive questions not to heap blame on the parents. No prosecutor would dream of prosecuting. The sole purpose of the enquiry is to establish whether either or both parents and doctors have come under a legal duty to Jodie, as I conclude they each have, to procure and to carry out the operation which will save her life. If so then performance of their duty to Jodie is irreconcilable with the performance of their duty to Mary. Certainly it seems to me that if this court were to give permission for the operation to take place, then a legal duty would be imposed on the doctors to treat their patient in her best interests, that is, to operate upon her. Failure to do so is a breach of their duty. To omit to act when under a duty to do so may be a culpable omission. Death to Jodie is virtually certain to follow (barring some unforeseen intervention). Why is this not killing Jodie? ...

... The first important feature is that the doctors cannot be denied a right of choice if they are under a duty to choose. They are under a duty to Mary not to operate because it will kill Mary, but they are under a duty to Jodie to operate because not to do so will kill her. It is important to stress that it makes no difference whether the killing is by act or by omission. That is a distinction without a difference: see Lord Lowry in *Bland* at p 877. There are similar opinions in the other speeches. Lord Browne-Wilkinson said at p 885G:

> Finally, the conclusion I have reached will appear to some to be almost irrational. How can it be lawful to allow a patient to die slowly, though painlessly, over a period of weeks from lack of food but unlawful to produce his immediate death by lethal injection, thereby saving his family from yet another ordeal to add to the tragedy that has already struck them? I find it difficult to find a moral answer to that question. But it is undoubtedly the law
>
> ...

Lord Mustill said at p 887C:

> The acute unease which I feel by adopting this way (drawing a crucial distinction between acts and omissions) through the legal and ethical maze is I believe due in an important part to the sensation that however much the terminologies may differ the ethical status of the two courses of action is for all relevant purposes indistinguishable.

The [Archbishop of Westminster, who was permitted to make written submissions] would agree. He tells us that:

> To aim at ending an innocent person's life is just as wrong when one does it by omission as when one does it by a positive act.

Liability for omission based on holding an office

R v Dytham [1979] QB 722 (CA)

[**Lord Widgery CJ** read the following judgment of the court prepared by **Shaw LJ:**] The appellant was a police constable in Lancashire. On 17 March 1977 at about one o'clock in the morning he was on duty in uniform and was standing by a hot-dog stall in Duke Street, St Helens. A Mr Wincke was inside the stall and a Mr Sothern was by it. Some 30 yards away was the entrance to Cindy's Club. A man named Stubbs was ejected from the club by a bouncer. A fight ensued in which a number of men joined. There arose cries and screams and other indications of great violence. Mr Stubbs became the object of a murderous assault. He was beaten and kicked to death in the gutter outside the club. All this was audible and visible to the three men at the hot-dog stall. At no stage did the appellant make any move to intervene or any attempt to quell the disturbance or to stop the attack on the victim. When the hubbub had died down he adjusted his helmet and drove away. According to the other two at the hot-dog stall, he said that he was due off and was going off.

His conduct was brought to the notice of the police authority. As a result he appeared on 10 October 1978 in the Crown Court at Liverpool to answer an indictment which was in these terms:

... the charge against you is one of misconduct of an officer of justice, in that you ... misconducted yourself whilst acting as an officer of justice in that you being present and a witness to a criminal offence, namely a violent assault upon one ... Stubbs by three others deliberately failed to carry out your duty as a police constable by wilfully omitting to take any steps to preserve the Queen's Peace or to protect the person of the said ... Stubbs or to arrest or otherwise bring to justice [his] assailants.

On arraignment the appellant pleaded not guilty and the trial was adjourned to 7 November. On that day before the jury was empanelled counsel for the appellant took an objection to the indictment by way of demurrer. The burden of that objection was that the indictment as laid disclosed no offence known to the law. Neill J ruled against the objection and the trial proceeded. The defence on the facts was that the appellant had observed nothing more than that a man was turned out of the club. It was common ground that in that situation his duty would not have required him to take any action. The jury were directed that the crucial question for their consideration was whether the appellant had seen the attack on the victim. If he had, they could find him guilty of the offence charged in the indictment. The jury did return a verdict of guilty. Hence this appeal which is confined to the matters of law raised by the demurrer pleaded at the court of trial.

At the outset of his submissions in this court counsel for the appellant conceded two matters. The first was that a police constable is a public officer. The second was that there does exist at common law an offence of misconduct in a public office.

From that point the argument was within narrow limits though it ran deep into constitutional and jurisprudential history. The effect of it was that not every failure to discharge a duty which devolved on a person as the holder of a public office gave rise to the common law offence of misconduct in that office. As counsel for the appellant put it, non-feasance was not enough. There must be a malfeasance or at least a misfeasance involving an element of corruption. In support of this contention a number of cases were cited from 18th and 19th century reports. It is the fact that in nearly all of them the misconduct asserted involved some corrupt taint; but this appears to have been an accident of circumstance and not a necessary incident of the offence. Misconduct in a public office is more vividly exhibited where dishonesty is revealed as part of the dereliction of duty. Indeed in some cases the conduct impugned cannot be shown to have been misconduct unless it was done with a corrupt or oblique motive ...

In the present case it was not suggested that the appellant could not have summoned or sought assistance to help the victim or to arrest his assailants. The charge as framed left this answer open to him. Not surprisingly he did not seek to avail himself of it, for the facts spoke strongly against any such answer. The allegation made was not of mere non-feasance but of deliberate failure and wilful neglect. This involves an element of culpability which is not restricted to corruption or dishonesty but which must be of such a degree that the misconduct impugned is calculated to injure the public interest so as to call for condemnation and punishment. Whether such a situation is revealed by the evidence is a matter that a jury has to decide. It puts no heavier burden on them than when in more familiar contexts they are called on to consider whether driving is dangerous or a publication is obscene or a place of public resort is a disorderly house ...

The judge's ruling was correct. The appeal is dismissed.

Liability for omission based on accidentally creating a dangerous situation

R v Miller [1983] 2 AC 161 (HL)

Lord Diplock: My Lords, the facts which give rise to this appeal are sufficiently narrated in the written statement made to the police by the appellant Miller. That statement ... reads:

> Last night I went out for a few drinks and at closing time I went back to the house where I have been kipping for a couple of weeks. I went upstairs into the back bedroom where I've been sleeping. I lay on my mattress and lit a cigarette. I must have fell to sleep because I woke up to find the mattress on fire. I just got up and went into the next room and went back to sleep. Then the next thing I remember was the police and fire people arriving. I hadn't got anything to put the fire out with so I just left it.

He was charged on indictment with the offence of 'arson contrary to s 1(1) and (3) of the Criminal Damage Act 1971'; the particulars of offence were that he:

> on a date unknown between 13 and 16 August 1980 without lawful excuse damaged by fire a house known as No 9, Grantham Road, Sparkbrook, intending to do damage to such property or recklessly as to whether such property would be damaged ...

... [T]he Court of Appeal ... certified that the following question of law of general public importance was involved:

> Whether the *actus reus* of the offence of arson is present when a defendant accidentally starts a fire and thereafter, intending to destroy or damage property belonging to another or being reckless as to whether any such property would be destroyed or damaged, fails to take any steps to extinguish the fire or prevent damage to such property by that fire?

The question speaks of *actus reus*. This expression is derived from Coke's brocard (3 Co Inst ch 1, fo 10), *actus non facit reum, nisi mens sit rea*, by converting incorrectly into an adjective the word reus which was there used correctly in the accusative case as a noun. As long ago as 1889 in *R v Tolson* 23 QBD 168 at 185, [1886–90] All ER Rep 26 at 36–37 Stephen J when dealing with a statutory offence, as are your Lordships in the instant case, condemned the phrase as likely to mislead, though his criticism in that case was primarily directed to the use of the expression *mens rea*. In the instant case, as the argument before this House has in my view demonstrated, it is the use of the expression *actus reus* that is liable to mislead, since it suggests that some positive act on the part of the accused is needed to make him guilty of a crime and that a failure or omission to act is insufficient to give rise to criminal liability unless some express provision in the statute that creates the offence so provides.

My Lords, it would I think be conducive to clarity of analysis of the ingredients of a crime that is created by statute, as are the great majority of criminal offences today, if we were to avoid bad Latin and instead to think and speak (as did Stephen J in those parts of his judgment in *R v Tolson* to which I referred at greater length in *Sweet v Parsley* [1970] AC 132 at 162–63) about the conduct of the accused and his state of mind at the time of that conduct, instead of speaking of *actus reus* and *mens rea*.

The question before your Lordships in this appeal is one that is confined to the true construction of the words used in particular provisions in a particular statute, *viz* s 1(1) and (3) of the Criminal Damage Act 1971. Those particular provisions will fall to be construed in the light of general principles of English criminal law so well established that it is the practice of parliamentary draftsmen to leave them unexpressed in criminal statutes, on the confident assumption that a court of law will treat those principles as intended by Parliament to be applicable to the particular offence unless expressly modified or excluded. But this does not mean that your Lordships are doing any more than construing the particular statutory provisions. These I now set out:

(1) A person who without lawful excuse destroys or damages any property belonging to another intending to destroy or damage any such property or being reckless as to whether any such property would be destroyed or damaged shall be guilty of an offence ...

(3) an offence committed under this section by destroying or damaging property by fire shall be charged as arson.

This definition of arson makes it a 'result-crime' in the classification adopted by Professor Gordon in his work *The Criminal Law of Scotland*, 2nd edn, 1978. The crime is not complete unless and until the conduct of the accused has caused property belonging to another to be destroyed or damaged.

In the instant case property belonging to another, the house, was damaged; it was not destroyed. So in the interest of brevity it will be convenient to refer to damage to property and omit reference to destruction. I should also mention, in parentheses, that in this appeal your Lordships are concerned only with the completed crime of arson, not with related inchoate offences such as attempt or conspiracy to destroy or damage property belonging to another, to which somewhat different considerations will apply. Nor does this appeal raise any question of 'lawful excuse'. None was suggested.

The first question to be answered where a completed crime of arson is charged is: 'Did a physical act of the accused start the fire which spread and damaged property belonging to another (or did his act cause an existing fire, which he had not started but which would otherwise have burnt itself out harmlessly, to spread and damage property belonging to another)?' I have added the words in brackets for completeness. They do not arise in the instant case; in cases where they do, the accused, for the purposes of the analysis which follows, may be regarded as having started a fresh fire.

The first question is a pure question of causation; it is one of fact to be decided by the jury in a trial on indictment. It should be answered 'No' if, in relation to the fire during the period starting immediately before its ignition and ending with its extinction, the role of the accused was at no time more than that of a passive bystander. In such a case the subsequent questions to which I shall be turning would not arise. The conduct of the parabolical priest and Levite on the road to Jericho may have been indeed deplorable, but English law has not so far developed to the stage of treating it as criminal; and if it ever were to do so there would be difficulties in defining what should be the limits of the offence.

If, on the other hand the question, which I now confine to: 'Did a physical act of the accused start the fire which spread and damaged property belonging to another?' is answered 'Yes', as it was by the jury in the instant case, then for the purpose of the further questions the answers to which are determinative of his guilt of the offence of arson, the conduct of the accused, throughout the period from immediately before the moment of ignition to the completion of the damage to the property by the fire, is relevant; so is his state of mind throughout that period.

Since arson is a result-crime the period may be considerable, and during it the conduct of the accused that is causative of the result may consist not only of his doing physical acts which cause the fire to start or spread but also of his failing to take measures that lie within his power to counteract the danger that he has himself created. And if his conduct, active or passive, varies in the course of the period, so may his state of mind at the time of each piece of conduct. If at the time of any particular piece of conduct by the accused that is causative of the result, the state of mind that actuates his conduct falls within the description of one or other of the states of mind that are made a necessary ingredient of the offence of arson by s 1(1) of the Criminal Damage Act 1971 (ie intending to damage property belonging to another or being reckless as to whether such property would be damaged) I know of no principle of English criminal law that would prevent his being guilty of the offence created by that subsection. Likewise I see no rational ground for excluding from conduct capable of giving rise to criminal liability, conduct which consists of failing to take measures that lie within one's power to counteract a danger that one has oneself created, if at the time of such conduct one's state of mind is such as constitutes a necessary ingredient of the offence. I venture to think that the habit of lawyers to talk of *actus reus*, suggestive as it is of action rather than inaction, is responsible for any erroneous notion that failure to act cannot give rise to criminal liability in English law.

No one has been bold enough to suggest that if, in the instant case, the accused had been aware at the time that he dropped the cigarette that it would probably set fire to his mattress and yet had taken no steps to extinguish it he would not have been guilty of the offence of arson, since he would have damaged property of another being reckless whether any such property would be damaged.

I cannot see any good reason why, so far as liability under criminal law is concerned, it should matter at what point of time before the resultant damage is complete a person becomes aware that he has done a physical act which, whether or not he appreciated that it would at the time when he did it, does in fact create a risk that property of another will be damaged; provided that, at the moment of awareness, it lies within his power to take steps, either himself or by calling for the assistance of the fire brigade if this be necessary, to prevent or minimise the damage to the property at risk.

Let me take first the case of the person who has thrown away a lighted cigarette expecting it to go out harmlessly, but later becomes aware that, although he did not intend it to do so, it has, in the event, caused some inflammable material to smoulder and that unless the smouldering is extinguished promptly, an act that the person who dropped the cigarette could perform without danger to himself or difficulty, the inflammable material will be likely to burst into flames and damage some other person's property. The person who dropped the cigarette deliberately refrains from doing anything to extinguish the smouldering. His reason for so refraining is that he intends that the risk which his own act had originally created, though it was only subsequently that he became aware of this, should fructify in actual damage to that other person's property; and what he so intends, in fact occurs. There can be no sensible reason why he should not be guilty of arson. If he would be guilty of arson, having appreciated the risk of damage at the very moment of dropping the lighted cigarette, it would be quite irrational that he should not be guilty if he first appreciated the risk at some later point in time but when it was still possible for him to take steps to prevent or minimise the damage.

In that example the state of mind involved was that described in the definition of the statutory offence as 'intending' to damage property belonging to another. This state of mind necessarily connotes an appreciation by the accused that the situation that he has by his own act created involves the risk that property belonging to another will be damaged. This is not necessarily so with the other state of mind, described in the definition of the statutory offence as 'being reckless as to whether any such property would be damaged'. To this other state of mind I now turn; it is the state of mind which is directly involved in the instant case. Where the state of mind relied on by the prosecution is that of 'intending', the risk of damage to property belonging to another created by the physical act of the accused need not be such as would be obvious to anyone who took the trouble to give his mind to it; but the accused himself cannot form the intention that it should fructify in actual damage unless he himself recognises the existence of some risk of this happening. In contrast to this, where the state of mind relied on is 'being reckless', the risk created by the physical act of the accused that property belonging to another would be damaged must be one that would be obvious to anyone who had given his mind to it at whatever is the relevant time for determining whether the state of mind of the accused fitted the description 'being reckless whether such property would be damaged': see *R v Caldwell* [1982] AC 341, 352; see also *R v Lawrence* [1982] AC 510 at 526 for a similar requirement in the mental element in the statutory offence of reckless driving.

In *R v Caldwell* this House was concerned with what was treated throughout as being a single act of the accused, viz starting a fire in the ground floor room of a residential hotel which caused some damage to it; although, if closer analysis of his conduct, as distinct from his state of mind, had been relevant, what he did must have been recognised as consisting of a series of successive acts. Throughout that sequence of acts, however, the state of mind of Caldwell remained unchanged, his acknowledged intention was to damage the hotel and to revenge himself on its owner, and he pleaded guilty to an offence under s 1(1) of the 1971 Act; the question at issue in the appeal was whether in carrying out this avowed intention he was reckless whether the life of another would be thereby endangered, so as to make him guilty also of the more serious offence under s 1(2). This House did not have to consider the case of an accused who although he becomes aware that, as the result of an initial act of his own, events have occurred that present an obvious risk that property belonging to another will be damaged, only becomes aware of this at some time after he has done the initial act. So the precise language suggested in *Caldwell* as appropriate in summing up to a jury in the ordinary run of cases under s 1(1) of the Criminal Damage Act 1971 requires some slight adaptation to make it applicable to the particular and unusual facts of the instant case.

My Lords, just as in the first example that I took the fact that the accused's intent to damage the property of another was not formed until, as a result of his initial act in dropping the cigarette, events had occurred which presented a risk that another person's property would be damaged, ought not under any sensible system of law to absolve him from criminal liability, so too in a case where the relevant state of mind is not intent but recklessness I see no reason in common sense and justice why, *mutatis mutandis*, a similar principle should not apply to impose criminal liability on him. If in the former case he is criminally liable because he refrains from taking steps that are open to him to try to prevent or minimise the damage caused by the risk he has himself created and he so refrains because he intends such damage to occur, so in the latter case, when, as a result of his own initial act in dropping the cigarette, events have occurred which would have made it obvious to anyone who troubled to give his mind to them that they presented a risk that another person's property would be damaged, he should likewise be criminally liable if he refrains from taking steps that lie within his power to try and prevent the damage caused by the risk that he himself has created, and so refrains either because he has not given any thought to the possibility of there being any such risk or because, although he has recognised that there was some risk involved, he has nonetheless decided to take that risk.

My Lords, in the instant case the prosecution did not rely on the state of mind of the accused as being reckless during that part of his conduct that consisted of his lighting and smoking a cigarette while lying on his mattress and falling asleep without extinguishing it. So the jury were not invited to make any finding as to this. What the prosecution did rely on as being reckless was his state of mind during that part of his conduct after he awoke to find that he had set his mattress on fire and that it was smouldering, but did not then take any steps either to try to extinguish it himself or to send for the fire brigade, but simply went into the other room to resume his slumbers, leaving the fire from the already smouldering mattress to spread and to damage that part of the house in which the mattress was.

The recorder, in his lucid summing up to the jury (they took 22 minutes only to reach their verdict), told them that the accused, having by his own act started a fire in the mattress which, when he became aware of its existence, presented an obvious risk of damaging the house, became under a duty to take some action to put it out. The Court of Appeal upheld the conviction, but its *ratio decidendi* appears to be somewhat different from that of the recorder. As I understand the judgment, in effect it treats the whole course of conduct of the accused, from the moment at which he fell asleep and dropped the cigarette onto the mattress until the time the damage to the house by fire was complete, as a continuous act of the accused, and holds that it is sufficient to constitute the statutory offence of arson if at any stage in that course of conduct the state of mind of the accused, when he fails to try to prevent or minimise the damage which will result from his initial act, although it lies within his power to do so, is that of being reckless whether property belonging to another would be damaged.

My Lords, these alternative ways of analysing the legal theory that justifies a decision which has received nothing but commendation for its accord with common sense and justice have, since the publication of the judgment of the Court of Appeal in the instant case, provoked academic controversy. Each theory has distinguished support. Professor J C Smith espouses the 'duty theory' (see [1982] Crim LR 526 at 528); Professor Glanville Williams who, after the decision of the Divisional Court in *Fagan v Metropolitan Police Comr* [1969] 1 QB 439 appears to have been attracted by the duty theory, now prefers that of the continuous act (see [1992] Crim LR 773). When applied to cases where a person has unknowingly done an act which sets in train events that, when he becomes aware of them, present an obvious risk that property belonging to another will be damaged, both theories lead to an identical result; and, since what your Lordships are concerned with is to give guidance to trial judges in their task of summing up to juries, I would for this purpose adopt the duty theory as being the easier to explain to a jury; though I would commend the use of the word 'responsibility', rather than 'duty' which is more appropriate to civil than to criminal law since it suggests an obligation owed to another person, ie the person to whom the endangered property belongs, whereas a criminal statute defines combinations of conduct and state of mind which render a person liable to punishment by the state itself.

While in the general run of cases of destruction or damage to property belonging to another by fire (or other means) where the prosecution relies on the recklessness of the accused, the direction recommended by this House in *R v Caldwell* [1982] AC 341 is appropriate, in the exceptional case, (which is most likely to be one of arson and of which the instant appeal affords a striking example) where the accused is initially unaware that he has done an act that in fact sets in train events which, by the time the accused becomes aware of them, would make it obvious to anyone who troubled to give his mind to them that they present a risk that property belonging to another would be damaged, a suitable direction to the jury would be: that the accused is guilty of the offence under s 1(1) of the Criminal Damage Act 1971 if, when he does become aware that the events in question have happened as a result of his own act, he does not try to prevent or reduce the risk of damage by his own efforts or if necessary by sending for help from the fire brigade and the reason why he does not is either because he has not given any thought to the possibility of there being any such risk or because having recognised that there was some risk involved he has decided not to try to prevent or reduce it.

So, while deprecating the use of the expression *actus reus* in the certified question, I would answer that question 'Yes' and would dismiss the appeal.

Lord Keith of Kinkel, Lord Bridge of Harwich, Lord Brandon of Oakwood and **Lord Brightman** all agreed with Lord Diplock.

Where the defendant is absolved from any duty

R v Smith [1979] Crim LR 251 (Birmingham Crown Court)

The deceased had a medical condition which gave her a ' blown-up ' appearance, and had given her a marked aversion to doctors and medical treatment. After the birth of her first child she declared that she would not go into hospital again, and so she deceived both her GP and her family as to both the date her second child was due and the medical arrangements for the birth. The child was delivered at home by S, her husband. She concealed her third pregnancy from everyone until 22 December 1977, when she told S that it was due at the end of January. She commenced labour in the early morning of December 28, and S delivered the child, which was still-born. The body was secreted by S and the deceased in a cupboard. After the birth the deceased was unwell and S looked after her – both falsely told the deceased's mother that she was receiving medical attention. S wanted to call a doctor, but the deceased would not allow him to do so till Saturday 31 December. He did not tell the receptionist at the surgery of the full circumstances of the illness and the doctor did not come.

In the afternoon of the same day S phoned again. A locum called, but the deceased died of puerperal fever before he arrived. Medical evidence was that she could have been saved had a doctor been called before that Saturday.

S was charged with (1) manslaughter of his wife on 31 December; (2) concealment of birth on 28 December. On the second count his defence was that they did not intend to conceal the birth permanently but would have told the police when they felt up to it. The judge directed the jury that this amounted to a defence to the charge. The judge in his summing-up directed that it had to be proved that in reckless disregard of his duty to care for the deceased's health, S failed to get medical attention, and that as a direct result of that failure she died.

'Reckless disregard' meant that, fully appreciating that she was so ill that there was a real risk to her health if she did not get help, S did not do so, either because he was indifferent, or because he deliberately ran a wholly unjustified and unreasonable risk. It was accepted that he was not indifferent – the evidence was that they were a devoted couple and that he stayed with her all the time when she was ill. It was also accepted that she did not want a doctor called, and the jury had to balance the weight that it was right to give to this wish against her capacity to make rational decisions. In addition it had been proved that the 'reckless disregard' led to the death and that had S acted differently on 31 December, his wife's life would have been saved.

The jury convicted on the second count but could not agree on the charge of manslaughter and were discharged from giving a verdict.

Airedale National Health Service Trust v Bland [1993] 1 All ER 82 (HL)

Anthony Bland was injured in the Hillsborough Stadium disaster. He suffered irreversible brain damage and was diagnosed as being in a persistent vegetative state (PVS). Expert medical evidence was to the effect that there was no hope of recovery. The Airedale NHS Trust, with the support of Bland's parents, sought a declaration that the doctors treating Bland might lawfully discontinue all life-sustaining treatment and medical treatment except that required to enable Bland to die without unnecessary distress. The Official Solicitor appealed to the House of Lords against the granting of the declaration on the basis that the withdrawal of life support treatment would amount to murder.

> **Lord Goff:** I agree that the doctor's conduct in discontinuing life support can properly be categorised as an omission It is true that it may be difficult to describe what the doctor actually, does as an omission, for example where he takes some positive step to bring the life support to an end. But discontinuation of life support is, for present purposes, no different from not initiating life support in the first place. in each case, the doctor is simply allowing his patient to die in the sense that lie is desisting from taking a step which might, in certain circumstances, prevent his patient front dying as a result of his pre-existing condition: and as a matter of

general principle an omission such as this will not be unlawful unless it constitutes a breach of duty to the patient. I also agree that the doctor's conduct is to be differentiated from that of, for example, an interloper who maliciously switches off a life support machine because, although the interloper may perform exactly the same act as the doctor who discontinues life support, his doing so constitutes interference with the life-prolonging treatment then being administered by the doctor. Accordingly, whereas the doctor, in discontinuing life support, is simply allowing his patient to die of his pre-existing condition, the interloper is actively intervening to stop the doctor from prolonging the patient's life, and such conduct cannot possibly he categorised as an omission ... If the justification for treating a patient who lacks tile capacity to consent lies in the fact that the treatment is provided in his best interests, it must follow that the treatment may, and indeed ultimately should, be discontinued where it is no longer in his best interests to provide it. The question which lies at the heart of the present case is, as I see it, whether on that principle the doctors responsible for the treatment and care of Anthony Bland can justifiably discontinue the process of artificial feeding upon which the prolongation of his life depends.

It is crucial for the understanding of this question that the question itself should he correctly formulated. The question is not whether the doctor should take a course which will kill his patient, or even take a course which has the effect of accelerating his death. The question is whether the doctor should or should not continue to provide his patient with medical treatment or care which, if continued, will prolong his patient's life. The question is sometimes put in striking or emotional terms, which can be misleading. For example, in the case of a life support system, it is sometimes asked: should a doctor be entitled to switch it off, or to pull the plug? And then it is asked: can it be in the best interests of the patient that a doctor should be able to switch the life support system off, when this will inevitably result in the patient's death? Such an approach has rightly been criticised as misleading ... This is because the question is not whether it is in the best interests of the patient that he should die. The question is whether it is in the best interests of the patient that his life should be prolonged by the continuance of this form of medical treatment or care.

The correct formulation of the question is of particular importance in a case such as the present, where the patient is totally unconscious and where there is nô hope whatsoever of any amelioration of his condition. In circumstances such as these, it may be difficult to say that it is in his best interests that the treatment should be ended. But, if the question is asked, as in my opinion it should be, whether it is in his best interests that treatment which has the effect of artificially prolonging his life should be continued, that question can sensibly be answered to the effect that it is not in his best interests to do so.

Lord Mustill: I turn to an argument which in my judgment is logically defensible and consistent with the existing law. In essence it turns the previous argument on its head by directing the inquiry to the interests of the patient, not in the termination of life but in the continuation of his treatment. It runs as follows. (i) The cessation of nourishment and hydration is an omission not an act. (ii) Accordingly, the cessation will not be a criminal act unless the doctors are under a present duty to continue the regime. (iii) At the time when Anthony Bland came into the care of the doctors decisions had to be made about his care which he was unable to make for himself ... Since the possibility that he might recover still existed his best interests required that he should be supported in the hope that this would happen. These best interests justified the application of the necessary regime without his consent. (iv) All hope of recovery has now been abandoned. Thus, although the termination of his life is not in the best interests of Anthony Bland, his best interests in being kept alive have also disappeared, taking with them the justification for the non-consensual regime and the correlative duty to keep it in being. (v) Since there is no longer a duty to provide nourishment and hydration a failure to do so cannot be a criminal offence.

My Lords, I must recognise at once that this chain of reasoning makes an unpromising start by transferring the morally and intellectually dubious distinction between acts and omissions into a context where the ethical foundations of the law are already open to question. The opportunity for anomaly and excessively fine distinctions, often depending more on the way in which the problem happens to be stated than on any real distinguishing features, has been exposed by many commentators ... All this being granted, we are still forced to take the law as we find it and try to make it work. Moreover, although in cases near the borderline the categorisation of conduct will be exceedingly hard, I believe that nearer the periphery there will be many instances which fall quite clearly into one category rather than the other ... I therefore consider the argument to be soundly based. Now that the time has come when Anthony Bland has no further interest in being kept alive, the necessity to do so, created by his inability to make a choice, has gone; and the justification for the invasive care and treatment together with the duty to provide it have also gone. Absent a duty, the omission to perform what had previously been a duty will no longer be a breach of the criminal law.

Lord Keith, Lord Lowry and **Lord Browne-Wilkinson** all concurred that the appeal should be dismissed.

Notes and queries

1   To what extent did the court in *Smith* proceed on the basis that the defendant was under no duty to summon assistance for his wife provided she was capable of making a rational decision regarding medical treatment for herself? Does this mean that the duty arises once she ceases to be capable of rational judgment? If, by that point, she has suffered irreparable harm in the sense that medical treatment will not avail her, and the defendant fails to summon help, can it be said that his omission is the cause of her death?

CODIFICATION AND LAW REFORM PROPOSALS

The Criminal Code team's draft Code of 1985 did contain a codification of the law relating to criminal liability for omissions, but these provisions were eventually excluded from the Law Commission's draft Code Bill published in 1989. Clause 17 of the 1989 Bill does, however, make clear that results may be caused by omission. As the commentary to the Bill explains:

> The ... Bill therefore defines homicide offences in terms of causing death rather than of killing ; and other offences against the person similarly require the causing

of relevant harms. It seems to us to be desirable to draft some other offences at least (most obviously, offences of damage to property) in the same way, in order to leave fully open to the courts the possibility of so construing the relevant (statutory) provisions as to impose liability for omissions. For to prefer 'cause death' to 'kill' while retaining 'destroy or damage property' might be taken to imply an intention to exclude all liability for omissions in the latter case [Vol II, para 7.13].

In its report *Legislating the Criminal Code* (Law Com 218), the Law Commission extend this approach to its proposals for a number of non-fatal offences against the person, clause 19(1) of the Bill contained in that report stating that:

An offence to which this section applies may be committed by a person who, with the result specified for the offence, omits to do an act that he is under a duty to do at common law. Where this section applies to an offence a person may commit an offence if, with the result specified for the offence, he omits to do an act that he is under a duty to do at common law; and accordingly references to acts include references to omissions.

The issue of whether or not a duty arose would remain to be determined by the common law. The *Miller* principle is codified with some amendments by cl 31 of the Draft Criminal Law Bill as follows:

Where it is an offence to be at fault in causing a result, a person who lacks the fault required when he does an act that may cause, or does cause, the result, he nevertheless commits the offence if being aware that he has done the act and that the result may occur or, as the case may be, has occurred and may continue, and with the fault required, he fails to take reasonable steps to prevent the result occurring or continuing and it does occur or continue.

The commentary on this provision indicates that D would be under a duty to take measures that lie within his power to counteract the danger he has inadvertently created – see Law Com 218, para 41.3. The Home Office draft Offences Against the Person Bill also contains a similar measure in clause 16 as regards the commission of the offences provided for in that Bill.

Further reading

G Williams, 'What should the Code do about omissions' (1987) 7 Legal Studies 92

A Ashworth, 'The scope of criminal liability for omission' (1989) 105 LQR 424

G Williams, 'Criminal omissions – the conventional view' (1991) 107 LQR 86

A Smart, 'Criminal responsibility for failing to do the impossible' (1987) 103 LQR 532

CHAPTER 3

CAUSATION

Some criminal offences, such as murder and wounding, are referred to as 'result crimes' on the basis that establishing the *actus reus* involves proof that the defendant caused the prohibited result (that is, the death of the victim, or the wounding) both as a matter of fact and as a matter of law. In effect the prosecution must establish a chain of causation between the defendant's act (or in some cases omission) and the prohibited consequence. As will be seen, it may be possible for a defendant to provide evidence that the chain of causation has been broken by a *novus actus interveniens* (new intervening act), in which case liability for the completed crime cannot be established, although the defendant might still bear liability for having attempted to commit the offence; see further Chapter 12. The majority of case extracts in this chapter are drawn from cases that involve defendants charged with murder or manslaughter. This is not surprising given that homicide cases are likely to throw up interesting and novel problems of causation. It should be borne in mind, however, that the general principles of causation enunciated by the courts are of application to the vast majority of result crimes.

CAUSATION IN FACT

The first step in establishing a chain of causation is for the prosecution to prove that the defendant's act or omission is a cause in fact of the prohibited result. This is normally done by applying the 'but for' test. The question asked is: 'But for the defendant's act or omission would the result have occurred?' If the answer is 'no' causation in fact is established. If the answer is 'yes', it means that the result would have occurred in any event – thus the defendant's act or omission was not a cause in fact of the result.

R v White [1908–10] All ER Rep 340 (CA)

The defendant placed poison in his mother's drink. She was found dead on the sofa a little later. The expert evidence revealed that she had died from some external cause such as fright or heart failure before the poison could take effect. The defendant was convicted of attempted murder and appealed unsuccessfully against his conviction.

> **Bray J**: [The defendant] ... therefore, perfectly well knew the deadly character of this poison, and supposed that a very small quantity would produce an instant effect. Upon consideration of all the evidence, including the denial of the prisoner that he had put anything into the wine glass at all, we are of opinion that there was sufficient evidence to warrant the jury also in coming to the conclusion that the appellant put the cyanide in the glass with intent to murder his mother.

The next point made was that, if he put it there with that intent, there was no attempt at murder; that the jury must have acted upon a suggestion of the learned judge in his summing tip that this was one, the first or some later, of a series of doses which he intended to administer and so cause her death by slow poisoning, and if they did act on that suggestion there was no attempt at murder, because the act of which he was guilty – the putting of poison in the wine glass – was a completed act and could not be and was not intended by the appellant to have the effect of killing her at once. It could not kill unless it were followed by other acts which he might never have done. There seems no doubt that the learned judge in effect did tell the jury that, if this was a case of slow poisoning, the appellant would be guilty of the attempt to murder. We are of opinion that this direction was right, and that the completion or attempted completion of one of a series of acts intended by a man to result in killing is an attempt to murder even although this completed act would not, unless followed by the other acts, result in killing. it might be the beginning of the attempt, but would none the less be an attempt. While saying this, we must say also that we do not think it likely the jury acted on this suggestion, because there was nothing to show that the administration of small doses of cyanide of potassium, to the would have a cumulative effect; we think it much more likely, having regard statement made by the prisoner to the witness Carden, that the appellant supposed he had put sufficient poison in the glass to kill her. This, of course, would be an attempt to murder ...

CAUSATION IN LAW: BASIC PRINCIPLES

Whether or not the defendant has caused the prohibited result as a matter of law is a question that will be determined by the jury in the light of the trial judge's directions as to the relevant law. In the vast majority of cases no specific direction is required. It will be sufficient for the prosecution to show that the defendant's act was more than a merely negligible cause of the prohibited result. As the following case extracts indicate that are a number of ways in which the basic approach to causation in law can be expressed. It would normally be legitimate to ask whether the prohibited result was a reasonably foreseeable consequence of the defendant's act or omission. Alternatively, where there is evidence to suggest that there might have been a *novus actus interveniens*, the courts have endorsed an approach that involves asking whether or not the defendant's act or omission was the operating and substantial cause of the prohibited consequence.

R v Notman [1994] Crim LR 518 (CA)

Facts: The defendant was acquitted of affray and convicted of assault occasioning actual bodily harm. The defendant and others entered a shop from which he had been banned and created a disturbance. A police officer arrived and the defendant charged at him. The officer moved out of the way and put out his leg to stop the defendant, thereby sustaining an injury to his ankle. The recorder directed the jury that the conduct of the defendant must have been a substantial cause of the officer's injury for them to convict. It was argued on appeal that the recorder should not have used the expression 'a substantial cause', but should have directed the jury in accordance with the test in *Roberts* (1971) 56 Cr App R 95.

Held:

(1) The case was on all fours with *Hennigan* (considered below). In that case it was said that the expression 'a substantial cause' was convenient to indicate to the jury that the cause must have been more than just *de minimis*, which was the only necessary qualification. It also avoided the necessity to go into the details of legal causation and remoteness.

(2) The test set out in *Roberts* (considered below: was the injury the natural result of what the assailant said and did, in the sense that it was something that could reasonably have been foreseen as the consequence of what he was saying and doing?) did not invalidate the simple direction given by the trial judge in that case (was the harm 'as a result' of the assailant's act?). The test in *Roberts* is not one always to be applied and about which there should always be a direction.

What constitutes a 'substantial' cause?

R v Hennigan [1971] 3 All ER 133 (CA)

Lord Parker CJ: ... In view of the point that is made, it is really unnecessary to go into the facts in full in this case. Quite shortly what happened was that a Mrs Lowe driving a Vauxhall car with two passengers was emerging from a road called Old Road in order to cross the Wigan to Ashton Road and go into Nicol Road opposite. Old Road and Nicol Road were minor roads and indeed there was a 'Give way' sign where Mrs Lowe was approaching. The evidence was that she stopped at the entrance and then moved forward, and her evidence was that she had looked to her left towards Wigan and that the only traffic that she saw was a long way down by a railway bridge. However, she had only just got astride the middle of the road when a Ford Cortina driven by the appellant from Wigan towards Ashton crashed into her broadside and unfortunately as a result Mrs Lowe's two passengers were killed.

There was a considerable body of evidence that the appellant was driving at a fast speed; the estimates went up to 80 miles an hour, and almost immediately before the accident he appears to have overtaken a Jaguar, regaining his side of the road and then crashing into Mrs Lowe's car. It at once occurs to one that if this was a civil action, Mrs Lowe might be held substantially to blame, emerging from a minor road, because she clearly was at fault; on the other hand the appellant in a restricted area at night – it was 11.00 pm – was clearly going too fast, and dangerously too fast.

The trouble that has arisen in this case is in regard to a direction that the judge gave when the jury, after retirement, came back and asked a question. In the course of the summing up he told the jury that it must be shown that the appellant's manner of driving caused the collision and that the collision caused the death. He said this:

It is admitted by the defence here very properly that the death of both Mr Twiss and Miss Twiss was the result of the collision, so the only issue you have to try is whether it is established, first of all, that the manner of his driving his car was dangerous, and, second, if it was, that that dangerous driving on his part was a substantial cause of the collision which is admitted resulted in the death of those two people.

A little later he said addressing the jury:

You then say: 'If I think it was dangerous was it a substantial cause – not necessarily the whole cause – was it a substantial cause of the collision which caused the death?'

Then as I said the jury returned for a further direction, and they had probably been considering this from the point of view of blameworthiness as in a civil action. They asked: 'We would like further guidance on what you mean by "substantial", my Lord.' The judge then said:

'Substantial' means that it is not a remote cause of the death, but it is an appreciable cause of the death. It is rather like this: in a collision between two motor cars there may be both drivers each 50% to blame, and each would be a substantial cause of the collision. If on the other hand you get a situation where you can say that one of the drivers was four-fifths to blame and the other was one-fifth, you can say: 'I don't regard one-fifth as being a substantial cause of the accident; if it is as low as that then the fellow who really caused the accident was the one who is four-fifths to blame'. It is hard to define, but it means the real cause as opposed to being a minimal cause. Do you follow me? Would you like to retire again?

Then the foreman, clearly indicating what was in his mind, said: 'There is some doubt as to whether we can apportion blame'. The trial judge quite rightly said:

You have only one man before you, and you are not concerned in any civil claim or with compensation. All you have to find is whether [the appellant] in your charge, was guilty of dangerous driving which was a substantial cause of the death of these two people, and I hope I have explained 'substantial' to you effectively.

What is said, as the court understands it, is that that conveyed the impression to the jury that they could find the appellant guilty if he was only little more than one-fifth to blame. The court would like to emphasise this, that there is of course nothing in s 1 of the Road Traffic Act 1960 which requires the manner of the driving to be a substantial cause, or a major cause, or any other description of cause, of the accident. So long as the dangerous driving is a cause and something more than *de minimis*, the statute operates. What has happened in the past is that judges have found it convenient to direct the jury in the form that it must be, as in one case it was put, the substantial cause ...

Although the word does not appear in the statute, it is clearly a convenient word to use to indicate to the jury that it must be something more than *de minimis*, and also to avoid possibly having to go into details of legal causation, remoteness and the like. That appears from the further direction of the trial judge, who in terms said that it must not be remote, and that it must be a real cause as opposed to being a minimal cause. It is perhaps unfortunate that he dealt with the matter in the illustration he gave on the basis of apportioning blame, but when one analyses it, it is quite clear that the direction, if anything, was much too favourable to the appellant in that the court is quite satisfied that even if he was in this case only one-fifth to blame, he was a cause of the death of these two people. In these circumstances the appeal is dismissed.

R v Cato and Others [1976] 1 WLR 110 (CA)

Lord Widgery CJ: ... The victim, as I have said, was a young man called Anthony Farmer. The events leading up to his death occurred on 25 July 1974. On that day Cato and Farmer had been in each other's company for most of the day. The evidence suggests certain intervals when they were apart, but by and large they seem to have been together all that day, and they spent much of the day with Morris and Dudley as well. All four of them at that time were living at a house called 34 Russell Street, and on 25 July their activities brought them to the Crown public house where they were until closing time, and after closing time they went back to 34 Russell Street.

There were others living in the house. They went to bed, and the four (that is to say, Cato, Morris, Dudley and the deceased Farmer) remained downstairs for a time. The moment came when Farmer produced a bag of white powder and some syringes and invited the others to have a 'fix' with him; and so they did. The white powder was put in its bag on the mantelpiece, the syringes were distributed amongst the four who were to participate, and the procedure which they adopted (which may or may not be a common one) was to pair off so that each could do the actual act of injection into the other half of his pair. Following this procedure Morris and Dudley paired off together and so did Cato and Farmer (the deceased). All four had a number of injections following this procedure, but the time came when Dudley and Morris went to bed, leaving Cato and Farmer downstairs in the sitting room. Cato and Farmer continued to give each other these injections from time to time right through the night.

The actual method, which I have probably described sufficiently already, may deserve a moment's repetition because so much hinges on it. The method, as I have already indicated, was that each would take his own syringe. He would fill it to his own taste with whatever mixture of powder and water he thought proper. He would then give his syringe to the other half of his pair – in this case Farmer would give his syringe to Cato – and the other half of the pair would conduct the actual act of injection. It is important to notice that the strength of the mixture to be used was entirely dictated by the person who was to receive it because he prepared his own syringe; but it is also to be noticed that the actual act of injection was done by the other half of the pair, which of course has a very important influence on this case when one comes to causation.

When the following morning came Farmer and Cato were still downstairs. They were apparently fast asleep, although everybody thought they were well enough at 8 am when they were seen. But as the next hour or two passed it became apparent that they were both in difficulties. Cato indeed was having difficulty in breathing, and probably his life was saved only because somebody gave him some rudimentary first aid. No one was able to do the same for Farmer, and by 11 am Farmer was dead. The cause of death was that his respiratory system ceased to function consequent on intoxication from drugs ... Of course behind the whole question of the sufficiency of evidence of causation is the fact that it was not necessary for the prosecution to prove that the heroin was the only cause. As a matter of law, it was sufficient if the prosecution could establish that it was a cause, provided it was a cause outside the *de minimis* range, and effectively bearing on the acceleration of the moment of the victim's death.

When one has that in mind it is, we think, really possible to say if the jury had been directed to look for heroin as a cause, not *de minimis* but a cause of substance, and they came back with a verdict of not guilty, the verdict could really be described as a perverse one. The whole background of the evidence was the other way and there certainly was ample evidence, given a proper direction, on which a charge of manslaughter could be supported.

But what about the proper direction? It will be noted that in none of the versions which I have quoted of the judge's direction on this point, nor in any of those which I have not quoted which appear in the summing up, is there any reference to it being necessary for the cause to be a substantial one. It is said in clear terms in one of the six questions that the jury can consider whether the administration of the heroin was a cause or contributed to or accelerated the death, and in precise terms the word 'contributed' is not qualified to show that a substantial contribution is required.

Counsel for Cato, whose eagle eye misses nothing, sees here, and seeks to exploit here, what is a misdirection on the part of the trial judge. In other words, taking the judge's words literally, it would be possible for the jury to bring in a verdict of guilty of manslaughter even though the contribution was not of substance.

Before pursuing that, it is worth reminding oneself that some of the more recent *dicta* in the textbooks about this point do not support as strongly as was once the case the theory that the contribution must be substantial.

In Smith and Hogan, *Criminal Law*, 3rd edn, 1973, p 217 there is this rather interesting extract:

> It is commonly said by judges and writers that, while the accused's act need not be the sole cause of the death, it must be a substantial cause. This appears to mean only that a minute contribution to the cause of death will not entail responsibility. It may therefore be misleading to direct a jury that D is not liable unless his conduct was a 'substantial' cause. Killing is merely an acceleration of death and factors which produce a very trivial acceleration will be ignored.

Whether that be so or not, and we do not propose to give that passage the court's blessing today at all events, if one looks at the circumstances of the present case with any real sense of reality, we think there can be no doubt that when the judge was talking about contribution the jury knew perfectly well that he was talking about something more than the mere *de minimis* contribution. We have given this point particular care in our consideration of the case because it worried us to some extent originally, but we do feel in the end, having looked at all the circumstances, that there could not have been any question in this case of the jury making the mistake of thinking that the contribution would suffice if it were *de minimis*. Therefore in our judgment there is no substance in the attack of counsel for Cato on the basis of causation, whether it be an attack on the available evidence or on the trial judge's treatment of that evidence ...

R v Kimsey [1996] Crim LR 35 (CA)

Facts: The appellant was convicted of causing death by dangerous driving. A close friend of the appellant overtook him and the two engaged in a high-speed chase with the appellant driving a few feet from the rear of his friend's car. Both cars had just overtaken another car at 75 mph, when the friend's car swerved on to the verge. The prosecution evidence was that the appellant overtook his friend at that point and struck her car, either because she swerved back to the right, or because he pulled to the left as he overtook. The friend, not in control of her car, struck an oncoming car, and was killed. One of her tyres was underinflated, which could have led to the car being difficult to control. The appellant's case was that the friend had lost control before his car hit hers and the first collision did not have any effect on her loss of control, which in turn led to the second, fatal collision. The prosecution case was that the appellant's driving had caused the friend's loss of control and the first collision, which in turn led to the fatal collision, or alternatively that his driving encouraged her to drive too fast and lose control; or that by driving so closely behind, when she did lose control, the first collision occurred, occasioning further loss of control. The recorder told the jury that they did not have to be sure that the appellant's driving 'was the principal, or a substantial, cause of the death, as long as you are sure that it was a cause and that there was something more than a slight or a trifling link'.

On appeal, it was argued that it was wrong to say that the cause did not have to be a substantial cause.

Held, dismissing the appeal, that the test in *Hennigan* (1971) 55 Cr App R 262 was whether the contribution of the dangerous driving to the death was more than minute. To use the expression 'a substantial cause' is no doubt a convenient way of putting the test to the jury, as was suggested in that case. But the jury may well give the word 'substantial' a larger meaning. The recorder's reference to a 'slight or trifling link' was a permissible and useful way to avoid the term de minimis. His direction was faithful to the logic of *Hennigan*.

NOVUS ACTUS INTERVENIENS – CAN THE CHAIN OF CAUSATION BE BROKEN BY THE ACTIONS OF THE VICTIM?

Refusing medical treatment

R v Blaue [1975] 1 WLR 1411 (CA)

Lawton LJ: ... The victim was a young girl aged 18. She was a Jehovah's Witness. She professed the tenets of that sect and lived her life by them. During the late afternoon of 3 May 1974 the appellant came into her house and asked her for sexual intercourse. She refused. He then attacked her with a knife inflicting four serious wounds. One pierced her lung. The appellant ran away. The girl staggered out into the road. She collapsed outside a neighbour's house. An ambulance took her to hospital, where she arrived at about 7.30 pm. Soon afterwards she was admitted to the intensive care ward. At about 8.30 pm she was examined by the surgical registrar who quickly decided that serious injury had been caused which would require surgery. As she had lost a lot of blood, before there could be an operation there would have to be a blood transfusion. As soon as the girl appreciated that the surgeon was thinking of organising a blood transfusion for her, she said that she should not be given one and that she would not have one. To have one, she said, would be contrary to her religious beliefs as a Jehovah's Witness. She was told that if she did not have a blood transfusion she would die. She said that she did not care if she did die. She was asked to acknowledge in writing that she had refused to have a blood transfusion under any circumstances. She did so. The Crown admitted at the trial that had she had a blood transfusion when advised to have one she would not have died. She did so at 12.45 am the next day. The evidence called by the Crown proved that at all relevant times she was conscious and decided as she did deliberately, and knowing what the consequences of her decision would be. In his final speech to the jury, counsel for the Crown accepted that the girl's refusal to have a blood transfusion was a cause of her death. The prosecution did not challenge the defence evidence that the appellant was suffering from diminished responsibility.

Towards the end of the trial and before the summing up started counsel on both sides made submissions as to how the case should be put to the jury. Counsel then appearing for the appellant invited the judge to direct the jury to acquit the appellant generally on the count of murder. His argument was that the girl's refusal to have a blood transfusion had broken the chain of causation between the stabbing and her death. As an alternative he submitted that the jury should be left to decide whether the chain of causation had been broken. Counsel for the Crown submitted that the judge should direct the jury to convict, because no facts were in issue and when the law was applied to the facts there was only one possible verdict, ie manslaughter by reason of diminished responsibility ...

There have been two cases in recent years which have some bearing on this topic: *R v Jordan* (1956) 40 Cr App R 152 and *R v Smith* [1959] 2 QB 35 ... We share Lord Parker CJ's opinion in Smith that Jordan should be regarded as a case decided on its own special facts and not as an authority relaxing the common law approach to causation ...

The physical cause of death in this case was bleeding into the pleural cavity arising from the penetration of the lung. This had not been brought about by any decision made by the deceased girl but by the stab wound.

Counsel for the appellant tried to overcome this line of reasoning by submitting that the jury should have been directed that if they thought the girl's decision not to have a blood transfusion was an unreasonable one, then the chain of causation would have been broken. At once the question arises – reasonable by whose standards? Those of Jehovah's Witnesses? Humanists? Roman Catholics? Protestants of Anglo-Saxon descent? The man on the Clapham omnibus? But he might well be an admirer of Eleazar who suffered death rather than eat the flesh of swine (see 2 *Maccabees*, Chapter 6 vv 18–31) or of Sir Thomas Moore who, unlike nearly all his contemporaries, was unwilling to accept Henry VIII as Head of the

Church of England. Those brought up in the Hebraic and Christian traditions would probably be reluctant to accept that these martyrs caused their own deaths.

As was pointed out to counsel for the appellant in the course of argument, two cases, each raising the same issue of reasonableness because of religious beliefs, could produce different verdicts depending on where the cases were tried. A jury drawn from Preston, sometimes said to the most Catholic town in England, might have different views about martyrdom to one drawn from the inner suburbs of London ... It has been the policy of the law that those who use violence on other people must take their victims as they find them. This in our judgment means the whole man, not just the physical man. It does not lie in the mouth of the assailant to say that his victim's religious beliefs which inhibited her from accepting certain kinds of treatment were unreasonable. The question for decision is what caused her death. The answer is the stab wound. The fact that the victim refused to stop this end coming about did not break the causal connection between the act and death.

If a victim's personal representatives claim compensation for his death the concept of foreseeability can operate in favour of the wrongdoer in the assessment of such compensation; the wrongdoer is entitled to expect his victim to mitigate his damage by accepting treatment of a normal kind: see *Steele v George & Co Ltd* [1942] AC 497. As counsel for the Crown pointed out, the criminal law is concerned with the maintenance of law and order and the protection of the public generally. A policy of the common law is applicable to the settlement or tortious liability between subjects may not be, and in our judgment is not, appropriate for the criminal law.

The issue of the cause of death in a trial for either murder or manslaughter is one of fact for the jury to decide. But if, as in this case, there is no conflict of evidence and all the jury has to do is to apply the law to the admitted facts, the judge is entitled to tell the jury what the result of that application will be. In this case the judge would have been entitled to have told the jury that the appellant's stab wound was an operative cause of the death. The appeal fails.

Lawton LJ: It has long been the policy of the law that those who use violence on other people must take their victims as they find them. This in our judgment means the whole man, not just the physical man. It does not lie in the mouth of the assailant to say that his victim's religious beliefs which inhibited him from accepting certain kinds of treatment were unreasonable.

See further *R v Holland* (1841) 2 Mood & R 351.

Aggravating the condition caused by defendant's act or omission

R v Dear [1996] Crim LR 595 (CA)

Facts: The appellant appealed against his conviction of murder. The prosecution case was that, following allegations by the appellant's 12 year old daughter that the deceased had sexually interfered with her, the appellant had slashed the deceased repeatedly with a Stanley knife, and that he had died two days later as a result of the wounds inflicted. The appellant's case was that he had been provoked, but that in any event the chain of causation had been broken between his actions and the death because the deceased had committed suicide either by reopening his wounds or, the wounds having reopened themselves, by failing to take steps to staunch the consequent blood flow. It was argued on the appeal that the suicide of the deceased would have been a *novus actus interveniens* and that the judge had misdirected the jury on the issue of causation.

Held, dismissing the appeal, that the real question in the case was, as the judge had correctly directed the jury, whether the injuries inflicted by the appellant were an operating and significant cause of the death. That had been enunciated as the correct approach in *Smith* [1959] 2 QB 35; *Blaue* [1975] 1 WLR 1411; *Malcherek* [1981] 1 WLR 690; *Cheshire* (1991) 93 Cr App R 251, and Smith and Hogan, *Criminal Law*, 7th edn. It would not be helpful to juries if the law required them to decide causation in a case such as the present by embarking on an analysis of whether a victim had treated himself with mere negligence or gross neglect, the latter breaking but former not breaking the chain of causation between the defendant's wrongful act and the victim's death. It would be a retrograde step if the niceties of apportionment of fault and causation in the civil law, and the roles which the concepts of *novus actus interveniens* and foreseeability did or should play in causation, were to invade the criminal law. In the present case the cause of the deceased's death was bleeding from the artery which the defendant had severed. Whether or not the resumption or continuation of that bleeding was deliberately caused by the deceased, the jury were entitled to find that the appellant's conduct made an operative and significant contribution to the death.

A positive supervening voluntary act by the victim

R v Armstrong [1989] Crim LR 149 (St Albans Crown Court)

Facts: The defendant, a drug addict, supplied to the victim, who had already consumed a potentially lethal quantity of alcohol, heroin and the means by which to mix and inject the heroin. There was no evidence that the defendant had injected the heroin into the victim. The case proceeded upon the assumption that the victim had injected himself. Shortly after injecting himself, the victim died.

The defendant was charged, *inter alia*, with manslaughter. At the trial the Crown called a pathologist and a toxicologist: the former opined that death was caused primarily by the deceased's alcohol intake and said that it was 'possible' that heroin had been a contributory cause; the latter initially expressed a different view but deferred to the pathologist's opinion.

It was submitted at the close of the Crown's case (1) that there was no or insufficient evidence that heroin had been a substantial cause of death, alternatively (2) that if heroin did cause death, the deceased injecting himself was a *novus actus interveniens* breaking the chain of causation flowing from the defendant's acts.

Held, upholding the submissions: (1) that if the expert could not be sure that heroin caused the deceased's death, the jury could not be and (2) that the alternative submission was well-founded. Regard was had to *Cato* (1976) 62 Cr App R 41 and *Dalby* (1982) 74 Cr App R 348: the facts proved were closest to *Dalby*.

Notes and queries

1 In *R v Dalby* [1982] 1 All ER 916, the defendant supplied drugs to the deceased who consumed them with fatal consequences. The Court of Appeal allowed Dalby's appeal, *inter alia*, on the ground that the act of supply did not cause 'direct harm' to the deceased. This aspect of the decision was subsequently approved by the Court of Appeal in *R v Goodfellow* (1986) 83 Cr App R 23. For extracts from these cases see further Chapter 15.

2 In *R v Kennedy* [1999] Crim LR 65 the defendant, at the request of the deceased, supplied the deceased with a syringe containing heroin. The deceased proceeded to injected himself with the mixture and died from the effect of the drug shortly afterwards. The defendant's appeal against his conviction for manslaughter, based on the contention that the deceased has caused his own death by self-injection, was dismissed. The Court of Appeal sought to distinguish the case from *Dalby* on the basis that the defendant had not simply supplied the drug but had also prepared the syringe and handed it to the deceased. The decision is, with respect, highly questionable. What the deceased did was to deliberately risk his own life – this is not an unlawful act. Hence the defendant could not be said to be assisting or encouraging an unlawful act.

3 In determining whether self-administration of drugs by the deceased is a *novus actus interveniens* to what extent should the courts take into account the knowledge of the deceased? How should the courts view the self-administration where the deceased is a child, a mental defective, or an adult who has been misled as to the nature of the substance?

The victim's actions in seeking to escape from the defendant

R v Roberts (1971) 56 Cr App R 95 (CA)

Facts: The victim of the alleged assault had been at a party. She left the party at about 3 am, having agreed to travel with the appellant in his car to what he said was another party in Warrington. After they had driven out of Warrington in the direction of Liverpool, she asked the appellant where the party was, and he said that they were going to Runcorn. They took a curious route to Runcorn, and eventually, she said, they stopped on what seemed like a big cinder track. The time by then was apparently about 4 am. Then, she said, 'He just jumped on me. He put his hands up my clothes and tried to take my tights off. I started to fight him off, but the door of the car was locked and I could not find the catch. Suddenly he grabbed me and then he drove off and I started to cry and asked him to take me home. He told me to take my clothes off and, if I did not take my clothes off, he would let me walk home, so I asked him to let me do that. He said, that if he did, he would beat me up before he let me go. He said that he had done this before and had got away with it and he started to pull my coat off. He was using foul language.' And then she said that she told him, 'I am not like that', and he said something like, 'You are all like that'. Then he drove on. 'Again', said the girl, 'he tried to get my coat off, so I got hold of my handbag and I jumped out of the car. When I opened the door, he said something and revved the car up and I jumped out. The next thing I remember he was backing towards me and so I ran to the nearest house. He backed and shouted and then he drove off', and then she remembered being in the lady's house. She said she was taken to hospital, where she was treated for some concussion and for some grazing, and was detained in hospital for three days. The defendant was charged with assault occasioning actual bodily harm.

> **Stephenson LJ**: ... [The jury] had to consider: was the appellant guilty of occasioning [the victim] actual bodily harm? Of course, for that to be established, it had to be established that he was responsible in law and in fact for her injuries caused by leaving in a hurry the moving car ...
>
> We have been ... referred to ... *Beech* (1912) 7 Cr App R 197, which was a case of a woman jumping out of a window and injuring herself ... In that case the Court of Criminal Appeal (at p 200) approved the direction given by the trial judge in these terms: 'Will you say whether the conduct of the prisoner amounted to a threat of causing injury to this young woman, was the act of jumping the natural consequence of the conduct of the prisoner, and was the grievous bodily harm the result of the conduct of the prisoner?' That, said the court, was a proper direction as far as the law went, and they were satisfied that there was evidence before the jury of the prisoner causing actual bodily harm to the woman. 'No-one could say,' said Darling J when giving the judgment of the court, 'that if she jumped from the window it was not a natural consequence of the prisoner's conduct. It was a very likely thing for a woman to do as the result of the threats of a man who was conducting himself as this man indisputably was.'
>
> This court thinks that that correctly states the law ...
>
> ... The test is: Was it [the action of the victim which resulted in actual bodily harm] the natural result of what the alleged assailant said and did, in the sense that it was something that could reasonably have been foreseen as the consequence of what he was saying or doing? As it was put in one of the old cases, it had got to be shown to be his act, and if of course the victim does something so 'daft', in the words of the appellant in this case, or so unexpected, not that this particular assailant did not actually foresee it but that no reasonable man could be expected to foresee it, then it is only in a very remote and unreal sense a consequence of his assault, it is really occasioned by a voluntary act on the part of the victim which could not reasonably be foreseen and which breaks the chain of causation between the assault and harm or injury.

R v Williams and Another [1992] 1 WLR 380 (CA)

Stuart-Smith LJ: ... The facts were these. On 15 June 1989 the deceased, John Shephard, was hitch-hiking to a free festival at Glastonbury. He was picked up in a car driven by Williams; Davis and the co-accused Bobat were passengers. After some five miles, while the car was travelling at about 30 mph, the deceased jumped from the car, and died from head injuries caused by falling onto the road.

The key issue in the case was whether anything had happened in the car, and, if so, what, to cause him to jump. The prosecution case was that this was a planned robbery of the hitch-hiker, conceived before the deceased got into the car and involving all three occupants, and that the deceased met his death trying to escape. The deceased, John Shephard, was 28. He smoked cannabis quite often. At the post mortem cannabinoids were found in his blood, consistent with his having smoked one or two joints. The psychiatric evidence was that the cannabis would not have caused him to act in an irrational manner.

A Mr Brickell was driving behind the car (a Toyota) in which the deceased had been given a lift. He noticed that the car was drifting across the road and narrowly missed an oncoming lorry but he saw nothing untoward going on inside the car. Suddenly the rear nearside door opened, someone looked out and then jumped from the car into the path of Mr Brickell's car. At the same time an object went up in the air, almost certainly the deceased's wallet. The door closed and the car sped away ...

Davis's appeal

In the forefront of Mr Perry's submission on behalf of Davis is the contention that the judge misdirected the jury on the law relating to manslaughter where death follows a threat of violence in that he failed to give them any guidance on the question of causation.

... [I]n some cases, and in our judgment this is one of them, it is necessary to give the jury a direction on causation, and explain the test by which the voluntary act of the deceased may be said to be caused by the accused's act and not a *novus actus interveniens*, breaking the chain of causation between the threat of violence and the death. There must be some proportionality between the gravity of the threat and the action of the deceased in seeking to escape from it ...

The necessary causal link can be traced through the old cases and also the judgments of Stephenson LJ in *R v Roberts* (1971) 56 Cr App R 95 and *R v Mackie* (1973) 57 Cr App R 453 ...

In *R v Roberts* (1971) 56 Cr App R 95 the complainant had jumped from a moving car because she said the appellant had assaulted and threatened her. The appellant was convicted of assault occasioning actual bodily harm. The issue was one of causation. In giving the judgment of the court Stephenson LJ said (at 102):

> The test is: Was it the natural result of what the alleged assailant said and did, in the sense that it was something that could reasonably have been foreseen as the consequence of what he was saying or doing? As it was put in one of the old cases, it had got to be shown to be his act, and if of course the victim does something so 'daft', in the words of the appellant in this case, or so unexpected, not that this particular assailant did not actually foresee it but that no reasonable man could be expected to foresee it, then it is only in a very remote and unreal sense a consequence of his assault, it is really occasioned by a voluntary act on the part of the victim which could not reasonably be foreseen and which breaks the chain of causation between the assault and the harm or injury.

In *R v Mackie* 57 Cr App R 453 the Crown's case was that the victim, a child of three, was fleeing from fear of his father's violence and fell downstairs and was killed. Stephenson LJ, after citing the case to which we have just referred, said (at 459):

> Where the injuries are not fatal, the attempt to escape must be the natural consequence of the assault charged, not something which could not be expected, but something which any reasonable and responsible man in the assailant's shoes would have foreseen. Where the injuries are fatal, the attempt must be the natural consequence of an unlawful act and that unlawful act 'must be such as all sober and reasonable people would inevitably recognise must subject the other person to, at least, the risk of some harm resulting therefrom, albeit not serious harm ...

It is plain that in fatal cases there are two requirements. The first, as in non-fatal cases, relates to the deceased's conduct, which would be something that a reasonable and responsible man in the assailant's shoes would have foreseen. The second, which applies only in fatal cases, relates to the quality of the unlawful act, which must be such that all sober and reasonable people would inevitably recognise must subject the other person to some harm resulting therefrom albeit not serious harm. It should be noted that the headnote is inaccurate and tends to confuse these two limbs.

The harm must be physical harm. Where the unlawful act is a battery, there is no difficulty with the second ingredient. Where however the unlawful act is merely a threat unaccompanied and not preceded by any actual violence, the position may be more difficult. In the case of a life-threatening assault, such as pointing a gun or knife at the victim, all sober and reasonable people may well anticipate some physical injury through shock to the victim, as for example in *R v Daweson* (1985) 81 Cr App R 150, where the victim died of a heart attack following a robbery in which two of the appellants had been masked, armed with a replica gun and pickaxe handles. But the nature of the threat is of importance in considering both the foreseeability of harm to the victim from the threat and the question whether the deceased's conduct was proportionate to the threat, that is to say that it was within the ambit of reasonableness and not so daft as to make it his one voluntary act which amounted to a *novus actus interveniens* and consequently broke the chain of causation. It should of course be borne in mind that a victim may in the agony of the moment do the wrong thing.

In this case there was an almost total lack of evidence as to the nature of the threat. The prosecution invited the jury to infer the gravity of the threat from the action of the deceased. The judge put it this way:

> ... what he was frightened of was robbery, that this was going to be taken from him by force, and the measure of the force can be taken from his reaction to it. The prosecution suggest that if he is prepared to get out of a moving car, then it was a very serious threat involving him in the risk of, as he saw it, serious injury.

In our judgment that was a wholly impermissible argument and was simply a case of the prosecution pulling itself up by its own bootstraps.

Moreover in a case of robbery the threat of force is made to persuade the victim to hand over money: if the money is handed over actual violence may not eventuate. The jury should consider two questions: first, whether it was reasonably foreseeable that some harm, albeit not serious harm, was likely to result from the threat itself; and, second, whether the deceased's reaction in jumping from the moving car was within the range of responses which might be expected from a victim placed in the situation which he was. The jury should bear in mind any particular characteristic of the victim and the fact that in the agony of the moment he may act without thought and deliberation ...

R v Corbett [1996] Crim LR 594 (CA)

Facts: The appellant was convicted of manslaughter. The victim was a mentally handicapped man of 26 who suffered from time to time with mental illness and had problems with high alcohol consumption. The appellant and the victim had been drinking all day. At about 9.30 pm the appellant had an argument with the victim and started to hit and head-butt him. The victim ran away and fell into the gutter where he was struck by a passing car and killed. In the course of his summing up the judge gave a direction on manslaughter and told the jury that they had to consider whether what the victim had done was within the foreseeable range. The judge referred to the fact that the victim had been immensely drunk and asked the jury to decide whether what the victim had done was something that might be expected as a reaction of somebody in that state. On appeal counsel for the appellant contended that the judge should have told the jury that the Crown had to prove the death occurred as *the* natural consequence of what the defendant had done and that if there had been scope for any other consequence the Crown would not have discharged the burden of proof on them.

Held, dismissing the appeal, the judgment in *Roberts* (1971) 56 Cr App R 95 at 102 undermined the submission made by counsel for the appellant because it clearly envisaged a foreseeable range of consequences and held that it would only be a daft reaction on the part of a victim which would be beyond that range and which would thus break the chain of causation. Here the judge had emphasised to the jury that the victim's reaction had to be in the foreseeable range.

Notes and queries

1   *R v Majoram* [2000] Crim LR 372 confirms that the issue of causation is to be assessed objectively. There is no need to prove that the defendant had any foresight of the harmful consequences in order to establish causation. For these purposes the reasonable person does not share any of the defendant's personal attributes. In the course of his judgment Roch LJ cited with approval the passage from *R v Roberts* (above) to the effect that the chain of causation would be broken if P did something so unexpected it might be described as 'daft'.

2   The doctrine that the defendant should take his victim as he finds him or her, as expressed in *Blaue*, would suggest that even a 'daft' action by the victim should not break the chain of causation. To what extent can this apparent contradiction be resolved by arguing that: (i) *Blaue* is to be preferred because

it is the later case; (ii) the 'take your victim as you find him or her' doctrine is part of the *ratio* of *Blaue*; (iii) *Blaue* is preferable as a matter of public policy (ie the defendant should not be absolved because of the unforeseen 'peculiarities' of the victim).

NOVUS ACTUS INTERVENIENS – CAN THE CHAIN OF CAUSATION BE BROKEN BY THE ACTIONS OF A THIRD PARTY?

Police officers

R v Pagett (1983) 76 Cr App R 279 (CA)

Facts: In the early hours of one morning on the first floor of a block of flats where he lived, the appellant, who was armed with a shotgun and cartridges, shot at police officers who were attempting to arrest him for various serious offences. The appellant had with him a 16 year old girl who was pregnant by him, and against her will used her body to shield him from any retaliation by the officers. The officers in fact returned the appellant's fire and as a result the girl was killed. The appellant was charged, inter alia, with her murder.

> **Robert Goff LJ**: ... [I]t was pressed upon us by Lord Gifford [counsel for the appellant] that there either was, or should be, a comparable rule of English law, whereby, as a matter of policy, no man should be convicted of homicide (or, we imagine, any crime of violence to another person) unless he himself, or another person acting in concert with him, fired the shot (or, we imagine, struck the blow) which was the immediate cause of the victim's death (or injury).
>
> No English authority was cited to us in support of any such proposition, and we know of none. So far as we are aware, there is no such rule in English law; and, in the absence of any doctrine of constructive malice, we can see no basis in principle for any such rule in English law. Lord Gifford urged upon us that, in a case where the accused did not, for example, fire the shot which was the immediate cause of the victim's death, he will inevitably have committed some lesser crime, and that it would be sufficient that he should be convicted of that lesser crime. So, on the facts of the present case, it would be enough that the appellant was convicted of the crime of attempted murder of the two police officers, DS Sartain and DC Richards. We see no force in this submission. In point of fact, it is not difficult to imagine circumstances in which it would manifestly be inadequate for the accused merely to be convicted of a lesser offence; for example, a man besieged by armed terrorists in a house might attempt to make his escape by forcing some other person to act as a shield, knowing full well that that person would in all probability be shot, and possibly killed, in consequence. For that man merely to be convicted of an assault would, if the person he used as a shield were to be shot and killed, surely be inadequate in all the circumstances; we can see no reason why he should not be convicted at least of manslaughter. But in any event there is, so far as we can discern, no basis of legal principle for Lord Gifford's submission. We are therefore unable to accept it.

In our judgment, the question whether an accused person can be held guilty of homicide, either murder or manslaughter, of a victim the immediate cause of whose death is the act of another person must be determined on the ordinary principles of causation, uninhibited by any such rule of policy as that for which Lord Gifford has contended. We therefore reject the second ground of appeal.

We turn to the first ground of appeal, which is that the learned judge erred in directing the jury that it was for him to decide *as a matter of law* whether by his unlawful and deliberate acts the appellant caused or was a cause of Gail Kinchen's death ...

We have no intention of embarking in this judgment on a dissertation of the nature of causation, or indeed of considering any matters other than those which are germane to the decision of the issues now before us. Problems of causation have troubled philosophers and lawyers throughout the ages; and it would be rash in the extreme for us to trespass beyond the boundaries of our immediate problem. Our comments should therefore be understood to be confined not merely to the criminal law, but to cases of homicide (and possibly also other crimes of violence to the person); and it must be emphasised that the problem of causation in the present case is specifically concerned with the intervention of another person (here one of the police officers) whose act was the immediate cause of the death of the victim, Gail Kinchen.

In cases of homicide, it is rarely necessary to give the jury any direction on causation as such. Of course, a necessary ingredient of the crimes of murder and manslaughter is that the accused has by his act caused the victim's death. But how the victim came by his death is usually not in dispute. What is in dispute is more likely to be some other matter: for example, the identity of the person who committed the act which indisputably caused the victim's death; or whether the accused had the necessary intent; or whether the accused acted in self-defence, or was provoked. Even where it is necessary to direct the jury's minds to the question of causation, it is usually enough to direct them simply that in law the accused's act need not be the sole cause, or even the main cause, of the victim's death, it being enough that his act contributed significantly to that result. It is right to observe in passing, however, that even this simple direction is a direction of law relating to causation, on the basis of which the jury are bound to act in concluding whether the prosecution has established, as a matter of fact, that the accused's act did in this sense cause the victim's death. Occasionally, however, a specific issue of causation may arise. One such case is where, although an act of the accused constitutes a *causa sine qua non* of (or necessary condition for) the death of the victim, nevertheless the intervention of a third person may be regarded as the sole cause of the victim's death, thereby relieving the accused of criminal responsibility. Such intervention, if it has such an effect, has often been described by lawyers as a *novus actus interveniens*. We are aware that this time-honoured Latin term has been the subject of criticism. We are also aware that attempts have been made to translate it into English; though no simple translation has proved satisfactory, really because the Latin term has become a term of art which conveys to lawyers the crucial feature that there has not merely been an intervening act of another person, but that act was so independent of the act of the accused that it should be regarded in law as the cause of the victim's death, to the exclusion of the act of the accused. At the risk of scholarly criticism, we shall for the purposes of this judgment continue to use the Latin term.

Now the whole subject of causation in the law has been the subject of a well-known and most distinguished treatise by Professors Hart and Honore, *Causation in the Law*. Passages from this book were cited to the learned judge, and were plainly relied upon by him; we, too, wish to express our indebtedness to it. It would be quite wrong for us to consider in this judgment the wider issues discussed in that work. But, for present purposes, the passage which is of most immediate relevance is to be found in Chapter 12, in which the learned authors consider the circumstances in which the intervention of a third person, not acting in concert with the accused, may have the effect of relieving the accused of criminal responsibility. The criterion which they suggest should be applied in such circumstances is whether the intervention is voluntary, ie whether it is 'free, deliberate and informed'. We resist the temptation of expressing the judicial opinion whether we find ourselves in complete agreement with that definition; though we certainly consider it to be broadly correct and supported by authority. Among the examples which the authors give of non-voluntary conduct, which is not effective to relieve the accused of responsibility, are two which are germane to the present case, viz a reasonable act performed for the purpose of self-preservation, and an act done in performance of a legal duty.

There can, we consider, be no doubt that a reasonable act performed for the purpose of self-preservation, being of course itself an act caused by the accused's own act, does not operate as a *novus actus interveniens*. If authority is needed for this almost self-evident proposition, it is to be found in such cases as *Pitts* (1842) C & M 284, and *Curley* (1909) 2 Cr App R 96. In both these cases, the act performed for the purpose of self-preservation consisted of an act by the victim in attempting to escape from the violence of the accused, which in fact resulted in the victim's death. In each case it was held as a matter of law that, if the victim acted in a reasonable attempt to escape the violence of the accused, the death of the victim was caused by the act of the accused. Now one form of self-preservation is self-defence; for present purposes, we can see no distinction in principle between an attempt to escape the consequences of the accused's act, and a response which takes the form of self-defence. Furthermore, in our judgment, if a reasonable act of self-defence against the act of the accused causes the death of a third party, we can see no reason in principle why the act of self-defence, being an involuntary act caused by the act of the accused, should relieve the accused from final responsibility for the death of the third party. Of course, it does not necessarily follow that the accused will be guilty of the murder, or even of the manslaughter, of the third party; though in the majority of cases he is likely to be guilty at least of manslaughter. Whether he is guilty of murder or manslaughter will depend upon the question whether all the ingredients of the relevant offence have been proved; in particular, on a charge of murder, it will be necessary that the accused had the necessary intent ...

No English authority was cited to us, nor we think to the learned judge, in support of the proposition that an act done in the execution of a legal duty, again of course being an act itself caused by the act of the accused, does not operate as a *novus actus interveniens* ... Even so, we agree with the learned judge that the proposition is sound law, because as a matter of principle such an act cannot be regarded as a voluntary act independent of the wrongful act of the accused. A parallel may be drawn with the so-called 'rescue' cases in the law of negligence, where a wrongdoer may be held liable in negligence to a third party who suffers injury in going to the rescue of a person who has been put in danger by the defendant's negligent act. Where, for example, a police officer in the execution of his duty acts to prevent a crime, or to apprehend a person suspected of a crime, the case is surely *a fortiori*. Of course, it is inherent in the requirement that the police officer, or other person, must be acting in the execution of his duty that his act should be reasonable in all the circumstances: see s 3 of the Criminal Law Act 1967. Furthermore, once again we are only considering the issue of causation. If intervention by a third party in the execution of a legal duty, caused by the act of the accused, results in the death of the victim, the question whether the accused is guilty of the murder or manslaughter of the victim must depend on whether the necessary ingredients of the relevant offence have been proved against the accused, including in particular, in the case of murder, whether the accused had the necessary intent.

The principles which we have stated are principles of law. This is plain from, for example, the case of *Pitts* (1842) C & M 284, to which we have already referred. It follows that where, in any particular case, there is an issue concerned with what we have for convenience called *novus actus interveniens*, it will be appropriate for the judge to direct the jury in accordance with these principles. It does not however follow that it is accurate to state broadly that causation is a question of law. On the contrary, generally speaking causation is a question of fact for the jury. Thus in, for example, *Towers* (1874) 12 Cox C C 530, the accused struck a woman; she screamed loudly, and a child whom she was then nursing turned black in the face, and from that day until it died suffered from convulsions. The question whether the death of the child was caused by the act of the accused was left by the judge to the jury to decide as a question of fact. But that does not mean that there are no principles of law relating to causation, so that no directions on law are ever to be given to a jury on the question of causation. On the contrary, we have already pointed out one familiar direction which is given on causation, which is that the accused's act need not be the sole, or even the main, cause of the victim's death for his act to be held to have caused the death. His Lordship referred to *Blaue* [1975] 1 WLR 1411.

This was plainly a statement of a principle of law. Likewise, in cases where there is an issue whether the act of the victim or of a third party constituted a *novus actus interveniens*, breaking the causal connection between the act of the accused and the death of the victim, it would be appropriate for the judge to direct the jury, of course in the most simple terms, in accordance with the legal principles which they have to apply. It would then fall to the jury to decide the relevant factual issues which, identified with reference to those legal principles, will lead to the conclusion whether or not the prosecution have established the guilt of the accused of the crime of which he is charged ...

There is however one further aspect of the present case to which we must advert. On the evidence, Gail Kinchen was not just an innocent bystander killed by a shot fired from the gun of a police officer who, acting in reasonable self-defence, fired his gun in response to a lethal attack by the appellant: though on those facts alone it would, in our opinion, have been open to the jury to convict the appellant of murder or manslaughter. But if, as the jury must have found to have occurred in the present case, the appellant used Gail Kinchen by force and against her will as a shield to protect him from shots fired by the police, the effect is that he committed not one but two unlawful acts, both of which were dangerous – the act of firing at the police, and the act of holding Gail Kinchen as a shield in front of him when the police might well fire shots in his direction in self-defence. Either act could in our judgment, if on the principles we have stated it was held to cause the death of Gail Kinchen, constitute the *actus reus* of the manslaughter or, if the necessary intent were established, murder of Gail Kinchen by the appellant, even though the shot which killed her was fired not by the appellant but by the police officer.

In the light of these principles, we do not consider that any legitimate criticism can be made, on behalf of the appellant, of the direction given by the learned judge to the jury on the issue of causation in the present case ...

Notes and queries

1 To what extent do you think the police might have been grossly negligent in returning fire in the circumstances described in *Pagett*? If gross negligence on the part of a police officer had been established would this have constituted a *novus actus interveniens*? See the consideration of gross negligence on the part of doctors in *R v Cheshire*, considered below.

2 See further *R v Watson* [1989] 1 WLR 684, considered in Chapter 15. Suppose D burgles P's house, and there is evidence that P dies of a heart attack several hours later, the attack being brought on by P's exertions in making his property safe. Do P's actions amount to a *novus actus interveniens*. Alternatively, what if the medical evidence indicates that the heart attack was brought on by the stress of dealing with the police inquiries following the burglary? Can the activities of the police be seen as a *novus actus interveniens*?

Doctors

R v Jordan (1956) 40 Cr App R 152 (CA)

Hallett J: ... The facts of the case, so far as I need refer to them, are as follows. The appellant, together with three other men, all serving airmen of the United States Forces, were charged with the murder of a man named Beaumont as the result of a disturbance which arose in a cafe at Hull. Beaumont was stabbed with a knife. There was no evidence that any one of the other three men used a knife on Beaumont or was acting in concert with the man who did use the knife, and accordingly Byrne J, who tried the case, directed the acquittal of those three men. With regard to the appellant it was ultimately conceded by Mr Veale, who appeared for him in the court below and in this court, that he did use the knife and stab Beaumont. Beaumont was admitted to hospital very promptly and the wound was stitched up, but nonetheless he died not many days after. In those circumstances the appellant was tried for murder. Various defences were raised, accident, self-defence, provocation and stabbing in the course of a quarrel. On all of those defences the direction of the learned judge is not in any way challenged and the jury rejected them.

Mr Veale told us, with his usual frankness, that the original intention of the defence was not to lodge an appeal, but certain information reached the United States authorities and the defence became in a position to put forward further evidence, and in particular the evidence of two doctors, Dr Keith Simpson and Mr Blackburn, whose standing is beyond question ...

The further evidence is said to show that death was not, to use words of Byrne J, 'consequent upon the wound inflicted'. On the contrary, both the doctors called are of opinion that, from the medical point of view, it cannot be described as caused by the wound at all. Whether from the legal point of view it could be described as caused by the wound is a more doubtful question ...

... There were two things other than the wound which were stated by these two medical witnesses to have brought about death. The stab wound had penetrated the intestine in two places, but it was mainly healed at the time of death. With a view to preventing infection it was thought to administer an antibiotic, terramycin.

It was agreed by the two additional witnesses that that was the proper course to take, and a proper dose was administered. Some people, however, are intolerant to terramycin, and Beaumont was one of those people. After the initial doses he developed diarrhoea, which was only properly attributable, in the opinion of those doctors, to the fact that the patient was intolerant to terramycin. Thereupon the administration of terramycin was stopped, but unfortunately the very next day the resumption of such administration was ordered by another doctor and it was recommenced the following day. The two doctors both take the same view about it. Dr Simpson said that to introduce a poisonous substance after the intolerance of the patient was shown was palpably wrong. Mr Blackburn agreed.

Other steps were taken which were also regarded by the doctors as wrong – namely the intravenous introduction of wholly abnormal quantities of liquid far exceeding the output. As a result the lungs became waterlogged and pulmonary oedema was discovered. Mr Blackburn said that he was not surprised to see that condition after the introduction of so much liquid, and that pulmonary oedema leads to bronchopneumonia as an inevitable sequel, and it was from bronchopneumonia that Beaumont died.

We are disposed to accept it as the law that death resulting from any normal treatment employed to deal with a felonious injury may be regarded as caused by the felonious injury, but we do not think it necessary to examine the cases in detail or to formulate for the assistance of those who have to deal with such matters in the future the correct test which ought to be laid down with regard to what is necessary to be proved in order to establish causal connection between the death and the felonious injury. It is sufficient to point out here that this was not normal treatment. Not only one feature, but two separate and independent features, of treatment were, in the opinion of the doctors, palpably wrong and these produced the symptoms discovered at the post mortem examination which were the direct and immediate cause of death, namely the pneumonia resulting from the condition of oedema which was found.

The question then is whether it can be said that, if that evidence had been before the jury, it ought not to have, and in all probability would not have, affected their decision. We recognise that the learned judge, if this matter had been before him, would have had to direct the jury correctly on how far such supervening matters could be regarded as interrupting the chain of causation; but we felt that in the end it would have been a question of fact for the jury depending on what evidence they accepted as correct and the view they took on that evidence. We feel no uncertainty at all that, whatever direction had been given to the jury and however correct it had been, the jury would have felt precluded from saying that they were satisfied that death was caused by the stab wound.

For these reasons we come to the conclusion that the appeal must be allowed and the conviction set aside.

R v Smith [1959] 2 QB 35 (CA)

Facts: The appellant, Thomas Joseph Smith, a private soldier in the King's Regiment, took part in a fight between a company of his regiment and a company of the Gloucestershire Regiment, who were sharing barracks in Germany, on the night of 13 April 1958. Three men of the Gloucesters received stab wounds. One of them subsequently died.

Lord Parker CJ: ... The second ground concerns a question of causation. The deceased man in fact received two bayonet wounds, one in the arm and one in the back. The one in the back, unknown to anybody, had pierced the lung and caused haemorrhage. There followed a series of unfortunate occurrences. A fellow member of his company tried to carry him to the medical reception station. On the way he tripped over a wire and dropped the deceased man. He picked him up again, went a little farther, and fell apparently a second time, causing the deceased man to be dropped onto the ground. Thereafter he did not try a third time but went for help, and ultimately the deceased man was brought into the reception station. There, the medical officer, Captain Millward, and his orderly were trying to cope with a number of other cases, two serious stabbings and some minor injuries, and it is clear that they did not appreciate the seriousness of the deceased man's condition or exactly what had happened. A transfusion of saline solution was attempted and failed. When his breathing seemed impaired he was given oxygen and artificial respiration was applied, and in fact he died after he had been in the station about an hour, which was about two hours after the original stabbing. It is now known that having regard to the injuries which the man had in fact suffered, his lung being pierced, the treatment that he was given was thoroughly bad and might well have affected his chances of recovery. There was evidence that there is a tendency for a wound of this sort to heal and for the haemorrhage to stop. No doubt his being dropped on the ground and having artificial respiration applied would halt or at any rate impede the chances of healing. Further, there were no facilities whatsoever for blood transfusion, which would have been the best possible treatment. There was evidence that if he had received immediate and different treatment, he might not have died. Indeed, had facilities for blood transfusion been available and been administered, Dr Camps, who gave evidence for the defence, said that his chances of recovery were as high as 75%.

In these circumstances Mr Bowen urges that not only was a careful summing up required but that a correct direction to the court would have been that they must be satisfied that the death of Private Creed was a natural consequence and the sole consequence of the wound sustained by him and flowed directly from it. If there was, says Mr Bowen, any other cause, whether resulting from negligence or not, if, as he contends here, something happened which impeded the chance of the deceased recovering, then the death did not result from the wound. The court is quite unable to accept that contention. It seems to the court that if at the time of death the original wound is still an operating cause and a substantial cause, then the death can properly be said to be the result of the wound, albeit, that some other cause of death is also operating. Only if it can be said that the original wounding is merely the setting in which another cause operates can it be said that the death does not result from the wound. Putting it in another way, only if the second cause is so overwhelming as to make the original wound merely part of the history can it be said that the death does not flow from the wound ...

Mr Bowen placed great reliance on a case decided in this court of *R v Jordan* (1956) 40 Cr App R 152 and in particular on a passage in the headnote which says: '... that death resulting from any normal treatment employed to deal with a felonious injury may be regarded as caused by the felonious injury, but that the same principle does not apply where the treatment employed is abnormal.' Reading those words into the present case, Mr Bowen says that the treatment that this unfortunate man received from the moment that he was struck to the time of his death was abnormal. The court is satisfied that *Jordan's* case was a very particular case depending upon its exact facts. It incidentally arose in this court on the grant of an application to call further evidence, and leave having been obtained, two well-known medical experts gave evidence that in their opinion death had not been caused by the stabbing but by the introduction of terramycin after the deceased had shown that he was intolerant to it, and by the intravenous introduction of abnormal quantities of liquid. It also appears that at the time when that was done the stab wound which had penetrated the intestine in two places had mainly healed. In those circumstances the court felt bound to quash the conviction because they could not say that a reasonable jury properly directed would not have been able on that to say that there had been a break in the chain of causation; the court could only uphold the conviction in that case if they were satisfied that no reasonable jury could have come to that conclusion.

In the present case it is true that the judge-advocate did not in his summing up go into the refinements of causation. Indeed, in the opinion of this court he was probably wise to refrain from doing so. He did leave the broad question to the court whether they were satisfied that the wound had caused the death in the sense that the death flowed from the wound, albeit that the treatment he received was in the light of after-knowledge a bad thing. In the opinion of this court that was on the facts of the case a perfectly adequate summing up on causation; I say 'on the facts of the case' because, in the opinion of the court, they can only lead to one conclusion: a man is stabbed in the back, his lung is pierced and haemorrhage results; two hours later he dies of haemorrhage from that wound; in the interval there is no time for a careful examination, and the treatment given turns out in the light of subsequent knowledge to have been appropriate and, indeed, harmful. In those circumstances no reasonable jury or court could, properly directed, in our view possibly come to any other conclusion than that the death resulted from the original wound. Accordingly, the court dismisses this appeal.

R v Malcherek; R v Steel [1981] 1 WLR 690 (CA)

In these conjoined appeals both appellants had attacked women causing their victims serious injuries. In both cases the victims were placed on life support machines. In both cases doctors treating the victims decided to switch off the machines on the basis that there was no prospect of recovery. The appellants contended that the actions of the doctors in each case should have been regarded as a *novus actus interveniens* breaking the chain of causation in law between the attacks and the deaths.

> **Lord Lane CJ**: ... This is not the occasion for any decision as to what constitutes death. Modern techniques have undoubtedly resulted in the blurring of many of the conventional and traditional concepts of death. A person's heart can now be removed altogether without death supervening; machines can keep the blood circulating through the vessels of the body until a new heart can be implanted in the patient, and even though a person is no longer able to breathe spontaneously a ventilating machine can, so to speak, do his breathing for him, as is demonstrated in the two cases before us. There is, it seems, a body of opinion in the medical profession that there is only one true test of death and that is the irreversible death of the brain stem, which controls the basic functions of the body such as breathing. When that occurs it is said the body has died, even though by mechanical means the lungs are being caused to operate and some circulation of blood is taking place.
>
> We have had placed before us, and have been asked to admit, evidence that in each of these two cases the medical men concerned did not comply with all the suggested criteria for establishing such brain death. Indeed, further evidence has been suggested and placed before us that those criteria or tests are not in themselves stringent enough. However, in each of these two cases there is no doubt that whatever test is applied the victim died; that is to say, applying the traditional test, all body functions, breathing and heartbeat and brain function came to an end, at the latest, soon after the ventilator was disconnected.
>
> The question posed for answer to this court is simply whether the judge in each case was right in withdrawing from the jury the question of causation. Was he right to rule that there was no evidence on which the jury could come to the conclusion that the assailant did not cause the death of the victim?
>
> The way in which the submissions are put by counsel for Malcherek on the one hand and by counsel for Steel on the other is as follows: the doctors, by switching off the ventilator and the life support machine, were the cause of death or, to put it more accurately, there was evidence which the jury should have been allowed to consider that the doctors, and not the assailant, in each case may have been the cause of death.
>
> In each case it is clear that the initial assault was the cause of the grave head injuries in the one case and of the massive abdominal haemorrhage in the other. In each case the initial assault was the reason for the medical treatment being necessary. In each case the medical treatment given was normal and conventional. At some stage the doctors must decide if and when treatment has become otiose. This decision was reached, in each of the two cases here, in circumstances which have already been set out in some detail. It is no part of the task of this court to inquire whether the criteria, the Royal Medical College confirmatory tests, are a satisfactory code of practice. It is no part of the task of this court to decide whether

the doctors were, in either of these two cases, justified in omitting one or more of the so called 'confirmatory tests'. The doctors are not on trial; Steel and Malcherek respectively were.

There are two comparatively recent cases which are relevant to the consideration of this problem. The first is *R v Jordan* (1956) 40 Cr App R 152 ...

In the view of this court, if a choice has to be made between the decision in *R v Jordan* and that in *R v Smith*, which we do not believe it does (*R v Jordan* being a very exceptional case), then the decision in *R v Smith* is to be preferred.

The only other case to which reference has been made, it having been drawn to our attention by counsel for Steel, is *R v Blaue* [1975] 1 WLR 1411 ...

There is no evidence in the present case here that at the time of conventional death, after the life support machinery was disconnected, the original wound or injury was other than a continuing, operating and indeed substantial cause of the death of the victim, although it need hardly be added that it need not be substantial to render the assailant guilty. There may be occasions, although they will be rare, when the original injury has ceased to operate as a cause at all, but in the ordinary case if the treatment is given *bona fide* by competent and careful medical practitioners, then evidence will not be admissible to show that the treatment would not have been administered in the same way by other medical practitioners. In other words, the fact that the victim has died, despite or because of medical treatment for the initial injury given by careful and skilled medical practitioners, will not exonerate the original assailant from responsibility for the death. It follows that so far as the ground of appeal in each of these cases relates to the direction given on causation, that ground fails. It also follows that the evidence which it is sought to adduce now, although we are prepared to assume that it is both credible and was not available properly at the trial (and a reasonable explanation for not calling it at the trial has been given), if received could, under no circumstances, afford any ground for allowing the appeal.

The reason is this. Nothing which any of the two or three medical men whose statements are before us could say would alter the fact that in each case the assailant's actions continued to be an operating cause of the death. Nothing the doctors could say would provide any ground for a jury coming to the conclusion that the assailant in either case might not have caused the death. The furthest to which their proposed evidence goes, as already stated, is to suggest, first, that the criteria or the confirmatory tests are not sufficiently stringent and, second, that in the present case they were in certain respects inadequately fulfilled or carried out. It is no part of this court's function in the present circumstances to pronounce on this matter, nor was it a function of either of the juries at these trials. Where a medical practitioner adopting methods which are generally accepted comes *bona fide* and conscientiously to the conclusion that the patient is for practical purposes dead, and that such vital functions as exist (for example, circulation) are being maintained solely by mechanical means, and therefore discontinues treatment, that does not prevent the person who inflicted the initial injury from being responsible for the victim's death. Putting it in another way, the discontinuance of treatment in those circumstances does not break the chain of causation between the initial injury and the death.

Although it is unnecessary to go further than that for the purpose of deciding the present point, we wish to add this thought. Whatever the strict logic of the matter may be, it is perhaps somewhat bizarre to suggest, as counsel have impliedly done, that where a doctor tries his conscientious best to save the life of a patient brought to hospital *in extremis*, skilfully using sophisticated methods, drugs and machinery to do so, but fails in his attempt and therefore discontinues treatment, he can be said to have caused the death of the patient.

For these reasons we do not deem it either necessary under s 23(2) of the Criminal Appeal Act 1968 nor desirable or expedient under s 23(1) to receive the proposed evidence of the doctors which, in statement form, has been placed before us. Likewise, there is no ground for saying that the judge in either case was wrong in withdrawing the issue of causation from the jury. It follows that the appeal of Malcherek is dismissed. It now remains to consider the application in the case of Steel in so far as it relates to the matters other than causation ...

R v Cheshire [1991] 1 WLR 844 (CA)

Beldam LJ: ... At about midnight on 9/10 December 1987 the appellant was in the 'Ozone' fish and chip shop in Greenwich when he became involved in an argument with Trevor Jeffrey, the deceased. The appellant produced a handgun and fired it at the ceiling. The deceased grappled with him but the appellant fired two more shots. They were fired at the deceased at close range. One bullet entered the top of the thigh and shattered the thigh bone. The other entered the deceased's stomach. The appellant fled from the shop, and an ambulance and the police were summoned. The deceased was taken to the accident and emergency department of the Greenwich District Hospital. There, in the early hours of the morning, he underwent surgery. Both bullets had caused extensive damage. The thigh injury was cleaned, the bone joined and his leg placed in traction. There was substantial damage in the abdominal cavity, which was contaminated. A fairly extensive bowel resection and wound toilet was carried out and he was given blood transfusions. In due course he was transferred to the intensive care unit. He there developed respiratory problems and his breathing had to be maintained by a ventilator using a tube placed in the windpipe. A week later this tube was replaced by a tracheotomy tube, which remained in place for the next four weeks. His condition did not improve and after a marked deterioration on Christmas Day a further operation to explore his abdomen was carried out.

From time to time he suffered from chest infections, from vomiting and from discharges from the abdominal wound and it was not until 2 February 1988 that he began to show improvement. During his time in intensive care the deceased's lungs had become congested and filled with fluid and he suffered considerable difficulty with breathing. On 8 February he again complained of difficulty in breathing and it was at first thought that this was a recurrence of the problem with his lungs. An X-ray was taken but it showed no recurrence of lung trouble. Whilst in intensive care the deceased had on several occasions shown signs of anxiety and a tentative diagnosis was made that the intermittent problem with his breathing of which he complained after 8 February was due to attacks of anxiety. He was seen by several doctors of differing experience during the ensuing week. He was probably seen by Mr Harrison, the consultant general surgeon at Greenwich District Hospital, on one occasion. He was also seen by the surgical registrar, Mr Saunders, and the orthopaedic registrar. Later, on the evening of 14 February, he complained of further difficulty with breathing and was attended by a house surgeon, Dr Clare Jones. Dr Jones had qualified in the summer of 1987 and had been a medical houseman for six months before becoming house surgeon on 1 February. She was worried about the deceased's condition and sat with him for three-quarters of an hour recording in the notes that he was making a noise through his respiratory passages which she described as 'stridor'. The deceased's condition deteriorated and the medical registrar was called. Urgent resuscitation, including cardiac massage, was given but the deceased died shortly after midnight.

At post mortem it was found that the deceased's windpipe had become obstructed due to narrowing near the site of the tracheotomy scar. Such a condition is a rare but not unknown complication of intubation of the windpipe. The deceased's windpipe had become so narrowed that even a small amount of mucus could block it and cause asphyxiation.

The experienced pathologist who conducted the post mortem gave evidence that the immediate cause of death was cardio-respiratory arrest:

due to a condition which was produced as a result of treatment to provide an artificial airway in the treatment of gunshot wounds of the abdomen and leg.

And he said:

in other words, I give as the cause of death cardio-respiratory arrest due to gunshot wounds of the abdomen and leg.

For the appellant it was conceded that the sequence of events which had led to the deceased's death was that described by the pathologist but a consultant surgeon, Mr Eadie, gave it as his opinion that by 8 February 1988 the wounds of the thigh and the abdomen no longer threatened the life of the deceased and his chances of survival were good. In his view:

The cause of his death was the failure to recognise the reason for his sudden onset and continued breathlessness after the 18 February [and the] severe respiratory obstruction, including the presence of stridor [on 14 February] ...

The doctors who examined and treated the deceased in the week before his death ought to have diagnosed the serious clinical condition from which he was suffering. Mr Eadie was particularly critical of the failure to appreciate the serious implications of 'stridor' on the evening of 14 February. The deceased would not have died if his condition had been diagnosed and properly treated. The doctors had been negligent and this was the cause of his death ...

One question for the jury at trial therefore was whether the Crown had proved, so that they were sure, that the shots fired by the appellant had caused the deceased's death ...

A case in which the facts bear a close similarity to the case with which we are concerned is *R v Evans and Gardiner (No 2)* [1976] VR 523. In that case the deceased was stabbed in the stomach by the two applicants in April 1974. After operation the victim resumed an apparently healthy life but nearly a year later, after suffering abdominal pain and vomiting and undergoing further medical treatment, he died. The cause of death was a stricture of the small bowel, a not uncommon sequel to the operation carried out to deal with the stab wound inflicted by the applicants. It was contended that the doctors treating the victim for the later symptoms ought to have diagnosed the presence of the stricture, that they had been negligent not to do so and that timely operative treatment would have saved the victim's life.

The Supreme Court of Victoria held that the test to be applied in determining whether a felonious act has caused a death which follows, in spite of an intervening act, is whether the felonious act is still an operating and substantial cause of the death.

The summing up to the jury had been based on the passage already quoted from Lord Parker CJ's judgment in *R v Smith* and the Supreme Court indorsed a direction in those terms. It commented upon the limitations of *R v Jordan* and made observations of the difference between the failure to diagnose the consequence of the original injury and cases in which medical treatment has been given which has a positive adverse effect on the victim. It concluded (at 528):

> But in the long run the difference between a positive act of commission and an omission to do some particular act is for these purposes ultimately a question of degree. As an event intervening between an act alleged to be felonious and to have resulted in death, and the actual death, a positive act of commission or an act of omission will serve to break the chain of causation only if it can be shown that the act or omission accelerated the death, so that it can be said to have caused the death and thus to have prevented the felonious act which would have caused death from actually doing so.

Later in the judgment the court said (at 534):

> In these circumstances we agree with the view of the learned trial judge expressed in his report to this court that there was a case to go to the jury. The failure of the medical practitioners to diagnose correctly the victim's condition, however, inept or unskilful, was not the cause of death. It was the blockage of the bowel which caused death and the real question for the jury was whether that blockage was due to the stabbing. There was plenty of medical evidence to support such a finding, if the jury chose to accept it.

It seems to us that these two passages demonstrate the difficulties in formulating and explaining a general concept of causation but what we think does emerge from this and the other cases is that when the victim of a criminal attack is treated for wounds or injuries by doctors or other medical staff attempting to repair the harm done, it will only be in the most extraordinary and unusual case that such treatment can be said to be so independent of the acts of the accused that it could be regarded in law as the cause of the victim's death to the exclusion of the accused's acts.

Where the law requires proof of the relationship between an act and its consequences as an element of responsibility, a simple and sufficient explanation of the basis of such relationship has proved notoriously elusive.

In a case in which the jury have to consider whether negligence in the treatment of injuries inflicted by the accused was the cause of death we think it is sufficient for the judge to tell the jury that they must be satisfied that the Crown have proved that the acts of the accused caused the death of the deceased, adding that the accused's act need not be the sole cause or even the main cause of death, it being sufficient that his acts contributed significantly to that result. Even though negligence in the treatment of the victim was the immediate cause of his death, the jury should not regard it as excluding the responsibility of the accused unless the negligent treatment was so independent of his acts, and in itself so potent in causing death, that they regard the contribution made by his acts as insignificant.

It is not the function of the jury to evaluate competing causes or to choose which is dominant provided they are satisfied that the accused's acts can fairly be said to have made a significant contribution to the victim's death. We think the word 'significant' conveys the necessary substance of a contribution made to the death which is more than negligible ...

R v Mellor [1996] 2 Cr App R 245

Schiemann LJ: ... The deceased was 71 years old and was attacked by some hooligans at 11.15 pm on 15 January 1994. He was taken to hospital suffering from bruising to the eyes, a damaged nose, and complaining of chest pain and a pain in his right shoulder. He died in hospital two days later. The defence of Mr Mellor who gave evidence was twofold:

1   He was not the man who attacked Mr Sims.

2   The substantial cause of Mr Sims's death was not the beating which he had received from the hooligan who attacked him but rather the actions and inactions of the hospital ...

The immediate cause of death was broncho-pneumonia which, upon the evidence, was brought on directly by the injuries inflicted by the appellant. Those injuries were certainly the cause of death. Probably if the appellant had been administered sufficient oxygen in time, the broncho-pneumonia would not have been fatal, and therefore the failure to administer sufficient oxygen could be regarded as a cause of death. It was asserted on behalf of the appellant, and supported by expert evidence, that the failure to administer sufficient oxygen in time amounted to negligence or incompetence in the care of Mr Sims in hospital.

The question for the trial judge was how he should frame his direction to the jury in these circumstances. The question was debated with counsel before leading counsels' final speeches and the case of *Cheshire* [1991] 1 WLR 844, was considered.

In homicide cases, where the victim of the alleged crime does not die immediately, supervening events will occur which are likely to have some causative effect leading to the victim's death; for example, a delay in the arrival of the ambulance, a delay in resuscitation, the victim's individual response to medical or surgical treatment, and the quality of medical, surgical and nursing care. Sometimes such an event may be the result of negligence or mistake or bad luck. It is a question of fact and degree in each case for the jury to decide, having regard to the gravity of the supervening event, however caused, whether the injuries inflicted by the defendant were a significant cause of death.

The onus on the Crown is to make the jury sure that the injuries inflicted by the defendant were a significant cause of death. However, the Crown has no onus of establishing that any supervening event was not a significant cause of death or that there was no medical negligence in the deceased's treatment.

If the issue of medical negligence is raised, the jury must have regard to the evidence adduced on the issue. If they conclude that there was or may have been medical negligence, they must have regard to that conclusion when answering the all-important question: 'Has the Crown proved that the injuries inflicted by the defendant were a significant cause of death?' In appropriate cases the jury can be told that there may be a number of significant causes leading to a victim's death. So as long as the Crown proves that the injuries inflicted by the defendant were at least a significant, if not the only, cause of death that will be sufficient to prove the nexus between injury and death ...

His Lordship referred to *R v Cheshire* (above) and *R v Pagett* (above) and continued:

> In our judgment, Beldam LJ (in *Cheshire*) was not intending to put any gloss on Goff LJ's suggested direction in *Pagett*, which was not a medical negligence case, but relating it to a medical negligence case. He made it clear at the end of the passage which we have cited that the question for the jury was whether they were satisfied that the accused's acts significantly contributed to the victim's death. That was the question for the jury in the present case.
>
> What the Crown had to prove in the present case were the injuries inflicted by the appellant significantly contributed to Mr Sims's death. There was no onus whatever on the Crown to negative medical negligence. Equally, there was no onus on the appellant to establish medical negligence. However, if negligence was established it was a factor to be taken into account by the jury in deciding whether the Crown had established that, notwithstanding this negligence, the injures inflicted by the appellant had significantly contributed to Mr Sims's death. In the event of a jury being sure that medical negligence has been negatived by the Crown as a significant contributory cause of death, the medical negligence factor would be out of the equation.
>
> In our judgment, it is undesirable in most cases for juries to be asked to embark upon the question of whether medical negligence as a significant contributory cause of death has been negatived because it diverts the jury from the relevant question, namely has the accused's act contributed significantly to the victim's death? ...
>
> An appropriate, but we do not suggest the only appropriate, form of words on the particular facts of this case would have been:
>
> > You must acquit the defendant of murder unless the Crown has made you sure that the injuries that he inflicted contributed significantly to Mr Sims's death. Provided you are sure of that, it matters not whether incompetence or mistake in treatment at the hospital may have also contributed significantly to the death.
>
> In our judgment, if the medical/causation issue had been put in this way there could only have been one answer. The evidence was overwhelming that having regard to the extent and nature of the injuries inflicted upon the 71 year old Mr Sims those injuries significantly contributed to his death less than two days later ...

ACT OF GOD AS A *NOVUS ACTUS INTERVENIENS*

This is an event which is entirely unforeseen and entirely unconnected with the accused's act. If it would have been sufficient on its own to bring about the consequence in question, it breaks the chain of causation.

Southern Water Authority v Pegrum and Pegrum [1989] Crim LR 442 (DC)

Facts: The respondents were charged with an offence contrary to s 31(1) of the Control of Pollution Act 1974, causing polluting matter (pig effluent) to enter a stream. The respondents reared pigs; effluent produced by the pigs was held initially in tanks and then transferred by gravity into a lagoon constructed for the purpose. The lagoon itself was emptied of liquid content for use as manure several times a year and of sediment annually. In the winter of 1987, after heavy rain, a blocked drain resulted in rain water flowing into the lagoon. A fissure developed at the top of one side of the lagoon and polluting liquid escaped, finding its way into a stream and eventually into a river. The magistrates found that the overflow from the lagoon was caused by an act of God – the ingress of rainwater – and that it was unnecessary to consider whether the respondents were negligent either in not inspecting the drain or discovering the overflow promptly enough or in not providing an adequate drain. They further found that the blocked drain causing the ingress of rainwater was an intervening event 'breaking the chain of causation'. They dismissed the information and the prosecutor appealed by way of case stated.

Held, allowing the appeal and remitting the case with a direction to convict, the following principles applied: (1) where the defendant conducts some active operation involving the storage, use or creation of material capable of polluting a river should it escape, then if it does escape and pollute, the defendant is liable if he 'caused' that escape; (2) the question of causation is to be decided in a common sense way; (3) a defendant may be found to have caused that escape even though he did not intend that escape and even though the escape happened without his negligence; (4) it is a defence to show that the cause of the escape was the intervening act of a third party or act of God or *vis major* which are the *novus actus interveniens* defences to strict civil liability referred to in *Rylands v Fletcher* (1868) LR 3 HL 330; (5) in deciding whether the intervening cause affords a defence the test is whether it was of so powerful nature that the conduct of the defendant was not a cause at all, but was merely part of the surrounding circumstances. On the facts of the present case, the active operations or positive acts of the respondents were the storage and re-use of the effluent which resulted in the formation of the toxic sediment which polluted the stream. The magistrates erred in finding that the ingress of rainwater was an act of God; an act of God is an operation of natural forces so unpredictable as to excuse a defendant all liability for its consequences. The quantity of rain could not properly be regarded in itself as an act of God and in any event the ingress of rainwater into the lagoon was the result of the overflow from the blocked drain. Although unpredictable and unforeseeable operation of animate forces can amount to an act of God (see *Carstairs v Taylor* (1870) LR 6 Exch 217), there was no factual basis for such finding in the present case. The respondents submitted that the blocked drain was an effective intervening cause relegating the respondent's effluent operation to a mere surrounding circumstance; it was sought to distinguish *Alphacell Ltd v Woodward* [1972] AC 824 on the basis that in that case the blockage and breakdown was within the system of the 'active operations' which led to the creation and storage of the pollutant, while in the present case the drainage system was nothing to do with the system for storing and using the effluent. That factual difference made no difference in law. The submission must fail on a proper understanding of the strict liability established by s 31. It would defeat the object of the legislation if a landowner who chooses to keep on his land matter capable of polluting should it escape is liable for the non-negligent breakdown of the system for dealing with the matter but is not liable for the non-negligent breakdown of another system (in the present case drainage) within his control and utilised for his purpose.

CODIFICATION AND LAW REFORM PROPOSALS

Clause 17 of the draft Code Bill seeks to restate the common law position regarding causation. It provides:

> 17(1) Subject to subsections (2) and (3), a person causes a result which is an element of an offence when:
>
> (a) he does an act which makes a more than negligible contribution to its occurrence; or
>
> (b) he omits to do an act which might prevent its occurrence and which he is under a duty to do according to the law relating to the offence.

Regarding *novus actus interveniens*, cl 17(2) states:

> A person does not cause a result where, after he does such an act or makes such an omission, an act or event occurs:
>
> (a) which is the immediate and sufficient cause of the result;
>
> (b) which he did not foresee; and
>
> (c) which could not in the circumstances reasonably have been foreseen.

The commentary on the draft code Bill observes:

> [Clause 17(2)] appears to restate satisfactorily for criminal law the principles which determine whether intervening acts or events are sufficient to break the chain of causation ... According to this provision a person will still be liable if his intended victim suffers injury in trying to escape from the threatened attack unless the victim has done something so improbable that it can properly be said not to have been reasonably foreseeable. Equally, liability for homicide will be unaffected if the victim refuses medical treatment for a wound caused by the defendant. Even if the refusal could be said to unforeseeable, it is not sufficient in itself to cause the victim's death – in such a case, to use the language of the cases, the original wound is still the 'operating and substantial cause' of death [Vol II, para 7.17].

Further reading

HLA Hart and AM Honore, *Causation in the Law*, 2nd edn, 1985, Oxford: OUP

H Benyon, 'Causation, omissions and complicity' [1987] Crim LR 539

G Williams, '*Finis* for *novus actus*?' (1989) 48 CLJ 391

A Norrie, 'A critique of criminal causation' (1991) 54 MLR 685

JE Stannard, 'Medical treatment and the chain of causation' (1993) JCL 88

CHAPTER 4

MENS REA: THE MENTAL ELEMENT

The term *mens rea* (or fault element, as it is some time referred to) refers to the state of mind of the accused at the time of the commission of the *actus reus* of an offence. The traditional maxim is '*actus non facit reum nisi mens sit rea*': the act is not guilty unless the mind is also guilty. The only offences for which this is not a requirement are offences of 'strict liability' (as to which, see Chapter 5). This chapter examines the general principles of *mens rea*. The *mens rea* required for specific offences is dealt with as appropriate in subsequent chapters. Certain defences effectively involve a denial of *mens rea*, for example where the defendant raises issues such as insanity, diminished responsibility, intoxication or mistake. These too are dealt with in separate chapters.

INTENTION

For a range of offences, both statutory and common law, intention on the part of the defendant is the fault element that has to be established by the prosecution. As the following material demonstrates defining intention has proved to be a difficult task – one that has occupied the House of Lords on at least five occasions since 1975.

In simple terms there are two types of intent. The first requires proof of purpose, that is, that it was the defendant's purpose to bring about a prohibited consequence. The second is based on evidence indicating the extent to which the defendant foresaw the prohibited consequence as resulting from his act or omission. In *DPP v Smith* [1961] AC 290 the House of Lords held that a defendant could be presumed to have foreseen the natural and probable consequences of his actions (that is, if a reasonable person would have foreseen the result then it could be presumed that the defendant had). The effect of *Smith* was reversed by s 8 of the Criminal Justice Act 1967 which provides:

A court or jury, in determining whether a person has committed an offence:

(a) shall not be bound in law to infer that he intended or foresaw a result of his actions by reason only of its being a natural and probable consequence of those actions; but

(b) shall decide whether he did intend or foresee that result by reference to all the evidence, drawing such inferences from the evidence as appear proper in the circumstances.

As a result of s 8 a jury cannot conclude that the defendant *must* have foreseen a consequence simply because it was the natural and probable consequence of his act or omission. The fact that something is the natural and probable consequence of the defendant's act or omission is, however, evidence from which it may be inferred that the defendant intended that result to occur. One of the major difficulties facing the House of Lords in this regard has been determining the degree of foresight that could be equated with intention.

R v Moloney [1985] 1 AC 905 (HL)

Lord Bridge of Harwich: ... My Lords, in the early hours of 22 November 1981, the appellant fired a single cartridge from a 12-bore shotgun. The full blast of the shot struck the appellant's stepfather, Patrick Moloney, in the side of the face at a range of about six feet and killed him instantly ... [following conviction for murder] ... The [Court of Appeal] certified that a point of law of general public importance was involved in their decision in the following terms:

> Is malice aforethought in the crime of murder established by proof that when doing the act which causes the death of another the accused either: (a) intends to kill or do serious harm; or (b) foresees that death or serious harm will probably occur, whether or not he desires either of those consequences?

... The true and only basis of the appellant's defence that he was guilty, not of murder, but of manslaughter, was encapsulated in the two sentences in his statement: 'I didn't aim the gun. I just pulled the trigger and he was dead.' The appellant amplified this defence in two crucial passages in his evidence. He said: 'I never deliberately aimed at him and fired at him intending to hurt him or to aim close to him intending to frighten him'. A little later, he said he had no idea in discharging the gun that it would injure his father. 'In my state of mind I never considered that the probable consequence of what I might do might result in injury to anybody. It was just a lark' ...

The golden rule should be that, when directing a jury on the mental element necessary in a crime of specific intent, the judge should avoid any elaboration or paraphrase of what is meant by intent, and leave it to the jury's good sense to decide whether the accused acted with the necessary intent, unless the judge is convinced that, on the facts and having regard to the way the case has been presented to the jury in evidence and argument, some further explanation or elaboration is strictly necessary to avoid misunderstanding. In trials for murder or wounding with intent, I find it very difficult to visualise a case where any such explanation or elaboration could be required, if the offence consisted of a direct attack on the victim with a weapon, except possibly the case where the accused shot at A and killed B, which any first-year law student could explain to a jury in the simplest of terms. Even where the death results indirectly from the act of the accused, I believe the cases that will call for a direction by reference to foresight of consequences will be of extremely rare occurrence. I am in full agreement with the view expressed by Viscount Dilhorne that, in *R v Hyam* [1975] AC 55 at 82 itself, if the issue of intent had been left without elaboration, no reasonable jury could have failed to convict. I find it difficult to understand why the prosecution did not seek to support the conviction, as an alternative to their main submission, on the ground that there had been no actual miscarriage of justice.

I do not, of course, by what I have said in the foregoing paragraph, mean to question the necessity, which frequently arises, to explain to a jury that intention is something quite distinct from motive or desire. But this can normally be quite simply explained by reference to the case before the court or, if necessary, by some homely example. A man who, at London Airport, boards a plane which he knows to be bound for Manchester, clearly intends to travel to Manchester, even though

Manchester is the last place he wants to be and his motive for boarding the plane is simply to escape pursuit. The possibility that the plane may have engine trouble and be diverted to Luton does not affect the matter. By boarding the Manchester plane, the man conclusively demonstrates his intention to go there, because it is a moral certainty that that is where he will arrive ...

In one sense I should be happy to adopt in its entirety the qualified negative answer proposed by my noble and learned friend on the Woolsack to the certified question in *R v Hyam* [1975] AC 55 at 79, because, if I may say so, it seems to me to be supported by the most convincing jurisprudential and philosophical arguments to be found in any of the speeches in *R v Hyam*. But I have to add at one that there are two reasons why I cannot regard it as providing practical guidance to judges who have to direct juries in the rare cases where foresight of probable consequences must be canvassed with the jury as an element which should affect their conclusion on the issue of intent.

First, I cannot accept that the suggested criterion that the act of the accused, to amount to murder, must be 'aimed at someone' as explained in *DPP v Smith* [1961] AC 290 by Viscount Kilmuir LC at 327 is one which would be generally helpful to juries ... I believe this criterion would create more doubts than it would resolve.

Second, I believe that my noble and learned friend, Lord Hailsham of St. Marylebone LC's inclusion in the mental element necessary to a conviction of murder of 'the intention to expose a potential victim', *inter alia*, to 'a serious risk that ... grievous bodily harm will ensue from his acts' ([1975] AC 55, 79) comes dangerously near to causing confusion with at least one possible element in the crime of causing death by reckless driving, and by inference equally of motor manslaughter, as identified by Lord Diplock in the later case of *R v Lawrence* [1982] AC 510, 526, 527, where the driving was such 'as to create an obvious and serious risk of causing physical injury to some other person' and the driver 'having recognised that there was some risk involved, had nonetheless gone on to take it'. If the driver, overtaking in a narrow country lane in the face of an oncoming cyclist, recognises and takes not only 'some risk' but a serious risk of hitting the cyclist, is he to be held guilty of murder ...

I am firmly of opinion that foresight of consequences, as an element bearing on the issue of intention in murder, or indeed any other crime of specific intent, belongs, not to the substantive law, but to the law of evidence ...

In the rare cases in which it is necessary to direct a jury by reference to foresight of consequences, I do not believe it is necessary for the judge to do more than invite the jury to consider two questions. First, was death or really serious injury in a murder case (or whatever relevant consequence must be proved to have been intended in any other case) a natural consequence of the defendant's voluntary act? Second, did the defendant foresee that consequence as being a natural consequence of his act? The jury should then be told that if they answer yes to both questions it is a proper inference for them to draw that he intended that consequence ...

R v Hancock and Shankland [1986] 1 AC 455 (HL)

Lord Scarman: ... In the dark hours of the early morning of 30 November 1984 Mr David Wilkie was driving his taxi along the Heads of the Valley Road. As he approached the bridge over the road at Rhymney he was killed when two lumps of concrete hit the car. The two lumps, a block and a post, had been dropped from the bridge as he approached it.

Mr Wilkie's passenger was a miner going to work. Mr Hancock and Mr Shankland were miners on strike, and strongly objected to Mr Wilkie's passenger going to work. That morning they had collected the block and the post from nearby, had brought them to the bridge under which the Heads of the Valley Road runs through a cutting, and had placed them on the parapet on the side facing towards the Rhymney roundabout. They then awaited the arrival of a convoy escorting the miner on his way to work ... As the convoy neared the bridge, the concrete block struck the taxi's windscreen. The post struck the carriageway some 4ft 8in from the nearside verge. Before, however, the post subsided on the ground, it was hit by the taxi. The taxi skidded out of control, coming to rest on the embankment. Mr Wilkie died from the injuries he received in the wrecking of the taxi by the two lumps of concrete ...

The defence was simple enough: that the two men intended to block the road, to stop the miner going to work, but not to kill or to do serious bodily harm to anyone ... [The trial judge directed the jury in accordance with the guidelines given by the House of Lords in *R v Moloney* [1985] AC 905. The Court of Appeal expressed disquiet over those guidelines, in that they offered the jury no assistance as to the relevance or weight of the probability factor in determining whether they should, or could properly, infer from foresight of a consequence the intent to bring about that consequence.] ... The question for the House is, therefore, whether the Moloney guidelines are sound. In *Moloney* the *ratio decidendi* was that the judge never properly put to the jury the defence, namely that the accused was unaware that the gun was pointing at his stepfather. The House, however, held it necessary in view of the history of confusion in this branch of the law to attempt to clarify the law relating to the establishment of the mental element necessary to constitute the crime of murder and to lay down guidelines for assisting juries to determine in what circumstances it is proper to infer intent from foresight. The House certainly clarified the law. First, the House cleared away the confusions which had obscured the law during the last 25 years laying down authoritatively that the mental element in murder is a specific intent, the intent to kill or to inflict serious bodily harm. Nothing less suffices: and the jury must be sure that the intent existed when the act was done which resulted in death before they can return a verdict of murder.

Second, the House made it absolutely clear that foresight of consequences is no more than evidence of the existence of the intent; it must be considered, and its weight assessed, together with all the evidence in the case. Foresight does not necessarily imply the existence of intention, though it may be a fact from which when considered with all the other evidence a jury may think it right to infer the necessary intent ...

Third, the House emphasised that the probability of the result of an act is an important matter for the jury to consider and can be critical in their determining whether the result was intended ...

It is only when Lord Bridge of Harwich turned to the task of formulating guidelines that difficulty arises. It is said by the Court of Appeal that the guidelines by omitting any express reference to probability are ambiguous and may well lead a jury to a wrong conclusion. The omission was deliberate. Lord

Bridge omitted the adjective 'probable' from the time-honoured formula 'foresight of the natural and probable consequences of his acts' because he thought that 'if a consequence is natural, it is really otiose to speak of it as also being probable' [1985] AC 905 at 929B. But is it? ...

... My Lords, I very much doubt whether a jury without further explanation would think that 'probable' added nothing to 'natural'. I agree with the Court of Appeal that the probability of a consequence is a factor of sufficient importance to be drawn specifically to the attention of the jury and to be explained. In a murder case where it is necessary to direct a jury on the issue of intent by reference to foresight of consequences the probability of death or serious injury resulting from the act done may be critically important. Its importance will depend on the degree of probability: if the likelihood that death or serious injury will result is high, the probability of that result may, as Lord Bridge of Harwich noted and the Lord Chief Justice emphasised, be seen as overwhelming evidence of the existence of the intent to kill or injure. Failure to explain the relevance of probability may, therefore, mislead a jury into thinking that it is of little or no importance and into concentrating exclusively of the causal link between the act and its consequence. In framing his guidelines Lord Bridge of Harwich [1985] AC 905, 929G, emphasised that he did not believe it necessary to do more than to invite the jury to consider his two questions. Neither question makes any reference (beyond the use of the word 'natural') to probability. I am not surprised that when in this case the judge faithfully followed this guidance the jury found themselves perplexed and unsure. In my judgment, therefore, the *Moloney* guidelines as they stand are unsafe and misleading. They require a reference to probability. They also require an explanation that the greater the probability of a consequence the more likely it is that the consequence was foreseen and that if that consequence was foreseen the greater the probability is that that consequence was also intended. But juries also require to be reminded that the decision is theirs to be reached upon a consideration of all the evidence.

Accordingly, I accept the view of the Court of Appeal that the *Moloney* guidelines are defective. I am, however, not persuaded that guidelines of general application, albeit within a limited class of case, are wise or desirable ...

I fear that their elaborate structure may well create difficulty. Juries are not chosen for their understanding of a logical and phased process leading by question and answer to a conclusion but are expected to exercise practical common sense. They want help on the practical problems encountered in evaluating the evidence of a particular case and reaching a conclusion. It is better, I suggest, notwithstanding my respect for the comprehensive formulation of the Court of Appeal's guidelines, that the trial judge should follow the traditional course of a summing up. He must explain the nature of the offence charged, give directions as to the law applicable to the particular facts of the case, explain the incidence and burden of proof, put both sides' cases making especially sure that the defence is put; he should offer help in understanding and weighing up all the evidence and should make certain that the jury understand that whereas the law is for him the facts are for them to decide. Guidelines, if given, are not to be treated as rules of law but as a guide indicating the sort of approach the jury may properly adopt to the evidence when coming to their decision on the facts.

In a case where foresight of a consequence is part of the evidence supporting a prosecution submission that the accused intended the consequence, the judge, if he thinks some general observations would help the jury, could well, having in mind s 8 of the Criminal Justice Act 1967, emphasise that the probability, however high, of a consequence is only a factor, though it may in some cases be a very significant factor, to be considered will all the other evidence in determining whether the accused intended to bring it about. The distinction between the offence and the evidence relied on to prove it is vital. Lord Bridge's speech in Moloney made the distinction crystal clear: it would be a disservice to the law to allow his guidelines to mislead a jury into overlooking it.

For these reasons I would hold that the *Moloney* guidelines are defective and should not be used as they stand without further explanation. The laying down of guidelines for use in directing juries in cases of complexity is a function which can be usefully exercised by the Court of Appeal. But it should be done sparingly, and limited to cases of real difficulty. If it is done, the guidelines should avoid generalisation so far as is possible and encourage the jury to exercise their common sense in reaching what is their decision on the facts. Guidelines are not rules of law: judges should not think that they must use them. A judge's duty is to direct the jury in law and to help them upon the particular facts of the case.

Accordingly, I would answer the certified question in the affirmative and would dismiss the appeal ...

Lord Keith of Kinkel, **Lord Roskill**, **Lord Brightman** and **Lord Griffiths** agreed with Lord Scarman.

R v Nedrick [1986] 1 WLR 1025 (CA)

Lord Lane CJ: ... The case for the Crown was that the appellant had a grudge against a woman called Viola Foreshaw, as a result of which, after threats that he would 'burn her out', he went to her house in the early hours of 15 July 1984, poured paraffin through the letter-box and on to the front door and set it alight. He gave no warning. The house was burnt down and one of Viola Foreshaw's children, a boy aged 12 called Lloyd, died of asphyxiation and burns.

After a number of interviews during which he denied any responsibility, the appellant eventually confessed to the police that he had started the fire in the manner described, adding, 'I didn't want anyone to die, I am not a murderer; please tell the judge; God knows I am not a murderer'. When asked why he did it, he replied, 'Just to wake her up and frighten her'.

The appellant's defence, rejected by the jury, was that he had neither started the fire nor made any admissions to that effect.

The sole effective ground of appeal is that the judge misdirected the jury on the intent necessary to establish a charge of murder ...

What then does a jury have to decide so far as the mental element in murder is concerned? It simply has to decide whether the defendant intended to kill or do serious bodily harm. In order to reach that decision the jury must pay regard to all the relevant circumstances, including what the defendant himself said and did.

In the great majority of cases a direction to that effect will be enough, particularly where the defendant's actions amounted to a direct attack upon his victim, because in such cases the evidence relating to the defendant's desire or motive will be clear and his intent will have been the same as his desire or motive. But in some cases, of which this is one, the defendant does an act which is manifestly dangerous and as a result someone dies. The primary desire or motive of the defendant may not have been to harm that person, or indeed anyone. In that situation what further directions should a jury be given as to the mental state which they must find to exist in the defendant if murder is to be proved?

We have endeavoured to crystallise the effect of their Lordships' speeches in *R v Moloney* and *R v Hancock* in a way which we hope may be helpful to judges who have to handle this type of case ...

When determining whether the defendant had the necessary intent, it may therefore be helpful for a jury to ask themselves two questions:

(1) How probable was the consequence which resulted from the defendant's voluntary act?

(2) Did he foresee that consequence?

If he did not appreciate that death or serious harm was likely to result from his act, he cannot have intended to bring it about. If he did, but thought that the risk to which he was exposing the person killed was only slight, then it may be easy for the jury to conclude that he did not intend to bring about that result. On the other hand, if the jury are satisfied that at the material time the defendant recognised that death or serious harm would be virtually certain (barring some unforeseen intervention) to result from his voluntary act, then that is a fact from which they may find it easy to infer that he intended to kill or do serious bodily harm, even though he may not have had any desire to achieve that result.

Where the charge is murder and in the rare cases where the simple direction is not enough, the jury should be directed that they are not entitled to infer the necessary intention, unless they feel sure that death or serious bodily harm was a virtual certainty (barring some unforeseen intervention) as a result of the defendant's actions and that the defendant appreciated that such was the case.

Where a man realises that it is for all practical purposes inevitable that his actions will result in death or serious harm, the inference may be irresistible that he intended that result, however little he may have desired or wished it to happen. The decision is one for the jury to be reached upon a consideration of all the evidence.

R v Woollin [1999] 1 AC 82 (HL)

Lord Steyn:

The case in a nutshell

The appellant lost his temper and threw his three month old son on to a hard surface. His son sustained a fractured skull and died. The appellant was charged with murder. The Crown did not contend that the appellant desired to kill his son or to cause him serious injury. The issue was whether the appellant nevertheless had the intention to cause serious harm. The appellant denied that he had any such intention. Subject to one qualification, the Recorder of Leeds summed up in accordance with the guidance given by Lord Lane, CJ in *Nedrick* ... But towards the end of his summing up the judge directed the jury that if they were satisfied that the appellant –

must have realised and appreciated when he threw that child that there was a substantial risk that he would cause serious injury to it, then it would be open to you to find that he intended to cause injury to the child and you should convict him of murder.

The jury found that the appellant had the necessary intention; they rejected a defence of provocation; and they convicted the appellant of murder ...

The Court of Appeal certified the following questions as of general importance:

1   In murder, where there is no direct evidence that the purpose of a defendant was to kill or to inflict serious injury on the victim, is it necessary to direct the jury that they may only infer an intent to do serious injury, if they are satisfied:

    (a)   that serious bodily harm was a virtually certain consequence of the defendant's voluntary act, and

    (b)   that the defendant appreciated that fact?

2   If the answer to question 1 is 'yes,' is such a direction necessary in all cases or is it only necessary in cases where the sole evidence of the defendant's intention is to be found in his actions and their consequence to the victim.

On appeal to your Lordships' House the terrain of the debate covered the correctness in law of the direction recommended by Lord Lane CJ in *Nedrick* and, if that direction is sound, whether it should be used only in the limited category of cases envisaged by the Court of Appeal. And counsel for the appellant renewed his submission that by directing the jury in terms of substantial risk the judge illegitimately widened the mental element of murder.

The directions of the judge on the mental element

... it is necessary to set out the judge's relevant directions of law with a brief explanation of the context and implications. The judge reminded the jury that the Crown did not allege an intention to kill. He accordingly concentrated on intention to do really serious bodily harm. He further reminded the jury that the Crown accepted that the defendant did not want to cause the child serious injuries. The judge then directed the jury as follows:

In looking at this, you should ask yourselves two questions and I am going to suggest that you write them down. First of all, how probable was the consequence which resulted from his throw, the consequence being, as you know, serious injury? How probable was the consequence of serious injury which resulted from his throw? Secondly, did he foresee that consequence in the second before or at the time of throwing? The second question is of particular importance, members of the jury, because he could not have intended serious harm could he, if he did not foresee the consequence and did not appreciate at the time that serious harm might result from his throw? If he thought, or may have thought, that in throwing the child he was exposing him to only the slight risk of being injured, then you would probably readily conclude that he did not intend to cause serious injury, because it was outside his contemplation that he would be seriously injured. But the defence say here that he never thought about the consequence at all when he threw the child. He did not give it a moment's thought. Again, if that is right, or may be right, you may readily conclude that he did not appreciate that serious harm would result. *It follows from that, if that is how you find, that you cannot infer that he intended to do Karl really serious harm unless you are sure that serious harm was a virtual certainty from what he was doing and he appreciated that that was the case.* So, members of the jury, that is how you should approach this question – and it is a vital question in the case. Are we sure that the prosecution have established that the defendant intended to cause Karl serious harm at the time that he threw him? (My emphasis added.)

The first two questions identified by the judge appear in Lord Lane's guidance in *Nedrick* ... The [emphasised] passage is a classic direction in accordance with *Nedrick* ... After an overnight adjournment the judge continued his summing up. He returned to the mental element which had to be established in order to find the appellant guilty of murder. On this occasion the judge did not use the *Nedrick* direction. Instead the judge directed the jury as follows:

If you think that he had not given any thought to the consequences of what he was doing before he did it, then the Crown would have failed to prove the necessary intent, the intent to cause really serious harm, for murder and you should acquit him of murder and convict him of manslaughter. If, on the other hand, you reject that interpretation and are quite satisfied that he was aware of what he was doing and must have realised and appreciated when he threw that child that there was a substantial risk that he would cause serious injury to it, then it would be open to you to find that he intended to cause injury to the child and you should convict him of murder.

It is plain, and the Crown accepts, that a direction posing an issue as to appreciation of a 'substantial risk' of causing serious injury is wider than a direction framed in terms of appreciation of a 'virtual certainty (barring some unforeseen intervention).' If Lord Lane correctly stated the law in *Nedrick*, the judge's direction in terms of substantial risk was wrong. But the Crown argued ... that *Nedrick* was wrongly decided or, alternatively, that the principle as enunciated by Lord Lane does not apply to the present case.

The premises of the appeal

The first premise of any examination of the issues raised by this appeal is that it is at present settled law that a defendant may be convicted of murder if it is established (1) that he had an intent to kill or (2) that he had an intent to cause really serious bodily injury: *R v Cunningham* [1982] AC 566. In regard to (2) the intent does not correspond to the harm which resulted, ie, the causing of death. It is a species of constructive crime ... Secondly, I approach the issues arising on this appeal on the basis that it does not follow that 'intent' necessarily has precisely the same meaning in every context in the criminal law. The focus of the present appeal is the crime of murder.

The problem facing the Court of Appeal in Nedrick

In *Hancock* Lord Scarman did not express disagreement with the test of foresight of a probability which is 'little short of overwhelming' as enunciated in *Moloney*. Lord Scarman also did not express disagreement with the law underlying Lord Lane's model direction in *Hancock* which was based on a defendant having 'appreciated that what he did was highly likely to cause death or really serious bodily injury.' Lord Scarman merely said that model directions were generally undesirable. Moreover, Lord Scarman thought that where explanation is required the jury should be directed as to the relevance of probability without expressly stating the matter in terms of any particular level of probability. The manner in which trial judges were to direct juries was left unclear. Moreover, in practice juries sometimes ask probing questions which cannot easily be ignored by trial judges. For example, imagine that in a case such as *Hancock* the jury sent a note to the judge to the following effect:

> We are satisfied that the defendant, though he did not want to cause serious harm, knew that it was probable that his act would cause serious bodily harm. We are not sure whether a probability is enough for murder. Please explain.

One may alter the question by substituting 'highly probable' for 'probable'. Or one may imagine the jury asking whether a foresight of a 'substantial risk' that the defendant's act would cause serious injury was enough. What is the judge to say to the jury? *Hancock* does not rule out an answer by the judge but it certainly does not explain how such questions are to be answered. It is well known that judges were sometimes advised to deflect such questions by the statement that 'intention' is an ordinary word in the English language. That is surely an unhelpful response to what may be a sensible question. In these circumstances it is not altogether surprising that in *Nedrick* the Court of Appeal felt compelled to provide a model direction for the assistance of trial judges ...

The direct attack on Nedrick

It is now possible to consider the Crown's direct challenge to the correctness of *Nedrick*. First, the Crown argued that *Nedrick* prevents the jury from considering all the evidence in the case relevant to intention. The argument is that this is contrary to the provisions of s 8 of the Criminal Justice Act 1967 [set out above] ...

Paragraph (a) [of s 8] is an instruction to the judge and is not relevant to the issues on this appeal. The Crown's argument relied on paragraph (b) which is concerned with the function of the jury. It is no more than a legislative instruction that in considering their findings on intention or foresight the jury must take into account all relevant evidence ... *Nedrick* does not prevent a jury from considering all the evidence: it merely stated what state of mind (in the absence of a purpose to kill or to cause serious harm) is sufficient for murder. I would therefore reject the Crown's first argument.

In the second place the Crown submitted that *Nedrick* is in conflict with the decision of the House in *Hancock*. Counsel argued that in order 'to bring some coherence to the process of determining intention Lord Lane specified a minimum level of foresight, namely virtual certainty'. But that is not in conflict with the decision in *Hancock* which, apart from disapproving Lord Bridge's 'natural consequence' model direction, approved *Moloney* in all other respects. And in *Moloney* Lord Bridge said that if a person foresees the probability of a consequence as little short of overwhelming, this 'will suffice to establish the necessary intent.' Nor did the House in *Hancock* rule out the framing of model directions by the Court of Appeal for the assistance of trial judges. I would therefore reject the argument that the guidance given in *Nedrick* was in conflict with the decision of the House in *Hancock*.

The Crown did not argue that as a matter of policy foresight of a virtual certainty is too narrow a test in murder. Subject to minor qualifications, the decision in *Nedrick*, was widely welcomed by distinguished academic writers ... It is also of interest that it is very similar to the threshold of being aware 'that it will occur in the ordinary course of events' in the Law Commission's draft Criminal Code ... Moreover, over a period of twelve years since *Nedrick* the test of foresight of virtual certainty has apparently caused no practical difficulties. It is simple and clear. It is true that it may exclude a conviction of murder in the often cited terrorist example where a member of the bomb disposal team is killed. In such a case it may realistically be said that the terrorist did not foresee the killing of a member of the bomb disposal team as a virtual certainty. That may be a consequence of not framing the principle in terms of risk taking. Such cases ought to cause no substantial difficulty since immediately below murder there is available a verdict of manslaughter which may attract in the discretion of the court a life sentence. In any event, as Lord Lane eloquently argued in a debate in the House of Lords, to frame a principle for particular difficulties regarding terrorism 'would produce corresponding injustices which would be very hard to eradicate': *Hansard* (HL Debates), 6 November 1989, col 480. I am satisfied that the *Nedrick* test, which was squarely based on the decision of the House in *Moloney*, is pitched at the right level of foresight.

The argument that Nedrick *has limited application*

The Court of Appeal held that the phrase 'a virtual certainty' should be confined to cases where the evidence of intent is limited to admitted actions of the accused and the consequences of those actions. It is not obligatory where there is other evidence to consider. The Crown's alternative submission on the appeal was to the same effect. This distinction would introduce yet another complication into a branch of the criminal law where simplicity is of supreme importance. The distinction is dependent on the vagaries of the evidence in particular cases. Moreover, a jury may reject the other evidence to which the Court of Appeal refers. And in preparing his summing up a judge could not ignore this possibility. If the Court of Appeal's view is right, it might compel a judge to pose different tests depending on what evidence the jury accepts. For my part, and with the greatest respect, I have to say that this distinction would be likely to produce great practical difficulties. But, most importantly, the distinction is not based on any principled view regarding the mental element in murder. Contrary to the view of the Court of Appeal, I would also hold that s 8(b) of the Act of 1967 does not compel such a result.

In my view the ruling of the Court of Appeal was wrong. It may be appropriate to give a direction in accordance with *Nedrick* in any case in which the defendant may not have desired the result of his act. But I accept the trial judge is best placed to decide what direction is required by the circumstances of the case.

The disposal of the present appeal

It follows that judge should not have departed from the *Nedrick* direction. By using the phrase 'substantial risk' the judge blurred the line between intention and recklessness, and hence between murder and manslaughter. The misdirection enlarged the scope of the mental element required for murder. It was a material misdirection. At one stage it was argued that the earlier correct direction 'cured' the subsequent incorrect direction. A misdirection cannot by any means always be cured by the fact that the judge at an earlier or later stage gave a correct direction. After all, how is a jury to choose between a correct and an incorrect direction on a point of law? If a misdirection is to be corrected, it must be done in the plainest terms ...

That is, however, not the end of the matter. For my part, I have given anxious consideration to the observation of the Court of Appeal that, if the judge had used the phrase 'a virtual certainty,' the verdict would have been the same. In this case there was no suggestion of any other ill-treatment of the child. It would also be putting matters too high to say that on the evidence before the jury it was an open-and-shut case of murder rather than manslaughter. In my view the conviction of murder is unsafe. The conviction of murder must be quashed.

The status of Nedrick

In my view Lord Lane's judgment in *Nedrick* provided valuable assistance to trial judges. The model direction is by now a tried-and-tested formula. Trial judges ought to continue to use it. On matters of detail I have three observations, which can best be understood if I set out again the relevant part of Lord Lane's judgment. It was as follows:

> (*A*) When determining whether the defendant had the necessary intent, it may therefore be helpful for a jury to ask themselves two questions. (1) How probable was the consequence which resulted from the defendant's voluntary act? (2) Did he foresee that consequence? If he did not appreciate that death or serious harm was likely to result from his act, he cannot have intended to bring it about. If he did, but thought that the risk to which he was exposing the person killed was only slight, then it may be easy for the jury to conclude that he did not intend to bring about that result. On the other hand, if the jury are satisfied that at the material time the defendant recognised that death or serious harm would be virtually certain (barring some unforeseen intervention) to result from his voluntary act, then that is a fact from which they may find it easy to infer that he intended to kill or do serious bodily harm, even though he may not have had any desire to achieve that result. (*B*) Where the charge is murder and in the rare cases where the simple direction is not enough, the jury should be directed that they are not entitled to infer the necessary intention, unless they feel sure that death or serious bodily harm was a virtual certainty (barring some unforeseen intervention) as a result of the defendant's actions and that the defendant appreciated that such was the case. (*C*) Where a man realises that it is for all practical purposes inevitable that his actions will result in death or serious harm, the inference may be irresistible that he intended that result, however little he may have desired or wished it to happen. The decision is one for the jury to be reached upon a consideration of all the evidence. (Lettering added.)

First, I am persuaded by the speech of my noble and learned friend, Lord Hope of Craighead, that it is unlikely, if ever, to be helpful to direct the jury in terms of the two questions set out in (A). I agree that these questions may detract from the clarity of the critical direction in (B). Secondly, in their writings previously cited Glanville Williams, JC Smith and Andrew Ashworth observed that the use of the words 'to infer' in (B) may detract from the clarity of the model direction. I agree. I would substitute the words 'to find.' Thirdly, the first sentence of (C) does not form part of the model direction. But it would always be right for the judge to say, as Lord Lane put it, that the decision is for the jury upon a consideration of all the evidence in the case.

The certified questions

Given my conclusions the certified questions fall away.

Notes and queries

1 What is the difference between inferring intention and finding intention?

2 What is to be made of Lord Steyn's observation that he approached the issues arising on the appeal 'on the basis that it does not follow that "intent" necessarily has precisely the same meaning in every context in the criminal law'? Does he mean that some offences require 'purpose' type intent? Or does he mean that intent might have a different meaning when used, for example, in the context of offences against the person? Is it conceivable that intent, in the context of intention to do grievous bodily harm contrary to s 18 of the Offences Against the Person Act 1861 (see further Chapter 16), would have a different meaning to that enunciated in *Woollin*? Given that intent to do grievous bodily harm will suffice for murder this (one hopes) seems unlikely.

Codification and law reform proposals

A proposed codification of intention can be found in cl 18(b) of the draft Criminal Code Bill (DCCB). The Law Commission subsequently published its proposals for reform of offences against the person (not including homicide) in *Offences Against the Person and General Principles* (Law Com 218). The draft Criminal Law Bill (DCLB) attached to that report provided for a somewhat amended definition of intention in cl 1. The most recent reform proposals are to be found in the draft Bill attached to the Home Office consultation paper *Violence: Reforming the Offences Against the Person Act 1861*, published in February 1998.

Clause 14 of the Home Office Bill proposes the following:

14(1) A person acts intentionally with respect to a result if –

(a) it is his purpose to cause it, or

(b) although it is not his purpose to cause it, he knows that it would occur in the ordinary course of events if he were to succeed in his purpose of causing some other result.

...

(3) A person intends an omission to have a result if –

(a) it is his purpose that the result will occur, or

(b) although it is not his purpose that the result will occur, he knows that it would occur in the ordinary course of events if he were to succeed in his purpose that some other result will occur.

Note that this proposed definition would only apply for the purposes of the Bill, hence it raises the prospect of intention having a different meaning in respect of other offences such as murder or criminal damage. This is clearly not a satisfactory state of affairs. If the *mens rea* for murder were to remain as 'intention to cause serious harm' it would be absurd if intent had one meaning in the context of murder, and another where the offence charged was intentionally causing serious harm under the proposed Bill.

RECKLESSNESS

For the vast majority of offences where *mens rea* has to be proved, recklessness will suffice. For offences such as 'simple' criminal damage contrary to s1(1) of the Criminal Damage Act 1971, assault, malicious wounding, or deception intention or recklessness will suffice. What meaning then is to be attributed to the term 'reckless'? On the one hand it can be seen as a fault element that justifies conviction notwithstanding that the defendant foresaw a prohibited consequence as something less than a virtually certain consequence of his act or omission – for example where the defendant foresaw that a certain harm might result. As will be seen from the extracts that follow, however, the debate in recent years has centred around the extent to which a defendant can be described as reckless notwithstanding the fact that he has not realised the risk of harm that could result from his act or omission.

Subjective recklessness

Although some would question the attribution of broad labels such as subjective or objective when describing fault elements, the subjective species of recklessness requires proof that the defendant was aware of the risk that a given harm might result from his actions. The modern authority for such an approach to recklessness is the Court of Appeal's decision in *R v Cunningham* (see below).

R v Morrison (1989) 89 Cr App R 17 (CA)

Lord Lane CJ: ... The other type of recklessness is that defined by Byrne J in the Court of Criminal Appeal in *Cunningham* (1957) 41 Cr App R 155, [1957] 2 QB 396 ... Byrne J in *Cunningham*, having set out the various cases under the 1861 Act, said at 159 and 399 respectively:

> We have considered those cases, and we have also considered, in the light of those cases, the following principle which was propounded by the late Professor CS Kenny in the first edition of his *Outlines of Criminal Law* published in 1902 and repeated at p 186 of the 16th edition edited by Mr JW Cecil Turner and published in 1952: 'In any statutory definition of a crime, malice must be taken not in the old vague sense of wickedness in general but as requiring either (1) An actual intention to do the particular kind of harm that in fact was done; or (2) [this is the important passage] recklessness as to whether such harm should occur or not (ie the accused has foreseen that the particular kind of harm might be done and yet has gone on to take the risk of it). It is neither limited to nor does it indeed require any ill will towards the person injured.'

We think that this is an accurate statement of the law.

Objective recklessness

Metropolitan Police Commissioner v Caldwell [1982] AC 343; [1981] 1 All ER 961 (HL)

Lord Diplock: My Lords, the facts that gave rise to this appeal are simple. The respondent had been doing work for the proprietor of a residential hotel. He considered that he had a grievance against the proprietor. One night he got very drunk and in the early hours of the morning he decided to revenge himself on the proprietor by setting fire to the hotel, in which some 10 guests were living at the time. He broke a window and succeeded in starting a fire in a ground floor room; but fortunately it was discovered and the flames were extinguished before any serious damage was caused. At his trial he said that he was so drunk at the time that the thought that there might be people in the hotel whose lives might be endangered if it were set on fire had never crossed his mind ...

The question of law certified for the opinion of this House was:

> Whether evidence of self-induced intoxication can be relevant to the following questions: (a) whether the defendant intended to endanger the life of another; and (b) whether the defendant was reckless as to whether the life of another would be endangered, within the meaning of s 1(2)(b) of the Criminal Damage Act 1971.

The question recognises that under s 1(2)(b) there are two alternative states of mind as respects endangering the life of another, and that existence of either of them on the part of the accused is sufficient to constitute the *mens rea* needed to convert the lesser offence under s 1(1) into the graver offence under s 1(2). One is intention that a particular thing should happen in consequence of the *actus reus*, viz, that the life of another person should be endangered (this was not relied on by the prosecution in the instant case). The other is recklessness whether that particular thing should happen or not. The same dichotomy of *mentes reae*, intention and recklessness, is to be found throughout the section; in subsection (1) and paragraph (a) of subsection (2) as well as in paragraph (b); and 'reckless' as descriptive of a state of mind must be given the same meaning in each of them ...

My Lords, the restricted meaning that the Court of Appeal in *R v Cunningham* had placed upon the adverb 'maliciously' in the Malicious Damage Act 1861 in cases where the prosecution did not rely upon an actual intention of the accused to cause the damage that was in fact done, called for a meticulous analysis by the jury of the thoughts that passed through the mind of the accused at or before the time he did the act that caused the damage, in order to see on which side of a narrow dividing line they fell. If it had crossed his mind that there was a risk that someone's property might be damaged but, because his mind was affected by rage or excitement or confused by drink, he did not appreciate the seriousness of the risk or trusted that good luck would prevent its happening, this state of mind would amount to malice in the restricted meaning placed upon that term by the Court of Appeal; whereas if, for any of these reasons, he did not even trouble to give his mind to the question whether there was any risk of damaging the property, this state of mind would not suffice to make him guilty of an offence under the Malicious Damage Act 1861.

Neither state of mind seems to me to be less blameworthy than the other; but if the difference between the two constituted the distinction between what does and what does not in legal theory amount to a guilty state of mind for the purposes of a statutory offence of damage to property, it would not be a practicable distinction for use in a trial by jury. The only person who knows what the accused's mental processes were is the accused himself – and probably not even he can recall them accurately when the rage or excitement under which he acted has passed, or he has sobered up if he were under the influence of drink at the relevant time. If the accused gives evidence that because of his rage, excitement or drunkenness the risk of particular harmful consequences of his acts simply did not occur to him, a jury would find it hard to be satisfied beyond reasonable doubt that his true mental process was not that, but was the slightly different mental process required if one applies the restricted meaning of 'being reckless as to whether' something would happen, adopted by the Court of Appeal in *R v Cunningham*.

My Lords, I can see no reason why Parliament when it decided to revise the law as to offences of damage to property should go out of its way to perpetuate fine and impracticable distinctions such as these, between one mental state and another. One would think that the sooner they were got rid of, the better ...

... 'Reckless' as used in the new statutory definition of the *mens rea* of these offences is an ordinary English word. It had not by 1971 become a term of legal art with some more limited esoteric meaning than that which it bore in ordinary speech, a meaning which surely includes not only deciding to ignore a risk of harmful consequences resulting from one's acts that one has recognised as existing, but also failing to give any thought to whether or not there is any such risk in circumstances where, if any thought were given to the matter, it would be obvious that there was.

If one is attaching labels, the latter state of mind is neither more nor less 'subjective' than the first. But the label solves nothing. It is a statement of the obvious; *mens rea* is, by definition, a state of mind of the accused himself at the time he did the physical act that constitutes the *actus reus* of the offence; it cannot be the mental state of some non-existent, hypothetical person.

Nevertheless, to decide whether someone has been 'reckless' as to whether harmful consequences of a particular kind will result from his act, as distinguished from his actually intending such harmful consequences to follow, does call for some consideration of how the mind of the ordinary prudent individual would have reacted to a similar situation. If there were nothing in the circumstances that ought to have drawn the attention of an ordinary prudent individual to the possibility of that kind of harmful consequence, the accused would not be described as 'reckless' in the natural meaning of that word for failing to address his mind to the possibility; nor, if the risk of the harmful consequences was so slight that the ordinary prudent individual on due consideration of the risk would not be deterred from treating it as negligible, could the accused be described as 'reckless' in its ordinary sense if, having considered the risk, he decided to ignore it. (In this connection the gravity of the possible harmful consequences would be an important factor. To endanger life must be one of the most grave.) So to this extent, even if one ascribes to 'reckless' only the restricted meaning, adopted by the Court of Appeal in *R v Stephenson* [1979] QB 695 and *R v Briggs* (Note) [1977] 1 WLR 605, of foreseeing that a particular kind of harm might happen and yet going on to take the risk of it, it involves a test that would be described in part as 'objective' in current legal jargon. Questions of criminal liability are seldom solved by simply asking whether the test is subjective or objective.

In my opinion, a person charged with an offence under s 1(1) of the Criminal Damage Act 1971 is 'reckless as to whether or not any such property would be destroyed or damaged' if (1) he does an act which in fact creates an obvious risk that property will be destroyed or damaged and (2) when he does the act he either has not given any thought to the possibility of there being any such risk or has recognised that there was some risk involved and has nonetheless gone on to do it. That would be a proper direction to the jury; cases in the Court of Appeal which held otherwise should be regarded as overruled.

Where the charge is under s 1(2) the question of the state of mind of the accused must be approached in stages, corresponding to paragraphs (a) and (b). The jury must be satisfied that what the accused did amounted to an offence under s 1(1), either because he actually intended to destroy or damage the property or because he was reckless (in the sense that I have described) as to whether it might be destroyed or damaged. Only if they are so satisfied must the jury go on to consider whether the accused also either actually intended that the destruction or damage of the property should endanger someone's life or was reckless (in a similar sense) as to whether a human life might be endangered.

Turning now to the instant case, the first stage was eliminated by the respondent's plea of guilty to the charge under s 1(1). Furthermore he himself gave evidence that his actual intention was to damage the hotel in order to revenge himself on the proprietor. As respects the charge under s 1(2) the prosecution did not rely on an actual intent of the respondent to endanger the lives of the residents but relied on his having been reckless whether the lives of any of them would be endangered. His act of setting fire to it was one which the jury were entitled to think created an obvious risk that the lives of the residents would be endangered; and the only defence with which your Lordships are concerned is that the respondent had made himself so drunk as to render him oblivious of that risk. If the only mental state capable of constituting the necessary *mens rea* for an offence under s 1(2) were that expressed in the words 'intending by the destruction or damage to endanger the life of another', it would have been necessary to consider whether the offence was to be classified as one of 'specific' intent for the purposes of the rule of law which this House affirmed and applied in *R v Majewski* [1977] AC 443; and this it plainly is. But this is not, in my view, a relevant inquiry where 'being reckless as to whether the life of another would be thereby endangered' is an alternative mental state that is capable of constituting the necessary *mens rea* of the offence with which he is charged.

The speech of Lord Elwyn-Jones LC in *R v Majewski* [1977] AC 443, 475, with which Lord Simon, Lord Kilbrandon and I agreed, is authority that self-induced intoxication is no defence to a crime in which recklessness is enough to constitute the necessary *mens rea*. The charge in *Majewski* was of assault occasioning actual bodily harm and it was held by the majority of the House, approving *R v Venna* [1976] QB 421 at 428, that recklessness in the use of force was sufficient to satisfy the mental element in the offence of assault. Reducing oneself by drink or drugs to a condition in which the restraints of reason and conscience are cast off was held to be a reckless course of conduct and an integral part of the crime. Lord Elwyn-Jones

LC accepted at 475 as correctly stating English law the provision in s 2.08 (2) of the American Model Penal Code:

> When recklessness establishes an element of the offence, if the actor, due to self-induced intoxication, is unaware of a risk of which he would have been aware had he been sober, such unawareness is immaterial.

So, in the instant case, the fact that the respondent was unaware of the risk of endangering the lives of residents in the hotel owing to his self-induced intoxication, would be no defence if that risk would have been obvious to him had he been sober ...

I would give the following answers to the certified question: (a) If the charge of an offence under s 1(2) of the Criminal Damage Act 1971 is framed so as to charge the defendant only with 'intending by the destruction or damage [of the property] to endanger the life of another', evidence of self-induced intoxication can be relevant to his defence. (b) If the charge is, or includes, a reference to his 'being reckless as to whether the life of another would thereby be endangered', evidence of self-induced intoxication is not relevant.

Lord Keith of Kinkel and **Lord Roskill** concurred. **Lord Edmund Davies** and **Lord Wilberforce** agreed that the appeal should be dismissed but disagreed with the reasoning of the majority of the relevance of the defendant's intoxication to the issue of recklessness.

R v Lawrence [1982] AC 510 (HL)

The respondent driver appealed against his conviction for causing death by reckless driving. The House of Lords considered the meaning of the word reckless as used in the Road Traffic Act 1972.

> **Lord Diplock**: My Lords ... this House has very recently had occasion in *R v Caldwell* ... to give close consideration to the concept of recklessness as constituting *mens rea* in criminal law ... The conclusion reached by the majority was that the adjective 'reckless' when used in a criminal statute, ie the Criminal Damage Act 1971, had not acquired a special meaning as a term of legal art, but bore its popular or dictionary meaning of careless, regardless, or heedless of the possible harmful consequences of one's acts. The same must be true of the adverbial derivative 'recklessly'.
>
> The context in which the word 'reckless' appears in s 1 of the Criminal Damage Act 1971 differs in two respects from the context in which word 'recklessly' appears in ss 1 and 2 of the Road Traffic Act 1972, as now amended. In the Criminal Damage Act 1971 the *actus reus*, the physical act of destroying or damaging property belonging to another, is in itself a tort. It is not something that one does regularly as part of the ordinary routine of daily life, such as driving a car or a motor cycle. So there is something out of the ordinary to call the doer's attention to what he is doing and its possible consequences, which is absent in road traffic offences. The other difference in context is that in s 1 of the Criminal Damage Act 1971 the *mens rea* of the offences is defined as being reckless as to whether particular harmful consequences would occur, whereas in ss 1 and 2 of the Road Traffic Act 1972, as now amended, the possible harmful consequences of which the driver must be shown to have been heedless are left to be implied from

the use of the word 'recklessly' itself. In ordinary usage 'recklessly' as descriptive of a physical act such as driving a motor vehicle which can be performed in a variety of different ways, some of them entailing danger and some of them not, refers not only to the state of mind of the doer of the act when he decides to do it but also qualifies the manner in which the act itself is performed. One does not speak of a person acting 'recklessly', even though he has given no thought at all to the consequences of his act, unless the act is one that presents a real risk of harmful consequences which anyone acting with reasonable prudence would recognise and give heed to. So the *actus reus* of the offence under ss 1 and 2 is not simply driving a motor vehicle on a road, but driving it in a manner which in fact creates a real risk of harmful consequences resulting from it. Since driving in such a manner as to do no worse than create a risk of causing inconvenience or annoyance to other road users constitutes the lesser offence under s 3, the manner of driving that constitutes the *actus reus* of an offence under ss 1 and 2 must be worse than that; it must be such as to create a real risk of causing physical injury to someone else who happens to be using the road or damage to property more substantial than the kind of minor damage that may be caused by an error of judgment in the course of parking one's car ...

I turn now to the *mens rea*. My task is greatly simplified by what has already been said about the concept of recklessness in criminal law in *R v Caldwell* [1982] AC 341. Warning was there given against adopting the simplistic approach of treating all problems of criminal liability as soluble by classifying the test of liability as being either 'subjective' or 'objective'. Recklessness on the part of the doer of an act does presuppose that there is something in the circumstances that would have drawn the attention of an ordinary prudent individual to the possibility that his act was capable of causing the kind of serious harmful consequences that the section which creates the offence was intended to prevent, and that the risk of those harmful consequences occurring was not so slight that an ordinary prudent individual would feel justified in treating them as negligible. It is only when this is so that the doer of the act is acting 'recklessly' if before doing the act, he either fails to give any thought to the possibility of there being any such risk or, having recognised that there was such risk, he nevertheless goes on to do it.

In my view, an appropriate instruction to the jury on what is meant by driving recklessly would be that they must be satisfied of two things:

First, that the defendant was in fact driving the vehicle in such a manner as to create an obvious and serious risk of causing physical injury to some other person who might happen to be using the road or of doing substantial damage to property; and

Second, that in driving in that manner the defendant did so without having given any thought to the possibility of there being any such risk or, having recognised that there was some risk involved, had nonetheless gone on to take it.

It is for the jury to decide whether the risk created by the manner in which the vehicle was being driven was both obvious and serious and, in deciding this, they may apply the standard of the ordinary prudent motorist as represented by themselves.

If satisfied that an obvious and serious risk was created by the manner of the defendant's driving, the jury are entitled to infer that he was in one or other of the states of mind required to constitute the offence and will probably do so; but regard must be given to any explanation he gives as to his state of mind which may displace the inference ...

R v Reid [1992] 1 WLR 793 (HL)

The appellant was convicted of causing death by reckless driving. He appealed unsuccessfully to the House of Lords, the appeal providing the House with the opportunity to reassess its previous decisions in *Caldwell* and *Lawrence*.

Lord Keith of Kinkel: My Lords, the question principally debated at the hearing of this appeal was whether the formulation by Lord Diplock in *R v Lawrence* [1982] AC 510 at 525–26 of the meaning of 'driving recklessly' in s 1 of the Road Traffic Act 1972 (as amended) was incorrect, so that the decision in that case should be departed from under the 1966 practice statement (see Note [1966] 1 WLR 1234). It was argued for the appellant that the formulation was mistaken in respect that Lord Diplock expressed the *mens rea* for the statutory offence as including not only a state of mind where the accused drove as he did recognising that his action created a risk of injury or of substantial damage to property but nevertheless went on to take that risk, but also a state of mind where the accused drove as he did without giving any thought to the possibility of there being any such risk, notwithstanding that the risk was obvious (see [1982] AC 510 at 526–27). In truth, so it was maintained, it was only the former state of mind which constituted the relevant *mens rea*. In common with my noble and learned friends Lord Ackner and Lord Goff of Chieveley I am satisfied that, for the reasons they give, the argument is unsound. Lord Diplock described the *actus reus* of the offence as driving a vehicle in such a manner as to create an obvious and serious risk of causing physical injury to some other person who might happen to be using the road or of doing substantial damage to property. The important thing here is that the risk created must be an obvious and serious one. No criticism has been or could be made of that. The precise state of mind of a person who drives in the manner indicated must in the vast majority of cases be quite incapable of ascertainment. Absence of something from a person's mind is as much part of his state of mind as its presence. Inadvertence to risk is no less a subjective state of mind than is disregard of a recognised risk. If there is nothing to go upon apart from what actually happened, the natural inference is that the driver's state of mind was one or other of those described by Lord Diplock. It would, however, be quite impossible for any juryman to say which it was, and in particular for him to be satisfied beyond reasonable doubt that it was the first state of mind rather than the second. So logically, if only the first state of mind constituted the relevant *mens rea*, it would be impossible ever to get a conviction. There is no room for doubt, in my opinion, that a large proportion of drivers who drive in such a manner as to create the relevant sort of risk do so without giving any thought to the possibility of risk. Indeed, the very attempt to exclude such drivers from the ambit of the statutory offence recognises that this must be so. Driving a motor vehicle is potentially an extremely dangerous activity, requiring a high degree of self-discipline. Those who fail to display the requisite degree of self-discipline through failing to give any thought to the possibility of the serious risks they are creating may reasonably be regarded as no less blameworthy than those who consciously appreciate a risk but nevertheless go on to take it. The word 'reckless' in its ordinary meaning is apt to embrace the former category no less than the latter, and I feel no doubt that Parliament by its use intended to cover both of them.

The substance of Lord Diplock's formulation of a specimen jury direction is accordingly apt, in my opinion, to cover the generality of cases. But I do not rule out that in certain cases there may be special circumstances which require it to be modified or added to, for example where the driver acted under some understandable and excusable mistake or where his capacity to appreciate risks was adversely affected by some condition not involving fault on his part. There may also be cases where the driver acted as he did in a sudden dilemma created by the actions of others. The specific certified question as to whether the jury should always be directed in the *ipsissima verba* of Lords Diplock's formulation I would answer in the negative. In some cases when the only relevant issue is one of disputed fact it may not be necessary to use it at all. In others it may require to be modified or adapted to suit the circumstances of the case ...

Lord Goff of Chieveley: My Lords ... I think it right that I should at this stage set out the passage from Lord Diplock's speech in *R v Lawrence* ... This definition of the *mens rea* (which mirrors Lord Diplock's definition in *R v Caldwell* [1982] AC 341 at 354 of the *mens rea* of recklessness in s 1 of the Criminal Damage Act 1971) has proved to be most controversial. It has provoked a very hostile reaction from some of our leading academic lawyers specialising in criminal law. Their view has been that the mental element in crimes involving recklessness should be restricted to the second of the two alternatives referred to by Lord Diplock, viz disregarding a recognised risk, which is usually called the subjective test. The first of these two alternative formulations, viz acting without giving any thought to the possibility of there being any risk of the relevant kind, they have rejected as contrary to principle and contrary to previous Court of Appeal authority (see, in particular, *R v Stephenson* [1979] QB 695, a decision under the Criminal Damage Act 1971, disapproved in *R v Caldwell*).

The central question in this appeal is whether, in cases concerned with driving recklessly, your Lordships' House should reject Lord Diplock's alternative form of recklessness and restrict that concept to the so-called subjective approach. It came as no surprise that Mr Michael Hill QC, for the appellant Mr Reid, placed this submission at the forefront of his argument, seeking to persuade your Lordships to reconsider *R v Lawrence* and, in so far as the decision extended the mental element in cases of recklessness beyond the category of disregarding a recognised risk, to exercise the power under the 1966 practice statement (see Note [1966] 1 WLR 1234) to hold that it was wrongly decided and, on that basis, to allow the appeal.

In order to consider the submission advanced by Mr Hill for the appellant, it is first necessary to ascertain precisely what led to the formulation of Lords Diplock's specimen direction in *R v Lawrence*, and in particular to his introduction of his first alternative form of the mental element in recklessness in that case. I am anxious not to indulge in long quotations from Lord Diplock's speeches in *R v Caldwell* and *R v Lawrence* so I will summarise, as best I can, the steps to his reasoning. Central to his reasoning in *R v Caldwell* [1982] AC 341 at 351–55 was the idea that recklessness, in its ordinary meaning, covers a whole range of states of mind, from failing to give any thought to whether there is any risk of the relevant kind, to recognising the existence of the risk and nevertheless deciding to ignore it. From this it followed that to concentrate on one type of recklessness (disregarding a recognised risk) to the exclusion of others would impose an unnaturally narrow meaning upon the word; and, since disregarding a recognised risk was not necessarily more blameworthy than failing to give any thought to the possibility of risk, to restrict recklessness to the former meaning was undesirable as a matter of policy. Furthermore, to require a jury to convict a defendant of recklessness only if he had in fact foreseen the relevant risk and nevertheless disregarded it was in reality to impose an impossible task upon juries, since in real life disregarding a recognised risk and failing to address one's mind to the possibility of risk are states of mind which shade into each other and in many cases are very difficult, if not impossible, to segregate and so identify in any particular case. To the suggestion that disregarding a recognised risk constituted a test of *mens rea* which was subjective (and therefore acceptable as a criterion of blameworthiness), whereas failing to address one's mind to the possibility of risk was essentially objective and therefore not acceptable, Lord Diplock's response was to disparage the use of the terms 'subjective' and 'objective', and to assert that in any event both criteria were, in their different ways, subjective. Even so he recognised that, before a man could be held to have been reckless, there must have been something which ought to have drawn the attention of an ordinary prudent person to the possibility of the relevant harm occurring; and he laid down the further requirement that the ordinary prudent person would not, on consideration, have treated the risk as negligible.

In *R v Lawrence* [1982] AC 510 at 525–26 Lord Diplock developed this reasoning to render it more appropriate to the rather different case of driving recklessly. He considered that, in ordinary usage, the word 'recklessly' as descriptive of a physical act such as driving a motor vehicle not only refers to the state of mind of the driver, but also qualifies the manner in which his act of driving is performed. In his opinion, the *actus reus* of such an offence must be driving the vehicle in a manner which in fact creates a real risk of harm. Furthermore, since driving recklessly must be intended to be worse than merely careless driving punishable under s 3 of the same Act, it must be such as to create a risk of damage more substantial than the kind of minor damage associated with an error of judgment. It was his reasoning in *R v Caldwell* together with his further reasoning in *R v Lawrence*, which led him to formulate the specimen direction in *R v Lawrence* which I have already quoted.

Now the fundamental reason for the academic hostility to *R v Caldwell* and *R v Lawrence* lies in the perception that the appropriate definition of the mental element in recklessness is to be found in the idea of acting in disregard of a recognised risk. Thus, in cl 5.12 of the draft Criminal Code (*Legislating the Criminal Code: Offences Against the Person and General Principles* (Law Commission Consultation Paper 122) (1992)), of which Professor Smith is the leading draftsman, we find the following definition of recklessness:

> ... a person acts ... 'recklessly' with respect to: (1) a circumstance when he is aware of a risk that it exists or will exist; (2) a result when he is aware of a risk that it will occur; and it is, in the circumstances known to him, unreasonable to take the risk.

Likewise, we find Professor Glanville Williams asserting in para 5.1 of his *Textbook of Criminal Law*, 2nd edn, 1983, p 96, that recklessness 'normally involves conscious and unreasonable risk-taking'. This is generally accepted as constituting a form of recklessness. But the question is whether this is the only form which recklessness is understood to take, and indeed whether recklessness should properly be understood to take only one form. This is the point on which Lord Diplock challenged academic opinion, by embracing within the concept of recklessness his alternative category. It is evident from his reasoning that he would include within this alternative category cases where the defendant's perception is impaired by drink or by blind rage or by some other excitement, with the result that he fails to give any thought to the possibility of such risk. But there may well be other cases. For example, the defendant's state of mind may be such that he does not care whether any such risk exists or not, which has been described as an attitude of indifference, or of not caring less. Such a state of mind does not necessarily involve awareness of risk ... In other cases, the defendant's state of mind may be one of wilful blindness, where he simply closes his mind to the possibility of risk. In yet other case, perhaps the most common, the defendant simply does not think about the matter at all, perhaps because he is acting impetuously on the spur of the moment without addressing his mind to the possibility of risk.

It is not difficult to give examples of cases of this kind in the context of driving. I can for example see no difficulty in envisaging a driver who drives at high speed in traffic or in a built-up area or both, just not caring whether any risk of personal injury or damage to other vehicles exists or not. It does not matter whether in such a case he is indifferent to the existence of the risk, or whether he has closed his mind to any such thing; the point is that in such circumstances he may not even address his mind to the possibility of risk. Likewise, when driving down the motorway many of us must have seen small groups of motorcyclists weaving in and out of the traffic at enormous speeds, with their eyes apparently glued to their speedometers to see how fast they are going. Again, these young men may very well not even address their minds to the possibility of risk, concentrating only on the speed at which they are travelling. Then there are the young joyriders who take other people's cars, often fast cars such as GTIs, and drive them at high speed around housing estates. They, too, may well give no thought to the possibility of risk to other people or other vehicles in the vicinity. These are everyday examples of cases which we have either seen ourselves on the road or have read about in the newspapers. I cannot help thinking that in ordinary speech all these people would be described as driving recklessly. Certainly, I do not think that ordinary people would regard it as a relevant inquiry to ascertain whether these drivers had in fact addressed their minds to the possibility of risk before they could be said to have acted recklessly. Indeed, I would go further and say that this category of recklessness on the roads may well be as prevalent as the category in which the driver actually foresees the risk and decides to disregard it. This is because on the roads decisions to act, for example to overtake or to go for a gap, are often split-second decisions which may be taken virtually without thought. In retrospect after the event, a driver may say, 'Yes, I did think about it and I did realise that there was a risk'; but he may be just as likely, if not more likely, to say, 'I am afraid that I just did not think but, if I had done, I would have realised that there was a risk'. In circumstances such as these, an enquiry into the existence of actual foresight of the risk would seem to be unrealistic for the purpose of assessing blameworthiness or criminality. Indeed, it can be argued with force that, in many cases of failing to think, the degree of blameworthiness to be attached to the driver can be greater than that to be attached in some cases to the driver who recognised the risk and decided to disregard it. This is because the unspoken premise which seems to me to underlie Lord Diplock's statement of the law in *R v Lawrence* (and perhaps also in *R v Caldwell*) is that the defendant is engaged in an activity which he knows to be potentially dangerous. Every driver knows that driving can be dangerous; and if when a man is in fact driving dangerously in the sense described by Lord Diplock, he does not even address his mind to the possibility of risk, then, in the absence of special circumstances (to which I will refer later) it is right that he should, if the risk was obvious, be held to have been driving recklessly, even though he was not in fact aware of the risk. It cannot be right that in such circumstances he should be able to shelter behind his ignorance, or be given preferred treatment as compared with another person who, having recognised and considered the risk, has wrongly decided to disregard it. If the policy underlying this category of recklessness were to be explained to a jury, I would be surprised if they had difficulty in understanding it ...

It follows that in cases of driving recklessly (with which your Lordships are here concerned), I find myself to be in respectful agreement with the conclusion of Lord Diplock, that recklessness cannot sensibly be restricted to the so-called subjective test, but must be extended to embrace cases where the defendant has failed to give any thought to the possibility of risk ... I recognise that it has been suggested that, if this is right, driving recklessly cannot be so sharply differentiated from careless driving, ie driving without due care and attention, as it would be if the purely subjective test were to be adopted as the sole criterion of recklessness, in which case a clear distinction could be drawn between cases where the defendant was aware of the risk and nevertheless disregarded it, and cases where the defendant failed to advert to the relevant risk. But the answer to this criticism is, I believe, as follows. First, as I have already said, we have to recognise that there are cases where, although the defendant is unaware of the risk, his conduct coupled with his state of mind is such that, in ordinary speech, he can properly be described as driving recklessly. Second, these cases can be differentiated from mere careless driving, because they are cases in which the defendant's driving would be described as dangerous in the sense that he was driving in such a manner as to create a serious risk of causing physical injury to other people or substantial damage to other people's property, and yet he did not even address his mind to the possibility of there being any such risk. This is different from a case where, for example, momentary inadvertence happens incidentally to create a risk; for the recklessness arises from the combination of the dangerous character of the driving coupled with failure by the driver even to address his mind to the possibility of risk. I for my part see no real difficulty, in practice, in perceiving a sufficiently clear differentiation between cases of this kind and cases of driving without due care and attention, which we see happening so often on the roads and of which many of us may, I fear, be guilty from time to time. Take the simple case of a man driving his car on the motorway in a group of other cars, all travelling at say 60 mph, and he fails for a moment or so to keep his eye on the car in front – perhaps his attention is caught by a pretty girl in the car alongside – with the result that he does not notice that the car in front has had to brake suddenly and he drives straight into it causing it damage. This is a classic case of careless driving; I do not think that on these simple facts anybody would say that he was driving recklessly. This is not a case of a man driving dangerously (in the sense described by Lord Diplock) and nevertheless failing to address his mind to the possibility of risk; it is a case of a man who failed to drive with due care and attention, and no more ...

Lord Browne-Wilkinson: ... In the present context, I would have thought that the correct usage of the word 'subjective' is to connote a requirement that the offence is committed only if the mental state of the accused himself, as opposed to the mental state of the reasonable man, were such as to satisfy the requirements of *mens rea* for that offence. An objective test, on the other hand, would be satisfied if it could be shown that the state of mind of a reasonable man in those circumstances would satisfy the requirements of *mens rea* for that offence.

That being my understanding of the words, I am puzzled by the criticism of the direction in *R v Lawrence* that it lays down an objective test since in my judgment it plainly does not. First, the answer given by this House to the first question posed in *Lawrence* – '*mens rea* is involved in the offence of driving recklessly' – shows that it is not an absolute offence. Lord Diplock in his speech when dealing with *mens rea* refers to the necessary mental state of the accused himself ...

As I understand the criticisms of *R v Lawrence*, they are founded on the proposition that 'recklessness' requires it to be shown that the defendant was aware of the risk and disregarded it, which I shall call 'advertence'. It is said that a 'couldn't care less' attitude in which the defendant does not address his mind at all to whether or not there is a risk (non-advertence) is not sufficient. Non-advertence is characterised by the critics as being not subjective. In my judgment this is to confuse the issue; both advertence and non-advertence to risk are states of mind of the defendant himself. Therefore the test is, on my terminology, subjective in both cases ...

Elliott v C [1983] 1 WLR 939 (DC)

Glidewell J: This is an appeal by way of case stated from Kent Justices ... who ... found the defendant not guilty of a charge ... that she on 16 June 1982, without lawful excuse had destroyed by fire a shed and its contents, intending to destroy such property or being reckless as to whether such property would be destroyed, contrary to s 1(1) of the Criminal Damage Act 1971.

The shed was the property of a Mr Walter Davies. It was a large wooden shed, and stood at the bottom of the garden of Mr Davies's home. In it he stored tools, various paints, and turpentine or white spirit.

The defendant was a schoolgirl who had reached the age of 14 years in May 1982. She lived with her foster-mother and was in a remedial class at school. On the evening of 15 June 1982, the defendant went out with an older girl friend. She hoped to stay the night in the friend's home, but was not able to do so. The defendant did not return to her own home but stayed out all night, not sleeping for the whole night.

At about 5 am on 16 June 1982, the defendant entered Mr Davies's garden shed. She found the white spirit in its plastic container. She poured white spirit onto the carpet on the floor of the shed and threw two lighted matches onto the spirit, the second of which ignited. The fire immediately flared up out of control and the defendant left the shed.

A Mr Hubbard, who was delivering milk in the area, saw the defendant in the vicinity at about 5.40 am, and a few minutes later saw the shed on fire and raised the alarm.

The police arrested the defendant at her home at 8 am on 16 June 1982, on suspicion of arson and two offences of burglary. She was cautioned in the presence of her foster-mother and made no reply. She was taken to Whitstable Police Station and placed in the cells, where she slept until about 3 pm on the afternoon of the same day.

At 3 pm on 16 June 1982, the defendant was interviewed by two police officers in the presence of her foster-mother. After caution she admitted that she had entered the shed, put spirit on the floor, and set fire to it. She said that she did not know why she had set fire to the shed and that she had 'just felt like it'. She said that she had had the matches with her when she entered the shed, and that after she had set fire to the shed she had run out into the road and had been seen by the milkman. She agreed to make a written statement under caution, in which she admitted entering the shed and setting fire to it.

Although the wording of the information, following the wording of s 1(1) of the Criminal Damage Act 1971, alleged that the defendant destroyed by fire the shed 'intending to destroy such property or being reckless as to whether such property would be destroyed', at the hearing before the justices the contention on behalf of the prosecutor, was not that the evidence proved an intention to destroy the property but that it did prove that the defendant was reckless as to whether the property would be destroyed ...

... [Counsel for the prosecutor] submits that the phrase [in *R v Caldwell* [1982] AC 341] 'creates an obvious risk' means that the risk is one which must have been obvious to a reasonably prudent man, not necessarily to the particular defendant if he or she had given thought to it. It follows, says [counsel], that if the risk is one which would have been obvious to a reasonably prudent person, once it has also been proved that the particular defendant gave no thought to the possibility of there being such a risk, it is not a defence that because of limited intelligence or exhaustion she would not have appreciated the risk even if she had thought about it ...

That [this] submission is correct is to my mind ... put beyond a peradventure by two later decisions of the House of Lords. [His Lordship then referred to *R v Lawrence (Stephen)* [1982] AC 510 and to *R v Miller* [1983] 2 AC 161 and continued:]

In the light of these last two authorities, we are in my judgment bound to hold that the word 'reckless' in s 1 of the Criminal Damage Act 1971 has the meaning ascribed to it by [counsel for the prosecutor] ...

The questions posed [by the justices] in the case are:

1   Whether properly directing ourselves and upon a true construction of s 1(1) of the Criminal Damage Act 1971 we were correct in our interpretation of the meaning of reckless, namely that a defendant should only be held to have acted recklessly by virtue of his failure to give any thought to an obvious risk that property would be destroyed or damaged, where such risk would have been obvious to him if he had given any thought to the matter?

2   Whether properly directing ourselves on the evidence we could properly have come to our decision that the [defendant] had acted neither intentionally nor recklessly in destroying by fire the shed and its contents?

I would answer 'No' to both questions, and allow the appeal.

Robert Goff LJ: I agree with the conclusion reached by Glidewell J, but I do so simply because I believe myself constrained to do so by authority ...

[His Lordship summarised the facts and noted that the defendant] gave no thought at the time when she started the fire to the possibility of there being a risk that the shed and its contents would be destroyed [and that this] risk would not have been obvious to her or have been appreciated by her if she had given thought to the matter. I add that these conclusions were reached by the justices, having regard to the age and understanding of the defendant, her lack of experience of dealing with inflammable spirit, and the fact that she must have been tired and exhausted at the time ...

Plainly, she did destroy the shed and its contents by fire; plainly, too, she did so without lawful excuse. But was she reckless as to whether the shed and its contents would be destroyed?

His Lordship then referred to *R v Caldwell* [1982] AC 341 and cited the *dictum* of Lord Diplock at 354.

Now, if that test is applied literally in the present case, the conclusion appears inevitable that, on the facts found by the justices, the defendant was reckless whether the shed and contents would be destroyed; because first she did an act which created an obvious risk that the property would be destroyed, and second she had not given any thought to the possibility of there being any such risk.

Yet, if I next pause ... and ask myself the question: would I, having regard only to the ordinary meaning of the word, consider this girl to have been, on the facts found, reckless whether the shed and contents would be destroyed, my answer would, I confess, be in the negative. This is not a case where there was a deliberate disregard of a known risk of damage or injury of a certain type or degree; nor is it a case where there was mindless indifference to a risk of such damage or injury ... nor is it even a case where failure to give thought to the possibility of the risk was due to some blameworthy cause, such as intoxication. This is a case where it appears that the only basis on which the accused might be held to have been reckless would be if the appropriate test to be applied was purely objective – a test which might in some circumstances be thought justifiable in relation to certain conduct (eg reckless driving) ... But such a test does not appear at first sight to be appropriate to a crime such as that under consideration in the present case, especially as recklessness in that crime has to be related to a particular consequence. I therefore next ask myself the question whether I can, consistently with the doctrine of precedent, sensibly interpreted, legitimately construe or qualify the principle stated by Lord Diplock in *R v Caldwell* [1982] AC 341 so as to accommodate what I conceive to be the appropriate result on the facts of the present case, bearing in mind that those facts are very different from the facts under consideration by the House of Lords in *R v Caldwell*, where the defendant had set fire to a hotel when in a state of intoxication.

... I find it striking that the justices, in reaching their conclusion in the present case, have done so ... by imposing on Lord Diplock's statement of principle a qualification ... that a defendant should only be regarded as having acted recklessly by virtue of his failure to give any thought to an obvious risk that property would be destroyed or damaged, where such risk would have been obvious to him if he had given any thought to the matter. However, having studied Lord Diplock's speech, I do not think it would be consistent with his reasoning to impose any such qualification. I say that not only because this qualification does not appear in terms in his conclusion ... but also because ...

earlier in his speech ... Lord Diplock expressly adverted to the fact that [Professor Kenny's] definition presupposed that 'if thought were given to the matter by the doer before the act was done, it would have been apparent to him that there was a real risk of its having the relevant harmful consequences'. It seems to me that, having expressly considered that element in Professor Kenny's test, and having (as I think) plainly decided to omit it from his own formulation of the concept of recklessness, it would not now be legitimate for an inferior court, in a case under this particular subsection, to impose a qualification which had so been rejected by Lord Diplock himself. It follows that for that reason alone I do not feel able to uphold the reasoning of the justices in the present case. But I wish to add that, for my part, I doubt whether this qualification can be justified in any event. Where there is no thought of the consequences, any further enquiry necessary for the purposes of establishing guilt should *prima facie* be directed to the question why such thought was not given, rather than to the purely hypothetical question of what the particular person would have appreciated had he directed his mind to the matter ...

In these circumstances, I agree that the questions must be answered as proposed by Glidewell J, and that the appeal must be allowed.

Notes and queries

1   What was the point of imposing liability on a defendant who would not have been aware of the 'obvious risk' even if she had stopped to consider the risks involved? How was the imposition of *Caldwell* recklessness supposed to model her behaviour?

2   In *R v R (Stephen Malcolm)* (1984) 79 Cr App R 334, the Court of Appeal again rejected the contention that the test for recklessness in criminal damage cases ought to be amended so as to ask whether a person of the age of the defendant and with his characteristics which might be relevant to his ability to foresee the risk, would have appreciated the risk. In doing so the court noted that the House of Lords had dismissed a petition by the defendant in *Elliot v C* for leave to appeal. Ackner LJ observed that this was 'just the sort of point (if it was a valid one) which we would have expected the House of Lords to have desired to have dealt with, thus clearing up the position, when they had the opportunity to do so when considering whether or not to give leave [in *Elliot v C*] ... But they did not take that opportunity. We do not think that we should seek by this subtlety to avoid applying principles which we also have difficulty accepting. We respectfully share the regrets voiced by Robert Goff LJ that in essence "recklessness" has now been construed synonymously with "carelessness"'.

3   Any uncertainty as to the objective nature of the test for perception of risk in *Caldwell* was removed by the Court of Appeal in *R v Sangha* [1988] 1 WLR 519, where Tucker J observed (in relation to a case of arson): '... In our judgment, when consideration is given whether an act of setting fire to something creates an obvious and serious risk of damaging property and thereby endangering the life of another, the test to be applied is this: is it proved that an ordinary prudent bystander would have perceived an

obvious risk that property would be damaged and that life would thereby be endangered? The ordinary prudent bystander is not deemed to be invested with expert knowledge relating to the construction of the property, nor to have the benefit of hindsight. The time at which his perception is material is the time when the fire is started.'

4   Why is a man who drives his car whilst distracted by the sight of a 'pretty girl' (see *R v Reid*) not reckless?

5   Parliament has since replaced the offence of causing death by reckless driving with the offence of causing death by dangerous driving. What is the significance of the substitution of the word 'dangerous' for 'reckless'? Will it make convictions easier to come by? Does it make clear that the fault element is totally objective? Does it suggest that the House of Lords in *Lawrence* was trying to achieve a laudable result by the wrong means (that is, judicial activism to bring careless drivers within the scope of the offence of reckless driving)?

6   It seems fair to assume that Lord Diplock was attempting, in *Caldwell* and *Lawrence*, to send out a message that failure to advert to an obvious risk could give rise to criminal liability. Is there any deterrent effect to such decisions? Do members of the general public know about these rulings? If so do they alter their behaviour as a result, or are defendants only aware of the scope of recklessness when they find themselves convicted of offences where *Caldwell* applies?

7   Significantly, *Caldwell* recklessness has now effectively been confined to the offence of criminal damage. In *W (A Minor) v Dolbey* (1989) 88 Cr App R 1 (DC), Robert Goff LJ (on the issue of whether or not the *Lawrence* (1981) and *Caldwell* (1981) approach to recklessness was appropriate in relation to offences that could be committed 'maliciously' such as malicious wounding contrary to s 20 of the Offences Against the Person Act 1861) observed:

> ... in my judgment ... Lord Diplock was concerned to distinguish the meaning of the word 'maliciously' as used in the Offences Against the Person Act 1861 from the meaning of the word 'reckless' as used in s 1 of the Criminal Damage Act 1971. No guidance can be derived from the definition of the latter word in Lord Diplock's speech in the consideration of the problem in the present case. It also follows that it was the view of Lord Diplock that *Cunningham* was still good law so far as the subject-matter of that case was concerned, and that what he was saying in *Caldwell* was not considered by him to have any impact on either the decision or the reasoning in that case. So we can put on one side the definition of 'reckless' in *Caldwell* and it follows from what Lord Diplock said that we are simply concerned with the meaning of the word 'maliciously' used as a term of art, as he put it, in criminal law.

See further *R v Savage; R v Parmenter* [1992] AC 699 – considered in Chapter 16. The courts also have made clear that *Caldwell* has no application to rape – see *R v Satnam; R v Kewal* (considered in Chapter 17), and it cannot, almost by definition, apply to deception offences. It may still have some application in the area of unlawful act manslaughter where the unlawful act causing death is criminal damage – see further Chapter 15).

THE LACUNA IN RECKLESSNESS

The 'lacuna' argument runs thus: if a defendant, before acting, shows that he stopped to consider a risk, and genuinely concluded that there was no risk, he cannot be found to be reckless under either the objective or subjective approaches, if the risk materialises. This is because he has given thought to the risk, and thus falls outside the scope of *Caldwell* recklessness, and he did not believe he was taking a risk, hence he falls outside the scope of *Cunningham* recklessness. As the following extracts indicate. The lacuna is real, but the task facing a defendant who seeks to put himself within it is not inconsiderable.

Chief Constable of Avon and Somerset v Shimmen (1986) 84 Cr App R 7 (DC)

Taylor J: ... The charge against the defendant was that on 15 February 1985, in the City of Bristol, without lawful excuse, he destroyed property belonging to Maskreys Ltd, namely a plate-glass window of the value of £495, intending to destroy such property or being reckless as to whether such property would be destroyed, contrary to s 1(1) of the Criminal Damage Act 1971. The justices found the following facts, *inter alia*.

The defendant had, on the relevant evening, been in the company of four friends. They had been in a public house and later they went to a club. During the evening, the defendant consumed a quantity of alcohol. He and his four friends left the club together and made their way along the road to a position outside Maskrey's shop. There the defendant and one of his friends, David Woodhouse, were laughing, joking, and larking around. Woodhouse pushed the defendant who then started flailing his arms and legs, contriving not to make any contact with Mr Woodhouse. Mr Woodhouse issued a warning to the defendant that he might one day hurt someone. The defendant assured Woodhouse that he had everything under control and, to prove it, he made as if to strike the window with his foot. His foot, however, did make contact with the window and broke it. The defendant was the holder of a green belt and yellow belt in the Korean art of self-defence. He was a skilled and experienced practitioner of that art.

It was conceded that he had no intent to break the window. But the prosecutor's contention was that his act amounted to recklessness and that he ought to be convicted on that ground. The defendant contended that by reason of the skill which he had, he had satisfied himself that the window would not break and that he was, in those circumstances, not reckless. The court was, as one would expect, referred to the leading authorities on the nature of recklessness. They are two decisions of the House of Lords. The first is *R v Caldwell* [1982] AC 341. The second is *R v Lawrence* [1982] AC 510 ...

The justices were of the opinion that an obvious and serious risk was created by the defendant's conduct. They accepted the argument that the inference that he was in one or other of the necessary states of mind required to constitute the offence could be displaced in his case by virtue of his evidence relating to his expertise in the science of martial arts ... They made the finding that the defendant perceived there could be a risk of damage, but after considering such risk concluded that no damage would result. They therefore dismissed the charge.

The question posed for this court is as follows: were we correct in law to decide that the defendant should not be regarded as reckless as to whether or not property would be destroyed or damaged if he does an act which in fact creates an obvious risk that property will be destroyed or damaged and having considered the circumstances subjectively concludes that no damage will result from that act?

... [I]t seems to me that on the findings of the justices and more particularly, as I shall indicate in a moment, on the evidence which they exhibited to their case, this defendant did recognise the risk. It was not a case of his considering the possibility and coming to the conclusion that there was no risk. What he said to the justices in cross-examination should be quoted. He said: 'I thought I might break the window but then I thought I will not break the window ... I thought to myself, the window is not going to break'. A little later on he said: 'I weighed up the odds and thought I had eliminated as much risk as possible by missing by two inches instead of two millimetres'.

The specific finding of the justices ... was as follows:

> ... the defendant perceived there could be a risk of damage but after considering such risk concluded that no damage would result.

It seems to me that what this case amounts to is as follows; that this defendant did perceive, which is the same as Lord Diplock's word 'recognise' [in *Caldwell*], that there could be a risk, but by aiming off rather more than he normally would in this sort of display, he thought he had minimised it and therefore no damage would result. In my judgment, that is far from saying that he falls outside the state of mind described by Lord Diplock in these terms: '... has recognised that there was some risk involved and has nonetheless gone on to do it' ...

R v Merrick [1995] Crim LR 802 (CA)

Facts: The appellant was convicted of damaging property being reckless as to whether life was endangered contrary to s 1(2) of the Criminal Damage Act 1971. It was the appellant's practice to visit householders to whose property certain old cable television cabling was attached, and ask if they were receiving wayleave payments from the owner of the cables, with whom he had fallen out. If they were not, he offered to collect payments, and if they were not made, he would, with the householder's consent, remove the cable and ancillary equipment. A number of counts of criminal damage relating to such cabling and equipment were withdrawn from the jury, the appellant's defence being reasonable excuse in the form of the householder's consent. In respect of the count on which he was convicted, he had, with the householder's written consent, removed a piece of equipment known as a repeater box. In doing so, he inevitably left a live electrical cable exposed. He then proceeded to put the cable in plastic bags, buried it under rubble and cemented it over.

At trial, he said in his evidence that he knew that the repeater box was attached to the mains and had come prepared with material to make good the damage. To leave the cable exposed would, he knew, have been dangerous. The cable had been left entirely exposed for a period of six minutes. He did not believe there was any risk of endangering life at any stage, and he would not have undertaken the work if he had not been competent to do so. The judge ruled that as a matter of law, any precautions designed to eliminate the risk of endangering life must, to provide a defence, be taken before the damage was caused. As a result of the ruling the appellant changed his plea to guilty.

On appeal, it was argued that the defendant fell outside the definition of recklessness set out in *Caldwell* [1982] AC 341. He had not failed to consider the risk (he had thought about it), and nor had he acted recognising the existence of a risk (he had decided there was no risk). Counsel relied on *Chief Constable of Avon and Somerset v Shimmen* (1987) 84 Cr App R 7.

Held, dismissing the appeal, there is a clear distinction between avoiding a risk and taking steps to remedy a risk which has already been created. If a defendant is to successfully contend that the taking of certain steps has prevented him from falling within the definition of recklessness, then those steps must be directed towards preventing the risk at all, rather than at remedying it once it has arisen. The appellant accepted that he had created a risk by exposing the cable, and that it remained exposed for six minutes. Although he said he took reasonable precautions to eliminate the danger, by then he was inevitably remedying a risk that he had already created rather than preventing the risk which arose when the live wire was exposed.

R v Reid [1992] 1 WLR 793 (HL)

Lord Goff of Chieveley: ... It has been pointed out that, although Lord Diplock's two categories of recklessness taken together have the effect that, in most cases where the defendant is driving dangerously in the sense I have described, he will in fact be driving recklessly, nevertheless there are cases in which this is not so. This may occur where the defendant considers the possibility of risk but nevertheless concludes that there is none. But we have to remember that, *ex hypothesi*, the defendant is driving dangerously in the sense I have described; and in practice his evidence that in such circumstances he thought that there was no risk is only likely to carry weight if he can point to some specific fact as to which he was mistaken and which, if true, would have excluded the possibility of risk which might occur if, for example, as my noble and learned friend Lord Ackner has pointed out, he misunderstood in good faith some direction or instruction, or if he drove the wrong way down a one-way street at a normal speed in the mistaken belief that it was a two-way street. If that was indeed the case, his driving might well not be described as reckless, though such cases are likely to be rare. It has been suggested that there is therefore a 'loophole' or 'lacuna' in Lord Diplock's definition of recklessness. I feel bound to say that I myself regard these expressions as misleading. The simple fact is that Lord Diplock was concerned to define driving recklessly, not dangerous driving; and it is not in every case where the defendant is in fact driving dangerously that he should be held to be driving recklessly, although in most cases the two will coincide. Another example where they may not coincide would occur where a driver who, while driving, is afflicted by illness or shock which impairs his capacity to address his mind to the possibility of risk; it may well not be right to describe him as driving recklessly in such circumstances. Likewise (as my noble and learned friend has pointed out), if a driver takes evasive action in an emergency, his action may involve the taking of a risk which is regarded as justified in the special circumstances, so that he cannot be described as driving recklessly. Such cases, which again are likely to be rare, can be dealt with if and when they arise. It is however unnecessary to consider any such case on the present appeal.

Lord Browne-Wilkinson: ... As to the so called 'loophole' or 'lacuna' in Lord Diplock's direction ... [t]here may be cases where, despite the defendant being aware of the risk and deciding to take it, he does so because of a reasonable misunderstanding, sudden disability or emergency which render it inappropriate to characterise his conduct as being reckless. Lord Diplock in *R v Lawrence* was not seeking to lay down a test applicable to all cases and the facts in the present case do not fall within this special category ...

Notes and queries

1   Why should a 'sudden disability' enable a defendant to escape a finding that he was reckless whereas a permanent one (for example, learning difficulties as in *Elliot v C*) cannot be taken into account?

Codification and law reform proposals

The Home Office Consultation Paper *Violence: Reforming the Offences Against the Person Act 1861* proposes the following definition of recklessness (for the purposes of the proposed offences against the person set out in the Bill):

14(2) A person acts recklessly with respect to a result if he is aware of a risk that it will occur and it is unreasonable to take that risk having regard to the circumstances as he knows or believes them to be.

...

(4) A person is reckless whether an omission will have a result if he is aware of a risk that the result will occur and it is unreasonable to take that risk having regard to the circumstances as he knows or believes them to be.

The notes to Bill provide:

3.11 ... The Government welcomes this as giving a greater clarity and certainty to the criminal law, and accepts the Law Commission's conclusion that it is appropriate to have a subjective rather than objective definition of recklessness for offences against the person. The Government recognises that a different definition will apply to other criminal behaviour, such as criminal damage, but is satisfied that this reflects the present state of the law ...

As this passage indicates, cl 14 as regards recklessness reflects, with minor amendments, the proposed codification of recklessness put forward in the 1989 Draft Code Bill. The commentary to the DCCB is, therefore, still instructive in this regard:

8.17 'Recklessly'. Clause 18(c) provides that a person acts 'recklessly' with respect to a circumstance when he is aware of a risk that it exists or will exist, and with respect to a result when he is aware of a risk that it will occur, it being, in either case, 'in the circumstances known to him, unreasonable to take the risk'. The use thus proposed for 'reckless' and related words is the same as that which we proposed in our Mental Element Report.

8.18 Recent House of Lords' decisions have given 'reckless' and 'recklessly' a wider meaning than that proposed by clause 18(c). The leading case of *Caldwell* ... concerned the Criminal Damage Act 1971 ... *Lawrence* applied *Caldwell* in interpreting the offence of driving recklessly. It was indeed soon afterwards declared in a manslaughter case that 'reckless' should be given 'the same meaning' (that is, the *Caldwell* meaning) 'in relation to all offences which involve recklessness' as one of the elements unless Parliament has otherwise ordained' ... but the contrary view prevailed in the Court of Appeal in relation to the statutory definition of rape, in the light of the modern history of that offence.

8.19 Explanation of the narrower definition. If the *Caldwell* concept of giving no thought to the possibility of there being a risk, where the risk is in fact obvious, is to be a basis of liability for some offences governed by the Code, the Code ought to have a term to express it. But the question that must first be faced is whether 'reckless' should be used in the Code to express this concept as well as that of the actor's recognising 'that there [is] some risk involved and ... nevertheless [going] on to do' the act which creates the risk. We are sure that it should not and we adhere to the narrower meaning for the term which we recommended in our Mental Element Report and which seemed to have become the judicially accepted meaning before *Caldwell*. Our reasons are as follows:

(i) The Code needs a term, for use as necessary in the specification of offences, which refers only to the unreasonable taking of a risk of which the actor is aware. Such conscious risk-taking is the preferred minimum fault element for most serious modern offences. This appears, for example, from recommendations of the Criminal Law Revision Committee on offences against the person and on sexual offences from the recently enacted public order offence and from the modern history of the law of rape.

(ii) Before *Caldwell*, 'reckless' had become the conventional term by which to refer to this narrower type of fault. We do not know of an acceptable alternative.

(iii) We understand that trial courts have experienced considerable difficulties in using the complex *Caldwell* definition of recklessness. That definition in effect describes two kinds of fault. Even if both kinds were to be needed for some offences, they need not be conveyed by a single Code expression. We believe, indeed, that it may be of advantage to prosecutors and to sentencing courts to be able to distinguish, by means of a discriminating language, between different modes of committing the same offence.

8.20 The 'subjectivist' approach to criminal liability. 'Knowledge', 'intention' and 'recklessness' (and cognate words) are terms used throughout the draft Bill with the meanings given by clause. The modern English criminal law tradition tends to require a positive state of mind with respect to the various external elements of an offence of any seriousness; and the three key terms are the obvious terms, because of their familiarity in criminal law usage, by which to refer to some of the most common states of mind required. Although this 'subjectivist' tradition is not without its critics, we are proposing a Code that stays within the mainstream of English criminal law. But in doing so we do not exclude the possibility that Parliament may hereafter wish to create offences constructed upon a different foundation of liability. The group of House of Lords' cases led by *Caldwell* can, indeed, be interpreted as having placed some serious offences upon such a different foundation. It will, of course, be open to Parliament to pursue the line followed by those cases by rejecting or modifying the fault requirements proposed for particular offences in Part II of our draft Bill and by providing further key terms to supplement the three that we have defined.

8.21 The Code team, in their Bill, did in fact provide a term ('heedlessness') to convey the extended sense of recklessness laid down in *Caldwell*. We have not found occasion to use that expression in the definitions of offences in Part 11 of our Bill but it remains available if there should prove to be a use for it.

OTHER FAULT TERMS

Some statutory offences have fault elements denoted by the use of specific terms. Some of the more common ones are considered in the following extracts.

Wilfully

R v Sheppard [1981] AC 394 House of Lords

Lord Diplock: My Lords, the appellants ('the parents') were convicted in the Crown Court at Northampton of an offence under s 1(1) of the Children and Young Persons Act 1933 of wilfully neglecting their infant child, Martin, between 1 July 1978 and 29 January 1979 in a manner likely to cause him unnecessary suffering or injury to health.

The child, who had been a slow developer, died, at the age of 16 months, on 28 January 1979 of hypothermia associated with malnutrition, a condition which increases the susceptibility of infants to hypothermia. If Martin had received timely medical attention his life might well have been saved. For five days or more before his death he had probably suffered from gastroenteritis which had caused him to vomit up and so fail to ingest the food that had been offered to him; but the details of such symptoms of serious illness as were apparent during the period before his death do not affect the question which falls to be decided by your Lordships in this appeal and is a question of law alone.

The gravamen of the charge against the parents was that they had failed to provide Martin with adequate medical aid on several occasions during the seven months to which the charge related and, in particular, during the week immediately preceding his death. In the light of the trial judge's instructions given to the jury as to the law applicable to the offence charged, it can safely be inferred from the verdicts of guilty that the jury found (1) that injury to Martin's health had in fact been caused by the failure by each of the parents to have him examined by a doctor in the period prior to his death and (2) that any reasonable parents, ie parents endowed with ordinary intelligence and not indifferent to the welfare of their child, would have recognised from the manifest symptoms of serious illness in Martin during that period that a failure to have him examined by a doctor might well result in unnecessary suffering or injury to his health.

The parents, a young couple aged 20 and 22 respectively, occupied poor accommodation, particularly as respects heating, where the family, which included another (older) child, subsisted on a meagre income. They would appear, on the evidence, to have been of low intelligence. Their real defence, if it were capable of amounting to a defence in law, was that they did not realise that the child was ill enough to need a doctor; they had observed his loss of appetite and failure to keep down his food, but had genuinely thought that this was due to some passing minor upset to which babies are prone, from which they recover naturally without medical aid and which medical treatment can do nothing to alleviate or to hasten recovery.

We do not know whether the jury would have thought that this explanation of the parents' failure to have Martin examined by a doctor might be true. In his instructions the judge had told the jury that to constitute the statutory offence with which the parents were charged it was unnecessary for the Crown to prove that at the time when it was alleged the parents should have had the child seen by a doctor either they in fact knew that their failure to do so involved a risk of causing him unnecessary suffering or injury to health or they did not care whether this was so or not. Following a line of authority by appellate courts that was binding on him, the trial judge treated the offence as one of strict liability and told the jury that the test of the parents' guilt was objective only: 'Would a reasonable parent, with knowledge of the facts that were known to the accused, appreciate that failure to have the child examined was likely to cause him unnecessary suffering or injury to health?' That was the question that the jury by their verdict answered Yes, not any question as to the parents' own state of mind.

The Court of Appeal, regarding themselves as bound by the same line of authority, felt compelled to dismiss the parents' appeal, but expressed their opinion that the law on this subject was worthy of review by your Lordships' House and gave the parents leave to appeal. They certified as the point of law of general public importance involved in their decision to dismiss the appeal: 'What is the proper direction to be given to a jury on a charge of wilful neglect of a child under s 1 of the Children and Young Persons Act 1933 as to what constitutes the necessary *mens rea* of the offence?'

The relevant provisions of s 1 are in the following terms:

(1) If any person who has attained the age of 16 years and has the custody, charge, or care of any child or young person under that age, wilfully assaults, ill-treats, neglects, abandons, or exposes him, or causes or procures him to be assaulted, ill-treated, neglected, abandoned, or exposed, in a manner likely to cause him unnecessary suffering or injury to health (including injury to or loss of sight, or hearing, or limb, or organ of the body, and any mental derangement), that person shall be guilty of a misdemeanour, and shall be liable: (a) on conviction on indictment, to a fine, or alternatively, or in addition thereto, to imprisonment for any term not exceeding two years ...

(2) For the purposes of this section: (a) a parent or other person legally liable to maintain a child or young person shall be deemed to have neglected him in a manner likely to cause injury to his health if he has failed to provide adequate food, clothing, medical aid or lodging for him, or if, having been unable otherwise to provide such food, clothing, medical aid or lodging, he has failed to take steps to procure it to be provided under enactments applicable in that behalf ...

The presence of the adverb 'wilfully' qualifying all five verbs, 'assaults, ill-treats, neglects, abandons, or exposes', makes it clear that any offence under s 1 requires *mens rea*, a state of mind on the part of the offender directed to the particular act or failure to act that constitutes the *actus reus* and warrants the description 'wilful'. The other four verbs refer to positive acts, 'neglect' refers to failure to act, and the judicial explanation of the state of mind denoted by the statutory expression 'wilfully' in relation to the doing of a positive act is not necessarily wholly apt in relation to a failure to act at all. The instant case is in the latter category, so I will confine myself to considering what is meant by wilfully neglecting a child in a manner likely to cause him unnecessary suffering or injury to health.

In construing the statutory language it is not always appropriate and may often be misleading to dissect a compound phrase and to treat a particular word or words as intended to be descriptive only of the *mens rea* of the offence and the remainder as defining only the *actus reus*. But s 1 of the 1933 Act contains in subsection (2)(a) a clear indication of a dichotomy between 'wilfully' and the compound phrase 'neglected him [the child] in a manner likely to cause injury to his health'. When the fact of failure to provide adequate food, clothing, medical aid or lodging has been established, the deeming provision applies only to that compound phrase; it still leaves the prosecution with the burden of proving the required *mens rea*, the mental element of 'wilfulness' on the part of the accused.

The *actus reus* of the offence with which the accused were charged in the instant case does not involve construing the verb 'neglect', for the offence fell within the deeming provision; and the only question as respects the *actus reus* was: did the parents fail to provide for Martin in the period before his death medical aid that was in fact adequate in view of his actual state of health at the relevant time? This, as it seems to me, is a pure question of objective fact to be determined in the light of what has become known *by the date of the trial* to have been the child's actual state of health at the relevant time. It does not depend on whether a reasonably careful parent, with knowledge of those facts only which such a parent might reasonably be expected to observe for himself, would have thought it prudent to have recourse to medical aid. The concept of the reasonable man as providing the standard by which the liability of real persons for their actual conduct is to be determined is a concept of civil law, particularly in relation to the tort of negligence; the obtrusion into criminal law of conformity with the notional conduct of the reasonable man as relevant to criminal liability, though not unknown (eg in relation to provocation sufficient to reduce murder to manslaughter), is exceptional, and should not lightly be extended: see *Andrews v DPP* [1937] AC 576 at 582–83. If failure to use the hypothetical powers of observation, ratiocination and foresight of consequences possessed by this admirable but purely notional exemplar is to constitute an ingredient of a criminal offence it must surely form part not of the *actus reus* but of the *mens rea*.

It does not, however, seem to me that the concept of the reasonable parent, what he would observe, what he would understand from what he had observed and what he would do about it, has any part to play in the *mens rea* of an offence in which the description of the *mens rea* is contained in the single adverb 'wilfully'. In the context of doing to a child a positive act (assault, ill-treat, abandon or expose) that is likely to have specified consequences (to cause him unnecessary suffering or injury to health), 'wilfully', which must describe the state of mind of the actual doer of the act, may be capable of bearing the narrow meaning that the wilfulness required extends only to the doing of the physical act itself which in fact results in the consequences described, even though the doer thought that it would not and would not have acted as he did had he foreseen a risk that those consequences might follow. Although this is a possible meaning of 'wilfully', it is not the natural meaning even in relation to positive acts defined by reference to the consequences to which they are likely to give rise; and, in the context of the section, if this is all the adverb 'wilfully' meant it would be otiose. Section 1(1) would have the same effect if it were omitted; for even in absolute offences (unless vicarious liability is involved) the physical act relied on as constituting the offence must be wilful in the limited sense, for which the synonym in the field of criminal liability that has now become the common term of legal art is 'voluntary'.

So much for 'wilfully' in the context of a positive act. To 'neglect' a child is to omit to act, to fail to provide adequately for its needs, and, in the context of s 1 of the 1933 Act, its physical needs rather than its spiritual, educational, moral or emotional needs. These are dealt with by other legislation. For reasons already given the use of the verb 'neglect' cannot, in my view, of itself import into the criminal law the civil law concept of negligence. The *actus reus* in a case of wilful neglect is simply a failure, for whatever reason, to provide the child whenever it in fact needs medical aid with the medical aid it needs. Such a failure as it seems to me could not be properly described as 'wilful' unless the parent *either* (1) had directed his mind to the question whether there was some risk (though it might fall far short of a probability) that the child's health might suffer unless he were examined by a doctor and provided with such curative treatment as the examination might reveal as necessary, and had made a conscious decision, for whatever reason, to refrain from arranging for such medical examination, *or* (2) had so refrained because he did not care whether the child might be in need of medical treatment or not.

As regards the second state of mind, this imports the concept of recklessness which is a common concept in *mens rea* in criminal law. It is not to be confused with negligence in the civil law of tort (see *Andrews v Director of Public Prosecutions* [1937] AC 576 at 582–83). In speaking of the first state of mind I have referred to the parent's knowledge of the existence of some risk of injury to health rather than of a probability. The section speaks of an act or omission that is 'likely' to cause unnecessary suffering or injury to health. This word is imprecise. It is capable of covering a whole range of possibilities from 'it's on the cards' to 'it's more probable than not'; but, having regard to the ordinary parent's lack of skill in diagnosis and to the very serious consequences which may result from failure to provide a child with timely medical attention, it should in my view be understood as excluding only what would fairly be described as highly unlikely ...

To give to s 1(1) of the 1933 Act the meaning which I suggest it bears would not encourage parents to neglect their children nor would it reduce the deterrent to child neglect provided by the section. It would afford no defence to parents who do not bother to observe their children's health or, having done so, do not care whether their children are receiving the medical examination and treatment that they need or not; it would involve the acquittal of those parents only who through ignorance or lack of intelligence are genuinely unaware that their child's health may be at risk if it is not examined by a doctor to see if it needs medical treatment. And, in view of the abhorrence which magistrates and juries feel for cruelty to helpless children, I have every confidence that they would not readily be hoodwinked by false claims by parents that it did not occur to them that an evidently sick child might need medical care.

In the instant case it seems likely that on the evidence the jury, if given the direction which I have suggested as correct, would have convicted one or both of the accused; but I do not think it possible to say with certainty that they would. It follows that in my opinion these appeals must be allowed and that the certified question should be answered: 'The proper direction to be given to a jury on a charge of wilful neglect of a child under s 1 of the Children and Young Persons Act 1933 by failing to provide adequate medical aid is that the jury must be satisfied (1) that the child did in fact need medical aid at the time at which the parent is charged with failing to provide it (the *actus reus*) and (2) either that the parent was aware at that time that the child's health might be at risk if it was not provided with medical aid or that the parent's unawareness of this fact was due to his not caring whether his child's health was at risk or not (the *mens rea*).'

Maliciously

R v Cunningham [1957] 2 QB 396 (CA)

Byrne J: The appellant was convicted at Leeds Assizes upon an indictment framed under s 23 of the Offences Against the Person Act, 1861, which charged that he unlawfully and maliciously caused to be taken by Sarah Wade a certain noxious thing, namely, coal gas, so as thereby to endanger the life of the said Sarah Wade ...

The facts were not really in dispute, and in a statement to a police officer the appellant said: 'All right, I will tell you. I was short of money, I had been off work for three days, I got eight shillings from the gas meter. I tore it off the wall and threw it away.' Although there was a stop tap within two feet of the meter the appellant did not turn off the gas, with the result that a very considerable volume of gas escaped, some of which seeped through the wall of the cellar and partially asphyxiated Mrs Wade, who was asleep in her bedroom next door, with the result that her life was endangered.

... The act of the appellant was clearly unlawful and therefore the real question for the jury was whether it was also malicious within the meaning of s 23 of the Offences Against the Person Act 1861 ...

With the utmost respect to the learned judge, we think it is incorrect to say that the word 'malicious' in a statutory offence merely means wicked. We think the judge was, in effect, telling the jury that if they were satisfied that the appellant acted wickedly – and he had clearly acted wickedly in stealing the gas meter and its contents – they ought to find that he had acted maliciously in causing the gas to be taken by Mrs Wade so as thereby to endanger her life.

In our view it should have been left to the jury to decide whether, even if the appellant did not intend the injury to Mrs Wade, he foresaw that the removal of the gas meter might cause injury to someone but nevertheless removed it. We are unable to say that a reasonable jury, properly directed as to the meaning of the word 'maliciously' in the context of s 23, would without doubt have convicted.

The meaning of the word 'malicious' is considered further in the context of non-fatal offences against the person in Chapter 16.

Knowingly

R v Ellis, Street and Smith (1987) 84 Cr App R 235 (CA)

O'Connor LJ: ... All three appellants accepted that they participated in importing large quantities of cannabis into this country concealed in secret compartments in motor cars. They were indicted in the ordinary form for being knowingly concerned in the fraudulent evasion of the prohibition on the importation of a controlled drug contrary to s 170(2) of the Customs and Excise Management Act 1979. The particulars of offence were that on the relevant dates they were in relation to a class B controlled drug, namely in the case of Ellis and Street 29.3 kilogrammes and in the case of Smith 24.85 kilogrammes of cannabis, 'knowingly concerned in the fraudulent evasion of the prohibition on importation imposed by s 3(1) of the Misuse of Drugs Act 1971'.

In both cases the defendants as they then were pleaded not guilty and at once asked for a ruling as to whether they had a defence in law if the facts were that they knew that they were participating in the importation of prohibited goods but believed that the goods were pornographic goods which they knew to be subject to a prohibition and which were in fact subject to a prohibition.

In both cases the trial judges, holding themselves bound by the decision of this court in *Hennessey* (1979) 68 Cr App R 419, ruled that they had no defence in law on those assumed facts. Thereupon they changed their pleas to guilty and were sentenced.

Mr Shaw has appeared for all three appellants in this court. He accepted that these three cases could not be distinguished from *Hennessey*. In a carefully thought-out, concise and lucid argument, for which we express our gratitude, he submitted that Hennessey is no longer good law because it cannot stand with subsequent decisions in the House of Lords.

Before we turn to *Hennessey* it is necessary to start the consideration of the law by looking at *Hussain* [1969] 2 QB 567 ...

In *Hussain* the defendant was a seaman on a ship which came into Liverpool. In his cabin customs officers found a secret compartment in the bulkhead full of cannabis. In due course he said, and this was his defence, that while he was in his cabin the first officer and a carpenter had come there and threatened him. They had opened up the bulkhead to create the secret compartment, had put something in it, he did not know what it was, and had told him that if he said anything about it they would cut him up. So that on analysis his defence was that he did not know what was in the secret compartment. His real defence was duress. He was indicted on two counts, one an offence against what was then s 304 of the Customs and Excise Act 1952, which is the same offence as that indicated here under s 170(2) of the 1979 Act, and the other a count of possessing a controlled drug. He was convicted of both. In the Court of Appeal Widgery LJ, as he then was, gave the judgment of the court. In the summing up the chairman had directed the jury that the phrase they had to consider was 'being knowingly concerned in a fraudulent evasion of the prohibition against importation of cannabis resin'. At 451 and 571 respectively Widgery LJ said:

> Then he proceeded to go through that phrase in some detail; he pointed out there was a prohibition against the importation of cannabis (which was not

disputed); and he further pointed out that there was an importation of cannabis in the present case: any difficulties on the law in that regard having disappeared in the course of the trial. He then proceeded: 'The question is: Has it been proved that the defendant was knowingly concerned in that operation? ... Knowingly concerned in that operation means that he was co-operating with the smugglers, if I may so put it, and it does not matter if he did not know precisely the nature of the goods the smugglers were dealing with. He would be just as guilty if he had thought they were dealing with brandy, for instance, but what has to be proved is that he was knowingly and to that extent consciously and deliberately concerned in co-operating in what he must have known was an operation of smuggling or getting prohibited goods into this country.' ... Two main complaints are made against that passage in the summing up. First of all, it is said that the learned chairman was wrong in saying that the Crown did not have to prove that the accused knew that cannabis was the subject of the importation. It is submitted on behalf of the appellant that proof of knowledge on the part of the accused that the goods being smuggled were cannabis was part of the obligation of the prosecution, and since the learned chairman had directed that it was not necessary for the accused to know precisely the nature of the goods there was a misdirection. The court is not prepared to accept that submission. It seems perfectly clear that the word 'knowingly' in the section in question is concerned with knowing that a fraudulent evasion of a prohibition in respect of goods is taking place. If, therefore, the accused knows that what is afoot is the evasion of a prohibition against importation and he knowingly takes part in that operation, it is sufficient to justify his conviction, even if he does not know precisely what kind of goods are being imported. It is, of course, essential that he should know that the goods which are being imported are goods subject to a prohibition. It is essential he should know that the operation with which he is concerning himself is an operation designed to evade that prohibition and evade it fraudulently. But it is not necessary he should know the precise category of the goods the importation of which has been prohibited. Accordingly, in our judgment, there is nothing in that point taken on behalf of the appellant.

There is a clear statement of the law construing s 304 of the 1952 Act. The 1979 Act was a consolidating statute and, as will appear later in our judgment, there is no difference to be made in construing s 170.

Hussain was in 1969. In 1978 came *Hennessey* (1979) 68 Cr App R 419. In *Hennessey* the defence raised was what in shorthand can be called the 'blue-film' defence, namely that although there was a large quantity of cannabis concealed in the motor car the defendant said he thought he was bringing in obscene material. It was exactly the same as this case. Lawton LJ, who gave the judgment of the court, had this to say about it, at 422:

Customs officers searched his car and found ... cannabis resin ... Hennessey said, 'I don't know anything about them'. About a month later he made a written statement in which he said that he thought he was bringing back 'blue' films to England and the context in which he said it showed that he knew that what he claimed to be bringing back was a prohibited import. This was the basis of his defence at his trial. It did not succeed.

At the foot of p 422 Lawton LJ said this:

> Mr Godfrey on behalf of Hennessey submitted that Judge Abdela had misdirected the jury. He told the jury what the relevant section of the Customs and Excise Act 1952, namely s 304(b), provided and went on at pp 5–6 of the transcript of the summing up as follows: 'You can see from the terms in which the statement of offence is set out that the crux of the matter is, in fact, being knowingly concerned in the fraudulent evasion of a prohibition. Now this is where I have to correct Mr Godfrey when he was addressing you about the question of knowledge and I noticed that one or two of you were taking down what he said and I must correct it. "Knowingly" in this section of this statute is concerned with knowing that a fraudulent evasion of a prohibition in respect of goods is taking place. It is not a question of knowing whether you have got a particular commodity in your pocket or container or car and there is quite a considerable amount of legal authority for that proposition. If, therefore, an accused person knows that what is afoot is the evasion of a prohibition against importation and he knowingly takes part in that operation, it is sufficient to justify his conviction under this section of the Act, even if he does not know precisely what kind of goods are being imported.' By directing the jury in these terms Judge Abdela was following, as he told the jury he was, the judgment of Widgery LJ (as he then was) in *Hussain* (above). In that case the appellant had submitted that the trial judge should have directed the jury that the prosecution had to prove that the accused knew what was the subject of the prohibited importation. Mr Godfrey made the same submission in this case. The court in *Hussain* rejected the submission. Mr Godfrey boldly submitted that this court had been wrong to do so and that we should not follow Hussain. We intend to follow it for the best of reasons, it was correctly decided. On his own story Hennessey did know that he was concerned in a fraudulent evasion of a prohibition in relation to goods. In plain English he was smuggling goods. It matters not for the purpose of conviction what the goods were as long as he knew that he was bringing into the United Kingdom goods which he should not have been bringing in. Hennessey's appeal against conviction is dismissed.

In 1983 the case of *Taaffe* (1983) Cr App R 82 came before this court. *Taaffe* had this difference. In that case the defendant, when he was found to have a lot of cannabis stowed in the spare tyre of his motor car and a lot more strapped to his body, said that he thought that what he was bringing into this country was currency, and that he thought that currency was prohibited. In fact, there was no prohibition on bringing currency into this country. It was in those circumstances that *Taaffe* came to this court because once again the trial judge had ruled that those facts afforded no defence, relying on the decisions in *Hussain* (above) and *Hennessey* (above) ...

In the House of Lords *R v Taaffe* [1984] AC 539 is an important case in the present circumstances. It is necessary to look shortly at the argument. First of all, we must point out that the members of the House in *Taaffe* were Lord Fraser of Tullybelton, Lord Scarman, Lord Roskill, Lord Bridge of Harwich and Lord Brightman. It is particularly important to note that Lord Scarman and Lord Bridge were members of the House ...

It is important that Lord Rawlinson of Ewell who appeared for the defendant made the following submissions, at 542:

(1) The requisite element of *mens rea* that arises in offences against s 170(2) is imparted by the word 'knowingly' and governs all the material elements of the offence. (2) An offence under s 170(2) may be committed in one or more of three ways, as set out in paragraphs (a), (b) and (c). The essence of an offence under s 170(2)(a), (b), (c) is not merely a fraudulent evasion of a regulation; rather, the essence of the offence is being 'knowingly concerned' in any fraudulent evasion of a regulation. (3) It is not sufficient for the commission of an offence to be 'involved in a smuggling operation'. For a person to be convicted of an offence, he must be knowingly concerned in (a) a fraudulent evasion, or attempt thereat, of (b) a prohibition or restriction in force. (4) There is no issue as to the state of the defendant's mind on any question of reasonableness of belief or recklessness, for, on the agreed facts, he (1) mistakenly believed that the packages, etc contained money and (2) mistakenly believed money to be subject to a prohibition. (5) Had a jury accepted those facts, he could not have been 'knowingly concerned' as to the fraudulent evasion of the prohibition of drugs.

I now come to the important submission made, which is:

(6) It is immaterial that a person charged under this section is mistaken as to the particular prohibition that he breaches or whether the goods that he carried are dutiable. Certainly, where a person knows that the goods hidden are subject to a prohibition and he designs to evade that prohibition fraudulently, it is not necessary that he should know the precise category of goods nor the precise prohibition: see *Hussain*. (7) That does not, however, arise in this case, since the goods that the defendant believed that he was carrying and that he believed to be prohibited were not in fact prohibited.

Lastly, Lord Rawlinson said in his argument at 544D:

The House is fixed with the agreed facts. It should not be led into interpreting 'knowingly' lightly. The first part of subsection (2) governs any offence created. People may be involved in smuggling operations innocently. 'Knowingly' is the word most apt to introduce an element of *mens rea*. It is the clearest word that Parliament could have used to indicate that requirement. *Hussain* (above) and *Hennessey* (above) are to be distinguished because there the defendants did have the *mens rea*; they did believe that there was a fraudulent evasion. If the defendant here honestly believed (and it is an agreed fact that he did) that he was bringing money into the country, which is not an offence, how can it be said that he was knowingly concerned in the fraudulent evasion of the prohibition on the importation of a controlled drug? To believe that he was bringing in coffee (prohibited) would not be a defence.

It is in the light of those submissions that Lord Scarman dealt with the appeal quite shortly in his speech. He read the certified question at 546:

When a defendant is charged with an offence, contrary to s 170(2) of the Customs and Excise Management Act 1979, of being knowingly concerned in the fraudulent evasion of the prohibition on the importation of a controlled drug, does the defendant commit the offence where he: (a) imports prohibited drugs into the United Kingdom; (b) intends fraudulently to evade a prohibition on importation; but (c) mistakenly believes the goods to be money and not drugs; and (d) mistakenly believes that money is the subject of a prohibition against importation?

In effect, the learned recorder answered the question in the affirmative and the Court of Appeal in the negative.

There was no trial: for the respondent changed his plea to guilty after the learned recorder's ruling. On his appeal against conviction, the judgment of the Court of Appeal was delivered by Lord Lane CJ. The judgment recites the history of the case and the assumptions upon which a decision had to be taken. It is unnecessary to burden the House with a repetition of what is there so clearly set forth.

Lord Lane CJ construed the subsection under which the respondent was charged as creating not an offence of absolute liability but an offence of which an essential ingredient is a guilty mind. To be 'knowingly concerned' meant, in his judgment, knowledge not only of the existence of a smuggling operation but also that the substance being smuggled into the country was one the importation of which was prohibited by statute. The respondent thought he was concerned in a smuggling operation but believed that the substance was currency. The importation of currency is not subject to any prohibition. Lord Lane concluded: '(The respondent) is to be judged against the facts that he believed them to be. Had this indeed been currency and not cannabis, no offence would have been committed.' Lord Lane went on to ask this question: 'Does it make any difference that the (respondent) thought wrongly that by clandestinely importing currency he was committing an offence?' The Crown submitted that it does. The court rejected the submission: the respondent's mistake of law could not convert the importation of currency into a criminal offence: and importing currency is what it had to be assumed that the respondent believed he was doing. My Lords, I find the reasoning of the Lord Chief Justice compelling. I agree with his construction of s 170(2) of the Act of 1979: and the principle that a man must be judged upon the facts as he believes them to be is an accepted principle of the criminal law when the state of a man's mind and his knowledge are ingredients of the offence with which he is charged ...

How does Mr Shaw seek to escape from the situation? He submitted that the true ratio of *Hussain* is not that the defendant mistakenly thought he was bringing in some other prohibited material, as in *Hennessey* and in *R v Taaffe* and in the present cases, but that in *Hussain* the defendant was simply not concerned at all with what it was, that he did not care what the material was; and that in those circumstances *Hussain* can be distinguished from *Hennessey* and from these cases. The difficulty about that argument is that it seems to us when the history of *Hussain*, through *Hennessey*, through *R v Shivpuri* is examined, it is the passage from Widgery LJ's judgment which we have cited at the beginning of this judgment that remains in full force (ie (1969) 53 Cr App R 448, 451; [1969] 2 QB 567, 571). That shows that 'knowingly' in the section in question is concerned with knowing that a fraudulent evasion of a prohibition in respect of goods is taking place. It seems to us that it cannot make any difference whether a particular defendant says: 'I don't know what the goods were; I only know they were prohibited' or a defendant says: 'I didn't know what the goods in fact were. I thought that they were some other prohibited goods' (*Hennessey*). The House of Lords having had the opportunity in *R v Shivpuri* to take up Lord Scarman's question in *R v Taaffe* as to whether Hennessey was correctly decided, did not deal with it. Therefore *Hennessey* as we have already said remains good law ...

CHILDREN AND PROOF OF *MENS REA*

A child under the age of 10 cannot incur criminal liability. This is established by s 50 of the Children and Young Persons Act 1933, which provides: 'It shall be conclusively presumed that no child under the age of 10 can be guilty of an offence.' Prior to 1998 it was the case that, in respect of a child between the ages of 10 and 14, *mens rea* would only be established if the defendant knew that what he had done was wrong – sometimes referred to as 'mischievous discretion'. This operated as a rebuttable presumption against a child between the ages of 10 and 14 having *mens rea*. Section 34 of the Crime and Disorder Act 1998 Act abolished the presumption as follows:

> The rebuttable presumption of criminal law that a child aged 10 or over is incapable of committing an offence is hereby abolished.

T v United Kingdom; V v United Kingdom (1999) The Times, 17 December

The European Court of Human Rights was asked to rule upon whether or not the imposition of criminal liability on children as young as 10 years of age amounted to a breach of the European Convention on Human Rights.

> **European Court of Human Rights**: Pursuant to section 50 of the Children and Young Persons Act 1933 ('the 1933 Act') as amended by section 16(1) of the Children and Young Persons Act 1963, the age of criminal responsibility in England and Wales is ten years, below which no child can be found guilty of a criminal offence. The age of ten was endorsed by the Home Affairs Select Committee (composed of Members of Parliament) in October 1993 (Juvenile Offenders, Sixth Report of the Session 1992–93, Her Majesty's Stationary Office) ... The United Nations Standard Minimum Rules for the Administration of Juvenile Justice (the Beijing Rules) ... were adopted by the United Nations General Assembly on 29 November 1985. These Rules are not binding in international law ... They provide, as relevant:
>
> > 4.1 In those legal systems recognising the concept of the age of criminal responsibility for juveniles, the beginning of that age shall not be fixed at too low an age level, bearing in mind the facts of emotional, mental and intellectual maturity.
>
> *Commentary*: The minimum age of criminal responsibility differs widely owing to history and culture. The modern approach would be to consider whether a child can live up to the moral and psychological components of criminal responsibility; that is, whether a child, by virtue of her or his individual discernment and understanding, can be held responsible for essentially antisocial behaviour. If the age of criminal responsibility is fixed too low or if there is no lower age limit at all, the notion of criminal responsibility would become meaningless. In general, there is a close relationship between the notion of responsibility for delinquent or criminal behaviour and other social rights and responsibilities (such as marital status, civil majority, etc).
>
> Efforts should therefore be made to agree on a reasonable lowest age limit that is applicable.
>
> ... The age of criminal responsibility is seven in Cyprus, Ireland, Switzerland and Liechtenstein; eight in Scotland; thirteen in France; fourteen in Germany, Austria,

Italy and many Eastern European countries; fifteen in the Scandinavian countries; sixteen in Portugal, Poland and Andorra; and eighteen in Spain, Belgium and Luxembourg.

... The applicant alleged that the cumulative effect of the age of criminal responsibility, the accusatorial nature of the trial, the adult proceedings in a public court, the length of the trial, the jury of twelve adult strangers, the physical lay-out of the courtroom, the overwhelming presence of the media and public, the attacks by the public on the prison van which brought him to court and the disclosure of his identity, together with a number of other factors linked to his sentence gave rise to a breach of Article 3.

He submitted that, at ten years old, the age of criminal responsibility in England and Wales was low compared with almost all European countries, in the vast majority of which the minimum age of responsibility was thirteen or higher. He contended, moreover, that there was a clear developing trend in international and comparative law towards a higher age of criminal responsibility ... He accepted that it was in principle possible for a State to attribute criminal responsibility to a child as young as ten without violating that child's rights under Article 3. However, it was then incumbent on such a State to ensure that the procedures adopted for the trial and sentencing of such young children were modified to reflect their age and vulnerability.

... The Government denied that the attribution of criminal responsibility to the applicant and his trial in public in an adult court breached his rights under Article 3.

With regard to the age of criminal responsibility, they submitted that the practice amongst the Contracting States was very varied, with ages ranging from seven in Cyprus, Ireland, Liechtenstein and Switzerland, to eighteen in a number of other States. There were no international principles laying down a specific age for criminal responsibility: Article 40(3) of the UN Convention required States to adopt a minimum age but imposed no specific such age. The Beijing Rules relied upon by the applicant were not binding under international law; the Preamble invited States to adopt them but left it up to States to decide whether or not to do so.

... The Court has considered first whether the attribution to the applicant of criminal responsibility in respect of acts committed when he was ten years old could, in itself, give rise to a violation of Article 3. In doing so, it has regard to the principle, well established in its case-law that, since the Convention is a living instrument, it is legitimate when deciding whether a certain measure is acceptable under one of its provisions to take account of the standards prevailing amongst the Member States of the Council of Europe ...

... In this connection, the Court observes that, at the present time there is not yet a commonly accepted minimum age for the imposition of criminal responsibility in Europe. While most of the Contracting States have adopted an age-limit which is higher than that in force in England and Wales, other States, such as Cyprus, Ireland, Liechtenstein and Switzerland, attribute criminal responsibility from a younger age. Moreover, no clear tendency can be ascertained from examination of the relevant international texts and instruments ... Rule 4 of the Beijing Rules which, although not legally binding, might provide some indication of the existence of an international consensus, does not specify the age at which criminal responsibility should be fixed but merely invites States not to fix it too low, and Article 40(3)(a) of the UN Convention requires States Parties to establish a minimum age below which children shall be presumed not to have the capacity to infringe the criminal law, but contains no provision as to what that age should be.

The Court does not consider that there is at this stage any clear common standard amongst the member States of the Council of Europe as to the minimum age of criminal responsibility. Even if England and Wales is among the few European jurisdictions to retain a low age of criminal responsibility, the age of ten cannot be said to be so young as to differ disproportionately from the age-limit followed by other European States. The Court concludes that the attribution of criminal responsibility to the applicant does not in itself give rise to a breach of Article 3 of the Convention.

CORPORATIONS AND PROOF OF *MENS REA*

Where parliament creates regulatory schemes, such as those that seek to prevent pollution, ensure minimum building standards, or ensure the quality of foodstuffs sold for public consumption, it often reinforces compliance by creating criminal offences that can be charged against those causing prohibited results. In many cases the parties subject to these regulations will be corporations rather than real people. The concept of *mens rea* is, of course, one that has developed in relation to the human mind, not the artificial legal identity of the corporation. In order to avoid the difficulty of establishing *mens rea* on the part of a corporation, many regulatory offences operate on the basis of strict liability – that is, liability without fault; see further Chapter 5.

Where, however, a corporation is charged with an offence requiring proof of fault the question arises as to how that can be established. Which officer of the corporation is to be deemed to be the 'controlling mind' of the corporation? Is it a question of seniority? Can the *mens rea* of several managers be aggregated to provide a 'composite' *mens rea* for the corporation as a whole? The issue has particularly come to the fore in the context of corporate liability for manslaughter – a matter considered in Chapter 15. The following extracts concern the general principles of identifying corporate *mens rea*.

R v ICR Haulage Ltd [1944] KB 551 (CA)

Stable J: The question before us is whether a limited company can be indicted for a conspiracy to defraud. Section 33 of the Criminal Justice Act 1925, removed certain procedural obstacles which had hitherto existed in connection with the trial of criminal offences alleged against corporations. This section did not enlarge the ambit of a company's criminal responsibility, but provided machinery for simplifying its enforcement.

It was conceded by counsel for the company that a limited company can be indicted for some criminal offences, and it was conceded by counsel for the Crown that there were some criminal offences for which a limited company cannot be indicted. The controversy centred round the question where and on what principle the line must be drawn and on which side of the line an indictment such as the present one falls. Counsel for the company contended that the true principle was that an indictment against a limited company for any offence involving as an essential ingredient *mens rea* in the restricted sense of a dishonest or criminal mind, must be bad for the reason that a company, not being a natural person, cannot have a mind honest or otherwise, and that, consequently, though in certain circumstances it is civilly liable for the fraud of its officers, agents or servants, it is immune from criminal process. Counsel for the Crown contended that a limited company, like any other entity recognised by the law, can as a general rule be indicted for its criminal acts which from the very necessity of the case must be performed by human agency and which in given circumstances become the acts of the company, and that for this purpose there was no distinction between an intention or other function of the mind and any other form of activity.

The offences for which a limited company cannot be indicted are, it was argued, exceptions to the general rule arising from the limitations which must inevitably attach to an artificial entity, such as a company. Included in these exceptions are the cases in which, from its very nature, the offence cannot be committed by a corporation, as, for example, perjury, an offence which cannot be vicariously committed, or bigamy, an offence which a limited company, not being a natural person, cannot commit vicariously or otherwise. A further exception, but for a different reason, comprises offences of which murder is an example, where the only punishment the court can impose is corporal, the basis on which this exception rests being that the court will not stultify itself by embarking on a trial in which, if a verdict of guilty is returned, no effective order by way of sentence can be made. In our judgment these contentions of the Crown are substantially sound, and the existence of these exceptions, and it may be that there are others, is by no means inconsistent with the general rule ...

In support of the contention of the Crown we were referred to a number of authorities. The earliest of these to which we think it necessary to refer is *Pharmaceutical Society v London and Provincial Supply Association* 5 App Cas 857, 869. The decision in that case, which was earlier than the Interpretation Act 1889, was that the words 'person' in the Act then under consideration did not include an incorporated company. Lord Blackburn, however, said at 869:

> But I may also say now, in order to avoid coming back to it, that I do not feel the least difficulty arising from what seems to have troubled some of the learned judges in the court below. If this word does include a corporation – I quite agree that a corporation cannot, in one sense, commit a crime – a corporation cannot be imprisoned, if imprisonment be the sentence for the crime; a corporation cannot be hanged or put to death if that be the punishment for the crime; and so, in those senses a corporation cannot commit a crime. But a corporation may be fined, and a corporation may pay damages; and therefore I must totally dissent, notwithstanding what Bramwell LJ said, or is reported to have said, upon the supposition that a body corporate or a corporation that incorporated itself for the purpose of publishing a newspaper could not be tried and fined, or an action for damages brought against it for a libel; or that a corporation which commits a nuisance could not be convicted of the nuisance or the like. I must really say that I do not feel the slightest doubt upon that part of the case. If you could get over the first difficulty of saying that the word 'person' here may be construed to include an artificial person, a

corporation, I should not have the least difficulty upon those other grounds which have been suggested.

Lord Blackburn's emphatic expression of opinion that a limited company can be indicted and convicted for publishing a criminal libel was later accepted by the Court of Appeal in *Triplex Safety Glass Co Ltd v Lancegaye Safety Glass Co Ltd* [1939] 2 KB 395, where it was held that a limited company was entitled to object to answering an interrogatory on the ground that the answer would tend to incriminate it. As an actual condition of mind amounting to express malice may be an element in the offence of libel, it is plain that the Court of Appeal decided that, whatever the principle may be that fixes the line between those offences for which a limited company can and those for which it cannot be indicted, it is not the presence or absence in the human agent of a particular condition of mind. It would be unreasonable to suppose that a limited company can be indicted for a criminal libel only in those cases in which express malice is not proved, or that it could defeat a prosecution by proving that its duly authorised agent was, in fact, actuated by malice.

The latest authority is the *DPP v Kent and Sussex Contractors Ltd* [1944] KB 146. A limited company was charged with offences under a Defence of the Realm Regulation which involved an intent to deceive. The justices dismissed the informations on the ground that a body corporate could not be guilty of the offences charged in as much as an act of will or state of mind which could not be imputed to a corporation was implicit in the commission of these offences. On a case stated to a Divisional Court this conclusion of law on the part of the justices was held to be erroneous, and the case was remitted to them to hear and determine. It is clear that the state of mind involved was a dishonest state of mind, namely an intention to deceive and that the state of mind was an essential element in the offence. There is a distinction between that case and the present, in that there the offences were charged under a regulation having the effect of a statute, whereas here the offence is a common law misdemeanour, but, in our judgment, this distinction has no material bearing on the question we have to decide. Lord Caldecote CJ said, at 151: 'the real point we have to decide ... is whether a company is capable of an act of will or of a state of mind, so as to be able to form an intention to deceive or to have knowledge of the truth or falsity of a statement', and after dealing with a number of authorities, he proceeds, at 155:

> The offences created by the regulation are those of doing something with intent to deceive or of making a statement known to be false in a material particular. There was ample evidence, on the facts as stated in the special case, that the company, by the only people who could act or speak or think for it, had done both these things, and I can see nothing in any of the authorities to which we have been referred which requires us to say that a company is incapable of being found guilty of the offences with which the respondent company was charged.

In his judgment in the same case MacNaghten J says as follows:

> It is true that a corporation can only have knowledge and form an intention through its human agents, but circumstances may be such that the knowledge and intention of the agent must be imputed to the body corporate ... If the responsible agent of a company, acting within the scope of this authority, puts forward on its behalf a document which he knows to be false and by which he

intends to deceive, I apprehend that according to the authorities that my Lord has cited, his knowledge and intention must be imputed to the company.

With both the decision in that case and the reasoning on which it rests, we agree.

In our judgment, both on principle and in accordance with the balance of authority, the present indictment was properly laid against the company, and the learned commissioner rightly refused to quash. We are not deciding that in every case where an agent of a limited company acting in its business commits a crime the company is automatically to be held criminally responsible. Our decision only goes to the invalidity of the indictment on the face of it, an objection which is taken before any evidence is led and irrespective of the facts of the particular case. Where in any particular case there is evidence to go to a jury that the criminal act of an agent, including his state of mind, intention, knowledge or belief is the act of the company, and, in cases where the presiding judge so rules, whether the jury are satisfied that it has been proved, must depend on the nature of the charge, the relative position of the officer or agent, and the other relevant facts and circumstances of the case. It was because we were satisfied on the hearing of this appeal that the facts proved were amply sufficient to justify a finding that the acts of the managing director were the acts of the company and the fraud of that person was the fraud of the company, that we upheld the conviction against the company, and, indeed, on the appeal to this court no argument was advanced that the facts proved would not warrant a conviction of the company assuming that the conviction of the managing director was upheld and that the indictment was good in law.

Tesco Ltd v Nattrass [1972] AC 153 (HL)

Lord Reid: My Lords, the appellants own a large number of supermarkets in which they sell a wide variety of goods. The goods are put out for sale on shelves or stands, each article being marked with the price at which it is offered for sale. The customer selects the articles he wants, takes them to the cashier, and pays the price. From time to time the appellants, apparently by way of advertisement, sell 'flash packs' at prices lower than the normal price. In September 1969 they were selling Radiant washing powder in this way. The normal price was 3s 11d but these packs were marked and sold at 2s 11d. Posters were displayed in the shops drawing attention to this reduction in price.

These prices were displayed in the appellants' shop at Northwich on 26 September. Mr Coane, an old age pensioner, saw this and went to buy a pack. He could only find packs marked 3s 11d. He took one to the cashier who told him that there were none in stock for sale at 2s 11d. He paid 3s 11d and complained to an inspector of weights and measures. This resulted in a prosecution under the Trade Descriptions Act 1968 and the appellants were fined £25 and costs.

Section 11(2) provides:

If any person offering to supply any goods gives, by whatever means, any indication likely to be taken as an indication that the goods are being offered at a price less than that at which they are in fact being offered he shall, subject to the provisions of this Act, be guilty of an offence.

It is not disputed that that section applies to this case. The appellants relied on s 24(1) which provides:

In any proceedings for an offence under this Act it shall, subject to subsection (2) of this section, be a defence for the person charged to prove: (a) that the commission of the offence was due to a mistake or to reliance on information supplied to him or to the act or default of another person, an accident or some other cause beyond his control; and (b) that he took all reasonable precautions and exercised all due diligence to avoid the commission of such an offence by himself or any person under his control.

The relevant facts as found by the magistrates were that on the previous evening a shop assistant, Miss Rogers, whose duty it was to put out fresh stock, found that there were no more of the specially marked packs in stock. There were a number of packs marked with the ordinary price so she put them out. She ought to have told the shop manager, Mr Clement, about this, but she failed to do so. Mr Clement was responsible for seeing that the proper packs were on sale, but he failed to see to this although he marked his daily return 'all special offers OK'. The magistrates found that if he had known about this he would either have removed the poster advertising the reduced price or given instructions that only 2s 11d was to be charged for the packs marked 3s 11d.

Section 24(2) requires notice to be given to the prosecutor if the accused is blaming another person and such notice was duly given naming Mr Clement.

In order to avoid conviction the appellants had to prove facts sufficient to satisfy both parts of s 24(1) of the Act of 1968. The magistrates held that they: '... had exercised all due diligence in devising a proper system for the operation of the said store and by securing so far as was reasonably practicable that it was fully implemented and thus had fulfilled the requirements of s 24(1)(b).'

But they convicted the appellants because in their view the requirements of s 24(1)(a) had not been fulfilled: they held that Clement was not 'another person' within the meaning of that provision.

The Divisional Court held that the magistrates were wrong in holding that Clement was not 'another person'. The respondent did not challenge this finding of the Divisional Court so I need say no more about it than that I think that on this matter the Divisional Court was plainly right. But that court sustained the conviction on the ground that the magistrates had applied the wrong test in deciding that the requirements of s 24(1)(b) had been fulfilled. In effect that court held that the words 'he took all reasonable precautions ...' do not mean what they say: 'he' does not mean the accused, it means the accused and all his servants who were acting in a managerial or supervisory capacity. I think that earlier authorities virtually compelled the Divisional Court to reach this strange construction. So the real question in this appeal is whether these earlier authorities were rightly decided.

But before examining those earlier cases I think it necessary to make some general observations.

Over a century ago courts invented the idea of an absolute offence. The accepted doctrines of the common law put them in a difficulty. There was a presumption that when Parliament makes the commission of certain acts an offence it intends that *mens rea* shall be a constituent of that offence whether or not there is any reference to the knowledge or state of mind of the accused. And it was and is held to be an invariable rule that where *mens rea* is a constituent of any offence the burden of proving *mens rea* is on the prosecution. Some day this House may have to re-examine that rule, but that is another matter. For the protection of purchasers or consumers Parliament in many cases made it an offence for a trader to do certain things. Normally those things were done on his behalf by his servants and cases arose where the doing of the forbidden thing was solely the fault of a servant, the master having done all he could to prevent it and being entirely ignorant of its having been done. The just course would have been to hold that, once the facts constituting the offence had been proved, *mens rea* would be presumed unless the accused proved that he was blameless. The courts could not, or thought they could not, take that course. But they could and did hold in many such cases on a construction of the statutory provision that Parliament must be deemed to have intended to depart from the general rule and to make the offence absolute in the sense that *mens rea* was not to be a constituent of the offence.

This has led to great difficulties. If the offence is not held to be absolute the requirement that the prosecutor must prove *mens rea* makes it impossible to enforce the enactment in very many cases. If the offence is held to be absolute that leads to the conviction of persons who are entirely blameless: an injustice which brings the law into disrepute. So Parliament has found it necessary to devise a method of avoiding this difficulty. But instead of passing a general enactment that it shall always be a defence for the accused to prove that he was no party to the offence and had done all he could to prevent it, Parliament has chosen to deal with the problem piecemeal, and has in an increasing number of cases enacted in various forms with regard to particular offences that it shall be a defence to prove various exculpatory circumstances.

In my judgment the main object of these provisions must have been to distinguish between those who are in some degree blameworthy and those who are not, and to enable the latter to escape from conviction if they can show that they were in no way to blame. I find it almost impossible to suppose that Parliament or any reasonable body of men would as a matter of policy think it right to make employers criminally liable for the acts of some of their servants but not for those of others and I find it incredible that a draftsman, aware of that intention, would fail to insert any words to express it. But in several cases the courts, for reasons which it is not easy to discover, have given a restricted meaning to such provisions. It has been held that such provisions afford a defence if the master proves that the servant at fault was the person who himself did the prohibited act, but that they afford no defence if the servant at fault was one who failed in his duty of supervision to see that his subordinates did not commit the prohibited act. Why Parliament should be thought to have intended this distinction or how as a matter of construction these provisions can reasonably be held to have that meaning is not apparent.

In some of these cases the employer charged with the offence was a limited company. But in others the employer was an individual and still it was held that he, though personally entirely blameless, could not rely on these provisions if the fault which led to the commission of the offence was the fault of a servant in failing to carry out his duty to instruct or supervise his subordinates.

Where a limited company is the employer difficult questions do arise in a wide variety of circumstances in deciding which of its officers or servants is to be identified with the company so that his guilt is the guilt of the company.

I must start by considering the nature of the personality which by a fiction the law attributes to a corporation. A living person has a mind which can have knowledge or intention or be negligent and he has hands to carry out his intentions. A corporation has none of these: it must act through living persons, though not always one or the same person. Then the person who acts is not speaking or acting for the company. He is acting as the company and his mind which directs his acts is the mind of the company. There is no question of the company being vicariously liable. He is not acting as a servant, representative, agent or delegate. He is an embodiment of the company or, one could say, he hears and speaks through the persona of the company, within his appropriate sphere, and his mind is the mind of the company. If it is a guilty mind then that guilt is the guilt of the company. It must be a question of law whether, once the facts have been ascertained, a person in doing particular things is to be regarded as the company or merely as the company's servant or agent. In that case any liability of the company can only be a statutory or vicarious liability.

In *Lennard's Carrying Co Ltd v Asiatic Petroleum Co Ltd* [1915] AC 705 the question was whether damage had occurred without the 'actual fault or privity' of the owner of a ship. The owners were a company. The fault was that of the registered managing owner who managed the ship on behalf of the owners and it was held that the company could not dissociate itself from him so far as to say that there was no actual fault or privity on the part of the company. Viscount Haldane LC said, at 713, 714:

> For if Mr Lennard was the directing mind of the company, then his action must, unless a corporation is not to be liable at all, have been an action which was the action of the company itself within the meaning of s 502 ... It must be upon the true construction of that section in such a case as the present one that the fault or privity is the fault or privity of somebody who is not merely a servant or agent for whom the company is liable upon the footing *respondeat superior*, but somebody for whom the company is liable because his action is the very action of the company itself.

Reference is frequently made to the judgment of Denning LJ in *HL Bolton (Engineering) Co Ltd v T J Graham and Sons Ltd* [1957] 1 QB 159. He said, at 172:

> A company may in many ways be likened to a human body. It has a brain and nerve centre which controls what it does. It also has hands which hold the tools and act in accordance with directions from the centre. Some of the people in the company are mere servants and agents who are nothing more than hands to do the work and cannot be said to represent the mind or will. Others are directors and managers who represent the directing mind and will of the company, and control what it does. The state of mind of these managers is the state of mind of the company and is treated by the law as such.

In that case the directors of the company only met once a year, they left the management of the business to others, and it was the intention of those managers which was imputed to the company. I think that was right. There have been attempts to apply Lord Denning's words to all servants of a company whose work is brain work, or exercise some managerial discretion under the direction of superior officers of the company. I do not think that Lord Denning intended to refer to them. He only referred to those who 'represent the directing mind and will of the company, and control what it does'.

I think that it is right for this reason. Normally the board of directors, the managing director and perhaps other superior officers of a company carry out the functions of management and speak and act as the company. Their subordinates do not. They carry out orders from above and it can make no difference that they are given some measure of discretion. But the board of directors may delegate some part of their functions of management giving to their delegate full discretion to act independently of instructions from them. I see no difficulty in holding that they have thereby put such a delegate in their place so that within the scope of the delegation he can act as the company. It may not always be easy to draw the line but there are cases in which the line must be drawn. *Lennard's* case [1915] AC 705 was one of them.

In some cases the phrase *alter ego* has been used. I think it is misleading. When dealing with a company the word *alter* is I think misleading. The person who speaks and acts as the company is not *alter*. He is identified with the company. And when dealing with an individual no other individual can be his *alter ego*. The other individual can be a servant, agent, delegate or representative but I know of neither principle nor authority which warrants the confusion (in the literal or original sense) of two separate individuals ...

[Where a statute introduces a] defence if the accused proved that 'he used all due diligence' I think that it [means] what it [says]. As a matter of construction I can see no ground for reading in 'he and all persons to whom he has delegated responsibility'. And if I look to the purpose and apparent intention of Parliament in enacting this defence I think that it was plainly intended to make a just and reasonable distinction between the employer who is wholly blameless and ought to be acquitted and the employer who was in some way at fault, leaving it to the employer to prove that he was in no way to blame.

What good purpose could be served by making an employer criminally responsible for the misdeeds of some of his servants but not for those of others? It is sometimes argued – it was argued in the present case – that making an employer criminally responsible, even when he has done all that he could to prevent an offence, affords some additional protection to the public because this will induce him to do more. But if he has done all he can how can he do more? I think that what lies behind this argument is a suspicion that magistrates too readily accept evidence that an employer has done all he can to prevent offences. But if magistrates were to accept as sufficient a paper scheme and perfunctory efforts to enforce it they would not be doing their duty – that would not be 'due diligence' on the part of the employer.

Then it is said that this would involve discrimination in favour of a large employer like the appellants against a small shopkeeper. But that is not so. Mr Clement was the 'opposite number' of the small shopkeeper and he was liable to prosecution in this case. The purpose of this Act must have been to penalise those at fault, not those who were in no way to blame.

The Divisional Court decided this case on a theory of delegation. In that they were following some earlier authorities, but they gave far too wide a meaning to delegation. I have said that a board of directors can delegate part of their functions of management so as to make their delegate an embodiment of the company within the sphere of the delegation. But here the board never delegated any part of their functions. They set up a chain of command through regional and district supervisors, but they remained in control. The shop managers had to obey their general directions and also take orders from their superiors. The acts or omissions of shop managers were not acts of the company itself.

In my judgment the appellants established the statutory defence. I would therefore allow this appeal.

Lord Morris of Borth-y-Gest: ... My Lords, we are here only concerned with the question whether the company committed an offence. If the nature of the offence under s 11(2) was such that, under the perhaps rather exceptional principle already referred to, the company could be held to be guilty of it – it would only be guilty if it failed to prove one of the defences available under s 24(1). If it is accepted that 'the commission of the offence' was due to 'the act or default of another person' then the company would have a defence (and so be entitled to be acquitted) if it further proved that it (ie the company) 'took all reasonable precautions and exercised all due diligence to avoid the commission' of the offence either by itself or by any person under its control. It is here that it is important to remember that it is the criminal liability of the company itself that is being considered. In general criminal liability only results from personal fault. We do not punish people in criminal courts for the misdeeds of others. The principle of respondeat superior is applicable in our civil courts but not generally in our criminal courts. So the sole issue in the present case is whether 'the company' took all reasonable precautions and exercised all due diligence. We are not concerned to express any opinion as to whether some other or which other person was by reason of the terms of s 11 and of s 23 guilty of an offence.

How, then, does a company take all reasonable precautions and exercise all due diligence? The very basis of s 24 involves that some contraventions of the Act may take place and may be contraventions by persons under the control of the company even though the company itself has taken all reasonable precautions and exercised all due diligence and that the company will not be criminally answerable for such contraventions. How, then, does a company act? When is some act the act of the company as opposed to the act of a servant or agent of the company (for which, if done within the scope of employment, the company will be civilly answerable)? In *Lennard's Carrying Co Ltd v Asiatic Petroleum Co Ltd* [1915] AC 705 Viscount Haldane LC said, at 713:

> My Lords, a corporation is an abstraction. It has no mind of its own any more than it has a body of its own; its active and directing will must consequently be sought in the person of somebody who for some purposes may be called an agent but who is really the directing mind and will of the corporation, the very ego and centre of the personality of the corporation. That person may be under the direction of the shareholders in general meeting; that person may be the board of directors itself, or it may be, and in some companies it is so, that that person has an authority co-ordinate with the board of directors given to him under the articles of association, and is appointed by the general meeting of the company, and can only be removed by the general meeting of the company.

Within the scheme of the Act now being considered an indication is given (which need not necessarily be an all-embracing indication) of those who may personify 'directing mind and will' of the company. The question in the present case becomes a question whether the company as a company took all reasonable precautions and exercised all due diligence. The magistrates so found and so held.

The magistrates found and held that 'they' (ie the company) had satisfied the provisions of s 24(1)(b). The reason why the Divisional Court felt that they could not accept that finding was that they considered that the company had delegated its duty to the manager of the shop. The manager was, they thought, 'a person whom the appellants had delegated in respect of that particular shop their duty to take all reasonable precautions and exercise all due diligence to avoid the commission' of an offence. Though the magistrates were satisfied that the company had set up an efficient system there had been 'a failure by someone to whom the duty of carrying out the system was delegated properly to carry out that function'.

My Lords, with respect I do not think that there was any feature of delegation in the present case. The company had its responsibilities in regard to taking all reasonable precautions and exercising all due diligence. The careful and effective discharge of those responsibilities required the directing mind and will of the company. A system had to be created which could rationally be said to be so designed that the commission of offences would be avoided. There was no delegation of the duty of taking precautions and exercising diligence. There was no such delegation to the manager of a particular store. He did not function as the directing mind or will of the company. His duties as the manager of one store did not involve managing the company. He was one who was being directed. He was one who was employed but he was not a delegate to whom the company passed on its responsibilities. He had certain duties which were the result of the taking by the company of all reasonable precautions and of the exercising by the company of all due diligence. He was a person under the control of the company and on the assumption that there could be proceedings against him, the company would by s 24(1)(b) be absolved if the company had taken all proper steps to avoid the commission of an offence by him. To make the company automatically liable for an offence committed by him would be to ignore the subsection. He was, so to speak, a cog in the machine which was devised: it was not left to him to devise it. Nor was he within what has been called the 'brain area' of the company. If the company had taken all reasonable precautions and exercised all due diligence to ensure that the machine could and should run effectively then some breakdown due to some action or failure on the part of 'another person' ought not to be attributed to the company or to be regarded as the action or failure of the company itself for which the company was to be criminally responsible. The defence provided by s 24(1) would otherwise be illusory ...

Lord Pearson: ... Clearly the Divisional Court's decision was based on the theory of 'delegation'. One has to examine the meaning of the word 'delegation' in relation to the facts of this case and the provision of ss 11(2) and 24 Trade Descriptions Act 1968. In one sense the meaning is as wide as the principle of the master's vicarious liability for the acts and omissions of his servants acting within the scope of their employment. In this sense the master can be said to 'delegate' to every servant acting on his behalf all duties which the servant has to perform. But that cannot be the proper meaning here. If the company 'delegated' to Miss Rogers the duty of filling the fixture with appropriate packets of washing powder, and 'delegated' to Mr Clement the duty of supervising the proper filling of fixtures and the proper exhibition or withdrawal of posters proclaiming reduced prices, then any master whether a company or an individual, must be vicariously liable for all the acts and omissions of all its or his servants acting on its or his behalf. That conclusion would defeat the manifest object of s 24 which is to enable defendants to avoid vicarious liability where they were not personally at fault. Section 24 requires a dividing line to be drawn between the master and any other person. The defendant cannot disclaim liability for an act or omission of his ego or his alter ego. In the case of an individual defendant, his ego is simply himself, but he may have an alter ego. For instance, if he has only one shop and he appoints a manager of that shop with full discretion to manage it as he thinks fit, the manager is doing what the employer would normally do and may be held to be the employer's alter ego. But if the defendant has hundreds of shops, he could not be expected personally to manage each one of them and the manager of one of his shops cannot in the absence of exceptional circumstances be considered his alter ego. In the case of a company, the ego is located in several persons, for example, those mentioned in s 20 of the Act or other persons in a similar position of direction or general management. A company may have an alter ego, if those persons who are or have its ego delegate to some other person the control and management, with full discretionary powers, of some section of the company's business. In the case of a company, it may be difficult, and in most cases for practical purposes unnecessary, to draw the distinction between its ego and its alter ego, but theoretically there is that distinction.

Mr Clement, being the manager of one of the company's several hundreds of shops, could not be identified with the company's ego nor was he an *alter ego* of the company. He was an employee in a relatively subordinate post. In the company's hierarchy there were a branch inspector and an area controller and a regional director interposed between him and the board of directors.

It was suggested in the argument of this appeal that in exercising supervision over the operations in the shop Mr Clement was performing functions of management and acting as a delegate and *alter ego* of the company. But supervision of the details of operations is not normally a function of a higher management: it is normally carried out by employees at the level of foremen, chargehands, overlookers, floor managers and 'shop' managers (in the factory sense of 'shop') ...

Meridian Global Funds Management Asia v Securities Commission
[1995] 3 WLR 413 (PC)

Through two of its employees (Koo and Ng) the appellant company, Meridian Global Funds Management Asia, acquired a controlling interest in another company (Euro-National Corporation Ltd). In doing so the appellant company failed to comply with s 20 of the (New Zealand) Securities Amendment Act 1988, which required any person who became a substantial security holder in another company to give notice of the fact. Notwithstanding that the activities of Koo and Ng had not been authorised by the appellant company, the Court of Appeal in New Zealand held that Koo's knowledge was attributable to the appellant company under the 'directing mind and will' doctrine. The Privy Council dismissed the company's appeal.

Lord Hoffmann: Any proposition about a company necessarily involves a reference to a set of rules. A company exists because there is a rule (usually in a statute) which says that a *persona ficta* shall be deemed to exist and to have certain of the powers, rights and duties of a natural person. But there would be little sense in deeming such a *persona ficta* to exist unless there were also rules to tell one what acts were to count as acts of the company. It is therefore a necessary part of corporate personality that there should be rules by which acts are attributed to the company. These may be called 'the rules of attribution'.

The company's primary rules of attribution will generally be found in its constitution, typically the articles of association, and will say things such as 'for the purpose of appointing members of the board, a majority vote of the shareholders shall be a decision of the company' or 'the decisions of the board in managing the company's business shall be the decisions of the company'. There are also primary rules of attribution which are not expressly stated in the articles but implied by company law, such as:

> ... the unanimous decision of all the shareholders in a solvent company about anything which the company under its memorandum of association has power to do shall be the decision of the company: see *Multinational Gas and Petrochemical Co v Multinational Gas and Petrochemical Services Ltd* [1983] Ch 258.

These primary rules of attribution are obviously not enough to enable a company to go out into the world and do business. Not every act on behalf of the company could be expected to be the subject of a resolution of the board or a unanimous decision of the shareholders. The company therefore builds upon the primary rules of attribution by using general rules of attribution which are equally available to natural persons, namely, the principles of agency. It will appoint servants and agents whose acts, by a combination of the general principles of agency and the company's primary rules of attribution, count as the acts of the company. And having done so, it will also make itself subject to the general rules by which liability for the acts of others can be attributed to natural persons, such as estoppel or ostensible authority in contract and vicarious liability in tort.

It is worth pausing at this stage to make what may seem an obvious point. Any statement about what a company has or has not done, or can or cannot do, is necessarily a reference to the rules of attribution (primary and general) as they apply to that company. Judges sometimes say that a company 'as such' cannot do anything; it must act by servants or agents. This may seem an unexceptionable, even banal, remark. And of course the meaning is usually perfectly clear. But a reference to a company 'as such' might suggest that there is something out there called the company of which one can meaningfully say that it can or cannot do something. There is in fact no such thing as the company as such ... only the applicable rules. To say that a company cannot do something means only that there is no one whose doing of that act would, under the applicable rules of attribution, count as an act of the company.

The company's primary rules of attribution together with the general principles of agency, vicarious liability and so forth are usually sufficient to enable one to determine its rights and obligations. In exceptional cases, however, they will not provide an answer. This will be the case when a rule of law, either expressly or by implication, excludes attribution on the basis of the general principles of agency or vicarious liability. For example, a rule may be stated in language primarily applicable to a natural person and require some act or state of mind on the part of that person 'himself'. as opposed to his servants or agents. This is generally true of rules of the criminal law, which ordinarily impose liability only for the *actus reus* and *mens rea* of the defendant himself. How is such a rule to be applied to a company?

One possibility is that the court may come to the conclusion that the rule was not intended to apply to companies at all; for example, a law which created an offence for which the only penalty was community service. Another possibility is that the court might interpret the law as meaning that it could apply to a company only on the basis of its primary rules of attribution, ie, if the act giving rise to liability was specifically authorised by the resolution of the board or an unanimous agreement of the shareholders. But there will be many cases in which neither of these solutions is satisfactory; in which the court considers that the law was intended to apply to companies and that, although it excludes ordinary vicarious liability, insistence on the primary rules of attribution would in practice defeat that intention. In such a case, the court must fashion a special rule of attribution for the particular substantive rule. This is always a matter of interpretation: given that it was intended to apply to a company, how was it intended to apply? Whose act (or knowledge, or state of mind) was *for this purpose* intended to count as the act etc of the company? One finds the answer to this question by applying the usual canons of interpretation, taking into account the language of the rule (if it is a statute) and its content and policy.

The fact that the rule of attribution is a matter of interpretation or construction of the relevant substantive rule is shown by the contrast between two decisions of the House of Lords, *Tesco Supermarkets Ltd v Nattrass* [1972] AC 153 and *In Re Supply of Ready Mixed Concrete (No 2)* [1995] 1 AC 456 ... [In the latter case] ... a restrictive arrangement in breach of an undertaking by a company to the Restrictive Practices Court was made by executives of the company acting within the scope of their employment. The board knew nothing of the arrangement; it had in fact given instructions to the company's employees that they were not to make such arrangements. But the House of Lords held that for the purposes of deciding whether the company was in contempt, the act and state of mind of an employee who entered into an arrangement in the course of his employment should be attributed to the company. This attribution rule was derived from a construction of the undertaking against the background of the Restrictive Trade Practices Act 1976: such undertakings by corporations would be worth little if the company could avoid liability for what its employees had actually done on the ground that the board did not know about it. As Lord Templeman said, at p 465, an uncritical transposition of the construction in *Tesco Supermarkets Ltd v Nattrass* [1972] AC 153:

> ... would allow a company to enjoy the benefit of restrictions outlawed by Parliament and the benefit of arrangements prohibited by the courts provided that the restrictions were accepted and implemented and the arrangements were negotiated by one or more employees who had been forbidden to do so by some superior employee identified in argument as a member of the 'higher management' of the company or by one or more directors of the company identified in argument as 'the guiding will' of the company.

Against this background of general principle, their Lordships can return to Viscount Haldane LC. In *Lennard's Carrying Co Ltd v Asiatic Petroleum Co Ltd* [1915] AC 705 the substantive provision for which an attribution rule had to be devised was s 502 of the Merchant Shipping Act 1894 (57 & 58 Vict c 60), which provided a shipowner with a defence to a claim for the loss of cargo put on board his ship if he could show that the casualty happened 'without his actual fault or privity'. The cargo had been destroyed by a fire caused by the unseaworthy condition of the ship's boilers. The language of s 502 excludes vicarious liability; it is clear that in the case of an individual owner, only his own fault or privity can defeat the statutory protection. How is this rule to be applied to a company? Viscount Haldane LC rejected the possibility that it did not apply to companies at all or (which would have come to the same thing) that it required fault or privity attributable under the company's primary rules. Instead, guided by the language and purpose of the section, he looked for the person whose functions in the company, in relation to the cause of the casualty, were the same as those to be expected of the individual shipowner to whom the language primarily applied. Who in the company was responsible for monitoring the condition of the ship, receiving the reports of the master and ship's agents, authorising repairs etc? This person was Mr Lennard, whom Viscount Haldane LC, at 713–714, described as the 'directing mind and will' of the company. It was therefore his fault or privity which s 502 attributed to the company.

Because *Lennard's Carrying Co Ltd* does not seem to have done anything except own ships, there was no need to distinguish between the person who fulfilled the function of running the company's business in general and the person whose functions corresponded, in relation to the cause of the casualty, to those of an individual owner of a ship. They were one and the same person. It was this coincidence which left Viscount Haldane LC's speech open to the interpretation that he was expounding a general metaphysic of companies. In *HL Bolton (Engineering) Co Ltd v TJ Graham &Sons Ltd* [1957] 1 QB 159 Denning LJ certainly regarded it as a generalisation about companies 'as such' when, in an equally well known passage, at 172, he likened a company to a human body: 'It has a brain and nerve centre which controls what it does. It also has hands which hold the tools and act in accordance with directions from the centre.'

But this anthropomorphism, by the very power of the image, distracts attention from the purpose for which Viscount Haldane LC said, at 713, he was using the notion of directing mind and will, namely to apply the attribution rule derived from s 502 to the particular defendant in the case:

> For if Mr Lennard was the directing mind of the company, then his action must, unless a corporation is not to be liable at all, have been an action which was the action of the company itself *within the meaning of section 502* ... (Emphasis supplied.)

The true nature of the exercise became much clearer, however, in later cases on the Merchant Shipping Act 1894. In *The Truculent* [1952] P 1, an action to limit liability for damage caused by collision under s 503, which also required the owner of the ship which caused the collision to show that the casualty happened without his 'actual fault or privity', the offending ship was a Royal Navy submarine. Her collision with a fishing vessel had been caused by the inadequate system of navigation lights then carried by submarines. Willmer J held that for this purpose the 'directing mind and will' of the Crown, which owned the submarine, was the Third Sea Lord, to whom the Board of Admiralty had entrusted the function of supervising such matters as the systems of navigation lights carried by warships. That function was one which an individual owner of a ship would be expected to fulfil. in *The Lady Gwendolen* [1965] P 294 the owners of the ship were Arthur Guinness, Son & Co (Dublin) Ltd. The collision occurred because the master, in accordance with his custom, had taken his vessel laden with stout up the Mersey Channel to Liverpool at full speed in dense fog without more than the odd casual glance at his radar. Owning ships was a very subsidiary part of the company's activities. It had a traffic department which managed the ships under the general supervision of a member of the board who was a brewer and took no interest in the safety of their navigation. The manager of the traffic department knew about railways but took equally little interest in ships. The marine superintendent, one beneath him in the hierarchy, failed to observe that the master of *The Lady Gwendolen* was given to dangerous navigation although, as Willmer LJ said, at 338:

> It would not have required any very detailed examination of the engine room records in order to ascertain that *The Lady Gwendolen* was frequently proceeding at full speed at times when the deck log was recording dense fog.

In applying s 503 of the Merchant Shipping Act 1894, Sellers LJ said of the company, at 333:

> In their capacity as shipowners they must be judged by the standard of conduct of the ordinary reasonable shipowner in the management and control of a vessel or of a fleet of vessels.

The court found that a reasonable shipowner would have realised what was happening and given the master proper instruction in the use of radar. None of the people in the company's hierarchy had done so.

It is difficult to see how, on any reasonable construction of s 503, these findings would not involve the actual fault or privity of Guinness. So far as anyone in the hierarchy had functions corresponding to those to be expected of an individual owner, his failure to discharge them was attributable to the company. So far as there was no such person, the superior management was at fault in failing to ensure that there was. In either case, the fault was attributable to the company. But the Court of Appeal found it necessary to identify a 'directing mind and will' of the company and lodged it in the responsible member of the board or (in the case of Willmer LJ) the railway expert who managed the traffic department.

Some commentators have not been altogether comfortable with the idea of the Third Sea Lord being the directing mind and will of the Crown or the traffic manager being the directing mind and will of Guinness. Their Lordships would agree that the phrase does not fit the facts of *The Truculent* [1952] P 1 or *The Lady Gwendolen* [1965] P 294 as happily as it did those of *Lennard's* case [1915] AC 705. They think, however, that the difficulty has been caused by concentration on that particular phrase rather than the purpose for which Viscount Haldane LC was using it. It will often be the most appropriate description of the person designated by the relevant attribution rule, but it might be better to acknowledge that not every such rule has to be forced into the same formula.

Once it is appreciated that the question is one of construction rather than metaphysics, the answer in this case seems to their Lordships to be as straightforward as it did to Heron J. The policy of s 20 of the Securities Amendment Act 1988 is to compel, in fast-moving markets, the immediate disclosure of the identity of persons who become substantial security-holders in public issuers. Notice must be given as soon as that person knows that he has become a substantial security-holder. In the case of a corporate security-holder, what rule should be implied as to the person whose knowledge for this purpose is to count as the knowledge of the company? Surely the person who, with the authority of the company, acquired the relevant interest. Otherwise the policy of the Act would be defeated. Companies would be able to allow employees to acquire interests on their behalf which made them substantial security-holders but would not have to report them until the board or someone else in senior management got to know about it. This would put a premium on the board paying as little attention as possible to what its investment managers were doing. Their Lordships would therefore hold that upon the true construction of s 20(4)(e), the company knows that it has become a substantial security-holder when that is known to the person who had authority to do the deal. It is then obliged to give notice under s 20(3). The fact that Koo did the deal for a corrupt purpose and did not give such notice because he did not want his employers to find out cannot in their Lordships' view affect the attribution of knowledge and the consequent duty to notify.

It was therefore not necessary in this case to inquire into whether Koo could have been described in some more general sense as the 'directing mind and will' of the company. But their Lordships would wish to guard themselves against being understood to mean that whenever a servant of a company has authority to do an act on its behalf, knowledge of that act will for all purposes be attributed to the company. It is a question of construction in each case as to whether the particular rule requires that the knowledge that an act has been done, or the state of mind with which it was done, should be attributed to the company. Sometimes, as in *In re Supply of Ready Mixed Concrete (No 2)* [1995] 1 AC 456 and this case, it will be appropriate. Likewise in a case in which a company was required to make a return for revenue purposes and the statute made it an offence to make a false return with intent to deceive, the Divisional Court held that the *mens rea* of the servant authorised to discharge the duty to make the return should be attributed to the company: see *Moore v I Bresler Ltd* [1944] 2 All ER 515. On the other hand, the fact that a company's employee is authorised to drive a lorry does not in itself lead to the conclusion that if he kills someone by reckless driving, the company will be guilty of manslaughter. There is no inconsistency. Each is an example of an attribution rule for a particular purpose, tailored as it always must be to the terms and policies of the substantive rule.

AG's Ref (No 2 of 1999) [2000] 3 All ER 182

[The appeal arose out of a failed prosecution of a rail operating company in respect of the deaths of several passengers following a train crash involving the company's trains. For the full facts see the extract in Chapter 15 dealing with corporate manslaughter. The following extracts concern the basis upon which the courts would seek to identify the *mens rea* of a corporate body.]

Rose LJ: The court's opinion is sought in relation to two questions referred by the Attorney General under s 36 of the Criminal Justice Act 1972. [The second of these is] ... Can a non-human defendant be convicted of the crime of manslaughter by gross negligence in the absence of evidence establishing the guilt of an identified human individual for the same crime? ...

As to question (2), Mr Lissack [for the Attorney General] accepted that policy considerations arise. Large companies should be as susceptible to prosecution for manslaughter as one-man companies. Where the ingredients of a common law offence are identical to those of a statutory offence there is no justification for drawing a distinction as to liability between the two and the public interest requires the more emphatic denunciation of a company inherent in a conviction for manslaughter. He submitted that the ingredients of the offence of gross negligence manslaughter are the same in relation to a body corporate as to a human being, namely grossly negligent breach of a duty to a deceased causative of his death. It is, he submitted, unnecessary and inappropriate to inquire whether there is an employee in the company who is guilty of the offence of manslaughter who can be properly be said to have been acting as the embodiment of the company. The criminal law of negligence follows the civil law of negligence as applied to corporations: the only difference is that, to be criminal, the negligence must be gross. Of the three theories of corporate criminal liability, namely vicarious liability, identification and personal liability, it is personal liability which should here apply. In the present case, it would have been open to the jury to convict if they were satisfied that the deaths occurred by reason of a gross breach by the defendant of its personal duty to have a safe system of train operation in place. The identification theory, attributing to the company the mind and will of senior directors and managers, was developed in order to avoid injustice: it would bring the law into disrepute if every act and state of mind of an individual employee was attributed to a company which was entirely blameless (see *Tesco Supermarkets Ltd v Nattrass* [1971] 2 All ER 127 at 130–31, [1972] AC 153 at 169 *per* Lord Reid and *Canadian Dredge and Dock Co Ltd v R* (1985) 1 SCR 662 at 701 *per* Estey J of the Supreme Court of Canada). Its origins lay in the speech of Viscount Haldane LC in *Lennard's Carrying Co Ltd v Asiatic Petroleum Co Ltd* [1915] AC 705 at 713, [1914–15] All ER Rep 280 at 283 and it was developed by the judgment of Denning LJ in *HL Bolton Engineering Co Ltd v TJ Graham & Sons Ltd* [1956] 3 All ER 624 at 630, [1957] 1 QB 159 at 172 and *Tesco Supermarkets Ltd v Nattrass* ...

Before turning to Mr Lissack's submission in relation to personal liability it is convenient first to refer to the speech of Lord Hoffmann in *Meridian Global Funds Management Asia Ltd v Securities Commission* ... on which Mr Lissack relied as the lynchpin of this part of his argument. It was a case in which the chief investment officer and senior portfolio manager of an investment management company, with the company's authority but unknown to the board of directors and managing director, used funds managed by the company to acquire shares, but failed to comply with a statutory obligation to give notice of the acquisition to the Securities Commission. The trial judge held that the knowledge of the officer and manager should be attributed to the company and the Court of Appeal of New Zealand upheld the decision on the basis that the officer was the directing mind and will of the company. The Privy Council dismissed an appeal. Lord Hoffmann, giving the judgment of the Privy Council, said that the company's primary rules of attribution were generally found in its constitution or implied by company law ... But, in an exceptional case, where the application of those principles would defeat the intended application of a particular provision to companies, it was necessary to devise a special rule of attribution ... Lord Hoffmann went on to comment that it was not necessary in that case to inquire whether the chief investment officer could be described as the 'directing mind and will' of the company. He said:

> It is a question of construction in each case as to whether the particular rule requires that the knowledge that an act has been done, or the state of mind in which it was done, should be attributed to the company.

Mr Lissack's submission that personal liability on the part of the company is capable of arising in the present case was based on a number of authorities in addition to the *Meridian* case.

In *R v British Steel plc* [1995] 1 WLR 1356 the defendant was prosecuted, as was the present defendant, for a breach of ss 3(1) and 33(1)(a) of the 1974 Act. A worker was killed because of the collapse of a steel platform during a re-positioning operation which a competent supervisor would have recognised was inherently dangerous. The defence was that the workmen had disobeyed instructions and, even if the supervisor was at fault, the company at the level of its directing mind had taken reasonable care. An appeal against conviction was dismissed by the Court of Appeal, Criminal Division. The judgment was given by Steyn LJ who said (at 1362–63):

> ... counsel for British Steel plc concedes that it is not easy to fit the idea of corporate criminal liability only for acts of the 'directing mind' of the company into the language of section 3(1). We would go further. If it be accepted that Parliament considered it necessary for the protection of public health and safety to impose, subject to the defence of reasonable practicability, absolute criminal liability, it would drive a juggernaut through the legislative scheme if corporate employers could avoid criminal liability where the potentially harmful event is committed by someone who is not the directing mind of the company ... That would emasculate the legislation.

In a commentary on this decision Professor Sir John Smith QC said in relation to the 'directing mind' argument ([1995] Crim LR 655):

> Where a statutory duty to do something is imposed on a particular person (here an 'employer') and he does not do it, he commits the *actus reus* of an offence. It may be that he has failed to fulfil his duty because his employee or agent has failed to carry out his duties properly but this is not a case for vicarious liability. If the employer is held liable, it is because he, personally, has failed to do what the law requires him to do and he is personally, not vicariously liable. There is no need to find someone – in the case of a company, the 'brains' and not merely the 'hands' – for whose act the person with the duty be held liable. The duty on the company in this case was 'to ensure' – ie to make certain – that persons are not exposed to risk. They did not make it certain. It does not matter how; they were in breach of their statutory duty and, in the absence of any requirement for *mens rea*, that is the end of the matter.

Mr Lissack also relied on *Re Supply of Ready Mixed Concrete (No 2)* [1995] 1 All ER 135, [1995] 1 AC 456 where the House of Lords held companies liable for a breach of the restrictive trade practices legislation where their local managers had entered into price fixing and market sharing agreements in defiance of clear instructions from the board of directors and without their knowledge. Lord Templeman said that to permit a company to escape liability by forbidding its employees to do the acts in question would allow it:

> ... to enjoy the benefit of restriction outlawed by Parliament and the benefit of arrangements prohibited by the courts provided that the restrictions were accepted and implemented and the arrangements negotiated by one or more employees who had been forbidden to do so by some superior employee identified in argument as a member of the 'higher management' of the company or by one or more of the directors of the company identified in

argument as 'the guiding will' of the company.' (See [1995] 1 All ER 135 at 141–42, [1995] 1 AC 456 at 465.)

In *R v Associated Octel Ltd*, in a prosecution under s 3 of the 1974 Act, the defendant's conviction was upheld by the House of Lords. Lord Hoffmann, in a speech with which the other members of the House agreed, said that s 3 imposed a duty towards persons not in employment on the employer himself defined by the conduct of his undertaking (see [1996] 4 All ER 846 at 850, [1996] 1 WLR 1543 at 1547). In *R v Gateway Foodmarkets Ltd* [1997] 3 All ER 78 the Court of Appeal, Criminal Division reached a similar conclusion in relation to s 2(1) of the same Act in relation to employees.

Mr Lissack submitted that, in accordance with the speech of Lord Hoffmann in the *Meridian* case, the choice of the appropriate theory depends on the ingredients of the offence itself, and the requirements of both retribution and deterrence point to corporate liability where death is caused through the company's gross negligence. He relied on a passage in Steyn LJ's judgment in *R v British Steel plc* [1995] 1 WLR 1356 at 1364 where there is reference to the promotion of 'a culture of guarding against the risks to health and safety by virtue of hazardous industrial operations'.

Mr Lissack advanced two subsidiary submissions. First, if, contrary to his primary submission, a corporation cannot be convicted unless an employee embodying the company can be identified as guilty of manslaughter, the presence of such an employee can be inferred: he relied on a passage in the speech of Lord Hoffmann in *Meridian Global Funds Management Asia Ltd v Securities Commission* [1995] 3 All ER 918 at 927, [1995] 2 AC 500 at 510 which seems to us to afford no support whatever for this submission. We reject it.

Secondly, he suggested that aggregation has a role to play, ie where a series of venial management failures are aggregated and cumulatively amount to gross negligence, a company may be convicted. There is a tentatively expressed passage in Smith and Hogan p 186, based on an analogy with civil negligence, which supports this suggestion. But there is no supporting and clear contrary judicial authority – see *R v HM Coroner for East Kent ex p Spooner, R v HM Coroner for East Kent ex p Rohan* (1987) 88 Cr App R 10 at 16–17 *per* Bingham LJ:

> A case against a personal defendant cannot be fortified by evidence against another defendant. The case against a corporation can only be made by evidence properly addressed to showing guilt on the part of the corporation as such.

The Law Commission are against introducing the concept of aggregation (see Law Com No 237, para 7.33). We reject the suggestion that aggregation has any proper role to play.

For the defendant, Mr Caplan submitted, in relation to question (2), that *R v Adomako* [1994] 3 All ER 79, [1995] 1 AC 171 was not concerned with corporate liability. It is necessarily implicit in the Law Commission's recommendation, in Law Com No 237, that Parliament should enact a new offence of corporate killing, that the doctrine of identification still continues to apply to gross negligence manslaughter since *R v Adomako*. *Tesco Supermarkets Ltd v Nattrass* [1971] 2 All ER 127, [1972] AC 153 is still authoritative (see *Seaboard Offshore Ltd v Secretary of State for Transport* [1994] 2 All ER 99, [1994] 1 WLR 541) and it is impossible to find a company guilty unless its alter ego is identified. None of the authorities since *Tesco Supermarkets Ltd v Nattrass* relied on by Mr Lissack supports the demise of the doctrine of identification: all are concerned with statutory construction of different substantive offences and the appropriate rule of attribution was decided having regard to the legislative intent, namely whether Parliament intended companies to be liable. There is a sound reason for a special rule of attribution in relation to statutory offences rather than common law offences, namely there is, subject to a defence of reasonable practicability, an absolute duty imposed by the statutes. The authorities on statutory offences do not bear on the common law principle in relation to manslaughter. Lord Hoffmann's speech in the *Meridian* case is a restatement not an abandonment of existing principles: see, for example, *Tesco Supermarkets Ltd v Nattrass* [1971] 2 All ER 127 at 156, [1972] AC 153 at 200 *per* Lord Diplock: '... there may be criminal statutes which on their true construction ascribe to a corporation criminal responsibility for the acts of servants and agents who would be excluded by the test that I have stated ...' (viz those exercising the powers of the company under its articles of association). The Law Commission's proposals were made after the *Meridian* and *British Steel* cases. Identification is necessary in relation to the *actus reus*, ie whose acts or omissions are to be attributed to the company, and *R v Adomako*'s objective test in relation to gross negligence in no way affects this. Furthermore, the civil negligence rule of liability for the acts of servants or agents has no place in the criminal law – which is why the identification principle was developed. That principle is still the rule of attribution in criminal law whether or not *mens rea* needs to be proved.

Codification and law reform proposals

The DCCB has provisions, cll 30 and 31, that seek to codify and clarify the common law relating to the imposition of criminal liability on corporations – see also the commentary in Vol II, paras 10.1–10.25. Since then, however, the focus of reform proposals has shifted to the area of corporate liability for manslaughter. The current reform proposals are considered in Chapter 15.

COINCIDENCE OF *ACTUS REUS* AND *MENS REA*

Establishing criminal liability normally involves the prosecution in proving that there was a coincidence of the *actus reus* and the *mens rea* for the offence in question. In the vast majority of cases the coincidence is evident from the facts. In some cases, however, the courts have had to deal with arguments based on non-coincidence and, as the following extracts indicate, they have responded by developing a somewhat elastic concept of coincidence.

Thabo Meli and Others v R [1954] 1 WLR 228 (PC)

Lord Reid: The four appellants in this case were convicted of murder ... The appeal which has been heard by this Board dealt with two matters: first, whether the conclusions of the learned judge on questions of fact were warranted: and, second, whether, on a point of law, the accused are entitled to have the verdict quashed.

On the first matter, there really is no ground for criticising the learned judge's treatment of the facts. It is established by evidence, which was believed and which is apparently credible, that there was a preconceived plot on the part of the four accused to bring the deceased man to a hut and there to kill him, and then fake an accident, so that the accused should escape the penalty for their act. The deceased man was brought to the hut. He was there treated to beer and was at least partially intoxicated; and he was then struck over the head in accordance with the plan of the accused. Witnesses say that while the deceased was seated and bending forward he was struck a heavy blow on the back of the head with a piece of iron like the instrument produced at the trial. But a post mortem examination showed that his skull had not been fractured and medical evidence was to the effect that a blow such as the witnesses described would have produced more severe injuries than those found at the post mortem examination. There is at least doubt whether the weapon which was produced as being like the weapon which was used could have produced the injuries that were found, but it may be that this weapon is not exactly similar to the one which was used, or it may be that the blow was a glancing blow and produced less severe injuries than those which one might expect. In any event, the man was unconscious after receiving the blow, but he was not then dead. There is no evidence that the accused then believed that he was dead, but their Lordships are prepared to assume from their subsequent conduct that they did so believe; and it is only on that assumption that any statable case can be made for this appeal. The accused took out the body, rolled it over a low krantz or cliff, and dressed up the scene to make it look like an accident. Obviously, they believed at that time that the man was dead, but it appears from the medical evidence that the injuries which he received in the hut were not sufficient to cause the death and that the final cause of his death was exposure when he was left unconscious at the foot of the krantz.

The point of law which was raised in this case can be simply stated. It is said that two acts were done: first, the attack in the hut; and, second, the placing of the body outside afterwards; and that they were separate acts. It is said that, while the first act was accompanied by *mens rea*, it was not the cause of death; but that the second act, while it was the cause of death, was not accompanied by *mens rea*; and on that ground, it is said that the accused are not guilty of murder, though they may have been guilty of culpable homicide. It is said that the *mens rea* necessary to establish murder is an intention to kill, and that there could be no intention to kill when the accused thought that the man was already dead, so their original intention to kill had ceased before they did the act which caused the man's death. It appears to their Lordships impossible to divide up what was really one series of acts in this way. There is no doubt that the accused set out to do all these acts in order to achieve their plan, and as parts of their plan; and it is much too refined a ground of judgment to say that, because they were under a misapprehension at one stage and thought that their guilty purpose had been achieved before, in fact, it was achieved, therefore they are to escape the penalties of the law. Their Lordships do not think that this is a matter which is susceptible of elaboration. There appears to be no case, either in South Africa or England, or for that matter elsewhere, which resembles the present. Their Lordships can find no difference relevant to the present case between the law of South Africa and the law of England; and they are of opinion that by both laws there can be no separation such as that for which the accused contend. Their crime is not reduced from murder to a lesser crime merely because the accused were under some misapprehension for a time during the completion of their criminal plot.

Their Lordships must, therefore, humbly advise Her Majesty that this appeal should be dismissed.

AG's Ref (No 4 of 1980) [1981] 1 WLR 705 (CA)

Ackner LJ: This is a reference to the court by the Attorney General of a point of law seeking the opinion of the court pursuant to s 36 of the Criminal Justice Act 1972. It raises yet again the problem of the supposed corpse, and the facts, which I take from the terms of the reference itself, are inevitably macabre.

The deceased was the fiancée of the accused and for some months before her death they had lived together in a maisonette consisting of two floors of a house connected by two short flights of carpeted wooden stairs. The deceased was employed locally and was last seen at work on 17 January 1979 at about 5 pm. Thereafter no one, other than the accused, ever saw her alive again.

The deceased met her death on 18 January 1979, although this fact was not known until over three weeks later when the defendant so informed a friend. His account, the first of a number, was that in the course of an argument on the evening of 17 January he had slapped her on the face causing her to fall downstairs and bang her head. He said that he had then put her to bed but discovered next morning that she was dead. He then took her body to his home town and buried her.

On the following day, 14 February, he gave his second account, telling the same friend that after the deceased had 'fallen downstairs' he had dragged her upstairs by a piece of rope tied round her neck. He subsequently cut up her body with a saw before burying it. The next day, on the advice of his friend, the accused went to see a superior and gave an account similar to the one he had given his friend.

We now come to the statements which he made to the police. On 27 February, having consulted solicitors, the accused was interviewed by the police at his solicitors' office. He began by giving the police substantially the same account that he had given to his friend and his superior but added that instead of burying the deceased he had 'dumped' the various parts of her body on a tip. At the police station later that day he amplified his statement by saying that the incident when the deceased 'fell downstairs' occurred at about 7 pm on 17 January and that it was the following day, when he found her motionless, that he pulled her upstairs by a rope around her neck and then cut up her body in the bathroom. On the following day after much questioning by the police he changed his account stating that everything had happened on Thursday 18 January at about 7 am. This is what he then said happened. (1) He and the deceased had an argument on the landing in the course of which each slapped the other; he seized the deceased and shook her hard; she dug her nails into him and he pushed her away instinctively, causing her to fall backwards over the handrail, down the stairs head first onto the floor. (2) He went downstairs immediately to find her motionless and on a very cursory examination discovered no pulse, and no sign of breath but frothy blood coming from her mouth. (3) Almost immediately thereafter he dragged her upstairs by a rope tied around her neck, placed her in the bath and cut her neck with a penknife to let out her blood, having already decided to cut up her body and dispose of the pieces.

He agreed that his previous account was untrue and he made a detailed voluntary statement along the lines set out in (1), (2) and (3) above describing how subsequently he had cut up and disposed of her body.

In the course of these interviews at the police station, after the defendant had given his revised account, the following conversation took place:

Officer: How long was it from the time that she went backwards over the handrail to when you started pulling her up the stairs with a piece of rope around her neck?

Accused: I went downstairs when she went backwards. I looked at her, tried her pulse. I tried to lift her and she wee'd, so I put her down again. Then two girls went past [the glass fronted door] so I covered the door with the blanket. Then I got the piece of rope and pulled her up the stairs.

Officer: When did you decide you were going to cut the body up and dispose of it?

Accused: Just before I pulled her up the stairs.

Later he was questioned by the officer:

Q: Is it correct that you hauled [her] to the bathroom, and put her into the bath and then cut her neck with a knife to let the blood out and these were all a continuous series of events?

A: Yes, they all happened together.

Subsequently the police discovered evidence which corroborated the accused's account of how, where and when he had cut up the body. They also found the saw he had used and the shopkeeper who sold it to him. However, the body of the deceased was never found, only some minute fragments of bone, which were discovered in the maisonette. There was thus no expert evidence as to the cause of death. The deceased died either as a result of being pushed and thus caused to fall backwards over the handrail and backwards down the stairs head first onto the floor, or by being strangled with the rope, or having her throat cut. The Crown conceded that it was not possible for them to prove whether the deceased died as the result of the 'fall' downstairs or from what the accused did to the deceased thereafter.

The indictment charged the accused with (1) manslaughter, (2) obstructing the coroner in the execution of his duty, and (3) preventing the burial of a corpse.

The accused pleaded guilty to the third count, the Crown offered no evidence on the second and the trial proceeded on the count of manslaughter.

At the close of the Crown's case counsel for the accused stated that he proposed to submit that on the facts proved there was no case of manslaughter capable of going to the jury. It is not easy to follow from the transcript the exact basis of his submissions, but what he appears to have been contending was that (a) it was not possible for the jury to be sure what caused the deceased's death and (b) whether the death was caused as a result of her 'fall' down the stairs or from what the accused subsequently did, believing her to be dead, in neither event was there a *prima facie* case of manslaughter.

The judge, although expressing his reluctance to accept that the accused could be in a better position as a result of his dismembering the body of the deceased, appeared to have been very concerned at what he described as 'an insuperable problem of sentencing', were the accused to be convicted of manslaughter. He expressed the view that the real criminality of the accused's behaviour was in disposing of the body, a view which this court is unable to accept. These views appear to have influenced his decision, which was to withdraw the case from the jury and to direct an acquittal on the ground that the Crown had failed to prove the cause of the death of the deceased.

On the above facts this reference raises a single simple question, viz if an accused kills another by one or other of two or more different acts each of which, if it caused the death, is a sufficient act to establish manslaughter, is it necessary in order to found a conviction to prove which act caused the death? The answer to that question is No, it is not necessary to found a conviction to prove which act caused the death. No authority is required to justify this answer, which is clear beyond argument, as was indeed immediately conceded by counsel on behalf of the accused.

What went wrong in this case was that counsel made jury points to the judge and not submissions of law. He was in effect contending that the jury should not convict of manslaughter if the death had resulted from the 'fall', because the push which had projected the deceased over the handrail was a reflex and not a voluntary action, as a result of her digging her nails into him. If, however, the deceased was still alive when he cut her throat, since he then genuinely believed her to be dead, having discovered neither pulse nor sign of breath, but frothy blood coming from her mouth, he could not be guilty of manslaughter because he had not behaved with gross criminal negligence. What counsel and the judge unfortunately overlooked was that there was material available to the jury which would have entitled them to have convicted the accused of manslaughter, whichever of the two sets of acts caused her death. It being common ground that the deceased was killed by an act done to her by the accused and it being conceded that the jury could not be satisfied which was the act which caused the death, they should have been directed in due course in the summing up, to ask themselves the following questions: (1) Are we satisfied beyond reasonable doubt that the deceased's 'fall' downstairs was the result of an intentional act by the accused which was unlawful and dangerous? If the answer was No, then they would acquit. It the answer was Yes, then they would need to ask themselves a second question, namely (2) Are we satisfied beyond reasonable doubt that the act of cutting the girl's throat was an act of gross criminal negligence? If the answer to that question was No, then they would acquit, but if the answer was Yes, then the verdict would be guilty of manslaughter. The jury would thus have been satisfied that, whichever act had killed the deceased, each was a sufficient act to establish the offence of manslaughter.

The fact of this case did not call for a 'series of acts direction' following the principle in *Thabo Meli v R* ...

R v Le Brun [1992] 1 QB 61 (CA)

Lord Lane CJ: ... The facts giving rise to the charge were these. In September 1989 the appellant, who was then serving in the Royal Navy, was living at an address in Plymouth with his wife, who was the victim in the present case. They went out for the evening to some friends, the Cartwrights, on 23 September 1989. They left the house of the friends in the early hours at about 2 am. They did not have very far to go to their own home. They had been drinking. They were both described as merry, but neither, it was said, was drunk.

It was only two or three minutes' walk to get to their own home. But during that short journey it is quite plain that a heated argument developed between the two of them. To come to the end of the story, after a short interval, which was really only sufficient for the friends whose house they had visited to have tidied up the house, taken the dog for a walk and prepared for bed, the appellant returned to the Cartwrights, banged on the door and shouted 'It's Joannie ... she's collapsed. There's blood everywhere. Get an ambulance.'

In fact the wife (as I shall call her now) was lying near the top of some steps leading from the pathway to their home. She had sustained two wounds to her head: a fracture to the back of the skull and a severe injury to her chin which had produced what might be described as a star shaped wound. That wound had broken the jaw and caused bleeding into the joints on each side. She had sustained also a bruise on the outer edge of the lip on the left, a fracture to both wings of the hyoid bone at the top of the neck. As can be seen from the photographs, there was a good deal of blood at the scene and – a matter of some importance – some hair, which had plainly been pulled by the roots out of her scalp, was lying at the scene. The cause of death was bruising to the brain which in its turn had been caused by the fracture to the back of the skull.

There was abundant evidence from the neighbours of the argument which had taken place between these two. For example Mrs Luke whose house overlooked the area where the incident took place, heard a man sounding very angry and aggressive, plainly wanting a woman (the wife in this case) to go into the house. Indeed it is plain from her evidence and from the evidence of other eye witnesses or other witnesses who heard what was going on, that one reason for the altercation between these two was the woman's wish not to go into the house and the man's wish that she should.

Mrs Luke saw two people arguing. Eventually she heard a thump and a moan and saw the woman kneeling against the metal railing and the man taking hold of her with a hand on her head. She next saw the woman lying on the ground, the man telling her to get up and then pulling her by the arms or shoulders towards the road. It then seemed to her that he let go of her. So she fell and her head hit the ground and that thump could be heard.

Mr Hislop, whose evidence is referred to by the judge in his summing up, said that the man was shouting 'get on home', and the woman was saying 'get off me'. They were saying that sort of thing repeatedly and there was a lot of swearing, he said, from both of them. He said that he went to the window and saw a man and a woman struggling in the middle of the road, pulling and pushing at each other. He tried to pull her in the direction which it emerged was the direction of the appellant's house and she resisted. Further evidence was given by a Mrs Bradford, whose evidence had certain unsatisfactory features about it.

There was medical evidence from a pathologist and also an expert in dental and facial injuries. The effect of that evidence was that the injury to the back of the skull would have to have been caused by the body falling at least from waist height. The importance of that evidence was that there was one witness who had said that the head had been lifted an inch or two from the ground and let fall. On the pathological evidence it seems that that would not have been sufficient to cause the fracture to the back of the skull which in its turn was responsible for the death ...

When the police arrived at the scene they found the appellant in a hysterical state trying to revive his wife. He was arrested. He continued to struggle on his way to the police station, shouting that he wanted to see his wife. He said that she had slipped on the steps and hit her head. He had not touched her. When interviewed he declined to answer any questions.

He gave evidence at the trial. He said the two of them had been happy when they left the house of the Cartwrights, but an argument which became heated developed as they made their way towards home. He had asked his wife for the house keys which she had. She was standing by the railings at the steps. She would not give him the keys. He tried to persuade her. He took hold of her arm, whereupon she shouted 'get off me', as one of the witnesses had heard. He started walking back to the house away from her, and all of a sudden he heard a scream, a thud behind him, he turned round and saw the deceased on the ground. He told her to get up. She seemed to be unconscious. He described how he had tried to lift her, but she had slipped from his hold and had fallen. Eventually he held her upright against himself, with her legs trailing along the ground, and tried to drag her backwards, but she slipped through his arms so that her back and then her head hit the roadway. He then realised she was seriously hurt and went for help. He never hit her, he said. He did not know how she had sustained her injuries. He had tried to revive her and then all he had wanted to do was to get her home ...

Problems of causation and remoteness of damage are never easy of solution. We have had helpful arguments from both counsel on this point, the point in the present case being, to put it in summary before coming to deal with it in more detail, that the intention of the appellant to harm his wife one way or another may have been separated by a period of time from the act which in fact caused the death, namely the fact of her falling to the ground and fracturing her skull. The second incident may have taken place without any guilty mind of the part of the appellant.

The authors of Smith and Hogan, *Criminal Law*, 6th edn, 1988, p 320, say:

> An intervening act by the original actor will not break the chain of causation so as to excuse him, where the intervening act is part of the same transaction, but it is otherwise if the act which causes the *actus reus* is part of a completely different transaction. For example, D, having wounded P, visits him in hospital and accidentally infects him with smallpox of which he dies.

The problem in the instant case can be expressed in a number of different ways, of which causation is one. Causation on the facts as the jury in this case must have found them – I say at the best from the point of view of the appellant – is in one sense clear. Death was caused by the victim's head hitting the ground as she was being dragged away by the appellant. The only remoteness was that between the initial unlawful blow and the later moment when the skull was fractured causing death.

The question can be perhaps framed in this way. There was here an initial unlawful blow to the chin delivered by the appellant. That, again on what must have been the jury's finding, was not delivered with the intention of doing really serious harm to the wife. The guilty intent accompanying that blow was sufficient to have rendered the appellant guilty of manslaughter, but not murder, had it caused death. But it did not cause death. What caused death was the later impact when the wife's head hit the pavement. At the moment of impact the appellant's intention was to remove her, probably unconscious body to avoid detection. To that extent the impact may have been accidental. May the earlier guilty intent be joined with the later non-guilty blow which caused death to produce in the conglomerate a proper verdict of manslaughter?

It has usually been in the previous decisions in the context of murder that the problem has arisen. We have had our attention directed to a Privy Council case, *Meli v R* [1954] 1 WLR 228 ...

That decision of course is not binding upon us. It is of very persuasive authority and it was adopted by another division of this court in 1975 in *R v Moore* [1975] Crim LR 229.

However, it will be observed that the present case is different from the facts of those two cases in that death here was not the result of a preconceived plan which went wrong, as the case in those two decisions which were have cited. Here the death, again assuming the jury's finding to be such as it must have been, was the result of an initial unlawful blow, not intended to cause serious harm, in its turn causing the appellant to take steps possibly to evade the consequences of his unlawful act. During the taking of those steps he commits the *actus reus* but without the *mens rea* necessary for murder or manslaughter. Therefore the *mens rea* is contained in the initial unlawful assault, but the *actus reus* is the eventual dropping of the head on to the ground.

Normally the *actus reus* and *mens rea* coincide in point of time. What is the situation when they do not? Is it permissible, as the prosecution contend here, to combine them to produce a conviction for manslaughter? ...

It seems to us that where the unlawful application of force and the eventual act causing death are parts of the same sequence of events, the same transaction, the fact that there is an appreciable interval of time between the two does not serve to exonerate the defendant from liability. That is certainly so where the appellant's subsequent actions which caused death, after the initial unlawful blow, are designed to conceal his commission of the original assault.

It would be possible to express the problem as one of causation. The original unlawful blow to the chin was a *causa sine qua non* of the later *actus reus*. It was the opening event in a series which was to culminate in death: the first link in the chain of causation, to use another metaphor. It cannot be said that the actions of the appellant in dragging the victim away with the intention of evading liability broke the chain which linked the initial blow with the death.

In short, in circumstances such as the present, which is the only concern of this court, the act which causes death, and the necessary mental state to constitute manslaughter, need not coincide in point of time ...

AG's Ref (No 3 of 1994) [1997] 3 All ER 936

The facts are set out in extracts below dealing with the issue of transferred malice. **Lord Mustill** began by rehearsing what he saw as the 'established rules' of liability for homicide, including the rule that *mens rea* and *actus reus* should coincide.

The existence of an interval of time between the doing of an act by the defendant with the necessary wrongful intent and its impact on the victim in a manner which leads to death does not in itself prevent the intent, the act and the death from together amounting to murder, so long as there is an unbroken causal connection between the act and the death.

If authority is needed for this obvious proposition it may be found in *R v Church* ... and *R v Le Brun* ...

Lord Hope: As Lord Lane CJ observed in *R v Le Brun* ... following *R v Church* ... the act which caused the death and the mental state which is needed to constitute manslaughter need not coincide in point of time. So to this extent as least it may be said to be immaterial that the child was not alive when the defendant stabbed the mother with the intention which was needed to show that he was committing an unlawful act. It is enough that the original unlawful and dangerous act, to which the required mental state is related, and the eventual death of the victim are both part of the same sequence of events.

TRANSFERRED MALICE

Under the doctrine of transferred malice if A fires a gun at B, intending to kill him, and he misses, but succeeds in killing a bystander C, A cannot deny that he had the *mens rea* for murder. This could be explained by saying that the identity of the victim in homicide is no part of the *mens rea* (that is, the *mens rea* is intention to kill or do grievous bodily harm to a person – not a named individual). It can also, however, be expressed in terms of the 'malice' aimed at B being transferred to the actual victim, C. The same principle applied to property offences.

R v Pembliton (1874) LR 2 CCR 119

Lord Coleridge CJ: I am of opinion that the conviction should be quashed. The facts of the case are that there was fighting going on in the streets of Wolverhampton near the prosecutor's house, and the prisoner, after fighting for some time, separated himself from the crowd and threw a stone, which missed the person he aimed at, but struck and broke a window, doing damage to the extent of upwards of £5. The question is, whether under an indictment for unlawfully and maliciously injuring the property of the owner of the plate-glass window, these facts will support the indictment when coupled with the other facts found by the jury, that the prisoner threw the stone at the people intending to strike one or more of them, but not intending to break a window. I am of opinion that the evidence does not support the conviction. The indictment is under the 24 and 25 Vict c 97, s 51, which deals with malicious injuries to property, and the section expressly says that the act is to be unlawful and malicious. There is also the 58th section, which makes it immaterial whether the offence has been committed from malice against the owner of the property or otherwise, that is, from malice against someone not the owner of the property. In both these sections it seems to me that what is intended by the statute is a wilful doing of an intentional act. Without saying that if the case had been left to them in a different way the conviction could not have been supported, if, on these facts the jury had come to a conclusion that the prisoner was reckless of the consequence of his act, and might reasonably have expected that it would result in breaking the window, it is sufficient to say that the jury have expressly found the contrary. I do not say anything to throw doubt on the rule under the common law in cases of murder which has been referred to, but the principles laid down in such cases have no application to the statutable offence we have to consider.

R v Latimer (1886) 17 QB 359 (CCR)

Facts: The defendant aimed a blow with his belt at one person, striking him slightly. The belt also struck someone else, causing a severe wound. The court had to decide whether A can be guilty of unlawfully wounding C where A intends to strike B but strikes C instead.

Lord Coleridge CJ: ... It is common knowledge that a man who has an unlawful and malicious intent against another, and, in attempting to carry it out, injures a third person, is guilty of what the law deems malice against the person injured, because the offender is doing an unlawful act, and has that which the judges call general malice, and that is enough ... [His Lordship then referred to *R v Hunt* 1 Moo CC 93 and said:] There a man intended to injure A, and said so, and, in the course of doing it, stabbed the wrong man, and had clearly malice in fact, but no intention of injuring the man who was stabbed. He intended to do an unlawful act, and in the course of doing it the consequence was that somebody was injured ...

Lord Esher MR: I am of the same opinion. The only case which could be cited against the well-known principle of law applicable to this case was *R v Pembliton* (1874) Law Rep 2 CC 119, but, on examination, it is found to have been decided on this ground, viz that there was no intention to injure any property at all. It was not a case of attempting to injure one man's property and injuring another's, which would have been wholly different.

Bowen LJ: I am of the same opinion. It is quite clear that the act was done by the prisoner with malice in his mind. I use the word 'malice' in the common law sense of the term, viz a person is deemed malicious when he does an act which he knows will injure either the person or property of another. The only case that could be cited for the prisoner is *R v Pembliton* (1874) Law Rep 2 CC 119, which was founded not upon malice in general, but upon a particular form of malice, viz malicious injury to property; and the court held that though the prisoner might have been acting maliciously in the common law sense of the term, he was not malicious in the sense of the Act directed against malicious injury to property. That decision does not apply to a case under the Act where the indictment is for injury to the person. *R v Pembliton* might have been ground for an argument of some plausibility if the prisoner meant to strike at a pane of glass and had hit a person. It might have been that the malice in that case was not enough. But when, as here, an intent to injure a person is proved, that is enough.

Manisty J: I will add only a few words, for all has been said that could be said, but the facts of this case, no doubt, raise an exceedingly important question, for the man Chapple, whom the prisoner intended to strike, and who was struck, with the belt, was standing close by the woman, and the belt bounded off and struck the prosecutrix. It seems to me that the first and second findings of the jury are quite sufficient to justify the verdict, for they find that the blow was unlawful and malicious, and that it wounded the prosecutrix. That being so, the third finding does not entitle the prisoner to acquittal. The third finding is that the striking of the prosecutrix was purely an accident, and so it was in one sense. The prisoner did not intend to strike her, but in the unlawful and malicious act of striking Chapple the prisoner did unlawfully and maliciously wound the prosecutrix, and the third finding is quite immaterial.

AG's Ref (No 3 of 1994) [1997] 3 All ER 936

Lord Mustill: My Lords ... As will appear, the events which founder the appeal were never conclusively proved at the trial, but are assumed to have been as follows. At the time in question a young woman M was pregnant, with between 22 and 24 weeks of gestation. According to the present state of medical knowledge if her baby had been born after 22 weeks it would not have had any significant of prospect of survival. Two further weeks would have increased the chance to about 10 per cent. The pregnancy was, however, proceeding normally, and the risk that it would fail to continue to full term and be followed by an uneventful birth was very small indeed. Sadly, however, the natural father B quarrelled with M and stabbed her in the face, back and abdomen with a long-bladed kitchen knife in circumstances raising a *prima facie* inference that he intended to do her grievous bodily harm. M was admitted to hospital for surgical treatment and was later discharged in an apparently satisfactory state, still carrying the baby. Unfortunately, some 17 days after the incident M went into premature labour. The baby, named S, was born alive. The birth was still grossly premature, although by that time the chance that the baby would survive had increased to 50 per cent. Thereafter S lived for 121 days, when she succumbed to broncho-pulmonary dysplasia from the effects of premature birth. After her birth it was discovered that one of the knife cuts had penetrated her lower abdomen. The wound needed surgical repair, but it is agreed that this 'made no provable contribution to her death'.

The case for the Crown at the trial of B was that the wounding of M by B had set in train the events which caused the premature birth of S and hence her failure to achieve the normal prospect of survival which she would have had if the pregnancy had proceeded to full term. In this sense, therefore, we must assume that the wounding of M, at a time when S was a barely viable foetus, was the reason why she later died when she did.

Meanwhile, B had been prosecuted for an offence of wounding the mother with intent to cause her grievous bodily harm, had pleaded guilty and had been sentenced to a term of four years' imprisonment.

After S died he was charged again, this time with the murder of S, to which he pleaded not guilty. At his trial a submission was advanced that on the evidence no criminal offence relating to S was proved. In a considered ruling the trial judge upheld that submission, as regards the offences of both murder and manslaughter. I leave aside the first submission for the defence, to the effect that causation between the wounding of the mother, the premature birth and the subsequent death of S had not been established on the evidence. This failed before the judge and has not been renewed. The gist of the ruling lay in the law, and was to the effect that both the physical and the mental elements of murder were absent. There was no relevant *actus reus*, for the foetus was not a live person; and the cause of the death was the wounding of the mother, not of S. As to *mens rea* again there was none. When B stabbed the mother he had no intent to kill or do serious harm to any live person other than the mother, or to do any harm at all to the foetus. The Crown could not make good this deficiency by reliance on the concept of 'transferred malice', for this operates only where the *mens rea* of one crime causes the *actus reus* of the same crime, albeit the result is in some respects unintended. Here, the intent to stab the mother (a live person) could not be transferred to the foetus (not a live person), an organism which could not be the victim of a crime of murder.

As to the alternative verdict of manslaughter the judge was at first exercised by the possibility that since the stabbing of M was an unlawful and dangerous act which led to the death of S a conviction could be sustained even though the act was not aimed at the ultimate victim: see *R v Mitchell* [1983] QB 741. In the end, however, he was persuaded that this approach could not be sustained where there was at the material time no victim capable of dying as a direct and immediate result.

Accordingly, the trial judge directed the jury to acquit the defendant.

Considering that this ruling should be reviewed the Attorney General referred the matter to the opinion of the Court of Appeal under s 36 of the Criminal Justice Act 1972. The point of law referred was as follows:

1.1 Subject to the proof by the prosecution of the requisite intent in either case: whether the crimes of murder or manslaughter can be committed where unlawful injury is deliberately inflicted: (i) to a child *in utero*; (ii) to a mother carrying a child *in utero* where the child is subsequently born alive, enjoys an existence independent of the mother, thereafter dies and the injuries inflicted while *in utero* either caused or made a substantial contribution to the death.

1.2 Whether the fact that the death of the child is caused solely as a consequence of injury to the mother rather than as a consequence of direct injury to the foetus can negative any liability for murder or manslaughter in the circumstances set out in question 1.1.

... In the result, the [Court of Appeal] answered the first of the referred questions in the affirmative, adding, at 598:

The requisite intent to be proved in the case of murder is an intention to kill or cause really serious bodily injury to the mother, the foetus before birth being viewed as an integral part of the mother. Such intention is appropriately modified in the case of manslaughter.

The court answered the second question in the negative, provided the jury is satisfied that causation is proved. The accused person now brings the matter before this House, and maintains that the answers given to both questions were wrong, and that the ruling of the trial judge was right ...

(a) Established rules

The able arguments of counsel were founded on a series of rules which, whatever may be said about their justice or logic, are undeniable features of the criminal law today. I will begin by stating them. Next, I shall describe two different ways in which the arguments for the Crown build on these rules, and will follow with reasons for rejecting one of these quite summarily. Closer examination is needed for the other, to see whether its historical origins are sound. Finally, an attempt will be made to see whether a principled answer can be given to the questions posed by the Attorney General. I perceive the established rules to be as follows ...

[In Rule 1 Lord Mustill summarised the *mens rea* for murder.] ... 2 If the defendant does an act with the intention of causing a particular kind of harm to B, and unintentionally does that kind of harm to V, then the intent to harm B may be added to the harm actually done to V in deciding whether the defendant has committed a crime towards V.

This rule is usually referred to as the doctrine of 'transferred malice', a misleading label but one which is too firmly entrenched to be discarded. Nor would it possible now to question the rule itself, for although the same handful of authorities are called up repeatedly in the texts they are constantly cited without disapproval ... Counsel rightly did not seek to deny the existence of the rule although, here again, it will be necessary to examine its rationale ... [Rule 3 dealt with the proposition that a foetus could not be the victim of a crime of violence; Rule 4 with coincidence of *actus reus* and *mens rea*; and Rule 5 with the proposition that violence towards a foetus that results in harm suffered by the baby once born can give rise to criminal liability.]

I prefer, so far as binding authority permits, to start afresh, and to do so by reference to the second of the arguments advanced by the Attorney General. This builds on the rules stated above by the following stages. If D struck X intending to cause her serious harm, and the blow, in fact, caused her death, that would be murder (Rule 1). If she had been nursing a baby Y which was accidentally struck by the blow and consequently died, that would also be murder (Rules 1 and 2). So, also, if an evil-doer had intended to cause harm but not death to X by giving her a poisoned substance and the substance was, in fact, passed on by X to the baby, which consumed it and died as a result (Rules 1, 2, and 3). Again, it would have been murder if the foetus had been injured *in utero* and had succumbed to the wound after being born alive (Rules 1, 2, 4 and 5). It is only a short step to make a new rule, adding together the malice towards the mother, the contemporaneous starting of a train of events, and the coming to fruition of those events in the death of the baby after being born alive.

My Lords, the attractions of this argument are plain, not least its simplicity. But for my part I find it too dependent on the piling up of old fictions, and too little on the reasons why the law takes its present shape. To look for these reasons is not, to use an expression sometimes met, 'legal archaeology' for its own sake. Except in those cases, of which the present is not one, where the rationale of the existing law is plain on its face, the common law must build for the future with materials from the past. One cannot see where a principle should go without an idea of where it has come from ...

I turn to the second rule, of 'transferred malice.' For present purposes this is more important and more difficult. Again, one must look at its origins to see whether they provide a theme which can be applied today. Three of them are familiar. Taking Lord Coke's example of the glancing arrow we have seen how one explanation of the poacher's responsibility founded on the notion of risk. The person who committed a crime took the chance that the outcome would be worse than he expected. Amongst many sources one can find the idea in *Russell on Crime*, 4th edn (1845), p 739:

> If an action, unlawful in itself, be done deliberately, and with the intention of mischief or great bodily harm to particular individuals, or of mischief indiscriminately, fall where it may, and death ensue or beside the original intention of the party, it will be murder.

In a later edition (1855, p 759) this was exemplified by cases of particular malice to one individual falling by mistake upon another. In support are cited *R v Saunders* (1573) 2 Plowd 473 (a poisoned apple intended for the mother but given to the child) and Gore 9 Co Rep 81 (medicine poisoned by the wife to kill her husband and consumed by the apothecary to prove his innocence); also 1 Hawkins PC, c 31, 545 and 1 Hale 436. As already suggested, this doctrine does survive in some small degree today, but as the foundation of a modern doctrine of transferred malice broad enough to encompass the present case it seems to me quite unsupportable.

Secondly, there is the reversed burden of proof whereby the causing of death is prima facie murder, unless it falls within one of the extenuating categories recognised by the institutional writers. Again, this concept is long out-of-date. Nobody could seriously think of using it to make new law.

Third, there was the idea of 'general malice', of an evil disposition existing in the general and manifesting itself in the particular, uniting the aim of the offender and the result which his deeds actually produced. According to this theory, there was no need to 'transfer' the wrongful intent from the intended to the actual victim; for since the offender was (in the words of Blackstone) 'an enemy to all mankind in general', the actual victim was the direct object of the offender's enmity. Plainly, this will no longer do, for the last vestiges of the idea disappeared with the abolition of the murder/felony doctrine.

What explanation is left: for explanation there must be, since the 'transferred malice' concept is agreed on both sides to be sound law today? The sources in more recent centuries are few. Of the two most frequently cited the earlier is *R v Pembliton* ... The ancient origins of this argument need no elaboration, and indeed the report of the argument as it developed showed that it was based on a conception of general malice. The interventions in argument are instructive. After the prosecutor had relied on the fact that the prisoner was actuated by malice, Blackburn J responded: 'But only of a particular kind, and not against the person injured.' Later, in reply to a reliance on a passage from *Hale* the same judge said:

> Lord Coke, 3 Inst, p 56, puts the case of a man stealing deer in a park, shooting at the deer, and by the glance of the arrow killing a boy that is hidden in a bush, and calls this murder; but can anyone say that ruling would be adopted now?

This most learned of judges continued:

> I should have told the jury that if the prisoner knew there were windows behind, and that the probable consequence of his act would be to break one of them, that would be evidence for them of malice.

The conviction was quashed. It is sufficient to quote briefly from the judgment of Blackburn J:

> We have not now to consider what would be malice aforethought to bring a given case within the common law definition of murder; here the statute says that the act must be unlawful and malicious ... the jury might perhaps have found on this evidence that the act was malicious, because they might have found that the prisoner knew that the natural consequence of his act would be to break the glass, and although that was not his wish, yet he was reckless whether he did it or not; but the jury have not so found ...

This decision was distinguished in *R v Latimer* ... [see above] ... [members of the court] ... were able to distinguish *Pembliton* which, as Bowen LJ put the matter: 'was founded not upon malice in general but on a particular form of malice, viz, malicious injury to property. ...

My Lords, I find it hard to base a modern law of murder on these two cases. The court in Latimer was, I believe, entirely justified in finding a distinction between their statutory backgrounds and one can well accept that the answers given, one for acquittal, the other for conviction, would be the same today. But the harking back to a concept of general malice, which amounts to no more than this, that a wrongful act displays a malevolence which can be attached to any adverse consequence, has long been out of date. And to speak of a particular malice which is 'transferred' simply disguises the problem by idiomatic language. The defendant's malice is directed at one objective, and when after the event the court treats it as directed at another object it is not recognising a 'transfer' but creating a new malice which never existed before. As Dr Glanville Williams pointed out (*Criminal Law*, the General Part, 2nd edn (1961), p 184) the doctrine is 'rather an arbitrary exception to general principles.' Like many of its kind this is useful enough to yield rough justice, in particular cases, and it can sensibly be retained notwithstanding its lack of any sound intellectual basis. But it is another matter to build a new rule upon it.

I pause to distinguish the case of indiscriminate malice from those already discussed, although even now it is sometimes confused with them. The terrorist who hides a bomb in an aircraft provides an example. This is not a case of 'general malice' where under the old law any wrongful act sufficed to prove the evil disposition which was taken to supply the necessary intent for homicide. Nor is it transferred malice, for there is no need of a transfer. The intention is already aimed directly at the class of potential victims of which the actual victim forms part. The intent and the *actus reus* completed by the explosion are joined from the start, even though the identity of the ultimate victim is not yet fixed. So also with the shots fired indiscriminately into a crowd. No ancient fictions are needed to make these cases of murder ...

The fourth rule is an exception to the generally accepted principle that *actus reus* and *mens rea* must coincide. A continuous act or continuous chain of causes leading to death is treated by the law as if it happened when first initiated. The development of this into the fifth rule, which links an act and intent before birth with a death happening after a live delivery, causes a little more strain, given the incapacity of the foetus to be the object of homicide. If, however, it is possible to interpret the situation as one where the mental element is directed, not to the foetus but to the human being when and if it comes into existence, no fiction is required.

My Lords, the purpose of this enquiry has been to see whether the existing rules are based on principles sound enough to justify their extension to a case where the defendant acts without an intent to injure either the foetus or the child which it will become. In my opinion they are not. To give an affirmative answer requires a double 'transfer' of intent: first from the mother to the foetus and then from the foetus to the child as yet unborn. Then one would have to deploy the fiction (or at least the doctrine) which converts an intention to commit serious harm into the *mens rea* of murder. For me, this is too much. If one could find any logic in the rules I would follow it from one fiction to another, but whatever grounds there may once have been have long since disappeared. I am willing to follow old laws until they are overturned, but not to make a new law on a basis for which there is no principle.

Moreover, even on a narrower approach the argument breaks down. The effect of transferred malice, as I understand it, is that the intended victim and the actual victim are treated as if they were one, so that what was intended to happen to the first person (but did not happen) is added to what actually did happen to the second person (but was not intended to happen), with the result that what was intended and what happened are married to make a notionally intended and actually consummated crime. The cases are treated as if the actual victim had been the intended victim from the start. To make any sense of this process there must, as it seems to me, be some compatibility between the original intention and the actual occurrence, and this is, indeed, what one finds in the cases. There is no such compatibility here. The defendant intended to commit and did commit an immediate crime of violence to the mother. He committed no relevant violence to the foetus, which was not a person, either at the time or in the future, and intended no harm to the foetus or to the human person which it would become. If fictions are useful, as they can be, they are only damaged by straining them beyond their limits. I would not overstrain the idea of transferred malice by trying to make it fit the present case.

Codification and law reform proposals

The Law Commission's Report *Legislating the Criminal Code: Offences Against the Person and General Principles* (1993) (Law Com 218) sought to codify the doctrine of transferred malice – see cl 32. A slightly amended version now appears in the draft Offences Against the Person Bill appended to the Home Office Consultation Paper, cl 17 of which provides:

17(1) This section applies in determining whether a person is guilty of an offence under this Act.

(2) A person's intention or awareness of a risk that his act will cause, a result in relation to a person capable of being the victim of the offence must be treated as an intention to cause or (as the case may be) awareness of a risk that his act cause, that result in relation to any other person affected by his act.

(3) A person's intention, or awareness of a risk, that his omission will have a result in relation to a person capable of being the victim of the offence must be treated as an intention or (as the case may be) awareness of a risk that his omission will have that result in relation to any other person affected as a result of his omission.

Given the close similarity between the Law Commission's proposed cl 32 in Law Com 218, and the provisions in the Home Office Bill, it is instructive to note the commentary on the transferred malice clause originally provided in Law Com 218.

42.1 Clause 25 of the Bill accompanying LCCP 122 restated, in the most general terms and not only in relation to offences against the person, the common law doctrine known as 'transferred intent' (subsection (1)), and provided a corresponding rule for 'transferred' defences. We received very little comment on the clause, and are satisfied, in particular, that the formulation of subsection (1) accurately represents the current law. Both subsections appear unchanged in clause 32 of the final draft Bill. Accordingly, the following explanation of the clause repeats in substance that which we gave in LCCP 122 ...

42.3 The clause assumes that the specified result, such as serious injury, or damage to property belonging to another, is an element of a specific offence. If the actor does not cause such a result, the external elements of the offence with which he is charged are not made out. Accordingly, no question of criminal liability arises. It is only when the external elements of the offence charged have been caused by the defendant that the second question arises, of whether he acted with the fault required for that offence. This clause provides that if he acted with that fault, it can be transferred. What is required is a concurrence of fault in relation to the result specified for the offence and the occurrence of such a result, although not in relation to the same person or thing.

42.4 The equivalent clause in the Draft Code referred in terms to 'recklessness' and not, like the draft in LCCP 122 or clause 32 of the Criminal Law Bill, to 'awareness of a risk'. 'Recklessness' will have a prescribed meaning under the Bill for the purposes of offences against the person, but will continue to have its other meaning or meanings in other contexts. It is therefore necessary to avoid the term in a provision of general application. The only state of mind, other than intention, with which the subsection needs to deal is awareness of a risk. It is this aspect of recklessness that may call for 'transfer'. The provision is not needed in relation to the limb of *Caldwell* recklessness concerned with failure to advert to an obvious risk. In order to apply that limb to (for example) the causing of damage to the property actually affected, it is sufficient to ask: was there an obvious risk that that property (or such property) would be damaged and did the defendant fail to advert to that risk? It is irrelevant that there was a risk to other property of which the defendant should have been, but was not, aware.

42.5 Awareness of a relevant risk does not alone establish recklessness. It is necessary also that the risk be one that it was unreasonable to take in the circumstances known to the actor. If a defendant unreasonably took a known risk in relation to X, the risk-taking in relation to Y that the subsection treats as having occurred must similarly be unreasonable before recklessness is established in relation to Y Conversely if, in the circumstances known to the defendant, it was reasonable to take the risk in relation to X that he knowingly took, the taking of the risk in relation to Y that he is treated as having knowingly taken can hardly be regarded as reckless.

42.6 Clause 32(2) enables a person who affects an uncontemplated victim to rely on a defence that would have been available to him if he had affected the person or thing he had in contemplation. The provision will be useful for the avoidance of doubt.

Further reading

ACE Lynch, 'The mental element in the *actus reus*' (1982) 98 LQR 109

AP Simester and W Chan, 'Intention thus far' [1997] Crim LR 704

A Norrie, 'After *Woollin*' [1999] Crim LR 532

LH Leigh, 'Recklessness after *Reid*' (1993) 56 MLR 208

S Gardner, 'Recklessness refined' (1993) 109 LQR 21

A Halpin, 'Definitions and directions: recklessness unheeded' (1998) 18 Legal Studies 294

CHAPTER 5

STRICT LIABILITY

There are certain offences where a defendant can be convicted notwithstanding that he did not have any *mens rea*. These offences are generally referred to as offences of strict liability. To say that these offences do not require proof of any *mens rea* may, however, be too sweeping. There are offences where no fault element at all arises – it is perhaps better to classify these as offences of absolute liability. Many so called strict liability offences do in fact require some *mens rea* in relation to some elements of the offence. The significant factor is that there may be some elements of the *actus reus* in relation to which no *mens rea* is required. When dealing with a statutory offence that is silent as to *mens rea* the task of the court lies in determining whether or not Parliament actually intended the offence to operate without proof of fault. The exercise is, largely, one of statutory interpretation. As the following extracts indicate, the factors taken into account by the courts can be summarised as follows:

(a) There is a presumption in favour of *mens rea* – that is, even if the statute is silent as to *mens rea* the courts will assume that some is required unless there is evidence to the contrary.

(b) The presumption in favour of *mens rea* can be rebutted by express wording in the statute or by necessary implication.

(c) The presumption in favour of *mens rea* is stronger where the offence is truly criminal – as opposed to merely regulatory. Factors such as the stigma attaching to a conviction and the penalty imposed will be significant here.

(d) The presumption in favour of *mens rea* may be rebutted by the subject matter of the offence, for example where the prohibition relates to a grave social danger or matter of public concern.

(e) The presumption in favour of *mens rea* is less likely to be rebutted where there is little evidence that the imposition of strict liability will help to achieve the aims and objects of the legislation.

THE PRESUMPTION IN FAVOUR OF *MENS REA*: READING THE STATUTE AS A WHOLE

Sweet v Parsley [1970] AC 132 (HL)

Lord Morris of Borth-y-Gest: My Lords, it has frequently been affirmed and should unhesitatingly be recognised that it is a cardinal principle of our law that *mens rea*, an evil intention or a knowledge of the wrongfulness of the act, is in all ordinary cases an essential ingredient of guilt of a criminal offence. It follows from this that there will not be guilt of an offence created by statute unless there is *mens rea* or unless Parliament has by the statute enacted that guilt may be established in cases where there is no *mens rea*.

To this effect were the words of Wright J in *Sherras v De Rutzen* [1895] 1 QB 918 and in *Derbyshire v Houliston* in [1897] 1 QB 772. In the judgment of the Privy Council in *Lim Chin Aik v R* [1963] AC 160 the principle was amply expressed. It was said, at 172: 'That proof of the existence of a guilty intent is an essential ingredient of a crime at common law is not at all in doubt'.

But as Parliament is supreme, it is open to Parliament to legislate in such a way that an offence may be created of which someone may be found guilty though *mens rea* is lacking. There may be cases in which, as Channell J said in *Pearks, Gunston and Tee Ltd v Ward* [1902] 2 KB 1 at 11:

> ... the legislature has thought it so important to prevent the particular act from being committed that it absolutely forbids it to be done; and if it is done the offender is liable to a penalty whether he had any *mens rea* or not, and whether or not he intended to commit a breach of the law.

Thus in diverse situations and circumstances and for any one of a variety of reasons Parliament may see fit to create offences and make people responsible before criminal courts although there is an absence of *mens rea*. But I would again quote with appreciation (as I did in *Warner's* case [1969] 2 AC 256) the words of Lord Goddard CJ, in *Brend v Wood* (1946) 175 LT 306 at 307, when he said:

> It is of the utmost importance for the protection of the liberty of the subject that a court should always bear in mind that, unless a statute, either clearly or by necessary implication, rules out *mens rea* as a constituent part of a crime, the court should not find a man guilty of an offence against the criminal law unless he has a guilty mind.

The intention of Parliament is expressed in the words of an enactment. The words must be looked at in order to see whether either expressly or by necessary implication they displace the general rule or presumption that *mens rea* is a necessary prerequisite before guilt of an offence can be found. Particular words in a statute must be considered in their setting in the statute and having regard to all the provisions of the statute and to its declared or obvious purpose. In 1842 in *AG v Lockwood* (1842) 9 M & W 378, 398 Alderson B said:

> The rule of law, I take it, upon the construction of all statutes ... is, whether they be penal or remedial, to construe them according to the plain, literal and grammatical meaning of the words in which they are expressed, unless that construction leads to a plain and clear contradiction of the apparent purpose of the Act, or to some palpable and evident absurdity.

It must be considered, therefore, whether by the words of a penal statute it is either express or implied that there may be a conviction without *mens rea* or, in other words, whether what is called an absolute offence is created ...

The inquiry must be made, therefore, whether Parliament has used words which expressly enact or impliedly involve that an absolute offence is created. Though sometimes help in construction is derived from noting the presence or the absence of the word 'knowingly', no conclusive test can be laid down as a guide in finding the fair, reasonable and common sense meaning of language. But in considering whether Parliament has decided to displace what is a general and somewhat fundamental rule it would not be reasonable lightly to impute to Parliament an intention to create an offence in such a way that someone could be convicted of it who by all reasonable and sensible standards is without fault ...

The question must always be: what has Parliament enacted? That is the question in the present case and to that I now turn. The wording of s 5 of the Dangerous Drugs Act 1965, is as follows:

If a person:

(a) being the occupier of any premises, permits those premises to be used for the purpose of smoking cannabis or cannabis resin or of dealing in cannabis resin (whether by sale or otherwise); or

(b) is concerned in the management of any premises used for any such purpose as aforesaid,

he shall be guilty of an offence against this Act.

The words are nearly the same as and presumably were derived from words in s 5 of the Dangerous Drugs Act 1920, concerning opium.

In the present case the appellant was charged with being concerned in the management of certain premises situate at Fries Farm which were used for the purpose of smoking cannabis or cannabis resin. I need not recite the facts which are set out in the case stated.

It was for the prosecution to prove the guilt of the appellant. It was found by the magistrates that the appellant had no knowledge whatsoever that cannabis had been smoked in the house. The prosecution contended that guilt can be established of the offence created by s 5(b) if a person is concerned in the management of premises in which cannabis is in fact smoked. The consequence was acknowledged and indeed asserted that if some person managed a hostel containing, say, 50–100 rooms, and if on one day in one room an occupant smoked one cannabis cigarette without the knowledge of the persons managing, they would have no defence to a charge under s 5(b). If Parliament has so enacted, then the law must be enforced. But I am sure that that is not what Parliament has decreed.

If someone is concerned in management there must at least be knowledge of what it is that is being managed: otherwise there could be no concern in it. If someone is concerned in the management of a building containing a number of separately let residential flats the concern in such case would be in the arrangements for the lettings and in the arrangements relating to lifts or staircases or the structure of the building as a whole. The concern would be in the management of premises used for residential purposes. In the ordinary course of things the landlord or the manager would have no right of entry into a flat and would have no concern with any normal, reasonable and lawful activity within a flat. If a tenant, who was a non-smoker, had a guest one day who smoked a pipe of tobacco in the flat, it would be a strained and unnatural use of language to describe the flat which the tenant rented as being premises used for the purpose of smoking. It would be equally strained and unnatural to describe the landlord or his agent as being concerned in the management of premises used for the purpose of smoking. If on an isolated occasion a tenant gave a showing of some cinematograph films to his friends, it would be unreasonable to describe the manager of the flats (who had no occasion to know of the film showing) as being one who was concerned in the management of premises used for the purpose of exhibiting films.

If a tenant took sugar with his tea it would be fanciful to describe the flat as premises used for the purpose of putting sugar into tea.

It seems to me, therefore that the words 'premises ... used for the purpose of smoking cannabis' are not happily chosen if they were intended to denote premises in which at any time cannabis is smoked. In my opinion, the words 'premises ... used for the purpose of ...' denote a purpose which is other than quite incidental or casual or fortuitous: they denote a purpose which is or has become either a significant one or a recognised one though certainly not necessarily an only one. There is no difficulty in appreciating what is meant if it is sad that premises are used for the purposes of a dance hall or a billiard hall or a bowling alley or a hairdressing saloon or a cafe. A new or additional use might, however, arise. It might happen that a house let as a private dwelling might come to be used as a brothel or for the purposes of prostitution. A room let for private occupation might come to be the resort of a number of people who wished to smoke opium so that the time would come when the room could rationally be described as a room used for the purpose of smoking opium.

The words 'concerned in the management of any premises used for the purpose of' are, in my view, to be considered together and as one phrase. Even so the phrase may be capable of two meanings. It could denote the management of premises used for a certain purpose in the sense that the management is limited to management in respect of the premises themselves. It could denote the management of premises used for a certain purpose in the sense that the management was concerned either additionally or perhaps separately with the purpose for which the premises were used. Thus, if someone is said so to be concerned in the management of premises used for the purpose of dancing, he could be someone concerned only in the management of the premises themselves, or he could be someone who additionally or possibly separately was concerned with the dancing. On either approach and with an ordinary use of words, it would seem to me that the person would be one who would have and would need to have knowledge of the use of the premises for the particular purpose ...

For the reasons that I have indicated I consider that on a fair reading of the phrase 'concerned in the management of premises used for the purpose of' a link is denoted between management and user for a purpose. To say that someone is concerned in the management of premises used for the purpose of smoking cannabis involves, in my view, that his management is with knowledge that the premises are so used. The wording of s 5(b) contains positive indications that *mens rea* is an essential ingredient of an offence. Even if, contrary to my view, it is not affirmatively enacted that there must be *mens rea* I cannot read the wording as enacting that there need not be *mens rea*. I find it wholly impossible to say that the statute has either clearly, or by necessary implication, ruled out *mens rea* as a constituent part of guilt.

On the findings of the magistrates it follows that the appellant was not guilty. I would, therefore, allow the appeal. Accordingly, in my view, the case should be remitted to the Divisional Court with a direction to quash the conviction.

Pharmaceutical Society of Great Britain v Storkwain Ltd
[1986] 1 WLR 903 (HL)

Lord Goff of Chieveley: My Lords, this appeal is concerned with a question of construction of s 58 of the Medicines Act 1968. Section 58(2)(a) of the Act provides:

(2) Subject to the following provisions of this section:

    (a) no person shall sell by retail, or supply in circumstances corresponding to retail sale, a medicinal product of a description, or falling within a class specified in an order under this section except in accordance with a prescription given by an appropriate practitioner ...

By s 67(2) of the Act of 1968, it is provided that any person who contravenes, *inter alia*, s 58 shall be guilty of an offence. The question which has arisen for decision in the present case is whether, in accordance with the well-organised presumption, there are to be read into s 58(2)(a) words appropriate to require *mens rea*, on the principle stated in *R v Tolson* (1889) 23 QBD 168, and *Sweet v Parsley* [1970] AC 132.

The matter has arisen in the following way. On 2 February 1984, informations were preferred by the prosecutor, the Pharmaceutical Society of Great Britain, against the defendants, Storkwain Ltd, alleging that the defendants had on 14 December 1982 unlawfully sold by retail certain medicines. It was alleged that they unlawfully sold by retail, to a person purporting to be Linda Largey, 200 Physeptone tablets and 50 Ritalin tablets; and that they unlawfully sold by retail, to a person purporting to be Thomas Patterson, 50 ampoules of Physeptone and 30 Valium tablets. All these medicines are substances controlled under Article 3(1)(b) of the Medicines (Prescription only) Order 1980 (SI 1980/1921); and the informations alleged in each case that the sale was not in accordance with a prescription issued by an appropriate practitioner, contrary to s 58(2) and s 67(2) of the Act of 1968. Before the magistrate, the evidence (which was all agreed) was to the effect that the medicines were supplied under documents which purported to be prescriptions signed by a doctor, Dr Irani, of Queensdale Road, London; but that subsequent inquiries revealed that the prescriptions were both forgeries. It was submitted on behalf of the defendants that the presumption of *mens rea* applied to the prohibition in s 58(2)(a) of the Act of 1981; and that, the medicines having been supplied by the defendants on the basis of prescriptions which they believed in good faith and on reasonable grounds to be valid prescriptions, the informations should be dismissed. The magistrate accepted that submission and accordingly dismissed the informations; but he stated a case for the opinion of the High Court, the question for the opinion of the court being whether or not *mens rea* was required in the case of a prosecution under ss 58(2) and 67(2) of the Medicines Act 1968. On 2 May 1985, a Divisional Court (Farquharson and Tudor Price JJ) answered the question in the negative, and accordingly allowed the appeal of the prosecutor and directed that the case should be remitted to the magistrate with a direction to convict. The Divisional Court certified the following point of law as being of general public importance:

Whether the prosecution has to prove *mens rea* where an information is brought under s 58(2)(a) of the Medicines Act 1968, where the allegation is that the supply of prescription only drugs was made by the [defendants] in accordance with a forged prescription and without fault on their part.

From that decision, the defendants now appeal with leave of your Lordships' House, the Divisional Court having refused leave ...

For the defendants, Mr Fisher submitted that there must, in accordance with the well-recognised presumption, be read into s 58(2)(a) words appropriate to require *mens rea* in accordance with *R v Tolson* (1889) 23 QBD 168; in other words, to adopt the language of Lord Diplock in *Sweet v Parsley* [1970] AC 132, 163, the subsection must be read subject to the implication that a necessary element in the prohibition (and hence in the offence created by the subsection together with s 67(2) of the Act of 1968) is the absence of belief, held honestly and upon reasonable grounds, in the existence of facts which, if true, would make the act innocent. He further submitted, with reference to the speech of Lord Reid in *Sweet v Parsley*, at 149, that the offence created by s 58(2)(a) and s 67(2) of the Act of 1968 was not to be classified as merely an offence of a quasi-criminal character in which the presumption of *mens rea* might more readily be rebutted, because in his submission the offence was one which would result in a stigma attaching to a person who was convicted of it, especially as Parliament had regarded it as sufficiently serious to provide that it should be triable on indictment, and that the maximum penalty should be two years' imprisonment. He also submitted that, if Parliament had considered that a pharmacist who dispensed under a forged prescription in good faith and without fault should be convicted of the offence, it would surely have made express provision to that effect; and that the imposition of so strict a liability could not be justified on the basis that it would tend towards greater efficiency on the part of pharmacists in detecting forged prescriptions. Finally, he referred your Lordships to the Misuse of Drugs Act 1971. Under s 4(1) and (3) of that Act, it is an offence to supply a controlled drug to another; but it is provided in s 28 that (subject to an immaterial exception) it shall be a defence for the accused to prove that he neither knew of nor suspected nor had reason to suspect the existence of some fact alleged by the prosecution which it is necessary for the prosecution to prove if he is to be convicted of the offence charged. Mr Fisher submitted that it would be anomalous if such a defence were available in the case of the more serious offence of supplying a controlled drug to another, but that the presumption of *mens rea* should be held inapplicable in the case of the offence created by ss 58(2)(a) and 67(2) of the Act of 1968.

I am unable to accept Mr Fisher's submission, for the simple reason that it is, in my opinion, clear from the Act of 1968 that Parliament must have intended that the presumption of *mens rea* should be inapplicable to s 58(2)(a). First of all, it appears from the Act of 1968 that, where Parliament wished to recognise that *mens rea* should be an ingredient of an offence created by the Act, it has expressly so provided. Thus, taking first of all offences created under provisions of Part II of the Act of 1968, express requirements of *mens rea* are to be found both in s 45(2) and in s 46(1), (2) and (3) of the Act. More particularly, in relation to offences created by Part III and Parts V and VI of the Act of 1968, s 121 makes detailed provision for a requirement of *mens rea* in respect of certain specified sections of the Act, including ss 63–65 (which are contained in Part 3), but significantly not s 58, nor indeed ss 52 and 53 ... It is very difficult to avoid the conclusion that, by omitting s 58 from those sections to which s 121 is expressly made applicable, Parliament intended that there should be no implication of a requirement of *mens rea* in s 58(2)(a). This view is fortified by subsections (4) and (5) of s 58 itself. Subsection (4)(a) provides that any order made by the appropriate ministers for the purposes of s 58 may provide that s 58(2)(a) or (b), or both, shall have effect subject to such exemptions as may be specified in the order. From this subsection alone it follows that the ministers, if they think it right, can provide for exemption where there is no *mens rea* on the part of the accused. Subsection (5) provides that any exemption conferred by an order in accordance with subsection (4)(a) may be conferred subject to such conditions or limitations as may be specified in the order. From this it follows that if the ministers, acting under subsection (4), were to confer an exemption relating to sales where the vendor lacked the requisite *mens rea* they may nevertheless circumscribe their exemption with conditions and limitations which render the exemption far narrower than the implication for which Mr Fisher contends should be read into the statute itself. I find this to be very difficult to reconcile with the proposed implication.

It comes as no surprise to me, therefore, to discover that the relevant order in force at that time, the Medicines (Prescription Only) Order 1980, is drawn entirely in conformity with the construction of the statute which I favour. It is unnecessary, in the present case, to consider whether the relevant articles of the Order may be taken into account in construing s 58 of the Act of 1968; it is enough, for present purposes, that I am able to draw support from the fact that the ministers, in making the Order, plainly did not read s 58 as subject to the implication proposed by Mr Fisher. So, for example, Article 11 of the order (which is headed 'Exemption in cases involving another's default') reads as follows:

> The restrictions imposed by s 58(2)(a) (restrictions on sale and supply) shall not apply to the sale or supply of a prescription only medicine by a person who, having exercised all due diligence believes on reasonable grounds that the product sold or supplied is not a prescription only medicine, where it is due to the act or default of another person that the product is a product to which s 58(2)(a) applies.

This provision which, by including the words 'having exercised due diligence', provides for a narrower exemption than that which Mr Fisher has submitted should be read by implication into the statute, in the limited circumstances specified in the concluding words of the paragraph, is plainly inconsistent with the existence of any such implication. Likewise, Article 13(1) provides that, for the purposes of s 58(2)(a), a prescription only medicine shall not be taken to be sold or supplied in accordance with a prescription given by a practitioner unless certain specified conditions are fulfilled. Those conditions, which are very detailed, are set out in Article 13(2); and they all presuppose the existence of a valid prescription. Furthermore, Article 13(3) provides:

> The restrictions imposed by s 58(2)(a) (restrictions on sale and supply) shall not apply to a sale or supply of a prescription only medicine which is not in accordance with a prescription given by an appropriate practitioner by reason only that a condition specified in paragraph (2) is not fulfilled, where the person selling or supplying the prescription only medicine, having exercised all due diligence believes on reasonable grounds that that condition is fulfilled in relation to that sale or supply.

So here again we find a provision which creates an exemption in narrower terms than that which Mr Fisher submits is to be found, by implication, in s 58(2)(a) itself. It follows that Article 13, like Article 11, of the Order is inconsistent with the existence of any such implication.

For these reasons, which are substantially the same as those which are set out in the judgments of Farquharson and Tudor Price JJ in the Divisional Court [1985] 3 All ER 4, I am unable to accept the submissions advanced on behalf of the defendants. I gratefully adopt as my own the following passage from the judgment of Farquharson J, at 10:

It is perfectly obvious that pharmacists are in a position to put illicit drugs and perhaps other medicines on the market. Happily this rarely happens but it does from time to time. It can therefore be readily understood that Parliament would find it necessary to impose a heavier liability on those who are in such a position, and make them more strictly accountable for any breaches of the Act.

I would therefore answer the certified question in the negative, and dismiss the appeal with costs.

B v DPP [2000] 1 All ER 833

[**Lord Steyn** began by rehearsing the facts:] On 19 August 1997 a girl aged 13 years was a passenger on a bus in Harrow. The appellant, who was aged 15 years, sat next to her. The appellant asked the girl several times to perform oral sex with him. She repeatedly refused. The appellant was charged with inciting a girl under 14 to commit an act of gross indecency contrary to section 1(1) of the Indecency with Children Act 1960. In January 1998 the appellant stood trial at the Harrow Youth Court. Initially, the appellant pleaded not guilty. The primary facts, as well as the fact that the appellant honestly believed that the girl was over 14 years, were admitted. The defence argued that on the admitted facts the appellant was entitled to be acquitted. The prosecution submitted that the offence was one of strict liability. The justices were asked to rule whether the appellant's state of mind could constitute a defence to the charge. They ruled that it could not. As a result of this ruling the appellant changed his plea to guilty. In law his plea of guilty constituted a conviction. The justices imposed a supervision order on the appellant for 18 months. The justices were asked to state a case, and they did so. The case stated set out the primary facts. The admitted facts did not cover the question whether the appellant had reasonable grounds for his belief. And there was no finding on this point. The case stated raised the question of law of the correct interpretation of section 1(1) of the Act of 1960. The appellant appealed by way of case stated to the Divisional Court. In three separate judgments the Divisional Court (Brooke LJ, Tucker and Rougier JJ) affirmed the ruling of the justices and dismissed the appeal ...

His Lordship then considered the extent to which the offence in question could be read as one that imposed strict liability.

The correct approach

My Lords, it will be convenient to turn to the approach to be adopted to the construction of section 1(1) of the Act of 1960. While broader considerations will ultimately have to be taken into account, the essential point of departure must be the words of section 1(1). The language is general and nothing on the face of section 1(1) indicates one way or the other whether section 1(1) creates an offence of strict liability. In enacting such a provision Parliament does not write on a blank sheet. The sovereignty of Parliament is the paramount principle of our constitution. But Parliament legislates against the background of the principle of legality ... Recently, in *R v Secretary of State for the Home Department ex p Simms* [1999] 3 WLR 328 the House applied the principle to subordinate legislation: see in particular the speeches of Lord Hoffmann (at 341F–G), myself (at 340G–H) and Lord Browne-Wilkinson (at 330E). In *ex p Simms* Lord Hoffmann explained the principle as follows (at 341F–G):

But the principle of legality means that Parliament must squarely confront what it is doing and accept the political cost. Fundamental rights cannot be overridden by general or ambiguous words. This is because there is too great a risk that the full implications of their unqualified meaning may have passed unnoticed in the democratic process. In the absence of express language or necessary implication to the contrary, the courts therefore presume that even the most general words were intended to be subject to the basic rights of the individual.

This passage admirably captures, if I may so, the rationale of the principle of legality. In successive editions of his classic work Professor Sir Rupert Cross cited as the paradigm of the principle the '"presumption" that *mens rea* is required in the case of statutory crimes': *Statutory Interpretation* 3rd edn (1995), p 166. Sir Rupert explained that such presumptions are of general application and are not dependent on finding an ambiguity in the text. He said they 'not only supplement the text, they also operate at a higher level as expressions of fundamental principles governing both civil liberties and the relations between Parliament, the executive and the courts. They operate as constitutional principles which are not easily displaced by a statutory text'. In other words, in the absence of express words or a truly necessary implication, Parliament must be presumed to legislate on the assumption that the principle of legality will supplement the text. This is the theoretical framework against which section 1(1) must be interpreted. It is now necessary to examine the practical application of the principle as explained by the House in *Sweet v Parsley* ... Lord Reid drew a distinction between 'a truly criminal act' and acts which are not truly criminal in any real real sense, but are 'acts which in the public interest are prohibited under a penalty': at 149F ... he said that in cases of truly criminal acts it is wrong to take into account 'no more than the wording of the Act and the character and seriousness of the mischief which constitutes the offence': at 150A ...

Counsel for the Crown accepted that the approach as outlined in *Sweet v Parsley*, and in particular in the speech of Lord Reid, is an authoritative and accurate statement of the law. It is only necessary to refer one further decision. In *Lim Chin Aik v R* [1963] AC 160, at 174, the Privy Council observed that in considering how the presumption can be displaced 'it is not enough in their Lordships' opinions merely to label the statute as one dealing with a grave social evil and from that to infer that strict liability was intended'. Their Lordships no doubt had in mind that the prevalence of even a grave social evil does not necessarily throw light on the question of what technique was adopted to combat the evil, viz the creation of an offence of strict liability or an offence of which *mens rea* is an ingredient.

Concentrating still on the wording of section 1(1) of the Act of 1960, I now address directly the question whether the presumption is *prima facie* applicable. Two distinctive features of section 1(1) must be taken in to account. First, the *actus reus* is widely defined. Unlike the position under sections 14 and 15 of the Act of 1956, an assault is not an ingredient of the offence under section 1(1). Any act of gross indecency with or towards a child under the age of 14, or incitement to such an act, whether committed in public or private, is within its scope. The subsection is apt to cover acts of paedophilia and all responsible citizens will welcome effective legislation in respect of such a great social evil. But it also covers any heterosexual or homosexual contact between teenagers if one of them is under 14. And the *actus reus* extends to incitement of a child under 14: words are enough. The subsection therefore extends to any verbal sexual overtures between teenagers if one of them is under 14 ... For the law to criminalise such conduct of teenagers by offences of strict liability would be far reaching and controversial. The second factor is that section 1(1) creates an offence of a truly criminal character. It was initially punishable on indictment by a custodial term of up to two years and by subsequent amendment the maximum term has been increased to ten years' imprisonment. Moreover, as Lord Reid observed in *Sweet v Parsley* (at 146H) 'a stigma still attaches to any person convicted of a truly criminal offence, and the more serious or more disgraceful the offence the greater the stigma.' Taking into account the cumulative effect of these two factors, I am persuaded that, if one concentrates on the language of section 1(1), the presumption is *prima facie* applicable. It is, however, now necessary to examine weighty contrary arguments based on the broader context in which section 1(1) must be seen. Since counsel for the Crown adopted as part of his argument the reasoning of the Divisional Court, and in particular the reasoning of Rougier J, it is unnecessary to summarise the judgments. Instead I propose to examine directly the major planks of the reasoning contained in the judgments of the Divisional Court and in the submissions of counsel for the Crown. But I would respectfully record my tribute to the careful and elegant judgments in the Divisional Court ...

[Turning to the legislative policy underpinning the 1956 and 1960 Acts] Counsel for the Crown next submitted that a necessary implication negativing *mens rea* as an ingredient of the offence is to be found in the general legislative policy of the Act of 1956 to protect girls under the age of 16: see sections 5, 6, 14, 15, 26 and 28. It is undoubtedly right that there is a clear legislative policy prohibiting the sexual exploitation of girls. It is unquestionably a great social evil as Lord Hutton has so clearly explained. Whatever can be done sensibly and justly to stamp it out ought to be done.

The real question is: what does this policy tell us about the critical question whether section 1(1) is an offence of strict liability or not? It is not enough to label the statute as one dealing with a grave social evil and from that to infer that strict liability was intended ... Moreover, upon analysis the argument is far from compelling. It infers from the premise of the legislative policy directed against the mischief a conclusion that the legislature gave clear expression to a choice of the solution of creating an offence of strict liability rather than an offence containing *mens rea* as an ingredient. The cardinal principle of construction described by Lord Reid in *Sweet v Parsley* is not to be displaced by such speculative considerations as to the chosen legislative technique. I would reject this argument.

Prince's case

Counsel for the Crown also relied on what he described as a principle of construction established in *R v Prince* (1875) LR 2 CCR 154. In *Prince* the defendant was convicted under a Victorian statute of unlawfully taking an unmarried girl under the age of 16 out the possession of her father. The defendant bona fide and on reasonable grounds believed that the girl was over 16. The judge referred the question of the availability of the defence to the Court for Crown Cases Reserved. The court consisted of 16 judges. The prisoner was not represented. By a majority of 15 to 1 the court held that there was no such defence. The leading judgment was given by Blackburn J with the concurrence of nine other judges. Blackburn J relied strongly on a drafting flaw in sections 50 and 51 of the Offences Against the Person Act 1861. The two sections respectively provided for offences of sexual intercourse with a girl under ten (section 50) and above the age of ten years and under the age of twelve years (section 51). The first was a felony and the latter a misdemeanour. Blackburn J produced what Professor Sir Rupert Cross in a magisterial article described as a 'knock-out' argument: 'Centenary reflections on *Prince's* case' (1975) 91 LQR 540. The passage in Blackburn's J judgment reads as follows:

> It seems impossible to suppose that the intention of the legislature in those two sections could have been to make the crime depend upon the knowledge of the prisoner of the girl's actual age. It would produce the monstrous result that a man who had carnal connection with a girl, in reality not quite ten years old, but whom he on reasonable grounds believed to be a little more than ten, was to escape altogether. He could not, in that view of the statute, be convicted of the felony, for he did not know her to be under ten. He could not be convicted of the misdemeanour, because she was in fact not above the age of ten. It seems to us that the intention of the legislature was to punish those who had connection with young girls, though with their consent, unless the girl was in fact old enough to give a valid consent. The man who has connection with a child, relying on her consent, does it at his peril, if she is below the statutable age. The 55th section, on which the present case arises, uses precisely the same words as those in sections 50 and 51, and must be construed in the same way.

Eventually the distinction between felonies and misdemeanours was abolished and the drafting flaw in the earlier legislation no longer exists. The principal ground of the decision of Blackburn J has disappeared. It is true that Bramwell B gave a separate judgment in which seven judges concurred. This judgment is largely based on the view that the defendant was guilty in law because if the facts had been as he supposed he would have acted immorally. For the further reasons given by Sir Rupert Cross in his article one can be confident that the reasoning of Bramwell B., if tested in a modern court, would not be upheld: see also *DPP v Morgan* [1976] AC 182, at 238, *per* Lord Fraser of Tullybelton; and the valuable discussion by Brooke LJ of the context of *Prince's* case: at 130B–32B. Significantly, Prince's case was cited in *Sweet v Parsley* but was not mentioned in any of the judgments. The view may have prevailed that it was not necessary to overrule it because its basis had gone and that the principle laid down in *Sweet v Parsley* would in future be the controlling one. In any event, I would reject the contention that there is a special rule of construction in respect of age-based sexual offences which is untouched by the presumption as explained in *Sweet v Parsley*.

Lord Nicholls:

The construction of section 1 of the Indecency with Children Act 1960

In section 1(1) of the Indecency with Children Act 1960 Parliament has not expressly negatived the need for a mental element in respect of the age element of the offence. The question, therefore, is whether, although not expressly negatived, the need for a mental element is negatived by necessary implication. 'Necessary implication' connotes an implication which is compellingly clear. Such an implication may be found in the language used, the nature of the offence, the mischief sought to be prevented and any other circumstances which may assist in determining what intention is properly to be attributed to Parliament when creating the offence.

I venture to think that, leaving aside the statutory context of section 1, there is no great difficulty in this case. The section created an entirely new criminal offence, in simple unadorned language. The offence so created is a serious offence. The more serious the offence, the greater is the weight to be attached to the presumption, because the more severe is the punishment and the graver the stigma which accompany a conviction. Under section 1 conviction originally attracted a punishment of up to two years' imprisonment. This has since been increased to a maximum of ten years' imprisonment. The notification requirements under Part I of the Sex Offenders Act 1997 now apply, no matter what the age of the offender: see Schedule 1, paragraph 1(1)(b). Further, in addition to being a serious offence, the offence is drawn broadly ('an act of gross indecency'). It can embrace conduct ranging from predatory approaches by a much older paedophile to consensual sexual experimentation between precocious teenagers of whom the offender may be the younger of the two. The conduct may be depraved by any acceptable standard, or it may be relatively innocuous behaviour in private between two young people. These factors reinforce, rather than negative, the application of the presumption in this case. The purpose of the section is, of course, to protect children. An age ingredient was therefore an essential ingredient of the offence. This factor in itself does not assist greatly. Without more, this does not lead to the conclusion that liability was intended to be strict so far as the age element is concerned, so that the offence is committed irrespective of the alleged offender's belief about the age of the 'victim' and irrespective of how the offender came to hold this belief. Nor can I attach much weight to a fear that it may be difficult sometimes for the prosecution to prove that the defendant knew the child was under fourteen or was recklessly indifferent about the child's age. A well known passage from a judgment of that great jurist, Sir Owen Dixon, in *Thomas v R* (1937) 59 CLR 279, 309, bears repetition:

> The truth appears to be that a reluctance on the part of courts has repeatedly appeared to allow a prisoner to avail himself of a defence depending simply on his own state of knowledge and belief. The reluctance is due in great measure, if not entirely, to a mistrust of the tribunal of fact – the jury. Through a feeling that, if the law allows such a defence to be submitted to the jury, prisoners may too readily escape by deposing to conditions of mind and describing sources of information, matters upon which their evidence cannot be adequately tested and contradicted, judges have been misled into a failure steadily to adhere to principle. It is not difficult to understand such tendencies, but a lack of confidence in the ability of a tribunal correctly to estimate evidence of states of mind and the like can never be sufficient ground for excluding from inquiry the most fundamental element in a rational and humane criminal code.

Similarly, it is far from clear that strict liability regarding the age ingredient of the offence would further the purpose of section 1 more effectively than would be the case if a mental element were read into this ingredient. There is no general agreement that strict liability is necessary to the enforcement of the law protecting children in sexual matters. For instance, the draft criminal code bill prepared by the Law Commission in 1989 proposed a compromise solution. Clauses 114 and 115 of the bill provided for committing or inciting acts of gross indecency with children aged under thirteen or under sixteen. Belief that the child is over sixteen would be a defence in each case: see the Law Commission, *Criminal Law, A Criminal Code for England and Wales*, Vol 1, *Report and draft Criminal Code Bill*, p 81 (Law Com 177).

Is there here a compellingly clear implication that Parliament should be taken to have intended that the ordinary common law requirement of a mental element should be excluded in respect of the age ingredient of this new offence? Thus far, having regard especially to the breadth of the offence and the gravity of the stigma and penal consequences which a conviction brings, I see no sufficient ground for so concluding.

Indeed, the Crown's argument before your Lordships did not place much reliance on any of the matters just mentioned. The thrust of the Crown's argument lay in a different direction: the statutory context. This is understandable, because the statutory background is undoubtedly the Crown's strongest point. The Crown submitted that the law in this field has been regarded as settled for well over one hundred years, ever since the decision in *R v Prince* (1875) LR 2 CCR 154. That well known case concerned the unlawful abduction of a girl under the age of sixteen. The defendant honestly believed she was over sixteen, and he had reasonable grounds for believing this. No fewer than fifteen judges held that this provided no defence. Subsequently, in *R v Maughan* (1934) 24 Cr App R 130 the Court of Criminal Appeal (Lord Hewart CJ, Avory and Roche JJ) held that a reasonable and honest belief that a girl was over sixteen could never be a defence to a charge of indecent assault. The court held that this point had been decided in *R v Forde* (1923) 17 Cr App R 99. The court also observed that in any event the answer was to be found in *Prince's* case. Building on this foundation Mr Scrivener QC submitted that the Sexual Offences Act 1956 was not intended to change this established law, and that section 1 of the Indecency with Children Act 1960 was to be read with the 1956 Act. The preamble to the 1960 Act stated that its purpose was to make 'further' provision for the punishment of indecent conduct towards young people. In this field, where Parliament intended belief as to age to be a defence, this was stated expressly: see, for instance, the 'young man's defence' in section 6(3) of the 1956 Act.

This is a formidable argument, but I cannot accept it. I leave on one side Mr. O'Connor QC's sustained criticisms of the reasoning in *Prince's* case and Maughan's case. Where the Crown's argument breaks down is that the motley collection of offences, of diverse origins, gathered into the Sexual Offences Act 1956 displays no satisfactorily clear or coherent pattern. If the interpretation of section 1 of the Act of 1960 is to be gleaned from the contents of another statute, that other statute must give compelling guidance. The Act of 1956 as a whole falls short of this standard. So do the two sections, sections 14 and 15, which were the genesis of section 1 of the Act of 1960.

Accordingly, I cannot find, either in the statutory context or otherwise, any indication of sufficient cogency to displace the application of the common law presumption. In my view the necessary mental element regarding the age ingredient in section 1 of the Act of 1960 is the absence of a genuine belief by the accused that the victim was fourteen years of age or above. The burden of proof of this rests upon the prosecution in the usual way. If Parliament considers that the position should be otherwise regarding this serious social problem, Parliament must itself confront the difficulties and express its will in clear terms. I would allow this appeal.

I add a final observation. As just mentioned, in reaching my conclusion I have left on one side the criticisms made of *Prince's* case and *Maughan's* case. Those cases concerned different offences and different statutory provisions. The correctness of the decisions in those cases does not call for decision on the present appeal. But, without expressing a view on the correctness of the actual decisions in those cases, I must observe that some of the reasoning in *Prince's* case is at variance with the common law presumption regarding *mens rea* as discussed above. To that extent, the reasoning must be regarded as unsound. For instance, Bramwell B (at p 174) seems to have regarded the common law presumption as ousted because the act forbidden was 'wrong in itself'. Denman J (at p 178) appears to have considered it was 'reasonably clear' that the Act of 1861 was an Act of strict liability so far as the age element was concerned. On its face this is a lesser standard than necessary implication. And in the majority judgment, Blackburn J reached his conclusion by inference from the intention Parliament must have had when enacting two other, ineptly drawn, sections of the Act. But clumsy parliamentary drafting is an insecure basis for finding a necessary implication elsewhere, even in the same statute. *Prince's* case, and later decisions based on it, must now be read in the light of this decision of your Lordships' House on the nature and weight of the common law presumption.

Lord Hutton: ... the Act of 1960 is an appendix to the Act of 1956, and the wording of sections 5 and 6 of the 1956 Act relating respectively to intercourse with a girl under thirteen and to intercourse with a girl under sixteen, but with the latter section providing in subsection (3) for 'the young man's defence', makes it plain that the offence under section 5 is an offence of strict liability. Therefore it is clear that in the Act of 1956 Parliament intended that there should be strict liability when a man had sexual intercourse with a girl under thirteen, and accordingly it can be argued that it is in accordance with the intention of Parliament that there should be strict liability when a person is guilty of gross indecency towards a child under fourteen. The second point is that in addition to section 6(3) there are a number of sections in the Act of 1956 which expressly provide for a defence of mistake. In the case of intercourse with a woman who is a defective section 7(2) provides a defence if the man does not know and has no reason to suspect the woman to be a defective. The same applies to the offence of procurement of a defective: see section 9(2). The same defence applies to indecent assault on a woman defective: see Section 14(4). The same defence is available in respect of permitting a defective to use premises for intercourse or causing or encouraging the prostitution of a defective: see section 27(2) and section 29(2). Therefore the Crown can argue with considerable force that when Parliament intends that there should be a defence of mistake it makes express provision for this defence, so that where there is no express provision for such a defence the statute by implication intends that the defence will not be available. This point is well stated by Tucker J in his judgment at p 127H:

> I deduce from all these statutory provisions that it is the clear intention of Parliament to protect young children and to make it an offence to commit offences against children under a certain age whether or not the defendant knows of the age of the victim, and that it was intended that, save where expressly provided, a mistaken or honest belief in the victim's age should not afford a defence.

Therefore I consider that it would be reasonable to infer that it was the intention of Parliament that liability under section 1(1) of the Act of 1960 should be strict so that an honest belief as to the age of the child would not be a defence. But the test is not whether it is a reasonable implication that the statute rules out *mens rea* as a constituent part of the crime – the test is whether it is a necessary implication. Applying this test, I am of opinion that there are considerations which point to the conclusion that it is not a necessary implication. One is that the various provisions of the Act of 1956 have not been drafted to give effect to a consistent scheme but are a collection of diverse provisions derived from a variety of sources: ... A further consideration is that in *Sweet v Parsley* Lord Reid stated at p 149D:

> It is also firmly established that the fact that other sections of the Act expressly require *mens rea*, for example because they contain the word 'knowingly', is not in itself sufficient to justify a decision that a section which is silent as to *mens rea* creates an absolute offence.

Whilst, as I have stated, I think there is force in the view expressed by Blackburn J at pp 171–72 of *R v Prince*, I am of opinion that to the extent that Prince's case can be viewed as establishing a general rule that mistake as to age does not afford a defence in age-based sexual offences, that rule cannot prevail over the presumption stated by this House in *Sweet v Parsley*.

Therefore, for the reasons which I have stated, I would allow this appeal and I would answer the first certified question in the negative. For the reasons which have been stated by my noble and learned friend Lord Steyn, and with which I agree, I would answer part (a) of the second certified question in the affirmative, and I would answer part (b) by stating that the burden of proof rests on the Crown once the defendant has raised some evidence before the jury or magistrates that he or she honestly believed the child was over fourteen.

I am conscious that the decision by this House to allow this appeal may make it more difficult to convict those who are guilty of an offence under Section 1(1) of the Act of 1960 and thus reduce the protection given to children, but I have come to the conclusion that as Parliament has failed to state by express provision or by necessary implication that *mens rea* as to age is not necessary, the legal presumption stated by Lord Reid that *mens rea* is required must be applied. If Parliament regards the decision in this case as giving rise to undesirable consequences it will be for it to change the law, and I share the regret of Brooke LJ expressed in his judgment at p 136A–H that Parliament does not take account of the expert advice which it has received over the years from the Criminal Law Revision Committee and the Law Commission, and does not address its mind, in enacting legislation creating or restating criminal offences, to the issue whether *mens rea* should be a constituent part of the offences and does not state in clear terms whether or not *mens rea* is required.

THE SERIOUSNESS OF THE OFFENCE: STIGMA AND PUNISHMENT VERSUS MERELY REGULATORY

Alphacell Ltd v Woodward [1972] AC 824 (HL)

The appellant company had been convicted, under the Rivers (Prevention of Pollution) Act 1951, of the offence of causing or knowingly permitting to enter a stream 'any poisonous, noxious or polluting matter' (s 2(1)(a)). The following extracts focus upon the extent to which the imposition of strict liability can be justified where the prohibition is essentially regulator in substance, as opposed to 'truly criminal'.

Viscount Dilhorne: ... This Act, in my opinion, is one of those Acts to which my noble and learned friends, Lord Reid and Lord Diplock, referred in *Sweet v Parsley* [1970] AC 132, 149, 163 which, to apply the words of Wright J in *Sherras v De Rutzen* [1895] 1 QB 918, 922 deals with acts which 'are not criminal in any real sense, but are acts which in the public interest are prohibited under a penalty'.

What, then, is meant by the word 'caused' in the subsection? If a man, intending to secure a particular result, does an act which brings that about, he causes that result. If he deliberately and intentionally does certain acts of which the natural consequence is that certain results ensue, may he not also be said to have caused those results even though they may not have been intended by him? I think he can, just as he can be said to cause the result if he is negligent, without intending that result ...

We have not here to consider what the position would be if pollution were caused by an inadvertent and unintentional act without negligence. In such case it might be said that the doer of the act had not caused the pollution although the act had caused it. Here the acts done by the appellants were intentional. They were acts calculated to lead to the river being polluted if the acts done by the appellants, the installation and operation of the pumps, were ineffective to prevent it. Where a person intentionally does certain things which produce a certain result, then it can truly be said that he has caused that result, and here in my opinion the acts done intentionally by the appellants causes the pollution ...

Lord Salmon: My Lords ... The appellants contend that, even if they caused the pollution, still they should succeed since they did not cause it intentionally or knowingly or negligently. Section 2(1)(a) of the Rivers (Prevention of Pollution) Act 1951 is undoubtedly a penal section. It follows that if it is capable of two or more meanings then the meaning most favourable to the subject should be adopted. Accordingly, so the argument runs, the words 'intentionally' or 'knowingly' or 'negligently' should be read into the section immediately before the word 'causes'. I do not agree. It is of the utmost public importance that our rivers should not be polluted. The risk of pollution, particularly from the vast and increasing number of riparian industries, is very great. The offences created by the Act of 1951 seem to me to be prototypes of offences which 'are not criminal in any real sense, but are acts which in the public interest are prohibited under a penalty': *Sherras v De Rutzen* [1895] 1 QB 918, *per* Wright J at 922, referred to with approval by my noble and learned friends, Lord Reid and Lord Diplock, in *Sweet v Parsley* [1970] AC 132, at 149, 162. I can see no valid reason for reading the word 'intentionally', 'knowingly' or 'negligently' into s 2(1)(a) and a number of cogent reasons for not doing so. In the case of a minor pollution such as the present, when the justices find that there is no wrongful intention or negligence on the part of the defendant, a comparatively nominal fine will no doubt be imposed. This may be regarded as a not unfair hazard of carrying on a business which may cause pollution on the banks of a river. The present appellants were fined £20 and ordered to pay, in all, £24 costs. I should be surprised if the costs of pursuing this appeal to this House were incurred for the purpose of saving these appellants £44.

If this appeal succeeded and it were held to be the law that no conviction could be obtained under the Act of 1951 unless the prosecution could discharge the often impossible onus of proving that the pollution was caused intentionally or negligently, a great deal of pollution would go unpunished and undeterred to the relief of many riparian factory owners. As a result, many rivers which are now filthy would become filthier still and many rivers which are now clean would lose their cleanliness. The legislature no doubt recognised that as a matter of public policy this would be most unfortunate. Hence s 2(1)(a) which encourages riparian factory owners not only to take reasonable steps to prevent pollution but to do everything possible to ensure that they do not cause it ...

Wings Ltd v Ellis [1985] AC 272 (HL)

Lord Scarman: My Lords, this appeal turns on the construction properly to be put upon a few ordinary English words in the context of s 14 of the Trade Descriptions Act 1968. Put very shortly, the basic issue between the parties is whether upon its proper construction s 14(1)(a) creates an offence of strict, or more accurately, semi-strict, liability or is one requiring the existence of full *mens rea*. The issue has provoked elaborate and subtle legal argument between the parties before the Divisional Court and in your Lordships' House. But the point is, or ought to be, a short one, arising, as it does, upon the words of a statute passed to protect the public in a way the public can understand.

Section 14, so far as material, is in these terms:

(1) It shall be an offence for any person in the course of any trade or business:

(a) to make a statement which he knows to be false; or

(b) recklessly to make a statement which is false;

as to any of the following matters, that is to say: (1) the provision in the course of any trade or business of any services, accommodation or facilities ...

The respondent company was charged with two offences under the section. The first, to which the appeal relates, was an offence under s 14(1)(a) of making a statement which the company knew to be false as to the provision which it offered to its customers of certain hotel accommodation. The statement was alleged to have been made on 13 January 1982, the date on which a customer, Mr Wade, having read it in a brochure published by the respondent company booked a holiday for his wife and himself in reliance upon it. The second, which is not the subject of an appeal to the House, was an offence under s 14(1)(b) of recklessly making a false statement in respect of the same offer. This charge related to the same booking but arose from a photograph said in the brochure to be a photograph of the hotel bedroom, which it was not. The Plymouth justices convicted the company on both charges. The Divisional Court allowed the company's appeal against both convictions. The prosecutor now, with the leave of the House, appeals only against the quashing of the first conviction.

The Divisional Court certified that the case involved the following point of law of general public importance:

Whether a defendant may properly be convicted of an offence under s 4(1)(a) of the Trade Descriptions Act 1968 where he had no knowledge of the falsity of the statement at the time of its publication but knew of the falsity at the time when the statement was read by the complainant.

As will later appear, the statement (admittedly false) was contained in a brochure prepared and published without knowledge of its falsity by the respondent company in May 1981, but not read by the complainant until 13 January 1982, by which time (admittedly) the respondent company knew it was false. The two issues, therefore, which arise in the appeal are both points of construction. The first is whether, as the respondent contends, the offence is knowingly to make a false statement or whether the offence can be committed without knowledge of the making of the statement. The second point raises the question: what is meant by the words 'make a statement' in their statutory context? What constitutes a statement upon the proper construction of s 14(1)(a)? Did the respondent company make a statement on 13 January 1982?

The details of the charge laid under s 14(1)(a) were that on 13 January 1982 (the prosecution tied its case to this date) the defendant in the course of its business made a statement, which it knew to be false, as to the nature of the accommodation at the Seashells Hotel, Negombo, Sri Lanka, namely that the bedrooms were air-conditioned, whereas in truth they were not. The statement consisted of the use of two code letters 'AC' in the description of the hotel's accommodation published by the defendant in its brochure 'Wings Faraway Holidays Winter Oct 1981 – April 1982'.

The defendant (hereinafter called the respondent or respondent company) is a body corporate engaged in the business of providing holidays on a package deal basis. The business is entrepreneurial in character, a service industry: the company arranges for the travel to and from the holiday destination and for the accommodation to be provided by others. Business, as between company and holidaymaker, is done on the basis of a written description of what is on offer. The description is usually contained, as in this case, in an attractively written and illustrated brochure published by the company well in advance of the holiday season and widely distributed to travel agents through whom it becomes available and is seen by interested members of the public. The brochure is, therefore, as in this case, the document from which the holidaymaker is invited to choose his holiday and upon the faith of the descriptions contained in which he makes his choice. The print run of a brochure may, as in this case, go into hundreds of thousands of copies. Most inquiries from the public reach the company through travel agents who pass them on to the company, as also in this case, by telephone. The holidaymaker tells the travel agent his selection, and the travel agent phones it through to the company, a member of whose sales staff, as also in this case, makes the booking.

The justices found that the respondent published the brochure containing the false statement relied on in this case in May 1981. At that time no one in the respondent company knew that it was false. It was an innocent error, the source of which has never been traced. The error was, however, discovered before 1 June 1981 by which time the brochure had already been given a wide distribution. The brochure was not however, withdrawn: indeed, it would have been impossible to recall all copies. Nor were 'errata' slips distributed – again because they would not have reached everyone into whose hands the brochure had come. But the company did prepare and on 1 June 1981 despatched to their sales staff a memorandum instructing them to amend their own copies of the brochure by deleting the code letters 'AC'. The memorandum further instructed the sales staff to inform travel agents and customers of the error whenever a booking was sought to be made for the Seashells Hotel holiday. A letter was also sent in June 1981 to customers who had already booked a Seashells holiday informing them that the bedrooms were not air-conditioned.

The letter, of course, never went to Mr Wade who did not make his booking until 13 January 1982. He made the booking through a Plymouth travel agent who telephoned a member of the respondent company's sales staff who accepted it. Under the instruction of 1 June 1981 the member of staff should have informed the travel agent of the error in description. The justices made no finding as to whether she did or did not do so, although they ventured the comment in their case stated that 'the travel agent might well have known'. It certainly was not found as a fact that he did. But the justices did find unequivocally that Mr Wade was never informed of the lack of air-conditioning at the hotel and that he selected the holiday from the brochure in reliance upon its uncorrected false statement that the bedrooms were air-conditioned. Mr Wade and his wife went on the holiday on 3 March 1982, found to their discomfort that the bedroom was not air-conditioned and, not surprisingly, complained to the trading standards officer on their return home.

It is no exaggeration to say that the social impact of the class of business which I have described and in which the respondent company is engaged has been immense. It has brought about a dramatic change in the lifestyle of millions. People rely on the brochures issued by the companies engaged in this highly competitive business when choosing their annual holidays abroad. Some, like Mr and Mrs Wade in this case, choose to travel great distances to far-away places very different from anything which they have experienced at home upon their faith in a description which they have read in a brochure but which they cannot check.

The Trade Descriptions Act 1968 is plainly a very important safeguard for those members of the public (and they run into millions) who choose their holidays in this way. If the protection is not to be undermined, the Act must be widely known (as indeed it is), easily understood (as, having heard the arguments in this case, I fear that it may not be), and must be of general application save in situations specifically excepted by the statute itself. The Act is not based on the law of contract or tort. It operates by prohibiting false descriptions under the pain of penalties enforced through the criminal courts. But it is not a truly criminal statute. Its purpose is not the enforcement of the criminal law but the maintenance of trading standards. Trading standards, not criminal behaviour, are its concern.

Its prohibitions include false trade descriptions applied to goods (s 1); misleading indications as to the price of goods (s 11); false representations as to royal approval or awards (s 12); and false statements as to the nature of services, accommodation, or facilities provided in the course of business (s 14). It provides for certain defences to be available, two of which could have been relevant in this case. They are defences made available under ss 23 and 24, to which I shall return later. Neither section was invoked at the hearing before the justices, who consequently made no finding upon either of them. Indeed, it was argued by the respondent in your Lordships' House that neither was applicable to an offence charged under s 14.

The Act, of course, to be of any value at all in modern conditions, has to cover trades and businesses conducted on a large scale by individual proprietors, by firms, and by bodies corporate. The day-to-day business activities of large enterprises, whatever their legal structure, are necessarily conducted by their employees, and particularly by their sales staff. It follows that many of the acts prohibited by the Act will be the acts of employees done in the course of the trade or business and without the knowledge at the time of those who direct the business. It will become clear that the Act does cover such acts when one comes to consider the terms of the two statutory defences to which I have already referred. The Act also makes specific provision consistent with this view of its operation in respect of businesses carried on by bodies corporate. Section 20 provides that where an offence has been committed by a body corporate and was committed with the consent or is attributable to the neglect of a director or other officer of the company, he 'as well as the body corporate' is guilty of the offence ...

My Lords, the subject-matter and structure of the Act make plain that the Act belongs to that class of legislation which prohibits acts which 'are not criminal in any real sense, but are acts which in the public interest are prohibited under a penalty', as Wright J put it in *Sherras v De Rutzen* [1895] 1 QB 918, 922. In construing the offence-creating sections of the Act it will, therefore, be necessary to bear in mind that it may well have been the intention of the legislature 'in order to guard against the happening of the forbidden thing, to impose a liability upon a principal even though he does not know of, and is not a party to, the forbidden act done by his servant': see *per* Viscount Reading CJ in *Mousell Brothers Ltd v London and North-Western Railway Co* [1917] 2 KB 836, 844.

While, however, the subject-matter of the Act is such that the presumption recognised by Lord Reid in *Sweet v Parsley* [1970] AC 132, 148G as applicable to truly criminal statutes 'that Parliament did not intend to make criminals of persons who were in no way blameworthy in what they did' is not applicable to this Act, it does not necessarily follow that merely because an offence-creating section in the Act is silent as to *mens rea* its silence must be construed as excluding *mens rea*. As Lord Reid said, at 149, in the absence of a clear indication that an offence is intended to be an absolute offence one must examine all relevant circumstances in order to establish the intention of Parliament ... At the end of the day the question whether an offence created by statute requires *mens rea*, guilty knowledge or intention, in whole, in part, or not at all, turns on the subject-matter, the language and the structure of the Act studied as a whole, on the language of the particular statutory provision under consideration construed in the light of the legislative purpose embodied in the Act, and on 'whether strict liability in respect of all or any of the essential ingredients of the offence would promote the object of the provision': *Gammon's* case at 16 and see *Sweet v Parsley* [1970] AC 132, 163, *per* Lord Diplock ...

PRESUMPTION IN FAVOUR OF *MENS REA* REBUTTED BY SUBJECT MATTER: THE NEED TO PROTECT SOCIETY

Gammon (Hong Kong) Ltd v AG of Hong Kong [1985] 1 AC 1 (PC)

Lord Scarman: ... The issue in the appeal is whether the offences charged are offences of strict liability or require proof of *mens rea* as to their essential facts.

The first appellant, Gammon (Hong Kong) Ltd ('the company') is a contractor registered under the Ordinance and was carrying out building works at a site known as Marine Lot No 3, Queen's Road Central, Hong Kong. The second and third appellants were employees of the company, being respectively the project manager and site agent for the works.

The appellants were charged under subsection (2A) and (2B) of s 40 of the Ordinance. It is necessary to set out in full the two subsections:

(2A) Any person for whom any building works, street works, lift works or escalator works are being carried out and any authorised person, registered structural engineer, registered contractor, registered lift contractor or registered escalator contactor directly concerned with any such works who: (a) permits or authorises to be incorporated in or used in the carrying out of any such works any material which: (1) are defective or do not comply with the provisions of this Ordinance; (2) have not been mixed, prepared, applied, used, erected, constructed, placed or fixed in the manner required for such material under this Ordinance; (b) diverges or deviates in any material way from any work shown in a plan approved by the Building Authority under this Ordinance; or (c) knowingly misrepresents a material fact in any plan, certificate, form or notice given to the Building Authority under this Ordinance, shall be guilty of an offence and shall be liable on conviction to a fine of $250,000 and to imprisonment for three years.

(2B) Any person (whether or not an authorised person, a registered structural engineer or a registered contractor) directly concerned with any site formation works, piling works, foundation works or other form of building works who: (a) carries out or has carried out such works, or authorises or permits or has authorised or permitted such works to be carried out, in such manner that it causes injury to any person or damage to any property; or (b) carries out or has carried out such works, or authorises or permits or has authorised or permitted such works to be carried out, in such manner as is likely to cause a risk of injury to any person or damage to any property, shall be guilty of an offence and shall be liable on conviction to a fine of $250,000 and to imprisonment for three years.

The company was charged with a material deviation from an approved plan in contravention of subsection (2A)(b), and with carrying out works in a manner likely to cause risk or injury or damage in contravention of subsection (2B)(b). The second and third appellants were charged under subsection (2B)(b): it was charged against the second appellant that, being the company's manager, he carried out the works, and against the third appellant that he permitted the works to be carried out, in a manner likely to cause risk of injury or damage ...

The facts relevant to the issue can be very briefly summarised. The company had delegated the fulfilment of its obligations under the Ordinance on the site to the second and third appellants: it is accepted, therefore, that the company is vicariously responsible if either of them contravened or failed to comply with the provisions of the Ordinance. If either of them committed an offence in the course of his employment, the company has also offended and is liable to the penalties imposed by the Ordinance.

The offending act, which is the basis of all the charges, was the removal of part of the lateral support system on the site; a system which was required in the interest of safety by plans approved by the building authority. The removal was a 'deviation of substance' from the plans; and it is to be assumed for the purpose of the appeal (for it is not admitted by the appellants) that the removal was likely to cause a risk of injury or damage ...

In their Lordships' opinion, the law relevant to this appeal may be stated in the following propositions ...: (1) there is a presumption of law that *mens rea* is required before a person can be held guilty of a criminal offence; (2) the presumption is particularly strong where the offence is 'truly criminal' in character; (3) the presumption applies to statutory offences, and can be displaced only if this is clearly or by necessary implication the effect of the statute; (4) the only situation in which the presumption can be displaced is where the statute is concerned with an issue of social concern, and public safety is such an issue; (5) even where a statute is concerned with such an issue, the presumption of *mens rea* stands unless it can also be shown that the creation of strict liability will be effective to promote the objects of the statute by encouraging greater vigilance to prevent the commission of the prohibited act.

The Ordinance

Their Lordships turn to consider the purpose and subject matter of the Ordinance. Its overall purpose is clearly to regulate the planning, design and construction of the building works to which it relates in the interests of safety. It covers a field of activity where there is, especially in Hong Kong, a potential danger to public safety. And the activity which the Ordinance is intended to regulate is one in which citizens have a choice as to whether they participate or not. Part IV (s 40) of the Ordinance makes it very clear that the legislature intended that criminal sanctions for contraventions of the Ordinance should be a feature of its enforcement. But it is not to be supposed that the legislature intended that any of the offences created by the Ordinance should be offences of strict liability unless it is plain, from a consideration of the subject matter of the Ordinance and of the wording of the particular provision creating the offence, that an object of the Ordinance, eg the promotion of greater vigilance by those having responsibility under the Ordinance, would be served by the imposition of strict liability ...

Put in positive terms, the conclusion of the Board is that it is consistent with the purpose of the Ordinance in its regulation of the works to which it applies that at least some of the criminal offences which it creates should be of strict liability. It is a statute the subject-matter of which may properly be described as 'the regulation of a particular activity involving potential danger to public health [and] safety ... in which citizens have a choice as to whether they participate or not': *per* Lord Diplock in *Sweet v Parsley* [1970] AC 132, 163.

Whether, therefore, a particular provision of the statute creates an offence of full *mens rea* or of strict liability must depend upon the true meaning of the words of the particular provision construed with reference to its subject-matter and to the question whether strict liability in respect of all or any of the essential ingredients of the offence would promote the object of the provision ...

Subsections (2A) and (2B)

Their Lordships now turn to consider the two subsections in detail and separately; for it does not follow that, if one subsection should create an offence of strict liability, the other must also do so. But first a few observations on certain features common to both.

The first common feature is that both subsections have a characteristic of which Lord Reid spoke in *Sweet v Parsley* [1970] AC 132, 149. The specific provisions subsections (2A)(b) and (2B)(b) belong to that:

> ... multitude of criminal enactments where the words of the Act simply make it an offence to do certain things but where everyone agrees that there cannot be a conviction without proof of *mens rea* in some form?

Each provision clearly requires a degree of *mens rea*, but each is silent as to whether it is required in respect of all the facts which together constitute the offence created. The issue here is, therefore, a narrow one. Does subsection (2A)(b) require knowledge of the materiality of the deviation? Does subsection (2B)(b) require knowledge of the likelihood of risk of injury or damage?

The second common feature is that each provision appears in a section which creates many other offences, the wording of some, though not all, of which clearly requires full *mens rea*.

A third common feature is that the maximum penalties for the offences which they create are heavy: a fine of $250,000 and imprisonment for three years. There is no doubt that the penalty indicates the seriousness with which the legislature viewed the offences.

The first of these features raises the determinative question in the appeal. Their Lordships will, therefore, consider it later in respect of each subsection.

The second feature, in their Lordships' opinion, proves nothing. One would expect a wide range of very different offences in a statute which establishes a comprehensive system of supervision and control over a great range of complicated works in diverse circumstances. And it can be said with equal force that a feature of s 40 is that in many cases where *mens rea* is required it expressly says so, and that, where a defence of reasonable excuse or lack of knowledge is to be available, it makes express provision to that end: examples may be seen in subsections (1B), (1C), (2A)(c), (2C), (6), (7) and (7A).

The severity of the maximum penalties is a more formidable point. But it has to be considered in the light of the Ordinance read as a whole. For reasons which their Lordships have already developed, there is nothing inconsistent with the purpose of the Ordinance in imposing severe penalties for offences of strict liability. The legislature could reasonably have intended severity to be a significant deterrent, bearing in mind the risks to public safety arising from some contraventions of the Ordinance. Their Lordships agree with the view on this point of the Court of Appeal. It must be crucially important that those who participate in or bear responsibility for the carrying out of works in a manner which complies with the requirements of the Ordinance should know that severe penalties await them in the event of any contravention or non-compliance with the Ordinance by themselves or by anyone over whom they are required to exercise supervision or control.

Subsection (2A)

This provision applies to building owners, authorised persons (ie architects, surveyors, structural engineers), registered structural engineers and registered contractors. It is thus confined to persons bearing responsibility for the decision to undertake works and for their supervision and control. There is plainly an element of *mens rea* in the offences it creates: the wording of subparagraphs (a) and (b) does no make clear how far *mens rea* extends: the wording of subparagraph (c) reveals an offence of full *mens rea* ...

The wording of subparagraph (b) clearly requires knowledge of the approved plan and of the fact of deviation. But in their Lordships' view it would be of little use in promoting public safety if it also required proof of knowledge of the materiality of the deviation. As it was put on behalf of the Attorney General, if the offence requires knowledge of the materiality of the deviation to be proved, the defendant is virtually judge in his own cause. The object of the provision is to assist in preventing material deviations from occurring. If a building owner, an authorised or a registered person is unaware of the materiality of the deviation which he authorises (and knowledge of the deviation is necessary), he plainly ought to be. He is made liable to criminal penalties because of the threat to public safety arising from material deviations from plans occurring within the sphere of his responsibility. The effectiveness of the Ordinance would be seriously weakened if it were open to such a person to plead ignorance of what was material. In the words ... of the Court of Appeal: 'it therefore behoves the incompetent to stay away and the competent to conduct themselves with proper care'.

Subsection (2B)

The construction of subsection (2B)(b) is more difficult, but their Lordships are satisfied that it imposes strict liability for substantially the same reasons as those which have led them to this conclusion in respect of subsection (2A)(b). The offence created clearly requires a degree of *mens rea*. A person cannot carry out works or authorise or permit them to be carried out in a certain manner unless he knows the manner which he is employing, authorising, or permitting. The appellants laid great emphasis on the reference to permitting as an indication of full *mens rea*. They referred their Lordships to *James and Son Ltd v Smee* [1955] 1 QB 78. But their Lordships agree with the answer of the Court of Appeal to this point:

> We would therefore hold that the word 'permitting' in s 40(2B)(b) does not by itself import *mens rea* in the sense of intention to cause a likelihood of risk of injury or knowledge that such likelihood would result but does require that the defendant shall have had a power to control whether the *actus reus* (the carrying out of the works in the manner which in fact causes a likelihood of risk of injury) shall be committed or not ...

Their Lordships find some support for their view that subsection (2B)(b) is an offence of strict liability in the wording of the offence created by (2B)(a). The wording of (a) points to strict liability, once injury or damage has in fact been caused. Anyone who has carried out authorised or permitted work to be carried out in a manner which has in fact caused injury or damage is caught ...

R v Blake [1997] 1 All ER 963 (CA)

The appellant was convicted of using a station for wireless telegraphy without a licence.

Hirst LJ: ... [T]here was no dispute that [the appellant] knew he was using the broadcasting apparatus in the studio. His defence was that he believed he was making demonstration tapes at the time and so did not know that he was, in fact, transmitting.

The question which the [trial judge] had to decide on ... was whether, as the prosecution contended, the offence created by s 1(1) of the Wireless Telegraphy Act 1949 is an absolute offence of strict liability, or whether, as the defence contended, the prosecution needed to establish *mens rea* ...

Section 1(1) provides, so far as relevant, as follows:

> *Licensing of wireless telegraphy* – No person shall establish or use any station for wireless telegraphy or instal or use any apparatus for wireless telegraphy except under the authority of a licence in that behalf granted under this section ... and any person who establishes or uses any station for wireless telegraphy or instals or uses any apparatus for wireless telegraphy except under and in accordance with such a licence shall be guilty of an offence under this Act ...

[His Lordship then quoted from the judgment of Lord Scarman in *Gammon (Hong Kong) Ltd v AG of Hong Kong* [1985] AC 1 at 14, and noted the creation of additional offences by the Broadcasting Act 1990 and noted that the penalty was increased, from 3 months' imprisonment and/or a fine up to £100, to six months' imprisonment and/or a fine up to the statutory maximum (following summary trial) or 2 years' imprisonment and/or a fine (following trial on indictment).] ...

The solution to this case ... clearly lies in the application of the five principles laid down by Lord Scarman in the *Gammon* case. In our judgment, since throughout the history of s 1(1), an offender has been potentially subject to a term of imprisonment, the offence is 'truly criminal' in character, and it follows ... that the presumption in favour of *mens rea* is particularly strong. However, it seems to us manifest that the purpose behind making unlicensed transmissions a serious criminal offence must have been one of social concern in the interests of public safety ... since undoubtedly the emergency services and air traffic controllers were using radio communications in 1949, albeit in a much more rudimentary form than nowadays. No doubt the much greater sophistication of these modes of communication, and the wider prevalence of pirate radio stations 40 years on, led to the substantial increase in the penalty in 1990.

Clearly, interference with transmissions by these vital public services poses a grave risk to wide sections of the public. We, therefore, consider that the test laid down in para (4) in the *Gammon* case is met.

Furthermore, we are satisfied that the test in para (5) is also met, since the imposition of an absolute offence must surely encourage greater vigilance on the part of those establishing or using a station, or installing or using the apparatus, to avoid committing the offence, eg in the case of users by carefully checking whether they are on air; it must also operate as a deterrent. The case is thus in our judgment, *mutatis mutandis*, comparable with *R v Wells Street Metropolitan Stipendiary Magistrate ex p Westminster City Council* [1986] 1 WLR 1046 [where the Divisional Court applied the principles laid down in *Gammon* and concluded that s 55(1) of the Town and Country Planning Act 1971, which prohibited the execution of various works to a listed building, was an absolute offence], perhaps *a fortiori*, since here public safety is the main consideration and, in our view, a consideration of paramount importance ...

So ... it is incumbent upon the prosecution to establish that the defendant knew he was making use of the apparatus, but they need not show that he was doing it with a guilty mind. Thus, for example, if a remark made by a bystander near the studio was accidentally picked up by the microphone and broadcast, the bystander would not be liable.

In these circumstances, we are satisfied that s 1(1) does create an absolute offence and it follows that this appeal will be dismissed.

WHETHER THE IMPOSITION OF STRICT LIABILITY HELPS TO ACHIEVE THE LEGISLATIVE PURPOSE

Sherras v De Rutzen [1895] 1 QB 918 (QBD)

Day J: I am clearly of opinion that this conviction ought to be quashed. This police constable comes into the appellant's public house without his armlet, and with every appearance of being off duty. The house was in the immediate neighbourhood of the police station, and the appellant believed, and he had very natural grounds for believing, that the constable was off duty. In that belief he accordingly served him with liquor. As a matter of fact, the constable was on duty; but does that fact make the innocent act of the appellant an offence? I do not think it does. He had no intention to do a wrongful act; he acted in the *bona fide* belief that the constable was off duty. It seems to me that the contention that he committed an offence is utterly erroneous ...

Wright J: I am of the same opinion. There are many cases on the subject, and it is not very easy to reconcile them. There is a presumption that *mens rea*, an evil intention, or a knowledge of the wrongfulness of the act, is an essential ingredient in every offence; but that presumption is liable to be displaced either by the words of the statute creating the offence or by the subject-matter with which it deals, and both must be considered: *Nichols v Hall* Law Rep 8 CP 322. One of the most remarkable exceptions was in the case of bigamy. It was held by all the judges, on the statute 1 Jac 1, c 11, that a man was rightly convicted of bigamy who had married after an invalid Scotch divorce, which had been obtained in good faith, and the validity of which he had no reason to doubt: *Lolley's* case R & R 237. Another exception, apparently grounded on the language of a statute, is *Prince's* Case Law Rep 2 CC 154, where it was held by 15 judges against one that a man was guilty of abduction of a girl under 16, although he believed, in good faith and on reasonable grounds, that she was over that age. Apart from isolated and extreme cases of this kind, the principal classes of exceptions may perhaps be reduced to three. One is a class of acts which, in the language of Lush J in *Davies v Harvey* Law Rep 9 QB 433, are not criminal in any real sense, but are acts which in the public interest are prohibited under a penalty. Several such instances are to be found in the decisions on the Revenue Statutes, eg *AG v Lockwood* 9 M & W 378, where the innocent possession of liquorice by a beer retailer was held an offence. So under the Adulteration Acts, *R v Woodrow* 15 M & W 404, as to innocent possession of adulterated tobacco; *Fitzpatrick v Kelly* Law Rep 8 QB 337 and *Roberts v Egerton* Law Rep 9 QB 494 as to the sale of adulterated food ...

... Another class comprehends some, and perhaps all, public nuisances: *R v Stephens* Law Rep 1 QB 702 where the employer was held liable on indictment for a nuisance caused by workmen without knowledge and contrary to his orders ... Last, there may be cases in which, although the proceeding is criminal in form, it is really only a summary mode of enforcing a civil right: see *per* Williams and Willes JJ in *Morden v Porter* 7 CB (NS) 641; 29 LJ (MC) 213, as to unintentional trespass in pursuit of game; *Lee v Simpson* 3 CB 871, as to unconscious dramatic piracy; and *Hargreaves v Diddams* Law Rep 10 QB 582, as to a *bona fide* belief in a legally impossible right to fish. But, except in such cases as these there must in general be guilty knowledge on the part of the defendant, or of someone whom he has put in his place to act for him, generally, or in the particular matter, in order to constitute an offence. It is plain that if guilty knowledge is not necessary, no care on the part of the publican could save him from a conviction ... since it would be as easy for the constable to deny that he was on duty when asked, or to produce a forged permission from his superior officer, as to remove his armlet before entering the public house. I am, therefore, of opinion that this conviction ought to be quashed.

Lim Chin Aik v R [1963] AC 160 (PC)

Lord Evershed: ... What should be the proper inferences to be drawn from the language of the statute or statutory instrument under review – in this case of ss 6 and 9 of the Immigration Ordinance? More difficult, perhaps, still, what are the inferences to be drawn in a given case from the 'subject-matter with which [the statute or statutory instrument] deals'?

Where the subject-matter of the statute is the regulation for the public welfare of a particular activity – statutes regulating the sale of food and drink are to be found among the earliest examples – it can be and frequently has been inferred that the legislature intended that such activities should be carried out under conditions of strict liability. The presumption is that the statute or statutory instrument can be effectively enforced only if those in charge of the relevant activities are made responsible for seeing that they are complied with. When such a presumption is to be inferred, it displaces the ordinary presumption of *mens rea* ...

But it is not enough in their Lordships' opinion merely to label the statute as one dealing with a grave social evil and from that to infer that strict liability was intended. It is pertinent also to inquire whether putting the defendant under strict liability will assist in the enforcement of the regulations. That means that there must be something he can do, directly or indirectly, by supervision or inspection, by improvement of his business methods or by exhorting those whom he may be expected to influence or control, which will promote the observance of the regulations. Unless this is so, there is no reason in penalising him, and it cannot be inferred that the legislature imposed strict liability merely in order to find a luckless victim ...

Where it can be shown that the imposition of strict liability would result in the prosecution and conviction of a class of persons whose conduct could not in any way affect the observance of the law, their Lordships consider that, even where the statute is dealing with a grave social evil, strict liability is not likely to be intended.

Their Lordships apply these general observations to the Ordinance in the present case. The subject-matter, the control of immigration, is not one in which the presumption of strict liability has generally been made. Nevertheless, if the courts of Singapore were of the view that unrestricted immigration is a social evil which it is the object of the Ordinance to control most rigorously, their Lordships would hesitate to disagree. That is a matter peculiarly within the cognisance of the local courts. But [counsel for the Crown] was unable to point to anything that the appellant could possibly have done so as to ensure that he complied with the regulations. It was not, for example, suggested that it would be practicable for him to make continuous inquiry to see whether an order had been made against him. Clearly one of the objects of the Ordinance is the expulsion of prohibited persons from Singapore, but there is nothing that a man can do about it if, before the commission of the offence, there is no practical or sensible way in which he can ascertain whether he is a prohibited person or not.

[Counsel], therefore, relied chiefly on the text of the Ordinance and their Lordships return, accordingly, to the language of the two material sections. It is to be observed that the Board is here concerned with one who is said (within the terms of s 6(3)) to have 'contravened' the subsection by 'remaining' in Singapore (after having entered) when he had been 'prohibited' from entering by an 'order' made by the Minister containing such prohibition. It seems to their Lordships that, where a man is said to have contravened an order or an order of prohibition, the common sense of the language presumes that he was aware of the order before he can be said to have contravened it. Their Lordships realise that this statement is something of an oversimplification when applied to the present case; for the 'contravention' alleged is of the unlawful act, prescribed by subsection (2) of the section, of remaining in Singapore after the date of the order of prohibition. Nonetheless it is their Lordships' view that, applying the test of ordinary sense to the language used, the notion of contravention here alleged is more consistent with the assumption that the person charged had knowledge of the order than the converse. But such a conclusion is in their Lordships' view much reinforced by the use of the word 'remains' in its context. It is to be observed that if the respondent is right a man could lawfully enter Singapore and could thereafter lawfully remain in Singapore until the moment when an order of prohibition against his entering was made; that then, instanter, his purely passive conduct in remaining – that is, the mere continuance, quite unchanged, of his previous behaviour, hitherto perfectly lawful – would become criminal. These considerations bring their Lordships clearly to the conclusion that the sense of the language here in question requires for the commission of a crime thereunder *mens rea* as a constituent of such crime; or at least that there is nothing in the language used which suffices to exclude the ordinary presumption. Their Lordships do not forget the emphasis placed by [counsel] on the fact that the word 'knowingly' or the phrases 'without reasonable cause' or 'without reasonable excuse' are found in various sections of the Ordinance (as amended) but find no place in the section now under consideration – see, for example, ss 16(4), 18(4), 19(2), 29, 31(2), 41(2) and 56(d) and (e) of the Ordinance. In their Lordships' view the absence of such a word or phrase in the relevant section is not sufficient in the present case to prevail against the conclusion which the language as a whole suggests. In the first place, it is to be noted that to have inserted such words as 'knowingly' or 'without lawful excuse' in the relevant part of s 6(3) of the Act would in any case not have been sensible. Further, in all the various instances where the word or phrase is used in the other sections of the Ordinance before-mentioned the use is with reference to the doing of some specific act or the failure to do some specific act as distinct from the mere passive continuance of behaviour theretofore perfectly lawful. Finally, their Lordships are mindful that in the *Sherras* case [1895] 1 QB 918 itself the fact that the word 'knowingly' was not found in the subsection under consideration by the court but was found in another subsection in the same section was not there regarded as sufficient to displace the ordinary rule.

Their Lordships have accordingly reached the clear conclusion, with all respect to the view taken in the courts below, that the application of the rule that *mens rea* is an essential ingredient in every offence has not in the present case been ousted by the terms or subject-matter of the Ordinance, and that the appellant's conviction and sentence cannot stand ...

Sweet v Parsley [1970] AC 132 (HL)

The facts are given in the earlier extract at the beginning of this chapter. The following passage indicates that strict liability ought not to be imposed on those who cannot take action to prevent a prohibited circumstance arising.

Lord Morris of Borth-y-Gest: It is said that the intention of Parliament was to impose a duty on all persons concerned in the management of any premises to exercise vigilance to prevent the smoking of cannabis. If that had been the intention of Parliament different words would have been used. It would be possible for Parliament to enact, though it would be surprising if it did, that if anyone should at any time smoke cannabis on any premises, then all those concerned in the management of those premises, whether they knew of the smoking or not, should automatically be guilty of a criminal offence. Yet this is in effect what it is now said that Parliament has enacted. The implications are astonishing. Parliament would not only be indirectly imposing a duty upon persons concerned in the management of any premises requiring them to exercise complete supervision over all persons who enter the premises to ensure that no one of them should smoke cannabis, but Parliament would be enacting that the persons concerned in the management would become guilty of an offence it, unknown to them, someone by surreptitiously smoking cannabis eluded the most elaborately devised measures of supervision. There would not be guilt by reason of anything done nor even by reasons of any carelessness, but by reason of the unknown act of some unknown person whom it had not been found possible to control. When the range of possible punishments is remembered the unlikelihood that Parliament intended to legislate in such way becomes additionally apparent.

Lord Pearce: My Lords, the prosecution contend that any person who is concerned in the management of premises where cannabis is in fact smoked even once, is liable, though he had no knowledge and no guilty mind. This is, they argue, a practical act intended to prevent a practical evil. Only by convicting some innocents along with the guilty can sufficient pressure be put upon those who make their living by being concerned in the management of premises. Only thus can they be made alert to prevent cannabis being smoked there. And if the prosecution have to prove knowledge or *mens rea*, many prosecutions will fail and many of the guilty will escape. I find that argument wholly unacceptable.

The notion that some guilty mind is a constituent part of crime and punishment goes back far beyond our common law. And at common law *mens rea* is a necessary element in a crime. Since the Industrial Revolution the increasing complexity of life called into being new duties and crimes which took no account of intent. Those who undertake various industrial and other activities, especially where these affect the life and health of the citizen, may find themselves liable to statutory punishment regardless of knowledge or intent, both in respect of their own acts or neglect and those of their servants. But one must remember that normally *mens rea* is still an ingredient of any offence. Before the court will dispense with the necessity for *mens rea* it has to be satisfied that Parliament so intended. The mere absence of the word 'knowingly' is not enough. But the nature of the crime, the punishment, the absence of social obloquy, the particular mischief and the field of activity in which it occurs, and the wording of the particular section and its context, may show that Parliament intended that the act should be prevented by punishment regardless of intent or knowledge.

Viewing the matter of these principles, it is not possible to accept the prosecution's contention. Even granted that this were in the public health class of case, such as, for instance, are offences created to ensure that food shall be clean, it would be quite unreasonable. It is one thing to make a man absolutely responsible for all his own acts and even vicariously liable for his servants if he engages in a certain type of activity. But it is quite another matter to make him liable for persons over whom he has no control. The innocent hotel-keeper, the lady who keeps lodgings or takes paying guests, the manager of a cinema, the warden of a hostel, the matron of a hospital, the house-master and matron of a boarding school, all these, it is conceded, are, on the prosecution's argument, liable to conviction the moment that irresponsible occupants smoke cannabis cigarettes. And for what purpose is this harsh imposition laid on their backs? No vigilance by night or day can make them safe. The most that vigilance can attain is advance knowledge of their own guilt. If a smell of cannabis comes from a sitting room, they know that they have committed the offence. Should they then go at once to the police and confess their guilt in the hope that they will not be prosecuted? They may think it easier to conceal the matter in the hope that it may never be found out. For if, though morally innocent, they are prosecuted they may lose their livelihood, since thereafter, even though not punished, they are objects of suspicion. I see no real, useful object achieved by such hardship to the innocent. And so wide a possibility of injustice to the innocent could not be justified by any benefit achieved in the determent and punishment of the guilty. If, therefore, the words creating the offence are as wide in their application as the prosecution contend, Parliament cannot have intended an offence to which absence of knowledge or *mens rea* is no defence ...

Notes and queries

1 The corollary to the argument that there is no point in imposing strict liability upon a defendant who could not have taken action to avoid liability is that strict liability can be justified where D has a choice as to whether participate in a particular trade or activity. A trader serving food to the public is regarded as having accepted the risk of liability for selling contaminated food, even where he has no knowledge of the contamination, as an occupational hazard. If he thinks such liability is unfair he should engage in a less hazardous trade. The purpose of strict liability in such cases is to ensure vigilance and to prevent the courts being flooded with 'unmeritorious' defences based on lack of knowledge. As Lord Russell CJ observed in *Parker v Alder* [1899] 1 QB 20, when referring to the imposition of strict liability on a defendant selling adulterated milk:

> Now, assuming that the respondent was entirely innocent morally, and had no means of protecting himself from the adulteration of this milk in the course of transit, has he committed an offence against the Acts? I think that he has.

When the scope and object of these Acts are considered, it will appear that if he were to be relieved from responsibility a wide door would be opened for evading the beneficial provisions of this legislation ... This is one of the class of cases in which the legislature has, in effect, determined that *mens rea* is not necessary to constitute the offence ...

2   The 'implausible defence' issue was obviously a factor in the court's ruling in *R v Bradish* (1990) 90 Cr App R 271, where the appellant was convicted of possessing a prohibited weapon contrary to s 5(1) of the Firearms Act 1968. He had contended that he had not known that the container in his possession was a CS gas canister. Auld J observed:

... the possibilities and consequences of evasion would be too great for effective control, even if the burden of proving lack of guilty knowledge were to be on the accused. The difficulty of enforcement, when presented with such a defence, would be particularly difficult where there is a prosecution for possession of a component part of a firearm or prohibited weapon, as provided for by sections 1 and 5 when read with section 57(1) of the 1968 Act. It would be easy for an accused to maintain, lyingly but with conviction, that he did not recognise the object in his possession as part of a firearm or prohibited weapon. To the argument that the innocent possessor or carrier of firearms or prohibited weapons or parts of them is at risk of unfair conviction under these provisions there has to be balanced the important public policy behind the legislation of protecting the public from the misuse of such dangerous weapons. Just as the Chicago-style gangster might plausibly maintain that he believed his violin case to contain a violin, not a sub-machine gun, so it might be difficult to meet a London lout's assertion that he did not know an unmarked plastic bottle in his possession contained ammonia rather than something to drink.'

3   In *Harrow LBC v Shah* [1999] 3 All ER 302, the Divisional Court held that a defendant could be convicted of selling a lottery ticket to a person under the age of 16, even though there was no fault established on the part of the defendant retailer. Mitchell J observed that the imposition of strict liability would '... unquestionably encourage greater vigilance in preventing the commission of the prohibited act' and that '... no sort of stigma attaches to [the] offence ... '.

CODIFICATION AND LAW REFORM PROPOSALS

Clause 20 of the draft Criminal Code Bill provides as follows:

20(1) Every offence requires a fault element of recklessness with or respect to each of its elements other than fault elements, unless otherwise provided.

As the commentary in Vol II explains:

An enactment creating an offence should ordinarily specify the fault required for the offence or expressly provide that the offence is one of strict liability in respect of one or more identified elements. It is necessary, however, to have a general rule for the interpretation of any offence the definition of which does not state, in respect of one or more elements, whether fault is required or what degree of fault is required. The absence of a consistent rule of interpretation has been a regrettable source of uncertainty in English law ... We considered a suggestion that the clause should seek to make the presumption displaceable only by express provision requiring some fault other than recklessness, or stating that no fault is required, with respect to an element of an offence. We do not think that this would be appropriate. We are mindful of the 'constitutional platitude' pointed out by Lord Ackner in *Hunt* [1987] AC 352 at 380 that the courts must give effect to what Parliament has provided not only 'expressly' but also by 'necessary implication'. If the terms of a future enactment creating an offence plainly implied an intention to displace the presumption created by clause 20(1), the courts would no doubt feel obliged to give effect to that intention even if the present clause were to require express provision for the purpose [Vol II, paras 8.25–8.28].

Further reading

DJ Lanham, '*Larsonneur* revisited' [1976] Crim LR 276

L Leigh, *Strict and Vicarious Liability*, 1982, London: Sweet & Maxwell

G Richardson, 'Strict liability for regulatory crime: the empirical research' [1987] Crim LR 295

BS Jackson, '*Storkwain*: a case study in strict liability and self-regulation' [1991] Crim LR 892

CHAPTER 6

MISTAKE

Although it is common to hear mistake spoken of as a substantive defence in criminal law, in reality a defendant pleading mistake is almost always denying that he had the *mens rea* for the offence with which he has been charged. On this basis it is likely to be the case that mistake is the most commonly pleaded 'defence' in criminal law. It is possible to identify three categories of defence argument based on mistake.

(a) Where the defendant claims that he did not know that a particular activity was prohibited by law, that is, mistake of law.

(b) Where a defendant makes a mistake of fact. The key here is to distinguish between relevant and irrelevant mistakes.

- If D burgles A's house mistaking it for P's, he has made a mistake of fact but not one that has any relevance in terms of denying the *mens rea* of the offence.

- If D points a gun at P and pulls the trigger, wrongly believing the gun to be unloaded, with the result that P suffers injuries, D has again made a mistake of fact, but not one that necessarily denies the *mens rea* for the offence. D may not have intended to injure P, but he may still be regarded as reckless in not having checked whether or not the gun was loaded before pulling the trigger. In effect this type of mistake is a denial of foresight of consequences.

- D fires his gun at what he believes to be a small deer. In fact it is poacher who dies from the resultant injuries. D has made a mistake of fact, but this time it relates to an element of the offence that the prosecution has to prove – that is, on a murder charge the prosecution has to prove that D intended to kill or do grievous bodily harm to a human being. If D's mistake of fact leads him to believe he is shooting at an animal, and he therefore acts with intent to attack an animal, he lacks the *mens rea* for the offence. The mistake is evidence that D lacked the *mens rea*. As the extracts below indicate, the debate here has centred around whether D should be judged on the facts as he believes them to be, or whether D should only be able to rely on a mistake of fact that the reasonable person would have made.

(c) D may make a mistake of fact that leads him to believe in the existence of justificatory or exculpatory circumstances. For example he may mistakenly believe that P is consenting to what would otherwise be an indecent assault, or D may mistakenly believe that P is about to attack him, leading D to use force on P that would be justified as self-defence if the facts were as D believed them to be; this aspect of mistake is considered further in Chapters 14, 16 and 17.

MISTAKE OF LAW

Secretary of State for Trade v Hart [1982] 1 WLR 481 (DC)

Woolf J: This is a case stated by a metropolitan stipendiary magistrate in respect of his adjudication whilst sitting at Wells Street, on 7 April 1981, when he dismissed two informations which had been preferred against the defendant by the prosecutor, the Secretary of State for Trade and Industry. The first of those two offences related to the fact that the defendant in the case of a company (AMF Ashby Metal Fabrications Ltd) of which he was a director and secretary, acted as an auditor when he knew he was disqualified for such appointment. The second offence was similar in nature in that he had acted as auditor of a company called Auger Safety Equipment Ltd, knowing that he was disqualified for appointment as auditor of a company in that he was also a director of that company. The offences were alleged to be contrary to s 161(2) of the Companies Act 1948 and s 13 of the Companies Act 1976.

The fact that the defendant, during the relevant period, had acted as auditor of those companies, at a time when he was disqualified as alleged in the information, was not in dispute before the magistrate. The only matter that was in issue was whether or not the defendant had the necessary *mens rea* to constitute the offences which were alleged ...

The defendant had contended, before the magistrate, that he was not guilty because he was ignorant of the statutory provisions which made him disqualified as a matter of law from holding the office of auditor of the respective companies. The Secretary of State is concerned that such ignorance is treated as amounting to a defence in law, and I can well understand that concern because of the important part the auditor plays in company law. He is relied upon to act as a watch-dog in relation to the affairs of companies and clearly it is very much in the public interest that persons should not act as auditors at a time when they are as a matter of fact disqualified from so acting. However, it has to be remembered that the defendant was charged with a criminal offence and therefore it is, in my view, necessary to answer the question which is raised by the case stated, by reference to the relevant statutory provisions ...

[The] position has now been radically changed by the provisions of s 13 of the Companies Act 1976. Subsection (1) of that Act deals with persons who are qualified for appointment as auditors. Subsection (5) provides:

> No person shall act as auditor of a company at a time when he knows that he is disqualified for appointment to that office; and if an auditor of a company to his knowledge becomes so disqualified during his term of office he shall thereupon vacate his office and give notice in writing to the company that he has vacated it by reason of such disqualification.

Subsection (5) therefore creates the disqualification which arises as a result of persons holding particular offices. It is significant that the provisions of subsection (5) are very different in terms to those of s 161(2) of the Act of 1948. Section 161 of the Act of 1948 contained an absolute prohibition certain persons holding the office of appointment as an auditor of a company. Subsection (5) puts it in a different way: 'No person shall act as auditor of a company at a time when he knows that he is disqualified for appointment ...' and requires a person who becomes aware that he is so disqualified to vacate the office and give notice of that matter. Section 13(6) of the Act of 1976 widens the categories of persons who could be guilty of a criminal offence in relation to this matter. It provides:

> Any person who acts as auditor in contravention of subsection (5) above or fails without reasonable excuse to give notice of vacating his office as required by that subsection shall be guilty of an offence and liable on conviction on indictment to a fine and on summary conviction to a fine not exceeding £40 for every day during which the contravention continues.

It is subsections (5) and (6) that this court is primarily concerned with in answering the question posed by this appeal. Mr Moses, on behalf of the Secretary of State, argues that when subsection (5) and subsection (6) are read together the position is one where a person is guilty of an offence under those provisions if he knows the facts of circumstances which cause him to be disqualified but nonetheless acts as an auditor. He contends that it is not necessary for a person charged with an offence under those subsections also to know that as a matter of law he is disqualified. He submits that it is sufficient if he knows the facts and circumstances, because like anyone else a person acting as an auditor should be aware of the provisions of law which deal with the disqualification for an appointment to the office of auditor.

This is, however, as I have already pointed out, a criminal offence which is created by s 13(5) and (6). In my view it is at least equally consistent with the ordinary meaning of the words which are used in those subsections, that their effect is that a person is not guilty of an offence and is not disqualified from acting as an auditor unless he in fact knows not only the relevant facts but also that in consequence of the facts he is disqualified by the law for appointment to the office. The words in their ordinary interpretation are wholly consistent with a view of the subsections which means that a person in the position of the defendant must be aware of the statutory restrictions which exist against his holding the appointment ...

Ormrod LJ: ... We have to begin by construing the relevant section which, as Woolf J has pointed out, is the combined effect of subsections (5) and (6) of s 13 of the Companies Act 1976. We have to construe those words in the context of the Act itself and to a limited extent in relation to the legislative history, which in this case strikes me as quite important.

Up until 1976, it was not a criminal offence for an officer (or a company director or secretary) to act as auditor of the company if he were otherwise qualified to do so. The fact that he was disqualified had possibly various effects from a civil point of view, but it was not a criminal offence. It was, however, a criminal offence from 1948 onwards (and perhaps earlier) for a body corporate to act as an auditor to a company, and subsection (5) of s 161 of the Act of 1948 imposed a fine of £100 on a body corporate which so acted.

In 1976 it was presumably considered necessary to insert, in the process of 'topping up' the qualifications for auditors, a provision which made it a criminal offence to act in contravention of the section dealing with the qualifications. The language which Parliament has chosen to use seems to me to be explicit, straightforward and quite simple. [His Lordship read s 13(5) and continued:]

Subsection (6) makes it an offence to act in contravention of subsection (5). In other words, the offence, as was correctly set out in the information, is that the defendant acted as an auditor of a company at a time when he knew that he was disqualified for that appointment. And interpreting the language quite simply, it seems to me to indicate that the defendant is not guilty of a criminal offence unless he knew that he was disqualified.

If that means that he is entitled to rely on ignorance of the law as a defence, in contrast to the usual practice and the usual rule, the answer is that the section gives him that right. Whether it does so intentionally or not is another matter. Whether it is easy for anyone to prove or establish that, in the defendant's position, he did not know he was disqualified, will be problematical.

But in this case the facts are unusual. The magistrate who heard the facts, and who saw the defendant give his evidence, accepted him as a person who gave a true and honest account of his position, however improbable it may seem, and accordingly he acquitted the defendant. In my judgment he was fully entitled to do so ...

AG's Ref (No 1 of 1995) [1996] 1 WLR 970 (CA)

Lord Taylor of Gosforth CJ: ... This is a reference by the Attorney General (No 1 of 1995) under s 36 of the Criminal Justice Act 1972.

On 22 November 1994 the respondents were convicted in the Crown Court at Teesside of a number of offences under s 35 of the Banking Act 1987. They were sentenced to a term of imprisonment. The offences involved fraudulent inducements to make deposits.

They were, however, acquitted on the trial judge's directions of two counts charged under s 3(1) of the Banking Act 1987. The judge withdrew those counts from the jury's considerations following submissions at the conclusion of the case for the Crown. Her Majesty's Attorney General now seeks the option of this court on points of law, namely:

(1) Whether on a charge against a company director of consenting to the acceptance of a deposit contrary to ss 3 and 96 of the Banking Act 1987, ignorance of the law as to the requirement of the authorisation of the Bank of England is a defence; and

(2) what *mens rea* is required to be proved to show 'consent'.

The terms of the two relevant sections of the Banking Act 1987 are as follows, so far as is relevant. Section 3(1):

No person shall ... accept a deposit in the course of carrying on ... a business which for the purposes of this Act is a deposit-taking business unless that person is an institution for the time being authorised by the Bank [of England] under ... this Act.

Section 96(1):

Where an offence under this Act committed by a body corporate is proved to have been committed with the consent or connivance of, or to be attributable to any neglect on the part of any director, manager, secretary or other similar officer of the body corporate, or any person who was purporting to act in any such capacity, he, as well as the body corporate, shall be guilty of that offence ...

It is convenient for completeness to refer also to s 96(4), which provides:

In any proceedings for an offence under this Act it shall be a defence for the person charged to prove that he took all reasonable precautions and exercised all due diligence to avoid the commission of such an offence by himself or any person under his control.

The facts of the present case can be shortly stated. The respondents were directors of a company trading in the north of England. It was a small company dealing in insurance and investment brokerage. The first respondent, F was the chairman. He ran the business. He and his wife were the only directors. The second respondent, B was his right-hand man and acted as a *de facto* director.

There was evidence that from 1987 onwards the company was accepting deposits in the course of carrying on a deposit-taking business and that both were men who were directly concerned in that activity. Large sums of money were deposited, amounting to some £750,000 in total. In order to induce such deposits the respondents told a number of the depositors that the money would be lent on as bridging loans for which the company would hold charges as security. In fact the money thus raised was being diverted into a night club venture. When that venture failed in 1989, most of the money was lost. It was in respect of the representations made by respondents to the depositors that the charges which were proved against the respondents were based.

The company was not authorised by the bank to accept deposits. In February 1992 the respondents were arrested and in October 1992 they were charged. Following their arrest interviews were sought with the two respondents. They declined to answer questions. However, in September 1992 the second respondent volunteered an interview. Towards the end of it the detective sergeant asked the second respondent what explanation he could give for the unlicensed deposit-taking of the company. In the course of questioning it emerged from the second respondent that he had no idea that in order to take people's money on deposit or to take people's money on investment you have to be licensed by the Bank of England.

The two counts in question were specimen offences. Count 1 related to Mrs B. She had originally invested a total of about £20,000 through the company. She said that at some point after her initial investment the second respondent offered her 17% on her money and the respondents had carte blanche from her to invest the money where it would get 17%. The money was then deposited in the company's 'bridging fund'. The deposit was evidenced by a document called a 'property bridging bond' which was signed by the second respondent. It referred to an 'investment', which the prosecution said was truly a deposit, of £19,210 on 25 November 1988 at a flat rate interest of 17%. The first respondent later acknowledged in a letter dated 27 December 1989 that Mrs B had been offered participation in the bridging fund scheme with fixed interest.

Count 2 concerned Mr and Mrs G who placed £54,511 in the company's bridging fund via an intermediary. That transaction was evidenced by an agreement with the company signed by the second respondent, which was found at the first respondent's house.

At the end of the prosecution case the defence submitted that there was no case to answer on these two counts. It was argued on their behalf that in order to be guilty of consenting to the offence by the company a defendant director must be aware of the relevant facts. If the director was not aware that the business is as a matter of fact deemed to be a deposit-taking business for the purposes of the Act, he cannot give informed consent and therefore cannot consent to the acceptance of the deposit in contravention of s 3 ...

On behalf of the Attorney General, Mr Worsley submits that the judge's rulings and observations to the jury were incorrect. He relies on the well-known principle that ignorance of the law is no excuse. That proposition is not, and indeed could not be, in dispute. The issue on this reference is as to what state of mind has to be established against the accused to make him guilty of 'consenting' under s 96(1).

Mr Worsley submits that if a person mentioned in that subsection knows the facts which constitute the offence under s 3(1) committed by the body corporate and consents to that body's affairs being carried on in accordance with those facts, he is guilty of the offence under s 96(1), subject to any defence he may have under s 96(4). It is no defence to say 'I had no idea it was an offence to carry on that business without authorisation from the bank'.

Mr Worsley relies upon *dicta* in two cases. *Johnson v Youden* [1950] 1 KB 544 was a case in the Divisional Court concerned with aiding and abetting. Lord Goddard CJ said, at 546:

> If a person knows all the facts and is assisting another person to do certain things, and it turns out that the doing of those things constitutes an offence, the person who is assisting is guilty of aiding and abetting that offence, because to allow him to say, 'I knew all those facts but I did not know that an offence was committed', would be allowing him to set up ignorance of the law as a defence.

That passage was expressly approved in the decision of the House of Lords in *R v Churchill (No 2)* [1967] 2 AC 224, a conspiracy case. Viscount Dilhorne, with whom all the other members of the Appellate Committee agreed, said at 237:

> The question is, 'What did they agree to do?'. If what they agreed to do was, on the facts known to them, an unlawful act, they are guilty of conspiracy and cannot excuse themselves by saying that, owing to their ignorance of the law, they did not realise that such an act was a crime.

Mr Collier's submission reflected in the judge's rulings was that unless the accused directors were shown to have addressed their minds specifically to the absence of authorisation or, as it has been called throughout these proceedings, a licence from the Bank of England, they could not be guilty of consenting under s 96(1) ...

... Mr Collier referred the court to *Secretary of State for Trade and Industry v Hart* [1982] 1 WLR 481 upon which the judge relied ... In our judgment that case was crucially different from the present one. There, knowledge of the unlawfulness of his acting as an auditor was an ingredient of the offence which had to be proved against the defendant.

Here, we are satisfied that the correct approach is that suggested on behalf of the Attorney General. A director who knows that acts which can only be performed by the company if it is licensed by the bank, are being performed when in fact no licence exists and who consents to that performance is guilty of the offence charged. The fact that he does not know it is an offence to perform them without a licence, ie ignorance of the law, is no defence.

Mr Collier's suggestion that the director must actively have addressed his mind to the question of licences is wholly unreal. If the two directors, who were wholly responsible for the company's business activity, were ignorant of the need for a licence it can readily be inferred that they knew they did not have one. The concept of a director who is ignorant of the law requiring a licence, focusing his mind on the question of whether he has or has not obtained one is wholly academic. Had anyone approached the defendant directors and asked: 'Have you a licence or authorisation from the Bank of England?' the ready answer would have been 'No', probably supplemented by 'I did not know I needed one'. There would have been no need for a search, an inquiry or a focusing of the mind. Since the question had not occurred to them they would know that the company did not have one.

The ignorance of the law on the point necessarily must in the context of this case point to the knowledge that the company is operating unlicensed. That is not to say that s 96(1) creates an absolute offence in respect of directors. There could, for example, in a company with a number of directors responsible for different limbs of the company's business, be a director who believed the licence had been obtained and was not therefore consenting to the offences committed by the company. That was not the situation here. In our view the judge was wrong to withdraw counts 1 and 2 from the jury.

Our answers to the two questions posed are as follows: (1) No. (2) A defendant has to be proved to know the material facts which constitute the offence by the body corporate and to have agreed to its conduct of its business on the basis of those facts.

Notes and queries

1 A mistake of law will normally only amount to a defence if it is a mistake as to civil law, not criminal law. For example, it is a defence to say 'I thought that I was – as a matter of civil law – the legal owner of the property I damaged' (as in *R v Smith* [1974] QB 354, considered in Chapter 23) but it is not a defence to say 'I thought that a wild creature could not be "property" for the purposes of theft' (cf s 4(4) of the Theft Act 1968).

2 A defendant charged with theft will be able to argue that he was not dishonest if, when he appropriated the property belonging to another he did so in the honest belief that he had the right in law to take the property. Note that he does not have to provide evidence of any such right, it suffices that he believes he has the right. In this sense his mistake as to his civil law rights can provide a shield against criminal liability; see further Chapter 19.

3 A defendant who, through mental illness, is unaware that an activity is prohibited by the criminal law could be entitled to rely on the defence of insanity – see further Chapter 7.

4 Suppose D wants to fix a distinctive mascot to the front of his car and enquires at the local police station as to whether this would be lawful. The duty officer advises him that it would be lawful. D is later stopped by the police and prosecuted because the mascot contravenes a provision in the relevant road traffic legislation. Can D plead mistake of law as a defence? Would there be any public law argument to the effect that he had a legitimate expectation that he would not be prosecuted?

MISTAKE OF FACT RELATING TO AN ELEMENT
OF THE OFFENCE CHARGED

DPP v Morgan [1976] AC 182 (HL)

Lord Hailsham of St Marylebone: ... Although each appellant was originally separately represented, their appeals raise the same point, and they were accorded single representation before this House. The question certified as being of general public importance by the Court of Appeal, and the only point of principle raised on their behalf is:

> Whether, in rape, the defendant can properly be convicted notwithstanding that he in fact believed that the woman consented if such belief was not based on reasonable grounds.

The question arises in the following way. The appellant Morgan and his three co-appellants, who were all members of the RAF, spent the evening of 15 August 1973 in one another's company. The appellant Morgan was significantly older than the other three, and considerably senior to them in rank. He was, as I have said, married to the alleged victim, but not, it seems, at the time habitually sleeping in the same bed. At this time, Mrs Morgan occupied a single bed in the same room as her younger son aged about 11 years, and by the time the appellants arrived at Morgan's house, Mrs Morgan was already in bed and asleep, until she was awoken by their presence.

According to the version of the facts which she gave in evidence, and which was evidently accepted by the jury, she was aroused from her sleep, frog-marched into another room where there was a double bed, held by each of her limbs, arms and legs apart, by the four appellants, while each of the three young appellants in turn had intercourse with her in the presence of the others during which time the other two committed various lewd acts on various parts of her body. When each had finished and had left the room, the appellant Morgan completed the series of incidents by having intercourse with her himself.

According to Mrs Morgan she consented to none of this and made her opposition to what was being done very plain indeed. In her evidence to the court, she said that her husband was the first to seize her and pull her out of bed. She then 'yelled' to the little boy who was sleeping with her to call the police, and later, when the elder boy came out on the landing, she called to him also to get the police, and 'screamed'. Her assailants, however, covered her face and pinched her nose, until she begged them to let her breathe. She was held, wrists and feet, 'dragged' to the neighbouring room, put on the bed where the various incidents occurred. At this stage she was overcome by fear of 'being hit'. There was never a time when her body was free from being held. When it was all over she grabbed her coat, ran out of the house, drove straight to the hospital and immediately complained to the staff of having been raped. This last fact was fully borne out by evidence from the hospital.

In their evidence in court, the appellants made various damaging admissions which certainly amounted to some corroboration of all this. They admitted that some degree of struggle took place in the bedroom, that Mrs Morgan made some noise which was forcibly suppressed, and that she was carried out forcibly into the other bedroom, and that her arms and legs were separately held. In addition to this, Mrs Morgan's evidence was far more fully corroborated by a number of statements (each, of course, admissible only against the maker) which virtually repeated Mrs Morgan's own story but in far greater and more lurid detail. Of course, the appellants repudiated their statements in the witness box, saying that the words were put into their mouths by the police, even though at least one was written out in the hand of the maker of the statement. I think it likely to the extent of moral certainty that the jury accepted that these statements were made as alleged and contained the truth. But I need not rest my opinion on this, since the undeniable fact is that the jury accepted, after an impeccable summing up and adequate corroboration, that Mrs Morgan was telling the truth in her evidence. I mention all these details simply to show, that if, as I think plain, the jury accepted Mrs Morgan's statement in substance there was no possibility whatever of any of the appellants holding any belief whatever, reasonable or otherwise, in their victim's consent to what was being done.

The primary 'defence' was consent. I use the word 'defence' in inverted commas, because, of course, in establishing the crime of rape, the prosecution must exclude consent in order to establish the essential ingredients of the crime. There is no burden at the outset on the accused to raise the issue. Nevertheless, at the close of the prosecution case the appellants had a formidable case to answer, and they answered by going into the witness box and swearing to facts which, if accepted, would have meant, not merely that they reasonably believed that Mrs Morgan had consented, but that, after she entered the bedroom where the acts of intercourse took place, she not merely consented but took an active and enthusiastic part in a sexual orgy which might have excited unfavourable comment in the court of Caligula or Nero.

All four appellants explained in the witness box that they had spent the evening together in Wolverhampton, and by the time of the alleged offence had had a good deal to drink. Their original intention had been to find some women in the town but, when this failed, Morgan made the surprising suggestion to the others that they should all return to his home and have sexual intercourse with his wife. According to the three younger appellants (but not according to Morgan who described this part of their story as 'lying') Morgan told them that they must not be surprised if his wife struggled a bit, since she was 'kinky' and this was the only way in which she could get 'turned on'. However this may be, it is clear that Morgan did invite his three companions home in order that they might have sexual intercourse with his wife and, no doubt, he may well have led them in one way or another to believe that she would consent to their doing so. This, however, would only be a matter predisposing them to believe that Mrs Morgan consented, and would not in any way establish that, at the time, they believed she did consent whilst they were having intercourse.

I need not enter into the details of what the appellants said happened after they arrived at the house. As I have said they admitted that some degree of struggle took place in the wife's bedroom. But all asserted that after she got into the double bedroom she not merely consented to but actively co-operated with and enjoyed what was being done. She caressed and masturbated their private parts, she licked their private parts, she made noises and 'moans' of pleasure. When it was all over she said, 'Have you all had a go?', but not in a sarcastic sense. In other words, she was actively participating in a sexual orgy, and was anxious to see that each of the participants had enjoyed himself as much as she.

The choice before the jury was thus between two stories each wholly incompatible with the other, and in my opinion it would have been quite sufficient for the judge, after suitable warnings about the burden of proof, corroboration, separate verdicts and the admissibility of the statements only against the makers, to tell the jury that they must really choose between the two versions, the one of a violent and unmistakable rape of a singularly unpleasant kind, and the other of active co-operation in a sexual orgy, always remembering that if in reasonable doubt as to which was true they must give the appellants the benefit of it. In spite of the valiant attempts of counsel to suggest some way in which the stories could be taken apart in sections and give rise in some way to a situation which might conceivably have been acceptable to a reasonable jury in which, while the victim was found not to have consented, the appellants, or any of them could conceivably either reasonably or unreasonably have thought she did consent, I am utterly unable to see any conceivable half-way house. The very material which could have introduced doubt into matter of consent goes equally to belief and vice versa. As the judge's summing up, so far as relevant to this point, was wholly impeccable, and as the jury obviously accepted the victim's story in its substance there is in my view no conceivable way in which a miscarriage of justice can have taken place and therefore no possibility of quashing these convictions, even though, as I shall show, the substantial question of principle should be answered in favour of the appellants' contention.

The certified question arises because counsel for the appellants raised the question whether, even if the victim consented, the appellants may not have honestly believed that she did. As I have pointed out, the question was wholly unreal, because if there was reasonable doubt about belief, the same material must have given rise to reasonable doubt about consent, and vice versa. But, presumably because, at that stage, the jury's view of the matter had not been sought, the matter was left to them, as the appellants complain, in a form which implied that they could only acquit if the mistaken belief in consent was reasonable, and it was not enough that it should be honest. This ruling was originally made at the close of the case for the prosecution, but, as it was subsequently embodied in the summing up, it is sufficient to refer to this. I will quote the principal passage *in extenso* from the record.

His Lordship then quoted from the summing up, in the course of which the trial judge directed the jury that where a defendant says that he believed that the woman was consenting to sexual intercourse, 'his belief must be a reasonable belief; such a belief as a reasonable man would entertain if he applied his mind and thought about the matter ...'.

... [It was submitted on behalf of the appellants that an] honest belief in consent ... is enough. It matters not whether it be also reasonable ... [T]he appellants contend [that] ... the fact to be refuted by the prosecution is honesty and not honesty plus reasonableness ...

If ... it is necessary for any belief in the woman's consent to be 'a reasonable belief' before the defendant is entitled to an acquittal, it must either be because the mental ingredient in rape is not 'to have intercourse and to have it without her consent' but simply 'to have intercourse' subject to a special defence of 'honest and reasonable belief', or alternatively to have intercourse without a reasonable belief in her consent ... [I]n my view each [of these alternatives] is open to insuperable objections of principle. No doubt it would be possible, by statute, to devise a law by which intercourse, voluntarily entered into, was an absolute offence, subject to a 'defence' of belief whether honest or honest and reasonable, of which the 'evidential' burden is primarily on the defence and the 'probative' burden on the prosecution. But in my opinion such is not the crime of rape as it has hitherto been understood. The prohibited act in rape is to have intercourse without the victim's consent. The minimum *mens rea* or guilty mind in most common law offences, including rape, is the intention to do the prohibited act ...

His Lordship held that the trial judge had correctly stated the law when he said:

... Further, the prosecution has to prove that each defendant intended to have sexual intercourse with this woman without her consent. Not merely that he intended to have intercourse with her but that he intended to have intercourse without her consent. Therefore, if the defendant believed or may have believed that Mrs Morgan consented to him having sexual intercourse with her, then there would be no such intent in his mind and he would not be guilty of the offence of rape, but such a belief must be honestly held by the defendant in the first place ...

The only qualification I would make to [this part of the] direction of the learned [judge] ... is the refinement ... that if the intention of the accused is to have intercourse *nolens volens*, that is recklessly and not caring whether the victim be a consenting party or not, that is equivalent on ordinary principles to an intent to do the prohibited act without the consent of the victim ...

Once one has accepted, what seems to me abundantly clear, that the prohibited act in rape is non-consensual sexual intercourse, and that the guilty state of mind is an intention to commit it, it seems to me to follow as a matter of inexorable logic that there is no room either for a 'defence' of honest belief or mistake, or of a defence of honest and reasonable belief and mistake. Either the prosecution proves that the accused had the requisite intent, or it does not. In the former case it succeeds, and in the latter it fails. Since honest belief clearly negatives intent, the reasonableness or otherwise of that belief can only be evidence for or against the view that the belief and therefore the intent was actually held, and it matters not whether, to quote Bridge J [giving the judgment of the Court of Appeal in the present case], 'the definition of a crime includes no specific element beyond the prohibited act' ...

... I am content to rest my view of the instant case on the crime of rape by saying that it is my opinion that the prohibited act is and always has been intercourse without consent of the victim and the mental element is and always has been the intention to commit that act, or the equivalent intention of having intercourse willy-nilly not caring whether the victim consents or no. A failure to prove this involves an acquittal because the intent, an essential ingredient, is lacking. It matters not why it is lacking if only it is not there, and in particular it matters not that the intention is lacking only because of a belief not based on reasonable grounds ...

For the above reasons I would answer the question certified in the negative, but would apply the proviso to s 2(1) of the Criminal Appeal Act 1968 on the ground that no miscarriage of justice has or conceivably could have occurred. In my view, therefore these appeals should be dismissed.

Lord Cross of Chelsea and **Lord Fraser of Tullybelton** delivered concurring speeches.

Lord Simon of Glaisdale and **Lord Edmund-Davies** dissented.

B v DPP [2000] 1 All ER 833

For the facts see the extract in Chapter 5.

Lord Nicholls:

Reasonable belief or honest belief

The existence of the presumption is beyond dispute, but in one respect the traditional formulation of the presumption calls for re-examination. This respect concerns the position of a defendant who acted under a mistaken view of the facts. In this regard, the presumption is expressed traditionally to the effect that an honest mistake by a defendant does not avail him unless the mistake was made on reasonable grounds. Thus, in *R v Tolson* (1889) 23 QBD 168, 181, Cave J observed:

> At common law an honest and reasonable belief in the existence of circumstances, which, if true, would make the act for which a prisoner is indicted an innocent act has always been held to be a good defence. This doctrine is embodied in the somewhat uncouth maxim *'actus non facit reum, nisi mens sit rea'*. Honest and reasonable mistake stands on the same footing as absence of the reasoning faculty, as in infancy, or perversion of that faculty, as in lunacy ... So far as I am aware it has never been suggested that these exceptions do not equally apply in the case of statutory offences unless they are excluded expressly or by necessary implication.

The other judges in that case expressed themselves to a similar effect. In *Bank of New South Wales v Piper* [1897] AC 383, 389–90, the Privy Council likewise espoused the 'reasonable belief' approach:

> ... the absence of *mens rea* really consists in an honest and reasonable belief entertained by the accused of facts which, if true, would make the act charged against him innocent.

In *Sweet v Parsley* [1970] AC 132, 163, Lord Diplock referred to a general principle of construction of statutes creating criminal offences, in similar terms:

> ... a general principle of construction of any enactment, which creates a criminal offence, [is] that, even where the words used to describe the prohibited conduct would not in any other context connote the necessity for any particular mental element, they are nevertheless to be read as subject to the implication that a necessary element in the offence is the absence of a belief, held honestly and upon reasonable grounds, in the existence of facts which, if true, would make the act innocent.

The 'reasonable belief' school of thought held unchallenged sway for many years. But over the last quarter of a century there have been several important cases where a defence of honest but mistaken belief was raised. In deciding these cases the courts have placed new, or renewed, emphasis on the subjective nature of the mental element in criminal offences. The courts have rejected the reasonable belief approach and preferred the honest belief approach. When *mens rea* is ousted by a mistaken belief, it is as well ousted by an unreasonable belief as by a reasonable belief. In the pithy phrase of Lawton LJ in *R v Kimber* [1983] 1 WLR 1118, 1122, it is the defendant's belief, not the grounds on which it is based, which goes to negative the intent. This approach is well encapsulated in a passage in the judgment of Lord Lane CJ in *R v Williams (Gladstone)* (1984) 78 Cr App R 276, 281:

> The reasonableness or unreasonableness of the defendant's belief is material to question of whether the belief was held by the defendant at all. If the belief was in fact held, its unreasonableness, so far as guilt or innocence is concerned, is neither here nor there. It is irrelevant. Were it otherwise, the defendant would be convicted because he was negligent in failing to recognise that the victim was not consenting ... and so on.

Considered as a matter of principle, the honest belief approach must be preferable. By definition the mental element in a crime is concerned with a subjective state of mind, such as intent or belief. To the extent that an overriding objective limit ('on reasonable grounds') is introduced, the subjective element is displaced. To that extent a person who lacks the necessary intent or belief may nevertheless commit the offence. When that occurs the defendant's 'fault' lies exclusively in falling short of an objective standard. His crime lies in his negligence. A statute may so provide expressly or by necessary implication. But this can have no place in a common law principle, of general application, which is concerned with the need for a mental element as an essential ingredient of a criminal offence.

The traditional formulation of the common law presumption, exemplified in Lord Diplock's famous exposition in *Sweet v Parsley*, cited above, is out of step with this recent line of authority, in so far as it envisages that a mistaken belief must be based on reasonable grounds. This seems to be a relic from the days before a defendant in a criminal case could give evidence in his own defence. It is not surprising that in those times juries judged a defendant's state of mind by the conduct to be expected of a reasonable person.

I turn to the recent authorities. The decision which heralded this development in criminal law was the decision of your Lordships' House in *Director of Public Prosecutions v Morgan* [1976] AC 182. This was a case of rape. By a bare majority the House held that where a defendant had sexual intercourse with a woman without her consent but believing she did consent, he was not guilty of rape even though he had no reasonable grounds for his belief. The intent to commit rape involves an intention to have intercourse without the woman's consent or with a reckless indifference to whether she consents or not. It would be inconsistent with this definition if an honest belief that she did consent led to an acquittal only when it was based on reasonable grounds. One of the minority, Lord Edmund-Davies, would have taken a different view had he felt free to do so. In *R v Kimber* [1983] 1 WLR 1118, a case of indecent assault, the Court of Appeal applied the approach of the majority in *Morgan's* case. The guilty state of mind was the intent to use personal violence to a woman without her consent. If the defendant did not so intend, he was entitled to be found not guilty. If he did not so intend because he believed she was consenting, the prosecution will have failed to prove the charge, irrespective of the grounds for the defendant's belief. The court disapproved of the suggestion made in the earlier case of *R v Phekoo* [1981] 1 WLR 1117, 1127, that this House intended to confine the views expressed in *Morgan's* case to cases of rape.

This reasoning was taken a step further in *R v Williams (Gladstone)* (1984) 78 Cr App R 276. There the Court of Appeal, presided over by Lord Lane CJ, adopted the same approach in a case of assault occasioning actual bodily harm. The context was a defence that the defendant believed that the person whom he assaulted was unlawfully assaulting a third party. In *Beckford v R* [1988] AC 130 a similar issue came before the Privy Council on an appeal from Jamaica in a case involving a defence of self-defence to a charge of murder. The Privy Council applied the decisions in *Morgan's* case and *Williams'* case. Lord Griffiths said, at 144:

> If then a genuine belief, albeit without reasonable grounds, is a defence to rape because it negatives the necessary intention, so also must a genuine belief in facts which if true would justify self-defence be a defence to a crime of personal violence because the belief negatives the intent to act unlawfully.

Lord Griffiths also observed, at a practical level, that where there are no reasonable grounds to hold a belief it will surely only be in exceptional circumstances that a jury will conclude that such a belief was or might have been held. Finally in this summary, in *Blackburn v Bowering* [1994] 1 WLR 1324, the Court of Appeal, presided over by Sir Thomas Bingham MR, applied the same approach to the exercise by the court of its contempt jurisdiction in respect of an alleged assault on officers of the court while in the execution of their duty.

The Crown advanced no suggestion to your Lordships that any of these recent cases was wrongly decided. This is not surprising, because the reasoning in these cases is compelling. Thus, the traditional formulation of the common law presumption must now be modified appropriately. Otherwise the formulation would not be an accurate reflection of the current state of the criminal law regarding mistakes of fact. Lord Diplock's *dictum* in *Sweet v Parsley* [1970] AC 132, 163, must in future be read as though the reference to reasonable grounds were omitted.

I add one further general observation. In principle, an age-related ingredient of a statutory offence stands on no different footing from any other ingredient. If a man genuinely believes that the girl with whom he is committing a grossly indecent act is over fourteen, he is not intending to commit such an act with a girl under fourteen ...

Lord Steyn: ... the following supplementary certified questions arise: (a) Must the belief be held on reasonable grounds? (b) On whom does the burden of proof lie? Counsel for the Crown did not argue, in the alternative, that the belief must be held on reasonable grounds. Nevertheless, I initially regarded such a requirement as an acceptable solution. A basis for this view would be Lord Diplock's observation in *Sweet v Parsley*. This view is however contrary to the way in which our criminal law has subsequently developed. In *DPP v Morgan* ... the House of Lords held by a majority of three to two that when a defendant had sexual intercourse with a woman without her consent, genuinely believing that she did consent, he was not guilty of rape, even if he had no reasonable grounds for his belief. The importance of this decision for the coherent development of English law was not immediately appreciated. The next stage in the development was the decision of the Court of Appeal in *R v Williams* ... Holding that the jury had been materially misdirected, the Court of Appeal, applying the logic of *Morgan*, held that if the defendant believed, reasonably or not, in the existence of facts which would justify the force used in self-defence, he did not intend to use unlawful force. The decision in *Williams* was followed and approved and applied by the Privy Council in *Beckford* ... It was held that if the defendant honestly believed the circumstances to be such as would, if true, justify his use of force to defend himself from attack and the force was no more than reasonable to resist the attack, he was entitled to be acquitted of murder; since the intent to act unlawfully would be negatived by his belief, however mistaken or unreasonable. *Morgan* was described as the 'a landmark decision in the development of the common law': *Beckford v R* at 145C. There has been a general shift from objectivism to subjectivism in this branch of the law. It is now settled as a matter of general principle that mistake, whether reasonable or not, is a defence where it prevents the defendant from having the *mens rea* which the law requires for the crime with which he is charged. It would be in disharmony with this development now to rule that in respect of a defence under subsection 1(1) of the Act of 1960 the belief must be based on reasonable grounds. Moreover, if such a special solution were to be adopted, it would almost certainly create uncertainty in other parts of the criminal law. It would be difficult to confine it on a principled basis to subsection 1(1). I would answer question (a) in the negative.

MISTAKE OF FACT RELATING TO THE AVAILABILITY OF A DEFENCE

For mistake relating to circumstances justifying the use of force in self-defence see Chapter 14. For mistake as to consent see Chapter 16 (assaults) and Chapter 17 (indecent assault).

Notes and queries

1   What is the test for mistake where the offence requires *Caldwell* recklessness? Where an offence can be committed with what may be called 'objective recklessness' (that is, failure to appreciate an obvious risk – see *Caldwell* [1982] AC 341, dealt with in Chapter 4) is it the case that a mistake can only amount to a defence if a reasonable person could have made the same mistake as the accused? See *R v S* (1983) 78 Cr App R 149 (rape); *R v Kimber* [1983] 1 WLR 1118 (indecent assault); *Chief Constable of Avon and Somerset v Shimmen* (1986) 84 Cr App R 7 and *R v Merrick* [1995] Crim LR 802 (criminal damage).

2   Section 1 of the Sexual Offences (Amendment) Act 1976 provides that the presence or absence of reasonable grounds for a belief that the victim was consenting to sexual intercourse is a matter to which the jury shall have regard in considering whether the accused did in fact hold that belief.

3   Where a defendant makes a mistake of fact because he has, of his own volition, reduced himself to a state of intoxication, the mistake will not avail him if he is charged with a crime of basic intent – see further Chapter 8.

CODIFICATION AND LAW REFORM PROPOSALS

Clause 21 of the draft Criminal Code Bill (DCCB) provides:

21(1) Ignorance or mistake as to a matter of law does not affect liability to conviction of an offence except –

(a) where so provided; or

(b) where it negatives a fault element of the offence

The commentary to these clauses explains:

8.29 There is abundant authority that the accused's ignorance of the offence he is alleged to have committed or his mistake as to its application, will not relieve him of liability. This principle appears to be an absolute one. So it seems appropriate to make explicit in the Code one of the best known maxims of the common law. The effect will be to preclude any attempt to stimulate judicial recognition of exceptions to the general rule by reliance on clause 45(c), under which common law defences can be developed, but only if they are not inconsistent with other Code provisions.

8.30 The Code team in their Report drew attention to the case for the recognition of a defence of excusable mistake of law, particularly where the act that constitutes an offence has been done in reliance upon a statement of law made by a competent court or a responsible official. Such a defence, as the team acknowledged, could only be introduced in the light of a major law reform exercise involving detailed consideration and extensive consultation. We have not been able to undertake such an exercise in the context of the present project.

8.31 *Express defence of ignorance or mistake of law.* Paragraph (a) contemplates the possibility that such a defence might be provided in relation to a particular offence. Examples are likely to be rare.

8.32 *Ignorance or mistake negativing a fault element.* 'Ignorance of the law is no defence' is a popular aphorism with a good deal of power to mislead. It therefore seems worthwhile to state, in paragraph (b), the truth that a mistake as to the law, equally with one as to fact, can be the reason why a person is not at fault in the way prescribed for an offence. A simple example occurs where a person destroys property in the mistaken belief that it is his own to do with as he wishes. He does not intentionally or recklessly destroy property belonging to another within the meaning of clause 180.

The specific issue of non-publication of the criminal law, in so far as it relates to orders provided for in statutory instruments, is dealt with by cl 46 of the DCCB, which provides:

46(1) A person is not guilty of an offence consisting of a contravention of a statutory instrument if –

(a) at the time of his act the instrument has not been issued by Her Majesty's Stationery Office; and

(b) by that time reasonable steps have not been taken to bring the purport of the instrument to the notice of the public, or of persons likely to be affected by it, or of that person.

(2) The burden of proving the matter referred to in subsection (1)(a) is on the defendant.

This proposal effectively reproduces s 3(2) of the Statutory Instruments Act 1946 in the style of the DCCB.

CHAPTER 7

SANE AND INSANE AUTOMATISM

The imposition of criminal liability is based on a number of presumptions, in particular that the acts of the defendant which cause a prohibited result or conduct were freely willed and voluntary, in the sense that the defendant was aware of his actions and able to control them. If there is evidence of involuntariness it may provide a partial or complete answer to a prosecution. For these purposes involuntariness should be distinguished from mere reluctance or compulsion. Where a defendant is forced by a third party, or indeed by circumstances, to commit an offence he may have a defence of duress or necessity – see further Chapter 13. This chapter looks at the strategies open to a defendant who claims that he was unaware of his actions at the time of the offence alleged. As will be seen the defence that can be raised by the defendant in such circumstances will depend, to a large extent on the cause of his lack of consciousness and the extent to which he is seen, by the prosecution and the court, as representing a threat to the safety of others.

SANE AUTOMATISM

A defendant who raises the defence of sane automatism is claiming that he was unaware of his actions and thus unable to control them. In that sense his actions were involuntary. If the defence succeeds it amounts to a complete defence. Involuntariness can obviously be seen as a denial of *actus reus*, but if one accepts that voluntariness is an aspect of *actus reus* as well, in the sense that an act is only *reus* if it is voluntary, the defence could also succeed where the offence alleged is one of strict liability.

Hill v Baxter [1958] 1 QB 277 (DC)

Lord Goddard CJ: This special case stated by justices for the County Borough of Brighton concerns two informations preferred against the respondent, the first for the dangerous driving of a motor vehicle contrary to s 11(1) of the Road Traffic Act, 1930, and the second for failing to conform to a Halt sign contrary to s 49(b) of the Act. The facts found by the justices are that at 10.45 pm on the evening of 12 April this year the respondent drove a motor van along Springfield Road, Brighton, in a westerly direction and where that road crosses Beaconsfield Road he ignored an illuminated Halt sign, drove across the road junction at a fast speed and came into collision with a car which was being driven northwards in Beaconsfield Road. The respondent's van then carried on for a short distance and overturned. A police constable arrived and found the respondent in a dazed condition and at the hospital to which he was taken he said:

> I remember being in Preston Circus going to Withdean. I don't remember anything else until I was searching for my glasses. I don't know what happened.

The justices found that to be in Springfield Road on the way to Withdean from Preston Circus involved a substantial and unnecessary detour but that the respondent must have exercised skill in driving in order to reach Springfield Road by whatever route he took. The justices apparently accepted the respondent's evidence and found that he remembered nothing from the time when he was at Preston Circus till the accident had happened. They were of opinion that the respondent was not conscious of what he was doing after leaving Preston Circus and to this finding they add the words 'with the implication that he was not capable of forming any intention as to his manner of driving'. They dismissed the informations, accepting a submission that loss of memory could only be attributed to the respondent being overcome by illness without warning ...

The first thing to be remembered is that the statute contains an absolute prohibition against driving dangerously or ignoring Halt signs. No question of mens rea enters into the offence; it is no answer to a charge under those sections to say 'I did not mean to drive dangerously' or 'I did not notice the Halt sign'. The justices' finding, that the respondent was not capable of forming any intention as to the manner of driving, is really immaterial. What they evidently meant was that the respondent was in a state of automatism ...

I agree that there may be cases where the circumstances are such that the accused could not really be said to be driving at all. Suppose he had a stroke or an epileptic fit, both instances of what may properly be called acts of God; he might well be in the driver's seat even with his hands on the wheel but in such a state of unconsciousness that he could not be said to be driving. A blow from a stone or a swarm of bees I think introduces some conception akin to *novus actus interveniens*. In this case, however, I am content to say that the evidence falls far short of what would justify a court holding that this man was in some automatous state. There was no evidence that he was suffering from anything to account for what is so often called a 'black-out' and which probably, if genuine, is epileptic in origin ...

The degree of involuntariness required for automatism

AG's Ref (No 2 of 1992) [1994] QB 91 (CA)

Lord Taylor of Gosforth CJ: ... The point is defined in the reference as follows: 'Whether the state described as "driving without awareness" should, as a matter of law, be capable of founding a defence of automatism.' This formulation relates to expert evidence given in the particular case. However, we take the point more generally to raise the question: 'What are the requirements and limits of the defence of automatism?'

On 6 September 1991 in the Crown Court at Worcester, the respondent was acquitted after a five-day trial of two offences of causing death by reckless driving.

On 16 April 1991 the respondent, who was a professional heavy-goods-lorry driver, drove his lorry from Lincolnshire to Liverpool between the hours of 10 am and 4 pm. At about 6 pm he set off again, driving south on the M6 and then on the M5. Throughout the day he had taken appropriate breaks to comply with regulations. He ate a full meal at a service station between 10 and 10.30 pm. He stopped at another service station later and put on an extra coat. He then drove a further 22 miles before the accident occurred. After junction 6 on the M5, the motorway narrowed from three to two lanes. On passing junction 7, the respondent steered, apparently deliberately, on to the hard shoulder. He drove some 700 metres along that shoulder with only inches to spare on either side before crashing into a stationary white van. The van had its hazard lights flashing and in front of it was a recovery vehicle with rotating yellow lights. Standing between the two vehicles were the two victims who received fatal injuries as the van was pushed into the recovery vehicle. Marks on the road showed that braking had occurred only at the very last moment. The respondent had been driving for over six hours out of the preceding 12 and had covered 343 miles.

It was the prosecution case that the respondent had been overcome by sleep at the wheel. In the course of a lengthy interview with the police, he ultimately acknowledged that he was tired but had decided to push on to the next service station and must have fallen asleep.

Both the prosecution and the defence had obtained expert evidence. For the defence, there was a report from Professor Brown, a chartered psychologist and assistant director of the Medical Research Council's Applied Psychology Unit in Cambridge. The Crown had obtained a report from Professor Horne, director of the Sleep Research Laboratory at Loughborough University. It was agreed by counsel that the evidence of each of these experts should be adduced and the judge admitted it. Professor Horne was called as part of the prosecution case. The respondent did not give evidence but relied upon Professor Brown's expert testimony which is central to this reference.

Professor Brown described to the court a condition known as 'driving without awareness' and on the basis of his evidence it was contended for the defence that the respondent was in a state of automatism at the time of the accident and was therefore not to be regarded as driving at all. Professor Horne did not accept Professor Brown's analysis. However, the judge in summing up to the jury left the defence of automatism based upon Professor Brown's evidence as an issue properly open for the jury's consideration.

It is common ground that, for the purposes of this reference, the court should proceed on the basis of Professor Brown's evidence at its highest. He said that 'driving without awareness' is not a scientific term but a provisional, or interim, descriptive phrase coined at a conference he had attended. He said that there are two essential components to the act of driving: collision avoidance and steering within highway lanes. In a state of 'driving without awareness', the driver's capacity to avoid a collision ceases to exist. This is because repetitive visual stimuli experienced on long journeys on straight, flat, featureless motorways can induce a trance-like state in which the focal point of forward vision gradually comes nearer and nearer until the driver is focusing just ahead of his windscreen. He therefore fails to see further ahead in the central field of vision. However, peripheral vision continues to send signals which are dealt with subconsciously and enable the driver to steer within highway lanes.

Professor Brown said this condition can occur insidiously without the driver being aware it is happening. However, he also said that usually a driver would 'snap out' of the condition in response to major stimuli appearing in front of him. Thus flashing lights would usually cause him to regain full awareness. Professor Brown was unable to explain why that had not happened in the present case. In fact, the respondent told the police when interviewed that he had seen the flashing lights some quarter of a mile before reaching them. Professor Brown was also unable to explain why the respondent should have steered, apparently deliberately, onto the hard shoulder.

Despite his phrase 'driving without awareness', Professor Brown agreed that the driver's body would still be controlling the vehicle, that there would be subconscious motivation to his steering and that although 'largely unaware of what was happening ahead' and 'largely unaware of steering either' the unawareness was not total. Asked if nothing intrudes into the driver's consciousness when he is in this state, the professor said: 'I would not go so far as to say nothing, but very little'. There must, as a matter of common sense, be some awareness if, as Professor Brown accepted, the driver will usually be caused to 'snap out' of the condition by strong stimuli noticed by his eyes.

Against this evidential background, the recorder directed the jury as follows:

> Professor Brown ... has told you that in his opinion [the respondent] was driving in a state which he describes as 'driving without awareness' in which he moved onto the hard shoulder, mistaking it for the nearside lane, and then continued steering subconsciously until a fraction of a second before the collision. Indeed, Professor Brown's view was that that state of driving without awareness had persisted for quite a long time and had included not only that last half mile, but had included the manoeuvre at junction 6 illustrated in the photograph some miles before. As a matter of law I direct you that if, because of this state of driving without awareness, [the respondent's] consciousness was, or may have been, so impaired that his mind did not control his action, he is not guilty of the offence and it is for the prosecution to make you sure that that was not his condition.

The contention on behalf of the Attorney General is that on the evidence given by Professor Brown, even taken at its highest, there was no basis for leaving the defence of automatism to the jury.

[Counsel for the Attorney General] submits that automatism as a defence in a driving case arises only where there is such total destruction of voluntary control that the defendant cannot be said to be driving at all. He cited *Hill v Baxter* [1958] 1 QB in which Lord Goddard CJ said at 283:

> I agree that there may be cases where the circumstances are such that the accused could not really be said to be driving at all. Supposed he had a stroke or an epileptic fit, both instances of what may properly be called acts of God; he might well be in the driver's seat even with his hands on the wheel, but in such a state of unconsciousness that he could not be said to be driving.

Pearson J at 286, gave as examples an epileptic fit, a coma, a blow on the head from a stone thrown up from the roadway and an attack by a swarm of bees so that the driver is:

> prevented from exercising any directional control over the vehicle, and any movement of his arms and legs are solely caused by the action of the bees. In each of these cases it can be said that at the material time he is not driving and, therefore, not driving dangerously. Then suppose that the man in the driving seat falls asleep. After he has fallen asleep he is no longer driving, but there was an earlier time at which he was falling asleep and therefore failing to

perform the driver's elementary and essential duty of keeping himself awake and therefore he was driving dangerously.

In *Bratty v AG for Northern Ireland* [1963] AC 386, a defence of automatism due to an attack of psychomotor epilepsy was raised. Lord Denning said of the *actus reus*, at 409:

> No act is punishable if it is done involuntarily: and an involuntary act in this context – some people nowadays prefer to speak of it as 'automatism' – means an act which is done by the muscles without any control by the mind, such as a spasm, a reflex action or a convulsion; or an act done by a person who is not conscious of what he is doing, such as an act whilst suffering from concussion or whilst sleep-walking.

The extent of the loss of control is crucial in the present case. [Counsel for the Attorney General] referred to three other authorities in support of his proposition that automatism requires there to be total destruction of voluntary control and that impairment or reduction of voluntary control is insufficient.

Watmore v Jenkins [1962] 2 QB 572 was a decision by a court of five judges in a case where the defendant was a diabetic and sought to raise automatism due to hypoglycaemia as a defence to driving charges. Giving the judgment of the court, Winn J said, at 586:

> It is ... a question of law what constitutes a state of automatism. It is salutary to recall that this expression is no more than a modern catchphrase which the courts have not accepted as connoting any wider or looser concept than involuntary movement of the body or limbs of a person.

Later, at p 587, he referred to the need for 'such a complete destruction of voluntary control as could constitute in law automatism'.

Second, [counsel for the Attorney General] relies on *Roberts v Ramsbottom* [1980] 1 WLR 823, a civil case in which the defendant driver sought to rely on automatism due to a stroke. Neill LJ said, at p 831G: '... I am not concerned with the total loss of consciousness but with a clouding or impairment of consciousness.' He then referred, *inter alia*, to *Watmore v Jenkins* [1962] 2 QB 572 and *Hill v Baxter* [1958] 1 QB 277 and concluded:

> I am satisfied that in a civil action a similar approach should be adopted. The driver will be able to escape liability if his actions at the relevant time were wholly beyond his control. The most obvious case is sudden unconsciousness. But if he retained some control, albeit imperfect control, and his driving, judged objectively, was below the required standard, he remains liable. His position is the same as a driver who is old or infirm. In my judgment unless the facts establish what the law recognises as automatism the driver cannot avoid liability on the basis that owing to some malfunction of the brain his consciousness was impaired. [Counsel] put the matter accurately, as I see it, when he said: 'One cannot accept as exculpation anything less than total loss of consciousness'.

The third case relied upon by [counsel for the Attorney General] is *Broome v Perkins* [1987] RTR 321, where again a driver charged with careless driving relied on an attack of hypoglycaemia as creating automatism. Glidewell LJ referred to *Bratty's* case [1963] AC 386 and to *Watmore v Jenkins* [1962] 2 QB 572. He said [1987] RTR 321 at 330:

The question which is posed in the case can be rephrased to ask: 'On the evidence, could the justices properly conclude that the defendant was not conscious of what he was doing and that his actions were involuntary and automatic throughout the whole of the five-mile journey over which the erratic driving was observed?' If, during a part or parts of that journey, they were satisfied his actions were voluntary and not automatic, at those times he was driving ... When driving a motor vehicle, the driver's conscious mind receives signals from eyes and ears, decides on the appropriate course of action as a result of those signals, and gives directions to the limbs to control the vehicle. When a person's actions are involuntary and automatic his mind is not controlling or directing his limbs.

[Counsel for the respondent] concedes that he can find no authority which runs counter to the principle illustrated by those three cases. Moreover, he conceded that despite Professor Brown's phrase 'driving without awareness', the professor's description of the condition showed that it amounts only to reduced or imperfect awareness. There remains the ability to steer the vehicle straight. There is also usually a capacity to react to stimuli appearing in the road ahead. In the present case the respondent admitted he had actually seen the flashing lights a quarter of a mile from the scene ...

We were referred to a number of decisions drawing a distinction between insane automatism and non-insane automatism: see *R v Quick* [1973] QB 910; *R v Sullivan* [1984] AC 156; *R v Hennessy* [1989] 1 WLR 287; and *R v Burgess* [1991] 2 QB 92.

The effect of those decisions is that if the defence of automatism is said to arise from internal causes so as to bring the defendant within the *M'Naghten Rules* (see *M'Naghten's* case), then if it succeeds the verdict should be one of not guilty by reason of insanity. An epileptic seizure, in *R v Sullivan*, a stress disorder, prone to recur and lacking the features of novelty or accident, in *R v Hennessy*, and sleep-walking, in *R v Burgess*, were all regarded as internal causes. If, however, automatism is said to arise from an external cause, for example a stone hitting the driver on the head, then a successful defendant is entitled to be acquitted.

Here, [counsel for the respondent] argues that the precipitating cause of the condition described by Professor Brown was the external factor of motorway conditions. However that may be, the proper approach is that prescribed by Lord Lane CJ in *R v Burgess* [1991] 2 QB 92 at 96:

Where the defence of automatism is raised by a defendant, two questions fall to be decided by the judge before the defence can be left to the jury. The first is whether a proper evidential foundation for the defence of automatism has been laid. The second is whether the evidence shows the case to be one of insane automatism, that is to say, a case which falls within the *M'Naghten* Rules, or one of non-insane automatism.

The first of those questions is the one raised by this reference. In our judgment, the 'proper evidential foundation' was not laid in this case by Professor Brown's evidence of 'driving without awareness'. As the authorities cited above show, the defence of automatism requires that there was a total destruction of voluntary control of the defendant's part. Impaired, reduced or partial control is not enough. Professor Brown accepted that someone 'driving without awareness' within his description, retains some control. He should be able to steer the vehicle and usually to react and return to full awareness when confronted by significant stimuli.

Accordingly, in our judgment the recorder ought not to have left the issue of automatism to the jury in this case and the answer to the point of law as formulated is, 'No'.

Conditions giving rise to automatism

Bratty v AG for Northern Ireland [1963] AC 386 (HL)

Lord Denning: My Lords, in the case of *Woolmington v DPP* [1935] AC 462, 482 Viscount Sankey LC said that 'when dealing with a murder case the Crown must prove (a) death as the result of a voluntary act of the accused and (b) malice of the accused'. The requirement that it should be a voluntary act is essential, not only in a murder case, but also in every criminal case. No act is punishable if it is done involuntarily; and an involuntary act in this context – some people nowadays prefer to speak of it as 'automatism' – means an act which is done by the muscles without any control by the mind, such as a spasm, a reflex action or a convulsion; or an act done by a person who is not conscious of what he is doing, such as an act done whilst suffering from concussion or whilst sleep-walking. The point was well put by Stephen J in 1889: 'Can anyone doubt that a man who, though he might be perfectly sane, committed what would otherwise be a crime in a state of somnambulism, would be entitled to be acquitted? And why is this? Simply because he would not know what he was doing'; see *R v Tolson* (1889) 23 QBD 168, 187. The term 'involuntary act' is, however, capable of wider connotations: and to prevent confusion it is to be observed that in the criminal law an act is not to be regarded as an involuntary act simply because the doer does not remember it. When a man is charged with dangerous driving, it is no defence for him to say 'I don't know what happened. I cannot remember a thing'; see *Hill v Baxter* [1958] 1 QB 277. Loss of memory afterwards is never a defence in itself, so long as he was conscious at the time; see *Russell v HM Advocate* [1946] SC (J) 37; *R v Podola* [1960] 1 QB 325. Nor is an act to be regarded as an involuntary act simply because the doer could not control his impulse to do it. When a man is charged with murder and it appears that he knew what he was doing, but he could not resist it, then his assertion 'I couldn't help myself' is no defence in itself; see *AG for South Australia v Brown* [1960] AC 432: though it may go towards a defence of diminished responsibility, in places where that defence is available; see *R v Byrne* [1960] 2 QB 396: but it does not render his act involuntary so as to entitle him to an unqualified acquittal. Nor is an act to be regarded as an involuntary act simply because it is unintentional or its consequences are unforeseen. When a man is charged with dangerous driving, it is no defence for him to say, however truly, 'I did not mean to drive dangerously'. There is said to be an absolute prohibition against that offence, whether he had a guilty mind of not; see *Hill v Baxter* [1958] 1 QB 277 at 282 by Lord Goddard CJ. But even though it is absolutely prohibited, nevertheless he has a defence if he can show that it was an involuntary act in the sense that he was unconscious at the time and did not know what he was doing, see *HM Advocate v Ritchie* 1926 S C (J) 45, *R v Minor* (1955) 15 WWR (NS) 433 and *Cooper v McKenna ex p Cooper* [1960] Qd LR 406.

Another thing to be observed is that it is not every involuntary act which leads to a complete acquittal. Take first an involuntary act which proceeds from a state of drunkenness. If the drunken man is so drunk that he does not know what he is doing, he has a defence to any charge, such as murder or wounding with intent, in which a specific intent is essential, but he is still liable to be convicted of manslaughter or unlawful wounding for which no specific intent is necessary, see *Beard's* case [1920] AC 479 at 494, 498, 504 ...

My Lords, I think that the difficulty is to be resolved by remembering that, whilst the *ultimate* burden rests on the Crown of proving every element essential in the crime, nevertheless in order to prove that the act was a voluntary act, the Crown is entitled to rely on the *presumption* that every man has sufficient mental capacity to be responsible for his crimes: and that if the defence wish to displace that presumption they must give some evidence from which the contrary may reasonably be inferred. Thus a drunken man is presumed to have the capacity to form the specific intent necessary to constitute the crime, unless evidence is given from which it can reasonably be inferred that he was incapable of forming it; see the valuable judgment of the Court of Justiciary in *Kennedy v HM Advocate* 1944 SC (J) 171, 177 which was delivered by Lord Normand. So also it seems to me that a man's act is presumed to be a voluntary act unless there is evidence from which it can reasonably be inferred that it was involuntary. To use the words of Devlin J, the defence of automatism 'ought not to be considered at all until the defence has produced at least *prima facie* evidence'; see *Hill v Baxter* [1958] 1 QB 277, 285; and the words of North J in New Zealand 'unless a proper foundation is laid'; see *R v Cottle* [1958] NZLR 999 at 1025. The necessity of laying the proper foundation is on the defence: and if it is not so laid, the defence of automatism need not be left to the jury, any more than the defence of drunkenness (*Kennedy v HM Advocate* 1944 SC (J) 171), provocation (*R v Gauthier* (1943) 29 Cr App R 113, CCA) or self-defence (*R v Lobell* [1957] 1 QB 547) need be.

What, then, is a proper foundation? The presumption of mental capacity of which I have spoken is a provisional presumption only. It does not put the legal burden on the defence in the same way as the presumption of sanity does. It leaves the legal burden on the prosecution, but nevertheless, until it is displaced, it enables the prosecution to discharge the ultimate burden of proving that the act was voluntary. Not because the presumption is evidence itself, but because it takes the place of evidence. In order to displace the presumption of mental capacity, the defence must give sufficient evidence from which it may reasonably be inferred that the act was involuntary. The evidence of the man himself will rarely be sufficient unless it is supported by medical evidence which points to the cause of the mental incapacity. It is not sufficient for a man to say 'I had a black-out': for 'black-out' as Stable J said in *Cooper v McKenna ex p Cooper* 'is one of the first refuges of a guilty conscience and a popular excuse'. The words of Devlin J in *Hill v Baxter* should be remembered: 'I do not doubt that there are genuine cases of automatism and the like, but I do not see how the layman can safely attempt without the help of some medical or scientific evidence to distinguish the genuine from the fraudulent.' When the only cause that is assigned for an involuntary act is drunkenness, then it is only necessary to leave drunkenness to the jury, with the consequential directions, and not to leave automatism at all. When the only cause that is assigned for it is a disease of the mind, then it is only necessary to leave insanity to the jury and not automatism. When the cause assigned is concussion or sleep-walking, there should be some evidence from which it can reasonably be inferred before it should be left to the jury. If it is said to be due to concussion, there should be evidence of a severe blow shortly beforehand. If it is said to be sleep-walking, there should be some credible support for it. His mere assertion that he was asleep will not suffice.

Once a proper foundation is thus laid for automatism, the matter becomes at large and must be left to the jury. As the case proceeds, the evidence may weigh first to one side and then to the other: and so the burden may appear to shift to and fro. But at the end of the day the legal burden comes into play and requires that the jury should be satisfied beyond reasonable doubt that the act was a voluntary act.

R v Quick and Paddison [1973] 1 QB 910 (CA)

Lawton LJ: ... In their broadest aspects these appeals raise the question as to what is meant by the phrase 'a defect of reason from disease of the mind' within the meaning of the *M'Naghten* Rules. More particularly the question is whether a person who commits a criminal act while under the effect of hypoglycaemia can raise a defence of automatism, as the defendants submitted was possible, or whether such a person must rely on a defence of insanity if he wishes to relieve himself of responsibility for his acts, as Bridge J ruled.

The defendants were both employed at Farleigh Mental Hospital, Flax Bourton, Somerset. Quick was a charge nurse, Paddison a state enrolled nurse. At the trial it was not disputed that at about 4 pm on 27 December 1971, one Green, a paraplegic spastic patient, unable to walk, was sitting in Rosemount Ward at the hospital, watching television. Quick was on duty; Paddison had gone off duty at 2 pm but was still present in the ward. Half an hour later, Green had sustained two black eyes, a fractured nose, a split lip which required three stitches and bruising of his arm and shoulders. There was undisputed medical evidence that these injuries could not have been self-inflicted.

The prosecution's case was that Quick had inflicted the injuries on Green and that Paddison had been present aiding and abetting him, not by actual physical participation, but by encouragement. On arraignment Quick pleaded not guilty. At the close of the evidence, following a ruling by the judge as to the effect in law of the evidence relied upon by Quick to support a defence of automatism, he pleaded guilty to count 2 of the indictment. The judge's ruling was to the effect that that evidence could only be relied upon to support a defence of insanity.

The evidence upon which the judge ruled came partly from witnesses for the prosecution and partly from Quick's own evidence and that of a consultant physician, Dr Cates, who was called on his behalf ... In the course of his own evidence Quick said that he could not remember assaulting Green. He admitted that he had been drinking and that his drinks had included whisky and a quarter of a bottle of rum. He also said that he was, and had been since the age of seven, a diabetic and that that morning he had taken insulin as prescribed by his doctor. After taking insulin he had had a very small breakfast and no lunch. Dr Cates said that on 12 or more occasions Quick had been admitted to hospital either unconscious or semi-conscious due to hypoglycaemia, which is a condition brought about when there is more insulin in the bloodstream than the amount of sugar there can cope with. When this imbalance occurs, the insulin has much the same effect as an excess of alcohol in the human body. At the onset of the imbalance the higher functions of the mind are affected. As the effects of the imbalance become more marked, more and more mental functions are upset; and unless an antidote is given (and a lump of sugar is an effective one) the sufferer can relapse into coma. In the later stages of mental impairment a sufferer may become aggressive and violent without being able to control himself or without knowing at the time what he was doing or having any recollection afterwards of what he had done. The following answer by Dr Cates sums up his evidence about hypoglycaemia and his opinion as to whether Quick could have been doing what he was proved to have been doing in the course of a suggested hypoglycaemic reaction:

> If a patient is going unconscious with a falling blood sugar, for a while he will be aggressive, for a while he will be more than aggressive, for a while he may start being physically violent and then he will be in a semi-conscious state when he could be struggling and resisting people's efforts to give him sugar. Then he may have a fit, then he may stay deeply unconscious for quite a while. It would sound from the evidence that this man developed an increasing effect of a falling blood sugar from some time in the afternoon till when he collapsed after the episode of attack. At least the events fit with that.

Dr Cates said that on three or four occasions while in hospital under treatment for diabetes Quick had behaved violently when his blood sugar had got too low.

As is well known, insulin is prescribed by doctors in order to ensure that only the requisite amount of sugar is in the patient's bloodstream; but from time to time the sugar level may get too low. Dr Cates said that there were a number of causes for that. The doctor may have prescribed too much insulin; the patient may have eaten too little or have been overactive. He accepted that on the occasion when Green was attacked, Quick's own conduct that day might well have caused a severe fall in blood sugar.

At the trial and before this court it was accepted by the prosecution that the evidence to which we have referred was enough to justify an issue being left to the jury whether Quick could be held responsible for what he had done to Green. If the jury were to accept the evidence relied on by Quick, what should their verdict be? Quick's counsel submitted, 'not guilty'; Sir Joseph Moloney on behalf of the Crown submitted that it should be 'not guilty by reason of insanity'.

The judge ruled in favour of the Crown. As Quick did not want to put forward a defence of insanity, after consulting with his counsel, he pleaded guilty to count 2. As that plea had been made as a result of the judge's ruling, it was accepted by the prosecution before this court that if that ruling was adjudged to be wrong it would not be a bar to an appeal by Quick against his conviction ...

Our examination of such authorities as there are must start with *Bratty v AG for Northern Ireland* [1963] AC 386, because the judge ruled as he did in reliance on that case. Bratty had been accused of the murder of a young girl. He put forward three defences; first, that at the material time he was in a state of automatism by reason of suffering from an attack of psychomotor epilepsy; second, that he was guilty only of manslaughter since he was incapable of forming an intent on the ground that his mental condition was so impaired and confused and he was so deficient in reason that he was not capable of forming such intent; and third, that he was insane. The trial judge left the issue of insanity to the jury (which they rejected) but refused to leave the other two issues. The House of Lords adjudged on the evidence in *Bratty's* case that he had been right to rule as he did, but accepted that automatism as distinct from insanity could be a defence if there was a proper foundation in the evidence for it. In this case, if Quick's alleged condition could have been caused by hypoglycaemia and that condition, like psychomotor epilepsy, was a disease of the mind, then Bridge J's ruling was right. The question remains, however, whether a mental condition arising from hypoglycaemia does amount to a disease of the mind. In *Bratty v AG for Northern Ireland* [1963] AC 386, all their Lordships based their speeches on the basis that such medical evidence as there was pointed to Bratty suffering from a 'defect of reason from disease of the mind' and nothing else. Lord Denning discussed in general terms what constituted a disease of the mind. [His Lordship then quoted from the speech of Lord Denning at 412.]

If [Lord Denning's] opinion is right and there are no restricting qualifications which ought to be applied to it, Quick was setting up a defence of insanity. He may have been at the material time in a condition of mental disorder manifesting itself in violence. Such manifestations had occurred before and might recur. The difficulty arises as soon as the question is asked whether he should be detained in a mental hospital. No mental hospital would admit a diabetic merely because he had a low blood sugar reaction; and common sense is affronted by the prospect of a diabetic being sent to such a hospital, when in most cases the disordered mental condition can be rectified quickly by pushing a lump of sugar or a teaspoonful of glucose into the patient's mouth.

The 'affront to common sense' argument, however, has its own inherent weakness, as Sir Joseph Moloney pointed out. If an accused is shown to have done a criminal act while suffering from a 'defect of reason from disease of the mind', it matters not whether the condition of the mind is curable or incurable, transitory or permanent: see *per* Devlin J in *R v Kemp* [1957] 1 QB 399, 407. If the condition is transitory, the Secretary of State may have a difficult problem of disposal; but what happens to those found not guilty by reason of insanity is not a matter for the courts ...

Applied without qualification of any kind, Devlin J's statement of the law would have some surprising consequences. Take the not uncommon case of the rugby player who gets a kick on the head early in the game and plays on to the end in a state of automatism. If, while he was in that state, he assaulted the referee, it is difficult to envisage any court adjudging that he was not guilty by reason of insanity. Another type of case which could occur is that of the dental patient who kicks out while coming round from an anaesthetic. The law would be in a defective state if a patient accused of assaulting a dental nurse by kicking her while regaining consciousness could only excuse himself by raising the defence of insanity.

In *Hill v Baxter* [1958] 1 QB 277, the problem before the Divisional Court was whether the accused had put forward sufficient evidence on a charge of dangerous driving to justify the justices adjudging that he should be acquitted, there having been no dispute that at the time when his car collided with another one he was at the driving wheel. At the trial the accused had contended that he became unconscious as a result of being overcome by an unidentified illness. The court (Lord Goddard CJ, Devlin and Pearson JJ) allowed an appeal by the prosecution against the verdict of acquittal. In the course of examining the evidence which had been put forward by the accused the judges made some comments of a general nature. Lord Goddard CJ at 282, referred to some observations of Humphreys J in *Kay v Butterworth* (1945) 61 TLR 452 which seemed to indicate that a man who became unconscious while driving due to the onset of a sudden illness should not be made liable at criminal law and then said at 283:

> I agree that there may be cases where the circumstances are such that the accused could not really be said to be driving at all. Suppose he had a stroke or an epileptic fit, both instances of what may properly be called acts of God; he might well be in the driver's seat even with his hands on the wheel, but in such a state of unconsciousness that he could not be said to be driving ... In this case, however, I am content to say that the evidence falls far short of what would justify a court holding that this man was in some automatous state.

Lord Goddard CJ did not equate unconsciousness due to a sudden illness, which must entail the malfunctioning of the mental processes of the sufferer, with disease of the mind, and in our judgment no one outside a court of law would. In *Hill v Baxter* [1958] 1 QB 277, 285, Devlin J accepted that some temporary loss of consciousness arising accidentally (the italics are ours) did not call for a verdict based on insanity. It is not clear what he meant by 'accidentally'. The context suggests that he may have meant 'unexpectedly' as can happen with some kinds of virus infections. He then said at 285:

> But if disease is present, the same thing may happen again, and therefore, since 1800, the law has provided that persons acquitted on this ground should be subject to restraint.

If that be right anyone suffering from a tooth abscess, who knows from past experience that he reacts violently to anaesthetics because of some constitutional bodily disorder which can be attributed to disease, might have to go on suffering or take the risk of being found insane unless he could find a dentist who would be prepared to take the risk of being kicked by a recovering patient. It seems to us that the law should not give the words 'defect of reason from disease of the mind' a meaning which would be regarded with incredulity outside a court ...

In this quagmire of law seldom entered nowadays save by those in desperate need of some kind of a defence, *Bratty v AG for Northern Ireland* [1963] AC 386, 403, 412, 414 provides the only firm ground. Is there any discernible path? We think there is. Judges should follow in a common sense way their sense of fairness. This seems to have been the approach of the New Zealand Court of Appeal in *R v Cottle* [1958] NZLR 999, 1011 and of Sholl J in *R v Carter* [1959] VR 105, 110. In our judgment no help can be obtained by speculating (because that is what we would have to do) as to what the judges who answered the House of Lords' questions in 1843 meant by disease of the mind, still less what Sir Matthew Hale meant in the second half of the 17th century. A quick backward look at the state of medicine in 1843 will suffice to show how unreal it would be to apply the concepts of that age to the present time. Dr Simpson had not yet started his experiments with chloroform, the future Lord Lister was only 16 and laudanum was used and prescribed like aspirins are today. Our task has been to decide what the law means now by the words 'disease of the mind'. In our judgment the fundamental concept is of a malfunctioning of the mind caused by disease. A malfunctioning of mind of transitory effect caused by the application to the body of some external factor such as violence, drugs, including anaesthetics, alcohol and hypnotic influences cannot fairly be said to be due to disease. Such malfunctioning unlike that caused by a defect of reason from disease of the mind, will not always relieve an accused from criminal responsibility. A self-induced incapacity will not excuse (see *R v Lipman*

[1970] 1 QB 152), nor will one which could have been reasonably foreseen as a result of either doing, or omitting to do something, as, for example, taking alcohol against medical advice after using certain prescribed drugs, or failing to have regular meals while taking insulin. From time to time difficult borderline cases are likely to arise. When they do, the test suggested by the New Zealand Court of Appeal in *R v Cottle* is likely to give the correct result, viz, can this mental condition be fairly regarded as amounting to or producing a defect of reason from disease of the mind?

In this case Quick's alleged mental condition, if it ever existed, was not caused by his diabetes but by his use of the insulin prescribed by his doctor. Such malfunctioning of his mind as there was, was caused by an external factor and not by a bodily disorder in the nature of a disease which disturbed the working of his mind. It follows in our judgment that Quick was entitled to have his defence of automatism left to the jury and that Bridge J's ruling as to the effect of the medical evidence called by him was wrong. Had the defence of automatism been left to the jury, a number of questions of fact would have had to be answered. If he was in a confused mental condition, was it due to a hypoglycaemic episode or to too much alcohol? If the former, to what extent had he brought about his condition by not following his doctor's instructions about taking regular meals? Did he know that he was getting into a hypoglycaemic episode? If yes, did he not use the antidote of eating a lump of sugar as he had been advised to do? On the evidence which was before the jury Quick might have had difficulty in answering these questions in a manner which would have relieved him of responsibility for his acts. We cannot say, however, with the requisite degree of confidence, that the jury would have convicted him. It follows that his conviction must be quashed on the ground that the verdict was unsatisfactory.

If Quick's conviction is quashed, what happens to Paddison's having regard to the fact that he was said to have aided an abetted Quick? The quashing of Quick's conviction amounts in law to an acquittal. Can Paddison be deemed to have aided and abetted someone who has been adjudged 'not guilty'? As a general proposition of law, the answer to this question is a qualified 'yes'. The facts of each case, however, have to be considered and in particular what is alleged to have been done by way of aiding and abetting. In this case the allegation against Paddison was encouraged by conduct. The case against him was that he knew what Quick was going to do and encouraged him to do it by getting the other patients out of the way. If Quick acted without conscious volition, it is most unlikely that Paddison would have known what he intended to do. The quashing of Quick's conviction in our judgment introduced an element of unreality into the verdict against Paddison. It follows that that verdict too must be quashed as being unsatisfactory.

R v Bingham [1991] Crim LR 433 (CA)

Facts: Following arrest for shoplifting, the defendant, a diabetic, was charged with theft of a can of Coke and sandwiches, worth £1.16, at a time when he had £90 in his pocket. He had paid for one can of Coke, and was stopped on leaving the store, following which he replied to questions with 'no comment'. His defence was automatism based on the claim that, at the time, he was suffering from hypoglycaemia and was unaware of his actions. The judge refused to leave that defence to the jury.

Held, allowing the appeal, the arguments put to the judge failed to distinguish between hyperglycaemia and hypoglycaemia, the former being too much sugar in the blood, and the latter too little. Hyperglycaemia might raise difficult problems about the *M'Naghten* Rules and verdicts of not guilty by reason of insanity. Hypoglycaemia was not caused by the initial disease of diabetes, but by the treatment in the form of too much insulin, or by insufficient quality or quantity of food to counterbalance the insulin. Generally speaking, that would not give rise to a verdict of not guilty by reason of insanity but would, if it were established and showed that the necessary intent was or might be lacking, provide a satisfactory defence to an alleged crime such as theft, due to lack of *mens rea*. Those simple facts would be plain to anyone who troubled to read *Quick* (1973) 57 Cr App R and *Hennessy* [1989] 1 WLR 287. In the present case, the problem was hypoglycaemia and the judge had to decide whether, on the evidence, there was a *prima facie* case for the jury to decide whether the defendant was suffering from its effects and, if so, whether the Crown had shown that he had the necessary intent under the Theft Act. It was not doubted that the defendant was a diabetic and there was evidence that he might have been suffering from the effects of a low blood sugar level at the relevant time. That evidence should have been left to the jury.

Notes and queries

1   In *R v T* [1990] Crim LR 256, the court accepted evidence that post-traumatic stress disorder could give rise to automatism. By contrast, in *R v Sandie Smith* [1982] Crim LR 531, evidence of severe pre-menstrual tension was not accepted as giving rise to automatism. Aside from the issue of whether there was sufficient evidence of automatism in the latter case, the determining factor was the court's desire to exercise some jurisdiction over the accused. If a plea of automatism is successful the defendant is free to go – the courts cannot compel him or her to receive treatment for the condition giving rise to the automatism.

Self-induced automatism

R v Bailey [1983] 1 WLR 760 (CA)

Griffiths LJ: ... The appellant is a diabetic and has been so for some 30 years. He requires to take insulin to control his condition. His defence at the trial was that he was acting in a state of automatism caused by hypoglycaemia.

In early January 1982, the woman with whom the appellant had been living for the previous two years left him and formed an association with the victim, Mr Harrison. At about 7 pm on 20 January 1982, the appellant, seeming upset, visited Mr Harrison at his home. They had a cup of tea and discussed the matter. After 10 or 15 minutes the appellant said that he felt unwell and asked Mr Harrison to make him some sugar and water, which the appellant drank. About 10 minutes later the appellant started to leave. He then said that he had lost his glove and that it might be down the side of the chair on which he had been sitting. Mr Harrison bent down to look and the appellant struck him on the back of the head with an iron bar, which was a case opener about 18 inches long. The appellant remained there holding the iron bar. Mr Harrison ran from the house. His wound required 10 stitches.

The Crown's case was that although it was theoretically possible, from a medical point of view, for there to have been a temporary loss of awareness due to hypoglycaemia, as the appellant claimed, this was not what had happened. On the contrary, it was contended that the appellant, upset and jealous about Mr Harrison's relationship with his girlfriend, had armed himself with the iron bar and gone to Mr Harrison's house with the intention of injuring him ...

Automatism resulting from intoxication as a result of a voluntary ingestion of alcohol or dangerous drugs does not negative the mens rea necessary for crimes of basic intent, because the conduct of the accused is reckless and recklessness is enough to constitute the necessary *mens rea* in assault cases where no specific intent forms part of the charge: see *R v Majewski* [1977] AC 443, 476 in speech of Lord Elwyn Jones LC and in the speech of Lord Edmund-Davies where he said, at p 496, quoting from Stroud, *Mens Rea*, 1914, p 115:

> The law therefore establishes a conclusive presumption against the admission of proof of intoxication for the purpose of disproving *mens rea* in ordinary crimes. Where this presumption applies, it does not make 'drunkenness itself' a crime, but the drunkenness is itself an integral part of the crime, as forming together with the other unlawful conduct charged against the defendant, a complex act of criminal recklessness.

The same considerations apply where the state of automatism is induced by the voluntary taking of dangerous drugs: see *R v Lipman* [1970] 1 QB 152 where a conviction for manslaughter was upheld, the appellant having taken LSD and killed his mistress in the course of an hallucinatory trip. It was submitted on behalf of the Crown that a similar rule should be applied as a matter of public policy to all cases of self-induced automatism. But it seems to us that there may be material distinctions between a man who consumes alcohol or takes dangerous drugs and one who fails to take sufficient food after insulin to avert hypoglycaemia.

It is common knowledge that those who take alcohol to excess or certain sorts of drugs may become aggressive or do dangerous or unpredictable things, they may be able to foresee the risks of causing harm to others but nevertheless persist in their conduct. But the same cannot be said without more of a man who fails to take food after an insulin injection. If he does appreciate the risk that such a failure may lead to aggressive, unpredictable and uncontrollable conduct and he nevertheless deliberately runs the risk or otherwise disregards it, this will amount to recklessness. But we certainly do not think that it is common knowledge, even among diabetics, that such is a consequence of a failure to take food and there is no evidence that it was known to this appellant. Doubtless he knew that if he failed to take his insulin or proper food after it, he might lose consciousness, but as such he would only be a danger to himself unless he put himself in charge of some machine such as a motor car, which required his continued conscious control.

In our judgment, self-induced automatism, other than that due to intoxication from alcohol or drugs, may provide a defence to crimes of basic intent. The question in each case will be whether the prosecution have proved the necessary element of recklessness. In cases of assault, if the accused knows that his actions or inaction are likely to make him aggressive, unpredictable or uncontrolled with the result that he may cause some injury to others and he persists in the action or takes no remedial action when he knows it is required, it will be open to the jury to find that he was reckless ...

In the present case the recorder never invited the jury to consider what the appellant's knowledge or appreciation was of what would happen if he failed to take food after his insulin or whether he realised that he might become aggressive. Nor were they asked to consider why the appellant had omitted to take food in time. They were given no direction on the elements of recklessness. Accordingly, in our judgment there was also a misdirection in relation to the second count in the indictment of unlawful wounding.

But we have to consider whether, notwithstanding these misdirections, there has been any miscarriage of justice and whether the jury properly directed could have failed to come to the same conclusion. As Lawton LJ said in *Quick's* case at 922 [*R v Quick* (1973) QB 910], referring to the defence of automatism, it is a 'quagmire of law seldom entered nowadays save by those in desperate need of some kind of a defence'. This case is no exception. We think it very doubtful whether the appellant laid a sufficient basis for the defence to be considered by the jury at all. But even if he did we are in no doubt that the jury properly directed must have rejected it. Although an episode of sudden transient loss of consciousness or awareness was theoretically possible it was quite inconsistent with the graphic description that the appellant gave to the police both orally and in his written statement. There was abundant evidence that he had armed himself with the iron bar and gone to Mr Harrison's house for the purpose of attacking him because he wanted to teach him a lesson and because he was in the way ...

Codification and law reform proposals

The draft Criminal Code Bill proposes the following as its codification of the defence of sane automatism:

33(1) A person is not guilty of an offence if –

(a) he acts in a state of automatism, that is, his act –

(i) is a reflex, spasm or convulsion; or

(ii) occurs while he is in a condition (whether of sleep, unconsciousness, impaired consciousness or otherwise) depriving him of effective control of the act, and

(b) the act or condition is the result neither of anything done or omitted with the fault required for the offence nor of voluntary intoxication.

(2) A person is not guilty of an offence by virtue of an omission to act if –

(a) he is physically incapable of acting in the way required; and

(b) his being so incapable is the result neither of anything done or omitted with the fault required for the offence nor of voluntary intoxication.

The commentary on this clause in Vol II of Law Com 177 provides as follows:

11.1 'Automatism' has been referred to as 'a modern catch-phrase' to describe 'an involuntary movement of the body or limbs of a person.' In general a person is not criminally liable for such a movement or its consequences. On one analysis an 'involuntary movement' is not an 'act'. In Code terms, however, even an unconscious movement of a person is an 'act', but one done 'in a state of automatism'. This permits flexible use of the word 'act' as a key term in the Code and makes 'a state of automatism' also available as a Code expression. The word 'involuntary' is not needed – happily, in view of the variable use to which it tends to be put.

11.2 Limited function of subsection (1). The main function of clause 33 (1) is to protect a person who acts in a state of automatism from conviction of an offence of strict liability. It is conceded that he does 'the act' specified for the offence; but the clause declares him not guilty. One charged with an offence requiring fault in the form of failure to comply with a standard of conduct may also have to rely on the clause. On the other hand, a state of automatism will negative a fault requirement of intention or knowledge or (normally) recklessness; so a person charged with an offence of violence against another, or of criminal damage, committed when he was in a condition of impaired consciousness, does not rely on this clause for his acquittal but on the absence of the fault element of the offence.

11.3 Conditions within the subsection. Subsection (1)(a) refers to acts of two kinds:

(i) an act over which the person concerned, although conscious, has no control: the ' reflex, spasm or convulsion'. Such an act would rarely, if ever, be the subject of a prosecution;

(ii) an act over which the person concerned does not have effective control because of a 'condition' of 'sleep, unconsciousness, impaired consciousness or otherwise'. We believe that the references to 'impaired consciousness', and to deprivation of 'effective' control are justified both on principle and by some of the leading cases. The governing principle should be that a person is not guilty of an offence if, without relevant fault on his part, he cannot choose to act otherwise than as he does. The acts of the defendants in several cases have been treated as automatons although it is far from clear, and even unlikely, that they were entirely unconscious when they did the acts and although it cannot confidently be said that they exercised no control, in any sense of that phrase, over their relevant movements.

11.4 The case law, however, is not consistent. In *Broome v Perkins*, D drove five miles home, very erratically, in a hypoglycaemic state. The evidence was that he may well not have been conscious of what he was doing. The Divisional Court directed a conviction of driving without due care and attention, on the ground that D's mind must have reacted to stimuli, made decisions (to swerve, brake, restart after stopping) and given directions to his limbs. His actions were regarded as not 'involuntary' or 'automatic'. Yet it seems clear that D's condition was such that he could not choose to behave otherwise than as he did. Cases such as those we have mentioned above appear not to have been referred to. Finding it necessary to choose between the authorities, we propose a formula under which we expect (and indeed hope) that a person in the condition of the defendant in *Broome v Perkins* would be acquitted (subject to the question of prior fault).

11.5   Prior fault. Subsection (1)(b) excepts from the protection of the subsection cases in which the state of automatism itself is the result of relevant fault on the part of the person affected or of voluntary intoxication. A person charged with an offence that may be committed by negligence can be convicted if his state of automatism was the result of his own negligent conduct. Under clause 22 (1)(a) a person who was unaware of a risk by reason of voluntary intoxication is credited, when charged with an offence of recklessness, with the awareness that he would have had if sober; and clause 33 (1)(b) ensures that he cannot escape liability for the offence by a plea of automatism. Paragraph (b) is intended to produce the same results as the common law.

11.6   Physical incapacity. Subsection (2) provides the necessary corresponding rules for a case in which physical incapacity prevents the doing of that which there is a duty to do. The law does not condemn a person for not doing what cannot possibly be done – unless, once again, it is in a relevant way his fault that he cannot possibly do it.

INSANE AUTOMATISM

In broad terms, a criminal court may be concerned with the issue of insanity at two stages. First, was the defendant insane at the time of the alleged offence? Secondly, is the defendant fit to stand trial? Where it is accepted on both sides that D was insane at the time of the offence, or is unfit to stand trial, the court will nevertheless have to investigate whether or not the defendant committed the *actus reus* of the offence charged. The purpose of this exercise is to ensure that the defendant is only detained where there is evidence that he actually committed the *actus reus* alleged; see further the Criminal Procedure (Insanity and Unfitness to Plead) Act 1991, and *AG's Ref (No 3 of 1998)* [1999] 3 All ER 40.

Insanity is a general defence in criminal law and can be raised, if the defendant so wishes, in relation to minor offences; see *R v Horseferry Road Magistrates' Court ex p K* [1997] QB 23. As the defence involves a denial of *mens rea* it will not avail a defendant charged with a strict liability offence; see *DPP v H* (1997) *The Times*, 2 May.

Where the defence of insanity is established the jury, in accordance with the Criminal Procedure (Insanity) Act 1964, can return a 'special verdict' of not guilty by reason of insanity.

The test for insane automatism

M'Naghten's case (1843) 10 Cl & F 200

Daniel McNaghten was acquitted of shooting Sir Robert Peel's secretary, in what today would probably be termed a state of paranoia. The question of insanity and criminal responsibility was the subject of debate in the legislative chamber of the House of Lords. The House invited the judges of the courts of common law to answer five abstract questions on the subject of insanity as a defence to criminal charges. The answer to the second and third of these questions combined was given to Tindal CJ on behalf of all the judges, except Maule J, and constituted what have become known as the *M'Naghten* Rules.

> **Tindal CJ**: ... The jurors ought to be told in all cases that every man is to be presumed to be sane, and to possess a sufficient degree of reason to be responsible for his crimes, until the contrary be proved to their satisfaction; and that to establish a defence on the ground of insanity, it must be clearly proved that, at the time of the committing of the act, the party accused was labouring under such a defect of reason, from disease of the mind, as not to know the nature and quality of the act he was doing; or, if he did know it, that he did not know he was doing what was wrong.

It will be noted from the above that the rules envisage the defendant's defect of reason as manifesting itself in one of two ways – automatism, or a failure to appreciate that the actions were 'wrong'. This latter manifestation of insanity is considered later in this chapter. The defendant is presumed to be sane unless he proves (and the burden is on him to show), on the balance of probabilities, that he was insane at the time of the alleged offence. It follows that the jury do not have be satisfied beyond reasonable doubt that the defendant was insane; it is sufficient that they are satisfied that it is more likely than not that he was insane at the relevant time: see *Sodeman v The King* [1936] 2 All ER. Note that in *R v Clarke* [1972] 1 All ER 219, Ackner J observed: '... The *M'Naghten* Rules relate to accused persons who by reason of a disease of the mind are deprived of the power of reasoning. They do not apply and never have applied to those who retain the power of reasoning but who in moments of confusion or absent-mindedness fail to use their powers to the full.'

Disease of the mind for the purposes of insanity

R v Kemp [1957] 1 QB 399 (Devlin J, Bristol Assizes)

Devlin J: ... The facts of the case in relation to which this point has to be considered are that the accused, who is charged with causing grievous bodily harm to his wife, struck her during the night with a hammer with such violence as to inflict a grievous wound. The accused is an elderly man of excellent character and he and his wife have always been thought to be a devoted couple, and it seems that there is strong evidence to show that the act was entirely motiveless and irrational. I say strong evidence to show, though that is a matter which the jury will have in due course to decide: for the purpose of my ruling I assume that in accordance with the evidence to which I have referred, the act was committed, as the doctors on all sides think it was, while the accused was in a mental condition which made him not responsible for his actions. Their view upon this – and all three are agreed – is that he did the act, as he says he did, not knowing anything about it and that he has not any real memory of it. It is not merely a question of his striking his wife when in some mental derangement, nor appreciating that what he was doing was wrong; it is a case in the view of all three doctors in which he was not conscious at the time that he did the act, that he picked up the hammer or that he was striking his wife with it ...

It is common ground on the evidence that the accused was suffering from a physical disease, namely arteriosclerosis, or hardening of the arteries. It had not reached – and this, I think, is clear from the evidence, at any rate I assume so for this purpose – the stage at which the accused was showing any general sign of mental trouble. Apart from a depression, not an irrational depression, produced by his poor state of health, there were no signs of mental trouble ...

I shall say by way of commencement that there is, according to the evidence, no general medical opinion upon what category of diseases are properly to be called diseases of the mind. Both doctors have expressed their views, but they have expressed their views as personal views and not ones for which they can call in aid any general body of medical opinion. Doctors' personal views, of course, are not binding upon me. I have to interpret the rules according to the ordinary principles of interpretation, but I derive help from their interpretations in as much as they illustrate the nature of the disease and the matters which from the medical point of view have to be considered in determining whether or not it is a disease of the mind.

The broad submission that was made to me on behalf of the accused was that this is a physical disease and not a mental disease; arteriosclerosis is a physical condition primarily and not a mental condition. But that argument does not go so far as to suggest that for the purpose of the law diseases that affect the mind can be divided into those that are physical in origin and those that are mental in origin. There is such a distinction medically. I think it is recognised by medical men that there are mental diseases which have an organic cause, there are disturbances of the mind which can be traced to some hardening of the arteries, to some degeneration of the brain cells or to some physical condition which accounts for mental derangement. It is also recognised that there are diseases functional in origin where it is not possible to point to any physical cause but simply to say that there has been a derangement of the functioning of the mind, such as melancholia, schizophrenia and many other of those diseases which are usually handled by psychiatrists. This medical distinction is not pressed as part of the argument for the accused in this case, and I think rightly. The distinction between the two categories is quite irrelevant for the purposes of the law, which is not concerned with the origin of the disease or the cause of it but simply with the mental condition which has brought about the act. It does not matter, for the purposes of the law, whether the defect of reason is due to a degeneration of the brain or to some other form of mental derangement. That may be a matter of importance medically, but it is of no importance to the law, which merely has to consider the state of mind in which the accused is, not how he got there.

The distinction that emerges from the evidence of Dr Gibson and which has been argued by [counsel for the accused] is a different one. It is that this is something which is capable of becoming a mental disease but has not yet become one. It has not created any degeneration of the brain and the argument is that it is merely interfering temporarily with the working of the brain by cutting off the supply of blood in the same way as concussion might, or something of that sort. I am invited to say that this disease at this stage is purely physical; when it interferes with the brain cells so that they degenerate, it then becomes a disease of the mind. This would be a very difficult test to apply for the purposes of the law. I should think it would be a matter of great difficulty medically to determine precisely at what point degeneration of the brain sets in, and it would mean that the verdict depended upon a doubtful medical borderline.

The law is not concerned with the brain but with the mind, in the sense that 'mind' is ordinarily used, the mental faculties of reason, memory and understanding. If one read for 'disease of the mind' 'disease of the brain', it would follow that in many cases pleas of insanity would not be established because it could not be proved that the brain had been affected in any way, either by degeneration of the cells or in any other way. In my judgment the condition of the brain is irrelevant and so is the question of whether the condition of the mind is curable or incurable, transitory or permanent. There is no warranty for introducing those considerations into the definition in the *M'Naghten* Rules. Temporary insanity is sufficient to satisfy them. It does not matter whether it is incurable and permanent or not.

I think that the approach of [counsel for the Crown] to the definition in the rules is the right one. He points out the order of the words 'a defect of reason, from disease of the mind'. The primary thing that has to be looked for is the defect of reason. 'Disease of the mind' is there for some purpose, obviously, but the prime thing is to determine what is admitted here, namely whether or not there is a defect of reason. In my judgment, the words 'from disease of the mind' are not to be construed as if they were put in for the purpose of distinguishing between diseases which have a mental origin and diseases which have a physical origin, a distinction which in 1843 was probably little considered. They were put in for the purpose of limiting the effect of the words 'defect of reason'. A defect of reason is by itself enough to make the act irrational and therefore normally to exclude responsibility in law. But the rule was not intended to apply to defects of reason caused simply by brutish stupidity without rational power. It was not intended that the defence should plead: 'Although with a healthy mind he nevertheless had been brought up in such a way that he had never learned to exercise his reason, and therefore he is suffering from a defect of reason'. The words ensure that unless the defect is due to a diseased mind and not simply to an untrained one there is insanity within the meaning of the rule.

Hardening of the arteries is a disease which is shown on the evidence to be capable of affecting the mind in such a way as to cause a defect, temporarily or permanently, of its reasoning, understanding and so on, and so is in my judgment a disease of the mind which comes within the meaning of the rules ...

R v Sullivan [1984] 1 AC 156 (HL)

Lord Diplock: My Lords, the appellant, Mr Sullivan, a man of blameless reputation, has the misfortune to have been a lifelong sufferer from epilepsy. There was a period when he was subject to major seizures known as grand mal; but, as a result of treatment which he was receiving as an out-patient of the Maudsley Hospital from 1976 onwards, these major seizures had, by the use of drugs, been reduced by 1979 to seizures of less severity known as petit mal; or psychomotor epilepsy, though they continued to occur at a frequency of one or two per week.

One such seizure occurred on 8 May 1981, when Mr Sullivan, then aged 51, was visiting a neighbour, Mrs Killick, an old lady aged 86 for whom he was accustomed to perform regular acts of kindness. He was chatting there to a fellow visitor and friend of his, a Mr Payne aged 80, when the epileptic fit came on. It appears likely from the expert medical evidence about the way in which epileptics behave at the various stages of a petit mal seizure that Mr Payne got up from the chair to help Mr Sullivan. The only evidence of an eyewitness was that of Mrs Killick, who did not see what had happened before she saw Mr Payne lying on the floor and Mr Sullivan kicking him about the head and body, in consequence of which Mr Payne suffered injuries severe enough to require hospital treatment.

As a result of this occurrence Mr Sullivan was indicted upon two counts: the first was of causing grievous bodily harm with intent contrary to s 18 of the Offences Against the Person Act 1861; the second of causing grievous bodily harm contrary to s 20 of that Act. At his trial, which took place at the Central Criminal Court before Judge Lymbery and a jury, Mr Sullivan pleaded not guilty to both counts. Mrs Killick's evidence that he had kicked Mr Payne violently about the head and body was undisputed and Mr Sullivan himself gave evidence of his history of epilepsy and his absence of all recollection of what had occurred at Mrs Killick's flat between the time that he was chatting peacefully to Mr Payne there and his return to the flat somewhere else to find that Mr Payne was injured and that an ambulance had been sent for. The prosecution accepted his evidence as true. There was no cross-examination.

Counsel for Mr Sullivan wanted to rely upon the defence of automatism or, as Viscount Kilmuir LC had put it in *Bratty v AG for Northern Ireland* [1963] AC 386, 405, 'non-insane' automatism; that is to say, that he had acted unconsciously and involuntarily in kicking Mr Payne, but that when doing so he was not 'insane' in the sense in which that expression is used as a term of art in English law, and in particular in s 2 of the Trial of Lunatics Act 1883, as amended by s 1 of the Criminal Procedure (Insanity) Act 1964. As was decided unanimously by this House in *Bratty*, before a defence of non-insane automatism may properly be left to the jury, some evidential foundation for it must be laid.

The evidential foundation that counsel laid before the jury in the instant case consisted of the testimony of two distinguished specialists from the neuro-psychiatry epilepsy unit at the Maudsley Hospital, Dr Fenwick and Dr Taylor, as to the pathology of the various stages of a seizure due to psychomotor epilepsy. Their expert evidence, which was not disputed by the prosecution, was that Mr Sullivan's acts in kicking Mr Payne had all the characteristics of epileptic automatism at the third or post-ictal stage of petit mal; and that in view of his history of psychomotor epilepsy and hospital records of his behaviour during previous seizures, the strong probability was that Mr Sullivan's acts of violence towards Mr Payne took place while he was going through that stage.

The evidence as to the pathology of a seizure due to psychomotor epilepsy can be sufficiently stated for the purposes of this appeal by saying that after the first stage, the prodram, which precedes the fit itself, there is a second stage, the ictus, lasting a few seconds, during which there are electrical discharges into the temporal lobes of the brain of the sufferer. The effect of these discharges is to cause him in the post-ictus stage to make movements which he is not conscious that he is making, including, and this was a characteristic of previous seizures which Mr Sullivan had suffered, automatic movements of resistance to anyone trying to come to his aid. These movements of resistance might, though in practice they very rarely would, involve violence ...

The *M'Naghten* Rules have been used as a comprehensive definition for this purpose by the courts for the last 140 years. Most importantly, they were so used by this House in *Bratty v AG for Northern Ireland* [1963] AC 386. That case was in some respects the converse of the instant case. Bratty was charged with murdering a girl by strangulation. He claimed to have been unconscious of what he was doing at the time he strangled the girl and he sought to run as alternative defences non-insane automatism and insanity. The only evidential foundation that he laid for either of these pleas was medical evidence that he might have been suffering from psychomotor epilepsy which, if he were, would account for his having been unconscious of what he was doing. No other pathological explanation of his actions having been carried out in a state of automatism was supported by evidence. The trial judge first put the defence of insanity to the jury. The jury rejected it; they declined to bring in the special verdict. Thereupon, the judge refused to put to the jury the alternative defence of automatism. His refusal was upheld by the Court of Criminal Appeal of Northern Ireland and subsequently by this House ...

In the instant case, as in *Bratty*, the only evidential foundation that was laid for any finding by the jury that Mr Sullivan was acting unconsciously and involuntarily when he was kicking Mr Payne, was that when he did so he was in the post-ictal stage of seizure of psychomotor epilepsy. The evidential foundation in the case of Bratty, that he was suffering from psychomotor epilepsy at the time he did the act with which he was charged, was very weak and was rejected by the jury; the evidence in Mr Sullivan's case, that he was so suffering when he was kicking Mr Payne, was very strong and would almost inevitably be accepted by a properly directed jury. It would be the duty of the judge to direct the jury that if they did accept that evidence the law required them to bring in a special verdict and none other. The governing statutory provision is to be found in s 2 of the Trial of Lunatics Act 1883. This says 'the jury shall return a special verdict ...'

My Lords, I can deal briefly with the various grounds on which it has been submitted that the instant case can be distinguished from what constituted the *ratio decidendi* in *Bratty v AG for Northern Ireland* [1963] AC 386, and that it falls outside the ambit of the *M'Naghten* Rules.

First, it is submitted that the medical evidence in the instant case shows that psychomotor epilepsy is not a disease of the mind, whereas in *Bratty* it was accepted by all the doctors that it was. The only evidential basis for this submission is that Dr Fenwick said that in medical terms to constitute a 'disease of the mind' or 'mental illness', which he appeared to regard as interchangeable descriptions, a disorder of brain functions (which undoubtedly occurs during a seizure in psychomotor epilepsy) must be prolonged for a period of time usually more than a day; while Dr Taylor would have it that the disorder must continue for a minimum of a month to qualify for the description 'a disease of the mind'.

The nomenclature adopted by the medical profession may change from time to time; *Bratty* was tried in 1961. But the meaning of the expression 'disease of the mind' as the cause of 'a defect of reason' remains unchanged for the purposes of the application of the *M'Naghten* Rules. I agree with what was said by Devlin J in *R v Kemp* [1957] 1 QB 399, 407, that 'mind' in the *M'Naghten* Rules is used in the ordinary sense of the mental faculties of reason, memory and understanding. If the effect of a disease is to impair these faculties so severely as to have either of the consequences referred to in the latter part of the rules, it matters not whether the aetiology of the impairment is organic, as in epilepsy, or functional, or whether the impairment itself is permanent or is transient and intermittent, provided that it subsisted at the time of commission of the act. The purpose of the legislation relating to the defence of insanity, ever since its origin in 1800, has been to protect society against recurrence of the dangerous conduct. The duration of a temporary suspension of the mental faculties of reason, memory and understanding, particularly if, as in Mr Sullivan's case, it is recurrent, cannot on any rational ground be relevant to the application by the courts of the *M'Naghten* Rules, though it may be relevant to the course adopted by the Secretary of State, to whom the responsibility for how the defendant is to be dealt with passes after the return of the special verdict of 'not guilty by reason of insanity'.

To avoid misunderstanding I ought perhaps to add that in expressing my agreement with what was said by Devlin J in *Kemp*, where the disease that caused the temporary and intermittent impairment of the mental faculties was arteriosclerosis, I do not regard that learned judge as excluding the possibility of non-insane automatism (for which the proper verdict would be a verdict of 'not guilty') in cases where temporary impairment (not being self-induced by consuming drink or drugs) resulted from some external physical factor such as a blow on the head causing concussion or the administration of an anaesthetic for therapeutic purposes. I mention this because in *R v Quick* [1973] QB 910, Lawton LJ appears to have regarded the ruling in *Kemp* as going as far as this. If it had done, it would have been inconsistent with the speeches in this House in *Bratty* [1963] AC 386, where *Kemp* was alluded to without disapproval by Viscount Kilmuir LC at 403, and received the express approval of Lord Denning at 411. The instant case, however, does not in my view afford an appropriate occasion for exploring possible causes of non-insane automatism.

The only other submission in support of Mr Sullivan's appeal which I think it necessary to mention is that, because the expert evidence was to the effect that Mr Sullivan's acts in kicking Mr Payne were unconscious and thus 'involuntary' in the legal sense of that term, his state of mind was not dealt with by the *M'Naghten* Rules at all, since it was not covered by the phrase 'as not to know the nature and quality of the act he was doing'. Quite apart from being contrary to all three speeches in this House in *Bratty v AG for Northern Ireland* [1963] AC 386, this submission appears to me, with all respect to counsel, to be quite unarguable. Dr Fenwick himself accepted it as an accurate description of Mr Sullivan's mental state in the post-ictal stage of a seizure. The audience to whom the phrase in the *M'Naghten* Rules was addressed consisted of peers of the realm in the 1840s when a certain orotundity of diction had not yet fallen out of fashion. Addressed to an audience of jurors in the 1980s it might more aptly be expressed as 'He did not know what he was doing'.

My Lords, it is natural to feel reluctant to attach the label of insanity to a sufferer from psychomotor epilepsy of the kind to which Mr Sullivan was subject, even though the expression in the context of a special verdict of 'not guilty by reason of insanity' is a technical one which includes a purely temporary and intermittent suspension of the mental faculties of reason, memory and understanding resulting from the occurrence of an epileptic fit. But the label is contained in the current statute, it has appeared in this statute's predecessors ever since 1800. It does not lie within the power of the courts to alter it. Only Parliament can do that. It has done so twice; it could do so once again ...

R v Hennessy [1989] 1 WLR 287 (CA)

Lord Lane: ... The facts which gave rise to the charges, so far as material, were these. On Thursday 28 May 1987, two police constables, Barnes and Grace, were on duty in St Leonards-on-Sea on the Sussex coast, among other things looking for a Ford Granada car which had been stolen. They found the car. It was unattended. They kept it under watch. As they watched they saw the appellant get into the car, switch on the headlights and ignition, start the car and drive off. The appellant at the wheel of the car correctly stopped the car at a set of traffic lights which were showing red against him. PC Grace then went over to the car as it was stationary, removed the ignition keys from the ignition lock, but not before the appellant had tried to drive the motor car away and escape from the attention of the policeman. The appellant was put in the police car. On the way to the police station an informal conversation about motor vehicles took place between the appellant and the police officers, in particular about the respective merits of the new Rover motor car and the Ford Sierra. Indeed, the appellant appeared to PC Barnes not only to be fully in possession of his faculties but to be quite cheerful and intelligent. Indeed he went so far as to say to the police officer that if he had only got the car, which he was in the process of removing, into the open road, he would have given the policemen a real run for their money.

However after having been at the police station for a time, the appellant was at a later stage escorted by PC Barnes to hospital. He seemed to be normal when he left the cell block at the police station, but when he arrived at the hospital he appeared to be dazed and confused. He complained to the sister in the casualty ward that he had failed to take his insulin and indeed had had no insulin since the previous Monday when he should have had regular self-injection doses. He was given insulin, with which he injected himself, and the hospital discharged him and he was taken back to the police station.

The appellant gave evidence to the effect that he had been a diabetic for about 10 years. He needed, in order to stabilise his metabolism, two insulin injections on a daily basis, morning and afternoon. The amount required would depend on factors such as stress and eating habits. He was on a strict carbohydrate diet. At the time of the offence he said he had been having marital and employment problems. His wife had submitted a divorce petition some time shortly before, and he was very upset. He had not been eating and he had not been taking his insulin. He remembered very few details of the day. He could recall being handcuffed and taken to the charge room at the police station. He remembered being given insulin at the hospital and injecting himself and he remembers feeling better when he got back to the police station afterwards. He said he did not recall taking the car ...

The defence to these charges accordingly was that the appellant had failed to take his proper twice-a-day dose of insulin for two or three days and at the time the events in question took place he was in a state of automatism and did not know what he was doing. Therefore it is submitted that the guilty mind, which is necessary to be proved by the prosecution, was not proved, and accordingly that he was entitled to be acquitted.

The judge took the view, rightly in our view, that the appellant, having put his state of mind in issue, the preliminary question which he had to decide was whether this was truly a case of automatism or whether it was a case of legal 'insanity' within the *M'Naghten* Rules ... He concluded that it was the latter, and he so ruled, whereupon the appellant changed his plea to guilty and was sentenced to the terms of imprisonment suspended which we have already mentioned. The judge then certified the case fit for appeal in the terms which I have already described.

The *M'Naghten* Rules in the earlier part of the last century have in many ways lost their importance; they certainly have lost the importance they once had, but they are still relevant in so far as they may affect the defence of automatism. Although the rules deal with what they describe as insanity, it is insanity in the legal sense and not in the medical or psychological sense ...

The importance of the rules in the present context, namely the context of automatism, is this. If the defendant did not know the nature and quality of his act because of something which *did not* amount to defect of reason from disease of the mind then he will probably be entitled to be acquitted on the basis that the necessary criminal intent which the prosecution has to prove is not proved. But, if, on the other hand, his failure to realise the nature and quality of his act was due to a defect of reason from disease of the mind, then in the eyes of the law he is suffering from insanity, albeit *M'Naghten* insanity ...

The question in many cases, and this is one such case, is whether the function of the mind was disturbed on the one hand by disease or on the other hand by some external factor. The matter was discussed, as counsel for the appellant has helpfully pointed out to us, by the House of Lords in *R v Sullivan* ... [see above] ... The point was neatly raised in *R v Quick, R v Paddison* ...

Thus in *R v Quick* the fact that his condition was, or may have been, due to the injections of insulin meant that the malfunction was due to an external factor and not to the disease. The drug it was that caused the hypoglycaemia, the low blood sugar. As suggested in another passage of the judgment of Lawton LJ, hyperglycaemia, high blood sugar, caused by an inherent defect and not corrected by insulin is a disease, and if, as the defendant was asserting here, it does cause a malfunction of the mind, then the case may fall within the *M'Naghten* Rules.

The burden of the argument of counsel for the appellant to us is this. It is that the appellant's depression and marital troubles were a sufficiently potent external factor in his condition to override, so to speak, the effect of the diabetic shortage of insulin on him. He refers us not only to the passage which I have already cited in *R v Quick*, but also to a further passage in *Hill v Baxter* [1958] 1 QB 277 at 285 which is part of the judgment of Devlin J, sitting with Lord Goddard CJ and Pearson J, in the Divisional Court of Queen's Bench Division. It reads as follows:

> I have drawn attention to the fact that the accused did not set up a defence of insanity. For the purposes of the criminal law there are two categories of mental irresponsibility, one where the disorder is due to disease and the other where it is not. The distinction is not an arbitrary one. If disease is not the cause, if there is some temporary loss of consciousness arising accidentally, it is reasonable to hope that it will not be repeated and that it is safe to let an acquitted man go entirely free. If, however, disease is present, the same thing may happen again and therefore since 1800 the law has provided that persons acquitted on this ground should be subject to restraint.

That is the submission made by counsel as a basis for saying the judge's decision was wrong and that this was a matter which should have been decided by the jury.

In our judgment, stress, anxiety and depression can no doubt be the result of the operation of external factors, but they are not, it seems to us, in themselves separately or together external factors of the kind capable in law of causing or contributing to a state of automatism. They constitute a state of mind which is prone to recur. They lack the feature of novelty or accident, which is the basis of the distinction drawn by Lord Diplock in *R v Sullivan*. It is contrary to the observations of Devlin J, to which we have just referred in *Hill v Baxter*. It does not, in our judgment, come within the scope of the exception 'some external physical factor such as a blow on the head ... or the administration of an anaesthetic ... ' (see *R v Sullivan* [1984] AC 156 at 172) ...

R v Burgess [1991] 1 QB 92 (CA)

Lord Lane CJ: On 20 July 1989 in the Crown Court at Bristol before Judge Sir Ian Lewis and a jury the appellant was found not guilty by reason of insanity on a charge of wounding with intent. He was ordered to be admitted and detained in such hospital as the Secretary of State should direct.

He now appeals against that verdict by certificate of the trial judge under s 12 of the Criminal Appeal Act 1968.

The appellant did not dispute the fact that in the early hours of 2 June 1988 he had attacked Katrina Curtis hitting her on the head first with a bottle when she was asleep, then with a video recorder and finally grasping her round the throat. She suffered a gaping 3 cm laceration to her scalp requiring sutures.

His case was that he lacked the *mens rea* necessary to make him guilty of the offence, because he was 'sleep-walking' when he attacked Miss Curtis. He was, it was alleged, suffering from 'non-insane' automatism and he called medical evidence, in particular from Dr d'Orban and Dr Eames, to support that contention.

The prosecution on the other hand contended that this was not a case of automatism at all, but that the appellant was conscious of what he was doing. If, contrary to that contention, he was not conscious of what he was doing, then the case fell within the *M'Naghten* Rules, and accordingly the verdict should be not guilty by reason of insanity. The prosecution called an equally eminent expert in the shape of Dr Fenwick.

Where the defence of automatism is raised by a defendant two questions fall to be decided by the judge before the defence can be left to the jury. The first is whether a proper evidential foundation for the defence of automatism has been laid. The second is whether the evidence shows the case to be one of insane automatism, that is to say a case which falls within the *M'Naghten* Rules, or one of non-insane automatism.

The judge in the present case undertook that task and on the second question came to the conclusion that (assuming the appellant was not conscious at the time of what he was doing), on any view of the medical evidence so far as automatism was concerned, it amounted to evidence of insanity within the *M'Naghten* Rules and not merely to evidence of non-insane automatism.

The sole ground of appeal is that the ruling was wrong.

The jury then had to decide on the basis of the judge's direction, which of course followed his ruling, whether the appellant was conscious when he struck Miss

Curtis, in which case the verdict would be guilty, or whether he was not guilty by reason of insanity. As already indicated, they came to the latter conclusion.

The facts required setting out in a little more detail.

Miss Curtis occupied the flat immediately above that of the appellant. The two were on friendly terms. They were in the habit of watching video tapes together in her flat. She realised that the appellant was probably in love with her. She did not wish to allow their relationship to develop beyond mere friendship. The appellant was then 32 years of age. He was sexually inexperienced and of a somewhat solitary disposition. He had always behaved impeccably towards her and had made no physical advances. He had hopes that her friendship towards him might develop into something deeper.

On the evening in question the appellant came up to her flat with the video tapes. They had one glass of Martini each. There is no suggestion of any intoxication. Having watched one video tape, she fell asleep on the sofa. The next thing she knew was that something hard had hit her on the head. This must have been about one to one and a half hours later, so it seems. She woke up, dazed, to find herself surrounded by broken glass and confronted by the appellant with the video recorder held up high, clearly intending to bring it down on her head, which he did. He was speaking loudly. He seemed vicious and angry – quite out of character. She fell to the floor, whereupon he put a hand round her throat. With great presence of mind, she managed to say, 'I love you Bar', whereupon he appeared to come to his senses and to show great anxiety for what he had done. He later telephoned for an ambulance. It seems that he must have unplugged the video recorder detaching the various leads and then carried it round to where Miss Curtis lay ...

[His Lordship quoted the material part of the *M'Naghten* Rules (set out at the start of this chapter) and went on:]

The reason for the finding of not guilty in these circumstances is of course the absence of the intent which must be proved to accompany the defendant's actions before guilt can be established.

What the law regards as insanity for the purposes of these enactments may be far removed from what would be regarded as insanity by a psychiatrist.

There can be no doubt but that the appellant, on the basis of the jury's verdict, was labouring under such a defect of reason as not to know what he was doing when he wounded Miss Curtis. The question is whether that was from 'disease of the mind'.

The first point that has to be understood is that the phrase is 'disease of the mind' and not 'disease of the brain' ...

The appellant plainly suffered from a defect of reason from some sort of failure (for lack of a better term) of the mind causing him to act as he did without conscious motivation. His mind was to some extent controlling his actions, which were purposive rather than the result simply of muscular spasm, but without his being consciously aware of what he was doing. Can it be said that that 'failure' was a *disease* of the mind rather than a defect or failure of the mind not due to disease? That is the distinction, by no means always easy to draw, upon which this case depends, as others have depended in the past.

One can perhaps narrow the field of enquiry still further by eliminating what are sometimes called the 'external factors' such as concussion caused by a blow on the head. There were no such factors here. Whatever the cause may have been, it was an 'internal' cause. The possible disappointment or frustration caused by unrequited love is not to be equated with something such as concussion. On this aspect of the case, we respectfully adopt what was said by Martin JA giving the judgment of the court in the Ontario Court of Appeal in *R v Rabey* (1977) 17 OR (2d) 1 at 17, 22, which was approved by a majority in the Supreme Court of Canada (see [1980] 2 SCR 513 at 519 where the facts bore a similarity to those in the instant case although the diagnosis was different):

> Any malfunctioning of the mind, or mental disorder having its source primarily in some subjective condition or weakness internal to the accused (whether fully understood or not), may be a 'disease of the mind' if it prevents the accused from knowing what he is doing, but transient disturbances of consciousness due to certain specific external factors do not fall within the concept of disease of the mind ... In my view, the ordinary stresses and disappointments of life which are the common lot of mankind do not constitute an external cause constituting an explanation for a malfunctioning of the mind which takes it out of the category of a 'disease of the mind'. To hold otherwise would deprive the concept of an external factor of any real meaning.

This distinction between 'internal' and 'external' factors appears in the speech of Lord Diplock in *R v Sullivan* [1984] AC 156 at 172 [from which his Lordship then quoted].

What help does one derive from the authorities as to the meaning of 'disease' in this context? Lord Denning in *Bratty v AG for Northern Ireland* [1963] AC 386 at 412 said:

> On the other hand discussed by Devlin J, namely what is a 'disease of the mind' within the *M'Naghten* Rules, I would agree with him that this is a question for the judge. The major mental diseases, which the doctors call psychoses, such as schizophrenia, are clearly diseases of the mind. But in *R v Charlson* [1955] 1 WLR 317, Barry J seems to have assumed that the other diseases such as epilepsy or cerebral tumour are not diseases of the mind, even when they are such as to manifest themselves in violence. I do not agree with this. It seems to me that any mental disorder which has manifested itself in violence and is prone to recur is a disease of the mind. At any rate it is the sort of disease for which a person should be detained in hospital rather than be given an unqualified acquittal.

It seems to us that if there is a danger of recurrence that may be an added reason for categorising the condition as a disease of the mind. On the other hand, the absence of the danger of recurrence is not a reason for saying that it cannot be a disease of the mind. Subject to that possible qualification, we respectfully adopt Lord Denning's suggested definition.

There have been several occasions when during the course of judgments in the Court of Appeal and the House of Lords observations have been made, obiter, about the criminal responsibility of sleep-walkers, where sleep-walking had been used as a self-evident illustration of non-insane automatism ...

One turns then to examine the evidence upon which the judge had to base his decision and for this purpose the two medical experts called by the defence are the obvious principal sources. Dr d'Orban in examination-in-chief said:

> On the evidence available to me, and subject to the results of the tests when they became available, I came to the same conclusion as Dr Nicholas and Dr Eames, whose reports I had read, and that was that [the appellant's] actions had occurred during the course of a sleep disorder.

He was asked, 'Assuming this is a sleep-associated automatism, is it an internal or external factor?' He answered: 'In this particular case, I think that one would have to see it as an internal factor.'

Then in cross-examination:

> Q: Would you go so far as to say that it was liable to recur?
>
> A: It is possible for it to recur, yes.
>
> Judge Lewis: Is this a case of automatism associated with a pathological condition or not?
>
> A: I think the answer would have to be Yes, because it is an abnormality of the brain function, so it would be regarded as a pathological condition.

Dr Eames in cross-examination agreed with Dr d'Orban as to the internal rather than the external factor. He accepted that there is a liability to recurrence of sleepwalking. He could not go so far as to say that there is no liability of recurrence of serious violence but he agreed with the other medical witnesses that there is no recorded case of violence of this sort recurring.

The prosecution, as already indicated, called Dr Fenwick, whose opinion was that his was not a sleep-walking episode at all. If it was a case where the appellant was unconscious of what he was doing, the most likely explanation was that he was in what is described as a hysterical dissociative state. That is a state in which, for psychological reasons, such as being overwhelmed by his emotions, the person's brain works in a different way. He carries out acts of which he has no knowledge and for which he has no memory. It is quite different from sleep-walking.

He then went on to describe features of sleep-walking. This is what he said:

> First, violent acts in sleep-walking are very common. In just an exposure of one day to a sleep-walking clinic, you will hear of how people are kicked in bed, hit in bed, partially strangled – it is usually just arms round the neck, in bed, which is very common. Serious violence fortunately is rare. Serious violence does recur, or certainly the propensity for it to recur is there, although there are very few cases in the literature – in fact I know of none – in which somebody has come to court twice for a sleep-walking offence. This does not mean that sleep-walking violence does not recur; what it does mean is that those who are associated with the sleeper take the necessary precautions. Finally, should a person be detained in hospital? The answer to that is: Yes, because sleep-walking is treatable. Violent night terrors are treatable. There is a lot which can be done for the sleep-walker, so sending them to hospital after a violent act to have their sleep-walking sorted out makes good sense.

Dr Fenwick was also of the view that in certain circumstances hysterical dissociative states are also subject to treatment.

It seems to us that on th[e] evidence the judge was right to conclude that this was an abnormality or disorder albeit transitory, due to an internal factor, whether functional or organic, which had manifested itself in violence. It was a disorder or abnormality which might recur, though the possibility of it recurring in the form of serious violence was unlikely. Therefore, since this was a legal problem to be decided on legal principles, it seems to us that on those principles the answer was as the judge found it to be. It does however go further than that. Dr d'Orban, as already described, stated it as his view that the condition would be regarded as pathological. Pathology is the science of diseases. It seems therefore that in this respect at least there is some similarity between the law and medicine ... This appeal must accordingly be dismissed.

RELATIONSHIP BETWEEN SANE AND INSANE AUTOMATISM

Bratty v AG for Northern Ireland [1963] AC 386 (HL)

Viscount Kilmuir LC: ... To establish the defence of insanity within the *M'Naghten* Rules the accused must prove on the preponderance of probabilities, first a defect of reason from a disease of the mind, and, second, as a consequence of such a defect, ignorance of the nature and quality (or the wrongfulness) of the acts. We have to consider a case in which it is sought to do so by medical evidence to the effect that the conduct of the accused might be compatible with psychomotor epilepsy, which is a disease of the mind affecting the reason, and that psychomotor epilepsy could cause ignorance of the nature and quality of the acts done, but in which the medical witness can assign no other cause for that ignorance. Where the possibility of an unconscious act depends on, and only on, the existence of a defect of reason from disease of the mind within the *M'Naghten* Rules, a rejection by the jury of this defence of insanity necessarily implies that they reject the possibility.

The Court of Criminal Appeal also took the view that where the alleged automatism is based solely on a disease of the mind within the *M'Naghten* Rules, the same burden of proof rests on the defence whether the 'plea' is given the name of insanity or automatism. I do not think that statement goes further than saying that when you rely on insanity as defined by the Rules you cannot by a difference of nomenclature avoid the road so often and authoritatively laid down by the courts.

What I have said does not mean that, if a defence of insanity is raised unsuccessfully, there can never, in any conceivable circumstances, be room for an alternative defence based on automatism. For example, it may be alleged that the accused had a blow on the head, after which he acted without being conscious of what he was doing or was a sleep-walker. There might be a divergence of view as to whether there was a defect of reason from disease of the mind (compare the curious position which arose in *R v Kemp* [1957] 1 QB 399). The jury might not accept the evidence of a defect of reason from disease of the mind, but at the same time accept the evidence that the prisoner did not know what he was doing. If the jury should take that view of the facts they would find him not guilty. But it should be noted that the defence would only have succeeded because the necessary foundation had been laid by positive evidence which, properly considered, was evidence of something other than a defect of reason from disease of the mind. In my opinion, this analysis of the two defences (insanity and automatism) shows that where the only cause alleged for the unconsciousness is a defect of reason from disease of the mind, and that cause is rejected by the jury, there can be no room for the alternative defence of automatism. Like the Court of Criminal Appeal, I cannot therefore accept the submission that the whole of the evidence directed to the issue of insanity should have been left to the jury to consider whether there was automatism due to another cause. It was conceded before this House, and this is stated in the judgment of the Court of Criminal Appeal, that there was nothing to show or suggest that there was any other pathological cause for automatism.

Lord Denning ... if the involuntary act proceeds from a disease of the mind, it gives rise to a defence of insanity, but not to a defence of automatism. Suppose a crime is committed by a man in a state of automatism or clouded consciousness due to a recurrent disease of the mind. Such an act is no doubt involuntary, but it does not give rise to an unqualified acquittal, for that would mean that he would be let at large to do it again. The only proper verdict is one which ensures that the person who suffers from the disease is kept secure in a hospital so as not to be a danger to himself or others. That is, a verdict of guilty but insane.

Once you exclude all the cases I have mentioned, it is apparent that the category of involuntary acts is very limited. So limited, indeed, that until recently there was hardly any reference in the English books to this so-called defence of automatism ... In striking contrast to *Charlson's* case [1955] 1 WLR 317, is *R v Kemp* [1957] 1 QB 399. A devoted husband of excellent character made an entirely motiveless and irrational attack upon his wife. He struck her violently with a hammer. He was charged with causing her grievous bodily harm. It was found that he suffered from hardening of the arteries which might lead to a congestion of blood in the brain. As a result of such congestion, he suffered a temporary lack of consciousness, so that he was not conscious that he picked up the hammer or that he was striking his wife with it. It was therefore an involuntary act. Note again the important point – no plea of insanity was raised but only the defence of automatism. Nevertheless, Devlin J put insanity to the jury. He held that hardening of the arteries was a 'disease of the mind' within the *M'Naghten* Rules and he directed the jury they ought so to find. They accordingly found Kemp guilty but insane.

My Lords, I think that Devlin J was quite right in *Kemp's* case in putting the question of insanity to the jury, even though it had not been raised by the defence. When it is asserted that the accused did an involuntary act in a state of automatism, the defence necessarily puts in issue the state of mind of the accused man: and thereupon it is open to the prosecution to show what his true state of mind was. The old notion that only the defence can raise a defence of insanity is now gone. The prosecution are entitled to raise it and it is their duty to do so rather than allow a dangerous person to be at large ...

Upon the other point discussed by Devlin J, namely what is a 'disease of the mind' within the *M'Naghten* Rules, I would agree with him that this is a question for the judge. The major mental diseases, which the doctors call psychoses, such as schizophrenia, are clearly diseases of the mind. But in *Charlson's* case, Barry J seems to have assumed that other diseases such as epilepsy or cerebral tumour are not diseases of the mind, even when they are such as to manifest themselves in violence. I do not agree with this. It seems to me that any mental disorder which has manifested itself in violence and is prone to recur is a disease of the mind. At any rate it is the sort of disease for which a person should be detained in hospital rather than be given an unqualified acquittal.

It is to be noticed that in *Charlson's* case and *Kemp's* the defence raised only automatism, not insanity. In the present case the defence raised both automatism and insanity. And herein lies the difficulty because of the burden of proof. If the accused says he did not know what he was doing, then, so far as the defence of automatism is concerned, the Crown must prove that the act was a voluntary act, see *Woolmington's* case. But so far as the defence of insanity is concerned, the defence must prove that the act was an involuntary act due to disease of the mind, see *M'Naghten's* case (1843) 10 Cl & F 200, 210, HL ...

This brings me to the root question in the present case: Was a proper foundation laid here for the defence of automatism, apart from the plea of insanity? There was the evidence of George Bratty himself that he could not remember anything because 'this blackness was over me'. He said 'I did not realise exactly what I was doing', and added afterwards 'I didn't know what I was doing. I didn't realise anything.' He said he had four or five times previously had 'feelings of blackness' and frequently headaches. There was evidence, too, of his odd behaviour at times, his mental backwardness and his religious leanings. Added to this there was the medical evidence. Dr Sax, who was called on his behalf, said that there was a possibility that he was suffering from psychomotor epilepsy. It was, he said, practically the only possibility that occurred to him. Dr Walker, his general practitioner, said you could not leave the possibility out of account. Dr Robinson, a specialist, who gave evidence on behalf of the Crown, said he thought it was extremely unlikely that it was an epileptic attack, but could not rule it out. All the doctors agreed that psychomotor epilepsy, if it exists, is a defect of reason due to disease of the mind: and the judge accepted this view. No other cause was canvassed.

In those circumstances, I am clearly of opinion that, if the act of George Bratty was an involuntary act, as the defence suggested, the evidence attributed it solely to a disease of the mind and only defence open was the defence of insanity. There was no evidence of automatism apart from insanity. There was, therefore, no need for the judge to put [non-insane automatism] to the jury. And when the jury rejected the defence of insanity, they rejected the only defence disclosed by the evidence ...

Notes and queries

1   To what extent is the distinction between diabetes as a disease of the mind resulting in insanity (see *Hennessy*, above) and lack of insulin as an external factor giving rise to automatism (*Bingham*, above) sustainable and credible?

2   As the above extracts indicate, the issue of insanity often arises not because the defendant has raised the defence, but because the trial judge indicates that it is the only defence, on the facts, that he is willing to leave to the jury.

3   Given that a defendant charged with murder who suffers from a mental illness will now plead diminished responsibility (see further Chapter 15), why would any defendant charged with a lesser offence actively seek to raise the issue of insanity? Would a defendant not be better advised simply to plead guilty?

Where the defendant did not realise his actions were wrong

As indicated above, the defence of insanity may be available to a defendant who was aware of his actions but, because of his defect of reason, did not realise that his actions were wrong. The issue here has been as to the correct interpretation of the word 'wrong'. Does it mean morally wrong, or legally wrong? Earlier cases such as *R v Codere* (1916) 12 Cr App R 21 suggested that a defendant might not be able to avail himself of the defence of insanity, even where he was unaware that his actions were contrary to law, if he nevertheless realised that his conduct was wrong according to the ordinary standards adopted by reasonable persons. As will be seen below, *R v Windle* suggests that it is sufficient that the defendant was unaware that his actions were illegal.

R v Windle [1952] 2 QB 526 (CA)

Facts: The appellant was convicted of the murder of his wife. He was a man, 40 years of age, of little resolution and weak character, and was married to a woman 18 years his senior. His married life was very unhappy; his wife was always speaking of committing suicide and the doctors who gave evidence at the trial were of opinion, from the history of the case, that she was certifiably insane. The appellant frequently discussed his home life with his workmates, until, as one of them said, they were sick and tired of hearing about it. Eventually a workmate said to the appellant, 'Give her a dozen aspirins', and on the following day the appellant gave his wife 100 tablets. He sent for a doctor and told him that he had given his wife so many aspirins. She was taken to hospital, where she died. The appellant informed the police that he had given his wife 100 aspirins, and added: 'I suppose they will hang me for this?' At his trial a defence of insanity was put forward. A doctor was called for him who said that the appellant was suffering from a form of communicated insanity known as *folie à deux*. It was said that if a person was in constant attendance on another of unsound mind, in some way the insanity might be communicated to the attendant, so that, for a time at any rate, the attendant might develop a defect of reason or of mind. Rebutting medical evidence was allowed to be called for the prosecution, and the doctors called on either side expressed the opinion that the appellant, when administering the fatal dose of aspirin to his wife, knew that he was doing an act which the law forbade.

The trial judge, Devlin J, having heard the evidence, ruled that there was no evidence of insanity, as defined in the rules in *M'Naghten's* case (1843) 10 Cl & F 200, to be left to the jury. He accordingly withdrew that issue from them, and they found the appellant guilty of murder.

Lord Goddard CJ: ... In this particular case, the only evidence given on the issue of insanity was that of the doctor called by the appellant and of the prison doctor who was allowed to be called by the prosecution to rebut, if indeed it were necessary, any evidence which had been given. It was probably right that the prison doctor should be called as he had had the appellant under constant observation. Both the doctors gave their evidence in a way that commended itself to the judge, and both, without hesitation, expressed the view that the appellant knew, when administering this poison, for such as it was, to his wife, that he was doing an act which the law forbade. I need not put it higher than that.

It may well be that, in the misery in which he had been living, with this nagging and tiresome wife who constantly expressed the desire to commit suicide, he thought that she would be better out of this world than in it. He may have thought that it would be a kindly act to release her from what she was suffering from – or thought she was suffering from – but that the law does not permit. In the present case there was some exceedingly vague evidence that the appellant was suffering from a defect of reason. In the opinion of his own doctor, there was a defect of reason which he attributed to communicated insanity. In my opinion, if the only question in this case has been whether the appellant was suffering from a disease of the mind, I should say that that was a question which must have been left to the jury. That, however, is not the question.

... A man may be suffering from a defect of reason, but if he knows that what he is doing is 'wrong', and by 'wrong' is meant contrary to law, he is responsible. Mr Shawcross, in the course of his very careful argument, suggested that the word 'wrong', as it was used in the *M'Naghten* Rules, did not mean contrary to law but had some kind of qualified meaning, such as morally wrong, and that if a person was in such a state of mind through a defect of reason that, although he knew that what he was doing was wrong in law, he thought that it was beneficial or kind or praiseworthy, that would excuse him ...

... Counsel for the appellant argued that the *M'Naghten* Rules only applied to cases in which delusions were present. The court cannot agree with that. It is true that when the judges who formulated the rules were summoned by the House of Lords the occasion had special reference to *M'Naghten's* case, but ever since that date the rules have been generally applied in all cases of insanity, whatever the nature of the insanity or disease of the mind from which the person accused is suffering.

In the opinion of the court there is no doubt that in the *M'Naghten* Rules 'wrong' means contrary to law and not 'wrong' according to the opinion of one man or of a number of people on the question whether a particular act might or might not be justified. In the present case, it could not be challenged that the appellant knew that what he was doing was contrary to law, and that he realised what punishment the law provided for murder. That was the opinion of both the doctors who gave evidence ...

Notes and queries

1   Does the decision in *Windle* mean that a defendant, who knows his actions are wrong by all reasonable and civilised standards, but who is nevertheless unaware of the fact that they are prohibited by law, will be able to avail himself of the defence of insanity?

2   Suppose D kills P because he wrongly believes P is trying to kill him. Suppose that this belief springs from D's insane delusions. Would D be able to plead insanity? He believes he is acting in self-defence, hence he believes his actions are not unlawful. Is it true to say, therefore, that he is unaware that his actions are wrong?

3   Suppose D claims he was ordered by God to commit an offence of theft or criminal damage – does this amount to a plea of insanity? See further *R v Bell* [1984] Crim LR 685.

4   To what extent does the defence of insanity provide a defence based on ignorance of the criminal law?

Codification and law reform proposals

Clauses 34–40 of the draft Criminal Code Bill (DCCB) (Vol I of Law Com 177) propose significant reforms in its restatement of the law relating to a general defence of mental illness, as follows:

34 In this Act –

'mental disorder' means –

(a) severe mental illness; or

(b) a state of arrested or incomplete development of mind; or

(c) a state of automatism (not resulting only from intoxication) which is a feature of a disorder, whether organic or functional and whether continuing or recurring, that may cause a similar state on another occasion;

'return a mental disorder verdict' means –

(a) in relation to trial on indictment, return a verdict that the defendant is not guilty on evidence of mental disorder; and

(b) in relation to summary trial, dismiss the information on evidence of mental disorder;

'severe mental illness' means a mental illness which has one or more of the following characteristics –

(a) lasting impairment of intellectual functions shown by failure of memory, orientation, comprehension and learning capacity;

(b) lasting alteration of mood of such degree as to give rise to delusional appraisal of the defendant's situation, his past or his future, or that of others, or lack of any appraisal;

(c) delusional beliefs, persecutory, jealous or grandiose;

(d) abnormal perceptions associated with delusional misinterpretation of events;

(e) thinking so disordered as to prevent reasonable appraisal of the defendant's situation or reasonable communication with others;

'severe mental handicap' means a state of arrested or incomplete development of mind which includes severe impairment of intelligence and social functioning.

35 (1) A mental disorder verdict shall be returned if the defendant is proved to have committed an offence but it is proved on the balance of probabilities (whether by the prosecution or by the defendant) that he was at the time suffering from severe mental illness or severe mental handicap.

(2) Subsection (1) does not apply if the court or jury is satisfied beyond reasonable doubt that the offence was not attributable to the severe mental illness or severe mental handicap.

(3) A court or jury shall not, for the purposes of a verdict under subsection (1), find that the defendant was suffering from severe mental illness or severe mental handicap unless two medical practitioners approved for the purposes of section 12 of the Mental Health Act 1983 as having special experience in the diagnosis or treatment of mental disorder have given evidence that he was so suffering.

(4) Subsection (1), so far as it relates to severe mental handicap, does not apply to an offence under section 106(1), 107 or 108 (sexual relations with the mentally handicapped).

36 A mental disorder verdict shall be returned if –

(a) the defendant is acquitted of an offence only because, by reason of evidence of mental disorder or a combination of mental disorder and intoxication. it is found that he acted or may have acted in a state of automatism, or without the fault required for the offence, or believing that an exempting circumstance existed; and

(b) it is proved on the balance of probabilities (whether by the prosecution or by the defendant) that he was suffering from mental disorder at the time of the act.

37 A defendant may plead 'not guilty by reason of mental disorder'; and

(a) if the court directs that the plea be entered the direction shall have the same effect as a mental disorder verdict; and

(b) if the court does not so direct the defendant shall be treated as having pleaded not guilty.

38 (1) Whether evidence is evidence of mental disorder or automatism is a question of law.

(2) The prosecution shall not adduce evidence of mental disorder. or contend that a mental disorder verdict should be returned, unless the defendant has given or adduced evidence that he acted without the fault required for the offence, or believing that an exempting circumstance existed, or in a state of automatism, or (on a charge of murder) when suffering from mental abnormality as defined in section 57(2).

(3) The court may give directions as to the stage of the proceedings at which the prosecution may adduce evidence of mental disorder.

39 Schedule 2 has effect with respect to the orders that may be made upon the return of a mental disorder verdict, to the conditions governing the making of those orders, to the effects of those orders and to related matters.

40 A defendant shall not, when a mental disorder verdict is returned in respect of an offence and while that verdict subsists, be found guilty of any other offence of which, but for this section, he might on the same occasion be found guilty –

(a) on the indictment, count or information to which the verdict relates; or

(b) on any other indictment, count or information founded on the same facts.

The commentary explains the thinking behind these proposals:

Disability in relation to trial

11.7 *Reform proposals.* The defendant's mental disorder (or his being a deaf-mute) may operate as a bar to his trial on indictment or to the progress of his trial beyond the end of the prosecution case. If the defendant is found to be 'under disability' the court will order his admission to a hospital to be specified by the Secretary of State. The Committee on Mentally Abnormal Offenders (chairman: Lord Butler; hereafter called 'the Butler Committee') gave elaborate consideration to the law and procedure relating to disability and made important recommendations for reform. The Committee made a cogent case for change on a number of issues, including the extension of a disability procedure to the magistrates' court and the provision of flexible disposal powers in relation to a defendant under disability. But some of the Committee's procedural proposals were controversial. A consultative document issued by the Home Office in April 1978 referred in particular to serious doubts as to the practicability of a recommendation that if the defendant is found to be under disability there should nevertheless be a 'trial of the facts' – at once if there is no prospect of the defendant's recovering, or as soon (during periods of adjournment not exceeding six months in total) as he may prove unresponsive to treatment.

11.8 *Location in the Code.* We hope that the important matter of disability will be further considered as soon as possible with a view to reform. We do not, however, share the Code team's preference for including provisions on disability in Part 1 of the Code. It is true that the Butler Committee proposed that a finding of disability and an acquittal based on a mental disorder verdict should give rise to similar disposal powers. But compatibility between the two disposal regimes can be achieved without enacting the relevant provisions side by side. Those relating to disability are procedural in nature and in due course their proper place will be in the projected Part 111 of the Code.

Code provisions on mental disorder

11.9 *Butler Committee.* The Butler Committee proposed substantial reform of the law and procedure relating to the effect of mental disorder on criminal liability and the disposal of persons acquitted because of mental disorder. The necessity of incorporating in the projected Criminal Code an appropriate provision to replace the outdated 'insanity' defence was one justification given by the Committee for its review of the subject. We ourselves are persuaded that implementation of the Committee's proposals would greatly improve this area of the law. We have, however, found it necessary to suggest some important modifications of those proposals. Clauses 34 to 40 therefore aim to give effect to the policy of the Butler Committee as modified by us in ways that will be explained in the following paragraphs.

11.10 *The present 'insanity defence'.* Before considering the structure of the proposed law, it will be convenient to refer to that of the present law. The *M'Naghten* Rules together with statutory provisions, produce a 'special verdict' ('not guilty by reason of insanity') and the automatic committal of the acquitted person to a hospital to be specified by the Secretary of State, in two kinds of case.

(i) The first case is that where it is proved (rebutting the so-called 'presumption of sanity') that, because of 'a defect of reason, from disease of the mind', the defendant did not 'know the nature and quality of the act he was doing'. If the defendant 'did not know what he was doing', he must have lacked any fault required for the offence charged; so, in modern terms at least, this first element in the *M'Naghten* Rules has the appearance of a rule, not about guilt, but about burden of proof and disposal. The defendant should in any case be acquitted, but he must prove that he should be; and his acquittal is to be treated as the occasion for his detention as a matter of social defence.

(ii) The second case is that where, because of 'a defect of reason, from disease of the mind'. the defendant 'did not know he was doing what was wrong.' This is a case, then, in which the Rules afford a defence properly so called: a person who would otherwise be guilty is not guilty 'by reason of insanity'. But, once again, social defence requires his detention in hospital.

11.11 *Structure of the proposed provisions.* Clauses 35 and 36, following the structure proposed by the Butler Committee, are similarly concerned with two kinds of case, in each of which there is to be a verdict of acquittal in special form ('not guilty on evidence of mental disorder'). On the return of a mental disorder verdict the court would have flexible disposal powers, the availability of which would undoubtedly give clauses 35 and 36 greater practical importance than the insanity defence now has.

(a) Clause 35(1). In one case all the elements of the offence are proved but severe mental disorder operates as a true defence. This is equivalent to case (ii) above.

(b) Clause 36. In the other case an acquittal is inevitable because the prosecution has failed to prove that the defendant acted with the required fault (or to disprove his defence of automatism or mistake); but the reason for that failure is evidence of mental disorder, and it is proved that the defendant was indeed suffering from mental disorder at the time of the act. This differs from case (i) above in casting no burden on the defendant of proving his innocence.

11.12 *Summary trial.* The Butler Committee recommended that a magistrates' court should acquit on evidence of mental disorder in the same circumstances as a jury. Our clauses so provide. The general principles of the substantive criminal law applicable to offences triable either way must be the same whatever the mode of trial in the particular case. A defendant who lacked the fault required for the offence charged will of course be entitled to an acquittal wherever he is tried. And if severe mental illness or severe mental handicap at the time of the offence entails an acquittal on trial on indictment, it must do so also on summary trial. A defence of severe mental illness may, of course, make summary trial inappropriate. That is a consideration that could be taken care of by procedural provisions. But, assuming that mental disorder is capable of arising as an issue on summary trial, the Code must clearly provide for the same substantive consequences as on trial on indictment.

Clause 34: Mental disorder: definitions

11.13 *'Mental disorder'; 'severe mental illness'; 'severe mental handicap'.* These terms are considered below, in the context of the provisions in which they are crucial.

The Butler scheme renounces the outdated terms 'insanity' and 'disease of the mind'.

11. 14 *'Return a mental disorder verdict'*. Each of the situations defined in clauses 35(1) and 36 calls for the return of 'a mental disorder verdict' . The word 'verdict' is strictly speaking inapt to refer to the determination of a magistrates' court. But it greatly simplifies drafting to refer to the 'return' of a 'mental disorder verdict' as the relevant outcome of summary trial as of trial on indictment, and to explain that language in the definition section: a jury will declare that the defendant 'is not guilty on evidence of mental disorder'; the magistrates will 'dismiss the information on evidence of mental disorder.'

Clause 35: Case for mental disorder verdict: defence of severe disorder

11.15 Subsection (1) provides that even though he has done the act specified for the offence with the fault required, a defendant is entitled to an acquittal, in the form of a mental disorder verdict, if he was suffering from severe mental illness or severe mental handicap at the time. This implements the Butler Committee's conceptions with some modifications.

11.16 *Attributability of offence to disorder: a rebuttable presumption.* One aspect of the Committee's recommendation has proved controversial. The Committee acknowledged that –

> it is theoretically possible for a person to be suffering from a severe mental disorder which has in a causal sense nothing to do with the act or omission for which he is being tried;

but they found it 'very difficult to imagine a case in which one could be sure of the absence of any such connection'. They therefore proposed, in effect, an irrebuttable presumption that there was a sufficient connection between the severe disorder and the offence. This Proposal is understandable in view of the limitation of the defence to a narrow range of very serious disorders; and its adoption would certainly simplify the tasks of psychiatric witnesses and the court. Some people, however, take the view that it would be wrong in principle that a person should escape conviction if, although severely mentally ill, he has committed a rational crime which was uninfluenced by his illness and for which he ought to be liable to be punished. They believe that the prosecution should be allowed to persuade the jury (if it can) that the offence was not attributable to the disorder. We agree. Subsection (2) provides accordingly. We believe that it must improve the acceptability of the Butler Committee's generally admirable scheme as the basis of legislation.

11.17 *'Severe mental illness'* is defined in clause 34 in the terms proposed by the Butler Committee. Severe mental illness, for the purpose of this exemption from criminal liability, ought, in the Committee's view, to be closely defined and restricted to serious cases of psychosis (as that term is currently understood). The Committee recommended, as the preferable mode of definition, the identification of 'the abnormal mental phenomena which occur in the various mental illnesses and which when present would be regarded by common consent as being evidence of severity'. We believe that this symptomatic mode of definition has much to commend it. The psychiatric expert will give evidence in terms of strict 'factual tests', rather than of abstractions (such as 'disease of the mind' or 'severe mental illness' itself) or diagnostic labels. The method allocates appropriate functions to the law itself (in laying down the test of criminal responsibility), to the expert (in advising whether the test is satisfied) and to the tribunal of fact (in judging, by reference to the whole of the case, whether that advice is soundly given).

11.18 *Content of the definition.* We are grateful to the Section for Forensic Psychiatry of the Royal College of Psychiatrists for responding to our request for advice on the content of the definition of 'severe mental illness'. We are told that there was a suggestion, at the time of the Butler Committee's Report, that the list of symptoms in the definition might not be sufficiently comprehensive, but that this suggestion had had little support. Our advisers expressed their own satisfaction with the proposed criteria of severe mental illness and with the way in which they are expressed.

11.19 *'Severe mental handicap'* is defined in clause 34. The expression used by the Butler Committee was 'severe subnormality', which was defined in the Mental Health Act 1959, section 4, in terms apt for the Committee's purpose. But the expression 'severe mental impairment' has since replaced 'severe subnormality' in mental health legislation (the latter term having fallen out of favour). 'Severe mental impairment' has the following meaning:

> a state of arrested or incomplete development of mind which includes severe impairment of intelligence and social functioning and is associated with abnormally aggressive or seriously irresponsible conduct on the part of the person concerned.

This definition is not a happy one for present purposes; exemption from criminal liability on the ground of severe mental handicap ought not to be limited to a case where the handicap is associated with aggressive or irresponsible conduct. We therefore propose that the expression 'severe mental handicap' be used, with the same definition as 'severe mental impairment' down to the word 'functioning'. This will give effect to the Butler Committee's intentions and has the approval of our Royal College advisers.

11.20 *Burden of proof.* Subsection (1) permits proof of severe disorder by either prosecution or defendant. Normally it will be for the defendant to prove it, as his defence to the charge. This is as proposed by the Butler Committee. But there may he a case in which the defendant adduces evidence of mental disorder on an issue of fault or automatism and the prosecution responds with evidence of severe disorder and in such a case it may be the prosecution evidence (or a combination of prosecution and defence evidence) which results in a mental disorder verdict under clause 35(1).

11.21 *Evidence of severe disorder.* Subsection (3) provides that such evidence must be given by two appropriately qualified doctors, as recommended by the Butler Committee.

11.22 *Exception.* A severely mentally handicapped person cannot commit an offence under clause 106(1), 107 or 108 involving sexual relations with another such person. Subsection (4) ensures that such a person, if charged with one of those offences, receives an unqualified acquittal.

11.23 *Broad effect of the clause.* Evidence of mental disorder may be the reason why the court or jury is at least doubtful whether the defendant acted with the fault required for the offence. The Butler Committee recommended that, although in such a case there must be an acquittal, this acquittal should be in the qualified form 'not guilty on evidence of mental "disorder" where it is proved that the defendant was in fact suffering from mental disorder at the time of his act. Clause 36 gives effect to this recommendation, significantly modified by the adoption of a narrower meaning of 'mental disorder' than that proposed by the Committee.

11.24 *Cases covered by the clause.* The clause adapts the Committee's proposal to the conceptual structure of the Code. First, it provides that the mental disorder verdict is not to be returned unless evidence of mental disorder is the only reason for an acquittal. The provision must not affect a case in which the defendant is entitled to an acquittal on some additional ground having nothing to do with mental disorder. Secondly, it refers not only to absence of fault but also (a) to automatism and (b) to a belief in a circumstance of defence. (a) Automatism is mentioned because the acquittal of one who acted in a state of automatism is not grounded only in absence of 'fault' (see clause 33). (b) A person may commit an act of violence because of a deluded belief that he is under attack and must defend himself. Within the scheme of the Code – which draws a distinction between elements of offences (including fault elements) and defences – such a person would not, when relying on his delusion, be denying 'the fault required for the offence'. His mentally disordered belief must therefore be separately mentioned in the paragraph.

11.25 The clause deals also with the case where the defendant lacked the required fault because of the combined effects of mental disorder and intoxication. We have discussed this case in our comments on clause 22 (intoxication).

11.26 *'Mental disorder': the Butler Committee's proposal.* The Butler Committee proposed to adopt in principle the Mental Health Act definition of 'mental disorder' – namely, 'mental illness, arrested or incomplete development of mind, psychopathic disorder and any other disorder or disability of mind' – subject only to the exclusion of 'transient states not related to other forms of mental disorder and arising solely as a consequence of (a) the administration, maladministration or non-administration of alcohol, drugs or other substances or (b) physical injury.'

11.27 We are surprised that such an extremely wide definition, designed for the very different purposes of the Mental Health Act, should have been thought suitable as the basis of a qualified acquittal, subject only to the exclusion of certain 'transient states not related to other forms of mental disorder'. If this proposal were followed, the result might be to subject too many acquitted persons to a possibly stigmatising or distressing verdict and to inappropriate control through the courts' disposal powers. The cases attracting a mental disorder verdict under this clause should, we think, be strictly limited. We therefore exclude 'mental illness' (not being 'severe') and 'any other disorder or disability of mind' from our definition. We also exclude 'psychopathic disorder' as being, we believe, irrelevant to the existence of 'fault' in the technical sense.

11.28 *'Mental disorder': the proposed definition.* We define 'mental disorder' in clause 34 to include (only):

(a) 'severe mental illness' (as defined in the same section): the defendant who lacked fault, or believed in the existence of an exempting circumstance, because of a psychotic distortion of perception or understanding, will receive a mental disorder verdict and be amenable to the court's powers of restraint.

(b) 'arrested or incomplete development of mind': this category from the Mental Health Act definition of 'mental disorder' survives our amendment of the Butler Committee's proposal. We must, however, express a doubt as to whether it should do so. Some persons against whom fault cannot be proved might receive mental disorder verdicts, and become subject to the protective powers of the criminal courts, although under the present law they would receive unqualified acquittals. It may be thought more appropriate to leave any acquitted persons within this category who represent a danger to themselves or others to be dealt with under Part 11 of the Mental Health Act 1983.

(c) (in effect) pathological automatism that is liable to recur: it would not, we think, be acceptable to propose that the courts should lose all control over a person acquitted because of what is now termed 'insane automatism'. Paragraph (c) of our definition requires the 'state of automatism' (see clause 33 (1)) to be 'a feature of a disorder ... that may cause a similar state on another occasion'. This qualification confines the mental disorder verdict to those possibly warranting some form of control that the court can impose. It may nevertheless be felt by some that the paragraph includes too much. The Butler Committee wished, in particular, to protect from a mental disorder verdict a diabetic who causes a harm in a state of confusion after failing to take his insulin. We do not think, however, that there is a satisfactory way of distinguishing between the different conditions that may cause repeated episodes of disorder; nor do we think it necessary to do so. There is not, so far as we can see, a satisfactory basis for distinguishing between (say) a brain tumour or cerebral arteriosclerosis on the one hand and diabetes or epilepsy on the other. If any of these conditions causes a state of automatism in which the sufferer commits what would otherwise be an offence of violence, his acquittal should be 'on evidence of mental disorder'. Whether a diabetic so affected has failed to seek treatment, or forgotten to take his insulin, or decided not to do so, may affect the court's decision whether to order his discharge or to take some other course. What is objectionable in the present law is the offensive label of 'insanity' and the fact that the court is obliged to order the hospitalisation of the acquitted person, in effect as a restricted patient. With the elimination of these features under the Butler Committee's scheme, the verdict should not seem preposterous in the way that its present counterpart does.

11.29 *Burden of proof.* A mental disorder verdict under clause 36 will not be appropriate unless the court or jury is satisfied that the evidence of mental disorder that has prevented proof of fault – to take the most likely example – in fact establishes that he was suffering from such disorder. If the court or jury is not so satisfied, there will be an ordinary acquittal. As in the case of clause 35(1), proof may derive from prosecution or defence evidence, or indeed from a combination of the two. Clause 36 follows the Butter Committee in requiring the mental disorder to be proved on the balance of probabilities: but since the defendant is *ex hypothesi* entitled to an acquittal, there is an obvious argument for requiring proof beyond reasonable doubt of the case for exposing him, through a mental disorder verdict, to the disposal powers of the court.

Clause 37: Plea of 'not guilty by reason of mental disorder'

11.30 This clause gives effect (with a verbal amendment) to the Butler Committee's recommendation that a defendant should be allowed to plead 'not guilty on evidence of mental disorder'.

Clause 38: Evidence of mental disorder and automatism

11.31 *Question of law.* Subsection (1) puts it beyond doubt that it is the function of the court (and not, in particular, of medical witnesses) to interpret the definitions of 'automatism' and 'mental disorder' in clauses 33(1) and 34 respectively. The allocation of this function to the court is important for the purposes of clauses 33(1) and 36 as well as of subsection (2) of the present clause.

11.32 *Prosecution evidence.* The Butler Committee proposed that the prosecution should, as at present, be restrained from adducing evidence of mental disorder until the defendant raises an issue that justifies its doing so; but the Committee thought that, '[i]f the defendant admits doing the act and contests the case solely on his state of mind, it is right that all the evidence as to his state of mind can be given, and if the evidence is that he was mentally disordered when he did the act there should be a [mental disorder] verdict rather than an ordinary acquittal'. Subsections (2) and (3) give effect to these views.

11.33 *Notice of defence.* The Butler Committee proposed that the defence should be required to give notice of an intention 'to adduce psychiatric or psychological evidence on the mental element – whether in relation to the [mental disorder] verdict or the defence of automatism'; and the Code team included in their Bill a provision to give effect to this proposal in a modified form. Since then the Crown Court (Advance Notice of Expert Evidence) Rules 1987 have been made. The Code team's provision, in its application to trial on indictment, would substantially duplicate those Rules. In any case, we have elsewhere in our Bill forborne to offer rules requiring advance notice of defences. The subject merits further consideration in the present context, as does the Code team's further suggestions that the prosecution should (subject to judicial direction) be able to give evidence of mental disorder as part of its case in chief if a relevant defence has been notified.

Clause 39: Disposal after mental disorder verdict

11.34 *Proposal for flexible powers.* By far the most important aspect of the Butler Committee's scheme of reform was the proposal as to the consequences of a mental disorder verdict. The Committee recommended that the court be given quite flexible powers, including the power to order in-patient treatment in hospital (with or without a restriction order), out-patient treatment, certain forfeitures, or a driving disqualification, and the power to discharge the acquitted defendant without any order.

11.35 The details of this proposal no doubt still require consideration by the government departments concerned and it would not be realistic for us, without the benefit of necessary consultation, to offer a complete set of relevant provisions. We can only express the hope that this important reform will be undertaken without further delay. It should be clear that enactment of our clauses 35 and 36, providing for mental disorder verdicts, depends upon abolition of the mandatory consequences of the present equivalent verdict.

11.36 Clause 39 provides for a Schedule of provisions concerning the disposal of persons found not guilty on evidence of mental disorder.

Clause 40: Further effect of mental disorder verdict

11.37 This clause gives effect to a subsidiary recommendation of the Butler Committee.

Further reading

RD Mackay, 'Intoxication as a factor in automatism' [1982] Crim LR 146

RD Mackay, 'Fact and fiction about the insanity defence' [1990] Crim LR 247

RD Mackay and G Kearns, 'The continued underuse of unfitness to plead and the insanity defence' [1994] Crim LR 576

TH Jones, 'Insanity, automatism and the burden of proof on the accused' (1995) 111 LQR 475

CHAPTER 8

INTOXICATION

VOLUNTARY INTOXICATION

The rules governing the defence of intoxication are to be found at common law. Where a defendant, through his own volition, becomes intoxicated he may nevertheless have a partial or complete defence to the offence with which he is charged, depending on whether the offence is classified as being one of specific or basic intent. In general terms, where the offence is classified as requiring specific intent the defendant who successfully pleads the defence of intoxication will be acquitted of that specific intent crime, but convicted instead of the lesser included basic intent crime. Hence in a case where the defendant is charged with murder, he might be acquitted on the basis of his voluntary intoxication, but convicted instead of manslaughter. Similarly with an offence such as causing grievous bodily harm with intent contrary to s 18 of the Offences Against the Person Act 1861. The defendant might be acquitted under s 18 because of his intoxication but convicted of the lesser included basic intent crime of malicious wounding contrary to s 20 of the 1861 Act.

An intoxicant for these purposes is not limited to class A or class B drugs or alcohol, but can, in theory, extend to any substance which has the effect of altering the defendant's consciousness; see further *R v Hardie* [1985] 1 WLR 64, extracted below.

WHAT AMOUNTS TO A STATE OF INTOXICATION?

DPP v Beard [1920] AC 479

Lord Birkenhead LC (at p 499): ... where a specific intent is an essential element in the offence, evidence of a state of drunkenness rendering the accused incapable of forming such an intent should be taken into consideration in order to determine whether he had in fact formed the intent necessary to constitute the particular crime. If he was so drunk that he was incapable of forming the intent required he could not be convicted of a crime which was committed only if the intent was proved.

Notes and queries

1 In *R v Cole and Others* [1993] Crim LR 300, the Court of Appeal held that, whilst the defence of intoxication was made out if the defendant was incapable of forming the necessary intent, it was also made out where, even though the defendant was so capable, the intent was not actually formed.

2 *R v Bowden* [1993] Crim LR 380 makes clear that the fact that the defendant did something whilst drunk that he would not have done when sober did

not, of itself, give rise to the defence of intoxication. A drunken intent was nevertheless an 'intent'; see further *R v Kingston*, considered below.

3 Intoxication is regarded as voluntary if the defendant knowingly took alcohol or other intoxicating drugs. It is irrelevant that he might have misjudged the extent to which he would become intoxicated; see *R v Allen* [1988] Crim LR 698, below.

THE BASIC INTENT/SPECIFIC INTENT DICHOTOMY

DPP v Morgan [1976] AC 182

Lord Simon of Glaisdale (at p 216): By crimes of basic intent I mean those crimes whose definition expresses (or, more often, applies) a *mens rea* which does not go beyond the *actus reus*. The *actus reus* generally consists of an act and some consequence. The consequence may be closely connected with the act or remotely connected with it: but with a crime of basic intent the *mens rea* does not extend beyond the act and its consequence, however, remote, as defined in the *actus reus*.

Notes and queries
1 The problem with Lord Simon's explanation of the basic/specific intent dichotomy is that it is not borne out by practice. Murder is regarded as a specific intent crime, yet no one would claim that the *mens rea* – intention to kill – goes beyond the *actus reus* – killing. A simpler way of approaching the issue is to proceed on the basis that any crime for which recklessness would be sufficient *mens rea* can be regarded as a crime of basic intent for the purposes of the defence of intoxication.

THE RATIONALE FOR THE OPERATION OF THE DEFENCE OF INTOXICATION

R v Lipman [1970] 1 QB 152 (CA)

Widgery LJ: ... Both the defendant and the victim were addicted to drugs, and on the evening of 16 September 1967, both took a quantity of a drug known as LSD. Early on the morning of 18 September, the defendant, who is a United States citizen, hurriedly booked out of his hotel and left the country. On the following day, 19 September, the victim's landlord found her dead in her room. She had suffered two blows on the head causing haemorrhage of the brain, but she had died of asphyxia as a result of some eight inches of sheet having been crammed into her mouth.

The defendant was returned to this country by extradition proceedings, and at the trial he gave evidence of having gone with the victim to her room and there experienced what he described as an LSD 'trip'. He explained how he had the illusion of descending to the centre of the earth and being attacked by snakes, with which he had fought. It was not seriously disputed that he had killed the victim in the course of this experience, but he said he had no knowledge of what he was doing and no intention to harm her. He was charged with murder, but the jury evidently accepted that he lacked the necessary intention to kill or to do grievous bodily harm ...

For the purposes of criminal responsibility we see no reason to distinguish between the effect of drugs voluntarily taken and drunkenness voluntarily induced. [His Lordship then quoted from the speech of Lord Birkenhead in *DPP v Beard* [1920] AC 479, 499, 500 and from the speeches of Lord Denning in *Bratty v AG for Northern Ireland* [1963] AC 386, 410 and *AG for Northern Ireland v Gallagher* [1963] AC 349, 381. His Lordship went on to hold:] Those authorities show quite clearly, in our opinion, that it was well established that no specific intent was necessary to support a conviction for manslaughter based upon a killing in the course of an unlawful act and that, accordingly, self-induced drunkenness was no defence to such a charge.

In the case of manslaughter by neglect, however, it has been recognised that some mental element must be established ... [His Lordship quoted from the speech of Lord Atkin in *Andrews v DPP* [1937] AC 576, 582, 583 and from the judgment of Edmund Davis J in *R v Church* [1966] 1 QB 59, 69. He continued:] All that the judgment in *Church's* case says in terms is that whereas, formerly, a killing by any unlawful act amounted to manslaughter, this consequence does not now inexorably follow unless the unlawful act is one in which ordinary sober and responsible people would recognise the existence of risk.

... We can dispose of the present application by reiterating that when the killing results from an unlawful act of the prisoner no specific intent has to be proved to convict of manslaughter, and self-induced intoxication is accordingly no defence. Since in the present case the acts complained of were obviously likely to cause harm to the victim (and did, in fact, kill her) no acquittal was possible and the verdict of manslaughter, at the least, was inevitable ...

4 November 1969: The Appeal Committee of the House of Lords (Lord Wilberforce, Viscount Dilhorne and **Lord Pearson**) refused leave to appeal.

DPP v Majewski [1977] AC 443 (HL)

Lord Elwyn-Jones LC: My Lords, Robert Stefan Majewski appeals against his conviction on 7 November 1973, at Chelmsford Crown Court on three counts of assault occasioning actual bodily harm and three counts of assault on a police constable in the execution of his duty ...

The appellant's case was that when the assaults were committed he was acting under the influence of a combination of drugs (not medically prescribed) and alcohol, to such an extent that he did not know what he was doing and that he remembered nothing of the incidents that had occurred ...

The appeal raises issues of considerable public importance. In giving the judgment of the Court of Appeal Lawton LJ rightly observed, at 404, that:

> The facts are commonplace – indeed so commonplace that their very nature reveals how serious from a social and public standpoint the consequences would be if men could behave as the [appellant] did and then claim that they were not guilty of any offence.

Self-induced alcoholic intoxication has been a factor in crimes of violence, like assault, throughout the history of crime in this country. But voluntary drug taking with the potential and actual dangers to others it may cause has added a new dimension to the old problem with which the courts have had to deal in their endeavour to maintain order and to keep public and private violence under control. To achieve this is the prime purpose of the criminal law. I have said 'the courts', for most of the relevant law has been made by the judges. A good deal of the argument in the hearing of this appeal turned on that judicial history, for the crux of the case for the Crown was that, illogical as the outcome may be said to be, the judges have evolved for the purpose of protecting the community a substantive rule of law that, in crimes of basic intent as distinct from crimes of specific intent, self-induced intoxication provides no defence and is irrelevant to offences of basic intent, such as assault ...

What then is the mental element required in our law to be established in assault? This question has been most helpfully answered in the speech of Lord Simon of Glaisdale in *R v Morgan* [1976] AC 182, 216:

> ... I take assault as an example of a crime of basic intent where the consequence is very closely connected with the act. The *actus reus* of assault is an act which causes another person to apprehend immediate and unlawful violence. The *mens rea* corresponds exactly. The prosecution must prove that the accused foresaw that his act would probably cause another person to have apprehension of immediate and unlawful violence, or would possibly have that consequence, such being the purpose of the act, or that he was reckless as to whether or not his act caused such apprehension. This foresight (the term of art is 'intention') or recklessness is the *mens rea* in assault. For example of a crime of basic intent where the consequence of the act involved in the *actus reus* as defined in the crime is less immediate, I take the crime of unlawful wounding. The act is, say, the squeezing of a trigger. A number of consequences (mechanical, chemical, ballistic and physiological) intervene before the final consequence involved in the defined *actus reus* – namely, the wounding of another person in circumstances unjustified by law. But again here the *mens rea* corresponds closely to the *actus reus*. The prosecution must prove that the accused foresaw that some physical harm would ensue to another person in circumstances unjustified by law as a probable (or possible and desired) consequence of his act, or that he was reckless as to whether or not such consequence ensued.

How does the fact of self-induced intoxication fit into that analysis? If a man consciously and deliberately takes alcohol and drugs not on medical prescription, but in order to escape from reality, to go 'on a trip', to become hallucinated, whatever the description may be and thereby disables himself from taking the care he might otherwise take and as a result by his subsequent actions causes injury to another – does our criminal law enable him to say that because he did not know what he was doing he lacked both intention and recklessness and accordingly is entitled to an acquittal?

Originally the common law would not and did not recognise self-induced intoxication as an excuse. Lawton LJ spoke of the 'merciful relaxation' to that rule which was introduced by the judges during the 19th century, and he added, at 411:

Although there was much reforming zeal and activity in the 19th century, Parliament never once considered whether self-induced intoxication should be a defence generally to a criminal charge. It would have been a strange result if the merciful relaxation of a strict rule of law had ended, without any Parliamentary intervention, by whittling it away to such an extent that the more drunk a man became, provided he stopped short of making himself insane, the better chance he had of an acquittal ... The common law rule still applied but there were exceptions to it which Lord Birkenhead LC tried to define by reference to specific intent.

There are, however, decisions of eminent judges in a number of Commonwealth cases in Australia and New Zealand, (but generally not in Canada nor in the United States) as well as impressive academic comment in this country, to which we have been referred, supporting the view that it is illogical and inconsistent with legal principle to treat a person who of his own choice and volition has taken drugs and drink, even though he thereby creates a state in which he is not conscious of what he is doing, any differently from a person suffering from various medical conditions like epilepsy or diabetic coma and who is regarded by the law as free from fault. However our courts have for a very long time regarded in quite another light the state of self-induced intoxication. The authority which for the last half century has been relied upon in this context has been the speech of the Earl of Birkenhead LC in *DPP v Beard* [1920] AC 479, who stated at 494:

Under the law of England as it prevailed until early in the 19th century voluntary drunkenness was never an excuse for criminal misconduct; and indeed the classic authorities broadly assert that voluntary drunkenness must be considered rather an aggravation than a defence. This view was in terms based upon the principle that a man who by his own voluntary act debauches and destroys his will power shall be no better situated in regard to criminal acts than a sober man.

Lord Birkenhead LC made a historical survey of the way the common law, from the 16th century on, dealt with the effect of self-induced intoxication upon criminal responsibility. This indicates how, from 1819 on, the judges began to mitigate the severity of the attitude of the common law in such cases as murder and serious violent crime when the penalties of death or transportation applied or where there was likely to be sympathy for the accused, as in attempted suicide. Lord Birkenhead LC concluded at 499, that (except in cases where insanity is pleaded):

the law is plain beyond all question that in cases falling short of insanity a condition of drunkenness at the time of committing an offence causing death can only, when it is available at all, have the effect of reducing the crime from murder to manslaughter.

From this it seemed clear – and this is the interpretation which the judges have placed upon the decision during the ensuing half century – that it is only in the limited class of cases requiring proof of specific intent that drunkenness can exculpate. Otherwise in no case can it exempt completely from criminal liability ...

I do not for my part regard that general principle as either unethical or contrary to the principles of natural justice. If a man of his own volition takes a substance which causes him to cast off the restraints of reason and conscience, no wrong is done to him by holding him answerable criminally for any injury he may do while in that condition. His course of conduct in reducing himself by drugs and drink to that condition in my view supplies the evidence of *mens rea*, of guilty mind certainly sufficient for crimes of basic intent. It is a reckless course of conduct and recklessness is enough to constitute the necessary *mens rea* in assault cases: see *R v Venna* [1976] QB 421, *per* James LJ at 429. The drunkenness is itself an intrinsic, an integral part of the crime, the other part being the evidence of the unlawful use of force against the victim. Together they add up to criminal recklessness ...

My noble and learned friends and I think it may be helpful if we give the following indication of the general lines on which in our view the jury should be directed as to the effect upon the criminal responsibility of the accused of drink or drugs or both, whenever death or physical injury to another person results from something done by the accused for which there is no legal justification and the offence with which the accused is charged is manslaughter or assault at common law or the statutory offence of unlawful wounding under s 20, or of assault occasioning actual bodily harm under s 47 of the Offences Against the Person Act 1861.

In the case of these offences it is no excuse in law that, because of drink or drugs which the accused himself had taken knowingly and willingly, he had deprived himself of the ability to exercise self-control, to realise the possible consequences of what he was doing, or even to be conscious that he was doing it. As in the instant case, the jury may be properly instructed that they 'can ignore the subject of drink or drugs as being in any way a defence' to charges of this character ...

Lord Salmon: ... I accept that there is a degree of illogicality in the rule that intoxication may excuse or expunge one type of intention and not another. This illogicality is, however, acceptable to me because the benevolent part of the rule removes undue harshness without imperilling safety and the stricter part of the rule works without imperilling justice. It would be just as ridiculous to remove the benevolent part of the rule (which no one suggests) as it would be to adopt the alternative of removing the stricter part of the rule for the sake of preserving absolute logic. Absolute logic in human affairs is an uncertain guide and a very dangerous master. The law is primarily concerned with human affairs. I believe that the main object of our legal system is to preserve individual liberty. One important aspect of individual liberty is protection against physical violence.

If there were to be no penal sanction for any injury unlawfully inflicted under the complete mastery of drink or drugs, voluntarily taken, the social consequence could be appalling. That is why I do not consider that there is any justification for the criticisms which have been made of the Court of Appeal's decision in *R v Lipman* (extracted above) ... [offences] like manslaughter, are ... offences of basic intent and do not require the proof of any specific intent in order to establish guilt. According to our law as it has stood for about 150 years, in such cases evidence that the injuries were inflicted by a man not knowing what he was doing because he was intoxicated by drinks or drugs which he has voluntarily taken is wholly irrelevant. Certainly this rule seems, in practice, to have worked well without causing any injustice. The judge always carefully takes into account all the circumstances (which vary infinitely from case to case) before deciding which of the many courses open should be adopted in dealing with the convicted man.

If, as I think, this long-standing rule was salutary years ago when it related almost exclusively to drunkenness and hallucinatory drugs were comparatively unknown how much more salutary is it today when such drugs are increasingly becoming a public menace? My Lords, I am satisfied that this rule accords with justice, ethics and common sense, and I would leave it alone even if it does not comply with strict logic. It would, in my view, be disastrous if the law were changed to allow men who did what Lipman did to go free. It would shock the public, it would rightly bring the law into contempt and it would certainly increase one of the really serious menaces facing society today. This is too great a price to pay for bringing solace to those who believe that, come what may, strict logic should always prevail ...

Lord Russell of Killowen: ... There are those who consider that the pendulum should swing the whole way from the old attitude of the criminal law that self-induced intoxication was if anything an aggravation of the crime committed while under its influence, to an attitude whereunder if the intoxication deprives a man of the ability to appreciate what he was doing he cannot be held guilty of any crime at all, save one of absolute liability or in which drunkenness is itself a constituent element of the crime. A man who has no knowledge of what he does cannot, it is said, be a guilty man, whatever may have deprived him of that knowledge. There is, at least superficially, logic in that approach: but logic in criminal law must not be allowed to run away with common sense, particularly when the preservation of the Queen's Peace is in question. The ordinary citizen who is badly beaten up would rightly think little of the criminal law as an effective protection if, because his attacker had deprived himself of ability to know what he was doing by getting himself drunk or going on a trip with drugs, the attacker is to be held innocent of any crime in the assault. *Mens rea* has many aspects. If asked to define it in such a case as the present I would say that the element of guilt or moral turpitude is supplied by the act of self-intoxication reckless of possible consequences. (In the early history of the criminal law it was always recognised that intoxication not self-induced – the surreptitiously laced drink – gave rise to quite different considerations: and this was because it was not the man's 'fault'. And so nowadays.) If, however, the crime charged was, as described in *DPP v Beard* [1920] AC 479, one which required a 'specific intent' to constitute the crime, and the self-induced intoxication was such that he had not the required specific intent, the accused is not to be found guilty of that particular crime: though commonly there will be a lesser crime to which the intoxication – however mind-stealing – will be no defence: murder and manslaughter are such: assault causing grievous bodily harm with intent to cause grievous bodily harm, and assault causing grievous bodily harm or actual bodily harm is another example ...

WHAT IF A DEFENDANT DELIBERATELY INTOXICATES HIMSELF IN ORDER TO COMMIT A CRIME?

AG for Northern Ireland v Gallagher [1963] AC 349 (HL)

Lord Denning: My Lords, every direction which a judge gives to a jury in point of law must be considered against the background of facts which have been proved or admitted in the case. In this case the accused man did not give evidence himself. And the facts proved against him were:

> He had a grievance against his wife. She had obtained a maintenance order against him and had been instrumental in getting him detained in a mental hospital.

He had made up his mind to kill his wife. He bought a knife for the purpose and a bottle of whiskey – either to give himself Dutch courage to do the deed or to drown his conscience after it.

He did in fact carry out his intention. He killed his wife with the knife and drank much of the whiskey before or after he killed her.

There were only two defences raised on his behalf: (1) Insanity; (2) Drunkenness.

The Lord Chief Justice directed the jury that the *time* when they had to consider whether he was insane or not (within the *M'Naghten* Rules) was before he started on the bottle of whiskey. 'You should direct your attention', he said to them, 'to the state of his mind before he opened the bottle of whisky.' If he was sane at that time, he could not make good the defence of insanity 'with the aid of that bottle of whiskey'. Immediately after the jury retired, Mr Kelly took up this point of *time*. He suggested that it was inaccurate and inconsistent with the *M'Naghten* Rules. But the Lord Chief Justice adhered to his view. He declined to modify his charge to the jury on the matter. 'If I'm wrong', he said, 'I can be put right.' It was on this very point of *time* that the Court of Criminal Appeal reversed him. His direction was, they said, 'inconsistent with the *M'Naghten* Rules', which fix the crucial time as 'the time of the committing of the act', that is, the time of the killing and not at an earlier time.

The question is whether the direction of the Lord Chief Justice as to the *time* was correct. At least that is how I read the question posed by the Court of Criminal Appeal. It is complicated by the fact that, according to the medical evidence, the accused man was a psychopath. That does not mean that he was insane. But it sharpens the point of the question. He had a disease of the mind. It was quiescent before he started on the whiskey. So he was sane then. But the drink may have brought on an explosive outburst in the course of which he killed her. Can he rely on this self-induced defect of reason and put it forward as a defence of insanity?

My Lords, this case differs from all the others in the books in that the accused man, whilst sane and sober, before he took to the drink, had already made up his mind to kill his wife. This seems to me to be far worse – and far more deserving of condemnation – than the case of a man who, before getting drunk, has no intention to kill, but afterwards in his cups, whilst drunk, kills another by an act which he would not dream of doing when sober. Yet by the law of England in this latter case his drunkenness is no defence even though it has distorted his reason and his will power. So why should it be a defence in the present case? And is it made any better by saying that the man is a psychopath?

The answer to the question is, I think, that the case falls to be decided by the general principle of English law that, subject to very limited exceptions, drunkenness is no defence to a criminal charge, nor is a defect of reason produced by drunkenness. This principle was stated by Sir Matthew Hale in his *Pleas of the Crown*, 1, p 32, in words which I would repeat here: 'This vice' (drunkenness) 'both deprive men of the use of reason, and puts many men into a perfect, but temporary frenzy ... By the laws of England such a person shall have no privilege by this voluntary contracted madness, but shall have the same judgment as if he were in his right senses.'

This general principle can be illustrated by looking at the various ways in which drunkenness may produce a defect of reason:

a   It may impair a man's powers of perception so that he may not be able to foresee or measure the consequences of his actions as he would if he were sober. Nevertheless he is not allowed to set up his self-induced want of perception as a defence. Even if he did not himself appreciate that what he was doing was dangerous, nevertheless if a reasonable man in his place, who was not befuddled with drink, would have appreciated it, he is guilty: see *R v Meade* [1909] 1 KB 895, as explained in *DPP v Beard* ...

b   It may impair a man's power to judge between right or wrong, so that he may do a thing when drunk which he would not dream of doing while sober. He does not realise he is doing wrong. Nevertheless he is not allowed to set up his self-induced want of moral sense as a defence. In *Beard's* case Lord Birkenhead LC distinctly ruled that it was not a defence for a drunken man to say he did not know he was doing wrong.

The general principle which I have enunciated is subject to two exceptions:

1   If a man is charged with an offence in which a specific intention is essential (as in murder, though not in manslaughter), then evidence of drunkenness, which renders him incapable of forming that intention, is an answer: see *Beard's* case. This degree of drunkenness is reached when the man is rendered so stupid by drink that he does not know what he is doing (see *R v Moore* (1852) 3 Car & Kir 319), as where, at a christening, a drunken nurse put the baby behind a large fire, taking it for a log of wood (*Gentleman's Magazine*, 1748, p 570); and where a drunken man thought his friend (lying in his bed) was a theatrical dummy placed there and stabbed him to death (1951) *The Times*, 13 January. In each of those cases it would not be murder. But it would be manslaughter.

2   If a man by drinking brings on a distinct disease of the mind such as delirium tremens, so that he is temporarily insane within the *M'Naghten* Rules, that is to say, he does not at the time know what he is doing or that it is wrong, then he has a defence on the ground of insanity: see *R v Davis* (1881) 14 Cox CC 563 and *Beard's* case.

Does the present case come within the general principle or the exceptions to it? It certainly does not come within the first exception. This man was not incapable of forming an intent to kill. Quite the contrary. He knew full well what he was doing. He formed an intent to kill, he carried out his intention and he remembered afterwards what he had done. And the jury, properly directed on the point, have found as much, for they found him guilty of murder. Then does the case come within the second exception? It does not, to my mind, for the simple reason that he was not suffering from a disease of the mind brought on by drink. He was suffering from a different disease altogether. As the Lord Chief Justice observed in his summing up: 'If this man was suffering from a disease of the mind, it wasn't of a kind that is produced by drink.'

So we have here a case of the first impression. The man is a psychopath. That is, he has a disease of the mind which is not produced by drink. But it is quiescent. And whilst it is quiescent he forms an intention to kill his wife. He knows it is wrong but still he means to kill her. Then he gets himself so drunk that he has an explosive outburst and kills his wife. At that moment he knows what he is doing but he does not know it is wrong. So in that respect – in not knowing it is wrong – he has a defect of reason at the moment of killing. If that defect of reason is due to the drink, it is no defence in law. But if it is due to the disease of the mind, it gives rise to a defence of insanity. No one can say, however, whether it is due to the drink or to the disease. It may well be due to both in combination. What guidance does the law give in this difficulty? That is, as I see it, the question of general public importance which is involved in this case.

My Lords, I think the law on this point should take a clear stand. If a man, whilst sane and sober, forms an intention to kill and makes preparation for it, knowing it is a wrong thing to do, and then gets himself drunk so as to give himself Dutch courage to do the killing, and whilst drunk carries out his intention, he cannot rely on this self-induced drunkenness as a defence to a charge of murder, nor even as reducing it to manslaughter. He cannot say that he got himself into such a stupid state that he was incapable of an intent to kill. So also when he is a psychopath, he cannot by drinking rely on his self-induced defect of reason as a defence of insanity. The wickedness of his mind before he got drunk is enough to condemn him, coupled with the act which he intended to do and did so. A psychopath who goes out intending to kill, knowing it is wrong, and does kill, cannot escape the consequences by making himself drunk before doing it. That is, I believe, the direction which the Lord Chief Justice gave to the jury and which the Court of Criminal Appeal found to be wrong. I think it was right and for this reason I would allow the appeal.

I would agree, of course, that if before the killing he had discarded his intention to kill or reversed it – and then got drunk – it would be a different matter. But when he forms the intention to kill and without interruption proceeds to get drunk and carry out his intention, then his drunkenness is no defence and nonetheless so because it is dressed up as a defence of insanity. There was no evidence in this case of any interruption and there was no need for the Lord Chief Justice to mention it to the jury.

I need hardly say, of course, that I have here only considered the law of Northern Ireland. In England a psychopath such as this man might now be in a position to raise a defence of diminished responsibility under s 2 of the Homicide Act 1957 ...

IS ALL VOLUNTARY CONSUMPTION OF INTOXICANTS TO BE REGARDED AS RECKLESS?

R v Hardie [1985] 1 WLR 64 (CA)

Parker LJ: ... Shortly after 9.15 pm on 2 January 1982, fire broke out in a wardrobe in the bedroom of the ground floor flat at 55 Bassingham Road, London SW10. At that time there were in the flat the appellant, Mrs Jeanette Hardie, with whom the appellant had been living at the premises since May 1974, and who had changed her name to Hardie by deed poll in 1976, and her daughter Tonia. The upstairs flat was occupied by a Mrs Young. Shortly before 2 January, the appellant's relationship with Mrs Hardie had broken down and she had insisted that he must leave. He did not wish to do so, but on the morning of 2 January he packed a suitcase. At about lunchtime the appellant found two bottles of tablets in a cabinet. One contained Valium which Mrs Hardie had had in 1974 and the other tablets to assist urination.

The appellant's evidence in regard to this was that he had never taken Valium before, that he took one about 12 pm to calm him down for he was in a distressed state, that it did not have much effect, that he and Mrs Hardie had then gone shopping, that he had taken two more in front of her and she had said, 'take as many as you like, they are old stock and will do you no harm', that he taken two more shortly afterwards, that he may have taken two of the other tablets also, and that shortly thereafter on return to the house he had fallen into a deep sleep and could thereafter remember only periods. He was in fact collected from the flat by his mother and remained with her until returning to the flat again at 9.15 pm. It was not disputed that he must have started the fire for he was alone in the bedroom when it started. Having started it, he emerged, returned to the sitting room where were Mrs Hardie and Tonia and stayed there. Shortly afterwards Mrs Hardie heard sounds from the bedroom, went there and found smoke and flames coming from the wardrobe. There was evidence that before, at the time of and after the fire the appellant was exhibiting signs of intoxication and that such signs might have resulted from the taking of Valium some hours earlier.

The defence was that the appellant was so affected by the Valium that he could remember nothing about the fire and had not the necessary *mens rea* to constitute either of the offences charged. On the basis no doubt of *R v Majewski* [1977] AC 443 and *R v Caldwell* [1982] AC 341, the judge directed the jury in effect that, as the Valium was voluntarily self-administered, it was irrelevant as a defence and its effect could not negative *mens rea* ...

... It is clear from *R v Caldwell* [1982] AC 341 that self-induced intoxication can be a defence where the charge is only one specific intention. It is equally clear that it cannot be a defence where, as here, the charge included recklessness. Hence, if there was self-intoxication in this case the judge's direction was correct. The problem is whether, assuming that the effect of the Valium was to deprive the appellant of any appreciation of what he was doing it should properly be regarded as self-induced intoxication and thus no answer ...

R v Majewski was a case of drunkenness resulting from alcoholic consumption by the accused whilst under the influence of non-medically prescribed drugs. *R v Caldwell* [1982] AC 341 was a case of plain drunkenness. There can be no doubt that the same rule applies both to self-intoxication by alcohol and intoxication by hallucinatory drugs, but this is because the effects of both are well known and there is therefore an element of recklessness in the self-administration of the drug. *R v Lipman* [1970] 1 QB 152 is an example of such a case.

'Intoxication' or similar symptoms may, however, arise in other circumstances. In *R v Bailey (John)* [1983] 1 WLR 760 this court had to consider a case where a diabetic had failed to take sufficient food after taking a normal dose of insulin and struck the victim over the head with an iron bar. The judge directed the jury that the defence of automatism, ie that the mind did not go with the act, was not available because the incapacity was self-induced. It was held that his was wrong on two grounds (a) because on the basis of *R v Majewski* [1977] AC 443 it was clearly available to the offence embodying specific intent and (b) because although self-induced by the omission to take food it was also available to negative the other offence which was of basic intent only ...

In the present instance the defence was that the Valium was taken for the purpose of calming the nerves only, that it was old stock and that the appellant was told it would do him no harm. There was no evidence that it was known to the appellant or even generally known that the taking of Valium in the quantity taken would be liable to render a person aggressive or incapable of appreciating risks to others or have other side effects such that its self-administration would itself have an element of recklessness. It is true that Valium is a drug and it is true that it was taken deliberately and not taken on medical prescription, but the drug is, in our view wholly different in kind from drugs which are liable to cause unpredictability or aggressiveness. It may well be that the taking of a sedative or soporific drug will, in certain circumstances, be no answer, for example, in a case of reckless driving, but if the effect of a drug is merely soporific or sedative the taking of it, even in some excessive quantity, cannot in the ordinary way raise a conclusive presumption against the admission of proof of intoxication for the purpose of disproving *mens rea* in ordinary crimes, such as would be the case with alcoholic intoxication or incapacity or automatism resulting from the self-administration of dangerous drugs.

In the present case the jury should not, in our judgment, have been directed to disregard any incapacity which resulted or might have resulted from the taking of Valium. They should have been directed that if they came to the conclusion that, as a result of the Valium, the appellant was, at the time, unable to appreciate the risks to property and persons from his actions they should then consider whether the taking of the Valium was itself reckless. We are unable to say what would have been the appropriate direction with regard to the elements of recklessness in this case for we have not seen all the relevant evidence, nor are we able to suggest a model direction, for circumstances will vary infinitely and model directions can sometimes lead to more rather than less confusion. It is sufficient to say that the direction that the effects of Valium were necessarily irrelevant was wrong.

In *R v Bailey (John)* [1983] 1 WLR 760 the court upheld the conviction notwithstanding the misdirection, being satisfied that there had been no miscarriage of justice and that the jury properly directed could not have failed to come to the same conclusion. That is not so in the present case. Properly directed the jury might well have come to the same conclusion. There was, for example evidence that the Valium really did not materially affect the appellant at all at the relevant time, but we are quite unable to say that they must have come to the same conclusion ...

THE RELATIONSHIP BETWEEN INTOXICATION AND MISTAKE OF FACT

R v Woods (1982) 74 Cr App R 312 (CA)

Griffiths LJ: ... [The appellant's conviction of rape] arose out of a disgraceful incident on Saturday 29 September 1979. The victim, who was aged only 19, had been drinking at a club in Blackburn. I can summarise the facts by saying that after she left the club it was alleged that these young men had raped her one after the other.

The appellant made admissions of his part in it to the police. He said he had felt sick ever since it happened and he was disgusted with himself and asked if the girl was alright. When charged with rape he said that he was glad that he had been caught and he admitted that he had been attempting to have intercourse with the girl. He said, and no doubt this is true, it would never have happened if he had not been drunk. Forensic evidence showed that he had seminal staining on his underpants and there were fragments of grass on the outside of his jacket and a small amount of soil, all consistent with taking part in this rape in the car park.

At his trial he went back on those admissions and said in effect that he had so much to drink that he was not sure what had happened. He did not know whether he had raped her or not and did not realise that she was not consenting to anything that went on. The sole ground of this appeal is that the learned judge wrongly directed the jury that the appellant's self-induced intoxication afforded him no defence to the allegation that he was reckless as to whether the complainant consented to sexual intercourse.

[Counsel for the appellant] founded his submission upon the wording of s 1 of the Sexual Offences (Amendment) Act 1976. Subsection (1) provides:

> For the purposes of section 1 of the Sexual Offences Act 1956 (which relates to rape) a man commits rape if: (a) he has unlawful sexual intercourse with a woman who at the time of the intercourse does not consent to it; and (b) at the time he knows that she does not consent to the intercourse or he is reckless as to whether she consents to it; and references to rape in other enactments (including the following provisions of this Act) shall be construed accordingly.

[Counsel for the appellant] concedes that if the section ended there he could not pursue this appeal in the face of the decision of the House of Lords in *DPP v Majewski* [1977] AC 443, and in the very recent case of *Caldwell* [1981] 1 All ER 961. To show that he is correct to make his concession at that stage it is only necessary to read a short passage from the speech of Lord Diplock in *Caldwell*. [His Lordship then quoted the words of Lord Diplock at 967G.]

[Counsel for the appellant], however, relies upon the wording of subsection (2) which [then provided:]

> It is hereby declared that if at a trial for a rape offence the jury has to consider whether a man believed that a woman was consenting to sexual intercourse, the presence or absence of reasonable grounds for such a belief is a matter to which the jury is to have regard, in conjunction with any other relevant matters, in considering whether he so believed.

He submits that the language of this subsection is directing the jury to take into account a defendant's drunken state as a possible reasonable ground for his belief that a woman is consenting to intercourse.

As the law stood immediately before the passing of this Act self-induced intoxication was no defence to a crime of rape (see *DPP v Majewski*). If Parliament had intended to provide in future that a man whose lust was so inflamed by drink that he ravished a woman, should nevertheless be able to pray in aid his drunken state to avoid the consequences we would have expected them to have used the clearest words to express such a surprising result which we believe would be utterly repugnant to the great majority of people. We are satisfied that Parliament had no such intention and that this is clear from the use of the word 'relevant' in the subsection. Relevant means, in this context, legally relevant. The law, as a matter of social policy, has declared that self-induced intoxication is not a legally relevant matter to be taken into account in deciding as to whether or not a woman consents to intercourse.

Accordingly, the appellant's drunkenness was not a matter that the jury were entitled to take into consideration in deciding whether or not reasonable grounds existed for the appellant's belief that the woman consented to intercourse. The learned judge rightly directed the jury on this issue. In fact we believe that the object of subsection (2) is the very reverse of that contended by the appellant. It was not intended to make it easier for a man who rapes a woman to escape punishment by saying, in spite of the other evidence, that he thought she consented. The subsection directs the jury to look carefully at all the other relevant evidence before making up their minds on this issue ...

R v Fotheringham (1989) 88 Cr App R 206 (CA)

Facts: The appellant had been convicted of the rape of a 14 year old girl who had been baby-sitting for the appellant and his wife. The baby-sitter had been sleeping in the matrimonial bed. The defendant, who was drunk, got into bed with her and had sexual intercourse with her.

Watkins LJ: ... [The appellant's] defence, to put it as shortly as possible, was simply that he made an honest mistake. He mistook the 14 year old girl for his wife, entirely because he was so much under the influence of alcohol that he could not appreciate the difference ...

The ground of appeal is that the learned judge, when summing the matter up to the jury, was wrong in law to direct them to disregard the appellant's self-induced intoxication. In the circumstances this, it was submitted, left him with no real defence. He had admitted that his self-induced intoxication caused his mistake.

... The point of law which ... comes before us for resolution is whether it is a defence to a charge of rape ... that a defendant, as a result of self-induced intoxication, has an honest but mistaken belief that he was having conjugal relations ...

Counsel [for the appellant] had to recognise, as in fact he did, that where the issue in rape is consent, a defendant's self-induced intoxication is not a relevant matter which a jury are entitled to take into account in deciding whether there were reasonable grounds for the defendant's belief that the woman consented: see *R v Woods* (1982) 74 Cr App R 312 [*note*: the relevance of whether there are reasonable grounds for the defendant's belief is confined to the issue whether he in fact held that belief: s 1(2) Sexual Offences (Amendment) Act 1976]. Likewise he had to face the law, which is that 'self-induced intoxication is no defence to a crime in which recklessness is enough to constitute the necessary *mens rea*': see as to that the speech of Lord Diplock in *R v Caldwell* [1982] AC 341, 355, where Lord Diplock refers to *DPP v Majewski* [1977] AC 443, where it was held that rape is a crime of basic intent to which self-induced intoxication is no defence ...

[Counsel for the appellant] says that the mistake was as to the identification of the person with whom the appellant was having sexual intercourse ... But we are firmly of the view that mistake, as is consent, being a question of fact cannot be raised as a defence if, as here, it arises from self-induced intoxication. For that *O'Grady* [1987] QB 995 is very clear authority in our view ...

... [I]n rape self-induced intoxication is no defence, whether the issue be intention, consent or, as here, mistake as to the identity of the victim ...

In our judgment the judge was correct to rule as he did, namely ... 'But I must stress that ... you must ignore the effects of the drink that [the defendant] had taken, the seven or eight pints of lager which he has spoken about. The reasonable grounds are grounds which would be reasonable to a sober man.' In other words a mistake arising from self-induced intoxication is no defence in rape ...

R v Richardson and Irwin [1999] 1 Cr App R 392 (CA)

Clarke J: On May 29 1998 in the Crown Court at Guildford before Mr C Beaumont, sitting as a Recorder, and a jury, the appellants were convicted by a majority of 11 to one of inflicting grievous bodily harm contrary to section 20 of the Offences against the Person Act 1861. The Recorder imposed a community service order of 100 hours and each of the defendants was directed to pay compensation of £750 to the victim.

They now appeal against conviction by leave of the trial judge, who granted a certificate pursuant to section 1(2)(b) of the Criminal Appeal Act 1968 that the case was fit for appeal. The judge granted the certificate on the ground that:

> There was a Redirection in that the jury were directed that the intention of the defendant should be on the basis of a reasonable (ie not under the influence of drink) man and not (as they were) under the influence of drink.

The Recorder added that he did not agree that there was a Redirection but gave leave because he thought that the point was arguable.

The facts of the case can be shortly stated. Both appellants were at the material time students at Surrey University. The complainant, Simon Rose, was also a student at the university. There was evidence that the appellants, the complainant, and the other prosecution witnesses were all friends who regularly drank together at the university. The only possible exception was Nigel Richardson.

On the night in question it was effectively agreed in evidence that the appellants, the complainant and others had been drinking at the student union bar and returned to the appellant Irwin's accommodation. It was said that they had had four to five pints of lager. The accommodation consisted of a duplex flat in which one student occupied the lower floor and Irwin occupied a mezzanine floor up a flight of stairs.

When they arrived there they began joshing Irwin about a girlfriend of his who was also there. They also started what was apparently known as 'bundling', which the Recorder described as 'all jumping about and just regular sort of horseplay'. It was a regular occurrence among the group.

About 2 am the appellants, the complainant and another student, Dean Johnson, went up the stairs into Irwin's part of the accommodation. According to both the complainant and Dean Johnson, Irwin said, 'Let's get Simon over the edge'. There was something of a struggle, apparently all part of the horseplay. However, during the course of this the complainant was lifted over the edge of the balcony and was dropped, as a result of which he fell about 10 to 12 feet and suffered injuries which they must have concluded were really serious and thus grievous bodily harm.

The complainant alleged that that was done by the two appellants. The appellant Irwin agreed that they were the only two involved in it, although the appellant Richardson alleged that the fourth person present, Dean Johnson, was also involved. Irwin gave evidence shortly to this effect. He admitted that he was involved in the tussle which led to the complainant falling over the balcony. However, it was his case that such tussles were a regular occurrence among the group and that the complainant consented to it. It was further his evidence that it was not within any of their contemplations that the complainant should actually fall over the balcony, rather the complainant slipped out of his arms when he was seeking to hold him. Richardson did not give evidence but had admitted in interview that when Irwin had hold of the complainant he, Richardson, held his ankles. Richardson let go of Rose's ankles, and very shortly after that, a period which Richardson put in his interview at some three seconds, Irwin let go of his arms and the complainant fell.

[With regards to the charge under s 20 of the Offences against the Person Act 1861] a key issue before the jury was whether the appellants acted maliciously and the essential question in this appeal is whether the Recorder correctly directed the jury in this regard and, if he did not, whether the convictions are safe.

As we understand it, it was not the prosecution case that the appellants had intended to drop the complainant and cause him harm, but that they acted maliciously in the sense that they each actually foresaw that dropping the complainant would or might cause harm and that they nevertheless took the risk of doing so.

As we understand it, absent the effects of drink, it is common ground that in order to establish the offence under section 20 the prosecution had to prove that in the case of each defendant he either intended the dropping of the complainant to cause him some harm, or that he actually foresaw that it would or might do so: *R v Savage; Director of Public Prosecutions v Parmenter* (1992) 94 Cr App R 193, [1992] 1 AC 699, HL, *per* Lord Ackner at 214, and 751 where he said this:

> Therefore in order to establish an offence under section 20 the prosecution must prove either the defendant intended or that he actually foresaw that his act would cause harm.

As so often, the instant case is complicated by the fact that the appellants had had a good deal to drink. It was therefore possible that the jury might conclude that they did not actually foresee that the dropping of the complainant could cause him injury, if only because they did not foresee the risk of dropping him. The reason that they did not do so was the amount of drink which they had consumed.

It appears to us *to be* clear on the authorities that in considering what *each* defendant actually foresaw the jury must disregard the fact that the appellants had been drinking.

... In *Director of Public Prosecutions v Majewski* ... the House of Lords did not give guidance as to how juries should be directed in cases such as this. However, in *R v Caldwell* (1981) 73 Cr App R 13, [1982] AC 341, HL, although the House was there considering a different question, namely the test of recklessness under section 1(2) of the Criminal Damage Act 1971, Lord Diplock said at pp 21 and 355:

> The speech of the Lord Chancellor, Lord Elwyn-Jones in *Majewski* ... is authority that self-induced intoxication is no defence to a crime in which

recklessness is enough to constitute the necessary *mens rea* ... Reducing oneself by drink or drugs to a condition in which the restraints of reason and conscience are cast off was held to be a reckless course of conduct and an integral part of the crime. The Lord Chancellor accepted as correctly stating English law the provision in paragraph 2.08(2) of the American Model Penal Code: 'When recklessness establishes an element of the offence, if the actor, due to self-induced intoxication, is unaware of a risk of which he would have been aware had he been sober such unawareness is immaterial.' So in the instant case, the fact that the respondent was unaware of the risk of endangering the lives of residents in the hotel owing to his self-induced intoxication, would be no defence if that risk would have been obvious to him had he been sober.

The matter was expressly considered by the Courts-Martial Appeal Court in *Aitken, Bennet and Barson* (1992) 95 Cr App R 304. In that case the judge advocate had directed the court in this way at p 308:

> ... you must be satisfied so that you feel sure that each defendant, when he did the act, either foresaw that it might cause some injury, not necessarily serious injury, or wound to some person; in other words, he or she does not have to foresee the particular type of wound or injury which resulted, but foresaw that he might cause some injury, albeit of a minor nature – that is the first – or would have foreseen that the act might cause some injury, had he not been drinking.

It was submitted that the last part of that direction, namely 'would have foreseen that the act might cause some injury, had he not been drinking', was a direction, having regard to the reasoning in *Parmenter*. The court ... considered the matter in considerable detail. It held that the House of Lords in *Parmenter* did not intend to go behind the clear dicta in *Majewski*, which we have quoted. Its conclusion was that the judge advocate's direction with regard to what it called 'self-induced intoxication' was correct.

It follows that in the instant case, if the matter was to be raised at all, the Recorder should have given a direction to like effect ...

There were a number of issues which the jury had to consider. As we understand it Mr Dunlop opened the case on the basis that the jury had to sure that each defendant foresaw the risk that Mr Rose might fall or be dropped and sustain harm. He did not invite the jury to consider the case the alternative basis that the particular defendant might not have actually foreseen harm, but that he would have done so if he had not been drinking. That would of course have been a less favourable formulation from the defendant's point of view than the one in fact advanced. The prosecution's final speech was also put on the basis of actual foresight and it was that case which the defence speeches were designed to meet. We see no reason why the prosecution should not confine the way in which it put the case in the way described. However the Recorder introduced the alternative into his summing up. In our judgment it would have been better if before doing so he had indicated his intention to counsel before they addressed the jury so that they might take that possibility into account in their addresses to the jury.

It follows from the conclusions which we have stated that, as we see it, the Recorder should have directed the jury along these lines, which seem to us to be consistent with the standard judicial Studies Board directions:

The complainant, Rose, suffered bodily harm because he slipped or was dropped from the top of the stairwell. No question of self-defence arises. To convict either defendant you must be sure: (1) that he alone or with the other defendant put Rose into the position from which he slipped or was dropped; (2) that Rose did not consent to being put there; (3) that he realised that Rose did not consent; (4) that his actions in putting Rose there were deliberate, ie not accidental; (5) that when doing this either (a) he realised that Rose might slip or be dropped and thus sustain some degree of bodily harm, albeit of a minor character, or (b) would have realised that had he not been drinking.

Questions (3) and (5)(a) are about the defendant's state of mind. When considering both you must take account of the evidence that the defendant's mind was affected by alcohol. In relation to question (3) you cannot convict if you find that the defendant did mistakenly believe or might have mistakenly believed that Rose did consent. Take the evidence of his consumption of alcohol into account when considering this. Similarly in relation to question (5)(a) you cannot convict if you find that the defendant did not realise or might not have realised that Rose might slip or be dropped and be injured. Here too you must take account of the evidence of the defendant's consumption of alcohol into account. In the same way the alcohol consumed by Rose bears on question (2).

There was, in our judgment, no need to mention the word recklessness. It is to be noted that if question (5)(b) was to be included it asks not about what the reasonable man would have realised, but what the defendant would have realised. In this case, as Mr Edwards has pointed out, the defendants were not hypothetical reasonable men, but university students.

Notes and queries

1   In his speech in *DPP v Majewski* (above) Lord Elwyn-Jones refers to a defendant who voluntarily consumes intoxicants and thereby '... disables himself from taking the care he might otherwise take ...'. Does this mean that a defendant, charged with a basic intent crime, who became intoxicated through his own volition, can still escape liability where there is evidence that, even if he had been sober at the time the *actus reus*, he would not have been aware of the risk of the prohibited consequence occurring? In *R v Cullen* [1993] Crim LR 936, the Court of Appeal held, in respect of a self-intoxicated defendant charged with aggravated criminal damage, that the prosecution would either have to prove that he would have been aware of the risk of damage if he had been sober, or that the risk would have been obvious to the reasonable prudent bystander (that is, *Caldwell* recklessness would be enough). See further *R v Richardson and Irwin* (above), which suggests that even in respect of basic intent crimes, the jury should be asked to consider whether the defendant would have been aware of the risk in question had he been sober – assuming it is an offence to which *Cunningham* recklessness applies.

2   In *R v O'Grady* [1987] 1 QB 995, the Court of Appeal held that, where a defendant makes a mistake of fact causing him to believe that he is justified in using force to defend himself, and that mistake arises from his voluntary

intoxication, he is not entitled to rely on self-defence. In this respect the court further held that no distinction was to be made between offences of basic or specific intent – see further Chapter 14).

3   Can *R v Richardson and Irwin* be reconciled with *R v Woods* and *R v Fotheringham*? Why should a an intoxicated mistake as to consent to rough play be any different from an intoxicated mistake as to consent to sexual intercourse?

INVOLUNTARY INTOXICATION

Following the 'logic' of *DPP v Majewski* (above) a defendant who commits the *actus reus* of an offence whilst in a state of intoxication brought about the by involuntary consumption of intoxicants should escape liability on the basis that he was not at fault in becoming intoxicated. The common law has not, however, adopted an entirely logical response to this problem. Where the effect of the involuntary intoxication is that the defendant was in a state of automatism at the time the actus reus was committed, which might be the case, for example, where a third party surreptitiously places LSD in the defendant's food, the defendant should escape liability entirely. The third party could be charged as the principal offender acting through an innocent agent.

Where the defendant is in a state of involuntary intoxication falling short of automatism he can still avail himself of the defence of intoxication in respect of specific intent crimes, following the principles laid down in *DPP v Majewski*, above. If such a defendant is charged with a basic intent crime he would be advised to rely on both *DPP v Majewski* and *R v Hardie* to the effect that he was not 'reckless' in becoming intoxicated, hence there is no prior fault on which to base liability.

MISTAKE AS TO THE NATURE OF THE SUBSTANCE CONSUMED

R v Allen [1988] Crim LR 698 (CA)

Facts: The appellant was convicted of buggery and indecent assault. It was the appellant's alternative line of defence that if, contrary to his basic assertion that he was not the attacker, he was so drunk at the time that he was not responsible for his actions and was in effect acting in a state of automatism; and that that drunken condition was due to his involuntarily having imbibed a quantity of alcohol which he was not responsible for consuming. The appellant gave evidence that he had consumed some drink in a public house and had later been given wine by a friend. He had not realised that the wine had a high alcohol content. The second line of defence was not left to the jury by the judge. The appellant appealed against conviction on the ground that the judge erred in ruling that involuntary drunkenness could not be a defence to a crime of non-specific intent.

Held, dismissing the appeal, the judge was correct in ruling that there was no evidence before him that the drinking was other than voluntary. Further, where an accused knows that he is drinking alcohol, such drinking does not become involuntary for the reason alone that he may not know the precise nature or strength of the alcohol that he is consuming.

INVOLUNTARY CONSUMPTION OF INTOXICANTS FALLING SHORT OF INTOXICATION

R v Kingston [1995] 2 AC 355 (HL)

Lord Mustill: My Lords, this appeal concerns the effect on criminal liability of involuntary intoxication ...

The relevant facts are simple. The respondent was in dispute over business matters with a couple named Foreman, who employed Penn to obtain damaging information which they could use against the respondent, who is a homosexual with paedophiliac predilections. As part of this plan Penn invited the youth to his room. According to the evidence given by the youth at the trial he remembered nothing between a time when he was sitting on the bed and when he woke up, still in Penn's room, the following morning. It was the case for the prosecution, which the jury by their verdict on the second count must have accepted, that the boy fell asleep because Penn had secretly given him a soporific drug in a drink. On the same evening the respondent went to the room where the youth lay unconscious. He and Penn indulged in gross sexual acts with him. As part of the plan Penn made a recording of what was going on, and also took some photographs ...

At the outset of the trial counsel for the respondent foreshadowed a defence on the lines that as part of the plan Penn had secretly administered drugs not only to the boy but also to the respondent. It was not said, and in the light of the recordings and photographs could not have been said, that the consequence was to make the respondent, like the boy, insensible; nevertheless his case was he had suffered effects which annulled the criminal liability which his acts would otherwise have involved ...

... [T]here are three grounds on which the respondent might be held free from criminal responsibility. First, that his immunity flows from general principles of the criminal law. Second, that this immunity is already established by a solid line of authority. Finally, that the court should, when faced with a new problem, acknowledge the justice of the case and boldly create a new common law defence.

It is clear from the passage already quoted that the Court of Appeal [which allowed Kingston's appeal] adopted the first approach. The decision was explicitly founded on general principle. There can be no doubt what principle the court relied upon, for at the outset the court [1994] QB 81, 87, recorded the submission of counsel for the respondent:

> The law recognises that, exceptionally, an accused person may be entitled to be acquitted if there is a possibility that although his act was intentional, the intent itself arose out of circumstances for which he bears no blame.

The same proposition is implicit in the assumption by the court that if blame is absent the necessary *mens rea* must also be absent.

My Lords, with every respect I must suggest that no such principle exists or, until the present case, had ever in modern times been thought to exist. Each offence consists of a prohibited act or omission coupled with whatever state of mind is called for by the statute or rule of the common law which create the offence. In those offences which are not absolute the state of mind which the prosecution must prove to have underlain the act or omission – the 'mental element' – will in the majority of cases be such as to attract disapproval. The mental element will then be the mark of what may properly be called a 'guilty mind'. The professional burglar is guilty in a moral as well as a legal sense; he intends to break into the house to steal, and most would confidently assert that this is wrong. But this will not always be so. In respect of some offences the mind of the defendant and still less his moral judgment, may not be engaged at all. In others, although a mental activity must be the motive power for the prohibited act or omission the activity may be of such a kind or degree that society at large would not criticise the defendant's conduct severely or even criticise it at all. Such cases are not uncommon. Yet to assume that contemporary moral judgments affect the criminality of the act, as distinct from the punishment appropriate to the crime one proved, is to be misled by the expression *mens rea*, the ambiguity of which has been the subject of complaint for more than a century. Certainly, the *mens* of the defendant must usually be involved in the offence; but the epithet *rea* refers to the criminality of the act in which the mind is engaged, not to its moral character ...

I would therefore reject that part of the respondent's argument which treats the absence of moral fault on the part of the appellants as sufficient in itself to negative the necessary mental element of the offence ...

... His second ground is more narrow, namely that involuntary intoxication is already recognised as a defence by authority which the House ought to follow ...

[His Lordship discussed the older authorities, and then went on:] There is, however, another line of authority to be considered, for it is impossible to consider the exceptional case of involuntary intoxication without placing it in the context of intoxication as a whole. The area of the law is controversial, as regards the content of the rules, their intellectual foundations, and their capacity to furnish a practical and just solution. Since the law was not explored in depth during the arguments and since it is relevant only as part of the background it is better not to say any more about it than is strictly necessary. Some consideration of the law laid down in *R v Majewski* [1977] AC 443 is however inevitable. As I understand the position it is still the law that in the exceptional case where intoxication causes insanity the *M'Naghten* Rules (*M'Naghten's* case (1843) 10 Cl & F 200) apply: see *DPP v Beard* [1920] AC 479, 501 and *AG for Northern Ireland v Gallagher* [1963] AC 349. Short of this, it is no answer for the defendant to say that he would not have done what he did had he been sober, provided always that whatever element of intent is required by the offence is proved to have been present. As was said in *R v Sheehan* [1975] 1 WLR 739, 744c, 'a drunken intent is nevertheless an intent'. As to proof of intent, it appears that at least in some instances self-induced intoxication can be taken into account as part of the evidence from which the jury draws its conclusions; but that in others it cannot. I express the matter in this guarded way because it has not yet been decisively established whether for his purpose there is a line to be drawn between offences of 'specific' and of 'basic' intent. That in at least some cases a defendant cannot say that he was so drunk that he could not form the required intent is however clear enough. Why is this so? The answer must I believe be the same as that given in other common law jurisdictions: namely that such evidence is excluded as a matter of policy ...

There remains the question by what reasoning the House put this policy into effect. As I understand it two different rationalisations were adopted. First that the absence of the necessary consent is cured by treating the intentional drunkenness (or more accurately, since it is only in the minority of cases that the drinker sets out to make himself drunk, the intentional taking of drink without regard to its possible effects) as a substitute for the mental element ordinarily required by the offence. The intent is transferred from the taking of drink to the commission of the prohibited act. The second rationalisation is that the defendant cannot be heard to rely on the absence of the mental element when it is absent because of his own voluntary acts. Borrowing an expression from a far distant field it may be said that the defendant is estopped from relying on his self-induced incapacity.

Your Lordships are not required to decide how these two explanations stand up to attack, for they are not attacked here. The task is only to place them in the context of an intoxication which is not voluntary. Taking first the concept of transferred intent, if the intoxication was not the result of an act done with an informed will there is no intent which can be transferred to the prohibited act, so as to fill the gap in the offence. As regards the 'estoppel' there is no reason why the law should preclude the defendant from relying on a mental condition which he had not deliberately brought about. Thus, once the involuntary nature of the intoxication is added the two theories of *Majewski* fall away, and the position reverts to what it would have been if *Majewski* [1977] AC 443 had not been decided, namely that the offence is not made out if the defendant was so intoxicated that he could not form an intent. Thus, where the intoxication is involuntary *Majewski* does not subtract the defence of absence of intent; but there is nothing in *Majewski* to suggest that where intent is proved involuntary intoxication adds a further defence ...

To recognise a new defence of this type would be a bold step. The common law defences of duress and necessity (if it exists) and the limited common law defence of provocation are all very old. Since counsel for the appellant was not disposed to emphasise this aspect of the appeal the subject was not explored in argument, but I suspect that the recognition of a new general defence at common law has not happened in modern times. Nevertheless, the criminal law must not stand still, and if it is both practical and just to take this step, and if judicial decision rather than legislation is the proper medium, then the courts should not be deterred simply by the novelty of it. So one must turn to consider just what defence is now to be created. The judgment under appeal implies five characteristics:

1   The defence applies to all offences, except perhaps to absolute offences. It therefore differs from defences such as provocation and diminished responsibility.

2   The defence is a complete answer to a criminal charge. If not rebutted it leads to an outright acquittal, and unlike provocation and diminished responsibility leaves no room for conviction and punishment for a lesser offence. The underlying assumption must be that the defendant is entirely free from culpability.

3   It may be that the defence applies only where the intoxication is due to the wrongful act of another and therefore affords no excuse when, in circumstances of no greater culpability, the defendant has intoxicated himself by mistake (such as by shortsightedly taking the wrong drug). I say that this may be so, because it is not clear whether, since the doctrine was founded in part on the dictum of Park J in *Pearson's* case, 2 Lew 144, the 'fraud or stratagem of another' is an essential element, or whether this was taken as an example of a wider principle.

4   The burden of disproving the defence is on the prosecution.

5   The defence is subjective in nature. Whereas provocation and self-defence are judged by the reactions of the reasonable person in the situation of the defendant, here the only question is whether this particular defendant's inhibitions were overcome by the effect of the drug. The more susceptible the defendant to the kind of temptation presented, the easier the defence is to establish.

My Lords, since the existence or otherwise of the defence has been treated in argument at all stages as a matter of existing law the Court of Appeal had no occasion to consider the practical and theoretical implications of recognising this new defence at common law, and we do not have the benefit of its views. In their absence, I can only say that the defence appears to run into difficulties at every turn. In point of theory, it would be necessary to reconcile a defence of irresistible impulse derived from a combination of innate drives and external disinhibition with the rule that irresistible impulse of a solely internal origin (not necessarily any more the fault of the offender) does not in itself excuse although it may be a symptom of a disease of the mind: *AG for South Australia v Brown* [1960] AC 432. Equally, the state of mind which founds the defence superficially resembles a state of diminished responsibility, whereas the effect in law is quite different. It may well be that the resemblance is misleading, but these and similar problems must be solved before the bounds of a new defence can be set.

On the practical side there are serious problems. Before the jury could form an opinion on whether the drug might have turned the scale witnesses would have to give a picture of the defendant's personality and susceptibilities, for without it the crucial effect of the drug could not be assessed; pharmacologists would be required to describe the potentially disinhibiting effect of a range of drugs whose identity would, if the present case is anything to go by, be unknown; psychologists and psychiatrists would express opinions, not on the matters of psychopathology familiar to those working within the framework of the Mental Health Acts but on altogether more elusive concepts. No doubt as time passed those concerned could work out techniques to deal with these questions. Much more significant would be the opportunities for a spurious defence. Even in the field of road traffic the 'spiked' drink as a special reason for not disqualifying from driving is a regular feature. Transferring this to the entire range of criminal offences is a disturbing prospect. The defendant would only have to assert, and support by the evidence of well-wishers, that he was not the sort of person to have done this kind of thing, and to suggest an occasion when by some means a drug might have been administered to him for the jury to be sent straight to the question of a possible disinhibition. The judge would direct the jurors that if they felt any legitimate doubt on the matter – and by its nature the defence would be one which the prosecution would often have no means to rebut – they must acquit outright, all questions of intent, mental capacity and the like being at this stage irrelevant.

My Lords, the fact that a new doctrine may require adjustment of existing principles to accommodate it, and may require those involved in criminal trials to learn new techniques, is not of course a ground for refusing to adopt it, if that is what the interests of justice require. Here, however, justice makes no such demands for the interplay between the wrong done to the victim, the individual characteristics and frailties of the defendant, and the pharmacological effects of whatever drug may be potentially involved can be far better recognised by a tailored choice from the continuum of sentences available to the judge than by the application of a single yea-or-nay jury decision. To this, there is one exception. The mandatory life sentence for murder, at least as present administered, leaves no room for the trial judge to put into practice an informed and sympathetic assessment of the kind just described. It is for this reason alone that I have felt any hesitation about rejecting the argument for the respondent. In the end however I have concluded that this is not a sufficient reason to force on the theory and practice of the criminal law an exception which would otherwise be unjustified. For many years mandatory sentences have impelled juries to return merciful but false verdicts, and have stimulated the creation of partial defences such as provocation and diminished responsibility whose lack of a proper foundation has made them hard to apply in practice. I do not think it right that the law should be further distorted simply because of this anomalous relic of the history of the criminal law.

All this being said, I suggest to your Lordships that the existing work of the Law Commission in the fields of intoxication could usefully be enlarged to comprise questions of the type raised by this appeal, and to see whether by statute a merciful, realistic and intellectually sustainable solution could be newly created. For the present, however, I consider that no such regime now exists, and that the common law is not a suitable vehicle for creating one ...

CODIFICATION AND LAW REFORM PROPOSALS

Clause 22 of the draft Criminal Code Bill (DCCB) (see Law Com No 177 Vol I) sought to codify *Majewski* with some minor clarifications. Although the defence of intoxication has been the subject of a much more searching review by the Law Commission since, see its Consultation Paper (LCCP 127) and the Report *Legislating the Criminal Code: Intoxication and Criminal Liability* (Law Com 229), the Home Office Offences Against the Persons Bill (see clause 19) adopts the approach adopted in clause 22 – hence it is reproduced here along with the commentary from Law Com 173 Vol II.

Clause 22 of the DCCB provides:

22(1) Where an offence requires a fault element of recklessness (however described), a person who was voluntarily intoxicated shall be treated –

(a) as having been aware of any risk of which he would have been aware had he been sober;

(b) as not having believed in the existence of an exempting circumstance (where the existence of such a belief is in issue) if he would not have so believed had he been sober.

(2) Where an offence requires a fault element of failure to comply with a standard of care, or requires no fault, a person who was voluntarily intoxicated shall be treated as not having believed in the existence of an exempting circumstance (where the existence of such a belief is in issue) if a reasonable sober person would not have so believed.

(3) Where the definition of a fault element or of a defence refers, or requires reference, to the state of mind or conduct to be expected of a reasonable person, such person shall be understood to be one who is not intoxicated.

(4) Subsection (1) does not apply –

  (a) to murder (to which section 55 applies); or

  (b) to the case (to which section 36 applies) where a person's unawareness or belief arises from a combination of mental disorder and voluntary intoxication.

(5) (a) 'Intoxicant' means alcohol or any other thing which, when taken into the body, may impair awareness or control.

  (b) 'Voluntary intoxication' means the intoxication of a person by an intoxicant which he takes, otherwise than properly for a medicinal purpose, knowing that it is or may be an intoxicant.

  (c) For the purposes of this section, a person 'takes' an intoxicant if he permits it to be administered to him.

(6) An intoxicant, although taken for a medicinal purpose, is not properly so taken if –

  (a)(i) it is not taken on medical advice; or

    (ii) it is taken on medical advice but the taker fails then or thereafter to comply with any condition forming part of the advice; and

  (b) the taker is aware that the taking, or the failure, as the case may be, may result in his doing an act capable of constituting an offence of the kind in question;

  and accordingly intoxication resulting from such taking or failure is voluntary intoxication.

(7) Intoxication shall be taken to have been voluntary unless evidence is given, in the sense stated in section 13(2), that it was involuntary.

The commentary in Vol II Law Com 177 states:

Clause 22: Intoxication

8.33 This clause provides for the effect of intoxication upon the liability of a person who causes the external elements of an offence. It aims to reproduce the present law on this topic with modifications recommended by the Criminal Law Revision Committee. It is a somewhat complex clause because it restates relatively complex law. We have kept it as simple as possible by omitting aspects of the corresponding clause in the Code team's Bill that we regarded as strictly speaking redundant (as we explain below). The provision of a simpler clause on intoxication could only result from a major law reform exercise. That was not in question as an aspect of the present project. But, like the majority of the Criminal Law Revision Committee, we are not in any case persuaded that the law as stated in clause 22 would be seriously unsatisfactory.

8.34 *Involuntary intoxication; offences requiring intention, knowledge, etc.* The legal position in relation to situations not referred to by clause 22 is to be deduced from the rest of the Code, read with the enactment creating the offence charged. Thus, the clause has nothing to say about evidence of involuntary intoxication, which is accordingly to be treated like any other evidence tending to show that the defendant lacked the fault required for the offence charged. If the evidence shows no more than that the defendant more readily gave way to passion or temptation than he would have done if he had been sober, it may be a mitigating factor but it will not be a defence. Again, when the offence charged requires proof of intention, knowledge or belief, evidence of voluntary intoxication is to be treated like any other evidence tending to show that the defendant lacked the state of mind in question. This is presently the position in relation to any offence classified as an offence of 'specific intent'. And once again, with such an offence as with any other, intoxication will have no bearing on liability to conviction if it merely affected the defendant's emotional reaction or reduced his inhibitions. There is no need for express provision on these matters.

8.35 *Offences of recklessness.* So far as proof of the fault element of an offence is concerned, the law at present has a special rule for the effect of voluntary intoxication where the offence charged is one of so-called 'basic intent'. We agree with the view of the Criminal Law Revision Committee that this should be replaced by a rule, modelled upon the corresponding provision of the American Law Institute's Model Penal Code, relating to any offence requiring a fault element of recklessness. Subsection (1)(a) provides that a person who was voluntarily intoxicated is to be treated, for the purposes of such an offence, as having been aware of any risk of which he would have been aware had he been sober. Subsection (1) applies to an offence requiring recklessness 'however described'. So, for example, if any offences requiring 'malice' survive the enactment of the Code, they will be governed by the subsection since 'maliciously' is satisfied by proof of recklessness, as defined in clause 18(c); and the same will be true of any offences enacted after the Code which employ the concept of recklessness but use different terminology to describe it.

8.36 Subsection (1) applies to an offence requiring a fault element of recklessness even where it also requires, expressly or by implication, an element of intention or knowledge. So, for example, any charge of rape no doubt implies an allegation of an intention to have sexual intercourse; but paragraph (a) nonetheless applies to an alleged 'fault element of recklessness' constituted by the defendant's having been aware that the woman was not consenting to the intercourse.

8.37 A defendant who was intoxicated may, however, deny that he intended to do any act at all, having no control over, or awareness of, his movements. Charged with recklessly causing serious personal harm by beating a woman, he says that because of his drugged condition he was unconscious. Clause 33

(1)(b) makes it clear that he cannot rely on his condition as a 'state of automatism' if it arose from voluntary intoxication. He is to be treated as having beaten the woman, being aware of any risk of causing harm of which he would have been aware had he been sober.

8.38   *Belief in exempting circumstances.* Just as a person may, because of intoxication, lack the state of mind required for an offence, so he may have the state of mind required for a defence – as when, being drunk, he mistakenly believes that P is making a murderous attack on him and retaliates, as he supposes, in self-defence. As with the fault elements of offences, we believe that it is unnecessary to refer in this clause to the relevant effect of involuntary intoxication. Evidence of involuntary intoxication will, without special provision, be treated like any other evidence tending to show that the defendant held any belief or had any other state of mind which is an element of a defence.

8.39   Where intoxication is voluntary, its effect depends on the fault element of the offence charged. Subsection (1)(b) follows the recommendation of the Criminal Law Revision Committee:

> ... in offences in which recklessness constitutes an element of the offence, if the defendant because of a mistake due to voluntary intoxication holds a belief which, if held by a sober man, would be a defence to the charge but which the defendant would not have held had he been sober, the mistaken belief should be immaterial.

8.40   A slightly stricter rule must apply to offences not requiring a fault element of recklessness. Subsection (2) therefore provides that, where the offence charged involves a fault element of failure to comply with a standard of care, or requires no fault, the defendant is to be treated as not having believed in the existence of an exempting circumstance if a reasonable sober person would not have so believed.

8.41   In *Jaggard v Dickinson* [1981] QB 527 [see Chapter 23] the defendant was allowed to rely on a drunken belief that she was damaging property belonging to a person who would consent to her doing so. The effect of subsection (1)(b) is to reverse this decision. This is justified, not only on the ground that it follows from the Committee's recommendations, but also because that decision creates an anomalous distinction (between mistake as to the non-existence of an element of an offence and mistake as to the existence of a circumstance affording a defence) which it would be wrong to perpetuate in the Code.

8.42   *Mistake and offences requiring intention.* The same anomaly would be introduced if the Code were to adopt a *dictum* of the Court of Appeal in *O'Grady* to the effect that a defendant, on a charge of an offence of 'specific intent' equally with one of 'basic intent', would not be able to rely upon evidence of an intoxicated mistaken belief in an occasion for self-defence. The court was concerned that one who kills because of a drunken mistake should not be 'entitled to leave the court without a stain on his character'. But a conviction of manslaughter will of course be available (and similarly, in a case of serious personal harm, a conviction of an offence of recklessly causing such harm); and it would, we believe, be unthinkable to convict of murder a person who thought, for whatever reason, that he was acting to save his life and who would have been acting reasonably if he had been right. Moreover, the Code should if possible provide consistently for all defences; it would not he appropriate to try to devise a special rule for self-defence alone, or generally for the use of force in public or private defence (clause 44) or in defence of property (clause 185). In all the circumstances we are satisfied that the *dictum* referred to must be ignored in framing the present clause. The result is consistent with the view of the Criminal Law Revision Committee on this topic.

8.43 *Intoxication and reasonableness.* It would seem obvious that, when the law prescribes a standard of reasonable behaviour, this must relate to the standard to be expected of a sober person. But the fact that the point has been argued in the Court of Appeal in two modern case suggests the desirability of including in the Code the principle that those cases establish, to avoid the matter being reopened. The principle is stated in subsection (3). In *R v Young* [1984] 1 WLR 654 the Court of Appeal thought that, in determining whether a person 'has reason to suspect', it is 'an unnecessary gloss to introduce the concept of the reasonable man'. It is, however, impossible to state a principle concerning intoxication or sobriety without a reference to a person. It does not necessarily follow that the judge need refer to such a person in directing the jury, though it may sometimes be convenient to do so.

8.44 *Exceptions from subsection (1): (a) murder.* Murder has to be excepted (by subsection (4)(a)) from the application of subsection (1) because the fault required by clause 54(b) ('A person who causes the death of another ... intending to cause serious personal harm and being aware that he may kill') is a variety of recklessness. If murder were not excepted, a person who, because of intoxication, was unaware that he might kill might be treated as being aware of that risk and so liable to conviction of murder. This would be a departure from long established law and from the recommendation of the Criminal Law Revision Committee. The exception reproduces existing law in accordance with that recommendation. It is justified because manslaughter, being punishable with life imprisonment, is sufficient to protect the public interest.

8.45 *(b) Voluntary intoxication and mental disorder in combination.* The courts have accepted that a person's unawareness or mistaken belief may be due to a combination of voluntary intoxication and mental disorder. In *R v Burns* (1973) 58 Cr App R 364 where the defendant's unawareness may have been due partly to brain damage and partly to drink and drugs taken otherwise than on medical advice, the Court of Appeal held that he was entitled to an absolute acquittal. Yet neither of the concurrent causes alone would have entitled him to an absolute acquittal of the offence of 'basic intent' with which he was charged. Some such cases would be better dealt with by a mental disorder verdict under clause 36: the defendant is acquitted but made amenable to the special disposal powers available to the court. A mental disorder verdict will be returned (so long as clause 22 (1) does not apply) where the defendant was suffering at the time of the act from 'mental disorder' as defined in clause 34. The kind of mental disorder relevant in practice would be a state of automatism (not resulting only from the intoxication itself) that is associated with an underlying condition and likely to recur. A mental disorder verdict would be more satisfactory than an 'insanity' verdict under the present law because the court will have wide powers of disposal under the recommendations of the Butler Committee instead of being obliged to order indefinite detention of the offender. Subsection (4)(b) therefore provides that subsection (1) shall not apply in a case of combined intoxication and mental disorder.

8.46 *Definitions: (a) 'Intoxicant'.* It is desirable to define 'intoxicant' (and, by implication, 'intoxication') for the purposes of the Code because the meaning it has to bear, like its meaning under the existing law, is probably wider than that attributed to it in ordinary speech. There is only one aspect of intoxication which is relevant for present purposes and that is its effect on a person's awareness of circumstances and of the possible results of his conduct and on his ability to control his movements. Subsection (5)(a) therefore defines an intoxicant as anything which, when taken into the body, may impair awareness or control. The paragraph makes specific reference to alcohol not only because it is the most common intoxicant but also in order to direct the reader's mind more readily to the kind of effect envisaged. The definition is wide enough to include the vapour which is inhaled by a glue-sniffer as well as drugs taken orally or by injection.

(b) 'Voluntary intoxication'. When a person who takes an intoxicant knows that it is or may be an intoxicant his resulting intoxication is in general 'voluntary', as subsection (5)(b) provides. But it seems to be accepted in the present law that intoxication arising from the proper use of drugs for medicinal purposes does not have the consequences in the criminal law of voluntary intoxication; and this is clearly right in principle. A person who becomes voluntarily intoxicated may, without any further fault on his part, become guilty of serious crime. It would be entirely wrong that such a consequence should follow from acting either on medical advice or without medical advice but in all respects properly for a medicinal purpose.

(c) 'Takes' an intoxicant. In the interests of economy of statement, a person's permitting an intoxicant to be administered to himself is said by subsection (5)(c) to be a case of 'taking' it.

8.47 *When an intoxicant is not taken 'properly for a medicinal purpose'.* When drugs are taken on medical advice that advice may include conditions as to the circumstances in which the drug is to be taken. The effect of taking drugs and failing to comply with the conditions may be that the taker becomes intoxicated. If, in consequence of something he then does, he is charged with an offence requiring recklessness or a lower degree of fault, or with an offence of strict liability, the question arises whether the intoxication is 'voluntary' so as to attract the operation of subsection (1) or (2).

8.48 The same question arises where drugs are taken without specific medical advice but for a medicinal purpose and with similar results. As stated in the preceding paragraph, the answer is that it depends, in both types of case, on whether the drugs were taken 'properly' for a medicinal purpose (subsection (5)(b)). Subsection (6) explains that drugs taken on medical advice are properly taken unless (i) the taker fails to comply with the conditions of the advice and (ii) he is aware that he may as a result do an act capable of constituting an offence of the relevant kind. Drugs taken without medical advice but for a medicinal purpose are properly taken unless the taker is aware he may as a result do such an act.

8.49 Subsection (6) is based on the decisions of the Court of Appeal in *Bailey and Hardie (Paul Deverall)*. It appears from these decisions that what the taker of the drugs must be aware of in order to incur liability varies according to the nature of the offence charged. If he is charged with an offence of violence he must have been aware that he might behave aggressively. If he is charged with reckless driving it is sufficient that he was aware that his conscious control of what he was doing might be affected. This is expressed as a general principle that the defendant should be regarded as voluntarily intoxicated only if he was aware that his taking of the drugs (if not on medical advice), or his failure to comply with a condition of the advice under which he took them, might result in his doing an act capable of constituting an offence of the kind in question.

8.50 *Evidential burden as to nature of intoxication.* It would, we believe, be arguable, in the absence of special provision, that whenever there is evidence of the defendant's having been so intoxicated that he did not form the intention required for the offence charged, the burden lies on the prosecution to prove that the intoxication was 'voluntary' within the meaning of subsection (5)(b) (see clause 13 (1)(a)). We do not think that such a burden should rest on the prosecution in the absence of any evidence tending to show that the intoxication was involuntary. Subsection (7) therefore puts an evidential burden to that effect upon the defence.

8.51 The subsection does not go so far as to require the defence to prove that the intoxication was involuntary. The Code team included a provision imposing such a requirement in their Bill (in square brackets in view of their doubts about its correctness). They had regard in doing so to a recent provision to the same effect in section 6(5) of the Public Order Act 1986, based on a Law Commission recommendation. The question whether intoxication was involuntary, whenever it is relevant, will in effect be the question whether the defendant acted without the fault required for the offence charged or had a defence based on a belief that an exempting circumstance existed. We do not now think that it would be appropriate to place on the defence a burden of proving absence of fault or to distinguish, in respect of the incidence of the burden of proof, between a defence of mistaken belief that involuntary intoxication may exceptionally provide and other defences of general application. There was some support on consultation for abandonment of the Code team's bracketed provision; and relevant judicial statements appear to assume that the burden is on the prosecution.

Further reading

AR Ward, 'Making sense of self-induced intoxication' [1986] CLJ 247

G Virgo, 'Reconciling principle and policy' [1993] Crim LR 415

G Orchard, 'Surviving without *Majewski* – a view from down under' [1993] Crim LR 426

E Paton 'Reforming the intoxication rules: the Law Commission's Report' [1996] Crim LR 382

CHAPTER 9

ACCESSORIAL LIABILITY

Where two or more parties are involved in the commission of a criminal offence it may be necessary to distinguish between the principal offender (P) who commits the *actus reus* with the appropriate *mens rea*, and the accomplice(s) (A) who assist(s) in some way. In English criminal law accessorial liability tends to be derivative, in the sense that it is necessary to establish the principal's liability before considering what the accessories might be charged with.

An accomplice is one who aid, abets, counsels or procures the commission of an offence; see s 8 of the Accessories and Abettors Act 1861 which provides:

> Whosoever shall aid, abet, counsel or procure the commission of any misdemeanour, whether the same be a misdemeanour at common law or by virtue of any Act passed or to be passed, shall be liable to be tried, indicted and punished as a principal offender.

Section 44(1) of the Magistrates' Courts Act 1980 makes similar provision for summary offences (ie offences triable only in a magistrates' court).

THE *ACTUS REUS* OF PARTICIPATION: AID, ABET, COUNSEL AND PROCURE

AG's Ref (No 1 of 1975) [1975] QB 773 (CA)

Lord Widgery CJ: This case comes before the court on a reference from the Attorney General, under s 36 of the Criminal Justice Act 1972, and by his reference he asks the following question:

> Whether an accused, who surreptitiously laced a friend's drinks with double measures of spirits when he knew that his friend would shortly be driving his car home, and in consequence his friend drove with an excess quantity of alcohol in his body and was convicted of the offence under s 6(1) of the Road Traffic Act 1972, is entitled to a ruling of no case to answer on being later charged as an aider and abettor, counsellor and procurer, on the ground that there was no shared intention between the two, that the accused did not by accompanying him or otherwise positively encourage the friend to drive, or on any other ground.

... The present question has no doubt arisen because in recent years there have been a number of instances, where men charged with driving their motor cars with an excess quantity of alcohol in the blood have sought to excuse their conduct by saying that their drinks were 'laced', as the jargon has it; that is to say, some strong spirit was put into an otherwise innocuous drink and as a result the driver consumed more alcohol than he had either intended to consume or had the desire to consume. The relevance of all that is not that it entitles the driver to an acquittal because such driving is an absolute offence, but that it can be relied on as a special reason for not disqualifying the driver from driving. Hence no doubt the importance which has been attached in recent months to the possibility of this argument being raised in a normal charge of driving with excess alcohol.

The question requires us to say whether on the facts posed there is a case to answer and, needless to say, in the trial from which this reference is derived the judge was of the opinion that there was no case to answer and so ruled. We have to say in effect whether he is right.

The language in the section which determines whether a 'secondary party', as he is sometimes called, is guilty of a criminal offence committed by another embraces the four words 'aid, abet, counsel or procure'. The origin of those words is to be found in s 8 of the Accessories and Abettors Act 1861 ...

Thus, in the past, when the distinction was still drawn between felony and misdemeanour, it was sufficient to make a person guilty of a misdemeanour if he aided, abetted, counselled or procured the offence of another. When the difference between felonies and misdemeanours was abolished in 1967, s 1 of the Criminal Law Act 1967 in effect provided that the same test should apply to make a secondary party guilty either of treason or felony.

Of course it is the fact that in the great majority of instances where a secondary party is sought to be convicted of an offence there has been a contact between the principal offender and the secondary party. Aiding and abetting almost inevitably involves a situation in which the secondary party and the main offender are together at some stage discussing the plans which they may be making in respect of the alleged offence, and are in contact so that each knows what is passing through the mind of the other.

In the same way it seems to us that a person, who counsels the commission of a crime by another, almost inevitably comes to a moment when he is in contact with that other, when he is discussing the offence with that other and when, to use the words of the statute, he counsels the other to commit the offence.

The fact that so often the relationship between the secondary party and the principal will be such that there is a meeting of minds between them caused the trial judge in the case from which this reference is derived to think that this was really an essential feature of proving or establishing the guilt of the secondary party and, as we understand his judgment, he took the view that in the absence of some sort of meeting of minds, some sort of mental link between the secondary party and the principal, there could be no aiding, abetting or counselling of the offence within the meaning of the section.

So far as aiding, abetting and counselling are concerned we would go a long way with that conclusion. It may very well be, as I said a moment ago, difficult to think of a case of aiding, abetting or counselling when the parties have not met and have not discussed in some respects the terms of the offence which they have in mind. But we do not see why a similar principle should apply to procuring. We approach s 8 of the Act of 1861 on the basis that the words should be given their ordinary meaning, if possible. We approach the section on the basis also that if four words are employed here, 'aid, abet, counsel or procure', the probability is that there is a difference between each of those four words and the other three, because, if there were no such difference, then Parliament would be wasting time in using four words where two or three would do. Thus, in deciding whether that which is assumed to be done under our reference was a criminal offence we approach the section on the footing that each word must be given its ordinary meaning.

To procure means to produce by endeavour. You procure a thing by setting out to see that it happens and taking the appropriate steps to produce that happening. We think that there are plenty of instances in which a person may be said to procure the commission of a crime by another even though there is no sort of conspiracy between the two, even though there is no attempt at agreement or discussion as to the form which the offence should take. In our judgment the offence described in this reference is such a case.

If one looks back at the facts of the reference: the accused surreptitiously laced his friend's drink. This is an important element and, although we are not going to decide today anything other than the problem posed to us, it may well be that, in similar cases where the lacing of the drink or the introduction of the extra alcohol is known to the driver, quite different considerations may apply. We say that because, where the driver has no knowledge of what is happening, in most instances he would have no means of preventing the offence from being committed. If the driver is unaware of what has happened, he will not be taking precautions. He will get into his car seat, switch on the ignition and drive home and, consequently, the conception of another procuring the commission of the offence by the driver is very much stronger where the driver is innocent of all knowledge of what is happening, as in the present case where the lacing of the drink was surreptitious.

The second thing which is important in the facts set out in our reference is that, following and in consequence of the introduction of the extra alcohol, the friend drove with an excess quantity of alcohol in his blood. Causation here is important. You cannot procure an offence unless there is a causal link between what you do and the commission of the offence, and here we are told that in consequence of the addition of this alcohol the driver, when he drove home, drove with an excess quantity of alcohol in his body.

Giving the words their ordinary meaning in English, and asking oneself whether in those circumstances the offence has been procured, we are in no doubt that the answer is that it has. It has been procured because, unknown to the driver and without his collaboration, he has been put in a position in which in fact he has committed an offence which he never would have committed otherwise. We think that there was a case to answer and that the trial judge should have directed the jury that an offence is committed if it is shown beyond reasonable doubt that the defendant knew that his friend was going to drive, and also knew that the ordinary and natural result of the additional alcohol added to the friend's drink would be to bring him above the recognised limit of 80 milligrammes per 100 millilitres of blood.

It was suggested to us that, if we held that there may be a procuring on the facts of the present case, it would be but a short step to a similar finding for the generous host, with somewhat bibulous friends, when at the end of the day his friends leave him to go to their own homes in circumstances in which they are not fit to drive and in circumstances in which an offence ... is committed. The suggestion has been made that the host may in those circumstances be guilty with his guests on the basis that he has either aided, abetted, counselled or procured the offence.

The first point to notice in regard to the generous host is that that is not a case in which the alcohol is being put surreptitiously into the glass of the driver. That is a case in which the driver knows perfectly well how much he has to drink and where to a large extent it is perfectly right and proper to leave him to make his own decision.

Furthermore, we would say that, if such a case arises, the basis on which the case will be put against the host is, we think, bound to be on the footing that he has supplied the tool with which the offence is committed. This, of course is a reference back to such cases as those where oxy-acetylene equipment was bought by a man knowing it was to be used by another for a criminal offence: see *R v Bainbridge* [1960] 1 QB 129. There is ample and clear authority as to the extent to which supplying the tools for the commission of an offence may amount to aiding and abetting for present purposes.

Accordingly, so far as the generous host type of case is concerned we are not concerned at the possibility that difficulties will be created, as long as it is borne in mind that in those circumstances the matter must be approached in accordance with well-known authority governing the provision of the tools for the commission of an offence, and never forgetting that the introduction of the alcohol is not there surreptitious, and that consequently the case for saying that the offence was procured by the supplier of the alcohol is very much more difficult.

Our decision on the reference is that the question posed by the Attorney General should be answered in the negative.

AG v Able and Others [1984] 1 QB 795 (CA)

Woolf J: In this case, Her Majesty's Attorney General applies by originating summons for declaratory relief that, in the circumstances specified by him, the distribution of a booklet entitled 'A guide to self-deliverance', which is published by the executive committee of the Voluntary Euthanasia Society (which also used to be known as Exit), is unlawful as being either an offence or an attempted offence contrary to the provisions of s 2(1) of the Suicide Act 1961.

That Act, by s 1, abrogated the rule of law whereby it was a crime for a person to commit suicide. Section 2(1) provides:

> A person who aids, abets, counsels or procures the suicide of another, or an attempt by another to commit suicide, shall be liable on conviction on indictment to imprisonment for a term not exceeding 14 years.

The respondents to the summons, whose names were changed at the outset of the proceedings, are members of the executive committee of the society. The society is an unincorporated association of members. Its amended constitution recites the purposes for which the society was established. These are:

> (2) The society shall work for the legalisation of voluntary euthanasia and for the enactment and beneficial working of any other measure seeking to establish the right, within properly defined limits, to avoid suffering and to die peacefully. (3) The society shall publish and distribute a form of declaration enabling members and others to make known their wishes with regard to terminal and emergency treatment. (4) The society may take any other steps intended to promote a general acceptance and understanding of the principles of voluntary euthanasia. (5) The society may consider and evaluate questions relating to the avoidance of suffering and to peaceful death and may provide information and practical and other advice to members of mature years and reasonable length of membership (by, for example, publication and

distribution of a pamphlet or booklet) as to how most appropriately a prolonged and painful death can be avoided, and a life can be ended painlessly by someone hopelessly and painfully ill who has decided to embark on self-deliverance. (6) The society may carry our research in relation to all the above purposes and apply funds accordingly.

The respondents dispute the claim for relief on two main grounds. First, it is said that this is not a case in which it would be proper for the court to exercise its jurisdiction to grant declaratory relief, since it is for the criminal courts and not this court to apply the criminal law and if the law is unclear, the proper body to clarify the law is Parliament and not the courts. Second, they submit that the distribution of the booklet is not unlawful. The respondents go on to contend that if it is appropriate to grant declaratory relief, then a declaration should be granted that:

> No offence against s 2 of the Suicide Act is committed by publishing or supplying factual information about methods of committing suicide or arguments about the property of so doing, if its publisher or supplier (a) has no knowledge that the recipient has a present intention of committing suicide, or (b) lacks an intention to persuade a particular recipient to commit suicide, or (c) where the information or argument published is by its nature or by the circumstances attending its publication unlikely to precipitate suicidal attempts ...

... I consider it appropriate to proceed to consider whether, on the evidence which is before me, the Attorney General has established that he is entitled to the declaratory relief which he seeks. A starting point of such consideration must be the terms of s 2(1) itself. The intent of the subsection is clear. Section 1 of the Act having abrogated the criminal responsibility of the suicide, s 2(1) retains the criminal liability of an accessory at or before the fact. The nature of that liability has, however, changed. From being a participant in an offence of another, the accessory becomes the principal offender. This has the result that to attempt to 'aid, abet, counsel or procure the suicide of another, or an attempt by another to commit suicide' can be an offence even if the person concerned does not attempt to commit suicide: see *R v McShane* (1978) 66 Cr App R 97 and s 3 of the Criminal Attempts Act 1981. This is of significance in relation to the present issues because if the distribution of the booklet amounts to an offence under s 2(1) when the person to whom the booklet is distributed commits suicide or attempts to commit suicide, then the distribution to that person, if there is no attempt to commit suicide, could be an attempt to commit an offence under s 2(1) in the appropriate circumstances.

This being the general effect of s 2(1), the issue can be confined to considering whether to distribute the booklet to someone who commits suicide or attempts to commit suicide makes the distributor 'an accessory before the fact' to the suicide or attempted suicide, the position so far as the distributor is concerned being exactly the same as it would be if either suicide or attempted suicide were still a criminal offence.

Of the opening words of s 2(1), the words 'aids, abets' are normally regarded as referring to an accessory at the fact, and the words 'counsels or procures' to an accessory before the fact. However, it is not right to ignore the words 'aids, abets' in considering whether a person is an accessory before the fact.

As is pointed out in *Russell on Crime*, 12th edn, 1964, p 150, the conception of accessories before the fact is one of great antiquity and it cannot properly be understood without consideration of its history. Coke used both the word 'aide' and the word 'abetting' in dealing with accessories before the fact. Hale said in his *Pleas of the Crown*, 1778 edn, p 615: 'An accessory before, is he, that being absent at the time of the felony committed, doth yet procure, counsel, command, or abet another to commit a felony.'

Therefore, in the ordinary case, in deciding whether or not an offence has been committed, it is preferable to consider the phrase 'aids, abets, counsels or procures' as a whole. However, some of the previous decisions of the courts are explained by the fact that in the particular circumstances of that case, the court was considering only one part of the phrase.

The editor of *Russell* also provides assistance as to what is the 'bare minimum' which is necessary to constitute a person an accessory before the fact. At 151, it is stated that:

> ... the conduct of an alleged accessory should indicate (a) that he knew the particular deed was contemplated, and (b) that he approved of or assented to it, and (c) that his attitude in respect of it in fact encouraged the principal offender to perform – and I would here add 'or attempt to perform' – the deed.

In relation to the first minimum requirement, those responsible for publishing the booklet, because of its terms, would almost certainly know that a significant number of those to whom the booklet was intended to be sent would be contemplating suicide. They would not know precisely when, where or by what means the suicide was to be effected, if it took place, but this does not mean they cannot be shown to be accessories. As Lord Parker CJ said In *R v Bainbridge* [1960] 1 QB 129 at 134:

> If the principal does not totally and substantially vary the advice or the help and does not wilfully and knowingly commit a different form of felony altogether, the man who has advised or helped, aided or abetted, will be guilty as an accessory before the fact.

As the judge had directed the jury in that case: 'It must be proved he knew the type of crime which was in fact committed was intended.'

In relation to the second requirement, if the recipients of the booklet attempted to commit or committed suicide, the contents of the booklet indicate that the publishers approved or assented to their doing so. To conclude otherwise is inconsistent with the whole object of the booklet, which is to assist those who feel it necessary to resort to self-deliverance.

I turn, therefore, to the final minimum requirement. I have no doubt that in the case at least of certain recipients of the booklet, its contents would encourage suicide. Ignorance as to how to commit suicide must by itself be a deterrent. Likewise, the risks inherent in an unsuccessful attempt must be a deterrent. The contents of the booklet provide information as to methods which are less likely to result in an unsuccessful attempt. This assistance must encourage some readers to commit or attempt to commit suicide. This is clearly appreciated by the publishers, thus their care to control the persons to whom the booklet is to be sold and their advice as to the safe-keeping of the booklet.

I, therefore, have come clearly to the conclusion that there could be circumstances in which to supply the booklet could amount to an offence ...

The fact that the supply of the booklet could be an offence does not mean that any particular supply is an offence. It must be remembered that the society is an unincorporated body and there can be no question of the society committing an offence. Before an offence under s 2 can be proved, it must be shown that the individual concerned 'aided, abetted, counselled or procured' an attempt at suicide or a suicide and intended to do so by distributing the booklet. The intention of the individual will normally have to be inferred from facts surrounding the particular supply which he made. If, for example, before sending a copy of the booklet, a member of the society had written a letter, the contents of which were known to the person sending the booklet, which stated that the booklet was required because the member was intending to commit suicide, then, on those facts, I would conclude that an offence had been committed or at least an attempted offence contrary to s 2 of the Act. However, in the majority of cases, a member requesting the booklet will not make clear his intentions and the supply will be made without knowledge of whether the booklet is required for purposes of research, general information, or because suicide is contemplated. Is it, therefore, enough that in any particular case the person responsible for making the supply would appreciate that there is a real likelihood that the booklet is required by one of the substantial number of members of the society who will be contemplating suicide? It is as to this aspect of the case that there is the greatest difficulty and little assistance from the authorities.

[Counsel], on behalf of the society, contends that before a person can be an accessory, there must be a consensus between the accessory and the principal, and there can be no consensus where the alleged accessory does not even know whether the principal is contemplating (in this case) suicide. As, however, is pointed out in Smith and Hogan, *Criminal Law*, 4th edn, 1978, while counselling implies consensus, procuring and aiding do not. The editors say at 116:

> the law probably is that: (1) 'procuring' implies causation but not consensus; (2) 'abetting' and 'counselling' imply consensus but not causation; and (3) 'aiding' requires actual assistance but neither consensus nor causation.

As a matter of principle, it seems to me that as long as there is the necessary intent to assist those who are contemplating suicide to commit suicide if they decide to do so, it does not matter that the supplier does not know the state of mind of the actual recipient. The requirement for the necessary intent explains why in those cases where, in the ordinary course of business, a person is responsible for distributing an article, appreciating that some individuals might use it for committing suicide, he is not guilty of an offence. In the ordinary way, such a distributor would have no intention to assist the act of suicide. An intention to assist need not, however, involve a desire that suicide should be committed or attempted ...

Counsel for the respondents points out, and this I accept, that in some cases the booklet, far from precipitating someone to commit suicide, might have the effect of deterring someone from committing suicide when they might otherwise have done so. In such circumstances, he submits, it would be quite nonsensical to regard the supply of the booklet as being an attempted offence contrary to s 2. I agree, though I recognise that on one approach the result would be different. The reason why I agree with the submission is because, in such a case, the booklet has not provided any assistance with a view to a contemplated suicide. Such assistance is necessary to establish the *actus reus* for even the attempted offence.

There will also be cases where, although the recipient commits or attempts to commit suicide, the booklet has nothing to do with the suicide or the attempted suicide; for example, a long period of time may have elapsed between the sending of the booklet and the attempt. In such a case, again, I would agree with counsel for the respondents that there would not be a sufficient connection between the attempted suicide and the supply of the booklet to make the supplier responsible. This does not mean that it has to be shown that the suicide or attempted suicide would not have occurred but for the booklet. However, if 'procuring' alone is relied upon, this may be the case. As Lord Widgery CJ stated in *AG's Ref (No 1 of 1975)* [1975] QB 773, at 779–80:

> To procure means to produce by endeavour. You procure a thing by setting out to see that it happens and taking the appropriate steps to produce that happening ... You cannot procure an offence unless there is a causal link between what you do and the commission of the offence ...

However, you do not need to procure to be an accessory and the same close causal connection is not required when what is being done is the provision of assistance.

I therefore conclude that to distribute the booklet can be an offence. But, before an offence can be established to have been committed, it must at least be proved: (a) that the alleged offender had the necessary intent, that is, he intended the booklet to be used by someone contemplating suicide and intended that person would be assisted by the booklet's contents, or otherwise encouraged to attempt to take or take his own life; (b) that while he still had that intention he distributed the booklet to such a person who read it; and (c) in addition, if an offence under s 2 is to be proved, that such a person was assisted or encouraged by so reading the booklet to attempt to take or to take his own life, otherwise the alleged offender cannot be guilty of more than an attempt.

If these facts can be proved, then it does not make any difference that the person would have tried to commit suicide anyway. Nor does it make any difference, as the respondents contend, that the information contained in the booklet is already in the public domain. The distinguishing feature between an innocent and guilty distribution is that in the former case the distributor will not have the necessary intent, while in the latter case he will.

However, in each case it will be for a jury to decide whether the necessary facts are proved. If they are, then normally the offence will be made out. Nevertheless, even if they are proved, I am not prepared to say it is not possible for there to be some exceptional circumstance which means that an offence is not established.

The situations with which I have just sought to deal illustrate the problems in this case of granting any form of declaration to Her Majesty's Attorney General. However, as I am clearly of the view that the supply of this booklet can amount to an offence contrary to s 2, if the recipient commits or attempts to commit suicide, there can be no question of the respondents being granted a declaration ...

R v Calhaem [1985] 1 QB 808 (CA)

Parker LJ: ... The prosecution case was that the applicant had counselled or procured the commission of the offence by one Zajac, a private detective, on 23 February 1983. On 5 September 1983 Zajac pleaded guilty to the murder and was duly sentenced therefor. The prosecution case against the applicant was that she had hired Zajac to commit the murder in order to get rid of the victim, who had for some time had an affair with the applicant's solicitor, Mr Pigot, with whom she was infatuated; that she had made a down-payment to Zajac of some £5,000 at a meeting on 28 January 1983 and that he had thereafter committed the murder.

The principal witness for the prosecution was Zajac. He testified to the hiring, the receipt of the money, and the murder itself. He said that on the day of the murder he went to Mrs Rendell's house, having first ensured that her husband was out, taking with him a hammer, a knife, and a shotgun loaded with cartridges from which he had removed the shot, the gun being in a gift-wrapped parcel. He had, he said, no intention of killing Mrs Rendell, having decided in the preceding days not to do so. He had on arrival at the house rung the bell, and when Mrs Rendell came to the door he had asked her to sign for the gift-wrapped parcel. She went to get a pen, and when she returned and found him in the hall she screamed. He had intended to do no more than act out a charade, so that both Mrs Rendell and the applicant would think that an attempt had been made to murder her. However, when Mrs Rendell screamed, he said, he had gone berserk, hit her several times with the hammer and killed her. Thereafter, it appears, he had stabbed her in the neck with his knife.

The first point taken by Mr Carman on the applicant's behalf was that the judge had seriously misdirected the jury on the law as to the ingredients of the offence of counselling ... Put in summary form, the submission which was made was that (a) the Crown were bound by Zajac's evidence as to his state of mind before and at the time of the murder; (b) both procuring and counselling require a substantial causal connection between the acts of the secondary offender and the commission of the offence; and (c) on Zajac's evidence there was no causal connection, or at any rate no substantial causal connection.

So far as presently material, at the end of [this] submission ... the judge ruled as follows:

> In my judgment, therefore, the appropriate direction in this case is to this effect. 'To counsel' means to incite, solicit, instruct or authorise. The Crown have to prove that the defendant counselled Zajac in this sense to kill Mrs Rendell and that in fact Mrs Rendell was killed by Zajac in circumstances that amounted to murder, and that such killing was within the scope of that instruction or authorisation.

... The direction given by the judge was, Mr Carman submits, wrong in law. He should have directed the jury that, in the case of counselling as in the case of procuring, the counselling must be a 'substantial cause' ...

Such authority as there is does not, in our view, take the matter much further; although assistance as to the general approach is to be gained from *AG's Ref (No 1 of 1975)* [1975] QB 773 at 778 ...

> We must ... approach the question raised on the basis that we should give to the word 'counsel' its ordinary meaning, which is, as the judge said, 'advise', 'solicit', or something of that sort. There is no implication in the word itself that there should by any causal connection between the counselling and the offence. It is true that, unlike the offence of incitement at common law, the actual offence must have been committed, and committed by the person counselled. To this extent there must clearly be, first, contact between the parties, and, second, a connection between the counselling and the murder.

Equally, the act done must, we think, be done within the scope of the authority or advice, and not, for example, accidentally when the mind of the final murderer did not go with his actions. For example, if the principal offender happened to be involved in a football riot in the course of which he laid about him with a weapon of some sort and killed someone who, unknown to him, was the person whom he had been counselled to kill, he would not, in our view, have been acting within the scope of his authority; he would have been acting entirely outside it, albeit what he had done was what he had been counselled to do ...

The natural meaning of the word does not imply the commission of the offence. So long as there is counselling – and there was ample evidence in this case of that fact – so long as the principal offence is committed by the one counselled, and so long as the one counselled is acting within the scope of his authority, and not in the accidental way or some such similar way as I have suggested with regard to an incident in a football riot, we are of the view that the offence is made out ...

PRESENCE AT THE SCENE OF THE CRIME AND FAILING TO PREVENT THE COMMISSION OF OFFENCES

Normally, mere presence at the scene of a crime will not, of itself, result in a person being convicted as an accomplice to the offence in question. As the following extracts indicate, however, if presence at the scene of the crime encourages its commission, and the defendant is aware of this, it may be possible to impose accessorial liability. Similarly where a defendant is in a position of authority and has the right to prevent an activity taking place that he realises involves the commission of a criminal offence, his failure to intervene could lead to his being convicted as an accomplice to the offence.

R v Coney and Others (1882) 8 QBD 534

Cave J: ... The evidence was that on the 16 June last, at the close of Ascot races, Burke and Mitchell had engaged in a fight near the road from Ascot to Maidenhead; that a ring was formed with posts and ropes; that a large number of persons were present looking on, some of whom were undoubtedly encouraging the fight; that the men fought for some time; and that the three prisoners were seen in the crowd, but were not seen to do anything, and there was no evidence how they got there or how long they stayed there.

The chairman of quarter sessions directed the jury in the words of *Russell on Crimes*, Vol 1, p 818:

There is no doubt that prize-fights are illegal, indeed just as much so as that persons should go out to fight with deadly weapons, and it is not at all material which party strikes the first blow, and all persons who go to a prize-fight to see the combatants strike each other, and who are present when they do so are, in point of law, guilty of an assault.

And the chairman added, in the words of Littledale J, in *R v Murphy* 6 C & P 103: 'If they were not casually passing by, but stayed at the place, they encouraged it by their presence, although they did not say or do anything.'

... Now it is a general rule in the case of principals in the second degree that there must be participation in the act, and that, although a man is present whilst a felony is being committed, if he takes no part in it, and does not act in concert with those who commit it, he will not be a principal in the second degree merely because he does not endeavour to prevent the felony, or apprehend the felon ...

... Where presence may be entirely accidental, it is not even evidence of aiding and abetting. Where presence is *prima facie* not accidental it is evidence, but no more than evidence, for the jury ...

This summing up unfortunately appears to me capable of being understood in two different ways. It may mean either that mere presence unexplained is evidence of encouragement, and so of guilt, or that mere presence unexplained is conclusive proof of encouragement, and so of guilt. If the former is the correct meaning, I concur in the law so laid down, if the latter, I am unable to do so. It appears to me that the passage tending to convey the latter view is that which was read by the chairman in this case to the jury, and I cannot help thinking that the chairman believed himself, and meant to direct the jury, and at any rate I feel satisfied that the jury understood him to mean, that mere presence unexplained was conclusive proof of encouragement, and so of guilt; and it is on this ground I hold that this conviction ought not to stand.

Lopes J: ... I understand the ruling of the chairman to amount to this, that mere presence at a prize-fight, unexplained, is conclusive proof of aiding and abetting, even if there be no evidence that the person or persons so present encouraged, or intended to encourage the fight by his or their presence. I cannot hold, as a proposition of law, that the mere looking on is *ipso facto* a participation in or encouragement of a prize-fight. I think there must be more than that to justify a conviction for an assault. If, for instance, it was proved that a person went to a prize-fight, knowing it was to take place, and remained there for some time looking on, I think that would be evidence from which a jury might infer that such person encouraged, and intended to encourage, the fight by his presence. In the present case, the three prisoners were merely seen in the crowd, were not seen to do anything, and there was no evidence why or how they came there, or how long they stayed.

Applying the direction of the chairman to this state of facts, I think it was wrong.

Hawkins J: ... In summing up the case the chairman directed the jury that all persons who went to a prize-fight to see the combatants strike each other, and who were present when they did so, were, in point of law, guilty of an assault, for 'if they were not casually passing by, but stayed at the place, they encouraged it by their presence, although they did not do or say anything'. The jury, on that direction, found the defendants guilty, but they also found expressly that they were not aiding or abetting. The whole question, therefore, for us to determine, as a matter of law, is not whether voluntary presence at a prize-fight is evidence of an aiding and abetting, but whether inactive presence at a prize-fight as a voluntary spectator thereof, amounts of itself to such encouragement of it as to render a man amenable to the criminal law as an aider and abettor in that breach of the peace ...

In my opinion, to constitute an aider and abettor some active steps must be taken by word, or action, with the intent to instigate the principal, or principals. Encouragement does not of necessity amount to aiding and abetting, it may be intentional or unintentional, a man may unwittingly encourage another in fact by his presence, by misinterpreted words, or gestures, or by his silence, on non-interference, or he may encourage intentionally by expressions, gestures, or actions intended to signify approval. In the latter case he aids and abets, in the former he does not. It is no criminal offence to stand by, a mere passive spectator of a crime, even of a murder. Non-interference to prevent a crime is not itself a crime. But the fact that a person was voluntarily and purposely present witnessing the commission of a crime, and offered no opposition to it, though he might reasonably be expected to prevent and had the power so to do, or at least to express his dissent, might under some circumstances, afford cogent evidence upon which a jury would be justified in finding that he wilfully encouraged and so aided and abetted. But it would be purely a question for the jury whether he did so or not. So if any number of persons arrange that a criminal offence shall take place, and it takes place accordingly, the mere presence of any of those who so arranged it would afford abundant evidence for the consideration of a jury of an aiding and abetting ...

Huddleston B: ... The mere staying at the place where a fight is going on is not necessarily encouragement; the detective sent to report what is taking place and to bring the offenders to justice cannot be said to be encouraging what is going on; a person casually passing, but who stays to see what happens and interferes to prevent, or retires in disgust, or is hemmed in so that he cannot retire, cannot be said to be encouraging ... The finding of the jury was in fact one of not guilty. They bow with respect to the chairman's direction in point of law, but by adding that the prisoners were not aiding and abetting, I conclude that they intend to convey that by no act of theirs were they countenancing or encouraging the fight, a conclusion fully supported by the evidence in the case.

Manisty J: ... It is said that if the ruling of the chairman is not upheld a great impetus will be given to prize fighting. I do not share in that apprehension. It is well-settled law that every person who by his presence or otherwise encourages a fight, be it a prize or an ordinary fight, is guilty of a criminal offence, that is to say, of an assault or manslaughter, as the case may be, but it is for the jury in each particular case to say as a matter of fact whether the accused did by his presence or otherwise encourage the combatants to fight. To hold the contrary would, in my opinion, be erroneous in point of law, and very injurious in its consequences.

Suppose that the fight in question had resulted in the death of one of the combatants, then, if the direction given to the jury was right, every person who was in the crowd was in point of law guilty of manslaughter, though he neither spoke nor did anything, and notwithstanding that in the opinion of the jury he neither aided nor abetted the combatants. I cannot believe such is the law of England ...

Wilcox v Jeffery [1951] 1 All ER 464 (KBD)

Lord Goddard CJ: This is a case stated by the metropolitan magistrate at Bow Street Magistrates' Court before whom the appellant, Herbert William Wilcox, the proprietor of a periodical called 'Jazz Illustrated', was charged on an information that 'on 11 December 1949, he did unlawfully aid and abet one Coleman Hawkins in contravening Art 1(4) of the Aliens Order, 1920, by failing to comply with a condition attached to a grant of leave to land, to wit, that the said Coleman Hawkins should take no employment paid or unpaid while in the United

Kingdom, contrary to Art 18(2) of the Aliens Order, 1920'. Under the Aliens Order, Art 1(1), it is provided that:

> ... an alien coming ... by sea to a place in the United Kingdom: (a) shall not land in the United Kingdom without the leave of an immigration officer ...

It is provided by Art 1(4) that:

> An immigration officer, in accordance with general or special directions of the Secretary of State, may, by general order or notice or otherwise, attach such conditions as he may think fit to the grant of leave to land, and the Secretary of State may at any time vary such conditions in such manner as he thinks fit, and the alien shall comply with the conditions so attached or varied ...

If the alien fails to comply, he is to be in the same position as if he has landed without permission, ie he commits an offence.

The case is concerned with the visit of a celebrated professor of the saxophone, a gentleman by the name of Hawkins who was a citizen of the United States. He came here at the invitation of two gentlemen of the name of Curtis and Hughes, connected with a jazz club which enlivens the neighbourhood of Willesden. They, apparently, had applied for permission for Mr Hawkins to land and it was refused, but, nevertheless, this professor of the saxophone arrived with four French musicians. When they came to the airport, among the people who were there to greet them was the appellant. He had not arranged their visit, but he knew they were coming and he was there to report the arrival of these important musicians for his magazine. So, evidently, he was regarding the visit of Mr Hawkins as a matter which would be of interest to himself and the magazine which he was editing and selling for profit. Messrs Curtis and Hughes arranged a concert at the Princes Theatre, London. The appellant attended that concert as a spectator. He paid for his ticket. Mr Hawkins went on the stage and delighted the audience by playing the saxophone. The appellant did not get up and protest in the name of the musicians of England that Mr Hawkins ought not to be here competing with them and taking the bread out of their mouths or the wind out of their instruments. It is not found that he actually applauded, but he was there having paid to go in, and, no doubt, enjoying the performance, and then lo and behold, out comes his magazine with a most laudatory description, fully illustrated, of this concert. On those facts the magistrate has found that he aided and abetted.

Reliance is placed by the prosecution on *R v Coney* (1882) 8 QBD 534 which dealt with a prize-fight. This case relates to a jazz band concert, but the particular nature of the entertainment provided, whether by fighting with bare fists or playing on saxophones, does not seem to me to make any difference to the question which we have to decide. The fact is that a man is charged with aiding and abetting an illegal act, and I can find no authority for saying that it matters what that illegal act is, provided that the aider and abettor knows the facts sufficiently well to know that they would constitute an offence in the principal. In *R v Coney* the prize-fight took place in the neighbourhood of Ascot, and four or five men were convicted of aiding and abetting the fight. The conviction was quashed on the ground that the chairman had not given a correct direction to the jury when he told them that, as the prisoners were physically present at the fight, they must be held to have aided and abetted. That direction, the court held, was wrong, it being too wide. The matter was very concisely put by Cave J, whose judgment was fully concurred in by that great master of the criminal law, Stephen J. Cave J said (8 QBD 534 at 540):

> Where presence may be entirely accidental, it is not even evidence of aiding and abetting. Where presence is *prima facie* not accidental it is evidence, but no more than evidence, for the jury.

There was not accidental presence in this case. The appellant paid to go to the concert and he went there because he wanted to report it. He must, therefore, be held to have been present, taking part, concurring, or encouraging, whichever word you like to use for expressing this conception. It was an illegal act on the part of Hawkins to play the saxophone or any other instrument at this concert. The appellant clearly knew that it was an unlawful act for him to play. He had gone there to hear him, and his presence and his payment to go there was an encouragement. He went there to make use of the performance, because he went there, as the magistrate finds and was justified in finding, to get 'copy' for his newspaper. It might have been entirely different, as I say, if he had gone there and protested, saying: 'The musicians' union do not like you foreigners coming here and playing and you ought to get off the stage.' If he had booed, it might have been some evidence that he was not aiding and abetting. If he had gone as a member of a claque to try to drown the noise of the saxophone, he might very likely be found not guilty of aiding and abetting. In this case it seems clear that he was there, not only to approve and encourage what was done, but to take advantage of it by getting 'copy' for his paper. In those circumstances there was evidence on which the magistrates could find that the appellant aided and abetted, and for these reasons I am of opinion that the appeal fails.

R v Clarkson and Others [1971] 1 WLR 1402 (Courts-Martial Appeal Court)

Megaw LJ: ... It is unnecessary to go into much detail as to the disgraceful and shameful events which took place on the night of 9/10 May 1970 in which beyond all the appellants, as well as others, were concerned. On no view can the conduct of any of them be regarded as other than deplorable. The question, however, is whether their respective convictions for criminal offences can be sustained.

The relevant facts will be recited as briefly as possible. The victim of the offences was an 18 year old girl named Elke von Groen. On 9 May 1970 she, having recently come out of hospital where she had undergone an operation to her womb, went to a party at the barracks at Menden. At about midnight she left the party to go to see a soldier with whom she had in the past been familiar. She went to his room. He was not there but other soldiers were there. Eventually she went to another room, room 64, where the rapes occurred. There she was raped at least by Newton, by Holloway and by Marshall at one time or another between midnight and about 3.15 am. She was physically injured and her clothes were torn to shreds. To say that those who attacked her behaved like animals would be unjust to animals. At some time after the raping began and when she had been screaming and moaning, there were clustered outside the door of room 64 a number of men, including the three appellants, no doubt listening to what was going on inside. The only thing to be said in their favour is that they may have been in a drunken condition when their moral sense and sense of the requirements of human decency had left them. The door of room 64 opened and they, including the three appellants, in the words of a witness 'piled in' to the room. There is no doubt that they remained there for a considerable time and there is no doubt that during that time the unfortunate girl was raped. There is no doubt that some of those present actively assisted by helping to hold down the unfortunate girl. However, so far as the appellants Clarkson and Carroll are concerned, there was no evidence – no admissible evidence and therefore no evidence – of their having done any positive act to assist. There was no evidence – no admissible evidence – that either of them helped to hold down the girl ...

As has been said, there was no evidence on which the prosecution sought to rely that either the appellant Clarkson or the appellant Carroll had done any physical act or uttered any words which involved direct physical participation or verbal encouragement. There was no evidence that they had touched the girl, helped to hold her down, done anything to her, done anything to prevent others from assisting her or to prevent her from escaping, or from trying to ward off her attackers, or that they had said anything which gave encouragement to the others to commit crime or to participate in committing crime. Therefore, if there was here aiding and abetting by the appellants Clarkson or Carroll it could only have been on the basis of inferences to be drawn that by their very presence they, each of them separately as concerns himself, encouraged those who were committing rape. Let it be accepted, and there was evidence to justify this assumption, that the presence of those two appellants in the room where the offence was taking place was not accidental in any sense and that it was not by chance, unconnected with the crime, that they were there. Let it be accepted that they entered the room when the crime was committed because of what they had heard, which indicated that a woman was being raped, and they remained there.

R v Coney (1882) 8 QBD 534 decided that non-accidental presence at the scene of the crime is not conclusive of aiding and abetting. The jury has to be told by the judge, or as in this case the court-martial has to be told by the judge-advocate, in clear terms what it is that has to be proved before they can convict of aiding and abetting; what it is of which the jury or the court-martial, as the case may be, must be sure as matters of inference before they can convict of aiding and abetting in such a case where the evidence adduced by the prosecution is limited to non-accidental presence. [Having referred to the judgement of Hawkins J in *R v Coney* his Lordship continued:]

It is not enough, then, that the presence of the accused has, in fact, given encouragement. It must be proved that the accused intended to give encouragement; that he *wilfully* encouraged. In a case such as the present, more than in many other cases where aiding and abetting is alleged, it was essential that that element should be stressed; for there was here at least the possibility that a drunken man with his self-discipline loosened by drink, being aware that a woman was being raped, might be attracted to the scene and might stay on the scene in the capacity of what is known as a voyeur; and, while his presence and the presence of others might in fact encourage the rapers or discourage the victim, he himself, enjoying the scene or at least standing by assenting, might not intend that his presence should offer encouragement to rapers and would-be rapers or discouragement to the victim; he might not realise that he was giving encouragement; so that, while encouragement there might be, it would not be a case in which, to use the words of Hawkins J, the accused person 'wilfully encouraged'.

A further point is emphasised in passages in the judgment of the Court of Criminal Appeal in *R v Allan* [1965] 1 QB 130 at 135, 138. That was a case concerned with participation in an affray. Edmund Davies J, giving the judgment of the court, said:

> In effect, it amounts to this: that the learned judge thereby directed the jury that they were duty bound to convict an accused who was proved to have been present and witnessing an affray if it was also proved that he nursed an intention to join in if help were needed by the side which he favoured, and this notwithstanding that he did nothing by words or deeds to evince his intention and outwardly played the role of purely passive spectator. It was said that, if that direction be right, where A and B behave themselves to all outward appearances in an exactly similar manner, but it be proved that A had the intention to participate if needs be, whereas B had no such intention, then A must be convicted of being a principal in the second degree to the affray, whereas B should be acquitted. To do that, it is objected, would be to convict A on his thoughts, even though they found no reflection in his actions.

The other passage in the judgment is this:

> In our judgment, before a jury can properly convict an accused person of being a principal in the second degree to an affray, they must be convinced by the evidence that, at the very least, he by some means or other encouraged the participants. To hold otherwise would be, in effect, as counsel for the appellants rightly expressed it, to convict a man on his thoughts, unaccompanied by any physical act other than the fact of his mere presence.

From that it follows that mere intention is not in itself enough. There must be an intention to encourage; and there must also be encouragement in fact, in cases such as the present case.

So we come to what was said by the judge-advocate ...

The judge-advocate draws the analogy which is commonly drawn where direction is given of two persons jointly indicted, for example, of committing burglary. One actually enters the house and the other stands outside to keep watch. That analogy, in the view of this court, is misleading in relation to what was involved in the present case, for it presupposes a prior meeting of minds between the persons concerned as to the crime to be committed. The man who stands outside and does not go in is guilty of burglary; but it cannot in such a case properly be said that he has taken no active step in the commission of the offence. He has gone to the place where he is, and he has conducted himself as he does, as a part of the joint plan which, in its totality, is intended to procure commission of the crime.

In the view of this court the echo of that false analogy unfortunately continued throughout when the judge-advocate came to sum up the matter to the court-martial ...

Rubie v Faulkner [1940] 1 KB 571

Facts: The appellant, while in a motor vehicle driven by the holder of a provisional licence (a 'learner driver') who was driving under his supervision in accordance with reg 16(3)(a) of the Motor Vehicles (Driving Licences) Regulations 1937, was in a position to see that the driver was about to overtake another vehicle by pulling considerably to the offside at a pronounced bend of the road, but he neither said nor did anything to prevent it. An accident occurred and the driver was convicted of driving without due care and attention.

Lord Hewart CJ: ... The regulation contemplates a duty and the presence of a person, properly to be called a supervisor, who is to perform that duty, and the duty is obviously comprised in the task of supervision ...

In this court it appeared to be argued that, partly because the time occupied by the events leading to the accident had been short, the appellant was not called on to do or to say anything, but was justified in what the justices described as his 'passive conduct'. That argument gives the go-by to the obvious intention of the regulation. The condition on which the holder of a provisional licence is allowed to drive a motor vehicle on a highway is that he is under the supervision of an experienced driver. The very essence of the matter is that there should be a supervisor competent to supervise. The duty being clear on the face of the regulation, it was a pure question of fact for the justices to decide whether that duty had been performed.

It seems to me that it was open to the justices to find that the appellant, by his passive conduct in circumstances which required him to be active, if only by exclaiming 'Keep in!', failed to discharge the duty which he had undertaken, and thus was guilty of the offence with which he was charged. In my opinion, therefore, this appeal should be dismissed.

Hilbery J: I agree. The regulation is framed to make some provision for the protection of the public against the dangers to which they are exposed through a car being driven on the road by a driver who is still a learner and therefore assumed to be not fully competent. It is, I can only suppose, because a learner driver is assumed to be not fully competent that the regulation provides that a supervisor shall accompany him. This being so, the supervisor must be intended by the regulation to have the duty, by supervision, of making up as far as possible for the driver's incompetence. In other words, it is the supervisor's duty, when necessary, to do whatever can reasonably be expected to be done by a person supervising the acts of another to prevent that other from acting unskilfully or carelessly or in a manner likely to cause danger to others, and to this extent to participate in the driving.

In this case it was found that the supervisor could see the driver was about to do the unlawful act of which he was convicted and the magistrates found that the supervisor remained passive. There is no hint in the case that the supervisor in evidence ever asserted that he did anything. For him to refrain from doing anything when he could see that an unlawful act was about to be done, and his duty was to prevent an unlawful act if he could, was for him to aid and abet.

Tuck v Robson [1970] 1 WLR 741 (QBD)

Lord Parker CJ: This is an appeal by way of case stated from a decision of one of the magistrates of the magistrates' courts of the metropolis sitting at Lambeth, who convicted the appellant of an offence contrary to the licensing laws. The informations, three in number, alleged that on a certain day he being the licensee of certain premises aided and betted three customers to consume intoxicating liquor out of hours.

The relevant statutory provision is to be found in s 59(1) of the Licensing Act 1964, which, so far as it is material, provides:

> subject to the provisions of this Act, no person shall, except during the permitted hours: (a) himself or by his servant or agent sell or supply to any person in licensed premises ... any intoxicating liquor, whether to be consumed on or off the premises; or (b) consume in or take from such premises any intoxicating liquor.

Accordingly, if liquor is bought during permitted hours and is being consumed after the permitted hours, the consumer commits an offence and the licensee could only be guilty if anything of aiding and abetting.

What happened in the present case was that at 11.23 pm on 11 April 1969 police officers went into the Canterbury Arms public house in Maddocks Way, London SE17, of which the appellant was a joint licensee. At the time the police entered the main lights in the saloon bar had been extinguished, leaving those on behind the bar, and there was a barmaid standing behind the bar. In the saloon bar the police found 20 customers, 12 of whom were consuming intoxicating liquor, including the three involved in these three informations. They were drinking alcoholic drinks, some of them standing and others sitting at tables.

No consumption of intoxicating liquor is permitted on the premises after 11.10 pm and the justices found that at 11.00 pm the appellant had called 'time' and had switched off some of the main lights, and at 11.05 pm had called 'glasses please'.

Having done that, he went into the public bar to clear away glasses and assist customers from that part of the premises. He knew, so the finding is, that during that period from 11.10 pm until the time the police arrived at 11.23 pm, ie 13 minutes, that customers were consuming liquor in the saloon bar, and took no steps to stop them. Evidence was given of a conversation between the appellant and the police, during which the appellant said:

> I thought that if I called out 'time' and asked customers to leave, that is all I am required to do ...

As it seems to me, two things must be proved before an accused can be held to be guilty of aiding and abetting the commission of the offence: first, he must have full knowledge of the facts which constitute the offence. I interpose, there is no question of that here; there is a finding that the appellant knew full well that after 11.10 pm drink was being consumed. Second, there must be some form of voluntary assistance in the commission of the offence. Sometimes the word used is 'encouragement', and the real question here is how far inaction, passive tolerance, can amount to assistance so as to make the accused guilty of aiding and abetting ...

... Here is a licensee who is in control of his premises; he has full knowledge that liquor is being consumed after hours; he takes no steps in the matter other than to call 'time' and ask customers to leave, which he did at 11.00 pm, and as he himself puts it 'I thought that if I called out "time" and asked customers to leave, that is all I am required to do'.

The question as it seems to me is whether the magistrate, as a reasonable tribunal, was entitled in all the circumstances to draw the inference that here there was passive assistance in the sense of presence with no steps being taken to enforce his right either to eject the customers or at any rate to revoke their licence to be on the premises. In my judgment the magistrate was entitled to draw that inference, and accordingly I would dismiss this appeal.

R v JF Alford Transport Ltd; R v Alford; R v Payne [1997] 2 Cr App R 326

The appellant company, its managing director and transport manager, who were convicted of aiding and abetting offences under the Transport Act 1968. The court found that they had been aware that drivers employed by the company had been making false entries on tachograph records contrary to s 99(5) of the 1968 Act, and had not intervened to prevent the practice. Their appeals against conviction were allowed, on the basis that there was insufficient evidence of *mens rea* to be accomplices. Kennedy LJ, however, considered the extent to which failure to act could amount to giving positive encouragement:

> ... if the prosecution could show that the individual defendants, or either of them, knew that the drivers were illegally falsifying tachograph records, and if it could be shown that the individual defendants took no steps to prevent misconduct it was open to the jury in the absence of any alternative explanation, to infer that the individual defendant whom they happened to be considering, and thus the company, was positively encouraging what was going on ... [Counsel for the appellant] submitted that in [previous cases, such as *Tuck v Robson* and *Du Cros v Lambourne* [1907] 1 KB 40] it was critical that the aider and abettor was present at the time of the commission of the principal offence. In our judgment nothing turned on actual presence. What mattered was knowledge of the principal offence, the ability to control the action of the offender, and the deliberate decision to refrain from doing so ... in the context of the present case it would have to be proved that the defendant under consideration intended to do the acts which he knew to be capable of assisting or encouraging the commission of the crime, but he need not have intended that the crime be committed ... [T]hus if the management's reason for turning a blind eye was to keep the drivers happy rather than to encourage the production of false tachograph records that would afford no defence.

Notes and queries

1   Where a statute creates an offence aimed at protecting a class of people, a member of that class cannot be an accessory to such an offence, even if the offence is committed with his or her assistance, encouragement or consent; see further *R v Whitehouse* [1977] 1 QB 868 (considered in Chapter 10), and *R v Tyrrell* [1894] 1 QB 710. In the latter case the court had to consider whether it was an offence for 'a girl between the ages of 13 and 16 to aid and abet a male person in the commission of the misdemeanour of having unlawful carnal connection with her, or to solicit and incite a male person to commit that misdemeanour'.

Lord Coleridge CJ observed: 'The Criminal Law Amendment Act, 1885, was passed for the purpose of protecting women and girls against themselves ... it is impossible to say that the Act, which is absolutely silent about aiding or abetting, or soliciting or inciting, can have intended that the girls for whose protection it was passed should be punishable under it for the offences committed upon themselves.' Mathew J agreed, observing: '... I do not see how it would be possible to obtain convictions under the statute if the contention for the Crown were adopted, because nearly every section which deals with offences in respect of women and girls would create an offence in the woman or girl. Such a result cannot have been intended by the legislature. There is no trace in the statute of any intention to treat the woman or girl as criminal.'

THE *MENS REA* OF ACCOMPLICES

Some basic principles

As *Johnson v Youden and Others* (extracted below) indicates, an accomplice cannot be convicted without some evidence that he knew of the facts that constituted the offence. The difficulty, however, has been in determining just how precise the accomplice's *mens rea* must be. Where there is evidence that he was certain as to what the principal offender intended to do, liability is easy to establish. As can be imagined, however, many of those who are questioned about the role they might have had to play in the commission of an offence by another may be rather vague as to what they thought this other person might do. Hence the courts have had to develop a slightly different approach to *mens rea* where the liability of accomplices is concerned. Instead of concepts such as foresight, the courts have preferred expressions such as 'contemplation'. The problem remains, however. How likely must the commission of the offence by the principal offender have seemed to the accomplice to justify a court in concluding that accomplice had sufficient *mens rea* to be convicted as such?

Johnson v Youden and Others [1950] 1 KB 544 (DC)

Facts: One Dolbear, a builder, built a house under the authority of a licence granted under a Defence Regulation subject to a condition limiting the price for which the house might be sold to £1,025. The builder induced a purchaser to agree to pay for the house £250 in excess of the price permitted. That £250 was paid to the builder in advance. He then instructed a firm of solicitors, in which the three defendants were partners, to act for him in the sale. He concealed from the defendants the fact that he had received the additional £250, and the first two defendants did not know of it at any material time. On 6 April 1949, however, the purchaser's solicitors wrote a letter to the third defendant stating that they had not proceeded to completion because the builder was in breach of s 7 of the Building Materials and Housing Act 1945. The third defendant sought an explanation from the builder, who said that he had placed the £250 in question in a separate deposit account, and that it was to be spent on payment for work, as and when he would be able lawfully to execute it in the future, on the house on the purchaser's behalf. The third defendant accepted that explanation, and, having read the Act of 1945, formed the opinion that the payment of £250 was lawful and called on the purchaser to complete.

The builder was charged on information with offering to sell the house for a greater price than that permitted, contrary to s 7(1) of the Building Materials and Housing Act 1945; and informations were preferred against the three defendants charging them with aiding and abetting him in the commission of that offence.

On 5 July 1949, the builder was convicted, but the justices dismissed the three informations against the other defendants as they were of opinion that *mens rea* was a constituent of the offence of aiding and abetting an offence under s 7(1) of the Act of 1945. They found that the third defendant honestly believed the explanation given to him by the builder regarding the £250.

The prosecutor appealed.

Lord Goddard CJ: Before a person can be convicted of aiding and abetting the commission of an offence he must at least know the essential matters which constitute that offence. He need not actually know that an offence has been committed, because he may not know that the facts constitute an offence and ignorance of the law is not a defence. If a person knows all the facts and is assisting another person to do certain things, and it turns out that the doing of those things constitutes an offence, the person who is assisting is guilty of aiding and abetting that offence, because to allow him to say, 'I knew of all those facts but I did not know that an offence was committed', would be allowing him to set up ignorance of the law as a defence.

The reason why, in our opinion, the justices were right in dismissing the informations against the first two defendants is that they found, and found on good grounds, that they did not know of the matters which in fact constituted the offence; and, as they did not know of those matters, it follows that they cannot be guilty of aiding and abetting the commission of the offence.

With regard to their partner, the third defendant, a different state of affairs arises. His client, the builder, told him a story which, even if it were true, was on the face of it obviously a colourable evasion of the Act. The builder told him that he had received another £250, that he had placed the sum in a separate deposit account, 'and that it was to be spent on payment for work as and when he, the builder, would be lawfully able to execute it in the future on the house on behalf of the said purchaser'. It seems impossible to imagine that anyone could believe such a story. Who has ever heard of a purchaser putting money into the hands of the builder when he bought a house from him because he might want some work done thereafter? Surely, if the builder did not think that the purchaser could pay for the work, he would say: 'Will you pay something on account?' A story of that kind, on the face of it, is a mere colourable evasion of the Act.

It is more than likely, I think, that, in reading the Act, the third defendant did not read as carefully as he might have done s 7(5). If he had read that subsection carefully, I cannot believe that he – or indeed any solicitor, or even a layman – would not have understood that the arrangement which the builder said that he had made was just the kind of thing that subsection prohibited.

How could anybody say that the story which the builder told the third defendant was not a story with regard to a transaction with which the sale was associated? If that subsection had been read by the third defendant and appreciated by him, he would have seen at once that the extra £250 which the builder was obtaining was an unlawful payment; but unfortunately he did not realise it, but either misread the Act or did not read it carefully; and the next day he called on the purchaser to complete. Therefore he was clearly aiding and abetting the builder in the offence which the latter was committing.

The result is that, as far as the first two defendants are concerned, the appeal fails and must be dismissed; but as far as the third defendant is concerned, the case must go back to the justices with an intimation that an offence has been committed, and that he must be convicted.

National Coal Board v Gamble [1959] 1 QB 11 (QBD)

Facts: On 3 October 1957, an employee of a firm of hauliers took his lorry to a National Coal Board colliery, where it was filled with coal from a hopper and was then taken to a weighbridge, where the weighbridge operator (an employee of the NCB) weighed the lorry and its load and told the driver that the load was nearly four tons overweight. The driver, saying that he would risk taking the overload, took the weighbridge ticket from the weighbridge operator and left the colliery. He was subsequently stopped by the police. His employers were later convicted of contravening the Motor Vehicles (Construction and Use) Regulations 1955. The hauliers were collecting the coal for carriage to a power station, to whom the NCB were bound by contract to supply a bulk quantity of coal. The NCB were charged with aiding and abetting the hauliers in the commission of an offence.

> **Lord Goddard CJ**: ... In my opinion it is quite clear that neither side could have intended the property in the coal to pass when it was put from the hopper into the lorry. The quantity would have to be ascertained in order to enable the price to be ascertained. The lorry is then taken to the weighbridge to be weighed and in my opinion no sale takes place whereby the property is passed until the weighing is completed and assented to by the buyer, and this is shown by the handing to him and the acceptance by him of a weighbridge ticket. In my opinion, therefore, no property passes until the weighbridge ticket was accepted by Mallender [the lorry driver].
>
> As soon as Haslam [the weighbridge operator] weighed the coal he knew it was overweight and called Mallender's attention to that fact. From Mallender's answer he knew that Mallender intended to drive the overweighted lorry on the highway and with that knowledge he completed the sale and handed the weight ticket to Mallender whose duty then was to give it to the purchasers, namely the Central Electricity Authority. Haslam could, in my opinion, have refused to allow the overweight amount of 3 tons 18 cwts to leave the colliery. No specific amount had been asked for. The board were no doubt bound to deliver coal to the electricity authority under their contract, but were not bound to deliver any particular amount of coal at any particular moment.
>
> The justices drew the inference, and it was not disputed, that the Board were bound by contract to supply a bulk quantity of coal to the authority. It was urged on behalf of the Board that they had no right to require Mallender to unload the coal or rather the excess, but with this I cannot agree. For the reasons I have already given the property had not passed until the delivery was completed, and it could only be completed by the weighing and the delivery and acceptance of the ticket.
>
> Suppose a purchaser took his lorry to the hopper and asked for 10 tons of coal or the Coal Board had offered to supply him with 10 tons of coal. Nobody would know how much the hopper delivered until it had been weighed. If it was found

that more than 10 tons had been put into the lorry it seems to me beyond question that the Board could insist upon the excess being taken out. Here no specific amount was asked for, but the Board, by their servant, knew that more had been put into the lorry than could be lawfully carried on the road and with that knowledge completed the sale. In my opinion that amounted to an aiding and abetting of the offence, as Haslam knew Mallender was going there and then to drive the lorry on the highway, in other words, a specific offence was contemplated ...

Devlin J: A person who supplies the instrument for a crime or anything essential to its commission aids in the commission of it; and if he does so knowingly and with intent to aid, he abets it as well and is therefore guilty of aiding and abetting. I use the words 'supplies' to comprehend giving, lending, selling, or any other transfer of the right of property ... In the transfer of property there must be either a physical delivery or a positive act of assent to a taking. But a man who hands over to another his own property on demand, although he may physically be performing a positive act, in law is only refraining from detinue. Thus in law the former act is one of assistance voluntarily given and the latter is only a failure to prevent the commission of the crime by means of a forcible detention, which would not even be justified except in the case of felony. Another way of putting the point is to say that aiding and abetting is a crime that requires proof of *mens rea*, that is to say, of intention to aid as well as of knowledge of the circumstances, and that proof of the intent involves proof of a positive act of assistance voluntarily done ...

It was contended on behalf of the Board that Haslam had no option after weighing but to issue the ticket for the amount then in the lorry. I think that this contention is unsound. In the circumstances of this case the loading must be taken as subject to adjustment; otherwise, if the contact were for a limited amount, the seller might make an over-delivery or an under-delivery which could not thereafter be rectified and the carrier might be contractually compelled to carry away a load in excess of that legally permitted. I think that the delivery of the coal was not completed until after the ascertained weight had been assented to and some act was done signifying assent and passing the property. The property passed when Haslam asked Mallender whether he intended to take the load and Mallender said he would risk it and when the mutual assent was, as it were, sealed by the delivery and acceptance of the weighbridge ticket. Haslam could therefore after he knew of the overload have refused to transfer the property in the coal.

This is the conclusion to which the justices came. Mr Thompson submits on behalf of the Board that it does not justify a verdict of guilty of aiding and abetting. He submits, first, that even if knowledge of the illegal purpose had been acquired before delivery began, it would not be sufficient for the verdict; and second, that if he is wrong about that, the knowledge was acquired too late, and the Board was not guilty of aiding and abetting simply because Haslam failed to stop the process of delivery after it had been initiated.

On his first point Mr Thompson submits that the furnishing of an article essential to the crime with knowledge of the use to which it is to be put does not of itself constitute aiding and abetting; there must be proved in addition a purpose or motive of the defendant to further the crime or encourage the criminal. Otherwise, he submits, there is no *mens rea*.

I have already said that in my judgment there must be proof of intent to aid. I would agree that proof that the article was knowingly supplied is not conclusive evidence of intent to aid ... But *prima facie* ... a man is presumed to intend the natural and probable consequences of his acts, and the consequence of supplying essential material is that assistance is given to the criminal. It is always open to the defendant, as in *R v Steane*, to give evidence of his real intention. But in this case the defence called no evidence. The *prima facie* presumption is therefore enough to justify the verdict, unless it is the law that some other mental element besides intent is necessary to the offence.

This is what Mr Thompson argues, and he describes the additional element as the purpose or motive of encouraging the crime. No doubt evidence of an interest in the crime or of an express purpose to assist it will greatly strengthen the case for the prosecution. But an indifference to the result of the crime does not of itself negative abetting. If one man deliberately sells to another a gun to be used for murdering a third, he may be indifferent about whether the third man lives or dies and interested only in the cash profit to be made out of the sale, but he can be still an aider and abettor. To hold otherwise would be to negative the rule that *mens rea* is a matter of intent only and does not depend on desire or motive ...

The case chiefly relied on by Mr Thompson was *R v Coney* (1882) 8 QBD 534. In that case the defendants were charged with aiding and abetting an illegal prize fight at which they had been present. The judgments all refer to 'encouragement', but it would be wrong to conclude from that that proof of encouragement is necessary to every form of aiding and abetting. Presence on the scene of the crime without encouragement or assistance is no aid to the criminal; the supply of essential material is. Moreover, the decision makes it clear that encouragement can be inferred from mere presence. Cave J, who gave the leading judgment, said of the summing up: 'It may mean either that mere presence unexplained is evidence of encouragement, and so of guilt, or that mere presence unexplained is conclusive proof of encouragement, and so of guilt. If the former is the correct meaning I concur in the law so laid down; if the latter, I am unable to do so'. This *dictum* seems to me to support the view I have expressed. If voluntary presence is *prima facie* evidence of encouragement and therefore of aiding and abetting, it appears to me to be *a fortiori* that the intentional supply of an essential article must be *prima facie* evidence of aiding and abetting.

As to Mr Thompson's alternative point, I have already expressed the view that the facts show an act of assent made by Haslam after knowledge of the proposed illegality and without which the property would not have passed. If some positive act to complete delivery is committed after knowledge of the illegality, the position in law must, I think, be just the same as if the knowledge had been obtained before the delivery had been begun. Of course, it is quite likely that Haslam was confused about the legal position and thought that he was not entitled to withhold the weighbridge ticket. There is no *mens rea* if the defendant is shown to have a genuine belief in the existence of circumstances which, if true, would negative an intention to aid ... But this argument, which might have been the most cogent available to the defence, cannot now be relied upon, because Haslam was not called to give evidence about what he thought or believed.

The fact that no evidence was called for the defence makes this case a peculiar one. We were told that the Board desired to obtain a decision on principle which would enable them to regulate their practice in the future. They therefore accepted responsibility for Haslam's act without going into any questions of vicarious liability; and they called no evidence in order, we were told, that the decision might be given on facts put against them as strongly as might be. What they wished to establish was that responsibility for overloaded lorries rested solely with the carrier and that the sale and delivery of the coal could not, if that was all that could be proved, involve them in a breach of the criminal law. For the reasons I have given I think that the law cannot be so stated and that the appeal should be dismissed.

Gillick v West Norfolk and Wisbech Area Health Authority and Department of Health and Social Security [1986] 1 AC 112 (HL)

Lord Fraser of Tullybelton: My Lords, the main question in this appeal is whether a doctor can lawfully prescribe contraception for a girl under 16 years of age, without the consent of her parents ...

In December 1980, the DHSS issued guidance on family planning services for young people ... which stated, or implied, that, at least in certain cases which were described as 'exceptional', a doctor could lawfully prescribe contraception for a girl under 16 without her parents' consent. Mrs Gillick, who is the mother of five daughters under the age of 16, objected to the guidance and she instituted the proceedings which have led to this appeal, and in which she claims a declaration ... that the advice given in the guidance was unlawful ...

Is a doctor who gives contraceptive advice or treatment to a girl under 16 without her parents' consent likely to incur criminal liability?

The submission was made to Woolf J on behalf of Mrs Gillick that a doctor who provided contraceptive advice and treatment to a girl under 16 without her parents' authority would be committing an offence under s 28 of the Sexual Offences Act 1956 by aiding and abetting the commission of unlawful sexual intercourse. When the case reached the Court of Appeal counsel on both sides conceded that whether a doctor who followed the guidelines would be committing an offence or not would depend on the circumstances. It would depend upon the doctor's intentions; this appeal is concerned with doctors who honestly intend to act in the best interests of the girl, and I think it is unlikely that a doctor who gives contraceptive advice or treatment with that intention would commit an offence under s 28. It must be remembered that a girl under 16 who has sexual intercourse does not thereby commit an offence herself, although her partner does: see the Sexual Offences Act 1956, ss 5 and 6. In any event, even if the doctor would be committing an offence, the fact that he had acted with the parents' consent would not exculpate him as Woolf J pointed out ([1984] QB 581, 595G). Accordingly, I regard this contention as irrelevant to the question that we have to answer in this appeal. Parker LJ in the Court of Appeal at 118a, dealt at some length with the provisions of criminal law intended to protect girls under the age of 16 from being seduced, and perhaps also to protect them from their own weakness. Parker LJ expressed his conclusion on this part of the case as follows at 137F–G:

It appears to me that it is wholly incongruous, when the act of intercourse is criminal, when permitting it to take place on one's premises is criminal and when, if the girl were under 13, failing to report an act of intercourse to the police would up to 1967 have been criminal, that either the department [or] the area health authority should provide facilities which will enable girls under 16 the more readily to commit such acts. It seems to me equally incongruous to assert that doctors have the right to accept the young, down, apparently, to any age, as patients, and to provide them with contraceptive advice and treatment without reference to their parents and even against their known wishes.

My Lords, the first of those two sentences is directed to the question, which is not in issue in this appeal, of whether contraceptive facilities should be available at all under the National Health Service for girls under 16. I have already explained my reasons for thinking that the legislation does not limit the duty of providing such facilities to women of 16 or more. The second sentence, which does bear directly on the question in the appeal, does not appear to me to follow necessarily from the first and with respect I cannot agree with it. If the doctor complies with the first of the conditions which I have specified, that is to say if he satisfies himself that the girl can understand his advice, there will be no question of his giving contraceptive advice to very young girls ...

Lord Scarman: ... If this case should be made good, the discussion of parental right is, of course, an irrelevance. If it be criminal or contrary to public policy to prescribe contraception for a girl under the age of 16 on the ground that sexual intercourse with her is unlawful and a crime on the part of her male partner, the fact that her parent knew and consented would not make it any less so. I confess that I find the submission based upon criminality or public policy surprising. So far as criminality is concerned, I am happy to rest on the judgment of Woolf J whose approach to the problem I believe to be correct. Clearly a doctor who gives a girl contraceptive advice or treatment not because in his clinical judgment the treatment is medically indicated for the maintenance of restoration of her health but with the intention of facilitating her having unlawful sexual intercourse may well be guilty of a criminal offence. It would depend, as my noble and learned friend, Lord Fraser of Tullybelton, observes, upon the doctor's intention – a conclusion hardly to be wondered at in the field of criminal law. The department's guidance avoids the trap of declaring that the decision to prescribe the treatment is wholly a matter of the doctor's discretion. He may prescribe only if she has the capacity to consent or if exceptional circumstances exist which justify him in exercising his clinical judgment without parental consent. The adjective 'clinical' emphasises that it must be a medical judgment based upon what he honestly believes to be necessary for the physical, mental, and emotional health of his patient. The *bona fide* exercise by a doctor of his clinical judgment must be a complete negation of the guilty mind which is an essential ingredient of the criminal offence of aiding and abetting the commission of unlawful sexual intercourse.

The public policy point fails for the same reason. It cannot be said that there is anything necessarily contrary to public policy in medical contraceptive treatment if it be medically indicated as in the interest of the patient's health: for the provision of such treatment is recognised as legitimate by Parliament: s 5 of the National Health Service Act 1977. If it should be prescribed for a girl under 16 the fact that it may eliminate a health risk in the event of the girl having unlawful sexual intercourse is an irrelevance unless the doctor intends to encourage her to have that intercourse. If the prescription is the *bone fide* exercise of his clinical judgment as to what is best for his patient's health, he has nothing to fear from the criminal law or from any public policy based on the criminality of a man having sexual intercourse with her.

It can be said by way of criticism of this view of the law that it will result in uncertainty and leave the law in the hands of the doctors. The uncertainty is the price which has to be paid to keep the law in line with social experience, which is that many girls are fully able to make sensible decisions about many matters before they reach the age of 16. I accept that great responsibilities will lie on the medical profession. It is, however, a learned and highly trained profession regulated by statute and governed by a strict ethical code which is vigorously enforced. Abuse of the power to prescribe contraceptive treatment for girls under the age of 16 would render a doctor liable to severe professional penalty. The truth may well be that the rights of parents and children in this sensitive area are better protected by the professional standards of the medical profession than by *a priori* legal lines of division between capacity and lack of capacity to consent since any such general dividing line is sure to produce in some cases injustice, hardship, and injury to health ...

R v Bainbridge [1960] 1 QB 129 (CA)

Facts: On the night of 30 October 1958 the Stoke Newington branch of the Midland Bank was broken into by cutting the bars of a window, the doors of the strong room and of a safe inside the strong room. This was done by a means of oxygen cutting equipment. The cutting equipment was left behind and it was later discovered that it had been bought by the appellant some six weeks earlier. The appellant was convicted of being an accessory before the fact to the burglary.

Lord Parker CJ: The case against him [the appellant] was that he had bought this cutting equipment on behalf of one or more of the thieves with the full knowledge that it was going to be used, if not against the Stoke Newington branch of the Midland Bank, at any rate for the purposes of breaking and entering premises.

The appellant's case, as given in his evidence, was this:

> True, I had bought this equipment from two different firms. I had gone there with a man called Shakeshaft to buy it for him. As a result of a conversation which I had with him I was suspicious that he wanted it for something illegal, I thought it was for breaking up stolen goods which Shakeshaft had received, and as a result in those purchases I gave false names and addresses, but I had no knowledge that the equipment was going to be used for any such purpose as it was used.

The complaint here is that Judge Aarvold, who tried the case, gave the jury a wrong direction in regard to what it was necessary for them to be satisfied of in order to hold the appellant guilty of being an accessory before the fact. The passages in question are these. He said:

> To prove that, the prosecution have to prove these matters: first of all they have to prove the felony itself was committed. Of that there is no doubt. That is not contested. Second, they have to prove the defendant, this man Bainbridge,

knew that a felony of that kind was intended and was going to be committed, and with that knowledge he did something to help the felons commit the crime. The knowledge that is required to be proved in the mind of this man Bainbridge is not the knowledge of the precise crime. In other words, it need not be proved he knew the Midland Bank, Stoke Newington branch, was going to be broken and entered and money stolen from that particular bank, but he must know the type of crime that was in fact committed. In this case it is a breaking and entering of premises and the stealing of property from those premises. It must be proved he knew that sort of crime was intended and was going to be committed. It is not enough to show that he either suspected or knew that some crime was going to be committed, some crime which might have been a breaking and entering or might have been disposing of stolen property or anything of that kind. That is not enough. It must be proved he knew the type of crime which was in fact committed was intended ...

Mr Simpson, who has argued this case very well, contends that that direction is wrong. As he puts it, in order that a man should be convicted of being accessory before the fact, it must be shown that at the time he bought the equipment in a case such as this he knew that a particular crime was going to be committed, and by a particular crime Mr Simpson means that the premises in this case which were going to be broken into were known to the appellant and contemplated by him, and not only the premises in question but the date when the breaking was going to occur; in other words, that he must know that on a particular date the Stoke Newington branch of the Midland Bank is intended to be broken into.

The court fully appreciates that it is not enough that it should be shown that a man knows that some illegal venture is intended. To take this case, it would not be enough if he knew – he says he only suspected – that the equipment was going to be used to dispose of stolen property. That would not be enough. Equally, this court is quite satisfied that it is unnecessary that knowledge of the particular crime which was in fact committed should be shown to his knowledge to have been intended, and by 'particular crime' I am using the words in the same way in which Mr Simpson used them, namely on a particular date and particular premises.

It is not altogether easy to lay down a precise form of words which will cover every case that can be contemplated but, having considered the cases and the law this court is quite clear that the direction of Judge Aarvold in this case cannot be criticised ...

Judge Aarvold in this case, in the passage to which I have referred, makes it clear that there must be not merely suspicion but knowledge that a crime of the type in question was intended, and that the equipment was bought with that in view. In his reference to the felony of the type intended it was, as he stated, the felony of breaking and entering premises and the stealing of property from those premises. The court can see nothing wrong in that direction ...

DPP for Northern Ireland v Maxwell [1978] 1 WLR 1350 (HL)

Lord Fraser of Tullybelton: My Lords, the appellant was convicted of, *inter alia*, two offences under s 3 of the Explosive Substances Act 1883. In count 1 he was charged with doing an act with intent to cause an explosion by a pipe bomb and in count 2 with possession of a pipe bomb. In fact, he did not physically do an act of placing the bomb in position, nor did he physically have the bomb in his possession, but he was a member of a gang of four or five men, acting in concert, other members of which conveyed the bomb to the place where they intended to explode it and placed it in position. The appellant's part in the enterprise was to act as guide by leading the way in his own motor car, while other members of the gang followed in another car. He led them to the Crosskeys Inn, where the bomb was placed and the fuse ignited. His part was important because the other members were strangers to the district, and he was familiar with the road.

In these circumstances, the answer to the question whether he was rightly convicted depends on the extent of his knowledge of the common plan when he took part in it. If he had known full details of the plan, the time, place and nature of the crimes intended, he would unquestionably be guilty as a principal because he had aided and abetted their commission. Even if he had not known the intended time and place, but had known the nature of the crimes that were planned, there would be no question of his guilt: see *R v Bainbridge* [1960] 1 QB 129. In the present case it was not proved that the appellant knew that a pipe bomb was to be used, nor that it was being carried in the second car, and the argument was that he was therefore not guilty of the crimes charged. The trial judge held that the appellant knew the men in the second car 'were going to attack the inn', but with great respect I have some doubt whether that finding is justified. It seems to me doubtful whether the proof went further than showing that the inn was the place to which the appellant was to guide the gang for the purpose of the operation, and that the inn might have been merely a convenient rendezvous for an attack on some other place nearby. But whether my doubt is justified or not it does not affect my view that the appellant was rightly convicted ...

In my opinion there is no substance in the argument for the appellant, having regard to the facts in this case. The appellant was a member of the Ulster Volunteer Force (UVF) and there was evidence from a police officer that the UVF had been responsible for various kinds of violent incidents, including murders and bombings of public houses and other premises owned by Roman Catholics. (The owner of the Crosskeys Inn was a Roman Catholic.) On the occasion in question, the appellant knew that he was being sent on a 'job'. The trial judge found that:

> As used by the accused the word 'job' is synonymous with military action which raises, having regard to the proven activities of the UVF, the irresistible inference [that] the attack would be one of violence in which people would be endangered or premises seriously damaged.

In my opinion it is clear that when the appellant was ordered, as his part in the job, to lead another car to the Crosskeys Inn, he must have contemplated that a violent attack of some kind was to be made either on the inn itself or on some neighbouring place. When he obeyed the order he must therefore have intended to assist in carrying out such an attack. Although he is not proved to have known exactly what form the attack was to take, whether a murder or a bombing of the premises, he must have known that either or both of these (and any form of attack which was practised by the UVF) was to be expected as the plan for that night. Further he must have known that the bombing of premises necessarily involved doing an act with intent to cause an explosion by explosive substances, and also being in possession of explosive substances. If he did not know the particular type of operation planned when he took part in it, he must have intended to assist in any one or more of these types of operations, with all that it necessarily involved, while being content to leave the choice of the actual operation to others, perhaps members of the gang or some higher commander. As Lowry LCJ expressed it in his judgment in the Court of Criminal Appeal: 'He was therefore in just the same situation, so far as guilty knowledge is concerned, as a man who had been given a list of jobs and told that one of them would be carried out.' He was guilty of any or all of the jobs on the list that were in fact carried out.

The possible extent of his guilt was limited to the range of crimes any of which he must have known were to be expected that night. Doing acts with explosives and possessing explosives were within that range and when they turned out to be crimes committed on that night he was therefore guilty of them. If another member of the gang had committed some crime that the appellant had no reason to expect, such as perhaps throwing poison gas into the inn, the appellant would not have been guilty of using poison gas.

The same reasoning applies to count 2, possession of the pipe bomb. The appellant must have known that use of such a bomb was to be expected, and he must have known that whatever weapon or device was to be used would almost certainly be carried in the second car ...

Lord Scarman: My Lords, I also would dismiss this appeal. The question it raises is as to the degree of knowledge required by law for the attachment of criminal responsibility to one who assists another (or others) to commit or attempt crime.

In *Johnson v Youden* ... the Divisional Court held that before a person can be convicted of aiding and abetting the commission of an offence he must at least know the essential matters which constitute the offence. He does not have to know that the facts constitute an offence: for ignorance of the law is no defence. In *R v Bainbridge* ... the [c]ourt ... held that it was not necessary that the accused should know the particular crime intended or committed by those whom he assisted, and upheld a direction in which the judge had made it clear that it was enough if the accused knew the type of crime intended ...

I think *R v Bainbridge* was correctly decided. But I agree with counsel for the appellant that in the instant case the Court of Criminal Appeal in Northern Ireland has gone further than the Court of Criminal Appeal for England and Wales found it necessary to go in *R v Bainbridge*. It is not possible in the present case to declare that it is proved, beyond reasonable doubt, that the appellant knew a bomb attack on the inn was intended by those whom he was assisting. It is not established therefore, that he knew the particular type of crime intended. The court, however, refused to limit criminal responsibility by reference to knowledge by the accused of the type or class of crime intended by those whom he assisted. Instead, the court has formulated a principle which avoids the uncertainties and ambiguities of classification. The guilt of an accessory springs, according to the court's formulation, 'from the fact that he contemplates the commission of one (or more) of a number of crimes by the principal and he intentionally lends his assistance in order that such a crime will be committed': *per* Lowry LCJ.

Lowry LCJ continues:

> The relevant crime must be within the contemplation of the accomplice and only exceptionally would evidence be found to support the allegation that the accomplice had given the principal a completely blank cheque.

The principle thus formulated has great merit. It directs attention to the state of mind of the accused: not what he ought to have in contemplation, but what he did have. It avoids definition and classification, while ensuring that a man will not be convicted of aiding an abetting any offence his principal may commit, but only one which is within his contemplation. He may have in contemplation only one offence, or several; and the several which he contemplates he may see as alternatives. An accessory who leaves it to his principal to choose is liable, provided always the choice is made from the range of offences from which the accessory contemplates the choice will be made. Although the court's formulation of the principle goes further than the earlier cases, it is a sound development of the law and in no way inconsistent with them. I accept it as good judge-made law in a field where there is no statute to offer guidance.

On the facts as found by the trial (there was no jury because of the Northern Ireland (Emergency Provisions) Act 1973), the appellant knew he was guiding a party of men to the Crosskeys Inn on a UVF military-style 'job', ie an attack by bomb, incendiary or bullet on persons or property. He did not know the particular type of offence intended, but he must have appreciated that it was very likely that those whom he was assisting intended a bomb attack on the inn.

If the appellant contemplated, as he clearly did, a bomb attack as likely, he must also have contemplated the possibility that the men in the car, which he was leading to the inn, had an explosive substance with them. Though he did not know whether they had it with them or not, he must have believed it very likely that they did. In the particular circumstances of this case, the inference that the two offences of possessing the explosive and using it with intent to cause injury or damage were within the appellant's contemplation is fully justified on the evidence. The appellant was rightly convicted, and I would dismiss his appeal.

Notes and queries

1 In *R v Lomas* (1913) 9 Cr App R 220, a burglary was committed by a man named King, who had used for the purpose a housebreaking implement known as a jemmy. He was convicted as a principal. On the day on which the burglary was committed the jemmy had been in the possession of the appellant who had originally received it from King. At King's request the appellant had returned it to him. The appellant was convicted of being an accessory before the fact (the terminology then used), but his conviction was quashed on appeal on the basis that he could not aid and abet by returning King's property to him as the appellant had been under a legal duty to deliver up the item. Compare this with the situation where A sells such an implement to knowing that P intends to use it to commit a burglary. In that case A will be an accomplice as he has no duty to sell the item to P.

Joint enterprise

Where two or more parties are acting together in pursuit of a common purpose they are described as being engaged in a joint enterprise. For example where A agrees that he will hold down the victim (V) whilst P, the principal, threatens V with a gun. There is no doubt that in such a case A will be an accomplice to the assault/actual bodily harm committed by P. Suppose, however, that P has loaded the gun and deliberately fires it, killing V. A's liability for murder, subject to any defences, seems tolerably clear. Can A also be charged with murder?

R v Powell and Daniels; R v English [1999] AC 1

Lord Hutton: My Lords, the appeals before your Lordships' House relate to the liability of a participant in a joint criminal enterprise when another participant in that enterprise is guilty of a crime, the commission of which was not the purpose of the enterprise.

In the case of Powell and Daniels the purpose of the joint enterprise was to purchase drugs from a drug dealer. Three men, including the two appellants, Powell and Daniels, went to purchase drugs from a drug dealer, but having gone to his house for that purpose, the drug dealer was shot dead when he came to the door. The Crown was unable to prove which of the three men fired the gun which killed the drug dealer, but it was the Crown case that if the third man fired the gun, the two appellants were guilty of murder because they knew that the third man was armed with a gun and realised that he might use it to kill or cause really serious injury to the drug dealer.

In the course of summing up to the jury at the trial the Recorder of London said:

> If B or C realised, without agreeing to such conduct being used, that A may kill or intentionally inflict serious injury and they nevertheless continue to participate with A in the venture, that will amount to a sufficient mental element for B or C to be guilty of murder if A with the requisite intent kills in the course of the venture. In those circumstances B and C have lent themselves to the enterprise and by so doing have given assistance and encouragement to A in carrying out an enterprise which they realised may involve murder. These are general principles which must be applied to the facts of this case.

Powell and Daniels were convicted of murder and their appeals were rejected by the Court of Appeal, and the question certified for the opinion of your Lordships' House is:

> Is it sufficient to found a conviction for murder for a secondary party to a killing to have realised that the primary party might kill with intent to do so or must the secondary party have held such intention himself?

The question certified in the appeals of Powell and Daniels ... raise the issue whether foresight of a criminal act which was not the purpose of the joint enterprise (in the case of Powell and Daniels the use of a gun ...) is sufficient to impose criminal liability for murder on the secondary party in the event that the jury find that the primary party used the weapon with intent to kill or cause really serious harm.

In the case of Powell and Daniels the Crown case was that the two appellants knew that the third man was armed with a gun, and the Crown accepted that if the jury did not find this knowledge the appellants would not be guilty of murder. But in the case of English the Crown case was that, even if he did not know that Weddle had a knife, English foresaw that Weddle would cause really serious injury to the police officer, and that this foresight was sufficient to impose criminal liability upon him for the murder. Accordingly the second question arises in the case of English and that question is, in essence, whether the secondary party is guilty of murder if he foresaw that the other person taking part in the enterprise would use violence that would cause really serious injury, but did not foresee the use of the weapon that was used to carry out the killing.

My Lords, the first question gives rise, in my opinion, to two issues. The first issue is whether there is a principle established in the authorities that where there is a joint enterprise to commit a crime, foresight or contemplation by one party to the enterprise that another party to the enterprise may in the course of it commit another crime, is sufficient to impose criminal liability for that crime if committed by the other party even if the first party did not intend that criminal act to be carried out. (I shall consider in a later part of this judgment whether the foresight is of a possibility or of a probability.) The second issue is whether, if there be such an established principle, it can stand as good law in the light of the decisions of this House that foresight is not sufficient to constitute the *mens rea* for murder in the case of the person who actually causes the death and that guilt only arises if that person intends to kill or cause really serious injury.

My Lords, I consider that there is a strong line of authority that where two parties embark on a joint enterprise to commit a crime, and one party foresees that in the course of the enterprise the other party may carry out, with the requisite *mens rea*, an act constituting another crime, the former is liable for that crime if committed by the latter in the course of the enterprise. This was decided by the Court of Appeal, constituted by five judges, in *R v Smith (Wesley)* [1963] 1 WLR 1200. In that case after an argument in a public-house, where the appellant and three other men had been causing a disturbance, the appellant and one of the other men went outside where they collected and threw bricks through the glass door of the premises, in order to 'tear up the joint.' While they were so doing, one of the remaining two men, who were still inside, continued the argument which developed into a fight in the course of which one of them, A, stabbed the barman with a knife, killing him. At the time of the stabbing the appellant was outside the premises, but he knew that the man who stabbed the barman was carrying the knife on his person. All four men were charged with murder. The trial judge directed the jury:

> Assuming that one of the four knifed the barman, assuming you are satisfied that it was done unlawfully in the course of an assault upon him, was [the appellant] taking part in a general attack on the bar directed in part at the barman, so as to make him a party to the general assault in some way upon [the deceased barman]? ... Manslaughter is unlawful killing without intent to kill or do grievous bodily harm. Anybody who is a party to an attack which results in an unlawful killing ... is a party to the killing.

The appellant was convicted of manslaughter.

In delivering the judgment of the Court of Appeal Slade J referred to the direction of the trial judge that: 'Anybody who is a party to an attack which results in an unlawful killing ... is a party to the killing.' Slade J then stated, at p 1205F:

> In the view of this court, that is a wholly unexceptionable direction upon the law except, of course, where the act can be said to be wholly outside the subject-matter of the concerted agreement. The terms 'agreement,' 'confederacy,' 'acting in concert,' and 'conspiracy,' all pre-suppose an agreement express or by implication to achieve a common purpose, and so long as the act done is within the ambit of that common purpose anyone who takes part in it, if it is an unlawful killing, is guilty of manslaughter. That does not mean that one cannot hypothesise a case in which there is an act which is wholly outside the scope of the agreement, in which case no doubt different considerations might apply; but the judge was not dealing with that case at all.

And, at p 1206F:

> The grounds of appeal in this case although worded in different ways really, as I understand them, amount to the same thing; that is, that the use of a knife by Atkinson in this case was a departure, that is to say, assuming against Smith, as must be assumed in the light of the jury's verdict, that he was a party to some concerted action being taken against the barman, he certainly was not a party to the use upon the barman of a knife which resulted in the barman's death. It is significant, as I have shown by reading Smith's own statement, that he knew that Atkinson carried a knife. Indeed, I think he knew that one of the other man carried a cut-throat razor. It must have been clearly *within the contemplation* of a man like Smith who, to use one expression, had almost gone berserk himself to have left the public-house only to get bricks to tear up the joint, that if the bar tender did his duty to quell the disturbance and picked up the night stick, anyone whom he knew had a knife in his possession, like Atkinson, might use it on the barman, as Atkinson did. *By no stretch of imagination, in the opinion of this court, can that be said to be outside the scope of the concerted action in this case.* In a case of this kind it is difficult to imagine what would have been outside the scope of the concerted action, possibly the use of a loaded revolver, the presence of which was unknown to the other parties; but that is not this case, and I am expressing no opinion about that. The court is satisfied that anything which is within the ambit of the concerted arrangement is the responsibility of each party who chooses to enter into the criminal purpose.

Therefore I consider that in *R v Smith* the Court of Appeal recognised that the secondary party will be guilty of unlawful killing committed by the primary party with a knife if he contemplates that the primary party may use such a weapon.

In *R v Anderson*; *R v Morris* [1966] 2 QB 110 the primary party (Anderson) killed the victim with a knife. The defence of the secondary party (Morris) was that even though he may have taken part in a joint attack with Anderson to beat up the victim, he did not know that Anderson was armed with a knife. In his summing up the trial judge told the jury that they could convict Morris of manslaughter even though he had no idea that Anderson had armed himself with a knife. The Court of Appeal held that this was a misdirection in respect of Morris and quashed his conviction for manslaughter.

In delivering the judgment of the Court of Appeal Lord Parker CJ accepted, at p 118, the principle formulated by Mr Geoffrey Lane QC (as he then was) on behalf of Morris:

> where two persons embark on a joint enterprise, each is liable for the acts done in pursuance of that joint enterprise, that that includes liability for unusual consequences if they arise from the execution of the agreed joint enterprise but (and this is the crux of the matter) that, if one of the adventurers goes beyond what had been tacitly agreed as part of the common enterprise, his co-adventurer is not liable for the consequences of that unauthorised act. Finally, he says it is for the jury in every case to decide whether what was done was part of the joint enterprise, or went beyond it and was in fact an act unauthorised by that joint enterprise.

As a matter of strict analysis there is, as Professor JC Smith pointed out in his commentary on *R v Wakely* [1990] Crim LR 119, 120, a distinction between a party to a common enterprise contemplating that in the course of the enterprise another party may use a gun or knife and a party tacitly agreeing that in the course of the enterprise another party may use such a weapon. In many cases the distinction will in practice be of little importance because as Lord Lane CJ observed in *R v Wakely*, at p 120, with reference to the use of a pick axe handle in a burglary, 'Foreseeability that the pick axe handle might be used as a weapon of violence was practically indistinguishable from tacit agreement that the weapon should be used for that purpose.' Nevertheless it is possible that a case might arise where a party knows that another party to the common enterprise is carrying a deadly weapon and contemplates that he may use it in the course of the enterprise, but, whilst making it clear to the other party that he is opposed to the weapon being used, nevertheless continues with the plan. In such a case it would be unrealistic to say that, if used, the weapon would be used with his tacit agreement. However it is clear from a number of decisions, in addition to the judgment of the Court of Appeal in *R v Smith* [1963] 1 WLR 1200, that as stated by the High Court of Australia in *McAuliffe v R* (1995) 69 ALJR 621, 624 (in a judgment to which I will refer later in more detail), 'The scope of the common purpose is to be determined by what was contemplated by the parties sharing that purpose.' Therefore when two parties embark on a joint criminal enterprise one party will be liable for an act which he contemplates may be carried out by the other party in the course of the enterprise even if he has not tacitly agreed to that act.

The principle stated in *R v Smith* was applied by the Privy Council in *Chan Wing-Siu v R* [1985] AC 168 in the judgment delivered by Sir Robin Cooke who stated, at p 175G:

> The case must depend rather on the wider principle whereby a secondary party is criminally liable for acts by the primary offender of a type which the former foresees but does not necessarily intend. That there is such a principle is not in doubt. It turns on contemplation or, putting the same idea in other words, authorisation, which may be express or is more usually implied. It meets the case of a crime foreseen as a possible incident of the common unlawful enterprise. The criminal culpability lies in participating in the venture with that foresight.

The principle stated by Sir Robin Cooke in *Chan Wing-Siu's* case was followed and applied in the judgment of the Court of Appeal in *R v Hyde* [1991] 1 QB 134, where Lord Lane CJ took account of Professor Smith's comment in *R v Wakeley* that there is a distinction between tacit agreement and foresight and made it clear that the latter is the proper test. In *Hui Chi-ming v R* [1992] 1 AC 34 the Privy Council again applied the principle stated by Sir Robin Cooke in *Chan Wing-Siu v R* and in delivering the judgment of the Board Lord Lowry stated, at p 53B:

> The defendant's second point relies on Sir Robin Cooke's use of the word 'authorisation' as a synonym for contemplation in the passage already cited from his judgment in *Chan Wing-Siu v R* [1985] AC 168, 175. Their Lordships consider that Sir Robin used this word—and in that regard they do not differ from counsel—to emphasise the fact that mere foresight is not enough: the accessory, in order to be guilty, must have foreseen the relevant offence which the principal may commit as a possible incident of the common unlawful enterprise and must, with such foresight, still have participated in the enterprise. The word 'authorisation' explains what is meant by contemplation, but does not add a new ingredient. That this is so is manifest from Sir Robin's pithy conclusion to the passage cited: 'The criminal culpability lies in participating in the venture with that foresight.

In *McAuliffe v R* (1995) 69 ALJR 621 the High Court of Australia has recently stated that the test for determining whether a crime falls within the scope of a joint enterprise is now the subjective test of contemplation and the court stated, at p 624:

> Each of the parties to the arrangement or understanding is guilty of any other crime falling within the scope of the common purpose which is committed in carrying out that purpose. Initially the test of what fell within the scope of the common purpose was determined objectively so that liability was imposed for other crimes committed as a consequence of the commission of the crime which was the primary object of the criminal venture, whether or not those other crimes were contemplated by the parties to that venture. However, in accordance with the emphasis which the law now places upon the actual state of mind of an accused person, the test has become a subjective one and the scope of the common purpose is to be determined by what was contemplated by the parties sharing that purpose.

There is therefore a strong line of authority that participation in a joint criminal enterprise with foresight or contemplation of an act as a possible incident of that enterprise is sufficient to impose criminal liability for that act carried out by another participant in the enterprise. I would add that, in my opinion, Lord Parker in *R v Anderson*; *R v Morris* [1966] 2 QB 110, having accepted the principle formulated by Mr Lane, made it clear in other parts of the judgment that he was not intending to depart from the principle in *R v Smith*, because immediately after stating Mr Lane's formulation Lord Parker said at p 119:

> In support of that, he refers to a number of authorities to which this court finds it unnecessary to refer in detail, which in the opinion of this court shows that at any rate for the last 130 or 140 years that has been the true position. This matter was in fact considered in some detail in *R v Smith (Wesley)*, heard by a court of five judges presided over by Hilbery J, in which Slade J gave the

judgment of the court. *R v Smith (Wesley)* was referred to at some length in the later decision in this court in *R v Betty*; it is unnecessary to go into that case in any detail. It followed the judgment of Slade J in *R v Smith* (Wesley), and it did show the limits of the general principle which Mr Lane invokes in the present case. In *R v Smith (Wesley)* the co-adventurer who in fact killed was known by the defendant to have a knife, and it was clear on the facts of that case that the common design involved an attack on a man, in that case a barman, in which the use of a knife would not be outside the scope of the concerted action. Reference was there made to the fact that the case might have been different if in fact the man using the knife had used a revolver, a weapon which he had, unknown to Smith. The court in *R v Betty* approved entirely of what had been said in *R v Smith (Wesley)*, and in fact added to it.

Later at p 120B I consider that Lord Parker applied the test of foresight when he stated:

> It seems to this court that to say that adventurers are guilty of manslaughter when one of them has departed completely from the concerted action of the common design and has suddenly formed an intent to kill and has used a weapon and acted in a way which no party to that common design could suspect is something which would revolt the conscience of people today.

Therefore I consider that the judgment in *R v Anderson* was not intended to constitute a departure from the principle stated in *R v Smith*, and that the acceptance of Mr Lane's test was regarded by the Court of Appeal as an alternative way of formulating the principle stated in *R v Smith*, although as Professor Smith has pointed out, as a matter of strict analysis, a distinction can be drawn between the two tests. The second issue which arises on these appeals is whether the line of authority exemplified by *R v Smith* and *Chan Wing-Siu* is good law in the light of the decisions of this House in *R v Moloney* [1985] AC 905 and *R v Hancock* [1986] AC 455. In the latter case Lord Scarman, referring to *Moloney*, stated, at p 471:

> First, the House cleared away the confusions which had obscured the law during the last 25 years laying down authoritatively that the mental element in murder is a specific intent, the intent to kill or to inflict serious bodily harm. Nothing less suffices: and the jury must be sure that the intent existed when the act was done which resulted in death before they can return a verdict of murder. Secondly, the House made it absolutely clear that foresight of consequences is no more than evidence of the existence of the intent; it must be considered, and its weight assessed, together with all the evidence in the case. Foresight does not necessarily imply the existence of intention, though it may be a fact from which, when considered with all the other evidence, a jury may think it right to infer the necessary intent. Lord Hailsham of St Marylebone LC put the point succinctly and powerfully in his speech in *R v Moloney* [1985] AC 905, 913: 'I conclude with the pious hope that your Lordships will not again have to decide that foresight and foreseeability are not the same thing as intention although either may give rise to an irresistible inference of such, and that matters which are essentially to be treated as matters of inference for a jury as to a subjective state of mind will not once again be erected into a legal presumption. They should remain, what they always should have been, part of the law of evidence and inference to be left to

the jury after a proper direction as to their weight, and not part of the substantive law.' Thirdly, the House emphasised that the probability of the result of an act is an important matter for the jury to consider and can be critical in their determining whether the result was intended.

In reliance upon *R v Moloney* and *R v Hancock* Mr Feinberg, on behalf of the appellants Powell and Daniels, submitted to this House, as he submitted to the Court of Appeal, that as a matter of principle there is an anomaly in requiring proof against a secondary party of a lesser *mens rea* than needs to be proved against the principal who commits the *actus reus* of murder. If foreseeability of risk is insufficient to found the *mens rea* of murder for a principal then the same test of liability should apply in the case of a secondary party to the joint enterprise. Mr Feinberg further submitted that it is wrong for the present distinction in mental culpability to operate to the disadvantage of a party who does not commit the *actus reus* and that there is a manifest anomaly where there is one test for a principal and a lesser test for a secondary party.

A similar argument had previously been rejected by the Court of Appeal in *R v Ward* (1986) 85 Cr App R 71 and in *R v Slack* [1989] QB 775. In *R v Ward*, Lord Lane CJ stated, at pp 76–77:

> It is submitted by Mr Steer in regard to that ground of appeal that the decisions of the House of Lords in *R v Moloney* and *R v Hancock* have had the effect of completely altering the law relating to joint enterprise. The way in which he put it was this. We asked him to dictate the submission so we could write it down. No man, he submits, can be convicted of murder unless it is specifically decided against him that he had a murderous intent and that could only be decided against him if the judge directed the jury that that was what they had to find. 'Each member of this court is bound to confess that he was unable to understand the submission. It is enough to say that we do not consider that the cases of *R v Moloney* and *R v Hancock* have had any effect at all upon the well-known and well-established principles of joint enterprise: in short, the principle set out in *R v Anderson; R v Morris* (1966) 50 Cr App R 216, [1966] 2 QB 110 still holds good ... We are told that the learned judge may have been equipped with the opinion of the Judicial Committee of the Privy Council in a case called *Chan Wing-Siu v R* [1985] AC 168. If that is so, the learned judge accurately reflected the view of their Lordships in that case in the passage which I have read. It was suggested by Mr Steer that the decision in that case, which came from Hong Kong, is not in accordance with the decisions of the House of Lords in *R v Moloney* and *R v Hancock*. We disagree. We think that what appears in that case, if we may say so respectfully, is good law.

In *R v Slack* [1989] QB 775, Lord Lane CJ stated, at p 780:

> *Chan Wing-Siu v R* [1985] AC 168 was considered and approved by this court in *R v Ward* (1986) 85 Cr App R 71. The appellant's submission in that case was that the decisions of the House of Lords in *R v Moloney* [1985] AC 905 and *R v Hancock* [1986] AC 455 had the effect of completely altering the law relating to joint enterprise; that no man can be convicted of murder unless it is specifically decided against him that he had a murderous intent; since intent had to be read against the decisions in *R v Moloney* [1985] AC 905 and *R v Hancock* [1986]

AC 455 the jury ought to be directed on the basis of those cases. This court in *R v Ward* (1986) 85 Cr App R 71 reiterated the passage from *R v Anderson*; *R v Morris* [1966] 2 QB 110, 118–19, cited above and went on to hold that *R v Moloney* [1985] AC 905 and *R v Hancock* [1986] AC 455 had had no effect on the well known and well established principles of joint enterprise.

As Lord Lane observed in *R v Slack*, p 780H, difficulties had arisen from the judgment of the Court of Appeal in *R v Barr* (1986) 88 Cr App R 362. It appears from the facts that violent acts by all three defendants, who were burglars, caused the death of the householder. The trial judge directed the jury as though it was not necessary for a defendant charged with murder to possess himself the necessary intent either to kill or do serious bodily harm to the victim: it was enough to convict him of murder if he contemplated that one of his co-defendants had one of these intents and that he foresaw the possibility of that intent being carried into effect by that person. The Court of Appeal held that this was a misdirection and quashed the convictions, Watkins LJ stating, at p 369:

> where it is appropriate to direct a jury upon foreseeability of consequence, the jury must be told that evidence of such foreseeability does no more than assist the jury to determine whether a defendant had at the requisite time an intention either to kill or to do serious harm to the victim. Unwittingly, the judge with regard to a time prior to the burglary, unaided by those authorities, because they were decided after he had directed the jury in the present case, seems to have directed them as though it was not necessary for a defendant charged with murder himself to possess one of the necessary intents: it was enough to convict him if he contemplated that one of his co-accused had one of those intents and that he no more than foresaw the possibility of that intent being carried into effect by that person.

I consider that the judge's summing up contained a misdirection to the extent that it could be read to suggest that participants in a joint venture which led to a killing would all be guilty of murder even if none of them possessed the intent to kill or do serious bodily harm. But I further consider, with respect, that the judgment of the Court of Appeal was erroneous to the extent that it suggests that if A kills with the requisite intent to kill or cause serious bodily harm, B a participant in the joint venture cannot be guilty of murder unless he also intends death or serious bodily harm to the victim.

Therefore the decision in *R v Barr* should not be followed in so far as it relates to the liability of a secondary party who is a participant in a joint enterprise.

In *R v Smith* [1988] Crim LR 616 it appears that *R v Ward* 85 Cr App R 71 was not cited to the Court of Appeal and its decision in that case, that specific intent to cause grievous bodily harm must be proved against a secondary party to convict him of that offence where the grievous bodily harm has been caused by another party to the joint enterprise to attack the victim, is also erroneous and should not be followed.

Before setting out the terms in which the Court of Appeal rejected the argument on behalf of the appellants Powell and Daniels based on *R v Moloney* [1985] AC 905 and *R v Hancock* [1986] AC 455 I would first refer to the rejection of another argument advanced on behalf of the appellants in reliance on the judgments of Woolf J at first instance and Lord Scarman in this House in *Gillick v West Norfolk and Wisbech Area Health Authority* [1984] QB 581; [1986] AC 112, 190E to the effect that whether or not a doctor who gives contraceptive advice or treatment to a girl under the age of 16 years could be guilty of aiding and abetting the commission of unlawful sexual intercourse would depend on his intention. The Court of Appeal rejected this argument in this case on the grounds that Gillick was a case where there was a civil claim for a declaration and the situations considered were remote from a common enterprise culminating in murder. My Lords, I agree, and I consider that a doctor exercising bona fide his clinical judgment cannot be regarded as engaging in a joint criminal enterprise with the girl.

Returning to the rejection in the Court of Appeal of the appellants' argument in reliance on *R v Moloney* and *R v Hancock*, Lord Taylor of Gosforth CJ stated, at p 22A:

> we feel bound to follow and apply the *Hyde* formulation having regard to the approval which it has received in a number of decisions in this court and to the fact that it is in accordance with the House of Lords' decision in *Maxwell*. If the result is an unacceptable anomaly, it must now be for the House of Lords or the legislature to say so.

My Lords, I recognise that as a matter of logic there is force in the argument advanced on behalf of the appellants, and that on one view it is anomalous that if foreseeability of death or really serious harm is not sufficient to constitute *mens rea* for murder in the party who actually carries out the killing, it is sufficient to constitute *mens rea* in a secondary party. But the rules of the common law are not based solely on logic but relate to practical concerns and, in relation to crimes committed in the course of joint enterprises, to the need to give effective protection to the public against criminals operating in gangs. As Lord Salmon stated in *R v Majewski* [1977] AC 443, 482E, in rejecting criticism based on strict logic of a rule of the common law, 'this is the view that has been adopted by the common law of England, which is founded on common sense and experience rather than strict logic'.

In my opinion there are practical considerations of weight and importance related to considerations of public policy which justify the principle stated in *Chan Wing-Siu* and which prevail over considerations of strict logic. One consideration is that referred to by Lord Lane CJ in *R v Hyde* [1991] 1 QB 134, 139C, where he cited with approval the observation of Professor Smith in his comment on *R v Wakeley*:

> If B realises (without agreeing to such conduct being used) that A may kill or intentionally inflict serious injury, but nevertheless continues to participate with A in the venture, that will amount to a sufficient mental element for B to be guilty of murder if A, with the requisite intent, kills in the course of the venture. As Professor Smith points out, B has in those circumstances lent himself to the enterprise and by so doing he has given assistance and encouragement to A in carrying out an enterprise which B realises may involve murder.

A further consideration is that, unlike the principal party who carries out the killing with a deadly weapon, the secondary party will not be placed in the situation in which he suddenly has to decide whether to shoot or stab the third person with intent to kill or cause really serious harm. There is, in my opinion, an argument of considerable force that the secondary party who takes part in a criminal enterprise (for example, the robbery of a bank) with foresight that a deadly weapon may be used, should not escape liability for murder because he, unlike the principal party, is not suddenly confronted by the security officer so that he has to decide whether to use the gun or knife or have the enterprise thwarted and face arrest. This point has been referred to in cases where the question has been discussed whether in order for criminal liability to attach the secondary party must foresee an act as more likely than not or whether it suffices if the secondary party foresees the act only as a possibility.

In *Chan Wing-Siu v R* [1985] AC 168 counsel for the Crown submitted, at p 172:

> Regard must be had to public policy considerations. Public policy requires that when a man lends himself to a criminal enterprise knowing it involves the possession of potentially murderous weapons which in fact are used by his partners with murderous intent, he should not escape the consequences to him of their conduct by reliance upon the nuances of prior assessment of the likelihood that such conduct will take place. In these circumstances an accomplice who knowingly takes the risk that such conduct might, or might well, take place in the course of that joint enterprise should bear the same responsibility for that conduct as those who use the weapons with the murderous intent.

Sir Robin Cooke stated, at p 177D:

> What public policy requires was rightly identified in the submissions for the Crown. Where a man lends himself to a criminal enterprise knowing that potentially murderous weapons are to be carried, and in the event they are in fact used by his partner with an intent sufficient for murder, he should not escape the consequences by reliance upon a nuance of prior assessment, only too likely to have been optimistic.

A somewhat similar viewpoint was stated by Professor Glanville Williams in *Criminal Law, The General Part*, 2nd edn, p 397 (cited by Stephen J in his judgment in the High Court of Australia in *Johns v R* (1980) 143 CLR 108, 119): 'It seems that a common intent to threaten violence is equivalent to a common intent to use violence, for the one so easily leads to the other.'

In *McAuliffe v R* (1995) 69 ALJR 621 the High Court of Australia referred to the decision in *Johns* and stated, at p 626:

> There was no occasion for the court to turn its attention to the situation where one party foresees, but does not agree to, a crime other than that which is planned, and continues to participate in the venture. However, the secondary offender in that situation is as much a party to the crime which is an incident of the agreed venture as he is when the incidental crime falls within the common purpose. Of course, in that situation the prosecution must prove that the individual concerned foresaw that the incidental crime might be committed and cannot rely upon the existence of the common purpose as establishing that state of mind. But there is no other relevant distinction. As Sir Robin Cooke observed, the criminal culpability lies in the participation in the joint criminal enterprise with the necessary foresight and that is so whether the foresight is that of an individual party or is shared by all parties. That is in accordance with the general principle of the criminal law that a person who intentionally assists in the commission of a crime or encourages its commission may be convicted as a party to it.

Therefore for the reasons which I have given I would answer the certified question of law in the appeals of Powell and Daniels and the first certified question in the appeal of English by stating that (subject to the observations which I make in relation to the second certified question in the case of English) it is sufficient to found a conviction for murder for a secondary party to have realised that in the course of the joint enterprise the primary party might kill with intent to do so or with intent to cause grievous bodily harm. Accordingly I would dismiss the appeals of Powell and Daniels.

Lord Mustill: My Lords ... Throughout the modern history of the law on secondary criminal liability (at least of the type with which this appeal is concerned) the responsibility of the secondary defendant has been founded on his participation in a joint enterprise of which the commission of the crime by the principal offender formed part. Any doubts on this score were set at rest by *R v Anderson*; *R v Morris* [1966] 2 QB 110 by reference to which countless juries have been directed over the years. As it seemed to me the House should not depart from this long-established principle without the strongest of reasons. The problem is to accommodate in the principle the foresight of the secondary party about what the main offender might do. Two aspects of this problem are simple. If S did not foresee what was actually done by P he is not liable for it, since it could not have been part of any joint enterprise. This is what the court decided in *R v Anderson*; *R v Morris*. Conversely, if S did foresee P's act this would always, as a matter of common sense, be relevant to the jury's decision on whether it formed part of a course of action to which both S and P agreed, albeit often on the basis that the action would be taken if particular circumstances should arise.

Intellectually, there are problems with the concept of a joint venture, but they do not detract from its general practical worth, which has proved itself over many years. In one particular situation there is, however, a problem which this time-honoured solution cannot solve. Namely, where S foresees that P may go too far; sincerely wishes that he will not, and makes this plain to P; and yet goes ahead, either because he hopes for the best, or because P is an overbearing character, or for some other reason. Many would say, and I agree, that the conduct of S is culpable, although usually at a lower level than the culpability of the principal who actually does the deed. Yet try as I may, I cannot accommodate this culpability within a concept of joint enterprise. How can a jury be directed at the same time that S is guilty only if he was party to an express or tacit agreement to do the act in question, and that he is guilty if he not only disagreed with it, but made his disagreement perfectly clear to P? Are not the two assertions incompatible?

At the same time the culpability of S ought to be reflected in some form of criminal liability, attracting some degree of punishment. If one rejects, for the reason just given, the idea of forcing it within the existing notion of a joint venture there remain only two alternatives. The first is to abandon that notion altogether, and employ in all cases a test of foreseeability as the direct route to a verdict. The second is to retain the concept of a joint venture in all those cases, forming the great majority, where on the facts it provides a complete test for whether S is or is not guilty of the crime which P actually committed. In the minority of cases where S ought to be guilty and yet cannot rationally be treated as party to an express or tacit agreement to commit the offence in question his culpability can be established by a different route, proposed by Sir Robin Cooke, delivering the opinion of the

Privy Council in *Chan Wing-Siu v R* [1985] AC 168, 175. Namely, that the culpability of S lies in his participation in the venture with foresight of the crime as a possible incident of the common unlawful enterprise.

My Lords, I had for my part preferred the second of these alternatives; for I did not favour the abandonment of a doctrine which has for years worked adequately in practice and its replacement by something which I conceived to be new, unless this step was strictly necessary; and I did not think it necessary, since the existing principles could be retained, in combination (for the exceptional cases) with the concept of wrongful participation in face of a known risk. This was indeed what I understood the law to be, after *Chan Wing-Siu v R* [1985] 1 AC 168; *Hui Chi-Ming v R* [1992] 1 AC 34 and *McAuliffe v R* (1995) 69 ALJR 621.

My Lords, given the importance of the topic I had originally prepared the draft of a speech containing a detailed historical analysis and a statement of the reasons which led me to prefer the second version of the law. Recognising, however, that the remainder of your Lordships see the matter differently I prefer that the draft should be withdrawn. There are some instances where the delivery of a minority opinion is a duty, the performance of which is not simply a matter of record, but also makes an important contribution to the future understanding and development of the law. This is not such a case. Doctrinally the differences may be considerable, but their practical significance is likely to be small, or perhaps even non-existent. What the trial judge needs is a clear and comprehensible statement of a workable principle, which he or she will find in the speech of my noble and learned friend, Lord Hutton; and the judge's task will not be helped in any way by a long exposition of a theory which might have prevailed, but in the event has not. This being so I am entirely willing to concur in the reasoning to which the remainder of your Lordships subscribe. This will, I suspect, require some judges to look again at the terms in which they have customarily directed juries, but the task should not be at all difficult to perform.

In conclusion I wish to express my wholehearted support for the observations of my noble and learned friend, Lord Steyn, in the latter part of his speech. Once again, an appeal to this House has shown how badly our country needs a new law of homicide, or a new law of punishment for homicide, or preferably both. The judges can do nothing about this, being held fast by binding authorities on the one hand and a mandatory statute on the other. Only Parliament has the powers, if it will choose to exercise them. It may not be a popular choice, but surely it is justice that counts.

Lord Steyn: My Lords, ... the established principle is that a secondary party to a criminal enterprise may be criminally liable for a greater criminal offence committed by the primary offender of a type which the former foresaw but did not necessarily intend. The criminal culpability lies in participating in the criminal enterprise with that foresight. Foresight and intention are not synonymous terms. But foresight is a necessary and sufficient ground of the liability of accessories. That is how the law has been stated in two carefully reasoned decisions of the Privy Council: see *Chan Wing-Sui v R* [1985] AC 168 and *Hui Chi-Ming v R* [1992] 1 AC 34. In a valuable article Professor Sir John Smith has recently concluded that there is no doubt that this represents English law: 'Criminal liability of accessories: law and law reform' (1997) 113 LQR 453, 455. And Lord Hutton has demonstrated in his comprehensive review of the case law that the law is as stated in the two Privy Council decisions. That does not mean that the established principle cannot be re-examined and, if found to be flawed, re-formulated. But the existing law and practice forms the starting point.

Counsel for the appellants argued that the secondary party to a criminal enterprise should only be guilty of a murder committed by the primary offender if the secondary party has the full *mens rea* sufficient for murder, ie an intent to kill or to cause really bodily harm. Their arguments fell into three parts, namely (1) that there is a disharmony between two streams of authority; (2) that the accessory principle involves a form of constructive criminal liability; and (3) that it is anomalous that a lesser form of culpability is sufficient for a secondary party than for the primary offender. The first part of the argument centred on the scope of decisions of the House of Lords in *R v Moloney* [1985] AC 905 and *R v Hancock* [1986] AC 455. Those decisions distinguish between foresight and intention and require in the case of murder proof of intention to kill or cause serious bodily injury. But those decisions were intended to apply to a primary offender only. The liability of accessories was not in issue. Plainly the House did not intend in those decisions to examine or pronounce on the accessory principle. The resort to authority must therefore fail.

That brings me to the second argument. If the application of the accessory principle results in a form of constructive liability that would be contrary to principle and it would be a defect in our criminal law. But subject to a qualification about the definition of the *mens rea* required for murder to which I will turn later, I would reject the argument that the accessory principle as such imposes a form of constructive liability. The accessory principle requires proof of a subjective state of mind on the party of a participant in a criminal enterprise, viz foresight that the primary offender might commit a different and more serious offence. Professor Sir John Smith, 'Criminal liability of accessories: law and law reform' (1997) 113 LQR 464, explained how the principle applies in the case of murder:

> Nevertheless, as the critics point out it is enough that the accessory is reckless, whereas, in the case of the principal, intention must be proved. Recklessness whether death be caused is a sufficient *mens rea* for a principal offender in manslaughter, but not murder. The accessory to murder, however, must be proved to have been reckless, not merely whether death might be caused, but whether murder might be committed: *he must have been aware, not merely that death or grievous bodily harm might be caused, but that it might be caused intentionally, by a person whom he was assisting or encouraging to commit a crime.* Recklessness whether murder be committed is different from, and more serious than, recklessness whether death be caused by an accident. The foresight of the secondary party must be directed to a real possibility of the commission by the primary offender in the course of the criminal enterprise of the greater offence. The liability is imposed because the secondary party is assisting in and encouraging a criminal enterprise which he is aware might result in the commission of a greater offence. The liability of an accessory is predicated on his culpability in respect of the greater offence as defined in law. It is undoubtedly a lesser form of *mens rea*. But it is unrealistic to say that the accessory principle as such imposes constructive criminal liability.

At first glance there is substance in the third argument that it is anomalous that a lesser form of culpability is required in the case of a secondary party, viz foresight of the possible commission of the greater offence, whereas in the case of the primary offender the law insists on proof of the specific intention which is an ingredient of the offence. This general argument leads, in the present case, to the particular argument that it is anomalous that the secondary party can be guilty of murder if he foresees the possibility of such a crime being committed while the primary can only be guilty if he has an intent to kill or cause really serious injury. Recklessness may suffice in the case of the secondary party but it does not in the case of the primary offender. The answer to this supposed anomaly, and other similar cases across the spectrum of criminal law, is to be found in practical and policy considerations. If the law required proof of the specific intention on the part of a secondary party, the utility of the accessory principle would be gravely undermined. It is just that a secondary party who foresees that the primary offender might kill with the intent sufficient for murder, and assists and encourages the primary offender in the criminal enterprise on this basis, should be guilty of murder. He ought to be criminally liable for harm which he foresaw and which in fact resulted from the crime he assisted and encouraged. But it would in practice almost invariably be impossible for a jury to say that the secondary party wanted death to be caused or that he regarded it as virtually certain. In the real world proof of an intention sufficient for murder would be well nigh impossible in the vast majority of joint enterprise cases. Moreover, the proposed change in the law must be put in context. The criminal justice system exists to control crime. A prime function of that system must be to deal justly but effectively with those who join with others in criminal enterprises. Experience has shown that joint criminal enterprises only too readily escalate into the commission of greater offences. In order to deal with this important social problem the accessory principle is needed and cannot be abolished or relaxed. For these reasons I would reject the arguments advanced in favour of the revision of the accessory principle.

Where the principal deliberately exceeds the scope of the joint enterprise

R v Powell and Daniels; R v English [1999] AC 1

Lord Hutton: My Lords ... In the case of English the purpose of the joint enterprise in which he and another young man, Weddle, took part was to attack and cause injury with wooden posts to a police officer, Sergeant Forth, and in the course of the attack Weddle used a knife with which he stabbed Sergeant Forth to death.

It was a reasonable possibility that English had no knowledge that Weddle was carrying a knife, and on this basis the learned trial judge, Owen J, stated in his summing up to the jury:

> If he did not know of the knife then you have to consider whether nevertheless he knew that there was a substantial risk that Weddle might cause some really serious injury with the wooden post which was used in the manner which you find it to have been used. So there is the question: 'Has the Prosecution proved'

– and this is an alternative, of course – 'that English joined in an unlawful attack on the sergeant realising at that time that there was a substantial risk that in that attack Weddle might kill or at least cause some really serious injury to the sergeant. If no, not guilty,

The judge then, in effect, directed the jury that if they answered that question in the affirmative they should find English guilty of murder.

Weddle and English were convicted of murder and their appeals were rejected by the Court of Appeal. English now appeals to your Lordships' House and the two questions certified for the opinion of the House are as follows:

(i) Is it sufficient to found a conviction for murder for a secondary party to a killing to have realised that the primary party might kill with intent to do so or with intent to cause grievous bodily harm or must the secondary party have held such an intention himself?

(ii) Is it sufficient for murder that the secondary party intends or foresees that the primary party would or may act with intent to cause grievous bodily harm, if the lethal act carried out by the primary party is fundamentally different from the acts foreseen or intended by the secondary party?

The second certified question in the appeal of English arises because of the last sentence in the following passage in the trial judge's summing up to the jury to which I have previously referred:

If he had the knife and English knew that Weddle had the knife, what would have been—must have been—in the mind of English, bearing in mind whatever condition you find that he was in as a result of drink? So you have to ask that question. If he did not know of the knife then you have to consider whether nevertheless he knew that there was a substantial risk that Weddle might cause some really serious injury with the wooden post which was used in the manner which you find it to have been used.

In *R v Hyde* [1991] 1 QB 134, as already set out, Lord Lane stated, at p 139C:

If B realises (without agreeing to such conduct being used) that A may kill or intentionally inflict serious injury, but nevertheless continues to participate with A in the venture, that will amount to a sufficient mental element for B to be guilty of murder if A, with the requisite intent, kills in the course of the venture.

However, in *Hyde* the attack on the victim took place without weapons and the Crown case was that the fatal blow to the victim's head was a heavy kick. The problem raised by the second certified question is that, if a jury is directed in the terms stated in Hyde, without any qualification (as was the jury in English), there will be liability for murder on the part of the secondary party if he foresees the possibility that the other party in the criminal venture will cause really serious harm by kicking or striking a blow with a wooden post, but the other party suddenly produces a knife or a gun, which the secondary party did not know he was carrying, and kills the victim with it.

Mr Sallon, for the appellant, advanced to your Lordships' House the submission (which does not appear to have been advanced in the Court of Appeal) that in a case such as the present one where the primary party kills with a deadly weapon, which the secondary party did not know that he had and therefore did not foresee his use of it, the secondary party should not be guilty of murder. He submitted that to be guilty under the principle stated in *Chan Wing-Siu* the secondary party must foresee an act of the type which the principal party committed, and that in the present case the use of a knife was fundamentally different to the use of a wooden post.

My Lords, I consider that this submission is correct. It finds strong support in the passage of the judgment of Lord Parker in *R v Anderson; R v Morris* [1966] 2 QB 110, 120B which I have set out earlier, but which it is convenient to set out again in this portion of the judgment:

> It seems to this court that to say that adventurers are guilty of manslaughter when one of them has departed completely from the concerted action of the common design and has suddenly formed an intent to kill and has used a weapon and acted in a way which no party to that common design could suspect is something which would revolt the conscience of people today.

The judgment in *Chan Wing-Siu's* case [1985] AC 168 also supports the argument advanced on behalf of the appellant because Sir Robin Cooke stated, at p 175F: 'The case must depend rather on the wider principle whereby a secondary party is criminally liable for *acts by the primary offender of a type* which the former foresees but does not necessarily intend' [emphasis added].

There is also strong support for the appellant's submission in the decision of Carswell J (as he then was), sitting without a jury in the Crown Court in Northern Ireland, in *R v Gamble* [1989] NI 268. In that case the four accused were all members of a terrorist organisation, the Ulster Volunteer Force, who had a grievance against a man named Patton. The four accused entered upon a joint venture to inflict punishment upon him, two of them, Douglas and McKee, contemplating that Patton would be subjected to a severe beating or to 'kneecapping' (firing a bullet into his kneecap). In the course of the attack upon him Patton was brutally murdered by the other two accused. His throat was cut with a knife with great force which rapidly caused his death. In addition he was shot with four bullets, and two of the bullet wounds would have been fatal had his death not been caused by the cutting of his throat. Douglas and McKee had not foreseen killing with a knife or firing of bullets into a vital part of the body. It was argued, however, on behalf of the prosecution that the joint enterprise of committing grievous bodily harm, combined with the rule that an intent to cause such harm grounded a conviction for murder in respect of a resulting death, was sufficient to make the two accused liable for murder notwithstanding that they had not foreseen the actions which actually caused death. After citing the relevant authorities Carswell J rejected this argument and stated, at p 283F:

> When an assailant 'kneecaps' his victim, ie discharges a weapon into one of his limbs, most commonly into the knee joint, there must always be the risk that it will go wrong and that an artery may be severed or the limb may be so damaged that gangrene sets in, both potentially fatal complications. It has to be said, however, that such cases must be very rare among victims of what is an abhorrent and disturbingly frequent crime. Persons who take a part in inflicting injuries of this nature no doubt do not generally expect that they will endanger life, and I should be willing to believe that in most cases they believe that they are engaged in a lesser offence than murder. The infliction of

grievous bodily harm came within the contemplation of Douglas and McKee, and they might therefore be regarded as having placed themselves within the ambit of life-threatening conduct. It may further be said that they must be taken to have had within their contemplation the possibility that life might be put at risk. The issue is whether it follows as a consequence that they cannot be heard to say that the murder was a different crime from the attack which they contemplated, and so cannot escape liability for the murder on the ground that it was outside the common design. To accept this type of reasoning would be to fix an accessory with consequences of his acts which he did not foresee and did not desire or intend. The modern development of the criminal law has been away from such an approach and towards a greater emphasis on subjective tests of criminal guilt, as Sir Robin Cooke pointed out in *Chan Wing-Sui*. Although the rule remains well entrenched that an intention to inflict grievous bodily harm qualifies as the *mens rea* of murder, it is not in my opinion necessary to apply it in such a way as to fix an accessory with liability for a consequence which he did not intend and which stems from an act which he did not have within his contemplation. I do not think that the state of the law compels me to reach such a conclusion, and it would not in my judgment accord with the public sense of what is just and fitting.

In my opinion this decision was correct in that a secondary party who foresees grievous bodily harm caused by kneecapping with a gun should not be guilty of murder where, in an action unforeseen by the secondary party, another party to the criminal enterprise kills the victim by cutting his throat with a knife. The issue (which is one of fact after the tribunal of fact has directed itself, or has been directed, in accordance with the statement of Lord Parker in *R v Anderson; R v Morris* [1966] 2 QB 110, 120B) whether a secondary party who foresees the use of a gun to kneecap, and death is then caused by the deliberate firing of the gun into the head or body of the victim, is guilty of murder is more debatable although, with respect, I agree with the decision of Carswell J on the facts of that case.

Accordingly, in the appeal of English, I consider that the direction of the learned trial judge was defective (although this does not constitute a criticism of the judge, who charged the jury in conformity with the principle stated in *Hyde*) because in accordance with the principle stated by Lord Parker in *R v Anderson*, at p 120B, he did not qualify his direction on foresight of really serious injury by stating that if the jury considered that the use of the knife by Weddle was the use of a weapon and an action on Weddle's part which English did not foresee as a possibility, then English should not be convicted of murder. As the unforeseen use of the knife would take the killing outside the scope of the joint venture the jury should also have been directed, as the Court of Appeal held in *R v Anderson*, that English should not be found guilty of manslaughter.

On the evidence the jury could have found that English did not know that Weddle had a knife. Therefore the judge's direction made the conviction of English unsafe and in my opinion his appeal should be allowed and the conviction for murder quashed.

English was guilty of a very serious attack on Sergeant Forth, striking him a number of violent blows with a wooden post at the same time as Weddle attacked him with a wooden post. Therefore English was fully deserving of punishment for that attack, but it is unnecessary for your Lordships to give any further consideration to this point as English has already served a number of years in detention pursuant to the sentence of the trial judge.

I have already stated that the issue raised by the second certified question in the appeal of English is to be resolved by the application of the principle stated by Lord Parker in *R v Anderson*, at p 120B. Having so stated and having regard to the differing circumstances in which the issue may arise I think it undesirable to seek to formulate a more precise answer to the question in case such an answer might appear to prescribe too rigid a formula for use by trial judges. However I would wish to make this observation: if the weapon used by the primary party is different to, but as dangerous as, the weapon which the secondary party contemplated he might use, the secondary party should not escape liability for murder because of the difference in the weapon, for example, if he foresaw that the primary party might use a gun to kill and the latter used a knife to kill, or vice versa.

In conclusion I would wish to refer to a number of other points which arise from the submissions in these appeals. The first issue is what is the degree of foresight required to impose liability under the principle stated in *Chan Wing-Siu* [1985] AC 168. On this issue I am in respectful agreement with the judgment of the Privy Council in that case that the secondary party is subject to criminal liability if he contemplated the act causing the death as a possible incident of the joint venture, unless the risk was so remote that the jury take the view that the secondary party genuinely dismissed it as altogether negligible.

Secondly, as the Privy Council also stated in *Chan Wing-Siu*, in directing the jury the trial judge need not adopt a set of fixed formulae, and the form of the words used should be that best suited to the facts of the individual case. In this judgment I have cited two passages from the judgment of Lord Parker in *R v Anderson; R v Morris* [1966] 2 QB 110. One passage commences at p 118F, the second passage commences at p 120B. Trial judges have frequently based their directions to the jury in respect of the liability of a secondary party for an action carried out in a joint venture on the first passage. There is clearly no error in doing so. However in many cases there would be no difference in result between applying the test stated in that passage and the test of foresight, and if there would be a difference the test of foresight is the proper one to apply. I consider that the test of foresight is a simpler and more practicable test for a jury to apply than the test of whether the act causing the death goes beyond what had been tacitly agreed as part of the joint enterprise. Therefore, in cases where an issue arises as to whether an action was within the scope of the joint venture, I would suggest that it might be preferable for a trial judge in charging a jury to base his direction on the test of foresight rather than on the test set out in the first passage in *R v Anderson; R v Morris*. But in a case where, although the secondary party may have foreseen grievous bodily harm, he may not have foreseen the use of the weapon employed by the primary party or the manner in which the primary party acted, the trial judge should qualify the test of foresight stated in *R v Hyde* [1991] 1 QB 134 in the manner stated by Lord Parker in the second passage in *Anderson v Morris*.

As I have already observed in referring to the decision in *R v Gamble* [1989] NI 268, in applying the second passage in *R v Anderson* there will be cases giving rise to a fine distinction as to whether or not the unforeseen use of a particular weapon or the manner in which a particular weapon is used will take a killing outside the scope of the joint venture, but this issue will be one of fact for the common sense of the jury to decide.

Notes and queries

1 A principal offender may deliberately exceed the scope of the common design by committing the acts agreed, but in relation to a different victim. Hence in *R v Saunders and Archer* (1573) 2 Plowd 473, A supplied S with poison, concealed in a roasted apple, so that S could kill his wife. S gave the apple to his wife who, instead of eating it herself, gave it to their young daughter, who consumed the apple and died. S was present throughout this chain of events. It was held that by deliberately allowing his daughter to die, rather than his wife, S had exceeded the scope of the common design between S and A. See *R v Leahy* [1985] Crim LR 99, for a more modern application of this doctrine.

2 A agrees to supply P with a gun so that P can carry out a murder, P not specifying who the victim will be. In the event P shoots A's partner V, killing her. A is distraught at this turn of events. Can A claim that he would not have agreed to P killing V, had he known that P intended V as his victim? *R v Reardon* [1999] Crim LR 392 suggests not. The appellant supplied the principal offender with a knife in order to 'finish off' one of the two victims that P had already shot. P used the knife to kill both of his victims. The appellant's conviction as an accomplice to both murders was upheld.

3 If P accidentally exceeds the scope of the joint enterprise A will normally be an accomplice to the prohibited consequences that result. For example, if A agrees to hold V down whilst P takes V's wallet and V dies of shock, P may be guilty of manslaughter , and A guilty of manslaughter as an accomplice. The death of V is an accidental consequence of P carrying out the agreed plan. See *R v Betts and Ridley* (1930) 22 Cr App R 148; and *R v Baldessare* (1930) 22 Cr App R 70.

4 Uncertainty remains as regards the extent to which the principal's use of a weapon other than that contemplated by the accomplice results in the principal exceeding the scope of the common design. In *R v Uddin* [1998] 2 All ER 744, the appellant was involved in a group attack on S who was stabbed to death. The principal offender was convicted of murder, and the appellant was convicted of murder as an accomplice.

Beldam LJ observed (at p 751):

> In deciding whether the actions [of the principal are of an entirely different type to those contemplated by the accomplice] the use by [the principal] of a weapon is a significant factor. If the character of the weapon, eg its propensity to cause death is different from any weapon used or contemplated by the others and if it is used with specific intent to kill, the others are not responsible for the death unless it is proved that they knew or foresaw the likelihood of the use of such a weapon.

In practice it will be for the jury to determine whether the weapon used by the principal is sufficiently different from that contemplated by the accomplice for there to be a departure from the joint enterprise, but it can be imagined how difficulties might arise where, for example, the agreement is to hit the victim with bare fists and the principal kicks him whilst wearing steel-capped boots. Are the boots a fundamentally different type of weapon?

5   P may use the weapon contemplated by A, and with intent contemplated by A, but in a way that causes more life threatening injuries than those contemplated by A. For example A and P agree that P will attack V with a baseball bat and cause grievous bodily harm by breaking P's arms. In the event P attacks V with the baseball bat, intending to cause V grievous bodily harm, by striking V on the head. V dies from his injuries. P may be convicted of murder, and A (in theory) could be convicted as an accomplice, given his *mens rea*. Can it not be argued, however, in the light of *Gamble* (see above) that by choosing to attack V and causing more life threatening GBH, P deliberately departed from the common design? See further *R v Bamborough* [1996] Crim LR 744, where the Court of Appeal proceeded on the basis that it would be sufficient, in order to substantiate A's conviction for murder as an accomplice, that he had contemplated grievous bodily harm as a possible incident of the common design, the court not being overly concerned at how A might have foreseen the grievous bodily harm being caused by P.

Residual liability for manslaughter where the principal is convicted of murder

R v Dunbar and Others [1988] Crim LR 693 (CA)

Facts: The appellant was convicted of manslaughter. Her co-defendants were convicted of murder. It was the prosecution case that the appellant had incited her co-defendants to murder her former lover. The victim died after being hit on the head with a metal bar; the cause of death was asphyxiation when the metal bar used to garotte her with such force that her voice box was shattered. The appellant denied inciting murder; she admitted that she may have expressed a wish to see the victim dead but claimed that was rambling associated with drink and drugs. She had suspected that the co-defendants planned to burgle the victim's flat and that in the course of the burglary some violence might be done to her former lover. The appellant appealed against conviction on the ground that the verdict of manslaughter was not open to the jury.

Held, allowing the appeal and quashing the conviction, the jury's verdict must have been reached upon the basis that while the appellant contemplated the use of some unlawful violence, short of the infliction of grievous bodily harm, one or other or both of her co-defendants must have gone beyond the scope of that design and used the extreme violence which was intended to cause grievous bodily harm or death. The judge's direction in the appellant's case did not deal with that situation (or with) the appropriate verdict of not guilty should the jury find the second and/or third defendant went beyond what was contemplated by the appellant. On the facts of the case there were only two verdicts open to the jury, guilty or not guilty of murder. If, as the Crown contended, she was a party to an agreement to kill, she was guilty of murder. If she was a party to an agreement to inflict some harm, short of grievous bodily harm, then she was guilty of neither murder nor manslaughter. The victim's killing and the manner of the killing could not be within the ambit of the agreement to which the appellant was a party, if the ambit was confined on her part to an intention that only some harm should befall the deceased, albeit not death or really serious injury. The issues involved could not be distinguished from those adumbrated by Widgery LJ in *Lovesey and Peterson* (1969) 53 Cr App R 461. The judge failed to remind the jury of the law as laid down in *Anderson and Morris* (1966) 50 Cr App R 216 and followed in *Lovesey and Peterson* (1969) 53 Cr App R 461. The result of that non-direction was that the jury returned a verdict which was not open to them.

R v Stewart and Schofield [1995] 3 All ER 159 (CA)

Hobhouse LJ: In *R v Reid* (1975) 62 Cr App R 109 at 112 Lawton LJ, delivering the judgment of the court, said:

> When two or more men go out together in joint possession of offensive weapons such as revolvers and knives and the circumstances are such as to justify an inference that the very least they intend to do with them is to use them to cause fear in another, there is, in our judgment, always a likelihood that, in the excitement and tensions of the occasion, one of them will use his weapon in some way which will cause death or serious injury. If such injury was not intended by the others, they must be acquitted of murder; but having started out on an enterprise which envisaged some degree of violence, albeit nothing more than causing fright, they will be guilty of manslaughter.

It has been argued on behalf of the appellants in this case, with the support of the authors of Smith and Hogan, *Criminal Law*, 7th edn, 1992, p 146, that this statement of the law cannot stand with other decisions of the Court of Appeal and should not be regarded as good law ...

On the evening of Thursday 23 January 1992 Mr Dada, a 60 year old Pakistani, was in his shop, the Popular Delicatessen in Wilmslow Road, Withington. During the early evening two young women, Dawn Rothwell and Heather Stewart, went into the shop. They bought some cigarettes. Whilst there, Stewart noticed Mr Dada removing some money from the till and putting it into his pocket. After they had left the shop and were walking along the road they met Lambert, who was known to Stewart. He was driving a car and Schofield was with him. Stewart told them about what she had seen in the shop and suggested that they should rob Mr Dada of the cash which they had seen him put in his pocket. They agreed. The four of them then drove back to near the shop, where Lambert, Schofield and Stewart got out. Rothwell stayed in the car and did not take any further part. There was evidence that the trio took out of the car a scaffolding bar and a knife. Lambert put on a balaclava and a long coat. Whilst Schofield kept watch outside, the other two went into the shop. On the evidence that the jury must have accepted, Lambert had the bar and Stewart had the knife. The upshot was that Mr Dada was viciously beaten with the bar, seriously injured, and a relatively small amount of cash was stolen from him. He died a few days later in hospital as a result of the injuries he had received; these included four skull fractures. The money taken from Mr Dada was less than £100 cash. After the incident the three ran off to the car where the money was divided up.

Both Stewart and Schofield had answered questions at interview but only Stewart gave evidence at the trial. Schofield had admitted knowledge of the weapons with which Lambert and Stewart were armed. Stewart said she did not know but the jury must have disbelieved her. They both said that they had not contemplated that Mr Dada would be more than threatened. They did not know at that time that Lambert was a person who was deeply motivated by racial hatred or would be liable to use such excessive violence ...

They said it went far beyond anything that they contemplated or that they had any reasons to contemplate. His attack on Mr Dada was motivated not by the needs of the robbery but by vicious racial hatred and was so excessive that it did not form part of any joint enterprise upon which the three of them engaged. They said that the jury should not be satisfied that they were parties to the unlawful killing of Mr Dada ...

The primary ground of appeal of the appellants is:

> Having regard to the decision of the Court of Criminal Appeal in *R v Anderson and Morris* [1966] 2 QB 110 and notwithstanding the subsequent authority of *R v Reid (Barry)* (1975) 62 Cr App R 109, it is not open to a jury which acquits a secondary party of murder to convict him of manslaughter in the alternative, where the principal is guilty of murder ...

Joint enterprise

The allegation that a defendant took part in the execution of a crime as a joint enterprise is not the same as an allegation that he aided, abetted, counselled or procured the commission of that crime. A person who is a mere aider or abettor etc is truly a secondary party to the commission of whatever crime it is that the principal has committed although he may be charged as a principal. If the principal has committed the crime of murder, the liability of the secondary party can only be a liability for aiding and abetting murder. In contrast, where the allegation is joint enterprise, the allegation is that one defendant participated in the criminal act of another. This is a different principle. It renders each of the parties to a joint enterprise criminally liable for the acts done in the course of carrying out that joint enterprise. Where the criminal liability of any given defendant depends upon the further proof that he had a certain state of mind, that state of mind must be proved against that defendant. Even though several defendants may, as a result of having engaged in a joint enterprise, be each criminally responsible for the criminal act of one of those defendants done in the course of carrying out the joint enterprise, their individual criminal responsibility will, in such a case, depend upon what individual state of mind or intention has been proved against them. Thus, each may be a party to the unlawful act which caused the victim's death. But one may have had the intent either to kill him or to cause him serious harm and be guilty of murder, whereas another may not have had that intent and may be guilty only of manslaughter.

Mens rea

An allegation that a defendant was part of a criminal joint enterprise with others includes an allegation that he was aware of the character of the joint enterprise in which he was joining and foresaw that the relevant criminal acts were liable to be involved. Thus, the allegation of joint enterprise involves an allegation concerning the state of the defendant's mind at the time of his participation in the joint enterprise. Normally the fact that the defendant had the state of mind sufficient to prove his guilt of the offence charged is proved by proof that he was a party to the joint enterprise in the course of which the criminal acts were committed. But joint enterprises vary. They may have a purpose, say the infliction of grievous bodily harm, which corresponds to the specific intent for a particular crime, say murder or an offence contrary to s 18 of the Offences Against the Person Act 1861, in which case participation in the joint enterprise will prove the relevant *mens rea*. But in other cases the purpose of the joint enterprise may have been more limited and the relevant criminal liability may only have arisen from some undesired consequence. Provided that the joint enterprise is proved in relation to the relevant acts, then it is not an answer that consequences of those acts were unusual or unexpected. Even if unusual or unexpected consequences arose from the execution of the plan, each participant is responsible for those consequences. In such cases the liability of an individual defendant may depend upon whether his intention at the time the act was done included an intention that the consequences should follow. A defendant who had that intention may have a more serious criminal liability than one who did not. This is because the *mens rea* for the more serious offence can by proved against the one but not against the other.

Archbold

The analysis which we have shortly summarised is that followed by the editors of Archbold and by way of summary we are content to adopt what they say:

> A person who is a party to a joint enterprise, the pursuance of which results in the causing of another's death may be criminally liable for that death either on the basis that he is guilty of murder or on the basis that he is guilty of manslaughter. It is fundamental to a conviction of either offence that the accused must have been a party to the act which caused death. The application of the law concerning joint enterprise in cases of homicide in practice raises two problems, (1) whether in the circumstances the accused was party to the act which caused death; (2) if he was, whether his state of mind was such as to make him guilty of murder or of manslaughter.

The editors go on to refer to *R v Richards, R v Stober* (1992) 96 Cr App R 258 in which it was recognised that difference pleas might be accepted from defendants involved in a joint enterprise on this basis. The editors also treat *R v Reid* (1975) 62 Cr App R 109 and *R v Betty* (1963) 48 Cr App R 6 as exemplifying and confirming their analysis.

The authorities

The main case upon which [counsel for Schofield] founded his submission was *R v Anderson and Morris* [1966] 2 QB 110. But like him we will start with *R v Betty*. Betty and another man were charged with manslaughter and both were convicted. The killing arose out of a fight in which they were both involved. Their defences at trial were self-defence. But Betty also argued that in truth his co-defendant had murdered the victim and that this meant that he, Betty, should not have been convicted of manslaughter. The Court of Criminal Appeal rejected that argument, saying that the point was covered by an earlier decision of a five-judge court, *R v Smith* [1963] 1 WLR 1200 at 1205–06, in which the court had expressly approved the direction:

> Anybody who is a party to an attack which results in an unlawful killing which results in death is a party to the killing ... Only he who intended that unlawful and grievous bodily harm should be done is guilty of murder. He who intended only that the victim should be unlawfully hit and hurt will be guilty of manslaughter if death results.

The court dismissed Betty's appeal. They applied *R v Smith* and held that the point raised was no defence unless the unlawful act which resulted in death was not done in the court of the joint enterprise.

In *R v Anderson and Morris* the court was again a five-judge court. Two men had been involved in an attack on a man. One of the men, Anderson, stabbed him with a knife and killed him. The other man, Morris, said that he had not known that Anderson was going to use a knife. Anderson was convicted of murder and Morris of manslaughter. Morris's appeal was allowed because the trial judge had directed the jury that neither the fact that Morris had not known about the knife nor the fact that Anderson did an act outside the common design to which Morris was a party could provide Morris with a defence to manslaughter. This was a clear misdirection. The court approved and adopted the submission of Mr Lane QC, counsel for Morris, that whilst a party to a joint enterprise would be liable for the acts done in pursuance of the joint enterprise, including:

> liability for unusual consequences if they arise from the execution of the agreed joint enterprise but ... if one of the adventurers goes beyond what has been tacitly agreed as part of the common enterprise, his co-adventurer is not liable for the consequences of that unauthorised act. (See [1966] 2 QB 110 at 221.)

The court did not question in *R v Smith* and *R v Betty* (by which they were anyway bound). What they did was to confirm and stress the need for the Crown, if it seeks to rely upon joint enterprise, to prove that the criminal act was done as part of the joint enterprise ...

In *R v Lovesey*, *R v Peterson* [1970] 1 QB 352, following *R v Anderson and Morris* and applying the '*Lane*' formulation, the court refused to substitute a verdict of manslaughter for an unsatisfactory conviction for murder because they considered that the degree of violence used led to the conclusion that if the acts were within the common design it had to be murder and, if they were not, there was no other basis for any finding of guilt.

R v Reid 62 Cr App R 109 was decided in 1975. The court included Lane LJ, who had been involved in both the previously cited cases and must have had them fully in mind. Three men, alleged by the Crown to be supporters of the IRA, armed with weapons, went to the house of an army officer at night. When he opened the door one of them shot him. Two were convicted of murder; the third, Reid, was acquitted of murder but convicted of manslaughter. His defence had been that he was not part of the joint venture but had gone along with them in order to see whether the other two were really IRA terrorists, which he did not believe they were. The judge had given the jury direction on manslaughter based upon *R v*

Church [1966] 1 QB 59. The appeal of Reid was based upon the factual submission that on the evidence it must have been murder or nothing. The court rejected that submission. They stressed the common possession of the weapons. Lawton LJ said (62 Cr App R 109 at 112):

> If men carrying offensive weapons – indeed deadly – weapons go to a man's house in the early hours of the morning for no discernible lawful purpose, they must, in our judgment, intend to do him harm of some kind, and the very least kind of harm is causing fright by threats to use them.

Having cited *R v Anderson and Morris*, they asked (at 112):

> Was O'Connaill's deliberate firing of the revolver 'a mere unforeseen consequence' of the unlawful possession of offensive weapons? We adjudge it was.

There then followed the passage quoted at the outset of this judgment. They dismissed Reid's appeal.

It is not possible to suggest that this decision was in any way *per incuriam*. Unless it is inconsistent with other binding authority, it is binding upon us.

R v Penfold (1979) 71 Cr App R 4 did not involve the use of weapons, but the court held that the fact that one defendant used excessive violence during a robbery, killing the victim, did not preclude a conviction for manslaughter on the basis of joint enterprise. The court strongly commented upon the need to proceed on the basis of realistic inferences as to what was to be contemplated by those involved in crimes of violence and not to be drawn into unrealistic theoretical distinctions. This echoed the language in *R v Reid* ...

A case upon which [counsel for Schofield] has particularly relied, and which he says is inconsistent with *R v Reid* is *R v Dunbar* [1988] Crim LR 693 (for which we also have a transcript). The victim was a prostitute. She was found dead in the bath in her flat. She had been garrotted with a metal bar. She had also received other injuries. The evidence was that she had been killed by two burglars; they were convicted of murder. The case of the Crown was that they had been recruited by Dunbar, another prostitute. The allegation against her was, therefore, not that she had participated in a joint enterprise, but that she was an accessory before the fact and had counselled or procured the commission of the crime. She denied any incitement to murder. She knew that a burglary was being planned and appreciated that some minor violence might be done to the victim in the course of the burglary; she knew nothing about the intention to use an iron bar and did not contemplate any serious violence. She was acquitted of murder but convicted of manslaughter. The Court of Appeal, applying *R v Anderson and Morris* and *R v Lovesey, R v Peterson*, considered that the verdict of the jury was only consistent with the conclusion by the jury that:

> one or both of her co-defendants must have gone beyond the scope of that design and used the extreme violence which was intended to cause grievous bodily harm or death.

The court stressed that it was 'on the facts of this case' that they had concluded that there were only two verdicts open to the jury, guilty or not guilty of murder. The court also considered the summing up in her case to be defective because it did not sufficiently cover the law incorporated in the *Lane* formulation.

The transcript of the judgment of the Court of Appeal does not justify the conclusion that the law was being stated or applied in any different way from the earlier case. Leaving on one side defective directions of law by the trial judges, the distinction between the outcome of *R v Smith*, *R v Betty* and *R v Reid* on the one hand and *R v Anderson and Morris*, *R v Lovesey*, *R v Peterson* and *R v Dunbar* on the other is that a different view was taken of the facts of the cases and whether the act in question was, or was to be treated as being, within or without the scope of the joint enterprise. *R v Dunbar* is not authority for the proposition that the cases falling on the other side of the line were wrongly decided, nor for the proposition that, in a suitable case, a jury cannot properly find one participant in a joint enterprise guilty of murder and another of manslaughter. We do not agree with the views to the contrary expressed in the notes in the Criminal Law Review (see [1988] Crim LR 693 at 694–95) and in Smith and Hogan p 145; that discussion also does not seem to take account of the fact that *R v Dunbar* probably should not be categorised as a case of joint enterprise at all. *R v Hyde* [1991] 1 QB 134, a case of joint enterprise, however, illustrates and confirms that a joint enterprise to commit a non-violent crime, burglary, may become more serious if one participant continues appreciating that another may kill or intentionally inflict serious injury; a conviction for murder on that basis was upheld.

Finally, we should refer to the advice of the Judicial Committee delivered by Lord Lowry in *Hui Chi-Ming v R* [1992] 1 AC 34 which involved a group attack on a man in the course of which one of the attackers used a piece of piping and the man was killed. The fatal blow was struck by a man who had been acquitted of murder at an earlier trial but convicted of manslaughter. At the appellant's trial the Crown's case was that it had, nevertheless, been a case of a joint enterprise to inflict serious harm or kill. The appellant was convicted of murder. The main discussion related to what common enterprise was necessary to prove the *mens rea* for murder; *R v Hyde* was followed. But for present purposes the interest in the case is that the trial judge had directed the jury ([1992] 1 AC 34 at 46):

> If on the other hand, you are satisfied that the accused was present and that he shared an intention with his companions that the victim should be assaulted and caused some injury, but some injury less than some really serious bodily injury, then he would not be guilty of murder but he would be guilty of manslaughter. If you conclude that it was a reasonable possibility that the accused though present did not share any intention with the others that the victim should in any way be assaulted, then he would be entitled to an acquittal.

These directions recognised that, although the victim may have been murdered by another participant in the joint venture, the appellant, although a participant in a joint venture with others, may have lacked the *mens rea* for murder but could still be guilty of manslaughter. They were implicitly approved by Lord Lowry ([1992] 1 AC 34 at 47).

The authorities do not support the appellants' submission. There is no suggestion that *R v Reid* was wrongly decided nor that there is an inconsistency between what Lawton LJ there said and what was said in *R v Anderson and Morris* by Lord Parker CJ. The distinction between the various cases is that, as one would expect, in different factual situations there may be different verdicts open to a jury. The latest case, *Hui Chi-Ming v R*, confirms again that it is possible that a person may be a party to a joint enterprise which leads to death and be guilty of manslaughter although the actual killer may be guilty of murder.

Conclusion

The directions given by Morland J in the present case disclose no error of law. The verdicts of manslaughter were properly open to the jury and were correctly left to them. It is possible to identify a number of confusions in the appellants' arguments and, it appears, in the academic comment. Cases of joint enterprise, properly so termed, should not be confused with cases of counselling or procuring. It may often be the case that the proof of a defendant's *mens rea* is sufficiently proved by proof of this participation in the joint enterprise; the cases cited emphasise this. But it does not follow that this will, or must, always be the case. It is possible that a defendant, whilst being a participant in a joint enterprise and responsible for the unintended consequences of acts done in the course of carrying out that joint enterprise, may lack a specific intent possessed by another participant. In any given case the issue may arise what was the scope of the joint enterprise; depending upon what answer is given to that question, a further question may arise where a crime of specific intent is charged, what was the state of mind of the defendant. The *mens rea* of the defendant may be proved by either method, by proof of participation in a joint enterprise having the requisite character, or, where the joint enterprise proved does not have that character, by proof of a specific intent. Where proof of participation in the joint enterprise during the course of which the relevant act was done is considered to prove only the *mens rea* appropriate to a lesser offence, only the lesser crime will have been proved against that defendant, although the act in question may have involved the commission of a more serious crime by another against whom a specific intent can be proved.

The question whether the relevant act was committed in the course of carrying out the joint enterprise in which the defendant was a participant is a question of fact not law. If the act was not so committed then the joint enterprise ceases to provide a basis for a finding of guilt against such a defendant. He ceases to be responsible for the act. This is the fundamental point illustrated by *R v Anderson and Morris* and *R v Lovesey*, *R v Peterson*. But it does not follow that a variation in the intent of some of the participants at the time the critical act is done precludes the act from having been done in the course of carrying out the joint enterprise, as is illustrated by *R v Betty* and *R v Reid*.

The appeals against conviction must accordingly be dismissed.

18 May 1995: the Appeal Committee of the House of Lords (**Lord Keith of Kinkel, Lord Lloyd of Berwick** and **Lord Hoffmann**) refused leave to appeal.

R v Perman [1996] 1 Cr App R 24 (CA)

Roch LJ: ... The jury were concerned with events which occurred on 22 February 1993 at a newsagent's shop in Hammersmith. Both the appellant and his co-defendant lived in that part of London. The evidence indicated that on that evening the co-defendant had taken drugs and alcohol. He was carrying a loaded single-barrelled 12-bore shotgun, the barrel of which had been cut down to just under 11 inches and the stock of which had been shortened to resemble a pistol grip. The appellant had taken two Valium tablets that evening which had been given him by his co-defendant. The appellant knew the co-defendant had a gun when he and the co-defendant left the appellant's home some time after 5 pm. They went to a public house at which it would seem the co-defendant took heroin and where they both drank alcohol. From there they went into a shop in King Street owned by a Mr Kumar so that the co-defendant could buy cigarettes. In that shop the appellant had taken a Cadbury's cream egg without paying for it. Mr Kumar saw him do that and became angry, and the co-defendant told the appellant to put the egg back as Mr Kumar's shop was the place where his family shopped. The co-defendant apologised to Mr Kumar for the appellant's behaviour.

From Mr Kumar's shop they walked some distance, deciding to go to an off-licence in Goldhawk Road to buy some beer. That off-licence was chosen because the appellant knew that he would be served although he was under age. Before reaching there, the co-defendant and the appellant entered the newsagent's shop of a Cyril Fernando in which the co-defendant produced his gun and threatened people in the shop with it. The co-defendant took the money from the till, both notes and coins. Cigarettes were handed over. At some point Mr Cyril Fernando, his wife and his brother, Luigi, and Luigi's wife were able to leave the shop through a rear storeroom, leaving in the shop a man called Nath Banda, who was there waiting for the Fernando family to close their shop because he, Nath Banda, was to have supper with the Fernandoes that evening. It is clear that the co-defendant turned his attention to Nath Banda and that the shotgun was fired with the muzzle at a distance of approximately 18 inches from Mr Banda's stomach, inflicting a fatal wound.

The appellant gave evidence to the jury. He told the jury that as they were going to the off-licence, his co-defendant suddenly said that he wanted cigarettes and went across the road into Mr Fernando's shop. He, the appellant, thought it odd that his co-defendant, who had just bought cigarettes in Mr Kumar's shop should want more cigarettes, and consequently he followed his co-defendant into the shop. They did not enter the shop together. The appellant's face was not covered in any way. He could see that his co-defendant was robbing the shop with the gun out. It was the co-defendant who took the money and who asked for the cigarettes and took them. His co-defendant had thrown some cigarettes at him which may have hit him. He, the appellant, might have bent down, but he did not bend down to pick the coins up off the floor that had spilled from the drawer of the till. He might have picked up some cigarettes. He turned and left the shop, walked round the corner into West Croft Square and some 10 yards or so further. Then he decided to go back to see what was going on. As he reached the shop window on the corner, the gun went off. The appellant denied in his evidence that he was acting as a look out. Although he knew that the co-defendant had a gun, he did not know the gun was loaded. Indeed, he did not know that his co-defendant had ammunition for the gun. He had never seen ammunition or heard of the co-defendant having ammunition. We observe that the Crown called evidence which contradicted this part of the appellant's evidence to the jury, namely the witnesses Cotton and Flemming.

The co-defendant had come flying out of the shop saying that it was an accident and had run past him. Momentarily he, the appellant, had considered whether to go back into the shop or whether to run away, and he had run away because he did not want to be blamed for anything. They had both run back to the appellant's home by a back way. Once at the appellant's home the co-defendant had told him that it was an accident; the gun just went off. They had persuaded the appellant's mother to take them to the flat of the co-defendant's girlfriend in North London, where both of them had spent the night and stayed until the early afternoon of the next day.

He had not had any of the proceeds of the robbery. He told the jury that he had had no idea that his co-defendant was going into the shop in order to commit a robbery. He knew that his co-defendant had the gun, but not that it was loaded. He believed it to be unloaded. He did not participate in the robbery at all ...

The Crown's case against the appellant was that there was a joint enterprise between the appellant and his co-defendant to rob this newsagent's, that the appellant had known that his co-defendant had a gun and would use it to threaten and intimidate those in the shop and that in the shop the appellant had played an active, albeit minor, part in the robbery. The unlawful use of the gun had been part of and within the scope of the joint enterprise. Consequently the appellant was guilty of manslaughter, although in the circumstances of the case the Crown did not seek conviction of the appellant on the charge of murder. The appellant's case, as we have already observed, was simply that there was no such joint enterprise and that he had not taken any part at all in the robbery ...

Because of the conclusion we have reached on the third ground of appeal, it is unnecessary for us to reach a concluded view on Mr Robertson's second ground. We would simply raise the question whether once the criminal activity contemplated in a joint enterprise has commenced, it is possible for a party to the joint enterprise to withdraw, and whether it is ever open to a party to a joint enterprise to say that he is not criminally responsible for all that is done in that criminal activity which is within the scope of the joint enterprise. In this case, saying that the appellant withdrew may be no more than another way of saying that the robbery of Mr Banda was outside the scope of the original joint enterprise. Certainly most of the instances given in Smith and Hogan, 7th edn p 153, of withdrawal, are cases of withdrawal from a joint enterprise before the start of the contemplated criminal activity ...

In the present case, if the appellant did not know that the gun was loaded, and believed that it was unloaded, the scope of the joint enterprise in which he joined was the robbery of those in the shop by the putting of such persons as were in the shop in fear by the use of an unloaded and therefore innocuous gun. The appellant's knowledge that the gun was loaded was crucial to the Crown's case, because if it were proved that he knew the gun was loaded then he was party to a joint enterprise in which those in the shop were to be threatened with a lethal weapon, that is to say were to be subjected to the obvious risk of that weapon being fired in the excitement and tensions of the occasion. That would make him guilty of manslaughter, as is demonstrated by the case of *Reid*.

A joint enterprise to cause fright or hysteria through threats being made with an unloaded and innocuous gun was not sufficient to found a conviction of manslaughter in the circumstances of this case. It was, of course, sufficient to found convictions in respect of the counts of robbery and possession of an offensive weapon with intent. Nevertheless, the judge directed that the defence to the manslaughter count was the same as the defence to the counts of robbery and possession of the offensive weapon with intent. Here again the implication was that even if the appellant did not know the gun was loaded, and believed it to be unloaded, he would be not guilty of murder but he would be guilty of all the other charges he faced, including manslaughter. The true distinction between the appellant being guilty of murder and the appellant being guilty of manslaughter in the circumstances of this case was not the appellant's knowledge that the gun was loaded but the appellant's knowledge that the co-defendant was likely to use the loaded gun to kill or cause grievous bodily harm on the one hand, or was simply going to use the loaded gun to frighten on the other. We conclude that there was here a material misdirection in respect of count 4 ...

R v Gilmour [2000] 2 Cr App R 407

G appealed successfully against his conviction as an accomplice to murder. He had driven members of a terrorist organisation to a house on the basis that it was to be firebombed. Three young boys living in the house were killed in the ensuing fire. The Court of Appeal of Northern Ireland held that as G had not foreseen the risk that anyone would suffer death or grievous bodily harm, he could not be an accomplice to murder. A conviction for manslaughter could be substituted, however, as G had contemplated the unlawful acts, that is, the petrol bombing, that had caused the deaths.

Carswell LCJ: ... The issue then is whether [Gilmour] can be found guilty of manslaughter on the first three counts, on the basis that if the principals had thrown the petrol bomb into the house without the intention of killing or inflicting grievous bodily harm on any person they would have properly been convicted of that offence. It was argued on behalf of the appellant that if he did not share the intention of the principals he should not be found guilty of either murder or manslaughter, in the same way as if the principals go outside the contemplated acts involved in the joint enterprise the accessory cannot be convicted of either offence: see ... *R v Powell and English* ...

The issue is discussed in Blackstone's *Criminal Practice* ... in which the example is posed where the principal and accessory agree that the principal will post an incendiary device to the victim, the accessory contemplating only superficial injuries but the principal foreseeing and hoping that the injuries will be serious or fatal. The principal will be guilty of murder and the accessory will not. The editors conclude that the accessory should in such a case be convicted of manslaughter, because the act done by the principal is precisely what was envisaged.

In our opinion this is the correct principle to apply in the present case. The appellant foresaw that the principals would carry out the act of throwing a petrol bomb into the house, but did not realise that in so doing they intended to kill or do grievous bodily harm to the occupants. To establish that a person charged as an accessory to a crime of specific intent is guilty as an accessory it is necessary to prove that he realised the principal's intention ... The line of authority represented by such cases as *Anderson and Morris* [19661 2 QB 110, approved in *R v Powell and English*, deals with situations where the principal departs from the contemplated joint enterprise and perpetrates a more serious act of a different kind unforeseen by the accessory. In such cases it is established that the accessory is not liable at all for such unforeseen acts. It does not follow that the same result should follow where the principal carries out the very act contemplated by the accessory, though the latter does not realise that the principal intends a more serious consequence from the act.

We do not consider that we are obliged by authority to hold that the accessory in such a case must be acquitted of manslaughter as well as murder. The cases in which an accessory has been found not guilty both of murder and manslaughter all concern a departure by the principal from the *actus reus* contemplated by the accessory, not a difference between the parties in respect of the *mens rea* of each. In such cases the view has prevailed that it would be wrong to hold the accessory liable when the principal committed an act which the accessory did not contemplate or authorise. We do not, however, see any convincing policy reason why a person acting as an accessory to a principal who carries out the very deed contemplated by both should not be guilty of the degree of offence appropriate to the intent with which lie so acted. It is of course conceivable, as is suggested in Blackstone ... that in some cases the nature of the principal's *mens rea* may change the nature of the act committed by him and take it outside the type of act contemplated by the accessory, but it does not seem to us that the existence of such a possibility affects the validity of the basic principle which we have propounded. A verdict of guilty of manslaughter on this basis was upheld by the Court of Appeal in *Stewart and Schofield* (above) ... Even if there may be ground for criticism of some of the propositions enunciated in the court's judgment, the principle accepted as its basis is in our view sustainable.

Notes and queries

1   A and P agree that P will attack V with an iron bar whilst A acts as a look-out. They agree that P will only wound V. P attacks V intending to cause grievous bodily harm and V dies from his injuries. P is convicted of murder. On the basis of *R v Stewart and Schofield* (above) A will be an accomplice to manslaughter. Why is it that P's decision to use the iron bar with more deadly intent than that agreed between A and P is not a deliberate departure from the scope of the joint enterprise?

PROBLEMS WITH ACCESSORIAL LIABILITY

No *actus reus* on the part of the principal offender

Thornton v Mitchell [1940] 1 All ER 339 (KBD)

Lord Hewart LCJ: In my opinion, it is quite clear that this appeal must be allowed. Informations were preferred by the respondent, a superintendent of police, against a certain motor driver, one Hollinrake, for driving a motor vehicle – that is to say, an omnibus – without due care and attention, contrary to s 12(1) of the Road Traffic Act 1930, and also against the same driver for driving a motor vehicle – that is to say, a motor omnibus – without reasonable consideration for other persons using the road. At the same time, the bus conductor was charged as an aider and abettor. The information alleged that Hollinrake did unlawfully drive the motor vehicle without due care and attention, and that the present appellant, who was a bus conductor, unlawfully did aid, abet counsel and procure Hollinrake to do and commit that offence. There was a further charge against the bus conductor under the second information, whereby the driver was charged with driving 'without reasonable consideration for other persons using the road'. In the result, the justices dismissed the two charges against the driver, but convicted the appellant of unlawfully aiding, abetting counselling and procuring the driver to do and commit the offence of driving without due care and attention, contrary to s 12(1). They say in para 8:

> We, being of opinion that the conductor [had been very negligent], held that he was guilty of aiding and abetting, counselling and procuring the said Hollinrake to drive without due care and attention, and accordingly we inflicted a fine.

In my opinion, this case is *a fortiori* upon *Morris v Tolman* [1923] 1 KB 166, to which our attention has been directed. I will read one sentence from the judgment of Avory J at 171:

> ... in order to convict, it would be necessary to show that the respondent was aiding the principal, but a person cannot aid another in doing something which that other has not done.

That, I think is the very thing which these justices have decided that this bus conductor did. In one breath they say that the principal did nothing which he should not have done, and in the next breath they hold that the bus conductor aided and abetted the driver in doing something which had not been done or in not doing something which he ought to have done. I really think that, with all respect to the ingenuity of counsel for the respondent, the case is too plain for argument, and this appeal must be allowed and the conviction quashed.

R v Loukes [1996] 1 Cr App R 444 (CA)

Auld LJ: ... Mr Loukes and his brother, Ian Loukes, were partners in a haulage contractors. Mr Loukes's role in the business was to oversee the maintenance and servicing by the firm's mechanics of its fleet of vehicles. Ian Loukes drove some of the vehicles and had other responsibilities, but none of them included the servicing of vehicles. Ronnie Kennedy was one of the firm's drivers.

On 10 July 1993 Mr Kennedy was driving an ERF tipper truck of the firm along the northbound carriageway of the M1. Part of the prop shaft broke free and flew across the crash barrier into the path of a vehicle travelling in the southbound carriageway, killing its driver. The police examined the vehicle, and as a result Mr Kennedy was charged with causing death by dangerous driving, and Mr Loukes and his brother were charged with aiding, abetting, counselling or procuring that offence.

At the trial the prosecution case against Mr Loukes was that he caused the truck to be driven by Mr Kennedy when he, Mr Loukes, knew or ought to have known that it was in a dangerous state. PC Logan, an accident investigation officer, gave evidence about the truck's transmission system of which the prop shaft was a part. He said that the system had several pre-accident defects which, together, had caused lateral movements in the sliding joints of the system, which in turn had caused the prop shaft to become loose and fly off ...

As to the mechanics of the prop shaft breaking free, PC Logan's opinion was that the nut had become loose and had eventually become detached from the flange, allowing the flange to move partly away from the shaft, hence the worn splines and grooves on the shaft. He said that he would have expected that last damage to have occurred about four hours before the castellated nut worked its way completely free of the flange, allowing the prop shaft to break away. He added that during that period of loosening of the nut there would have been additional noise and vibration detectable to the driver. His conclusion in summary was that an examination of the underside of the vehicle before the accident would have revealed the defects in the flange, and that it would have been obvious there was a danger of that part of the prop shaft breaking free and causing an accident ...

At the close of the prosecution case the judge upheld submissions of no case to answer on behalf of Ian Loukes and Ronnie Kennedy, but rejected a similar submission on behalf of Mr Loukes.

Mr Loukes did not give evidence or call any witnesses. His defence, as presented by his counsel to the jury, was that, although the truck had been in a dangerous state, there was no evidence that the defects alleged to have been dangerous and to have caused the accident, did cause it, and, in any event, no evidence that he had known of its dangerous state.

The first ground of appeal is that the judge, having directed the jury to acquit Mr Kennedy of the principal offence, misdirected the jury by directing them that Mr Loukes could be found guilty of the secondary offence. His case, in reliance on the well-known authority of *Thornton v Mitchell* [1940] 1 All ER 339, is that the judge directed the acquittal of Mr Kennedy because there was no evidence that he had committed the *actus reus* of the offence, and that, therefore, he, Mr Loukes, could not be convicted of procuring it. He accepts, in reliance on *Millward* [1994] Crim LR 527, that if the judge properly directed the acquittal of Mr Kennedy only for want of evidence of *mens rea*, he, Mr Loukes, could be convicted of the secondary offence.

The principle upon which the court proceeded in *Millward* was that the procurer of another to commit the *actus reus* of an offence may be convicted of procuring it even if that other is not guilty of it for want of *mens rea*. The critical question here is 'What is the *actus reus* of the new offence of causing death by dangerous driving?'

Mr Loukes was charged with aiding, abetting, counselling or procuring Mr Kennedy to cause death by dangerous driving, contrary to ss 1 and 2A(2) of the Road Traffic Act 1988, as amended on 1 July 1992 by the Road Traffic Act 1991. The effect of that amendment was to substitute the offence of causing death by dangerous driving for that of causing death by reckless driving. The material provisions of ss 1 and 2A of the 1988 Act read:

1 A person who causes the death of another by driving a mechanically propelled vehicle dangerously on a road or other public place is guilty of an offence.

2A(1) For the purposes of s 1 ... above a person is to be regarded as driving dangerously if (and, subject to subsection (2) below, only if):

(a) the way he drives falls far below what would be expected of a competent and careful driver, and

(b) it would be obvious to a competent and careful driver that driving in that way would be dangerous.

(2) A person is also to be regarded as driving dangerously for the purposes of s 1 ... if it would be obvious to a competent and careful driver that driving the vehicle in its current state would be dangerous.

(3) ... in determining ... what would be ... obvious to ... a competent and careful driver in a particular case, regard shall be had not only to the

circumstances of which he could be expected to be aware but also to any circumstances shown to have been within the knowledge of the accused.

By reference to ss 1 and 2A(2), the principal offence charged, giving rise to the secondary charge against Mr Loukes, was that Mr Kennedy caused death by driving the vehicle when it would have been obvious to a competent and careful driver that to do so in its then state would be dangerous ...

It is implicit in the judge's ruling on the submission on behalf of Mr Loukes that he did not regard the *actus reus* as including any element of constructive knowledge of a notional competent and careful driver. In his definition of the *actus* he was clearly influenced by the decision of this court in *Millward*, a case concerning the procuring of the former offence of causing death by reckless driving, the recklessness relating to a defect in the vehicle and not to the manner of driving. The court there held that the *actus reus* of the principal offence lay in the taking of the vehicle on the road in a defective condition so as to cause death. It held that a procurer could be found guilty even though the driver was not, and that the *mens rea* of the procurer lay in the causing of that *actus reus* knowing of the vehicle's defective condition, whether or not it was or should have been known to the driver. The decision has been expressly approved by another division of this court in *Wheelhouse* [1994] Crim LR 756. As Professor Sir John Smith observed in a commentary in [1994] Crim LR 528–30, it:

... breaks new ground, being the first case to decide that procuring the *actus reus* of an offence is itself that offence ...

The drafting of the new provisions is tortuous, but their intent is plain, namely that a driver is guilty of an offence if, measured by an objective standard, his driving is dangerous. The standard might be said to be one of constructive blameworthiness, namely a constructive knowledge of danger – what should have been obvious to him because it would have been obvious to a competent and careful driver who also knew what he did. This is close to the first, alternative part of the *Lawrence* test of recklessness applicable to the former offence of reckless driving, namely driving in a way so as to create an obvious risk of danger without having given any thought to it. See *R v Lawrence* [1982] AC 510 HL, *per* Lord Diplock at p 526e. We say 'close to' because of the logical uncertainty that that formula left as to the relevance of what was or what should have been in the mind of a person accused of reckless driving and the tangled jurisprudence to which the formula gave rise ...

The purpose of the 1991 amendment was to resolve that uncertainty by introducing a wholly objective test and thus an absolute offence. In our view, it has achieved that. *Mens rea* plays no part in the principal offence. Proof of guilt depends on an objective standard of driving, namely what would have been obvious to a competent and careful driver. The accused driver's state of mind is relevant only if and to the extent that it attributes additional knowledge to the notional competent and careful driver. See the commentary to *Woodward* [1995] Crim LR 487; and the commentary to *Skelton* [1995] Crim LR 635. It should be noted too that the threshold of proof is high. It must be shown that the defect was 'obvious' to a 'competent and careful driver'. It is not enough to show in the case of such a driver that, say, if he had examined the vehicle by going underneath it, he would have seen the defect. See *Strong* [1995] Crim LR 428.

The effect of the judge's ruling in withdrawing from the jury the case against Mr Kennedy was that there was no dangerous driving here because, not only was there no evidence that he knew of the dangerous condition, but also – the critical test – no evidence that it would have been obvious to a competent and careful driver. It follows that the effect, though not the form, of the judge's ruling was that there was no evidence of the commission of the *actus reus* of the offence.

Where does that conclusion leave the conviction of Mr Loukes as an alleged procurer of a non-existent offence? We do not consider *Millward* to be of help in the new statutory context. It was essential to the decision in that case that there was evidence of the commission of the *actus reus*. Scott Baker J, giving the judgment of the court, said:

> ... the *actus reus* ... was the taking of the vehicle in the defective condition on the road so as to cause the death.

For reasons we have given, the *actus reus* of the new offence of dangerous driving is broader, its criterion being the objective one of obviousness to a competent and careful driver, whether or not supplemented by any particular knowledge of the accused driver. In the offence of reckless driving, there was scope for consideration of *mens rea*, however faint on the first alternative in the *Lawrence* test, and it was certainly an element of the second alternative. Here there is no room for it.

Accordingly, we are of the view that the *Millward* principle does not enable conviction of an alleged procurer of causing death by dangerous driving where the dangerous driving as defined in s 2A(2) has not been established. In our view, this case is governed by *Thornton v Mitchell*. A man cannot be convicted of procuring an offence where the *actus reus* is not established. That is enough to dispose of the appeal in Mr Loukes's favour ...

... [F]or the reasons that we have given, we allow the appeal on the first ground, that Mr Loukes could not procure an offence, the *actus reus* of which – all of the offence in this case – has not been committed. The case of *Millward* [1994] Crim LR 527 was decided after the change in the law, and the problem that the court had to consider there does not appear to have been considered in the Road Traffic Review Report (the North Report), Department of Transport and Home Office 1988, the Government White Paper, *The Road User and the Law*, February 1989 (Cmd 576) or in the passage of the Bill which became the 1991 Act through Parliament. If we are correct in our interpretation of the new provisions, a person who, knowing of the dangerous state of a vehicle, procures another, innocent of that dangerous state, to drive it, and where there is no evidence that that state would have been obvious to a competent and careful driver, will escape conviction. In our view, that injustice can only be cured by legislation ...

Principal offender lacks *mens rea* or has less *mens rea* than the accomplice

R v Cogan and Leak [1976] 1 QB 217 (CA)

Lawton LJ: ... The indictment in the statement of offence charged Cogan with rape and Leak as 'being aider and abettor to the same offence'. The particulars of offence against Cogan were in common form. As against Leak they were as follows: 'at the same time and place did aid and abet counsel and procure John Rodney Cogan to commit the said offence'.

The victim of the conduct which the prosecution submitted was rape by both defendants was Leak's wife, a slightly built young woman in her early 20s. They had been married in 1969. There had been many quarrels and some violence. On 9 July 1974, Leak came home in the evening under the influence of alcohol. He asked his wife for money. She refused to give him any. Shortly afterwards he attacked her. He knocked her down and while she was on the floor he kicked her many times. She sustained numerous bruises on her back and hip. At his trial he pleaded guilty to this assault.

The next day Leak came home at about 6 pm with Cogan. Both had been drinking. Leak told his wife that Cogan wanted to have sexual intercourse with her and that he, Leak, was going to see she did. She was frightened of him and what he might do, as well she might have been. He made her go upstairs where he took her clothes off and lowered her on to a bed. Cogan then came into the room. Leak asked him twice whether he wanted sexual intercourse with her. On both occasions he said that he did not. Leak then had sexual intercourse with her in the presence of Cogan. When he had finished, Leak again asked Cogan if he wanted sexual intercourse with his wife. This time Cogan said he did. He asked Leak to leave the room but he refused to do so. Cogan then had sexual intercourse with Mrs Leak. Her husband watched. While all this was going on for most of the time, if not all, Mrs Leak was sobbing. She did not struggle when Cogan was on top of her but she did try to turn away from him. When he had finished, he left the room. Leak then had intercourse with her again and behaved in a revolting fashion to her. When he had finished he joined Cogan and the pair of them left the house to renew their drinking. Mrs Leak dressed. She went to a neighbour's house and then to the police. The two defendants were arrested about three-quarters of an hour later. Both made oral and written statements. Leak did not give evidence.

Leak's statement amounted to a confession that he had procured Cogan to have sexual intercourse with his wife. He admitted that while Cogan was having sexual intercourse with her she was 'sobbing on and off not all the time'. There was ample evidence from the terms of his statement that she had not consented to Cogan having intercourse with her. The whole tenor of this statement was that he had procured Cogan to do what he did in order to punish her for past misconduct. He intended that she should be raped and that Cogan's body should provide the physical means to an end.

Cogan, in his written statement, admitted that he had had sexual intercourse with Mrs Leak at Leak's suggestion and that while he was on top of her she had been upset and had cried. At the trial Cogan gave evidence that he thought Mrs Leak had consented. The basis of his belief was what he had heard from her husband about her. The drink he had had seems to have been a reason, if not the only one, for mistaking her sobs and distress for consent ...

Cogan's appeal against conviction was based on the ground that the decision of the House of Lords in *R v Morgan* [1976] AC 182 applied. It did. There is nothing more to be said. It was for this reason that we allowed the appeal and quashed his conviction.

Leak's appeal against conviction was based on the proposition that he could not be found guilty of aiding and abetting Cogan to rape his wife if Cogan was acquitted of that offence as he was deemed in law to have been when his conviction was quashed: see s 2(3) of the Criminal Appeal Act 1968 ...

... [H]ere one fact is clear – the wife had been raped. Cogan had had sexual intercourse with her without her consent. The fact that Cogan was innocent of rape because he believed that she was consenting does not affect the position that she was raped.

Her ravishment had come about because Leak had wanted it to happen and had taken action to see that it did by persuading Cogan to use his body as the instrument for the necessary physical act. In the language of the law the act of sexual intercourse without the wife's consent was the *actus reus*: it had been procured by Leak who had the appropriate *mens rea*, namely his intention that Cogan should have sexual intercourse with her without her consent. In our judgment it is irrelevant that the man whom Leak had procured to do the physical act himself did not intend to have sexual intercourse with the wife without her consent. Leak was using him as a means to procure a criminal purpose.

Before 1861 a case such as this, pleaded as it was in the indictment, might have presented a court with problems arising from the old distinctions between principals and accessories in felony. Most of the old law was swept away by s 8 of the Accessories and Abettors Act 1861 and what remained by s 1 of the Criminal Law Act 1967. The modern law allowed Leak to be tried and punished as a principal offender. In our judgment he could have been indicted as a principal offender ...

Had Leak been indicted as a principal offender, the case against him would have been clear beyond argument. Should he be allowed to go free because he was charged with 'being aider and abettor to the same offence'? If we are right in our opinion that the wife had been raped (and no one outside a court of law would say that she had not been), then the particulars of offence accurately stated what Leak had done, namely he had procured Cogan to commit the offence. This would suffice to uphold the conviction. We would prefer, however, to uphold it on a wider basis. In our judgment convictions should not be upset because of mere technicalities of pleading in an indictment. Leak knew what the case against him was and the facts in support of that case were proved. But for the fact that the jury thought that Cogan in his intoxicated condition might have mistaken the wife's sobs and distress for expressions of her consent, no question of any kind would have arisen about the form of pleading. By his written statement Leak virtually admitted what he had done. As Judge Chapman said in *R v Humphreys* [1965] 3 All ER 689, 692:

> It would be anomalous if a person who admitted to a substantial part in the perpetration of a misdemeanour as aider and abettor could not be convicted on his own admission merely because the person alleged to have been aided and abetted was not or could not be convicted.

In the circumstances of this case it would be more than anomalous: it would be an affront to justice and to the common sense of ordinary folk ...

R v Millward [1994] Crim LR 527 (CA)

Facts: The appellant was convicted of aiding, abetting, counselling or procuring another person to cause death by reckless driving. The prosecution case was that the appellant had given one of his employees instructions which involved him using a tractor belonging to the appellant to tow a trailer on a main road. The tractor's hitch was poorly maintained and during the journey the trailer became detached and hit a car, causing the death of a passenger. The recklessness alleged was confined to the state of the hitch mechanism, and the appellant was said to have procured the offence by his instructions to his employee. It was argued on appeal that there was no reported case of a procurer being convicted following the acquittal of a principal offender. Further, in the instant case, the word 'reckless' imported a mental element into the *actus reus* of the offence. The acquittal thus implied that the *actus reus* had not been committed.

Held, dismissing the appeal:

1   A passage in Blackstone's *Criminal Practice* was approved, to the effect that an accessory can be liable provided that there is the *actus reus* of the principal offence even if the principal offender is entitled to be acquitted because of some defence personal to him. Procuring does not require a joint intention between accessory and principal. The procurer may, therefore, be convicted where the principal lacks the necessary *mens rea*.

2   In the instant case, the *actus reus* was taking of the vehicle in its defective condition on to the road so as to cause the death. It was procured by the appellant.

3   The *ratio* of *Thornton v Mitchell* [1940] 1 All ER 339 was that the driver did not commit the *actus reus* of careless driving, the offence in that case. He relied on the conductor's signals.

4   *Cogan and Leak* [1976] QB 217 was, contrary to the submissions of the defence, essentially a case of procuring rather than aiding and abetting, and could not be distinguished from the present case.

Principal offender has a defence not available to the accomplice

R v Bourne [1939] 1 KB 687 (CA)

Lord Goddard CJ: The appellant was indicted before Hallett J at the last assizes for Worcestershire and convicted of aiding and abetting his wife to commit the offence commonly called bestiality. The circumstances were such that nobody can approach this case without feeling the utmost repulsion, and indeed the learned judge thought it right, and I think he was quite right, to have a special report on the sanity of the appellant before he tried him. Without going into more of the revolting facts of this case than one can help, the appellant, who is only 28 years of age, his wife being a year or two younger, compelled her on two occasions to submit to the insertion of the male organ of a dog which he had excited into her vagina. That such a man should be allowed to be at large is almost intolerable and dreadful. Though he denied the offence when he went into the witness box, he had admitted it to the police. He had gone to the police to inquire where his wife and children were. The police meantime had been informed of what had been going on, I suppose on complaint by the wife, and they told him what had been suggested and he made a full confession to them, saying he admitted he had been a brute to his wife ...

The case against the appellant was that he was a principal in the second degree to the crime of buggery which was committed by his wife, because if a woman has connection with a dog, or allows a dog to have connection with her, that is the full offence of buggery. She may be able to show that she was forced to commit the offence. I will assume that the plea of duress could have been set up by her on the evidence, and in fact we have allowed Mr Green to argue this case on the footing that the wife would have been entitled to be acquitted on the ground of duress. The learned judge left no question to the jury on duress, but the jury have found that she did not consent ... I am willing to assume for the purpose of this case, and I think my brethren are too, that if this woman had been charged herself with committing the offence, she could have set up the plea of duress, not as showing that no offence had been committed, but as showing that she had no *mens rea* because her will was overborne by threats of imprisonment or violence so that she would be excused from punishment. But the offence of buggery whether with man or beast does not depend upon consent; it depends on the act, and if an act of buggery is committed, the felony is committed.

A point is raised here that the appellant was charged with being not merely an accessory before the fact but with being an aider and abettor. So he was, because the charge is: 'you being present aided and abetted, counselled and procured ...'

In the opinion of the court, there is no doubt that the appellant was properly indicted for being a principal in the second degree to the commission of the crime of buggery. That is all that it is necessary to show. The evidence was, and the jury by their verdict have shown they accepted it, that he caused his wife to have connection with a dog, and if he caused his wife to have connection with a dog he is guilty, whether you call him an aider and abettor or an accessory, as a principal in the second degree. For that reason, this appeal fails and is dismissed.

R v Howe and Others [1987] 1 AC 417 (HL)

For the facts see Chapter 13.

Lord Mackay of Clashfern: ... In dismissing the appeals the court certified [*inter alia*, the following point of law] of general public importance ... namely: ...

(2) Can the one who incites or procures by duress another to kill or to be a party to a killing be convicted of murder if that other is acquitted by reason of duress?...

... Clarkson's appeal is concerned with the second question in respect of which he contends that if Burke was acquitted by reason of duress he could not be convicted of murder as one who had incited or procured by duress Burke to kill or to be a party to a killing ...

Question 2

I turn now to the second certified question. In the view that I take on question one the second does not properly arise. However, I am of opinion that the Court of Appeal reached the correct conclusion upon it as a matter of principle.

Giving the judgment of the Court of Appeal Lord Lane CJ said [1986] QB 626 at 641–42:

> The judge based himself on a decision of this court in *R v Richards* [1974] QB 776. The facts in that case were that Mrs Richards paid two men to inflict injuries on her husband which she intended should 'put him in hospital for a month'. The two men wounded the husband but not seriously. They were acquitted of wounding with intent but convicted of unlawful wounding. Mrs Richards herself was convicted of wounding with intent, the jury plainly, and not surprisingly, believing that she had the necessary intent, though the two men had not. She appealed against her conviction on the ground that she could not properly be convicted as accessory before the fact to a crime more serious than that committed by the principals in the first degree. The appeal was allowed and the conviction for unlawful wounding was substituted. The court followed a passage from Hawkins' *Pleas of the Crown*, Vol 2 c 29, para 15: 'I take it to be an uncontroverted rule that [the offence of the accessory can never rise higher than that of the principal]; it seeming incongruous and absurd that he who is punished only as a partaker of the guilt of another, should be adjudged guilty of a higher crime than the other.'

James LJ delivering the judgment in *R v Richards* [1974] QB 776 said at 780: 'If there is only one offence committed, and that is the offence of unlawful wounding, then the person who has requested that offence to be committed, or advised that that offence be committed, cannot be guilty of a graver offence than that in fact which was committed.' The decision in *R v Richards* has been the subject of some criticism. Counsel before us posed the situation where A hands a gun to D informing him that it is loaded with blank ammunition only and telling him to go and scare X by discharging it. The ammunition is in fact live, as A knows, and X is killed. D is convicted only of manslaughter, as he might be on those facts. It would seem absurd that A should thereby escape conviction for murder. We take the view that *R v Richards* was incorrectly decided, but it seems to us that it cannot properly be distinguished from the instant case.

I consider that the reasoning of Lord Lane CJ is entirely correct and I would affirm his view that where a person has been killed and that result is the result intended by another participant, the mere fact that the actual killer may be convicted only of the reduced charge of manslaughter for some reason special to himself does not, in my opinion in any way, result in a compulsory reduction for the other participant ...

Withdrawal by an accomplice

As the following extracts indicate, a party who has a change of mind and wishes to withdraw from a joint enterprise must communicate to the other parties his intention to withdraw from the enterprise and must do in sufficient time before the commission of the offence:

R v Becerra and Cooper (1975) 62 Cr App R 212 (CA)

Roskill LJ: ... The facts were horrifying for they reveal acts of brutality almost unequalled even in this day and age. On 13 June 1974, in the early hours of the morning, these appellants and the third man entered this old lady's house at 8 Gore Terrace, Swansea, intending to steal some money that they had been told, as a result of a conversation in a public house, she kept in a drawer in her kitchen. It was said – whether truthfully or not does not matter – she might have as much as £4,000 there.

When they entered this house through the old lady's bedroom window, the applicant Becerra was carrying a clasp knife which had according to undisputed evidence, a handle 4 and a half and a blade 3 and a half inches long; and once that knife blade was opened, it remained rigid until a lever on the handle was released. The evidence was beyond question that Cooper knew that Becerra had that knife, and indeed Cooper borrowed it to cut the telephone wires leading to the house.

It is not necessary to go through the details, but some of the story must be related. Cooper climbed in through the window. The old lady began to switch her bedside light on and off. Cooper went over to her. He punched her, knelt and jumped on her, and covered her head with a pillow. Becerra and the third man followed Cooper. On Cooper's instructions the third man, somewhat reluctantly, took over the holding of the pillow over the old lady's face and Becerra cut the wires of the telephone by the side of the bed with the knife I have already mentioned.

Cooper then took Becerra's knife in his left hand and went out into the hall, going towards the kitchen. Why he took that knife and why he was given that knife was matter of acute controversy at the trial. Mr Lewis, who was the occupier of a first floor flat in the house came downstairs, obviously having been aroused by what he heard was going on. Becerra and the third man heard him, climbed out of the window and ran away. Cooper tried the back door, but it was locked and so he turned back and was confronted by Lewis. There was a struggle in which beyond question Lewis was stabbed four times on the left-hand side of his body and one of the stab wounds was 3 and a half inches deep and penetrated the right ventricle of his heart and he died. Cooper then made his escape through the window leaving the knife behind.

Only by the mercy of providence was the old lady not killed by the brutal treatment which she received. But she was greatly shocked and an innocent tenant of this house lost his life. Mrs Francis herself was in such a state of shock that she was unable to speak and the medical evidence showed she had bruising on her chest and face. Mercifully there was no damage to her central nervous system.

The basic prosecution case against Becerra and Cooper was that they had entered into a common agreement to use such force as was necessary against anyone in the house to get the money or to avoid identification or arrest. It was urged that this common agreement included the use, if necessary, of the knife to inflict serious bodily injury, if not death, and it was alleged that Cooper, in furtherance of that common agreement, murdered Lewis with the knife in his left hand while he pinioned Lewis from behind with his right arm around Lewis's shoulder ...

... It was argued in the alternative on behalf of Becerra, that ... Becerra had open to him a second line of defence, namely that – I hope I do Mr Owen's argument on the second ground no injustice if I put it this way – whatever Cooper did immediately before and at the time of the killing of Lewis, Becerra had by then withdrawn from that common design and so should not be convicted of the murder of Lewis, even though the common design had previously been that which I have stated ...

It is necessary, before dealing with that argument in more detail, to say a word or two about the relevant law. It is a curious fact, considering the number of times in which this point arises where two or more people are charged with criminal offences, particularly murder or manslaughter, how relatively little authority there is in this country upon the point. But the principle is undoubtedly of long standing.

Perhaps it is best first stated in *Saunders and Archer* (1577) 2 Plowd 473 (in the 18th year of the first Queen Elizabeth) at 476, in a note by Plowden, thus: '... for if I command one to Kill JS and before the Fact done I go to him and tell him that I have repented, and expressly charge him not to kill JS and he afterwards kills him, there I shall not be Accessory to this Murder, because I have countermanded my first Command, which in all Reason shall discharge me, for the malicious Mind of the Accessory ought to continue to do ill until the Time of the Act done, or else he shall not be charged; but if he had killed JS before the Time of my Discharge or Countermand given, I should have been Accessory to the Death, notwithstanding my private Repentance.'

The next case to which I may usefully refer is some 250 years later, but over 150 years ago: *Edmeads and Others* (1828) 3 C & P 390, where there is a ruling of Vaughan B at a trial at Berkshire Assizes, upon an indictment charging Edmeads and others with unlawfully shooting at gamekeepers. At the end of his ruling the learned Baron said on the question of common intent at 392, 'that is rather a question for the jury; but still, on this evidence, it is quite clear what the common purpose was. They all draw up in lines, and point their guns at the gamekeepers, and they are all giving their countenance and assistance to the one of them who actually fires the gun. If it could be shown that either of them separated himself from the rest, and showed distinctly that he would have no hand in what they were doing, the objection would have much weight in it.'

I can go forward over 100 years. Mr Owen (to whose juniors we are indebted for their research into the relevant Canadian and United States cases) referred us to several Canadian cases, to only one of which is it necessary to refer in detail, a decision of the Court of Appeal of British Columbia in *Whitehouse (alias Savage)* (1941) 1 WWR 112. I need not read the headnote. The Court of Appeal held that the trial judge concerned in that case, which was one of murder, had been guilty of misdirection in his direction to the jury on this question of 'withdrawal'. The matter is, if I may most respectfully say so, so well put in the leading judgment of Sloan JA, that I read the whole of the passage at pp 115 and 116: 'Can it be said on the facts of this case that a mere change of mental intention and a quitting of the scene of the crime just immediately prior to the striking of the fatal blow will absolve those who participate in the commission of the crime by overt acts up to that moment from all the consequences of its accomplishment by the one who strikes in ignorance of his companions' change of heart? I think not. After a crime has been committed and before a prior abandonment of the common enterprise may be found by a jury there must be, in my view, in the absence of exceptional circumstances, something more than a mere mental change of intention and physical change of place by those associates who wish to dissociate themselves from the consequences attendant upon their willing assistance up to the moment of the actual commission of that crime. I would not attempt to define too closely what must be done in criminal matters involving participation in a common unlawful purpose to break the chain of causation and responsibility. That must depend upon the circumstances of each case but it seems to me that one essential element ought to be established in a case of this kind: Where practicable and reasonable there must be timely communication of the intention to abandon the common purpose from those who wish to dissociate themselves from the contemplated crime to those who desire to continue in it. What is 'timely communication' must be determined by the facts of each case but where practicable and reasonable it ought to be such communication, verbal or otherwise, that will serve unequivocal notice upon the other party to the common unlawful cause that if he proceeds upon it he does so without the further aid and assistance of those who withdraw. The unlawful purpose of him who continues alone is then his own and not one in common with those who are no longer parties to it nor liable to its full and final consequences.' The learned judge then went on to cite a passage from Hale's *Pleas of the Crown* 618 and the passage from *Saunders and Archer* to which I have already referred.

In the view of each member of this court, that passage, if we may respectfully say so, could not be improved upon and we venture to adopt it in its entirety as a correct statement of the law which is to be applied in this case.

The last case, an English one, is *Croft* [1944] 1 KB 295, a well known case of a suicide pact where, under the old law, the survivor of a suicide pact was charged with and convicted of murder. It was sought to argue that he had withdrawn from the pact in time to avoid liability (as the law then was) for conviction for murder.

The Court of Criminal Appeal, comprising Lawrence J (as he then was), Lewis and Wrottesley JJ dismissed the appeal and upheld the direction given by Humphreys J to the jury at the trial. Towards the end of the judgment Lawrence J said at pp 297 and 298:

> ... counsel for the appellant complains – although I do not understand that the point had ever been taken in the court below – that the summing up does not contain any reference to the possibility of the agreement to commit suicide having been determined or countermanded. It is true that the learned judge does not deal expressly with that matter except in a passage where he says: 'Even if you accept his statement in the witness box that the vital and second shot was fired when he had gone through that window, he would still be guilty of murder if she was then committing suicide as the result of an agreement which they had mutually arrived at that that should be the fate of both of them, and it is no answer for him that he altered his mind after she was dead and did not commit suicide himself.' ... The authorities, such as they are, show in our opinion, that where a person has acted as an accessory before the fact, in order that he should not be held guilty as an accessory before the fact, he must give express and actual countermand or revocation of the advising, counselling, procuring, or abetting which he had given before.

It seems to us that those authorities make plain what he law is which has to be applied in the present case.

We therefore turn back to consider the direction which the learned judge gave in the present case to the jury and what was the suggested evidence that Becerra had withdrawn from the common agreement. The suggested evidence is the use by

Becerra of the words 'Come on, let's go', coupled, as I said a few moments ago, with his act in going out through the window. The evidence, as the judge pointed out, was that Cooper never heard that nor did the third man. But let it be supposed that that was said and the jury took the view that it was said.

On the facts of this case, in the circumstances then prevailing, the knife having already been used and being contemplated for further use when it was handed over by Becerra to Cooper for the purpose of avoiding (if necessary) by violent means the hazards of identification, if Becerra wanted to withdraw at that stage, he would have to 'countermand', to use the word that is used is some of the cases or 'repent' to use another word so used, in some manner vastly different and vastly more effective than merely to say 'Come on, let's go' and go out through the window.

It is not necessary, on this application, to decide whether the point of time had arrived at which the only way in which he could effectively withdraw, so as to free himself from joint responsibility for any act Cooper thereafter did in furtherance of the common design, would be physically to intervene so as to stop Cooper attacking Lewis, as the judge suggested, by interposing his own body between them or somehow getting in between them or whether some other action might suffice. That does not arise for decision here. Nor is it necessary to decide whether or not the learned judge was right or wrong, on the facts of this case, in that passage which appears at the bottom of p 206, which Mr Owen criticised: 'and at least take all reasonable steps to prevent the commission of the crime which he had agreed the others should commit.' It is enough for the purposes of deciding this application to say that under the law of this country as it stands, and on the facts (taking them at their highest in favour of Becerra), that which was urged as amounting to withdrawal from the common design was not capable of amounting to such withdrawal. Accordingly Becerra remains responsible, in the eyes of the law, for everything that Cooper did and continued to do after Becerra's disappearance through the window as much as if he had done them himself.

Cooper being unquestionably guilty of murder, Becerra is equally guilty of murder. Mr Owen's careful argument must therefore be rejected and the application by Becerra for leave to appeal against conviction fails ...

R v Whitefield (1983) 79 Cr App R 36 (CA)

Dunn LJ: ... The facts of the burglary were as follows. Between 4 pm on 3 November and 11 pm on 5 November 1982, a quantity of goods were taken from a flat in London SE16 when the occupier was away. On his return the latter reported the matter to the police. On 23 November the police interviewed the appellant after two other persons (Anthony Gallagher and Helen Coffey) had been arrested and charged with the burglary. Contemporaneous notes of the interviews were made and signed by the appellant. The appellant stated at the interview that he never took part in the burglary, but admitted telling Gallagher one evening that the flat that was next to his own was unoccupied. He also admitted that he had agreed to break into the flat with Gallagher by way of his own flat and balcony. They discussed how the property should be disposed of and the proceeds divided. Subsequently the appellant decided that he would not take part, and so informed Gallagher before the burglary took place. However he knew that the burglary was to take place on a particular night. He heard it being committed, but did nothing to prevent it. He denied having spoken to Gallagher since the burglary. He had received none of the property or proceeds from its disposal ...

The law upon withdrawal is stated in *Becerra and Cooper* ... and *Grundy* [1977] Crim LR 543. So far as material to the facts of this case, the law may be shortly stated as follows. If a person has counselled another to commit a crime, he may escape liability by withdrawal before the crime is committed, but it is not sufficient that he should merely repent or change his mind. If his participation is confined to advice or encouragement, he must at least communicate his change of mind to the other, and the communication must be such as 'will serve unequivocal notice upon the other party to the common unlawful cause that if he proceeds upon it he does so without the aid and assistance of those who withdraw'. (See the Canadian case of *Whitehouse* [1941] 1 WWR 112, 116 *per* Sloan JA, approved in *Becerra and Cooper* and *Grundy*.)

In this case there was, if the jury accepted it, evidence in the answers given by the appellant to the police that he had served unequivocal notice on Gallagher that if he proceeded with the burglary he would do so without the aid or assistance of the appellant. In his ruling the judge stated that such notice was not enough, and that in failing to communicate with the police or take any other steps to prevent the burglary he remained 'liable in law for what happened, for everything that was done that night'. In the judgment of this court, in making that statement the judge fell into an error of law. The direct result of it was that the appellant changed his plea to one of guilty. A change of plea founded upon an error of law by the judge cannot stand, and the conviction must be quashed and the appeal allowed ...

R v Rook [1993] 1 WLR 1005 (CA)

Lloyd LJ: ... The case concerns a so-called contract killing. Afsar was a taxi driver in Nottingham. He wished to be rid of his wife, Shaheen. On Tuesday 19 December 1989 he met the appellant, Armstrong, and a man called Barker, when they hired his taxi. During the journey there was some conversation. Afsar asked whether the appellant wanted to earn some money. A friend of his, said Afsar, wanted to have a woman beaten up. As the conversation continued, it became clear that the 'friend' wanted the woman murdered. There was some discussion between the appellant, Afsar and Armstrong about money. The appellant named a price of £20,000. The price agreed was £15,000 cash, and £5,000 worth of jewellery which the woman would be wearing. Afsar said it was to be a murder on credit. In the event he paid no more than £50.

Barker said he wanted nothing to do with it; so the following day, Wednesday 20 December 1989, the appellant recruited Leivers. He said to Leivers: 'Look Mark, it's murder.' Leivers replied: 'Yea, it's all right. I'll be there.' It was arranged that Afsar would pick up the other three at about 4.30 pm. They drove to Colwick Park, by the side of the lake. There was some discussion between all four as to how the murder should be committed. Afsar said that when they were ready he would bring the woman in his car. It was agreed that the murder would take place the following day.

On the evening of Wednesday 20 December there was a further discussion between the appellant, Armstrong and Leivers about the method of killing. They decided to use a knife and a piece of wood. Armstrong said that he wanted some money 'up front'. The appellant said that they would need money in order to buy new clothes after the murder.

On Thursday 21 December 1989 Afsar drove Armstrong and Leivers to Colwick Park, and dropped them as arranged. The appellant could not be found. Afsar went back to collect Shaheen. When he returned, Armstrong and Leivers dragged her from the car and killed her most brutally. Her body was found in the lake the next day.

The appellant was interviewed and made certain admissions. He also gave evidence at the trial. His defence was that he never intended the woman to be killed. He hoped to get some money from Afsar 'up front', and then disappear. At first he 'tagged along' to see how serious the others were. He was not sure whether they would go through with it or not. Then he tried to stall them, because he never intended to go through with it himself. Finally, on the Thursday, he deliberately absented himself. He said he thought that, if he were not there, Armstrong and Leivers would not go ahead without him ...

... Mr Maxwell QC [for the appellant] submits that where a person has given assistance, for example by providing a gun, in circumstances which would render him liable as a secondary party if he does not withdraw, then in order to escape liability he must 'neutralise' his assistance. He must, so it was said, break the chain of causation between his act of assistance, and the subsequent crime, by recovering the gun, or by warning the victim to stay away, or by going to the police. Mr Hockman submits, on the other hand, that the Crown must prove that the defendant continued ready to help until the moment the crime is committed; and if there is doubt as to the defendant's state of mind on the day in question, or his willingness to provide further help if required, then the jury must acquit.

As between these two extreme views, we have no hesitation in rejecting the latter. In *R v Croft* [1944] KB 295 the surviving party of a suicide pact was held to be guilty of murder. Lawrence J, giving the judgment of the court, said ([1944] KB 295 at 298):

> The authorities, however, such as they are, show, in our opinion, that the appellant, to escape being held guilty as an accessory before the fact must establish that he expressly countermanded or revoked the advising, counselling, procuring or abetting which he had previously given.

In *R v Whitehouse* [1941] 1 WWR 112 at 114 Sloan JA said:

> Can it be said on the facts of this case that a mere change of mental intention and a quitting of the scene of the crime just immediately prior to the striking of the fatal blow will absolve those who participate in the commission of the crime by overt acts up to that moment from all the consequences of its accomplishment by the one who strikes in ignorance of his companions' change of heart? I think not. After a crime has been committed and before a prior abandonment of the common enterprise may be found by a jury there must be, in my view, in the absence of exceptional circumstances, something more than a mere mental change of intention and physical change of place by those associates who wish to dissociate themselves from the consequences attendant upon their willing assistance up to the moment of the actual commission of that crime. I would not attempt to define too closely what must be done in criminal matters involving participation in a common unlawful purpose to break the chain of causation and responsibility. That must depend upon the circumstances of each case but it seems to me that one essential element ought to be established in a case of this kind: Where practicable and

reasonable there must be timely communication of the intention to abandon the common purpose from those who wish to dissociate themselves from the contemplated crime to those who desire to continue in it. What is 'timely communication' must be determined by the facts of each case but where practicable and reasonable it ought to be such communication, verbal or otherwise, that will serve unequivocal notice upon the other party to the common unlawful cause that if he proceeds upon it he does so without the further aid and assistance of those who withdraw. The unlawful purpose of him who continues alone is then his own and not one in common with those who are no longer parties to it nor liable to its full and final consequences.

In *R v Becerra* ... this court approved that passage as a correct statement of the law. The facts of *R v Becerra* were that the victim was killed in the course of a burglary. The appellant had provided the knife shortly before the murder. The court held that the appellant's sudden departure from the scene of the crime with the words 'Come on, let's go' was an insufficient communication of withdrawal. So the appellant's conviction as a secondary party to the murder was upheld. In *R v Whitefield* (1983) 79 Cr App R 36 at 39–40 Dunn LJ stated the law as follows:

> If a person has counselled another to commit a crime, he may escape liability by withdrawal before the crime is committed, but it is not sufficient that he should merely repent or change his mind. If his participation is confined to advice or encouragement, he must at least communicate his change of mind to the other, and the communication must be such as 'will serve unequivocal notice upon the other party to the common unlawful cause that if he proceeds upon it he does so without the aid and assistance of those who withdraw'.

In the present case the appellant never told the others that he was not going ahead with the crime. His absence on the day could not possibly amount to 'unequivocal communication' of his withdrawal. In his evidence-in-chief, in a passage already quoted, he said that he made it quite clear to himself that he did not want to be there on the day. But he did not make it clear to the others. So the minimum necessary for withdrawal from the crime was not established on the facts. In these circumstances, as in *R v Becerra*, it is unnecessary for us to consider whether communication of his withdrawal would have been enough, or whether he would have had to take steps to 'neutralise' the assistance he had already given.

Mr Maxwell rightly drew our attention to a sentence in the judgment of Sloan JA, already quoted, where he refers to the service of notice on the other party that if he proceeds he does so without *further* aid from those who withdraw. This may suggest that aid *already* afforded need not be neutralised. We agree with Mr Maxwell that this attaches too much importance to a single word. But that is as far as we are prepared to go in this case. We are not prepared, as at present advised, to give our approval to his proposition in its extreme form. In *Criminal Law: The General Part*, 2nd edn, 1961, para 127, Glanville Williams quotes a graphic phrase from an American authority (*Eldredge v US* (1932) 62 F 2d 449, *per* McDermott J): 'A declared intent to withdraw from a conspiracy to dynamite a building is not enough, if the fuse has been set; he must step on the fuse.' It may be that this goes too far. It may be that it is enough that he should have done his best to step on the fuse. Since this is as much a question of policy as a question of law, and since it does not arise on the facts of the present case, we say no more about it ...

R v Baker [1994] Crim LR 444 (CA)

Facts: A man with the same name as the deceased had earlier been robbed in his own home and there was evidence that the deceased had paid the robbers to commit the offence. He was called out one night and killed with two knives belonging to the appellant. Witnesses said that the appellant had said that he had done the killing. At trial, a co-defendant gave evidence in his own defence which implicated the appellant. He said that on the night of the killing, the appellant said he wanted to see Sam, which was the nickname of the deceased, because, he said, the appellant had been a party to the robbery. They went to waste ground where he expected the appellant to have a word with Sam but instead he attacked him and went mad, stabbing him repeatedly. Death was caused by 48 stab wounds, each of which was fatal. The appellant's evidence was that he knew that his co-defendant was a violent man who had kicked and punched him previously and threatened to finish him off. He and others had told him that Sam was going to the police about the robbery and wanted him to go with them to see Sam. He went out of fear, and they took his knives. Once on the open ground, the co-defendant handed the appellant a knife and told him to kill Sam. He then went berserk and was waving the other knife at the appellant, who was petrified. The appellant swung the knife which penetrated Sam somewhere near the shoulder or the throat, Sam staggered back and the co-defendant went on screaming for the appellant to kill Sam and so he swung the knife twice more. He did not know where it went in. The appellant then passed the knife back to the co-defendant and said 'I'm not doing it'. He did not touch Sam again but moved a short distance away and turned his back. He then heard more thuds caused by the others continuing to stab Sam. He then saw him on the ground.

The defence was that insofar as he was involved in any joint enterprise, it was a joint enterprise to do serious harm to Sam but not to kill him, and he did it under duress. It could not be proven that any of the three stab wounds he had inflicted would have killed Sam or that they did kill him. That he passed over the knife and thereafter disassociated himself from what the others did meant that the joint enterprise had come to an end. The witnesses were tainted by their close relationship with the co-defendant.

Held: It would be considered how far in practice a direction to the jury to consider a s 18 count would have benefited or might have benefited the appellant. The defence would have relied on duress by the co-defendant but if that had succeeded there would have been a complete acquittal. The risk that the jury might be unwilling to acquit him completely and should therefore have been allowed to consider convicting on a lesser charge presupposed that they would convict him after satisfying themselves that he did not act under duress. In that situation, according to his story, the appellant was told by the co-defendant to kill Sam and stabbed him three times before turning away and saying that he wasn't doing it. He then stayed there until Sam was on the ground dead or dying, whereupon he left with the other two. If that account were accepted by the jury the court was far from confident that the appellant, by his words and actions, had effectively put an end to the joint enterprise so that he had no criminal responsibility for what happened after the three stab wounds which he inflicted. The words 'I'm not doing it' and the turning around and moving a few feet away were far from unequivocal notice that the appellant was wholly disassociating himself from the entire enterprise. The words were quite capable of meaning no more than 'I will not myself strike any more blows'. They were not an unequivocal indication that he did not intend to take any further part in any further assault on Sam and indeed he did no more than withdraw by a few feet (see *Becerra* (1976) 62 Cr App R 212; *Rook* [1993] 1 WLR 1005).

Notes and queries

1 In *R v Mitchell* [1999] Crim LR 496, the Court of Appeal held that a distinction was to be drawn between pre-planned and spontaneous violence, in the sense that where violence was pre-planned, communication of withdrawal from the planned violence was necessary for that withdrawal to be effective. Where the violence was spontaneous communication of the intention to withdraw was not necessarily required. Is this distinction justifiable?

CODIFICATION AND LAW REFORM PROPOSALS

The most recent review of the law relating to accessorial liability is contained in the Law Commission's Consultation Paper *Assisting and Encouraging Crime* (LCCP No 131). Set out below is the Commission's review of the options for reform of liability for assisting in the commission of crime. For details of the review and proposed reforms of the law relating to the encouragement of crime, see Chapter 10.

Assisting and Encouraging Crime (LCCP No 131)

The future structure of the law

4.8 Two, separate but interrelated, matters must be discussed. First, the nature, and proper analysis, of the conduct to be covered by the law of assisting and encouraging crime. Second, whether there should be maintained the present distribution of that law between accessory liability on the one hand and the inchoate offence of incitement on the other hand.

Types of accessory conduct

4.9 Until very recently, the conduct that constitutes aiding and abetting had been thought to fall into one of two, albeit sometimes overlapping, categories: conduct that encourages or influences the perpetrator; and conduct that helps the perpetrator to carry out the offence. It was not possible to regard that as a complete or accurate statement of the present law, because such analytical questions have never been definitively confronted in the common law authorities; and the question has in any event been clouded in recent years by the insistence in *AG's Reference (No 1 of 1975)* that each of the words aid, abet, counsel, or procure used in section 8 of the Accessories and Abettors Act 1861 denotes a separate head of accessoryship.

4.10 However, commentators not bound by particular legislative accidents have been clear that accessoryship or complicity has basically two natures:

> Two kinds of actions render the secondary party liable for the criminal actions of the primary party: intentionally influencing the decision of the primary party to commit a crime, and intentionally helping the principal actor commit the crime, where the helping actions themselves constitute no part of the actions prohibited by the definition of the crime ...

We agree with that general view. It accurately distinguishes the two different types of conduct that constitute accessoryship, and clarity in expounding a law of accessoryship or secondary liability will only be achieved if this distinction is recognised as the foundation of the law. The remainder of this Consultation Paper proceeds on the basis that our subject matter consists mainly of two, separate, activities: assisting crime; and encouraging crime.

4.11 That decision necessarily implies that the approach in *AG's Ref (No 1 of 1975)* must be abandoned, and section 8 of the 1861 Act is consigned to history. We are quite clear that that is the only sensible approach to these recent developments in the law. The case is, we have to say with respect, an historical aberration, that gives section 8 a weight and significance that were clearly not intended by the legislature, and which had been rejected by previous authority. But it is not merely the misinterpretation of the statutory provisions, but also, and more importantly, the complications to which that approach has led that make it imperative for a new start to be made.

Aiding and abetting and incitement

4.12 During our work we have not become aware of any good reason why there should be separate chapters of the law dealing with aiding and abetting (including the 'counselling and procuring' aspects of aiding and abetting) on the one hand; and incitement on the other hand. The textbooks merely note that the two concepts are different, in that aiding and abetting is a form of, albeit derivative, principal liability for a crime actually committed; whilst incitement is a form of inchoate liability. The requirements of the two very similar forms of liability have never been rationally considered together, outside the straitjacket of their different historical origins. In what follows we will assume that a single set of rules should be developed to cover all cases of assisting and encouraging crime, without the present structural distinction between aiding and abetting and incitement.

Assisting and encouraging

4.13 We therefore address the problems of law reform by assuming that there should be two new offences, to take the place both of the present law of aiding and abetting and of the present law of incitement.

4.14 The separate consideration of assisting crime on the one hand and encouraging crime on the other' enables us to isolate, and to confine to their proper sphere, some of the most pressing policy issues on which we seek the views of consultees. That is because two of the most important issues arise in connection with assisting, rather than with encouraging, crime. First, the question of whether assisting should become an inchoate offence, in the sense that the assister may be guilty even if the principal crime is not in the event committed. Second, the question of whether the mental state of an assister necessary for conviction should be expressed in terms of purpose that the principal crime be committed; or, as in the present law of aiding and abetting, merely in terms that the accessory is liable when he does an act of assistance and is aware that the principal may be going to act with the fault required for the principal offence.

4.15 These are not live issues in respect of encouraging crime. The terms of the proposed offence of encouraging crime that we submit for consideration are broadly the same as the rules of the present offence of incitement. An inciter or encourager's *mens rea*, in terms of purpose that the principal offence should be committed, follows naturally and inevitably from the nature of his conduct. The very description of that conduct as having encouraged, provoked, incited, stirred up or cheered on the commission of a crime presupposes a desire on the encourager's part that that crime should be committed. Nor has there ever been thought to be difficulty about incitement as an inchoate offence. If D positively encourages P to commit a crime, it has never been questioned that D should be guilty of the offence of incitement even if, for whatever reason, P did not in the event commit the offence incited. It has long been accepted that positively to encourage another to commit a crime is a sufficiently undesirable act to be punishable by the law whether or not the crime encouraged is in fact committed.

4.16 The issues identified in paragraph 4.14 above are, however, contested and difficult questions in relation to assisting crime. That activity, as part of the present law of aiding and abetting, is at the moment only itself criminal if the principal crime is in fact committed, though many weighty commentators have urged that that rule should be changed. At the, same time, however, something far less than purpose that the principal crime should be committed suffices in the present law to convict an assister of aiding and abetting.

4.17 It will therefore be convenient if we discuss the proposed offence of assisting crime separately from the proposed offence of encouraging crime. Within that discussion we will confront the major policy questions just referred to. We will then, more briefly, discuss the offence of encouraging crime; and then a range of difficult, but less central, issues that are common both to assisting and to encouraging crime.

ASSISTING CRIME

An inchoate offence of assisting?

4.18 We take first the question of whether assisting crime should become an inchoate offence, liability for which will attach even if the principal crime is not committed. This issue does not arise when D assists at and during the actual commission of the crime by P, in the manner of the old principal in the second degree, since there the principal crime will always necessarily either be committed or be in the course of commission. The problem relates only to assistance given in advance of the principal crime, or at least away from its actual or believed place of commission.

4.19 We have already set out, in paragraphs 3.17–3.26 above, the many difficulties caused in the present law by the requirement that liability for assistance, as opposed to encouragement, can only attach if the principal crime is actually committed: difficulties that many commentators have urged should be avoided by the creation of an offence of inchoate assistance. Those difficulties are of two different kinds.

4.20 First, problems of social policy associated with law enforcement. it may be thought clearly undesirable and antisocial for D to give active assistance towards the commission of a crime; and it may be thought unsatisfactory that the law enforcement agencies have to wait until that crime is actually committed before they can intervene to control the conduct of assisters. To that extent the present law may be thought ineffective. Second, however, the absence of an offence of inchoate aiding has caused the rules both of aiding and abetting itself, and of related parts of the law, to be significantly distorted, in order to provide for cases in which prosecution for inchoate aiding would be the more natural remedy. To that extent, the law may be thought undesirably wide and vague.

4.21 Concern about the distortions created in the law is not limited to the difficulty thereby caused in stating the law clearly and on the basis of consistent principle, though that problem is severe enough. Rather, such developments appear to indicate an unexpressed belief, correct or not, that cases that seem naturally to be ones of inchoate assistance should be legally punishable. Thus, the *Bainbridge* rule is impossible to reconcile with any requirement of knowledge on the part of the accessory as to the crime actually committed but appears tolerable because the 'accessory' was willing to provide assistance towards another, uncommitted, crime; one who provides assistance for an escape from prison that is foiled before it takes place is in reality an inchoate aider, and the authorities should be able, and perhaps indeed obliged, to prosecute him as such, and not have to fall back on the vaguer and less immediate offence of conspiracy; and the conduct of people who simply provide instruments to be used in committing crimes, but with indifference as to whether those crimes are in fact committed, is more naturally, and more accurately, described as assistance rather than incitement.

4.22 That courts and prosecutors have been forced into these expedients in recent years may be thought to indicate the existence of a gap in the present law of accessoryship. In the cases mentioned, the anti-social nature of the accused's conduct consists in the assistance that he seeks or is willing to give towards the commission of crime. It would produce a clearer and more principled solution to the problem that such conduct poses if it were proceeded against, if at all, as a case of assisting, rather than as incitement, conspiracy, or, in the *Bainbridge* type of case, as a distorted version of the orthodox law of accessoryship.

4.23 We therefore share the view of other commentators that serious consideration must be given to the introduction of an offence of inchoate assisting. A good deal will, of course, depend on the precise definition of that offence, and of the mental element that has to be established in order to convict of it. We have concluded, however, that that issue should be discussed as part of the general requirements of a single offence of assisting crime, with the same rules to apply whether or not the principal crime is actually committed. We take that view because, far from the inclusion of inchoate aiding distorting the terms of an offence of assisting crime, it will in fact cause discussion of that offence to focus on the proper issues.

4.24 That may at first sight seem surprising. However, the conclusion that an accessory's liability is, even in the present law, essentially inchoate in nature springs directly from analysis of the conduct that founds that liability in law. An accessory's legal fault is complete as soon as his act of assistance is done, and acts thereafter by the principal, in particular in committing or not committing the crime assisted, cannot therefore add to or detract from that fault. Moreover, it is not the present law, and it is logically impossible that it should become the law, that the accessory must cause the commission of the principal crime; and for that reason also the actual occurrence of the principal crime is not taken into account in assessing the accessory's culpability. Even under the present law, therefore, where the principal crime has to be committed before accessory liability can attach, the conditions for the liability of the accessory should be, indeed can only be, assessed at the time of, and in relation to, that act of assistance. Thus, the issues as to, for instance, the purpose or awareness of the shopkeeper who sells the known burglar the screwdriver can only be assessed at the point of sale, when, in relation to the eventually completed principal crime, his liability undoubtedly' remains 'inchoate'. His subsequent awareness or purpose, when or after the principal crime is actually committed, cannot affect the legal status or culpability of an act that he has already completed.

4.25 Even under the present law, therefore, the requirement that the principal crime should actually be committed adds nothing to the analysis of accessory liability, and does not serve as any sort of principled limitation on that liability. Rather, it serves as an additional condition for liability, that may, however, enable some 'assisters' to escape conviction, possibly in a quite erratic and unmeritorious fashion.

4.26 An inchoate offence of assisting, if it is to be created at all, should therefore logically cover the whole of the law of assisting, and not be simply a special offence used only when the principal crime is not committed. In the most usual case the act of assistance will only come to light, or be thought to be worth prosecuting, where the principal crime has in fact been committed. In practice, therefore, to put assisting on an inchoate basis is unlikely greatly to extend the reach of the law; and, indeed, the clarification and limitation of the mental element in the offence of assisting that is made possible by concentration on the actual intentions and beliefs of the assister will certainly reduce some of the vaguer and potentially intrusive aspects of the present law.

4.27 That said, however, at least in theory a law of inchoate assisting will create liability in cases that some readers may at first sight find surprising. In the next section we therefore set out in broad terms what the potential reach of such a law would be; indicate what might be seen as the objections to such a law, on the one hand, and the objections to not adopting such a law on the other hand; and particularly invite the comments of consultees.

4.28 We have to sound one note of warning. Because of the importance of this issue we put it at an early stage of our discussion, before descending into the details of a possible inchoate offence of assisting. In so doing, we have to mention some aspects of that offence that are expounded in much fuller detail later in the paper. Readers may therefore wish to suspend final judgement until they have seen the whole of the discussion of the proposed offence of assisting, and only then return to the question of whether that offence should be placed on an inchoate basis.

Objections to an inchoate offence of assisting

Preliminary: the broad characteristics of the offence

4.29 We have noted in paragraph 4.27 above that liability for assisting on an inchoate basis may produce results that, viewed objectively, appear surprising or undesirable. Those problems cannot be properly considered without a clear view of the full range of cases to which an offence of inchoate assisting might extend. In this sub-section, therefore, in order to assist critical assessment of the possibility of an inchoate offence, we set out what we consider, subject to consultation, to be the limits of the new offence of assisting, and give examples of cases to which it would extend if it were to be placed on an inchoate basis.

4.30 Readers may find it convenient to refer to the provisional definition of the new offence that is set out in semi-statutory form in paragraph 4.99 below. We consider, subject to consultation, that the new offence should apply to assistance in the commission of all statutory or common law offences; that 'assistance' should be understood in a broad common sense manner, but should exclude any such assistance by mere omission; that any such act of assistance, even of a trivial nature, should come within the offence; and that the nature and legal categorisation of the offence assisted should be identified, but not necessarily the time, place or other details of the offence.

4.31 A further important and difficult question concerns the mental element of the new offence. As already indicated in connection with the present law, there are two competing candidates: that the accessory should have as his purpose that the principal crime be committed; and that, as is the present law, he should merely have some form of awareness that the principal crime may be committed. In this paper we provisionally propose that, if 'awareness' is to be the test, it should at least be expressed in terms of the accessory's knowledge or belief that the principal crime is to be committed, in order to avoid the outcome, entirely possible under the present law, of convicting an assister who merely suspects that what he does may be of assistance towards a criminal offence. However, even after that amendment there are strong arguments in favour of limiting the offence of assistance to cases where it is the assister's purpose that the principal offence should be committed. Consultees' views as to the appropriateness of an inchoate offence of assisting may well be affected by whether that offence requires purpose, or only knowledge or belief, as to the commission of the principal crime.

4.32 For the purposes of the instant discussion, however, we will make the working assumption that it will suffice for liability for assisting an offence that the assister knows or believes that he is assisting the principal to do something that, if completed, would constitute the commission by that principal of an identified offence. On that approach, it is possible to formulate some extreme cases that could potentially fall under the new offence. Thus:

> D, a publican, or a generous host, believes that P is going to leave the premises in his car, but continues to ply him with drink to an extent that puts him well over the statutory limit. P does not in the event drive home.

D agrees to pay P, a builder doing repairs to his house, in cash rather than by cheque, believing that P wants payment in this form to assist him in defrauding the Inland Revenue. P in fact makes a proper return to the Revenue, either because he so intended all along, or because he suddenly realises the consequences of fraud.

D sells P oxyacetylene equipment, believing that P intends to commit a burglary using it. P does not commit the burglary: either because he is arrested at the scene of the crime; or because he thinks better of it; or because he never intended to do so.

D gives P advice as to how to circumvent the alarm system at a Bank, believing that P is going to use the advice to assist him to commit a burglary there. Because the advice is incorrect, P is unable to commit the burglary.

4.33 In all these cases, the principal crime has not taken place and therefore on one view no, or no sufficient, harm has occurred. That leads to objections at various levels of generality to an offence of inchoate assisting, which we consider in the following sections.

Non-intervention by the criminal law

4.34 This objection simply says that in cases where the principal crime has not been committed, and in particular in cases of the type referred to in paragraph 4.32 above, it is simply inappropriate for the criminal law to intervene. It may well be admitted that in each such case the conduct of D is much less than admirable. He is willing to do something that he thinks will assist the commission of a criminal offence, and thus actively and positively infringes the social obligation of a citizen to support, or at least not to attack, the law. But in the event, for whatever reason, the principal crime has not been committed; and it may therefore be thought inappropriate, unduly intrusive, or a waste of resources to bring the assister within the ambit of the criminal law. It can also be argued that where no substantive, principal offence has in fact occurred, the criminal law should be slow to intervene to impose constraints on behaviour, and indeed punishment. Comparisons might be drawn in this respect with the law of attempt, where the principal who fails to commit his crime will not be open to control by the law unless he has done an act more than merely preparatory to the commission of that crime.

4.35 Consultees will no doubt wish to bear these considerations in mind when commenting on the proposals in this paper. Two observations might, however, be ventured at this stage.

4.36 First, an inchoate offence of assisting does not, any more than does the inchoate offence of attempt, or of incitement, punish for thoughts alone. In all these cases the defendant must have acted on the strength of his beliefs, and have been ready so to act in a way that would, if his beliefs were correct, constitute, or (in the case of accessory liability) assist the commission of, conduct deemed by the law to be criminal. In some cases, such as the hypothetical cases suggested in paragraph 4.32 above, that may produce liability for conduct that, viewed 'objectively' (that is, without reference to the accused's beliefs and intentions), appears to be innocuous. In the parallel case of attempt, however, Parliament has determined that liability should attach to actions taken on the strength of the accused's beliefs even though, in truth, commission of the completed crime was an impossibility. And the House of Lords has recently stressed that liability in attempt should indeed be judged on the basis of the accused's intent and his carrying of those intentions into action, and not according to whether what he does is objectively innocent. Consultees may wish to have that parallel in mind when considering the practical impact, and justification in policy terms, of an inchoate offence of assisting.

4.37 Second, and more pragmatically, if the offence of assisting is not put on an inchoate basis, the law has no way of meeting the difficulties that are at present caused by the rule that there cannot be a conviction in respect of any form of assistance unless the crime sought to be aided is actually committed. Consultees may wish to consider whether any objections that they see to an inchoate offence of assistance outweigh the need to find a solution for the problems of the present law.

Comparison with the unconvicted principal

4.38 A further particular objection is that an inchoate offence of assisting could produce results that are, at least on the face of them, inconsistent and, thus, unfair. Thus, D provides equipment to P for P to use in a burglary on the following day. P is arrested, or repents, as he leaves D's house with the kit. P has committed neither burglary nor attempted burglary, and is liable for no preparatory offence in relation to that burglary; but D will be liable, for inchoate assistance in that burglary. In practice, D would be unlikely to be prosecuted, and it might in any event be difficult to prove his liability, but the theoretical implications of such a case must nonetheless be considered.

4.39 The first thing to say about this case is that the concern that it, at first sight, very understandably generates is in reality about having a law against assisting crime at all; or at least, a law against assisting any crime that was to take place in the future, as opposed to the limited liability for immediate assistance of the old principal in the second degree. In any case of assistance, and not just cases of inchoate assistance, the aider's act is complete, and culpable, once he has given the assistance, and it is for that that he is censured. In the case given in paragraph 4.38 above, D has done something that the law forbids, P has not. Under the present law it is a matter of chance, so far as D is concerned, whether he becomes guilty, that chance depending entirely on whether P commits the principal crime. If D is convicted of accessoryship, his conviction will depend entirely on what he did at his house, and what his mental state was then, and not on what his mental state was when P was actually committing the principal crime. If, despite fulfilling all those requirements, D is exculpated because and only because P happens to be arrested on his way to the burglary, that would seem to be the irrational outcome. And it is hard to see that such an outcome has any fairness in it if one compares the position of D with another alleged accessory, D2, who may have provided the same help in exactly similar circumstances to P2 but, unlike D, is convicted because P2 did go on to commit a crime.

4.40 Second, there may be very different reasons why P does not commit the crime. He may succeed in not committing the crime because he is inefficient, or because he is prevented by outside forces from carrying out his plans. In such a case he is simply lucky, and has no moral virtue on his side. It is very difficult to see that there is any unfairness or irrationality in saying that D, who is also criminally culpable, should in that case still be proceeded against for the criminal act that he has already completed. Again, the irrationality is if anything that of the present law, that in effect says that because P has been fortunate, so must D be also.

4.41 However, there may be more respectable, principled, reasons why P does not commit the crime, since he may abandon his plans either through prudence or through remorse. Here again, however, there is no rational reason why D should also escape liability for his act of (inchoate) assistance, merely because P repents before committing the crime. Such a unilateral act on P's part does not count for merit on the part of D. But what if P's act is not unilateral, but the failure to commit the principal offence is brought about by an intervention on the part of D?

4.42 With a strict law of inchoate liability, such acts will not avail D, because his own crime will already be complete. Such concerns can, however, be accommodated, albeit with some recognition of the need to allow commonsense and social policy to prevail over the demands of strict logic, by providing a defence of withdrawal even in the case of an inchoate inciter. Such defence as already exists in aiding and abetting is already difficult to reconcile with the doctrinal basis of that offence, since even though an accessory's liability does not at present crystallise until the commission of the principal offence, the accessory may have done all that depends on him for liability well before that commission takes place; but nevertheless considerations of social policy have prevailed, in order to encourage repentance on his part. We therefore consider in paragraphs 4.132ff below how such considerations should similarly be deployed in the case of the wider offence of assisting crime that we envisage. Such consideration will also enable the arguments in favour of a defence of withdrawal to be directed at the conduct that at present falls under the crime of incitement. Because incitement is a separate, inchoate, offence, withdrawal has never been thought relevant to it; but the policy arguments are just the same there as in the case of the assisting, or counselling, that falls under aiding and abetting.

Excessive width and vagueness

4.43 The other principal concern expressed about an offence of inchoate aiding is that, by removing the need to link the act of aiding to an actually committed principal offence, it will make the requirements for liability unduly vague and uncertain.

4.44 Such concerns are far from negligible. They have, however, to be confronted in the case of any inchoate offence, the clearest example of the working out of these general matters of principle being found in the law of attempt. What is necessary is that the rules applying to accessory conduct in the future should be formulated with these issues of principle clearly in mind. That will mean in particular, and as in the law of attempt, that the mental element required for conviction is clearly defined; and that sufficient action, and not merely thought, on the part of the accessory will have to be established before a conviction can be obtained.

4.45 We have attempted to observe these principles when making the provisional proposals that follow for the general law of assisting and encouraging crime. We venture to suggest that an approach along these lines is more likely to produce a fair and effective system than is reliance, as a controlling factor, on the need to show the actual commission of the principal crime. It will not be overlooked in that connection that in at least one area of the present law, the Bainbridge type of cases, the requirement of commission of the principal crime has, far from producing certainty, in fact introduced substantial vagueness into the law because of the need, in order to catch cases of significant wrongdoing, to escape from the unreal straitjacket that that requirement imposes.

4.46   We therefore proceed to discuss the elements of the offence of assisting crime on the basis that that offence will be of an inchoate nature: that is, that it can be committed whether or not the principal crime assisted is itself committed. As we have made plain, we particularly seek the comment of consultees as to whether that is the right course to adopt. We also invite consultees who consider that the offence should not be placed on an inchoate basis to indicate how, if at all, that affects their view of the constituents of the offence.

ASSISTING CRIME

The physical element of the offence

4.47   The basic definition of the conduct to be controlled by this part of the law is somewhat simpler to state than the physical element of incitement or encouragement. In the Draft Code we used the expression 'assist' as a basic and comprehensive term to indicate the form of conduct sought to be controlled, which we did not think required, or indeed admitted of, definition or expansion. We pointed out that the word is used, and has not presented any difficulties of definition, in other penal statutes, notably in the offences of assisting in the retention of stolen goods under section 22 of the Theft Act 1968.

4.48   We remain of that view; though we now invite comment, as in the Draft Code exercise we could not, as to whether 'assisting' is a sufficient and satisfactory concept for use in defining this part of the law.

4.49   So stated, any act that assists the commission of crime will, subject to *mens rea*, itself be criminal. We recognise that that might be thought to state the law in dangerously wide terms; that such concerns would largely disappear if the mental element necessary for conviction as an assister were narrowly defined. This would be particularly the case if it were to be required, as in the case of the Model Penal Code, that the assister act with the purpose or objective that a principal crime should be committed. This formulation would solve many of the (often hypothetical) cases that have caused concern because it is difficult to see any legitimate objection to criminalising, for instance, a shopkeeper who sells a screwdriver to a known burglar if *his purpose* in so doing is that burglary should take place.

4.50   However, there are strong and legitimate reasons for thinking that liability for complicity in criminal activity should not be so limited: most obviously, that a person who acts in a fashion that he knows will assist in the commission of crime, without having the commission as his purpose, nonetheless behaves in a clearly anti-social fashion. This dilemma cannot be resolved without balancing the desirability of checking such behaviour; and the possible limitations that might be placed on a law that attached liability to knowing assistance; against the possibly very wide ambit of a law that punished all cases of knowing assistance.

4.51   However, the balance can only be struck after full consideration of the implications of a law that did not limit liability to those whose purpose is to facilitate the commission of criminal offences. The competing merits of the two approaches to the *mens rea* of an assister referred to in paragraphs 4.49–4.50 above are fully discussed below, and consultees' advice is sought on them. Here we are concerned with what should be the physical elements of the offence. It is desirable to consider those issues in their widest application, and thus, at this stage, to forego the luxury of solving the undoubted policy problems presented by some aspects of that question by recourse to a narrow definition of the mental element required for liability for assisting crime. With that approach in mind, we now discuss some particular aspects of 'assistance'.

Advice as assistance

4.52   To quote the commentary on the Draft Code, a person assists another to commit an offence when, for example, he supplies tools or labour or information to the principal, or when he does any other act which facilitates the offence. 'Assistance' therefore includes advice as to how to commit a crime, as well as aid in a more physical form. Such advice may of course also, and perhaps often, be construable as encouragement, but in the present context we consider advice merely as a form of assistance.

4.53   There is little doubt that under the present law the provision of advice may constitute a form of aiding and abetting. That law has been strongly criticised because it 'gives too great an extension to criminal complicity. If the writer of the letter was guilty the first time his information was used, he would be guilty the nth time, which is absurd'. This problem is not limited to advice: multiple crimes by P, or others, with the same jemmy provided by D might be thought to pose the same problem. We doubt, however, whether in either case the problem is as extreme as is suggested: and in our view it is certainly not sufficiently difficult to justify the complete exclusion of the giving of advice from the category of assistance in crime.

4.54   First, some of the apparent oddity under the present law may stem from the requirement of regarding the accessory as a party to the crime actually committed, and thus as a party to each crime actually committed. Reason may feel strained by saying that D, by one piece of advice, 'committed' a hundred burglaries. However, the offence to reason is caused by the treating of D as a party to the eventual principal offences, rather than inculpating him for his original anti-social act of advice. The reshaping of accessory liability in inchoate form will ensure that liability is focused on that original act. Second, as Woolf J pointed out in Able, advice, to ground liability, must be given with the necessary *mens rea*: which, even if it does not involve purpose that the principal crime be committed, on any view will require at least awareness that that crime may be committed with the use of the advice.

4.55   On that basis, therefore, we are unpersuaded (though we invite comment) that advice on how to commit crimes should not be included within the potential category of complicity by assistance. However, to treat information or advice as a category of assistance for the purpose of the law of complicity as is presently assumed to be the law, provokes two more general reflections on which it will be necessary to comment further. The first is that if we are concerned with inchoate assisting it is necessary to define carefully the alleged offence or offences in respect of which the criminal advice is proffered: in other words, to be certain that the conduct of P about which D advised was sufficiently identified as being criminal in nature. That is a general problem, for assistance in the sense of help as well as for advice, to which we return in paragraphs 4.57ff below.

4.56 Secondly, the social reasons for including mere advice within criminal facilitation may appear more obviously attractive in some cases than in others. Perhaps an extreme example is the contrast between terrorist manuals describing methods of creating explosions with the booklet published by the Voluntary Euthanasia Society. However, accessory, and any other inchoate, liability is justifiable primarily because it assists and supports conduct that has been identified by the law as sufficiently anti-social to be categorised as criminal. It is not the obvious function of the law of accessory liability to discriminate, in terms of relative seriousness, between different forms of crime. However, we consider below whether there should be made available specific defences to exculpate those who provide assistance for criminal acts in circumstances that are, in general social terms, innocuous or of positive social benefit.

The offence assisted

4.57 As in the present law, the principal offence relevant to accessory liability is to be identified according to the accessory's knowledge or belief in respect of the principal's actions. We suggest that the offence assisted will be sufficiently identified if the accessory is required to know or believe, first, that the principal is committing acts that constitute the commission of a crime or intends to commit acts that, if carried through, would constitute the commission of a crime; and, second, that his, the accessory's, acts assist or will assist the principal in the commission of that crime. A number of points arise on that formulation.

4.58 Where the crime is actually in progress at the time of the assistance, for instance in the common case of D keeping watch whilst P commits the actual burglary, the identification of that crime will not cause difficulty. Where the principal crime is in the future, it would in our view be unreasonably restrictive to require knowledge or belief on the part of D in all the detail that would be necessary in order to indict the principal crime. In particular, it should not be required that D can necessarily state the time or place of the principal crime, or identify its victim. However, he should be shown to have known or believed P's future course of action in sufficient detail for it to be possible in charging him to identify the branch of the criminal law that P's conduct would infringe. Thus, if P asked D to supply him with gelignite, or to drive him to a particular location, D must be shown to have believed that P intended to use the gelignite, or to engage at the location in conduct that would in law amount to, for example, 'burglary', 'unlawfully causing an explosion', 'murder' or 'unlawful wounding'. If a principal crime cannot be identified in that way, in our view it makes the law too imprecise to retain the possibility of accessory liability. Without identification of the principal crime, suppliers and assisters would be liable to be convicted simply on the basis of a belief on their part that the other party was going to do something unlawful, but they did not know what.

4.59 We have spoken above in terms of the legal category into which the principal's acts fall. The accessory need not, of course, know what that legal category is, or the reasons in law that make the principal's conduct criminal, any more than the principal himself need know that his conduct is illegal. What the accessory has to know or believe are the facts that do or would constitute the commission of a crime by the principal.

4.60 Those facts include, except in the case of an offence of strict liability on the part of the principal, the mental state or *mens rea* necessary for conviction of the principal crime. Again, that will normally not give rise to any difficulty. Where the crime is in the actual course of commission at the time of the assistance, P's state of mind should be clear to D. Where assistance is given in advance, D will be inculpated according to his understanding of P's future intentions; so in the normal case he will only be inculpated where he understands that P will intentionally commit a criminal act. There might, however, be cases where D knew that P intended to commit the *actus reus* of a crime, but mistakenly believed in the existence of circumstances that would make P's act non-criminal. In such cases D should not be liable for complicity. Examples are:

> P asks D to keep watch outside a house which P was to enter to retrieve goods which, P falsely told D, belonged to P himself. D therefore believed that P's removal of the goods would be honest and thus, in law, not theft.

> D sees P fighting with X. D holds down Y, a friend of X, in order to prevent his restraining P. D believes, wrongly, that P is acting in reasonable self-defence, so that on the facts as D believes them to be P would be committing no crime.

> D provides a pass that entitles P to gain access to a public building. The pass is, unknown to D, a forgery. In presenting the pass P would commit an offence under section 3 of the Forgery and Counterfeiting Act 1981 if he knew or believed the pass to be false. P knows of the forgery, and thus commits the offence, but the state of D's knowledge is such that he believes P to be innocent.

> P and D are babysitting in X's house while he is out for the evening. P informs D that she wishes to borrow a book belonging to X, which is on the top shelf and can only be reached by D. D gets the book down for her, and she puts it in her bag. While D believes that she will bring the book back after she has read it, P actually intends to keep it permanently.

4.61 We have spoken above of 'the principal', who will normally be a particular person identified by name by D. We do not, however, think that that should be a necessary precondition of liability. We may give an example adapted from the facts of the conspiracy case of Hollinshead. D1 manufactures devices for use in defrauding the electricity authorities, which he knows can only be used for that purpose. He supplies them to D2, expecting and intending that D2 should sell them to people who wish and intend to use the devices for that dishonest purpose. In that case D1 believes that the ultimate purchasers will commit the criminal offence by use of the boxes, and knows that the boxes will assist in the commission of that offence. He does not know who the principals will be; but he knows that they will exist, since they are the only 'market' for his boxes. In such a case, provided, importantly, that the requirements of knowledge and belief on the part of D1 are fulfilled, it would seem entirely right that he should be convicted of assisting, even though he cannot specify the names of the ultimate offenders, or when exactly they are going to commit their offences.

4.62　Where the principal offence is one of strict liability, the only factor that the accessory has to be aware of, in order to be aware of the existence of the principal offence, is the commission by the principal of the forbidden act: because the definition of the principal offence consists of the commission of that act, and no more. That has given rise to some discussion as to whether, when one is considering the *mens rea* of the accessory, something less than knowledge or belief in the forbidden circumstances on his part should be sufficient to convict him of accessoryship. We discuss that question further, as part of our consideration of *mens rea* issues, in paragraph 4.89 below.

4.63　The need to identify the principal offence, together with the possibility of liability on an inchoate basis, will resolve the *Bainbridge* problem. Where a principal offence other than that expected by D is committed by P, the question will be whether, at the time at which D gave his assistance, any future offence was sufficiently identified as the object of that assistance. That we suggest to be a more precise, and fairer, basis on which to convict D than the erratic comparison of the expected and the actual conduct of the principal that the present law forced on the court in *Bainbridge* itself.

A *de minimis* principle for assistance?

4.64　To say that any act of 'assistance' is *prima facie* sufficient to ground liability opens the prospect of such liability in cases where the assister's contribution might be thought very slight: 'for example, a prosecution for facilitating an offence of Sunday trading by giving a shop assistant a lift to the illegally open DIY on a rainy Sunday'. Like Mr Spencer, we do not favour the avoidance of the apparent oddity of that outcome by limiting the assistance (or indeed the encouragement) offences to indictable or otherwise 'serious' offences. If certain types of 'assistance' are not sufficient to incur criminal liability, that should be so irrespective of the nature of the criminal conduct perpetrated. Moreover, the example has force not so much because it relates to a principal activity which not everybody thinks it wise to criminalise, but, more pressingly, because the act of assistance seems remote from the actual commission of the principal crime. Thus, it is not the shop assistant, but the supermarket chain who are his employers, who make the sales that breach section 47 of the Shops Act 1950. The employers will no doubt open for business, albeit with marginally less convenience and efficiency, and make illegal sales, whether or not this particular assistant arrives for work; and many other factors, including cooperation by suppliers of services and of the goods to be sold, not to mention the presence of customers, are necessary before the prohibited supply can take place.

4.65　The possibility of what might be acts incidental to or remote from the commission of the principal offence attracting accessory liability appears to have been one of the reasons ... for the original draft of the Model Penal Code having required that an accessory's acts should have substantially facilitated the commission of the principal offence. This expression or, we would think, any similar expression seeking to introduce the same type of limitation raises difficult issues of judgement, not least because it is not possible to require a causal connection between the act of assistance and the commission of the principal crime. There are also difficult issues of policy: in particular in the assumption that some actions that as a matter of fact assist in the commission of crime can nonetheless be excused as insignificant. It would seem to be considerations of this sort that led the American Law Institute to abandon the requirement of substantial facilitation of the principal offence in favour of the simple giving of aid in its commission.

4.66 It should be noted, however, that that change in the MPC formulation took place at the same time as the MPC adopted the requirement that D should have had the purpose of promoting or facilitating the commission of the principal offence. This is therefore yet another case where restriction of the ambit of complicity to acts of the complicitor done with the purpose that the principal crime should be committed would solve a problem of excessive width of the law. Where it is D's purpose in giving assistance that the principal crime should be committed, he cannot legitimately claim to be exculpated on the ground that his assistance was in the event not substantial.

4.67 A final decision on the present point can perhaps, therefore, only be taken in the light of the discussion of whether purpose, or merely awareness, should be the mental requirement for complicity. The potential width of a physical element in an offence of complicity stated only in terms of assistance is clearly a material factor in that debate. Even, however, if it were to be concluded that awareness that conduct will be of assistance should indeed be sufficient to create liability in the offence of complicity, it might still be considered that any conduct that is legitimately described as assisting the commission of a crime should come within the reach of this offence. We however invite comment on that point, and on whether the definition of 'assistance' should be qualified to apply only to 'substantial', 'material' or other limited types of assistance.

4.68 A case which requires particular attention is where the assistance is remote from the commission of a principal crime, for example where D assists someone who is himself merely committing an accessory or inchoate offence. To adapt the example given above, this would occur if D gives a lift to work to an employee of a company supplying goods to the supermarket trading illegally on Sunday. There are in our view good reasons of policy why generally such cases should not attract criminal liability. Since those reasons reach more widely than problems about the definition of 'assistance', the issue is discussed separately in paragraphs 4.180–4.184 below.

Omissions as 'assistance'

4.69 Is there, and should there be, an offence of assisting the commission of a criminal offence by a mere omission? In the Draft Code the Commission considered that the present law could not be stated less broadly than that

> Assistance or encouragement includes assistance or encouragement arising from a failure by a person to take reasonable steps to exercise any authority or to discharge any duty he has to control the relevant acts of the principal in order to prevent the commission of the offence.

4.70 This formulation merely states the type of conduct that can potentially amount to assistance or encouragement, if as a matter of fact the conduct has that effect. It does not state that failure to exercise authority necessarily makes a person in authority an accomplice. Nevertheless, we are satisfied that it is unsatisfactory as a statement of a reformed law of complicity. In the Draft Code it was necessary to reproduce the structure of the present law in which, within the general category of 'aiding and abetting', assistance and encouragement are simply two different forms of what is, in law, the same activity, each therefore governed by exactly the same rules. It is however clear that passivity and omission have very different implications according to whether they are considered as a form of assistance, or as a form of encouragement.

4.71 'Assistance', in the normal sense that we think the word should be given, extends to any conduct on the part of D that, as a matter of fact, makes it easier for P to commit the principal offence. We do not think that that concept will be difficult to apply in cases where the alleged assistance consists of positive conduct on D's part: supplying tools for use in the principal crime; giving advice on how to commit a crime; driving P to the scene of the offence; or positively misleading or obstructing the police or other law enforcement agents. However, if that legal category of assistance can include 'conduct' consisting of a merely passive failure to act the obligations placed on D appear to be uncertain of definition; unreasonably wide; and inconsistent with other principles governing the criminal law.

4.72 Those objections can be illustrated from the statement of the present law contained in clause 27(3) of the Draft Code. The duties there referred to may not even be confined to legal, rather than merely social or moral, duties. But even if the duties referred to are so confined, it Would seem to follow from the citizen's general, if somewhat undefined, duty to assist the police, or at least from the citizen's undoubted authority to use such force as is reasonable in the prevention of crime, that any failure on the part of D to intervene to prevent the commission of a crime by P would convict D of complicity in that crime. And, in more specific cases, D can find himself obliged, in order to avoid an accusation of assisting the commission of an offence, to take very positive action. The clearest example is perhaps *Tuck v Robson*, where a landlord was convicted of aiding and abetting his customers to consume liquor after permitted hours. He had called 'time', and asked the customers to leave, but there was held nonetheless to be 'passive assistance in the sense of presence with no steps being taken to enforce his right either to eject the customers or at any rate to revoke their licence to be on the premises.' It is doubtful whether the landlord was under any duty to eject his customers, apart from that imposed ex post facto by the law of complicity. However, he clearly had 'authority' to remove them, based on his control of the premises; as the car-owner in *Du Cros v Lambourne* had authority, based on his ownership, to require the speeding driver of the car to slow down. In each case it would seem that failure to exercise, or rather to attempt to exercise, that authority was enough to convict D as an assister.

4.73 Some of the uncertainty of the law turns on whether, in these and similar cases, D's conduct can naturally be described as 'assistance' at all. However, the natural meaning of that word does not exclude cases of inaction; and if (as we provisionally propose)' the general law should require only awareness on the part of the defendant of the assisting nature of his conduct, then many cases of inaction would *prima facie* fall within this offence. A general law of complicity that extended to merely passive assistance would, however, be burdensome, because it would place obligations of law enforcement on those who, under rules of law completely unconnected with the crimes in question, had a duty or even merely authority to act to impede the commission of a principal crime. The law importantly recognises that restraint should be exercised in imposing criminal liability for a mere omission, though opinion differs as to how far and on what basis that restraint does and should extend. It would however seem reasonable that that restraint should in particular be exercised when determining the limits of liability for an inchoate offence. Our judgement, on which we invite comment, is therefore that a general offence of assisting crime would be extended too far if it were applied to cases where the accused had afforded assistance' in the commission of a principal crime simply by failing to discharge a duty or exercise an authority that, if acted on, would or might have prevented the commission of the offence.

4.74 Nor do we see, any more than did the Commission when formulating the Draft Code, any way of reasonably limiting liability for 'passive assistance' to a specific range of cases. The general objections to this head of liability are in our view too great, and the number of cases in which it would be even arguably desirable to enforce it are too few, for attempts to produce a limited version of passive assistance to be justifiable. We therefore provisionally conclude that the offence of assisting in the commission of crime should be limited to positive acts of assistance on the part of the accused.

4.75 'Encouragement' raises different issues. As we will indicate below, encouragement is by its nature limited to cases where it is the object or intention of D that P should commit the principal crime; and in such cases it is much more clearly arguable that any conduct properly described as encouraging or stirring up P to the commission of crime should fall within the law of complicity, even though the encouraging conduct consists of what might be characterised as mere omission on D's part. We will therefore return to this issue when we consider the separate head of complicity liability, based on encouragement rather than assistance, that we discuss in paragraphs 4.143ff below.

THE MENTAL ELEMENT OF THE OFFENCE

Purpose or awareness?

4.76 The controversy in the present law as to whether the accessory must have the commission of the principal crime as his purpose has been discussed at length earlier in this paper. On the basis of that discussion, the issues for the future structure of the law can be dealt with comparatively shortly; bearing in mind that we are here concerned only with assisting, and not with encouraging, the commission of crime.

4.77 If D had to have as his purpose the commission of a crime by P, many of the concerns that have been expressed as to the possibly excessive width of a law of complicity would resolve themselves. Thus, if D provides P with a jemmy with the purpose that P should commit a burglary using it; or D permits an overloaded lorry to leave his premises because it is his purpose that it should be driven on the road, and not merely because he wants to sell more coal with complete indifference to what happens to the coal or how it is transported; or a doctor provides contraceptives to a fifteen year old girl for the purpose of removing her lover's inhibitions from intercourse, and not merely as a precaution against pregnancy should that intercourse occur; then there is unlikely to be concern on policy grounds about any of those defendants being convicted of complicity. Somewhat similarly, even if D's assistance seems of only minimal help towards the commission of the principal crime, doubts about convicting D of complicity are likely to be stilled if that assistance was given with the purpose of bringing about the commission of the crime.

4.78   However if, as is the present law, all that is required is awareness on the part of D that his acts might assist in the commission of the principal offence, then the law of complicity reaches a wide variety of activities, some at least of which might not instinctively be thought appropriately visited with criminal liability.

4.79   The choice between these two differing approaches is one of policy, on which we seek the views of consultees, and on which we do not think it appropriate, at this stage, to express any concluded opinion. However, in seeking those views we venture to draw attention to some considerations that we think relevant to the decision.

Should indifference to the commission of crime excuse?

4.80   First, to limit liability to cases where it was the accused's purpose to promote the commission of the principal crime would, necessarily, exclude cases where the accused knew that he was in fact assisting the principal in the commission of a crime, but was merely indifferent as to whether or not that crime was in fact committed. That would mean that, in particular, one who supplied goods or services that he knew were to be used in crime, but did so purely for the motive of gain and not specifically to promote the commission of the crime, would himself commit no offence. It is far from obvious that that outcome is correct, either from the point of view of justice or from the point of view of social protection. It might well be thought that those who willingly and knowingly assist in crime should be liable to punishment, not least as some means of impeding the commission of the crimes that they would otherwise assist in; and that they act for profit should hardly be a reason for excusing them.

Special cases to be excluded?

4.81   Second, a law based on mere awareness of the criminal intentions of the principal would necessarily encompass some at least who acted not in order to promote their own interests but for higher purposes. Those cases may, however, be accommodated by providing specific defences in particular cases of assistance. Some such defences have been suggested, though with uncertain status and in uncertain terms, under the present law. We review below what specific cases might be exempted from liability under a law of assisting that went wider than cases of purpose on the part of the accomplice, and how those cases might be defined. We invite comment not only on the defences so formulated, but also on whether, if those and perhaps other defences were available, a general test of liability, based more broadly on awareness rather than purpose, might be more acceptable.

The test of knowledge or belief

4.82   Third, if the test for the mental element of the assisting offence is to be broader than purpose that the principal offence be committed, that test must be defined with some care. We consider that the law would in any event be too broad if it were formulated in terms of, or in terms that could be interpreted as requiring only suspicion as to the principal's intentions. That consideration is particularly relevant to supply of assistance 'in the ordinary course of business': for instance, the sale of a screwdriver or the provision of a taxi ride to a person known or thought to be a professional burglar. In such a case, D may well legitimately suspect that P will use the assistance given to him in one of his burglaries; but it seems too restrictive of ordinary activities to make supply criminal on the basis simply of suspicion of the use to which the supply is to be put.

4.83 We accordingly suggest that if the law were to be formulated in terms of 'awareness' the test should be that the accessory knows or believes that the principal is using or will use the assistance in the commission of a crime. 'Knowing or believing' is a concept already familiar in the law from its use to describe the necessary state of mind of a person charged with handling stolen goods under section 22 of the Theft Act 1968. It has been stressed, admittedly after some different and more elaborate approaches to that section, that 'knowledge or belief' are words of ordinary usage, which in normal circumstances can be simply applied by the jury without further elaboration. This branch of the law also recognises that mere suspicion, or the presence of suspicious circumstances, does not suffice to establish the existence of belief.

4.84 The belief that, in complicity by assistance, the accused must be shown to hold is that the principal crime will, not merely may, be committed: because a belief as to a future possibility collapses into mere suspicion.

The practical effect of the 'belief' test

4.85 It may be objected that to require belief, rather than merely suspicion, on the part of an accessory encourages the turning of a blind eye to criminality, or may exculpate those who ignore the obvious. That, of course, is very much the other side of the coin from the contention that only those whose purpose is the commission of the principal offence should be convicted of complicity. However, the reality is that suspicious circumstances known to the accused are evidence of belief, particularly if the accused enters into transactions in such circumstances on a number of occasions; and where such an accused is a willing and regular supplier of assistance in criminal activities juries can be relied on to deal realistically with claims that he suspected, but had no belief about, the use to which his assistance was to be put. To quote a commentator from another jurisdiction: 'The person most likely to be caught by this part of the law is the recurrent supplier in suspicious circumstances, and there is no reason why he should not be'. The belief test will, however, exclude from liability for complicity those who conduct ordinary businesses, even with suspect customers, and that again is in our view a proper limitation on the law.

4.86 We would also suggest that the operation, and the benefits, of the belief test are easier to appreciate when it is remembered that the offence of complicity that we propose will be inchoate in nature, complete once the act of assistance is done. Under the present law, when the issue of complicity only arises for consideration if the principal crime is actually committed, the accessory's mental state has nonetheless still to be assessed at the moment when he actually provides the assistance. That concentration on the commission of the principal crime may, however, make it all too easy to assume that, at the earlier stage of providing what proved in the event to be assistance towards the commission of a crime, the accessory must have known that that crime would be committed. We venture to suggest that, under an offence that looks only at facts existing at the time of the provision of the advice, materials or other help, it is easier to see that the accused must be judged according to his mental state at that time; and that, broadly put, his fault is based on willingness to assist in the commission of crime, whether or not in the event a crime is actually committed with the assistance that he provides.

The 'shopping-list' case

4.87   A test couched in terms of purpose that a particular crime should be committed, and a test in terms of belief that a particular crime will be committed, both equally fail to catch what has been described as the 'shopping list' case, exemplified by *DPP v Maxwell* where the accessory knows or believes that his actions will assist in the commission of one of a number of possible crimes, but he does not know which one. In *Maxwell* itself, the accused had driven members of a terrorist organisation to premises of a person to whom they were opposed, knowing that some form of terrorism was to be perpetrated there, but not knowing whether it was intended to be damage by bombing to the premises, murder of the occupiers, or lesser assaults upon them.

4.88   It would in our view make unduly vague the definition of the 'offence' that the accessory has to contemplate if this case were sought to be contained within a single formula covering all cases of accessory liability. If this were done the accessory would only be required to believe that there was to be committed acts that would be 'criminal', without having to show any belief on his part as to the specific characteristics of those acts that would make them criminal. We therefore consider that special provision should be made for cases such as *Maxwell*. The basic test should remain that the accessory knows or believes that his conduct will assist the principal in the commission of a specific crime. However, the accessory should also be liable where he knows or believes that his conduct will assist the principal in the commission of one of a number of such specific crimes, but does not know in which of those specific crimes his assistance will in fact be used.

The principal's *mens rea*: a special rule for crimes of strict liability?

4.89   We referred in paragraph 4.62 above to the issue, much debated in theoretical discussions of the present law, of whether in the case of offences of strict liability the rule should be relaxed that the accessory must, at the least, believe in the present or future existence of the elements constituting the principal offence.

4.90   The case round which discussion traditionally centres is *Callow v Tillstone*. A butcher relied on a certificate of fitness for human consumption given negligently by a veterinary surgeon, and offered unsound meat for sale. He was found liable for the (strict liability) offence of exposing unsound meat for sale, but the surgeon's negligence was insufficient to incriminate him as an abettor in the sale. It has been strongly argued that it is unjust and anomalous, and an impediment to the effective implementation of the social policy that lies behind the creation of strict liability offences, if a negligently culpable secondary party, who could be regarded as primarily responsible for the actions of the principal, may go unpunished. To avoid that anomaly, it is argued, negligence on the part of the accessory should suffice for his conviction.

4.91 We invite comment on this suggestion, but for our part we see difficulties in developing the law in that manner. That is principally because caution should be exercised in creating offences of negligence, which in our view have to be justified on the basis of a careful analysis of the social and law enforcement need for imposing such liability in the particular circumstances of each case. Such assessment is, of necessity, precluded by the imposition of a rule of negligence liability that extends over all offences of strict liability, whatever the status and role in those offences of the accessory. It is also quite unclear why, if law enforcement requires the imposition of negligence liability on accessories to crimes of strict liability, that rationale should not extend also to *mens rea* crimes. Those crimes, as a category, are to be presumed to be at least as deserving of deterrence by stringent rules of accessory liability as are principal crimes of strict liability. If the approach of the present law to accessory responsibility in strict liability offences is thought to create anomalies in particular cases, those anomalies are in our present view more appropriately cured by the imposition of express and limited liability, as *principals*, on those who are culpably involved in activities that have been prohibited by statute.

The alternative: 'purpose' as the *mens rea* of assisting crime

4.92 The foregoing paragraphs assume that knowledge or belief as to the principal's present or future commission of the crime assisted should suffice to convict of the offence of assisting crime. There is, however, a different possible view.

4.93 If accessory liability were to attach only in cases where it could be shown that the assister's purpose in giving help was that the principal crime should be committed, then, as we pointed out in paragraph 4.77 above, many of the objections, on grounds of potentially excessive width, to an offence of assistance would fall away. Thus, it is difficult to think that there would be serious objection to a rule that forbade even minor assistance towards a criminal end; or which forbade a doctor from providing contraceptives that might assist in unlawful intercourse; if in both cases the defendant had acted with the purpose of bringing about the commission of the crime. The law would also be made simpler: because if it is a precondition to liability that the accused must have the commission of the principal crime as his purpose there would be little justification or need for the special defences that exempt difficult cases from the general rule of liability on the grounds of mere knowledge of or belief in the principal's criminal intentions.

4.94 A further argument in favour of limiting the offence of assisting crime to cases where it is the accused's purpose that the principal offence should be committed is that that might make it appear more acceptable to place the offence on an inchoate basis. It may simply seem more acceptable that defendants, for instance in the examples suggested in paragraph 4.32 above, should be convicted of assisting when the principal crime has not been committed if they gave their assistance with the purpose that that crime should be committed, and not merely in a state of knowing indifference as to whether the principal crime took place or not.

4.95 We therefore specifically invite comment on whether the offence of assisting crime should be limited to cases where it is the assister's purpose that the principal crime should be committed.

4.96 It will be appreciated that such a rule would exclude from liability many cases where there might be thought to be strong reasons for the law to intervene. For instance, the regular supplier of goods or of transport, who well knows that they are to be used for criminal purposes, but is merely interested in making a profit on the sale; or, more generally, commercial suppliers who would positively prefer the completed crime not to take place, so long as they obtain payment, since that may make their part in the affair less likely to be detected.

4.97 We invite comment on whether, if such cases were to be excluded from liability by a general 'purpose' rule, there should nonetheless be special provisions that inculpated some of the assisters referred to in paragraph 4.96 above albeit that they could only be shown to have acted in the knowledge or belief that crimes were being or would be committed. The identification of the appropriate categories for such a rule, and the justification of imposing liability in those categories rather than others, is a matter of some difficulty. For instance, the liability might be limited to those who provide what could be 'equipment' for use in crime; or to those who provide transport to the scene of a crime; or to those who do any act for gain or reward. We do not ourselves see any of those categories as self-evidently standing out from acts of assistance generally, and foresee some considerable problems of legislative definition. However, we invite comment from those who reject the general test of knowledge or belief on the part of the, accessory as to whether they consider that it would be desirable, and practical, to adopt that test in any, and if so what, special categories of assistance.

4.98 We have already pointed out that if 'purpose' that the principal crime should be committed were to be adopted as the general test for liability on the part of an assister, then it will not be necessary to consider many of the further rules, and in particular the provision of special defences, that are thought to be required by the 'knowledge or belief' test. In order to enable discussion of those latter rules, therefore, it will be convenient if we proceed from this point on the basis of the knowledge or belief test; while not forgetting that we particularly invite comment on whether that test is correct.

Our provisional definition of the offence of assisting crime

4.99 We hope that it may assist readers in critically reviewing the discussion in this section if we set out in something like statutory form the basic definition of the offence that results from it. We suggest

(1) A person commits the offence of assisting crime if he

(a) knows or believes that another ('the principal') is doing or causing to be done, or will do or cause to be done, acts that do or will involve the commission of an offence by the principal; and

(b) knows or believes that the principal, in so acting,, does or will do so with the fault required for the offence in question; and

(c) does any act ... that he knows or believes assists or will assist the principal in committing that offence.

(2) Assistance includes giving the principal advice as to commit the offence, or as to how to avoid detection or apprehension before or during the commission of the offence.

(3) A person does not assist the commission of an offence for the purposes of this section if all that he does is to fail to prevent or impede the commission of that offence.

(4) 'Offence' in sub-paragraphs (a)–(c) of sub-section (1) above means the breach of a specified prohibition laid down by statute or the common law; but, provided the defendant knows or believes sufficient facts to show that such a breach is taking place or will take place, he need not know the time, place or other details of the offence.

(5) A person also commits an offence under this section if he knows or believes that the principal intends to commit one of a number of offences and does any act that he knows or believes will assist the principal in committing whichever of those offences the principal in fact intends.

Defences to an offence of assisting crime

4.100 The normal 'general' defences, applying throughout the criminal law, will apply also to this offence. In this section we consider rather what defences or, perhaps more accurately expressed, exemptions from liability ought to be provided in the specific case of criminal assistance. As we have already observed, such exemptions are most likely to be thought necessary if the general definition of such an offence includes all cases where the provider of assistance does so in the belief that the principal is committing or will commit a crime. Within that general rule, different considerations may apply in those cases where the accessory's purpose in providing his assistance is to bring about the commission of the principal crime. We deal specifically with such cases in paragraphs 4.138–4.140 below. Many of the issues have already been raised in our discussion of the resent law.

Persons involved in statutory offences

4.101 The present defence, based on *Tyrrell*, is very uncertain in its content, but it would seem to be limited to those who, although technically aiders and abettors of a statutory offence, can be identified as the 'victim' intended to be protected by the enactment creating the offence. We were forced to put the defence in that limited form when stating the present law in the Draft Code; and that formulation has led to elaborate and technical interpretative speculation as to whether or not Parliament can be taken to have seen a particular category of persons as 'victims' of the particular statutory offence under consideration.

4.102 Not only must such speculation be put to rest, but also, in our provisional view, the defence or exemption should be stated much more widely than at present. Many statutory offences are so defined as to require the participation of two people before they can be committed: obvious examples include offences of sale, which require a buyer before they can be committed; and the offence of carrying on an unregistered care home for old or disabled persons under section 2 of the Registered Homes Act 1984, which would seem to need the assistance of the inmates before it can be committed. Where Parliament has created such an offence, but has not seen fit at the same time to impose principal liability on those who assist in the acts that constitute the offence, we do not think that those people should be even theoretically at risk under the law of complicity.

4.103 We therefore propose a rule, in terms similar to those recommended by the Commission's Working Party in 1972, that a person is not guilty of complicity by assisting an offence if the offence is so defined that his conduct is inevitably incidental to its commission and that conduct is not made criminal by that offence.

4.104 That rule will, we think, apply only in the case of statutory crimes, because there does not appear to be any common law crime defined in such a way as to make the participation of another party inevitably incidental to its commission. The rule will mainly affect what are sometimes regarded as 'regulatory', non-indictable, offences, such as offences of sale; but, as the discussion of the present and more limited law has shown, it would also extend to sexual offences of some gravity.

4. 105 It is, again, important to point out that this rule applies only to complicity by assistance. Some difficulty was seen both by the Working Party, and by the Commission itself when formulating the Draft Code, in a rule that exculpated from liability a 'victim', or incidental party, who had nonetheless initiated or encouraged the commission of the offence. That would indeed be the effect of a rule such as that here under consideration if applied to the present law of accessoryship, since it would exempt the alleged accessory from the 'counselling' as well as from the 'aiding' limb of aiding and abetting. The rule that we propose is however restricted to what our predecessors saw as its most clearly justified role, the limitation of liability for mere assistance. We discuss separately below' whether any such rule should also apply in cases where the accessory has encouraged or initiated the commission of the offence.

Employees

4.106 A further category of persons who might well be thought to be unjustifiably at risk under a crime of assisting that required only belief that the principal crime was being committed, and who are indeed at risk under the present law, are the employees of individuals or, more usually, companies that break certain kinds of statutory prohibitions. The problem can be demonstrated from the example discussed in paragraph 4.64 above, of the motorist giving a lift to a shop assistant travelling to work at an illegally opened DIY store. The example was originally formulated in the light of concern for the position of the motorist; but if the motorist is potentially liable for assisting the unlawful sale, the shop assistant must be also.

4.107 We believe (though we invite comment on the point) that in such a case there would be strong objections to the shop assistant being even theoretically at risk of liability for complicity. However, the formulation of an effective and properly limited exemption in such a case poses some problems. The related rule that we propose in paragraph 4.103 does not clearly exclude from liability employees who merely assist the principal in the course of their employment, not least since an offence of, for instance, 'sale' is not expressed in such a way as necessarily to require the assistance of an employee of the seller, as opposed to the presence of a buyer. Nor should there be a blanket rule exempting all assistance given in the course of employment: one has only to think of the bodyguards of a violent professional criminal or, less dramatically, the bookkeepers of a fraudulent loan business to see the impossibility of such a rule.

4.108 We have indicated that, in general, we do not think that it is desirable to have different regimes for complicity liability according to whether the principal offence is indictable or only summary in nature. However, we think that that distinction might legitimately be employed to achieve in practical terms the protection that we seek for employees, that they should not find themselves threatened with criminal liability just because the business that employs them has used their services as employees when breaking regulatory or statutory rules. We therefore provisionally propose that an employee should not be liable for complicity by assistance in a summary offence committed by his employer in respect of acts that he does within the course of his employment.

4.109 In the case of more serious offences, where the exemption will not apply, we recognise that employees may be put in the situation where they have to disobey their employer in order to avoid liability for complicity. However, that in itself is no cause of objection: indeed, one of the reasons for having a law of complicity at all is to deter all potential assisters, and not merely employees, from giving assistance in criminal enterprises. The limited rule that we provisionally propose in paragraph 4.108 above however seeks to recognise one type of case in which that general objective may be thought legitimately to yield to the problems caused to an employee by law-breaking conduct on the part of his employer.

4.110 The foregoing discussion is couched solely in terms of exempting an employee from complicity in offences committed by his employer. We provisionally consider, however, that, so long as this defence is limited to cases of complicity in summary offences, the exemption should also extend to persons whose acts of assistance towards the commission of summary offences by third parties are done in the course of their employment. For instance, P seeks to acquire premises that he intends to use as a common lodging house, but without registering with the local housing authority, the use thus involving a summary offence under sections 402 and 408(1)(a) of the Housing Act 1985. In seeking and acquiring those premises he employs the services of D1, an estate agent, and D2, a solicitor. Not only D1 and D2, but also the members of their staff who actually handle the transaction, are aware of P's unlawful intentions. It would seem on balance to go too far to inculpate the staff members, who were simply carrying out their employer's instructions, as complicitors.

4.111 That said, we should emphasise two further points. First, where the principal offence is indictable, the balance between crime prevention, and the putting of undue burdens on employees, would seem to come down in favour of the deterrent effect of requiring the employee not to obey instructions that involve him in assisting in serious crime, in the same way as we have suggested that this dilemma should be resolved in the case of serious offences committed by the employer. Thus, for instance, we do not think that it should be an excuse for a shop assistant who administers a sale of equipment that he knows or believes is going to be used in a burglary that he was only doing his job. Secondly, in the example given in 4.110 above, as at present advised we see no objection to the employers, D1 and D2, being liable for complicity, provided they have the required knowledge of P's intentions, even though the offences in question are only summary. We revert to the question of whether there should be a general exemption from the law of complicity when the principal offence is summary only in paragraphs 4.171ff below. We suggest there that those who knowingly assist in what may be quite serious regulatory offences should be controlled by this branch of the law.

4.112 This defence or exception would, again, apply only in the case of complicity by assistance. Different considerations apply in the case of complicity by encouragement, which we discuss in paragraph 4.143ff below.

Supply in the ordinary course of business

4.113 A type of case that is frequently cited as needing to be excluded from complicity liability is that of 'ordinary business supply'. Thus, the taxi driver who takes a fare to the scene of the crime; the Coal Board that in *NCB v Gamble* supplied the coal that constituted the illegal load; and the wholesalers who sell goods to DIY companies who are going to retail them on Sunday; are all actually or very arguably guilty of complicity under the present law.

4.114 If the law of assisting crime were to be reformed to require purpose on the part of the assister that the principal crime should be committed, these cases are unlikely to cause problems. Such suppliers are unlikely to have as their positive purpose the commission of crime, as opposed to the making of a profit for themselves. If they do have that purpose there seems no reason why they should not be held liable for complicity. However, if the general test is to be merely whether the supplier knows or believes that the goods supplied will be used in the commission of a crime, then some at least of the concern expressed about the present law will remain.

4.115 It should however be noted that the formulation of the *mens rea* that we have suggested might be appropriate for a reformed law excludes cases of mere *suspicion* that an offence will be committed. That, we would suggest, eases much of the concern that has been expressed about the width of the present law, which may well require nothing more than suspicion or recklessness on the part of the accessory as to the criminal intentions of the principal. A balance has to be struck between the social interest in inhibiting crime by cutting off its materials and the social and personal interest in not unduly inhibiting the conduct of business by the imposition of criminal sanctions. Once belief as to the principal's criminality is required on the part of the supplier, he would seem to place himself in a position where the public interest in crime prevention should prevail, if he continues to supply in those circumstances.

4.116 The potential liability of accessories in general having been limited in that way, it is far from clear that there are any legitimate grounds of policy for conferring further exemptions from liability on 'business' suppliers; or, indeed, that those who have expressed concern on this issue would argue that there are such policy grounds. For our part, though we invite comment, we see great difficulty in any suggestion that, within the context of a properly limited law of complicity, those who otherwise fulfil the requirements of that law should be excused because they act for mercantile or financial motives. Indeed, from the point of view of discouraging or inhibiting the commission of the principal crime, it might be thought desirable that 'business' suppliers, above all others, should be deterred from providing the means of crime.

'Social' assistance

4.117 The concern about 'business' suppliers has been extended to what might be called by 'social' assisters, who do acts that assist the future commission of criminal offences in the course of what are otherwise ordinary and legitimate social activities. Examples include the man who pulls his friend's car out of a ditch to enable it to be driven away, after noting that it is so damaged as to be unroadworthy; or the over-generous host who plies with drink to the point of unlawful intoxication a guest whom he knows is going to drive himself home.

4.118 Such cases push to its limits a law of complicity based on belief as to the future commission of a crime and not on a requirement of purpose. It is far less obvious that there is here what we have suggested to be the proper and desirable need to inhibit business suppliers. A rule that abolished the whole of the law of complicity in the case of summary offences' would avoid some of the oddest-seeming examples of 'social' complicity, including those quoted in the preceding paragraph but, the law having decided that summary offences are indeed crimes, it is far from clear that the offence of assisting should never apply to them. Nor can we envisage any rational categorisation by which cases of the type here under discussion could be exempted from a law of complicity that otherwise extended to them.

4.119 As against these concerns, however, there are certainly good reasons for arguing that respect for the law, and the desirability of discouraging law-breaking, makes it legitimate to criminalise any conduct that knowingly assists the commission of a crime; bearing in mind in particular that, under the formulation that we envisage, belief in the future commission of a crime, and not merely suspicion as to the future, will be required to convict an accessory. It may well be thought that such considerations may legitimately prevail even though they make criminal some conduct that is, on one view, a normal pan of social life; and even though, for those and other reasons, such conduct is not likely on many occasions to be detected, or to be prosecuted.

4.120 We therefore particularly invite views on whether it is acceptable that the law of complicity by assistance should extend as far as the cases envisaged as possible in this section; and whether those who find such cases inappropriately ones of complicity can propose, as to date we have not been able to do, any categorisation that would effectively exclude the types of cases, but only those cases, that they find anomalous. Commentators will no doubt wish to bear this problem in mind when considering two more general issues, namely whether complicity by assistance should be limited to cases where it is the accessory's purpose that the principal crime should be committed; and whether liability for complicity as a whole should be limited to complicity in indictable, or in some other category of 'serious', offences.

Defences associated with 'good motive'

4.121 We referred in paragraphs 2.59–2.62 above to the possibility that, contrary to the general principles of the criminal law, it is at the moment a defence in respect of conduct that would otherwise involve accessory liability to show that D's acts were done with a good motive. Although we invite comment on this point, we do not think that such a defence is either necessary or desirable.

There is in effect no authority for it; its limits are obscure and would give rise to much argument and uncertainty; and if the mental element of assisting crime is properly defined, so that there is in every case required at least a belief on the part of D that what he does will assist P to commit a crime, then a defence of this degree of generality does not seem necessary to avoid hard cases.

4.122 That is not to say, however, that there may not be particular cases, such as those that we considered when drawing up the Draft Code, in which a more specific defence, based on particular types of good motive, should be provided. We mention such possible defences, on all of which we again invite comment, in paragraphs 4.123–4.137 below.

Law enforcement

4.123 No such defence is formally recognised in the present law. However, in the Draft Code we suggested the possibility of a defence in terms that a person should not be guilty as an accessory by reason of anything that he does with the purpose of preventing the commission of the principal offence. The case that we had in mind was that of the police informer or undercover agent who does acts that in fact assist the commission of an offence but whose purpose is to frustrate its commission.

4.124 At present, persons in such a case will escape liability if, perhaps entirely irrespective of their own law enforcement efforts, the principal offence is not in fact committed. Under a law that attaches liability at the moment the act of assistance is performed, such a defence is perhaps even more necessary. We suggest, for comment, that it might appropriately have the following more detailed content.

4.125 If the defence is to be effective, it will have to be expressed in fairly wide terms, to exempt any act of assistance that is performed during or as part of attempts to prevent the commission of the principal offence. Thus, for instance, it may be necessary, in order for D to maintain his 'cover', for him to drive members of the gang that he has joined to the scene of the crime, before informing the police of their whereabouts with a view to their arrest. That act of assistance in itself is, fairly clearly, not directed at the prevention of the commission of the crime, but we suggest that it should benefit from this defence if it is part of an overall course of conduct on the part of D that is so directed.

4.126 Provided that D's overall purpose is the prevention of crime, it should not be necessary to be too demanding, after the event, as to the appropriateness of the measures that he takes to fulfil that purpose. Weight should therefore be given to D's judgment: it should be enough that he believes that his act of assistance is necessary as part of the implementation of his purpose of preventing the commission of the principal crime.

4.127 The foregoing discussion limits the defence to acts of assistance in the particular crime that it is D's purpose to prevent. We however invite views on whether the defence should go even further, to exculpate assistance in any crime in the course of seeking to prevent the commission of an offence. The type of case that we have in mind is as follows. D joins in the preparations for a bank robbery, with a view to frustrating its actual commission. In order to make his involvement in those preparations for the robbery seem genuine to the principal offenders, D agrees to assist in a burglary to acquire equipment for use in the robbery. We appreciate that that case poses considerably more problems than cases of the type discussed in paragraph 4.125 above. There is nothing in the law to suggest that if D actually committed the burglary as a principal, with the same motive, he would or should be excused. That perhaps indicates that the present rule should be regarded as a particular limitation on accessoryship, as a recognition that the social fault of assisting a criminal is mitigated or removed by efforts to prevent that assistance being effective in the commission of the principal crime; rather than as an expression of a more general social principle or excuse. We also recognise that there must be stringent limits on the extent to which, in particular, police officers should be permitted to commit criminal acts, of any sort, with impunity.

4.128 Although the principal beneficiaries of a 'law enforcement' defence may be police officers, or those working under police supervision, notably as informers, we do not think that the defence should be formally limited to such cases. However, it may be noted that citizens who give assistance in criminal schemes as part of a law enforcement operation entered into entirely on their own initiative may find some difficulty in establishing that law enforcement was indeed their purpose in so acting.

Acts with the purpose of limiting harmful consequences

4.129 This defence, which has many affinities with the defence of law enforcement, is almost as obscure as that defence as to its status in the present law. In the Draft Code we formulated it as applying to anything done by the accused

> with the purpose of avoiding or limiting any harmful consequences of the offence and without the purpose of furthering its commission.

We pointed out that such a defence seems to have been in the minds of those of their Lordships who rejected the possibility of criminal liability on the part of the doctor in *Gillick*, without having been expressly formulated as such; and we continued:

> The generalisation that acts [done for the sole purpose of containing the harm done by the principal] do not attract criminal liability seems plainly right although, perhaps unsurprisingly, authority for it is lacking. We should perhaps refer to some topical examples. The supply of condoms to prisoners, or of sterile hypodermic needles to drug abusers, if done solely for the purpose of limiting the risk that the prisoners or addicts will be infected by the AIDS virus as a result of anticipated acts of buggery or injection, would, on that ground alone if on no other, not attract accessory liability for any offences that those acts might involve.

4.130 We continue to be of that opinion. We recognise that in such cases there would be unlikely to be pressure for prosecution; and that in the cases mentioned there might be considerable doubt as to whether D's acts had in fact assisted the unlawful intercourse or drug abuse. Nevertheless, we consider that in cases that fall within the formulation offered by the Draft Code there should be a simple and clear ground of defence for those who act in a responsible fashion to prevent the ill-effects of crimes committed by others, without the need to argue the more difficult aspects of the general law of accessoryship.

4.131 Both in the case of the limitation of harmful consequences and, in particular, in the case of law enforcement, much of the information on which the defence rests will be in the exclusive knowledge of the accused: to take the most obvious example, the need perceived by him to act in a certain manner as part of his overall endeavour to prevent crime. We therefore invite views as to whether in either case an accused relying on the defence should bear an evidential burden.

Withdrawal

4.132 There is no doubt that a defence of withdrawal exists in the present law of aiding and abetting, involving the taking of counter-measures between the act of assistance and the commission of the principal crime. The terms and limitations of this defence are, however, unclear, and withdrawal has never been thought to be an available defence in cases of incitement.

4.133 It has been suggested that a defence of withdrawal is particularly required in respect of an offence of *inchoate* aiding, since before the principal crime is committed the aider may be in a position to reverse the real damage in which he has involved himself, the commission of that crime; and if he is in a position to reverse that damage he should be encouraged to try to do so. In truth, however, exactly the same point arises under the present law. Even in the present law of aiding and abetting the accessory's fault is complete as soon as his act of assistance is complete, his criminal liability thereafter depending on what may be the complete accident of whether or not the principal crime is in fact committed. In both cases, the arguments for allowing a defence of withdrawal are essentially pragmatic, the social value of encouraging the reversal of the accessory's acts of assistance overriding the logic that applies to accessoryship the general rule of law that repentance once the crime has been committed is no defence, however much it may be a matter of mitigation.

4.134 If, as we propose, assistance and encouragement are treated separately, it is possible to consider the terms of this defence much more clearly and rationally than under the current law, where aiding and counselling are regarded as sub-classes of a single category of aiding and abetting. That has led to expression of the current law in terms of a single concept of 'countermand'. This is a concept which is difficult to apply, and it produces, perhaps, results which are unduly favourable to the accused, in a case where D has provided assistance, and not merely encouragement, towards P's criminal enterprise.

4.135 In the case of assistance, we consider that such a defence should only be available if the assister takes all reasonable steps to prevent the commission of the crime towards which he has assisted. That requirement in our view gives proper effect to the balance between the need to recognise that the accused, by giving assistance towards a criminal act, has already engaged in seriously antisocial behaviour; and the pragmatic consideration that assisters who repent while there is still time should be given positive encouragement to prevent the commission of a further antisocial act, on the part of their principal.

4.136 What are 'all *reasonable* steps' will depend on the circumstances of the case. In *Rook* the Court of Appeal said, *obiter*, that the suggestion that 'A declared intent to withdraw from a conspiracy to dynamite a building is not enough, if the fuse has been set; he must step on the fuse, might go too far. 'It may be that it is enough that he should have done his best to step on the fuse.' The court described this as a question of policy as much as of [the current] law. As to what the law should be, however, we agree that what should be required are reasonable efforts on the part of the defendant rather than necessarily success in preventing the crime. It would not normally, we think, be reasonable to expect a defendant to expose himself to serious additional risk, or to create the likelihood of further offences occurring: for instance, by physically intervening to try to stop an armed robbery on a bank, when he had previously provided information to the robbers about how the security arrangements at the bank could be circumvented. The most obvious step in such circumstances is that the defendant should inform the police of the planned offence, with sufficient detail to enable them to intervene. However, while we invite views on this point, we are not as at present advised minded to propose that notification of the police should be a necessary condition of the defence of withdrawal.

4.137 In the case of *encouragement* to commit a crime, somewhat different considerations apply. Since the nub of the defendant's fault is encouragement and not assistance, it may be enough that the encouragement is countered by (sufficiently forceful) discouragement. We pursue that matter when dealing generally with our proposals as to encouragement in paragraphs 4.168–4.169 below.

Cases where it is the defendant's purpose that the principal offence should be committed

4.138 We have stressed that a number of the potential defences discussed above are most obviously necessary in cases where the defendant is merely aware that his conduct will assist in the commission of a crime, without it being his purpose in acting that that crime should be committed. Where the commission of the principal crime can be shown to have been the defendant's purpose, it is difficult or impossible to apply reasoning that supports a possible defence of employment; 'ordinary course of business'; or 'social' assistance; and our provisional conclusion is that those defences should not be available in such a case. That is also the case in respect of the defences of law enforcement and limitation of harmful consequences. indeed, where the defendant's purpose is that the principal crime should be committed it is difficult to see that his conduct can also be described as falling within the basic requirements of either of those defences.

4.139 We also incline to the view that the defence of incidental involvement in statutory offences' should not be available, or at least should only be available in a very limited range of cases, if the 'victim' had as his purpose the commission of the principal offence. The defence that we propose is wide in its ambit, including not only sexual offences that were in issue in *Tyrrell* but a range of cases in which the 'assister' is merely the purchaser of illegally sold goods or the otherwise innocent participant in other types of unlicensed or illegal operations. If he seeks to bring about the commission of these offences the need to protect him from liability falls away. However, there may be a difference in respect of offences such as that in issue in *Tyrrell* itself, unlawful carnal knowledge of a girl under the age of sixteen, where it can be said that the statute was passed to protect women and girls against themselves, such protection perhaps extending to cases where they positively seek the commission of the offence against them. We therefore invite comment on whether this defence should be available in respect of some offences even to assisters who have the commission of those offences as their purpose; and, if so, what specific offences or types of offences should be covered.

4.140 The considerations discussed in the preceding two paragraphs do not apply to the defence of withdrawal, since that defence turns on steps taken by the defendant to rectify the effects of his complicity, rather than on circumstances that excuse his complicity in the first place. It may be noted, however, that a person who originally had as his purpose the commission of the principal offence may need to be more active than others before he can be deemed to have taken all reasonable steps to prevent its commission.

Other possible defences

4.141 In the Draft Code the Commission, in an attempt to reflect one of the more obscure parts of the current law, formulated a defence in terms of doing an act of assistance in the belief that the defendant is under an obligation so to act. This 'defence' is extremely difficult to express in other than very vague terms and, as stated, is in our view insupportable. Whatever protection such a defence would legitimately provide is better and more precisely to be found in the various more limited defences already discussed. We do not see this defence as forming an element in a reformed law.

4.142 We believe that we have reviewed in paragraphs 4.100–4.137 above all the cases that might reasonably be considered potentially to provide a defence to 'assistance' liability. However, we invite comment on whether there are any other cases that ought to be considered, and what respondents' grounds are for taking that view.

...

Procurement

4.192 According to the view of section 8 of the Accessories and Abettors Act 1861 that was adopted in *AG's Ref (No 1 of 1975)*, 'procurement' is a type of aiding and abetting distinct from either aiding or counselling. We have provisionally concluded that the approach of *AG's Ref (No 1)* should be abandoned. That does not mean, however, that there may not be cases that should fall within the law of complicity, but which cannot be accommodated, or at least cannot be accommodated without distortion, within the two offences of assisting and of encouraging crime; and which might be better treated under a separate offence expressed in terms of procurement.

4.193 In *AG's Ref (No 1)* the court considered 'procurement' to be the head of liability available to meet the unusual case where there was no 'meeting of minds' between the accessory and the principal: there, D 'laced' P's drink, causing him to commit the (strict liability) offence of driving with excess blood alcohol. Although it is arguable that that conduct could be described as 'assisting' on D's part we think that it could cause misunderstanding if the offence as defined in paragraph 4.99 above were applied to this case. 'Assistance' more naturally applies to the case where D's help is given towards an enterprise in which P was aware he was engaged. P does not need to know of the assistance: to take the example that we gave in the Code Report, D 'assists' where, knowing that P has made plans to murder X, he takes steps unknown to P to ensure that X is not warned of the danger. However the particular case of 'procurement' arises where P is not only unaware of the 'assistance', but also is unaware that he is doing the act that constitutes the principal crime; so that it is plausible to say, as in the example just given it is not, that D 'caused' the commission of that crime.

4.194 Nor in a case such as that just mentioned is it correct to say that D 'encouraged' P to commit the offence. Quite apart from the linguistic oddity of saying that A encourages B to do an act of which B is unaware, there may well in such a case be no actual communication between P and D: as indeed was so in *AG's Ref (No 1)* and in the other recent 'lacing' case of *Blakely and Sutton*. That conflicts with the requirement of the present law of incitement, which we think should be retained in a new offence of encouragement, that the 'encouragement' must be brought to the attention of the principal.

4.195 Offences of strict liability are virtually the only offences, and certainly the only significant offences, that P can commit without knowing what he is doing, which would seem to be the only circumstance in which the present problem arises. The present offence of procurement covers cases where D is reckless as to the commission of such a crime by P as well as where the commission of the crime is D's purpose, and that would seem to be correct: where D laces P's drink to an extent that puts P over the legal limit of intoxication, D is culpable if he knows that P may drive as well as where he has as his purpose that P should drive while intoxicated.

4.196 These no doubt rare cases can be met by a provision to the effect that where an offence can be committed without fault on the part of the principal a person commits the offence of procurement if he does any act with the intent that it should bring about, or being reckless whether that act will bring about, the commission of that offence by another. We invite comment on this provisional proposal.

4.197 There are a number of statutory offences of procurement, principally procurement of vulnerable person. As in relation to the general law of complicity just discussed, 'procure' implies the causation by the endeavours of the accused. However, in these cases what is procured, intercourse outside marriage, is not itself criminal. Such offences are therefore not affected by the proposals that we make here.

Joint enterprise

4.198 We discussed the present law on the doctrine of 'joint enterprise', and the considerable difficulties in formulating its limits, in paragraphs 2.108–2.124 above. Not the least of those difficulties is that the doctrine has developed with only somewhat haphazard consideration of how it relates to the law of aiding and abetting. However, properly considered, the present doctrine of joint enterprise extends beyond liability for aiding and abetting. D may be liable under this doctrine if he participates in an unlawful 'venture' while contemplating a real and substantial risk that a *collateral* crime may be committed by P in the course of the venture; in the most usual case, accompanying P on a stealing expedition contemplating that P may use violence on someone encountered during the expedition. It may however also be noted that, although the reported cases have tended to involve ventures which are clearly criminal, such as burglary, the extent to which other enterprises, which less obviously threaten further criminal acts, might fulfil the requirements of 'joint enterprise', is at present unresolved.

4.199 If it were to be accepted that the law of complicity should be reformed along the lines proposed in this Paper, with emphasis on the proof of acts of assistance with awareness of the principal crime, or knowing encouragement of that crime, and with the formulation of specific and limited special defences; then the justification, and need, to retain the further doctrine of joint enterprise comes into serious question. In most cases at present discussed under the heading of joint enterprise, the requirements of liability for assisting or encouraging crime will in fact be fulfilled. In particular, the present requirement in joint enterprise that D should foresee a real and substantial risk of P's commission of the principal crime ensures that D would not avoid the 'awareness' requirement in the offence of assisting crime. But there may be cases where, although D has joined the venture, with that level of awareness, he cannot properly be said in fact to have assisted in, or to have encouraged, the commission of the collateral crime by his companion: for instance, if P assaults a householder who unexpectedly returns to the house while D is upstairs ransacking the bedroom. We invite comment on whether, in such circumstances, D should be responsible only for the crimes that he has actually assisted or encouraged; and, with a clear and distinct law governing those activities, whether it is necessary to have to fall back on the vaguer common law rules of joint enterprise.

4.200 We invite comment, therefore, on whether, if the new offences of assisting and encouraging crime were to be adopted the doctrine of joint enterprise should be abolished. We however particularly invite comment as to whether there are thought to be cases that would not be brought within the new offences but which consultees consider should nevertheless be addressed by the present doctrine of joint enterprise or by some variation upon it.

4.201 A particular issue may be thought to arise in that respect in relation to the law of murder. The application of the doctrine of joint enterprise to the present law of murder has produced undoubted anomalies, but those anomalies are partly at least attributable to the retention of intention to cause grievous bodily harm as part of the *mens rea* of murder. If the new offence of assisting crime' were applied to this case, it would be necessary for the assister to know or believe that the principal was going to commit the *actus reus* of the offence, that is to kill; and know or believe that the principal would do so intending either to kill or to cause serious harm. If the 'assister' fell short of either of those requirements he might however be guilty of assisting in an assault committed by the principal in the course of killing. It may well be thought that that would be the right outcome, and that the present law extends liability for complicity in murder too widely. However, we invite comment on whether there should be special rules as to the liability of those who assist in acts on the part of others that result in the commission of murder.

The guilty accessory and the innocent principal

4.202 Cases can easily be imagined which look like the assistance or encouragement of 'crime', but which do not in fact fall within the rules already discussed because no principal crime has been committed: for instance, D encourages P, an eight-year old child, to steal from a shop; or, to adapt the facts of *Curr*, D encourages and assists P to make a claim on a public fund that is in fact, unknown to P, false; or D makes a room available to P so that P can have intercourse with Miss X, whom P believes to be under sixteen, but who is in fact over sixteen.

4.203 Such cases may often entail *principal* liability on the part of D through the operation of the doctrine of innocent agency. Thus, in the case of the use of a child under the age of criminal responsibility to remove goods from a shop, D himself may well by that agency have dishonestly appropriated the goods so as to be guilty of theft. That solution is however not available where it is not possible to say, as a matter of fact, that D has committed the *actus reus* of the principal offence. For instance, the fact of sexual intercourse assumes intercourse by the actual actor and not by proxy, and therefore D, the panderer, cannot be guilty of rape or unlawful intercourse when the intercourse is actually committed by P. And, on a somewhat different level, boys under eighteen cannot be guilty of buying alcohol 'on' licensed premises when they send an adult into the public house to make the purchase for them.

4.204 However, in many cases where even the doctrine of innocent agency cannot be used to convict the principal, inability to convict the non-acting accessory does not, in our view, give rise to serious concern. If it is desired to impose criminal liability on a careless giver of directions to a bus-driver, or on youths who find an ingenious way of circumventing the drafting of the Licensing Acts,' then the statutory offences involved should be extended, in the light of the policy of that particular statutory regime, to encompass them as principals. The suggested gaps in the law that continue to give concern cannot, however, be dismissed so easily, since they are cases, admittedly infrequent in their appearance at least in the law reports, where the 'accessory' appears to be seriously morally culpable, and there is no statutory offence that can easily be adapted to include his conduct.

4.205 The problems of the present law were described in paragraphs 2.43–2.46 above. Broadly speaking, we are concerned with cases where what the 'principal' does, in his particular state of mind, does not amount to a criminal offence on his part, and therefore neither in the present law of accessoryship nor in the law that we propose can it be the foundation of liability for complicity in crime; but that innocence on the principal's part is brought about only because of a state of mind culpably induced by the 'accessory'. That will be the case, conspicuously, either where the principal has a defence of duress resulting from threats by the accessory or where the principal is acting under a mistake of fact induced by the accessory.

4.206 In the Draft Code we sought to reflect what appears to be the law as envisaged in *Cogan and Leak* by treating such cases as an extended and special category of innocent agency. We cannot however recommend that solution as part of a law reform project. The solution through innocent agency is, however, highly artificial. It simply is not the case that Mr Leak had 'intercourse' with his wife through the agency of Mr Cogan, or that Mr Bourne had connection with the dog; and it strains the patience of the jurors who have to decide these cases to ask them to proceed on what purports to be a factual basis, but which in truth goes against all proper description of the acts that took place. If such cases are to be addressed at all, a special rule, which acknowledges the structurally secondary nature of the morally guilty party's involvement, must be produced.

4.207 A prime danger of such a rule is that, in its anxiety to meet cases of the type just discussed, it will reach too far. For that reason, we doubt whether it can be right (though we invite views on the point) to adopt a general rule that would attach liability for 'the abetting or counselling of a mere *actus reus*'. The physical element of many crimes is expressed in very general terms, the acts in question only coming within the legitimate control of the criminal law if performed in a criminal state of mind. For instance, the ... decision in *Gomez* has demonstrated the wide range of acts that are included within 'appropriation' in theft. We cannot think that it would be right to create 'accessory' liability in any case where a person encouraged such an act, even though the actor himself lacked, or was believed by the encourager to lack, any state of mind that would make his act criminal. Rather, we suggest the following approach.

4.208 The first option is simply to do nothing. It might well be argued that the problem is sufficiently limited in occurrence for what are necessarily going to be somewhat complicated provisions not to be justified.

4.209 If that view does not commend itself, we suggest that the emphasis should be on the *encouragement* by D of acts by P. We doubt very much whether the particular objection to D's conduct that is thought to require a response on the law's part will ever arise in a case where D has merely assisted, and not positively encouraged, P's acts. And that particular objection essentially arises when there has been either threats or deceit on D's part. We therefore provisionally propose that there should be a special offence of encouragement, where D solicits, etc, acts on P's part which if performed will only fail to involve the commission of an offence by P because either

(i) P can adduce a defence of duress based on threats made to him by D; or

(ii) P is acting under a mistake of fact and that mistake has been intentionally brought about by D.

4.210 This approach would catch cases like *Bourne* and *Cogan and Leak*. It would also impose liability on the facts of a case like Curr if the 'Mr Big' had persuaded the claimants that they were entitled to payments from public funds when in fact they were not. However, it would not, we think, extend the law unduly widely in other directions. We however ask for critical comment on this approach to what the present law has found to be an intractable problem.

Further reading

DJ Lanham, 'Accomplices and withdrawal' (1981) 97 LQR 575

JN Spencer, 'Trying to help another person commit a crime', in P Smith (ed), *Criminal Law: Essays in Honour of JC Smith*, 1987, London: Butterworths

RA Duff, 'Can I help you? Accessorial liability and the intention to assist' (1990) 10 Legal Studies 165

G Williams, 'Letting offences happen' [1990] Crim LR 780

KJM Smith, 'The Law Commission Consultation Paper on *Complicity: A Blueprint for Rationalisation*' [1994] Crim LR 239

GR Sullivan, 'Fault elements and joint enterprise' [1994] Crim LR 252

N Padfield, 'Assisting and encouraging crime' [1994] 58 JCL 297

JC Smith, 'Criminal liability of accessories: law and law reform' (1997) 113 LQR 453

CMV Clarkson, 'Complicity, *Powell* and manslaughter' [1998] Crim LR 556

CHAPTER 10

INCHOATE OFFENCES – INCITEMENT

To incite another to commit a criminal offence is itself an offence at common law. The offence requires proof that:

(a) The incitor communicated his incitement to an incitee.

(b) The act incited would be an offence if carried out by the incitee.

(c) The incitee was aware of the facts that would make the conduct incited an offence.

(d) The incitor intended to communicate the incitement.

(e) The incitor intended the incitement to be acted upon.

In addition to the common law offence Parliament has, from time to time, created statutory offences of incitement where the conduct incited would not, of itself, involve the commission of a criminal offence. Examples include incitement to racial hatred, and incitement to disaffection amongst troops.

ELEMENTS OF INCITEMENT

As Lord Denning observed in *Race Relations Board v Applin* [1973] QB 815, at 825G: '[It was] suggested that to "incite" means to urge or spur on by advice, encouragement, and persuasion, and not otherwise. I do not think the word is so limited, at any rate in this context. A person may "incite" another to do an act by threatening or by pressure, as well as persuasion.'

Normally D will be seeking to incite a particular incitee, but an incitement can be unilateral, for example where it forms part of an advertisement or broadcast; see *R v Most* (1881) 7 QBD 244.

Invicta Plastics Ltd and Another v Clare [1976] RTR 251 (DC)

Park J: These two defendants appeal by way of case stated from Hertfordshire Justices sitting at St Albans against convictions on 15 January 1975 of four offences of incitement to use unlicensed apparatus for wireless telegraphy, contrary to s 1(1) of the Wireless Telegraphy Act 1949. That section, as amended, provides, *inter alia*:

> No person shall ... use any apparatus for wireless telegraphy except under the authority of a licence in that behalf granted by the Secretary of State ... and any person who ... uses any apparatus for wireless telegraphy except under and in accordance with such a licence shall be guilty of an offence ...

The company, Invicta Plastics Ltd, were the manufacturers of a device called 'Radatec', and the defendant, Mr Jones-Fenleigh, was the chairman of the company. According to the case, Radatec is apparatus for wireless telegraphy within the meaning of the Act of 1949. It operates on the frequency range which is allocated to a number of radio services, including radio amateurs and the police in pursuance of their responsibilities in law enforcement.

By regulation 3 of the Wireless Telegraphy (Broadcast Licence Charges and Exemptions) Regulations 1970 the licence is not required for the use of wireless telegraphy apparatus used only for the reception of messages sent from authorised broadcasting stations and licensed amateur stations. Accordingly, s 1(1) of the Act of 1949 prohibits the use of apparatus for wireless telegraphy for the interception of radio communications not intended for the general use of the public except under the authority of a licence. Signals transmitted by the police in pursuance of their responsibility in law enforcement in connection with speeding offences are not intended for reception by the general public and a licence for their reception would not be granted except to authorised members of the public.

The facts giving rise to these charges are that the prosecutor bought a copy of a magazine called *What Car*. It contained an advertisement covering one-third of a page which used the words:

> You ought to know more about Radatec.

We have in fact seen a copy of it. It included a picture taken from behind the driver of a motor car travelling along a road and showed a 40 mph restriction sign immediately ahead of the car; it also showed the Radatec device attached to the top of the windscreen near the driving mirror. That advertisement forms the basis of the first two charges against the defendants. The prosecutor wrote to the address given in the advertisement and received in return two documents: namely, a slip giving the name of the stockist nearest to his address from which he could obtain Radatec, and a leaflet describing the Radatec X band receiver. The contents of the leaflet are fully set out in the case; they form the basis of the other two charges of incitement. I need only refer to some sentences. It begins with the words:

> The Radatec unit gives advance warning of X band transmissions in the vicinity. This band covers transmission from radio amateurs, police radar speed traps, commercial airport radar, military airport radar and commercial shipping navigational radar. The majority of X band transmissions are not intended for public use and, therefore, their deliberate reception is illegal unless licensed by the Post Office. However, no licence is required to receive amateur radio transmissions. As the Radatec is a broadly tuned receiver, it will intercept transmissions from any of the above sources. This need give no cause for concern since accidental reception of other transmissions while listening for amateur radio transmissions is not an offence. It is illegal to employ the Radatec specifically for the reception of, for instance, police radar transmissions. Admission of such an intentional mode of employment would doubtless lead to prosecution. Ownership of a Radatec unit is absolutely legal.

Then, under the heading 'operating features' is this sentence:

> As you approach the transmitting source, the tone of the Radatec will change to a high-pitched whine, diminishing again as you pass out of range.

In the next paragraph are the words:

> Detection ranges of up to half a mile have been noted.

The first question which the justices had to decide was whether a person who used the Radatec in his motor car without a licence from the Secretary of State would be using apparatus for wireless telegraphy contrary to s 1 of the Act of 1949. On the evidence before them they decided that such a person would be committing such an offence. There is no submission to this court that the justices were wrong in coming to that conclusion. So, on the first summons, which concerned the company, the question was whether the company by the advertisement in the magazine incited its readers to commit an offence under the Act ...

It is submitted on behalf of the company that, before the offence of incitement could be committed by means of the advertisement, there had to be in it an incitement to use the device which was advertised; that, if not, any matter in the advertisement would not constitute incitement, as it would not be sufficiently proximate to the offence alleged to have been incited; and that, as the advertisement merely encouraged readers to find out more about the device, it did not amount to incitement in fact or in law.

I think that it is necessary to look at the advertisement as a whole. Approaching it in this way, I have come to the conclusion that the company did incite a breach of the Act by means of the advertisement. I think, therefore, that justices were right to convict the company of this offence.

It is conceded that on the other summons against the company the case is much stronger because it depends upon the view taken by the justices of the pamphlet. [Counsel for the defendants], in the course of his argument, conceded that this pamphlet would amount to incitement except for two sentences, which I have read, which he submits amount to 'disclaimers'. Those two sentences are those where the pamphlet states that the majority of X band transmissions are not intended for public use and, therefore, their deliberate reception is illegal unless licensed by the Post Office, and where it states that it is illegal to employ Radatec specifically for the reception of, for instance, police radar transmissions.

Again, looking at the pamphlet as a whole, as the justices did, it is plain that from the words used readers were being persuaded and incited to use the Radatec device. In my view, therefore, the justices were also right to convict the company on that charge...

The conduct incited must be such as would constitute an offence if carried out by the incitee

R v Whitehouse [1977] QB 868 (CA)

Scarman LJ: ... The indictment which the defendant faced in 1976 was an indictment charging him with incitement to commit incest, and the particulars of the offence charged were that he, on a date unknown between 1 December 1975 and 10 February 1976, unlawfully incited a girl then aged 15, who was to his and her knowledge his daughter, to have sexual intercourse with him. To that count he pleaded guilty, as also to a second count charging incitement to commit incest, but on a different occasion, and he pleaded guilty to that as well.

When the court saw those two counts framed in the way I have just described, we queried whether it was an offence known to law and we doubted whether it was because a girl aged 15 is incapable of committing the crime of incest. Later in this judgment it will be necessary to look at the terms of s 11 of the Sexual Offences Act

1956 but that shortly is the effect of the section so far as material to the issue in this case ...

We turn now to consider whether the indictment disclosed an offence known to the law. The count standing by itself does disclose such an offence because the count merely alleges incitement to commit incest. But when one goes on to the particulars one sees that the defendant is charged with inciting his daughter, a girl aged 15, to commit incest with him. The Crown recognises that there are difficulties in the drafting of the indictment. The Crown recognises that under s 11 of the Sexual Offences Act 1956 a girl aged 15 cannot commit incest. The relevant subsection is (1) and I read it:

> It is an offence for a woman of the age of 16 or over to permit a man whom she knows to be her ... father ... to have sexual intercourse with her by her consent.

It is of course accepted by the Crown that at common law the crime of incitement consists of inciting another person to commit a crime. When one looks at this incitement in the light of the particulars of the offence pleaded, one sees that it is charging the defendant with inciting a girl to commit a crime which in fact by statute she is incapable of committing. If therefore the girl was incapable of committing the crime alleged, how can the defendant be guilty of the common law crime of incitement? The Crown accepts the logic of that position and does not seek in this court to rely on s 11 of the Act of 1956 or to suggest that this man could be guilty of inciting his daughter to commit incest, to use the old phrase, as a principal in the first degree. But the Crown says that it is open to them upon this indictment to submit that it covers the offence of inciting the girl to aid and abet the man to commit the crime of incest upon her. Section 10 of the Act of 1956 makes it an offence for a man to have sexual intercourse with a woman whom he knows to be his daughter, and the Crown says that upon this indictment it is possible to say that the defendant has committed an offence known to the law, the offence being that of inciting his daughter under the age of 16 to aid and abet him to have sexual intercourse with her.

All this is clearly very strange and we will come to the problem of the substantive law a little later. At this stage, we have to ask ourselves whether the indictment framed in the terms to which I have referred can conceivably encompass the offence which the Crown now says is known to the law, that is to say, the offence of inciting this girl to aid and abet this man to have unlawful sexual intercourse with her. The Crown, accepting that the indictment is most ineptly drafted, nevertheless submits that under the broad principles governing the drafting and amendment of indictments all is cured by the existence of a plea of guilty. It will be obvious from the somewhat tortuous language in which it has been necessary to explain what the offence is that is said to be known to the law, that it would be a very odd-looking indictment indeed, and would certainly bear not even a faint resemblance to the particulars as pleaded.

[Counsel] for the defendant has understandably submitted that, however flexible be the rules allowing amendment, the language of this indictment is too far away from what the Crown says is the offence charged, to be able to encompass it. We think there is much to be said for that submission, but we are prepared to assume, for the purposes of this appeal, that the indictment can be cured, and accordingly we now read the indictment as an indictment charging this man with the offence of inciting a girl of 15 to aid and abet him to commit incest with her.

Is there such an offence known to the law? The difficulty arises from two features of the law to which I have already referred. First, at common law the crime of incitement consists of inciting another person to commit a crime ... The second difficult feature of the law is s 11 of the Act of 1956 to which I have already referred. A woman under the age of 16 cannot commit the crime of incest. But, says the Crown, a man can commit incest, and so they go on to make their submission that a girl of 15 can aid and abet him to do so.

There is no doubt of the general principle, namely that a person, provided always he or she is of the age of criminal responsibility, can be guilty of aiding or abetting a crime even though it be a crime which he or she cannot commit as a principal in the first degree. There are two famous illustrations in the books of this principle. A woman can aid and abet a rape so as herself to be guilty of rape, and a boy at an age where he is presumed impotent can nevertheless aid and abet a rape ...

But what if the person alleged to be aiding and abetting the crime is herself the victim of the crime? This poses the short question with which this appeal is concerned. Before we consider it we would comment that, if indeed it be the law that this girl aged 15 can be guilty of incest as the aider and abettor of a man who is seeking to have intercourse with her, then one has the strange situation that, although she cannot be guilty of the crime of incest under the section which formulates the conditions under which a woman may be found guilty of that crime, yet through this doctrine of aiding and abetting she can be guilty of the offence when it is committed by a man. That is an odd conclusion, but not necessarily to be rejected because of its oddity.

The important matters in our judgment are these. First this girl, aged 15, belongs to a class which is protected, but not punished, by ss 10 and 11 of the Sexual Offences Act 1956, and second the girl is alleged to be the victim of this notional crime. The whole question has an air of artificiality because nobody is suggesting either that the father has committed incest with her or that she has aided and abetted him to commit incest upon her. What is suggested is that the father has committed the crime of incitement because by his words and conduct he has incited her to do that which, of course, she never has done.

The question in our judgment is determined by authority. It is, strictly speaking, persuasive authority only because it deals with a different Act of Parliament, but it is a decision by a strong court which has declared a principle which is as applicable to the statutory provision with which we are concerned as to that with which that case was concerned. The case is *R v Tyrrell* [1894] 1 QB 710. It was a decision of the Court of Crown Cases Reserved and it was a five-judge court, consisting of Lord Coleridge CJ, Mathew, Grantham, Lawrence and Collins JJ. The headnote reads as follows:

> It is not a criminal offence for a girl between the ages of 13 and 16 to aid and abet a male person in committing, or to incite him to commit, the misdemeanour of having unlawful carnal knowledge of her contrary to s 5 of the Criminal Law Amendment Act 1885.

... In our judgment it is impossible, as a matter of principle, to distinguish *R v Tyrrell* from the present case. Clearly the relevant provisions of the Sexual Offences Act 1956 are intended to protect women and girls. Most certainly, s 11 is intended to protect girls under the age of 16 from criminal liability, and the Act as a whole exists, in so far as it deals with women and girls exposed to sexual threat, to protect them. The very fact that girls under the age of 16 are protected from criminal liability for what would otherwise be incest demonstrates that this girl who is said to have been the subject of incitement was being incited to do something which, if she did it, could not be a crime by her.

One can only avoid that conclusion if one can pray in aid the doctrine of aiding and abetting and apply it to the crime committed by a man under s 10. But *R v Tyrrell* makes it clear that to do that would be to impose criminal liability upon the persons whom Parliament has intended should be protected, not punished.

We have therefore come to the conclusion, with regret, that the indictment does not disclose an offence known to the law because it cannot be a crime on the part of this girl aged 15 to have sexual intercourse with her father, though it is of course a crime, and a very serious crime, on the part of the father. There is here incitement to a course of conduct, but that course of conduct cannot be treated as a crime by the girl. Plainly a gap or lacuna in the protection of girls under the age of 16 is exposed by this decision. It is regrettable indeed that a man who importunes his daughter under the age of 16 to have sexual intercourse with him but does not go beyond incitement cannot be found guilty of a crime ...

Note: It is now an offence, under s 54(1) of the Criminal Law Act 1977, for a man to incite to have sexual intercourse with him a girl under the age of 16 whom he knows to be his granddaughter, daughter or sister.

The incitee must know of the facts that constitute the offence

R v Curr [1968] 2 QB 944 (CA)

Fenton Atkinson J: ... The facts shortly were these, that he was in fact a trafficker in family allowance books. His method was to approach some married woman who had a large family of children and lend her money on the security of her family allowance book. A woman would borrow from him, let us say, £6 and would sign three of the vouchers in her family allowance book to the value of, let us say, £9, and hand over the book to him as security. He then had a team of women agents whom he sent out to cash the vouchers, and he would pocket the proceeds in repayment of the loans and thereafter return the books. He admitted quite freely in evidence that he had done, as he put it, 40 to 80 books a week, and he said, in February 1966, he had between three and five women agents assisting him in this matter, and when he was arrested he had about 80 family allowance books in his possession. He agreed quite frankly that he knew he was not legally entitled to receive these payments, and that it could be risky; in dealing with the husband of one of the women concerned he said: 'When you're doing business like this, you should keep your big mouth shut'. So it is quite plain that the dealings of this man were highly objectionable, and the assistant recorder who tried the case clearly had very strong views about it; on two occasions in his summing up he spoke of preying on these women with large families, and he finished up his direction to the jury with words to this effect: 'If you are getting interest at 800% per annum it is not bad, is it? That is what the prosecution say here, that the whole system was corrupt', and the language there used was no whit too strong.

But the very nature of the case being bound to arouse strong prejudice in the mind of any right-thinking juror, for that reason it was all the more important to put the law on each count clearly to the jury, and to make sure that the defence was clearly put before them ...

... [The defendant was charged] that on a day unknown [he] unlawfully 'solicited a woman unknown to obtain on his behalf from HM's Postmaster General the sum of £2 18s on account of an allowance knowing that it was not properly receivable by her' ...

[The relevant legislation, the Family Allowances Act 1945, contained a section headed] 'Penalty for obtaining or receiving payment wrongfully' [which provided:]

> If any person: ... (b) obtains or receives any such sum as on account of an allowance, either as in that person's own right or as on behalf of another, knowing that it was not properly payable, or not properly receivable by him or her; that person shall be liable on summary conviction to imprisonment for a term not exceeding three months or to a fine not exceeding £50 or to both such imprisonment and such fine.

[Defence counsel's] argument was that if the woman agent in fact has no guilty knowledge, knowing perhaps nothing of the assignment, or supposing that the defendant was merely collecting for the use and benefit of the woman concerned, then she would be an innocent agent, and by using her services in that way the defendant would be committing the summary offence himself, but would not be inciting her to receive money knowing that it was not receivable by her. He contends that it was essential to prove, to support this charge, that the woman agent in question in this transaction affecting a Mrs Currie knew that the allowances were not properly receivable by her. [Prosecuting counsel's] answer to that submission was that the woman agent must be presumed to know the law, and if she knew the law, she must have known, he contends, that the allowance was not receivable by her ...

The argument is that in no other circumstances may an agent lawfully collect for the use and benefit of the book holder, and [counsel for the prosecution] was ready to contend, for example, that if a mother with, say, eight children to look after at home asks a neighbour to go and collect her allowance for her, and the neighbour does so, the neighbour would be committing an offence under the 1945 Act, and the mother would be guilty of the offence of soliciting. We are by no means satisfied that any agent who collects with the full authority of the book holder and for her use and benefit would commit an offence under that subsection. There appears to be no express prohibition, certainly we were referred to no express prohibition, in the Family Allowance Act 1945, or any orders making such collection unlawful. On the evidence, the Post Office in practice appears to allow this to be done in certain cases; in our view there can be situations, or may be situations, in which an agent, however well she may know the statute and regulations, could properly suppose that her action in receiving an allowance of this kind was lawful.

In our view the prosecution argument here gives no effect to the word 'knowing' in the 1945 Act, and in our view the defendant could only be guilty if the woman solicited, that is, the woman agent sent to collect the allowance, knew that the action she was asked to carry out amounted to an offence. As has already been said, the defendant himself clearly knew that his conduct in the matter was illegal and contrary to the 1945 Act, but it was essential in our view for the jury to consider the knowledge, if any, of the woman agent. The assistant recorder dealt with this count be referring to soliciting as follows: 'Solicited means encouraged or incited another person to go and draw that money which should have been paid, you may think, to Mrs Currie'. He later dealt with ignorance of the law being no excuse. He went on to deal with statutory offences, under the Family Allowances Act 1945, telling the jury in effect that, apart from the case of sickness, nobody else could legally receive these allowances, and then went on to consider the position of the defendant, asking the rhetorical question whether he could be heard to say with his knowledge of this matter and his trafficking in these books that it was not known to be wrong to employ an agent to go and collect the family allowance. But the assistant recorder never followed that with the question of the knowledge of the woman agents, and in the whole of the summing up dealing with this matter he proceeded on the assumption that either guilty knowledge in the woman agent was irrelevant, or, alternatively, that any woman agent must be taken to have known that she was committing an offence under the Act.

If the matter had been left on a proper direction for the jury's consideration, they might well have thought that the woman agents, other than Mrs Nicholson, whom they acquitted, must have known very well that they were doing something wrong; some of them were apparently collecting as many as 10 of these weekly payments. But the matter was never left to them for their consideration, and here again, so it seems to this court, there was a vital matter where the defence was not left to the jury at all and there was no sufficient direction; it would be quite impossible to say that on a proper direction the jury must have convicted on this count ...

Notes and queries

1 In *Curr*, did the court treat the knowledge of the incitees as part of the *actus reus* that had to be established, or is the court saying that the incitor must know that the incitee will be acting with the necessary *mens rea*? Consider further *DPP v Armstrong* [2000] Crim LR 379, where A incited J (where J, unknown to A, was an undercover police officer) to supply child pornography. A was acquitted on the basis that there could be no liability for incitement unless J had parity of *mens rea* – on the facts J had no intention of supplying the pictures. Allowing the prosecutor's appeal the Divisional Court held that strict parity of *mens rea* was not required in incitement cases. J knew of the facts that would constitute the offence even though he had no intention of supplying the material requested. Had J done what was requested by A, J would have been committing an offence.

2 By virtue of s 5(7) of the Criminal Law Act 1977, incitement to commit the offence of conspiracy, whether statutory or common law, ceases to be an offence.

INCITEMENT AND IMPOSSIBILITY

As will be seen from the following extracts, the courts have elected to apply the common law rules on impossibility, as laid down in *DPP v Nock* [1978] AC 979 (extracted in Chapter 11) to the offence of common law conspiracy.

R v Fitzmaurice [1983] QB 1083 (CA)

Neill J: On 22 July 1981, Robert Fitzmaurice was convicted at the Central Criminal Court of unlawfully inciting three men, Terence Bonham, James Brown and Steven Brown to commit robbery by robbing a woman at Bow ...

The facts of the case were unusual. They have been set out in a convenient form in an agreed statement of facts as follows:

(1) On 28 September 1978, Bonham, James Brown and Steven Brown were arrested in Bow in a green van. Bonham was the driver and the Browns were each armed with an imitation firearm. All had sleeve masks and there was a pickaxe handle in the van.

(2) Bonham and the others believed that they were there to carry out a wages snatch from a woman walking from her place of work to the bank. A security van was due to visit the National Westminster Bank in Bow Road at that time, and police officers had received information from the appellant's father that a robbery on the security van had been planned. All three were subsequently charged with conspiracy to rob a person on the basis of their account that they were there to rob a woman of money on her way to the bank and not the security van. At their trial they pleaded guilty to the conspiracy count and were sentenced to imprisonment.

(3) Subsequent investigations revealed that the three men were victims of a trick by the appellant's father, and had been set up to carry out a robbery by him so that he and his accomplice Skipp could collect the reward money for informing the police of an intended raid on the security van. That information was false and the invention of the appellant's father.

(4) The appellant's father asked the appellant if he could find someone to carry out a robbery. The appellant approached Bonham and informed him of the proposed robbery, describing it as a 'wages snatch'. The appellant brought Bonham to an address where the appellant's father outlined the plan. The plan was to snatch wages from a woman carrying money from a factory to a bank in Bow, east London. The appellant offered to participate, but was excluded. Bonham agreed to the plan. Later Bonham, who had recruited the two Browns, visited Bow with the appellant's father, but not the appellant. They saw a woman, in fact Skipp's girlfriend, walking from the factory to the bank. She was carrying a bag. The following week the appellant's father took Bonham and the two Browns to Bow again and pointed out where the getaway car would be left. On the day appointed, Bonham and the others met the appellant's house. Imitation guns and masks were distributed. Bonham and the others left the premises and were subsequently arrested. The appellant believed throughout that the robbery plan was genuine and agreed to accept £200 and a television for his part.

(5) On 5 June 1981 Bonham had his conviction for conspiracy set aside by the Court of Appeal on the grounds that the crime which he had conspired to commit was impossible of fulfilment. O'Connor LJ said:

> However morally culpable, the truth is that these three men had been fraudulently induced to agree to commit a crime which could not be committed in the strict sense; they were themselves the victims of a different conspiracy to which they were not parties.

In support of the appellant's appeal to this court, [counsel for the appellant] put forward two submissions: (a) that the trial judge had misdirected the jury as to the meaning of 'incitement'; and (b) that the appellant could not be guilty of inciting other men to commit a crime which in fact could not be committed.

On his first submission, [counsel for the appellant] drew our attention to a passage in the summing up where the judge said:

> The word 'incitement' is a word which is used in widely differing circumstances. A person can incite another to envy or hatred. A person can also be incited to loyalty and patriotism. Here, the charge is that the accused incited Mr Bonham to commit a crime. Now, the original approach by the defendant to Mr Bonham is not denied. There is no dispute about the fact that the defendant approached Mr Bonham, and it was an approach to him to commit a crime. There is no question about that. The defendant does not deny that Mr Bonham was an old friend of his, and that he knew at the time that he was out of work and needed money. You may conclude that an approach to Mr Bonham in those circumstances by the defendant, whether it was a suggestion, a proposal or a request, was an approach that embodied naturally the promise of reward, that if he engaged in the enterprise he would get money. That prospect, you may think, was the most persuasive factor in the approach. If you take that view, then clearly you may think that there was incitement to commit the crime, in the broad sense I have indicated.

[Counsel for the appellant] criticised this passage on the basis that it provided an unsatisfactory and inadequate definition of incitement because the judge did not sufficiently instruct the jury as to the necessity of proof that the appellant had persuaded or encouraged the commission of the robbery. He submitted that there was a clear distinction between the mere procurement of a crime and incitement. Procuration, he said, did not necessarily involve any persuasion or counselling of a third party by the defendant to commit the crime. Similarly, said [counsel], a person may be liable as an accessory before the fact, for example, by providing the tools for a crime, but, in the absence of any proof of persuasion to commit the crime, he will not be guilty of incitement ...

We have considered this submission in the context of the present case. In our judgment the judge gave a perfectly adequate definition to deal with the facts which the jury had to consider. We are satisfied that in some cases a person who is deputed to collect men together to take part in a crime may well not be guilty of incitement. For example, his role may be limited to informing certain named individuals that the planner of the enterprise would like to see them. But in the present case the judge could point to the fact that Bonham was out of work and needed money. The suggestion, proposal or request was accompanied by an implied promise of reward. Indeed, by using the words 'That proposal, you may think, was the most persuasive factor in the approach', the judge rightly focused the attention of the jury on the element of persuasion which it was necessary for the prosecution to prove. We therefore see no reason to fault the judge's summing up in this respect.

[Counsel's] second submission, however, is at first sight more formidable. Incitement is one of the three inchoate offences, incitement, conspiracy and attempt. [Counsel] argued that there was no logical basis for treating the three offences differently when considering their application in circumstances where the complete offence would be impossible to commit, and that therefore the court should apply the principles laid down by the House of Lords in the case of attempts in *R v Smith (Roger)* [1975] AC 476 and in the case of conspiracy in *DPP v Nock* [1978] AC 979 ...

In our view ... the right approach in a case of incitement is the same as that which was underlined by Lord Scarman in *DPP v Nock* [1978] AC 979 when he considered the offence of conspiracy. In every case it is necessary to analyse the evidence with care to decide the precise offence which the defendant is alleged to have incited. Lord Scarman said, at 995:

> The indictment makes plain that the Crown is alleging in this case a conspiracy to commit a crime: and no one has suggested that the particulars fail to disclose an offence known to the law. But the appellants submit, and it is not disputed by the Crown, that the agreement as proved was narrower in scope than the conspiracy charged. When the case was before the Court of Appeal, counsel on both sides agreed that the evidence went to prove that the appellants agreed together to obtain cocaine by separating it from the other substance or substances contained in a powder which they had obtained from one of their co-defendants, a Mr Mitchell. They believed that the powder was a mixture of cocaine and lignocaine, and that they would be able to produce cocaine from it. In fact the powder was lignocaine hydrochloride, an anaesthetic used in dentistry, which contains no cocaine at all. It is impossible to produce, by separation or otherwise, cocaine from lignocaine ...
>
> The trial judge in his direction to the jury, and the Court of Appeal in their judgment dismissing the two appeals, treated this impossibility as an irrelevance. In their view the agreement was what mattered: and there was plain evidence of an agreement to produce cocaine, even though unknown to the two conspirators it could not be done. Neither the trial judge nor the Court of Appeal thought it necessary to carry their analysis of the agreement further. The trial judge described it simply as an agreement to produce cocaine. The Court of Appeal thought it enough that the prosecution had proved 'an agreement to do an act which was forbidden by s 4 of the Misuse of Drugs Act 1971'. Both descriptions are accurate, as far as they go. But neither contains any reference to the limited nature of the agreement proved; it was an agreement upon a specific course of conduct with the object of producing cocaine, and limited to that course of conduct. Since it could not result in the production of cocaine, the two appellants by pursuing it could not commit the statutory offence of producing a controlled drug.

In our view these words suggest the correct approach at common law to any inchoate offence. It is necessary in every case to decide on the evidence what was the course of conduct which was (as the case may be) incited or agreed or attempted. In some cases the evidence may establish that the persuasion by the inciter was in quite general terms whereas the subsequent agreement of the conspirators was directed to a specific crime and a specific target. In such cases where the committal of the specific offence is shown to be impossible it may be quite logical for the inciter to be convicted even though the alleged conspirators (if not caught by s 5 of the Criminal Attempts Act 1981) may be acquitted. On the other hand, if B and C agree to kill D and A, standing beside B and C, though not intending to take any active part whatever in the crime, encourages them to do so, we can see no satisfactory reason, if it turns out later that D was already dead, why A should be convicted of incitement to murder whereas B and C at common law would be entitled to an acquittal on a charge of conspiracy. The crucial question is to establish on the evidence the course of conduct which the alleged inciter was encouraging.

We return to the facts of the instant case. [Counsel for the appellant] submitted that the 'crime' which Bonham and the two Browns were being encouraged to commit was a mere charade. The appellant's father was not planning a real robbery at all and therefore the appellant could not be found guilty of inciting the three men to commit it. In our judgment, however, the answer to [counsel's] argument is to be found in the facts which the prosecution proved against the appellant. As was made clear by [counsel for the Crown], the case against the appellant was based on the steps he took to recruit Bonham. At that stage the appellant believed that there was to be a wages snatch and he was encouraging Bonham to take part in it. As [counsel] put it, 'The appellant thought he was recruiting for a robbery not for a charade'. It is to be remembered that the particulars of offence in the indictment included the words 'by robbing a woman at Bow'. By no stretch of the imagination was that an impossible offence to carry out and it was that offence which the appellant was inciting Bonham to commit.

For these reasons, therefore we are satisfied that the appellant was rightly convicted. The appeal is dismissed.

R v Sirat (1986) 83 Cr App R 41 (CA)

Parker LJ: ... The charges on the indictment were as follows:

Count 1: soliciting to murder contrary to s 4 of the Offences Against the Person Act 1861.

Particulars of offence: Mohammed Sirat between the 15th and 21st days of August 1984 solicited encouraged persuaded or endeavoured to persuade Mohammed Bashir to murder Raquia Begum by the act of Mohammed Bashir and/or by the acts of another or others.

Count 2: incitement to cause grievous bodily harm.

Particulars of offence: Mohammed Sirat Between the 15th and 21st days of August 1984 unlawfully incited Mohammed Bashir to cause grievous bodily harm to Raquia Begum by the acts of Mohammed Bashir and/or by the acts of another or others.

The facts may be shortly stated. Between Thursday 16 August 1984, and Monday 20 August, both dates inclusive, the appellant had four meetings with Mr Bashir, the last of which was recorded by the police, to whom Mr Bashir had reported after the first two had taken place. It is unnecessary to set out the details of the conversations. It is sufficient to say that they plainly showed that the appellant desired the death of his wife or, if not that, her serious injury, and that he was urging Bashir to (1) either kill or injure her himself, or (2) pay a man who was in fact non-existent to do so, or (3) procure the result, whether by doing the deed himself or by paying someone else, not necessarily the non-existent man, to do so.

At the close of the prosecution case it was submitted on behalf of the appellant that (1) there was no such offence in law as inciting a person to counsel or abet a third person to commit an offence, and (2) there was not sufficient evidence to go to the jury that the appellant had incited Bashir himself to murder or cause grievous bodily harm to the appellant's wife. The judge rightly rejected the second of those two submissions and no complaint is made as to that.

We are now only indirectly concerned with the ruling on the first submission; for what now matters is not the ruling itself but the subsequent direction to the jury which was based on it. Of this complaint is made. In the only ground of appeal which was pursued it is contended that the learned judged erred in law 'in directing the jury that if the defendant urged the witness Bashir to incite a third man to cause grievous bodily harm to the defendant's wife the defendant was guilty of the offence charged in count 2 of the indictment and in rejecting a submission by defence counsel that there was no such offence in law as inciting a person to counsel or abet a third person to commit an offence'.

There is no doubt that at common law incitement to commit a crime is an offence. This being so, it follows logically that if A incites B to incite C to commit a crime, eg to wound D, A is guilty of incitement to commit a crime, namely incitement. This however is subject to the qualification that if C is non-existent, being either dead or fictional, A would not be guilty, because he would be inciting the commission of an impossible crime. B cannot incite C, because C does not exist. On the basis of *Fitzmaurice* [1983] QB 1083, the judge rightly so directed the jury. Hence, since the jury convicted on count 2, it follows that they must have concluded that the appellant had not urged Bashir to get the fictional man and no other to do the deed.

With regard to the remaining possibilities, the essence of the learned judge's directions appears from the following passages in his summing up:

> If a man wants a murder to be committed and he tries to persuade somebody else to commit it or he tries to persuade that second person to get a third person to commit it, then the first man is guilty of the crime of incitement ... incitement to murder.

> If you are sure that in reality the effect of what he was saying to Bashir was this, 'I want you to get her seriously injured, do it yourself or get the white man from Leeds to do it', then what Sirat was proposing was a possibility because the white man from Leeds was only one way in which he was making his proposal. Another, on the basis that I am putting it to you, was that Bashir might do it himself and that was obviously possible, so in that event he would be guilty of count 2 and, equally, if the effect of what he was saying was this, 'I want you to get her seriously injured, get the white man from Leeds to do it if you like, get somebody else to do it if you like, so long as you get somebody', if that is the effect of what he was saying, then once again the serious injury which he wanted brought about would be a possibility and he would then be guilty of count 2.

Similarly with count 2, you have to be sure before you can convict him that he desired his wife to be seriously injured and that he tried to persuade Bashir to bring about her serious injury in a way which was, in fact, possible.

In principle there is nothing wrong with these directions, but complication is introduced by the provisions of the Criminal Law Act 1977. Section 1 of that Act created the statutory offence of conspiracy and s 5(1), subject to exceptions which do not matter, abolished the offence of conspiracy at common law. Section 5(7) then provided: 'Incitement and attempt to commit the offence of conspiracy (whether the conspiracy incited or attempted would be an offence at common law or under s 1 above or any other enactment) shall cease to be offences'. If, therefore, A incites B to agree with C that C will wound D, A's incitement of B is by statute not an offence.

There is, in our view, no doubt that one possible view of the evidence was that the appellant was inciting Bashir to agree, with either the non-existent man or anyone else who would do it at the right price, that such person should cause grievous bodily harm to the appellant's wife. It is therefore clearly possible that the jury may have convicted him of something which by statute is no longer an offence. Moreover, as was accepted by the prosecution, they may have convicted him of an offence with which he was not charged, namely incitement to incite to cause grievous bodily harm, whereas the prosecution charged incitement to cause grievous bodily harm.

This being so, we allowed the appeal on two grounds: (a) that the appellant may have been convicted of an offence of which he was not charged, and (b) that he may have been convicted of an offence which does not exist.

Lest there be any doubt, we do not intend to indicate that the common law offence of inciting to incite no longer exists. Where however the facts are that the accused's incitement of B is actually to enter into an agreement with C for the commission of a crime, it would in our judgment be impossible to hold that the accused can be guilty of incitement, on the ground that B must of necessity propose the crime to C on the way to making the agreement. Whether other forms of incitement to incite survive will fall for decision when the question arises. It may appear to be absurd that, where a person is inciting actual agreement to be made for the commission of a crime, he should be guilty of no offence, but that where he does not seek actual agreement but mere encouragement he should be guilty. This however is not necessarily absurd, for there may well be circumstances where there is no question of an agreement being sought but where the particular form of incitement is more effective than any attempt to secure agreement.

Notes and queries

1 In *R v Pickford* [1995] 1 Cr App R 420, the appellant contested his conviction for inciting his son to have sexual intercourse with his (the appellant's) wife, on the basis that, at the time of the alleged offence, the appellant's son would have been under the age of 14, and thus presumed at common law, to have been incapable of having sexual intercourse (a presumption since abolished by statute). The essence of the appeal was that the appellant had been charged with inciting a non-existent crime. Dismissing the appeal, the court noted that the common law presumption of incapacity existed to protect young boys in respect of crimes committed by them, not to protect adults

committing offences against them. As Laws J observed: 'The reasons for the presumption, however they may have been articulated in the old cases, cannot begin to justify its application in a case where the boy is not the perpetrator of the offence, but its victim. Accordingly, the appellant in the present case would rightly have been found guilty of inciting the mother to have intercourse with her son, even if it were plain beyond argument that he was under 14 at the time ...'

2   In *DPP v Armstrong* (above), A had contended that the offence he had incited was impossible to carry out as the incitee (unknown to A at the relevant time) was an undercover police office who would never have supplied the pornography requested by A. This argument was rejected by the Divisional Court on the basis that the incitee could have had access to and supplied the material if he had wanted to. J could have supplied the material had he so wished.

3   As part of the government's response to concerns over 'sexual tourism' – principally the sexual exploitation of children in countries overseas facilitated by individuals in the United Kingdom – Parliament enacted the Sexual Offences (Conspiracy And Incitement) Act 1996. Section 2 of the Act applies where:

2(1) ...

(a) any act done by a person in England and Wales would amount to the offence of incitement to commit a listed sexual offence but for the fact that what he had in view would not be an offence triable in England and Wales,

(b) the whole or part of what he had in view was intended to take place in a country or territory outside the United Kingdom, and

(c) what he had in view would involve the commission of an offence under the law in force in that country or territory.

The term 'listed sexual offence' is defined in the Schedule to the Sexual Offences (Conspiracy and Incitement) Act 1996:

- rape (s 1 of the Sexual Offences Act 1956), but only if the victim has not attained the age of 16

- intercourse with a girl under the age of 13 (s 5 of the Sexual Offences Act 1956)

- intercourse with a girl under the age of 16 (s 6 of the Sexual Offences Act 1956)

- buggery (s 12 of the Sexual Offences Act 1956), but only if the victim has not attained the age of 16

- indecent assault on a girl (s 14 of the Sexual Offences Act 1956), provided that the victim has not attained the age of 16

- indecent assault on a boy (s 15 of the Sexual Offences Act 1956), provided that the victim has not attained the age of 16

- indecent conduct towards a young child (s 1 of the Indecency with Children Act 1960)

If these conditions are satisfied, what the defendant had in view is to be treated as that listed sexual offence for the purpose of any charge of incitement brought in respect of that act, and any such charge is accordingly triable in England and Wales (s 2(2)). Under s 2(3) any act of incitement by means of a message (however communicated) is to be treated as done in England and Wales if the message is sent or received in England and Wales.

4   The scope of the domestic courts' jurisdiction over incitement to commit offences abroad was further extended by the coming into force of provisions of the Criminal Justice Act 1993, on 1 June 1999. Under the 1993 Act courts in England and Wales have jurisdiction over what are referred to as 'Group B' offences – this includes incitement to commit a range of offences abroad involving dishonest and fraudulent conduct – provided the conduct incited would amount to an offence triable by the courts in England and Wales were the conduct incited to be carried out within the jurisdiction.

CODIFICATION AND LAW REFORM PROPOSALS

The Law Commission's Consultation Paper *Assisting and Encouraging Crime* (LCCP No 131) outlines some radical reforms in relation to incitement – essentially the abolition of the offence and its replacement with a new offence of 'encouraging crime'. These proposals should be read in the context of the Law Commission's views as to reforming accessorial liability generally, set out in Chapter 9.

Encouraging Crime

Introduction

4.143 In this section we set out our provisional proposals for the second aspect of the new law, dealing with the encouragement, rather than the assistance, of crime. We envisage this part of the new law covering the ground that at the moment is addressed not only by the 'counselling' element in aiding and abetting but also by the present law of incitement. The separation of encouragement from assistance enables a clearer and more precise approach to some of the policy issues that affect the law on encouraging crime, freed from the present need to formulate rules that cover both the aiding and the counselling aspects of aiding and abetting. At the same time, however, it will be convenient at many stages of the discussion to compare the proposed law on encouragement with that already suggested for assisting and helping, both to demonstrate common features and to demonstrate how the two types of complicity differ.

An inchoate offence

4.144 We have indicated our provisional conclusion that the offence of assisting crime should in future be put on an inchoate basis, in that the actual commission of the crime assisted should not be a precondition to liability. Incitement, however, has always been regarded as an inchoate offence, committed by, and complete in, the act of incitement itself. We see no reason why that rule should be changed for the offence of encouraging crime that we envisage as taking the place of incitement; and there is no reason in the current law, apart from historical accident, why the counselling component of aiding and abetting should be handled differently from incitement in this respect.

4.145 We will therefore proceed on the basis that the offence of encouraging crime will be complete once the act of encouragement is completed with the necessary *mens rea*; and will not depend on the actual commission by the principal (as it is convenient to continue to call him) of the crime encouraged. That arrangement however demands that care is taken in defining both what is sufficient to constitute an act of 'encouragement' and what the objective of the encourager must be: elements that have not always been analysed with sufficient clarity in discussions of the present law of incitement.

The conduct constituting the offence

4.146 Under the present law, if 'abet' and 'counsel' are, following the ruling in *AG's Reference (No 1 of 1975)*, to be given their ordinary meaning, then mere encouragement of the commission of a crime, as well as the narrower concept of the instigation of that activity, would seem to be covered by the offence of aiding and abetting. To satisfy the present crime of incitement 'an element of persuasion or pressure' on the part of the inciter may be necessary, but the law on the point is far from clear. What is needed in the reformed law is a formula that adequately encapsulates, and limits, the activity that is sought to be prohibited.

4.147 The policy questions are (i) whether the defendant must be shown to have initiated or caused the principal's intention to commit the principal crime; and (ii) even in cases where the defendant did not initiate the principal's criminal intentions, whether he must be shown to have influenced or attempted to influence those intentions by persuasion or exhortation. These issues arise most clearly where the principal has already determined to commit the principal offence, and the defendant merely gives agreeing support to that determination; but the decision as to whether, in those circumstances, the defendant should himself be criminally liable decides the limits of the whole law of encouraging crime.

4.148 Our provisional conclusion, on which we invite comment, is that the law should extend to all those who give encouragement and moral support to the commission of a crime, whether or not that encouragement has the effect of changing the principal's mind, or is intended to change the principal's mind, in the direction of the commission of that crime. There are reasons both of practicality and of principle for that view.

4.149 First, it would be extremely difficult to distinguish, with the certainty necessary for a criminal conviction, between a case where D influenced or persuaded P to commit a principal crime; and a case where D merely encouraged or supported P in the commission of that crime. There would be infinite room for allegation and argument that P would have committed the crime in any event; or had already made up his mind to do so before receiving D's encouragement; or that D's encouragement was only one of many factors influencing P's decision. Such allegations would be very easy to make and very difficult to counter: to the extent that the law of encouraging crime might well become a dead letter.

4.150 Second, however, quite apart from the practicalities of the matter, to encourage others to go ahead and commit crimes that they have already decided on, and to support them in that determination, is objectionable in itself in any law-abiding system. Even one who has decided to commit a crime may repent before he actually acts; encouragement from others may inhibit such repentance. And more generally, to give encouragement to those who are committing or thinking of committing crimes conflicts with the citizen's duty of upholding the law, and creates an antisocial atmosphere in which criminal activity is made to appear regular and praiseworthy.

4.151 We therefore proceed on the basis that encouragement to commit a crime should be enough to constitute this offence, and that it should not be necessary to show that the defendant initiated or caused either the commission of that crime or the principal's plans to commit it. Such would already appear to be the law in respect of the abetting and counselling aspects of aiding and abetting, so far as it is possible to identify any rules specifically addressing those activities. It would also appear to be the case that, despite the language in which the offence of incitement is sometimes described, there is no requirement that the inciter should in fact be the motive force in the commission of the principal crime.

4.152 The uncertainty of the limits of the present law is caused by the absence of any authoritative definition either of the counselling element in aiding and abetting or of the crime of incitement. It is therefore necessary to consider carefully how the new offence should be described and defined, in order to capture the policy approach suggested above. For reasons that will become apparent, that question is best addressed at the same time as the question of the mental element of the offence, to which we now turn.

The mental element of the offence

4.153 The general policy issue, much debated in connection with assisting, as to whether the defendant must have the commission of the principal crime as his purpose, should be much easier to resolve in the case of encouraging crime. That is because the whole notion of encouraging, inciting or exhorting the commission of a crime presupposes that the encourager wishes that crime to be committed. As Ashworth puts it, in connection with the present offence of incitement:

> The-fault element in incitement is that D should intend the substantive offence to be committed and should know the facts and circumstances specified by that offence. This is unlikely to cause a problem in most cases, since someone who either encourages or exerts pressure on another person to commit an offence will usually, by definition, intend that offence to be committed.

> Subject, therefore, to some subtleties of definition, considered below, there should be no danger of conduct that merely happens to fortify P in his criminal inclinations, without that being D's intention or purpose, falling within the ambit of a crime of 'encouragement.'

4.154 In our view (though we invite comment) that is the correct policy position for the law to take. We are concerned here only with exhortation or encouragement, and not with conduct that actually assists in the commission of an offence. If D's conduct can truly be said to assist the commission of crime, and he is aware that that is so, then there are strong arguments for imposing legal inhibitions upon it, even though the giving of such assistance was not D's purpose. Where, however, D's conduct is not of assistance to P, but merely emboldens or fortifies P in committing a crime, it seems to extend the law too far to make D's conduct itself criminal, unless D intended it to have that effect. Examples can easily be cited. Thus, D might publish an article criticising the use of animals in scientific experiments, that inspires P to cause criminal damage at a particular laboratory; or a politician criticises the policy of the police in their use of the 'breathalyser' powers, which causes one of his listeners to determine to resist such approaches, if needs be by force, on the next occasion that they are made to him. If D's remarks can in truth be analysed as encouraging or persuading others to commit such crimes, then he should be convicted. It is quite a different matter if the commission of crime is the unlooked-for outcome of his comments on a matter of public interest.

4.155 Within those policy assumptions, there are a few comparatively detailed issues of practical definition. First, the conduct encouraged must be a definable crime, and (we suggest) it should be necessary, as in the present law of incitement, that the encourager is aware of the elements, both physical and mental, that make the principal's conduct criminal. To be liable, therefore, he should have to be shown to have encouraged a defined category of criminal conduct on the part of the principal, without necessarily descending to specificities as to the place, time or detailed circumstances in which that conduct is to take place. He should also know or believe that the principal, when he acts, will do so in a mental state that will render his action criminal. These issues seem to us to be the same as arise in relation to assisting crime, and we refer the reader to the discussion of them in paragraphs 4.57–4.62 above.

4.156 Second, the requirement or assumption of purpose or intention on the part of the encourager has been seen as causing some difficulty in the (no doubt rare) case where the encourager or inciter acts under duress. D is caused, by the threats of terrorists, to persuade his son P to plant a bomb on an airliner. The last thing that D wants to happen is the death of the passengers and crew, though that is the inevitable outcome of the bombing. However, this problem is easily avoided, as Williams suggests, by recognising that what D must intend, and what he clearly does intend through his decision, however reluctant, to exercise encouragement towards P, is the commission of the crime by P, in the terms suggested in paragraph 4.155 above.

Omissions as encouragement

4.157 We discussed in paragraphs 4.69–4.74 the problems caused for the present law of complicity by omissions to exercise a right of control over the activities of law-breakers; and by 'mere presence' at the scene of a crime. It will be recalled that our provisional conclusion, as to the general offence of assistance, is that the accused should merely need to be aware, and not necessarily intend, that his acts are of assistance in the commission of crime. Because of the broader potential reach of that offence, therefore, we suggested that it could become oppressively wide if extended to omissions, as opposed to positive action.

4.158 The case of encouragement is, however, different in a number of respects. Many of the leading cases in the present law concern encouragement rather than assistance: for instance, the spectators who cheer an illegal prize-fight; or criminals present in a vehicle driven by P, whose conduct is intended by them to fortify P in driving dangerously to help them avoid arrest. In these cases the question, one of fact, is whether D's conduct can truly be described as 'encouragement', and is intended by D to be such. If D in truth encourages P to commit crimes it does not seem unreasonable, or to make the law dangerously wide, if it encompasses conduct that could also be described as an omission, or a failure to perform a duty. We say conduct that could also be described as an omission because it will be very rare for mere inactivity on the part of D to constitute an act of encouragement: the spectators must not merely be casual bystanders, but must be there to cheer; the passengers must not be merely accidentally in the vehicle, but must be there as part of a common understanding with and support of the activities of the driver. But where such people do intend to encourage the criminal activities of others, then this offence should extend to them.

Our provisional definition of the offence of encouraging crime

4.159 At the stage of a Consultation Paper we are not drafting a Bill, but we hope that, as in the case of assisting crime, it may assist critical assessment of these suggestions to offer a fairly precise formulation of the new offence.

4.160 In the Draft Code, when considering the present crime of incitement separately from aiding and abetting, we retained the word 'incite'. We doubt, however, whether that word is appropriate for the new offence. 'Incite', in its normal meaning, has somewhat instigatory connotations, thus limiting the new offence more narrowly than we provisionally, consider desirable. We rejected the simple word 'encourage' because of a fear expressed by one of the Code scrutiny groups about its ambiguity. 'Encourage' or 'encouraged', used without further expansion, can refer either to the act of encouragement, or to the fact that a person was actually encouraged. Thus, it is a perfectly natural use of language to say 'The company has been encouraged by the poor performance of its competitors'; but the present offence is not intended to extend to such non-purposive, accidental influence or support. And, on the other side of the coin, the simple use of the word 'encourage' might be thought to require that the principal had in fact been encouraged or influenced in committing the principal crime: which is neither the present law, nor what we think that the law ought to be.

4.161 Despite these problems, however, we consider that 'encouragement' best captures the nature of the activity that the law should seek to control. The, perhaps marginal, objections just discussed can be met by clearly defining the elements of the offence so as to remove ambiguity. First, it can be made plain that actual influence need not be exerted on the principal. Second, a requirement that the defendant must intend or have as his purpose the commission of the principal crime will ensure that casual or accidental 'encouragement' does not fall within this offence.

4.162 Thus explained, 'encouragement' is in our view both a necessary and a sufficient description of the conduct aimed at by the new offence. However, it may be considered desirable to mention some other common activities that also fall within this offence, even though, strictly speaking, they are all cases of encouragement. Thus, commanding or soliciting the commission of crime will be a common form of the new offence and perhaps should be specifically mentioned, even though one who can be called a commander or solicitor must in ordinary usage also necessarily be an encourager of the principal's conduct.

4.163 We therefore suggest, for critical comment,

    (1) A person commits the offence of encouraging crime if he

        (a) solicits, commands or encourages another ('the principal') to do or cause to be done an act or acts which, if done, will involve the commission of an offence by the principal; and

        (b) intends that that act or those acts should be done by the principal; and

        (c) knows or believes that the principal, in so acting, will do so with the fault required for the offence in question.

    (2) The solicitation, command or encouragement must be brought to the attention of the principal, but it is irrelevant to the person's guilt whether or not the principal reacts to or is influenced by the solicitation, command or encouragement.

    (3) The defendant need not know the identity of the principal, nor have any particular principal or group of principals in mind, provided that he intends his communication to be acted on by any person to whose attention it comes.

    (4) 'Offence' in sub-paragraphs (a) and (c) of sub-section (1) above means the breach of a specified prohibition laid down by statute or the common law; but for the purposes of this section the defendant may solicit, command or encourage the commission of such an offence without intending that it should be committed at a specific time or place.

4.164 This formulation may appear a little elaborate, but in our view it is safer to spell out the intended effect of the law in particular situations of difficulty, rather than rely for the solution of those problems on general and necessarily vague assumptions about the implications of 'incitement' or 'encouragement'. We put it forward as the basis for comment on the limits of the offence of encouraging crime.

Defences to an offence of encouraging crime

Introduction

4.165 As in the case of assisting crime, we now consider whether the offence of encouraging crime requires the creation of defences special to that offence, over and above the general common law and statutory defences that apply throughout the criminal law.

4.166 Many of the defences discussed in connection with assisting crime are, in our view, not appropriate for consideration in connection with encouraging crime. That is because such defences are primarily or wholly designed to meet cases in which the defendant is aware that he is assisting the commission of a current or future crime, but does not have the commission of that crime as his purpose. We therefore take the view, as we did in respect of those cases of assisting crime in which it is the accessory's intention or purpose that the principal crime should be committed, that the defences of employment; 'ordinary course of business'; 'social' assistance; law enforcement; and limitation of harmful consequences; are inappropriate in respect of a case of encouragement. In the first two cases, the policy reasons for affording relief to one who knowingly but non-purposively assists do not apply to one who encourages; in the other cases, the factual circumstances that have to be established for the defence even to be considered do not seem to exist where the accessory has encouraged the commission of the crime.

Persons involved in statutory offences

4.167 As in the case of assisting crime, this defence raises more difficult issues. In most cases, it will be simply inappropriate to extend the defence to an encourager. For instance, the situation of the after-hours purchaser of drink does not seem to be deserving of sympathy if he can be shown to have encouraged, rather than merely to have been the passive beneficiary of, the landlord's illegal sale. We therefore see no good reason for the present defence to be applied generally in cases of encouraging crime. However, as in the case of assisting crime we recognise that there may be cases, conspicuously those of sexual offences against minors, where the 'victim' should be exculpated even though she encouraged rather than merely assisted in the commission of the offence. We therefore invited comment, as we did in connection with assisting crime, as to what offences might be covered by such a rule.

Withdrawal

4.168 Since incitement is a separate offence, the defence of withdrawal, potentially recognised in respect of counselling as in respect of all the other elements of aiding and abetting, is not available in cases of incitement. There is however no obvious policy reason why that should be so; and with the replacement of both incitement and counselling by a new offence of encouraging crime the matter can be considered afresh.

4.169 The pragmatic considerations in favour of recognising effective repentance and counter-measures before the principal crime is committed apply equally in the case of encouragement as in the case of assistance. In stating the law in respect of the counselling element of aiding and abetting for the purposes of the Draft Code we tentatively suggested that the defence of withdrawal was available if the accessory either countermanded his encouragement with a view to preventing the commission of the principal offence; or took all reasonable steps with a view to preventing its commission. We provisionally consider that those are the correct formulations for a defence of withdrawal applied to a new offence of encouragement. We do, however, invite comment on whether it should be sufficient that the encourager subsequently does one or other of the acts of countermanding his encouragement or taking steps to prevent the commission of the principal offence. it seems arguable that where it is possible for him to do so, the encourager should not only countermand his encouragement but also take steps to prevent the offence, most conspicuously by enabling the police to intervene.

...

Impossibility

4.174 It was originally the law that, if the other requirements of the offence are fulfilled, a person could be guilty of incitement even though the crime incited was impossible of the decisions on attempt in *Haughton v Smith*, and on conspiracy in *DPP v Nock*, that it was a principle of the common law applying to all inchoate offences, and therefore to incitement, that if the principal crime envisaged was impossible of commission there could be no liability for an inchoate offence in respect of it. The question does not arise in the present law of aiding and abetting, because of the requirement that the principal offence be actually committed; but since we envisage both of the new offences of encouraging and of aiding crime as being inchoate in nature it must be reconsidered here.

4.175 Much depends, in the present law of incitement, on the specificity with which the principal crime is envisaged, and on whether that crime is truly impossible. Thus, the conviction in *McDonough* was explained in *Fitzmaurice* on the grounds that 'though there may have been no stolen goods or no goods at all which were available to be received at the time of the incitement, the offence of incitement to receive stolen goods could nevertheless be proved because it was not impossible that at the relevant time in the future the necessary goods would be there'; and in *Fitzmaurice* itself the principle that the Court of Appeal recognised did not lead to an acquittal because, although the robbery that D incited P to take part in was (unknown to D) a charade, and never intended to take place, it was not impossible for such a robbery to have occurred.

4.176 Such fine distinctions indicate the difficulty of applying the *Fitzmaurice* rule. More fundamentally, however, we question whether the rule is sound as a matter of principle. The same rule, as applied in the case of attempt and of conspiracy, has been reversed by statute; and it seems likely that a similar step would have been taken in respect of incitement but for a mistaken belief that the common law principle enunciated in *DPP v Nock* did not extend to that crime. The rationale of these legislative interventions was that the justification for the existence of inchoate offences lies in the anti-social and criminal intentions or inclinations of the secondary party, which he carries into action; and those intentions are none the less culpable because they are based on mistaken beliefs about the relevant facts. Similarly, the offence of assisting crime is based on the defendant's knowledge or belief that what he does will assist in the commission of a crime; and the offence of encouraging crime on the defendant's intention that a crime should be committed by others. While we invite comment on this point, as at present advised we see no reason why, if the defendant fulfils those requirements, he should escape liability because the commission of that crime is, unknown to him, impossible.

4.177 The particular structure of assisting and of encouraging crime however raises one issue that has no direct parallel with those considered in relation to 'impossible' attempts, and which must be commented on separately. Both of the new offences will require knowledge or belief on the part of the defendant as to the legally culpable state of mind of the principal. What then of offences that are 'impossible' not in the sense discussed in connection with attempt, that the *actus reus* cannot in fact be committed; but in the sense that the principal does not in fact have the culpable state of mind necessary for the offence, though the 'accessory' believes that to be the case?

4.178 The point can be illustrated by cases that are the converse of those used in paragraph 4.60 above to illustrate the basic principle that the accessory is not liable if he, wrongly, believes the principal to be acting innocently. For instance, D might keep watch while P removed property from X's house, not realising that P claimed ownership of the property and thus was not or might not be acting dishonestly; or D provides a document for use by P which D knows to be a forgery but which, unknown to D, P thinks to be genuine. Such problems will hardly be frequent in practice. It is unlikely that in these or similar cases the true state of P's mind will not be known to D. And, if such cases did arise, they would be unlikely to be detected or prosecuted. Nonetheless, we must resolve the issue of principle of whether it should be possible to convict of assisting or encouraging crime where the defendant has the necessary belief as to the principal's culpable state of mind, but that belief is in fact false.

4.179 While we ask for separate comment on this point, our provisional view is that the principle should hold good in this case, and that the essence of the new offences, like any other inchoate offences, is the anti-social and criminal intentions of the defendant. The implementation of those intentions remains, therefore, something of which the law should take notice even in cases where actual assistance in the commission of crime is impossible because the intended principal, contrary to the belief of his would-be accessory, lacks the necessary criminal intent.

CHAPTER 11

INCHOATE OFFENCES – CONSPIRACY

At its most simple, a conspiracy is an agreement between two or more persons on a course of conduct that will culminate in the commission of a criminal offence. Originally a common law offence, since the enactment of the Criminal Law Act 1977 the vast majority of criminal conspiracies are now charged as offences contrary to s 1(1) of that Act, although, as will be seen, certain common law forms of conspiracy survived the coming into force of the 1977 Act.

STATUTORY CONSPIRACY

Criminal Law Act 1977

1(1)   Subject to the following provisions of this part of this Act, if a person agrees with any other person or persons that a course of conduct shall be pursued which, if the agreement is carried out in accordance with their intentions, either:

(a) will necessarily amount to or involve the commission of any offence or offences by one or more of the parties to the agreement; or

(b) would do so but for the existence of facts which render the commission of the offence or any of the offences impossible,

he shall be guilty of conspiracy to commit the offence or offences in question.

1(2)   Where liability for any offence may be incurred without knowledge on the part of the person committing it of any particular fact or circumstance necessary for the commission of the offence, a person shall nevertheless not be guilty of conspiracy to commit that offence by virtue of subsection (1) above unless he and at least one other party to the agreement intend or know that the fact or circumstance shall or will exist at the time when the conduct constituting the offence is to take place.

The *actus reus* of statutory conspiracy

The *actus reus* of conspiracy is the agreement: *R v Gill* (1993) 97 Cr App R 215 (CA). This agreement is usually proved by evidence of acts carried out to fulfil the agreement: see *R v Cooper* (extracted below). Nevertheless, because it is the agreement itself which amounts to the conspiracy, it does not matter if the acts actually carried out differ from those agreed: see *R v Bolton* (1992) 94 Cr App R 74.

R v Cooper and Compton [1947] 2 All ER 701 (CA)

Humphreys J: These two appellants were tried at the Central Criminal Court on an indictment which contained nine counts. The first count was a charge of conspiracy to steal. The second, third, fourth and fifth counts alleged that in four separate cases the appellants had been guilty of robbing four separate persons, that is, forcing them to give their money or goods as the result of threats and owing to fear. The next four counts charged that in those same cases they had stolen the money of those four persons, simple larceny.

The main ground of this appeal is put well in the grounds of appeal. The jury found a verdict of guilty on the first count. They found a verdict of not guilty on each and all of the remaining counts, and it is argued in support of the appeals that in those circumstances a verdict of not guilty on the substantive counts 2 and 9 leaves the first count unsupported by sufficient, or any, evidence ...

... The jury ... returned the verdict of guilty on the first count and not guilty on each of the others ...

... All we can say is that the jury has said in terms: 'We are not satisfied with the case for the prosecution on counts 2–9. We are satisfied with the case for the prosecution on count 1.'

Is it possible that this court can uphold that verdict as being reasonable? In a great many cases there is no doubt that a verdict of guilty of conspiracy, but not guilty of the particular acts charged, is a perfectly proper and reasonable one. In such cases it would be wrong not to insert in the indictment a charge of conspiracy. Criminal lawyers know it often happens that, while a general conspiracy to do such a thing as to steal is likely to be inferred by the jury from the evidence, it may be that the evidence of the particular acts constituting the larcenies charged in the indictment are supported by rather nebulous evidence. That is a case where the jury may say, and very likely will say, not guilty of larceny but guilty of being concerned with others to commit larceny ...

In the present case it appears that to us that there was no necessity from any point of view for the insertion of any charge of conspiracy. A verdict of guilty could only be supported if the jury believed the general story, and the general story was told by four different persons, each of whom, if he was believed, proved conclusively a charge of stealing ...

R v Bolton (1992) 94 Cr App R 74 (CA)

Facts: The defendant was charged with conspiracy to procure the execution of valuable securities by deception. The appeal concerned the question whether it mattered that the defendant expected a cheque but in fact money was transferred by electronic means.

Woolf LJ: ... [His Lordship referred to *R v Siracusa* (1990) 90 Cr App R 340, *R v Anderson* [1986] AC 27 and *R v Reed* [1982] Crim LR 819.] In the latter case Donaldson LJ said:

> ... A and B agree to drive from London to Edinburgh in a time which can be achieved without exceeding the speed limits, but only if the traffic which they encounter is exceptionally light. Their agreement will not necessarily involve the commission of any offence, even if it is carried out in accordance with their intentions, and they do arrive ... within the agreed time. Accordingly the agreement does not constitute the offence of statutory conspiracy.

[Woolf LJ went on to say:] there can be a distinction between the manner in which the conspirators intend to achieve their objective and how that objective is in fact achieved. Taking the example given by Donaldson LJ in the case of *Reed*, if A and B agree and intend to drive from London to Edinburgh in excess of the speed limit because they expect heavy traffic, the fact that it proves unnecessary for them to do so because the traffic is light does not avoid them being guilty of conspiracy. Their agreement was to do something which necessarily would involve the commission of an offence, namely exceeding the speed limit and they embarked on the commission of that offence. So in this case, if Roger Bolton and his co-conspirators agree dishonestly etc to procure the building societies to make a mortgage advance by executing a valuable security and this was what they set out to achieve, it would not mean the conspirators were not guilty of conspiracy, if contrary to what they intended, the building societies happened always to use a method of advancing the mortgage moneys which did not involve the use of a valuable security. In the case of conspiracy as opposed to the substantive offence, it is what is agreed to be done and not what was in fact done which is all important ...

R v Griffiths [1966] 1 QB 589 (CA)

Paull J: ... In the opening the case for the prosecution, Mr Morris said: 'This is the story of a large-scale fraud', and a little later said: 'It is the case for the Crown that they each conspired together with Griffiths and Booth in this fraud but not with each other'. Construed strictly, these words mean that there were a number of different conspiracies and not one conspiracy, for in law all must join the one agreement, each with the others, in order to constitute one conspiracy. They may join in at various times, each attaching himself to that agreement; any one of them may not know all the other parties but only that there are other parties; any one of them may not know the full extent of the scheme to which he attaches himself. But what each must know is that there is coming into existence, or is in existence, a scheme which goes beyond the illegal act or acts which he agrees to do ...

The matter can be illustrated quite simply. I employ an accountant to make out my tax return. He and his clerk are both present when I am about to sign the return. I notice an item in my expenses of £100 and say: 'I don't remember incurring this expense'. The clerk says: 'Well, actually I put it in. You didn't incur it, but I didn't think you would object to a few pounds being saved.' The accountant indicates his agreement to this attitude. After some hesitation I agree to let it stand. On those bare facts I cannot be charged with 50 others in a conspiracy to defraud the Exchequer of £100,000 on the basis that this accountant and his clerk have persuaded 500 other clients to make false returns, some being false in one way, some in another, or even all in the same way. I have not knowingly attached myself to a general agreement to defraud. Similarly, the Post Office clerk who agrees to alter a date stamp in a case where a bookmaker has been swindled must know that the alteration is to be used for a fraudulent purpose. He therefore joins a scheme to defraud that bookmaker, of whom he may not have heard, but he cannot be indicted, merely because he has agreed to alter that stamp, on a charge of a conspiracy to alter date stamps and cheat bookmakers all over the country ...

Notes and queries

1   Certain persons cannot be guilty of conspiracy – notably the intended victim of the conspiracy and children under the age of 10. Similarly, a person cannot be guilty of conspiracy if the only other parties to the conspiracy are

his spouse; a child under the age of 10; or the intended victim; see further s 2 of the 1977 Act.

2   In *Practice Note* [1977] 2 All ER 540, Lord Widgery CJ at the sitting of the court announced the following practice direction made after consultation with the judges of the Queen's Bench Division:

(1) In any case where an indictment contains substantive counts and a related conspiracy count, the judge should require the prosecution to justify the joinder, or, failing justification, to elect whether to proceed on the substantive or on the conspiracy counts.

(2) A joinder is justified for this purpose if the judge considers that the interests of justice demands it.

3   Where D1 and D2 are charged with conspiracy, the acquittal of D1 does not necessarily mean that D2 must be acquitted as well. Under s 5 of the Criminal Law Act 1977, the court will have regard to whether or not, in all the circumstances of the case, the conviction of D2 is inconsistent with the acquittal of D1.

The *mens rea* of statutory conspiracy

To be convicted of conspiracy a defendant must clearly intend to agree, but the courts have had difficulty with the question of the extent to which a defendant must actually be shown to have intended that the agreement be carried out, particularly where he himself intends to play no part in the execution of the agreement. Whilst Lord Bridge in *Anderson* (below) thought a conspirator would have to intend to play some part in carrying out the agreement, the Court of Appeal in *Siracusa* (below) quickly clarified this by explaining that the only mens rea required was an intention to agree that other parties to the conspiracy should carry out the agreed course of conduct.

R v Anderson [1986] AC 27 (HL)

Lord Bridge of Harwich: ... In June 1981 the appellant and Ahmed Andaloussi were both in custody on remand in Lewes prison. Andaloussi was awaiting trial on charges of very serious drug offences and was rightly believed by the appellant to have large sums of money at his disposal. The appellant was on remand in connection with some entirely different matter. He spent one night in the same cell as Andaloussi. The appellant was then confidently expecting that in a short time he would be, as in the event he was, released on bail. During the night they spent together the appellant agreed with Andaloussi to participate in a scheme to effect Andaloussi's escape from prison. Other participants in the scheme were to be Ahmed Andaloussi's brother Mohammed and Mohammed Assou. They were to maintain contact with Ahmed in prison after the appellant's release. The appellant was to be paid £20,000 for his part in the escape scheme. It is not clear, nor is it significant for the purpose of any issue arising in the appeal, how far details of the escape plan were worked out at the initial meeting in prison between the appellant and Ahmed Andaloussi. What is clear is that either at that meeting or after the appellant's release from prison and after one or more meetings between the appellant and Assou, it was agreed that the appellant would purchase and supply diamond wire, a cutting agent capable of cutting through metal bars, to be smuggled into the prison by Assou or Mohammed Andaloussi to enable Ahmed Andaloussi to escape from his cell. Further steps in the escape plan were to include the provision of rope and a ladder to enable Ahmed Andaloussi to climb on to the roof of an industrial building in the prison and thence over the main wall, transport to drive him away from the prison and safe accommodation where he could hide.

What happened in the event was that the appellant received from Assou a payment of £2,000 on account of the agreed fee of £20,000. Shortly after this the appellant was injured in a road accident and thereafter took no further step in pursuance of the escape plan. His admitted intention, however, was to acquire the diamond wire and give it to Assou. His further intention, according to the version of the facts which we must for present purposes accept, was then to insist that before he would proceed further he should be paid a further £10,000 on account, on receipt of which he would have left the country and gone to live in Spain, taking no further part in the scheme to effect Andaloussi's escape ...

The Court of Appeal, having dismissed his appeal, certified that their decision involved a point of law of general public importance in terms which can conveniently be divided into two parts, since, in truth, there are two separate questions involved:

(1) Is a person who 'agrees' with two or more others, who themselves intend to pursue a course of conduct which will necessarily involve the commission of an offence, and who has a secret intention himself to participate in part only of that course of conduct, guilty himself of conspiracy to commit that offence under s 1(1) of the Criminal Law Act 1977?

(2) If not, is he liable to be indicted as a principal offender under s 8 of the Accessories and Abettors Act 1861? ...

The Criminal Law Act of 1977, subject to exceptions not presently material, abolished the offence of conspiracy at common law. It follows that the elements of the new statutory offence of conspiracy must be ascertained purely by interpretation of the language of s 1(1) of the Act of 1977. For purposes of analysis it is perhaps convenient to isolate the three clauses each of which must be taken as indicating an essential ingredient of the offence as follows: (1) 'if a person agrees with any other person or persons that a course of conduct shall be pursued' (2) 'which will necessarily amount to or involve the commission of any offence or offences by one or more of the parties to the agreement' (3) 'if the agreement is carried out in accordance with their intentions'.

Clause (1) presents, as it seems to me, no difficulty. It means exactly what it says and what it says is crystal clear. To be convicted, the party charged must have agreed with one or more others that 'a course of conduct shall be pursued'. What is important is to resist the temptation to introduce into this simple concept ideas derived from the civil law of contract. Any number of persons may agree that a course of conduct shall be pursued without undertaking any contractual liability. The agreed course of conduct may be a simple or an elaborate one and may involve the participation of two or any larger number of persons who may have agreed to play a variety of roles in the course of conduct agreed.

Again, clause (2) could hardly use simpler language. Here what is important to note is that it is not necessary that more than one of the participants in the agreed course of conduct shall commit a substantive offence. It is, of course, necessary that any party to the agreement shall have assented to play his part in the agreed course of conduct, however innocent in itself, knowing that the part to be played by one or more of the others will amount to or involve the commission of an offence.

It is only clause (3) which presents any possible ambiguity. The heart of the submission for the appellant is that in order to be convicted of conspiracy to commit a given offence the language of clause (3) requires that the party charged should not only have agreed that a course of conduct shall be pursued which will necessarily amount to or involve the commission of that offence by himself or one or more other parties to the agreement, but must also be proved himself to have intended that that offence should be committed. Thus, it is submitted here that the appellant's case that he never intended that Andaloussi should be enabled to escape from prison raised an issue to be left to the jury, who should have been directed to convict him only if satisfied that he did so intend. I do not find it altogether easy to understand why the draftsman of this provision chose to use the phrase 'in accordance with their intentions'. But I suspect the answer may be that this seemed a desirable alternative to the phrase 'in accordance with its terms', or any similar expression, because it is a matter of common experience in the criminal courts that the 'terms' of a criminal conspiracy are hardly ever susceptible of proof. The evidence from which a jury may infer a criminal conspiracy is almost invariably to be found in the conduct of the parties. This was so at common law and remains so under the statute. If the evidence in a given case justifies the inference of an agreement that a course of conduct should be pursued, it is a not inappropriate formulation of the test of the criminality of the inferred agreement to ask whether the further inference can be drawn that a crime would necessarily have been committed if the agreed course of conduct had been pursued in accordance with the several intentions of the parties. Whether that is an accurate analysis or not, I am clearly driven by consideration of the diversity of roles which parties may agree to play in criminal conspiracies to reject any construction of the statutory language which would require the prosecution to prove an intention on the part of each conspirator that the criminal offence or offences which will necessarily be committed by one or more of the conspirators if the agreed course of conduct is fully carried out should in fact be committed. A simple example will illustrate the absurdity to which this construction would lead. The proprietor of a car hire firm agrees for a substantial payment to make available a hire car to a gang for use in a robbery and to make false entries in his books relating to the hiring to which he can point if the number of the car is traced back to him in connection with the robbery. Being fully aware of the circumstances of the robbery in which the car is proposed to be used he is plainly a party to the conspiracy to rob. Making his car available for use in the robbery is as much part of the relevant agreed course of conduct as the robbery itself. Yet, once he has been paid, it will be a matter of complete indifference to him whether the robbery is in fact committed or not. In these days of highly organised crime the most serious statutory conspiracies will frequently involve an elaborate and complex agreed course of conduct in which many will consent to play necessary but subordinate roles, not involving them in any direct participation in the commission of the offence or offences at the centre of the conspiracy. Parliament cannot have intended that such parties should escape conviction of conspiracy on the basis that it cannot be proved against them that they intended that the relevant offence or offences should be committed.

There remains the important question whether a person who has agreed that a course of conduct will be pursued which, if pursued as agreed, will necessarily amount to or involve the commission of an offence, is guilty of statutory conspiracy irrespective of his intention, and, if not, what is the *mens rea* of the offence. I have no hesitation in answering the first part of the question in the negative. There may be many situations in which perfectly respectable citizens, more particularly those concerned with law enforcement, may enter into agreements that a course of conduct shall be pursued which will involve commission of a crime without the least intention of playing any part in furtherance of the ostensibly agreed criminal objective, but rather with the purpose of exposing and frustrating the criminal purpose of the other parties to the agreement. To say this is in no way to encourage schemes by which police act, directly or through the agency of informers, as agents provocateurs for the purpose of entrapment. That is conduct of which the courts have always strongly disapproved. But it may sometimes happen, as most of us with experience in criminal trials well know, that a criminal enterprise is well advanced in the course of preparation when it comes to the notice either of the police or of some honest citizen in such circumstances that the only prospect of exposing and frustrating the criminals is that some innocent person should play the part of an intending collaborator in the course of criminal conduct proposed to be pursued. The mens rea implicit in the offence of statutory conspiracy must clearly be such as to recognise the innocence of such a person, notwithstanding that he will, in literal terms, be obliged to agree that a course of conduct be pursued involving the commission of an offence.

I have said already, but I repeat to emphasise its importance, that an essential ingredient in the crime of conspiring to commit a specific offence or offences under s 1(1) of the Act of 1977 is that the accused should agree that a course of conduct be pursued which he knows must involve the commission by one or more of the parties to the agreement of that offence or those offences. But, beyond the mere fact of agreement, the necessary *mens rea* of the crime is, in my opinion, established if, and only if, it is shown that the accused, when he entered into the agreement, intended to play some part in the agreed course of conduct in furtherance of the criminal purpose which the agreed course of conduct was intended to achieve. Nothing less will suffice; nothing more is required.

Applying this test to the facts which, for the purposes of the appeal, we must assume, the appellant, in agreeing that a course of conduct be pursued that would, if successful, necessarily involve the offence of effecting Andaloussi's escape from lawful custody, clearly intended, by providing diamond wire to be smuggled into the prison, to play a part in the agreed course of conduct in furtherance of that criminal objective. Nether the fact that he intended to play no further part in attempting to effect the escape, nor that he believed the escape to be impossible, would, if the jury had supposed they might be true, have afforded him any defence.

In the result, I would answer the first part of the certified question in the affirmative and dismiss the appeal. Your Lordships did not find it necessary to hear argument directed to the second part of the certified question and it must, therefore, be left unanswered.

R v Siracusa (1990) 90 Cr App R 340 (CA)

O'Connor LJ: ... The case arises out of the operations of an organisation of smugglers engaged in moving massive quantities of heroin from Thailand and cannabis from Kashmir to Canada via England. The scheme was simple. The drugs were to be housed in secret compartments in selected items of locally produced furniture, which would be included in substantial shipments of furniture. The object of passing the consignments through England was to support the manifests to be presented to the Canadian customs declaring the country of origin of the goods as England.

On 13 December 1984 a consignment of 52 packing cases of furniture from India consigned to Elongate Ltd arrived at Felixstowe. Customs officers found in some articles of furniture cannabis with a street value of £0.5 million in England and £3 million in Canada. They repacked and waited and watched. The consignment was cleared by shipping agents and delivered to a warehouse, Unit 5, Batsworth Road, Mitcham. The customs moved in on 18 December 1984, seized the consignment and arrested Siracusa and a man named Gaultieri. Unit 5 is a spacious warehouse. There was nothing in it except the 52 cases of furniture and a fork-lift truck. The work in hand was the painting out of the Indian shipping marks with black paint.

On 28 May 1985, a consignment of 84 packing cases of furniture from Thailand consigned to Ital Provisions Ltd arrived at Southampton. Customs officers found in some articles of furniture heroin with a street value of £15 million in England and £75 million in Canada. They repacked some of the heroin and waited and watched. The consignment was not delivered in this country, but transshipped and left for Canada on 8 June 1985.

After delivery in Canada on 21 June 1985, enforcement officers moved in, seized the consignment and arrested three men. It was found that they had gone unerringly to the cases containing the pieces in which heroin was concealed. In England, Monteleone, Luciani and Di Carlo were arrested on 21 June 1985 ...

The appellants contend that ... the prosecution had to prove against each defendant that he knew that the Kashmir operation involved cannabis and that the Thailand operation involved heroin ...

His Lordship referred to the speech of Lord Bridge in *R v Anderson* [1986] AC 27 and commented:

... We think it obvious that Lord Bridge cannot have been intending that the organiser of a crime who recruited others to carry it out would not himself be guilty of conspiracy unless it could be proved that he intended to play some active part himself thereafter ...

The present case is a classic example of such a conspiracy. It is the hallmark of such crimes that the organisers try to remain in the background and more often than not are not apprehended. Second, the origins of all conspiracies are concealed and it is usually quite impossible to establish when or where the initial agreement was made, or when or where other conspirators were recruited. The very existence of the agreement can only be inferred from overt acts. Participation in a conspiracy is infinitely variable: it can be active or passive. If the majority shareholder and director of a company consents to the company being used for drug smuggling carried out in the company's name by a fellow director and minority shareholder, he is guilty of conspiracy. Consent, that is the agreement or adherence to the agreement, can be inferred if it is proved that he knew what was going on and the intention to participate in the furtherance of the criminal purpose is also established by his failure to stop the unlawful activity. Lord Bridge's dictum does not require anything more.

His Lordship then referred to the *dictum* of Lord Bridge that:

.... an essential ingredient in the crime of conspiring to commit a specific offence or offences under s 1(1) of the Act of 1977 is that the accused should agree that a course of conduct be pursued which he knows must involve the commission by one or more of the parties to the agreement of that offence or those offences.

And O'Connor LJ went to observe that:

Lord Bridge plainly does not mean that the prosecution have to prove that persons who agree to import prohibited drugs into this country know that the offence which will be committed will be in contravention of s 170(2) of the Customs and Excise Management Act. He is not to be taken as saying that the prosecution must prove that the accused knew the name of the crime. We are satisfied that Lord Bridge was doing no more than applying the words of s 1 of the Criminal Law Act 1977, namely that when the accused agreed to the course of conduct, he knew that it involved the commission of an offence.

The *mens rea* sufficient to support the commission of a substantive offence will not necessarily be sufficient to support a charge of conspiracy to commit that offence. An intent to cause grievous bodily harm is sufficient to support the charge of murder, but is not sufficient to support a charge of conspiracy to murder or of attempt to murder.

We have come to the conclusion that if the prosecution charge a conspiracy to contravene s 170(2) of the Customs and Excise Management Act by the importation of heroin, then the prosecution must prove that the agreed course of conduct was the importation of heroin. This is because the essence of the crime of conspiracy is the agreement and in simple terms, you do not prove an agreement to import heroin by proving an agreement to import cannabis.

We are confident that in coming to this conclusion, we are not making the enforcement of the anti-drug laws more difficult. If the facts suggest that the agreement was to import prohibited drugs of more than one class that can be appropriately laid because s 1(1) of the Criminal Law Act expressly provides for the agreed course of conduct to involve the commission of more than one offence ...

Yip Chiu-Cheung v R [1994] 3 WLR 514 (PC)

Lord Griffiths: ... The prosecution case was based primarily on the evidence of Philip Needham who was an undercover drug enforcement officer of the United States of America and named in the indictment as a co-conspirator. The other conspirator, referred to in the indictment as a person unknown, was introduced to Needham by the defendant under the name of Hom.

In outline Needham's evidence was that he had a series of meetings in Thailand with the defendant, at one of which Hom also took part, at which it was arranged that Needham would act as a courier to carry five kilos of heroin from Hong Kong to Australia, travelling by air.

The arrangement was that Needham would fly to Hong Kong on 22 October 1989 under the name of Larsen, where he would be met by the defendant. He would then stay at the Nathan Hotel in Kowloon for a few days and then fly on to Australia with five kilos of heroin supplied by the defendant. For this service he would be paid US $16,000. In fact Needham did not fly to Hong Kong on 22 October because the flight was delayed and he missed the rescheduled flight. Needham said he had no way of contacting the defendant in Hong Kong and had been advised by the Hong Kong authorities that the Nathan Hotel would be a dangerous place for him to stay. Needham therefore proceeded no further with the plan, and did not go to Hong Kong.

The defendant was arrested in Hong Kong on 15 November, a piece of paper with the name Larsen was found in the defendant's possession and it was admitted that he had come to the airport to meet Needham's flight on 22 October.

Needham said that throughout his dealings with the defendant and Hom he kept the authorities in Hong Kong and Australia informed of the plans and they agreed that he would not be prevented from carrying the heroin out of Hong Kong and into Australia. It was obviously the intention to try to identify and arrest both the suppliers and the distributors of the drug ...

On the principal ground of appeal it was submitted that the trial judge and the Court of Appeal were wrong to hold that Needham, the undercover agent, could be a conspirator because he lacked the necessary mens rea or guilty mind required for the offence of conspiracy. It was urged upon their Lordships that no moral guilt attached to the undercover agent who was at all times acting courageously and with the best of motives in attempting to infiltrate and bring to justice a gang of criminal drug dealers. In these circumstances it was argued that it would be wrong to treat the agent as having any criminal intent, and reliance was placed upon a passage in the speech of Lord Bridge of Harwich in *R v Anderson* [1986] AC 27, 38–39; but in that case Lord Bridge was dealing with a different situation from that which exists in the present case. There may be many cases in which undercover police officers or other law enforcement agents pretend to join a conspiracy in order to gain information about the plans of the criminals, with no intention of taking any part in the planned crime but rather with the intention of providing information that will frustrate it. It was to this situation that Lord Bridge was referring in *R v Anderson*. The crime of conspiracy requires an agreement between two or more persons to commit an unlawful act with the intention of carrying it out. It is the intention to carry out the crime that constitutes the necessary mens rea for the offence. As Lord Bridge pointed out, an undercover agent who has no intention of committing the crime lacks the necessary mens rea to be a conspirator.

The facts of the present case are quite different. Nobody can doubt that Needham was acting courageously and with the best of motives; he was trying to break a drug ring. But equally there can be no doubt that the method he chose and in which the police in Hong Kong acquiesced involved the commission of the criminal offence of trafficking in drugs by exporting heroin from Hong Kong without a licence. Needham intended to commit that offence by carrying the heroin through the customs and on to the aeroplane bound for Australia.

Neither the police, nor customs, nor any other members of the executive have any power to alter the terms of the ordinance forbidding the export of heroin, and the fact that they may turn a blind eye when the heroin is exported does not prevent it from being a criminal offence ...

Naturally, Needham never expected to be prosecuted if he carried out the plan as intended. But the fact that in such circumstances the authorities would not prosecute the undercover agent does not mean that he did not commit the crime albeit as part of a wider scheme to combat drug dealing.

The judge correctly directed the jury that they should regard Needham as a conspirator if they found that he intended to export the heroin ...

COMMON LAW CONSPIRACY

Although s 5(1) of the Criminal Law Act 1977 states that it has the effect of abolishing common law conspiracy, s 5(2) provides that this '... does not affect the offence of conspiracy at common law so far as it relates to conspiracy to defraud'. Subsection (3) goes on to preserve common law conspiracy to corrupt public morals or outrages public decency.

Conspiracy to defraud

There are two types of conspiracy to defraud. One involves agreeing dishonestly to deprive a person of something to which he is entitled or to which he might be entitled; no actual deception need be proved. See *Scott v Metropolitan Police Commissioner* [1975] AC 819 and *R v Hollinshead* [1985] AC 975.

The other form, which does require proof of deception, consists of dishonestly deceiving a person into acting contrary to his public duty. See, for example, *Welham v DPP* [1961] AC 103 and *R v Moses* [1991] Crim LR 617.

Scott v Metropolitan Police Commissioner [1975] AC 818 (HL)

Viscount Dilhorne: ... The Court of Appeal certified that a point of law of general public importance was involved in the decision to dismiss the appeal against conviction on count 1, namely:

> Whether, on a charge of conspiracy to defraud, the Crown must establish an agreement to deprive the owners of their property by deception; or whether it is sufficient to prove an agreement to prejudice the rights of another or others without lawful justification and in circumstances of dishonesty ...

In this case it is not necessary to decide that a conspiracy to defraud may exist even though its object was not to secure a financial advantage by inflicting an economic loss on the person at whom the conspiracy was directed. But for myself I see no reason why what was said by Lord Radcliffe in relation to forgery should not equally apply in relation to conspiracy to defraud.

In this case the accused bribed servants of the cinema owners to secure possession of films in order to copy them and in order to enable them to let the copies out on hire. By so doing Mr Blom-Cooper conceded they inflicted more than nominal damage to the goodwill of the owners of the copyright and distribution rights of the films. By so doing they secured for themselves profits which but for their actions might have been secured by those owners just as in *R v Button* 3 Cox CC 229 the defendants obtained profits which might have been secured by their employer. In the circumstances it is, I think, clear that they inflicted pecuniary loss on those owners ...

Reverting to the questions certified by the Court of Appeal, the answer to the first question is in my opinion in the negative. I am not very happy about the way in which the second question is phrased although the word 'prejudice' has been not infrequently used in this connection. If by 'prejudice' is meant 'injure', then I think the answer to that question is yes, for in my opinion it is clearly the law that an agreement by two or more by dishonesty to deprive a person of something which is his or to which he is or would be or might be entitled and an agreement by two or more by dishonesty to injure some proprietary right of his, suffices to constitute the offence of conspiracy to defraud.

In my opinion this appeal should be dismissed.

Lord Diplock: My Lords, I have had the advantage of reading the speech of my noble and learned friend, Viscount Dilhorne. I agree with it. The authorities he cites and others cited in the speeches in this House in the contemporaneous appeal in *R v Withers* [1975] AC 751, in my view, established the following propositions: ...

(2) Where the intended victim of a 'conspiracy to defraud' is a private individual the purpose of the conspirators must be to a cause the victim economic loss by depriving him of some property or right, corporeal or incorporeal, to which he is or would or might become entitled. The intended means by which the purpose is to be achieved must be dishonest. They need not involve fraudulent misrepresentation such as is needed to constitute the civil tort of deceit. Dishonesty of any kind is enough.

(3) Where the intended victim of a 'conspiracy to defraud' is a person performing public duties as distinct from a private individual it is sufficient if the purpose is to cause him to act contrary to his public duty, and the intended means of achieving this purpose are dishonest. The purpose need not involve causing economic loss to anyone.

In the instant case the intended victims of the conspiracy to defraud were private individuals. The facts bring it squarely within proposition 2 above. The dishonest means to be employed were clandestine bribery.

I would dismiss the appeal.

R v Hollinshead [1985] 1 AC 975 (HL)

Lord Roskill: ... The Court of Appeal (Criminal Division) certified two points of law as of general public importance:

1   If parties agree (a) to manufacture devices whose only use is fraudulently to alter electricity meters and (b) to sell those devices to a person who intends merely to re-sell them and not himself to use them, does that agreement constitute a common law conspiracy to defraud?

2   Alternatively, is such an agreement properly charged as a statutory conspiracy to aid, abet counsel or procure persons unknown to commit offences under s 2 of the Theft Act 1978? ...

His Lordship quoted from the speech of Lord Bridge of Harwich in *R v Ayres* [1984] AC 447 and continued:

I therefore turn to consider whether it was necessary for the prosecution in order to secure a conviction on count 2 to aver and prove a dishonest agreement actually to use the black boxes so as to defraud the intended victims, various electricity boards ...

The real question ... is whether in order to secure conviction on count 2 it was necessary to aver and prove a dishonest agreement by the respondents actually to use the black boxes, the submission being that it was not enough to show only an intention that such a dishonest use should follow their dishonest manufacture and sale ...

His Lordship referred to a number of authorities including *AG's Ref (No 1 of 1982)* [1983] QB 751, concerning a dishonest agreement to produce, label and distribute bottles of whiskey so as to represent them as containing whiskey of a well known brand which in fact they did not contain, and said:

In my view the respondents were liable to be convicted of conspiracy to defraud because they agreed to manufacture and sell and thus put into circulation dishonest devices, the sole purpose of which was to cause loss just as the former defendants in the case just referred to would, apart from the jurisdictional problem, have been liable to be convicted to defraud because they agreed dishonestly to produce, label and distribute bottles of whiskey, the sole purpose of the sale of which was to defraud potential purchasers of those bottles ...

In the result I would allow the appeals, answer certified question 1 'Yes' and certified question 2 'No'. I would restore the convictions of the respondents on count 2 ...

Welham v DPP [1961] AC 103 (HL)

Lord Radcliffe: ... Now, I think that there are one or two things that can be said with confidence about the meaning of this word 'defraud'. It requires a person as its object: that is, defrauding involves doing something to someone. Although in the nature of things it is almost invariably associated with the obtaining of an advantage for the person who commits the fraud, it is the effect upon the person who is the object of the fraud that ultimately determines its meaning. This is nonetheless true because since the middle of the last century the law has not required an indictment to specify the person intended to be defrauded or to prove intent to defraud a particular person.

Second, popular speech does not give, and I do not think ever has given, any sure guide as to the limits of what is meant by 'to defraud'. It may mean to cheat someone. It may mean to practise a fraud on someone. It may mean to deprive someone by deceit of something which is regarded as belonging to him or, though not belonging to him, as due to him or his right. It passes easily into metaphor, as does so much of the English natural speech. Murray's *New English Dictionary* instances such usages as defrauding a man of his due praise or his hopes. Rudyard Kipling in the First World War wrote of our 'angry and defrauded young'. There is nothing in any of this that suggests that to defraud is in ordinary speech confined to the idea of depriving a man by deceit of some economic advantage or inflicting upon him some economic loss.

Has the law ever so confined it? In my opinion there is no warrant for saying that it has ...

Of course, as I have said, in 99 cases out of 100 the intent to deceive one person to his prejudice merely connotes the deceiver's intention of obtaining an advantage for himself by inflicting a corresponding loss upon the person deceived. In all such cases the economic explanation is sufficient. But in that special line of cases where the person deceived is a public authority or a person holding a public office, deceit may secure an advantage for the deceiver without causing anything that can fairly be called either a pecuniary or an economic injury to the person deceived. If there could be no intent to defraud in the eyes of the law without an intent to inflict a pecuniary or economic injury, such cases as these could not have been punished as forgeries at common law, in which an intent to defraud is an essential element of the offence, yet I am satisfied that they were regularly so treated ...

Lord Denning: ... If a drug addict forges a doctor's prescription so as to enable him to get drugs from a chemist, he has, I should have thought, an intent to defraud, even though he intends to pay the chemist the full price and no one is a penny the worse off ...

... It has long been ruled that it is no answer to a charge of forgery to say that there was no intent to defraud any particular person, because a general intent to defraud is sufficient to constitute the crime. So also it is no answer to say that there was no intent to defraud the recipient, if there was intent to defraud somebody else: see *R v Taylor* (1779) 1 Leach 214 ...

R v Moses and Ansbro [1991] Crim LR 617 (CA)

Facts: The two appellants were charged with conspiracy to defraud by facilitating applications by immigrants to get work permits, notwithstanding that they were barred from so doing by a passport stamp. The first step was obtaining a National Insurance number, which required attendance with documents for checking and the completion of form CF8. An applicant whose passport bore a stamp prohibiting him from working would be refused a National Insurance number. It was alleged that the appellants conspired to ensure that such applications were not turned down by withholding from the departmental supervisors the existence of the stamp in the applicants' passports. They obtained blank CF8 forms, the first appellant completed them and the second appellant signed them and obtained a countersignature from another member of staff, withholding the evidence that the applicant was barred from working. Thus, the CF8s were successfully introduced into the system and the risk of the applications being turned down avoided.

Held, on appeal, dismissing the appeals, in by-passing the system, they were practising a deception on the department by causing the CF8s to enter the system as though they had been properly processed. It was clear that they intended that the department should treat the applications as regular in form and in compliance with procedure. They recognised that had the proper procedures been followed there was at least a chance that the applications would fail. This was a conspiracy to defraud. Officers of the department who played a part in processing the applications which, on their true facts, ought not to have been processed, were acting contrary to their public duty, and where the intended victim of a conspiracy to defraud was a person performing public duties, it was sufficient if the purpose was to cause him to contravene that duty, and the intended means of achieving it were dishonest. The purpose need not involve causing economic loss to anyone (see the *dictum* in *Scott* (1974) 60 Cr App R 124 at 131). The department was entitled to decide how the National Insurance contributions scheme should be administered, both locally and nationally, and it was not accepted that it was not defrauded by the circumvention of the system.

R v Landy [1981] 1 WLR 355 (CA)

Lawton LJ: ... What the prosecution had to prove was a conspiracy to defraud which is an agreement dishonestly to do something which will or may cause loss or prejudice to another. The offence is one of dishonesty. This is the all-important ingredient which must be stressed by the judge in his directions to the jury and must not be minimised in any way. There is always a danger that a jury may think that proof of an irregularity followed by loss is proof of dishonesty. The dishonesty to be proved must be in the minds and intentions of the defendants. It is to their states of mind that the jury must direct their attention. What the reasonable man or the jurors themselves would have believed or intended in the circumstances in which the defendants found themselves is not what the jury have to decide; but what a reasonable man or they themselves would have believed or intended in similar circumstances may help them to decide what in fact individual defendants believed or intended. An assertion by a defendant that throughout a transaction he acted honestly does not have to be accepted but has to be weighed like any other piece of evidence. If that was the defendant's state of mind, or may have been, he is entitled to be acquitted. But if the jury, applying their own notions of what is honest and what is not, conclude that he could not have believed that he was acting honestly, then the element of dishonesty will have been established. What a jury must not do is to say to themselves: 'If we had been in his place we would have known we were acting dishonestly so he must have known he was'. What they can say is: 'We are sure he was acting dishonestly because we can see no reason why a man of his intelligence and experience would not have appreciated, as right-minded people would have done, that what he was doing was dishonest'. In our judgment this is the way *R v Feely* [1973] QB 530 should be applied in cases where the issue of dishonesty arises. It is also the way in which the jury should have been directed in this case but, unfortunately, they were not ...

Wai Yu-Tsang v R [1992] 1 AC 269 (PC)

Lord Goff of Chieveley: ... [*Welham v DPP* [1961] AC 103] establishes that the expression 'intent to defraud' is not to be given a narrow meaning, involving an intention to cause economic loss to another. In broad terms, it means simply an intention to practise a fraud on another, or an intention to act to the prejudice of another man's right ...

His Lordship then referred to *R v Scott* [1975] AC 819 and to the speech of Lord Diplock and said:

With the greatest respect to Lord Diplock, their Lordships consider this categorisation to be too narrow. In their opinion, in agreement with the approach of Lord Radcliffe in *Welham v DPP* [1961] AC 103, the cases concerned with persons performing public duties are not to be regarded as a special category in the manner described by Lord Diplock, but rather as exemplifying the general principle that conspiracies to defraud are not restricted to cases of intention to cause the victim economic loss ...

... In *R v Allsop* 64 Cr App R 29 what the defendant agreed to do was to present the company with false particulars, in reliance upon which, as he knew, the company would decide whether to enter into hire-purchase transactions. It is then necessary to consider whether that could constitute a conspiracy to defraud, notwithstanding that the defendant's underlying purpose or motive was not to damage any economic interest of the company but to ensure that the transaction went through so that he would earn his commission. Their Lordships can see no reason why such an agreement should not be a conspiracy to defraud the company, substantially for the reasons given by the Court of Appeal. The defendant was, for his own purposes, dishonestly supplying the company with false information which persuaded it to accept risks which it would or might not have accepted if it had known the true facts. Their Lordships cannot see why this was not an agreement to practise a fraud on the company because ... it was a dishonest agreement to employ a deceit which imperilled the economic interests of the company ...

... Their Lordships are ... reluctant to allow this part of the law to become enmeshed in a distinction, sometimes artificially drawn, between intention and recklessness. The question whether particular facts reveal a conspiracy to defraud depends upon what the conspirators have dishonestly agreed to do, and in particular whether they have agreed to practise a fraud on somebody. For this purpose it is enough for example that, as in *R v Allsop* and in the present case, the conspirators have dishonestly agreed to bring about a state of affairs which they realise will or may deceive the victim into so acting, or failing to act, that he will suffer economic loss or his economic interests will be put at risk. It is however important in such a case, as the Court of Appeal stressed in *R v Allsop*, to distinguish a conspirator's intention (or immediate purpose) dishonestly to bring about such a state of affairs from his motive (or underlying purpose). The latter may be benign to the extent that he does not wish the victim or potential victim to suffer harm; but the mere fact that it is benign will not of itself prevent the agreement from constituting a conspiracy to defraud. Of course, if the conspirators were not acting dishonestly, there will have been no conspiracy to defraud; and in any event their benign purpose (if it be such) is a matter which, if they prove to be guilty, can be taken into account at the stage of sentence ...

Conspiracy to corrupt public morals; conspiracy to outrage public decency

The existence of these offences was confirmed by the House of Lords in *Shaw v DPP* [1962] AC 220 and *Knuller v DPP* [1973] AC 435 and, as indicated above, their existence has been preserved by s 5(3) of the Criminal Law Act 1977. These offences have been interpreted very restrictively. In essence, 'corrupting public morals' involves undermining the very fabric of society; 'outraging public decency' means going considerably further than shocking reasonable people.

Shaw v DPP [1962] AC 220 (HL)

Lord Tucker: ... The first count charged the appellant in the following terms:

Statement of offence: conspiracy to corrupt public morals

Particulars of offence: Frederick Charles Shaw on divers days between the first day of October 1959 and 23 July 1960, within the jurisdiction of the Central Criminal Court conspired with certain persons who inserted advertisements in issues of a magazine entitled 'Ladies Directory' numbered 7, 7 revised, 8, 9, 10 and a supplement thereto, and with certain other persons whose names are unknown, by means of the said magazine and the said advertisements to induce readers thereof to resort to the said advertisers for the purposes of fornication and of taking part in ... other disgusting and immoral acts and exhibitions with intent thereby to debauch and corrupt the morals as well of youth as of divers other liege subjects of Our Lady the Queen and to raise and create in their minds inordinate and lustful desires ...

... It has for long been accepted that there are some conspiracies which are criminal although the acts agreed to be done are not *per se* criminal or tortious if done by individuals. Such conspiracies form a third class in addition to the well-known and more clearly defined conspiracies to do acts which are unlawful, in the sense of criminal or tortious, or to do lawful acts by unlawful means. Assuming that the corruption of public morals by the acts of an individual may not be criminal or tortious, does it follow that a conspiracy by two or more persons to this end is not indictable? The difficulty with regard to this third class of conspiracy has always been to define its limits or give a label which will include all its manifestations ...

It was further contended for the appellant that in any event the particulars in the indictment and the evidence adduced in support thereof were insufficient to support a conviction for conspiring to corrupt public morals. It was said that neither fornication nor prostitution are illegal and that, in any event, there is no precedent for holding that such conduct tends to corrupt and deprave adult males.

My Lords, I think that these were matters for the decision of the jury and that the learned judge was right in ruling that there was a case to be left to them. There was material in this case to support the view that some of the advertisements in the magazines indicated that the advertisers were willing to take part in acts of sexual perversion. This element was, I think, conclusive against the appellant's submission, but I am not to be taken as expressing the view that in the absence of this feature the case should have been withdrawn from the jury, who must be the final arbiters in such matters, as they are on the question of obscenity. They alone can adequately reflect the changing public view on such matters through the centuries ...

Lord Morris of Borth-y-Gest: My Lords, I have had the privilege of reading in advance the speeches which have been delivered by my noble and learned friend on the Woolsack and by my noble and learned friend Lord Tucker, and I am in agreement with them ...

I join ... with those of your Lordships who affirm that the law is not impotent to convict those who conspire to corrupt public morals ... [His Lordship went on to approve a statement in Kenny's *Outlines of Criminal Law*] that agreements by two or more persons may be criminal if they are agreements to do acts which are outrageously immoral or else are in some way extremely injurious to the public. There are certain manifestations of conduct which are an affront to and an attack upon recognised public standards of morals and decency, and which all well-disposed persons would stigmatise and condemn as deserving of punishment. The cases afford examples of the conduct of individuals which has been punished because it outraged public decency or because its tendency was to corrupt the public morals.

It is said that there is a measure of vagueness in a charge of conspiracy to corrupt public morals, and also that there might be peril of the launching of prosecutions in order to suppress unpopular or unorthodox views. My Lords, I entertain no anxiety on these lines. Even if accepted public standards may to some extent vary from generation to generation, current standards are in the keeping of juries, who can be trusted to maintain the corporate good sense of the community and to discern attacks upon values that must be preserved. If there were prosecutions which were not genuinely and fairly warranted juries would be quick to perceive this ...

Lord Hodson: My Lords, I am in full agreement with the speeches by my noble and learned friend on the Woolsack, and by my noble and learned friend Lord Tucker, and wish only to add a few sentences on the first count.

I am wholly satisfied that there is a common law misdemeanour of conspiracy to corrupt public morals. The judicial precedents which have been cited show conclusively to my mind that the courts have never abandoned their function as *custodes morum* by surrendering to the legislature the right and duty to apply established principles to new combinations of circumstances ...

That prostitution is not a punishable offence does not involve that it is regarded as a lawful activity ... I do not see why any reason why a conspiracy to encourage fornication and adultery should be regarded as outside the ambit of conspiracy to corrupt public morals ...

Since a criminal indictment is followed by the verdict of a jury it is true that the function of *custos morum* is in criminal cases ultimately performed by the jury, by whom, on a proper direction, each case will be decided. This I think is consonant with the course of the development of our law. One may take, as an example, the case of negligence where the standard of care of the reasonable man is regarded as fit to be determined by the jury. In the field of public morals it will thus be the morality of the man in the jury-box that will determine the fate of the accused, but this should hardly disturb the equanimity of anyone brought up in the traditions of our common law ...

Knuller (Publishing, Printing and Promotions) Ltd v DPP [1973] AC 435 (HL)

Lord Reid: My Lords, the accused took part in publishing a magazine which contained a wide variety of material thought to be of interest to those holding 'progressive' views. Much of this material is unobjectionable. Some would be distasteful to many people, some is more objectionable. In this case we are only concerned with some columns of advertisements appearing on inner pages of the magazine. These columns are headed 'Males'. In most cases these advertisements were inserted by homosexuals and their express purpose was to attract answers from persons who would indulge in homosexual practices with the advertisers. Sometimes persons answering the advertisements were to communicate directly with the advertisers. Sometimes they were to send their answers to the magazine and the answers were then forwarded to the advertisers ...

The first count charges a conspiracy to corrupt public morals. The particulars given are that between January and May 1969 the accused conspired together and with persons inserting the advertisements by means of the advertisements 'to induce readers thereof to meet those persons inserting such advertisements for the purpose of sexual practices taking place between male persons and to encourage readers thereof to indulge in such practices, with intent thereby to debauch and corrupt the morals as well of youth as of divers other liege subjects of Our Lady the Queen'.

It was decided by this House in *Shaw v DPP* [1962] AC 220 that conspiracy to corrupt public morals is a crime known to the law of England. So if the appellants are to succeed on this count, either this House must reverse that decision or there must be sufficient grounds for distinguishing this case. The appellants' main argument is that we should reconsider that decision; alternatively they submit that it can and should be distinguished.

I dissented in *Shaw's* case. On reconsideration I still think that the decision was wrong and I see no reason to alter anything which I said in my speech. But it does not follow that I should now support a motion to reconsider the decision. I have said more than once in recent cases that our change of practice in no longer regarding previous decisions of this House as absolutely binding does not mean that whenever we think that a previous decision was wrong we should reverse it. In the general interest of certainty in the law we must be sure that there is some very good reason before we so act. We were informed that there had been at least 30 and probably many more convictions of this new crime in the 10 years which have elapsed since *Shaw's* case was decided, and it does not appear that there has been manifest injustice or that any attempt has been made to widen the scope of the new crime. I do not regard our refusal to reconsider *Shaw's* case as in any way justifying any attempt to widen the scope of the decision and I would oppose any attempt to do so. But I think that however wrong or anomalous the decision may be it must stand and apply to cases reasonably analogous unless or until it is altered by Parliament.

I hold that opinion the more strongly in this case by reason of the nature of the subject-matter we are dealing with. I said in *Shaw's* case [1962] AC 220, 275 and I repeat that Parliament and Parliament alone is the proper authority to change the law with regard to the punishment of immoral acts. Rightly or wrongly the law was determined by the decision in *Shaw*. Any alteration of the law as so determined must in my view be left to Parliament ...

Although I would not support reconsidering *Shaw's* case I think that we ought to clarify one or two matters. In the first place conspiracy to corrupt public morals is something of a misnomer. It really means to corrupt the morals of such members of the public as may be influenced by the matter published by the accused.

Next I think that the meaning of the word 'corrupt' requires some clarification. One of my objections to the *Shaw* decision is that it leaves too much to the jury. I recognise that in the end it must be for the jury to say whether the matter published is likely to lead to corruption. But juries, unlike judges, are not expected to be experts in the use of the English language and I think that they ought to be given some assistance ...

... I think that the jury should be told in one way or another that although in the end the question whether matter is corrupting is for them, they should keep in mind the current standards of ordinary decent people.

I can now turn to the appellants' second argument. They say that homosexual acts between adult males in private are now lawful so it is unreasonable and cannot be the law that other persons are guilty of an offence if they merely put in touch with one another two males who wish to indulge in such acts. But there is a material difference between merely exempting certain conduct from criminal penalties and making it lawful in the full sense. Prostitution and gaming afford examples of this difference ...

I find nothing in the Act to indicate that Parliament thought or intended to lay down that indulgence in these practices is not corrupting. I read the Act as saying that, even though it may be corrupting, if people choose to corrupt themselves in this way that is their affair and the law will not interfere. But no licence is given to others to encourage the practice. So if one accepts *Shaw's* case as rightly decided it must be left to each jury to decide in the circumstances of each case whether people were likely to be corrupted. In this case the jury were properly directed and it is impossible to say that they reached a wrong conclusion. It is not for us to say whether or not we agree with it. So I should dismiss the appeal as regards the first count.

The second count is conspiracy to outrage public decency, the particulars, based on the same facts, being that the accused conspired with persons inserting lewd disgusting and offensive advertisements in the magazine 'by means of the publication of the said magazine containing the said advertisements to outrage public decency'.

The crucial question here is whether in this generalised form this is an offence known to the law. There are a number of particular offences well-known to the law which involve indecency in various ways but none of them covers the facts of this case. We were informed that a charge of this character has never been brought with regard to printed matter on sale to the public. The recognised offences with regard to such matter are based on its being obscene, ie likely to corrupt or deprave. The basis of the new offence, if it is one, is quite different. It is that ordinary decent-minded people who are not likely to become corrupted or depraved will be outraged or utterly disgusted by what they read. To my mind questions of public policy of the utmost importance are at stake here.

I think that the objections to the creation of this generalised offence are similar in character to but even greater than the objections to the generalised offence of conspiracy to corrupt public morals.

In upholding the decision in *Shaw's* case we are, in my view, in no way affirming or lending any support to the doctrine that the courts still have some general or residual power either to create new offences or so to widen existing offences as to make punishable conduct of a type hitherto not subject to punishment. Apart from some statutory offences of limited application, there appears to be neither precedent nor authority of any kind for punishing the publication of written or printed matter on the ground that it is indecent as distinct from being obscene. To say that published matter offends against public decency adds nothing to saying that it is indecent. To say, as is said in this charge, that it outrages public decency adds a new factor: it seems to me to mean no more than that the degree of indecency is such that decent members of the public who read material will not merely feel shocked or disgusted but will feel outraged. If this charge is an attempt to introduce something new into the criminal law it cannot be saved because it is limited to what a jury might think to be a high degree of indecency ...

I must now consider what the effect would be if this new generalised crime were held to exist. If there were in any book, new or old, a few pages or even a few sentences which any jury could find to be outrageously indecent, those who took part in its publication and sale would risk conviction. I can see no way of denying to juries the free hand which *Shaw's* case gives them in cases of conspiracy to corrupt public morals. There would be no defence based on literary, artistic or scientific merit. The undertaking given in Parliament with regard to obscene publications would not apply to this quite different crime. Notoriously many old words, commonly regarded as classics of the highest merit, contain passages which many a juryman might regard as outrageously indecent. It has been generally supposed that the days for bowdlerising the classics were long past, but the introduction of this new crime might make publishers of such works think twice. It may be said that no prosecution would ever be brought except in a very bad case. But I have expressed on previous occasions my opinion that a bad law is not defensible on the ground that it will be judiciously administered. To recognise this new crime would go contrary to the whole trend of public policy followed by Parliament in recent times. I have no hesitation in saying that in my opinion the conviction of the accused on the second count must be quashed ...

Lord Morris of Borth-y-Gest: ... The point of law which the Court of Appeal certified as being of general importance was:

> whether an agreement by two or more persons to insert advertisements in a magazine whereby adult male advertisers seek replies from other adult males who are prepared to consent to commit homosexual acts with them in private, is capable of amounting to the offence of conspiracy to corrupt public morals ...

I agree ... with Fenton Atkinson LJ when he said in the Court of Appeal [1972] 2 QB 179, 187 that:

> it was for the jury to say whether by present-day standards, which they were there to represent, these advertisements were in their view corrupting of public morals even though Parliament had provided that acts of this kind between consulting male adults should no longer be a crime.

I pass, then, to consider the second main submission on behalf of the appellants. It was urged that *Shaw's* case [1962] AC 220 should now be reconsidered. I reject this submission primarily because, in my view, *Shaw's* case was correctly decided. Even had I been of a different opinion I would nevertheless consider it wholly inappropriate now to review the decision. Such a course would not, in my view, be warranted or desirable within the ambit of the statement made in this House on 26 July 1966 [*Practice Statement (Judicial Precedent)* [1966] 1 WLR 1234]. That statement drew attention to the especial need for certainty as to the criminal law. It was clearly held in *Shaw's* case that there had been and that there continued to be as part of the criminal law of England the offence of conspiracy to corrupt public morals. The decision established that fact with certainty. If any person had previously had doubts as to this their doubts were removed. There are some who regret that there should be such an offence and who would wish to change the law: their course is to persuade Parliament to change it. Once this House in its judicial capacity was satisfied that the offence was known to and existed as part of the law it would neither have been proper nor would it have been within its judicial province to proclaim or to suggest that the law should be forgotten or ignored or that its force should be denied. The decision in *Shaw's* case was made nearly 11 years ago. We were told that in one period of four years since that time there had been over 30 prosecutions for conspiracy to corrupt public morals: we do not know how many in total there have been. Those prosecutions were for an offence which this House had authoritatively laid down to be a part of our criminal law. It is accepted that all relevant authorities were examined before this House came to its decision. There comes a stage when further disputation should cease ...

It has sometimes been asserted that in his speech in *Shaw's* case Viscount Simonds was proclaiming that the courts had power to extend the sphere of the law by devising new extensions of the operations of the criminal law; his use of the words 'residual power' is pointed to as a basis of what is asserted. In my view, the sustained reasoning of his speech refutes the assertion. In the first place, he expressly and firmly repudiated any notion that there is in the judges a right to create new criminal offences. He held, in agreement with Lord Tucker, that the offence of conspiracy to corrupt public morals was an offence known to the common law. He then proceeded to demonstrate that if offending acts do reveal a conspiracy to corrupt public morals it is not to be said that no offence has been committed merely because the particular acts are novel or unprovided for or are unprecedented. He pointed out that Parliament from time to time by legislative acts alters the common law but that yet there are 'unravished remnants' of it. The residual power to which he referred is the power 'where no statute has yet intervened to supersede the common law, to superintend those offences which are prejudicial to the public welfare' ([1962] AC 220, 268). The reasoning is directed to the enforcement of the common law to the extent that its power may reach: the reasoning disclaims the existence of an arbitrary power to refashion the common law ...

Lord Simon of Glaisdale: ... It follows, in my view, that your Lordships should follow *Shaw v DPP* on the matter as to which it constituted a direct authority: namely, that the offence of conspiracy to corrupt public morals is part of the criminal law of England ... [T]here are some suggestions in the speeches in *Shaw v DPP* that the courts have still some role to play in the way of general superintendence of morals. This was a phrase used in various 18th and 19th century cases, 'superintendence of' meaning 'jurisdiction over'. Whatever may have been the position in the 18th century – and there is more than one clear indication that the courts of common law then assumed that they were fitted for and bound to exercise such a role – I do not myself believe that such is any part of their present function. As will appear, I do not think that 'conspiracy to corrupt public morals' invites a general tangling with codes of morality ... [I]t has [also] been suggested that the speeches in *Shaw v DPP* indicated that the courts retain a residual power to create new offences. I do not think they did so. Certainly, it is my view that the courts have no more power to create new offences than they have to abolish those already established in the law; both tasks are for Parliament. What the courts can and should do (as was truly laid down in *Shaw v DPP*) is to recognise the applicability of established offences to new circumstances to which they are relevant. [Next] I have already indicated my view that *Shaw v DPP* is not authority for the proposition that male homosexualism, or even its facilitation or encouragement, are themselves as a matter of law corrupting of public morals. It is for the jury to decide as a matter of fact whether the conduct alleged to be the subject-matter of the conspiracy charged is in any particular case corrupting of public morals. Last, it was suggested in argument before your Lordships that, if *Shaw v DPP* were not overruled, it would be open to juries to convict if they thought that the conduct in question was liable to 'lead morally astray'. But all that was decided in *Shaw v DPP* was that, in the general context of the whole of the summing up in that case, the use of the phrase 'lead morally astray' was not a misdirection. *Shaw v DPP* must not be taken as an authority that 'corrupt public morals' and 'lead morally astray' are interchangeable expressions. On the contrary, 'corrupt' is a strong word. The *Book of Common Prayer*, following the Gospel, has '... where rust and moth doth corrupt'. The words 'corrupt public morals' suggest conduct which a jury might find to be destructive of the very fabric of society ...

Turning to the second count, conspiracy to outrage public decency, Lord Simon said:

The following questions, therefore, arise on this part of the case: (1) is there a general common law offence of outraging public decency, or only the particular offences which the cases establish? (2) Is there a common law offence of conspiring to outrage public decency? ...

His Lordship reviewed the authorities and said:

I think that the authorities establish a common law offence of conduct which outrages public decency.

If there is a common law offence of conduct which outrages public decency, a conspiracy to outrage public decency is also a common law offence, as an agreement to do an illegal act. In *Shaw v DPP* [1962] AC 220, 267, Viscount Simonds seems to have considered that the conduct there in question was indictable also as a conspiracy 'to affront public decency'.

In my view, counsel for the appellants was right to concede that there is a common law offence of conspiring to outrage public decency ...

R v Gibson [1990] 2 QB 619 (CA)

Lord Lane CJ: ... Richard Norman Gibson and Peter Sebastian Sylveire were convicted ... of outraging public decency, contrary to common law ...

The facts of the case were unusual, but simple, Sylveire ran an art gallery called the Young Unknowns Gallery in the Cut, London SE1. Displayed in that gallery was an article which had been assembled by Gibson. The article consisted of a model's head to each ear of which was attached an earring. The earring was made out of a freeze-dried human foetus of three or four months' gestation. The foetus was attached to the ear by means of a ring fitting tapped into the skull of the foetus, and the upper end of that fitting was attached to the lobe of the model's ear.

The gallery was in a parade of shops. The general public was invited to and had access to the gallery during the exhibition. No payment was required for entry. Gibson had, apparently unknown to his co-defendant, done some advertising promotion of this particular article, with the result that the police and press were on the scene not long after the exhibition had opened its doors. The gallery charged a commission on any works which were sold to members of the public.

The article in question was one of 41 items which had been selected for display out of a much larger number by Sylveire. It was Exhibit No 9, and was described in the catalogue as 'Human Earrings'. Although it was not suggested that Sylveire had taken active steps to publicise this particular exhibit, there was no doubt that the more people who attended the gallery, the better pleased Sylveire would be, and the greater would be the likelihood of selling exhibits ...

The first question to decide then is whether there is an offence at common law of outraging public decency. The answer to that question is to be found in the speech of Lord Simon of Glaisdale in *Knuller (Publishing, Printing and Promotions) Ltd v DPP* [1973] AC 435, 493:

> Fourth, my noble and learned friend, Lord Morris of Borth-y-Gest, in *Shaw v DPP* [1962] AC 200 where, though there was no count of conspiracy to outrage decency, most of the cases were reviewed, said at 292: 'The cases afford examples of the conduct of individuals which has been punished because it outraged public decency ...' And my noble and learned friend, Lord Reid, though dissenting on the main issue, said at 281: 'I think that they [the authorities] establish that it is an indictable offence to say or do or exhibit anything in public which outrages public decency, whether or not it also tends to corrupt and deprave those who see or hear it'.

Lord Morris of Borth-y-Gest and Lord Kilbrandon seem to have agreed with that view.

The point is not taken before us that no such offence exists. We respectfully agree with their Lordships in *Knuller* that it does ...

... [W]here the charge is one outraging public decency, there is no requirement that the prosecution should prove an intention to outrage ... If the publication takes place, and if it is deliberate, there is, in the words of Lord Russell in *R v Lemon* [1979] AC 617, 657–58: 'no justification for holding that there is no offence when the publisher is incapable for some reason particular to himself of agreeing with the jury on the true nature of the publication' ...

Notes and queries

1   In cases where there is an overlap between statutory conspiracy and conspiracy to defraud, the prosecution can make a choice as to which form of conspiracy should be charged. As s 12 of the Criminal Justice Act 1987 provides, the fact that a statutory conspiracy could be charged (ie an agreement to commit a criminal offence) does not preclude a charge of conspiracy to defraud being brought.

Conspiracy to commit a crime abroad

The courts in England and Wales have always had jurisdiction at common law to try a defendant for conspiracy to commit murder, regardless of whether or not the murder was planned to occur with the jurisdiction. This was recognised by Parliament in enacting s 1 (4) of the Criminal Law Act 1977 which provides:

> In this part of this Act 'offence' means an offence triable in England and Wales, except that it includes murder notwithstanding that the murder in question would not be so triable if committed in accordance with the intentions of the parties to the agreement.

This should now be read subject to the provisions of the Criminal Justice (Terrorism and Conspiracy) Act 1998, the provisions of which repeal those aspects of the Sexual Offences (Conspiracy and Incitement) Act 1996, and the Criminal Justice Act 1993, in so far as those enactments dealt with the extra-territorial jurisdiction of the domestic courts in respect of conspiracy.

Criminal Justice (Terrorism and Conspiracy) Act 1998

5 (1) The following section shall be inserted after section 1 of the Criminal Law Act 1977 (conspiracy) –

'Conspiracy to commit offences outside the United Kingdom

(1A)– (1) Where each of the following conditions is satisfied in the case of an agreement, this Part of this Act has effect in relation to the agreement as it has effect in relation to an agreement falling within section 1(1) above.

(2) The first condition is that the pursuit of the agreed course of conduct would at some stage involve – (a) an act by one or more of the parties, or (b) the happening of some other event, intended to take place in a country or territory outside the United Kingdom.

(3) The second condition is that that act or other event constitutes an offence under the law in force in that country or territory.

(4) The third condition is that the agreement would fall within section 1(1) above as an agreement relating to the commission of an offence but for the fact that the offence would not be an offence triable in England and Wales if committed in accordance with the parties' intentions.

(5) The fourth condition is that –

(a) a party to the agreement, or a party's agent, did anything in England and Wales in relation to the agreement before its formation, or

(b) a party to the agreement became a party in England and Wales (by joining it either in person or through an agent), or

(c) a party to the agreement, or a party's agent, did or omitted anything in England and Wales in pursuance of the agreement.

(6) In the application of this Part of this Act to an agreement in the case of which each of the above conditions is satisfied, a reference to an offence is to be read as a reference to what would be the offence in question but for the fact that it is not an offence triable in England and Wales.

(7) Conduct punishable under the law in force in any country or territory is an offence under that law for the purposes of this section, however it is described in that law.

(8) Subject to subsection (9) below, the second condition is to be taken to be satisfied unless, not later than rules of court may provide, the defence serve on the prosecution a notice –

    (a) stating that, on the facts as alleged with respect to the agreed course of conduct, the condition is not in their opinion satisfied,

    (b) showing their grounds for that opinion, and

    (c) requiring the prosecution to show that it is satisfied.

(9) The court may permit the defence to require the prosecution to show that the second condition is satisfied without the prior service of a notice under subsection (8) above.

(10) In the Crown Court the question whether the second condition is satisfied shall be decided by the judge alone, and shall be treated as a question of law for the purposes of –

    (a) section 9(3) of the Criminal Justice Act 1987 (preparatory hearing in fraud cases), and

    (b) section 31(3) of the Criminal Procedure and Investigations Act 1996 (preparatory hearing in other cases).

(11) Any act done by means of a message (however communicated) is to be treated for the purposes of the fourth condition as done in England and Wales if the message is sent or received in England and Wales.

(12) In any proceedings in respect of an offence triable by virtue of this section, it is immaterial to guilt whether or not the accused was a British citizen at the time of any act or other event proof of which is required for conviction of the offence.

(13) References in any enactment, instrument or document (except those in this Part of this Act) to an offence of conspiracy to commit an offence include an offence triable in England and Wales as such a conspiracy by virtue of this section (without prejudice to subsection (6) above).

(14) Nothing in this section –

    (a) applies to an agreement entered into before the day on which the Criminal Justice (Terrorism and Conspiracy) Act 1998 was passed, or

    (b) imposes criminal liability on any person acting on behalf of, or holding office under, the Crown.

(2) At the end of section 4 of that Act (restrictions on the institution of proceedings) there shall be added –

(5) Subject to subsection (6) below, no proceedings for an offence triable by virtue of section 1A above may be instituted except by or with the consent of the Attorney General.

(6) The Secretary of State may by order provide that subsection (5) above shall not apply, or shall not apply to any case of a description specified in the order.

(7) An order under subsection (6) above –

    (a) shall be made by statutory instrument, and

    (b) shall not be made unless a draft has been laid before, and approved by resolution of, each House of Parliament.

IMPOSSIBILITY AS A DEFENCE TO CONSPIRACY

Section 1(1)(b) of the Criminal Law Act 1977 effectively removes the defence of impossibility in respect of any charge alleging a statutory conspiracy. For common law conspiracy, the defence of impossibility remains as detailed below in *DPP v Nock*.

DPP v Nock [1978] AC 979 (HL)

Lord Scarman: ... Five persons, including the two appellants, David Michael Nock and Kevin Charles Alsford, appeared at the Snaresbrook Crown Court on 5 January 1977, to answer an indictment charging them with a number of drug offences. Nock and Alsford were convicted upon several counts but your Lordships' House is concerned only with their conviction upon the first count in the indictment. It charged them (and others) with conspiracy to contravene s 4 of the Misuse of Drugs Act 1971. The section provides by subsection (1) that subject to regulations (which are of no present relevance) it shall not be lawful for a person to produce a controlled drug and by subsection (2) that it is an offence to produce a controlled drug in contravention of subsection (1). The particulars of offence, after being amended, were as follows:

> Kevin Charles Alsford, David Michael Nock [and three other named defendants] on divers days before 23 September 1975, conspired together and with other persons unknown to produce a controlled drug of Class A, namely cocaine.

The indictment makes plain that the Crown is alleging in this case a conspiracy to commit a crime: and no one has suggested that the particulars fail to disclose an offence known to the law. But the appellants submit, and it is not disputed by the Crown that the agreement as proved was narrower in scope than the conspiracy charged. When the case was before the Court of Appeal, counsel on both sides agreed that the evidence went to prove that the appellants agreed together to obtain cocaine by separating it from the other substance or substances contained in a powder which they had obtained from one of their co-defendants, a Mr Mitchell. They believed that the powder was a mixture of cocaine and lignocaine, and that they would be able to produce cocaine from it. In fact the powder was lignocaine hydrochloride, an anaesthetic used in dentistry, which contains no cocaine at all. It is impossible to produce, by separation or otherwise, cocaine from lignocaine. The agreement between the appellants was correctly summarised by the Court of Appeal, when certifying the point of law, as an agreement 'to pursue a course of action which could never in fact have produced cocaine'.

The appellants made a number of attempts – all of them, of course, unsuccessful – to extract cocaine from their powder. It was not until after they had been arrested and the powder seized by the police and sent for analysis that they learnt to their surprise that there was no way in which cocaine could be produced from it.

The trial judge in his direction to the jury, the Court of Appeal in their judgment dismissing the two appeals, treated this impossibility as an irrelevance. In their view the agreement was what mattered: and there was plain evidence of an agreement to produce cocaine, even though unknown to the two conspirators it could not be done. Neither the trial judge nor the Court of Appeal thought it necessary to carry their analysis of the agreement further. The trial judge described it simply as an agreement to produce cocaine. The Court of Appeal thought it enough that the prosecution had proved 'an agreement to do an act which was forbidden by s 4 of the Misuse of Drugs Act 1971'. Both descriptions are accurate, as far as they go. But neither contains any reference to the limited nature of the agreement proved: it was an agreement upon a specific course of conduct with the object of producing cocaine, and limited to that course of conduct. Since it could not result in the production of cocaine, the two appellants by pursuing it could not commit the statutory offence of producing a controlled drug. The appellants, who did get a chemist to take on the impossible job of extracting cocaine from the powder, may perhaps be treated as having completed their agreed course of conduct: if so, they completed it without committing the statutory offence. Perhaps, however, it would be more accurate to treat them as having desisted before they had completed all that they had agreed to do: but it makes no difference because, had they completed all that they had agreed to do, no cocaine would have been produced.

If, therefore, their agreement, limited as it was to a specific course of conduct which could not result in the commission of the statutory offence, constituted (as the Court of Appeal held) a criminal conspiracy, the strange consequence ensues, that by agreeing upon a course of conduct which was not criminal (or unlawful) the appellants were guilty of conspiring to commit a crime.

Upon these facts the appellants submit that the evidence reveals no 'conspiracy at large', by which they mean an agreement in general terms to produce cocaine if and when they could find a suitable raw material, but only the limited agreement, to which I have referred. Counsel for the appellants concedes that, if two or more persons decide to go into business as cocaine producers, or, to take another example, as assassins for hire (eg 'Murder Incorporated'), the mere fact that in the course of performing their agreement they attempt to produce cocaine from a raw material which could not possibly yield it or (in the second example), stab a corpse, believing it to be the body of a living man, would not avail them as a defence: for the performance of their general agreement would not be rendered impossible by such transient frustrations. But performance of the limited agreement proved in this case could not in any circumstances have involved the commission of the offence created by the statute.

The answer sought to be made by the Crown (and accepted by the Court of Appeal) is that the offence of conspiracy is committed when an agreement to commit, or to try to commit, a crime is reached, whether or not anything is, or can be, done to perform it. It is wrong, upon their view, to treat conspiracy as a 'preliminary' or 'inchoate' crime: for its criminality depends in no way upon its being a step towards the commission of the substantive offence (or, at common law, the unlawful act). Upon this view of the law the scope of agreement is irrelevant: all that is needed to constitute the crime is the intention to commit the substantive offence and the agreement to try to do so.

... In *Board of Trade v Owen* [1957] AC 602, 623–25 Lord Tucker, quoting with approval some observations from R S Wright J's little classic, *The Law of Criminal Conspiracies and Agreements* (1873) and some passages from Sir William Holdsworth's (somewhat larger) work, *The History of English Law,* accepted that the historical basis of the crime of conspiring to commit a crime (the case with which we are now concerned) was that it developed as an 'auxiliary' (RS Wright's word) to the law which creates the crime agreed to be committed. Lord Tucker accepted Holdsworth's comment (at 625) that 'it was inevitable therefore, as Stephen has said, that conspiracy should come to be regarded as a form of attempt to commit a wrong'. Lord Tucker concluded his survey with these words at 626:

> Accepting the above as the historical basis of the crime of conspiracy, it seems to me that the whole object of making such agreements punishable is to prevent the commission of the substantive offence before it has even reached the stage of an attempt ...

Lord Tucker, in whose opinion the other noble and learned Lords sitting with him concurred, by stressing the 'auxiliary' nature of the crime of conspiracy and by explaining its justification as being to prevent the commission of substantive offences, has placed the crime firmly in the same class and category as attempts to commit a crime. Both are criminal because they are steps towards the commission of a substantive offence. The distinction between the two is that, whereas a 'proximate' act is that which constitutes the crime of attempt, agreement is the necessary ingredient in conspiracy. The importance of the distinction is that agreement may, and usually will, occur well before the first step which can be said to be an attempt. The law of conspiracy thus makes possible an earlier intervention by the law to prevent the commission of the substantive offence. But the distinction has no relevance in determining whether the impossibility of committing the substantive offence should be a defence. Indeed upon the view of the law authoritatively explained and accepted in *Owen's* case [1957] AC 602, logic and justice would seem to require that the question as to the effect of the impossibility of the substantive offence should be answered in the same way, whether the crime charged be conspiracy or attempt ...

The Crown's argument, as developed before your Lordships, rests, in my judgment, upon a misconception of the nature of the agreement proved. This is a case not of an agreement to commit a crime capable of being committed in the way agreed upon, but frustrated by a supervening event making its completion impossible, which was the Crown's submission, but of an agreement upon a course of conduct which could not in any circumstances result in the statutory offence alleged, ie the offence of producing the controlled drug, cocaine ...

CODIFICATION AND LAW REFORM PROPOSALS

The Law Commission, in its Report *Criminal Law: Conspiracy to Defraud* (Law Com 228), concluded:

We believe that for practical reasons conspiracy to defraud performs a useful role in the present law of dishonesty, and we have concluded that it should remain intact pending our comprehensive review of the law. We have resolved that it would be inappropriate, at a time when we are about to re-examine the whole scheme of dishonesty offences, to make piecemeal recommendations for reform of other aspects of the law of dishonesty ... [para 1.20].

The Report went on, however, to consider some of the more significant criticisms of the offence of conspiracy to defraud as it currently stands.

B THE OFFENCE APPLIES TO AGREEMENTS TO DO LAWFUL ACTS

3.2 The first objection to conspiracy to defraud is that it runs counter to the principle established, in accordance with our recommendations,' in section 1 of the Criminal Law Act 1977-namely, that an act should not be criminal merely because more than one person is involved. Before 1977, an agreement to do an 'unlawful', though not criminal, act could amount to a criminal conspiracy, as could an agreement to do a lawful act by unlawful means.

3.3 Our recommendation that the object of a conspiracy should be limited to the commission of a substantive offence was originally put forward, 'very emphatically', as a provisional proposal in a working paper published in 1973. The proposal met with a very wide measure of approval on consultation. Conspiracy to defraud was retained, also in accordance with our recommendation,' as a temporary exception pending completion of a consideration of the extent of the offences which would be required in its place.

3.4 Many serious frauds involve more than one person, and the fact that a number of people are involved may be an aggravating factor. As Professor Sir John Smith has suggested, although it is 'of course illogical' to provide that it is an offence to conspire to do something which is not an offence:

... it is arguable that the requirement of conspiracy provides a desirable constraint on what would otherwise be too wide-ranging an offence. Few would want to make a criminal of the person who quite deliberately defers payment of his gas bill until he gets the threatening red reminder, even though he knows perfectly well that he is causing an unjustifiable loss to the Gas Board; but ... company directors ... who decide as a matter of policy to defer payment of their suppliers for long periods, being well aware of the damage they are doing, seem to fall into a quite different category. Of course, it is not only the fact of agreement which makes the conduct so serious – an individual in a large way of business might do the same – but it is a significant fact. Where there is no agreement the matter is likely to be trivial and the line between negligence and intention will be hard to draw. Where there is agreement, it is clearly intentional and likely to be substantial.

3.5 It remains true, none the less, that the existence of an agreement may be only one of a number of possible aggravating factors against which the seriousness of the criminal conduct is to be measured. Aggravating factors such as this usually affect the length or type of sentence rather than the issue of liability. To put the instant objection the other way: why should the absence of this particular aggravating factor mean that in some cases there should be no criminal liability at all?

3.6 We entirely accept that, as a matter of principle, this argument is valid; and that either it should be an offence to defraud or it should not be an offence for two or more persons to agree to do so. We explain below why we are unable, however, to recommend either option in the context of this report.

C   THE WIDTH OF THE OFFENCE

3.7 A second objection of principle to conspiracy to defraud is that the offence is too wide. There are two aspects to this objection. The first is that the offence is too wide because of its overlap with statutory conspiracy and with substantive offences, such as theft and obtaining by deception. We consider this in the following paragraphs. The second aspect is that it is too wide because the very broad scope of the offence means that it covers certain conduct which arguably ought not to be criminal at all ... On consultation there was no clear preponderance of opinion among respondents on the question whether, in either respect, the width of the offence was excessive.

3.8 Conduct sufficient to found conspiracy to defraud embraces almost every offence in the Theft Acts. In principle (the objection runs), overlapping offences should be avoided unless there is some reason which makes the overlap acceptable; and the objection is stronger where there is not merely an overlap but a total subsumption of other offences. Arguably, it allows too much discretion to prosecutors as to which charge to bring where either charge would be possible, but where only one of them is desirable in the circumstances.

3.9 The problem of overlap is not, however, confined to conspiracy to defraud. In particular, the effect of the recent decision of the House of Lords in *Gomez* is that almost every offence of obtaining property by deception automatically amounts also to theft. The question of overlap generally, and not only in relation to conspiracy to defraud, will fall for consideration in our forthcoming review of dishonesty offences. It should be borne in mind that, meanwhile, there are safeguards against injustice to defendants that may arise from an oppressive use of conspiracy to defraud.

D   THE VAGUE AND UNCERTAIN SCOPE OF THE OFFENCE

3.10   Another objection to conspiracy to defraud which may therefore be raised is that the boundaries of the offence are uncertain; that it offers insufficient guidance as to what can or cannot lawfully be done; and that it consequently infringes the principle that it should be possible to ascertain in advance whether any particular conduct would be criminal. On this view, the criminal law should have no place for an offence which is not sufficiently precise that it is possible to say with reasonable certainty whether any combination of facts constitutes the offence.

3.11 We have consistently favoured this approach. In a different context, we have said:

> Since 1973 the working papers and reports we have published have returned repeatedly to [the] theme that the criminal law must be both certain and accessible, and it has received widespread endorsement from those who have responded to our working papers. Thus in 1973 we said that it seemed to us not merely desirable, but obligatory, that legal rules imposing serious criminal sanctions should be stated with the maximum clarity that the imperfect medium of language could attain. The following year we repeated this principle in another Working Paper when we said that if legislation did not cover every kind of previously unidentified wicked conduct this was the inevitable price which had to be paid for an acceptable degree of certainty as to the conduct to be penalised by the law. Our view that this price was one which we believed to be worth paying was one which was supported by most of those who responded to that paper. When we were concerned with the task of codifying the old common law offences in the field of public order we said that a criminal code must define with precision what conduct it is which is a crime. And when we published our report on a Criminal Code we reiterated our view that codification of the criminal law was desirable not only as a matter of constitutional principle but also because it offered instrumental benefits in the way of greater accessibility, comprehensibility, consistency and certainty. This view was again strongly supported by those we consulted.

3.12 On the other hand, it may well be asked: if a person inflicts loss on another knowing that his conduct would be regarded as dishonest by the ordinary standards of reasonable and honest people, does he have a legitimate complaint if he is prosecuted for his behaviour? Moreover, in the light of *Gomez* dishonesty now does all the work in many cases of theft: the absence of dishonesty is, for example, the only reason why a shopper in a supermarket does not steal goods by removing them from the shelf. This will be one of the many issues examined in our review of dishonesty offences.

3.13 Although some aspects of conspiracy to defraud are undoubtedly vague in principle, on consultation we received little comment directed to the instant point; and while, of those few who did comment, some endorsed this criticism, the Serious Fraud Office did not accept that the offence is so uncertain as to be capable of covering conduct that should not be treated as criminal.

Further reading

I Dennis, 'The rationale of criminal conspiracy' (1977) 93 LQR 39

CHAPTER 12

INCHOATE OFFENCES – ATTEMPTS

Until 1981 the offence of attempt was governed by the common law. With the enactment of the Criminal Attempts Act 1981 it has been placed on a statutory footing. Unlike the position with incitement and conspiracy there is no surviving form of common law attempt.

Section 1 of the Criminal Attempts Act 1981

(1) If, with intent to commit an offence to which this section applies, a person does an act which is more than merely preparatory to the commission of the offence, he is guilty of attempting to commit the offence.

(2) A person may be guilty of attempting to commit an offence to which this section applies even though the facts are such that the commission of the offence is impossible.

(3) In any case where:

   (a) apart from this subsection a person's intention would not be regarded as having amounted to an intent to commit an offence; but

   (b) if the facts of the case had been as he believed them to be, his intention would be so regarded,

   then for the purposes of subsection (1) above, he shall be regarded as having an intent to commit that offence.

ACTUS REUS: AN ACT WHICH IS MORE THAN MERELY PREPARATORY

Various tests of what constituted an attempt existed prior to the Criminal Attempts Act 1981. For example, whether the defendant had gone past the point of no return ('crossing the Rubicon'), and the 'uninterrupted series of acts' test set out in *Davey v Lee* [1968] 1 QB 366. However, pre-1981 case law is only persuasive; the correct approach is to give the words of the statute their ordinary and natural meaning. Was the act alleged 'more than merely preparatory to the commission of the offence'? See, for example, *R v Gullefer* [1990] 1 WLR 1063; *R v Jones* [1990] 1 WLR 1057; *AG's Ref (No 1 of 1992)* [1993] 1 WLR 274.

Section 4(3) of the Criminal Attempts Act 1981 provides:

Where, in proceedings against a person for an offence under s 1 above, there is evidence sufficient in law to support a finding that he did an act falling within subsection (1) of that section, the question whether or not his act fell within that subsection is a question of fact.

The effect is that if there is a *prima facie* case that the defendant did an act which was more than merely preparatory, the jury must be left to decide whether the act was indeed more than merely preparatory.

R v Gullefer [1990] 1 WLR 1063 (Note)

Lord Lane CJ: On 26 February 1986 before the Crown Court at Snaresbrook the appellant was convicted of attempted theft and sentenced to six months' imprisonment.

The judge certified that the case was fit for appeal on the ground that:

> ... a submission was made that the action alleged as constituting the attempt (as to which there was no dispute, because his action was filmed on video tape, which the jury and I saw) could not amount to an attempt to steal, even if the jury were satisfied that what the defendant did was done with the object of dishonestly receiving a sum of money equivalent to his stake from a bookmaker ...

The facts were as follows. On 5 March 1985 the appellant attended the Greyhound Racing Stadium at Romford. During the last race, as the dogs rounded the final bend, he climbed the fence on to the track in front of the dogs, waving his arms and attempting to distract them. His efforts were only marginally successful, and the stewards decided that it was unnecessary to declare 'no race'. Had they made such a declaration, by the rules the bookmakers would have been obliged to repay the amount of his stake to any punter, but would not have been liable to pay any winnings to those punters who would have been successful if the race had been valid.

When interviewed by the police the appellant said the reasons for his behaviour were partly that a year earlier he had lost a large bet at the stadium by reason of one of the stadium's staff leaning over the rails and distracting the dog on which he had gambled. He also admitted that he had attempted to stop the race because the dog on which he had staked £18 was losing. He hoped that by his actions the dogs would be distracted, that the stewards would declare 'no race' and that he would therefore recover his stake from the bookmaker ...

His Lordship quoted ss 1(1) and 4(3) of the Criminal Attempts Act and continued:

> Thus the judge's task is to decide whether there is evidence upon which a jury could reasonably come to the conclusion that the appellant had gone beyond the realm of mere preparation and had embarked upon the actual commission of the offence. If not, he must withdraw the case from the jury. If there is such evidence, it is then for the jury to decide whether the defendant did in fact go beyond mere preparation ...

> The first task of the court is to apply the words of the Act of 1981 to the facts of the case. Was the appellant still in the stage of preparation to commit the substantive offence, or was there a basis of fact which would entitle the jury to say that he had embarked on the theft itself? Might it properly be said that when he jumped on to the track he was trying to steal £18 from the bookmaker?

> Our view is that it could not properly be said that at that stage he was in the process of committing theft. What he was doing was jumping on to the track in an

effort to distract the dogs, which in its turn, he hoped, would have the effect of forcing the stewards to declare 'no race', which would in its turn give him the opportunity to go back to the bookmaker and demand the £18 he had staked. In our view there was insufficient evidence for it to be said that he had, when he jumped on to the track, gone beyond mere preparation.

So far at least as the present case is concerned, we do not think that it is necessary to examine the authorities which preceded the Act of 1981, save to say that the sections we have already quoted in this judgment seem to be a blend of various decisions, some of which were not easy to reconcile with others ...

It seems to us that the words of the Act of 1981 seek to steer a midway course. They do not provide, as they might have done, that the *R v Eagleton* test is to be followed, or that, as Lord Diplock suggested, the defendant must have reached a point from which it was impossible for him to retreat before the actus reus of an attempt is proved. On the other hand the words give perhaps as clear a guidance as is possible in the circumstances on the point of time at which Stephen's 'series of acts' begin. It begins when the merely preparatory acts come to an end and the defendant embarks upon the crime proper. When that is, will depend of course upon the facts in any particular case ...

R v Jones (Kenneth Henry) [1990] 1 WLR 1057 (CA)

Taylor LJ: read the following judgment of the court. This case raises a point of law as to the true construction of s 1 of the Criminal Attempts Act 1981 ...

The appellant, a married man, started an affair with a woman named Lynn Gresley in 1985. She lived with him in Australia during 1986. In September 1987, back in England, she began a relationship with the victim, Michael Foreman. She continued, however, to see the appellant to whom she was still very attached. In November 1987 she decided to break off the relationship with the appellant, but he continued to write to her, begging her to come back to him.

On 12 January 1988 the appellant applied for a shotgun certificate, and three days later bought two guns in company with two companions. He bought two more guns a few days later on his own. On 23 January he shortened the barrel of one of them and test fired it twice the following day.

The appellant told a colleague at work that he would be away on Tuesday 26 January. On 24 January he phoned Lynn Gresley in a distraught state. The next day he apologised, but she again refused his invitation to resume their relationship. The appellant then told his wife he had packed a bag as he was going to Spain to do some work on their chalet. On 26 January he left home dressed normally for work, saying he would telephone his wife as to whether he was leaving for Spain that evening.

That same morning, the victim, Michael Foreman, took his daughter to school by car as usual. After the child left the car, the appellant appeared, opened the door and jumped into the rear seat. He was wearing overalls, a crash helmet with the visor down, and was carrying a bag. He and the victim had never previously met. He introduced himself, said he wanted to sort things out and asked the victim to drive on. When they stopped on a grass verge, the appellant handed over a letter he had received from Lynn. Whilst the victim read it, the appellant took the sawn-off shotgun from the bag. It was loaded. He pointed it at the victim at range of some 10 to 12 inches. He said, 'You are not going to like this', or similar words. The victim grabbed the end of the gun and pushed it sideways and upwards. There was a struggle during which the victim managed to throw the gun out of the window. As he tried to get out, he felt a cord over his head pulling him back. He managed to break free and run away, taking the gun with him.

From a nearby garage he telephoned the police.

Meanwhile, the appellant drove off in the victim's car. He was arrested jogging away from it carrying his holdall. He said he had done nothing and only wanted to kill himself. His bag contained a hatchet, some cartridges and a length of cord. He also had a sharp kitchen knife which he threw away. In the appellant's car parked near the school was £1,500 sterling together with a quantity of French and Spanish money. The evidence showed that the safety catch of the shotgun had been in the on position. The victim was unclear as to whether the appellant's finger was ever on the trigger. When interviewed, the appellant declined to make any comment.

At the end of the prosecution case, after the above facts had been given in evidence, a submission was made to the judge that the charge of attempted murder should be withdrawn from the jury. It was argued that since the appellant would have had to perform at least three more acts before the full offence could have been completed, ie remove the safety catch, put his finger on the trigger and pull it, the evidence was insufficient to support the charge. There was a discussion as to the proper construction of s 1(1) of the Criminal Attempts Act 1981. After hearing full argument, the judge ruled against the submission and allowed the case to proceed on count 1. Thereafter, the appellant gave evidence. In the result, the jury convicted him unanimously of attempted murder. It follows that they found he intended to kill the victim.

The sole ground of appeal is that the judge erred in law in his construction of s 1(1) and ought to have withdrawn the case.

His Lordship then quoted s 1(1) and s 4(3) of the Criminal Attempts Act 1981.

[Counsel for the appellant] says that for about a century, two different tests as to the *actus reus* of attempt have been inconsistently applied by the courts. In *R v Eagleton* (1855) Dears CC 515, the defendant was charged with attempting to obtain money from the guardians of a parish by falsely pretending to the relieving officer that he had delivered loaves of bread of proper weight to the poor when in fact the loaves were underweight. In the course of giving the judgment of the court, Parke B said at 538:

Acts remotely leading towards the commission of the offence are not to be considered as attempts to commit it, but acts immediately connected with it are; and if, in this case, after the credit with the relieving officer for the fraudulent overcharge, any further step on the part of the defendant had been necessary to obtain payment, as the making out a further account or producing the vouchers to the board, we should have thought that the obtaining credit in account with the relieving officer would not have been sufficiently proximate to the obtaining the money. But, on the statement in this case, no other act on the part of the defendant would have been required. It was the last act, depending on himself towards the payment of the money, and therefore it ought to be considered as an attempt.

Accordingly, the test deriving from *R v Eagleton* was said to be the 'last act' test. It was adopted in a number of cases, eg *R v Robinson* [1915] 2 KB 342. In *DPP v Stonehouse* [1978] AC 55, 68, Lord Diplock referred to *R v Eagleton* as the *locus classicus*, adopted some of the words of Parke B and summarised them in the graphic phrase: 'In other words, the offender must have crossed the Rubicon and burnt his boats'.

The other test referred to by [counsel for the appellant] derives from Stephen's *Digest of the Criminal Law*, 9th edn, 1950, Chapter 4, art 29 where it was stated, at pp 24–25:

> An attempt to commit a crime is an act done with intent to commit that crime, and forming part of a series of acts, which would constitute its actual commission if it were not interrupted.

Lord Edmund-Davies noted in *Stonehouse's* case at 86, that Stephen's definition has been repeatedly cited with approval. He referred to its adoption in *Hope v Brown* [1954] 1 WLR 250, 253, and *Davey v Lee* [1968] 1 QB 366. It was also applied in *R v Linneker* [1906] 2 KB 99 where *Eagleton's* case was not cited.

In some cases, including three since the Act of 1981, both tests have been considered, and the court has found it unnecessary to decide between them, holding that the result in those cases would have been the same, whichever applied: see *R v Ilyas* (1984) 78 Cr App R 17; *R v Widdowson* (1986) 82 Cr App R 314 and *R v Boyle* (1986) 84 Cr App R 270 ...

... The Act of 1981 is a codifying statute. It amends and sets out completely the law relating to attempts and conspiracies. In those circumstances the correct approach is to look first at the natural meaning of the statutory words, not to turn back to earlier case law and seek to fit some previous test to the words of the section ...

[His Lordship then quoted with approval from the judgment of Lord Lane CJ in *R v Gullefer* (Note) [1990] 1 WLR 1063.]

... We do not accept [the appellant's] contention that s 1(1) of the Act of 1981 in effect embodies the 'last act' test derived from *R v Eagleton*. Had Parliament intended to adopt that test, a quite different form of words could and would have been used.

It is of interest to note that the Act of 1981 followed a report from the Law Commission on *Attempt, and Impossibility in Relation to Attempt Conspiracy and Incitement* (1980) Law Com No 102. At paragraph 2.47 the report states:

> The definition of sufficient proximity must be wide enough to cover two varieties of cases; first, those in which a person has taken all steps towards the commission of a crime which he believes to be necessary as far as he is concerned for that crime to result, such as firing a gun at another and missing. Normally such cases cause no difficulty. Second, however, the definition must cover those instances where a person has to take some further step to complete the crime, assuming that there is evidence of the necessary mental element on his part to commit it; for example, when the defendant has raised the gun to take aim at another but has not yet squeezed the trigger. We have reached the conclusion that, in regard to these cases, it is undesirable to recommend anything more complex than a rationalisation of the present law.

In paragraph 2.48 the report states:

The literal meaning of 'proximate' is 'nearest, next before or after (in place, order, time, connection of thought, causation, etc)'. Thus, were this term part of a statutory description of the *actus reus* of attempt, it would clearly be capable of being interpreted to exclude all but the 'final act'; this would not be in accordance with the policy outlined above.

Clearly, the draftsman of s 1(1) must be taken to have been aware of the two lines of earlier authority and of the Law Commission's report. The words 'an act which is more than merely preparatory to the commission of the offence' would be inapt if they were intended to mean 'the last act which lay in his power towards the commission of the offence'.

Looking at the plain natural meaning of s 1(1) in the way indicated by the Lord Chief Justice [in *R v Gullefer*], the question for the judge in the present case was whether there was evidence from which a reasonable jury, properly directed, could conclude that the appellant had done acts which were more than merely preparatory. Clearly his actions in obtaining the gun, in shortening it, in loading it, in putting on his disguise, and in going to the school could only be regarded as preparatory acts. But, in our judgment, once he had got into the car, taken out the loaded gun and pointed it at the victim with the intention of killing him, there was sufficient evidence for the consideration of the jury on the charge of attempted murder. It was a matter for them to decide whether they were sure those acts were more than merely preparatory. In our judgment, therefore, the judge was right to allow the case to go to the jury, and the appeal against conviction must be dismissed.

AG's Ref (No 1 of 1992) [1993] 1 WLR 274 (CA)

Lord Taylor of Gosforth CJ: This case comes before the court on a reference by Her Majesty's Attorney General under s 36 of the Criminal Justice Act 1972.

The respondent was charged with attempted rape and was acquitted by direction of the trial judge. In consequence of the judge's ruling, the Attorney General has referred a point of law for the opinion of this court. The point of law is stated thus:

> Whether, on a charge of attempted rape, it is incumbent upon the prosecution, as a matter of law, to prove that the defendant physically attempted to penetrate the woman's vagina with his penis.

... In *R v Jones (Kenneth Henry)* [1990] 1 WLR 1057 and again in *R v Campbell (Tony)* (1991) 93 Cr App R 350, this court made it clear that the words of the Act were to be applied in their plain and natural meaning, as the judge reminded himself in his first ruling. The words are not to be interpreted so as to reintroduce either of the earlier common law tests. Indeed one of the objects of the Act was to resolve the uncertainty those tests created ...

It is not, in our judgment, necessary, in order to raise a *prima facie* case of attempted rape, to prove that the defendant with the requisite intent had necessarily gone as far as to attempt physical penetration of the vagina. It is sufficient if there is evidence from which the intent can be inferred and there are proved acts which a jury could properly regard as more than merely preparatory to the commission of the offence. For example, and merely as an example, in the present case the evidence of the young woman's distress, of the state of her clothing, and the position in which she was seen, together with the respondent's acts of dragging her up the steps, lowering his trousers and interfering with her private parts, and his answers to the police, left it open to a jury to conclude that the respondent had the necessary intent and had done acts which were more than merely preparatory. In short that he had embarked on committing the offence itself.

For the reasons which we have endeavoured to give, we would answer the question posed in the reference, 'No'.

R v Geddes (1996) 160 JP 697 (CA)

Lord Bingham of Cornhill CJ: The background to the case may be shortly summarised. On 20 July 1994 the appellant went into the boys' lavatory block at Dorothy Stringer School, Brighton. He had no connection with the school and had no right to be there. At about midday a teacher saw him in the boys' lavatory and spoke to him. He had a rucksack with him. A woman police officer, who, by chance, was on the premises, saw him and shouted at him, but he left. In a cubicle in the lavatory block there was a cider can which had belonged to the appellant. In the course of leaving the school the appellant discarded his rucksack which was found in some bushes. Its contents included several articles: a large kitchen knife, some lengths of rope and a roll of masking tape. The appellant was arrested three days later. The teacher and some pupils from the school identified him.

The prosecution alleged that the presence of the cider can showed that the appellant had been inside a cubicle in the lavatory block. They further alleged that the contents of the rucksack could be used to catch and restrain a boy who entered the lavatory. The rope could have been used to tie the boy; the knife to frighten him; and the tape to cover his mouth to prevent him screaming.

The defence resisted the charge on the basis that the prosecution case was based on speculation. It was contested that the cider can showed that the appellant had been hiding in the cubicle, since he could well have entered the cubicle for normal purposes and left the cider can there. Alternatively, since the partitions of the lavatory did not extend from the floor to the ceiling, the can could have rolled or been thrown into the position where it was ultimately found. It was argued that there were other explanations for the contents of the rucksack ...

... The cases show that the line of demarcation between acts which are merely preparatory and acts which may amount to an attempt is not always clear or easy to recognise. There is no rule of thumb test. There must always be an exercise of judgment based on the particular facts of the case. It is, we think, an accurate paraphrase of the statutory test and not an illegitimate gloss upon it to ask whether the available evidence, if accepted, could show that a defendant has done an act which shows that he has actually tried to commit the offence in question, or whether he has only got ready or put himself in a position or equipped himself to do so.

In the present case ... there is not much room for doubt about the appellant's intention. Furthermore, the evidence is clearly capable of showing that he made preparations, that he equipped himself, that he got ready, that he put himself in a position to commit the offence charged. We question whether the cider can in the cubicle is of central importance, but would accept that in the absence of any explanation it could lead to the inference that the appellant had been in the cubicle. But was the evidence sufficient in law to support a finding that the appellant had actually tried or attempted to commit the offence of imprisoning someone? Had he moved from the realm of intention, preparation and planning into the area of execution or implementation? ... Here it is true that the appellant had entered the school; but he had never had any contact or communication with any pupil; he had never confronted any pupil at the school in any way ... [The] contents of the rucksack, which gave a clear indication as to what the appellant may have had in mind, but do not throw light on whether he had begun to carry out the commission of the offence [and so must be treated as irrelevant]. On the facts of this case we feel bound to conclude that the evidence was not sufficient in law to support a finding that the appellant did an act which was more than merely preparatory to wrongfully imprisoning a person unknown. In those circumstances we conclude that the appeal must be allowed and the conviction quashed.

Notes and queries

1   Section 1(4) of the Criminal Attempts Act 1981 expressly abolishes liability for attempted conspiracy and attempting to aid, abet, counsel or procure the commission of an offence. It is possible, however, to charge aiding and abetting an attempt – see *R v Dunnington* [1984] QB 472.

MENS REA: WITH INTENT TO COMMIT THE COMPLETED OFFENCE

The *mens rea* for an attempt is the intention to commit the complete offence; recklessness as to whether or not the prohibited consequence will occur is not enough: *R v Pearman* (1984) 80 Cr App R 259. Recklessness as to circumstances may still suffice, however; see *R v Khan* (below). It follows that the *mens rea* for an attempt is normally the same as the *mens rea* for the completed offence: *R v Millard* [1987] Crim LR 393; *R v Khan* [1990] 1 WLR 813; *AG's Ref (No 3 of 1992)* [1994] 1 WLR 409.

R v Pearman (1984) 80 Cr App R 259 (CA)

Facts: The appellant was charged with attempting to cause grievous bodily harm. He had driven his car at a police officer. His defence was that he did not intend to harm the police officer and did not foresee that his actions could cause serious injury to anybody.

Stuart-Smith J: ... This court, in the case of *Mohan* [1976] QB 1 dealt with the question of the mental element in an attempt before passing to that Act. It is not necessary to deal with the facts of the case. James LJ gave the judgment of the court. After reviewing the speeches of the House of Lords in *Hyam v DPP*, he said at p 11:

In our judgment, evidence of knowledge of likely consequences, or from which knowledge of likely consequences can be inferred, is evidence by which intent may be established but it is not in relation to the offence of attempt to be equated with intent. If the jury find such knowledge established, they may, and using common sense, they probably will find intent proved, but it is not the case that they must do so. An attempt to commit crime is itself an offence.

Often it is a grave offence. Often it is as morally culpable as the completed offence which is attempted but not in fact committed. Nevertheless it falls within the class of conduct which is preparatory to the commission of the crime and is one step removed from the offence which is attempted. The court must not strain to bring within the offence of attempt conduct which does not fall within the well-established bounds of the offence. On the contrary, the court must safeguard against extension of those bounds save by the authority of Parliament. The bounds are presently set requiring proof of specific intent, a decision to bring about, in so far as it lies within the accused's power, the commission of the offence which it is alleged the accused attempted to commit, no matter whether the accused desired that consequence of his act or not.

The last few words of that sentence, 'no matter whether the accused desired that consequence of his act or not', has given rise to debate amongst textbook writers as to what is meant by it, but it is clear from that passage that if the law is, as stated by James LJ in *Mohan* (above), still the same, that foresight of the consequences might be something from which the jury can infer intent, it is not to be equated with intent. We see no reason why the passing of the 1981 Act should have altered the law as to what is meant by the words 'intent'. The purpose of the Act was to deal with other matters rather than the content of the word 'intent'. We can see no reason why the judgment of the court in that case should not still be binding upon this court. It was, to some extent, based on the earlier decision of this court in *Whybrow* (1951) 35 Cr App R 141, where it was held that in the case of attempted murder although the *mens rea* for the completed offence of murder must be intent to kill or to cause really serious bodily harm, that was not sufficient in a case of attempted murder and it was necessary to prove the intent to kill.

As Parker LJ said in the course of argument, it would be an illogical conclusion and one offensive to common sense and offensive to any notion of an attempt if a man, who was in fact trying his best to avoid something coming about, could be guilty of an attempted offence simply because he foresaw that his actions might so involve him in committing it. It is offensive to common sense to suppose that simply because he could foresee it, he would be intending the offence to come about.

The words of James LJ which he used at the end of that passage, namely 'no matter whether the accused desired that consequence of his act of not', are probably designed to deal with a case where the accused has, as a primary purpose, some other object, for example, a man who plants a bomb in an aeroplane which he knows is going to take off, it being his primary intention that he should claim the insurance on the aeroplane when the freight goes down into the sea. The jury would not be put off from saying that he intended to murder the crew simply by saying that he did not want or desire to kill the crew, but that was something that he inevitably intended to do. Similarly, for example, a man who is cornered by the police when he is in a car may have the primary purpose of simply escaping from that situation. If he drives straight at the police officers at high speed, a jury is likely to conclude that he intended to injure a police officer and maybe cause him serious grievous bodily harm.

In the ordinary way, it would seem to this court to be sufficient for the judge to have told the jury that the Crown has to prove intent to cause grievous bodily harm on the part of the accused man ...

R v Millard and Vernon [1987] Crim LR 393 (CA)

Facts: The appellants were convicted of attempting to damage property, contrary to s 1(1) of the Criminal Attempts Act 1981. The particulars of the offence stated that they 'attempted to damage a wooden wall ... intending to damage [it] or being reckless as to whether [it] would be damaged'. They were football supporters who had repeatedly pushed against a wooden wall of a stand at a football ground. The prosecution alleged that they were trying to break the line of planking. The appellants denied pushing in unison and denied intending to damage the wall. The judge directed the jury that recklessness was an alternative to intention as an element of the substantive offence. The appellants appealed against conviction on the ground that recklessness – indifference to a known risk or failure to advert to an obvious risk – was incompatible with the intent required by s 1(1) of the 1981 Act.

Held, allowing the appeal and quashing the convictions, the result which would have been achieved by the full offence was damage to the stand. The prosecution had to show that it was this state of affairs which each appellant had decided to bring about. The judge was misled by the form of the indictment into offering a less stringent test. That was a material misdirection. Two different situations must be distinguished: (1) where the substantive offence consists simply of the act which constitutes the *actus reus*, the 'result', coupled with some element of volition, which may or may not amount to a full intent. The only question is whether the 'intent' to bring about the result called for by s 1(1) is to be watered down to such a degree, if any, as to make it correspond with the *mens rea* of the substantive offence. (2) The substantive offence does not consist of one result and one *mens rea*, but involves not only the underlying intention to produce the result, but also another state of mind directed to some circumstance or act which the prosecution must also establish in addition to proving the result. The substantive offence in the present case was in the first category. There was just one potential result, damage to the fence, and just one state of mind, the one which accompanied the acts said to have constituted the offence. There was no reason why the statutory requirement of an intent should be diluted by reference to the lower standard required by the substantive offence. There was nothing anomalous about a situation where, so far as the mental element is concerned, it is easier to prove the substantive offence than the attempt, eg murder and attempted murder.

Obiter: The problem in the second category could be illustrated by reference to the offence of attempted rape. As regards the substantive offence the 'result' is sexual intercourse with a woman. The offence is not established without proof of an additional circumstance (that is, that the woman did not consent) and a state of mind relative to that circumstance (that is, that the defendant knew she did not consent or was reckless as to whether she consented). In the offence of attempted rape, must the prosecution prove that the defendant intended the act to be non-consensual or should the jury be directed to consider two different states of mind, intent as to act and recklessness as to the circumstances? A similar problem may also arise where the additional matters to be proved relate not to some additional circumstance but to the method by which the result is achieved. An obvious example was causing death by reckless driving. Is it logically possible to attempt to commit the offence? *Mohan* [1976] QB 1 provided a partial answer; that intent bears its ordinary meaning and that the intent must be directed to the 'result' and not solely to the means of bringing about the result.

R v Khan [1990] 1 WLR 813 (CA)

Russell LJ: ... These appeals raise the short but important point of whether the offence of attempted rape is committed when the defendant is reckless as to the woman's consent to sexual intercourse. The appellants submit that no such offence is known to the law ...

In our judgment an acceptable analysis of the offence of rape is as follows: (1) the intention of the offender is to have sexual intercourse with a woman; (2) the offence is committed if, but only if, the circumstances are that: (a) the woman does not consent; and (b) the defendant knows that she is not consenting or is reckless as to whether she consents.

Precisely the same analysis can be made of the offence of attempted rape: (1) the intention of the offender is to have sexual intercourse with a woman; (2) the offence is committed if, but only if, the circumstances are that: (a) the woman does not consent; *and* (b) the defendant knows that she is not consenting or is reckless as to whether she consents.

The only difference between the two offences is that in rape sexual intercourse takes place whereas in attempted rape it does not, although there has to be some act which is more than preparatory to sexual intercourse. Considered in that way, the intent of the defendant is precisely the same in rape and in attempted rape and the *mens rea* is identical, namely an intention to have intercourse plus a knowledge of or recklessness as to the woman's absence of consent. No question of attempting to achieve a reckless state of mind arises; the attempt relates to the physical activity; the mental state of the defendant is the same. A man does not recklessly have sexual intercourse, nor does he recklessly attempt it. Recklessness in rape and attempted rape arises not in relation to the physical act of the accused but only in his state of mind when engaged in the activity of having or attempting to have sexual intercourse.

If this is the true analysis, as we believe it is, the attempt does not require any different intention on the part of the accused from that for the full offence of rape. We believe this to be a desirable result which in the instant case did not require the jury to be burdened with different directions as to the accused's state of mind, dependant on whether the individual achieved or failed to achieve sexual intercourse.

We recognise, of course, that our reasoning cannot apply to all offences and all attempts. Where, for example, as in causing death by reckless driving or reckless arson, no state of mind other than recklessness is involved in the offence, there can be no attempt to commit it.

In our judgment, however, the words 'with intent to commit an offence' to be found in s 1 of the 1981 Act mean, when applied to rape, 'with intent to have sexual intercourse with a woman in circumstances where she does not consent and the defendant knows or could not care less about her absence of consent'. The only 'intent', giving that word its natural and ordinary meaning, of the rapist is to have sexual intercourse. He commits the offence because of the circumstances in which he manifests that intent – ie when the woman is not consenting and he either knows it or could not care less about the absence of consent ...

Petition: The Appeal Committee of the House of Lords (**Lord Keith of Kinkel**, **Lord Brandon of Oakbrook** and **Lord Lowry**) dismissed petitions by Khan, Dhokia and Faiz for leave to appeal.

AG's Ref (No 3 of 1992) [1994] 1 WLR 409 (CA)

Schiemann J: The court has heard a reference made under s 36(1) of the Criminal Justice Act 1972. The point of law which has been referred to us was formulated as follows:

> Whether on a charge of attempted arson in the aggravated form contemplated by s 1(2) of the Criminal Damage Act 1971, in addition to establishing a specific intent to cause damage by fire, it is sufficient to prove that the defendant was reckless as to whether life would thereby be endangered.

The acquittals which have given rise to this reference had the following background according to the prosecution evidence. Following previous attacks upon their property the complainants maintained a night-time watch over their premises from a motor car (a Ford Granada). In the early hours of the morning the respondents came upon the scene in a vehicle. Inside this car, a Sierra, was a milk crate containing a number of petrol bombs, matches, a petrol can and some rags. As the Sierra approached the complainants, four inside their car and two persons on the pavement talking to them, a lighted petrol bomb was thrown towards them from the Sierra. The prosecution's case was that it was thrown at the Granada and its occupants. The petrol bomb in fact passed over the top of the Granada and smashed against the garden wall of a house a pavement's width away from the car. The Sierra accelerated away but crashed, and the respondents were arrested ...

So far as attempting to commit the ... offence [under s 1(1) of the Criminal Damage Act 1971] is concerned, in order to convict on such a charge it must be proved that the defendant: (a) did an act which was more than merely preparatory to the commission of the offence; and (b) did an act intending to damage any property belonging to another.

One way of analysing the situation is to say that a defendant, in order to be guilty of an attempt, must be in one of the states of mind required for the commission of the full offence, and did his best, as far as he could, to supply what was missing from the completion of the offence. It is the policy of the law that such people should be punished notwithstanding that in fact the intentions of such a defendant have not been fulfilled.

If the facts are that, although the defendant had one of the appropriate states of mind required for the complete offence, but the physical element required for the commission of the complete offence is missing, the defendant is not to be convicted unless it can be shown that he intended to supply the physical element. This was the state of affairs in *R v Millard and Vernon* [1987] Crim LR 393, of which we have seen the transcript. There the defendants were convicted of attempting to damage property. The particulars of the offence were that they 'attempted to damage a wooden wall at the ... stadium ... intending to damage the ... wall or being reckless as to whether the ... wall was damaged'. The trial judge directed the jury that recklessness was sufficient. Mustill LJ, delivering the judgment of the Court of Appeal, stated:

> The result which would have been achieved if the offence had been taken to fruition was damage to the stand ... the prosecution had to show ... that it was this state of affairs which each appellant had decided, so far as in him lay, to bring about.

In consequence, mere recklessness was not sufficient and the convictions were quashed.

We turn finally to the attempt to commit the aggravated offence [under s 1(2) of the Criminal Damage Act 1971]. In the present case, what was missing to prevent a conviction for the completed offence was damage to the property referred to in the opening lines of s 1(2) of the Act of 1981, what in the example of a crane, which we gave earlier in this judgment, we referred to as 'the first-named property'. Such damage is essential for the completed offence. If a defendant does not intend to cause such damage he cannot intend to commit the completed offence. At worst he is reckless as to whether the offence is committed. The law of attempt is concerned with those who are intending to commit crimes. If that intent cannot be shown, then there can be no conviction.

However, the crime here consisted of doing certain acts in a certain state of mind in circumstances where the first-named property and the second-named property were the same, in short where the danger to life arose from the damage to the property which the defendant intended to damage. The substantive crime is committed if the defendant damaged property in a state of mind where he was reckless as to whether the life of another would thereby be endangered. We see no reason why there should not be a conviction for attempt if the prosecution can show that he, in that state of mind, intended to damage the property by throwing a bomb at it. One analysis of this situation is to say that although the defendant was in an appropriate state of mind to render him guilty of the completed offence the prosecution had not proved the physical element of the completed offence, and therefore he is not guilty of the completed offence. If, on a charge of attempting to commit the offence, the prosecution can show not only the state of mind required for the completed offence but also that the defendant intended to supply the missing physical element of the completed offence, that suffices for a conviction. That cannot be done merely by the prosecution showing him to be reckless. The defendant must intend to damage property, but there is no need for a graver mental state than is required for the full offence ...

... What was missing in the present case was damage to the first-named property, without which the offence was not complete. The mental state of the defendant in each case contained everything which was required to render him guilty of the full offence. In order to succeed in a prosecution for attempt, it must be shown that the defendant intended to achieve that which was missing from the full offence.

Unless that is shown, the prosecution have not proved that the defendant intended to commit the offence. Thus in *R v Khan (Mohammed Iqbal)* [1990] 1 WLR 813 the prosecution had to show an intention to have sexual intercourse, and the remaining state of mind required for the offence of rape. In the present case, the prosecution had to show an intention to damage the first-named property, and the remaining state of mind required for the offence of aggravated arson ...

We answer [the question posed by the reference] in the affirmative.

We add that, in circumstances where the first-named property is not the same as the second-named property, in addition to establishing a specific intent to cause damage by fire to the first-named property, it is sufficient to prove that the defendant was reckless as to whether any second-named property was damaged and reckless as to whether the life of another would be endangered by the damage to the second-named property.

IMPOSSIBILITY

There are at least three forms of impossibility that a defendant charged with attempt may think will provide him with an answer to the charge. The first is impossibility of means; the second impossibility in fact; and the third, impossibility in law.

Impossibility of means has never been a defence as such. The fact that D does not use enough dynamite to blow open the doors of a safe, or that his arms are not long enough to reach the property he wants to steal, is irrelevant provided he has taken steps more than merely preparatory to the commission of the completed offence, with the necessary *mens rea*. Impossibility of fact, as for example where D fires a gun at P intending to kill him, only to discover that P had died an hour before, has presented some difficulties in the past, but is clearly now prevented from operating as any bar to liability for attempt, as *R v Shivpuri* (extracted below) indicates. Impossibility of law, where for example D handles goods that have (unknown to D), as a matter of law, ceased to be stolen, was for a time regarded as a bar to liability by the House of Lords (see *Haughton v Smith* [1973] 3 All ER 1109). The Criminal Attempts Act 1981, by virtue of s 1(2) and (3), makes clear that this decision has now been swept away leaving the defendant with no argument based on impossibility. In effect the only 'impossibility' argument that could now avail defendant charged with attempt is where he takes steps more than merely preparatory to committing what he wrongly believes to be an offence, for example an attempt to import the complete works of Shakespeare into the UK. Although he believes he is committing a crime, he cannot be charged with attempt as the offence only relates to offences known to law.

R v Shivpuri [1987] 1 AC 1 (HL)

Lord Hailsham of St Marylebone LC: My Lords, I have had the advantage of reading in draft the speech about to be delivered ... by my noble and learned friend, Lord Bridge of Harwich. Save for one relatively minor point I agree with it in its entirety and would dispose of this appeal as he proposes and for the reasons which he gives. I add a few remarks of my own for reasons which will appear ...

I must add, however, that even had I not been able to follow my noble and learned friend in interring *Anderton v Ryan* by using the *Practice Statement* of 1966, I would still have dismissed the instant appeal by distinguishing its facts from that case. Shortly, my reasoning would have been that the appellant was guilty on the clear wording of s 1(1) and 1(2) of the Act of 1981 and that no recourse was therefore necessary to the wording of s 1(3) which if so would be irrelevant.

I would have arrived at this conclusion by asking myself three simple questions to which the answers could only be made in one form. They are:

Q1: What was the intention of the appellant throughout?

A1: His intention throughout was to evade and defeat the customs authorities of the UK. He had no other intention. His motive was gain (the bribe of £1,000). But as I pointed out in *R v Hyam* [1975] AC 55 at 73 motive is not the same thing as intention.

Q2: Is the knowing evasion of the UK customs in the manner envisaged in the appellant's intent an offence to which s 1 of the Act of 1981 applies?

A2: Yes, see s 1(4).

Q3: Did the appellant do an act which was more than preparatory to the commission of the offence?

A3: Yes, for the reasons stated in the relevant paragraphs of my noble and learned friend's speech.

In this connection I do not feel it would have been necessary to invoke the doctrine of dominant and subordinate intention referred to by my noble and learned friend. The *sole* intent of the instant appellant from start to finish was to defeat the customs prohibition. In *Anderton v Ryan* [1985] AC 560 the only intention of Mrs Ryan was to buy a particular video cassette recorder at a knock-down price, and the fact that she believed it to be stolen formed no part of that intention. It was a belief, assumed to be false and not an intention at all. It was a false belief as to a state of fact, and, if it became an intention it was only the result of the deeming provisions of s 1(3) of the Act of 1981. Whether or not *Anderton v Ryan* was correctly decided, one has to go to s 1(3) to decide whether Mrs Ryan had committed a criminal attempt under the Act as the result of her belief, assumed to be false, that the video cassette recorder had in fact been stolen. Similarly, to my mind, the only intention of the lustful youth postulated by my noble and learned friends, Lord Roskill and Lord Bridge of Harwich, by way of example in *Anderton v Ryan* was to have carnal connection with a particular girl. One has to go to s 1(3) to discover whether or not a criminal attempt had been committed as the result of his false belief that she was under age.

By way of conclusion I have to say that I think it a pity that, as it emerged from Parliament, the Act of 1981 departed from the draft Bill attached to the Law Commission report *Criminal Law: Attempt, and Impossibility in Relation to Attempt, Conspiracy and Incitement* (1980) Law Com 102, which might have saved a lot of trouble. In particular the distinction which I have sought to draw above between the facts in *Anderton v Ryan* and the instant appeal would have been patently obvious and not to some extent controversial. In the second place it may perhaps have been inevitable, but is nonetheless unusual, that, in defining the prohibited act in s 1, the draftsman in both cases was driven to define the act by reference to an intent, instead, as is more usual in criminal jurisprudence, of defining the criminal intent by reference to a separately defined prohibited act. It is this feature of s 1 which, I believe, has caused the trouble, and once this road has been followed it was I believe impossible to avoid the disadvantages pointed out in paragraph 2.97 of the Law Commission's report to which my noble and learned friend has drawn attention.

In the circumstances I am happy that my noble and learned friend's conclusion has enabled the House to arrive at its destination without resorting to these, possibly excessively sophisticated, subtleties.

Lord Bridge of Harwich: My Lords, on 23 February 1984 the appellant was convicted at the Crown Court at Reading of two attempts to commit offences. The offences attempted were being knowingly concerned in dealing with (count 1) and in harbouring (count 2) a Class A controlled drug namely diamorphine, with intent to evade the prohibition of importation imposed by s 3(1) of the Misuse of Drugs Act 1971, contrary to s 170(1)(b) of the Customs and Excise Management Act 1979. On 5 November 1984 the Court of Appeal (Criminal Division) dismissed his appeal against conviction but certified that a point of law of general public importance was involved in their decision and granted leave to appeal to your Lordships' House.

The certified question granted on 13 November 1984 reads:

Does a person commit an offence under s 1 of the Criminal Attempts Act 1981 where, if the facts were as that person believed them to be, the full offence would have been committed by him, but where on the true facts of the offence which that person set out to commit was in law impossible, eg because the substance imported and believed to be heroin was not heroin but a harmless substance?

The facts plainly to be inferred from the evidence, interpreted in the light of the jury's guilty verdicts, may be shortly summarised. The appellant, on a visit to India, was approached by a man named Desai, who offered to pay him £1,000 if, on his return to England, he would receive a suitcase which a courier would deliver to him containing packages of drugs which the appellant was then to distribute according to instructions he would receive. The suitcase was duly delivered to him in Cambridge. On 30 November 1982, acting on instructions, the appellant went to Southall Station to deliver a package of drugs to a third party. Outside the station he and the man he had met by appointment were arrested. A package containing a powdered substance was found in the appellant's shoulder bag. At the appellant's flat in Cambridge, he produced to customs officers the suitcase from which the lining had been ripped out and the remaining packages of the same powdered substance. In answer to questions by customs officers and in a long written statement the appellant made what amounted to a full confession of having played his part, as described, as recipient and distributor of illegally imported drugs. The appellant believed the drugs to be either heroin or cannabis. In due course the powdered substance in the several packages was scientifically analysed and found not to be a controlled drug but snuff or some similar harmless vegetable matter ...

The certified question depends on the true construction of the Criminal Attempts Act 1981. That Act marked an important new departure since, by s 6, it abolished the offence of attempt at common law and substituted a new statutory code governing attempts to commit criminal offences. It was considered by your Lordships' House last year in *Anderton v Ryan* [1985] AC 560 after the decision in the Court of Appeal which is the subject of the present appeal. That might seem an appropriate starting point from which to examine the issues arising in this appeal. But your Lordships have been invited to exercise the power under the *Practice Statement (Judicial Precedent)* [1966] 1 WLR 1234 to depart from the reasoning in that decision if it proves necessary to do so in order to affirm the convictions appealed against in the instant case. I was not only a party to the decision in *Anderton v Ryan,* I was also the author of one of the two opinions approved by the majority which must be taken to express the House's *ratio.* That seems to me to afford a sound reason why, on being invited to re-examine the language of the statute in its application to the facts of this appeal, I should initially seek to put out of mind what I said in *Anderton v Ryan.* Accordingly I propose to approach the issue in the first place as an exercise in statutory construction, applying the language of the Act to the facts of the case, as if the matter were *res integra.* If this leads me to the conclusion that the appellant was not guilty of any attempt to commit a relevant offence, that will be the end of the matter. But if this initial exercise inclines me to reach a contrary conclusion, it will then be necessary to consider whether the precedent set by *Anderton v Ryan* bars that conclusion or whether it can be surmounted either on the ground that the earlier decision is distinguishable or that it would be appropriate to depart from it under the *Practice Statement.*

His Lordship quoted s 1 of the Criminal Attempts Act 1981 and continued:

Applying this language to the facts of the case, the first question to be asked is whether the appellant intended to commit the offences of being knowingly concerned in dealing with and harbouring drugs of Class A or Class B with intent to evade the prohibition on their importation. Translated into more homely language the question may be rephrased, without in any way altering its legal significance, in the following terms: did the appellant intend to receive and store (harbour) and in due course pass on to third parties (deal with) packages of heroin or cannabis which he knew had been smuggled into England from India? The answer is plainly yes, he did. Next, did he in relation to each offence, do an act which was more than merely preparatory to the commission of the offence? The act relied on in relation to harbouring was the receipt and retention of the packages found in the lining of the suitcase. The act relied on in relation to dealing was the meeting at Southall Station with the intended recipient of one of the packages. In each case the act was clearly more than preparatory to the commission of the intended offence; it was not and could not be more than merely preparatory to the commission of the actual offence, because the facts were such that the commission of the actual offence was impossible. Here then is the nub of the matter. Does the 'act which is more than merely preparatory to the commission of the offence' in s 1(1) of the Act of 1981 (the *actus reus* of the statutory offence of attempt) require any more than an act which is more than merely preparatory to the commission of the offence which the defendant intended to commit? Section 1(2) must surely indicate a negative answer; if it were otherwise, whenever the facts were such that the commission of the actual offence was impossible, it would be impossible to prove an act more than merely preparatory to the commission of that offence and subsections (1) and (2) would contradict each other.

This is very simple, perhaps oversimple, analysis leads me to the provisional conclusion that the appellant was rightly convicted of the two offences of attempt with which he was charged. But can this conclusion stand with *Anderton v Ryan*? The appellant in that case was charged with an attempt to handle stolen goods. She bought a video recorder believing it to be stolen. On the facts as they were to be assumed it was not stolen. By a majority the House decided that she was entitled to be acquitted. I have re-examined the case with care. If I could extract from the speech of Lord Roskill or from my own speech a clear and coherent principle distinguishing those cases of attempting the impossible which amount to offences under the statute from those which do not, I should have to consider carefully on which side of the line the instant case fell. But I have to confess that I can find no such principle.

Running through Lord Roskill's speech and my own in *Anderton v Ryan* [1985] AC 560 is the concept of 'objectively innocent' acts which, in my speech certainly, are contrasted with 'guilty acts'. A few citations will make this clear. Lord Roskill said at 580:

> My Lords, it has been strenuously and ably argued for the respondent that these provisions involve that a defendant is liable to conviction for an attempt even where his actions are innocent but he erroneously believes facts which, if true, would make those actions criminal, and further, that he is liable to such conviction whether or not in the event his intended course of action is completed.

He proceeded to reject the argument. At p 582 I referred to the appellant's purchase of the video recorder and said: 'Objectively considered, therefore, her purchase of the recorder was a perfectly proper commercial transaction'. A further passage from my speech proceeded, at pp 582–83:

> The question may be stated in abstract terms as follows. Does s 1 of the Act of 1981 create a new offence of attempt where a person embarks on and completes a course of conduct which is objectively innocent, solely on the ground that the person mistakenly believes facts which, if true, would make that course of conduct a complete crime? If the question must be answered affirmatively it requires convictions in a number of surprising cases: the classic case, put by Bramwell B in *R v Collins* (1864) 9 Cox CC 497, of the man who takes away his own umbrella from a stand, believing it not to be his own and with intent to steal it; the case of the man who has consensual intercourse with a girl over 16 believing her to be under that age; the case of the art dealer who sells a picture which he represents to be and which is in fact a genuine Picasso, but which the dealer mistakenly believes to be a fake. The common feature of all these cases, including that under appeal, is that the mind alone is guilty, the act is innocent.

I then contrasted the case of the man who attempts to pick the empty pocket, saying:

> Putting the hand in the pocket is the guilty act, the intent to steal is the guilty mind, the offence is appropriately dealt with as an attempt, and the impossibility of committing the full offence for want of anything in the pocket to steal is declared by [subsection (2)] to be no obstacle to conviction.

If we fell into error, it is clear that our concern was to avoid convictions in situations which most people, as a matter of common sense, would not regard as involving criminality. In this connection it is to be regretted that we did not take due note of paragraph 2.97 of the Law Commission's report *Criminal Law: Attempt, and Impossibility in Relation to Attempt, Conspiracy and Incitement* (1980) Law Com 102 which preceded the enactment of the Act of 1981, which reads:

> If it is right in principle that an attempt should be chargeable even though the crime which it is sought to commit could not possibly be committed, we do not think that we should be deterred by the consideration that such a change in our law would also cover some extreme and exceptional cases in which a prosecution would be theoretically possible. An example would be where a person is offered goods at such a low price that he believes that they are stolen, when in fact they are not; if he actually purchases them, upon the principles which we have discussed he would be liable for an attempt to handle stolen goods. Another case which has been much debated is that raised in argument by Bramwell B in *R v Collins* (1864) 9 Cox CC 497. If A takes his own umbrella, mistaking it for one belonging to B and intending to steal B's umbrella, is he guilty of attempted theft? Again, on the principles which we have discussed he would in theory be guilty, but in neither case would it be realistic to suppose that a complaint would be made or that a prosecution would ensue.

The prosecution in *Anderton v Ryan* itself falsified the Commission's prognosis in one of the 'extreme and exceptional cases'. It nevertheless probably holds good for other such cases, particularly that of the young man having sexual intercourse with a girl over 16, mistakenly believing her to be under that age, by which both Lord Roskill and I were much troubled.

However that may be, the distinction between acts which are 'objectively innocent' and those which are not is an essential element in the reasoning in *Anderton v Ryan* and the decision, unless it can be supported on some other ground, must stand or fall by the validity of this distinction. I am satisfied on further consideration that the concept of 'objective innocence' is incapable of sensible application in relation to the law of criminal attempts. The reason for this is that any attempt to commit an offence which involves 'an act which is more than merely preparatory to the commission of the offence' but for any reason fails, so that in the event no offence is committed, must *ex hypothesi*, from the point of view of the criminal law, be 'objectively innocent'. What turns what would otherwise, from the point of view of the criminal law, be an innocent act into a crime is the intent of the actor to commit an offence. I say 'from the point of view of the criminal law' because the law of tort must surely here be quite irrelevant. A puts his hand into B's pocket. Whether or not there is anything in the pocket capable of being stolen, if A intends to steal, his act is a criminal attempt; if he does not so intend, his act is innocent. A plunges a knife into a bolster in a bed. To avoid the complication of an offence of criminal damage, assume it to be A's bolster. If A believes the bolster to be his enemy B and intends to kill him, his act is an attempt to murder B; if he knows the bolster is only a bolster, his act is innocent. These considerations lead me to the conclusion that the distinction sought to be drawn in *Anderton v Ryan* between innocent and guilty acts considered 'objectively' and independently of the state of mind of the actor cannot be sensibly maintained.

Another conceivable ground of distinction which was to some extent canvassed in argument, both in *Anderton v Ryan* and in the instant case, though no trace of it appears in the speeches in *Anderton v Ryan*, is a distinction which would make guilt or innocence of the crime of attempt in a case of mistaken belief dependent on what, for want of a better phrase, I will call the defendant's dominant intention. According to the theory necessary to sustain this distinction, the appellant's dominant intention in *Anderton v Ryan* was to buy a cheap video recorder, her belief that it was stolen was merely incidental. Likewise in the hypothetical case of attempted unlawful sexual intercourse, the young man's dominant intention was to have intercourse with the particular girl; his mistaken belief that she was under 16 was merely incidental. By contrast, in the instant case the appellant's dominant intention was to receive and distribute illegally imported heroin or cannabis.

Whilst I see the superficial attraction of this suggested ground of distinction, I also see formidable practical difficulties in its application. By what test is a jury to be told that a defendant's dominant intention is to be recognised and distinguished from his incidental but mistaken belief? But there is perhaps a more formidable theoretical difficulty. If this ground of distinction is relied on to support the acquittal of the appellant in *Anderton v Ryan*, it can only do so on the basis that her mistaken belief that the video recorder was stolen played no significant part in her decision to buy it and therefore she may be acquitted of the intent to handle stolen goods. But this line of reasoning runs into head-on collision with s 1(3) of the Act of 1981. The theory produces a situation where, apart from the subsection, her intention would not be regarded as having amounted to any intent to commit an offence. Section 1(3)(b) then requires one to ask whether, if the video recorder had in fact been stolen, her intention would have been regarded as an intent to handle stolen goods. The answer must clearly be yes, it would. If she had bought the video recorder knowing it to be stolen, when in fact it was, it would have availed her nothing to say that her dominant intention was to buy a video recorder because it was cheap and that her knowledge that it was stolen was merely incidental. This seems to me fatal to the dominant intention theory.

I am thus led to the conclusion that there is no valid ground on which *Anderton v Ryan* can be distinguished. I have made clear my own conviction, which as a party to the decision (and craving the indulgence of my noble and learned friends who agreed in it) I am the readier to express, that the decision was wrong. What then is to be done? If the case is indistinguishable, the application of the strict doctrine of precedent would require that the present appeal be allowed. Is it permissible to depart from precedent under the *Practice Statement (Judicial Precedent)* [1966] 1 WLR 1234 notwithstanding the especial need for certainty in the criminal law? The following considerations lead me to answer that question affirmatively. First, I am undeterred by the consideration that the decision in *Anderton v Ryan* was so recent. The *Practice Statement* is an effective abandonment of our pretention to infallibility. If a serious error embodied in a decision of this House has distorted the law, the sooner it is corrected the better. Second, I cannot see how, in the very nature of the case, anyone could have acted in reliance on the law as propounded in *Anderton v Ryan* in the belief that he was acting innocently and now find that, after all, he is to be held to have committed a criminal offence. Third, to hold the House bound to follow *Anderton v Ryan* because it cannot be distinguished and to allow the appeal in this case would, it seems to me, be tantamount to a declaration that the Act of 1981 left the law of criminal attempts unchanged following the decision in *R v Smith* [1975] AC 476. Finally, if, contrary to my present view, there is a valid ground on which it would be proper to distinguish cases similar to that considered in *Anderton v Ryan*, my present opinion on that point would not foreclose the option of making such a distinction in some future case.

I cannot conclude this opinion without disclosing that I have had the advantage, since the conclusion of the argument in this appeal, of reading an article by Professor Glanville Williams entitled 'The Lords and impossible attempts, or *quis custodiet ipsos custodes*?' [1986] CLJ 33. The language in which he criticises the decision in *Anderton v Ryan* is not conspicuous for it moderation, but it would be foolish, on that account, not to recognise the force of the criticism and churlish not to acknowledge the assistance I have derived from it.

I would answer the certified question in the affirmative and dismiss the appeal.

JURISDICTIONAL ISSUES

Section 1(4) of the Criminal Attempts Act 1981 provides that s 1 applies to '... any offence which, if it were completed, would be triable in England and Wales as an indictable offence ...'. One effect of this is that an attempt can comprise acts outside the jurisdiction that would have lead to the commission of the completed offence within the jurisdiction; see *DPP v Stonehouse* [1978] AC 55. Jurisdiction over attempts with a foreign element has been widened further by the provisions of the Criminal Justice Act 1993, which provides that courts in England and Wales have jurisdiction to deal with attempts to commit 'Class A' offences (defined in the 1993 Act as offences of dishonesty and fraud) provided certain conditions are met. It achieves this by inserting a s 1A after s 1 in the Criminal Attempts Act 1981:

Section 1A: Extended jurisdiction in relation to certain attempts

(1) If this section applies to an act, what the person doing the act had in view shall be treated as an offence to which section 1(1) above applies.

(2) This section applies to an act if –

    (a) it is done in England and Wales, and

    (b) it would fall within section 1(1) above as more than merely preparatory to the commission of a Group A offence but for the fact that that offence, if completed, would not be an offence triable in England and Wales.

(3) In this section 'Group A offence' has the same meaning as in Part 1 of the Criminal Justice Act 1993.

(4) Subsection (1) above is subject to the provisions of section 6 of the Act of 1993 (relevance of external law).

(5) Where a person does any act to which this section applies, the offence which he commits shall for all purposes be treated as the offence of attempting to commit the relevant Group A offence.

The commentary in *Blackstone's Criminal Practice*, 11th edn, at A6.38 observes:

The [Criminal Justice Act 1993] inserts a new s 1A in the Criminal Attempts Act 1981, supposedly to cover cases where the accused in England and Wales attempts to commit abroad something that would be a Group A offence, but for the fact that it is not triable under English law. This provision is fundamentally at odds with itself. If a Group A offence is instigated by conduct within England and Wales, that offence will inevitably be triable under English law. Section 1A is merely a trap for unwary prosecutors, who may be tempted to use it instead of s 1.

Further reading

B Hogan, 'The Criminal Attempts Act and attempting the impossible' [1984] Crim LR 584

JE Stannard, 'Making up for the missing element: a sideways look at attempts' (1987) 7 Legal Studies 194

KJM Smith, 'Proximity in attempt: Lord Lane's "midway course"' [1991] Crim LR 576

RA Duff, 'The circumstances of an attempt' [1991] CLJ 100

CHAPTER 13

DURESS AND NECESSITY

The common law has, for many years, recognised a defence of duress *per minas* – effectively duress through threats from a third party. The defendant is excused liability for certain crimes because he was forced to choose between, on the one hand, committing the criminal offence specified by X or, on the other, facing up to X's threat to kill or inflict grievous bodily harm if his demands were not met. More recently the courts have developed a common law defence of duress of circumstances where the compulsion to act may arise from something other than threats of death or grievous bodily harm. Uncertainty remains as to whether there is, at common law, a defence of necessity that is distinguishable from duress of circumstances and, if there is, what the requirements of such a defence might be.

DURESS *PER MINAS*

The need for a 'nominated crime'

R v Cole [1994] Crim LR 582 (CA)

Facts: The appellant's defence to robbing two building societies was his inability to repay money lenders, who had threatened him, hit him with a baseball bat, and threatened his girlfriend and child. At trial, the judge ruled that duress was only available where the threats were directed to the commission of the particular offence charged. Here, the threat related to the debt, and it was not contended that he was threatened with the unpleasant consequences if he did not commit the robbery.

Held, dismissing the appeal, two distinct defences had developed: duress by threats and duress of circumstances (necessity). The first applied when the threatener nominated the crime (*Hudson* (1972) 56 Cr App R 1; *DPP for Northern Ireland v Lynch* (1975) 61 Cr App R 6). The appellant could not rely on duress by threats since the money lenders had not stipulated that he commit robbery to meet their demands In the present case the imminent peril, which was a necessary precondition to the defence properly arising, was lacking. True, the appellant had said that he had no choice, and had to have the money by a particular time, but that fell short of the degree of directness and immediacy required of the link between the suggested peril and the offence charged. The connection between the threat and the criminal act was not close and immediate. Separating the two types of duress might on occasion appear to involve an imperfect logic, but the dichotomy was proposed to be continued in the draft Criminal Law Bill (Law Com 218). The court echoed the urgent call for legislation in *Hurst* (1994) *The Times*, 2 February, albeit provoked by rather different concerns than arose here. Meanwhile, this was not the time to give duress any wider ambit than had hitherto been recognised. Until all aspects of the defence had been put on a statutory footing, including as presently envisaged, shifting the burden of proof from the Crown to the accused, duress should be rigidly confined to its established present limits.

The nature of the threat directed at the defendant

The compulsion under which D acts must be a threat of death or grievous bodily harm; see *R v Graham* (extracted below). As Lord Simon observed in *DPP for Northern Ireland v Lynch* [1975] 1 All ER 913, 932: '... as a result of experience and human valuation, the law draws [a line] between threats to property and threats to the person ...' Although D may himself be the subject of the threats to kill or do grievous bodily harm, the defence is available where the threats are made to third parties, for example D's family; see further *R v Ortiz* (1986) 83 Cr App R 173, and *R v Harley and Murray* [1967] VR 526.

The imminence of the threat

R v Hudson and Taylor [1971] 2 QB 202 (CA)

Lord Parker CJ: ... On 6 April 1969, a fight took place in a Salford public house between one Wright and one Mulligan with the result that Wright was charged with wounding Mulligan. Each of the present appellants gave statements to the police and they were the principal prosecution witnesses at Wright's trial. Elaine Taylor is 19, and Linda Hudson is 17.

Wright's trial took place on 4 August 1969, but when called to give evidence the appellants failed to identify Wright as Mulligan's assailant. Taylor said that she knew no one called Jimmy Wright, and Hudson said that the only Wright she knew was not the man in the dock. Wright was accordingly acquitted and, in due course, the appellants were charged with perjury. At their trial they admitted that the evidence which they had given was false but set up the defence of duress. The basis of the defence was that, shortly after the fight between Wright and Mulligan, Hudson had been approached by a group of men including one Farrell who had a reputation for violence and was warned that if she 'told on Wright in court' they would get her and cut her up. Hudson passed this warning to Taylor who said that she had also been warned by other girls to be careful or she would be hurt. The appellants said in evidence that, in consequence of these threats, they were frightened and decided to tell lies in court in order to avoid the consequences which might follow if they testified against Wright. This resolve was strengthened when they arrived at court for Wright's trial and saw that Farrell was in the gallery.

The recorder directed the jury as a matter of law that the defence of duress was not open to the appellants in these circumstances ...

... Despite the concern expressed in Stephen's *History of the Criminal Law of England*, Vol 2, 1883, p 107 that it would be 'a much greater misfortune for society at large if criminals could confer [immunity] upon their agents by threatening them with death or violence if they refuse to execute their commands' it is clearly established that duress provides a defence in all offences including perjury (except possibly treason or murder as a principal) if the will of the accused had been overborne by threats of death or serious personal injury so that the commission of the alleged offence was no longer the voluntary act of the accused.

This appeal raises two main questions: first, as to the nature of the necessary threat and, in particular, whether it must be 'present and immediate'; second, as to the extent to which a right to plead duress may be lost if the accused has failed to take steps to remove the threat as, for example, by seeking police protection.

It is essential to the defence of duress that the threat shall be effective at the moment when the crime is committed. The threat must be a 'present' threat in the sense that it is effective to neutralise the will of the accused at that time. Hence an accused who joins a rebellion under the compulsion of threats cannot plead duress if he remains with the rebels after the threats have lost their effect and his own will has had a chance to re-assert itself: *R v M'Growther* (1746) Fost 13; *AG v Whelan* [1934] IR 518. Similarly a threat of future violence may be so remote as to be insufficient to overpower the will at that moment when the offence was committed, or the accused may have elected to commit the offence in order to rid himself of a threat hanging over him and not because he was driven to act by immediate and unavoidable pressure. In none of these cases is the defence of duress available because a person cannot justify the commission of a crime merely to secure his own peace of mind.

When, however, there is no opportunity for delaying tactics, and the person threatened must make up his mind whether he is to commit the criminal act or not, the existence at that moment of threats sufficient to destroy his will ought to provide him with a defence even though the threatened injury may not follow instantly, but after an interval. This principle is illustrated by *Subramaniam v Public Prosecutor* [1956] 1 WLR 965, when the appellant was charged in Malaya with unlawful possession of ammunition and was held by the Privy Council to have a defence of duress, fit to go to the jury, on his plea that he had been compelled by terrorists to accept the ammunition and feared for his safety if the terrorists returned.

In the present case the threats of Farrell were likely to be no less compelling, because their execution could not be effected in the courtroom, if they could be carried out in the streets of Salford the same night. In so far, therefore, as the recorder ruled as a matter of law that the threats were not sufficiently present and immediate to support the defence of duress we think that he was in error. He should have left the jury to decide whether the threats had overborne the will of the appellants at the time when they gave the false evidence.

[Counsel for the Crown], however, contends that the recorder's ruling can be supported on another ground, namely that the appellants should have taken steps to neutralise the threats by seeking police protection either when they came to court to give evidence, or beforehand. He submits on grounds of public policy that an accused should not be able to plead duress if he had the opportunity to ask for protection from the police before committing the offence and failed to do so. The argument does not distinguish cases in which the police would be able to provide effective protection, from those when they would not, and it would, in effect, restrict the defence of duress to cases where the person threatened had been kept in custody by the maker of the threats, or where the time interval between the making of the threats and the commission of the offence had made recourse to the police impossible. We recognise the need to keep the defence of duress within reasonable bounds but cannot accept so severe a restriction upon it. The duty, of the person threatened, to take steps to remove the threat does not seem to have arisen in an English case but, in a full review of the defence of duress in the Supreme Court of Victoria (*R v Harley and Murray* [1967] VR 526), a condition of raising the defence was said to be that the accused 'had no means, with safety to himself, of preventing the execution of the threat'.

In the opinion of this court it is always open to the Crown to prove that the accused failed to avail himself of some opportunity which was reasonably open to him to render the threat ineffective, and that upon this being established the threat in question can no longer be relied upon by the defence. In deciding whether such an opportunity was reasonably open to the accused the jury should have regard to his age and circumstances, and to any risks to him which may be involved in the course of action relied upon.

In our judgment the defence of duress should have been left to the jury in the present case, as should any issue raised by the Crown and arising out of the appellants' failure to seek protection ...

R v Abdul-Hussain and Others [1999] Crim LR 570 (CA)

Rose LJ: At the Central Criminal Court, on 31 October 1997, these appellants ... were convicted ... of hijacking, contrary to section 1(1) of the Aviation Security Act 1982 ... The appellants were all Shiite Muslims from Southern Iraq. Save for Hoshan, all had offended against the laws or regulations of the Saddam Hussein regime, from which they were fugitives. In the summer of 1996, they were living in Sudan and feared return to Iraq at the hands of the Sudanese authorities. Hoshan had a valid permit to reside in the United Kingdom and would have become entitled to a right of permanent settlement. He was free to travel to Middle Eastern countries and elsewhere. He helped Iraqis obtain false papers and in the bribing of officials. He appeared to have access to funds for that latter purpose.

In April 1996, he was in Jordan to assist a family called Macki, the eldest daughter of which he had arranged to marry. In Iraq, the father and two brothers in that family had been executed in horrifying circumstances, and all the women of the family had been imprisoned and tortured. They went with him, that is Hoshan, to the Sudan, in the belief that it would be easier to escape from that country. Hoshan believed that, because of his involvement in helping others, he was at risk of detection and deportation to Iraq, where he would probably be executed. Abdul-Hussain was under sentence of death, passed in Iraq in 1991, in his absence, following a confession extracted by torture. In 1996, that sentence of death had been reiterated. Aboud, Hasan and Maged Nagi had taken part in the Interfada, that is the unsuccessful uprising in Southern Iraq after the Gulf war. Aboud and Hasan had escaped from jail in Iraq. They had previously been hiding in Jordan. Muhssin had avoided service in the Iraqi army in the Gulf war and had been sentenced, in his absence, to 10 years and a very large fine for taking and selling a lorry. He believed that, if he were caught, he would be hanged at the Iraqi border.

Abdul-Hussain was related to the family of Macki. Maged Naji met Hoshan in Jordan. They feared detection by Iraqi agents. Sabah Naji had been deported from

Iraq in 1995 and was on a black list there and believed that, if he returned, he would face death.

The group made several attempts to leave Sudan using false passports. These were on each occasion rejected at Khartoum Airport but returned to them. Without success, they tried to obtain visas for other European countries. Some three weeks before the hijack to which, in a moment, we shall come, Sudanese security personnel had visited their apartment and taken away their passports. Hoshan had managed to get the documents back, but he was warned by the Sudanese that he would need to take steps to resolve the position of the group in Sudan. Hoshan also feared that the consequence of United Nation sanctions was that Khartoum airport might be closed.

On 8 August 1996, several members of the group watched a film about a hijack, which prompted an idea in their minds to hijack an aeroplane. Hoshan (who was the accepted leader) formulated the plans. Hasan had arrived in Khartoum in June 1995 and been sheltered by friends. He was making artificial flowers to earn money. He met Aboud a month before the hijack.

Aboud had tried, unsuccessfully, to get across the border to Libya. The two of them met Hoshan and agreed to join his scheme. Muhssin had been in the Sudan longer than anyone. He had succeeded in going to the Yemen, but had found himself unable otherwise to leave the Sudan. He had been approached to work as a spy for the security police, but he declined to do so and had been arrested as an overstayer. In July 1996, he was ordered to leave Sudan within a month. He agreed to join the scheme.

Everyone, by the end of August 1996, was an overstayer in Sudan. Hoshan alone did not have forged documents. All feared deportation to Iraq, or being handed over to the Iraqi embassy. All feared that, if either of those things happened, the next step would be torture and probable death.

At about 4 pm on 27 August 1996, at Khartoum Airport, the appellants boarded a Sudanese airbus bound for Amman in Jordan. They were equipped with plastic knives and plastic mustard bottles filled with salt. The plastic bottles, once on board, were wrapped in black tape and modified with plasticine to make them look like hand grenades.

Once the flight was in Egyptian airspace, Muhssin seized hold of an airhostess and threatened her with a plastic knife. He was overpowered by security officials. They, at that moment, thought he was acting on his own, but, at that stage, Maged Naji produced one of the imitation grenades and threatened to blow up the plane. Thereupon, Muhssin was released. The captain surrendered control of his aircraft to the appellants, and, thereafter, Muhssin remained on the flight deck with him holding a knife to his back.

Wholly independently of the activities of the appellants, there had gone on board a butcher who took with him his professional knives. They were placed elsewhere in the plane. Hoshan took possession of those knives and distributed them among the appellants. Several of the passengers who were believed to be security officials were tied up. One passenger who resisted was stabbed in the arm, and the judge concluded that Aboud was responsible for that injury.

Sabah Nagi declined to participate in the hijack. In particular, he refused to use his tie to tie up the airhostess. In consequence, he was himself tied up and gagged.

The intention was to divert the plane to London, but it had insufficient fuel and permission was given to land at Larnaca in Cyprus. There, the appellants declined to release the women and children. The atmosphere on board was very tense. Hoshan pretended to instruct the others to blow up the plane if there was any movement. Once it had been refuelled and permitted to take off, however, the atmosphere became conspicuously more calm. Eventually, it landed at Stansted Airport, in the early hours of 28th August, 12 hours after leaving Khartoum.

After negotiations for a period of some eight hours, the passengers and crew were released and the appellants surrendered.

In interview, Hoshan made full admissions of the plan to hijack the plane. He described how he had been living in England, trying to get his fiancee and her family out of, initially, Jordan and then the Sudan. He gave details about meeting the others, fleeing from the Iraqi authorities and the hijack plans. He described his role during the flight, though he denied responsibility for the stabbing. His account was largely supported by the other passengers and crew.

Muhssin denied taking part at first, but then he described how the plans were made and what had happened on board. He had the advantage of having been in the Iraqi air force, so he knew about aeroplanes and flight procedure, and that is why he had stayed with the captain.

Abdul-Hussain said he met the others only 10 days before, but he was a cousin of Hoshan. He had seen the film of the hijack and he had taken the tape on board to manufacture the imitation grenades. He said that he had carried a knife but did not have a grenade. He helped to tie up passengers. Aboud admitted he had taken part in the hijacking and had carried a knife. Hasan did not answer any questions. Maged Naji at first declined to answer, but then he said he had been party to the planning but was against the hijack, on the basis that they would be betrayed. He denied swearing an allegiance to the plan and said he had simply intended to travel to Amman as an ordinary passenger. When Muhssin was overpowered, he lost his temper, jumped up and shouted. But he did not have a grenade and he denied having threatened to blow up the plane. Afterwards, he said, he fell asleep, although he did sit by a door with a grenade at Hoshan's request. He said he had been facing execution in Iraq since in 1991.

Sabah Naji said that he had fled from Iraq in 1994, first to Jordan, and then to the Sudan. So far as the purchase of his air ticket was concerned, which was a central aspect of the case against him, he denied that Hoshan had bought it for him. He said it had been bought by a Sudanese woman. He said he was hoping to find work in Jordan. He was not a hijacker, but he knew three of them. At his retrial, Hasan gave evidence against Sabah Naji and said, indeed, that it was Sabah Naji who invited him, Hasan, to join the hijacking plan. There was evidence that Hoshan had bought all the tickets and Sabah Naji's tickets was numerically in the midst of the tickets which Hoshan had bought.

All the appellants, on arrival in this country, sought political asylum. It was accepted that, save in the case of Sabah Naji, all the appellants had hijacked the airliner. But it was said that the reason they had done so was as a last resort to escape death, either of themselves or of their families, at the hands of the Iraqi authorities. It is unnecessary for present purposes to rehearse the evidence which each of them gave before the jury. In substance, it accorded with the answers which they had given in interviews.

At the close of all the evidence, the trial judge, having heard submissions by counsel for the Crown and on behalf of all the appellants, ruled that the defence of necessity or duress of circumstances would not be left to the jury ... Mr Allen Newman QC, on behalf of Hoshan, in submissions adopted by counsel on behalf of all the other appellants, submitted to this court that the judge misdirected himself as to the law and was wrong to withdraw the defence of duress from the jury's consideration. Although there must be a nexus between the threat of death or serious injury and the criminal act, this nexus arises, he submitted on the authorities, from imminent peril not immediate threat or 'a virtually spontaneous reaction'. Imminent means impending threateningly, hanging over one's head, ready to overtake one, coming on shortly. Immediate means without intermediary, proximate, nearest, next.

Spontaneous, means voluntarily, without thought or premeditation, without external stimulus. The correct test, he submitted, is set out in *R v Martin* (1989) 88 Cr App R 343 at 345. Simon Brown J, giving the judgment of the court, said this: 'The principles may be summarised thus. First, English law does, in extreme circumstances, recognise a defence of necessity. Most commonly this defence arises as duress, that is pressure upon the accused's will from the wrongful threats or violence of another. Equally, however, it can arise from other objective dangers threatening the accused or others. Arising thus it is conveniently called 'duress of circumstances.' Secondly, the defence is available only if, from an objective standpoint, the accused can be said to be acting reasonably and proportionately in order to avoid a threat of death or serious injury. Thirdly, assuming the defence to be open to the accused on his account of the facts, the issue should be left to the jury, who should be directed to determine these two questions: first, was the accused or may he have been, impelled to act as he did because as a result of what he reasonably believed to be the situation he had good cause to fear that otherwise death or serious physical injury would result? Secondly, if so, may a sober person of reasonable firmness, sharing the characteristics of the accused, have responded to that situation by acting as the accused acted? If the answer to both those questions was yes, then the jury acquit: the defence of necessity would have been established. *R v Hudson and Taylor* ... Mr Newman submitted, is clear authority that, although there must be a threat operating on the actor's mind, a threat of future injury may suffice to support the defence of duress ... In *R v Cole* ... on which the trial judge relied, Simon Brown LJ, giving the judgment of the court, having referred to the Australian authority of *R v Loughnan* [1981] VR 443, in which the majority judgment draws no distinction between 'imminence' and 'immediacy', and all three judges refer to 'imminent peril' as an essential element of the defence of necessity, said this at p 10:

> Whichever formulation one applies, in our judgment it is perfectly plain that the present appellant cannot hope to bring himself within it. Considerations of proportionality aside, there was lacking here the situation of imminent peril which on any view is a necessary precondition to the defence properly arising. True, at one point of his interview with regard to the second robbery the appellant said: '... I had no choice really ... I couldn't go home that night again ... I had to have the money around that night by six o'clock.' Even that, however, the very high water mark of the appellant's case on urgency, in our judgment falls short of the degree of directness and immediacy required of the link between the suggested peril and the criminal offence charged. Certain it is,

as the trial judge pointed out, that the connection between threat and criminal act is by no means as close and immediate here as it was in Willer, Conway and Martin, the offence in each of those cases being virtually a spontaneous reaction to physical risk arising.

At p 12, Simon Brown LJ said this:

... until all aspects of this defence have been put on to a statutory footing, including as presently envisaged shifting the burden of proof with regard to it from the Crown to the accused, we believe that duress should be rigidly confined to its established present limits.

Mr Newman submitted that the passage in the judgment in *Cole*, at p 10, was obiter and, in so far as it is inconsistent with *Hudson and Taylor*, it was wrong and should not be followed by this court, which should follow *Hudson and Taylor*. Mr Newman accepted that imminence of peril is initially a question of law for the judge; but the evidence in the present case, he submitted, was such that, whether the judge misdirected himself or not, the jury should have been permitted to determine 'whether threats were so real and were at the relevant time so operative, and their effect so incapable of avoidance, that, having regard to all the circumstances, the conduct can be excused', *per* Lord Morris of Borth-y-Gest in *Lynch* at 675F. The analysis of principle in the speeches of the majority in *Lynch*, although not the actual decision as to the availability of the defence of duress to a person charged as an aider and abettor to murder, was approved by the House of Lords in *Howe* [1987] AC 417. It is necessary, briefly, to refer to some of the submissions on behalf of the other appellants. Mr Mansfield QC, for Abdul-Hussain, stressed that, as this appellant was the subject of two death sentences in Iraq, had his wife and children with him, had only recently reached Sudan in the course of flight, and was known by the Sudanese authorities to have a forged passport, his case, as the trial judge accepted, was the strongest on nexus, and should have been left to the jury, submitted Mr Mansfield, whatever the precise legal test. Mr Mansfield criticised the trial judge's reference, at p 23D of his ruling, to the 'very strict requirement' in the light of the highest authority, that duress is 'an extremely vague and elusive concept', see *per* Lord Simon of Glaisdale at 686A in *Lynch*, approved in *Howe* at 453G.

Mr Mansfield also criticised the five contingent steps identified by the trial judge, at p 23 of his ruling, as disconnecting the hijacking from the threats. Abdul-Hussain had already been detected in the Sudan as having forged documents. The judge's reference to decisions to arrest and deport, the act of deportation from the Sudan, and execution in Iraq suggests that duress would not become available until the firing squad were raising their rifles. This demonstrates, submitted Mr Mansfield, that 'a virtually spontaneous reaction' cannot be the proper test, and the 'instinctive reaction', to which the judge referred in summing up the matter to the jury, is even less appropriate. Mr Kershen QC, for Muhssin, submitted that the immediacy referred in *R v Dawson* [1978] VR 536 and *Loughnan*, and by Simon Brown LJ in *Cole*, refers to the immediacy of the threat of coercion, that is, there must be a present threat operating on the mind of the victim, although implementation of the threat may be delayed, as in *Hudson and Taylor*. A present threat, not to be carried out immediately, may give rise to duress if it is impossible or fruitless to invoke legal protection. Because the imminence of peril depends on a variety of factors, including the number, strength and status of those threatening, the hostility of the present environment and the prospects of escape to a friendly environment, it is the jury not the judge who should assess these. There will always be, submitted Mr Kershen, contingencies between threat and offence. In *Martin*, indeed, where the defendant drove while disqualified in response to his wife's threat to commit suicide, such contingent steps included the availability of a son who was qualified to drive. Mr Riza QC, on behalf of Maged Naji, submitted that the judge was wrong to categorise him as a volunteer, within the observations of Lord Lowry in *R v Fitzpatrick* [1977] NILR 20 at 30G and 31D, requiring moral innocence before duress can be invoked. Knowledge when he boarded the plane that a hijacking would be attempted which would probably fail did not give rise to a criminal act and was an insufficient basis on which to say that Naji had deliberately exposed himself to the risk of threat. In any event, voluntariness should have been left to the jury to decide.

He referred to *R v Shepherd* (1988) 86 Cr App R 47, at p 51, where reference is made to *R v Sharp* 85 Cr App R 212, in support of the proposition that a question of voluntary exposure is properly for the jury. For the Crown, Mr Hilliard emphasised the lack of precision in relation to the principles of duress, to which the House of Lords have drawn attention in *Howe* and *Lynch*. He also referred to the calls made three times in recent years by differently constituted divisions of this court for legislation to define the defence: in *Cole, R v Hurst* [1995] 1 Cr App R 82 and *R v Baker and Wilkins* [1997] Crim LR 497. He accepted that imminence and immediacy do not have the same meaning, and that imminent peril is an element in both forms of duress. But, he submitted, the move away from immediacy in *Hudson and Taylor*, which was a case of duress by threats, should not be extended to duress of circumstances. *Cole* was a duress of circumstances case, in that money had to be repaid within 2 hours after the robbery, and the observations of the court, at p 10, can therefore not be regarded as *obiter*. He submitted that, in this passage, the court was drawing a distinction between imminent peril applicable to both forms of duress, and immediacy and spontaneity, which limits duress of circumstances. He relies on a passage in *Loughnan* at p 448: '... if there is an interval of time between the threat and its expected execution it will be very rarely if ever that a defence of necessity can succeed.' He too relied on *Graham* as approved in *Howe* and reflected in *Martin*, as being the correct, largely objective, test. He submitted, boldly, that, as a matter of law aircraft hijacking, at least where the majority of passengers are innocent, is in the same category as murder and cannot ever be a proportionate response to any threat, however grave. More than 70 authorities were placed before the court. Of these, fewer than one-third were cited, and only a handful were of helpful significance.

In the light of the submissions made to us, we derive the following propositions from the relevant authorities:

1   Unless and until Parliament provides otherwise, the defence of duress, whether by threats or from circumstances, is generally available in relation to all substantive crimes, except murder, attempted murder and some forms of treason (*R v Pommell* [1995] 2 Cr App R 607 at 615C). Accordingly, if raised by appropriate evidence, it is available in relation to hijacking aircraft; although, in such cases, the terror induced in innocent passengers will generally raise issues of proportionality for determination, initially as a matter of law by the judge and, in appropriate cases, by the jury.

2   The courts have developed the defence on a case-by-case basis, notably during the last 30 years. Its scope remains imprecise (*Howe* [1987] AC 417, 453G–54C; *Hurst* [1995] 1 Cr App R 82 at 93D).

3   Imminent peril of death or serious injury to the defendant, or those to whom he has responsibility, is an essential element of both types of duress (see *Southwark LBC v Williams* [1971] 1 Ch 734, *per* Lord Justice Edmund-Davies at 746A; *Loughnan*, by the majority at 448 and the dissentient at 460; and *Cole* at p 10).

4   The peril must operate on the mind of the defendant at the time when he commits the otherwise criminal act, so as to overbear his will, and this is essentially a question for the jury (*Hudson and Taylor* at 4; and *Lynch* at 675F. It is to be noted that in *Hudson and Taylor* Lord Parker CJ presided over the court, whose reserved judgment was given by Widgery LJ (as he then was)).

5   But the execution of the threat need not be immediately in prospect (*Hudson and Taylor* at 425). If in *Cole* the court had had the advantage of argument, as to the distinction between imminence, immediacy and spontaneity which has been addressed to us, it seems unlikely that the second half of the paragraph at p 10 of the judgment which we have cited would have been so expressed. If, and in so far as anything said in *Cole* is inconsistent with *Hudson and Taylor*, we prefer and are, in any event, bound by *Hudson and Taylor*, as, indeed, was the court in *Cole*.

6   The period of time which elapses between the inception of the peril and the defendant's act, and between that act and execution of the threat, are relevant but not determinative factors for a judge and jury in deciding whether duress operates (*Hudson and Taylor*; *Pommell* at 616A).

7   All the circumstances of the peril, including the number, identity and status of those creating it, and the opportunities (if any) which exist to avoid it are relevant, initially for the judge, and, in appropriate cases, for the jury, when assessing whether the defendant's mind was affected as in 4 above. As Lord Morris of Borth-y-Gest said in *Lynch* at 675F in the passage previously cited, the issue in *Hudson and Taylor* was 'whether the threats were so real and were at the relevant time so operative and their effect so incapable of avoidance that, having regard to all the circumstances, the conduct of the girls could be excused.

8   As to 6 and 7, if Anne Frank had stolen a car to escape from Amsterdam and been charged with theft, the tenets of English law would not, in our judgment, have denied her a defence of duress of circumstances, on the ground that she should have waited for the Gestapo's knock on the door.

9   We see no reason of principle or authority for distinguishing the two forms of duress in relation to the elements of the defence which we have identified. In particular, we do not read the court's judgment in *Cole* as seeking to draw any such distinction.

10 The judgment of the court, presided over by Lord Lane CJ and delivered by Simon Brown LJ, in *Martin*, at 345 to 346 (already cited) affords, as it seems to us, the clearest and most authoritative guide to the relevant principles and appropriate direction in relation to both forms of duress. Subject to questions of continuance (which did not arise and as to which, see *Pommell* at 615D), it

clearly reflects Lord Lane's judgment in *R v Graham* (1981) 74 Cr App R 235 at 241, which was approved by the House of Lords in *Howe* in 458G. It applies a predominantly, but not entirely, objective test, and this court has recently rejected an attempt to introduce a purely subjective element divorced from extraneous influence (see *Roger and Rose*, 9th July 1997).

11 Clauses 25 and 26 of the Law Commission's draft Criminal Law Bill do not represent the present law. Accordingly, reference to those provisions is potentially misleading (see the forceful note by Professor Sir John Smith QC [1998] Crim LR 204, with which we agree). Applying these principles to the present case, we are satisfied that the learned judge was lead into error as to the applicable law. We have considerable sympathy with him. No submissions were addressed to him as to the distinction between imminence, immediacy and spontaneity, and he sought to follow the judgment of this court in *Cole*, where, likewise, no such submissions had been advanced. In our judgment, although the judge was right to look for a close nexus between the threat and the criminal act, he interpreted the law too strictly in seeking a virtually spontaneous reaction. He should have asked himself, in accordance with *Martin*, whether there was evidence of such fear operating on the minds of the defendants at the time of the hijacking as to impel them to act as they did and whether, if so, there was evidence that the danger they feared objectively existed and that hijacking was a reasonable and proportionate response to it. Had he done so, it seems to us it that he must have concluded that there was evidence for the jury to consider.

We stress that the prosecution did not seek to rely on a want of proportionality or to contend that duress was not capable of applying after the plane had landed at Larnaca. It follows that, in our judgment, in the light of how he was invited to approach the matter, the judge should have left the defence of duress for the jury to consider. Although the position of some of the defendants differed – in particular, Hoshan held documents which permitted him to travel freely and Maged Naji's case raised an additional argument in relation to voluntariness – we see no reason, for present purposes, to draw a distinction between the defendants. In relation to all of them, the jury should have been permitted to consider duress.

We express no view as to proportionality or the continued availability of duress after *Larnaca* because, as we have said, these matters were not relied on before the judge and because, more significantly, there is no sufficient material before us as to the evidence on these matters. In any event, having concluded, for the reasons given, that the judge was wrong to withdraw the defence from the jury, the convictions of the appellants at the first trial must be regarded as unsafe. Their appeals are therefore allowed and their convictions quashed. For the fourth time in five years this court emphasises the urgent need for legislation to define duress with precision.

The direction to the jury in cases of duress *per minas*

R v Graham [1982] 1 WLR 294 (CA)

Lord Lane CJ: ... The facts of the case were as follows. The appellant was the victim's husband. He is a practising homosexual. His wife was aware of this and indeed at the material time they were living in a bizarre *ménage à trois* with another homosexual called King. They were living in the flat above two other homosexuals, named Gillis and Minter, with whom the appellant occasionally had sexual relations. The appellant and King were jointly charged with the murder. King pleaded guilty. The appellant admitted playing an active part in the events leading to the killing and admitted seeking to conceal the killing after it had happened.

His defence was twofold: first, that he lacked the necessary intent, and he drew attention particularly to the drink and drugs he had taken; and, second, that whatever his intentional actions may have been, they were performed under duress because of his fear of King.

We are satisfied that the directions given to the jury by the trial judge, on the issues of murder and manslaughter, on joint enterprise and on the relevance of drink and drugs to those issues, were impeccable. Other minor complaints made in the notice of appeal are also without foundation. The only live issue is, as counsel for the appellant concedes, whether the direction to the jury on the question of duress was correct.

The evidence relevant to this issue was this. The appellant had suffered for some time from an anxiety state. He was taking Valium tablets on prescription. There was medical evidence to the effect that Valium, if taken in excess, would make him more susceptible to bullying, but that by mid-1980 he would have developed some tolerance to the drug. King was said to be a man of violence. There was evidence of altercations. In 1978 King had tipped the appellant and his wife off a settee because they were embracing and he was jealous. The appellant, it seems, knew of another incident in 1978 when some other woman had been assaulted by King and had had her ribs broken. In June 1980, said the appellant, King had 'swiped him over the head'.

On Friday 27 June 1980, the day before the killing, King attacked the wife with a knife. The appellant intervened and, for his trouble, cut his finger when he tried to grab the knife. As a result of this incident, the wife on the following day left and went to the appellant's mother's home. The appellant and King stayed behind and, together with the man Gillis, occupied their time in the flat drinking, talking and indulging in homosexual activities. The appellant said that he had a lot to drink during this time and had taken Valium tablets in excess of the quantity which had been prescribed for him. He also said that during the time that the three were together, he thought that King was going to attack him with a knife, but the incident came to nothing. Gillis left soon after midnight.

King then suggested getting rid of the wife once and for all. The two of them hatched a plan. The appellant telephoned his wife in the small hours, told her falsely that he had cut his wrists and asked her to come home at once. Meanwhile, King bandaged both of the appellant's wrists and he, the appellant, lay face down on the floor pretending to be seriously hurt. When the wife arrived, she knelt down beside the appellant to see how he was. King had the flex from a coffee percolator in his hands. He attempted unsuccessfully to put it round the wife's neck while she was kneeling. The appellant and his wife then both got up and King said: 'What's it feel like to know that you are going to die, Betty?' That remark was repeated. King then put the flex round the wife's neck and pulled it tight, hauling her off her feet onto his back as if she were a sack of coals. She put her hands up to the flex at her neck, whereupon King told the appellant to cut her fingers away. The appellant said in evidence that he picked up a knife but could not bring himself to use it. King thereupon put the wife on the floor, still holding the flex. He told the appellant to take hold of one end of it. The appellant said in evidence that he did so. He added that it was only in fear of King that he complied with the order. He said that, in any event, the plug at the end of the flex which he was holding came off as he exerted pressure on it. If that were the case, it would remain in doubt whether the appellant's act made any contribution to the death. It should, however, be noted that in the voluntary statement, which he made to the police, he had admitted pulling on the flex for about a minute. Whatever the precise sequence of events, it was beyond doubt that the ligature around the wife's neck was responsible for her death.

Thereafter, the appellant helped King to dispose of her body by wrapping it up, carrying her out of the flat and dumping it over an embankment. Each of the two men then took one of her earrings; the appellant rifled her handbag for anything he could find of use, and spread the rest of the contents near her body to make it look as though she had been robbed. He then made telephone calls suggesting that she had gone missing.

The Crown at the trial conceded that, on those facts, it was open to the defence to raise the issue of duress. In other words, they were not prepared to take the point that the defence of duress is not available to a principal in the first degree to murder. Consequently, the interesting question raised by the decisions in *Lynch v DPP for Northern Ireland* [1975] AC 653, and *Abbott v R* [1977] AC 755 was not argued before us. We do not have to decide it. We pause only to observe that the jury would no doubt have been puzzled to learn that whether the appellant was to be convicted of murder or acquitted altogether might depend on whether the plug came off the end of the percolator flex when he began to pull it ...

The direction which the judge gave to the jury required them to ask themselves two questions. First, a subjective question which the judge formulated thus: 'Was this man at the time of the killing taking part because he feared for his own life or personal safety as a result of the words or the conduct on the part of King, either personally experienced by him, or genuinely believed in by him?' Neither side in the present appeal has taken issue with the judge on this question. We feel, however, that for purposes of completeness, we should say that the direction appropriate in this particular case should have been in these words: 'Was this man at the time of the killing taking part because he held a well-grounded fear of death (or serious physical injury) as a result of the words or conduct on the part of King?' The bracketed words may be too favourable to the defendant. The point was not argued before us.

The judge then went on to direct the jury that if the answer to that first question was 'Yes', or 'He may have been', the jury should then go on to consider a second question importing an objective test of reasonableness. This is the issue which arises in this appeal. Counsel for the appellant contends that no second question arises at all; the test is purely subjective. He argues that if the appellant's will was in fact overborne by threats of the requisite cogency, he is entitled to be acquitted and no question arises as to whether a reasonable man, with or without his characteristics, would have reacted similarly.

Counsel for the Crown, on the other hand, submits that such dicta as can be found on the point are in favour of a second test; this time an objective test. He argues that public policy requires this and draws an analogy with provocation. He submits that while the judge was right to pose a second question, he formulated it too favourably to the appellant. The question was put to the jury in the following terms:

> Taking into account all the circumstances of the case, including the age, sex, sexual propensities and other characteristics personal to the defendant, including his state of mind and the amount of drink or drugs he had taken, was it reasonable for the defendant to behave in the way he did, that is to take part in the murder of his wife as a result of the fear present at the time in his mind? The test of reasonableness in this context is: would the defendant's behaviour in all the particular circumstances to which I have just referred reflect the degree of self-control and firmness of purpose which everyone is entitled to expect that his fellow citizens would exercise in society as it is today? ...

There is no direct binding authority on the questions whether the test is solely subjective or, if objective, how it is to be formulated ...

As a matter of public policy, it seems to us essential to limit the defence of duress by means of an objective criterion formulated in terms of reasonableness. Consistency of approach in defences to criminal liability is obviously desirable. Provocation and duress are analogous. In provocation the words or actions of one person break the self-control of another. In duress the words or actions of one person break the will of another. The law requires a defendant to have the self-control reasonably to be expected of the ordinary citizen in his situation. It should likewise require him to have the steadfastness reasonably to be expected of the ordinary citizen in his situation. So too with self-defence, in which the law permits the use of no more force than is reasonable in the circumstances. And, in general, if a mistake is to excuse what would otherwise be criminal, the mistake must be a reasonable one.

It follows that we accept counsel for the Crown's submission that the direction in this case was too favourable to the appellant. The Crown having conceded that the issue of duress was open to the appellant and was raised on the evidence, the correct approach on the facts of this case would have been as follows: (1) was the defendant, or may he have been, impelled to act as he did because, as a result of what he reasonably believed [on the need for the belief to be reasonable see now *R v Martin* below] King had said or done, he had good cause to fear that if he did not so act King would kill him or (if this is to be added) cause him serious physical injury? (2) if so, have the prosecution made the jury sure that a sober person of reasonable firmness, sharing the characteristics of the defendant, would not have responded to whatever he reasonably believed King said or did by taking part in the killing? The fact that a defendant's will to resist has been eroded by the voluntary consumption of drink or drugs is not relevant to this test.

We doubt whether the Crown was right to concede that the question of duress ever arose on the facts of this case. The words and deeds of King relied on by the defence were far short of those needed to raise a threat of the requisite gravity. However, the Crown having made the concession, the judge was right to pose the second objective question to the jury. His only error lay in putting it too favourably to the appellant.

R v Martin (David) [2000] 2 Cr App R 42

Mantell LJ: On 13 October 1998, at Maidstone Crown Court, David Paul Martin was convicted on two counts of robbery and after an adjournment for reports was sentenced to five years' imprisonment on each, it being ordered that those two sentences should be served concurrently. He now appeals against conviction by leave of the single judge. He has also an application for leave to appeal against sentence which is out of time, that matter having been referred to this court. We deal only for the moment with the appeal against conviction.

On 2 March 1998 at about 10.30 pm it is not disputed that the appellant went to a petrol station run by Texaco in Streatham High Street and robbed a gentleman who was working behind the counter by jumping on to the counter and wielding a hammer. He took away with him £45 and a packet of cigarettes. The following morning the appellant, again carrying a hammer, forced his way behind the counter of the Abbey National Building Society in Tunbridge Wells and stole over £4,000 ... In between the commission of those two robberies, which at the trial were never disputed, the appellant made phone calls to the police giving a clue as to the perpetrator of the first of the two robberies and in effect, so it is suggested, inviting the police to seek him out and arrest him.

The facts of the robberies never being in dispute, what defence was advanced on behalf of this appellant? It was the defence of duress. Once advanced, it became necessary for the crown to disprove that defence so as to make the jury sure that it did not arise. Put very briefly, the appellant was saying that he had been solicited by two ... men, one of whom was called 'junior', who were well known on the estate where he lived ... and they had prevailed upon him by serious threats to take part in each of the two robberies.

... The jury heard evidence from a consultant psychiatrist ... She told the jury that the appellant suffered from a psychiatric condition known as schizoid-affective state. A person suffering from the condition is more likely than others would be to regard things said to him as threatening and to believe that such threats would be carried out.

... The judge went on to direct the jury that ... whether the appellant's belief was reasonable or not was to be judged against the concept of the reasonable man not having the particular condition from which the appellant was suffering.

Mantell LJ referred to the definition of duress given by Lord Simon in *DPP v Lynch* [1975] AC 653, and the 'model' direction approved by the Court of Appeal in *R v Graham* (above), and continued:

It is to be observed that Lord Simon left open the question whether or not the fear had to be well grounded and whether the words 'reasonable belief' should be tested subjectively or objectively. The passage cited from *Graham* might suggest the latter. However, Lord Lane considered that duress and self-defence were analogous. It is now accepted that 'the test to be applied for self-defence is that a person may use such force as is reasonable in the circumstances as he honestly believes them to be in the defence of himself or another' (see *Beckford* [1988] AC 130, *per* Lord Griffiths at 145). The same subjective approach has been approved by this court in cases of duress of circumstances or duress of necessity (see *Cairns* [1999] 2 Cr App R 137). We cannot see that any distinction should be made in a case of straightforward duress by threat. It follows that in our view the learned judge was in error in directing the jury as he did with regard to the appellant's understanding or perception of the words alleged to have been used.

Relevance of the defendant's characteristics

R v Horne [1994] Crim LR 584 (CA)

Facts: The appellant, an employee of the DSS, conspired with others to make fraudulent claims for income support, totalling £17,741.22. He admitted creating the fictitious claims, saying he had been induced to do so by one of his co-conspirators, who offered him money, and said he would be looked after when the job had been done. He had been pressurised by telephone calls and visits to his home, had never been threatened directly with violence, but this person had implied that his brother, a drug dealer, knew a lot of people who could 'sort people out'. The issue at trial was whether the defence of duress had been negatived by the Crown. Following conviction, one of the grounds of appeal related to the judge's direction on duress and to his ruling that psychiatric evidence was inadmissible.

Held, dismissing the appeal, the judge directed the jury that the threats must have been such as would have driven a person of reasonable firmness to have behaved in the same way. A person of reasonable firmness was an average member of the public; not a hero necessarily, not a coward, just an average person. It was submitted for the appellant that the test was too narrowly stated. The classic statement of the law was laid down in *Graham* (1982) 74 Cr App R 235, which provided a two-limbed test. The first being subjective: was the defendant threatened with such violence that he acted as he did or might have been? The second, being objective, required the jury to consider whether a person of reasonable fairness, sharing the characteristics of the defendant and in his circumstances would have responded to the threat as he had done? That test was approved by the House of Lords in *Howe* [1987] AC 417, where one question was whether the defence of duress failed if the Crown proved that a person of reasonable firmness, sharing the characteristics of the defendant, would not have given way to the threats as he did. Lord Mackay cited with approval a passage from Lord Lane's judgment in *Howe* in the Court of Appeal [1986] 1 QB 626, and the relevant passage from *Graham*.

Counsel for the appellant submitted that the judge was wrong to construe the word 'characteristics' narrowly; it should be construed much more widely and should include such matters as the defendant's psychological characteristics.

During the trial, he had applied for leave to call a psychiatrist whose evidence was designed to show the jury that the appellant was a man who was unusually pliable and vulnerable to pressure. His report covered such matters as past history of giving way to bullying at school, and also expressed the view that his vulnerability was greater at the time of the offence due to the death of his father the previous year. However, it made clear that he had no history of psychiatric illness. In refusing to admit the evidence the judge considered *Graham* and *Howe* and said that if the word 'characteristics' was given the natural wide meaning it would include personal mental characteristics and if these were included the objective test would be undermined completely. Therefore, there must be a limited meaning in this context and it seemed to the judge it would include such things as age, sex, and serious physical disability, but he did not consider it included mental characteristics such as inherent weakness, vulnerability and susceptibility to threats. The history was inadmissible as hearsay and the doctor could not say whether the appellant was in fact threatened nor could he say whether he was affected by any threats which might have been made. The psychiatrist's opinion that the appellant was by nature pliable or vulnerable could not concern the jury because that would circumvent the objective test. The death of his father a year or more before the offences was something within the ordinary scope of human experience (see *Turner* (1974) 60 Cr App R 80).

In support of his argument that the judge was wrong, counsel relied on a passage from the Law Commission Report (No 83, para 228), which said that the personal characteristics of a defendant were most important. Threats directed against a weak, immature or disabled person might well be much more compelling than against a normal healthy person. However, that recommendation was not enacted by Parliament and did not represent the law. The court was bound by *Graham* and *Howe*, and Lord Lane's judgment in Graham did not comply with the suggestion of the Law Commission. The second limb of the test, which passed an objective test, required the jury to ask themselves whether a person of reasonable firmness, otherwise sharing the characteristics of the defendant, would or might have responded as he did to the threats to which he was subjected. If the standard for comparison was a person of reasonable firmness it must be irrelevant for the jury to consider any characteristics of the defendant which showed that he was not such a person, but was pliant or vulnerable to pressure. It would be a contradiction in terms to ask the jury this question, and then to ask them to take into account, as one of his characteristics, that he was pliant or vulnerable.

For the purposes of this appeal, evidence of personal vulnerability or pliancy falling short of psychiatric illness was not relevant.

R v Hegarty [1994] Crim LR 353 (CA)

Facts: At the appellant's trial for robbery, and possession of an imitation weapon, his defence was duress. He claimed that some Asian men who accommodated him when he was on the run later attacked him and threatened violence against his family unless he carried out the robberies. The Crown challenged the existence of the Asians or the threats. In support of the plea of duress the appellant sought to put before the court the evidence of two medical witnesses who would testify to his mental instability. He had a conviction for manslaughter of his wife on grounds of diminished responsibility, and the reports described him as 'emotionally unstable' and in a 'grossly elevated neurotic state'. The judge refused to admit the evidence, and on appeal following conviction it was contended that he was wrong. The primary contention was that the appellant's pre-existing mental condition made him vulnerable to threats.

Held, dismissing the appeal, the duress relied upon was duress by threats, but in some cases a defendant might be able to rely on 'duress by circumstances' (see *Conway* [1989] QB 290; *Martin* [1989] 1 All ER 652), and although not argued in this way it was proposed to consider whether the medical evidence could have been introduced on the basis that Hegarty might have been able to set up such a defence.

Duress by threats provided a defence to a charge of any offence other than murder (see *Howe* [1987] AC 417), attempted murder (see *Gotts* [1982] 2 AC 412) and some forms of treason. It was founded on public policy considerations (see *AG v Whelan* [1934] IR 518). The fact that the defendant's mind had been 'overborne' by the threats did not mean that he lacked the requisite intent to commit the crime (see *DPP for Northern Ireland v Lynch* [1975] AC 653, 703B). It followed that the law might have developed on the lines that, when considering duress, a purely subjective test should be applied, and it might well develop in this way in the future (see Law Com 218, para 29.14, November 1993, Cmnd 2370 and draft Criminal Law Bill, cl 25(2)).

As the law stood however the test was not purely subjective but required an objective test to be satisfied (*Howe*). The jury had to consider the response of a sober person of reasonable firmness 'sharing the characteristics of the defendant'. They could take account of age, sex and physical health, but it was open to consideration whether the shared characteristics could include a personality disorder of the kind suffered by the appellant. His counsel argued that the expert evidence was relevant to explain the reaction of a man like him to threats of violence to himself and his family, and admissible because the pathological aspects of his personality and the effect of his disorder on his behaviour were matters which lay outside the knowledge and experience of a judge and jury. Counsel referred to a passage in *Emery* (1993) 14 Cr App R (S) 394, 398 where Lord Taylor CJ said that: '... The question for the doctors was whether a woman of reasonable firmness with the characteristics of [the appellant], if abused in the manner which she said, would have had her will crushed so that she could not have protected her child.'

It was accepted that for the purposes of the subjective test medical evidence was admissible if the mental condition or abnormality was relevant and its effects lay outside the knowledge and experience of laymen. In the present case, the reports before the judge did not go that far, and the judge had to decide on the material before him.

There were no grounds for disturbing his decision. As the evidence was not admissible to explain the reaction of the appellant himself, it was clearly not admissible on the objective test. The passage cited could not be read in isolation, and it was not considered that Lord Taylor CJ intended to throw any doubt on the general rule which presently applied to cases of provocation and duress that the application of the objective test was a matter for the jury (see the speech of Lord Simon in *Camplin* [1978] AC 705). The medical evidence was not admissible as the law stood on the objective test in a case of duress. Further, as that test predicated a 'sober person of reasonable firmness' there was no scope for attributing to that hypothetical person as one of the characteristics of the defendant a pre-existing mental condition of being 'emotionally unstable' or in a 'grossly elevated neurotic state'.

That left consideration of whether the position would have been different had 'duress by circumstances' been asserted. It was plain from *Martin* that an objective test applied, and one of the questions to be addressed was whether a sober person of reasonable firmness, sharing the accused's characteristics, would have responded to the situation confronting him by acting as he did. The medical evidence in this case did not address that question. The judge was right to exclude it as inadmissible.

R v Flatt [1996] Crim LR 576 (CA)

Facts: The appellant was convicted on four counts of possession of drugs with intent. His defence was duress. He was addicted to crack cocaine and owed his supplier £1,500. Some 17 hours before the police searched his flat, the drug dealer told him to look after the drugs found, saying that if he did not, he would shoot the appellant's mother, grandmother and girlfriend.

On appeal, it was argued that the judge should have told the jury that, in assessing the response of the hypothetical person of reasonable firmness to the threats, they should have invested that person with the characteristic of being a drug addict.

Held, dismissing the appeal, that drug addiction was a self-induced condition, not a characteristic. There was no evidence that the appellant's addiction (or indeed that of anyone else) would have had an effect on a person's ability to withstand a threat from a drugs dealer. It was not sought to adduce psychiatric or other evidence to say that the appellant's ability to withstand threats was in any way weakened. It may well be that he felt under some obligation to look after the supplier's drugs.

R v Bowen [1997] 1 WLR 372 (CA)

Stuart-Smith LJ: On 2 August 1995 in the Crown Court at Luton the appellant was convicted of five counts of obtaining services by deception. He was subsequently sentenced to 18 months' imprisonment, concurrent on each count. He now appeals against his convictions with leave of the single judge.

The five counts were specimen counts reflecting a large number of incidents during the period January 1992 to June 1994. On some 40 occasions the appellant had visited shops selling electrical goods and obtained a large number of them by applying for 'instant credit'. On all occasions he had paid a proportion of the cost by way of deposit. He had not completed payment for any of the goods concerned. Payments were to be made in some cases by payment book and in others by direct debit. There was evidence that some of the direct debits had been cancelled by the appellant.

On all occasions he had given his correct name and bank details. On some occasions he had given his correct address; on others not. The total amount of credit obtained was about £20,000.

The appellant was arrested on 14 June 1994 as he attempted to buy a camcorder using the same method. He was interviewed at some length without a solicitor being present, though he had received some advice over the telephone. After some initial prevarication he told the officers that he had obtained a large number of goods that he subsequently sold and that, although he had made some payments for them, he stopped paying the finance company.

He was interviewed against on 10 August 1994 when details of the various agreements were put to him and he accepted that he had obtained the goods in question. He said that he had stopped paying for the credit because he could see little point in doing so when it was so easy and he had sold the goods as a way of making a 'quick buck'. He said that he had not realised that what he was doing was a criminal offence; he thought he was just getting himself into debt ...

Apart from an oblique reference to threats in these last two interviews there was no mention of the events which were to form the basis of his defence of duress. The Crown's case was that the appellant had no intention of paying the amounts of the credit outstanding in respect of any of the goods in question.

The appellant gave evidence; he accepted that he had obtained the goods on credit and had made few payments. He asserted that throughout the period he had acted under duress. He had been approached first by an acquaintance when buying a television for himself, and asked what was needed to obtain credit. Thereafter two men had accosted him in a public house, and he had been threatened by them that he and his family would be petrol-bombed if he did not obtain goods for them. On each occasion he was told what goods the men required. He was told that if he went to the police his family would be attacked. He said that he had not told the police this in interview because he was worried about the possible repercussions ...

The appeal is based on what [counsel for the appellant] submits was a misdirection in law in relation to the defence of duress ...

At the conclusion of the summing up [counsel for the appellant] submitted that the judge should have included in his direction that the sober person of reasonable firmness was someone who shared the defendant's characteristics. The judge accepted that he had not used this expression; he considered that he did not have to do so ...

[Counsel for the appellant] submits to this court that the judge was in error in omitting these words.

The classic statement of the law is to be found in the judgment of the Court of Appeal in *Graham* [1982] 1 WLR 294 at 299 ...

But the question remains, what are the relevant characteristics of the accused to which the jury should have regard in considering the second objective test? This question had given rise to considerable difficulty in recent cases. It seems clear that age and sex are, and physical health or disability may be, relevant characteristics.

But beyond that it is not altogether easy to determine from the authorities what others may be relevant ...

What principles are to be derived from [the] authorities? We think they are as follows:

(1) The mere fact that the accused is more pliable, vulnerable, timid or susceptible to threats than a normal person are not characteristics with which it is legitimate to invest the reasonable/ordinary person for the purpose of considering the objective test.

(2) The defendant may be in a category of persons who the jury may think less able to resist pressure than people not within that category. Obvious examples are age, where a young person may well not be so robust as a mature one; possibly sex, though many women would doubtless consider they had as much moral courage to resist pressure as men; pregnancy, where there is added fear for the unborn child; serious physical disability, which may inhibit self-protection; recognised mental illness or psychiatric condition, such as post-traumatic stress disorder leading to learned helplessness.

(3) Characteristics which may be relevant in considering provocation, because they relate to the nature of the provocation itself, will not necessarily be relevant in cases of duress. Thus homosexuality may be relevant to provocation if the provocative words or conduct are related to this characteristic; it cannot be relevant in duress, since there is no reason to think that homosexuals are less robust in resisting threats of the kind that are relevant in duress cases.

(4) Characteristics due to self-induced abuse, such as alcohol, drugs or glue sniffing, cannot be relevant.

(5) Psychiatric evidence may be admissible to show that the accused is suffering from mental illness, mental impairment or recognised psychiatric condition provided persons generally suffering from such condition may be more susceptible to pressure and threats and thus to assist the jury in deciding whether a reasonable person suffering from such a condition might have been impelled to act as the defendant did. It is not admissible simply to show that in the doctor's opinion an accused, who is not suffering from such illness or condition, is especially timid, suggestible or vulnerable to pressure and threats. Nor is medical opinion admissible to bolster or support the credibility of the accused.

(6) Where counsel wishes to submit that the accused has some characteristic which falls within (2) above, this must be made plain to the judge. The question may arise in relation to the admissibility of medical evidence of the nature set out in (5). If so, the judge will have to rule at that stage. There may, however, be no medical evidence, or, as in this case, medical evidence may have been introduced for some other purpose, eg to challenge the admissibility or weight of a confession. In such a case counsel must raise the question before speeches in the absence of the jury, so that the judge can rule whether the alleged characteristic is capable of being relevant. If he rules that it is, then he must leave it to the jury.

(7) In the absence of some direction from the judge as to what characteristics are capable of being regarded as relevant, we think that the direction approved in

R v Graham without more will not be as helpful as it might be, since the jury may be tempted, especially if there is evidence, as there was in this case, relating to suggestibility and vulnerability, to think that these are relevant. In most cases it is probably only the age and sex of the accused that is capable of being relevant. If so, the judge should, as he did in this case, confine the characteristics in question to these.

How are these principles to be applied in this case? [Counsel for the appellant] accepts, rightly in our opinion, that the evidence that the appellant was abnormally suggestible and a vulnerable individual is irrelevant. But she submits that the fact that he had, or may have had, a low IQ of 68 is relevant since it might inhibit his ability to seek the protection of the police. We do not agree. We do not see how low IQ, short of mental impairment or mental defectiveness, can be said to be a characteristic that makes those who have it less courageous and less able to withstand threats and pressure. Moreover, we do not think that any such submission as is now made, based solely on the appellant's low IQ, was ever advanced at the trial. Furthermore, it is to be noted that in two places the judge told the jury that if they thought the appellant passed the subjective test they should acquit him. We are quite satisfied that in the circumstances of this case the judge's direction was sufficient. He directed the jury to consider the only two relevant characteristics, namely age and sex. It would not have assisted them, and might well have confused them, if he had added, without qualification, that the person of reasonable firmness was one who shared the characteristics of the appellant. For these reasons, the appeal will be dismissed.

Notes and queries

1   Lord Lane CJ in *R v Graham* expresses the view that ' Provocation and duress are analogous'. To what extent does the law relating to duress have to be redrawn in the light of the House of Lords' ruling on the objective test for provocation in *R v Smith (Morgan)* [2000] 4 All ER 289 – considered in Chapter 15?

2   In *R v Martin* (above) it is to be noted that, as regards the objective stage of the test for duress, the trial judge had directed the jury in these terms: '... the second question is would a sober person of reasonable firmness with the defendant's characteristics of sex, age, any injury to leg found and the psychological condition of which I have spoken, [have] behaved in the same way and taken part in the offence.' Here the trial judge is allowing the jury to take into account the defendant's schizoid-affective state when applying the reasonable firmness part of the test. Is this condition compatible with the concept of the person of reasonable firmness?

The availability of the defence of duress *per minas*: murder and attempted murder

Duress is not a defence to murder, and this is so whether the accused is a principal offender or an accessory: see *R v Howe* (extracted below); similarly, duress is not available on a charge of attempted murder: see *R v Gotts* (extracted below).

R v Howe [1987] AC 417 (HL)

Lord Hailsham of St Marylebone LC: ... I take the facts of these truly horrible cases almost verbatim from the judgment of Lord Lane CJ [1986] QB 626 in the instant appeal. First, as to the case of Howe and Bannister, Murray and Bailey, the facts were as follows. At the time of the offences Howe and Bailey were 19, Bannister was 20 and Murray was 35. Howe had one minor conviction for motoring offences. Bannister had convictions for theft and burglary but none for violence. He was on probation. Bailey had convictions for burglary and theft. Murray had 25 previous court appearances, including two convictions for assault occasioning actual bodily harm, and in 1974 he had been convicted of assault with intent to rob and robbery in respect of which he had been sentenced to eight years' imprisonment.

Bannister met Murray in Risley Remand Centre. Howe and Bailey met in Stockport when Bailey was living in a hostel and Howe happened to be living next door with his grandmother. Murray came to visit Bailey when he was on six days' home leave from a sentence of two and a half years' imprisonment. Bailey introduced Howe to Murray. Lord Lane CJ continued, at pp 635–36:

> *Count 1: murder of Elgar.* The first victim was a 17 year old youth called Elgar. He was offered a job as a driver by Murray. On the evening of 10 October 1983 all five men were driven by Murray up into the hills between Stockport and Buxton, eventually stopping at some public lavatories at a remote spot called Goytsclough. Murray at some stage told both appellants in effect that Elgar was a 'grass', and that they were going to kill him. Bannister was threatened with violence if he did not give Elgar 'a bit of a battering'. From thenceforward Elgar, who was naked, sobbing and begging for mercy, was tortured, compelled to undergo appalling sexual perversions and indignities, he was kicked and punched. Bannister and Howe were doing the kicking and punching. The *coup de grâce* was executed by Bailey who strangled Elgar with a headlock. It is unnecessary to go into further details of the attack on Elgar which are positively nauseating. In brief the two appellants asserted that they had only acted as they did through fear of Murray, believing that they would be treated in the same way as Elgar had been treated if they did not comply with Murray's directions. The prosecution were content to assent to the proposition that death had been caused by Bailey strangling the victim, although the kicks and punches would have resulted in death moments later even in the absence of the strangulation. The body was hidden by the appellants and the other two men. On this basis the appellants were in the position of what would have earlier been principals in the second degree and duress was left to the jury as an issue on this count.
>
> *Count 2: murder of Pollitt.* Very much the same course of conduct took place as with Elgar. On 11 October 1983 the men picked up Pollitt, a 19 year old labourer, and took him to the same place where all four men kicked and punched the youth. Murray told Howe and Bannister to kill Pollitt, which they did by strangling him with Bannister's shoe lace. As the appellants were in the position of principals in the first degree, the judge did not leave duress to the jury on this count.
>
> *Count 3: conspiracy to murder Redfern.* The third intended victim was a 21 year old man. The same procedure was followed, but Redfern suspected that

something was afoot and managed with some skill to escape on his motorcycle from what would otherwise have inevitably been another horrible murder. The judge left the defence of duress to the jury on this charge of conspiracy to murder.

The grounds of appeal, which are the same in respect of each of these appellants, are as follows. That the judge erred in directing the jury (1) in respect of count 2, that the defence of duress was not available to a principal in the first degree to the actual killing; (2) in respect of counts 1 and 3, that the test as to whether the appellants were acting under duress contains an 'objective' element; that is to say, if the prosecution prove that a reasonable man in the position of the defendant would not have felt himself forced to comply with the threats, the defence fails ...

Lord Griffiths: ... For centuries it was accepted that English criminal law did not allow duress as a defence to murder. It was so stated in Hale's *Pleas of the Crown* (1736) Vol 1, p 51, repeated by Blackstone in his *Commentaries on the Laws of England*, 1857 edn, Vol 4, p 28, and so taught by all the authoritative writers on criminal law. It was accepted by those responsible for drafting the criminal codes for many parts of the British Empire and they provided, in those codes, that duress should not be a defence to murder. In *R v Tyler and Price* (1838) 8 C & P 616, Denman CJ told the jury in emphatic language that they should not accept a plea of duress that was put up in defence to a charge of murder against those who were not the actual killers. Fifty years later, in *R v Dudley and Stephens* (1884) 14 QBD 273, the defence of necessity was defined to the men who had killed the cabin boy and eaten him in order that they might survive albeit only Stephens was the actual killer. The reasoning that underlies that decision is the same as that which denies duress as a defence to murder. It is based upon the special sanctity that the law attaches to human life and which denies to a man the right to take an innocent life even at the price of his own or another's life.

There are surprisingly few reported decisions on duress but it cannot be gainsaid that the defence has been extended, particularly since the second war, to a number of crimes. I think myself it would have been better had this development not taken place and that duress had been regarded as a factor to be taken into account in mitigation as Stephen suggested in his *History of the Criminal Law of England* (1883) Vol 2, p 108. However, as Lord Morris of Borth-y-Gest said in *DPP for Northern Ireland v Lynch* [1975] AC 653, 670, it is too late to adopt that view. And the question now is whether that development should be carried a step further and applied to a murderer who is the actual killer, and if the answer to this question is no, whether there is any basis upon which it can be right to draw a distinction between a murderer who did the actual killing and a murderer who played a different part in the design to bring about the death of the victim ...

In *Abbot v R* [1977] AC 755, the majority in the Privy Council applied the law of duress in accordance with English authority and denied it as a defence to a murderer who took part in the actual killing. The minority would have extended the defence even to the actual killer, pointing out the illogicality of allowing it to the principal in the second degree or the aider and abettor and denying it to the principal in the first degree.

Since that time the whole question of duress has been studied by the Law Commission: see Law Commission Report, *Criminal Law, Report on Defences of General Application* (Law Com 83), dated 27 July 1977. The report sets out the arguments for and against the defence and deals in particular with whether it should apply to murder. They balanced the argument based upon the sanctity of human life that denies the defence to a murderer against the argument urged by the majority in *DPP for Northern Ireland v Lynch* [1975] AC 653, that the law should not demand more than human frailty can sustain. They preferred the latter argument and accordingly recommended that a defence of duress should be available to all crimes including murder ...

Against this background are there any present circumstances that should impel your Lordships to alter the law that has stood for so long and to extend the defence of duress to the actual killer? My Lords, I can think of none. It appears to me that all present indications point in the opposite direction. We face a rising tide of violence and terrorism against which the law must stand firm recognising that its highest duty is to protect the freedom and lives of those that live under it. The sanctity of human life lies at the root of this ideal and I would do nothing to undermine it, be it ever so slight.

On this question your Lordships should, I believe, accord great weight to the opinion of the Lord Chief Justice who by virtue of his office and duties is in far closer touch with the practical application of the criminal law and better able to evaluate the consequence of a change in the law than those of us who sit in this House. This is what Lord Lane CJ had to say in his judgment in this case [1986] QB 626, 641:

> It is true that to allow the defence to the aider and abettor but not to the killer may lead to illogicality, as was pointed out by this court in *R v Graham (Paul)* [1982] 1 WLR 294, where the question in issue in the instant case was not argued, but that is not to say that any illogicality should be cured by making duress available to the actual killer rather by removing it from the aider and abettor. Assuming that a change in the law is desirable or necessary, we may perhaps be permitted to express a view. The whole matter was dealt with *in extenso* by Lord Salmon in his speech in *Abbott v R* [1977] AC 755 to which reference has already been made. He dealt there with the authorities. It is unnecessary for us in the circumstances to repeat the citations which he there makes. It would, moreover, be impertinent for us to try to restate in different terms the contents of that speech with which we respectfully agree. Either the law should be left as it is or the defence of duress should be denied to anyone charged with murder, whether as a principal in the first degree or otherwise. It seems to us that it would be a highly dangerous relaxation in the law to allow a person who has deliberately killed maybe a number of innocent people, to escape conviction and punishment altogether because of a fear that his own life or those of his family might be in danger if he did not; particularly so when the defence of duress is so easy to raise and may be so difficult for the prosecution to disprove beyond reasonable doubt, the facts of necessity being as a rule known only to the defendant himself. That is not to say that duress may not be taken into account in other ways, for example, by the parole board. Even if, contrary to our views, it were otherwise desirable to extend the defence of duress to the actual killer, this is surely not the moment to make any such change, when acts of terrorism are commonplace and opportunities for mass murder have never been more readily to hand.

My Lords, in my view we should accept the advice of Lord Lane CJ and the judges who sat with him, and decline to extend the defence to the actual killer. If the defence is not available to the killer what justification can there be for extending it to others who have played their part in the murder. I can, of course, see that as a matter of common sense one participant in a murder may be considered less morally at fault than another. The youth who hero-worships the gangleader and acts as lookout man whilst the gang enter a jeweller's shop and kill the owner in order to steal is an obvious example. In the eyes of the law they are all guilty of murder, but justice will be served by requiring those who did the killing to serve a longer period in prison before being released on licence than the youth who acted as lookout. However, it is not difficult to give examples where more moral fault may be thought to attach to a participant in murder who was not the actual killer; I have already mentioned the example of a contract killing, when the murder would never have taken place if a contract had not been placed to take the life of the victim. Another example would be an intelligent man goading a weak-minded individual into a killing he would not otherwise commit.

It is therefore neither rational nor fair to make the defence dependent upon whether the accused is the actual killer or took some other part in the murder. I have toyed with the idea that it might be possible to leave it to the discretion of the trial judge to decide whether the defence should be available to one who was not the killer, but I have rejected this as introducing too great a degree of uncertainty into the availability of the defence. I am not troubled by some of the extreme examples cited in favour of allowing the defence to those who are not the killer such as a woman motorist being hijacked and forced to act as getaway driver, or a pedestrian being forced to give misleading information to the police to protect robbery and murder in a shop. The short, practical answer is that it is inconceivable that such persons would be prosecuted; they would be called as the principal witnesses for the prosecution.

As I can find no fair and certain basis upon which to differentiate between participants to a murder and as I am firmly convinced that the law should not be extended to the killer, I would depart from the decision of this House in *DPP for Northern Ireland v Lynch* [1975] AC 653 and declare the law to be that duress is not available as a defence to a charge of murder, or to attempted murder. I add attempted murder because it is to be remembered that the prosecution have to prove an even more evil intent to convict of attempted murder than in actual murder. Attempted murder requires proof of an intent to kill, whereas in murder it is sufficient to prove an intent to cause really serious injury.

It cannot be right to allow the defence to one who may be more intent upon taking a life than the murderer. This leaves, of course, the anomaly that duress is available for the offence of wounding with intent but not to murder if the victim dies subsequently. But this flows from the special regard that the law has for human life, it may not be logical but it is real and has to be accepted.

I do not think that your Lordships should adopt the compromise solution of declaring that duress reduces murder to manslaughter. Where the defence of duress is available it is a complete excuse. This solution would put the law back to lines upon which Stephen suggested it should develop by regarding duress as a form of mitigation. English law has rejected this solution and it would be yet another anomaly to introduce it for the crime of murder alone. I would have been more tempted to go down this road if the death penalty had remained for murder. But the sentence for murder, although mandatory and expressed as imprisonment for life, is in fact an indefinite sentence, which is kept constantly under review by the parole board and the Home Secretary with the assistance of the Lord Chief Justice and the trial judge. I have confidence that through this machinery the respective culpability of those involved in a murder case can be fairly weighed and reflected in the time they are required to serve in custody ...

R v Gotts [1992] 2 AC 412 (HL)

The appellant was convicted of attempted murder, the trial judge having rejected counsel for the appellant's submissions that duress was available as defence. The House of Lords (**Lord Keith** and **Lord Lowry** dissenting), dismissed the appeal.

Lord Jauncey: My Lords ... On appeal (*Director of Public Prosecutions for Northern Ireland v Lynch* [1975] AC 653), it was held by a majority of this House that the defence of duress was available to a person charged with murder as a principal in the second degree. In a dissenting judgment Lord Simon of Glaisdale referred, at p 687A, to the need for the law to draw a line somewhere and went on to pose the question: 'But if an arbitrary line is thus drawn, is not one between murder and traditionally lesser crimes equally justifiable?' It is, in my view, taking too much out of these observations to treat them as recognising the availability of the defence of duress to a charge of attempted murder.

In *Abbott v R* [1977] AC 755, the Privy Council by a majority held that on a charge of murder the defence of duress was not available to a principal in the first degree who took part in the actual killing. Mr Farrer relied on a passage from the dissenting judgment of Lord Wilberforce at p 772:

Director of Public Prosecutions for Northern Ireland v Lynch having been decided as it was, the most striking feature of the present appeal is the lack of any indication, in the judgment of the majority, why a flat declaration that in no circumstances whatsoever may the actual killer be absolved by a plea of duress makes for sounder law and better ethics. In truth, the contrary is the case. For example D attempts to kill P but, though injuring him, fails. When charged with attempted murder he may plead duress (*R v Fagan* (1974) unreported, 20 September, and several times referred to in *Lynch*). Later P dies and D is charged with his murder; if the majority of their Lordships are right, he now has no such plea available.

The observations as to attempted murder were *obiter* and I do not consider that *R v Fagan*, a Northern Irish case, which proceeded upon a concession by the Crown that the defence was available to a charge of attempted murder, can be treated as authoritative.

The last and most important of the three cases is *R v Howe* ... This case '[restored] the law to the condition in which it was almost universally thought not be prior to *Lynch*': *per* Lord Hailsham of Marylebone LC at p 430. Accordingly, duress is no defence to murder in whatever capacity the accused is charged with that crime.

My Lords, I share the view of Lord Griffiths that 'it would have been better had [the development of the defence of duress] not taken place and that duress had been regarded as a factor to be taken into account in mitigation as Stephen suggested in his *History of the Criminal Law of England*, Vol II, p 108': *R v Howe* [1987] AC 417, 439 – a view which was expressed in not dissimilar terms by Lord Hunter in the Scottish case of *Thomson v HM Advocate* (1983) SCCR 368, 372: 'I doubt whether – at any rate in the case of very serious crimes – it is sound legal policy ever to admit coercion as a full defence leading, if established, to acquittal.' At the time of the earlier writings on duress as a defence, offences against the person were much more likely to have involved only one or two victims. Weapons and substances capable of inflicting mass injury were not readily available to terrorists and other criminals as they are in the reputedly more civilised times in which we now live. While it is not now possible for this House to restrict the availability of defence of duress in those cases where it has been recognised to exist, I feel constrained to express the personal view that given the climate of violence and terrorism which ordinary law-abiding citizens have now to face Parliament might do well to consider whether that defence should continue to be available in the case of all very serious crimes. I am aware that in expressing this personal view I am at odds with the recommendations of the Law Commission Report, *Criminal Law Report on Defences of General Application* (1977) (Law Com 83), but I am also aware that during some 14 years since its publication Parliament has, perhaps advisedly, taken no action thereafter.

However, in this appeal there is no question of your Lordships being asked to deny the defence in circumstances where it has previously been held to be available. I have already expressed the opinion that earlier writings leave the matter at large. I do not consider that the obiter *dictum* of Lord Wilberforce in *Abbott v R* [1977] AC 755 to which I have already referred, supported as it is only by *R v Fagan*, 20 September 1974, which proceeded upon a concession, can be regarded as authoritative and there are no other observations in any of the three recent cases to a similar effect. There are, however, two obiter *dicta* in *R v Howe* [1987] AC 417 to which I must refer. Lord Hailsham, dealing with a defence argument as to the illogicality of allowing the defence of duress to a charge of attempted murder but not to one of murder, said, at p 432:

> More persuasive, perhaps, is the point based on the availability of the defence of duress on a charge of attempted murder, where the actual intent to kill is an essential prerequisite. It may be that we must meet this *casus omissus* in your Lordships' House when we come to it. It may require reconsideration of the availability of the defence in that case too.

I understand Lord Hailsham there to be accepting that the question was still open for decision by his House and that his use of the word 'reconsideration' was not intended to connote a change in established law. Lord Griffiths dealt with the matter more positively, at p 445:

> As I can find no fair and certain basis upon which to differentiate between participants to a murder and as I am firmly convinced that the law should not be extended to the killer, I would depart from the decision of this House in *Director of Public Prosecution for Northern Ireland v Lynch* [1975] AC 653 and declare the law to be that duress is not available as a defence to a charge of murder, or to attempted murder. I add attempted murder because it is to be remembered that the prosecution have to prove an even more evil intent to convict of attempted murder than in actual murder. Attempted murder requires proof of an intent to kill, whereas in murder it is sufficient to prove an

intent to cause really serious injury. It cannot be right to allow the defence to one who may be more intent upon taking a life than the murderer.

As the question is still open for decision by your Lordships it becomes a matter of policy how it should be answered. It is interesting to note that there is no uniformity of practice in other common law countries. The industry of Mr Miskin who appeared with Mr Farrer disclosed that in Queensland, Tasmania, Western Australia, New Zealand and Canada duress is not available as a defence to attempted murder but that it is available in almost all of the states of the United States of America. The reason why duress has for so long been stated not to be available as a defence to a murder charge is that the law regards the sanctity of human life and the protection thereof as of paramount importance. Does that reason apply to attempted murder as well as to murder? As Lord Griffiths pointed out in the passage to which I have just referred, an intent to kill must be proved in the case of attempted murder but not necessarily in the case of murder. Is there logic in affording the defence to one who intends to kill but fails and denying it to one who mistakenly kills intending only to injure? If I may give two examples:

(1a) A stabs B in the chest intending to kill him and leaves him for dead. By good luck B is found whilst still alive and rushed to hospital where surgical skill saves his life.

(1b) C stabs D intending only to injure him and inflicts a near identical wound. Unfortunately D is not found until it is too late to save his life.

I see no justification of logic or morality for affording a defence of duress to A who intended to kill when it is denied to C who did not so intend.

(2a) E plants in a passenger aircraft a bomb timed to go off in mid-flight. Owing to bungling it explodes while the aircraft is still on the ground with the result that some 200 passengers suffer physical and mental injuries of which many are permanently disabling, but no one is killed.

(2b) F plants a bomb in a light aircraft intending to injure the pilot before it takes off but in fact it goes off in mid-air killing the pilot who is the sole occupant of the airplane.

It would in my view be both offensive to common sense and decency that E, if he established duress, should be acquitted and walk free without a stain on his character notwithstanding the appalling results which he has achieved, whereas F who never intended to kill should, if convicted in the absence of the defence, be sentenced to life imprisonment as a murderer.

It is, of course, true that withholding the defence in any circumstances will create some anomalies but I would agree with Lord Griffiths (*R v Howe* [1987] AC 417, 444A) that nothing should be done to undermine in any way the highest duty of the law to protect the freedom and lives of those that live under it. I can therefore see no justification in logic, morality or law in affording to an attempted murderer the defence which is withheld from a murderer. The intent required of an attempted murderer is more evil than that required of a murderer and the line which divides the two offences is seldom, if ever, of the deliberate making of the criminal. A man shooting to kill but missing a vital organ by a hair's breadth can justify his action no more than can the man who hits that organ. It is pure chance that the attempted murderer is not a murderer and I entirely agree with what Lord Lane CJ [1991] 1 QB 660, 667 said: that the fact that the attempt failed to kill should not make any difference.

For the foregoing reasons I have no doubt that the Court of Appeal reached the correct conclusion and that the appeal should be dismissed.

Lord Lowry (dissenting): The foundation of the Crown's argument is that, accepting the sanctity of human life as the basis for denying the defence of duress in murder, both logic and morality demand that that defence must be withheld from one who tried (albeit unsuccessfully), and therefore *intended*, to kill, when one considers that in murder the defence is withheld not only from the deliberate killer but also from the killer who intended only to inflict very serious injury and from all principals in the second degree, whatever their *mens rea*. But the logic and, to some extent, also the morality of this proposition are open to attack, as follows.

1   Treason, too, is an excluded offence and it does not invariably involve killing or attempting or conspiring to kill. It is the ultimate crime against the state (a man-made, as distinct from a divinely ordained, offence).

2   The principle that a person ought to die himself rather than kill an innocent is attractive but does not touch the case in which the killer did not intend to cause death, nor does it touch a principal in the second degree either, if he merely intended the victim to suffer serious personal injury.

3   There is much authority to show that duress can be relevant which involves a threat not to the killer, but to others, in particular his wife and children, which fundamentally alters the moral problem: see *R v Brown and Morley* (1968) SASR 467, 498, *per* Bray CJ; *R v Harley and Murray* [1967] VR 526; *Abbott v R* [1977] AC 755, 767A and 769F, *per* Lord Salmon; *R v Howe* [1987] AC 417, 433, *per* Lord Hailsham of St Marylebone LC, and at p 453, *per* Lord Mackay of Clashfern, and also various statutory codes and the Law Commission's draft Bill on A Criminal Code for England and Wales (Vol 1, App A) (1989) (Law Com 177), the combined effect of which is to show that threats to harm others can be a basis for the defence of duress.

My Lords, I suggest that the only thing which can reconcile the anomalies that have been a prolific source of comment is the stark fact of death. Murder is a result related crime, as Lord Hailsham of St Marylebone LC and Lord Mackay of Clashfern both observed in *R v Howe* at pp 430 and 457. Thus, to exclude treason and murder relates the doctrine of duress to serious results (admittedly an unsuccessful attempt to subvert the government can itself be treason), namely, danger to the state or a crime committed with guilty intent and resulting in, but not necessarily aimed at, loss of life, and does not specially relate that doctrine to a scale of moral turpitude. It is founded on practical considerations and not on a moral value judgment: the recourse of moral values was found in Hale's explanation (*Pleas of the Crown*, Vol 1, p 51), which related only to murder (and certainly not to robbery) and which, even in relation to murder, did not serve to justify the law's attitude, since it did not cover the guilty causation of death while intending merely to injure.

Blackstone's explanation that crimes created by the laws of society are in relation to duress distinguished from natural offences, so declared by the law of God (*Commentaries on the Laws of England*, Vol IV, p 30), equally fails to satisfy, since treason is typically a crime created by the laws of society for its own protection and because the explanation does not contemplate a mere intent to injure.

I sympathise with the proposition that attempted murder should be recognised as an exempted crime. But from the point of view of deterrence this idea holds no special attraction. If one makes the somewhat artificial assumption (without which the principle of deterrence has no meaning) that a potential offender will know when the defence of duress is not available, one then has to realise that, whatever the law may be about *attempted* murder, one who sets out to kill under threat will be guilty of murder if he succeeds. Therefore the deterrent is in theory operative already. The moral position, too, is clouded, because *Director of Public Prosecutions for Northern Ireland v Lynch* [1975] AC 653 in this respect alone affirming the majority opinion of the Court of Criminal Appeal in Northern Ireland, affirmed that the offender, even when acting under duress, intends to commit the crime (of murder, not attempted murder). But his guilty intent is of a special kind: *coactus voluit*, as the Latin phrase has it. Thus the denial of the duress defence, based on moral principles, is not straightforward. It may not be just a case of the law saying: 'Although you did not succeed, you intended to kill. Therefore you cannot rely on duress.' The law might equally well say: 'As with other offenders who allege duress, your guilty intent was caused by threats. Therefore, since the intended victim did not die, you, like other offenders, can rely on those threats as a defence. If the victim had died in circumstances amounting to murder or if treason had been the crime, it would of course have been different.' This emphasises the point that murder is a result-related crime.

The choice is between the two views propounded by Lord Lane CJ [1991] 1 QB 660, 664F–G and 667B: (1) if the common law recognised that murder and treason were the only excepted crimes, then we are bound to accept that as the law, whether it seems a desirable conclusion or not; the fact that there is no binding decision on the point does not weaken a rule of the common law which has stood the test of time; or (2) we are not constrained by a common law rule or by authority from considering whether the defence of duress does or does not extend to the offence of attempted murder.

I consider that the view to be preferred is that which is contained in the first of these propositions and that to adopt the second would result in an unjustified judicial change in the law. It is only with diffidence that I would express an opinion on the criminal law which conflicts with that of such highly respected authorities as the present Lord Chief Justice and my noble and learned friend, Lord Griffiths, but on this occasion I feel obliged to do so. I proceed to give my reasons for this conclusion.

Both judges and textwriters have pointed out that the law on the subject is vague and uncertain. In *R v Brown and Morley* (1968) SASR 467, 479 the court mentioned 'the defence of duress, as to which there is little direct authority and much theoretical discussion'. And, speaking of compulsion, whether by a husband over a wife, by threats of injury or by necessity, Stephen said in his *History of the Criminal Law of England*, Vol II, at p 105:

> Of the three forms of compulsion above mentioned, I may observe generally that hardly any branch of the law of England is more meagre or less satisfactory than the law on this subject.

Your Lordships have seen that Professor Kenny expressed himself to the same effect in his *Outlines of Criminal Law*, 13th edn. There have, moreover, been few cases in which the doctrine of duress has been directly in issue either with regard to the offences in relation to which it may provide a defence or as to the kind of threatening conduct which may constitute duress. There has, for all that, been considerable discussion and debate. In such an atmosphere it is easy for the discussion to focus on what the law ought to be rather than on what it is, and that is an unsatisfactory basis for the exercise of criminal jurisdiction. But, in my opinion, this vagueness ought not to encourage innovation which makes a departure from the received wisdom even if that wisdom is imperfect. This is particularly true if the innovation is retrospective in effect, to the prejudice of an accused person.

Hale's philosophical explanation of withholding the duress defence (*Pleas of the Crown*, Vol 1, p 51) is not a good starting point for putting attempted murder in the category of murder and treason or for saying that it is in that category already. The intention of the offender is evil, but when the attempt has failed the sentence is variable, although someone who kills through compassion or who kills intending only to injure receives a fixed sentence (until recently a capital sentence). That a man who did not mean to kill can be found guilty of murder and will receive a mandatory life sentence is arguably a blot on our legal system but that is the law and this fact sets murder apart. Such a result is consistent with the traditional view that one who causes death when committing a felony (I exclude manslaughter) is guilty of murder. In *R v Stephenson* [1947] NI 110 the accused was charged with the murder of a woman on whom he performed an abortion but, on the verdict of the jury, was convicted of manslaughter. The principle on which Stephenson was charged, although outmoded, is further proof that murder is a result related crime.

Stephen (*History of the Criminal Law of England*, Vol II, p 108) – and many have agreed with him – thought that duress should not be a defence to any crime, but this view does not justify taking the most obvious candidate for exclusion from that defence any more than all the other offences below murder and treason which are listed in the code of 1879 and in relation to which your Lordships can safely say that the duress defence is available. Whatever one may say about the earlier days, attempted murder was a fully established and serious crime in 1861 and has been ever since.

To withhold in respect of every crime the defence of duress, leaving it to the court (or, in relation to fixed penalty crimes, the executive) to take mitigating circumstances into account, seems logical. But to withhold that defence only from a selected list of serious crimes (some of which incur variable penalties) is questionable from a sentencing point of view, as indeed the sentence in the present case shows. The defence is withheld on the ground that the crime is so odious that it must not be palliated: and yet, if circumstances are allowed to mitigate the punishment, the principle on which the defence of duress is withheld has been defeated.

The fact that the sentence for attempted murder is at large is, with respect to those who think otherwise, no justification for withholding the defence of duress. Quite the reverse, because it is the theoretical inexcusability of murder and treason which causes those crimes (the fixed penalty for which can be, mitigated only by the executive) to be deprived of the duress defence ... If the common law has had a policy towards duress heretofore, it seems to have been to go by the result and not primarily by the intent and, if a change of policy is needed with regard to criminal liability, it must be made prospectively by Parliament and not retrospectively by a court.

I am not influenced in favour of the appellant by the supposed illogicality of distinguishing between attempted murder on the one hand and conspiracy and incitement to murder on the other and I agree on this point with the view of Lord Lane CJ: short of murder itself, attempted murder is a special crime. But I am not swayed in favour of the Crown by the various examples of the anomalies which are said to result from holding that the duress defence applies to attempted murder. As Lord Lane CJ said, at p 668B, it would be possible to suggest anomalies wherever the line is drawn. The real logic would be to grant or withhold the duress defence universally.

Attempted murder, however heinous we consider it, was a misdemeanour. Until 1861 someone who shot and missed could suffer no more than two years' imprisonment and I submit that, when attempted murder became a felony, that crime, like many other serious felonies, continued to have available the defence of duress.

The availability of the defence of duress *per minas*: where a defendant voluntarily exposes himself to the risk of threats

R v Sharp [1987] 1 QB 853 (CA)

Lord Lane CJ: ... The circumstances which gave rise to the charge of murder were the culmination of what was in effect a series of armed robberies committed upon sub-post offices. They culminated in the Wraysbury offence which resulted in the death of the subpostmaster at that place.

Count 2, the Hounslow robbery, to which the appellant pleaded guilty, concerned the following facts, and they are of relevance to the main issue. At about midday on 23 August Alderson and Hussey, both of whom were armed with sawn-off shotguns in the company of the appellant held up a sub-post office in Hounslow. They wore wigs. Hussey threatened the wife of the postmaster, whereupon the postmaster himself pressed the alarm. All three then ran off to the getaway car empty handed, because they had not time, after the sounding of the alarm, to take any of the money which they had coveted. Hussey tried to fire his gun in the air in order to discourage anyone who was minded to pursue them. His first attempt to fire the gun failed, but his second attempt succeeded, and a pellet from that gun in fact hit Alderson, one of the other miscreants, in the ear.

The importance of that incident is this, that both Alderson and Sharp as a result of that knew the sort of man with whom they were associating in the commission of these offences and the predilection which Hussey had for loaded weapons. They must have known also that any attempt in the future by an unlucky postmaster to press the alarm button would be viewed by Hussey with disfavour to say the least.

On 14 September 1984 the sub-post office at Wraysbury, near Staines, was subject of a reconnaissance by the appellant and the two other men. Then they determined to attack the office. Alderson and Hussey once again carried loaded sawn-off shotguns. A further weapon, a pump action shotgun, was left in the getaway car. Hussey's gun was loaded with a particularly venomous sort of shot, namely buckshot. Sharp was responsible for locking the post office door after the three of them had entered.

Alderson moved towards the wife of the subpostmaster and Hussey went to the post office area of this little shop. Hussey then shot the subpostmaster in the head at close range: the ballistics expert thought about two or three feet. The unfortunate postmaster died instantly. As he fell, so money was scattered. Alderson took the opportunity to hit the subpostmaster's wife on the head with his gun three times. That was in order to try to stop her screaming, which, not surprisingly, she had started to do. Once outside, Alderson shot at the tyre of a parked vehicle which belonged to the subpostmaster in order plainly to impede anyone who might be minded to pursue them.

Hussey, as already stated, was convicted of murder. The jury, not unnaturally, rejected his contention that the gun may have been discharged by accident. Alderson at first denied that he had taken part in the matter at all, but eventually went on to admit his part in the affair and he was in due course convicted of manslaughter.

Sharp put forward the contention that he had been invited indeed to take part in these robberies and had willingly acceded to the invitation. He was the 'bagman', as he put it, the man carrying the bag in which the loot, if any would be contained. He regarded Hussey in the vernacular as a 'nutcase'. He, Sharp, did not wish any weapons to be used, so he said. He said that he panicked when he saw the guns being loaded into the car. He thought they were blanks, so he said. He wanted to pull out, but he lost his nerve and he carried on despite his wish to withdraw from the conspiracy, because Hussey pointed a gun at him and threatened to blow his head off if he did not carry on with the plan to rob the post office. He, Sharp, did not carry a gun. He said he had thought of sabotaging either the gun or the ammunition by using some salt, but he did not get the opportunity ...

... [Counsel for the appellant] now agrees that everything in this appeal depends upon whether the judge was correct or not in ruling that a defendant who has voluntarily joined a gang such as this cannot subsequently rely upon the defence of duress.

So we turn to examine the situation which lies behind [counsel's] submission to the judge, and again the submissions to this court, namely that the common law knows no such exception to the defence of duress. [Counsel for the appellant] realistically is the first to concede that pragmatically, to use his own word, and realistically, the judge's interpretation of the law was desirable, if not essential, if justice is to be done in circumstances such as existed in the present case. But he submits that it is not for this court, or indeed any other court, to usurp the function of Parliament and to introduce into the common law a rule which, in his submission, has never previously been held to form part of it.

No one could question that if a person can avoid the effects of duress by escaping from the threats, without damage to himself, he must do so. In other words if there is a moment at which he is able to escape, so to speak, from the gun being held at his head by Hussey, or the equivalent of Hussey, he must do so. It seems to us to be part of the same argument, or at least to be so close to the same argument as to be practically indistinguishable from it, to say that a man must not voluntarily put himself in a position where he is likely to be subjected to such compulsion.

... [W]e are fortified in the view which I indicate, which, to jump ahead, is that this is part of the common law and always has been, by certain matters which appear in the speeches of their Lordships in *DPP for Northern Ireland v Lynch* [1975] AC

653. Although *Lynch's* case has been the subject of certain adverse comment since the date of those speeches, nevertheless the passages to which we wish to refer have not, as far as we know, been the subject of criticism.

First of all in the speech of Lord Morris of Borth-y-Gest appears this passage, at 668:

> Where duress is in issue many questions may arise such as whether threats are serious and compelling or whether (as on the facts of the present case may specially call for consideration) a person the subject of duress could reasonably have extricated himself or could have sought protection or had what has been called a 'safe avenue of escape'. Other questions may arise such as whether a person is only under duress as a result of being in voluntary association with those whom he knew would require some course of action. In the present case, as duress was not left to the jury, we naturally do not know what they thought of it all.

A little later Lord Morris of Borth-y-Gest again said, at p 670:

> In posing the case where someone is 'really' threatened I use the word 'really' in order to emphasise that duress must never be allowed to be the easy answer of those who can devise no other explanation of their conduct nor of those who readily could have avoided the dominance of threats nor of those who allow themselves to be at the disposal and under the sway of some gangster-tyrant. Where duress becomes an issue courts and juries will surely consider the facts with care and discernment.

Here of course, I interpolate, Hussey was the archetypal gangster-tyrant.

I turn form Lord Morris of Borth-y-Gest to the speech of Lord Wilberforce, at 679:

> It is clear that a possible case of duress, on the facts, could have been made. I say 'a possible case' because there were a number of matters which the jury would have had to consider if this defence had been left to them. Among these would have been whether Meehan, though uttering no express threats of death or serious injury, impliedly did so in such a way as to put the appellant in fear of death or serious injury; whether, if so, the threats continued to operate throughout the enterprise; whether the appellant had voluntarily exposed himself to a situation in which threats might be used against him if he did not participate in a criminal enterprise (the appellant denied that he had done so); whether the appellant had taken every opportunity open to him to escape from the situation of duress. In order to test the validity of the judge's decision to exclude this defence, we must assume on this appeal that these matters would have been decided in favour of the appellant.

Finally, so far as the passages in favour of the contention which we are supporting are concerned, in the speech of Lord Simon of Glaisdale appears this passage, at p 687:

> I spoke of the social evils which might be attendant on the recognition of a general defence of duress. Would it not enable a gang leader of notorious violence to confer on his organisation by terrorism immunity from the criminal law? Every member of his gang might well be able to say with truth, 'It was as much as my life was worth to disobey'. Was this not in essence the plea of the appellant? We do not, in general, allow a superior officer to confer such immunity on his subordinates by any defence of obedience to orders: why

should we allow it to terrorists? Nor would it seem to be sufficient to stipulate that no one can plead duress as a defence who has put himself into a position in which duress could be exercised on himself ...

In other words, in our judgment, where a person has voluntarily, and with knowledge of its nature, joined a criminal organisation or gang which he knew might bring pressure on him to commit an offence and was an active member when he was put under such pressure, he cannot avail himself of the defence of duress ...

R v Shepherd (1988) 86 Cr App R 47 (CA)

Mustill LJ: ... The offences were all of a similar character. The appellant, in the company of a varying number of other men, would enter retail premises. Some would distract the shopkeeper, whilst others would carry away boxes of goods, usually cigarettes. In this simple way the thieves were able to make off with goods of very considerable value. Ultimately some of them, including the appellant, were caught. In the last of a series of interviews the appellant admitted what he had done, and pointed out to the police the premises concerned.

There was reason to believe that another man, whom we shall call P, was also involved in some of the offences, but he was not charged with any of them. P is a man with many convictions for offences of dishonesty and violence.

On these facts it would seem that the appellant had no choice but to plead guilty to all the charges. In the event however he sought to raise a defence on the following lines. He had originally been recruited to the joint enterprise by P. The very first of the offences took place during April 1986, and the appellant played a willing part. It was a stroke of great good fortune for the appellant that this offence was on the list of those taken into consideration, and was not the subject of a plea of guilty. But he was unnerved by the experience and wanted to give it up. He was however threatened by P with violence to himself and his family, and was compelled to carry on with the thefts and did so until he was caught some weeks later.

The story, which was not mentioned in the police records of his interviews, receives some colour from the undoubted fact that P was subsequently sent to prison for an assault on the appellant committed within the precincts of the court whilst the case was awaiting trial, and there was evidence of another assault on him at much the same time.

On the appellant's pleas of not guilty the matter came for trial in the Crown Court on 5 January 1987. We mention this date because it was some three months before another division of this court gave judgment in *Sharp* ... If the order of events had been different, and the guidance given in that judgment had been available to counsel and the learned assistant recorder, it may well be that a different course would have been adopted.

At all events what happened was this. Counsel for the appellant very properly informed the prosecution that the defence of duress was to be raised, and of the basis for it. Counsel for the prosecution intimated that he would contend that on the authorities the defence was unsound, even if the appellant's story were true, since his original participation in the joint venture had been voluntary. Since the validity of this argument would affect the scope of the evidence and cross-examination, it was thought proper to raise the question of the law at the outset in order to save a possible waste of time and cost. The learned assistant recorder agreed to this proposal, and after argument he ruled in favour of the prosecution.

In spite of this the appellant maintained his pleas, and gave evidence on his own behalf. For reasons which we do not follow, he was permitted to give his story of duress, even though the assistant recorder had already ruled that it was immaterial – as indeed he was to direct the jury when he reminded them of what the appellant had said. The story was not however tested in any way ...

The appellant now appeals, contending that the issue of duress should not have been withdrawn from the jury.

The basis for this contention, as it was developed in the course of the appeal, was substantially different from the argument presented at the trial. It was (and still is) accepted on behalf of the prosecution that duress may in appropriate circumstances be available as a defence to a person charged with offences such as the present. It was (and still is) accepted on behalf of the appellant that this defence is not available when the defendant has, to put the matter neutrally, voluntarily brought himself into the situation from which the duress has arisen. The problem concerns the breadth of this exception.

At the trial no recourse was had to authority beyond a very compressed account in *Archbold, Criminal Pleading, Evidence and Practice,* 42nd edn, para 17.58, of the judgment delivered by the Lord Chief Justice of Northern Ireland in *Fitzpatrick* [1977] NILR 20. This was relied on by counsel for the appellant in support of a submission that the accused forfeits the right to rely on duress only where he has joined an 'organisation' possessing some kind of formal, although illicit, structure such as has existed in Northern Ireland and elsewhere. The judge rejected this contention. Any doubts about whether he was right to do so have been laid to rest by *Sharp* (above), and we need say no more about this point. The exclusion from the defence of duress is undoubtedly capable of operating where the persons with whom the defendant involves himself are simply co-conspirators banded together for a single offence or a group of offences.

This was not however the only question of principle which arose on the facts which we have summarised. Does a voluntary participation in any joint criminal act entail that any act of duress thereafter committed by another participant is to be excluded from consideration when the defence is raised? Or is the exception to be more narrowly understood? ...

At the conclusion of the argument we had arrived at the following opinion:

(1) Although it is not easy to rationalise the existence of duress as a defence rather than a ground of mitigation, it must in some way be founded on a concession to human frailty in cases where the defendant has been faced with a choice between two evils.

(2) The exception which exists where the defendant has voluntarily allied himself with the person who exercises the duress must be founded on the assumption that, just as he cannot complain if he had the opportunity to escape the duress and failed to take it, equally no concession to frailty is required if the risk of duress is freely undertaken.

(3) Thus, in some instances it will follow inevitably that the defendant has no excuse: for example, if he has joined a group of people dedicated to violence as a political end, or one which is overtly ready to use violence for other criminal

ends. Members of so-called paramilitary illegal groups, or gangs of armed robbers, must be taken to anticipate what may happen to them if their nerve fails, and cannot be heard to complain if violence is indeed threatened.

(4) Other cases will be difficult. There is no need for recourse to extravagant examples. Common sense must recognise that there are certain kinds of criminal enterprises the joining of which, in the absence of any knowledge of propensity to violence on the part of one member, would not lead another to suspect that a decision to think better of the whole affair might lead him into serious trouble. The logic which appears to underlie the law of duress would suggest that if trouble did unexpectedly materialise, and if it put the defendant into a dilemma in which a reasonable man might have chosen to act as he did, the concession to human frailty should not be denied to him.

Having arrived at these conclusions on the argument addressed to us, it appeared to us plain there had been a question which should properly have been put to the jury and that the appeal must accordingly be allowed. We intimated that this would be so, whilst taking the opportunity to put our reasons in writing.

Naturally a proper scepticism would have been in order when the defence came to be examined at the trial, for there were many aspects on which the appellant could have been pressed. In particular, his prior knowledge of P would require investigation. At the same time the trial would not have been a foregone conclusion, since the concerted shoplifting enterprise did not involve violence to the victim either in anticipation or in the way it was actually put into effect. The members of the jury have had to ask themselves whether the appellant could be said to have taken the risk of P's violence simply by joining a shoplifting gang of which he was a member. Of course even if they were prepared to give the appellant the benefit of the doubt in this respect, an acquittal would be far from inevitable. The jury would have then to consider the nature and timing of the threats, and the nature and persistence of the offences, in order to decide whether the defendant was entitled to be exonerated. It may well be that, in the light of the evidence as it emerged, convictions would have followed. But the question was never put to the test. The issues were never investigated. The jury were left with no choice but to convict.

In these circumstances we saw no alternative but to hold that the convictions could not stand. The sentences necessarily fell away, leaving the fortunate appellant with no penalty attached to the first offence of which he was undeniably guilty, but which was not the subject of any charge.

That was the position at the conclusion of the argument. Since then we have been able to study a transcript of the ruling of the trial judge in *Sharp* (Kenneth Jones J), a ruling which was approved on appeal (see above) ...

This ruling, if we may say so, corresponds exactly with the view which we had independently formed. In the interests of accuracy it must be acknowledged that it was the ruling itself, rather than the whole of the passage in which it was expressed, which was the subject of the approval on appeal. Nevertheless the terms of the judgment delivered by the Lord Chief Justice were such as to make it clear, to our mind, that the approach of the trial judge was correct. In the context of that case, given the facts, such a conclusion was fatal to the appeal. Here, by contrast, it demonstrates that the issue ought to have been left to the jury ...

R v Ali [1995] Crim LR 303 (CA)

Facts: The appellant was convicted of robbery, having an imitation firearm with intent and possessing an imitation firearm when committing an offence. The appellant robbed a building society of £1,175, in the course of which he threatened cashiers with a gun. At trial he gave evidence that he had gone to Pakistan in 1987 and had become a heroin addict. One of the suppliers to whom he resorted was X, whom he refused to name but whom he knew to be a very violent person. He said the arrangement was that he would sell on the heroin he received from X and hand on the proceeds to him, as well as taking a certain amount for his own use. One day instead of selling on the bulk of the heroin, he used it all for his own purposes. That put him in debt to X, who threatened him and told him on several occasions that he would be shot. The appellant moved house, but X caught up with him, gave him a gun and told him he wanted the money the following day. The appellant was to get it from a bank or building society, otherwise he would be killed. The appellant was scared that X would return for him if he went to the police and so he committed the robbery. X took the money from him. On appeal, it was argued that the judge had not directed the jury correctly on the defence of duress, which was the burden of the appellant's case. The judge had posed four questions for the jury, the last of which was whether the appellant, in obtaining heroin from X and supplying it to others for gain, after he knew of X's reputation for violence, voluntarily put himself in a position where he knew that he was likely to be forced by X to commit a crime. It was submitted that it was not sufficient for the appellant knowing of X's reputation for violence, voluntarily to put himself in a position where he knew he was likely to be forced by X to commit a crime; the judge should have said 'forced by X to commit armed robbery'.

Held, dismissing the appeal, the jury could not have read the words 'a crime' as referring back to the drug dealing, as opposed to some crime other than that which was the common currency of the relationship between the appellant and X. The crux of the matter was knowledge in the defendant of either a violent nature to the gang or the enterprise which he had joined, or a violent disposition in the person or persons involved with him in the criminal activity he voluntarily joined. If a defendant voluntarily participated in criminal offences with a man 'X', whom he knows to be of a violent disposition and likely to require him to perform other criminal acts, he could not rely on duress if 'X' does so. The judge's summing up had expressed that proposition accurately. He had made it clear that, if there was no reason for a defendant to anticipate violence, then he would be entitled to rely on duress. But if he knew of a propensity for violence in those with whom he was working, then he could hardly rely on duress if they had threatened him with violence to make him do their bidding.

Notes and queries

1   Suppose D, a former member of a violent and ruthless criminal gang who has been 'going straight' for the last few years, is approached by X, a former partner in the criminal gang. X tells D that he must commit a burglary or D's family will be killed. Would D be able to avail himself of the defence of necessity?

2   It is not just membership of a criminal association that can prevent D from being allowed to rely on duress where he is threatened by fellow gang members. *R v Heath* (1999) *The Times*, 15 October indicates that D may be prohibited from relying on the defence where there is evidence that he voluntarily exposed himself to the risk of being subjected to such threats, for example by becoming indebted to a drugs dealer. The prosecution would need to provide evidence that D was aware that he might be have been putting himself at risk of being threatened with violence if he did not carry out specified offences (such as being a drugs courier) in order to 'clear his debt'. There is no need for the prosecution to prove that D knew what type of crime he might be compelled to commit.

DURESS OF CIRCUMSTANCES

As will be seen from the following extracts, the defence of duress of circumstance is effectively co-terminus with duress *per minas*, both in terms of the direction given to the jury and the offences in respect of which it is available (ie duress of circumstances cannot be raised as a defence to murder or attempted murder). What distinguishes the two forms of duress is the nature of the threat. With duress *per minas* X is saying to D 'Rob the bank or I'll kill you!'. With duress of circumstances, X need not specify the offence to be committed by D. D fears death or grievous bodily harm will occur simply because of X's words or actions (for example where X is a member of an angry mob gesticulating at D), and commits the offence in question (for example driving away in excess of the speed limit) in order to avoid such harm occurring. It may even be the case that D's compulsion arises from natural causes, where, for example D exceeds the speed limit, or drives with excess alcohol, because he needs to move his car from the vicinity of a blazing building.

R v Willer (1986) 83 Cr App R 225 (CA)

Watkins LJ: ... Mark Edward Willer is 19 years of age. He is of excellent character. He appeals against his conviction for reckless driving.

What happened to bring him to conviction was that at about half past nine in the evening of 24 April 1984 he and two school friends, Martin and Richard Jordan, were driving around the town of Hemel Hempstead in the appellant's Vauxhall Cavalier car. They heard a broadcast on the car's, what is known as, Citizen's Band radio. From what they heard, the appellant was persuaded to drive to a shopping precinct at Leverstock Green. There they expected to meet another enthusiast of

Citizen's Band radio. At one stage of the journey the appellant had to drive up a very narrow turning off a road called Green Lane in order to keep his assignment with the other enthusiast mentioned. As he made his way up what is called Leaside, which is, as we see from the photographs, an alleyway, he was suddenly confronted with a gang of shouting and bawling youths, 20–30 strong. He heard one of them shouting: 'I'll kill you Willer' and 'I'll kill you Jordan'. He stopped and tried to turn the car round. These youths surrounded him. They banged on the car. A youth called Smallpiece opened the rear door of the car and dived upon Richard Jordan who was sitting in the back of it. Martin Jordan, his brother, got out of the front seat to help. The appellant realised that the only conceivable way he could somehow escape from this formidable gang of youths, who were obviously bent upon doing further violence, was to mount the pavement on the right-hand side of Leaside and on the pavement to drive through a small gap into the front of the shopping precinct. That he did quite slowly, it was accepted, at about 10 mph.

Having gained the security, if that was what it could be called, of the front of the shopping precinct and moved somewhere in the vicinity of a car park which was there, he realised that he had lost one of his companions. So he turned the car round and drove very slowly, at 5 mph, back towards the gap and through it. He had to make a couple of turns in his search for his missing companion. All this time Smallpiece was in the back of the car fighting with Richard Jordan. With that going on the appellant drove to the local police station and reported the matter. For his pains he was prosecuted, a very surprising turn of events indeed.

He was charged with reckless driving. Very properly, so it seems to us, he chose trial by jury. He appeared at the Crown Court at St Albans on 16 April 1985. The trial was presided over by Mr Curwen, an assistant recorder. During the course of the trial an argument developed between the assistant recorder and counsel over the question as to whether or not the defence of necessity was available to the appellant. The assistant recorder ruled that it was not. The submissions were made very carefully, and authorities, some from America and Australia were referred to. We do not see the need to refer to them in this judgment. I say that because we doubt that the defence of necessity was in point here. There was however a very different defence available to the appellant to which I shall later return ...

Returning to how the appellant came to change his plea, one begins with the reasons advanced by the assistant recorder for declaring that the defence of necessity was not available to the appellant. He seems to have based himself upon the proposition, though saying that necessity was a defence known to English law, that it was not, albeit available to the appellant in respect of the journey through the gap into the car park in front of the shopping precinct, available to him upon the return journey because he was not at that stage being besieged by the gang of youths. We feel bound to say that it would have been for the jury to decide, if necessity could have been a defence at all in those circumstances, whether the whole incident should be regarded as one, or could properly be regarded as two separate incidents so as to enable them to say that necessity applied in one instance but not in the other. For that reason alone the course adopted by the assistant recorder was we think seriously at fault. Beyond that upon the issue of necessity we see no need to go further, for what we deem to have been appropriate in these circumstances to raise as a defence by the appellant was duress. The appellant in effect said: 'I could do no other in the face of this hostility than to take the right turn as I did, to mount the pavement and to drive through the gap out of further harm's way, harm to person and harm to my property'. Thus the offence of duress, it seems to us, arose but was not pursued. What ought to have happened therefore was that the assistant recorder upon those facts should have directed that he would leave to the jury the question as to whether or not upon the outward or the return journey, or both, the appellant was wholly driven by force of circumstance into doing what he did and did not drive the car otherwise than under that form of compulsion, ie under duress ...

R v Conway [1989] 1 QB 290 (CA)

Woolf LJ: ... The prosecution evidence was that on the day in question, 6 July 1987, two police officers were on duty in an unmarked police vehicle when they saw the appellant's motor car parked. The appellant was in the driving seat, there was a passenger in the front seat, and another passenger, named Giulio Tonna, in the rear seat. Tonna was known to the police officers as being the subject of a bench warrant and, having seen him in the appellant's car, they pulled their vehicle up alongside his car, blocking the vehicle, and one of the police officers leaned over towards the appellant, showed him his warrant card, and said to him: 'Police; wait there. I want to have a word with your passenger'. He then walked to the rear passenger door of the Rover to speak to Tonna, when he heard Tonna shout: 'Go, I am wanted', and, subsequently, 'It's the Old Bill, go, I am wanted', at which the appellant drove off at speed. The police officers followed and saw the appellant's car being driven in a way which would undoubtedly normally be regarded as reckless. The appellant's car performed a four-wheel skid around a corner, and drove down a very narrow road, in which there were cars parked on both sides, at speeds in excess of 40 mph. At one stage a car had to move on to the footway to avoid a collision. The appellant approached a junction on the wrong side of the road, forcing another car to swerve on to the pavement to avoid a collision. He also turned sharp left at a junction without stopping, cutting directly in front of a car on the near side, causing that car to perform an emergency stop, and drove through a 'No Entry' sign round a blind corner and along a one-way street until forced to stop by traffic coming in the opposite direction. He was then apprehended by the officers, but Tonna was no longer in the car, and when asked what he was doing he indicated that he wanted to avoid the police catching Tonna.

The appellant's evidence, which was supported by his witnesses, who included his passengers, differed substantially as to detail from that of the prosecution witnesses. The effect of the defence evidence is accurately summarised in the grounds of appeal, as follows:

A few weeks before 6 July Tonna had been in a vehicle when another man was shot by a 12-bore shotgun and severely injured and on that occasion Tonna was chased and narrowly escaped. That this event had occurred was not disputed by the prosecution. The appellant understood that Tonna was the main target and intended victim of that incident. Immediately before the alleged reckless driving, two young men in civilian clothes came running towards the vehicle and Tonna then screamed hysterically 'drive off'. The men never identified themselves as police officers, and the appellant drove off because he feared a fatal attack on Tonna. When he drove off the two persons whom he assumed to be intended attackers gave chase in a motor vehicle. It was only after he had dropped off Tonna and ceased driving that he realised the persons were police officers. At all times during the chase he had believed the two men were potential assassins. He did, however, deny many of the details of the alleged reckless driving, maintaining that although he drove at excessive speeds he did not carry out many of the dangerous manoeuvres alleged by the police. He accepted that nevertheless, were it not for the believed emergency, his manner of driving might well have been reckless. He was however petrified and when he saw the 'No Entry' sign he took no notice because he was in a panic ...

... [Counsel for the appellant] submits that the jury should have been given an additional direction. He says:

> The jury should be directed to consider whether the prosecution had proved beyond reasonable doubt that the appellant did not believe that he was acting in an emergency to save Tonna from serious bodily injury. If the jury found that the appellant so believed or may have so believed the jury should be directed to consider whether the manner of the appellant's driving was justified or excused having regard to the circumstances in which he drove.

Although [counsel] in his careful and helpful submissions was anxious not to put forward any proposition which was wider than was absolutely necessary for the purposes of this appeal, it appears from this suggested direction that what he is contending for is a defence of necessity based upon subjective belief which would justify what would otherwise amount to reckless driving. In doing this he is departing from the approach which was adopted by counsel who appeared for the appellant in the Crown Court. In submissions made at the end of the evidence and prior to the summing up counsel accepted that it would be 'impossible to run the defence of necessity in this particular case', and that the judge was not required to leave it to the jury. However, he contended that the jury nonetheless could consider whether the appellant's explanation was reasonable and, if it was, find him not guilty ...

We conclude that necessity can only be a defence to a charge of reckless driving where the facts establish 'duress of circumstances', as in *R v Willer* 83 Cr App R 225, ie where the defendant was constrained by circumstances to drive as he did to avoid death or serious bodily harm to himself or some other person.

As the editors point out in Smith and Hogan, *Criminal Law*, 6th edn, 1988, p 225, to admit a defence of 'duress of circumstances' is a logical consequence of the existence of the defence of duress as that term is ordinarily understood, ie 'do this or else'. This approach does no more than recognise that duress is an example of necessity. Whether 'duress of circumstances' is called 'duress' or 'necessity' does not matter. What is important is that, whatever it is called, it is subject to the same limitations as 'do this or else' species of duress. As Lord Hailsham of St Marylebone LC said in his speech in *R v Howe* [1987] AC 417 at 429:

> There is, of course, an obvious distinction between duress and necessity as potential defences; duress arises from the wrongful threats or violence of another human being and necessity arises from any other objective dangers threatening the accused. This, however, is ... a distinction without a relevant difference, since on this view of duress it is only that species of the genus of necessity which is caused by wrongful threats. I cannot see that there is any way in which a person of ordinary fortitude can be excused from the one type of pressure on his will rather than the other ...

It follows that a defence of 'duress of circumstances' is available only if from an objective standpoint the defendant can be said to be acting in order to avoid a threat of death or serious injury. The approach must be that indicated by Lord Lane CJ in *R v Graham (Paul)* [1982] 1 WLR 294 at 300 ...

Adopting the approach indicated by Lord Lane CJ, and not that argued by [counsel for the appellant], which involved a subjective element, we ask ourselves whether the judge in the Crown Court should have left the defence of 'duress of circumstances' to the jury, notwithstanding the submission made by his counsel that it was 'impossible to run the defence of necessity ... or indeed (to) leave it to the jury'.

On the facts alleged by the appellant we are constrained to hold that the judge was obliged to do so, notwithstanding his counsel's submission at the hearing... [H]is client's defence was that he drove as he did because he was in fear for his life and that of Tonna. Although it is unlikely that the outcome of the jury's deliberations would have been any different, they should have been directed as to the possibility that they could find the appellant not guilty because of duress of circumstances, although they were otherwise satisfied that he had driven recklessly ...

R v Martin [1989] 1 All ER 652 (CA)

Simon Brown J: ... The appellant now appeals against his conviction as of right on a pure point of law. The point is whether the defence of necessity is available to a charge of driving whilst disqualified when that driving occurs in circumstances such as the appellant was contending arose in his case. To those circumstances I shall come in a moment. In a private-room hearing before the appellant was arraigned, the judge held not. He concluded that, once it was established that the defendant was driving and that he was disqualified at the time, the offence was established. It was, in short, in those circumstances an absolute offence ...

The circumstances which the appellant desired to advance by way of defence of necessity were essentially these. His wife has suicidal tendencies. On a number of occasions before the day in question she had attempted to take her own life. On the day in question her son, the appellant's stepson, had overslept. He had done so to the extent that he was bound to be late for work and at risk of losing his job unless, so it was asserted, the appellant drove him to work. The appellant's wife was distraught. She was shouting, screaming, banging her head against a wall. More particularly, it is said she was threatening suicide unless the appellant drove the boy to work ...

The appellant's case on the facts was that he genuinely, and he would suggest reasonably, believed that his wife would carry out that threat unless he did as she demanded. Despite his disqualification he therefore drove the boy. He was in fact apprehended by the police within about a quarter of a mile of the house.

Sceptically though one may regard that defence on the facts (and there were, we would observe, striking difficulties about the detailed evidence when it came finally to be given before the judge in mitigation), the sole question before this court is whether those facts, had the jury accepted they were or might be true, amounted in law to a defence. If they did, then the appellant was entitled to a trial of the issue before the jury. The jury would of course have had to be directed properly on the precise scope and nature of the defence, but the decision on the facts would have been for them. As it was, such a defence was pre-empted by the ruling. Should it have been?

In our judgment the answer is plainly not. The authorities are now clear. Their effect is perhaps most conveniently to be found in the judgment of this court in *R v Conway* [1988] 3 WLR 1238. The decision reviews earlier relevant authorities.

The principles may be summarised thus: first, English law does in extreme circumstances recognise a defence of necessity. Most commonly this defence arises as duress, that is pressure on the accused's will from the wrongful threats or violence of another. Equally however it can arise from other objective dangers threatening the accused or others. Arising thus it is conveniently called 'duress of circumstances'.

Second, the defence is available only if, from an objective standpoint, the accused can be said to be acting reasonably and proportionately in order to avoid a threat of death or serious injury.

Third, assuming the defence to be open to the accused on his account of the facts, the issue should be left to the jury, who should be directed to determine these two questions: first, was the accused, or may he have been, impelled to act as he did because as a result of what he reasonably believed to be the situation he had good cause to fear that otherwise death or serious physical injury would result; second, if so, would a sober person of reasonable firmness, sharing the characteristics of the accused, have responded to that situation by acting as the accused acted? If the answer to both those questions was Yes, then the jury would acquit; the defence of necessity would have been established.

That the defence is available in cases of reckless driving is established by *R v Conway* itself and indeed by an earlier decision of the court in *R v Willer* (1986) 83 Cr App R 225. *R v Conway* is authority also for the proposition that the scope of the defence is no wider for reckless driving than for other serious offences. As was pointed out in the judgment, 'reckless driving can kill' (see [1988] 3 WLR 1238 at 1244).

We see no material distinction between offences of reckless driving and driving whilst disqualified so far as the application and scope of this defence is concerned. Equally we can see no distinction in principle between various threats of death; it matters not whether the risk of death is by murder or by suicide or indeed by accident. One can illustrate the latter by considering a disqualified driver being driven by his wife, she suffering a heart attack in remote countryside and he needing instantly to get her to hospital.

It follows from this that the judge quite clearly did come to a wrong decision on the question of law, and the appellant should have been permitted to raise this defence for what it was worth before the jury ...

DPP v Bell [1992] Crim LR 176 (DC)

Facts: The appellant was driving a car with an alcohol reading of 74 microgrammes/100 ml breath. He had been drinking with friends. Some trouble occurred which caused the appellant to run back to his car pursued by others. Finding himself outnumbered and in fear of serious personal injury he got into the car, reversed away and drove off for some distance down the road. In reversing he accidentally drove over one of his own passengers who had failed to get into the car in time. The magistrates' court convicted him of driving with excess alcohol but the Crown Court allowed his appeal against conviction on the basis of duress. The prosecutor appealed against the Crown Court decision by way of case stated.

Held, dismissing the appeal, it was clear that the defence of duress was made out where fear engendered by threats caused a person to lose complete control of his will (see *Willer* (1986) 83 Cr App R 225; *Ortiz* (1986) 83 Cr App R 173, 176, *per* Farquharson J). On the facts found by the Crown Court the appellant was in terror when he drove off and it was a hypothetical question whether he might have driven in the same way if he had not been in fear from the threats. A further important finding of fact was that he drove off only 'some distance' down the road and not, for example, all the way home so that the defence of duress/necessity continued to avail him. (*DPP v Jones* [1990] RTR 33 distinguished.) The prosecution had failed to negative the defence of duress.

DPP v Davis; DPP v Pittaway [1994] Crim LR 600 (DC)

Facts: The respondents were charged separately with driving with excess alcohol, contrary to s 5(1)(a) of the Road Traffic Act 1988. Magistrates dismissed the charges finding that, in each case, the defence of duress had been proved. The DPP appealed by way of case stated.

Davis: Magistrates found Davis had been suffering stress and anxiety when he had accepted an invitation to go for a meal with a male acquaintance. After the meal he returned to the other man's flat where he became the subject of an unwelcome homosexual advance. Magistrates found he feared for his life and had run from the flat. After breaking free from the other man's clutches, he had driven away. Magistrates applied a subjective test in deciding it was more likely than not that events had caused Davis to lose complete control of his will.

Pittaway: Pittaway had recently divorced her husband who had been violent towards her. Magistrates found that, as a result of the violence she was frightened of men. She formed a new relationship with the appellant. At a party, she and the appellant had a row, leading to an angry exchange of words outside the party and unspecified threats being made by the appellant. Magistrates found the respondent believed she would suffer immediate violence from the appellant and, although she ran to her house which was about 200 yards from the party, she decided instead to hide in her car. After five minutes or so, she drove 200 yards before being stopped. The appellant was not in the vicinity at the time.

Held, allowing both appeals and remitting the cases to the magistrates with a direction to convict, there was not evidence raising the defence of duress.

Davis: Although the defence of duress was subjective, it also had objective elements to it, namely whether there was good cause to fear death or serious injury would occur unless the respondent acted as he had done, and whether a sober person of reasonable firmness, sharing the respondent's characteristics, would have responded in the same way (*Graham* and *Howe*). The magistrates had focused on loss of will at the invitation of the prosecution, and this may have led them to overlook the objective elements. There was no finding that the respondent had been in fear of his life or serious injury at the moment he drove off, or that he continued to be frightened during the two miles he drove before being stopped. The only finding was that the respondent feared for his life when still in the flat. The magistrates did not consider whether there was good cause for the fear. Had they done so, it would have been impossible to conclude that the other man drawing near and undoing the respondent's shirt buttons could provide cause for such fear. Neither did the other man's attempts to pull the respondent from his car, which were accompanied by unspecified abuse but no actual blows.

The magistrates had also erred in deciding that it was not unreasonable for the respondent to drive two miles as it would have been difficult for him to stop. They should have considered whether it was necessary for him to continue driving.

Pittaway: The magistrates had again applied a subjective test, concerning themselves with the effect on the respondent of a man behaving violently towards her. They had not found that the threats amounted to threats of death or serious injury. They were wrong to apply a subjective test, and also wrong in considering whether the distance driven was reasonable, rather then necessary. Neither did they consider the significance of the respondent sitting in her car for five minutes, unpursued by the appellant, before driving off. They should have considered whether there was good cause for her to fear, which there was not.

R v Pommell [1995] 2 Cr App R 607 (CA)

Kennedy LJ: ... [T]he prosecution case was that at about 8 am on 4 June 1993 police officers entered the appellant's home to execute a search warrant. He was found lying in bed with a loaded gun in his right hand. He was asked if the gun was his and he replied, 'I took it off a geezer who was going to do some people some damage with it'. In the same bedroom police officers found a brown holdall containing ammunition. The appellant was arrested and interviewed. When interviewed he was asked to explain his possession of the gun, and he said:

> Last night someone come round to see me, this guy by the name of Erroll, and he had it with him with the intention to go and shoot some people because they had killed his friend and he wanted to kill their girlfriends and relatives and kids, and I persuade him, I took it off him and told him that it's not right to do that.

The appellant went on to say that Erroll had called between 12.30 am and 1 am and, after he left, the appellant took the gun upstairs and kept it from his girlfriend and took the bullets out of it. He appears to have achieved this by removing a loaded magazine containing 23 rounds. He then decided to wait until morning and decided to put the bullets back into it. To do this he must have inserted the loaded magazine back into the gun. He agreed that at the time of his arrest he was lying in bed with the gun against his leg because, he said, he did not want his girlfriend to see it. He said that he was going to hand the gun to his brother so that he could hand it to the police because his brother gets on with the police and had handed in guns in the past ...

We now turn to the events of 27 October 1993. In the course of an *ex parte* application as to discovery, prosecuting counsel advised the judge that the defence was going to be that the defendant had the weapon in his possession, holding it for another, so that the defence might be described as a defence of necessity. The judge said that he could not see that giving rise to an issue which it would be proper for a jury to consider, so the matter was explored further in open court. After arraignment, prosecuting counsel drew the attention of the judge to what the defendant had said in interview, and said that he understood that to be the basis of the defence. The judge said that he did not see any defence, and would need persuasion that a jury needed to be sworn. Defence counsel appears to have accepted that the judge should proceed on the basis that the contents of the interview were true. He drew the attention of the judge to the decision of this court in the case of *Martin* (1989) 88 Cr App R 343. There the court acknowledged that in extreme circumstances there can be a defence of necessity. Most commonly it arises when wrongful acts put pressure upon the accused, but it can arise from other objective dangers threatening the accused or others, then it is conveniently referred to as 'duress of circumstance'. Simon Brown J, as he then was, giving the judgment of the court, said:

> ... the defence is available only if, from an objective standpoint, the accused can be said to be acting reasonably and proportionately in order to avoid a threat of death or serious injury.

He went on to say that:

> ... assuming the defence to be open to the accused on his account of the facts, the *issue should be left to the jury*, who should be directed to determine these two questions: first, was the accused, or may he have been, impelled to act as he did because as a result of what he reasonably believed to be the situation he had good cause to fear that otherwise death or serious physical injury would result? Second, if so, may a sober person of reasonable firmness, sharing the characteristics of the accused, have responded to that situation by acting as the accused acted? If the answer to both questions was yes, then the jury would acquit: the defence of necessity would have been established. (The italics are ours.)

Martin had been charged with driving whilst disqualified, and asserted that he drove when he did because his wife, who was suicidal, threatened to kill herself. Obviously the circumstances of the present case are different and having had his attention drawn to the case of *Martin*, the trial judge said that in his view necessity could not be an issue here:

> ... because assuming that he was originally driven by necessity to take possession of it [the gun] ... his failure to go immediately to the police robs him of a defence ...

Before us there is substantially one ground of appeal. It is that the judge should not have ruled as he did and when he did in relation to the defence of necessity. [Counsel] for the appellant contends that the defence which he was seeking to advance should not have been so summarily dismissed. Evidence should have been called in the normal way, and then, if the evidence emerged as was anticipated, the judge should have left to the jury the issue of whether or not the defence of necessity was made out ...

... [W]e turn to consider the defence of necessity. There is an obvious attraction in the argument that if A finds B in possession of a gun which he is about to use to commit a crime, and if A is then able to persuade B to hand over the gun so that A may hand it to the police, A should not immediately upon taking possession of the gun become guilty of a criminal offence. However, if that is right, then in 1974, at least in the result, the case of *Woodage v Moss* was wrongly decided.

The strength of the argument that a person ought to be permitted to breach the letter of the criminal law in order to prevent a greater evil befalling himself or others has long been recognised (see, for example, Stephen's *Digest of Criminal Law*), but it has, in English law, not given rise to a recognised general defence of necessity, and in relation to the charge of murder, the defence has been specifically held not to exist (see *Dudley and Stephens* (1884) 14 QBD 273). Even in relation to other offences, there are powerful arguments against recognising the general defence. As Dickson J said in the Supreme Court of Canada in *Perka et al v R* (1985) 13 DLR (4th) 1 at 14:

> ... no system of positive law can recognise any principle which would entitle a person to violate the law because in his view the law conflicted with some higher social value.

The Criminal Code has specified a number of identifiable situations in which an actor is justified in committing what would otherwise be a criminal offence. To go beyond that and hold that ostensibly illegal acts can be validated on the basis of their expediency, would import an undue subjectivity into the criminal law. It would invite the courts to second-guess the legislature and to assess the relative merits of social policies underlying criminal prohibitions.

However, that does not really deal with the situation where someone commendably infringes a regulation in order to prevent another person from committing what everyone would accept as being a greater evil with a gun. In that situation it cannot be satisfactory to leave it to the prosecuting authority not to prosecute, or to individual courts to grant an absolute discharge. The authority may, as in the present case, prosecute because it is not satisfied that the defendant is telling the truth, and then, even if he is vindicated and given an absolute discharge, he is left with a criminal conviction which, for some purposes, would be recognised as such.

It was, as it seems to us, to meet this difficulty that the limited defence of duress of circumstances has been developed in English law in relation to road traffic offences. It was first recognised in *Willer* (1986) 83 Cr App R 225, where the accused drove onto a pavement and in and out of a shopping centre in order to escape a gang of youths seeking to attack him and his passenger. *Willer* was followed and applied in *Conway* (1989) 88 Cr App R 159, in which the Court of Appeal quashed a conviction on a charge of reckless driving. Having considered existing authorities, textbooks and the proposals of the Law Commission, the court in that case said at 164:

> ... it is still not clear whether there is a general defence of necessity or, if there is, what are the circumstances in which it is available.

In our judgment, that is still the position, but the court in *Conway* went on to say that necessity can be a defence to a charge of reckless driving where the facts establish duress of circumstances, that is to say when the defendant is constrained to drive as he did to avoid death or serious bodily harm to himself or some other person.

Then came *Martin*, a decision to which we referred earlier in this judgment, and *DPP v Bell* [1992] RTR 335, where the defendant, whose alcohol level was over the prescribed limit, was pursued to his car and, fearing serious injury, drove some distance down the road. The Crown Court allowed his appeal on the basis of duress of circumstances, and an appeal by way of case stated was dismissed. The Divisional Court particularly noted the finding of fact that the appellant drove only some distance down the road and not, for example, all the way home, so that the defence of duress of circumstances continued to avail him. In *DPP v Jones* [1990] RTR 33, it was held that any defence of necessity available to a driver would cease to be available if he drove for a longer period than necessary. Commenting on the case of *Bell*, Professor Sir John Smith has written:

> All the cases so far have concerned road traffic offences but there are no grounds for supposing that the defence is limited to that kind of case. On the contrary, the defence, being closely related to the defence of duress by threats, appears to be general, applying to all crimes except murder, attempted murder and some forms of treason ... (See [1992] Crim LR 176.)

We agree.

That leads us to the conclusion that in the present case the defence was open to the appellant in respect of his acquisition of the gun. The jury would have to be directed to determine the two questions identified in the passage which we have cited from the judgment in *Martin*. That leaves the question as to his continued possession of the gun thereafter. In our judgment, the test laid down in *Martin* is not necessarily the appropriate test for determining whether a person continues to have a defence available to him. For example, a person takes a gun off another in the circumstances in which this appellant says he did and then locks it away in a safe with a view to safeguarding it while the police are informed. When the gun is in the safe, the test laid down in *Martin* may not be satisfied: there would then be no immediate fear of death or serious injury. In our judgment, a person who has taken possession of a gun in circumstances where he has the defence of duress by circumstances must 'desist from committing the crime as soon as he reasonably can' (Smith and Hogan, *Criminal Law*, 7th edn, p 239). This test is similar to the test in *Jones*, to which we have already referred. In deciding whether a defendant acted reasonably, regard would be had to the circumstances in which he finds himself. Can it be said, in this case, that there was no evidence upon which a jury could have reached the conclusion that the appellant did desist, or may have desisted, as soon as he reasonably could? In answering this question, the jury would have to have regard to the delay that had occurred between, on the appellant's account, his acquisition of the gun and ammunition at 12.30 to 1 am, and the arrival of the police some hours later. The appellant has offered an explanation for that delay but, as it seems to us, the defence of duress of circumstances could not avail him once a reasonable person in his position would have known that the duress, in this case the need to obtain and retain the firearm, had ceased. In the present case the judge said that the failure of the appellant to go immediately to the police 'robs him of a defence'. We accept that in some cases a delay, especially if unexplained, may be such as to make it clear that any duress must have ceased to operate, in which case the judge would be entitled to conclude that even on the defendant's own account of the facts, the defence was not open to him. There would then be no reason to leave the issue to the jury. However, the situation does not seem to us to have been sufficiently clear cut to make that an appropriate step in the present case. In the first place, the delay of a few hours overnight might not be regarded as being unduly long and, second, the defendant did offer an explanation for it, therefore, in our judgment, the proposed defence should have been left to the jury.

We have considered whether the reloading of the gun and the fact that the appellant had the gun in his bed deprived him of the defence. Must a person who has acquired a gun in circumstances in which he has the defence of duress of circumstances not only desist from committing the offence as soon as he reasonably can but, in the meanwhile, act in a reasonable manner with the gun? The answer is that if he does not do so, it will be difficult for the court to accept that he desisted from committing the offence as soon as he reasonably could. Therefore, in our judgment, the acts of reloading and putting the gun in the bed do not of themselves deprive him of the defence, but are matters which may be taken into account by the jury in deciding the issues to which we have already made reference ...

Notes and queries

1   In *R v Martin* (above) the suicidal tendencies of the appellant's wife were accepted by the court as laying a foundation for the defence of duress of circumstances. Contrast this with *R v Rodger and Another* (1997) *The Times*, 30 July, where the Court of Appeal refused to allow a plea of duress of circumstance in respect of an appellant who had escaped from prison citing his own suicidal tendencies as the basis for the defence. The court held that the defence had to be based on something extraneous to the appellant.

A COMMON LAW DEFENCE OF NECESSITY?

Historically the courts have refused to accept that there could be a distinctive defence of necessity at common law. This reluctance, in part, explains the emergence of the defence of duress of circumstances and, it is submitted, the difficulty in explaining why the cases where duress of circumstance has been recognised might not also be seen as examples of necessity.

It may be possible to draw a distinction between duress of circumstance and necessity on the basis that, with the former, the defendant must show that he was 'constrained by circumstances' to act as he did (see *R v Conway*, above), or that he was 'impelled to act as he did' (see *R v Martin*, above). The latter defence, however, might be available to a defendant who, though not threatened himself, simply takes action which, although it involves the commission of a criminal offence, is the lesser of two evils in the situation as it presents itself to him. Developed along these lines there would be no need to show that the defendant had no choice but to act, or indeed that the evil he sought to avoid necessarily involved a threat of death or grievous bodily harm. As will have been seen from the extracts considered thus far, however, the courts are some way from identifying or accepting such a distinctive role for the a defence of necessity.

Necessity denied at common law

R v Dudley and Stephens [1884] 14 QBD 273

Lord Coleridge CJ: ... [T]his is clear, that the prisoners put to death a weak and unoffending boy upon the chance of preserving their own lives by feeding upon his flesh and blood after he was killed, and with the certainty of depriving him of any possible chance of survival. The verdict finds in terms that 'if the men had not fed upon the body of the boy they would probably not have survived', and that 'the boy being in a much weaker condition was likely to have died before them'. They might possibly have been picked up next day by a passing ship; they might possibly not have been picked up at all; in either case it is obvious that the killing of the boy would have been an unnecessary and profitless act. It is found by the verdict that the boy was incapable of resistance, and, in fact, made none; and it is not even suggested that his death was due to any violence on his part attempted against, or even so much as feared by, those who killed him ...

There remains to be considered the real question in the case – whether killing under the circumstances set forth in the verdict be or be not murder. The contention that it could be anything else was, to the minds of us all, both new and strange, and we stopped the Attorney General in his negative argument in order that we might hear what could be said in support of a proposition which appeared to us to be once dangerous, immoral, and opposed to all legal principle and analogy. All, no doubt, that can be said has been urged before us, and we are now to consider and determine what it amounts to. First it is said that it follows from various definitions of murder in books of authority, which definitions imply, if they do not state, the doctrine, that in order to save your own life you may lawfully take away the life of another, when that other is neither attempting nor threatening yours, nor is guilty of any illegal act whatever towards you or any one else. But if these definitions be looked at they will not be found to sustain this contention ...

... Now it is admitted that the deliberate killing of this unoffending and unresisting boy was clearly murder, unless the killing can be justified by some well-organised excuse admitted by the law. It is further admitted that there was in this case no such excuse, unless the killing was justified by what has been called 'necessity'. But the temptation to the act which existed here was not what the law has ever called necessity. Nor is this to be regretted. Though law and morality are not the same, and many things may be immoral which are not necessarily illegal, yet the absolute divorce of law from morality would be of fatal consequence; and such divorce would follow if the temptation to murder in this case were to be held by law an absolute defence of it. It is not so. To preserve one's life is generally speaking a duty, but it may be the plainest and the highest duty to sacrifice it. War is full of instances in which it is a man's duty not to live, but to die. The duty, in case of shipwreck, of a captain to his crew, to the crew to the passengers, of soldiers to women and children, as in the noble case of the Birkenhead; these duties impose on men the moral necessity, not the preservation, but of the sacrifice of their lives for others, from which in no country, least of all, it is to be hoped, in

England, will men ever shrink, as indeed, they have not shrunk. It is not correct, therefore, to say that there is any absolute or unqualified necessity to preserve one's life ... It is not needful to point out the awful danger of admitting the principle which has been contended for. Who is to be the judge of this sort of necessity? By what measure is the comparative value of lives to be measured? Is it to be strength, or intellect, or what? It is plain that the principle leaves to him who is to profit by it to determine the necessity which will justify him in deliberately taking another's life to save his own. In this case the weakest, the youngest, the most unresisting, was chosen. Was it more necessary to kill him than one of the grown men? The answer must be 'No':

> So spake the Fiend, and with necessity,
> The tyrant's plea, excused his devilish deeds.

It is not suggested that in this particular case the deeds were 'devilish', but it is quite plain that such a principle once admitted might be made the legal cloak for unbridled passion and atrocious crime. There is no safe path for judges to tread but to ascertain the law to the best of their ability and to declare it according to their judgment; and if in any case the law appears to be too severe on individuals, to leave it to the sovereign to exercise that prerogative of mercy which the constitution has intrusted to the hands fittest to dispense it.

It must not be supposed that in refusing to admit temptation to be an excuse for crime it is forgotten how terrible the temptation was; how awful the suffering; how hard in such trials to keep the judgment straight and the conduct pure. We are often compelled to set up standards we cannot reach ourselves, and to lay down rules which we could not ourselves satisfy. But a man has no right to declare temptation to be an excuse, though he might himself have yielded to it, nor allow compassion for the criminal to change or weaken in any manner the legal definition of the crime. It is therefore our duty to declare that the prisoners' act in this case was wilful murder, that the facts as stated in the verdict are no legal justification of the homicide; and to say that in our unanimous opinion the prisoners are upon this special verdict guilty of murder.

Necessity in disguise

The courts have, on occasion, declined to accept that there is a common law defence of necessity, but have relied upon the evidence of necessity to conclude that the defendant's actions were not, in the circumstances, unlawful.

R v Bourne [1939] 1 KB 687 (Central Criminal Court)

Facts: On 14 June 1938, the defendant performed an operation on the girl in question at St Mary's Hospital, and thereby procured her miscarriage. The following facts were also proved. On 27 April 1938, the girl, who was then under the age of 15, had been raped with great violence in circumstances which would have been most terrifying to any woman, let alone a child of 14, by a man who was in due course convicted of the crime. In consequence of the rape the girl became pregnant. Her case was brought to the attention of the defendant, who, after examination of the girl, performed the operation with the consent of her parents.

The defence put forward was that, in the circumstances of the case, the operation was not unlawful. The defendant was called as witness on his own behalf and stated that, after he had made careful examination of the girl and had informed himself of all the relevant facts of the case, he had come to the conclusion that it was his duty to perform the operation. In his opinion the continuance of the pregnancy would probably cause serious injury to the girl, injury so serious as to justify the removal of the pregnancy at a time when the operation could be performed without any risk to the girl and under favourable conditions.

Macnaghten J: ... The charge against Mr Bourne is made under s 58 of the Offences Against the Person Act 1861, that he unlawfully procured the miscarriage of the girl who was the first witness in the case ...

... That section is a re-enactment of earlier statutes, the first of which was passed at the beginning of the last century in the reign of George III (43 Geo 3, c 58, s 1). But long before then, before even Parliament came into existence, the killing of an unborn child was by the common law of England a grave crime: see Bracton, Book 3 (*De Corona*), fol 121. The protection which the common law afforded to human life extended to the unborn child in the womb of its mother. But, as in the case of homicide, so also in the case where an unborn child is killed, there may be justification for the act.

Nine years ago Parliament passed an Act called the Infant Life (Preservation) Act, 1929. Section 1(1) of the Act provides that 'any person who, with intent to destroy the life of a child capable of being born alive, by any wilful act causes a child to die before it has an existence independent of its mother, shall be guilty of felony, to wit, of child destruction, and shall be liable on conviction thereof on indictment to penal servitude for life: provided that no person shall be found guilty of an offence under this section unless it is proved that the act which caused the death of the child was not done in good faith for the purpose only of preserving the life of the mother'. It is true, as Mr Oliver has said, that this enactment provides for the case where a child is killed by wilful act at the time when it is being delivered in the ordinary course of nature; but in my view the proviso that it is necessary for the Crown to prove that the act was not done in good faith for the purpose only of preserving the life of the mother is in accordance with what has always been the common law of England with regard to the killing of an unborn child. No such proviso is in fact set out in s 58 of the Offences Against the Person Act 1861; but the words of that section are that any person who 'unlawfully' uses an instrument with intent to procure miscarriage shall be guilty of felony. In my opinion the word 'unlawfully' is not, in that section, a meaningless word. I think it imports the meaning expressed by the proviso in s 1(1) of the Infant Life (Preservation) Act 1929, and that s 58 of the Offences Against the Person Act 1861, must be read as if the words making it an offence to use an instrument with intent to procure a miscarriage were qualified by a similar proviso.

In this case, therefore, my direction to you in law is this: that the burden rests on the Crown to satisfy you beyond reasonable doubt that the defendant did not procure the miscarriage of the girl in good faith for the purpose only of preserving her life. If the Crown fails to satisfy you of that, the defendant is entitled by the law of this land to a verdict of acquittal. If, on the other hand, you are satisfied that what the defendant did was not done by him in good faith for the purpose only of preserving the life of the girl, it is your duty to find him guilty. It is said, and I think said rightly, that this is a case of great importance to the public and, more especially, to the medical profession; but you will observe that it has nothing to do with the ordinary case of procuring abortion to which I have already referred. In those cases the operation is performed by a person of no skill, with no medical qualifications, and there is no pretence that it is done for the preservation of the mother's life. Cases of that sort are in no way affected by the consideration of the question which is put before you today.

What then is the meaning to be given to the words 'for the purpose of preserving the life of the mother'? ...

... I think those words ought to be construed in a reasonable sense, and, if the doctor is of opinion, on reasonable grounds and with adequate knowledge, that the probable consequence of the continuance of the pregnancy will be to make the woman a physical or mental wreck, the jury are quite entitled to take the view that the doctor who, under those circumstances and in that honest belief, operates, is operating for the purpose of preserving the life of the mother ...

A LIMITED DEFENCE OF NECESSITY?

Re A (Children) (Conjoined Twins: Surgical Separation) [2000] 4 All ER 961

Ward LJ: It truly is a unique case. In a nutshell the problem is this. Jodie and Mary are conjoined twins. They each have their own brain, heart and lungs and other vital organs and they each have arms and legs. They are joined at the lower abdomen. Whilst not underplaying the surgical complexities, they can be successfully separated. But the operation will kill the weaker twin, Mary. That is because her lungs and heart are too deficient to oxygenate and pump blood through her body. Had she been born a singleton, she would not have been viable and resuscitation would have been abandoned. She would have died shortly after her birth. She is alive only because a common artery enables her sister, who is stronger, to circulate life sustaining oxygenated blood for both of them. Separation would require the clamping and then the severing of that common artery. Within minutes of doing so Mary will die. Yet if the operation does not take place, both will die within three to six months, or perhaps a little longer, because Jodie's heart will eventually fail. The parents cannot bring themselves to consent to the operation. The twins are equal in their eyes and they cannot agree to kill one even to save the other. As devout Roman Catholics they sincerely believe that it is God's will that their children are afflicted as they are and they must be left in God's hands. The doctors are convinced they can carry out the operation so as to give Jodie a life which will be worthwhile. So the hospital sought a declaration that the operation may be lawfully carried out. Johnson J granted it on 25 August 2000. The parents applied to us for permission to appeal against his order.

Ward LJ went on to conclude that the problem regarding the legality of the intervention by the doctors in the knowledge that they would kill the weaker of the two twins was to be resolved by resort to modified principles of self-defence – the relevant extracts are set out in Chapter 14.

Brooke LJ: We received some interesting and powerful submissions about the doctrine of necessity, and the ways in which it might be called in aid to justify the operation proposed by the doctors. Although for many years cases involving pleas of necessity were notable for their absence from our case law, the doctrine has recently been given a new lease of life by Lord Goff of Chieveley, first in *In Re F (Mental Patient: Sterilisation)* [1990] 2 AC 1, and more recently, in a speech with which the other members of the House of Lords agreed, in *R v Bournewood Community and Mental Health NHS Trust ex p L* [1999] 1 AC 458.

This doctrine is so obscure, and it has featured so seldom in our caselaw in the criminal courts, that I must describe it in considerable detail, and identify the problems it throws up, before I go on to decide whether it is permissible to apply it to the facts of the present case. In *In Re F* Lord Goff said at p 74A–C in the context of the law of tort:

> That there exists in the common law a principle of necessity which may justify action which would otherwise be unlawful is not in doubt. But historically the principle has been seen to be restricted to two groups of cases, which have been called cases of public necessity and cases of private necessity. The former occurred when a man interfered with another man's property in the public interest – for example (in the days before we would dial 999 for the fire brigade) the destruction of another man's house to prevent the spread of catastrophic fire, as indeed occurred in the Great Fire of London in 1666. The latter cases occurred when a man interfered with another's property to save his own person or property from imminent danger – for example, when he entered upon his neighbour's land without his consent, in order to prevent the spread of fire onto his own land.

Lord Goff then went on to consider a third group of cases, also founded upon the principle of necessity, which were concerned with actions taken by someone as a matter of necessity to assist another person without his consent. We are not, however, concerned in the present case with this application of the doctrine, because the law confers on the parents of an infant child the authority to consent on her behalf, and because there is also the residual right of consent vested in the court.

In *ex p L* Lord Goff had recourse to this doctrine again when holding that doctors were entitled to rely on it as the basis for their authority to care for compliant incapacitated patients of adult years and treat them without their consent. At the end of his speech in that case, he mentioned some old cases which authorised (in so far as this was shown to be necessary) the detention of those who were a danger, or potential danger, to themselves or others. He added (at p 490 C–D):

> I must confess that I was unaware of these authorities though, now that they have been drawn to my attention, I am not surprised that they should exist. The concept of necessity has its role to play in all branches of our law of obligations – in contract (see the cases on agency of necessity), in tort (see *In Re F (Mental Patient: Sterilisation)* [1990] 2 AC 1), and in restitution (see the sections on necessity in the standard books on the subject) and in our criminal law. It is therefore a concept of great importance. It is perhaps surprising, however, that the significant role it has to play in the law of torts has come to be recognised at so late a stage in the development of our law.

Public and private necessity in the criminal law In the present case we are concerned with what is said by some of those who appeared before us to be a case of private necessity in the eyes of the criminal law. Bracton, writing in the thirteenth century *On the Laws and Customs of England* (Selden Society Edition 1968, at Vol 2, 340–41) identified this type of necessity, in the context of the law of homicide, in these terms:

> Of necessity, and here we must distinguish whether the necessity was avoidable or not; if avoidable and he could escape without slaying, he will then be guilty of homicide; if unavoidable, since he kills without premeditated hatred but with sorrow of heart, in order to save himself and his family, since he could not otherwise escape [danger], he is not liable to the penalty for murder.

Five hundred years later the same concept of necessity, which still forms part of our law today, was expressed as follows by Lord Hale in his *Pleas of the Crown*, Vol 1, 51:

> ... but if he cannot otherwise save his own life, the law permits him in his own defence to kill the assailant; for by the violence of the assault, and the offence committed upon him by the assailant himself, the law of nature and necessity hath made him his own *protector cum debito moderamine inculpatae tutelae* as shall be further shewed, when we come to the chapter of homicide *se defendendo*.

Later in the same volume Hale identifies two kinds of necessity which justify homicide: necessity which is of a private nature, and the necessity which relates to the public justice and safety (with which we are not here concerned). He added (at p 478):

> The former is that necessity which obligeth a man to his own defence and safeguard, and this takes in these enquiries: (1) What may be done for the safeguard of a man's life ... As touching the first of these, viz homicide in defence of a man's own life, which is usually called *se defendendo* ... Homicide *se defendendo* is the killing of another person in the necessary defence of himself against him that assaults him.

Blackstone, in Volume IV of his *Commentaries on the Laws of England*, had recourse to the law of nature as the source of a person's authority to use proportionate force in self-defence, saying at p 30: 'In such a case [*viz* a violent assault] he is permitted to kill the assailant, for there the law of nature, and self-defence its primary canon, have made him his own protector.'

During the seventeenth century there were suggestions that the right of self-preservation extended beyond the right to use appropriate force in self-defence. Thus in his *Elements of the Common Laws of England* (1630) Lord Bacon wrote:

> Necessity is of three sorts – necessity of conservation of life, necessity of obedience, and necessity of the act of God or of a stranger. First, of conservation of life; if a man steal viands to satisfy his present hunger this is no felony nor larceny. So if divers be in danger of drowning by the casting away of some boat or barge, and one of them get to some plank, or on the boat's side to keep himself above water, and another to save his life thrust him from it, whereby he is drowned, this is neither *se defendendo* nor by misadventure, but justifiable.

Similar sentiments appear in Thomas Hobbes's *Leviathan* at p 157:

If a man by the terror of present death, be compelled to doe a fact against the Law, he is totally Excused, because no Law can oblige a man to abandon his own preservation. And supposing such a Law were obligatory; yet a man would reason thus, if I doe it not, I die presently; if I doe it, I die afterwards; therefore by doing it, there is time of life gained; Nature therefore compels him to the fact. When a man is destitute of food, or other thing necessary for his life, and cannot preserve himselfe any other way, but by some fact against the law; as if in a great famine he take the food by force, or stealth, which he cannot obtaine for mony nor charity; or in defence of his life, snatch away another mans Sword, he is totally Excused, for the reason next before alledged.

Both these extensions of the doctrine of necessity have been authoritatively disapproved as propositions of English law. For the disapproval of the idea that in order to save himself a man is entitled to deprive another of the place of safety he has already secured for himself, see *R v Dudley and Stephens* ... *per* Lord Coleridge CJ ... and *R v Howe* ... For the equally strong disapproval of the idea that if a starving beggar takes the law into his own hands and steals food he is not guilty of theft, see *Southwark LBC v Williams* [1971] 1 Ch 734 *per* Lord Denning MR at pp 743H–D and Edmund-Davies LJ at pp 745E–746C ... *R v Dudley and Stephens* ... has sometimes been taken as authority for the proposition that necessity can never under any circumstances provide a legal justification for murder. While it is true that a passage in the speech of Lord Hailsham in *R v Howe* [1987] 1 AC 417 at p 429C–D might be interpreted to this effect, in my judgment neither that passage nor a similar passage in Lord Mackay of Clashfern's speech at p 453 C–D displays any evidence that they had in mind a situation in which a court was invited to sanction a defence (or justification) of necessity on facts comparable to those with which we are confronted in the present case. I accept Miss Davies's submission that *R v Dudley and Stephens*, endorsed though it was by the House of Lords in *R v Howe*, is not conclusive of the matter.

Necessity: the recent studies by the Law Commission

We have also been shown how the Law Commission tackled this troublesome doctrine in the criminal law between 1974 and 1993. In 1974 a very experienced Working Party was brave enough to recommend codified proposals for a general defence of necessity (Law Commission Working Paper No 55, pp 38–39). Three years later the Commission itself retreated so far from this proposition that it recommended that there should be no general defence of necessity in any new Code, and that if any such general defence existed at common law it should be abolished (Law Com No 83 (1977), p 54). It felt that it would be much better if Parliament continued to create special defences of necessity, when appropriate. Because euthanasia was so controversial, and because the Criminal Law Revision Committee was engaged in work on offences against the person, the Commission thought it better to leave to that committee any questions relating to the provision of a defence in that area of the law.

This retreat, influenced by the responses it had received on consultation, particularly from practitioners (see pp 24–25), evoked a storm of protest from academic commentators (see, for instance, the articles entitled 'Necessity' by Glanville Williams [1978] Crim LR 12 and 'Proposals and counter proposals on the defence of necessity' by PHJ Huxley [1978] Crim LR 141, and the powerful criticism (to the effect that the proposals represented 'the apotheosis of absurdity') by Sir Rupert Cross in a Canadian university law journal cited by Professor Glanville Williams in a footnote on p 202 of the 2nd edn of his *Textbook on Criminal Law* (1983)).

Professor Williams returned to the topic of necessity in Chapter 26 of that book. He observed at p 602 that the main difficulty felt by the Law Commission appeared to have been in respect of certain 'human rights', whereas the doctrine of necessity was an expression of the philosophy of utilitarianism. He referred, however, to a suggestion by an American writer, Paul Robinson, to the effect that the recognition of important values did not entirely exclude a defence of necessity. In the determination of cases where those values did not appear, their existence could not affect the outcome, and even where they did appear, they could be given special weight in estimating the balance of interests.

In his powerful Section 26.3 ('Necessity as a reason for killing') Professor Williams addressed the issues with which we are confronted in this case. He began his treatment of the subject by saying that many people believed in the sanctity of life, and consequently believed that killing was absolutely wrong. It was for this reason, he said, that the defence of necessity, if allowed at all, was given very narrow scope in this area. He distinguished private defence from necessity (although the two overlapped) on the grounds that (unlike necessity) private defence involved no balancing of values, while on the other hand private defence operated only against aggressors (who, with rare exceptions, were wrongdoers) whereas the persons against whom action was taken by necessity might not be aggressors or wrongdoers. In this context, he mentioned *R v Bourne* [1939] 1 KB 687 (where Macnaghten J had suggested in his summing up that there might be a duty in certain circumstances to abort an unborn child to save the life of the mother), as an example of the defence of necessity, even though it was a case not of homicide but of feticide.

Professor Williams came to the heart of the matter at p 604:

Might this defence apply where a parent has killed his grossly malformed infant? Doubtless not. It may of course be argued that the value of such an infant's life, even to himself, is minimal or negative, and that if parents are obliged to rear him they may be disabled from having another and normal child. But it is not a case for applying the doctrine of necessity as usually understood. The child when born, unlike the fetus, is regarded as having absolute rights. Besides, there is no emergency. The usual view is that necessity is no defence to a charge of murder. This, if accepted, is a non-utilitarian doctrine; but in the case of a serious emergency is it wholly acceptable? If you are roped to a climber who has fallen, and neither of you can rectify the situation, it may not be very glorious on your part to cut the rope, but is it wrong? Is it not socially desirable that one life, at least, should be saved? Again, if you are flying an aircraft and the engine dies on you, it would not be wrong, but would be praiseworthy, to choose to come down in a street (where you can see you will kill or injure a few pedestrians), rather than in a crowded sports stadium. But in the case of cutting the rope you are only freeing yourself from someone who is, however involuntarily, dragging you to your death. And in the case of the aircraft you do not want to kill anyone; you simply minimise the slaughter that you are bound to do one way or the other. The question is whether you could deliberately kill someone for calculating reasons. We do regard the right to life as almost a supreme value, and it is very unlikely that anyone would be held to be justified in killing for any purpose except the saving of other life, or perhaps the saving of great pain or distress. Our revulsion against a deliberate killing is so strong that we are loth to consider utilitarian reasons for it. But a compelling case of justification of this kind is the action of a ship's captain in a wreck. He can determine who are to enter the first lifeboat; he can forbid overcrowding; and it makes no difference that those who are not allowed to enter the lifeboat will inevitably perish with the ship. The captain, in choosing who are to live, is not guilty of killing those who remain. He would not be guilty even though he kept some of the passengers back from the boat at revolver-point, and he would not be guilty even though he had to fire the revolver.

His Lordship went to consider the current recommendations of the Law Commission, contained in the Report *Offences Against the Person and General Principles* (Law Com 218, 1993), extracted below. He then turned to examine the work of academic writers on this topic.

> Those who prepared [Law Com 218] would have been familiar with a modern update of the 'two men on a plank' dilemma (which dates back to Cicero, *de Officiis*) and the 'two mountaineers on a rope' dilemma which was mentioned by Professor John Smith in his 1989 Hamlyn Lectures (published under the title *Justification and Excuse in the Criminal Law*). At the coroner's inquest conducted in October 1987 into the Zeebrugge disaster, an army corporal gave evidence that he and dozens of other people were near the foot of a rope ladder. They were all in the water and in danger of drowning. Their route to safety, however, was blocked for at least ten minutes by a young man who was petrified by cold or fear (or both) and was unable to move up or down. Eventually the corporal gave instructions that the man should be pushed off the ladder, and he was never seen again. The corporal and many others were then able to climb up the ladder to safety.

> In his third lecture, *Necessity and Duress*, Professor Smith evinced the belief at pp 77–78 that if such a case ever did come to court it would not be too difficult for a judge to distinguish *R v Dudley and Stephens*. He gave two reasons for this belief. The first was that there was no question of choosing who had to die (the problem which Lord Coleridge had found unanswerable in *R v Dudley and Stephens* at p 287) because the unfortunate young man on the ladder had chosen himself by his immobility there. The second was that unlike the ship's boy on the *Mignonette*, the young man, although in no way at fault, was preventing others from going where they had a right, and a most urgent need, to go, and was thereby unwittingly imperilling their lives.

> I would add that the same considerations would apply if a pilotless aircraft, out of control and running out of fuel, was heading for a densely populated town. Those inside the aircraft were in any event 'destined to die'. There would be no question of human choice in selecting the candidates for death, and if their inevitable deaths were accelerated by the plane being brought down on waste ground, the lives of countless other innocent people in the town they were approaching would be saved.

> It was an argument along these lines that led the rabbinical scholars involved in the 1977 case of conjoined twins to advise the worried parents that the sacrifice of one of their children in order to save the other could be morally justified. George J

Annas, *Siamese Twins: Killing One to Save the Other* (Hastings Center Report, April 1987 at p 27), described how they:

> ... reportedly relied primarily on two analogies. In the first, two men jump from a burning aeroplane. The parachute of the second man does not open, and as he falls past the first man, he grabs his legs. If the parachute cannot support them both, is the first man morally justified in kicking the second man away to save himself? Yes, said the rabbis, since the man whose parachute didn't open was 'designated for death'. The second analogy involves a caravan surrounded by bandits. The bandits demand a particular member of the caravan be turned over for execution; the rest will go free. Assuming that the named individual has been 'designated for death', the rabbis concluded it was acceptable to surrender him to save everyone else. Accordingly, they concluded that if a twin A was 'designated for death' and could not survive in any event, but twin B could, surgery that would kill twin A to help improve the chance of twin B was acceptable.

There is, however, no indication in the submission we received from the Archbishop of Westminster that such a solution was acceptable as part of the philosophy he espoused. The judge's dilemma in a case where he or she is confronted by a choice between conflicting philosophies was thoughtfully discussed by Simon Gardner in his article 'Necessity's newest inventions' (Oxford Journal of Legal Studies, Vol II, 125–35). He explored the possibility of rights-based justifications based on a principle that otherwise unlawful actions might be justified where the infraction was calculated to vindicate a right superior to the interest protected by the rule, but he was perplexed by the idea that judges in a democracy could make their own decisions as to what was right and what was wrong in the face of established law prohibiting the conduct in question. The whole article requires careful study, but its author concluded that in jurisdictions where rights were guaranteed, the judicial vindication of a guaranteed right would be seen as protecting democracy rather than contravening it. This consideration does not, however, assist us in a case where there are conflicting rights of apparently equal status and conflicting philosophies as to the priority, if any, to be given to either.

Before I leave the treatment afforded to the topic of necessity by modern academic writers of great distinction (there is a valuable contemporary summary of the issues in the Ninth Edition of Smith and Hogan's *Criminal Law* (1999) at pp 245–52), I must mention the section entitled 'Justifications, necessity and the choice of evils' in the 3rd edn (1999) of *Principles of Criminal Law* by Professor Andrew Ashworth. After referring to the facts of the Zeebrugge incident he said at pp 153–54:

> No English court has had to consider this situation, and it is clear that only the strongest prohibition on the taking of an innocent life would prevent a finding of justification here: in an urgent situation involving a decision between n lives and n + 1 lives, is there not a strong social interest in preserving the greater number of lives? Any residual principle of this kind must be carefully circumscribed; it involves the sanctity of life, and therefore the highest value with which the criminal law is concerned. Although there is a provision in the Model Penal Code allowing for a defence of 'lesser evil', it fails to restrict the application of the defence to cases of imminent threat, opening up the danger

of citizens trying to justify all manner of conduct by reference to overall good effects. The moral issues are acute: 'not just anything is permissible on the ground that it would yield a net saving of lives'. Closely connected with this is the moral problem of 'choosing one's victim', a problem which arises when, for example, a lifeboat is in danger of sinking, necessitating the throwing overboard of some passengers, or when two people have to kill and eat another if any of the three is to survive. To countenance a legal justification in such cases would be to regard the victim's rights as morally and politically less worthy than the rights of those protected by the action taken, which represents a clear violation of the principle of individual autonomy. Yet it is surely necessary to make some sacrifice, since the autonomy of everyone simply cannot be protected. A dire choice has to be made, and it must be made on a principle of welfare or community that requires the minimisation of overall harm. A fair procedure for resolving the problem – perhaps the drawing of lots – must be found. But here, as with self-defence and the 'uplifted knife' cases, one should not obscure the clearer cases where there is no need to choose a victim: in the case of the young man on the rope-ladder, blocking the escape of several others, there was no doubt about the person who must be subjected to force, probably with fatal consequences.

Necessity: the work of Parliament

I turn now from twentieth century academic writing and the work of the Law Commission and its specialist working parties to consider the way in which Parliament and the courts have addressed these issues.

So far as I am aware, Parliament has never even debated these issues in a general sense, in spite of the recommendations of the Law Commission and the increasingly insistent pleas for Parliamentary assistance which have been made by senior judges in the context of the rapidly developing new defence of 'duress of circumstances'. Parliament has, however, to an increasing extent included 'necessity' defences or justifications in modern offence-creating statutes, and where such provisions are present the Parliamentary intention is clear. In 1974 the Law Commission's Working Party identified such provisions in the Infant Life Preservation Act 1929 s 1(1), the Education Act 1944 s 39(2)(a), the Fire Services Act 1947 s 30(1), the Road Traffic (Regulation) Act 1967 s 79, the Abortion Act 1967 s 1(1) and the Road Traffic Act 1972 s 36(3). The Criminal Damage Act 1971 s 5(2)(b) provides another example from that period, and this statutory process has continued up to the present day, although, as is common with piecemeal law reform, the defences are not always framed along the same lines.

The Abortion Act provides a particularly good example of this process at work, expanding and clarifying the law for the benefit of the courts and for everyone else who, for whatever reason, needs to have recourse to the law in this controversial area. Before its enactment Macnaghten J in the case of *R v Bourne* derived a 'necessity' defence out of the word 'unlawfully' in Section 58 of the Offences against the Person Act 1861 ('Any person who unlawfully uses an instrument with intent to procure a miscarriage shall be guilty of felony'). Macnaghten J said at p 691 that he thought that the word 'unlawfully' imported the meaning expressed by the proviso in s 1(1) of the Infant Life Preservation Act 1929 ('Provided that no person shall be guilty of an offence under this section unless it is proved that the act which caused the death of the child was not done in good faith for the purpose only of preserving the life of the mother'). He went on to direct the jury at p 693:

> In such a case where a doctor anticipates, basing his opinion upon the experience of the profession, that the child cannot be delivered without the death of the mother, it is obvious that the sooner the operation is performed the better. The law does not require the doctor to wait until the unfortunate woman is in peril of immediate death. In such a case he is not only entitled, but it is his duty to perform the operation with a view to saving her life.

That, as I have observed earlier, was the common law defence of necessity at work when a judge was interpreting what he believed Parliament must have meant when it used the word 'unlawfully' in a codifying statute. Parliament's current intentions in this field are now clearly set out in the substituted Section 1(1) of the Abortion Act 1967. It would of course be very helpful, once Parliament has had the opportunity of considering the implications of the judgments in the present case, if it would provide similar assistance to the courts and to all other interested parties (and in particular parents and medical practitioners) as to what is legally permissible and what is not legally permissible in the context of separation surgery on conjoined twins. Parliament would of course now have to take account of the relevant provisions of the European Convention of Human Rights when formulating any new legislation.

Necessity: the courts and the defence of duress of circumstances

In addition to the major work that has been undertaken by Parliament in creating statutory excuses or justifications for what would otherwise be unlawful, the courts have also been busy in this field, at all events in those cases where a defendant maintains that he/she was irresistibly constrained by threats or external circumstances to do what he/she did.

So far as duress by threats is concerned, it was common ground between counsel that the solution to the present case is not to be found in the caselaw on that topic ... The work of academic writers and of the Law Commission has, however, led to one significant development in the common law. This lies in the newly identified defence of 'duress of circumstances'. The modern development of this defence began in the field of driving offences.

In *R v Kitson* (1955) 39 Cr App R 66 the defendant, who had had a lot to drink, went to sleep in the passenger seat of a car driven by his brother-in-law. When later charged with driving car under the influence of drink, he said in his defence that when he woke up, he found that the driving seat was empty, and the car was moving down a hill with the hand brake off. He managed to steer the car into a grass verge at the bottom of the hill. He was convicted of driving a car under the influence of drink, and when the Court of Criminal Appeal dismissed his appeal on the basis that the ingredients of the offence were made out, and he had undoubtedly been driving the car within the meaning of the Act, nobody suggested that he was entitled to rely on a defence of necessity or duress of circumstances.

Thirty years later, this potential line of defence first saw the light of day in *R v Willer* ... A similar issue arose in *R v Conway* [1989] QB 290, another case of reckless driving ... [Brooke LJ referred to *R v Martin, R v Pommell,* and *R v Abdul-Hussain* ... and continued]... I mention these ... to show that the Court of Appeal is now willing to entertain the possibility of a defence of duress even in a case as extreme as this if it is arguable that 'the will of the accused has been overborne by threats of death or serious personal injury so that the commission of the alleged defence was no longer [his] voluntary act' (see *R v Hudson* [1971] 2 QB 202 *per* Lord Parker CJ at p 206E). The defence is available on the basis that if it is established, the relevant actors have in effect been compelled to act as they did by the pressure of the threats or other circumstances of imminent peril to which they were subject, and it was the impact of that pressure on their freedom to choose their course of action that suffices to excuse them from criminal liability.

I have described how in modern times Parliament has sometimes provided 'necessity' defences in statutes and how the courts in developing the defence of duress of circumstances have sometimes equated it with the defence of necessity. They do not, however, cover exactly the same ground. In cases of pure necessity the actor's mind is not irresistibly overborne by external pressures. The claim is that his or her conduct was not harmful because on a choice of two evils the choice of avoiding the greater harm was justified.

Necessity: a Canadian perspective

In his judgment in *R v Pommell* Kennedy LJ cited an extract from the judgment of Dickson J, with which three other members of the Canadian Supreme Court agreed, in *Perka v R* 13 DLR (4th) 1. In that case a ship bound on a voyage between Columbia and Alaska was driven by mechanical breakdowns and deteriorating weather to seek refuge on the west coast of Vancouver Island. Canadian police officers boarded the ship and seized over 33 tons of cannabis marijuana, which would not have come within the jurisdiction of the Canadian courts but for the emergencies which forced the ship to seek shelter in Canadian waters.

It was not in issue in that case that necessity was a common law defence, since it was expressly preserved by section 7(3) of the Canadian Criminal Code. What was in issue was whether it was available to the defendants on the facts. Dickson J held that although the residual defence of necessity could not be conceptualised as a justification for wrong-doing, it might properly be identified as an excuse where someone does a wrongful act under pressure which, in the words of Aristotle's *Nichomachean Ethics*, 'overstrains human nature and which no one could withstand'. He was therefore concerned with that type of necessity which in modern English law would be characterised as 'duress of circumstances'.

In her judgment Wilson J cavilled at Dickson J's conclusion that the appropriate jurisdictional basis on which to premise the defence of necessity was exclusively that of excuse. She was firmly of the view that a door should be left open, in an appropriate case, for justification to be adopted as the jurisdictional basis of the defence. She said that an act might be said to be justified where an essential element of the offence was absent, whereas an act might be excused if all the elements of the offence were present but the jury was requested to exercise compassion for the accused's predicament in its evaluation of his claim that 'I could not help myself'. In making this distinction Wilson J drew on the recent writings of Professor GR Fletcher ('The individualisation of excusing conditions' 47 (1974) So Cal LR 1264 at 1269). She referred to some American cases as illustrations of situations where someone's criminally wrongful act was treated as 'normatively involuntary', and therefore blameless, in the particular circumstances in which he or she was situated.

She could see no reason why a court should not regard an act as justified on the grounds of necessity if it could say that the act was not only a necessary one but that it was also rightful rather than wrongful. She did not think that the fact that one act was done out of a sense of immediacy or urgency and another after some contemplation could serve to distinguish its quality in terms or right or wrong. Instead, she considered that any justification of a wrongful act must be premised on the need to fulfil a legal duty which was in conflict with the duty which the accused was charged with having breached. She gave two Canadian cases as examples. In *R v Walker* (1973) 48 CCC (2d) 126, it was held to be legitimate to break the law where it had been necessary to rescue someone to whom one owed a positive duty of rescue (because failure to act in such a situation might itself constitute a culpable act or omission: see *R v Instan* [1893] 1 QB 450). In *Morgentaler v R* [1976] 1 SCR 616 Laskin CJC (taking forward the thinking of Macnaghten J in *R v Bourne*) perceived a doctor's defence to an abortion charge as his legal duty to treat the mother rather than his alleged ethical duty to perform as unauthorised abortion.

At p 36 Wilson J said:

> ... [W]here necessity is involved as a justification for violation of the law, the justification must, in my view, be restricted to situations where the accused's act constitutes the discharge of a duty recognised by law. The justification is not, however, established simply by showing a conflict of legal duties. The rule of proportionality is central to the evaluation of a justification premised on two conflicting duties since the defence rests on the rightfulness of the accused's choice of one over the other.

She made it reasonably clear, however, that she could not conceive of any circumstances in which this application of the doctrine of necessity could be extended to provide justification of an act of homicide. Her recourse to the principle of the universality of rights showed that she envisaged that everyone was of equal standing in relation to their right to life. For this reason she went on to say at p 36:

> The assessment cannot entail a mere utilitarian calculation of, for example, lives saved and deaths avoided in the aggregate, but must somehow attempt to come to grips with the nature of the rights and duties being assessed. This would seem to be consistent with Lord Coleridge's conclusion that necessity can provide no justification for the taking of a life, such an act representing the most extreme form of rights violation. As discussed above, if any defence for such a homicidal act is to succeed, it would have to be framed as an excuse grounded on self-preservation. It could not possibly be declared by the court to be rightful.

I found this a valuable way of forcing us to think more clearly about the reasons why it is ever permissible to admit a defence drawn from what Lord Hailsham would describe as the genus of necessity as a means of establishing that a defendant is not in law guilty of a crime even though the requirements of *mens rea* (a guilty mind) and *actus reus* (a guilty act) appear to be satisfied. In the last resort, however, it does not provide the solutions we are seeking in the present case for three reasons. The first reason is that English criminal law does not make any clear-cut distinction between a justification and an excuse. As Professor John Smith said at p 12 of his first Hamlyn lecture in 1989,

Whether the act is one which society wants to be done, or merely tolerates, is a question which is not easy to answer if society has not expressed its wishes in the form of legislation or judicial decision. Not unnaturally there is a disagreement between the theorists. So far as the successful defendant is concerned, it matters not in the least whether the court, or anyone else, says that he is justified or merely excused; he is simply found not guilty in either event.

Secondly, as he points out at p 18 of that lecture, the distinction between those who save others out of a legal duty and those who do the same act for reasons which cannot be so characterised is not always very easy to sustain. Thirdly, Wilson J made it clear that she did not regard the analysis as available when someone's right to life was in question ...

... I have considered very carefully the policy reasons for the decision in *R v Dudley and Stephens*, supported as it was by the House of Lords in *R v Howe*. These are, in short, that there were two insuperable objections to the proposition that necessity might be available as a defence for the *Mignonette* sailors. The first objection was evident in the court's questions: Who is to be the judge of this sort of necessity? By what measure is the comparative value of lives to be measured? The second objection was that to permit such a defence would mark an absolute divorce of law from morality.

In my judgment, neither of these objections are dispositive of the present case. Mary is, sadly, self-designated for a very early death. Nobody can extend her life beyond a very short span. Because her heart, brain and lungs are for all practical purposes useless, nobody would have even tried to extend her life artificially if she had not, fortuitously, been deriving oxygenated blood from her sister's bloodstream.

It is true that there are those who believe most sincerely – and the Archbishop of Westminster is among them – that it would be an immoral act to save Jodie, if by saving Jodie one must end Mary's life before its brief allotted span is complete. For those who share this philosophy, the law, recently approved by Parliament, which permits abortion at any time up to the time of birth if the conditions set out in s 1(1)(d) of the Abortion Act 1967 (as substituted) are satisfied, is equally repugnant. But there are also those who believe with equal sincerity that it would be immoral not to assist Jodie if there is a good prospect that she might live a happy and fulfilled life if this operation is performed. The court is not equipped to choose between these competing philosophies. All that a court can say is that it is not at all obvious that this is the sort of clear-cut case, marking an absolute divorce from law and morality, which was of such concern to Lord Coleridge and his fellow judges.

There are sound reasons for holding that the existence of an emergency in the normal sense of the word is not an essential prerequisite for the application of the doctrine of necessity. The principle is one of necessity, not emergency: see Lord Goff (in *In Re F* at p 75D), the Law Commission in its recent report (Law Com No 218, paras 35.5–35.6), and Wilson J in *Perka* (at p 33).

There are also sound reasons for holding that the threat which constitutes the harm to be avoided does not have to be equated with 'unjust aggression', as Professor Glanville Williams has made clear in Section 26.3 of the 1983 edition of his book. None of the formulations of the doctrine of necessity which I have noted in this judgment make any such requirement: in this respect it is different from the doctrine of private defence.

If a sacrificial separation operation on conjoined twins were to be permitted in circumstances like these, there need be no room for the concern felt by Sir James Stephen that people would be too ready to avail themselves of exceptions to the law which they might suppose to apply to their cases (at the risk of other people's lives). Such an operation is, and is always likely to be, an exceptionally rare event, and because the medical literature shows that it is an operation to be avoided at all costs in the neonatal stage, there will be in practically every case the opportunity for the doctors to place the relevant facts before a court for approval (or otherwise) before the operation is attempted.

According to Sir James Stephen, there are three necessary requirements for the application of the doctrine of necessity: (i) the act is needed to avoid inevitable and irreparable evil; (ii) no more should be done than is reasonably necessary for the purpose to be achieved; (iii) the evil inflicted must not be disproportionate to the evil avoided.

Given that the principles of modern family law point irresistibly to the conclusion that the interests of Jodie must be preferred to the conflicting interests of Mary, I consider that all three of these requirements are satisfied in this case.

Finally, the doctrine of the sanctity of life respects the integrity of the human body. The proposed operation would give these children's bodies the integrity which nature denied them. For these reasons I, too, would dismiss this appeal.

Robert Walker LJ: The House of Lords has made clear that a doctrine of necessity does form part of the common law: see *Re F (Mental Patient: Sterilisation)* [1990] 2 AC 1 (especially in the speech of Lord Goff at pp 74–78) and *R v Bournewood Community and Mental Health Trust ex p L* [1999] 1 AC 458. In the latter case Lord Goff said (at p 490):

> The concept of necessity has its role to play in all branches of our law of obligations – in contract (see the cases on agency of necessity), in tort (see *In Re F (Mental Patient: Sterilisation)* [1990] 2 AC 1), and in restitution (see the sections on necessity in the standard books on the subject) and in our criminal law. It is therefore a concept of great importance. It is perhaps surprising, however, that the significant role it has to play in the law of torts has come to be recognised at so late a stage in the development of our law.

... Duress of circumstances can therefore be seen as a third or residual category of necessity, along with self-defence and duress by threats. I do not think it matters whether these defences are regarded as justifications or excuses. Whatever label is used, the moral merits of the defence will vary with the circumstances. The important issue is whether duress of circumstances can ever be a defence to a charge of murder ...

The special features of this case are that the doctors do have duties to their two patients, that it is impossible for them to undertake any relevant surgery affecting one twin without also affecting the other, and that the evidence indicates that both twins will die in a matter of months if nothing is done. Whether or not that is aptly described as duress of circumstances, it is a situation in which surgical intervention is a necessity if either life is to be saved.

I do not find any clear principle in *R v Howe*, *R v Gotts* or *R v Abdul-Hussain* which applies to the clinical dilemma which faces the doctors in this case. Like the other members of the court I have derived assistance from the minority judgment of Wilson J given in the Supreme Court of Canada in the case of *Perka and Other v R* ...

Wilson J's reference to a conflict of duties in relation to abortion must be treated with caution because of the well-established rule that English law (like Canadian law, but here differing markedly from the teaching of the Roman Catholic church) does not regard even a viable full-term fetus as a human being until fully delivered: see the account in *Rance v Mid-Downs HA* [1991] 1 QB 587, 617–23 to which I have already referred, and also *St George's Healthcare NHS Trust v S* [1999] Fam 26, 45–50. There is in law no real analogy between Mary's dependence on Jodie's body for her continued life, and the dependence of an unborn fetus on its mother.

In truth there is no helpful analogy or parallel to the situation which the court has to consider in this case. It is unprecedented and paradoxical in that in law each twin has the right to life, but Mary's dependence on Jodie is severely detrimental to Jodie, and is expected to lead to the death of both twins within a few months. Each twin's right to life includes the right to physical integrity, that is the right to a whole body over which the individual will, on reaching an age of understanding, have autonomy and the right to self-determination: see the citations from *Bland* collected in the *St George's Healthcare* case at pp 43–45.

In the absence of Parliamentary intervention the law as to the defence of necessity is going to have to develop on a case by case basis, as Rose LJ said in *R v Abdul-Hussain*. I would extend it, if it needs to be extended, to cover this case. It is a case of doctors owing conflicting legal (and not merely social or moral) duties. It is a case where the test of proportionality is met, since it is a matter of life and death, and on the evidence Mary is bound to die soon in any event. It is not a case of evaluating the relative worth of two human lives, but of undertaking surgery without which neither life will have the bodily integrity (or wholeness) which is its due. It should not be regarded as a further step down a slippery slope because the case of conjoined twins presents an unique problem.

There is on the facts of this case some element of protecting Jodie against the unnatural invasion of her body through the physical burden imposed by her conjoined twin. That element must not be overstated. It would be absurd to suggest that Mary, a pitiful and innocent baby, is an unjust aggressor. Such language would be even less acceptable than dismissing Mary's death as a 'side-effect'. Nevertheless, the doctors' duty to protect and save Jodie's life if they can is of fundamental importance to the resolution of this appeal.

CODIFICATION AND LAW REFORM PROPOSALS

The current views of the Law Commission are contained in *Offences Against the Person and General Principles* (Law Com 218, 1993). The draft Criminal Law Bill attached to the Report provides as follows:

Duress by threats: clause 25

25(1) No act of a person constitutes an offence if the act is done under duress by ... threats.

(2) A person does an act under duress by threats if he does it because he knows or believes –

   (a)   that a threat has been made to cause death or serious injury to himself or another if the act is not done, and

   (b)   that the threat will be carried out immediately if he does not do the act or, if not immediately, before he or that other can obtain official protection; and

   (c)   that there is no other way of preventing the threat being carried out,

   and the threat is one which in all the circumstances (including any of his personal circumstances that affect its gravity) he cannot reasonably be expected to resist.

   It is for the defendant to show that the reasons for his act was such knowledge or belief as is mentioned in paragraphs (a) to (c).

(3) This section applied in relation to omissions as it applies in relation to acts.

(4) This section does not apply to a person who knowingly and without reasonable excuse exposed himself to ... the risk of the threat made or believed to have been made.

   If the question arises whether a person knowingly and without reasonable excuse exposed himself to such a risk, it is for him to show that he did not.

The commentary in Law Com 218 is as follows:

The proposed defence

The threat

29.1   As we said at paragraph 18.5 of LCCP 122, the overwhelming tendency of the authorities as of modern codes, is to limit the defence [of duress by threats] to cases where death or serious injury is threatened ... Consultation strongly supported that limitation on the defence of duress, which is imposed by clause 25(2)(a) of the Criminal Law Bill.

The person threatened

29.2   There was very limited support for any formal limitation of the defence to cases in which the threat is to a limited class of person, such as the defendant's close relatives. We adhere to the view that the relevance of the closeness or otherwise of the relationship between the defendant and the person threatened is more appropriately catered for within the general test imposed by clause 25(2) of the Criminal Law Bill of whether 'the threat is one which in all the circumstances (including any of his personal characteristics that affect its gravity) he cannot reasonably be expected to resist'.

The possibility of official protection

29.3   The threat must be, or the defendant must believe that it is, one that will be carried out immediately, or before he (or the person under threat) can obtain official protection: Criminal Law Bill, clause 25(2)(b). This provision, by allowing the defence if the defendant believes that official protection will be ineffective, differs from previous treatments of the point.

29.4 Clause 26(3) of the Bill accompanying LCCP 122 provided that it would be immaterial that, in fact or as the actor believed, any available official protection would, or might be, ineffective ...

29.6 ... On careful re-examination, we are quite persuaded that no such provision as clause 26(3) should be retained. We would regard it as wholly unsatisfactory if a defendant who in every other respect qualified for the defence were to have it withheld because ineffective official protection was available, or because he or she had acted on the basis of an honest belief that such protection would be ineffective. The case of a wife committing perjury because subjected to duress by her husband, cited by one respondent in the context of *Hudson* is an obvious example of a case in which theoretical but not actual official protection might be available,

29.7 We have therefore removed clause 26(3) as inconsistent with the general approach of the rest of the defence, which has as its guiding principle the reasonable reaction of the defendant in the circumstances as he or she believed them to be. Clause 25(2)(b) of the Criminal Law Bill puts the matter beyond doubt by its reference to 'effective' official protection.

The actor's view of the facts

29.8 The emphasis in clause 26(2)(a) of the Bill accompanying LCCP 122 on the actor's *knowledge or belief* that a threat has been made reflected this latter aspect of the defence of duress. The actor is excused because he acted under the pressure of a threat. It is plainly not enough that a threat has been made, for example, to kill his child: he must know that it has been made. But the defence ought therefore equally to be available if the actor mistakenly believes the facts to be such that, were his belief correct, he would have the defence [see now *R v Martin* extracted above].

...

Is the threat one which the actor should resist?

29.11 Under present law, a threat of death or serious injury excuses the actor whose resistance it overcomes only if the threat might have overcome the resistance of 'a sober person of reasonable firmness, sharing the characteristics of the [actor]'. The actor is required to have 'the steadfastness reasonably to be expected of the ordinary citizen in his situation'. In paragraph 18.10 of LCCP 122 we invited views on the question whether this requirement of 'reasonable firmness' or 'steadfastness' should be maintained.

29.12 We quoted from our 1977 report that: 'Threats directed against a weak, immature or disabled person may well be much more compelling than the same threats directed against a normal healthy person'. The Court of Appeal in *Graham* accepted this approach in part when stating that the resistance to be expected was that of one 'sharing the characteristics of the defendant'. But the court added the requirement that the resistance match that of 'a sober person of reasonable firmness', seeking in this way to 'limit the defence ... by means of an objective criterion formulated in terms of reasonableness'. In LCCP 122 we continued to think, however, that the test should simply be whether in all the circumstances the person in question could reasonably be expected to have resisted the threat. We assumed that a person could not under this test rely upon his insobriety as a relevant circumstance; but at the same time, we were not convinced that a person's 'characteristics' can be distinguished in the way that the *Graham* test appears to contemplate. Relative timidity, for example, may be an inseparable aspect of a total personality that is in turn part cause and part product of its possessor's life situation; and thus may itself be one of the 'circumstances' in the light of which the pressure represented by the duress is to be assessed.

29.13 Clause 26(2)(b) of the Bill accompanying LCCP 122 therefore provided that the threat must be one 'which in all the circumstances (including any of his personal characteristics that affect its gravity) [the actor] cannot reasonably be expected to resist'. But since the *Graham* decision postdated our earlier consultation on this subject, we thought it right once again to seek views on this aspect of the defence.

29.14 On consultation, there was strong support for our view that the defence should apply where *the particular defendant in question* could not reasonably have been expected to resist the threat. We do not accept the contrary view, for which there was very little support, that the defence should be withheld from the 'objectively weak'. First, such an approach would be ineffectual as a means of law enforcement. If a person is in a condition that makes it unreasonable to expect him to resist, then he will not resist, and the fact that a different person in those circumstances might have resisted will not affect the matter. Second, the purpose of the defence is not to enforce unrealistically high standards of behaviour. Rather, the defence acknowledges that where the defendant could not reasonably have been expected to act otherwise he should not be convicted of a crime. Our view on this question therefore remains unchanged, as does the formulation now to be found in the closing words of clause 25(2) of the Criminal Law Bill.

...

Application of the defence to murder

...

The arguments of principle and the practical considerations

30.9 The arguments for and against extending the defence to murder appear to us to derive, some from principle, and others from concern for the practical implications of that step. We deal first with the issue of principle.

30.10 The moral argument against extending duress to murder remains that it cannot be right for the State to excuse deliberate killing even where the will of the defendant is overborne by the threat of death or serious injury to himself or another. According to this view, as reaffirmed in *Howe*, 'the special sanctity that the law attaches to human life ... denies to a man the right to take an innocent life even at the price of his own or another's life'. Rather than allow duress (or necessity) to excuse the taking of life, the law should 'set a standard of conduct which ordinary men and women are expected to observe': a standard, if necessary, of heroism and self-sacrifice, of which ordinary people are capable.

30.11 Powerful though that argument may appear to be, and deeply felt as it clearly is by a minority of those who responded to our consultation, we cannot adopt it. In our view, it is not only futile, but also wrong, for the criminal law to demand heroic behaviour. The attainment of a heroic standard of behaviour will always count for great merit; but failure to achieve that standard should not be met with punishment by the State. We emphasise that under our proposed formulation of the defence, it would only be available where, in the jury's view, the threat was such that the defendant could not reasonably have been expected to resist it. Criminal punishment, as opposed to moral exhortation, should not be used to try to achieve a standard of behaviour higher than that.

30.12 We also think it important to remember in this connection that the defence here under discussion is one of excuse and not justification. It is no part of our case for extending the defence of duress to murder to argue that deliberate killing may be, in certain circumstances, justified.

30.13 As we said in paragraph 30.7 above, we also respectfully agree with Lord Lowry's observation in *Gotts* that, since the defence of duress could arise in a case where the defendant was seeking to avoid the implementation of threats to third parties, the simple moral equation assumed by treating a defendant as one who kills to save his own life does not necessarily apply.

30.14 To the other arguments of principle for extending the defence of duress to murder, we would certainly add our rejection of the view that the absence of that defence can be sufficiently mitigated by exercise of executive discretion. We remain of the view expressed at paragraph 18.16(v) of LCCP 122, that reliance on executive discretion is not adequate in principle or in practice. Even if the prosecutor knows of a plea of duress, he may not be able, or think it proper, to judge its merits; and, apart from any other considerations, those responsible for considering a prisoner's release would have to judge his claim to have been coerced without the benefit of a proper trial of the issue.

30.15 The essence of the practical concern felt by those who oppose extension of the defence to murder was expressed by Lord Lane CJ in *Howe* and was strongly influential in the House of Lords in that case: duress is a defence most likely to arise in terrorist, gang or other organised crime offences and, particularly in such circumstances, 'the defence of duress is so easy to raise and may be so difficult for the prosecution to disprove beyond reasonable doubt, the facts of necessity being as a rule known only to the defendant himself'.

30.16 We feel the force of that concern, and did not lightly adopt the reply to it in LCCP 122 that the defence is not available to a member of a criminal or terrorist group; that the innocent tools of terrorists, on the other hand, should be excused if they could not have been expected to act otherwise; that such defendants should not be denied the right to raise a true defence because others may claim it falsely; and that the question whether the defendant was a terrorist or an innocent tool is a proper question for the jury and for the application of the normal burden of proof. On careful reconsideration, however, we think it important to separate within this reply the principle that the innocent should not be denied a true defence because others may abuse it from the view that the defendant should not bear the burden of proof. To the former principle we adhere. As to the latter question, we have already indicted our recognition that it is in the context of the extension of the defence to murder that the issue of burden of proof is most pressing. That is by no means to say that our reasons for recommending the reversal of the burden of proof should be, or are, confined to the context of murder. However, we are satisfied that the reversal of the burden of proof, together with the stringent requirements of the defence as we have formulated it, should be accepted as meeting the concerns here under discussion, in the case of murder as in the case of all other offences.

Duress as a complete defence

31.2 Leaving aside the rules that duress is not now a defence to murder or attempted murder, the arguments for reducing duress to a mitigatory factor seem to us to proceed essentially from a combination of principle and practical concern similar to that which led to the reaffirmation of those rules in *Howe* and *Gotts*. Once again, we deal first with the issue of principle.

31.3 The argument of principle against duress as a general defence also appears to us to be that the excuse afforded by it for any criminal act ought to be regarded as partial rather than complete, and that the taking of life is only the strongest and most important instance. In relation to that instance, we cited in LCCP 122 the criticism in *Howe* of the view that duress should reduce murder to manslaughter, and reaffirmed our own view of 1977 that it would be unjust for the defendant who fell within the stringent terms of our proposed defence to suffer the stigma of a conviction even for manslaughter. We think it important to bear in mind in this connection that the proposed defence would apply only where the defendant had acted because of a threat of serious injury or death which it was not reasonable for him to resist. As we have said, the view that the defendant should in these circumstances be convicted of manslaughter received little support on consultation. Not only do we adhere to our original view, but we explain in the next paragraph why we believe that the same principle applies *a fortiori* to all other offences.

31.4 We believe that if it is wrong even in respect of murder to condemn the defendant for not acting heroically rather than reasonably, it would be even more unjust to condemn defendants for lesser acts done under the same conditions. To censure and punish defendants who found themselves in such circumstances would bring the law into disrepute ... It would, in our view, be intolerable if, for instance, a wife whose husband threatened her with serious injury or death, and who as a result reasonably refused to give evidence against him, had nonetheless to be convicted of the offence of contempt.

31.5 The *practical* concerns underlying the suggestion that duress should cease to be a complete *defence might* appear to be the same as those which supported the reaffirmation by the House of Lords in *Howe* of the exclusion of that defence from the exceptional case of murder. Chief amongst those considerations, as we have seen in discussion of that question, was the view expressed by Lord Lane CJ in the Court of Appeal in that case, and which received considerable support in the House of Lords, that duress is a defence most likely to arise in terrorist, gang or other organised crime offences and, particularly in such circumstances, 'the defence of duress is so easy to raise and may be so difficult for the prosecution to disprove beyond reasonable doubt, the facts of necessity being as a rule known only to the defendant himself'. We explain below why we do not believe that it would be a rational or elective response to those considerations to treat duress as a mitigatory factor.

31.6 If, as we believe, the considerations just mentioned are of real weight, they need to be addressed by appropriate measures. As we have indicated, after careful reconsideration, we have reached the conclusion that the appropriate response, and the one which is right in principle bearing in mind the unique nature of duress, is that the defendant should bear the burden of proving that defence ... That, we suggest, is the correct approach, rather than that duress should cease to be a complete defence. We understand the concern that because allegations of duress are difficult to disprove, defendants who should not benefit from the defence may be able to do so. But if genuine duress is otherwise thought to be a proper ground for a complete defence to all offences, that conclusion should not be avoided, either in the case of murder, or in any other offence, out of the need to convict the defendant whose assertion of duress is false. The murderer who falsely asserts that he was acting under duress should be convicted of that offence and not of manslaughter. The defendant on any other charge, whose plea of duress is false, should not have his sentence reduced because of some trivial possibility that his plea might be genuine. Equally, it would not be just for the defendant who really *was acting under duress merely* to have his sentence reduced, and not acquitted altogether, for fear that the jury might be mistaken.

31.7 Further, and quite apart from compromise solutions adopted because of doubts about certainty of proof, we do not agree with the view that even *genuine duress ought* only to be a partial excuse, leading only to a reduction in sentence. Apart from its being wrong in principle, we believe this approach would be unworkable in practice. It is sometimes assumed that if the case fulfils the requirements of the defence, then no or a nominal penalty will be imposed. But judges with great experience of criminal trials have expressed scepticism that that chain of events will in fact occur. Nor, in logic, should it occur. If duress is rejected as a defence, that must be either because the defendant who acts under duress is in some way at fault, albeit only by not behaving heroically; or because there is some public policy reason for convicting him even though he is not at fault. If he is at fault, the law should mark his fault by a penalty, or at least should not assume that in no case will an effective penalty be imposed. If the reasons for rejecting duress as a defence are ones of public policy, it is hard to see that that policy is forwarded by a regime that assumes that convictions are to be purely nominal in nature; or, even more, that assumes that in some cases at least the law will not be enforced at all.

31.8 For all the reasons discussed above, we recommend, and clause 25 of the Criminal Law Bill provides, that duress by threats should remain a complete defence, and that it be extended to the case of murder.

Duress of circumstance: clause 26

26(1) No act of a person constitutes an offence if the act is done under duress of circumstances.

   (2) A person does an act under duress of circumstance if –

      (a) he does it because he knows or believes that it is immediately necessary to avoid death or serious injury to himself or another, and

(b) the danger that he knows or believes to exist is such that in all the circumstances (including any of his personal characteristics that affect its gravity) he cannot reasonably be expected to act otherwise.

It is for the defendant to show that the reason for his act was such knowledge or belief as is mentioned in paragraph (a).

(3) This section applies in relation to omissions as it applies in relation to acts.

(4) This section does not apply to a person who knowingly and without reasonable excuse exposed himself to the danger known or believed to exist.

If the question arises whether a person knowingly and without reasonable excuse exposed himself to that danger, it is for him to show that he did not.

(5) This section does not apply to –

(a) any act done in the knowledge or belief that a threat has been made to cause death or serious injury to himself or another ... or

(b) the use of force within the meaning of [clause 27 or 28] or an act immediately preparatory to the use of force, for the purposes mentioned in [clause 27 or 28].

The commentary in Law Com 218 is as follows:

DURESS OF CIRCUMSTANCES

35.1 Clause 27 of the Bill accompanying LCCP 122 provided a statutory formulation of the defence of duress of circumstances: where the accused acts to avoid an imminent danger of death or serious injury to himself or another, if in the circumstances he cannot reasonably be expected to act otherwise. LCCP 122, paragraphs 19.1–19.10, explained our approach to the clause. On consultation, we received very little adverse comment. The provision is accordingly retained as clause 26 of the Criminal Law Bill. The only change of substance reflected in that clause is the placing of the persuasive burden of proving the defence, on a balance of probabilities, on the defendant. This follows, as will be seen from the discussion in paragraphs 33.1–33.16 above, from our identical recommendation in relation to duress by threats. The following explanation of the clause is therefore substantially the same as that which appeared in LCCP 122.

The nature of the defence

Authority

35.2 Clause 27 of the Bill accompanying LCCP 122 provided a defence to one who acts to avoid an imminent danger of death or serious injury to himself or another, if in the circumstances he cannot reasonably be expected to act otherwise. The Court of Appeal has recently recognised the existence of such circumstances of defence on a number of occasions, in cases of reckless driving and of driving while disqualified. Nothing in these cases suggests that the defence is of narrower application than the defence of duress by threats. There is also impressive authority in other common law jurisdictions for a general defence.

Relation to duress by threats and to necessity

35.3 *Duress by threats.* Our inclusion of the defence of duress of circumstances in the Draft Code was based on the conviction that '[t]he impact of some situations of imminent peril upon persons affected by them is hardly different in kind from that of threats such as give rise to the defence of duress'. The effect of the situation on the actor's freedom to choose his course of action ought equally to provide him with an excuse for acting as he does. The analogy between 'threats' and other 'circumstances' promising an evil unless a crime is committed likewise influenced the Court of Appeal in naming the new defence 'duress of circumstances', and in modelling it closely upon duress by threats – by limiting the harm to be avoided to death or serious bodily harm and by adopting, with necessary modifications, the model jury direction laid down in *Graham*. Clause 26 of the Criminal Law Bill is generally designed to reflect the analogy with duress by threats.

35.4 *Necessity.* The relationship between duress and necessity is a difficult matter. Duress is sometimes spoken of as if it were a species of necessity, but the law recognises a defence of 'necessity' on a basis quite different from that which underlies the recognition of duress as a defence. The true basis of the duress defences, as we understand them, is that the actor has been in effect compelled to act as he does by the pressure of a human or other threat to which he himself is subject. It is the impact of that pressure on his freedom to choose his course of action that suffices to excuse him from criminal liability. In such cases, the threat must be such that he cannot reasonably be expected to resist it or (as it is put in clause 26 of the Criminal Law Bill in respect of duress of circumstances) to do otherwise than to commit the act that, absent the defence of duress, would be criminal. The gravity of the act committed may be relevant to the question whether the threat (death or serious injury for himself or another) understandably overcame the actor's natural reluctance to commit that act; but the defences do not depend on an objective comparison between the evil threatened and the harm committed to avoid it.

35.5 By contrast with the defences of duress just discussed, there appear to be some cases, more properly called cases of 'necessity', where the actor does not rely on any allegation that circumstances placed an irresistible pressure on him. Rather, he claims that his conduct, although falling within the definition of an offence, was not harmful because it was, in the circumstances, justified. Such claims, unlike those recognised by the duress defences, do seem to require a comparison between the harm that otherwise unlawful conduct has caused and the harm that that conduct has avoided; because if the latter harm was not regarded as the greater the law could not even consider accepting that the conduct was justified. Nor, fairly clearly, does the defence depend on any claim that the actor's will was 'overborne': on the contrary, the decision to do what, but for the exceptional circumstances, would be a criminal act may be the result of careful judgment, as in the case of the kind of professional decision referred to in the next paragraph.

35.6 Although the English courts have not expressly recognised a general doctrine of 'necessity', a case of high authority, *F v West Berkshire Health Authority*, provides an example of its operation in connection with the medical treatment of people who are unable to give a valid consent to it. In the circumstances of that case, the sterilisation of a mentally handicapped woman was held to be necessary in her own best interests. A perhaps more straightforward example is that given by Lord Goff in his judgment in the same case: 'a man who seizes another and forcibly drags him from the path of an oncoming vehicle, thereby saving him from injury or even death, commits no wrong'. In such cases there is no question of the defence depending on the actor's resistance being overcome, in the sense discussed in paragraph 29.11 above; rather, the courts decide that in all the circumstances the actor's, freely adopted, conduct was justified.

35.7 We therefore consider that, as part of the policy of retaining common law defences that we referred to in paragraphs 27.1–27.3 above, this specific defence of necessity should be kept open as something potentially separate from duress. That is provided for by clause 36(2) of the Criminal Law Bill, which expressly saves 'any distinct defence of necessity' when abrogating the common law defences of duress by threats and of circumstances.

Some details of the defence

The danger

35.8 The act done must be 'immediately necessary to avoid death or serious injury to [the actor] or another'. The act (reckless driving) in *Conway* was (allegedly) done to save the life of the defendant's passenger; in *Martin* it was claimed that the accused had to drive whilst disqualified to prevent his wife's suicide.

Other matters

35.9 As with duress by threats, the actor's knowledge of, or belief in the existence of, relevant circumstances is crucial. Consistently with that defence, the circumstances that clause 26 of the Criminal Law Bill requires to be taken into account include 'any of his personal characteristics that affect [the gravity of the danger]' (subsection (2)(b)). And a person who has voluntarily exposed himself to a danger cannot rely upon that danger as a ground of this defence (subsection (4)).

Application of the defence

35.10 As in the case of duress by threats, the balance of opinion on consultation was in favour of its application to murder. For the reasons we gave in LCCP 122, and which are repeat below, we remain of that view, and clauses 24 and 26 of the Criminal Law Bill so provide, by applying the defence to all offences.

35.11 The application of this defence to murder would in effect depart from the law as stated in *Dudley and Stephens*. ... Adoption of the clause now proposed would leave it to the jury to say whether in all the circumstances persons in the position of the defendants in *Dudley and Stephens*, assuming they believed their acts to be 'immediately necessary', could reasonably have been expected to act otherwise than as they did. This proposal would appear to stand or fall with the corresponding proposal for duress by threats: and we refer to the relevant discussion in that context.

Further reading

AWB Simpson, *Cannabilism and the Common Law*, 1984, Chicago: University of Chicago Press

A Brudner, 'A theory of necessity' (1987) 7 OJLS 338

J Horder, 'Occupying the moral high ground? The Law Commission on duress' [1994] Crim LR 334

Gardner J, 'Justifications and reasons', in AP Simester and ATH Smith (eds), *Harm and Culpability*, 1996, Oxford: OUP

KJM Smith, 'Duress and steadfastness: in pursuit of the unintelligible' [1999] Crim LR 363

Buchanan and Virgo, 'Duress and mental abnormality' [1999] Crim LR 517

CHAPTER 14

SELF-DEFENCE

At common law the scope of the defence of self-defence extends to using such force as is reasonable in the circumstances for the purposes of:

(1) self-defence;

(2) defence of another person;

(3) defence of property.

By virtue of s 3(1) of the Criminal Law Act 1967, reasonable force can also be used in the prevention of crime and in making a lawful arrest (see s 3(1) of the Criminal Law Act 1967).

Where an accused puts forward a defence, he bears what is known as an 'evidential' burden of proof in relation to it. This does *not* mean that he has to prove his defence to the satisfaction of the jury. All it means is that the accused has to adduce sufficient evidence of the defence for the judge or magistrates to decide that it is worthy of consideration. Thus, the 'legal' burden of proof is borne by the prosecution: it is for the prosecution to prove beyond reasonable doubt that the defence is negated. These rules apply whether the case is being tried in a magistrates' court or in the Crown Court. As Lord Slynn explained in *DPP (Jamaica) v Bailey* [1995] 1 Cr App R 257 (PC): '... hopeless defences which have no factual basis of support do not have to be left to the jury. But it is no less clear, in their Lordships' view, that if the accused's account of what happened includes matters which, if accepted, could raise a *prima facie* case of self-defence this should be left to the jury even if the accused has not formally relied upon self-defence.'

The concept of force is a broad one that can be left largely to the common sense of the jury – see *R v Renouf* [1986] 1 WLR 522. It can encompass threats as well as direct or indirect contact. As Milmo J observed in *R v Cousins* [1982] 1 QB 526 (CA): '... It is, of course, true that the charge against the appellant was not that he used force but that he threatened to use force. However, if force is permissible, something less, for example a threat, must also be permissible if it is reasonable in the circumstances.'

THE CONCEPT OF REASONABLE FORCE

Palmer v R [1971] AC 814 (PC)

Lord Morris of Borth-y-Gest: ... The only question that is raised for determination is whether in cases where on a charge of murder an issue of self-defence is left to the jury it will in all cases be obligatory to direct the jury that if they found that the accused while intending to defend himself had used more force than was necessary in the circumstances they should return a verdict of guilty of manslaughter ...

... Their Lordships conclude that there is no room for criticism of the summing up or of the conduct of the trial unless there is a rule that in every case where the issue of self-defence is left to the jury they must be directed that if they consider that excessive force was used in defence then they should return a verdict of guilty of manslaughter. For the reasons which they will set out, their Lordships consider that there is no such rule ...

On behalf of the appellant it was contended that if, where self-defence is an issue in a case of homicide, a jury came to the conclusion that an accused person was intending to defend himself, then an intention to kill or to cause grievous bodily harm would be negatived: so it was contended that if in such a case the jury came to the conclusion that excessive force had been used the correct verdict would be one of manslaughter: hence it was argued that in every case where self-defence is left to a jury they must be directed that there are the three possible verdicts, viz guilty of murder, guilty of manslaughter, and not guilty. But in many cases where someone is intending to defend himself he will have had an intention to cause serious bodily injury or even to kill, and if the prosecution satisfy the jury that he had one of these intentions in circumstances in which or at a time when there was no justification or excuse for having it, then the prosecution will have shown that the question of self-defence is eliminated. All other issues which on the facts may arise will be unaffected.

An issue of self-defence may of course arise in a range and variety of cases and circumstances where no death has resulted. The test as to its rejection or its validity will be just the same as in a case where death has resulted. In its simplest form the question that arises is the question: Was the defendant acting in necessary self-defence? If the prosecution satisfy the jury that he was not then all other possible issues remain ...

In their Lordships' view the defence of self-defence is one which can be and will be readily understood by any jury. It is a straightforward conception. It involves no abstruse legal thought. It required no set words by way of explanation. No formula need be employed in reference to it. Only common sense is needed for its understanding. It is both good law and good sense that a man who is attacked may defend himself. It is both good law and good sense that he may do, but may only do, what is reasonably necessary. But everything will depend upon the particular facts and circumstances. Of these a jury can decide. It may in some cases be only sensible and clearly possible to take some simple avoiding action. Some attacks may be serious and dangerous. Others may not be. If there is some relatively minor attack it would not be common sense to permit some action of retaliation which was wholly out of proportion to the necessities of the situation. If an attack is serious so that it puts someone in immediate peril then immediate defensive action may be necessary. If the moment is one of crisis for someone in imminent danger he may have to avert the danger by some instant reaction. If the attack is all over and no sort of peril remains then the employment of force may be by way of revenge or punishment or by way of paying off an old score or may be pure aggression. There may no longer be any link with a necessity of defence. Of all these matters the good sense of a jury will be the arbiter. There are no prescribed words which must be employed in or adopted in a summing up. All that is needed is a clear exposition, in relation to the particular facts of the case, of the conception of necessary self-defence. If there has been no attack then clearly there will have been no need for defence. If there has been attack so that defence is reasonably necessary it will be recognised that a person defending himself cannot weigh to a nicety the exact measure of his necessary defensive action. If a jury thought that in a moment of unexpected anguish a person attacked had only done what he honestly and instinctively thought was necessary that would be most potent evidence that only reasonable defensive action had been taken. A jury will be told that the defence of self-defence, where the evidence makes its raising possible, will only fail if the prosecution show beyond doubt that what the accused did was not by way of self-defence. But their Lordships consider, in agreement with the approach in the *De Freitas* case (1960) 2 WLR 523, that if the prosecution have shown that what was done was not done in self-defence then that issue is eliminated from the case. If the jury consider that an accused acted in self-defence or if the jury are in doubt as to this then they will acquit. The defence of self-defence either succeeds so as to result in an acquittal or it is disproved in which case as a defence it is rejected. In a homicide case the circumstances may be such that it will become an issue as to whether there was provocation so that the verdict might be one of manslaughter. Any other possible issues will remain. If in any case the view is possible that the intent necessary to constitute the crime of murder was lacking then that matter would be left to the jury ...

R v Shannon (1980) 71 Cr App R 192 (CA)

Ormrod LJ: ... [Counsel] for the appellant has criticised the learned judge's summing up on the basis of the well-known passage in the speech of Lord Morris of Borth-y-Gest giving the advice of the Privy Council in *Palmer v R* [1971] AC 814, 831 and 832. He submits that the learned judge overlooked one important sentence in that advice which reads thus: 'If a jury thought that in a moment of unexpected anguish a person attacked had only done what he honestly and instinctively thought was necessary, that would be most potent evidence that only reasonable defensive action had been taken.'

This proposition is, as it were, a bridge between what is sometimes referred to as 'the objective test', that is what is reasonable judged from the viewpoint of an outsider looking at a situation quite dispassionately, and 'the subjective test', that is the viewpoint of the accused himself with the intellectual capabilities of which he may in fact be possessed and with all the emotional strains and stresses to which at the moment he may be subjected.

The learned judge dealt fully with the relevant evidence and the law, and finally left this question to the jury: 'Has the prosecution satisfied you that Mr Shannon used more force than was reasonable in the circumstances; because that goes solely to the question: Did he lawfully kill Mr Meredith?' This summarises the burden of his direction to the jury. [Counsel for the appellant] argues that the judge ought to have invited the jury to consider whether the appellant, at the moment of stabbing, 'honestly and instinctively thought that this action was necessary' to his defence and to have told them that if they thought that that was right and provided an adequate reason for the stabbing, it would be strong evidence that only reasonable defensive action had been taken.

[Counsel for the appellant] in effect urged that the learned judge had concentrated so much on the state of the appellant's mind in relation to the intent necessary to establish the charge of murder that he had, unwittingly, obscured this subjective element in self-defence.

Taken in isolation it is not an easy concept to explain to a jury, or for a jury to understand and apply, although Lord Morris regarded the defence of self-defence as 'one which can and will be readily understood by any jury'. It is however easier to understand in its context and, if full justice is to be done to [counsel's] submission in this case, it is necessary to read what Lord Morris said *in extenso* at [1971] AC 814, 831, 832.

... The whole tenor of this statement of the law [ie what Lord Morris said] is directed to the distinction which has to be drawn between acts which are essentially defensive in character and acts which are essentially offensive, punitive, or retaliatory in character. Attack may be the best form of defence, but not necessarily in law. Counter-attack within limits is permissible; but going over to the offensive when the real danger is over is another thing. This, we think, is the distinction which Lord Morris was endeavouring to explain, and which he thought a jury would readily understand.

Various indicators are used by the judges to enable juries to make this crucial distinction. If the act or acts go beyond what the jury think reasonably necessary for defensive purposes, that points to the offensive rather than the defensive character of the act; if the attack is finished, the subsequent employment of force may be, in Lord Morris's words, 'by way of revenge or punishment or by way of paying off an old score or may be pure aggression'; if other people have come to the assistance of the person attacked before some act of violence is done to the assailant, this too may indicate that the victim has gone over to the offensive. But these are only indicators to be used by the jury in making their common sense assessment on the facts as they find them; they are not conclusive tests in themselves of self-defence on the one hand or of aggression on the other. This is where Lord Morris's references come in to 'a person defending himself cannot weigh to a nicety the exact measure of his necessary defensive action' and to such a person's 'honest and instinctive' belief that his act was necessary. These considerations, depending on the facts of the particular case, may have to be weighed by the jury before coming to their conclusion 'self-defence' or 'no self-defence'.

The learned judge, in the course of his summing up, used verbatim several extracts from Lord Morris's statement of the law *in Palmer v R* (above), but throughout the summing up, and at the end he left the jury with the bald question, 'Are you satisfied that the appellant used more force than was necessary in the circumstances?' without Lord Morris's qualification that if they came to the conclusion that the appellant honestly thought, without having to weigh things to a nicety, that what he did was necessary to defend himself, they should regard that as 'most potent evidence' that it was actually reasonably necessary. In other words, if the jury came to the conclusion that the stabbing was the act of a desperate man in extreme difficulties, with his assailant dragging him down by the hair, they should consider very carefully before concluding that the stabbing was an offensive and not a defensive act, albeit it went beyond what an onlooker would regard as reasonably necessary ...

In the judgment of this court the evidence of the appellant, if accepted by the jury, raised the questions (a) whether the stabbing was in fact the act of a desperate man trying to defend himself and to force his assailant to let go of his hair and (b) whether, although not reasonably necessary by an objective standard, nonetheless, to use Lord Morris's words, the appellant honestly and instinctively thought that it was; in which case his honest belief would be 'most potent evidence' that he had only taken defensive action; in other words, in the circumstances the stabbing was essentially defensive in character. The case for the prosecution, on the other hand, if accepted by the jury, was a perfect illustration of a man going over to the offensive and stabbing by way of revenge, punishment, retaliation or pure aggression.

The learned judge touched on this aspect of the matter when he was directing the jury on the issue of intent in relation to the charge of murder. At the end of the summing up he said this:

> If you think that he lashed out because he lost his temper, having been treated in this painful, humiliating, frightening way, then you may think – it is a matter for you – that because he lost his temper in those circumstances he gave little or no thought to what might be the consequences of lashing out and in those circumstances he did not form the intent suggested. That is the matter which you must consider, clearly. The more a man loses his temper, the less likely he may be to consider what are likely to be the consequences of his acts even though when he is in a balanced state of mind he realises that if you lash out with scissors and it lands and you do it with force then it is going to do a lot of personal injury.

But on the issue of self-defence he, effectively excluded the state of the accused's mind. In other words, by leaving that issue to the jury on the bald basis of 'Did the appellant use more force than was necessary in the circumstances?' the learned judge may have precluded the jury from considering the real issue, which, to paraphrase Lord Morris in *Palmer v R* (above) was: 'Was this stabbing within the conception of necessary self-defence judged by the standards of common sense, bearing in mind the position of the appellant at the moment of the stabbing, or was it a case of angry retaliation or pure aggression on his part?'

It is, we think, significant that in relation to intent, that is applying the test of what was in the accused's mind, the jury concluded that it was not murder but only manslaughter on the basis of no intent to cause really serious bodily harm, but seem to have excluded the appellant's state of mind in considering self-defence ...

R v Whyte [1987] 3 All ER 416 (CA)

Lord Lane CJ: ... The facts of the case were these. The appellant and his brother lived in an upstairs flat in a road called Pyrland Road, London N5. Their neighbours were a Mr and Mrs Holmes. Mr and Mrs Holmes owned a dog, which apparently was not fully house-trained. Mr and Mrs Holmes lived in the downstairs flat, but the appellant's flat and the Holmes's flat shared a common landing and it seems that the door leading to the upstairs flat was close to the door which led into the Holmes's flat. What happened was this. On the evening of 30 March Mr and Mrs Holmes were in a public house, and they met a man called Michael Khan, who had been an acquaintance of theirs for many years but whom they had not seen for some time. After they finished drinking in the public house they returned to the Holmes's flat.

Thereafter there is a sharp divergence in the account of what happened, because according to Mr Khan, who was the eventual victim of the incident, the appellant's voice was heard outside the flat. Mr Khan went to the door to see what was required. When he opened the door, according to Mr Khan, the appellant punched him and said: 'the dog's pissed against my door'. Mr Khan, according to him, tried to calm the appellant down because he was very agitated, but the appellant reached round into the door which led into his, the appellant's, premises, produced a lock-knife, the blade of which was already open, and tried to stab Mr Khan in the stomach. Mr Khan put his arm across his stomach to protect himself, and as a result the arm received the effect of the knife. It was very severely cut. Mr Khan, having blocked the blow in that way, punched the appellant and slammed the door, and that, according to Mr Khan, was the end of the incident.

The appellant was interviewed by the police. To the police he was uncommunicative. He declined to answer any of the questions which they posed to him. The account of the events which he gave at the trial was this. He said first of all that he had not deliberately stabbed Mr Khan at all. It remained to some degree a mystery in those circumstances how Mr Khan received the wound that he did. But his defence was that he was acting in self-defence of himself and also of his brother. He said that what happened was this. He said that there was a knock at his door. He opened the door, but before he did so, he placed his lock-knife, the six-inch blade of which he had already opened, in his back pocket. This was before the door was open at all. He opened the door and there was Mrs Holmes, who asked him to join her for a drink. At that moment, he said, Mr Khan stepped in front of him, though it is not quite clear why. The appellant, according to himself, said: 'The dog's pissed on the floor'. Mr Khan told him to calm down, but then Mr Khan made a gesture towards him which he endeavoured to avoid, but he did not avoid. In other words Mr Khan struck him on the face. The appellant then took out the knife, according to him, but dropped it on the floor. There was then a struggle. He managed to pick up the knife. He tried to push away Mr Khan, and in some way, which he could not explain, the knife had penetrated Mr Khan's arm. The appellant then threw away the knife and ran away from the flat. Eventually, having seen his solicitor some two days later, he went to see the police seven or eight days later.

Those were the two conflicting versions.

... What the judge said to the jury on the question of self-defence, having given them an impeccable direction on the general effect of that defence, was this:

> ... If a man does use violence and claims he was only violent in self-defence, he may only use such force to defend himself as was reasonable in all the circumstances. It is for you, the jury, to decide as a matter of common sense whether a blow with a knife was in self-defence, and if it was, if the use of a knife against a man who is not alleged to have been armed was reasonable ... So before you can convict Mr Whyte of either count 1 or count 2, you must be satisfied so that you are sure that Mr Whyte struck Mr Khan a blow with a knife as an assailant, and that the blow was not a blow in self-defence, or if it was, it was an unreasonable amount of force, having regard to the danger Mr Whyte himself was in at the hands of Mr Khan.

In most cases, where the issue is one of self-defence, it is necessary and desirable that the jury should be reminded that the defendant's state of mind, that is his view of the danger threatening him at the time of the incident, is material. The test of reasonableness is not, to put it at its lowest, a purely objective test.

We have been referred to two authorities. The first is an opinion of the Privy Council in *Palmer v R* [1971] AC 814 and the second is *R v Shannon* (1980) 71 Cr App R 192, a decision of this court which of course is binding on us. The effect of those two decisions seems to be this. A man who is attacked may defend himself, but may only do what is reasonably necessary to effect such a defence. Simple avoiding action may be enough if circumstances permit. What is reasonable will depend on the nature of the attack. If there is relatively a minor attack, it is not reasonable to use a degree of force which is wholly out of proportion to the demands of the situation. But if the moment is one of crisis for someone who is in imminent danger, it may be necessary to take instant action to avert that danger.

Although the test is what is sometimes called an objective one, yet nevertheless, to quote the words of Lord Morris in *Palmer v R* [1971] AC 814 at 832:

> If a jury thought that in a moment of unexpected anguish a person attacked had only done what he honestly and instinctively thought was necessary, that would be most potent evidence that only reasonable defensive action had been taken.

In *R v Shannon*, to which we have already referred, the trial judge had directed the jury to consider the question, 'Are you satisfied that the defendant used more force than necessary in the circumstances?' without going on to consider the qualification what the defendant may have done in a 'moment of unexpected anguish'. On the facts of *R v Shannon*, that was clearly a fatal flaw which led to the conviction being quashed.

The judge in the present case likewise omitted to mention the qualification which Lord Morris had suggested should be made and which *R v Shannon* says should be made in appropriate circumstances.

It is a trite observation, but nevertheless true, that the requirements of a summing up will depend on the particular facts of the case. Whereas on the facts of *R v Shannon* the court correctly held that the qualifying effect mentioned by Lord Morris should have been given, one has to look at this case to see whether it was similarly necessary here. The jury in convicting him of the s 18 offence must have come to the conclusion that he had deliberately stabbed Mr Khan with the knife, despite what he himself said. They were directed correctly on the question of accident. The appeal on that point has been abandoned. So the jury must have decided that the knife was deliberately used by the appellant on Mr Khan. At the very best, from the appellant's point of view, the jury must have come to the conclusion that he stabbed Mr Khan because Mr Khan had hit him in the face with his hand. Now I am assuming in favour of the appellant that the facts were, with that small amendment about accident, as the appellant himself stated them to be. It is highly likely that the jury entirely disbelieved the appellant.

Was it necessary in those circumstances that the judge should mention the qualifying factor as mentioned by Lord Morris? In our judgment it was not. There was no question raised by the appellant that he, acting in the agony of the moment, went too far, that he failed to weigh accurately the precise degree of the attack which he was suffering. It is perfectly plain that on any view the use of an already prepared knife, the blade having been extended, in circumstances such as this, could not possibly be reasonable under any circumstances, whether the direction in *Palmer v R* was given or not.

For those reasons we think that in this particular case it was not necessary for the judge to give the *Palmer* direction, although as a matter of abundance of caution he might perhaps have given it ...

Whether there is a duty to retreat from threatened violence

R v Julien [1969] 1 WLR 839 (CA)

Widgery LJ: ... The third point taken by counsel for the appellant is that the learned deputy chairman was wrong in directing the jury that before the appellant could use force in self-defence he was required to retreat. The submission here is that the obligation to retreat before using force in self-defence is an obligation which only arises in homicide cases. As the court understands it, it is submitted that if the injury results in death then the accused cannot set up self-defence except on the basis that he had retreated before he resorted to violence. On the other hand, it is said that where the injury does not result in death (as in the present case) the obligation to retreat does not arise. The sturdy submission is made that an Englishman is not bound to run away when threatened, but can stand his ground and defend himself where he is. In support of this submission no authority is quoted, save that counsel for the appellant has been at considerable length and diligence to look at the textbooks on the subject, and has demonstrated to us that the textbooks in the main do not say that a preliminary retreat is a necessary prerequisite to the use of force in self-defence. Equally, it must be said that the textbooks do not state the contrary either; and it is, of course, well-known to us all that for very many years it has been common form for judges directing juries where the issue of self-defence is raised in any case (be it a homicide case or not) that the duty to retreat arises. It is not, as we understand it, the law that a person threatened must take to his heels and run in the dramatic way suggested by counsel for the appellant; but what is necessary is that he should demonstrate by his actions that he does not want to fight. He must demonstrate that he is prepared to temporise and disengage and perhaps to make some physical withdrawal; and to the extent that that is necessary as a feature of the justification of self-defence, it is true, in our opinion, whether the charge is a homicide charge or something less serious. Accordingly, we reject counsel for the appellant's third submission ...

R v Bird [1985] 1 WLR 816 (CA)

Lord Lane CJ: ... The facts of the case are these. On 10 March 1984 the appellant was celebrating her 17th birthday. There was a party at a house in Harlow. Unhappily it was at that party that the events occurred which ended with her being sent to youth custody.

There was a guest at the party called Darren Marder, who was to be the victim of the events which occurred thereafter. He and the appellant had been friendly and had been going out together between about January and the middle of 1983. That close friendship had come to an end, but Marder arrived at the party with his new girlfriend and, for reasons which it is not necessary to explore, an argument broke out. After a great deal of bad language and shouting, the appellant told Marder to leave, and leave he did.

A little later he unwisely came back and a second argument took place together with a second exchange of obscenities between the two of them. What happened thereafter was the subject of dispute between the parties, though not so much dispute as often arises in these sudden events. The appellant poured a glassful of Pernod over Marder, and he retaliated by slapping her around the face. Further incidents of physical force took place between them. The appellant said that the time came when she was being held and held up against a wall, at which point she lunged at Marder with her hand, which was the hand, unhappily, which held the Pernod glass. The glass hit him in the face, broke, and his eye as a result was lost. It was a horrible event in the upshot, but of course she would not realise the extent to which she was going to cause injury to this young man.

The prosecution case was this, that Marder only slapped the appellant once and that was in order to calm her down, the commonly believed remedy for hysterics. The jury were accordingly invited to infer from that that she could not possibly have been acting in reasonable self-defence when she retaliated against that slap with a weapon as grave as a glass. Second, there was evidence of Marder, and also a Miss Bryant, who was his new girlfriend, that so far from showing remorse after the event the appellant said that she would do it again if the same situation arose. Third, there was the evidence of Mrs Sharpe, the owner of the house where the party was taking place, who said that after the incident the appellant had admitted to her, Mrs Sharpe, that she had slashed Marder in the face with a glass after he had punched her.

The appellant herself was interviewed by the police. She said that it was only afterwards that she realised that a glass was in her hand, the hand with which she struck the appellant.

The appellant gave evidence. She insisted that she had been acting in self-defence. She was being pushed. Marder had said to her that he would hit her if she did not shut up. He slapped her in the face, she was being held by him and thought the only thing for her to do was to strike back to defend herself. In the agony of the moment, so to speak, she did not realise that she was holding the glass. Those are the comparatively simple facts of the case.

The grounds of appeal are these. First of all, the judge was in error in directing the jury that before the appellant could rely on a plea of self-defence, it was necessary that she should have demonstrated by her action that she did not want to fight. That really is the essence of the appellant's case put forward by her counsel to this court ...

The court in *R v Julien* was anxious to make it clear that there was no duty, despite earlier authorities to the contrary, actually to turn round or walk away from the scene. But, reading the words which were used in that judgment, it now seems to us that they placed too great an obligation on a defendant in circumstances such as those in the instant case, an obligation which is not reflected in the speeches in *Palmer v R*.

The matter is dealt with accurately and helpfully in Smith and Hogan, *Criminal Law*, 5th edn, 1983, p 327 as follows:

> There were formerly technical rules about the duty to retreat before using force, or at least fatal force. This is now simply a factor to be taken into account in deciding whether it was necessary to use force, and whether the force was reasonable. If the only reasonable course is to retreat, then it would appear that

to stand and fight must be to use unreasonable force. There is, however, no rule of law that a person attacked is bound to run away if he can; but it has been said that: '... what is necessary is that he should demonstrate by his actions that he does not want to fight. He must demonstrate that he is prepared to temporise and disengage and perhaps to make some physical withdrawal.' It is submitted that it goes too far to say that action of this kind is necessary. It is scarcely consistent with the rule that it is permissible to use force, not merely to counter an actual attack, but to ward off an attack honestly and reasonably believed to be imminent. A demonstration by D [the defendant] at the time that he did not want to fight is, no doubt, the best evidence that he was acting reasonably and in good faith in self-defence; but it is no more than that. A person may in some circumstances so act without temporising, disengaging or withdrawing; and he should have a good defence.

We respectfully agree with that passage. If the defendant is proved to have been attacking or retaliating or revenging himself, then he was not truly acting in self-defence. Evidence that the defendant tried to retreat or tried to call off the fight may be a cast-iron method of casting doubt on the suggestion that he was the attacker or retaliator or the person trying to revenge himself. But it is not by any means the only method of doing that ...

R v McInnes [1971] 1 WLR 1600 (CA)

Edmund Davies LJ: ... The incident which led to the murder charge was of a kind only too frequently occurring in these days, namely a fracas between two perfect strangers which resulted in the violent death of one of them as the result of a knife wound. The appellant belonged to a group of youths commonly called 'greasers', who adopted a particular form of dress which includes leather jackets. Hostility generally exists between them and 'skinheads', who are youths differently dressed and having close-cropped heads. The deceased belonged to neither of these groups. The deceased was killed at about 9.30 pm on Saturday 22 August 1970, at a fair being held at Platt Fields in Manchester, and his death was caused by a knife wound in the left side of the body. The knife used had penetrated the heart. The wound was about 2 inches deep and about 3 feet 11 inches from the deceased's left heel ...

... We turn to the two criticisms advanced in relation to the manner in which the learned judge treated the topic of self-defence. Before doing this, however, it should again be observed that, while both prosecuting and defence counsel (very understandably in all the circumstances) dealt at length with this plea, it was one never advanced by the appellant himself in evidence. On the contrary, he insisted throughout that he never thrust the knife forward, and that the wounding and killing of the deceased were due to no aggressive action on his part.

The first criticism of the learned judge's treatment of self-defence is that he misdirected the jury in relation to the question of whether an attacked person must do all he reasonably can to retreat before he turns on his attacker. The direction given was in these terms:

In our law if two men fight and one of them after a while endeavours to avoid any further struggle and retreats as far as he can, and then when he can go no further turns and kills his assailant to avoid being killed himself, that homicide is excusable, but notice that to show that homicide arising from a fight was committed in self-defence it must be shown that the party killing had retreated as far as he could, or as far as the fierceness of the assault would permit him.

... In our judgment, the direction was expressed in too inflexible terms and might, in certain circumstances, be regarded as significantly misleading. We prefer the view expressed by the High Court of Australia (in *R v Howe* (1958) 100 CLR 448 at 462, 464, 469) that a failure to retreat is only an element in the considerations on which the reasonableness of an accused's conduct is to be judged (see *Palmer v R* [1971] 2 WLR 831 at 840), or, as it is put in Smith and Hogan's *Criminal Law*, 1969, 2nd edn, p 231:

> ... simply a factor to be taken into account in deciding whether it was necessary to use force, and whether the force used was reasonable.

The modern law on the topic was, in our respectful view, accurately set out in *R v Julien* [1969] 1 WLR 839 at 843 by Widgery LJ in the following terms:

> It is not, as we understand it, the law that a person threatened must take to his heels and run in the dramatic way suggested by counsel for the appellant; but what is necessary is that he should demonstrate by his actions that he does not want to fight. He must demonstrate that he is prepared to temporise and disengage and perhaps to make some physical withdrawal; and to the extent that that is necessary as a feature of the justification of self-defence, it is true, in our opinion, whether the charge is a homicide charge or something less serious.

In the light of the foregoing, how stands the direction given in the present case? Viewed in isolation, that is to say, without regard to the evidence adduced, it was expressed in too rigid terms. But the opportunity to retreat remains, as the trial judge said, 'an important consideration', and, when regard is had to the evidence as to the circumstances which prevailed, in our view it emerges with clarity that the appellant could have avoided this fatal incident with ease by simply walking or running away – as, indeed, he promptly did as soon as the deceased had been stabbed ...

Notes and queries

1   Once the threat has been removed, or subsided, the right to act in self-defence falls away. Hence in *Priestnall v Cornish* [1979] Crim LR 310, where the victim had retreated into his car after an altercation with the defendant following a road rage incident, and had therefore ceased to be a threat, the defendant was held not have been acting in self-defence in continuing to attack the victim as, by then, the defendant had had every means of retreat open to him.

Where the force used exceeds that which is reasonable

R v McInnes [1971] 1 WLR 1600 (CA)

Edmund Davies LJ: The final criticism levelled against the summing up is that the learned judge wrongly failed to direct the jury that, if death resulted from the use of excessive force by the appellant in defending himself against the aggressiveness of the deceased, the proper verdict was one of not guilty of murder but guilty of manslaughter. Certainly no such direction was given, and the question that arises is whether its omission constitutes a defect in the summing up.

The Privy Council decision in *Palmer v R* provides high persuasive authority which we, for our part, unhesitatingly accept, that there is certainly no rule that, in every case where self-defence is left to the jury, such a direction is called for. But where self-defence fails on the ground that the force used went clearly beyond that which was reasonable in the light of the circumstances as they reasonably appeared to the accused, is it the law that the inevitable result must be that he can be convicted of manslaughter only, and not of murder? It seems that in Australia that question is answered in the affirmative (see Professor Colin Howard's article, 'Two problems in excessive defence' (1968) 84 LQR 343), but not, we think, in this country. On the contrary, if self-defence fails for the reason stated, it affords the accused no protection at all. But it is important to stress that the facts on which the plea of self-defence is unsuccessfully sought to be based may nevertheless serve the accused in good stead. They may, for example, go to show that he may have acted under provocation or that, although acting unlawfully, he may have lacked the intent to kill or cause serious bodily harm, and in that way render the proper verdict one of manslaughter ...

Section 3(1) of the Criminal Law Act 1967 provides: 'A person may use such force as is reasonable in the circumstances in the prevention of crime ...' and in our judgment the degree of force permissible in self-defence is similarly limited. Deliberate stabbing was so totally unreasonable in the circumstances of this case, even on the appellant's version, that self-defence justifying a complete acquittal was not relied on before us, and rightly so. Despite the high esteem in which we hold our Australian brethren, we respectfully reject as far as this country is concerned the refinement sought to be introduced that, if the accused, in defending himself during a fisticuffs encounter, drew out against his opponent (who he had no reason to think was armed) the deadly weapon which he had earlier unsheathed and then 'let him have it', the jury should have been directed that, even on those facts, it was open to them to convict of manslaughter. They are, in our view, the facts of this case. It follows that in our judgment no such direction was called for ...

R v Clegg [1995] 1 AC 482 (HL)

Lord Lloyd of Berwick: My Lords, on the night of 30 September 1990 the appellant, Lee William Clegg, a soldier serving with the Parachute Regiment, was on patrol in Glen Road, West Belfast, when the driver of a stolen car and one of his passengers were shot and killed. Private Clegg was charged with murder of the passenger, and attempted murder of the driver. His defence was that he fired in self-defence. He was convicted on 4 June 1993, after a trial before Campbell J without a jury. His appeal to the Court of Appeal was dismissed. The Court of Appeal held that the firing of the shot which killed the passenger was, on the facts found by the judge, a grossly excessive and disproportionate use of force, and that any tribunal of fact properly directed would so have found. The certified question of law for your Lordships is whether a soldier on duty, who kills a person with the requisite intention for murder, but who would be entitled to rely on self-defence but for the use of excessive force, is guilty of murder or manslaughter.

The patrol consisted of 15 men under the command of Lieutenant Oliver. It was accompanied by a police constable from the Royal Ulster Constabulary. The purpose of the patrol was to catch joyriders. But this was not explained to Private Clegg. The patrol was divided into four teams or 'bricks'. Brick 11 formed a vehicle checkpoint at a bridge on the Glen Road about six miles west of Belfast. Brick 10A, consisting of Lieutenant Oliver, Private Clegg, Private Aindow and another, were moving down the road towards Belfast. Private Aindow was on the right-hand side of the road. The others were all on the left-hand side. Bricks 12 and 14 were still further down the road, around a corner. As the stolen car approached the bridge from the west, it was stopped by a member of Brick 11. The car then accelerated away in the centre of the road towards Brick 10A with its headlights full on. Someone in Brick 11 shouted to stop it. All four members of Brick 10A fired at the approaching car. Private Clegg's evidence was that he fired three shots at the windscreen, and a fourth shot into the side of the car as it was passing. He then replaced his safety-catch. According to Private Clegg he fired all four shots because he thought Private Aindow's life was in danger. However, scientific evidence showed, and the trial judge found as a fact, that Private Clegg's fourth shot was fired after the car had passed, and was already over 50 feet along the road to Belfast. It struck a rear-seat passenger, Karen Reilly, in the back. It was later found lodged beneath her liver. The judge found that Private Clegg's fourth shot was an aimed shot fired with the intention of causing death or serious bodily harm. Although another bullet passed through Karen Reilly's body, Private Clegg's fourth shot was a significant cause of the death.

In relation of the first three shots, the judge accepted Private Clegg's defence that he fired in self-defence or in defence of Private Aindow. But with regard to the fourth shot he found that Private Clegg could not have been firing in defence of himself or Private Aindow, since, once the car had passed, they were no longer in any danger.

Having rejected Private Clegg's defence in relation to the fourth shot, the judge went on to consider, as was his duty, whether there was any other defence open on the evidence, even though Private Clegg had not raised the defence himself. One possible defence was that Private Clegg fired the fourth shot in order to arrest the driver. Section 3(1) of the Criminal Law Act (Northern Ireland) 1967 provides:

> A person may use such force as is reasonable in the circumstances in the prevention of crime, or in effecting or assisting in the lawful arrest of offenders or suspected offenders or of persons unlawfully at large.

The judge held that there was insufficient evidence to raise such a defence. Accordingly he convicted Private Clegg of murder.

When the case reached the Court of Appeal, the court reviewed the whole of Private Clegg's evidence. In a number of his answers he had said that he fired to stop the driver of the car after it had, as he thought, struck Private Aindow. Accordingly there was, in the court's view, evidence on which the judge should have considered the defence under s 3 of the Act of 1967.

It should be noted in passing that the car did not, in fact, strike Private Aindow. The judge held that bruising found of Private Aindow's left leg was caused, not by the car, but by another soldier stamping on him in order to create the appearance that he had been struck by the car. In those circumstances, Private Aindow was charged with perverting the course of justice as well as attempted murder. He was convicted on the former count and sentenced to two years' imprisonment. His appeal on that count was dismissed.

Having held that there was evidence to raise the defence under s 3, the Court of Appeal went on to consider whether any miscarriage of justice had actually occurred by reason of the failure of the judge to consider that defence. Section 3 of the Act of 1967 allows a person to use 'such force as is reasonable in the circumstances'. So the question for the Court of Appeal was whether Private Clegg, in firing the fourth shot, used only such force as was reasonable in the circumstances, or whether the force which he used was excessive.

In the course of his cross-examination Private Clegg was asked whether he was aware of any circumstances which would have justified him in firing after the car had passed. He replied that he had no reason to fire at that stage.

> Q 29: And if you had fired any more you know of no justification for that action?
>
> A 29: That's correct. That's why I applied my safety-catch as the car went past me.

There was no suggestion in Private Clegg's evidence, as the Court of Appeal pointed out, that he thought that the driver was a terrorist, or that if the driver escaped he would carry out terrorist offences in the future. In those circumstances the use of lethal force to arrest the driver of the car was, in the court's view, so 'grossly disproportionate to the mischief to be averted' that any tribunal of fact would have been bound to find that the force used was unreasonable. It follows that if the defence under s 3 had been raised, which it was not, it would have failed. Accordingly, Private Clegg's appeal was dismissed ...

The point raised in the present case might have arisen for decision by your Lordships in *AG for Northern Ireland's Ref (No 1 of 1975)* [1977] AC 105. That case also concerned a soldier on patrol in Northern Ireland. He shot and killed an unarmed man, who ran away when challenged. The trial judge found that, unlike the present case, the prosecution had failed to prove that the soldier intended to kill or cause serious bodily harm, and further found that the homicide was justifiable under s 3 of the Act of 1967 on the ground that the use of force was reasonable in the circumstances. The questions for the opinion of the House were first whether, on the facts set out in the reference, the soldier had committed a crime at all and second whether, if so, the crime was murder or manslaughter. The House held that the first question was not a question of law at all, but a pure question of fact, which, on the facts proved at the trial, had been answered in favour of the soldier; and that the second question, though a question of law, did not arise on the facts. But it is to be observed that Viscount Dilhorne said in relation to the second question at 148:

> I now turn to the second point of law referred, whether if a crime was committed in the circumstances stated in the reference it was murder or manslaughter. The Attorney General indicated that he would like it to be held that it was manslaughter and, while I appreciated his reasons for doing so, I can find no escape from the conclusion that if a crime was committed, it was murder if the shot was fired with intent to kill or seriously wound. To hold that it could be manslaughter would be to make entirely new law. If a plea of self-defence is put forward in answer to a charge of murder and fails because excessive force was used though some force was justifiable, as the law now stands the accused cannot be convicted of manslaughter. It may be that a strong case can be made for an alteration of the law to enable a verdict of

manslaughter to be returned where the use of some force was justifiable but that is a matter for legislation and not for judicial decision.

... I do not find it necessary to go through the earlier English authorities relied on by counsel, since they were all reviewed at length by Lord Morris of Borth-y-Gest in *Palmer v R* [1971] AC 814. I respectfully agree with his analysis. Counsel did not advance any fresh arguments. In my opinion the law of England must now be taken to be settled in accordance with the decision of the Privy Council in that case. Thus, the consequence of the use of excessive force in self-defence will be the same in the law of England, Scotland, Australia, Canada and the West Indies. I consider later whether, despite this uniformity, some change in the law may, nevertheless, be desirable.

The second question is whether there is any distinction to be made between excessive force in self-defence and excessive force in the prevention of crime or in arresting offenders. In *AG for Northern Ireland's Ref (No 1 of 1975)* [1977] AC 105 Lord Diplock said, at 139, that the two cases were quite different. But I do not think it possible to say that a person who uses excessive force in preventing crime is always, or even generally, less culpable than a person who uses excessive force in self-defence; and even if excessive force in preventing crime were in general less culpable, it would not be practicable to draw a distinction between the two defences, since they so often overlap. Take, for example, the facts of the present case. The trial judge held that Private Clegg's first three shots might have been fired in defence of Private Aindow. But he could equally well have held that they were fired in the prevention of crime, namely to prevent Private Aindow's death being caused by dangerous driving. As is pointed out in Smith and Hogan, *Criminal Law*, 6th edn, 1988, p 244; 7th edn, 1992, p 255, the degree of permissible force should be the same in both cases. So also should the consequences of excessive force.

The third question is whether it makes any difference that Private Clegg was a member of the security forces, acting in the course of his duty ...

... In most cases of a person acting in self-defence, or a police officer arresting an offender, there is a choice as to the degree of force to be used, even if it is a choice which has to be exercised on the spur of the moment, without time for measured reflection. But in the case of a soldier in Northern Ireland, in the circumstances in which Private Clegg found himself, there is no scope for graduated force. The only choice lay between firing a high-velocity rifle which, if aimed accurately, was almost certain to kill or injure, and doing nothing at all.

It should be noticed that the point at issue here is not whether Private Clegg was entitled to be acquitted altogether, on the ground that he was acting in obedience to superior orders. There is no such general defence known to English law, nor was any such defence raised at the trial ... The point is rather whether the offence in such a case should, because of the strong mitigating circumstances, be regarded as manslaughter rather than murder. But so to hold would, as Viscount Dilhorne said in *AG for Northern Ireland's Ref (No 1 of 1975)* [1977] AC 105, 148, be to make entirely new law. I regret that under existing law, on the facts found by the trial judge, he had no alternative but to convict of murder ...

The Criminal law Act 1967

Section 3(1) of the Criminal Law Act 1967 provides:

> A person may use such force as is reasonable in the circumstances in the prevention of crime, or in effecting or assisting in the lawful arrest of offenders or suspected offenders or of persons unlawfully at large.

Whereas at common law it has been argued that the use of force to protect others requires proof of some nexus between the defendant and those he seeks to protect, under s 3 a defendant can use force to protect a complete stranger from a criminal attack as he will be using force to prevent the commission of a criminal offence. Similarly, at common law, a defendant can rely on self-defence to protect his property from attack. Under the statute the defendant could use reasonable force to protect anybody's property from criminal damage or theft.

Notes and queries

1 If D uses reasonable force to stop B (who is 9 years old) from attacking C, can D rely on s 3(1)? See the extract from *Re A* (below).

2 If D comes upon A attacking B and he uses reasonable force to restrain A, can he rely on s 3(1) if A is, in reality, defending himself from an attack by B?

Where the defendant mistakenly believes that force by way of self-defence is required

R v Williams [1987] 3 All ER 411 (CA)

Lord Lane CJ: ... The facts were somewhat unusual and were as follows. On the day in question the alleged victim, a man called Mason, saw a black youth seizing the handbag belonging to a woman who was shopping. He caught up with the youth and held him, he said with a view to taking him to a nearby police station, but the youth broke free from his grip. Mason caught the youth again and knocked him to the ground, and he then twisted one of the youth's arms behind his back in order to immobilise him and to enable him, Mason, so he said, once again to take the youth to the police station. The youth was struggling and calling for help at this time, and no one disputed that fact.

On the scene then came the appellant, who had only seen the latter stages of this incident. According to Mason he told the appellant first of all that he was arresting the youth for mugging the lady, and second, that he, Mason, was a police officer. That was not true. He was asked for his warrant card, which obviously was not forthcoming, and thereupon something of a struggle ensued between Mason on the one hand and the appellant and others on the other hand. In the course of these events Mason sustained injuries to his face, loosened teeth and bleeding gums.

The appellant put forward the following version of events. He said he was returning from work by bus when he saw Mason dragging the youth along and striking him again and again. He was so concerned about the matter that he rapidly got off the bus and made his way to the scene and asked Mason what on earth he was doing. In short he said that he punched Mason because he thought if he did so he would save the youth from further beating and what he described as torture ...

... [I]t is for the prosecution to eliminate the possibility that the appellant was acting under a genuine mistake of fact ...

One starts off with the meaning of the word 'assault'. 'Assault' in the context of this case, that is to say, using the word as a convenient abbreviation for assault and battery, is an act by which the defendant, intentionally or recklessly, applies unlawful force to the complainant. There are circumstances in which force may be applied to another lawfully. Taking a few examples: first, where the victim consents, as in lawful sports, the application of force to another will, generally speaking, not be unlawful. Second, where the defendant is acting in self-defence the exercise of any necessary and reasonable force to protect himself from unlawful violence is not unlawful. Third, by virtue of s 3 of the Criminal Law Act 1967, a person may use such force as is reasonable in the circumstances in the prevention of crime or in effecting or assisting in the lawful arrest of an offender or suspected offender or persons unlawfully at large. In each of those cases the defendant will be guilty if the jury are sure that first of all he applied force to the person of another, and secondly that he had the necessary mental element to constitute guilt.

The mental element necessary to constitute guilt is the intent to apply unlawful force to the victim. We do not believe that the mental element can be substantiated by simply showing an intent to apply force and no more.

What then is the situation if the defendant is labouring under a mistake of fact as to the circumstances? What if he believes, but believes mistakenly, that the victim is consenting, or that it is necessary to defend himself, or that a crime is being committed which he intends to prevent? He must then be judged against the mistaken facts as he believes them to be. If judged against those facts or circumstances the prosecution fail to establish his guilt, then he is entitled to be acquitted.

The next question is: does it make any difference if the mistake of the defendant was one which, viewed objectively by a reasonable onlooker, was an unreasonable mistake? In other words should the jury be directed as follows: 'Even if the defendant may have genuinely believed that what he was doing to the victim was either with the victim's consent or in reasonable self-defence or to prevent the commission of crime, as the case may be, nevertheless if you, the jury, come to the conclusion that the mistaken belief was unreasonable, that is to say that the defendant as a reasonable man should have realised his mistake, then you should convict him ...'

... The reasonableness or unreasonableness of the defendant's belief is material to the question of whether the belief was held by the defendant at all. If the belief was in fact held, its unreasonableness, so far as guilt or innocence is concerned, is neither here nor there. It is irrelevant. Were it otherwise, the defendant would be convicted because he was negligent in failing to recognise that the victim was not consenting or that a crime was not being committed and so on. In other words, the jury should be directed, first of all, that the prosecution have the burden or duty of proving the unlawfulness of the defendant's actions, second, that if the defendant may have been labouring under a mistake as to the facts he must be judged according to his mistaken view of the facts and, third, that that is so whether the mistake was, on an objective view, a reasonable mistake or not.

In a case of self-defence, where self-defence or the prevention of crime is concerned, if the jury come to the conclusion that the defendant believed, or may have believed, that he was being attacked or that a crime was being committed, and that force was necessary to protect himself or to prevent the crime, then the prosecution have not proved their case. If, however, the defendant's alleged belief was mistaken and if the mistake was an unreasonable one, that may be a powerful reason for coming to the conclusion that the belief was not honestly held and should be rejected.

Even if the jury come to the conclusion that the mistake was an unreasonable one, if the defendant may genuinely have been labouring under it, he is entitled to rely on it ...

Beckford v R [1988] AC 130 (PC)

Lord Griffiths: ... The defendant was a police officer who on 8 March 1983 was issued with a shotgun and ammunition and sent with a number of other armed police officers to a house at Greenvale Park in Manchester. The prosecution called no evidence to explain the circumstances in which this armed posse was sent out that morning but according to the defendant, in a statement he made from the dock, he and other police officers, including a Police Constable Reckord, were told by Deputy Superintendent Wilson that a report had been received from Heather Barnes that her brother Chester Barnes was terrorising her mother with a gun and that the police must come immediately to save her life. The defendant said that they were warned that the man appeared to be a dangerous gunman and that they must take special care. Heather Barnes, however, who was the first witness called by the prosecution, denied in cross-examination that she had made a telephone call to the police or that her brother Chester Barnes was armed ...

The prosecution case, based primarily on the evidence of Heather Barnes and a witness named Peart, was that the defendant armed with a shotgun and Police Constable Reckord, armed with a revolver, had aggressively entered the house whereupon the unarmed Chester Barnes had fled from the house, run across the yard, jumped over a wall and tried to hide by a pigsty on the adjoining common. Heather Barnes said the defendant had fired at her brother in the yard and then he and Police Constable Reckord had pursued him over the wall on to the common from whence she heard more shots. Peart said he saw Chester Barnes jump the wall pursued by the police. Later he saw Barnes hiding by a pigsty, he put his hands in the air and both police officers fired at him. He heard Barnes say 'do officer, don't shoot me, because me a cook' [sic]. He said Barnes had nothing in his hands, and when he fell after the first shots the defendant shot the deceased in the belly ...

At the conclusion of the defence case the only live issue for the jury was whether the prosecution had proved that the defendant had not killed in self-defence. The first ground of appeal before the Court of Appeal in Jamaica, and the only ground with which their Lordships are concerned, was that the trial judge had misdirected the jury on the issue of self-defence ...

It is accepted by the prosecution that there is no difference on the law of self-defence between the law of Jamaica and the English common law and it therefore falls to be decided whether it was correctly decided by the Court of Appeal in *R v Williams (Gladstone)* (1984) 78 Cr App R 276 that the defence of self-defence depends upon what the accused 'honestly' believed the circumstances to be and not upon the reasonableness of that belief ...

The common law recognises that there are many circumstances in which one person may inflict violence upon another without committing a crime, as for instance, in sporting contests, surgical operations or, in the most extreme example, judicial execution. The common law has always recognised as one of these circumstances the right of a person to protect himself from attack and to act in the defence of others and if necessary to inflict violence on another in so doing. If no more force is used than is reasonable to repel the attack such force is not unlawful and no crime is committed. Furthermore a man about to be attacked does not have to wait for his assailant to strike the first blow or fire the first shot; circumstances may justify a pre-emptive strike.

It is because it is an essential element of all crimes of violence that the violence or the threat of violence should be unlawful that self-defence, if raised as an issue in a criminal trial, must be disproved by the prosecution. If the prosecution fail to do so the accused is entitled to be acquitted because the prosecution will have failed to prove an essential element of the crime, namely that the violence used by the accused was unlawful.

If, then, a genuine belief, albeit without reasonable grounds, is a defence to rape because it negatives the necessary intention, so also must a genuine belief in facts which, if true, would justify self-defence, be a defence to a crime of personal violence because the belief negatives the intent to act unlawfully. Their Lordships therefore approve the following passage from the judgment of Lord Lane CJ in *R v Williams (Gladstone)* 78 Cr App R 276, 281, as correctly stating the law of self-defence:

> The reasonableness or unreasonableness of the defendant's belief is material to the question of whether the belief was held by the defendant at all. If the belief was in fact held, its unreasonableness, so far as guilt or innocence is concerned, is neither here nor there. It is irrelevant. Were it otherwise, the defendant would be convicted because he was negligent in failing to recognise that the victim was not consenting or that a crime was not being committed and so on. In other words the jury should be directed first of all that the prosecution have the burden or duty of proving the unlawfulness of the defendant's actions; second, if the defendant may have been labouring under a mistake as to the facts, he must be judged according to his mistaken view of the facts; third, that is so whether the mistake was, on an objective view, a reasonable mistake or not.

> In a case of self-defence, where self-defence or the prevention of crime is concerned, if the jury came to the conclusion that the defendant believed, or may have believed, that he was being attacked or that a crime was being committed, and that force was necessary to protect himself or to prevent the crime, then the prosecution have not proved their case. If, however, the defendant's alleged belief was mistaken and if the mistake was an unreasonable one, that may be a powerful reason for coming to the conclusion that the belief was not honestly held and should be rejected. Even if the jury come to the conclusion that the mistake was an unreasonable one, if the

defendant may genuinely have been labouring under it, he is entitled to rely upon it.

... There may be a fear that the abandonment of the objective standard demanded by the existence of reasonable grounds for belief will result in the success of too many spurious claims of self-defence. The English experience has not shown this to be the case. The Judicial Studies Board with the approval of the Lord Chief Justice has produced a model direction on self-defence which is now widely used by judges when summing up to juries. The direction contains the following guidance:

> Whether the plea is self-defence or defence of another, if the defendant may have been labouring under a mistake as to the facts, he must be judged according to his mistaken belief of the facts: that is so whether the mistake was, on an objective view, a reasonable mistake or not.

Their Lordships have heard no suggestion that this form of summing up has resulted in a disquieting number of acquittals. This is hardly surprising, for no jury is going to accept a man's assertion that he believed that he was about to be attacked without testing it against all the surrounding circumstances. In assisting the jury to determine whether or not the accused had a genuine belief, the judge will of course direct their attention to those features of the evidence that make such a belief more or less probable. Where there are no reasonable grounds to hold a belief it will surely only be in exceptional circumstances that a jury will conclude that such a belief was or might have been held ...

R v Oatridge (1992) 94 Cr App R 367 (CA)

Mustill LJ: ... The appellant and the deceased began to associate during 1988, and started to live together in July 1990. Their relationship seems always to have been stormy. The deceased was a diabetic. He is said to have been reasonable when sober, but he drank too much and on occasions failed to keep his blood sugar under control. He then became abusive and violent. There was ample evidence from other witnesses besides the appellant that there had been several instances when he had struck her. She herself spoke of occasions when he got hold of her by the neck. On the evening in question, 14 October 1990, the appellant had gone out for the evening with friends. She had a fair amount to drink. The deceased had also been drinking, much more heavily. He returned to their flat in the evening, very drunk. The appellant arrived soon afterwards by taxi. After an initial hesitation she went inside. A quarrel then broke out, in the course of which she stabbed him once with a knife, just below the sternum, severing a main pulmonary artery. A pathologist was to say at the trial that a moderate degree of force was required, and that it was unlikely that the deceased had fallen forward on to the knife. Soon after the incident the appellant called the emergency services. Ambulance workers, and later police officers, found the appellant in the flat with the deceased on the floor, either dying or dead. The knife was lying on a work surface. The police asked how he was stabbed. She said 'I stabbed him, he was at me, what else could I do ... He came in drunk, we had a fight. What could I do, I had to defend myself' ...

It is convenient to pause at this point to summarise the material law on self-defence, drawn from *Williams (Gladstone)* (1984) 78 Cr App R 276 and *Beckford v R* [1988] AC 130. In many cases of self-defence the following questions must be asked: (1) Was the defendant under actual or threatened attack by the victim? (2) If yes, did the defendant act to defend himself against this attack? (3) If yes, was his response commensurate with the degree of danger created by the attack? In answering this question allowance must of course be made for the fact that the defendant has to act in the heat of the moment and cannot be expected to measure his response exactly to the danger. (These questions are of course a considerable oversimplification, particularly since they omit reference to burden of proof. But they will suffice to illustrate the point at issue in the present appeal.) There are however occasions where a further question must be asked: (1a) Even if the defendant was not in fact under actual or threatened attack, did he nevertheless honestly believe that he was? (The relevance of the reasonableness of the supposed belief is explained by Lord Lane CJ in *Williams*, above, at pp 280, 281.) If this question is answered in the affirmative (or, more correctly, the prosecution does not establish that it should be answered in the negative), then the third question must be modified, so as to read: (3a) Was the response commensurate with the degree of risk which the defendant believed to be created by the attack under which he believed himself to be?

We return to the present case ...

In our opinion two questions arise on the appeal against the verdict of guilty. First, did the judge in fact give direction on mistaken belief? Second, if he did not should he have done so, in the light of the issues arising on the evidence? The first question does not bear elaborate analysis. Although there was a reference to honest belief, this was in the context of the 'agony of the moment' aspect of reasonable response, which is only indirectly linked with mistake as to the nature of the attack. The thrust of the summing up was, as the quoted passages will demonstrate, to point up the radical issue as to whether the deceased really was setting out to strangle the appellant, and the question whether she might honestly have believed that he was even if in fact he was not, was not explored at all. We are fortified in the view that when [counsel for the defendant] raised the question of subjective belief, [counsel] for the Crown submitted that any direction on the topic would have to include a reference to the effect of drink on the appellant's belief, the judge did not say anything further to the jury. As we understand the matter it was not disputed before us, or at any rate not disputed with any great vigour, that the summing up did not deal with honest mistake, and as the argument developed it emerged that the real question for decision was whether in the circumstances any such direction was required.

To this we now turn. In doing so we wish to make it quite plain from the outset that nothing we are about to say detracts from the principle, constantly emphasised by this court, that directions to a jury should be tailored to the occasion, and that the jury should not be burdened with propositions of law which have no practical bearing on the case. This will be so in many trials where self-defence is in issue. Often, the central question will be whether the acts relied upon as justifying the counter-attack took place as the defendant described them, and whether the circumstances rule out any possibility of mistake. If the defendant gives evidence that the victim attacked him with an axe in broad daylight and that after one blow had narrowly missed was preparing to deliver another, and where the witnesses for the prosecution deny that any such attack took place, it is pointless to confuse the jury with talk of subjective belief. Either there was an attack or there was not, and questions of mistake cannot come into it. So also if the fact and character of the attack are undisputed, and the defence turns on matters such as the proportionality of the response, or the possibility of escape. In all such cases it would be wrong for the judge to give such direction as the appellant contends for here, and the more so if (as frequently happens) the case is already complicated by the fact that defences of provocation, lack of intent and self-defence are all in play at once.

We therefore have to consider whether the possibility that the appellant mistook the victim's intentions towards her was sufficiently realistic for it to merit an express and distinct direction to the jury. This is not an easy task, since counsel appearing on the appeal differ as to their recollection of the way in which the case was conducted. Since of course no record exists of their closing submissions to the jury we thought it proper to postpone the delivery of judgment (the appellant being no longer in custody) whilst a transcript of the exchange with the judge after the jury retired was obtained, to see whether it cast any light on the problem. After a regrettably long delay this transcript is now available, but advances the matter very little further. All one can glean from it is that counsel for the defendant thought that honest mistake was a feasible middle ground between a rejection of the appellant's case that the victim was making as if to kill her, and an acceptance that this might be true.

We are therefore obliged to fall back on the evidence itself. Two points stand out: (1) Although the medical evidence suggests that the attack actually made was in pure physical terms not of great severity, it took place against the background of quite serious violence and threats of worse. (2) In one of the passages quoted the choice was not between a potentially lethal attack and a trifling assault. Even on the prosecution's case the victim tried unsuccessfully to get the appellant out of the front door by force, and then (being unsuccessful) grasped her by the throat.

It seems to us on these facts that the possibility of the appellant honestly believing that on this particular occasion the victim was really going to do what he had previously threatened – even if in fact this was not what he was going to do – was not so fanciful as to require its exclusion from the case as a piece of unnecessary clutter. This being so, although we respectfully endorse the learned judge's desire to keep the case as simple as possible, we consider that on this occasion he went too far. What the jury would have made of it if the point had been developed we cannot tell, but each of us considers that the jury might have felt that the possibility of mistake could not be excluded, in which case the question on proportionate response would have been crucially different. Thus, although conscious of differing from a judge of great experience who was present at the trial and had a chance to take the measure of it which we have not, we are constrained to hold that there was a misdirection. Since there can be no question of applying the proviso the appeal must be allowed.

R v Owino [1996] 2 Cr App R 128 (CA)

Collins J: ... The appellant and his wife had both been married before but were divorced when they first met in 1992 when they were working at a hospital in Kent, he as a doctor and she as a nurse. They were attracted and decided that they would get married.

The appellant was to move to a new post in London in 1993, and obtained a flat in Southgate. On 3 September 1993 they were married and went to live together at that flat. Very shortly after the marriage things began to go wrong. She said that he was extraordinarily jealous, and this led to arguments in which he treated her with physical violence. He said that she had a very violent temper and would blow up and go for him in a physical way, and that any violence that he did to her was purely in order to restrain her.

It is necessary to give a short account of the circumstances of each of the alleged assaults in order fully to follow the points made by Mr Mendelle on this appellant's behalf.

The first occurred on 2 October 1993 and resulted in the appellant's wife's wrist being fractured. Mrs Owino (she was referred to at trial by her maiden name of Miss Coulson) said that a row developed following a visit to the flat of the appellant's daughter by his previous marriage and, in the course of that argument, he grabbed her by the wrists, twisted her left wrist outwards, causing the ulna to break. She said that he refused to take her to hospital for some time, an allegation which was not supported by his daughter, who was called to give evidence.

There was evidence from the surgeon who treated her that the fracture was more likely to have been caused by a twist than a fall.

That was relevant because the appellant said that his wife had fallen off a chair when standing on it to reach for something in a cupboard in the kitchen when he was not even in the room, and it was that that caused her to break her wrist. That is indeed the story that she told various people, including the casualty officer when she went to hospital. Although some considerable time later in December, and of course when she gave her evidence, she said that the story was incorrect and that her husband had caused the fracture by twisting her wrist.

Count 2 related to an incident on 15 November. Miss Coulson alleged that the appellant had, in the course of an argument, punched her in the face a number of times, causing her to suffer a black eye. She undoubtedly did receive a black eye and she did attend hospital as a result. The hospital notes record that she could not recall what had happened because she was drunk. The appellant said that he saw the black eye the next morning. It had appeared overnight, and his wife told him that it had been caused when she had gone into the kitchen to get a glass of water and had unfortunately walked into the kitchen door.

Count 3 was an incident on 30 November 1993. There was an argument about sleeping arrangements. She said that this developed into him hitting her repeatedly about the head, causing her, among other things, to fear that she had damaged her eardrum. She telephoned the police.

Again she went to the hospital. She saw a Dr Shakani, who had photographs taken. There was a fresh bruise to the back of her head and old bruising to her left eye, her jaw and her arms, but the doctor said the bruising had 'several different ages' and was unlikely to have been caused, he thought, in merely restraining her.

The appellant's account was that they did have a quarrel in which they both pushed each other. She was screaming that she did not want him to sleep with her. She then calmed down. She woke him again at 3 am, wanting to talk to him. He refused to talk. She called him a 'selfish bastard' and began pushing and shoving him, and so he picked her up to take her from the room. She broke away and things calmed down. Any injuries she sustained were thus, if he was right, caused when he was using force to restrain her from attacking him.

After this incident she left him. She returned of her own volition in mid-December, about a fortnight or so later. There was no improvement in her temper, according to him, but they did spend Christmas together. She had been staying with her sister and had completed a list of matters which had aggravated the relationship. This did not include violence by him. Her explanation for that was that she was listing things which might create violence; she was not listing violent episodes themselves.

Finally, we come to count 4, which occurred on 3 January 1994. He was decorating the bathroom. There was a quarrel about her using the lavatory. This developed into a tussle of some sort. She said he hit her and threw her out of the flat, injuring her right thumb. Again, Dr Shakani was seen. He was not able to observe any new bruising, save for some reddening to the top of her back, but there were other bruises of variable age.

The appellant's case was that there had indeed been a quarrel. She made some very offensive remarks, and so he had lifted her up and put her out of the house.

Generally in the course of this interview with the police he denied any violence, with the exception of slaps, which were admitted towards the end of the interview, when he said:

> I don't deny she has bruises, but usually when Marie starts lunging, I usually hold her and that's where there is some pushing and falling. I don't deliberately hit her. I have never punched or kicked her or shoved her head against a wall or the floor. I've slapped her, yes; most I've done.

He denied that he had ever deliberately used violence to her except in those circumstances.

It is clear that in relation to counts 3 and 4, self-defence was being raised, the appellant's case being that any bruising suffered by his wife for which he was responsible was caused only by reasonable force used in restraining her and in preventing her from assaulting him. In those circumstances it was obviously incumbent upon the learned judge to give a full and proper direction as to the elements of self-defence and also to draw the jury's attention to the distinction between provocation by words or by conduct, which would not, and threats or actual attack which could raise an issue of self-defence. If there is material which raises this issue, the burden is of course on the prosecution to prove that the violence used was excessive and was not used in self-defence.

Unfortunately, the learned judge did not refer to self-defence at all in his summing up, and the jury retired shortly after 1 pm without any such direction being given to them. It was perfectly plain that such a direction ought to have been given ...

With the greatest of respect to the learned judge, if, as indeed was clear, the issue of self-defence had been raised on the evidence, he had a duty to put it to the jury and to direct the jury upon it. The fact, if it be a fact, that counsel had not specifically referred to self-defence in the course of their speeches was no reason for the learned judge not to deal with it in his summing up.

We are told by Mr Mendelle that he did not specifically use the word self-defence in the course of his submissions to the jury, nor, as we understand it, did counsel for the prosecution, Miss Kamill. But it was a matter, he says, that the jury were well aware of because the interview which the appellant had had with the police made it perfectly plain, in the passage to which we have already referred, that any violence that he had used to his wife was used only when he was restraining her when she was attacking or, perhaps, threatening to attack him. So, as we have said, in those circumstances, it was clearly necessary for the learned judge, whatever counsel may or may not have said, to have dealt with the matter in the course of his summing up. But the jury having sent the note, he then proceeded to deal with it.

Complaint is made by Mr Mendelle that he did not deal with it even then as adequately as he ought to have done. Mr Mendelle essentially submits that he failed to direct the jury, as he ought to have done, that any force used must be unlawful, in the sense that it must have been excessive – more than was reasonable for self-defence; and further, that the test of what was reasonable was subjective, in the sense that the defendant could not be convicted unless he intended to use force which was more than was necessary for lawful self-defence. He relies on the authority of *Scarlett* [1993] 4 All ER 629 to support that proposition.

Before I come to the case of *Scarlett* specifically, it is our view that the law does not go as far as Mr Mendelle submits that it does. The essential elements of self-defence are clear enough. The jury have to decide whether a defendant honestly believed that the circumstances were such as required him to use force to defend himself from an attack or a threatened attack. In this respect a defendant must be judged in accordance with his honest belief, even though that belief may have been mistaken. But the jury must then decide whether the force used was reasonable in the circumstances as he believed them to be.

Scarlett was a case where a landlord of a public house had been ejecting and perfectly lawfully and properly ejecting, a drunken customer from his public house. The allegation was that he had used excessive force in the course of ejecting him so that the customer fell down the steps of the entrance to the pub and unfortunately hit his head and was killed. What Mr Mendelle relies upon in the case of *Scarlett* is a passage at pp 295, 296 and p 636 of the respective reports, where Beldam LJ, giving the judgment of the court, said this:

> Where, as in the present case, an accused is justified in using some force and can only be guilty of an assault if the force used is excessive, the jury ought to be directed that he cannot be guilty of an assault unless the prosecution prove that he acted with the mental element necessary to constitute his action an assault, that is 'that the defendant intentionally or recklessly applied force to the person of another'. Further, they should be directed that the accused is not to be found guilty merely because he intentionally or recklessly used force which they consider to have been excessive. They ought not to convict him unless they are satisfied that the degree of force used was plainly more than was called for by the circumstances as he believed them to be and, provided he believed the circumstances called for the degree of force used, he is not to be convicted even if his belief was unreasonable.

In this case the learned judge gave no direction to the jury that the prosecution, to establish an assault, had to prove that the appellant intentionally or recklessly applied excessive force in seeking to evict the deceased.

The passage which we have cited could, if taken out of context, give rise to a suggestion that the submission by Mr Mendelle is well-founded. But what, in the context, the learned Lord Justice was really saying was, in our view, this: he was indicating that the elements of an assault involved the unlawful application of force. In the context of an issue of self-defence or reasonable restraint, which was what Scarlett was essentially about, then clearly a person would not be guilty of an assault unless the force used was excessive; and in judging whether the force used was excessive, the jury had to take account of the circumstances as he believed them to be. That is what is made clear in the first part of the sentence, which we will isolate and read again:

> They ought not to convict him unless they are satisfied that the degree of force used was plainly more than was called for by the circumstances as he believed them to be and, provided be believed the circumstances called for the degree of force used, he is not to be convicted even if his belief was unreasonable.

So far as the second half of the sentence is concerned, what we understand the learned Lord Justice to have been saying was that, in judging what he believed the circumstances to be, the jury are not to decide on the basis of what was objectively reasonable; and that even if he, the defendant, was unreasonable in his belief, if it was an honest belief and honestly held, that he is not to be judged by reference to the true circumstances. It is in that context that the learned Lord Justice talks about '[belief] that the circumstances called for the degree of force used', because clearly you cannot divorce completely the concept of degree of force and the concept of the circumstances as you believe them to be. In our judgment, that is effectively all that the learned Lord Justice was saying.

What he was not saying, in our view (and indeed if he had said it, it would be contrary to authority) was that the belief, however ill-founded, of the defendant that the degree of force he was using was reasonable, will enable him to do what he did. As Kay J indicated in argument, if that argument was correct, then it would justify, for example, the shooting of someone who was merely threatening to throw a punch, on the basis that the defendant honestly believed, although unreasonably and mistakenly, that it was justifiable for him to use that degree of force. That clearly is not, and cannot be, the law.

In truth, in the view of this court, the law was properly and adequately set out in the case of *Williams* [1984] 3 All ER 411, which was cited and referred to in *Scarlett* and the court in *Scarlett* was not going beyond what is set out in *Williams* ...

In the light of all that, we have to decide whether the direction given by the learned judge after the question was asked was adequate.

He told the jury that an assault was a deliberate, unlawful, hostile act committed against the person of another; he went on:

> If that occurs, you are entitled to defend yourself if attacked or if threatened with attack.

He then gave the classic direction in relation to self-defence. Unfortunately, he did not indicate that the burden was on the Crown to disprove self-defence. That was raised by Mr Mendelle, and the learned judge, that having been raised, said:

> You are absolutely right; I am grateful, members of the jury, self-defence is, of course, a plea of not guilty. In other words, 'I did not assault. I did not do what the Crown allege.' The burden is always on the Crown to prove their case and to establish that the force used or the restraint used was not reasonable in the circumstances. The burden shifts to the Crown to negative and destroy the defence of self-defence if it is put forward by a defendant. That was your point, was it not, Mr Mendelle?

Mr Mendelle: 'Yes.'

Mr Mendelle rightly criticises that because it indicates that there is a defence of self-defence and the burden shifts to the Crown. In one sense, of course, technically it does, because there is an evidential burden on the defence to raise the issue of self-defence in the first place. But it is not a helpful way of putting it.

Nonetheless, we have to ask ourselves whether, in the context of the direction as a whole, that really can have muddled the jury or led them to believe that there was any burden on the defence. In the light of the direction as a whole, we do not think that can reasonably have been the impression gained by the jury.

But it did not stop there, because the foreman of the jury then himself asked a question; he said:

> The question is about lifting people out of the room against their will while struggling.

That, clearly, was highly material on count 4 and may have been material too on count 3. The learned judge then said this:

> That must be a question of fact for you. You must look at all the circumstances of the case and you may say, 'In those circumstances, was that reasonable force?' Indeed, you must go further than that because it is not only whether it is reasonable force objectively looked at, it is whether or not the person so acting genuinely and instinctively believed it was other than reasonable force – genuinely believed that it was reasonable force, but it is upon the prosecution to establish that there was not such genuine belief. It is important to remember that.

That direction was, on the face of it, as favourable, in our view, as the defence could have hoped. Indeed it went further in favour of the defence than the law made necessary ...

Where the defendant's mistake regarding self-defence arises because he is intoxicated

R v O'Grady [1987] 1 QB 995 (CA)

Lord Lane CJ: ... The appellant was addicted to drinking large quantities of alcohol, as were the friends and acquaintances with whom he consorted, one of whom was McCloskey, the deceased man. On Thursday 26 September 1985, the appellant, McCloskey and another man called Brennan spent the day drinking. The appellant had drunk huge quantities of cider (some eight flagons), and he and Brennan and McCloskey repaired to the appellant's flat.

Early on Friday morning Brennan woke up to see that the appellant was covered in blood. 'We' – meaning McCloskey and himself – 'had a fight', said the appellant, 'and I felt him and he was cold.' The appellant went to the police station saying he wished to report a murder. He was medically examined. He had a number of cuts and bruises to the head, hands and legs which were consistent with (a) fighting and (b) grasping broken glass ...

... He said, 'I did not want to kill him. I wanted him alive, not dead. I had no enmity to him. If I had not hit him I would be dead myself.'

... How should the jury be invited to approach the problem? One starts with the decision of this court in *R v Williams (Gladstone)* (1984) 78 Cr App R 276, namely that where the defendant might have been labouring under a mistake as to the facts he must be judged according to that mistaken view, whether the mistake was reasonable or not. It is then for the jury to decide whether the defendant's reaction to the threat, real or imaginary, was a reasonable one. The court was not in that case considering what the situation might be where the mistake was due to voluntary intoxication by alcohol or some other drug.

We have come to the conclusion that where the jury are satisfied that the defendant was mistaken in his belief that any force or the force which he in fact used was necessary to defend himself and are further satisfied that the mistake was caused by voluntary induced intoxication, the defence must fail. We do not consider that any distinction should be drawn on this aspect of the matter between offences involving what is called specific intent, such as murder, and offences of so called basic intent, such as manslaughter. Quite apart from the problem of directing a jury in a case such as the present where manslaughter is an alternative verdict to murder, the question of mistake can and ought to be considered separately from the question of intent. A sober man who mistakenly believes he is in danger of immediate death at the hands of an attacker is entitled to be acquitted of both murder and manslaughter if his reaction in killing his supposed assailant was a reasonable one. What his intent may have been seems to us to be irrelevant to the problem of self-defence or no ...

This brings us to the question of public order. There are two competing interests. On the one hand the interest of the defendant who has only acted according to what he believed to be necessary to protect himself, and on the other hand that of the public in general and the victim in particular who, probably through no fault of his own, has been injured or perhaps killed because of the defendant's drunken mistake. Reason recoils from the conclusion that in such circumstances a defendant is entitled to leave the court without a stain on his character.

We find support for that view in the decision of the House of Lords in *R v Majewski* [1977] AC 443, and in particular in the speeches of Lord Simon of Glaisdale and Lord Edmund-Davies. [His Lordship quoted from the speech of Lord Simon at 476 and the speech of Lord Edmund-Davies at 492.]

His Lordship then referred to *R v Lipman* [1970] 1 QB 152 and went on to say that if the arguments put forward by the appellant in the present case were correct.

Lipman could successfully have escaped conviction altogether by raising the issue that he believed he was defending himself legitimately from an attack by serpents. It is significant that no one seems to have considered that possibility ...

Notes and queries

1   Where D makes a genuine mistake as to the need to act in self-defence he is judged on the facts as he believed them to be and, provided the force used was reasonable in the circumstances as he believed them to be, he will be acquitted – *Beckford*. If D is genuinely in a situation where he is justified in using force by way of self-defence, but makes a mistake as to the extent of the force required and uses more force than is reasonable, he has no defence *Clegg*. Is this fair?

SELF-DEFENCE AND NECESSITY

As will have been seen from the above extracts self-defence (whether at common law or under statute) arises where D claims that he was compelled to act to prevent a greater evil, whether this be harm to himself, others, harm to his property or the prevention of crime. The defence of necessity does not, of course, extend to killing another person in order to save one's own life. How can this be reconciled with the fact that the law allows D to kill another in self-defence? The answer lies, in part, in the status of the victim. In *R v Dudley and Stephens* (see Chapter 13) the cabin boy killed by the defendants was an 'innocent' party. Where D kills P in order to prevent a murderous attack by P, P ceases to be an 'innocent' party – in effect he becomes fair game. This can cause difficulties where P is under the age of criminal responsibility – in such cases is it really accurate to say that P is not 'innocent'? The following extract addresses the matter.

Re A (Children) (Conjoined Twins: Surgical Separation) [2000] 4 All ER 961

For the facts see Chapter 13. His Lordship considered whether operating to save one conjoined twin in the knowledge that it would cause the certain death of the other would offend the 'sanctity of life' principle.

> **Ward LJ**: The second reason why the right of choice should be given to the doctors is that the proposed operation would not in any event offend the sanctity of life principle. That principle may be expressed in different ways but they all amount to the same thing. Some might say that it demands that each life is to be protected from unjust attack. Some might say as the joint statement by the Anglican and Roman Catholic bishops did in the aftermath of the *Bland* judgment that because human life is a gift from God to be preserved and cherished, the deliberate taking of human life is prohibited except in self-defence or the legitimate defence of others. The Archbishop defines it in terms that human life is sacred, that is inviolable, so that one should never aim to cause an innocent person's death by act or omission. The reality here – harsh as it is to state it, and unnatural as it is that it should be happening – is that Mary is killing Jodie. That is the effect of the incontrovertible medical evidence and it is common ground in the case. Mary uses Jodie's heart and lungs to receive and use Jodie's oxygenated blood. This will cause Jodie's heart to fail and cause Jodie's death as surely as a slow drip of poison. How can it be just that Jodie should be required to tolerate that state of affairs? One does not need to label Mary with the American terminology which would paint her to be 'an unjust aggressor', which I feel is wholly inappropriate language for the sad and helpless position in which Mary finds herself. I have no difficulty in agreeing that this unique happening cannot be said to be unlawful. But it does not have to be unlawful. The six year old boy indiscriminately shooting all and sundry in the school playground is not acting unlawfully for he is too young for his acts to be so classified. But is he 'innocent' within the moral meaning of that word as used by the Archbishop? I am not qualified to answer that moral question because, despite an assertion – or was it an aspersion? – by a member of the Bar in a letter to *The Times* that we, the judges, are proclaiming some moral superiority in this case, I for my part would defer any opinion as to a child's

innocence to the Archbishop for that is his territory. If I had to hazard a guess, I would venture the tentative view that the child is not morally innocent. What I am, however, competent to say is that in law killing that six year old boy in self-defence of others would be fully justified and the killing would not be unlawful. I can see no difference in essence between that resort to legitimate self-defence and the doctors coming to Jodie's defence and removing the threat of fatal harm to her presented by Mary's draining her life-blood. The availability of such a plea of quasi self-defence, modified to meet the quite exceptional circumstances nature has inflicted on the twins, makes intervention by the doctors lawful.

CODIFICATION AND LAW REFORM PROPOSALS

The most recent examination of the use of force by way of defence has been in the context of the Law Commission's review of offences against the person *Legislating the Criminal Code: Offences Against the Person* (Law Com 218). Its proposals as regards the lawful use of force are set out in clauses 27–29 of the Criminal Law Bill attached to the report.

27(1) The use of force by a person for any of the following purposes, if only such as is reasonable in the circumstances as he believes them to be, does not constitute an offence –

(a) to protect himself or another from injury, assault or detention caused by a criminal act;

(b) to protect himself or (with the authority of that other) another from trespass to the person;

(c) to protect his property from appropriation, destruction or damage caused by a criminal act or from trespass or infringement;

(d) to protect property belonging to another from appropriation, destruction or damage caused by a criminal act or (with the authority of the other) from trespass or infringement; or

(e) to prevent crime or a breach of the peace.

(2) The expressions 'use of force' and 'property' in subsection (1) are defined and extended by sections 29 and 30 respectively.

(3) For the purposes of this section an act involves a 'crime' or is 'criminal' although the person committing it, if charged with an offence in respect of it, would be acquitted on the ground that –

(a) he was under ten years of age, or

(b) he acted under duress, whether by threats or of circumstances, or

(c) his act was involuntary, or

(d) he was in a state of intoxication, or

(e) he was insane, so as not to be responsible, according to law, for the act.

(4) The references in subsection (1) to protecting a person or property from anything include protecting him or it from its continuing; and the reference to preventing crime or a breach of the peace shall be similarly construed.

(5) For the purposes of this section the question whether the act against which force is used is of a kind mentioned in any of paragraphs (a) to (e) of subsection (1) shall be determined according to the circumstances as the person using the force ('D') believes them to be.

In the following provisions of this section references to unlawful or lawful acts are to acts. which are or are not of such a kind.

(6) Where an act is lawful by reason only of a belief or suspicion which is mistaken, the defence provided by this section applies as in the case of an unlawful act. unless –

(a) D knows or believes that the force is used against a constable or a person assisting a constable, and

(b) the constable is acting in the execution of his duty,

in which case the defence applies only if D believes the force to be immediately necessary to prevent injury to himself or another.

(7) The defence provided by this section does not apply to a person who causes conduct or a state of affairs with a view to using force to resist or terminate it.

But the defence may apply although the occasion for the use of force arises only because he does something he may lawfully do, knowing that such an occasion may arise.

28(1) The use of force by a person in effecting or assisting in a lawful arrest, if only such as is reasonable in the circumstances as he believes them to be, does not constitute an offence.

(2) The expression 'use of force' in subsection (1) is defined and extended by section 29.

(3) For the purposes of this section the question whether the arrest is lawful shall be determined according to the circumstances as the person 5 using the force believed them to be.

29(1) For the purposes of sections 27 and 28 –

(a) a person uses force in relation to another person or property not only where he applies force to, but also where he causes an impact on, the body of that person or that property;

(b) a person shall be treated as using force in relation to another person if –

(i) he threatens him with its use, or

(ii) he detains him without actually using it; and

(c) a person shall be treated as using force in relation to property if he threatens a person with its use in relation to property.

(2) Those sections apply in relation to acts immediately preparatory to the use of force as they apply in relation to acts in which force is used.

(3) A threat of force may be reasonable although the actual use of force would not be.

(4) The fact that a person had an opportunity to retreat before using force shall be taken into account, in conjunction with other relevant evidence, in determining whether the use of force was reasonable.

The commentary in the report provides the following rationale for these proposals:

Introduction

36.1 The Draft Code brought together for the first time various elements in the existing common law relating to the justifiable use of force, and expressed that part of the law in a rational statutory form. In LCCP 122 we provisionally proposed the statutory adoption of a similar clause, which would in effect codify the existing common law, and some related statutory additions, while at the same time eliminating some of the inconsistencies and uncertainties that have been produced by the unconnected development of different areas of the law.

36.2 It is, however, important to note that even the rationalised version of the common law that we proposed in LCCP 122, and which we recommend in this Report, does not cover all cases in which a person may use force against the person or property of another without incurring criminal liability. The law set out in the Criminal Law Bill covers a wide range of possible events, and seeks to define the circumstances in which the defence of justified use of force will apply with as much clarity as possible, in order to assist courts and other users in those cases where issues of the use of force for self-protection or cognate purposes most often arise ...

36.3 The most significant element in this part of the law is the present common law of self-defence. The basis of the present law of self-defence is that a person has a defence to a criminal charge if he acts to prevent the commission of an unjustifiable attack on himself or another, and the steps that he takes are reasonable in the circumstances as he believes them to be. The attack will often itself be criminal, but it need not necessarily be so in order to fulfil the requirements of the present law of self-defence. The present common law has a number of important features, which we stress here because they form the basis of the general statutory provision that we put forward in LCCP 122, and which is reproduced in substance in the Criminal Law Bill.

36.4 The essential justification of the defendant's acts is that he has acted for *self-protection*. No act that is done for motives of revenge, or in a spirit of informal punishment, can even potentially qualify for consideration under this defence.

36.5 The question for the jury is whether the defendant's acts of self-protection were reasonable in the circumstances that he believed to exist. That question has two distinct elements.

36.6 First, the defendant is judged according to the facts as he believed them to be. That was clearly established in the present law by the judgment of Lord Lane CJ in *Gladstone Williams* and further confirmed by the Privy Council in *Beckford v R*. This element, as Lord Lane pointed out, is of importance in eliminating the possibility that the accused was acting under a genuine mistake of fact. His Lordship emphasised that the reasonableness or unreasonableness of any belief alleged by the defendant is relevant to the question of whether the defendant held the belief at all: because if an unreasonable belief is alleged the jury are likely to have difficulty in thinking that the accused may be telling the truth. But, again to cite Lord Lane, 'If the belief was in fact held, its unreasonableness, so far as guilt or innocence is concerned, is neither here nor there'.

36.7   In his judgment the Lord Chief Justice referred to the recommendation of the CLRC in its Fourteenth Report that:

> The common law of self-defence should be replaced by a statutory defence providing that a person may use such force as is reasonable in the circumstances as he believes them to be in the defence of himself or any other person.

The court considered that that proposition already represented the common law. The statutory expression of the law of self-defence that we proposed in LCCP 122, and which we repeat in the Criminal Law Bill, therefore gives effect to the CLRC's desire that the defence should be put on a statutory footing, and incorporates the statement of the law that was considered to be correct both by the CLRC and by the court in *Gladstone Williams*.

36.8   In practice, the principle that the accused must be judged on the facts as he believed them to be is unlikely frequently to be decisive of the outcome of a case. It will not often be the case, and the jury are unlikely often to think, that the defendant may have mistakenly believed that, for instance, he or another person was about to be attacked, when a reasonable person in the defendant's position would not have so believed. But, for instance in a confused situation of brawling or disorder in a street or public house, or where there is a heated argument between two individuals, A may genuinely mistake B's raising of his hand as the immediate precursor of an attack on A, rather than as merely his seeking to emphasise a point or to summon help. Somewhat similarly, police officer A may wrongly and indeed unreasonably believe that B whom he is arresting is armed, and use the amount of force against him that would be reasonable if his belief were true; or he may make a mistake of identity, and think that B, an innocuous person, is C, a dangerous armed criminal. In such circumstances it would be unjust, as the Court of Appeal said in Gladstone Williams, if A, provided he did no more than would have been reasonably required to avoid an expected attack on himself, and not in a spirit of aggression or revenge, were to be exposed to criminal liability simply because of his mistaken or even negligent belief.

36.9   The second requirement of the present law of self-defence is that while, as emphasised in *Gladstone Williams*, the defendant is judged according to what he believed the circumstances to be, he will only be able to claim the benefit of this defence if he has acted (objectively) reasonably in the light of those circumstances. This requirement is equally as important as that just discussed. It is not for the defendant himself to adjudicate upon the reasonableness of the steps that he takes to prevent the offence, because that would unfairly and dangerously exculpate defendants who had an irresponsible, irrational or anti-social notion of the extent to which it is acceptable to react when threatened with attack. The reasonableness of the defendant's reaction is rather to be adjudicated upon by the jury, as a means of applying an external control to the conduct of persons who think themselves to be under attack.

The approach of the Criminal Law Bill

37.1   In LCCP 122 we proposed the adoption of the principles set out above, and their extension beyond the central case of self-defence to other cases where, in the present law, a defendant may be excused if he acts to protect valid personal and social interests: in particular, if he acts to protect property, or to prevent crime or in the arrest of offenders.

37.2   In these latter cases, the law is already broadly the same as that obtaining in the case of defence of the person. There are, however, some anomalies, and some unjustifiable gaps or uncertainties in the provision that the law currently makes. Clause 28 of the Bill that we submitted for consultation under LCCP 122 aimed to rationalise these problems, in line with the general principles of self-defence set out above. There was no significant dissent on consultation from that approach, which we have therefore felt justified in following through in the Criminal Law Bill. It may however be helpful if we summarise the gaps or illogicalities in the present law that clauses 27–30 of the Criminal Law Bill address.

37.3   The Criminal Damage Act 1971, section 5(2)(b), enables a person to rely on his purpose of protecting property as a 'lawful excuse' for the destruction of, or damage to, property belonging to another. The Criminal Law Act 1967, section 3(1), has been interpreted as providing a defence to a charge of reckless driving where a driver forces another car off the road in order to effect a person's arrest, at least where the 'force' used is 'reasonable in the circumstances'. But no provision at present identifies as a 'lawful excuse', for an act directed against property, the purpose of defending a person against unlawful force or of releasing a person from unlawful detention. Conversely, no provision at present expressly permits, in defence of property against an attack (as opposed to prevention of the crime that that attack may constitute), a use of force other than force directed against other property. The law is thus in need of the rationalisation provided by the Criminal Law Bill, since it ought surely to be made explicit that the purpose of protecting valuable property against vandalism is a defence to a use of modest force against the vandal; as, equally, it ought to be made explicit that force against property may be excusable when used in protection of a person as well as when used in protection of other property.

37.4   The Criminal Law Bill (together with amendments to the Criminal Damage Act) aims to improve further on existing law by providing consistently for the various purposes for which force may be lawfully used. The lawfulness of force used to protect a person against a violent attack ought not to depend upon whether its purpose is described as preventing the aggressor's crime or as the defence of the victim: the same act may have both purposes. But at present the use of force in the prevention of crime, as in effecting an arrest, is governed by section 3 of the Criminal Law Act 1967, and the use of force in self-defence or the defence of another is governed by the common law; and the principles are probably not quite the same.

37.5   A further important anomaly in the present law is that, as stressed in paragraph 36.9 above, the common law only allows such force in defence of the person as is objectively reasonable; whereas section 5(2)(b) of the Criminal Damage Act 1971 permits a person to damage or destroy another's property in order to protect his own property if he believes the means of protection that he employs to be reasonable. That cannot be right. It is anomalous that different, and less stringent, standards should apply when a person is defending his property than when he is defending his person, or defending another person; and it is in any event undesirable in any case, for the reasons suggested in paragraph 36.9 above, that the reasonableness of an accused's conduct should be judged by him rather than by objective external standards supervised by the court.

37.6   The Criminal Law Bill does not propose the complete repeal of section 5 of the Criminal Damage Act, and its replacement by the general provisions of the proposed new clauses. We think that it will be easier for those who have to deal with this chapter of the law if section 5, which has stood for twenty years, is retained as a special defence in cases of damage to property, even though it will substantially overlap with the new clause. That however is subject to the important qualification that the defence provided by the Criminal Damage Act should be amended to bring it into line, in respect of the requirement that the defendant's conduct should be objectively reasonable, and not merely reasonable in his own estimation, with the common law of self-defence that is described above. That step, which was proposed in LCCP 122,117 and not dissented from on consultation, is therefore provided for in the Criminal Law Bill .

37.7   On consultation on LCCP 122 there was no substantial disagreement with the approach contained in that Consultation Paper and outlined above. In particular, no respondent disagreed with the principle established in *Gladstone Williams* that the accused should be judged according to the circumstances that he believed to exist. We are therefore able with some confidence to put forward in the Criminal Law Bill a scheme that is in substance the scheme contained in LCCP 122 and, indeed, in the Draft Code.

37.8   Respondents to consultation did, however, make some valuable comments on the detailed drafting of the Bill annexed to LCCP 122, and our own further consideration has also caused us to review that draft in some respects. That has been done principally in order to clarify the application of the law in cases where people act under a mistake as to the other party's intentions, for instance where D mistakenly thinks that P is about to attack him or steal his property, and takes what would, if he were right, be reasonable pre-emptive action. Such cases may not arise, or be prosecuted, very frequently, but prosecutors and courts require guidance when they do.

37.9   Clauses 27–30 of the Criminal Law Bill set out a statement of the law in a form that is intended to give as complete guidance as is possible to police, prosecutors and the citizen in considering this part of the law, and to the courts in applying it ... these clauses bring what is in effect the present common law immediately and clearly to the attention of all those concerned with cases where self-defence or related matters are in issue. These basic provisions are grouped in clause 27. Provisions addressing special cases, and more detailed and explanatory matter, are placed in clauses 28–30.

37.10 The rest of this part of the Report comments on the provisions of those clauses. It will be convenient in that discussion to refer to the person using the force as 'D', and to the person against whom the force is used as 'P'.

PURPOSES FOR WHICH THE USE OF FORCE CAN BE JUSTIFIED

The concept of use of force

38.1 Clauses 27–30 of the Criminal Law Bill set out the circumstances in which the use of 'force' against the person or property of another will not constitute a criminal offence. The clauses apply generally, to all offences, though in practice they are most likely to come into play where self-defence is relied on as a defence to charges of assault or of the more serious offences against the person that are contained in clauses 2–4 of the Criminal Law Bill; and in cases of homicide.

38.2 The basic meaning of 'force' is not likely to cause difficulty, and the Criminal Law Bill contains no definition of this simple everyday concept. Some particular cases, including threats to use force, and the detention of a person without actually using force, are, however, dealt with in clause 29 of the Criminal Law Bill.

Types of conduct that may justify the use of force

38.3 The purposes for which the use of force may be justified, if the force is reasonable in the circumstances that D believes to exist, are listed in clause 27(1). A further purpose, the use of force in effecting or assisting in a lawful arrest, is, for the reasons explained in paragraph 38.31 below, separately set out in clause 28 of the Criminal Law Bill. It is important to note that all these categories are not mutually exclusive: for instance, where D acts to prevent P from assaulting him he will be simultaneously protecting himself from a criminal assault; and protecting himself from a tortious trespass; and seeking to prevent the commission of a crime by P. The question in any case will, therefore, be whether D's acts fall within any one of the categories listed in clauses 27 and 28.

38.4 In accordance with the basic requirement of the defence of self-defence, that was mentioned in paragraph 36.4 above, the essence of all these cases is that they should have as their motive the *protection* of persons or property, or the *prevention* of crime or breach of the peace.

38.5 We have endeavoured in the Criminal Law Bill to set out the various cases in a way that identifies for users the nature of, and justification for, the particular categories. For that reason, we have abandoned the use of the generalised concept of protection against 'unlawful' force or injury, in favour of separately identifying protection against criminal and against tortious acts ...

...

38.7 We now comment briefly on the cases listed in clause 27(1). In accordance with the current law as explained in paragraphs 36.6–36.8 above, whether a situation falls within one of the categories in which the use of force may be justified is to be determined according to the circumstances as the defendant,

D, believed them to be. That rule is stated explicitly in clause 27(5) of the Criminal Law Bill. If D knows or believes that the circumstances are such that P's acts do not fall into any of the categories of conduct against which force may *prima facie* be legitimately used, then he cannot claim the protection of this defence. But if he, even wrongly, believes that P's conduct is such that it would amount to a crime, or to a trespass against D, then it would seem wrong that he should be burdened with criminal liability if he reacts reasonably to protect person or property from a feared attack.

38.8 *'Self-defence'*. Paragraphs (a) and (b) reproduce the present law of self-defence, that was described in paragraphs 36.4–36.8 above. For reasons that are explained in paragraph 38.19ff below, it is convenient to deal separately with protection against criminal and against tortious interference with the person, though in all but the most unusual cases the two categories will overlap. The Bill's extended definition of 'force', as including force in relation to property, cures what might otherwise be a lacuna in the present law, where there is no explicit provision justifying acts directed at property for the purpose of defending a person from unlawful injury or detention.

38.9 Paragraphs (a) and (b) apply, as does the present law, to the reasonable defence of others, as well as to the defence of the person actually using the force; so for that reason it is not strictly accurate to describe the paragraphs as dealing with self-defence. One particular aspect of the use of force by D to protect a third party should however be noted.

38.10 Paragraph (b) addresses acts by P that are trespasses to the person but which are not or may not be a *criminal* act: principally where there is or may be doubt as to whether P's attack takes place with the mental element necessary for criminal liability. In respect of the protection of others from trespass, the Criminal Law Bill confirms the proposal of LCCP 122 that where an act of P directed against a third party is merely trespassory and not criminal, D should only be able to use force to prevent it with the agreement of that third party. This limitation on officious intermeddling in the affairs of others is perhaps of more practical importance in relation to acts done to protect the property of others, which we discuss in paragraph 38.15 below.

38.11 *Protection of property*. Where D is charged with criminal damage and his defence is that he was acting in defence of his own property, for instance where D kills P's dog that he claims was attacking his sheep, his liability will continue to be adjudicated on by the rules laid down under the Criminal Damage Act 1971. The provisions of paragraphs (c) and (d) of clause 27(1) of the Criminal Law Bill are however required to confirm, what is not expressly provided in the current law, that the same principles as apply in cases of self-defence extend also to the use of force against a person to protect property. What would be reasonable in such circumstances would, of course, be adjudicated upon in the light of the force having been used to protect property rather than a person: it being generally more reasonable to use serious force to protect a person than when merely property interests are at stake.

38.12 In respect of the non-criminal acts on the part of P to which the defence *prima facie* applies, we consider that 'trespass' as used in paragraphs (c) and (d) will better focus attention on the type of case in which this defence might properly arise than did the more general formula of 'unlawful appropriation, destruction or damage' that we proposed in LCCP 122.

38.13 Paragraphs (c) and (d) of clause 27(1) of the Criminal Law Bill do, however, refer, as did the LCCP 122 Bill, to 'infringement' of property That, together with the definition of 'property' in clause 30(1) of the Criminal Law Bill as including any right, interest or privilege over property, keeps this defence in line with the Criminal Damage Act, where the defence provided by section 5(2)(b) extends to the protection of an interest in property including, by section 5(4), any right or privilege in or over land. Under the Criminal Law Bill, therefore, reasonable force may be permissibly used to prevent unlawful interference with the exercise of such a right (for instance, an easement or a right to fish) rather than merely to protect the property itself.

38.14 The interest or right protected must, however, be in or over tangible property. We had originally, in LCCP 122, thought that the defence of reasonable use of force could appropriately, if in practice not very frequently, be applied in relation also to interferences with intangible property. However, it has been brought to our attention that the Copyright, Design and Patents Act 1988, while providing for certain acts of self-help on the part of a copyright owner, places strict limits on such acts. The decision to place limitations on the protection of intangible property even in the case of perhaps the paradigmatic example of such property, copyright, is, we think, an indication that Parliament sees legal action rather than the direct protection of rights as the appropriate course in such cases. We do not think it appropriate that we should potentially undermine that policy by extending the present defence to cases of protection of intangible property.

38.15 Clause 27(1)(d) of the Criminal Law Bill envisages the use of force by D to protect the property of a third party. Where that protection is against trespass or infringement of a non-criminal nature, D does not have the benefit of this defence unless he acts with the authority of the third party. That distinction seems to us to be a sensible one. Where D is intervening to prevent a criminal act, he should not have to seek the permission of another party; and in any event will have the protection of the defence of prevention of crime under clause 27(1)(e) of the Criminal Law Bill. Where, however, P's interference is objectionable only because it is tortious against a third party, and not against D, D should not be encouraged to intervene in that dispute unless he does so on behalf of the third party. At the same time, however, in cases of emergency, where D judges that he has to act without the authority of the third party, and without the opportunity to warn or question P about his activities, then D will be able to rely on the defence of necessity. Cases of such a sort, where P's activities do not constitute or threaten the commission of a crime, are likely to be rare. We think it right that before D intervenes in such non-criminal activity directed at a third party the element of urgent need that characterises the defence of necessity should be present.

38.16 *Prevention of crime.* Clause 27(1)(e) of the Criminal Law Bill, in respect of the prevention of crime, covers the same ground as section 3 of the Criminal Law Act 1967. It will replace that section in relation to criminal liability for the use of force for that purpose. Section 3 will continue in operation in respect of civil liability for the use of force.

38.17 This category of excuse will often overlap with those already discussed; since, as pointed out above, one who protects himself, or his or another's property, from criminal interference will almost necessarily also be preventing or terminating the commission of a crime. However, conversely, clause 27(1)(e) is not otiose, since D may act to prevent crime in circumstances where he is not protecting the person or property of himself or another: for instance, where D restrains P, who is clearly dangerously intoxicated, from driving P's motor vehicle.

38.18 *Breach of the peace.* Specific reference to prevention or termination of a breach of the peace is required because breach of the peace is a wider concept than 'crime', and prevention of such a breach of the peace is, particularly in public order situations, a common occasion for the legitimate use of force. Paragraph (e) makes it clear that it is not an offence to use reasonable force either to prevent a person's being put in fear of the kind that constitutes a breach of the peace, or to remove the cause of such fear where it already exists.

Defence against non-culpable acts: particular cases

38.19 There will occasionally arise cases where a person should have a defence of reasonable protection against the acts of another, although those acts are not in fact 'criminal' because of some particular circumstance, or some characteristic of his, that exculpates him from criminal liability. That lack of criminal liability on the part of the actor does not, however, reduce the threat that his acts pose to others. For instance a person may be attacked with a dagger by a nine year old child, or by a person suffering from severe mental illness; or P may be forced by threats made by X that afford him a defence of duress to make a murderous attack on D.

38.20 Often such acts will or may be tortious, even if not criminal, and therefore fall under clause 27(1)(b) of the Criminal Law Bill. However, there may be difficulties of fact in establishing the state of mind necessary for tortious liability in the case of infants or persons with mental disability; and the effect on tortious liability of duress operating on the defendant is far from clear. It is not acceptable that the determination of the criminal liability of persons who protect themselves from such attacks should, even in the rare cases where that question may arise, depend on complicated enquiries into the law of tort, and the possible failure of the defence of reasonable use of force because, for reasons that are perfectly valid within the law of tort, the attacker is not subject to civil liability.

38.21 To avoid these difficulties, the Criminal Law Bill provides that the defence will be available in a number of cases where the fact of what would otherwise be a criminal act occurs, but for particular reasons the actor would not be subject to criminal liability. [See clause 27(3)] ...

38.22 Paragraph [27(3)](c) is required to cover those cases where P, if charged, would be acquitted on grounds of 'automatism' or involuntary act. For instance, in the perhaps not very likely case of P attacking D while in a hypoglycaemic episode, or suffering from concussion, D should not incur criminal liability if he takes reasonable steps to defend himself. The reference to possible exculpation of P from criminal liability because of his intoxication is necessary principally to account for the special case, identified by the Court of Appeal in *Kingston*, where although P has the intent to commit the forbidden act, his conduct is not criminal because his ability to resist the desire to do that act was reduced or excluded by involuntary intoxication.

38.23 It should be emphasised that, in practice, it is not often likely to be necessary for D to have recourse to the special provisions of clause 27(3) in order to establish that the case falls within one of the categories listed in clause 27(1). That is because, as we explained in paragraph 38.7 above, those categories are assessed on the facts as D believes them to be. In most cases where D is attacked by a person who is under age, insane, acting in a state of automatism, or in the very limited circumstances where intoxication makes his act non-criminal, D will not have directed his mind to those special facts. He will know no more than the facts that, if they stood alone, would make the attack on him criminal in nature. Those facts justify him in morality and common sense and, by the operation of clause 27(1) of the Criminal Law Bill, in terms of criminal liability, in defending himself against an apparently criminal act. But D may in some cases know or believe the further facts that do or may render P's conduct non-criminal: perhaps the clearest example is likely to be where D knows that P is under ten years of age. It is only in such cases that clause 27(3) is necessary, to ensure that D can defend himself against acts that are 'criminal' in all respects except that, for a particular reason that happens to be known to D, P would not be convicted if charged in respect of them.

Defence against non-culpable acts: mistaken belief or suspicion

38.24 The cases dealt with above involve specific circumstances that exempt P from criminal liability for what may, nonetheless, be an attack against which D is entitled to defend himself or another. A problem of a more general nature arises where P would, if prosecuted, escape liability because he believed in circumstances that gave him a defence: often, the defence of reasonable use of force. We may give some examples of cases that could arise, in all of which D might legitimately wish or see the need to use force against P.

(i) P, a store-detective, wrongly thinks that D has not paid for goods that D is in the course of removing from the store. He attempts to arrest D. P has reasonable grounds for suspecting D to be committing theft, and therefore his arrest is lawful. D uses force to resist the arrest.

(ii) P comes upon a fight in the street between D and X. D is in fact lawfully attempting to make a 'citizen's arrest'. P, not realising that, and thinking that D is gratuitously attacking X, intervenes to restrain D. D in turn uses force to resist

(iii) P, a plain clothes police officer, is ordered to arrest X, a dangerous criminal. He mistakenly thinks that D is in fact X, and attempts to arrest him, using force that would be reasonable if he were arresting X. D resists, using force.

(iv) P knows that D is a supplier of controlled drugs. He wrongly thinks that D has a load of such drugs in his car, and is about to drive the car to hand the drugs over to a customer. P is in the process of disabling D's car, to prevent the supply of the drugs, when D comes on the scene, and uses force to prevent P from completing his work on the car.

(v) P is employed by X to demolish the garden shed at X's country cottage. P by mistake goes to the wrong house, X not being present, and starts to demolish the shed of D, X's next door neighbour. D intervenes to restrain P.

(vi) P takes the wrong overcoat from the cloakroom at a hotel. D, the cloakroom attendant, thinking that P is stealing the coat, attempts to take the coat from him by force.

38.25 As in the cases discussed in paragraph 38.23 above, it will normally not be necessary to have recourse to a special rule in order to deal justly with D's case. In most cases of the type exemplified above, D will not know the special facts that render P's acts non-criminal. For example, in case (ii) D is most likely to think, in the confusion of the melee in the street, that P is intervening unlawfully to assist X; or in case (iii) that P, who he does not know to be a police officer, is a thug making a criminal attack upon him. In these circumstances D will, under the general rule laid down by clause 27(1) of the Criminal Law Bill, be judged according to the reasonableness of his reaction in those believed circumstances.

38.26 What, however, if D knows of P's mistake? Then, in the circumstances as D believes them to be, P's actions are lawful. Nevertheless, it can hardly be right that the present defence should be withheld from D if he acts reasonably to protect himself or his property. In all the cases stated P's act is lawful only because of a mistake or suspicion on the part of P that is in fact incorrect. D is nonetheless put in a position of potential peril, that is not in any way lessened by P's error, and the fact D knows of the error should not shut him out from the defence.

38.27 This case is dealt with by clause 27(6) of the Criminal Law Bill, that provides that where an act potentially falling into one of the categories set out in clause 27(1) is lawful (according, as provided by clause 27(5), to the circumstances as D believes them to be) by reason only of a mistaken belief or suspicion on the part of the actor, then the defence of reasonable use of force will continue to be available in respect of steps taken in response to that act.

38.28 It should again be emphasised, however, that in none of these cases is D given carte blanche to use whatever force he pleases, just because the situation that he is facing comes potentially within the reach of the present defence. He must act reasonably in the circumstances as he believes them to be. If he knows that P is only acting as he does because of a mistake on P's part, it may often be reasonable initially not to use force at all to rectify the situation, but rather to explain to P the nature of his mistake. That would very likely be the case where P's error has caused him to interfere only with property, as in paragraph 38.24(vi) above. Where, however, P's mistake leads him to use force against D, there may not be time for, and it would not be reasonable to expect D to delay so that he can make, explanations. D should not in such circumstances find himself suffering criminal liability if all that he does is to act reasonably to secure his immediate protection.

38.29 The approach that we now recommend to these difficulties, as explained in paragraphs 38.22–38.28 above, relies on a narrower and more specific statutory formula than did the Bill presented for consultation under LCCP 122, which envisaged the acts of P being deemed to be 'unlawful' for the purpose of this defence if P 'lacked the fault required for the offence or believed that an exempting circumstance existed'. That formula would undoubtedly cover all the cases discussed above, but it would go much wider than them: because very many perfectly innocuous acts are criminal but for the fact that the actor lacks the fault required for criminal liability. Let us cite a simple case. D may hire his motor-car to P. P in driving another person's car away would be committing a crime were it not for the fact that by reason of D's permission he lacks the fault (dishonesty; and an intention permanently to deprive the owner) that is required for him to be guilty of theft. To include a case where D, wanting to break his contract, uses force to reverse his previous decision to lend the car to P within even the potential ambit of the present defence would be to deprive those having to make decisions about the application of the law of much of the guidance that it is the aim of the Criminal Law Bill to provide. It is true that in practice D would be unlikely to benefit from the defence, because where D knows that P's acts are innocent it can hardly ever be reasonable for him to use any force to interfere with those acts. We think, however, that the Criminal Law Bill should do as much as it can to state expressly the cases where the availability of the defence can even potentially arise, and not put all the burden on the ultimate test of whether D's action was reasonable.

Use of force in effecting or assisting in a lawful arrest

38.30 Section 3 of the Criminal Law Act 1967, referred to in paragraph 38.16 above, permits the use of reasonable force in effecting lawful arrest, as well as in the prevention of crime. That objective is, and has long been regarded as being, as much a proper occasion for the use of reasonable force as are the cases listed in clause 27(1) of the Criminal Law Bill that are discussed above.

38.31 It is, however, convenient to deal separately with this case, as is done in clause 28 of the Criminal Law Bill, because where D uses force to make a lawful arrest, the simple and single test of whether his conduct potentially falls within the present defence should be whether the arrest would have been lawful in the circumstances as he believed them to be. The somewhat elaborate provisions that are required in other cases, to elucidate those cases where D is reasonably protecting himself against acts that. in fact are or may not be objectively criminal, do not arise in this case.

38.32 It will therefore make for clarity if the simple rule in the arrest case is stated separately. This will be of particular importance in cases involving police officers. Clause 28 emphasises that the general rule that the criminality of a defendant's conduct is to be judged according to the circumstances as he believed them to be extends to protecting from criminal punishment conduct that is reasonable in effecting an arrest where the officer, or citizen, believes, even if mistakenly, that circumstances exist that would make the arrest lawful.

38.33 It may also be worth repeating that the only effect of this clause is to assist in determining whether the arrester commits a criminal offence by his use of force. Other provisions deal with, for instance, civil liability for that use of force [see Clause 28 of the Criminal Law Bill] ...

Other features of this defence

Force against a constable in the execution of his duty

...

39.2 [Clause 27(6)] ... is a special public policy exception to the general rule, described in paragraphs 38.26–38.27 above, that, where D knows of P's mistake, D may still take reasonable steps to resist P's attack on him. The exception applies where P, although mistaken, is a police constable acting in the execution of his duty. It can be illustrated from the most usual type of case in which the exception might arise.

39.3 Various provisions, notably in the Police and Criminal Evidence Act 1984 permit citizens, and in a wider range of circumstances constables, to make arrests on grounds of suspicion of commission of an offence, provided that the arrester has reasonable grounds for that suspicion. If such an arrest is attempted on D, who in fact knows that the suspicion is incorrect, he will, save where the special exception in respect of constables applies, have the defence provided by clause 27(5) and the first part of clause 27(6) of the Criminal Law Bill if he merely uses defensive force that is reasonable in the circumstances. Here again, as we suggested in paragraph 38.28 above, in many cases the reasonable reaction may be the giving of an explanation rather than the use of force: but if force is reasonably used to resist, D should not be criminally liable for so acting.

39.4 There are, however, special considerations where the arrester is a constable. If a constable making the arrest has reasonable grounds for his suspicion, even if that suspicion is mistaken, he is acting in accordance with his duty, and not unlawfully: see the provisions of the Police and Criminal Evidence Act 1984 referred to in paragraph 39.3 above. If D knows that the arrester is a constable, and for the reasons mentioned above the constable is in fact acting in the execution of his duty, the arrest may not be resisted even though the constable's suspicion is known by the person arrested to be mistaken. This special exception, in the case of force used against a person known to be a constable, who is in fact acting in the execution of his duty, accords with existing authority. It is usually thought to be justified or required by the need to encourage obedience to constables who are in fact (as the statement of the exception requires) acting in the execution of their duty. There was no substantial disagreement on consultation that that exception should be maintained.

39.5 Clause 27(6) further provides, however, that this principle does not hold where the person using force 'believes the force to be immediately necessary to prevent injury to himself or another'. For example, a constable, mistaking an innocent person for a dangerous armed criminal, may be about to use disabling or even lethal force to neutralise the imminent threat to himself or others that he believes the 'criminal' to represent. In these circumstances the innocent person may use reasonable force to save himself from injury if he believes that it is immediately necessary to do so. This rule probably coincides with existing law, and, again, it was not the subject of substantial challenge on consultation.

Must the use of force be, or be thought to be, immediately necessary?

39.6 In LCCP 122 we discussed at some length whether there should be a requirement that the defence is only available where the defendant fears or is subject to an immediate attack upon him. Such a requirement is in any event only appropriate for the particular case of self-defence; and even there it adds an unnecessary element of complication and formality, since in every case where there has been an element of 'pre-emptive' action by the defendant the court and jury will have to decide whether that action was reasonable in the circumstances.

39.7 We therefore provisionally proposed that no such express requirement should be contained in the Criminal Law Bill. Of those who addressed this matter on consultation the majority, including the General Council of the Bar and the Society of Public Teachers of Law, agreed with our provisional conclusion. We have therefore adopted that approach in the Bill, which includes no additional rule that the use of force by the defendant must, as a separate requirement, be shown to have been immediately necessary.

Preparatory acts

39.8 Clause 29(2) ensures that criminal liability (most obviously, under legislation prohibiting the possession of firearms and offensive weapons) will not attach to an act immediately preparatory to a use of force permitted by the clause.

'Self-induced' occasions for the use of force

39.9 The effect of the first part of clause 27(7) is that clause 27 provides no defence to a person who deliberately provokes the very attack against which he then defends himself. On the other hand, the second part of the subsection preserves the liberty of the citizen to go about his lawful business even if he knows that he is likely to be met by unlawful violence from others. If he does so and is attacked, he may defend himself.

Opportunity to retreat

39.10 Clause 29(4) restates the law on the significance of a defendant's having had an opportunity to retreat before using force. Although the fact that he had such opportunity is relevant to the court's or jury's consideration of whether his use of force was reasonable, it is not conclusive of the question and is simply to be taken into account together with other relevant evidence.

Circumstances unknown to and unsuspected by the actor

39.11 It follows from the requirement that the defendant be judged according to the circumstances as he believes them to be that he cannot rely on circumstances unknown to him that would in fact have justified acts on his part that were unreasonable on the facts as he perceived them. Although opinion was not unanimous on consultation, we think it right to maintain this long-standing common law rule. Citizens who react unreasonably to circumstances should not be exculpated by the accident of facts of which they were unaware.

Relation to other defences

Necessity and duress of circumstances

40.1 Cases may arise where it is felt unreasonable for a person to be put in peril of a criminal charge by doing acts to protect the person or property of himself or others, but where the circumstances do not fall even under the comparatively broadly expressed terms of the present defence. The present defence largely follows the present law by envisaging the use of force to avoid the consequences of a direct attack by another upon person or property. Cases will arise, however, where D needs to, and should properly, react to other types of danger. For instance, D may beat off, and thereby injure, a dog that is attacking him, or is attacking his or another's small child; or he may pull down another person's wall or fence in order to provide a fire-break against a fire that is threatening a residential area. Alternatively, the danger may accrue from another human being, but not take the form of any sort of direct or deliberate interference with D: for instance, P's entirely lawful driving of his motor-car may threaten a child that has carelessly run into the road.

40.2   Other instances of legitimate action by D which however fall outside the limits of the defence of justified use of force as defined in the Criminal Law Bill can easily be imagined. We have already mentioned, in paragraph 38.15 above, intervention in an emergency to protect another person's property, from non-criminal interference, but without the authority of that person. More generally, D may in some circumstances legitimately act to save P from himself, for instance if D restrains a small child to prevent him from wandering over a cliff or going too close to a fire. Few if any such cases would be seriously considered for prosecution. But if they were, in such cases, and in the examples suggested in paragraph 40.1 above, there remains available, as a safeguard, either the defence of duress of circumstances, under clause 26(1) of the Criminal Law Bill; or the developing defence of necessity, discussed in paragraphs 35.5–35.6 above. As we have already emphasised, the Criminal Law Bill's rationalisation of the defence of Justifiable Use of Force does not in any way affect the common law on those defences, just as they already cohabit with the existing common law defence of self-defence on which the defence of Justifiable Use of Force is based.

40.3   It would not be possible to adapt the defence of justified use of force to cover all such possible cases without producing a defence expressed in unduly wide terms, which would be in danger of taking the concept and defence of necessity further than the courts have yet seen fit to do. Extension of the defence of necessity is only appropriate on a case by case basis, in the context of such cases as are actually sought to be made the subject of criminal liability. The defence in the Criminal Law Bill, rather, provides for the application of clear and consistent principles in cases of the type that experience suggests are in practice most likely to be addressed by the criminal law, and in which guidance is required as to the appropriateness of the application of criminal sanctions.

Excessive self-defence

40.4   We refer to this matter here only to avoid possible misunderstanding. In accordance with our normal policy in drawing up the Draft Code we included in it the recommendation of the CLRC that where a person charged with murder *prima facie* would be able to rely on the defence of self-defence, but falls outside the ambit of that defence because he uses unreasonable force to defend himself, then, instead of losing the defence entirely, he should be convicted of manslaughter and not of murder. That is a special issue arising in the law of homicide, which is not covered in this Report, and on which we do not comment: the recommendation of the CLRC would clearly need thorough consideration in the context of a review of the law of homicide before it could be adopted. The issue has no effect at all on the general defence of reasonable use of force that we propose in this Report.

Further reading

C Harlow, 'Self-defence: public right or private privilege' [1974] Crim LR 528

M Giles, 'Self-defence and mistake: a way forward' (1990) 53 MLR 187

JC Smith, 'The right to life and the right to kill in law enforcement' (1994) 144 NLJ 354

CHAPTER 15

HOMICIDE

This chapter brings together material related to homicide, that is, the unlawful killing of a human being. The offences that come within the scope of homicide are:

- murder;
- voluntary manslaughter;
- involuntary manslaughter by an unlawful act;
- killing by gross negligence (including corporate manslaughter).

There are certain elements that are common to all murder and manslaughter cases – matters that have to be established by the prosecution if the case is to proceed.

THE VICTIM MUST BE A 'LIFE IN BEING'

The prosecution must prove that the victim in a murder or manslaughter case was a 'reasonable creature' – this means a creature capable of reasoning: that is, any human being. Many of the old cases that dealt with this issues arose out of botched abortions or deliveries, hence the term 'life in being' came to mean a child that had been fully expelled from its mother's body and capable of existence independent of its mother. With the introduction of statutory offences specifically designed to protect the unborn, in particular the Infant Life (Preservation) Act 1929, the matter has given rise to less litigation. The 1929 Act provides that any person who intentionally causes the death of a child capable of being born alive commits an offence carrying with it the possibility of life imprisonment. The Act contains a rebuttable presumption in s 1(2) that a child is capable of being born alive once 28 weeks of gestation have passed. If there was doubt, therefore, as to whether a child had been killed whilst *in utero*, or after having been born, the prosecution would simply proceed on the basis of alternative counts, murder and a charge under the 1929 Act. Two cases have, however, given rise to a consideration of the issue in the modern era, and are thus worthy of consideration on this point.

AG's Ref (No 3 of 1994) [1997] 3 All ER 936

For the facts see Chapter 4. Lord Mustill stated that his third established relating to homicide could be expressed thus:

> Except under statute an embryo or foetus in utero cannot be the victim of a crime of violence. In particular, violence to the foetus which causes its death in utero is not a murder.

The foundation authority is the definition by Sir Edward Coke of murder ... The proposition was developed by the same writer into examples of prenatal injuries as follows:

> If a woman be quick with child, and by a potion or otherwise killeth it in her womb; or if a man beat her, whereby the child dieth in her body, and she is delivered of a dead child; this is a great misprision, and no murder ...

It is unnecessary to look behind this statement to the earlier authorities, for its correctness as a general principle, as distinct from its application to babies expiring in the course of delivery or very shortly thereafter, has never been controverted ...

Lord Mustill then turned to consider the two arguments put forward by the Crown on this point.

> The decision of the Court of Appeal founded on the proposition that the foetus is part of the mother, so that an intention to cause really serious bodily injury to the mother is equivalent to the same intent directed towards the foetus. This intent could be added to the *actus reus*, constituted (as I understand it) by the creation of such a change in the environment of the foetus through the injury to the mother that the baby would be born at a time when, as events proved, it would not survive. I must dissent from this proposition for I believe it to be wholly unfounded in fact. Obviously, nobody would assert that once the mother had been delivered of S, the baby and her mother were in any sense 'the same'. Not only were they physically separate, but they were each unique human beings, though no doubt with many features of resemblance. The reason for the uniqueness of S was that the development of her own special characteristics had been enabled and bounded by the collection of genes handed down not only by M but also by the natural father. This collection was different from the genes which had enabled and bounded the development of M, for these had been handed down by her own mother and natural father. S and her mother were closely related but, even apart from differing environmental influences, they were not, had not been, and in the future never would be 'the same.' There was, of course, an intimate bond between the foetus and the mother, created by the total dependence of the foetus on the protective physical environment furnished by the mother, and on the supply by the mother through the physical linkage between them of the nutriments, oxygen and other substances essential to foetal life and development. The emotional bond between the mother and her unborn child was also of a very special kind. But the relationship was one of bond, not of identity. The mother and the foetus were two distinct organisms living symbiotically, not a single organism with two aspects. The mother's leg was part of the mother; the foetus was not.

> The only other ground for identifying the foetus with the mother that I can envisage is a chain of reasoning on the following lines. All the case law shows that the child does not attain a sufficient human personality to be the subject of a crime of violence, and in particular of a crime of murder, until it enjoys an existence separate from its mother; hence, whilst it is in the womb it does not have a human personality; hence it must share a human personality with its mother. This seems to me an entire *non sequitur*, for it omits the possibility that the foetus does not (for the purposes of the law of homicide and violent crime) have any relevant type of personality but is an organism *sui generis* lacking at this stage the entire range of characteristics both of the mother to which it is physically

linked and of the complete human being which it will later become. The argument involves one fiction too far, and I would reject it ...

The second argument: the foetus as a separate organism ...

I would, therefore, reject the reasoning which assumes that since (in the eyes of English law) the foetus does not have the attributes which make it a 'person' it must be an adjunct of the mother. Eschewing all religious and political debate I would say that the foetus is neither. It is a unique organism. To apply to such an organism the principles of a law evolved in relation to autonomous beings is bound to mislead ...

I turn to deal more briefly with the remaining rules. The third rule, it will be recalled, is that a foetus cannot be the victim of murder. I see no profit in an attempt to treat the medieval origins of this rule. It is sufficient to say that is established beyond doubt for the criminal law, as for the civil law (*Burton v Islington Health Authority* [1993] QB 204) that the child *en ventre sa mère* does not have a distinct human personality, whose extinguishment gives rise to any penalties or liabilities at common law.

Re A (Children) (Conjoined Twins) [2000] 4 All ER 961

For the facts see Chapter 13 – the following extract concerns the issue of whether or not Mary, the weaker of the two conjoined twins, who was incapable of independent existence, was to be regarded as a life in being for the purposes of the law of homicide.

Brooke LJ:

Is Mary a reasonable creature?

For the reasons given by Ward LJ and Robert Walker LJ, with which I agree, I am satisfied that Mary's life is a human life that falls to be protected by the law of murder. Although she has for all practical purposes a useless brain, a useless heart and useless lungs, she is alive, and it would in my judgment be an act of murder if someone deliberately acted so as to extinguish that life unless a justification or excuse could be shown which English law is willing to recognise.

In recent editions of *Archbold*, including the 2000 edition, the editors have suggested that the word 'reasonable' in Coke's definition (which they wrongly ascribe to Lord Hale in para 19.1) related to the appearance rather than the mental capacity of the victim and was apt to exclude 'monstrous births'. Spurred on by this suggestion, and because the present case broke so much novel ground, we explored with counsel some of the thinking of seventeenth century English philosophers in an effort to ascertain what Coke may have meant when he used the expression 'any reasonable creature' as part of his definition. We had in mind their absorbing interest in the nature of 'strange and deformed births' and 'monstrous births' (see Thomas Hobbes, *Elements of Law*, II.10.8, and John Locke, *An Essay Concerning Human Understanding*, III.III.17, III.VI.15 and 26 and III.XI.20).

In *AG's Ref (No 3 of 1994)* [1998] AC 245 Lord Mustill referred at p 254F to another statement in Coke's *Institutes*, not mentioned in that passage in *Archbold*, where after referring to prenatal injuries which lead to the delivery of a dead child, Coke writes (Co Inst Pt III, Ch 7, p 50):

if the childe be born alive, and dieth of the potion, battery, or other cause, this is murder; for in law it is accounted a reasonable creature, *in rerum natura*, when it is born alive.

In these circumstances I have no hesitation in accepting the submission by Miss Davies QC (whose assistance, as the friend of the court, was of the greatest value), which was in these terms:

> In *The Sanctity of Life and the Criminal Law* (1958), Professor Glanville Williams stated at p 31:
>
>> There is, indeed some kind of legal argument that a 'monster' is not protected even under the existing law. This argument depends upon the very old legal writers, because the matter has not been considered in any modern work or in any court judgment.

After discussing the meaning of the word 'monster' (which might originally have connoted animal paternity) he states at pp 33–34:

> Locked (Siamese) twins present a special case, though they are treated in *medical* works as a species of monster. Here the recent medical practice is to attempt a severance, notwithstanding the risks involved. Either the twins are successfully unlocked, or they die [emphasis added].

It is implicit in this analysis that the author is of the view that 'Siamese' twins are capable of being murdered and the *amicus curiae* supports this view.

Advances in medical treatment of deformed neonates suggest that the criminal law's protection should be as wide as possible and a conclusion that a creature in being was not reasonable would be confined only to the most extreme cases, of which this is not an example. Whatever might have been thought of as 'monstrous' by Bracton, Coke, Blackstone, Locke and Hobbes, different considerations would clearly apply today. This proposition might be tested in this way: suppose an intruder broke into the hospital and stabbed twin M causing her death. Clearly it could not be said that his actions would be outside the ambit of the law of homicide.

Modern English statute law has mitigated the prospective burden that might otherwise fall on the parents of severely handicapped children and their families if they are willing to avail themselves of its protection at any time up to the time the child (or children) is born. Section 1(1)(d) of the Abortion Act 1967, as substituted by s 37(1) of the Human Fertilisation and Embryology Act 1990, provides:

> Subject to the provisions of this section, a person shall not be guilty of an offence under the law relating to abortion when a pregnancy is terminated by a registered medical practitioner if two registered medical practitioners are of the opinion, formed in good faith ... that there is a substantial risk that if the child were born it would suffer from such physical or mental abnormalities as to be severely handicapped.

Once a seriously handicapped child is born alive, the position changes, and it is as much entitled to the protection of the criminal law as any other human being. The governing principle is sometimes described as the universality of rights. In the Canadian case of *Perka v R* 13 DLR (4th) 1 Wilson J said at p 31 that the principle of the universality of rights demands that all individuals whose actions are subjected to legal evaluation must be considered equal in standing.

It follows that unless there is some special exception to which we can have recourse, in the eyes of the law Mary's right to life must be accorded equal status with her sister Jodie's right to life. In this context it is wholly illegitimate to introduce considerations that relate to the quality, or the potential quality, of each sister's life.

THE DEFENDANT MUST BE SHOWN TO HAVE CAUSED THE DEATH IN FACT AND IN LAW

Murder and manslaughter are both result crimes, in the sense that the defendant must be proved to have caused the death of the victim in fact and in law. The chain of causation may be broken if there is evidence of a *novus actus interveniens*. These issues were considered in Chapter 3. It used to be the case that, for a person to be convicted of murder or manslaughter, the death of the victim had to occur within a year and a day of the act or omission which caused the death. Section 1 of the Law Reform (Year and a Day Rule) Act 1996, however, abolishes this rule. Section 2 of the Act provides instead:

Section 2 of the Law Reform (Year and a Day) Act 1996

(1) Proceedings to which this section applies may only be instituted by or with the consent of the Attorney General.

(2) This section applies to proceedings against a person for a fatal offence if:

    (a) the injury alleged to have caused the death was sustained more than three years before the death occurred; or

    (b) the person has previously been convicted of an offence committed in circumstances alleged to be connected with the death.

(3) In subsection (2) 'fatal offence' means:

    (a) murder, manslaughter, infanticide or any other offence of which one of the elements is causing a person's death; or

    (b) the offence of aiding, abetting, counselling or procuring a person's suicide.

An example of the operation of s 2(2)(b) would be where a person is convicted of causing grievous bodily harm and, after the conviction, the victim dies; in such a case, the consent of the Attorney General must be obtained before the person is prosecuted for murder (even if three years have not elapsed since the date of the assault).

THE SPECIFIC REQUIREMENTS OF MURDER

For a defendant to be convicted of murder he must have caused the death of a life in being and must be shown to have acted with the requisite *mens rea* – an intention to kill a human being, or an intention to cause a human being grievous bodily harm. The issue of causation was considered in Chapter 3. The nature of intention, particularly in the context of murder, was considered in Chapter 4, see in particular *R v Woollin* [1999] 1 AC 82. The term 'malice aforethought' is often used to denote the *mens rea* required for murder – see the classic definition of murder set out in Coke's *Institutes* (3 Co Inst 47): 'Murder is when a [person] ... unlawfully killeth ... any reasonable creature *in rerum natura* under the Queen's peace, with malice aforethought ... so as the party wounded or hurt, etc dies of the wound or hurt' – but it is submitted that, in the modern context, this phrase is likely to mislead. The defendant charged with murder does not need to have displayed any 'malice' towards his victim – it may, for example, be a mercy killing. Further, there is no need for the prosecution to prove that the killing was in any way premeditated or planned. All in all the phrase is best avoided.

Chapter 4 provides lengthy extracts from the key cases illustrating the development of the *mens rea* of murder in the modern era, through *R v Hancock* [1986] 1 All ER 641, *R v Nedrick* [1986] 1 WLR 1025 and *R v Woollin*. The following extracts concentrate on the extent to which the current law relating to the *mens rea* is considered rational and justifiable by the judiciary.

AG's Ref (No 3 of 1994) [1997] 3 All ER 936

Lord Mustill: My Lords murder is widely thought to be the gravest of crimes. One could expect a developed system to embody a law of murder clear enough to yield an unequivocal result on a given set of facts, a result which conforms with apparent justice and has a sound intellectual base. This is not so in England, where the law of homicide is permeated by anomaly, fiction, misnomer and obsolete reasoning. One conspicuous anomaly is the rule which identifies the 'malice aforethought' (a doubly misleading expression) required for the crime of murder not only with a conscious intention to kill but also with an intention to cause grievous bodily harm. It is, therefore, possible to commit a murder not only without wishing the death of the victim but without the least thought that this might be the result of the assault. Many would doubt the justice of this rule, which is not the popular conception of murder and (as I shall suggest) no longer rests on any intellectual foundation. The law of Scotland does very well without it, and England could perhaps do the same. It would, however, be fruitless to debate this here, since the rule has been established beyond doubt by *R v Cunningham* [1982] AC 566. This rule, which I will call the 'grievous harm' rule, is the starting point of the present appeal ...

Lord Mustill summarised the law thus:

1 It is sufficient to raise a *prima facie* case of murder (subject to entire or partial excuses such as self-defence or provocation) for it to be proved that the defendant did the act which caused the death intending to kill the victim or to cause him at least grievous bodily harm.

Although it will be necessary to look at the reasoning which founded this rule, it is undeniably a part of English law. (See *R v Vickers* [1957] 2 QB 664; *Hyam v DPP* [1975] AC 55; *R v Cunningham* [1982] AC 566.) Thus, if M had died as a result of the injuries received B would have been guilty of murdering her, even though in the everyday sense he did not intend her death ...

The materials for scrutinising the existing rules to see how they could be built upon to answer a problem like the present are therefore quite meagre. But an attempt must at least be made. I begin with the first rule. Three lines of thought, not identical but intertwined, seem to have gone to make it up. First there was a presumption that when one person killed another this was culpable homicide unless, in the words of East: *Pleas of the Crown*, (1803) Vol I, cap V, section 12), the defendant proved that there were circumstances of accident, necessity or infirmity; or in a later formulation, unless justified, excused or alleviated (Blackstone: *Commentaries on the Laws of England*, 17th edn (1830), pp 200–01); and, later still (according to Stephen's *Digest of Criminal Law* (1877), art 230) unless there existed excuse, justification or extenuation. This rule survived, perhaps only in terms of an evidential burden of proof, until surprisingly late. It was not until *Woolmington v DPP* [1935] AC 462 that it was finally expunged. For so long as it was current there was no chance of saying that an intent to cause really serious injury was insufficient to found an indictment for murder, for that high degree of wrongful intent took away the possibility of establishing a recognised excuse for the death which actually ensued.

The second theme was the obverse of the first. The wrongful intent was a demonstration of a general wickedness of mind which expressed itself in whatever specific intent was necessary to give the act in question a criminal character. In short, the wicked intent showed that the defendant was a bad man with a 'depraved inclination to mischief' (*Russell on Crime*, 4th edn (1865), p 740, citing Hale, *History of the Pleas of the Crown* (1736), Vol I, p 475 and East, *Pleas of the Crown* (1803), Cap V, section 18); and this inclination, if resulting in death, should not go unpunished.

Finally, there was a concept of risk. The doer of a wicked act took the chance that the consequences would be greater than he could foresee. His narrower subjective intent was not an answer to his responsibility for the unintended wider consequences. As Hawkins, *Pleas of the Crown*, 7th edn (1795), Vol I, section 51, put the matter in relation to deaths happening in the course of tumultuous assemblies, 'They must at their peril abide the event of their actions who wilfully engage in such bold disturbances of the public peace.' Again, at a later date *Russell on Crime*, 4th edn, p 742 explains Coke's pronouncement that a beating in anger which causes death is murder by the fact that 'what he did was *malum in se* and he must be answerable for all its consequences'.

It was, I believe, the coalescence of these three concepts which founded a doctrine more extreme than the grievous harm rule, under which an unintended death resulting from the commission or attempted commission of an offence of any kind or degree was treated as murder. This had its most notorious expression in the pronouncement of Coke (*Inst*, Pt III, ch 8, p 56):

> If the act be unlawful it is murder. As if A meaning to steal a deer in the park of B, shooteth at the deer, and by the glance of the arrow killeth a boy that is hidden in a bush: this is murder, for that the act was unlawful, although A had no intent to hurt the boy, nor knew not of him ... [so also if one] had shot at a cock or hen, or any tame fowl of another man's, and the arrow by mischance had killed a man, this had been murder, for the act was unlawful.

As Sir James Stephen would much later show (*History of the Criminal Law* (1883), Vol 3, pp 57–58), this doctrine was never securely founded on the authorities, but it left its mark for more than two centuries. The controversy over it in the institutional writers need not be resumed here. It is sufficient to say that it came to be perceived as morally odious, and subsided without any close analysis into the concept of felony/murder, not perhaps very different from a form of 'general malice', where the evil intent required was of a high degree. In this form it survived into modern times, although narrowed still further by confinement to crimes of violence *DPP v Beard* [1920] AC 479. It is indeed still part of the law in some common law jurisdictions. Finally, it was abolished in England by section 1 of the Homicide Act 1957.

My Lords, since the original concepts are no longer available to explain why an intent to cause grievous bodily harm will found a conviction for murder the reason must be sought elsewhere: for reason, in regard to such a grave crime, there must surely be. The obvious recourse is to ascribe this doctrine to the last vestiges of the murder/felony rule, and to see in it a strong example of that rule, for unlike the more extravagant early manifestations it offers at least some resemblance in nature and degree between the intended act and its unintended consequences. It would follow, therefore, that when the murder/felony rule was expressly abolished by section 1 of the Homicide Act 1957 the only surviving justification for the 'grievous harm' rule fell away, with nothing left. This proposition was indeed advanced soon after the 1957 Act in *R v Vickers* [1957] 2 QB 664, where it was dismissed out-of-hand. The same concept was developed in *Hyam v DPP* [1975] AC 55, where after close analysis it was adopted by Lord Diplock, and in a concurring speech by Lord Kilbrandon. The majority in the House did not agree. The question was raised again in *R v Cunningham* [1982] AC 566, and this time a decisive answer was given. The 'grievous harm' rule had survived the abolition of the murder/felony principle. The speeches show that it did so because a solid and long-lasting line of authority had decreed that this was the law, and the House saw no need to change a rule which answered practical needs.

My Lords, in a system based on binding precedent there could be no ground for doubting a long course of existing law, and certainly none which could now permit this House even to contemplate such a fundamental change as to abolish the grievous harm rule: and counsel rightly hinted at no such idea. But when asked to strike out into new territory it is, I think, right to recognise that the grievous harm rule is an outcropping of old law from which the surrounding strata of rationalisations have weathered away. It survives but exemplifies no principle which can be applied to a new situation.

R v Powell and Daniels; R v English [1999] AC 1

For the facts see Chapter 9.

Lord Steyn: That brings me to the qualification which I have foreshadowed. In English law a defendant may be convicted of murder who is in no ordinary sense a murderer. It is sufficient if it is established that the defendant had an intent to cause really serious bodily injury. This rule turns murder into a constructive crime. The fault element does not correspond to the conduct leading to the charge, ie the causing of death. A person is liable to conviction for a more serious crime than he foresaw or contemplated: see Glanville Williams, *Textbook of Criminal Law*, 2nd edn (1983), pp 250–51; Ashworth, *Principles of Criminal Law*, 2nd ed, pp 85 and 261; Card, Cross and Jones, *Criminal Law*, 12th ed (1992), pp 203–04. This is a point of considerable importance. The Home Office records show that in the last three years for which statistics are available mandatory life sentences for murder were imposed in 192 cases in 1994; in 214 cases in 1995; and in 257 cases in 1996. Lord Windlesham, writing with great Home Office experience, has said that a minority of defendants convicted of murder have been convicted on the basis that they had an intent to kill: *Responses to Crime*, Vol 3 (1996), at 342, n 29. That assessment does not surprise me. What is the justification for this position? There is an argument that, given the unpredictability whether a serious injury will result in death, an offender who intended to cause serious bodily injury cannot complain of a conviction of murder in the event of a death. But this argument is outweighed by the practical consideration that immediately below murder there is the crime of manslaughter for which the court may impose a discretionary life sentence or a very long period of imprisonment. Accepting the need for a mandatory life sentence for murder, the problem is one of classification. The present definition of the mental element of murder results in defendants being classified as murderers who are not in truth murderers. It happens both in cases where only one offender is involved and in cases resulting from joint criminal enterprises. It results in the imposition of mandatory life sentences when neither justice nor the needs of society require the classification of the case as murder and the imposition of a mandatory life sentence.

The observations which I have made about the mental element required for murder were not directly in issue in the appeals under consideration. But in the context of murder the application of the accessory principle, and the definition of murder, are inextricably linked. For that reason I have felt at liberty to mention a problem which was not addressed in argument. That counsel did not embark on such an argument is not altogether surprising. After all, in *R v Cunningham* [1982] AC 566 the House of Lords declined to rationalise and modernise the law on this point. Only Lord Edmund-Davies expressed the hope that the legislature would undertake reform: see p 583B–C. In my view the problem ought to be addressed. There is available a precise and sensible solution, namely, that a killing should be classified as murder if there is an intention to kill or an intention to cause really serious bodily harm coupled with awareness of the risk of death: 14th Report of the Law Revision Committee (1980), para. 31, adopted in the Criminal Code for England and Wales (Law Com 177, 1986), clause 54(1). This solution was supported by the House of Lords Select Committee on *Murder and Life Imprisonment*, HL Paper 78-1, 1989, para 68.

Re A (Children) (Conjoined Twins) [2000] 4 All ER 961

Ward LJ: It is obvious that the question whether or not this operation can be lawfully performed is crucial to the outcome of the appeal. What I confess I had not fully appreciated was how rooted in obscurity the answer to those difficulties was ...

Is there some immunity for doctors?

Archbold 2000: Criminal Pleading Evidence & Practice, para 19-38, states that:

> *Bona fide* medical or surgical treatment is not 'unlawful' and therefore death resulting therefrom does not amount to murder, even though death or serious injury is foreseen as a probable consequence. Nor does it amount to

manslaughter, unless the person giving the treatment has been guilty of 'gross negligence'.

No authority is given for this sweeping statement. It is true that in *Gillick* Lord Scarman said at p 190:

> The *bona fide* exercise by a doctor of his clinical judgment must be a complete negation of the guilty mind which is an essential ingredient of the criminal offence of aiding and abetting the commission of unlawful sexual intercourse.

Lord Mustill speaks of it in *Bland*. Yet hanging over *Bland* is the spectre of murder. To have crossed the Rubicon would have been to murder. I, therefore, approach the question of lawfulness of the proposed separation on the basis that, whatever immunity doctors do enjoy, they have no complete immunity. I have to be satisfied that in this case they will not be guilty of unlawfully killing Mary by active intervention – and perhaps of unlawfully killing Jodie by omitting to act in her interests if there is a duty upon them to do so ...

... It is sufficient for present purposes simply to note that, despite several attempts by the House of Lords to clarify the *mens rea* required to establish murder, 'the law of murder was in a state of disarray': *per* Lord Steyn in *R v Woollin* [1999] 1 AC 82, 91A. *Woollin* is binding upon us and, despite Mr Owen QC's submission that Article 2 of the European Human Rights Convention will require us to recast the definition, I do not propose to do so. Law which has long needed to be settled should be left to settle. The test I have to set myself is that established by that case. I have to ask myself whether I am satisfied that the doctors recognise that death or serious harm will be virtually certain (barring some unforeseen intervention) to result from carrying out this operation. If so, the doctors intend to kill or to do that serious harm even though they may not have any desire to achieve that result. It is common ground that they appreciate that death to Mary would result from the severance of the common aorta. Unpalatable though it may be – and Mr Whitfield contends it is – to stigmatise the doctors with 'murderous intent', that is what in law they will have if they perform the operation and Mary dies as a result.

The doctrine of double effect

This teaches us that an act which produces a bad effect is nevertheless morally permissible if the action is good in itself, the intention is solely to produce the good effect, the good effect is not produced through the bad effect and there is sufficient reason to permit the bad effect. It may be difficult to reconcile with *Woollin*. Nevertheless it seems to enjoy some approval from Lord Donaldson MR – see *In Re J* at p 46C – and Lord Goff – see *Bland* p 867C. I can readily see how the doctrine works when doctors are treating one patient administering pain-killing drugs for the sole good purpose of relieving pain, yet appreciating the bad side-effect that it will hasten the patient's death. I simply fail to see how it can apply here where the side-effect to the good cure for Jodie is another patient's, Mary's, death, and when the treatment cannot have been undertaken to effect any benefit for Mary ...

Brooke LJ: Next, the words 'intent to kill'. There is a technical difficulty about one aspect of the meaning of 'intention' in this context. It seems to me that the best way to describe it is to start with an extract from the Law Commission's 1993 Report on *Offences Against the Person and General Principles*, Law Com 218 at pp 8–10:

7.1 Clause 1(a) of the Criminal Law Bill [at p 90 of the report] provides for the purposes of the offences in Part I of the Bill that a person acts ... 'intentionally' with respect to a result when –

it is his purpose to cause it; or although it is not his purpose to cause that result, he knows that it would occur in the ordinary course of events if he were to succeed in his purpose of causing some other result.

...

7.4 In all but the most unusual cases, courts and juries will only be concerned with the basic rule in clause 1(a)(i) of the Criminal Law Bill: that a person acts intentionally with respect to a result when it is his purpose to cause that result.

7.5 The concept of purpose is ideally suited to express the idea of intention in the criminal law, because that law is concerned with results that the defendant causes by his own actions. These results are intentional, or intentionally caused, on his part, when he has sought to bring them about, by making it the purpose of his acts that they should occur...

7.6 ... [I]n almost all cases when they are dealing with a case of intention, courts will not need to look further than paragraph (i) of clause 1(a). Paragraph (ii) is however aimed at one particular type of case that, it is generally agreed, needs to be treated as a case of 'intention' in law, but which is not covered by paragraph (i) because the actor does not act in order to cause, or with the purpose of causing, the result in question.....

7.7 The point was formulated by Lord Hailsham of St Marylebone in *R v Hyam* [1975] AC 55, 74. A person must be treated as intending 'the means as well as the end and the inseparable consequences of the end as well as the means'. If he acts in order to achieve a particular purpose, knowing that that cannot be done without causing another result, he must be held to intend to cause that other result. The other result may be a pre-condition; as where D, in order to injure P, throws a brick through a window behind which he knows P to be standing; or it may be a necessary concomitant of the first result; as where ... D blows up an aeroplane in flight in order to recover on the insurance covering the cargo, knowing that the crew will inevitably be killed. D intends to break the window and he intends the crew to be killed.

7.8 There is, of course, no absolute certainty in human affairs. D's purpose might be achieved without causing the further result; P might fling up the window while the brick is in flight; the crew might make a miraculous escape by parachute. These, however, are only remote possibilities, as D (if he contemplates them at all) must know. The further result will occur, and D knows that it will occur, 'in the ordinary course of events'. This expression was used in Clause 18 of the [Law Commission's 1989 Draft Criminal Code Bill] to express the near-inevitability, as appreciated by the actor, of the further result.

In paragraph 7.2 of its report the Law Commission touched on some of the problems that existed in 1993 in this corner of the law. These problems were vividly described by Lord Steyn in his speech in the recent case of *R v Woollin* [1999] 1 AC 82 at pp 90E–93F, with which the other members of the House of Lords agreed. Apart from mentioning at p 91A the 'state of disarray' into which the House of Lords had plunged the law of murder in the case of *R v Hyam* [1975] AC 55, it is not necessary to go into any further detail about these problems. Suffice it to say that Lord Steyn restated the law along the lines suggested by the Law Commission six years earlier. The effect of his speech at p 96B–H is that in this rare type of case a judge should direct the jury in accordance with the following principles:

Where the charge is murder and in the rare cases where the simple direction is not enough, the jury should be directed that they are not entitled to find the necessary intention, unless they feel sure that death or serious bodily harm was a virtual certainty (barring some unforeseen intervention) as a result of the defendant's actions and that the defendant appreciated that such was the case ... Where a man realises that it is for all practical purposes inevitable that his actions will result in death or serious harm, the inference may be irresistible that he intended that result, however little he may have desired or wished it to happen.

Now that the House of Lords has set out the law authoritatively in these terms, an English court would inevitably find that the surgeons intended to kill Mary, however little they desired that end, because her death would be the virtually certain consequence of their acts, and they would realise that for all practical purposes her death would invariably follow the clamping of the common aorta.

The doctrine of double effect

We received interesting submissions from Mr Owen QC and Mr Whitfield in which they suggested that the doctrine of double effect would relieve the surgeons of criminal responsibility in these circumstances. This doctrine permits a doctor, in the best interests of his or her patient, to administer painkilling drugs in appropriate quantities for the purpose of relieving that patient's pain, even though the doctor knows that an incidental effect of the administration of these drugs will be to hasten the moment of death. In his speech in *Airedale NHS Trust v Bland*, Lord Goff, while describing the doctor's duty to act in the best interests of his patient, said at p 867C–E:

> It is this principle too which, in my opinion, underlies the established rule that a doctor may, when caring for a patient who is, for example, dying of cancer, lawfully administer painkilling drugs despite the fact that he knows that an incidental effect of that application will be to abbreviate the patient's life. Such a decision may properly be made as part of the care of the living patient, in his best interests; and, on this basis, the treatment will be lawful. Moreover, where the doctor's treatment of his patient is lawful, the patient's death will be regarded in law as exclusively caused by the injury or disease to which his condition is attributable.

In *In Re J* [1991] Fam 33 Lord Donaldson MR identified the relevant principles in these terms at p 46C–D:

> What doctors and the court have to decide is whether, in the best interests of the child patient, a particular decision as to medical treatment should be taken which as a side effect will render death more or less likely. This is not a matter of semantics. It is fundamental. At the other end of the age spectrum, the use of drugs to reduce pain will often be fully justified, notwithstanding that this will hasten the moment of death. What can never be justified is the use of drugs or surgical procedures with the primary purpose of doing so.

Mr Whitfield relied on these *dicta* in support of his argument that what matters in this context is the surgeon's 'primary purpose' (a phrase used by Ognall J in summing up to the jury in *R v Cox* 12 BMLR 38), and that the fact that Mary's accelerated death would be a secondary effect of the surgeon's actions would not justify his conviction for murder. He also referred us to the passage at pp 179–80 in an essay by Professor Ashworth, 'Criminal liability in a medical context: the treatment of good intentions', which is published in *Harm and Culpability* (edited by AP Simester and ATH Smith, Oxford, 1996). Mr Whitfield summarised Professor Ashworth's argument as follows: (i) the true meaning of intention is purpose; (ii) one may purpose ends or means; (iii) one does not purpose a side-effect; (iv) therefore a consequence, even if prohibited, is not intended if it is a side effect.

Mr Owen QC, for his part, referred us to a passage in the 2nd edn of *Medical Law*, in which Professors Ian Kennedy and Grubb criticise the doctrine of double effect in so far as it is advanced as negating the necessary elements of intention or causation for the crime of murder, saying at p 1207:

> The more appropriate analysis is as follows: the doctor by his act intends (on any proper understanding of the term) the death of his patient and by his act causes (on any proper understanding of the term) the death of his patient, but the intention is not culpable and the cause is not blameworthy because the law permits the doctor to do the act in question.

It is not necessary for the purpose of this case to decide authoritatively whether this is the correct analysis, answering as it does the anxieties about the manipulation of the law of causation expressed by Lord Mustill in *Airedale NHS Trust v Bland* [1993] AC 789 at pp 895D–896B. There are certainly some powerful dicta in support of a proposition that if a surgeon administers proper surgical treatment in the best interests of his or her patient and with the consent (except in an emergency) of the patient or his or her surrogate, there can be no question of a finding that the surgeon has a guilty mind in the eyes of the criminal law: see in particular *Gillick v West Norfolk and Wisbech Area Health Authority* [1986] 1 AC 112, *per* Lord Fraser of Tullybelton at pp 174G–175A and Lord Scarman at p 190F–G. The reason why it is not necessary to decide these matters now is that the doctrine of double effect can have no possible application in this case, as the judge rightly observed, because by no stretch of the imagination could it be said that the surgeons would be acting in good faith in Mary's best interests when they prepared an operation which would benefit Jodie but kill Mary.

In this context it is relevant to quote the second and third overarching moral considerations identified by the Archbishop of Westminster in his written submission:

> (b) A person's bodily integrity should not be involved when the consequences of so doing are of no benefit to that person; this is most particularly the case if the consequences are foreseeably lethal.

> (c) Though the duty to preserve life is a serious duty, no such duty exists when the only available means of preserving life involves a grave injustice. In this case, if what is envisaged is the killing of, or a deliberate lethal assault on, one of the twins, Mary, in order to save the other, Jodie, there is a grave injustice involved. The good end would not justify the means. It would set a very dangerous precedent to enshrine in English case law that it was ever lawful to kill, or to commit a deliberate lethal assault on, an innocent person that good may come of it, even to preserve the life of another.

It is of interest to note in this context that when the Catholic nurses at the Children's Hospital in Philadelphia consulted their archdiocesan authorities in a similar case in 1977 (with the sole distinguishing factor that the parents of the 'sacrificed' child were willing to consent to the operation once they had received favourable rabbinical advice) the comfort they received was based on the double effect doctrine. It was argued that the tying of the carotid artery was done not to terminate the life of the sacrificed twin but to preserve the life of the other twin by protecting it from the poisons that would built up in the sacrificed twin's blood after its death: see *Siamese Twins: Killing One to Save the Other*, by George J Annas (Hastings Center Report, April 1987, 27 at p 28) and *The Ethics of Caring for Conjoined Twins*, by David C Thomasma and others (Hastings Center Report, July–August 1996, 4 at p 9). I do not consider that this method of applying the doctrine of double effect would have any prospect of acceptance in an English court.

It follows from this analysis that the proposed operation would involve the murder of Mary unless some way can be found of determining that what was being proposed would not be unlawful. This, the fourth and final part of the investigation, is far the most difficult. It is worth noting at the outset that Miss Davies supported the contentions of Mr Whitfield and Mr Owen to the effect that what was proposed would not be unlawful. They were opposed by Mr Taylor (for the parents) and Mr Harris QC (instructed by the Official Solicitor on behalf of Mary). At the close of his final submissions on behalf of Mary, however, Mr Harris, acting on the Official Solicitor's express instructions, took us back to the final page of his original written argument to this court, which had ended in these terms:

> It is difficult to accommodate the proposed treatment which, notwithstanding the above comments, it is recognised the court may well consider to be desirable, within the framework of established legal principle. It might be argued that the basic principles of medical law cannot be applied to these facts. Existing case law is based upon the presumption of bodily integrity. John Locke's assertion that 'every Man has a Property in his own Person. This no Body has any Right to but himself' (*Two Treatises of Government*, 1690) which underpins much of the moral dialogue in this area is difficult to apply in the case of conjoined twins. Both twins' physical autonomy was compromised at birth with the result that they now have fundamentally inconsistent interests and needs. In these circumstances, the court may wish to explore the possibility of a development of the law to enable a doctor lawfully to undertake surgery to preserve the life and achieve the independence of one twin even though that may result in the death of the other provided that: (i) The actions of the doctor viewed objectively constitute a proportionate and necessary response to the competing interests viewed as a whole; and (ii) Such actions are approved in advance by the court. How any development of the law in this area might be reconciled with M's best interests and right to life is a question which it is easier to ask than answer.

This explicit encouragement by the Official Solicitor that we should explore the possibility of developing the law so as to enable such surgery to be undertaken lawfully was not at all unwelcome. We pointed out repeatedly to Mr Taylor and Mr Harris during the course of argument that if their contentions were correct, no separation surgery which would inevitably involve the sacrifice of one conjoined twin could ever lawfully take place, however ardently their parents wished one of their children to survive, and however severely compromised the condition of the other twin. It would also follow, if their arguments based on the effect of Article 2 of the European Convention on Human Rights (bolstered on this occasion by the written arguments of Mr David Anderson QC on behalf of the Pro-Life Alliance) are well-founded, that no separation surgery involving the sacrifice of a conjoined twin could take place in any of the member states of the Council of Europe. Mr Taylor and Mr Harris accepted, realistically, that this was indeed the effect of their submissions.

Robert Walker LJ: There are various ways in which English criminal law gives effect to the general intuitive feeling that a defendant should not be convicted of a serious crime unless he did the prohibited act intentionally and in circumstances in which he should be held responsible for the consequences. Many of these are concerned with cases (which can all be loosely called cases of necessity) where the defendant's freedom of choice has in one way or another been constrained by circumstances.

But if a defendant's action is of its nature certain, or virtually certain, to produce a harmful result, he cannot normally be heard to say that he did not intend that result. In *R v Woollin* [1999] 1 AC 82 an angry father threw his three month old son on to a hard surface. The child suffered a fractured skull and died. The father was convicted of murder but because of a misdirection the House of Lords allowed his appeal (substituting a verdict of guilty of manslaughter). That was the context in which their lordships approved (as part of a model direction to the jury) the passage at p 96:

> Where a man realises that it is for all practical purposes inevitable that his actions will result in death or serious harm, the inference may be irresistible that he intended that result, however little he may have desired or wished it to happen.

The decision of the House of Lords in *Woollin* has (it is to be hoped) finally resolved a debate as to the mental element requisite for murder ('malice aforethought' is the traditional but archaic phrase) which has been continuing intermittently since *DPP v Smith* [1961] AC 290, with legislative intervention in the form of s 8 of the Criminal Justice Act 1967. Mr Owen submitted that *Woollin* may have to be reconsidered in the light of the Human Rights Act 1998 and Article 2 of the European Convention on Human Rights. I would not accept that submission, if it were relevant, for reasons set out later in this judgment.

However the stark facts of *Woollin* and the speeches in the House of Lords in that case say nothing at all about the situation in which an individual acts for a good purpose which cannot be achieved without also having bad consequences (which may be merely possible, or very probable, or virtually certain). This is the doctrine (or dilemma) of double effect which has been debated by moral philosophers (as well as lawyers) for millennia rather than centuries. In one class of case the good purpose and the foreseen but undesired consequence (what Bentham called 'oblique intention') are both directed at the same individual. That can be illustrated by a doctor's duty to his patient. The doctor may in the course of proper treatment have to cause pain to the patient in order to heal him. Conversely he may in order to palliate severe pain, administer large doses of analgesics even though he knows that the likely consequence will be to shorten the patient's life. That was recognised by Lord Donaldson MR in the passage of his judgment in *Re J* which I have already cited (note its references to primary purpose and side effects; similar language was used by Ognall J in his summing up to the jury in *R v Cox* (1992), the case of the doctor who administered potassium chloride to a dying patient). Similarly Lord Goff referred in *Bland* (at p 867) to

... the established rule that a doctor may, when caring for a patient who is, for example, dying of cancer, lawfully administer painkilling drugs despite the fact that he knows that an incidental effect of that application will be to abbreviate the patient's life. Such a decision may properly be made as part of the care of the living patient, in his best interests; and, on this basis, the treatment will be lawful.

In these cases the doctrine of double effect prevents the doctor's foresight of accelerated death from counting as a guilty intention. This type of double effect cannot be relevant to conduct directed towards Mary unless the mere fact of restoring her separate bodily integrity, even at the moment of death, can be seen as a good end in itself and as something which ought to be achieved in the best interests of Mary as well as Jodie.

DEFENCES UNIQUE TO MURDER

There are four defences that are uniquely available to a defendant who is charged with murder. They are:

- diminished responsibility;
- provocation;
- infanticide;
- suicide pact.

All four operate as partial defences in the sense that, if they are made out, the defendant's liability is reduced from murder to manslaughter, thus avoiding the consequences of the mandatory life sentence for murder. Diminished responsibility and provocation are by far the more important of the four and are considered in more detail in the extracts that follow.

Infanticide

Infanticide was introduced as a defence by the Infanticide Act 1938, s 1 of which provides:

1(1) Where a woman by any wilful act or omission causes the death of her child being a child under the age of 12 months, but at the time of the act or omission the balance of her mind was disturbed by reason of her not having fully recovered from the effect of giving birth to the child or by reason of the effect of lactation consequent upon the birth of the child, then, notwithstanding that the circumstances were such that but for this Act the offence would have amounted to murder, she shall be guilty of [an offence], to wit of infanticide, and may for such offence be dealt with and punished as if she had been guilty of the offence of manslaughter of the child.

Suicide pact

Section 4(1) of the Homicide Act 1957 introduced the defence of suicide pact. It provides:

4(1) It shall be manslaughter, and shall not be murder, for a person acting in pursuance of a suicide pact between him and another to kill the other or be a party to the other being killed by a third person.

For these purposes a suicide pact is defined by s 4(3) as: '... a common agreement between two or more persons having for its object the death of all of them, whether or not each is to take his own life, but nothing done by a person who enters into a suicide pact shall be treated as done by him in pursuance of the pact unless it is done while he has the settled intention of dying in pursuance of the pact.'

Diminished responsibility

Diminished responsibility was introduced as a partial defence to murder by the Homicide Act 1957.

Section 2 of the Homicide Act 1957

(1) Where a person kills or is party to the killing of another, he shall not be convicted of murder if he was suffering from such abnormality of mind (whether arising from a condition of arrested or retarded development of mind or any inherent causes or induced by disease or injury) as substantially impaired his mental responsibility for his acts or omissions in doing or being a party to the killing.

(2) On a charge of murder, it shall be for the defence to prove that the person charged is by virtue of this section not liable to be convicted of murder.

(3) A person who but for this section would be liable, whether as principal or as accessory, to be convicted of murder shall be liable instead to be convicted of manslaughter.

(4) The fact that one party to a killing is by virtue of this section not liable to be convicted of murder shall not affect the question whether the killing amounted to murder in the case of any other party to it.

'Abnormality of the mind'

R v Byrne [1960] 2 QB 396 (CA)

Lord Parker CJ: The appellant was convicted of murder ... The victim was a young woman whom he strangled in the YWCA hostel, and after her death he committed horrifying mutilations upon her dead body. The facts as to the killing were not disputed, and were admitted in a long statement made by the accused. The only defence was that in killing his victim the accused was suffering from diminished responsibility as defined by s 2 of the Homicide Act 1957, and was accordingly, guilty not of murder but of manslaughter.

Three medical witnesses were called by the defence, the senior medical officer at Birmingham Prison and two specialists in psychological medicine. Their uncontradicted evidence was that the accused was a sexual psychopath, that he suffered from abnormality of mind, as indeed was abundantly clear from the other evidence in the case, and that such abnormality of mind arose from a condition of arrested or retarded development of mind or inherent causes. The nature of the abnormality of mind of a sexual psychopath, according to the medical evidence, is that he suffers from violent perverted sexual desires which he finds it difficult or impossible to control. Save when under the influence of his perverted sexual desires he may be normal. All three doctors were of opinion that the killing was done under the influence of his perverted sexual desires, and although all three were of opinion that he was not insane in the technical sense of insanity laid down in the *M'Naghten* Rules it was their view that his sexual psychopathy could properly be described as partial insanity ...

[Lord Parker CJ referred to the provisions of s 2 of the 1957 Act and continued:] 'Abnormality of mind', which has to be contrasted with the time-honoured expression in the *M'Naghten* Rules 'defect of reason', means a state of mind so different from that of ordinary human beings that the reasonable man would term it abnormal. It appears to us to be wide enough to cover the mind's activities in all its aspects, not only the perception of physical acts and matters, and the ability to form a rational judgment as to whether an act is right or wrong, but also the ability to exercise will power to control physical acts in accordance with that rational judgment. The expression 'mental responsibility for his acts' points to a consideration of the extent to which the accused's mind is answerable for his physical acts which must include a consideration of the extent of his ability to exercise will power to control his physical acts.

Whether the accused was at the time of the killing suffering from any 'abnormality of mind' in the broad sense which we have indicated above is a question for the jury. On this question medical evidence is no doubt of importance, but the jury are entitled to take into consideration all the evidence, including the acts or statements of the accused and his demeanour. They are not bound to accept the medical evidence if there is other material before them which, in their good judgment, conflicts with it and outweighs it.

The aetiology of the abnormality of mind (namely whether it arose from a condition of arrested or retarded development of mind or any inherent causes, or was induced by disease or injury) does, however, seem to be a matter to be determined on expert evidence.

Assuming that the jury are satisfied on the balance of probabilities that the accused was suffering from 'abnormality of mind' from one of the causes specified in parentheses in the subsection, the crucial question nevertheless arises: was the abnormality such as substantially impaired his mental responsibility for his acts in doing or being a party to the killing? This is a question of degree and essentially one for the jury. Medical evidence is, of course, relevant, but the question involves a decision not merely as to whether there was some impairment of the mental responsibility of the accused for his acts but whether such impairment can properly be called 'substantial', a matter upon which juries may quite legitimately differ from doctors.

Furthermore, in a case where the abnormality of mind is one which affects the accused's self-control the step between 'he did not resist his impulse' and 'he could not resist his impulse' is, as the evidence in this case shows, one which is incapable of scientific proof. *A fortiori* there is no scientific measurement of the degree of difficulty which an abnormal person finds in controlling his impulses. These problems which in the present state of medical knowledge are scientifically insoluble, the jury can only approach in a broad, common sense way. This court has repeatedly approved directions to the jury which have followed directions given in Scots cases where the doctrine of diminished responsibility forms part of the common law. We need not repeat them. They are quoted in *R v Spriggs* [1958] 1 QB 270. They indicate that such abnormality as 'substantially impairs his mental responsibility' involves a mental state which in popular language (not that of the *M'Naghten* Rules) a jury would regard as amounting to partial insanity or being on the borderline of insanity ...

... Inability to exercise will power to control physical acts, provided that it is due to abnormality of mind from one of the causes specified in parentheses in the subsection is, in our view, sufficient to entitle the accused to the benefit of the section; difficulty in controlling his physical acts depending on the degree of difficulty, may be. It is for the jury to decide on the whole of the evidence whether such inability or difficulty has, not as a matter of scientific certainty but on the balance of probabilities, been established, and in the case of difficulty whether the difficulty is so great as to amount in their view to a substantial impairment of the accused's mental responsibility for his acts. The direction in the present case thus withdrew from the jury the essential determination of fact which it was their province to decide ...

R v Sanders (1991) 93 Cr App R 245

The appellant was charged with the murder of his wife. He sought, unsuccessfully, to rely on the defence of diminished responsibility, supported by expert evidence. The Crown conceded that the appellant suffered from an abnormality of the mind, but contested the point as to whether or not it affected his responsibility for his actions. On appeal the appellant raised the point that the trial judge had failed to direct the jury expressly on the fact that the expert testimony had been unanimous in finding that the requirements of s 2(1) of the Homicide Act 1957 were satisfied. The appeal was dismissed.

Watkins LJ: We were referred to the following authorities. *Matheson* (1958) 42 Cr App R 145; [1958] 2 All ER 87, was a five judge court and it was held that where on a charge of murder a defence of diminished responsibility is relied on, and the medical evidence that diminished responsibility exists is uncontradicted and the jury return a verdict of guilty of murder, if there are facts entitling the jury to reject or differ from the opinions of the medical men the Court of Criminal Appeal will not interfere with the verdict unless it can be said that the verdict would amount to a miscarriage of justice. There may be cases where evidence of the conduct of the accused before, at the time of and after the killing may be a relevant consideration for the jury in determining this issue. Where, however, there is unchallenged medical evidence of abnormality of mind and consequent substantial impairments of mental responsibility and no facts or circumstances appear which can displace or throw doubt on that evidence a verdict of guilty of murder is one which cannot be supported having regard to the evidence within the meaning of s 4(1) of the Criminal Appeal Act 1907. In the course of the judgment of the court, which was given by the Lord Goddard CJ, he said at p 151 and p 89 respectively:

> Here it is said there was evidence of premeditation and undoubtedly there was, but an abnormal mind is as capable of forming an intention and desire to

kill as one that is normal; it is just what an abnormal mind might do. A desire to kill is quite common in cases of insanity ... Where a defence of diminished responsibility is raised, a plea of guilty to manslaughter on this ground should not be accepted; the issue must be left to the jury, as in the case of a defence of insanity.

It was complained in the perfected grounds in this case if not in the course of submissions to us that the judge had made no reference to premeditation being not necessarily inconsistent with diminished responsibility. That complaint was, we think, quite unjustified for the judge said of it in the green bundle at p 4C:

Even if the killing was premeditated, the doctors say that does not exclude or discount diminished responsibility as a defence, or in any way alter their opinions. Although Dr Holland accepted that if the killing was in fact premeditated that would mean that the defendant had not told him the truth. It is for you to assess that evidence and say what you make of it.

The next case which we were referred to was *Bailey* in 1961; reported in (1978) 66 Cr App R 31 [as a note, following *Walton v R*, below]. In that case a 17 year old youth was convicted of murder and sentenced to be detained at Her Majesty's pleasure. The Lord Chief Justice in giving the judgment of the court said at p 32:

This court has said on many occasions that of course juries are not bound by what the medical witness say, but at the same time they must act on evidence, and if there is nothing before them, no facts and no circumstances shown before them which throw doubt on the medical evidence, then that is all they are left with, and the jury, in those circumstances, must accept it. That was the effect of the decision of this court, sitting as a court of five judges, in the case of *Matheson* and as we understand it, nothing that this court said in the case of *Byrne* (1960) 44 Cr App R 246 throws any doubt upon what was said in *Matheson's* case.

In *Walton v R* (1978) 66 Cr App R 25; [1978] AC 788, a Privy Council case, in the course of giving the opinion of the Board, Lord Keith of Kinkel stated at p 30 and p 793:

These cases make clear that upon an issue of diminished responsibility the jury are entitled and indeed bound to consider not only the medical evidence but the evidence upon the whole facts and circumstances of the case. These include the nature of the killing, the conduct of the accused before, at the time of and after it and any history of mental abnormality. It being recognised that the jury on occasion may properly refuse to accept medical evidence, it follows that they must be entitled to consider the quality and weight of that evidence. As was pointed out by Lord Parker CJ in *Byrne* (1960) 44 Cr App R 246, 254 what the jury are essentially seeking to ascertain is whether at the time of the killing the accused was suffering from a state of mind bordering on but not amounting to insanity. That task is to be approached in a broad common sense way.

Finally, we were asked to look at *Kiszko* (1979) 68 Cr App R 62. In that case Bridge LJ, giving the judgment of the court, stated at p 69:

The most recent pronouncement on this subject, in a judgment of the Privy Council in the case of *Walton v R* (1978) 66 Cr App R 25 seems to us still to encapsulate the law entirely accurately and not to require any modification in the light of the provisions of s 2(1)(a) of the Criminal Appeal Act 1968. After referring to earlier authorities, the judgment delivered by Lord Keith of Kinkel is in these terms at p 30. ...

He then sets out the passage which I have already read. From these cases, in our opinion, two clear principles emerge where the issue is diminished responsibility. The first is that if there are no other circumstances to consider, unequivocal, uncontradicted medical evidence favourable to a defendant should be accepted by a jury and they should be so directed. The second is that where there are other circumstances to be considered the medical evidence, though it be unequivocal and uncontradicted, must be assessed in the light of the other circumstances. Turning again then to the summing up it is right to say that viewed in isolation the judge did not specifically refer to the medical evidence in the main passage of the summing up upon which Mr Gale concentrated his attention. Having dealt faultlessly, it is conceded, with the first two elements, namely abnormality of mind and whether that arose from inherent causes or disease, the judge went on in the orange bundle at p 9E:

As to the third element, was the abnormality of mind such as substantially impaired the defendant's mental responsibility for his acts? This question is one of degree. It is essentially one for you, the jury. You must approach this question also in a broad, common sense way. It means more than some trivial degree of impairment which does not make any appreciable difference to a person's ability to control himself, but it means, equally obviously, something less than total impairment. I can put that in a slightly different way. Substantial does not mean total, that is to say the mental responsibility need not be totally impaired, so to speak, destroyed altogether. It is something in between, and Parliament has left it to you, the jury, to say on the evidence, was the mental responsibility impaired and, if so, was it substantially impaired? The real issue, you may think, remember always that you decide this case, I do not so, is not whether the defendant was suffering from an abnormality of mind arising from inherent causes or induced by disease. The real question, you may think, the real issue is whether that abnormality of mind substantially impaired the defendant's mental responsibility for his acts.

Mr Gale [counsel for the appellant] relies heavily on the absence of reference to medical evidence there and in the early stages of the resumed summing up on the final day of the trial. Those passages simply cannot be viewed in isolation. There is, even in the passage relied upon, a reference to the evidence and in the green bundle at p 3 the learned judge had this to say:

As to diminished responsibility, the defendant relies upon two doctors, whose evidence I will remind you of, who say, in a word, that looking at all the defendant's circumstances, namely: his diabetes and its very considerable effect on him; his unemployment over two years, his deteriorating medical condition, particularly affecting his sight, his increasing dependency upon Mrs Sadlier; his deep affection for Mrs Sadlier and his realisation that he was losing her to another man; Mrs Sadlier's final rejection of him; the defendant's entirely genuine and very nearly successful suicide attempt; the defendant's depression and increasing preoccupation with Mrs Sadlier, his appetite, concentration and sleep being affected. Looking at all those matters, the doctors say that the defendant, at the time of the killing, was suffering from abnormality of mind arising from reactive depression which substantially impaired his mental responsibility for his acts in killing Mrs Sadlier. If you find that it is more likely than not that the doctors are right, having looked at all those circumstances, then the defendant will have established diminished responsibility and will thus be entitled to a verdict of manslaughter.

Having regard to that entirely correct direction we are satisfied that there is no substance whatever in the complaint that the judge did not direct the jury properly on the third element. That in our view he clearly did. We are also satisfied that the judge was not called upon to go further than he did with regard to the medical evidence, that is to say beyond reminding them, as he did, that it was so to speak all one way, that it was in the purely medical sense but it did not stand alone for the jury's consideration of the appellant's state of mind. It needs to be said anyway that the medical evidence was challenged upon certain of its assumptions by cross-examination. Regardless of that the jury had to bear in mind, among other matters, the manner of the killing, the contents of the will and the letters, when the last letter was written and certain admissions made by the appellant to the police in interview. We conclude that the summing up, without exception, was a model, to use Mr Gale's words, and therefore cannot in any way be complained of.

Notes and queries

1 According to Edmund Davies J in *R v Lloyd* [1967] 1 QB 175, whether or not a defendant's responsibility for his actions has been substantially impaired, as opposed to moderately, is a question of fact for the jury. As he put it: '... Substantial does not mean total, that is to say, the mental responsibility need not be totally impaired, so to speak, destroyed altogether. At the other end of the scale substantial does not mean trivial or minimal. It is something in between and Parliament has left it to ... juries to say on the evidence, was the mental responsibility impaired, and, if so, was it substantially impaired?'

2 The courts have tended to take a liberal view as to what can give rise to diminished responsibility. In *R v Reynolds* [1988] Crim LR 679, it was, in effect, accepted that pre-menstrual syndrome and postnatal depression could be causes. In *R v Hobson* (1997) *The Times,* 25 June, the Court of Appeal held that 'battered woman syndrome', having been included in the British classification of mental diseases recognised by the psychiatric profession, could form the basis of a plea of diminished responsibility.

3 Diminished responsibility will only be available as a defence where death has actually occurred, hence it is not available to a defendant charged with attempted murder; see *R v Campbell* [1997] Crim LR 495.

4 The fact that s 2(2) of the 1957 Act places the legal burden of proof on the defendant seeking to raise the defence of diminished responsibility has survived scrutiny under the Human Rights Act 1998. In *R v Lambert* [2001] 1 All ER 1014, the Court of Appeal confirmed that the sub-section did not require the defendant to prove any matter that could be said to be an element of the offence of murder. Placing the burden of proof on defendants as regards defences was not contrary to Art 6 of the European Convention on Human Rights; see further extracts on proof in Chapter 1.

Diminished responsibility and intoxication

R v Tandy [1989] 1 WLR 350 (CA)

The appellant was an alcoholic. She normally drank Cinzano. On one occasion, however, she consumed 90% of a bottle of vodka (which contains more alcohol than Cinzano). Later that day, she strangled her 11 year old daughter.

Watkins LJ: ... So in this case it was for the appellant to show:

(1) that she was suffering from an abnormality of mind at the time of the act of strangulation;

(2) that that abnormality of mind was induced by disease, namely the disease of alcoholism; and

(3) that the abnormality of mind induced by the disease of alcoholism was such as substantially impaired her mental responsibility for her act of strangling her daughter.

The principles involved in seeking answers to these questions are, in our view, as follows. The appellant would not establish the second element of the defence unless the evidence showed that the abnormality of mind at the time of the killing was due to the fact that she was a chronic alcoholic. If the alcoholism had reached the level at which her brain had been injured by the repeated insult from intoxicants so that there was gross impairment of her judgment and emotional responses, then the defence of diminished responsibility was available to her, provided that she satisfied the jury that the third element of the defence existed. Further, if the appellant were able to establish that the alcoholism had reached the level where although the brain had not been damaged to the extent just stated, the appellant's drinking had become involuntary, that is to say she was no longer able to resist the impulse to drink then the defence of diminished responsibility would be available to her, subject to her establishing the first and third elements, because if her drinking was involuntary, then her abnormality of mind at the time of the act of strangulation was induced by her condition of alcoholism.

On the other hand, if the appellant had simply not resisted an impulse to drink and it was the drink taken on the [day of the killing] which brought about the impairment of judgment and emotional response, then the defence of diminished responsibility was not available to the appellant.

... The appellant had chosen to drink vodka on the Wednesday rather than her customary drink of Cinzano. Her evidence was that she might not have had a drink at all on the Tuesday. She certainly did not tell the jury that she must have taken drink on the Tuesday or Wednesday because she could not help herself. She had been able to stop drinking at 6.30 pm on the Wednesday evening although her supply of vodka was not exhausted. Thus her own evidence indicated that she was able to exercise some control even after she had taken the first drink, contrary to the view of the doctors. There was the evidence of Dr Lawson that the appellant would have had the ability on that Wednesday to abstain from taking the first drink of the day ...

The three matters on which the appellant relies in the perfected grounds of appeal for saying that there was a misdirection can be dealt with shortly. As to the first, in our judgment the judge was correct in telling the jury that if the taking of the first drink was not involuntary, then the whole of the drinking on the Wednesday was not involuntary. Further, as we have pointed out, the appellant's own evidence indicated that she still had control over her drinking on that Wednesday after she had taken the first drink.

As to the second, the jury were told correctly that the abnormality of mind with which they were concerned was the abnormality of mind at the time of the act of strangulation and as a matter of fact by that time on that Wednesday the appellant had drunk 90% of the bottle of vodka.

On the third point, we conclude that for a craving for drinks or drugs in itself to produce an abnormality of mind within the meaning of s 2(1) of the Act of 1957, the craving must be such as to render the accused's use of drink or drugs involuntary ...

R v Gittens [1984] 1 QB 698 (CA)

The essential issue in this case was whether the abnormality of mind from which the appellant suffered when he killed his wife and stepdaughter was caused by the alcohol and drugs which he taken prior to the killing or whether it was due to inherent causes coupled with the drink and drugs.

Lord Lane CJ: ... Where alcohol or drugs are factors to be considered by the jury, the best approach is that adopted by the judge and approved by this court in *R v Fenton* (1975) 61 Cr App R 261. The jury should be directed to disregard what, in their view, the effect of the alcohol or drugs upon the defendant was, since abnormality of mind induced by alcohol or drugs is not (generally speaking) due to inherent causes and is not therefore within the section. Then the jury should consider whether the combined effect of the other matters which do fall within the section amounted to such abnormality of mind as substantially impaired the defendant's mental responsibility within the meaning of 'substantial' set out in *R v Lloyd* [1967] 1 QB 175.

R v Sanderson (1994) 98 Cr App R 325

The appellant was convicted of killing a woman – a Miss Glasgow. On appeal the court had to consider the proper approach to be taken where there was evidence to suggest that diminished responsibility might be caused by inherent factors, upbringing, and drug abuse.

Roch LJ: In this case there could not have been any real issue that the appellant, at the time he killed Miss Glasgow, was suffering from an abnormality of mind. He had no reason to want her death apart from his deluded beliefs for weeks. The way in which he inflicted death upon her and his subsequent behaviour all indicated that at the time his judgment and control over his emotions were not those of a normal mind. The first issue which arose on the medical evidence was the nature of that abnormality of mind: was it a paranoid psychosis, that is to say a serious disorder of the mind in which the appellant was suffering from fixed delusions centreing around some perverted idea which had some important bearing on his actions, or was he suffering from simple paranoia?

The second issue which arose out of the medical evidence was the cause of the abnormality of mind. Was the abnormality of mind due to inherent causes, the appellant's childhood and upbringing, possibly exacerbated by drug addiction, or simply a side effect or consequence of his drug-taking? It is now well established by authority that for abnormality of the mind to come within the subsection it must be caused by one of the matters listed in the subsection; that is to say it must arise from a condition of arrested or retarded development of mind – of which there is no suggestion in this case – or from inherent causes or be induced by disease or injury.

Dr Bowden's evidence was that the appellant did not have the mental illness of paranoid psychosis and that as far as he was aware medical science showed that the taking of heroin and cocaine could not injure the structures of the brain. Consequently, his evidence was to the effect that the appellant did not and had not had any injury or disease which could have induced the paranoia. Further, his evidence denied that the paranoia arose from inherent cause; it arose simply because the appellant used cocaine. There was no evidence that his use of cocaine was involuntary.

In those circumstances, in our judgment the Common Serjeant was quite correct to direct the jury that if they accepted the evidence of Dr Bowden and rejected that of Dr Coid the defence of diminished responsibility had to fail. In our judgment the jury could not have found that the appellant was suffering from an abnormality of mind within section 2(1) on the evidence of Dr Bowden. Consequently, the first ground of appeal fails.

The court considers that there is substance in the second and third submissions made by the appellant's counsel, and that for the reasons which we shall give shortly, the jury's verdict in this case is unsafe and unsatisfactory.

Cases of diminished responsibility can become difficult and confusing for a jury, and it is important that the judge in directing the jury should tailor his directions to suit the facts of the particular case. We think it will rarely be helpful to the jury to read to them section 2(1) in its entirety. Further, we consider that Annex F would have been of greater assistance had the words in brackets been confined to 'arising from any inherent cause or induced by disease', there being no evidence of arrested or retarded development or of injury.

The judge in his directions to the jury at p 9G, which we have already cited, then summarising the defendant's medical evidence and comparing it with the Crown's medical evidence, referred to the abnormality of mind arising from any inherent cause or disease on three occasions. In his final direction to the jury on diminished responsibility at the end of the summing up, the judge again referred to those two potential causes when he said:

Has the defendant proved that he was suffering from an abnormality of mind through inherent cause or induced by disease, that is to say a paranoid psychosis which is a mental illness, whether exacerbated by drugs or not?

Again the jury were being directed to consider whether the abnormality of mind arose either from inherent cause or was induced by disease. Further, that direction was so worded that the jury could understand the disease to be the mental illness of paranoid psychosis.

However, earlier in the summing up, the judge summarised Dr Coid's opinion in this way:

Dr Coid's opinion was this: 'The defendant was at the time of the killing and is now suffering from paranoid psychosis, a mental illness, forming incorrect and abnormal beliefs about other people. This was there already, irrespective of drug abuse. Although paranoid psychosis can be exacerbated by the use of cocaine over the years and much worse, nonetheless, quite apart from the drugs, paranoid psychosis, the mental illness, was there and that amounted to an abnormality of mind,' which is, when you call it inherent or resulting from disease.

We take it the last part should read: 'which it is, whether you call it inherent or resulting from disease.'

Thus the jury were being told Dr Coid was saying that the abnormality of mind was paranoid psychosis. In our opinion it was those apparently contradictory directions which must have given rise to the jury's questions. Although their questions are not free from ambiguity the jury were probably asking:

1   What is meant by induced by disease or injury, that is to say what does induced mean?

2   Is paranoid psychosis a disease or injury which can induce an abnormality of mind?

The judge interpreted the second question as being: 'Can a paranoid psychosis be induced by disease or injury?' and told the jury that he did not know; that 'nobody speaks of paranoid psychosis arising from disease of injury.' That was simply not correct.

The judge had summarised the appellant's doctor's evidence at p 9H:

It is said for the defence through Dr Coid that there was an underlying paranoid psychosis or mental illness which amounted to an abnormality of mind within the Act. It arose from an inherent cause or disease of long-standing.

Again, at p 23E in summarising Dr Coid's evidence the judge told the jury that Dr Coid was saying that paranoid psychosis amounted to an abnormality of mind which it was whether one said it arose from inherent cause or was induced by disease.

The judge should have sought clarification of the jury's questions, and then, if the real difficulty was whether the mental illness or paranoid psychosis was a disease within the meaning of the subsection, he should have directed them that the medical evidence they had was that this abnormality of mind was the mental illness of paranoid psychosis, if Dr Coid was right, and if Dr Coid was correct as to the aetiology of that mental illness, then it came within the words: 'arising from any inherent cause' and was therefore within the subsection. In our judgment the answers that the judge gave failed to answer the questions which we believe the jury were asking, and would, in any event have confused them rather than have helped them.

Mr Worsley for the Crown submits that the central issue was left to the jury. The judge finally left to the jury the substantive defence which the appellant was raising. The jury were being told, correctly, that if they accepted Dr Coid's evidence, then the defence, subject to their view on the second question set out in Annex F, would succeed, whereas if they preferred Dr Bowden's evidence, the defence failed. Thus, submits Mr Worsley, even if the questions had been clarified and direct answers given, the jury's verdict would have been the same. He invites us to apply the proviso.

To that submission, Mr Jones replied that the questions themselves showed that the jury were inclined to accept that there was a paranoid psychosis, ie Dr Coid's evidence, rather than Dr Bowden's simple paranoia resulting from the taking of cocaine. The jury's concern was whether the paranoid psychosis came within the subsection. The jury should have been directed that the paranoid psychosis described by Dr Coid could, as a matter of law, come within the subsection. Had that direction been given, the probable verdict would have been one of manslaughter.

We agree with that submission by Mr Jones.

Before concluding this judgment, the court pays tribute to the arguments of both counsel, and especially to the submissions of Mr Jones, who took us to the legislation on mental deficiency preceding the 1957 Act and two lines of authorities. The first was cases such as *Seers* (1984) 79 Cr App R 261, 264, on the nature and degree of impairment of mental responsibility which is within the section, and the second, cases where the defendant had been abusing drugs or alcohol, such as *Fenton* (1975) 61 Cr App R 261 and *Tandy* (1988) 87 Cr App R 45.

Mr Jones submitted that 'disease' in the phrase 'disease or injury' in section 2(1) meant 'disease of the mind' and was apt to cover mental illnesses which were functional as well as those which were organic. This interesting and difficult question does not, in our view, require an answer in this case. We content ourselves with observing that we did not find the pre-1957 Act authority particularly persuasive in deciding what is meant by 'disease or injury' in section 2(1) of the 1957 Act because those authorities were concerned with the meaning of words used by judges to delimit the special defence of insanity which originally resulted in a verdict of guilty by reason of insanity and lead to the defendant being sent to a secure mental institution. We incline to the view that that phrase 'induced by disease or injury' must refer to organic or physical injury or disease of the body including the brain, and that that is more probable because Parliament deliberately refrained from referring to the disease of, or injury to, the mind, but included as permissible causes of an abnormality of mind 'any inherent cause' which would cover functional mental illness.

For those reasons we allow this appeal, quash the conviction of murder and substitute the conviction of manslaughter.

Provocation

Provocation has a long history as a common law defence to murder – its origins are set out in the extracts from *R v Smith (Morgan)* that follow. Parliament has intervened in the shape of s 3 of the Homicide Act 1957, but this simply clarifies certain aspects of the defence. It does not place it on a statutory basis.

What for many years was regarded as the 'classic' definition of provocation is to be found in *R v Duffy* [1949] 1 All ER 932 (Note), where Lord Goddard CJ quoted with approval the direction given to the jury by the trial judge Devlin J: 'Provocation is some act, or series of acts, done by the dead man to the accused which would cause in any reasonable person, and actually causes in the accused, a sudden and temporary loss of self-control, rendering the accused so subject to passion as to make him or her for the moment not master of his mind ...'

Whilst this is a useful starting point, it will seen from the extracts that follow that this statement has since been modified in certain important respects by both statute (s 3 of the 1957 Act set out below) and judicial intervention.

Section 3 of the Homicide Act 1957

Where on a charge of murder there is evidence on which a jury can find that the person charged was provoked (whether by things done or by things said or by both together) to lose his self-control, the question whether the provocation was enough to make a reasonable man do as he did shall be left to be determined by the jury; and in determining that question the jury shall take into account everything both done and said according to the effect which, in their opinion, it would have on a reasonable man.

The development of the defence of provocation

In the course of his speech in *R v Smith (Morgan)*, Lord Hoffmann usefully summarised the historical background thus:

R v Smith (Morgan) [2000] 4 All ER 289

Lord Hoffmann: My Lords, it is impossible to read even a selection of the extensive modern literature on provocation without coming to the conclusion that the concept has serious logical and moral flaws. But your Lordships must take the law as it stands. Whatever your decision in this case, the result is not likely to be wholly satisfactory. The doctrine of provocation has always been described as a concession to human frailty and the law illustrates Kant's *dictum* that, from the crooked timber of humanity, nothing completely straight can be made. Nevertheless, I shall suggest to your Lordships that this appeal offers an opportunity, within the constraints imposed by history and by Parliament, to make some serviceable improvements.

The researches of Dr Horder (*Provocation and Responsibility*, 1992) show that although the doctrine has much earlier roots, it emerged in recognisably modern form in the late 17th and early 18th centuries. It comes from a world of Restoration gallantry in which gentlemen habitually carried lethal weapons, acted in accordance with a code of honour which required insult to be personally avenged by instant angry retaliation and in which the mandatory penalty for premeditated murder was death. To show anger 'in hot blood' for a proper reason by an appropriate response was not merely permissible but the badge of a man of honour. The human frailty to which the defence of provocation made allowance was the possibility that the man of honour might overreact and kill when a lesser retaliation would have been appropriate. Provided that he did not grossly overreact in the extent or manner of his retaliation, the offence would be manslaughter and execution avoided.

The situations which were considered to be proper occasions for anger reflected the code of honour of the time. The first full judicial discussion dates from the reign of Queen Anne. In *R v Mawgridge* (1707) Keil 119, a guest of the Lieutenant of the Tower of London quarrelled with his host over a woman, threw a bottle of wine at his head and then ran him through with a sword. The case was described by Holt CJ as being 'of great expectation' and was argued before all the judges. The court listed four categories of case which were 'by general consent' allowed to be sufficient provocations. The first was the quarrel which escalated from words to physical assault ('by pulling him by the nose, or filliping upon the forehead'): If the assaulted party drew his sword and immediately slew the other, it would be 'but manslaughter.' The second was a quarrel in which a friend of the person assaulted joined in and gave the deadly blow. The third was where someone took the part of a fellow-citizen who was being 'injuriously treated'. And the fourth was killing a man in the act of adultery with one's wife ('for jealousy is the rage of man and adultery is the highest invasion of property').

The 19th century judges had to adapt this law to a society of Victorian middle-class propriety. They changed it in two ways. First, they generalised the specific situations which the old law had regarded as sufficient provocation into a rule that whatever the alleged provocation, the response had to be 'reasonable.' In *R v Kirkham* (1837) 8 C & P 115, 119 Coleridge J told the jury that 'though the law condescends to human frailty, it will not indulge human ferocity. It considers man to be a rational being, and requires that he should exercise a reasonable control over his passions.' The 'reasonable man', as a test of the appropriate response, first appeared in *R v Welsh* (1869) 11 Cox CC 336, 339 in which Keating J said that provocation would be sufficient if it was 'something which might naturally cause an ordinary and reasonably minded man to lose his self-control and commit such an act'.

The second change was to shift the emphasis of the law from the question of whether the angry retaliation by the accused, though excessive, was in principle justified, to a consideration of whether the accused had lost his self-control. The Restoration view was that anger was right and proper. A killing 'in hot blood' was rational behaviour which, on account of emotional incontinence, had gone too far. But the nineteenth century judges preferred to look upon provocation as something which temporarily deprived the accused of his reason. As they knew virtually nothing about how the mind works or the relationship between emotion and rationality, they described the process in an equestrian metaphor drawn from Descartes. The emotions were depicted as an unruly horse and the reason as its rider who might, upon provocation, lose control. So in *R v Hayward* (1833) 6 C & P 157, 159 Tindal CJ said that the question was whether the provocation was so recent and strong that the prisoner was for the moment not 'master of his own understanding' or whether 'there had been time for the blood to cool and for reason to resume its seat.' Modern neurology has cast considerable doubt upon the accuracy of the metaphor (see Antonio Damasio, *Descartes' Error* (1996)) but the general concept of loss of self-control probably presents little difficulty to juries.

My Lords, both of these changes are reflected in the common law as it was settled in *Mancini* [1942] AC 1 and summarised by Devlin J in *Duffy* [1949] 1 All ER 932. They have caused problems in the modern law and I shall return to them when I have discussed the way the law was reformed by the Homicide Act 1957.

Determining whether or not the defence of provocation has been raised

R v Stewart [1995] 4 All ER 999 (CA)

Stuart-Smith LJ: ... It is now well established that even if the defence do not raise the issue of provocation, and even if they would prefer not to because it is inconsistent with and will detract from the primary defence, the judge must leave the issue for the jury to decide if there is evidence which suggests that the accused may have been provoked; and this is so even if the evidence of provocation is slight or tenuous in the sense that the measure of the provocative acts or words is slight: see *R v Rossiter* [1994] 2 All ER 752 and *R v Cambridge* [1994] 2 All ER 760, [1994] 1 WLR 971 ...

In our judgment, where the judge must, as a matter of law, leave the issue of provocation to the jury, he should indicate to them, unless it is obvious, what evidence might support the conclusion that the appellant lost his self-control ...

R v Acott [1997] 1 All ER 706 (HL)

Lord Steyn: ... The Court of Appeal (Criminal Division) certified that there was a point of law of general public importance involved in the decision to dismiss the appeal, namely:

> In a prosecution for murder, before the judge is obliged to leave the issue of provocation to the jury, must there be some evidence, either direct or inferential, as to what was either done or said to provoke the alleged loss of self-control? ...

... Strictly, the certified question need not be answered in order to dispose of the appeal. But it seems possible to summarise the legal position in terms which might be helpful. Section 3 is only applicable 'if there is evidence ... that the person charged was provoked (whether by things done or things said or by both together) to lose his self-control'. A loss of self-control caused by fear, panic, sheer bad temper or circumstances (eg a slow down of traffic due to snow) would not be enough. There must be some evidence tending to show that the killing might have been an uncontrolled reaction to provoking conduct rather than an act of revenge. Moreover, although there is no longer a rule of proportionality as between provocation and retaliation, the concept of proportionality is nevertheless still an important factual element in the objective inquiry. It necessarily requires of the jury an assessment of the seriousness of the provocation. It follows that there can only be an issue of provocation to be considered by the jury if the judge considers that there is some evidence of a specific act or words of provocation resulting in a loss of self-control. It does not matter from what source that evidence emerges or whether it is relied on at trial by the defendant or not. If there is such evidence, the judge must leave the issue to the jury. If there is no such evidence, but merely the speculative possibility that there had been an act of provocation, it is wrong for the judge to direct the jury to consider provocation. In such a case there is simply no triable issue of provocation ...

Counsel for the appellant invited your Lordships to go further and state what would be sufficient evidence of provocation to justify a trial judge in leaving the issue of provocation for the jury to consider. The invitation was attractively put.

But it must be rejected. What is sufficient in this particular context is not a question of law. Where the line is to be drawn depends on a judgment involving logic and common sense, the assessment of matters of degree and an intense focus on the circumstances of a particular case. It is unwise to generalise on such matters: it is a subject best left to the good sense of trial judges. For the same reason it is not useful to compare the facts of decided cases on provocation with one another.

For my part the certified question can be answered in the general way in which I have indicated. But the reasoning in this judgment is subject to the overriding principle that the legal burden rests on the Crown to disprove provocation on a charge of murder to the required standard of proof. In *Lee Chun-Chuen v R* [1963] AC 220 at 229 Lord Devlin summed up the legal position as follows:

> It is not of course for the defence to make out a *prima facie* case of provocation. It is for the prosecution to prove that the killing was unprovoked. All that the defence need do is to point to material which could induce a reasonable doubt.

That remains the position.

I would dismiss the appeal.

The 'subjective' stage: was there 'cooling time' between the provocation and the killing?

R v Ibrams and Gregory (1981) 74 Cr App R 154 (CA)

Facts: Ibrams was sharing a flat with his fiancée, Laura Adronik. An ex-boyfriend of Laura's, John Monk, was released from borstal and regularly visited the flat to bully and terrorise Ibrams and Adronik. On some occasions Gregory was also at the flat. On Sunday 7 October 1979 the police were contacted twice but did nothing. As it seemed that the police were not going to protect them, Ibrams, Adronik and Gregory felt that they had to protect themselves. On Wednesday 10 October they met together and drew up a plan for dealing with Monk. In essence, the plan was that they would get Monk drunk and he would be encouraged to go to bed with Adronik. Ibrams and Gregory would then enter the flat and attack Monk whilst he was in bed. This plan was carried out on Friday 12 October. The injuries inflicted by Ibrams and Gregory were so serious that Monk died of his injuries.

The trial judge, McNeill J, held that there was no evidence of provocation for the jury to consider. The Court of Appeal upheld this decision on the basis that the final incident of provocation had taken place several days before the attack on the deceased and that the attack had been planned in advance; accordingly, there was no evidence of the sudden and temporary loss of self-control necessary to establish provocation.

Lawton LJ: ... [His Lordship referred to the speech of Lord Diplock in *DPP v Camplin* [1978] AC 705 where Lord Diplock sets out the history of the law relating to provocation.] That history shows that, in the past at any rate, provocation and loss of self-control tended to be regarded by the courts as taking place with a very short interval of time between the provocation and the loss of self-control ... In our judgment, Lord Diplock clearly thought that the loss of self-control must occur at or about the time of the act of provocation ...

His Lordship then cited with approval part of the direction of Devlin J in *R v Duffy* [1949] 1 All ER 932:

> Indeed, circumstances which induce a desire for revenge are inconsistent with provocation, since the conscious formulation of a desire for revenge means that a person has had time to think, to reflect, and that would negative a sudden temporary loss of self-control, which is of the essence of provocation ...
>
> ... [The appellants] were masters of their minds when carrying [their plan] out, because they worked out the details with considerable skill; and in pursuing the plan as they did on the Friday night they were still masters of their own minds. They were doing what they had planned to do ... It follows ... that McNeill J was right in ruling that there was no evidence of loss of self-control ...

R v Ahluwalia [1992] 4 All ER 889 (CA)

Facts: The appellant, an Asian woman entered into an arranged marriage with the deceased. She had to endure several years of violence and abuse. Her husband regularly assaulted her; he had threatened to kill her; he taunted her with the fact that he was having an affair with another woman. During the evening of 8 May 1989 her husband threatened to beat her up and threatened to burn her face with an iron. That night, the appellant poured some petrol, which she had previously purchased, into a bucket (to make it easier to throw); she lit a candle on the gas cooker and carried the bucket and the candle upstairs, taking an oven glove for self-protection, and a stick. She went into her husband's bedroom, threw in some petrol, lit the stick with the candle and threw it into the room. Her husband suffered severe burns from which he died a few days later.

> **Lord Taylor CJ**: ... Section 3 of the Homicide Act 1957 did not provide a general or fresh definition of provocation which remains a common law not a statutory defence. The changes effected by the 1957 Act are conveniently summarised in Smith and Hogan, *Criminal Law*, 6th edn, 1988:
>
> (1) It made it clear that 'things said' alone may be sufficient provocation, if the jury should be of the opinion that they would have provoked a reasonable man ...
>
> (2) It took away the power of the judge to withdraw the defence from the jury on the ground that there was no evidence on which the jury could find that a reasonable man would have been provoked to do as the defendant did ...
>
> (3) It took away the power of the judge to dictate to the jury what were the characteristics of the reasonable man ...
>
> The phrase 'sudden and temporary loss of self-control' encapsulates an essential ingredient of the defence of provocation in a clear and readily understandable phrase. It serves to underline that the defence is concerned with the actions of an individual who is not, at the moment when he or she acts violently, master of his or her own mind ...
>
> ... [I]t is open to the judge, when deciding whether there is any evidence of provocation to be left to the jury and open to the jury when considering such evidence, to take account of the interval between the provocative conduct and the reaction of the defendant to it. Time for reflection may show that after the provocative conduct made its impact on the mind of the defendant, he or she kept

or regained self-control. The passage of time following the provocation may also show that the subsequent attack was planned or based on motives such as revenge or punishment, inconsistent with the loss of self-control and therefore with the defence of provocation. In some cases, such an interval may wholly undermine the defence of provocation; that, however, depends entirely on the facts of the individual case and is not a principle of law.

[Counsel for the appellant] referred to the phrase 'cooling-off period' which has sometimes been applied to an interval of time between the provocation relied upon and the fatal act. He suggests that although in many cases such an interval may indeed be a time for cooling and regaining self-control so as to forfeit the protection of the defence, in others the time lapse has an opposite effect. He submits, relying on expert evidence not before the trial judge, that women who have been subjected frequently over a period to violent treatment may react to the final act or words by what he calls a 'slow-burn' reaction rather than by an immediate loss of self-control.

We accept that the subjective element in the defence of provocation would not as a matter of law be negatived simply because of the delayed reaction in such cases, provided that there was at the time of the killing a 'sudden and temporary loss of self-control' caused by the alleged provocation. However, the longer the delay and the stronger the evidence of deliberation on the part of the defendant, the more likely it will be that the prosecution will negative provocation ...

R v Baillie [1995] 2 Cr App R 31

Henry LJ: On 19 February 1993, in the Crown Court at Northampton, before Ebsworth J the appellant was convicted of murder. He now appeals against conviction with the leave of the single judge. The appellant, who had no previous convictions, killed a drug dealer called Robert McCubbin. It was, as Mr Coward QC for the Crown told the jury, a case of a good man killing a bad man. It arose in this way. Mr Baillie had three sons in their mid to late teens. He had grown increasingly concerned as to their use of soft drugs. And where drugs are used, there is always the risk that the user will be tempted to supply them, because use can be an expensive pastime. McCubbin was one of the sources of their drugs. The appellant strongly disapproved of his sons' drug use, and of those that fed their habit.

On the day of the killing, 20 June 1992, the appellant was at work as a motor mechanic. A customer had given him a bottle of white rum, a good deal of which he had drunk at work. He then went to a public house, and then home, where he washed, shaved, and had more to drink. That afternoon, his house, where he lived with his sons, was filled with rumours. It seems that one of the sons had come under pressure from McCubbin to increase his purchase of drugs from McCubbin, presumably to retail some himself. His response had been to go elsewhere for his supply. McCubbin rightly or wrongly formed the impression that he was going to his, McCubbin's, supplier, direct, thus cutting him out. So the rumours were that McCubbin was extremely displeased, and that the appellant's sons 'were going to get a slap'. They were then in their mid to late teens. The appellant learned of those threats from his youngest son Kenneth who, according to the appellant, came to him in tears saying that the deceased had threatened him. The appellant, who by then was very drunk, set off in a rage to get McCubbin.

There was a sawn-off shotgun in the attic of his house. A friend had asked him to keep it there. After his arrest he told the police who the friend was, and he was arrested and sentenced for possession of the weapon. He went after McCubbin with that shotgun and with a cut-throat razor in his pocket. He took two of his sons with him, not apparently as reinforcements, but to show him where McCubbin lived. His car needed petrol, so he had to stop to fill up. His driving was affected by drink, and he had a minor accident. He parked his car openly as close to McCubbin's house as he could get, and he, with his two sons behind him, set off to walk through an alleyway through the housing estate to the door of that house. In the course of that short walk he fired the pump action shotgun, though it was not clear whether this was accidentally or deliberately. There was no concealment.

He knocked at the door. The deceased's son opened it. He pushed his way in. There was a confrontation with Robert McCubbin. He must have had the gun in one hand and his razor in another, because with the razor he inflicted terrible injuries to McCubbin, who fled out of the back of the house with blood pouring from him. The appellant pursued him, and fired the shotgun twice after him. It was not direct fire from these two ill-aimed shots that killed McCubbin but particles blasted from a wire mesh fence by the force of the shot. He went back to the house, said to the deceased's son: 'If your family ever fucks with us I'll be back, I'll do the same to you as your old man,' and, shouting over his shoulder, 'don't mess about with my boys.' He and his two sons walked back to their car and drove off. At about the same time McCubbin collapsed and died.

[The trial judge held that there was insufficient evidence of provocation and the appellant was convicted of murder.]

Lady Mallalieu [counsel for the appellant] points to the scheme of section 3 [of the Homicide Act 1957], under which the jury is the sole arbiter of the make-up of the reasonable man, and what would or would not have provoked him. She accepts, as she must, that on the wording of the section, provocation only comes into the picture where there is evidence fit for consideration by the jury that the defendant was, or might have been, suffering from a sudden and temporary loss of self-control at the time he did the fatal act. Here the judge ruled that there was *no* such evidence, and the question is whether she was right to do so.

The question is necessarily one of a value judgment, a matter of degree. The judge clearly expressed the view that in her *judgment* (our emphasis) this was not a case of provocation because any sudden or temporary loss of self-control must have ceased by the time of the fatal act. She so expresses it in the terms of her judgment: 'I am not persuaded ...', 'in my judgment ...', 'that seems to me to be ...'

It seems to us that that approach is too austere an approach for the purposes of section 3. Having regard to the clear intention of Parliament to move the test of provocation from the judge's province to that of the jury (while reserving to the judge a screening process), the provisions of that section must be construed paying proper and sensible regard to human frailty in answering the essential jury question. (See *DPP v Camplin* [1978] AC 705, 718H–719A where Lord Morris of Borth-y-Gest says:

> ... for many years past in cases where murder has been charged, it has been recognised by courts that there can be circumstances in which the accused person was so provoked that his unlawful act was held to amount to

manslaughter rather than to murder. Due and sensible regard to human nature and to human frailty and infirmity was being paid. In *Hayward* (1833) 6 C & P 157, 159 this result was said to be 'in compassion to human infirmity'.)

To the like effect in *Rossiter* (1992) 95 Cr App R 326, 332, Russell LJ said of section 3:

> The emphasis in that section is very much on the function of the jury as opposed to the judge. We take the law to be that wherever there is material which is capable of amounting to provocation, however tenuous it may be, the jury must be given the privilege of ruling on it.

Though the judge had the inestimable advantage over us of having herself heard the evidence, we do not believe that she can have applied that test here. We are dealing with threats to sons in their middle to late teens. We are dealing with threats by one who is supplying them with narcotics which may lead to the ruin of their lives quite independently of whether the actual physical threats are carried out or not. We are dealing with a father who, though no stranger to drink, behaved on this evening in a way apparently quite inconsistent with anything that he had done before. We are dealing with a case in which (depending on your view of the petrol stop) there was arguably no 'natural break' between the conversation with his son which caused him to go up to the attic to find the shotgun hidden there, and the shooting itself. Now, there are many and obvious difficulties in such a defence succeeding, but Lady Mallalieu has referred us to cases where the matter has been left to juries (and the defence has succeeded) even though there are the same qualities of the desire for revenge, as great a lapse of time, as much planning and as many of the features as point against a sudden and temporary loss of control. In our judgment, this is a matter which should have been left to the jury as being fit for their consideration. We say this while recognising that there are formidable, perhaps insuperable, obstacles in the jury arriving at a verdict of manslaughter because of provocation.

R v Thornton (No 2) [1996] 2 ALL ER 1023 (CA)

Lord Taylor of Gosforth CJ: ... [S]ince reliance is placed upon the appellant's suffering from a 'battered woman syndrome', we think it right to reaffirm the principle. A defendant, even if suffering from that syndrome, cannot succeed in relying on provocation unless the jury consider she suffered or may have suffered a sudden and temporary loss of self-control at the time of the killing.

That is not to say that a battered woman syndrome has no relevance to the defence of provocation. The severity of such a syndrome and the extent to which it may have affected a particular defendant will no doubt vary and is for the jury to consider. But it may be relevant in two ways. First, it may form an important background to whatever triggered the *actus reus*. A jury may more readily find there was a sudden loss of control triggered by even a minor incident, if the defendant has endured abuse over a period, on the 'last straw' basis. Second, depending on the medical evidence, the syndrome may have affected the defendant's personality so as to constitute a significant characteristic relevant (as we shall indicate) to the second question [ie whether the hypothetical reasonable woman possessing the appellant's characteristics would have reacted to the provocative conduct so as to do what the appellant did] the jury has to consider in regard to provocation.

The 'subjective' stage: looking at the history of events between the parties

R v Humphreys [1995] 4 All ER 889

Hirst LJ: This tempestuous relationship was a complex story, with several distinct and cumulative strands of potentially provocative conduct building up until the final encounter. Over the long term there was continuing cruelty, represented by the beatings and the continued encouragement of prostitution, and by the breakdown of the sexual relationship. On the first part of the night in question there was the threatened 'gang bang', and the drunkenness. Immediately before the killing, quite apart from the wounding verbal taunt, there was his [the deceased's] appearance in an undressed state, posing a threat of sex which she [the defendant] did not want and which he must have known she did not want, thus demonstrating potentially provocative conduct immediately beforehand not only by words but also by deeds. Finally of course there is the taunt itself, which was put forward as the trigger which caused the appellant's self-control to snap ... we consider that the guidance in the form of careful analysis of these strands should have been given by the judge so that the jury could clearly understand their potential significance.

The 'subjective' stage: can the provocation be 'self-induced'?

The defendant may rely on the defence of provocation even if he or she has been partly responsible for bringing that provocation about.

Edwards v R [1973] AC 648 (PC)

Lord Pearson: ... On principle it seems reasonable to say that:

(1) a blackmailer cannot rely on the predictable results of his own blackmailing conduct as constituting provocation sufficient to reduce his killing of the victim from murder to manslaughter, and the predictable results may include a considerable degree of hostile reaction by the person sought to be blackmailed, for instance vituperative words and even some hostile action such as blows with a fist;

(2) but if the hostile reaction by the person sought to be blackmailed goes to extreme lengths it might constitute sufficient provocation even for the blackmailer;

(3) there would in many cases be a question of degree to be decided by the jury ...

R v Johnson [1989] 1 WLR 740 (CA)

Watkins LJ: ... [His Lordship referred to the judgment of Lord Pearson in *Edwards v R* [1973] AC 648 at 658 and continued:] Those words cannot, we think, be understood to mean, as was suggested to us, that provocation which is 'self-induced' ceases to be provocation for the purposes of s 3 of the 1957 Act.

The relevant statutory provision being considered by the Privy Council was in similar terms to s 3. In view of the express wording of s 3, as interpreted in *DPP v Camplin*, which was decided after *Edwards v R*, we find it impossible to accept that the mere fact that a defendant caused a reaction in others, which in turn led him to lose his self-control, should result in the issue of provocation being kept outside a jury's consideration. Section 3 clearly provides that the question is whether things done or said or both provoked the defendant to lose his self-control. If there is any evidence that it may have done, the issue must be left to the jury. The jury would then have to consider all the circumstances of the incident, including all the relevant behaviour of the defendant, in deciding (a) whether he was in fact provoked and (b) whether the provocation was enough to make a reasonable man do what the defendant did ...

Notes and queries

1 Anything can be provocation – even the crying of a baby; see *R v Doughty* (1986) 83 Cr App R 319. The issue is whether the defendant's response to the provocation was reasonable. The more trivial the provocation, however, the less likely the jury are to believe that D actually was provoked at the time of the killing.

2 The defence of provocation is available to both the principal offender who is charged with murder, and an accomplice; see *R v Marks* [1998] Crim LR 676, although it seems likely that there would be considerable evidential difficulties in actually making out the defence.

The objective stage: what degree of self-control is to be expected from the defendant?

R v Camplin [1978] AC 705 (HL)

Lord Diplock: ... The respondent, Camplin, who was 15 years of age, killed a middle-aged Pakistani, Mohammed Lal Khan, by splitting his skull with a chapati pan, a heavy kitchen utensil like a rimless frying pan. At the time, the two of them were alone together in Khan's flat. At Camplin's trial for murder before Boreham J his only defence was that of provocation so as to reduce the offence to manslaughter. According to the story that he told in the witness box but which differed materially from that which he had told to the police, Khan had buggered him in spite of his resistance and had then laughed at him. Whereupon Camplin had lost his self-control and attacked Khan fatally with the chapati pan ...

The point of law of general public importance involved in the case has been certified as being:

> Whether on the prosecution for murder of a boy of 15, where the issue of provocation arises, the jury should be directed to consider the question under s 3 of the Homicide Act 1957 whether the provocation was enough to make a reasonable man do as he did by reference to a 'reasonable adult' or by reference to a 'reasonable boy of 15'.

My Lords, the doctrine of provocation in crimes of homicide has always represented an anomaly in English law. In crimes of violence which result in injury short of death, the fact that the act of violence was committed under provocation which had caused the accused to lose his self-control does not affect the nature of the offence of which he is guilty. It is merely a matter to be taken into consideration in determining the penalty which it is appropriate to impose.

Whereas in homicide provocation effects a change in the offence itself from murder for which the penalty is fixed by law (formerly death and now imprisonment for life) to the lesser offence of manslaughter for which the penalty is in the discretion of the judge ...

... [F]or the purposes of the law of provocation the 'reasonable man' has never been confined to the adult male. It means an ordinary person of either sex, not exceptionally excitable or pugnacious, but possessed of such powers of self-control as everyone is entitled to expect that his fellow citizens will exercise in society as it is today ... [N]ow that the law has been changed so as to permit of words being treated as provocation even though unaccompanied by any other acts, the gravity of verbal provocation may well depend upon the particular characteristics or circumstances of the person to whom a taunt or insult is addressed. To taunt a person because of his race, his physical infirmities or some shameful incident in his past may well be considered by the jury to be more offensive to the person addressed, however equable his temperament, if the facts on which the taunt is founded are true than it would be if they were not ...

In my opinion a proper direction to a jury on the question left to their exclusive determination by s 3 of the Act of 1957 would be on the following lines. The judge should state what the question is using the very terms of the section. He should then explain to them that the reasonable man referred to in the question is a person having the power of self-control to be expected of an ordinary person of the sex and age of the accused, but in other respects sharing such of the accused's characteristics as they think would affect the gravity of the provocation to him; and that the question is not merely whether such a person would in like circumstances be provoked to lose his self-control but also whether he would react to the provocation as the accused did ...

Lord Morris of Borth-y-Gest: ... It will first be for the court to decide whether, on a charge of murder, there is evidence on which a jury can find that the person charged was provoked to lose his self-control; thereafter, as it seems to me, all questions are for the jury. It will be for the jury to say whether they think that whatever was or may have been the provocation, such provocation was in their view enough to make a reasonable man do as the accused did: the jury must take into account everything both done and said according to the effect which they think there would have been on a reasonable man. Who then or what then is the 'reasonable man' who is referred to in the section? It seems to me that the courts are no longer entitled to tell juries that a reasonable man has certain stated and defined features. It is for the jury to consider all that the accused did: it is for them to say whether the provocation was enough to make a 'reasonable man' do as the accused did. The jury must take into account 'everything both done and said'. What do they think would have been the effect on a reasonable man? They must bring their 'collective good sense' to bear. As Lord Goddard CJ said in *R v McCarthy* [1954] 2 QB 105 at 112:

> No court has ever given, nor do we think ever can give, a definition of what constitutes a reasonable or an average man. That must be left to the collective good sense of the jury, and what no doubt would govern their opinion would be the nature of the retaliation used by the provoked person.

... If an impotent man were taunted about his impotence the jury would not today be told that an impotent man could not be a reasonable man as contemplated by the law. The jury would be entitled to decide that the accused man acted as 'a reasonable man' in being provoked as he was and in doing as he did.

It seems to me that as a result of the changes effected by s 3 a jury is fully entitled to consider whether an accused person, placed as he was, only acted as even a reasonable man might have acted if he had been in the accused's situation. There may be no practical difference between, on the one hand, taking a notional independent reasonable man but a man having the attributes of the accused and subject to all the events which surrounded the accused and then considering whether what the accused did was only what such a person would or might have done, and, on the other hand, taking the accused himself with all his attributes and subject to all the events and then asking whether there was provocation to such a degree as would or might make a reasonable man do what he (the accused) in fact did.

In my view it would now be unreal to tell a jury that the notional 'reasonable man' is someone without the characteristics of the accused: it would be to intrude into their province. A few examples may be given. If the accused is of particular colour or particular ethnic origin and things are said which to him are grossly insulting it would be utterly unreal if the jury had to consider whether the words would have provoked a man of different colour or ethnic origin, or to consider how such a man would have acted or reacted. The question would be whether the accused if he was provoked only reacted as even any reasonable man in his situation would or might have reacted. If the accused was ordinarily and usually a very unreasonable person, the view that on a particular occasion he acted just as a reasonable person would or might have acted would not be impossible of acceptance.

It is not disputed that the 'reasonable man' in s 3 could denote a reasonable person and so a reasonable woman. If words of grievous insult were addressed to a woman, words perhaps reflecting on her chastity or way of life, a consideration of the way in which she reacted would have to take account of how other women being reasonable women would or might in like circumstances have reacted. Would or might she, if she had been a reasonable woman, have done what she did?

In the instant case the considerations to which I have been referring have application to a question of age. The accused was a young man ... The jury had to consider whether a young man of about the same age as the accused but placed in the same situation as that which befell the accused could, had he been a reasonable young man, have reacted as did the accused and could have done what the accused did. For the reasons which I have outlined the question so to be considered by the jury would be whether they considered that the accused, placed as he was, and having regard to all the things that they found were said, and all the things that they found were done, only acted as a reasonable young man might have acted, so that, in compassion, and having regard to human frailty, he could to some extent be excused even though he had caused a death ...

Lord Simon of Glaisdale: ... In my judgment the reference to 'a reasonable man' at the end of [s 3 of the Homicide Act 1957] means 'a man of ordinary self-control'. If this is so the meaning satisfies what I have ventured to suggest as the reason for importing into this branch of the law the concept of the reasonable man – namely to avoid the injustice of a man being entitled to rely on his exceptional excitability or pugnacity or ill-temper or on his drunkenness ...

I think that the standard of self-control which the law requires before provocation is held to reduce murder to manslaughter is still that of the reasonable person (hence his invocation in s 3); but that, in determining whether a person of reasonable self-control would lose it in the circumstances, the entire factual situation, which includes the characteristics of the accused, must be considered ...

Making the objective test more subjective: what characteristics of the defendant can be taken into account when assessing the reasonableness of his response?

R v Dryden [1995] 4 All ER 987 (CA)

Lord Taylor of Gosforth CJ: ... The case attracted national notoriety since the offences were committed and recorded in a dramatic scene before the press and two film crews. On 29 June 1991, following a planning dispute, local authority employees went to the appellant's land in County Durham to demolish some buildings which he had erected. He shot and killed the principal planning officer of the local authority. He then attempted to kill the solicitor who had acted at various stages for the local authority, and in trying to do that he shot and wounded a BBC newsman and a police officer, wounding them with intent. There was, and could be, no dispute that the appellant had committed those acts since his actions were captured on film. However, there was disagreement between the Crown and the defence as to the appellant's responsibility for his acts. There were a number of doctors called to support, and in one instance reject, a defence of diminished responsibility. The jury were also invited to consider the defence of provocation ...

... [Counsel for the appellant] submits that, by using [the words 'You may think that a reasonable man is not exceptionally excitable or exceptionally eccentric – or indeed eccentric at all – or obsessed'] the judge not only failed to put forward eccentricity and obsession as characteristics which the jury ought to take into account; she excluded them from their consideration. He submits that they were characteristics which the judge ought to have referred specifically to the jury ...

... [Counsel for the appellant says] here one has somebody who was clearly marked off from the rest of the community; he was a man who was obsessive about particular things, and especially about the dispute over his land, which was central to his whole way of life, and he was, as one of the doctors indicated, vulnerable in regard to that matter. [Counsel] therefore submits that this was a characteristic which was permanent. It was something which marked off this appellant and distinguished him from the ordinary man of the community, and it was a factor which was specifically relevant to what happened in this case.

It was in regard to his obsession with his property and this dispute that the conduct of bringing the excavator to the scene was 'the last straw' in the build-up of stress upon the appellant.

We have come to the conclusion that this was a characteristic – the obsessiveness on the part of the appellant and his eccentric character – which ought to have been left to the jury for their consideration. We consider that they were features of his character or personality which fell into the category of mental characteristics and which ought to have been specifically left to the jury ...

R v Morhall [1996] 3 WLR 330 (HL)

Lord Goff of Chieveley: ... The circumstances in which the defendant killed the deceased are [as follows]: During the daytime on 7 June 1991 the deceased and one Donnellan had been taking the [defendant] to task over his glue-sniffing. At about 5 pm they were at his flat during an argument between the deceased and his girlfriend, also over his glue-sniffing of which she disapproved. She left. Later, the deceased and Donnellan went out a couple of times. The [defendant] was sniffing glue when they left and when they returned. By 10 pm, when they came back with some cider and beer, the [defendant] was 'high'. He was unsteady and his speech was affected. The deceased resumed nagging him about his glue-sniffing. At about 2 am the deceased went out and brought some food. Whilst the other two ate, the [defendant] carried on glue-sniffing. The deceased chided him again and then head-butted him. The [defendant] picked up a hammer and hit the deceased on the head. A fight ensued. It was broken up by Donnellan, who got the [defendant] to go to his bedroom. However, the deceased would not stop. He said, 'I am not having that, I am going to do him'. He went to the [defendant's] bedroom and Donnellan heard crashing and banging. When he went in the [defendant] was holding the commando dagger and the deceased said, 'The bastard has stabbed me'. Donnellan wrestled with the [defendant]. Meanwhile, the deceased had gone down to the next landing where he fell to the floor. He had been fatally stabbed.

... Judging from the speeches in *R v Camplin*, [the characteristic of glue-sniffing addiction] should indeed have been taken into account. Indeed, it was a characteristic of particular relevance, since the words of the deceased which were said to constitute provocation were directed towards the defendant's shameful addiction to glue-sniffing and his inability to break himself of it. Furthermore, there is nothing in the speeches in *R v Camplin* to suggest that a characteristic of this kind should be excluded from consideration ...

... In truth the expression 'reasonable man' or 'reasonable person' in this context can lead to misunderstanding. Lord Diplock described it (in *R v Camplin* at 716G) as an 'apparently inapt expression'. This is because the 'reasonable person test' is concerned not with ratiocination, nor with the reasonable man whom we know so well in the law of negligence (where we are concerned with reasonable foresight and reasonable care), nor with reasonable conduct generally. The function of the test is only to introduce, as a matter of policy, a standard of self-control which has to be complied with if provocation is to be established in law ... Lord Diplock himself spoke of 'the reasonable or ordinary person', and indeed to speak of the degree of self-control attributable to the ordinary person is (despite the express words of the statute) perhaps more apt, and certainly less likely to mislead, than to do so with reference to the reasonable person ... In my opinion it would be entirely consistent with the law as stated in s 3 of the Act of 1957, as properly understood, to direct the jury simply with reference to a hypothetical person having the power of self-control to be expected of an ordinary person of the age and sex of the defendant, but in other respects sharing such of the defendant's characteristics as they think would affect the gravity of the provocation to him ...

In truth, the mere fact that a characteristic of the defendant is discreditable does not exclude it from consideration, as was made plain by Lord Diplock in *R v Camplin* when he referred to a shameful incident in a man's past as a relevant characteristic for present purposes. Indeed, even if the defendant's discreditable conduct causes a reaction in another, which in turn causes the defendant to lose his self-control, the reaction may amount to provocation: see *Edwards v R* [1973] AC 648, a case concerned with a hostile reaction to his blackmailer by a man whom he was trying to blackmail, and *R v Johnson (Christopher)* [1989] 1 WLR 740 in which *Edwards v R* was followed and applied by the Court of Appeal ...

Of course glue-sniffing (or solvent abuse), like indulgence in alcohol or the taking of drugs, can give rise to a special problem in the present context, because it may arise in more than one way. First, it is well established that, in considering whether a person having the power of self-control to be expected of an ordinary person would have reacted to the provocation as the defendant did, the fact (if it be the case) that the defendant was the worse for drink at the time should not be taken into account, even though the drink would, if taken by him, have the effect of reducing an ordinary person's power of self-control. It is sometimes suggested that the reason for this exclusion is that drunkenness is transitory and cannot therefore amount to a characteristic. But I doubt whether that is right. Indeed some physical conditions (such as eczema) may be transitory in nature and yet can surely be taken into account if the subject taunts. In *R v Camplin* [1978] AC 705 at 726F, Lord Simon of Glaisdale considered that drunkenness should be excluded as inconsistent with the concept of the reasonable man in the sense of a man of ordinary self-control; but it has to be recognised that, in our society, ordinary people do sometimes have too much to drink. I incline therefore to the opinion that the exclusion of drunkenness in this context flows from the established principle that, at common law, intoxication does not of itself excuse a man from committing a criminal offence, but on one or other of these bases it is plainly excluded. At all events it follows that, in a case such as the present, a distinction may have to be drawn between two different situations. The first occurs where the defendant is taunted with his addiction (for example, that he is an alcoholic, or a drug addict, or a glue-sniffer), or even with having been intoxicated (from any cause) on some previous occasion. In such a case, however discreditable such a condition may be, it may where relevant be taken into account as going to the gravity of the provocation. The second is the simple fact of the defendant being intoxicated – being drunk, or high with drugs or glue – at the relevant time, which may not be so taken into account, because that, like displaying a lack of ordinary self-control, is excluded as a matter of policy ...

R v Smith (Morgan) [2000] 4 All ER 289

Lord Hoffmann: My Lords,

1 The facts

On a November evening in 1996 Morgan Smith received a visit from his old friend James McCullagh. They were both alcoholics and spent the evening in drinking and recrimination. Smith had grievances against McCullagh, some of which went back many years. The most recent was his belief that McCullagh had stolen the tools of his trade as a carpenter and sold them to buy drink. McCullagh's repeated denials only inflamed Smith further. A friend arrived to find the row in full swing. While the friend was using the lavatory, Smith took up a kitchen knife and stabbed McCullagh several times. One of the blows was fatal.

Smith was indicted on a charge of murder before Judge Coombe and a jury. His defences were, first, that he did not intend to kill or cause grievous bodily harm; secondly, that he was suffering from diminished responsibility and thirdly that he was acting under provocation. The jury rejected all three defences and convicted Smith of murder. It is accepted that no criticism can be made of the judge's summing-up on the first two defences. The question is whether he gave the jury the correct directions on the law of provocation.

2 The defence of provocation

As a result of the decision of the House of Lords in *Mancini v Director of Public Prosecutions* [1942] AC 1 the common law of provocation was tolerably well settled. First, the provocation had to be such as to temporarily deprive the person provoked of the power of self-control, as a result of which he committed the unlawful act which caused death. Secondly, the provocation had to be such as would have made a reasonable man act in the same way. These two requirements are commonly called the subjective and objective elements of the defence respectively. In *R v Duffy* [1949] 1 All ER 932 the gist of the defence was encapsulated by Devlin J ...

Two decisions of the House of Lords subsequent to Mancini added glosses to these principles. First, in *Holmes v Director of Public Prosecutions* [1946] AC 588 it was decided that mere words could not constitute provocation, whatever their effect upon the reasonable man might have been. Secondly, in *Bedder v Director of Public Prosecutions* [1954] 1 WLR 1119 it was decided that the 'reasonable man' is a wholly impersonal fiction to which no special characteristic of the accused should be attributed. The alleged provocation was that the victim, a prostitute, had taunted the accused for his impotence. The accused was in fact impotent but the House held that the jury had properly been directed to consider whether a reasonable man who was not impotent would have reacted in the same way.

On the recommendation of the Royal Commission on Capital Punishment (Cmd 8932, 1949–53), paras 151–52, the common law was amended by section 3 of the Homicide Act 1957 ...

This section plainly changed the law in two ways. First, it provided that if there was evidence that the accused was provoked to lose his self-control (the subjective element) then the question of whether the objective element was satisfied had to be left to the jury. The judge was not entitled, as he could at common law, to withdraw the issue from the jury if he thought there was no evidence upon which a jury could reasonably consider that the objective element might have been satisfied. Secondly, the jury could for this purpose take into account 'everything both said and done.' This removed any legal restriction on the kind of acts that could amount to provocation, such as the rule in *Holmes* [1946] AC 588 that words alone were insufficient.

The question which came before the House in *R v Camplin* [1978] AC 705 was whether by implication the section had also changed a third common law doctrine. This was the rule in *Bedder* [1954] 1 WLR 1119 which required the 'reasonable person' to be devoid of any particular characteristics. The accused was a youth of 15 who claimed that he had been provoked to kill an older man by sexual abuse and taunting. The judge had directed the jury that they should consider what effect the provocation would have had upon a reasonable person of full age. The House decided that since provocation by words was frequently directed at some characteristic of the accused, such as his past behaviour, disabilities or race, the change in the law which allowed such taunts or insults to constitute provocation would be ineffectual if the accused had to be assumed to lack such a characteristic. It was therefore decided that, at least for the purpose of considering the gravity of the provocation, the reasonable man should normally be assumed to share the relevant characteristics of the accused. Whether the decision went further and allowed the jury to take into account characteristics of the accused which affected his powers of self-control is the chief question in this appeal and, in order to answer it, I shall have to analyse the case later in more detail. It can however be said that *Camplin* [1978] AC 705 allowed at least one such characteristic to be taken into account, namely, the youth of the accused. The actual decision was that the jury should have been told to consider what the effect of the provocation would have been upon a person with the powers of self-control of a reasonable boy of 15 and not those of a grown-up.

The extent to which matters affecting the power of self-control should be taken into account divided the Judicial Committee of the Privy Council in *Luc Thiet Thuan v R* [1997] AC 131. The majority, in an opinion given by Lord Goff of Chieveley, decided that in principle the actual characteristics of the accused were relevant only to the gravity of the provocation. The only characteristics of the accused which could be attributed to the reasonable person for the purpose of expressing a standard of self-control were his or her age and sex. There had been evidence that the accused suffered from brain damage which made it difficult for him to control his impulses in response to minor provocation. But this was held irrelevant to the question of whether the objective element in the defence had been satisfied. The majority said that the English cases after *Camplin* (to some of which I shall later refer) which had held that the jury should be directed that they could take such matters into account, had been wrongly decided. Lord Steyn, in a minority opinion, said that the later cases were not inconsistent with *Camplin*, constituted a logical extension of its reasoning and were in accordance with justice and common sense.

3 The trial, summing-up and appeal

In the present case there was psychiatric evidence on both sides. It dealt mainly with the question of whether Smith was suffering from diminished responsibility but the expert witnesses also considered his susceptibility to react to provocation. A psychiatrist called by the defence, who had seen Smith in prison less than a fortnight after the offence, said that he was suffering from an abnormality of the mind, namely depression, which could reduce his 'threshold for erupting with violence.' Another said that he was suffering from clinical depression which made him 'more disinhibited', ie less able to control his reactions.

The judge gave a direction which, as it happens, was in accordance with the majority opinion in *Luc Thiet Thuan* [1997] AC 131, although the case does not appear to have cited to him. He told the jury that if they considered that the accused might have been suffering from a depressive illness, they should decide whether a man suffering from such illness, but with a reasonable man's powers of self-control, might have responded to McCullagh's behaviour by stabbing him to death. The fact that the depressive illness may have reduced Smith's own powers of self-control was 'neither here nor there' and should not be taken into account.

In *R v Campbell* [1997] 1 Cr App R 199 the Court of Appeal considered the majority opinion in *Luc Thiet Thuan v R* [1997] AC 131 and held that, unless your Lordships' House decided otherwise, it would continue to follow its earlier decisions and the minority opinion of Lord Steyn. In the Court of Appeal in the present case Potts J gave a careful judgment explaining why he considered that those decisions were correct. The court therefore allowed the appeal and substituted a verdict of manslaughter. But in view of the state of the authorities it gave leave to appeal and certified the following point of law of general public importance:

> Are characteristics other than age and sex, attributable to a reasonable man, for the purpose of section 3 of the Homicide Act 1957, relevant not only to the gravity of the provocation to him but also to the standard of self-control to be expected? ...

5 Proposals for reform

The Royal Commission on Capital Punishment (Cmd 8932, 1953), which reported in September 1953, before *Bedder v Director of Public Prosecutions* [1954] 1 WLR 1119 was decided, considered the law of provocation. It noted (at para 134) that the scope for alleviating the act of killing on the ground of provocation had been steadily limited by appellate courts, particularly by the concept of the impersonal reasonable man, but that

> the greater severity of the law has been tempered by leniency in its application. Judges have instructed juries in terms more favourable than the letter of the law would allow. Juries, sometimes with the encouragement of the judge, sometimes in the face of his direction, have returned verdicts of manslaughter where, as a matter of law, the most favourable interpretation of the evidence could scarcely justify them in doing so.

This state of affairs was, in the view of the Commission (at para 144), attributable to the single mandatory sentence for murder, which at that time was death.

> Provocation is in essence only an extenuating circumstance which in the case of lesser crimes ... does not alter the nature of the offence but is allowed for in the sentence. The rule of law that provocation may, within narrow bounds, reduce murder to manslaughter, represents an attempt by the courts to reconcile the preservation of the fixed penalty for murder with a limited concession to natural human weakness, but it suffers from the common defects of a compromise. The jury might fairly be required to apply the test of the 'reasonable man' in assessing provocation if the Judge were afterwards free to exercise his ordinary discretion and to consider whether the peculiar temperament or mentality of the accused justified mitigation of sentence. It is less easy to defend the application of the test in murder cases where the judge has no such discretion.

My Lords, the force of this criticism of the rigid impersonality of the 'reasonable man' test is only slightly reduced by the fact that the mandatory sentence for murder is now life imprisonment. It does not follow, however, that the abolition of the mandatory sentence would make the defence superfluous. It might still be thought desirable to allow the jury to decide whether provocation was a reason why the killing did not deserve the degree of moral condemnation and severity of sentence associated with the crime of murder: see paras 80–83 of the Report of the House of Lords Select Committee on *Murder and Life Imprisonment* (HL Paper 78-I

Session 1988–89). Why provocation should be the only ground upon which the jury should be allowed to express a moral judgment of this kind is a difficult question which would take me too far from my present purpose.

The Royal Commission on Capital Punishment concluded (at para 145) that it had no doubt that if the criterion of the reasonable man was strictly applied 'it would be too harsh in its application.' But in practice – 'the courts not infrequently give weight to factors personal to the prisoner in considering a plea of provocation.' The Home Secretary also took such matters into account in commuting death sentences. So the Commission made no recommendation for change. But it did recommend (at paras 151–52) that the rule that words could never constitute provocation should be abolished: 'the nature (as distinct from the degree) of provocation should be immaterial.' The issue should be left to the jury, which:

> can be trusted to arrive at a just and reasonable decision and will not hesitate to convict the accused of murder where he has acted on only slight provocation, whether by words or otherwise.

6 The construction of section 3

As I have already said, the issue in *Camplin* ... was whether, in addition to the two express changes in the law made by the statute concerning the provinces of judge and jury and the status of words as provocation, there was by necessary implication a change in the concept of the reasonable man as formulated in *Bedder* [1954] 1 WLR 1119. I shall in due course analyse the answer which the House gave to that question. But before doing so, I shall consider what seems to me, apart from authority, to have been the effect of the Act.

My Lords, if one reads the debates touching upon this subject in your Lordships House during the passage of the bill, there can be no doubt that Lord Kilmuir, the Lord Chancellor, was of opinion that the clause made no change in the concept of the reasonable man. That merely shows how unhelpful such debates often are as a guide to construction. Lord Kilmuir had not thought through the consequences of the changes made by the section in the way in which the House had to do in *Camplin*. If one approaches the question of construction in the orthodox way, namely by considering the language of the section against the background of the common law of provocation, one has to conclude that the concept of the reasonable man as a touchstone of the objective element could not have been intended to stay the same.

The reasons are to be found in both the other changes expressly made by the section. The first, namely the admission of words as a legitimate source of provocation, I have already mentioned. It was this reason which received the main emphasis in *Camplin*. But the other change, in the respective roles of judge and jury, was equally important. The Royal Commission, it will be remembered, said (at para 134) that a change in the law was unnecessary because juries, sometimes in the face of the judge's directions on the law, returned verdicts of manslaughter in cases in which justice appeared to require a concession to human frailty. That is to say, juries arrived at verdicts in favour of the accused which were contrary to law. The traditional way in which judges attempt to deflect the jury from a perverse verdict of this kind is to withdraw the issue. But section 3 was intended to deprive the judge of even this method of control. The jury was to be sovereign and have the power in theory as well as in practice to decide whether the objective element was satisfied.

I do not think it possible to attribute to Parliament, in making this change, any intention other than to legitimate the relaxation of the old law in those cases in which justice appeared to require it and to allow the jury in good conscience to arrive at a verdict which previously would have been perverse. In other words, the jury was given a normative as well as a fact-finding function. They were to determine not merely whether the behaviour of the accused complied with some legal standard but could determine for themselves what the standard in the particular case should be. In this way they could, as the Royal Commission said, 'give weight to factors personal to the prisoner' in cases in which it appeared unjust not to do so.

It follows, in my opinion, that it would not be consistent with section 3 for the judge to tell the jury as a matter of law that they should ignore any factor or characteristic of the accused in deciding whether the objective element of provocation had been satisfied. That would be to trespass upon their province. In a case in which the jury might consider that only by virtue of that characteristic was the act in question sufficiently provocative, the effect of such a direction would be to withdraw the issue of provocation altogether and this would be contrary to the terms of section 3.

If, therefore, the purpose of section 3 was to legitimate the normative role of the jury and free their consciences from the burden of having to give a perverse verdict in order to do justice, it must have had a corresponding effect upon the nature of the directions they were to be given by the judge. It is inconceivable that he was intended to instruct them according to the letter of the old law, in the expectation or even the hope that in an appropriate case his directions would be ignored. It meant, as I have said, that he could no longer tell them that they were obliged as a matter of law to exclude 'factors personal to the prisoner' from their consideration. But that did not mean that he was required to leave the jury at large and without any assistance in the exercise of their normative role. He could tell the jury that the doctrine of provocation included the principle of objectivity and that they should have regard to that principle in deciding whether the act in question was sufficiently provocative to be acceptable as a partial excuse.

The radical change which the Act made in the role of judge and jury was not something which had been recommended by the Royal Commission. Their view was that, apart from removing any restrictions on the acts which could amount to provocation, the law should stay the same. It is interesting however to notice that something very similar to section 3 had been recommended a century earlier by the Criminal Law Commissioners in their Second Report of 1846 ...

7 DPP v Camplin ...

... In the House of Lords Lord Diplock, with whom Lords Fraser of Tullybelton and Lord Scarman agreed, gave the leading judgment. Lord Diplock drew attention to the express changes which section 3 made to the nature of a provocative act and to the role of judge and jury. He noted (at [1978] AC 705, 716) that the 'reasonable man' had been preserved by the Act but said that it 'falls to be applied now in the context of a law of provocation that is significantly different from what it was before the Act was passed.' He pointed out, at p 717, that:

now that the law has been changed so as to permit of words being treated as provocation ... the gravity of verbal provocation may well depend upon the particular characteristics or circumstances of the person to whom a taunt or insult is addressed.

It would stultify this change in the law if the jury could not take into account 'all those factors which in their opinion would affect the gravity of taunts or insults when applied to the person to whom they are addressed'.

So far, the reasoning is concerned solely with the relevance of the characteristics or circumstances of the accused to the gravity of the provocation. But the actual facts in *Camplin* were not primarily concerned with a characteristic with affected the gravity of the provocation. It is true that the gravity of the alleged taunts and sexual abuse may have been affected by the accused's consciousness of his physical and intellectual inferiority in relation to the deceased. But the main case for the defence was that a 15 year old boy could not be expected to have the same powers of self-control as an adult. Lord Diplock acknowledged at pp 717–18, that:

in strict logic there is a transition between treating age as a characteristic that may be taken into account in assessing the gravity of the provocation addressed to the accused and treating it as a characteristic to be taken into account in determining what is the degree of self-control to be expected of the ordinary person with whom the accused's conduct is to be compared. But to require old heads upon young shoulders is inconsistent with the law's compassion to human infirmity to which Sir Michael Foster ascribed the doctrine of provocation more than two centuries ago. The distinction as to the purposes for which it is legitimate to take the age of the accused into account involves considerations of too great nicety to warrant a place in deciding a matter of opinion, which is no longer one to be decided by a judge trained in logical reasoning but is to be decided by a jury drawing on their experience of how ordinary human beings behave in real life.

This is a most important passage and I invite your Lordships' attention to the following points:

(1) Lord Diplock says that youth may be taken into account because the principle of compassion to human infirmity, as a jury drawing on their experience may apply it, requires one to do so. He does not say that the same principle of compassion is incapable of applying to any other characteristics which a jury might on similar grounds think should be taken into account. It would have been easy for him to have said that youth was for this purpose unique.

(2) Lord Diplock expressly rejects the distinction between the effect of age on the gravity of the provocation and on the power of self-control on the grounds that it is 'of too great nicety' for application by a jury. Again, there is nothing to suggest that this comment is not equally true of other characteristics. Since *Camplin*, there is a great deal of material which demonstrates that Lord Diplock's scepticism about whether the distinction could be made to work in practice was well founded.

(3) If age were to be the only case in which a particular characteristic could be taken into account as relevant to the expected power of self-control, it would be necessary to explain why it should be so singled out. The High Court of Australia, in *Stingel v R* (1990) 171 CLR 312, 330, said that it was because age is

a normal characteristic: 'the process of development from childhood to maturity is something which, being common to us all, is an aspect of ordinariness.' This explanation was embraced by Lord Goff of Chieveley in *Luc Thiet Thuan v R* [1997] AC 131, 140. It had, as I have said, been relied upon in *Camplin* by the Court of Appeal to distinguish *Bedder*. But the distinction between normal and abnormal characteristics was expressly rejected by Lord Diplock. He said (at p 718) that:

> The reasoning in *Bedder* would, I think, permit of this distinction between normal and abnormal characteristics, which may affect the powers of self-control of the accused; but for reasons that I have already mentioned the proposition stated in Bedder requires qualification as a consequence of the changes in the law effected by the Act of 1957. To try to salve what can remain of it without conflict with the Act could in my view only lead to unnecessary and unsatisfactory complexity in a question which has now become a question for the jury alone.

My Lords, the important passage which I have cited from Lord Diplock's speech provides in my view no support for the theory, widely advanced in the literature, that he was making a clear distinction between characteristics relevant to the gravity of the provocation and characteristics relevant to the power of self-control, with age (and possibly sex) as arbitrary exceptions which could be taken into account for the latter purpose. This interpretation depends principally upon what Lord Diplock described as 'a proper direction to the jury' which he gave at the end of his speech [see the extract from *DPP v Camplin*, above] ...

The references to age and sex have been taken to mean that in all cases these are the only matters which should be mentioned as relevant to the question of self-control. It seems to me clear, however, that Lord Diplock was framing a suitable direction for a case like *Camplin* [1978] AC 705 and not a one-size-fits-all direction for every case of provocation. A jury would be puzzled about why they were being asked to pay particular attention to the age and sex of the defendant if he was an ordinary adult. A number of writers and judges have thought that Lord Diplock was wrong to include the sex of the accused (see for example, *Stingel v R* (1990) 171 CLR 312, 331) and if the direction had been intended to be of general application, I would agree. But in my view Lord Diplock was only drawing attention to the fact that the hormonal development of male adolescents is different from that of females.

Finally, my Lords, I draw attention to the concluding sentence of Lord Diplock's speech, in which he summed up why he thought it would be wrong to direct the jury that they were not entitled to take into account the youth of the accused. It was because:

> So to direct them was to impose a fetter on the right and duty of the jury which the Act accords to them to act upon their own opinion on the matter.

This, in my view, goes to the heart of the matter and is in accordance with the analysis of the effect of section 3 which I have made earlier in my speech. The jury is entitled to act upon its own opinion of whether the objective element of provocation has been satisfied and the judge is not entitled to tell them that for this purpose the law requires them to exclude from consideration any of the circumstances or characteristics of the accused.

8 The gravity of provocation/self-control distinction

Although *DPP v Camplin* [1978] AC 705 does not in my opinion provide authoritative support for the distinction between gravity of provocation and powers of self-control, it has been adopted in Australia (*Stingel v R* (1990) 171 CLR 312); New Zealand (*R v Campbell* [1997] 1 NZLR 16 and *R v Rongonui* (2000) unreported, 13 April, Court of Appeal); Canada (*R v Hill* [1986] 1 SCR 313); and by the Privy Council for Hong Kong (*Luc Thiet Thuan v R* [1997] AC 131). It also has a good deal of academic support: see in particular Professor Ashworth's influential article 'The doctrine of provocation' [1976] CLJ 292–320, Jeremy Horder, 'Between provocation and diminished responsibility' (1999) 2 KCLJ 143–66 and Professor MJ Allen, 'Provocation's reasonable man: a plea for self-control' [2000] Journal of Criminal Law 216–44. It must therefore be considered on its own merits.

The theoretical basis for the distinction is that provocation is a defence for people who are, as Professor Ashworth put it, 'in a broad sense mentally normal': see [1976] CLJ at p 312. If they claim that they had abnormal characteristics which reduced their powers of self-control, they should plead diminished responsibility. There is a clear philosophical distinction between a claim that an act was at least partially excused as normal behaviour in response to external circumstances and a claim that the actor had mental characteristics which prevented him from behaving normally: see Sir Peter Strawson, 'Freedom and resentment', in *Free Will* (Watson, ed. 1982) at pp 64–67.

The difficulty about the practical application of this distinction in the law of provocation is that in many cases the two forms of claim are inextricably muddled up with each other. A good example is the recent New Zealand case of *R v Rongonui* (2000) unreported, 13 April, Court of Appeal. The accused was a woman with a history of violence against her, suffering from post-traumatic stress disorder. The alleged provocation was that a neighbour she was visiting to ask for help in babysitting her children had produced a knife – not in a threatening way, but sufficient to make her lose control of herself, seize the knife and stab the neighbour to death. The Court of Appeal agreed that it was very difficult in such a case to distinguish between the gravity of the provocation (the accused's previous experience of violence making the mere production of a knife a graver provocation than it would be to someone who had led a more sheltered life) and the accused's capacity for self-control which had been affected by the psychological stress of the violence she had suffered. Tipping J, giving one of the majority judgments which held that the New Zealand statute on provocation (section 169 of the Crimes Act 1961) mandated the application of the distinction, said that it required 'mental gymnastics.' Thomas J, who thought that the statute did not have to be construed so rigidly, said that most trial judges had seen:

> the glazed look in the jurors' eyes as, immediately after instructing them that it is open to them to have regard to the accused's alleged characteristic in assessing the gravity of the provocation, they are then advised that they must revert to the test of the ordinary person and disregard that characteristic when determining the sufficiency of the accused's loss of self-control.

Professor Stanley Yeo, in his recent book *Unrestrained Killings and the Law* (1998) at p 61 points out that the reason why jurors find the distinction so difficult is that it:

> bears no conceivable relationship with the underlying rationales of the defence of provocation ... The defence has been variously regarded as premised upon

the contributory fault of the victim and, alternatively, upon the fact that the accused was not fully in control of his or her behaviour when the homicide was committed. Neither of these premises requires the distinction to be made between characteristics of the accused affecting the gravity of the provocation from those concerned with the power of self-control.

Besides these practical difficulties in explaining the distinction to the jury, I think it is wrong to assume that there is a neat dichotomy between the 'ordinary person' contemplated by the law of provocation and the 'abnormal person' contemplated by the law of diminished responsibility. The Act of 1957 made a miscellany of changes of the law of homicide which can hardly be described as amounting to a coherent and interlocking scheme. Diminished responsibility as defined in section 2 ('such abnormality of mind ... as substantially impaired his mental responsibility for his acts and omissions ...') is a general defence which can apply whatever the circumstances of the killing and was introduced because of what was regarded as the undue strictness of the defence of insanity. Provocation is a defence which depends upon the circumstances of the killing and section 3 was introduced, as I have suggested, to legitimate the consideration by juries of 'factors personal to the prisoner'. If one asks whether Parliament contemplated that there might be an overlap between these two defences, I think that the realistic answer is that no one gave the matter a thought. But the possibility of overlap seems to me to follow inevitably from consigning the whole of the objective element in provocation to the jury. If the jury cannot be told that the law requires characteristics which could found a defence of diminished responsibility to be ignored in relation to the defence of provocation, there is no point in claiming that the defences are mutually exclusive.

There are in practice bound to be cases in which the accused will not be suffering from 'abnormality of mind' within the meaning of section 2 ('a state of mind so different from that of ordinary human beings that the reasonable man would term it abnormal': *R v Byrne* [1960] 2 QB 396, 403) but will nevertheless have mental characteristics (temporary or permanent) which the jury might think should be taken into account for the purposes of the provocation defence. The boundary between the normal and abnormal is very often a matter of opinion. Some people are entirely normal in most respects and behave unusually in others. There are people (such as battered wives) who would reject any suggestion that they were 'different from ordinary human beings' but have undergone experiences which, without any fault or defect of character on their part, have affected their powers of self-control. In such cases the law now recognises that the emotions which may cause loss of self-control are not confined to anger but may include fear and despair. Professor Ashworth, who argued in 1976 that diminished responsibility and provocation were logically mutually exclusive, was cautious enough to say ('The doctrine of provocation' [1976] CLJ 292, 314) that it was 'difficult to shed all one's misgivings about whether the law actually operates in this way.' I think not only that this scepticism was justified but also that section 3 prevents the judges from trying to force cases into logical dichotomies.

There is however one really serious argument in favour of the distinction between characteristics affecting the gravity of the provocation and characteristics affecting the power of self-control. This is the claim that, despite all its difficulties of application, it is the only way to hold the line against complete erosion of the objective element in provocation. The purpose of the objective element in provocation is to mark the distinction between (partially) excusable and inexcusable loss of self-control. As Lord Diplock said in *DPP v Camplin* [1978] AC 705, 717, the conduct of the accused should be measured against 'such powers of self-control as everyone is entitled to expect that his fellow citizens will exercise in society as it is today.' If there is no limit to the characteristics which can be taken into account, the fact that the accused lost self-control will show that he is a person liable in such circumstances to lose his self-control. The objective element will have disappeared completely.

My Lords, I share the concern that this should not happen. For the protection of the public, the law should continue to insist that people must exercise self-control. A person who flies into a murderous rage when he is crossed, thwarted or disappointed in the vicissitudes of life should not be able to rely upon his anti-social propensity as even a partial excuse for killing. In *Stingel v R* (1990) 171 CLR 312, for example, the accused was obsessively infatuated with a woman who had terminated their relationship. He became a stalker, following her about. She obtained a court order restraining him from approaching her. One evening after a party he found the woman in a car with another man. According to his own account, they were having sex. He went back to his own car, fetched a butcher's knife and came back and killed the man. His evidence conformed to the standard narrative which the legal requirement of 'loss of control' imposes on such defences:

> I was all worked up and feeling funny. It was like I was in a rage, almost to the stage where I felt dazed. It was like I really didn't know what happened until the knife went into him.

The High Court of Australia held that the judge was right to withdraw the issue of provocation from the jury on the ground that such conduct could not raise even a reasonable doubt as to whether the objective element in the defence had been satisfied. I respectfully agree. Male possessiveness and jealousy should not today be an acceptable reason for loss of self-control leading to homicide, whether inflicted upon the woman herself or her new lover. In Australia the judge was able to give effect to this policy by withdrawing issue from the jury. But section 3 prevents an English judge from doing so. So, it is suggested, a direction that characteristics such as jealousy and obsession should be ignored in relation to the objective element is the best way to ensure that people like Stingel cannot rely upon the defence.

9 The English cases

The first important English case after *DPP v Camplin* [1978] AC 705 was the judgment of Lord Lane CJ in *R v Newell* (1980) 71 Cr App R 331. He interpreted section 3 as meaning that the jury can be directed to take into account personal characteristics of the accused in relation to both the gravity of the provocation and the degree of self-control which could reasonably have been expected. It is true, as Lord Goff of Chieveley pointed out in *Luc Thiet Thuan v R* [1997] AC 131, 141–44, the Lord Chief Justice adopted the construction which had been given to a somewhat different statute in New Zealand. He approved a passage in *R v McGregor* [1962] NZLR 1069 in which North J had said:

The offender must be presumed to possess in general the power of self-control of the ordinary man, save in so far as his power of self-control is weakened because of some particular characteristic possessed by him.

But the course of the law in New Zealand has been a rather tangled story, as the judgments in *R v Rongonui* (2000) unreported, 13 April, Court of Appeal, reveal. I have already said enough to explain why I think that the construction of section 3 adopted by the Court of Appeal was in this respect correct, independently of any support which might be obtained from New Zealand. It is therefore inappropriate for me to undertake any analysis of the New Zealand cases or comment upon the construction which the courts have given to their statute. Nor can any direct assistance be obtained from Australia and Canada, where the objective standard remains a matter of law for the judge.

The construction adopted in *Newell* 71 Cr App R 331 was followed by Lord Taylor of Gosforth CJ in *R v Ahluwalia* [1992] 4 All ER 889, a case of a battered wife. He said that characteristics relating to the 'mental state or personality of an individual' such as the fact that a battered wife was suffering from post-traumatic stress disorder, could be taken into account. It is true that he recorded counsel for the appellant as having described this as a characteristic which the jury 'might think might affect the gravity of the provocation'. The same comment may be made about Lord Taylor's later judgment in *R v Dryden* [1995] 4 All ER 987. In that case the accused was convicted of murder after he had shot and killed a planning officer who was engaged in demolishing his bungalow pursuant to an enforcement notice. There was psychiatric evidence that the accused had developed an obsession about his planning problems. The Court of Appeal said that the obsessiveness and eccentricity of the defendant should have been left to the jury as 'mental characteristics' which they should take into account. In neither case, however, did Lord Taylor suggest that the jury should have been directed to have regard to these characteristics only insofar as they might have affected the gravity of the provocation and not insofar as they may have affected the accused's power of self-control. No doubt this omission was for the very good reason that, on the facts of both cases, no jury would have understood what such a distinction meant.

Finally, in *R v Campbell* [1997] 1 Cr App R 199 Lord Bingham of Cornhill CJ affirmed the principle of the earlier decisions, which he said represented 'a judicial response, born of everyday experience in criminal trials up and down the country, as to what fairness seems to require'.

My Lords, in the face of these views of three successive Lord Chief Justices, I would be most reluctant to advise your Lordships to turn back such a strong current of authority unless it was clearly inconsistent with the statute. But I do not think it is. On the contrary, it seems to me to reflect a realistic appreciation of what the statute has done.

10 Guiding the jury

My Lords, I think that some of the concern about the recent trend of authority in the English Court of Appeal has been due to the assumption that unless the judge can direct the jury that certain characteristics of the accused are legally irrelevant to the objective element in the defence, the jury may receive the impression that the law actually requires them to take such matters into account. The effect would be to encourage juries to find provocation on inappropriate grounds. Obviously, my Lords, there is always the risk that a jury may do so. That is the risk which Parliament took when it gave the jury an unfettered right to give effect to its own opinion on the objective element. But it considered that risk less likely to cause injustice than to confine the jury within the rules of law which had been developed about the notional characteristics of the reasonable man. In any case, I think that much can be done to reduce that risk if judges guide juries on this issue in a way which fully takes into account the difference which section 3 has made to their respective roles.

Before 1957 the judge had to direct the jury as to whether, if they found that some act had caused the accused to lose his self-control, that act was 'capable' of amounting to provocation. It would be so capable if the judge considered that a rational jury could find that it satisfied the objective element. If he did not, he would withdraw the issue by telling the jury that there was no evidence upon which they could properly find that the accused had acted under provocation. If, therefore, the judge left the issue to the jury, he would do so in terms which conveyed to them that they could rationally find that the objective element was satisfied.

The effect of section 3 is that once the judge has ruled that there is evidence upon which the jury can find that something caused the accused to lose self-control (compare *R v Acott* [1997] 1 WLR 306), he cannot tell the jury that the act in question was incapable of amounting to provocation. But that no longer involves any decision by the judge that it would be rational so to decide. For example, in *R v Doughty* (1986) 83 Cr App R 319 the Court of Appeal held that the judge had been wrong to direct the jury that the crying of 17 day old baby, which had caused its father to kill it by covering its head with cushions and kneeling on them, could not constitute a provocative act. Section 3 said that the jury were entitled to take into account 'everything both done and said.' I respectfully think that this construction of the Act was correct. But that does not mean that the judge should tell the jury that the crying of the baby was, in the traditional language, capable of amounting to provocation. This would give the jury the impression that the judge thought it would be rational and in accordance with principle to hold that the crying of the baby constituted an acceptable partial excuse for killing it. The point about section 3 is that it no longer matters whether the judge thinks so or not. He should therefore be able simply to tell the jury that the question of whether such behaviour fell below the standard which should reasonably have been expected of the accused was entirely a matter for them. He should not be obliged to let the jury imagine that the law now regards anything whatever which caused loss of self-control (whether an external event or a personal characteristic of the accused) as necessarily being an acceptable reason for loss of self-control.

11 The reasonable man

The main obstacle to directing the jury in a way which does not give such a false impression is the highly artificial way in which courts and writers have attempted to marry two discordant ideas: first, the old formula that the provocation must have been such as to cause a 'reasonable man' to act in the same way as the accused and, secondly, the rule in section 3 that no circumstances or characteristics should be excluded from the consideration of the jury. They have done so by telling the jury that certain characteristics are to be 'attributed' to the reasonable man. By such a combination, they have produced monsters like the reasonable obsessive, the reasonable depressive alcoholic and even (with all respect to the explanations of Lord Goff of Chieveley in *R v Morhall* [1996] 1 AC 90, 98) the reasonable glue-sniffer. Nor does it elucidate matters to substitute 'ordinary' for 'reasonable.' Quite apart from the question of whether the jury can understand what such concepts mean, it is bound to suggest to them that obsession, alcoholism and so forth are not merely matters which they are entitled in law to take into account but that, being 'attributed' to the reasonable man, they are qualities for which allowances must be made.

So, for example, in *R v Humphreys* [1995] 4 All ER 1008 there was a good deal of discussion as to whether 'attention seeking' and 'immaturity' were 'eligible characteristics' in the sense that they were to be attributed to (in that case) the reasonable woman. The Court of Appeal decided that they were. Similarly in *R v Dryden* [1995] 4 All ER 987, which I have already mentioned, the question was framed as being whether the obsessiveness and eccentricity of the defendant were 'mental characteristics' which the jury should attribute to the reasonable man. Professor MJ Allen, in the article to which I have referred in [2000] Journal of Criminal Law 216, 239, says with some force that this decision, 'endorsing obsession as a characteristic to attribute to the reasonable man should sound an alarm bell for all sexual partners.' If Dryden's obsession could be attributed to 'the reasonable man,' why not Stingel's?

My Lords, the concept of the 'reasonable man' has never been more than a way of explaining the law to a jury; an anthropomorphic image to convey to them, with a suitable degree of vividness, the legal principle that even under provocation, people must conform to an objective standard of behaviour which society is entitled to expect: see Lord Diplock in *Camplin* [1978] AC 705, 714. In referring to 'the reasonable man' section 3 invokes that standard. But I do not think that it was intended to require judges always to use that particular image, even in cases in which its use is more likely to confuse than illuminate. When Keating J in *R v Welsh* (1869) 11 Cox CC 336, 339 borrowed the *mot juste* which Baron Alderson had used in *Blyth v Birmingham Waterworks* (1856) 11 Exch 781, 784 to define negligence, he did not imagine that he was changing the law. He merely thought he had hit upon a felicitous way of explaining it. Whether he was right is perhaps questionable. Even before the Act of 1957, there had been expressions of doubt about the extent to which it really was a helpful way to explain the notion of objectivity in the particular context of provocation. The jury may have some difficulty with the notion that the 'reasonable man' will, even under severe provocation, kill someone else. But, my Lords, whatever the force of the earlier criticisms, the value of the image has been hopelessly compromised by the Act of 1957. This may not have been foreseen, just as many did not foresee the effect which the Act would have upon the concept of the reasonable man and the abandonment in *Camplin* [1978] AC 705 of the law laid down in *Mancini* [1941] AC 1 and *Bedder* [1954] 1 WLR 1119. But it seems to me now, since *Camplin*, impossible to avoid giving the jury a misleading, not to say unintelligible, account of the law when particular characteristics, sometimes highly unusual and even repulsive, are welded onto the concept of the reasonable man. I do not find it surprising that nine judges who gave written evidence to the House of Lords Select Committee on *Murder and Life Imprisonment* (HL Paper 78-I Session 1988–89) said that the reasonable man test was 'logically unworkable, or [rendered] the defence almost ineffective if it were strictly applied by juries.'

My Lords, I do emphasise that what has been rendered unworkable is not the principle of objectivity which (subject to the changes noted in *Camplin*) section 3 was plainly intended to preserve, but a particular way of explaining it. I am not suggesting that your Lordships should in any way depart from the legal principle embodied in section 3 but only that the principle should be expounded in clear language rather than by the use of an opaque formula.

In my opinion, therefore, judges should not be required to describe the objective element in the provocation defence by reference to a reasonable man, with or without attribution of personal characteristics. They may instead find it more helpful to explain in simple language the principles of the doctrine of provocation. First, it requires that the accused should have killed while he had lost self-control and that something should have caused him to lose self-control. For better or for worse, section 3 left this part of the law untouched. Secondly, the fact that something caused him to lose self-control is not enough. The law expects people to exercise control over their emotions. A tendency to violent rages or childish tantrums is a defect in character rather than an excuse. The jury must think that the circumstances were such as to make the loss of self-control sufficiently excusable to reduce the gravity of the offence from murder to manslaughter. This is entirely a question for the jury. In deciding what should count as a sufficient excuse, they have to apply what they consider to be appropriate standards of behaviour; on the one hand making allowance for human nature and the power of the emotions but, on the other hand, not allowing someone to rely upon his own violent disposition. In applying these standards of behaviour, the jury represent the community and decide, as Lord Diplock said in *Camplin* ([1978] AC 717), what degree of self-control 'everyone is entitled to expect that his fellow citizens will exercise in society as it is today.' The maintenance of such standards is important. As Viscount Simon LC said more than 50 years ago in *Holmes v DPP* [1946] AC 588, 601, 'as society advances, it ought to call for a higher measure of self-control'.

The general principle is that the same standards of behaviour are expected of everyone, regardless of their individual psychological make-up. In most cases, nothing more will need to be said. But the jury should in an appropriate case be told, in whatever language will best convey the distinction, that this is a principle and not a rigid rule. It may sometimes have to yield to a more important principle, which is to do justice in the particular case. So the jury may think that there was some characteristic of the accused, whether temporary or permanent, which affected the degree of control which society could reasonably have expected of him and which it would be unjust not to take into account. If the jury take this view, they are at liberty to give effect to it.

My Lords, I do not wish to lay down any prescriptive formula for the way in which the matter is explained to the jury. I am sure that if judges are freed from the necessity of invoking the formula of the reasonable man equipped with an array of unreasonable 'eligible characteristics,' they will be able to explain the principles in simple terms. Provided that the judge makes it clear that the question is in the end one for the jury and that he is not seeking to 'impose a fetter on the right and duty of the jury which the Act accords to them,' the guidance which he gives must be a matter for his judgment on the facts of the case.

12 The burden of proof

The burden is upon the prosecution to disprove provocation. This means that the prosecution must satisfy the jury that a version of the facts in which the accused was provoked could not reasonably be true. But the decision as to whether, having regard to the objective principle, those facts should count as sufficient provocation to reduce the offence to manslaughter has nothing to do with the burden of proof. The jury either think it does or they do not. It is irrelevant that they may think that a different jury could have taken a different view.

13 Conclusion

In my opinion the judge should not have directed the jury as a matter of law that the effect of Smith's depression on his powers of self-control was 'neither here nor there.' They should have been told that whether they took it into account in relation to the question of whether the behaviour of the accused had measured up to the standard of self-control which ought reasonably to have been expected of him was a matter for them to decide. For the above reasons and those given by my noble and learned friends Lord Slynn of Hadley and Lord Clyde, I would dismiss the appeal.

Lord Slynn: My Lords ... The exegisis of the defence of provocation together with the reasons for it and its development over three centuries in particular, though its origin is earlier, have been dealt with in detail by counsel for the Crown and for the respondent. That history has been further set out in decisions in your Lordships' House in *R v Camplin* [1978] AC 705, in *Luc Thiet Thuan v R* [1997] AC 131 and in the present case by my noble and learned friend Lord Hoffmann whose opinion I have had the advantage of reading in draft. I do not repeat that history. I agree with the conclusion of both my noble and learned friends Lord Hoffmann and Lord Clyde that the appeal should be dismissed and because of their detailed analysis of the issues involved and their citation of authority I state my own reasons more briefly.

The origin of the defence lay in the belief that if a man was so provoked as suddenly to lose all reason and self-control justice or 'compassion' required that there should be a verdict of manslaughter rather than of murder which attracted the death penalty. Certain categories of act, such as an insulting assault or seeing one's friend being grievously attacked, came to be recognised as constituting provocation. From the end of the 19th century and during the 20th century, however, the question became not only whether the provocation caused the loss of control which itself led to the fatal blow but also whether the jury considered that the provocation would have caused a reasonable man to lose his self-control *R v Welsh* (1869) 11 Cox 336.

The objective test of the reasonable man reached its high water-mark in your Lordships House in *Bedder v DPP* [1954] 1 WLR 1119. The House refused to accept that physical or mental infirmity could be regarded as material in considering whether a man had been provoked and whether a reasonable man could have lost his self-control in the circumstances.

It is agreed that section 3 of the Homicide Act 1957 was intended to and did change the position at common law; it also defined the defence of diminished responsibility. So in this case it is common ground that in considering whether the accused has been provoked to lose his self-control – sometimes described as the gravity of the provocation and said to be a subjective test – it is for the jury to take into account the personal characteristics of the accused. But the Crown contends that when the question is whether a reasonable man would have lost his self-control, personal characteristics, subject to very limited exceptions, must be excluded. Only in that way it is said can the test of a reasonable man objectively regarded be applied; only in that way can a uniform assessment be made. Departures from that approach destroy the concept of a reasonable man by whose standard of control the behaviour of the particular individual is to be judged.

The respondent says that this approach is unfair and unreal and not required by section 3. A person's response to provocation must be judged by comparison with a reasonable man having the same relevant characteristics as he has.

There are judicial decisions both ways. For example in *Luc Thiet Thuan v R* [1997] AC 131 the majority in the Privy Council and in *R v Morhall* [1996] 1 AC 90 the House of Lords underlined the need for an objective test in looking at the reasonable man. He must not be transformed into a replica of the individual defendant. In these two cases, it was however, accepted that personal characteristics could be taken into account when assessing the gravity of the provocation. On the other hand in *R v McGregor* [1962] NZLR 1069 and in a number of judgments of the Court of Appeal here it has been recognised, as it was by Lord Steyn dissenting in *Luc Thiet Thuan*, that in considering whether a reasonable man would have reacted as the accused did, some personal characteristics can be taken into account ... I cite by way of example only *R v Dryden* ... where Lord Taylor of Gosforth CJ said that the decision in *R v Camplin* ... was

clearly indicating that apart from the standard of self-control which is to be attributable to the reasonable man, other characteristics of the appellant should be taken into account in considering whether a reasonable man may have reacted in the way that the appellant did.

In *R v Ahluwalia* [1992] 4 All ER 889, 898, Lord Taylor said:

English cases concerned with the 'reasonable man' element of provocation, and examples given by judges, have tended to focus on physical characteristics. Thus age, sex, colour, race and any physical abnormality have been considered.

However, the endorsement of the New Zealand authority in *R v Newell* (1980) 71 Cr App R 331, shows that characteristics relating to the mental state or personality of an individual can also be taken into account by the jury, providing that they have the necessary degree of permanence ...

Much of the debate before your Lordships has centred on the precise effect of the decision of the House in *Camplin* [1978] AC 705. Lord Diplock made it clear, at p 716B, that the section was intended to mitigate in some degree 'the harshness of the common law of provocation as it had been developed in recent decisions in this House'. He said, at p 717 that a reasonable man

means an ordinary person of either sex, not exceptionally excitable or pugnacious, but possessed of such powers of self-control as everyone is entitled to expect that his fellow citizens will exercise in society as it is today... It would stultify much of the mitigation of the previous harshness of the common law in ruling out verbal provocation as capable of reducing murder to manslaughter if the jury could not take into consideration all those factors which in their opinion would affect the gravity of taunts or insults when applied to the person whom they are addressed. So to this extent at any rate the unqualified proposition accepted by this House in *Bedder v Director of Public Prosecutions* [1954] 1 WLR 1119 that for the purposes of the 'reasonable man' test any unusual physical characteristics of the accused must be ignored requires revision as a result of the passing of the Act of 1957.

Taking these passages into account it does not seem to me that Lord Diplock is saying that the question as to the reaction to provocation is wholly objective: on the contrary, he appears to me to be indicating that personal characteristics may be something the jury could take into account. He is certainly not limiting the characteristic which can be taken into account to age (or sex) – 'That he was only 15 years of age at the time of the killing is the relevant characteristic of the accused *in the instant case*' [emphasis added].

Lord Fraser of Tullybelton and Lord Scarman agreed with Lord Diplock. Lord Morris of Borth-y-Gest at p 721C said:

> In my view it would now be unreal to tell a jury that the notional 'reasonable man' is someone without the characteristics of the accused: it would be to intrude into their province ... The question would be whether the accused if he was provoked only reacted as even any reasonable man in his situation would or might have reacted.

Lord Simon of Glaisdale said at p 725D:

> But it is one thing to invoke the 'reasonable man' for the standard of self-control which the law requires: it is quite another to substitute some hypothetical being from whom all mental and physical attributes (except perhaps sex) have been abstracted.

Obviously if the only possible interpretation of section 3 were that the 'reactions of the reasonable man' test was wholly objective one would be bound to accept it whatever the consequences in particular cases. I am, however, satisfied that it is not the only possible construction of section 3, itself 'intended to mitigate in some degree the harshness of the common law of provocation as it had been developed by recent decisions in this House': *Camplin* [1978] AC 705, p 716B *per* Lord Diplock.

It important to bear in mind that the Section left the decision to the jury and took away the judge's power to direct the jury as to what characteristics of the accused could as a matter of law be taken into account and to withdraw the question from the jury on the basis of the judge's personal view. Judges must avoid imposing 'a fetter on the right and duty of the jury which the Act accords to them to act upon their own opinion on the matter': *Camplin*, p 718G *per* Lord Diplock ...

In *Camplin* it was asked in effect what could reasonably be expected of a 15 year old boy. In my view the section requires that the jury should ask what could reasonably be expected of a person with the accused's characteristics. This does not mean that the objective standard of what 'everyone is entitled to expect that his fellow citizens will exercise in society as it is today' is eliminated. It does enable the jury to decide whether in all the circumstances people with his characteristics would reasonably be expected to exercise more self-control than he did or put another way that he did exercise the standard of self-control which such persons would have exercised. It is thus not enough for the accused to say 'I am a depressive, therefore I cannot be expected to exercise control.' The jury must ask whether he has exercised the degree of self-control to be expected of someone in his situation.

It thus seems to me that the particular characteristics of the accused may be taken into account at both stages of the inquiry. I do not accept that the section intends the rigid distinction between the two parts of the inquiry for which the prosecution contends. As Lord Diplock said in *Camplin* at p 718A in respect even of the characteristic of age:

> The distinction as to the purposes for which it is legitimate to take the age of the accused into account involves considerations of too great nicety to warrant a place in deciding a matter of opinion, which is no longer one to be decided by a judge trained in logical reasoning but is to be decided by a jury drawing on their experience of how ordinary human beings behave in real life.

In this way the jury can legitimately 'give weight to factors personal to the prisoner in considering a plea of provocation,' a course they took in any event even when the stricter test was considered to apply. (Royal Commission on Capital Punishment Report (Cmd 8932, 1953), para 145).

I do not consider that the existence of section 2 defining the partial defence of diminished responsibility prevents this conclusion. The two defences are in any event different in important respects, not least that whereas provocation depends on a consideration of facts external to the accused, such as the acts of the deceased, the defence of diminished responsibility does not.

I accept that there may be difficult borderline cases as to which particular characteristics can be taken into account but the same is also true in applying the first part of the test. The second part of the test applied in the way I accept it should be applied has not caused insoluble difficulties in the Court of Appeal cases to which I have referred. Moreover the distinction being the 'objective' and the 'subjective' tests contended for by the prosecution is very difficult for a jury and I doubt whether it is really workable.

In my opinion justice requires that personal characteristics should be taken into account in the way I have indicated unless the section precludes it. In my view it does not. Accordingly I agree with the opinion of Lord Steyn in *Luc Thiet Thuan v R* [1997] AC 131. In my opinion the Court of Appeal in the various cases to which I have referred were right to take the view that personal characteristics other than age and sex could be taken into account when considering whether the reaction to the provocation was that of a reasonable man. It follows that I also agree with the judgment of Potts J on this point in the present case. I would accordingly dismiss the appeal.

Lord Clyde: My Lords ... In principle it is not easy to see how the plight of the individual accused can appropriately be taken into account if the standard of his conduct is to be tested by reference to an artificial concept remote from his own situation. The idea of provocation was no doubt born and bred in the context of a system which admitted capital punishment. That certainly added an edge to anxiety to secure that a fair and just treatment was afforded in cases of homicide. But the need for compassion may still hold where a distinction is preserved between the disposal for cases of murder and cases of manslaughter, and may indeed remain even if a formal distinction was removed.

One essential element for the availability of a plea of provocation has always been that the act be done in the heat of passion fired by the provocation before reason has returned. If, as by the passage of time, an initial passion has cooled and self-control has been regained, then the necessary connection between the provocation and the homicide which is alleged to have been prompted by it will be available to support the defence. It is of interest in the context of the present case to note that in considering whether the time was sufficient for reason to have returned account has been taken of the diminished intelligence of a particular accused. In *R v Lynch* (1832) 5 C & P 324, 325 Lord Tenterden in summing up said:

> If you think that there was not time and interval sufficient for the passion of a man proved to be of no very strong intellect to cool, and for reason to regain her dominion over his mind, then you will say that the prisoner is guilty only of manslaughter.

But for present purposes a more important consideration is that there should be a proportionality between the provocation and the response measured by what is acceptable to society. This element was recognised in *R v Kirkham* (1837) 8 C & P 115, 119 where Coleridge J observed that:

> though the law condescends to human frailty, it will not indulge human ferocity. It considers man to be a rational being, and requires that he should exercise a reasonable control over his passions.

The same concern was expressed in *R v Oneby* (1727) 2 Ld Raym 1485, 1496, where it was said of anger and passion 'which a man ought to keep under and govern.' But while society rightly expects that people should keep a rein over their passions, that expectation has to be seen against the realistic context of the variety of natures which mankind comprise. Some may be stoical or insensitive in the face of provocation and for them the problems to which this case gives rise may never occur. Others may require to make a solid conscious effort to restrain themselves in accordance with the requirements of society's expectations, and if they give way where they could and should have exercised a due restraint they may fail to qualify under the extenuation provided by the doctrine of provocation. Others may through no failure or shortcoming of their own be unable to achieve the level of control which could be met by others not similarly circumstanced. Examples of those with a post-natal depression or a personality disorder readily come to mind. It would seem to me unrealistic not to recognise the plight of such cases and refuse the compassion of the law to them.

But if the appellant is correct, it seems to me that there would be a serious risk of injustice being done in some cases where the homicide is due to provocation but the condition of the accused falls short of a mental abnormality. While I fully recognise the importance of not allowing the effects of a quarrelsome or choleric temperament to serve as a factor which may reduce the crime of murder to one of manslaughter, nevertheless I consider that justice cannot be done without regard to the particular frailties of particular individuals where their capacity to restrain themselves in the face of provocation is lessened by some affliction which falls short of a mental abnormality. It does not seem to me that it would be just if in assessing their guilt in a matter of homicide a standard of behaviour had to be applied to people which they are incapable of attaining. I would not regard it as just for a plea of provocation made by a battered wife whose condition falls short of a mental abnormality to be rejected on the ground that a reasonable person would not have reacted to the provocation as she did. The reasonable person in such a case should be one who is exercising a reasonable level of self-control for someone with her history, her experience and her state of mind. On such an approach a jury should be perfectly capable of returning a realistic answer and thus achieve a verdict which would fairly meet any peculiarities of the particular case consistently with the recognition of the importance of curbing temper and passion in the interest of civil order.

It is in the context of this relationship between the provocation and the homicide that the language of reasonableness has come to be adopted. An appeal to what is reasonable can be used as a test of the credibility of an assertion. The accused who asserts that he killed under provocation may be disbelieved on the ground that no one in his position would reasonably be provoked in the particular circumstances. Here the concept is of evidential significance. But in the context of the present statute the concept of reasonableness is adopted as a point of substance. It is to be used as a standard against which the conduct of the accused is to be measured. Two observations then fall to be made. One is that the use of the language of reasonableness appears to open the way to an analysis of the provocation on the one hand and the response to it on the other. One may talk of the reasonableness of the provocation which triggers the loss of self-control and the reasonableness of the response. But the exercise is essentially one of assessing the reasonableness of the relationship between them. There are no variables to be independently assessed in relation to either of the two elements in any given case. The response is always a constant; it is the homicide. The provocation may vary from case to case but the particular substance of it in any given case will be identifiable. It seems to me that the critical question is that of the proportionality between the provocation and the response. The gravity of the provocation, which prompts the loss of self-control, and the reasonableness of the response may both be aspects of the same question. It is useful to recall the language used by Devlin J in the directions which he gave in *R v Duffy* [1949] 1 All ER 932, which Lord Goddard quoted in the appeal in that case as providing as good a definition as he had read. In the course of the passage Devlin J noted two important things. The first was whether there had been time for passion to cool and to regain dominion over the mind. Then he continued:

> Secondly, in considering whether provocation has or has not been made out, you must consider the retaliation in provocation – that is to say, whether the mode of resentment bears some proper and reasonable relationship to the sort of provocation that has been given ...

The second observation is that the reference to reasonableness invites into the discussion the concept of the reasonable man. The idea of reasonableness was developed in *R v Welsh* (1869) 11 Cox 336 by Keating J who applied the concept to provocation, raising the question (at p 337) 'not merely whether there was passion, but whether there was reasonable provocation.' The introduction of the reasonable man appears in his summing up where he refers (p 538) to the possibility of attributing the accused's act to the violence of passion naturally arising from the provocation 'and likely to be aroused thereby in the breast of the reasonable man.' He later said:

> The law contemplates the case of a reasonable man, and requires that the provocation be such as that such a man might naturally be induced, in the anger of the moment, to commit the act.

But once the reasonable man was let loose on the law of provocation it became easy to advance to an increasingly objective approach to the matter. That advance can be traced from *Welsh* through such cases as *R v Alexander* (1913) 9 Cr App Rep 139, *R v Lesbini* [1914] 3 KB 1116, *R v Mancini* [1942] AC 1, and *Holmes v Director of Public Prosecutions* [1946] AC 588 to *Bedder v Director of Public Prosecutions* [1954] 1 WLR 1119, 1121 where it was affirmed that:

> infirmity of body or affliction of the mind of the assailant is not material in testing whether there has been provocation by the deceased to justify the violence used so as to reduce the act of killing to manslaughter.

The effect of the accused's impotence upon his mind was not the test; the jury required to consider the effect of the provocation upon a man without the particular physical qualities of the accused. It may be thought that the introduction of the reasonable man to this area of the law has added unnecessary obscurity to what ought to be a matter of relative simplicity; but he has been perpetuated in the formulation of the statutory provision. All the greater care is needed to secure that he does not lead the law into wonderland.

There is then a potential tension between the requirement of society that people should restrain their natural passions and the law's compassion for those who under the stress of provocation temporarily lose their self-control. This is not solved by recourse to the concept of the reasonable man. That concept may indeed make the solution the more elusive. At the one extreme a totally subjective approach effectively removes reference to any standard and flies in the face of the statute. At the other extreme the accused may be convicted of murder even although the jury believe that he was so provoked as to have lost his self-control, because they think that a reasonable man, who may be someone quite unlike the accused, would not have lose control in such circumstances. When what is at issue is the scale of punishment which should be awarded for his conduct it seems to me unjust that the determination should be governed not by the actual facts relating to the particular accused but by the blind application of an objective standard of good conduct.

Even those who are sympathetic with what may be described as an objective approach have to recognise that at its extreme it is unacceptable. So a concession is made for considerations of the age and sex of the accused. But then the problem arises why consideration should not be given to other characteristics. Some groups of people may be seen to be by nature more susceptible to provocation than others. Some races may be more hot-blooded than others. Nor do age or gender necessarily carry with them unusual levels of self-control or the lack of it. The problem is to identify where in the middle ground between these two extremes the line is to be drawn. It seems to me that the standard of reasonableness in this context should refer to a person exercising the ordinary power of self-control over his passions which someone in his position is able to exercise and is expected by society to exercise. By position I mean to include all the characteristics which the particular individual possesses and which may in the circumstances bear on his power of control other than those influences which have been self-induced. Society should require that he exercise a reasonable control over himself, but the limits within which control is reasonably to be demanded must take account of characteristics peculiar to him which reduce the extent to which he is capable of controlling himself. Such characteristics as an exceptional pugnacity or excitability will not suffice. Such tendencies require to be controlled. Section 3 requires that the accused should have made reasonable efforts to control himself within the limits of what he is reasonably able to do. This is not to destroy the idea of the reasonable man nor to reincarnate him; it is simply to clothe him with a reasonable degree of reality. But as the statute prescribes, the matter comes to be one of the circumstances of the case and the good sense of the jury. Although the statute expressly refers to a reasonable man it does not follow that in directing a jury on provocation a judge must in every case use that particular expression. The substance of the section may well be conveyed without necessarily importing the concept of a reasonable man.

Much of the debate in the appeal concerned the speeches in the important case of *R v Camplin* [1978] AC 705. There are five particular points which I take from that case. First, it was held that since provocation could now consist of words as well as actions any unusual characteristic of the accused which was the object of the provocative taunt had now to be recognised as relevant. So at least to that extent what had been said in *Bedder* [1954] 1 WLR 1119 required revision. I take this from the passage in the speech of Lord Diplock at p 717C–F.

Secondly, and more importantly, it is not only in relation to the gravity of the provocation that account may be taken of a relevant characteristic of the accused. Account may also be taken of a relevant characteristic in relation to the accused's power of self-control, whether or not the characteristic is the object of the provocation. In *Camplin* the relevant characteristic was the accused's age. But the provocation was not directed at his youthfulness. Lord Diplock recognised a lack of logic in extending the relevance of the characteristic from the gravity of the provocation to the power of self-control, but justified it on two grounds: first, the law's compassion to human infirmity, and second, the excessive difficulty for a jury to make the nice distinction between the relevance of the characteristic for the one purpose and not for the other. This is what I understand is intended by the important passage in Lord Diplock's speech at pp 717F–718B . It is echoed in the speech of Lord Simon of Glaisdale where he says at p 727F:

> But whether the defendant exercised reasonable self-control in the totality of the circumstances (which would include the pregnancy or the immaturity or the malformation) would be entirely a matter for consideration by the jury without further evidence. The jury would, as ever, use their collective common sense to determine whether the provocation was sufficient to make a person of reasonable self-control in the totality of the circumstances (including personal characteristics) act as the defendant did.

Thirdly, and associated with the point just made, while evidence may be admitted to show the existence of a particular characteristic, evidence is not admissible to show what effect such a characteristic might have on a person's self-control or whether the characteristic did in fact have an effect on the self-control of the accused in the circumstances of the case. That is left to the good sense of the jury.

Fourthly, the whole authority of the former cases, *Mancini* [1942] AC 1, *Holmes* [1946] AC 588 and *Bedder* [1954] 1 WLR 1119, should no longer be recognised. As Lord Diplock observed of *Camplin* [1978] AC 705, 718D:

To try to salve what can remain of it without conflict with the Act could in my view only lead to unnecessary and unsatisfactory complexity in a question which has now become a question for the jury alone.

Fifthly, so far as the 'reasonable man' is concerned that is to be understood as referring to the standard of reasonable behaviour expected of a person in the situation of and with the characteristics of the accused. It is here particularly that the context of the facts in *Camplin* have to be borne in mind. The House in that case was concerned with the problem of the young age of the accused. The precise words used in the suggested direction have to be read in the factual context of the particular case. The intention was not to limit the scope of provocation to the characteristics which featured in that case. The precise problem raised in the present case was not in issue. The policy which historically underlay the introduction of the reference to the 'reasonable man' was, as Lord Diplock explained at p 716, to prevent a person relying upon his own exceptional pugnacity or excitability as an excuse for loss of self-control. Lord Simon of Glaisdale echoed that view (at p 726) adding drunkenness to the list. All these matters may be seen as lying within the limits of a reasonable self-control and on that basis they should not be allowed to qualify as mitigating factors. But beyond that it seems to me that the person whom Lord Diplock had in mind when setting out his proposed direction to the jury at p 718 was a person who was not only of the same sex and age as the accused but also shared such of his or her characteristics as in the view of the jury would affect the gravity of the provocation to that particular person. He went on to explain that the question was not merely whether such a person would in like circumstances be provoked to lose his or her self-control but also whether he or she would react to the provocation as the accused did. I do not understand that a distinction is here being suggested between matters affecting the gravity of the provocation and matters affecting self-control. If the relevance of the characteristic in question had been limited to the gravity of the provocation the case would not have been decided in the way it was. Consistently with what he had said earlier I consider that the direction is intended to indicate the relevance of the accused's characteristics to his power of self-control. As Lord Simon of Glaisdale observed (at p 727):

> I think that the standard of self-control which the law requires before provocation is held to reduce murder to manslaughter is still that of the reasonable person (hence his invocation in section 3); but that, in determining whether a person of reasonable self-control would lose it in the circumstances, the entire factual situation, which includes the characteristics of the accused, must be considered.

From the arguments presented before us it seemed that some assistance might be found in the jurisprudence which has developed in New Zealand. In *Camplin* Lord Simon of Glaisdale stated (p 727):

> I think that the law as it now stands in this country is substantially the same as as that enacted in the New Zealand Crimes Act 1961, section 169(2), as explained by the Court of Appeal of New Zealand in *R v McGregor* [1962] NZLR 1069.

Section 169(2) provided:

> (2) Anything done or said may be provocation if

(a) In the circumstances of the case it was sufficient to deprive a person having the power of self-control of an ordinary person, but otherwise having the characteristics of the offender, of the power of self-control; and

(b) It did in fact deprive the offender of the power of self-control and thereby induced him to commit the act of homicide.

In *McGregor* North J presented a series of observations on the construction of the section. He noted that it required a fusion of the objective and subjective approaches and sought to resolve that by reference to the limitations to be placed upon the word 'characteristics.' In discussing that he excluded temporary or transitory factors, excitability or irascibility, and drunkenness. The characteristic must be such 'that it can fairly be said that the offender is thereby marked off or distinguished from the ordinary man of the community.' He then proceeded to a further point, that there must be 'a real connection between the nature of the provocation and the particular characteristic of the offender.'

That requirement, which was expressed in what I have referred to as the further point in the judgment, takes no account of the second of the points which I have already noted as arising from *Camplin* namely the desirability of avoiding the drawing of a distinction between the gravity of the provocation and the power of self-control in relation to the relevance of the particular characteristics of the accused and it was that aspect of the observations of North J which came to be further considered in *R v McCarthy* [1992] 2 NZLR 550. The passage in North J's judgment in *McGregor* which was quoted by Cooke J in *McCarthy* only begins with what I have referred to as the further point. His criticism is of the necessity to find that the provocation must be 'directed at' a particular characteristic. This element only adds an unjustifiable aggravation of the difficulty of applying the section. In that respect it seems to me that Cooke J was in effect following the guidance given in *Camplin*. Moreover he expressly stated that (p 558) that:

> A racial characteristic of the accused, his or her age or sex, mental deficiency, or a tendency to excessive emotionalism as a result of brain injury are, for the purposes of section 169(2)(a), examples of characteristics of the offender to be attributed to the hypothetical person. In a case where any of them apply, the ordinary power of self-control falls to be assessed on the assumption that the person has the same characteristics.

Later he observed that the question to be answered under section 169(2)(a) is 'whether a person with the accused's characteristics other than any lack of the ordinary power of self-control could have reacted in the same way.'

However during the course of the preparation of this speech my attention has been drawn to the recent decision of the Court of Appeal in New Zealand in *R v Janine Waiwera Rongonui* [13 April 2000] from which I understand that my reading of McCarthy may be incorrect. The majority of the judges in *Rongonui* adopted a more literal construction of section 162 whereby the special characteristics of the accused are relevant to the gravity of the provocation but not to the accused's self-control. If I have correctly understood the majority view, it appears that Lord Simon of Glaisdale's observation in *Camplin* on the substantial similarity between the law of England and the statutory provision in New Zealand is no longer apt. This may be an illustration of the danger of seeking assistance in the construction of one statutory provision by reference to another which is in different terms. It is also proper to bear in mind that the New Zealand statute did not include a provision for a defence of diminished responsibility and that may lead to differences in the application of the respective provisions. Examples of what might more readily be seen as falling under section 2 of the Act of 1957 may only be brought in New Zealand as examples of provocation.

The idea expressed in *McGregor* that the provocation required to be directed at the particular characteristics was taken up in *R v Newell* (1980) 71 Cr App R 331, but, as Lord Goff of Chieveley warned in *R v Morhall* [1996] 1 AC 90, 100, regard should now be had to the reservations about that case expressed in *McCarthy*. Certainly it should now be affirmed that while the fact that a taunt is directed at a particular characteristic is a relevant matter for consideration, provocation is by no means restricted in its scope to such situations. But, looking at the matter more broadly, it seems to me that over the last few years the English courts have followed the guidance of *Camplin* and the earlier part of the observations in *McGregor* in the cases where, like the present case, the provocation was not some taunt directed at some particular characteristic of the accused. In *R v Raven* [1982] Crim LR 51 the retarded development and low mental age of the accused were held to be relevant considerations in a case of provocation in the form of sexual assaults. In *R v Ahluwalia* [1992] 4 All ER 889 the court found no evidence of a post-traumatic stress disorder or battered woman syndrome which might have qualified as a characteristic as defined in *McGregor*; if there had been 'different considerations may have applied.' On the evidence there was nothing to support the proposition that the accused was marked off from the ordinary women of the community as having some altered personality or mental state. In *R v Dryden* [1995] 4 All ER 987 Lord Taylor of Gosforth CJ followed *Camplin* and the earlier part of the observations by North J in *McGregor* in holding that in the context of loss of self-control the obsessiveness and eccentricity of the accused were characteristics which should have been taken into account. In *R v Thornton (No 2)* [1996] 2 All ER 1023 the accused's personality disorder and the effect on her mental make-up of a period of abuse by the deceased were held relevant to the question (p 1031):

> whether the hypothetical reasonable woman possessing the accused's characteristics would have reacted to the provocative conduct so as to do what the appellant did.

If we were to allow the present appeal I do not think that we could avoid overturning a well-settled development of the criminal law to say nothing of the decision in Camplin from which the developments have proceeded. I am not persuaded that such a revolution in the law would be justified.

The appellant founds upon the decision of the majority in *Luc Thiet Thuan v R* [1997] AC 131. To criticise so recent a decision calls for hesitation as well as courage, but I have come to feel anxiety over the majority view in that case, at least so far as it may be thought to apply in England, in regard especially to three points. First, I am not persuaded that it sufficiently recognises that the decision in *Camplin* [1978] AC 705 extends beyond the matter of the gravity of the provocation to the matter of self-control. I have already referred to the passage in Lord Diplock's speech at pp 717–18 and I have already quoted the passage in the speech of Lord Simon of Glaisdale at p 727D. Secondly, while it is right to be cautious of finding assistance in the different terms of a different statute in a different jurisdiction, section 169 of the New Zealand statute was regarded by Lord Simon of Glaisdale as representing the law of England, and it has to be remembered that section 3 of the Act of 1957 is not seeking to define the whole law of provocation for England and Wales so that the case is not one of construing one statute by reference to another, but rather seeking guidance on the developing common law by reference to the attempt in New Zealand to enshrine it in statutory language. Furthermore, as I have already sought to explain, it is only the further part of the observations of North J which may call for qualification. The earlier passage remains as a useful source of guidance. Thirdly, considerable weight appears to have been placed upon a view expressed by Professor AJ Ashworth which is quoted at pp 104H–41A of the advice of the majority and which it is suggested may have influenced the decision in *Camplin*. But the idea that, as distinct from individual peculiarities which bear on the gravity of the provocation, individual peculiarities bearing on the accused's level of self-control should not be taken into account, commendable as that view may have been at the time when Professor Ashworth was writing, seems to me to be contrary to the decision which was taken in *Camplin* and which I have endeavoured to analyse already. Although the Court of Appeal are bound by their own line of authority and not required to make any choice between it and the decision in *Luc*, I am reassured by what appears to be a refusal of the Court of Appeal in *R v Campbell* [1997] 1 Cr App R 199 and *R v Parker* (unreported) 25 February 1997 to be moved to desert the position already established in English law.

I have had the opportunity of reading drafts of the speeches of my noble and learned friends Lord Slynn of Hadley and Lord Hoffmann. I agree with the views which they have expressed.

For the foregoing reasons I would dismiss the appeal.

Lord Millet (dissenting): My Lords, diminished responsibility and provocation are both partial defences to a charge of murder ... Although the defences are distinct, they may of course overlap, for a person with diminished responsibility may be provoked to lose his self-control and react in the same way as any one else. Accordingly, a jury may have to consider both defences, as they did in this case. But they are distinct defences nevertheless, for each has a necessary element which is absent from the other. The defence of diminished responsibility requires proof of diminished responsibility resulting from mental abnormality but not of provocation or loss of self-control. The defence of provocation requires disproof of loss of self-control induced by provocation but not of diminished responsibility or mental abnormality. Their underlying rationales are also very different. In the one case the jury are invited to say: 'You can't really call it murder: the poor man wasn't fully responsible for his actions.' The defence is the response of a civilised society to inadequacy. In the other, they are typically invited to say: 'You can't really call it murder. It was at least partly the victim's fault. Any one of us might have reacted in the same way if we had been in the defendant's shoes.' The defence is often described as a concession to human frailty.

But this is a reference to that human frailty to which we are all subject and of which the jury may be expected to take cognisance. It is not a reference to an infirmity peculiar to the accused, but to 'that human infirmity which is so general and almost universal as to render it proper to make allowances for it' and 'that loss of self-control which is natural to humanity': see the passage cited by my noble and learned friend Lord Hoffmann from the Second Report of the Criminal Law Commissioners of 1846.

My noble and learned friends Lord Hoffmann and Lord Hobhouse of Woodborough have analysed the history of the law of provocation and the authorities in detail, and I do not propose to traverse the ground again. But I would begin by recalling that while it is a necessary condition of the defence of provocation that the accused should have lost his self-control, this has never been sufficient. He must have been provoked to lose his self-control. In other words, it is not enough that he was temporarily not responsible for his actions; his loss of self-control must be attributable to something which is external to himself.

These requirements make up what has been described as the subjective element of the defence. But there is an additional requirement: the provocation must have been sufficient to cause a reasonable man to react in the same way. This is usually described as the objective element. In his monograph *Provocation and Responsibility* (1992) Dr Horder explains why it is of central importance in the defence of provocation, but Professor Ashworth (in his influential article in (1976) 35 CLJ 292) was the first academic writer to emphasise the link between the objective element and the moral basis of the defence. It goes to the sufficiency of the provocation. Only killings in response to grave provocation merit extenuation.

The need to satisfy the objective element was insisted on long before the Act of 1957, but it had been restrictively interpreted in a way which sometimes unjustly, and even absurdly, deprived an accused of the defence. Section 3 of the Act was enacted to remedy this. It provides that 'the question whether the provocation was enough to make a reasonable man do as he did shall be left to the jury' and that 'in determining that question the jury shall take into account everything both done and said according to the effect which in their opinion it would have had upon a reasonable man.'

As Lord Hoffmann observes, section 3 modified the law in two respects. First, if there was evidence on which the jury could properly find that the subjective element was satisfied, the question whether the objective element was satisfied must be left to the jury. Secondly, in determining that question, the jury must take into account 'everything both said and done'. Any rule of law, such the rule that words alone could not amount to provocation, was abolished. But some objective test of the sufficiency of the provocation was necessary if the requirement that the accused must have been provoked to lose his self-control was to be preserved. Otherwise, loss of self-control alone would be sufficient, for the accused could always say that he was provoked by something. Accordingly the objective element was retained and henceforth provided the sole test of the sufficiency of the provocation. There must be something said or done which the jury considers might provoke a reasonable man to react in the same way as the accused.

The expression 'the reasonable man' has a long and respectable ancestry in the law, but its use in section 3 is an unhappy one: (see *R v Camplin* [1978] AC 705, 716 where Lord Diplock referred to 'this apparently inapt expression'). It is not intended to invoke the concept of reasonable conduct: it can never be reasonable to react to provocation by killing the person responsible. Nor by pleading provocation does the accused claim to have acted reasonably. His case is that he acted unreasonably but only because he was provoked. But while this may not be reasonable it may be understandable, for even normally reasonable people may lose their self-control and react unreasonably if sufficiently provoked. It is this very human characteristic which the defence acknowledges. In this context, therefore, 'the reasonable man' simply means a person with ordinary powers of self-control. As Lord Goff of Chieveley explained in *R v Morhall* [1996] AC 90, 98:

> The function of the test is only to introduce as a matter of policy a standard of self-control which has to be complied with if provocation is to be established in law.

In *Camplin* [1978] AC 705, 726 Lord Simon of Glaisdale stated that 'the reasonable man' in section 3 means 'a man of ordinary self-control,' and Lord Diplock, at p 717, said that it means:

> an ordinary person of either sex, not exceptionally excitable or pugnacious, but possessed of such powers of self-control as everyone is entitled to expect that his fellow citizens will exercise in society as it is today.

In the present case Judge Coombe directed the jury in these terms. The Court of Appeal held that he was wrong to do so. There was evidence that the accused suffered from a depressive illness which reduced his powers of self-control. In these circumstances, the Court of Appeal ruled, he should have directed the jury that in his case 'the reasonable man' meant a man with the powers of self-control of a person suffering from such an illness; ie a person with less than normal powers of self-control.

My Lords, this approach requires the accused to be judged by his own reduced powers of self-control, eliminates the objective element altogether and removes the only standard external to the accused by which the jury may judge the sufficiency of the provocation relied on. By introducing a variable standard of self-control it subverts the moral basis of the defence, and is ultimately incompatible with a requirement that the accused must not only have lost his self-control but have been provoked to lose it; for if anything will do this requirement is illusory. It is also manifestly inconsistent with the terms of section 3. It makes it unnecessary for the jury to answer the question which section 3 requires to be left to them, viz whether the provocation was enough to make a reasonable man do as the accused did. It becomes sufficient that it made the accused react as he did. It substitutes for the requirement that the jury shall take into account everything both done and said according to the effect which in their opinion it would have on a reasonable man a different requirement by reference to the effect which it actually had on the accused. These tests are in truth no tests at all.

It is also inconsistent with Lord Diplock's description of the reasonable man in *Camplin* [1978] AC 705, for the reference to 'his fellow citizens' (in the plural) is deliberately intended to generalise the test and is plainly not a reference to persons possessing the abnormally reduced powers of self-control of the accused. I respectfully disagree with Lord Hoffmann's reformulation of the objective test: whether the defendant's behaviour fell below the standard which should reasonably have been expected of him, at least if this is taken to mean a person having only his own reduced powers of self-control. This would be inconsistent with Lord Diplock's reference, at p 717G, to 'the degree of self-control to be expected of the ordinary person with whom the accused's conduct is to be compared.' Moreover it is bound to confuse the jury, for the question is meaningless. How is the trial judge to answer the jury when they ask: 'what powers of self-control is everyone entitled to expect from a person who, according to the medical evidence, has no powers of self-control?' Or more bafflingly still, 'who has some undefined but less than normal powers of self-control'?

Lord Hobhouse has traced the development of the law since *Camplin* [1978] AC 705 and convincingly demonstrated that the approach adopted by the Court of Appeal in the present case cannot be supported by authority. I agree with his analysis that the present position is the result of a combination of errors, among which must be numbered the New Zealand jurisprudence, a mistaken desire to use the defence of provocation to cater for those who are mentally inadequate when this is properly the province of the defence of diminished responsibility, an inaccurate citation of the concluding words of section 3 which omits the words 'anything done or said', and an unjustified extrapolation from Lord Diplock's speech in *Camplin*.

The New Zealand legislation might have been understood as confirming the retention of the objective element. Unlike section 3 of the Act of 1957, section 169 of the Crimes Act 1961 of New Zealand did not merely modify certain aspects of the common law, but was a self-contained codification of the defence of provocation. It was obviously intended to, and probably did, reflect the law of England following the passage of the Act of 1957. It provided (*inter alia*) that:

> Anything done or said may be provocation if – (a) In the circumstances of the case it was sufficient to deprive a person having the power of self-control of an ordinary person, but otherwise having the characteristics of the offender, of the power of self-control.

This was clearly modelled on section 3 of the Act of 1957, but was a distinct improvement on its language, for by referring to 'a person having the power of self-control of an ordinary person' the New Zealand legislature avoided the 'apparently inapt' reference to the reasonable man. It was not, however, anticipating Lord Diplock's criticism of this expression in *Camplin* or Lord Goff's exposition of its meaning in this context in *Morhall* [1996] 1 AC 90. It was merely reproducing the language of the Criminal Code Act 1893 and the Crimes Act 1908 of New Zealand.

Both the Act of 1957 and the New Zealand statute require the sufficiency of the provocation to be determined by reference to the same external test, viz the degree of self-control of an ordinary person. But this is the only objective element which is present. In all other respects the jury must take the accused as they find him, warts and all. When considering whether a person of ordinary self-control would have been provoked to react as the accused did, the jury must have regard to what Lord Simon in *Camplin* called 'the entire factual situation.' The question for the jury is whether a person of ordinary self-control would have reacted as the accused reacted if he were similarly placed, that is to say, having the history, experiences, background, features and attributes of the accused. This is a question of opinion on which the jury may bring their collective experience and good sense to bear without further evidence: see *Camplin* at pp 716D, 720F–G, and 727G–H. Accordingly, I respectfully agree with Lord Hoffmann that the question is whether the defendant's behaviour fell below the standard which could reasonably be expected of him, but only if that is taken to mean of him exercising normal self-control.

Unhappily, the New Zealand statute used the word 'characteristics', and proceeded to invest the hypothetical ordinary man with all 'the characteristics of the offender' save for his power of self-control. In *Camplin* [1978] AC 705 Lord Diplock used much the same language. In suggesting how the judge should direct the jury, he said, at p 718:

> The judge should state what the question is, *using the very terms of the section*. He should then explain to them that the reasonable man referred to in the question is a person *having the power of self-control to be expected of an ordinary person of the sex and age of the accused, but in other respects sharing such of the accused's characteristics as they think would affect the gravity of the provocation to him* ... [emphasis added].

My noble and learned friends Lord Hoffmann and Lord Clyde consider that Lord Diplock's reference to the age and sex of the accused was not meant to be exhaustive. I respectfully disagree. I think he included 'sex' because he wished to emphasis that 'the reasonable man' was not gender-specific; he was certainly not suggesting that women *per se* have less self-control than men. He included the word 'age' because that was what the case was about. In relation to age, he acknowledged the 'logical transition' involved, but proceeded to justify it: the law should not 'require old heads upon young shoulders'. As the High Court of Australia observed in *R v Stingel* (1990) 171 ClR 312 this 'may be justified on grounds other than compassion, since the process of development from childhood to maturity is something which, being common to us all, is an aspect of ordinariness.' The jury can judge, from their own experience and good sense and without the assistance of expert evidence, whether the accused displayed the ordinary self-control of a person of his age. This approach is also justified by the rationale of the defence. The victim has only himself to blame if he expects a 15 year old to react to provocative words or conduct in the same way as an adult, and the law should not expect him to do so. But as Lord Goff said in *Luc Thiet Thuan v R* [1997] AC 131, 140:

> it is an entirely different question whether the mental infirmity of the defendant which impairs his power of self-control should be taken into account; and indeed it is difficult to see how it can be consistent with a person having the power of self-control of an ordinary person.

Unfortunately the use of the word 'characteristics' (which does not appear at all in section 3 and was probably not intended to have any particular significance in the New Zealand statute) has diverted attention from the true nature of the inquiry. Judges have seized on it to distinguish between those attributes of the accused which can properly be said to be 'characteristics' of his (with which the reasonable man must be invested) and his other attributes. They have distinguished between transient and permanent characteristics, between characteristics which are self-induced and those which are not, and between temperament and character on the one hand and mental illness on the other. It has finally led them to pose the certified question which asks in effect whether the jury should be directed that evidence which they must bear in mind when considering the gravity of the provocation should be disregarded when considering the requisite standard of self-control.

I think that the law has taken a wrong turning. It is time to restore a coherent and morally defensible role to the defence, and one which juries can understand. This can be achieved if it is recognised that the function of the 'reasonable man' is merely to provide an external standard by which the sufficiency of the provocation to bring about the defendant's response to it can be judged. That depends on a combination of two things: the gravity of the provocation and the requisite standard of self-control. A direction that the jury should have regard to evidence when considering the one and disregard it when considering the other is simply baffling. Such a direction is obviously undesirable if it can be avoided; I do not believe that it can ever be necessary.

The first question the jury must consider is whether the accused was provoked by something, whether done or said, into losing his self-control and reacting as he did. If he was, the next question is whether that something would or might have been sufficient to produce the like reaction in a person similarly placed but possessing the powers of self-control of an ordinary person. This does not require the jury to conjure up a picture of a hypothetical ordinary person or the judge to direct them which characteristics of the accused should be attributed to him and which should be disregarded. The question might perhaps be more easily answered if it were reformulated: would or might the provocation have produced the like reaction from the accused if he had exercised normal powers of self-control.

In my view it is confusing and unnecessary to direct the jury to have regard to evidence when considering the gravity of the offence and to disregard it when considering the requisite standard of self-control. It is confusing because they are two sides of the same coin. As Dr Horder observes, the function of the objective element is to identify provocation which is sufficiently grave to provide a moral warrant for the defendant's conduct. I think that it is also unnecessary. If the accused was taunted with (say) impotence, evidence of his impotence is relevant and admissible. It goes to the gravity of the provocation. But impotence does not affect a person's powers of self-control. The jury do not need to be told to disregard it when considering whether the objective element of the defence is satisfied. They can simply be reminded of the question and invited to consider whether a person in the situation in which the accused found himself, being impotent and being taunted with his impotence, but being possessed of normal powers of self-control, would or might react in the same way.

The position not in reality different where the accused was taunted with the very disability which had the effect of reducing his powers of self-control. In practice this is very unlikely to happen except in cases of obvious and self-induced disability like alcoholism, drug addiction or glue-sniffing. Your Lordships dealt with this situation in *R v Morhall* [1996] AC 90. Where, as in that case, the words which are said to constitute provocation were directed to the defendant's addiction, the jury should be directed to take it into account in considering whether a person with the ordinary person's power of self-control would react to the provocation as the accused did. While the addiction itself is relevant if the offensive words are directed to it, any effect of the addiction in reducing the defendant's powers of self-control is not. This does not require the judge to direct the jury to have regard to evidence for one purpose and disregard it for another. The jury must take account of the evidence that the accused was an addict, for that is part of the factual situation. But expert evidence that addiction may operate to reduce the addict's powers of self-control cannot be relevant to the question whether the accused exercised ordinary self-control.

The same applies to intoxication. This is not, in my opinion, because drunkenness is transient or self-induced, nor is it because it is in any way out of the ordinary, for as Lord Goff observed in *Morhall* at p 99 ordinary people sometimes have too much to drink. It is because the degree of self-control which the accused was capable of exercising when under the influence of drink is irrelevant to the question whether he exercised the requisite degree of self-control.

Addiction and chronic alcoholism are not transient states. The addict and the chronic alcoholic need treatment. They cannot cure themselves. While under the influence of drugs or drink they may be incapable of displaying ordinary powers of self-control. Yet this is no defence. Likewise a person's powers of self-control are affected by his personality and temperament. A man cannot help his personality or temperament any more than an addict can help his addiction. It is no use telling a bad-tempered man that he must control his temper. His temperament and personality are innate, not self-induced. Yet the defence of provocation is not available to the short-tempered or unusually excitable in circumstances where it would not be available to the even-tempered. In all these cases the jury must be satisfied that the provocation was sufficient to have caused a person with ordinary powers of self-control (which *ex hypothesi* the accused himself did not possess) to react as he did. I cannot see that it makes any difference that the defendant's inability to exercise an ordinary degree of self-control proceeds from depressive illness rather than chronic alcoholism or bad temper. This may seem hard, even unmerciful. But persons who cannot help what they do are intended to be catered for by the defence of diminished responsibility. The defence of provocation should be reserved for those who can and should control themselves, but who make an understandable and (partially) excusable response if sufficiently provoked.

Lord Hobhouse has convincingly demonstrated that the approach of the Court of Appeal in the present case is inconsistent with the English authorities and an understanding of the law shared by three successive Lord Chief Justices, Lord Parker, Lord Lane and Lord Taylor CJJ. We cannot adopt it without departing from *R v Morhall* [1996] AC 90, a unanimous decision of your Lordships' House not yet five years old, and without preferring Lord Steyn's dissenting opinion in *Luc Thiet Thuan* [1997] AC 131 to that of the majority.

Lord Steyn's dissenting opinion in the last-mentioned case is, as might be expected, extremely powerful, invoking as it does the pre-eminence of the dictates of justice over the promptings of legal logic. He instances three situations. The first is the woman suffering from post-natal depression. The second is the 'battered wife'. The third is the woman suffering from a personality disorder which makes her unusually prone to lose her self-control. In all three cases, Lord Steyn observes, the particular characteristic of the accused is potentially relevant only inasmuch as it affected the degree of self-control which she was capable of exercising.

With respect, I do not think that the case of the battered wife is affected by the issue in the present case. It is true that the treatment she received from her husband is only relevant insofar as it gradually wore down the natural inhibitions which would normally prevent her from resorting to violence. But, except from the fact that it usually produces a sudden and immediate reaction, that is how provocation works. It is a disinhibitor which overrides a person's natural inhibitions and causes him to lose his self-control.

The problem which faces the battered wife is in attributing her loss of self-control, not to its immediate cause (which may be trivial), but to the long history of ill-treatment which preceded it. Her difficulty arises from the fact that the defence is often seen in terms of 'a sudden and immediate loss of self-control'. In many situations this is a useful test for the jury to have in mind. The accused is unlikely to have lost his self-control by reason of provocation if he has had time to allow temper to cool and 'reason to resume her sway.' But in the case of the battered wife the test is unhelpful. There is no legal requirement that the defendant's reaction must be triggered by an event immediately preceding his loss of self-control: see *R v Chhay* (1994) 72 A Crim R 1, 9 *per* Gleeson CJ. The question for the jury is whether a woman with normal powers of self-control, subjected to the treatment which the accused received, would or might finally react as she did. This calls for an exercise of imagination rather than medical evidence, but it does not dispense with the objective element. It does not involve an inquiry whether the accused was capable of displaying the powers of self-control of an ordinary person, but whether a person with the power of self-control of an ordinary person would or might have reacted in the same way to the cumulative effect of the treatment which she endured. The more difficult question in such a case is likely to be whether she lost her self-control at all, or acted out of a pre-meditated desire for revenge. On this issue the jury may be assisted by expert evidence to the effect that ill-treatment can act as a disinhibitor, and that the defendant's outward calm and submissiveness may be deceptive; they may have masked inner turmoil and suppressed rage.

The other two cases should, in my opinion, normally be dealt with if at all by the defence of diminished responsibility. In both cases the disinhibiting factor is internal to the accused, and it is inappropriate to ascribe it to provocation. Post-natal depression is a common, and perhaps ordinary, product of child-birth; and it is tempting to equate it with age as an attribute of the ordinary person which the jury should take into account when considering the objective element in provocation. But I think that this is unsound. A woman suffering from post-natal depression may kill on trivial provocation or none at all. If the provocation is insufficient to cause a person of ordinary self-control to act as she did, then her actions are attributable to her depressive illness and not to the provocation.

I agree with Professor Ashworth in the article to which I have already referred (at p 312) that, while mitigation of the offences of those who are incapable of exercising ordinary self-control is desirable, the defence of provocation is not an appropriate vehicle. Where an individual who is congenitally incapable of exercising reasonable self-control is provoked by a petty affront, his loss of self-control must be ascribed to his own personality rather than to the provocation he received. In (1937) 37 Columbia LR 701, 1251, 1281 Wechsler and Michael write:

> Other things being equal, the greater the provocation [measured objectively], the more ground there is for attributing the intensity of the actor's passions and his lack of self-control on the homicidal occasion to the extraordinary character of the situation in which he was placed rather than to any extraordinary deficiency in his own character.

Professor Ashworth observes that the converse also holds true: where the provocation is objectively trivial, the defendant's loss of self-control should be attributed to his own deficiency rather than the provocation. He concludes that 'congenitally incapable individuals have an independent claim to mitigation,' and that 'the defence of provocation is for those who are in a broad sense mentally normal'. I agree with my noble and learned friend Lord Hobhouse that *R v Raven* [1982] Crim LR 51 was a plain case of diminished responsibility. The jury should not have been asked to consider the extent of self-control capable of being exercised by an 'ordinary' 22 year old with a mental age of nine.

I express no opinion whether post-natal depression, personality disorders, and chronic inability to exercise self-control can be brought within the restrictive language of section 2 of the Act of 1957. If they can, they should be dealt with as instances of diminished responsibility. If they cannot, the objective element of provocation should not be eroded and its moral basis subverted in order to provide a defence of diminished responsibility outside the limits within which Parliament has chosen to confine it.

I am not qualified to suggest, let alone lay down, any guide to the way in which the judge should explain matters to the jury. Everything will depend on the circumstances of the particular case, and those who preside over murder trials can call upon their great experience of the wide variety of contexts in which these problems arise. Where the jury has to consider both the defence of provocation and diminished responsibility, the judge will have to deal with them separately in his summing-up. How he does so will be a matter for him, but logic and ease of exposition would seem to require that the defence of provocation be ordinarily dealt with first, for the jury ought to consider whether the prosecution case is established before it turns to those matters where the burden of proof is on the accused. But even this must yield to the circumstances of the particular case and is a matter for the judgment of the trial judge.

So far as the defence of provocation is concerned, I have already indicated my own view that it is confusing, and should be unnecessary, to instruct the jury that particular evidence is relevant to the gravity of the provocation and not the degree of self-control which the law requires everyone to exercise. It should be sufficient to separate the two questions (whether the accused was provoked to lose his self-control and whether a person of ordinary self-control would have reacted as he did) and to marshal the evidence which is relevant to each. Evidence that the accused was congenitally or temporarily incapable of exercising self-control is relevant to the first question but not the second. It is likely to confuse the jury if they are asked to conjure up the picture of the hypothetical reasonable man with some (but not all) of the characteristics of the accused. It may sometimes assist the jury if the second question is reformulated: would the accused himself have reacted in the same way if he had exercised ordinary powers of self-control? The jury may find it helpful to have the moral basis of the defence explained to them. Where both provocation and diminished responsibility are left to the jury, it may be helpful to draw the distinction between internal and external factors, and to tell the jury that, if they are satisfied that the accused did not exercise ordinary self-control in the face of some trivial provocation because he was congenitally or otherwise incapable of doing so, then they must consider whether the defence of diminished responsibility is established. But everything will depend upon the circumstances of the particular case and must be a matter for the judgment of the trial judge. I would deprecate intervention by the appellate courts on the grounds that the judge's directions could have been improved.

In the present case I consider that Judge Coombe's summing up was sound and in accordance with law, and that it contained no material irregularity. The jury (not surprisingly) were unimpressed with the defence of provocation. They may well have taken the view that there was none. They must have taken the view that such provocation as there was, if any, was insufficient to cause an ordinary person to lose his self-control. I would allow the appeal and restore the conviction for murder.

Lord Hobhouse (dissenting): My Lords, this appeal raises a question of statutory construction. The provision to be construed is s 3 of the Homicide Act 1957 ... The question is how is the word 'reasonable' to be understood in this section. It is a question which has in the last 10 years given rise to repeated disputes before the courts ...

Thus, central to the issue of law raised by this appeal is the purpose for which the evidence of mental abnormality is being treated as relevant. It is common ground that s 3 and the common law of provocation require two questions to be answered. The first is the factual, or as some prefer to call it the 'subjective' question: Was the defendant provoked, whether by things said or done to lose his self-control and kill? Since this is a factual question, evidence of any mental or other abnormality which makes it more or less likely that the defendant lost his self-control is relevant and admissible, as is any evidence concerning the defendant which helps the understanding or assessment of the evidence of what occurred. In answering factual questions all relevant evidence is in principle admissible. For such purpose it does not matter whether the evidence relates to something which would be described as a 'characteristic' of the defendant. Thus, evidence may be relevant and therefore admissible that the defendant was at the time very drunk or under the influence of a hallucinogenic drug. Such evidence may of course cut either way. It may show that anything said or done did not affect the defendant's conduct which was simply due to his delusions. Or, it may show that something said or done which would not normally cause anyone to lose their self-control may have caused the defendant to do so.

The second question is what is called the 'objective' question. It is, in the words of s 3 'the question whether the provocation was enough to make a reasonable man do as the [defendant] did', taking 'into account everything both done and said according to the effect which ... it would have on a reasonable man.' This question itself contains two elements. The first is the assessment of the gravity of the provocation. The second is the assessment how a reasonable man would react to provocation of that gravity. The second element involves applying a standard of self-control. Essential to the understanding of the authorities and the issue on this appeal is the distinction between these two elements. It is well established and not in dispute that in assessing the gravity of the provocation everything both said and done must be taken into account and that this inevitably involves taking into account any peculiarity of the defendant which affects that gravity. What is in dispute on this appeal is whether in applying the standard of self-control the jury should apply a qualified standard to reflect the respondent's lack of capacity to exercise ordinary self-control.

The Court of Appeal accepted the respondent's submission that the standard of self-control should be the qualified one. [In] *Luc Thiet Thuan v R* ... [i]t was held that the section required the standard of self-control of an ordinary person not that of a person who only had an abnormal and deficient capacity for self-control. Lord Steyn dissented. Lord Steyn stated that he was deciding in accordance with the previous decisions of the English courts and by implication expressing the opinion that Lord Goff was not. Whether Lord Steyn's dissent did in truth accord with the earlier English authorities is in contention. It is an essential element in the correctness of his view of the law. Later judgments in the Court of Appeal have accepted Lord Steyn's view, referring to the earlier authorities but, it must be said, without themselves undertaking a close examination of what exactly was decided in them. My Lords, in this speech I will re-examine those authorities; I consider that, contrary to the view of Lord Steyn, they show that English law does not require that the jury be directed to visualise an ordinary (reasonable) man with abnormal (unreasonable) mental characteristics.

North J

One of the sources of confusion has been the citation in English cases of a judgment of North J in the New Zealand Court of Appeal in *R v McGregor* [1962] NZLR 1069. It was a substantial judgment impressively reviewing, partly *obiter*, various aspects of the law of provocation and expressing views about how the New Zealand Crimes Act 1961 should be construed. *Obiter*, he construed that Act in a way which superficially appears to conform to Lord Steyn's view of the point now in issue (p 1081). But various of the views of North J have been strongly criticised in New Zealand (Adams: *Criminal Law and Practice*) and must now be read subject to what was said by Cooke P in *R v McCarthy* [1992] 2 NZLR 550. The difficulties with what North J said include that it is not wholly self-consistent and is strongly coloured by the fact that there is no defence of diminished responsibility in the law of New Zealand and therefore is amenable to the argument that the law of provocation should indirectly fill the gap. For example, the conundrum raised by the New Zealand case *R v Rongonui* [unreported, 13 April 2000, NZ CA] is peculiar to New Zealand and the 'mental gymnastics' complained of by Tipping J would not be required by English law.

In order to follow the points which emerge from the authorities it is helpful to identify four points which arise in them. They can all be found referred to in the relevant passage from North J's judgment at pp 1081–82.

(1) 'Characteristics': This is a word emphasised by North J which has found its way into the English authorities although it is not used in s 3. Its purpose is restrictive. If attributes of the defendant are going to be taken into account, then it may be necessary to categorise attributes and hold that they must cross a threshold: they must amount to 'characteristics' of the defendant, not potentially transient states. Thus, North J said:

> the characteristic must be something definite ... and have also a sufficient degree of permanence to warrant its being regarded as something constituting part of the individual's character or personality. A disposition to be unduly suspicious or to lose one's temper readily will not suffice, nor will a temporary or transitory state of mind such as a mood of depression, excitability or irascibility.

(2) Relevance to the provocation: This too was emphasised by North J (at p 1082). Again its purpose is restrictive. He said:

> Special difficulties, however, arise when it becomes necessary to consider what purely mental peculiarities may be allowed as characteristics. In our opinion it is not enough to constitute a characteristic that the offender should merely in some general way be mentally deficient or weak-minded. To allow this to be said would, as we have earlier indicated, deny any real operation to the reference made in the section to the ordinary man, and it

would, moreover, go far towards the admission of a defence of diminished responsibility without any statutory authority in this country to sanction it. There must be something more, such as provocative words or acts directed to a particular phobia from which the offender suffers.

This is the point whether, for the purposes of the second question in s 3, the attribute of the defendant must be relevant to the provocation as such – as where it is the reason why the conduct is provocative at all or it aggravates the gravity of the provocation.

(3) Abnormality: Until the decision of the House of Lords in *R v Morhall* [1996] 1 AC 90, there was a view that any abnormal characteristic must be wholly ignored for the purpose of the second question in s 3 as being repugnant to the concept of the 'reasonable' man. (That had been the view of the Court of Appeal: [1993] 4 All ER 888, *per* Lord Taylor of Gosforth LCJ.) The view of North J had been that the characteristic had to be abnormal otherwise it was irrelevant and did not count: it must 'make the offender a different person from the ordinary run of mankind'.

(4) Self-control: This is the critical point. For the purpose of answering the second question, is it permissible to allege that the defendant lacked the ordinary power of self-control. North J, subject to the three important qualifications already mentioned, thought it did:

> The offender must be presumed to possess in general the power of self-control of the ordinary man, save in so far as his power of self-control is weakened because of some particular characteristic possessed by him.

It was in order to be able to say this that North J had effectively disregarded the plain words of the New Zealand statute – provocation 'sufficient to deprive a person, having the power of self-control of an ordinary person, but otherwise having the characteristics of the offender, of the power of self-control' – and had confessedly introduced limitations upon the characteristics of the defendant which could be relied on.

Anthropomorphism etc

My Lords, the view of English law relied upon by the respondent on this appeal is a recent phenomenon. It has emerged gradually from the opinion of North J over little more than a decade. But the seeds from which it has sprung can be detected further back. A root cause is the inveterate (and not wholly unmeritorious) tendency of common lawyers to anthropomorphise concepts. Thus the test of liability in negligence was explained by reference to 'the man on the Clapham omnibus'. When the phrase 'reasonable man' (coming from 19th century cases such as *R v Welsh* (1869) 11 Cox 336) is used in s 3, the common lawyer immediately tries to visualise and define some physical human being with identified characteristics (apparently both reasonable and unreasonable) whereas what the phrase is doing is identifying a concept, a standard of self-control. This standard is, as Lord Diplock and your Lordships' House have said in *R v Camplin* [1978] AC 705, 717, those 'powers of self-control as everyone is entitled to expect his fellow citizens will exercise in society as it is today'. Lord Taylor LCJ confirmed the point in *R v Dryden* [1995] 4 All ER at 997:

> The purpose of taking the reasonable man was to have a yardstick to measure the loss of self-control that will be permitted to found a defence of provocation.

In *R v Morhall* [1996] 1 AC at 90, 98, Lord Goff said:

> The function of the test is only to introduce as a matter of policy a standard of self-control which has to be complied with if provocation is to be established in law.

It is the anthropomorphic thinking and the artificialities to which it has given rise which have pervaded the more recent judgments of the Court of Appeal and been the primary cause of the confusions and errors which have led to a series of English cases in the decade before the present case came to the Court of Appeal and now a perceived conflict with a considered judgment of the Privy Council. If judges are encouraged or required to sum up to juries in artificial and self-contradictory anthropomorphic terms, it is no wonder that people are confused and critical. One can compare that with the simple and clearly understandable language used by Judge Coombe in the present case which is minimally anthropomorphic. Indeed, there is no complaint that the language of Judge Coombe was in any way obscure or incomprehensible. The complaint is that the jury will have understood his direction too well and therefore have excluded a factor in the respondent's favour which, it is said, they ought to have taken into account.

There have been other contributory factors to which I will have to draw attention in the course of this speech. They include a recurringly expressed sentiment that the function of the law of provocation is to show mercy for inadequates, drawing upon statements (eg *R v Hayward* (1833) 6 C & P 154 at 159 *per* Tyndal CJ) made over 150 years ago at a time when the rules of criminal evidence and procedure were radically different and the penalty for murder was death. This theme disregards that since then the concept of a reasonable standard of self-control has been developed in direct contradiction of such sentiments and that the significance of the sentiment was evaluated by the Royal Commission on Capital Punishment 1949–53 and the answer given by the Legislature, was to introduce into the English law of homicide the special defence of diminished responsibility. The absence of a consideration of the significance of s 2 of the Act of 1957 is a striking feature of most of the judgments on s 3.

Construing the 1957 Act in its context: diminished responsibility

The answer to the question raised by this appeal must be found by construing s 3 in its context. The context is primarily statutory. The Act of 1957 was an Act which made important changes to the law of homicide at a time when there was still the death penalty for murder. It followed on and represented the Legislature's response to the recommendations contained in the Report of the Royal Commission on Capital Punishment (Cmd 8932, 1953). The Royal Commission had had to consider the death penalty as it existed at that time in English law. This included the questions what unlawful killings should be treated as murder and what killings which would otherwise amount to murder should nevertheless be treated as manslaughter. Part II of the Act of 1957 retained the death penalty for certain categories of killing creating two categories of murder, capital and non-capital. It was not until the passing of the Murder (Abolition of Death Penalty) Act 1965 that murder ceased for all purposes to be a capital offence. However the mandatory sentence was preserved so that any murderer had to be sentenced to life imprisonment. Thus, at the time of the passing of the Act of 1957, murder was, in practical terms, a unique peace-time offence in the severity of the penalty which it carried and it has remained unique in that the sentence is mandatory. It must be recognised that these features of the crime of murder have given rise to distortions of ordinary principles of criminal law, distortions which are peculiar to the law of murder.

The Act of 1957 was an amending Act. It changed the existing law. Sections 1, 2 and 3 all emerged from the discussion in the Report of the Royal Commission ... Section 3, including the retention of the 'reasonable man' test, specifically derived from the recommendations of the Royal Commission as part of their review of all aspects of the existence of the death penalty. The Commission did not think that the introduction of the concept of diminished responsibility was justified although they carefully considered and recognised it merits. (See paragraphs 373–413.) Parliament however decided to introduce the defence, hence s 2. Both sections address the same question: the defendant's act was unjustified and unlawful but he may not have been fully responsible for his act.

... Section 2 of the Act of 1957 introduces the new defence ...

The striking thing about the present and similar cases is that the defendant is either unwilling to rely upon s 2 or, having done so, fails to satisfy the jury and wishes then to adopt a strained construction of s 3 in order to escape the burden of proof and introduce vaguer concepts not contemplated by either section. The present case has only come before the Court of Appeal and your Lordships' House because the jury, having heard the evidence and having been properly directed upon the law, rejected the defence under s 2. They were not satisfied that whatever degree of depressive illness the respondent was suffering from was such as substantially to impair his mental responsibility for the killing, that is to say, the actual killing with which he was charged taking into account the circumstances in which it occurred.

This is important because there seems in some quarters to be an implicit assumption that the assessment by a jury under s 2 is inadequate properly to allow for the defendant's abnormality of mind in relation to any killing which was contributed to by provocation. There is no reason to make this assumption. Further, it is contrary to the drafting of s 2 and to sections 2 and 3 read together. The brain damaged man has an abnormality of the mind. If it is of sufficient severity, in the opinion of the jury, to impair substantially his mental responsibility for killing his provoker, he will be found guilty of manslaughter, not murder, even if his action was not that of a reasonable man (indeed, one could say, because his action was not that of a reasonable man).

If the defendant is merely someone with a personality disorder, for example an exceptionally violent or immoral disposition, he will not be able to rely on s 2, nor will he be able to rely on s 3 if his response to the provocation was disproportionate. This is all in accord with the specific policy of the Act and the ordinary principles of criminal responsibility. Similarly, if the defendant suffered from an abnormality but the jury do not consider it to be sufficient substantially to impair his responsibility, he will not have a defence under s 2. This simply reflects the policy of the statute and it would be contrary to that policy to extend s 3 to give him the defence advisedly denied him by s 2.

One of the errors that have bedevilled some of the recent judicial statements in this part of the English law of homicide is the failure to take account of the interaction of sections 2 and 3 and appreciate that they not only show that the strained construction of s 3 is wrong but also that the perceived injustice which the strained construction is designed to avoid is in fact covered by an application of s 2 in accordance with its ordinary meaning. Section 2 is of course capable of applying in any situation and those situations include a killing by a defendant who has killed after losing his self-control. A defendant in this situation can contend that his conduct was not abnormal and require the prosecution to satisfy the jury that his loss of self-control was not the result of provocation or his response to it was not that of a reasonable man. Or, he can contend and seek to satisfy the jury on the balance of probabilities that he had an abnormality of the mind which in the circumstances substantially reduced his mental responsibility for what he did. A defendant can of course place both contentions before the jury, as the respondent did in this case. The jury can then return a verdict of manslaughter on the one or the other basis. But it is always open to the jury to conclude (as no doubt the jury did in the present case) that the defendant's response was objectively disproportionate and that his abnormality of mind did not suffice to impair his mental responsibility for what he had done.

This point was made by the Criminal Law Revision Committee and by Lord Simon of Glaisdale, by quotation, in *R v Camplin* [1978] AC 705, pp 726–27:

> In this country the law on this matter [provocation] has been indirectly affected by the introduction of the defence of diminished responsibility. It is now possible for a defendant to set up a combined defence of provocation and diminished responsibility, the practical effect being that the jury may return a verdict of manslaughter if they take the view that the defendant suffered from an abnormality of the mind *and* was provoked. In practice this may mean that a conviction of murder will be ruled out although the provocation was not such as would have moved a person of normal mentality to kill [Lord Simon's emphasis].

This very point had also been made by Lord Parker LCJ when giving the judgment of the Court of Appeal (which included Hilbery and Diplock JJ) in *R v Byrne* [1960] 2 QB 396, 402, recognising that the criterion of the reasonable man, 'that is to say, a man with a normal mind' ruled out the defence of provocation for a sexual psychopath with 'violent perverted sexual desires which he finds it difficult or impossible to control'. His only available defence was accordingly diminished responsibility under s 2. The judgment of Lord Parker and the decision in *Byrne* are strongly contradictory of the respondent's argument in the present case and the thesis that it is necessary and permitted to introduce abnormalities of mind into s 3.

The point can be similarly illustrated from Scottish law from which the statutory defence derives. The case in which diminished responsibility was first recognised as a defence, not merely as a ground for recommending mercy, was *Alex Dingwall* (1867) 5 Irv 466. The accused, Dingwall, was irreclaimably addicted to drink. He was weakminded but not insane. He had killed his wife with a carving knife, according to his account, after a quarrel because on Hogmanay she had hidden his supply of alcohol and his money. Whatever might now be the position in England, such facts would not then raise even an arguable case of provocation. Lord Deas directed the jury that they could return a verdict of culpable homicide not murder on the basis of his 'weakness of mind': 'the prisoner appeared not only to have been peculiar in his mental constitution, but to have had his mind weakened by successive attacks of disease' (p 479). In *HM Advocate v Robert Smith* (1893) 1 Adam 34, the accused was subjected to a course of taunting by his fellow workmen which so affected him that he eventually killed one of his tormentors. The taunts were described as 'altogether insufficient' to cause such a reaction in an ordinary man and this was regarded by Lord McClaren as indicating that his mind was displaced from its balance by the long course of provocation and he was convicted of culpable homicide on the ground of diminished responsibility. (See further Gordon: *Criminal Law*, 2nd edn, p 787.) In this case there was a causal link between the provocation and the accused's mental abnormality (point 2).

The defences of diminished responsibility and provocation are both recognised and are capable of operating separately. But, likewise, they can and very often do operate in conjunction. In English law by the Act of 1957 the two defences have been kept separate and are the subject of distinct provision – sections 2 and 3. But the two sections clearly form two parts of a legislative scheme for dealing with defendants who should not be treated as fully responsible for the death they have caused.

The context: the previous law

Turning now to s 3 itself, it is an amendment of the common law of provocation. At common law the burden of disproving provocation rests upon the prosecution. The section does not alter this. Nor does the section remove the requirement for there to be two constituents of the defence; indeed, the drafting of the section emphasises this requirement, specifying the two questions. The first is the purely factual question whether the defendant was provoked to lose his self-control. The second is the judgment whether the provocation was enough to make a reasonable man do as the defendant did. Section 3 changed the first constituent, the factual question, by adding 'whether by things done or by things said or by both together'. Prior to the Act, the loss of self-control had to be by reason of things done; things said were not as such enough even though they caused a loss of self-control. (*Holmes v DPP* [1946] AC 588.) The Royal Commission recommended that this rule be reversed (paragraphs 146 and following) and the Legislature agreed. As a consequence the second question had to be worded in the section so as also to include the direction that the jury when determining the second question should take into account 'everything both done and said'.

It is to be noted that neither the Royal Commission nor the Legislature saw any need to change the law in the manner which has since come into prominence. They retained the element of loss of self-control as a factual element of the defence of provocation. Historically, the relevant idea was to distinguish the motiveless killing. In *R v Duffy* [1949] 1 All ER 932, the elegantly compressed definition of Devlin J (which unfortunately also contained a troublesome elision of the first and second questions) included the words 'some act or a series of acts ... which ... actually caused in the accused a sudden and temporary loss of self-control'. This factual requirement has caused factual difficulties in relation to certain types of killing where the conduct of the deceased has had a long term cumulative effect which has caused the defendant to reach the point where he or she decides that he or she can take no more and kills the deceased. The most usually instanced example of such a case is that of the battered woman. She does not suddenly lose her self-control in the normal use of that term; she is driven in a controlled fashion to decide to kill. The problem that this presents has been discussed in a number of cases in the Court of Appeal, particularly *R v Thornton* [1992] 1 All ER 306, *R v Ahluwalia* [1992] 4 All ER 889, *R v Humphreys* [1995] 4 All ER 1008 and *R v Thornton (No 2)* [1996] 2 All ER 1023, and has been the primary subject of a written brief submitted to your Lordships by the interveners on this appeal. It also clearly influenced the dissent of Lord Steyn in *Luc Thiet Thuan* being the second example which he gave at the outset of his opinion (p 1048).

It must be stressed that this question is not raised by this appeal. The question whether or not a defendant did in fact lose his self-control is a question of fact: it is part of the factual first question. If the jury are satisfied that the defendant did not actually lose his self-control, that is an end of the defence. The second question, the question of judgment, does not arise. There may be scope for amending the law of murder in this respect, as in a number of others, but that amendment was not made by s 3 nor has it yet been made by any other Act of Parliament.

My Lords, I now turn to the second question, the question with which we are concerned. Section 3 altered the existing law here as well. It required that the question be left to and decided by the jury and not by the judge. Previously judges had been withdrawing consideration of the defence from the jury because in the judgment of the judge a reasonable man would not have been deprived of his self-control. But s 3 did not make any other alteration to the existing law save for the consequential change of wording (to which I have already referred) to take account of both things done and things said.

The 'reasonable man' test had been specifically considered by the Royal Commission (paragraphs 141 and following). They discussed the argument that:

> if the accused is mentally abnormal or is of subnormal intelligence or is a foreigner of more excitable temperament or is for some other reason particularly susceptible to provocation, it is neither fair nor reasonable to judge him by the standard of the ordinary Englishman.

They referred to and adopted the contrary argument that:

> It is a fundamental principle of the criminal law that it should be based on a generally accepted standard of conduct applicable to all citizens alike, and it is important that this principle should not be infringed. Any departure from it might introduce a dangerous latitude into the law.

They did not recommend any change in the law of provocation in this respect. In reaching this conclusion they expressly mentioned in paragraph 143 the relevance of the Scottish defence of diminished responsibility to the question of a provoked defendant who suffered from some mental abnormality not amounting to insanity, a topic to which they said they would revert (as they did) in a later chapter. The interrelation of the two concepts was not overlooked.

The Act of 1957 follows the same scheme. It preserves the 'reasonable man' test unchanged and separately introduces the new defence of diminished responsibility. The argument of the respondent on this appeal raises again the argument rejected by the Royal Commission and seeks to give the Act of 1957 an effect which it is patently not intended to have. Further, if the Legislature had intended to change the law in this respect, one would find some indication of it by a requirement that the jury were to be directed to take into account something which had previously been excluded – a reference to any abnormally deficient powers of self-control of the defendant. Instead the jury are required, in determining the second question, simply to 'take into account everything both done and said according to the effect which in their opinion it would have on a reasonable man'.

There is no problem about ascertaining what was the law on this aspect before 1957. In *R v Alexander* (1913) 9 Cr App R 139, 141, the court rejected the argument that a mentally deficient person who was provoked into killing a man by his red hair would be able to plead provocation. In *R v Lesbini* [1914] 3 KB 1116, the Court of Appeal had to consider the case of a man who 'was not of good mental balance, though not insane in the proper legal sense of the term' and refused to extend the defence of provocation and followed Alexander. The argument, said Lord Reading LCJ, at p 1120:

> substantially amounts to this, that the court ought to take into account different degrees of mental ability in the prisoners who come before it, and if one man's mental ability is less than another's it ought to be taken as a sufficient defence if the provocation given to that person in fact causes him to lose his self-control, although it would not otherwise be a sufficient defence because it would not be provocation which ought to affect the mind of a reasonable man.

The argument was emphatically rejected. Lord Reading's rejection was approved by the House of Lords in *Mancini v DPP* [1942] AC 1, *per* Viscount Simon LC at p 9:

> The test to be applied is that of the effect of the provocation on a reasonable man, as laid down by the Court of Criminal Appeal in *R v Lesbini*, so that an unusually excitable or pugnacious individual is not entitled to rely on provocation which would not have led an ordinary person to act as he did.

The argument rejected by Lord Reading is effectively the same as the argument which was rejected by the Royal Commission but has been repeated on this appeal. The Legislature in enacting s 3 likewise did not accept the argument in relation to provocation but, by introducing the defence of diminished responsibility in s 2, gave effect to it in a different way and to the extent Parliament thought proper.

The word 'reasonable' in s 3 was adopted by the draftsman of the statute from the earlier judicial terminology (eg *R v Welsh* (1869) 11 Cox 336). It was, and is, a concept used not infrequently in the criminal law to prevent a legitimate defence from becoming a licence to commit crimes. A straightforward example is the concept of acting reasonably in self-defence. Acting unreasonably in self-defence destroys the defendant's justification for deliberately injuring his attacker. Unless the defendant has acted in accordance with the standards of self-restraint to be expected of an ordinary citizen, his act remains criminal although in fact done in self-defence. Another, analogous, example is the rule that self-induced intoxication (although it may, if sufficiently extreme, provide evidence to negative a specific intent) does not provide an offender with a defence; he remains criminally responsible for his acts despite his drunkenness and his inability in that state fully to appreciate and control his conduct (eg *R v McCarthy* [1954] 2 QB 105). A further example is to be found in the law of duress where direct parallels have been drawn with the public policy and ordinary powers of self-control required in relation to provocation. (*R v Bowen* [1996] 2 Cr App R 157: 'The law requires the defendant to have the self-control of the ordinary citizen in his situation', *per*

Stuart-Smith LJ at p 162. This wording was drawn from the almost identical language of Lord Lane LCJ in *R v Graham* [1982] 1 WLR at 300 and Lord Mackay of Clashfern in *R v Howe* [1987] AC at 459.) These are rules of criminal policy. They do not have a perfect logic nor do they operate with complete precision. Their function is not to introduce some additional exemption from criminal responsibility: it is to impose a constraint upon the availability of what would otherwise be liable to become an exorbitant defence.

R v Camplin

Thus far there is nothing to support the respondent's argument. It has been rejected at every turn and has not been supported by the Act. However it is possible to see that the resurrection of the argument has partly derived from the drafting of s 3. When the alteration was made so as to enable provocation to be by words alone, inevitably peculiarities of the defendant became relevant. Physical provocation may affect all those subjected to it in a broadly similar way (except for the one-legged man who loses his crutch) and the reasonable man test was simpler to apply. But provocative words causing loss of self-control are far more likely to be specific to the defendant and his characteristics and will usually leave all others unmoved. How then, it is asked, can one answer the second question taking into account everything said 'according to the effect it would have on a reasonable man'? In *R v Morhall* [1996] 1 AC 90, the difficulty was caused by the fact that the defendant was a glue-sniffer who killed the man who was nagging him about his glue-sniffing. It is said, rhetorically, how can one have a reasonable glue-sniffer? It is a contradiction in terms just as is the idea of a reasonable drunkard.

The answer is that the role of the second question is being misunderstood. Its purpose is, as previously stated, to provide a standard of ordinary self-control so as to compare the reaction of the defendant as he was in fact provoked to lose his self-control with the reaction of a person with ordinary powers of self-control to provocation of equal gravity. Its purpose is not to create for the jury some impossible self-contradictory chimera designed ultimately to displace the concept of reasonableness altogether. The correct purpose was made clear by Lord Diplock in *R v Camplin* [1978] AC 705 in a speech with which the majority of their Lordships expressly agreed.

There were two particular points which gave rise to argument in *Camplin*. The first was that the defendant was only 15 at the time of the killing and the trial judge had taken it upon himself to direct the jury that 'reasonable man' must mean a man of full maturity and could not include a reasonable 15 year old boy. The second was that an argument was founded upon what had been said by Lord Simonds LC in *Bedder v DPP* [1954] 1 WLR 1119 before passing of the Act and at a time when provocative words had to be left out of account. With the concurrence of the House, he had said, at p 1123:

> It was urged upon your Lordships that the hypothetical reasonable man must be confronted with all the same circumstances as the accused and that this could not be fairly done unless he was also invested with the peculiar characteristics of the accused. But this makes nonsense of the test. Its purpose is to invite the jury to consider the act of the accused by reference to a certain standard or norm of conduct and with this object the 'reasonable' or the 'average' or the 'normal' man is invoked. If the reasonable man is then deprived in whole or in part of his reason or the normal man endowed with

abnormal characteristics, the test ceases to have any value. This is precisely the consideration which led this House in *Mancini's* case to say that an unusually excitable or pugnacious person is not entitled to rely on provocation which would not have led an ordinary person to act as he did.

The attribution of characteristics (be they normal or abnormal) of the defendant to the hypothetical reasonable man was an obvious source of confusion.

Lord Diplock stressed that s 3 recognised and retained the dual test for provocation. He also confirmed his agreement with Lord Simon of Glaisdale that evidence is not admissible upon the second question. He then stated, at p 717, the meaning of the phrase 'reasonable man' for the purposes of the law of provocation:

> It means an ordinary person of either sex, not exceptionally excitable or pugnacious' but possessed of such powers of self-control as everyone is entitled to expect that his fellow citizens will exercise in society as it is today.

Lord Diplock explained the effect of the change in the law made by s 3 in relation to provocative words:

> But so long as words unaccompanied by violence could not in law amount to provocation the relevant proportionality between provocation and retaliation was primarily one of degrees of violence. Words spoken to the accused before the violence started were not normally to be included in the proportion sum. But now that the law has been changed so as to permit of words being treated as provocation even though unaccompanied by any other acts, the gravity of verbal provocation may well depend upon the particular characteristics or circumstances of the person to whom a taunt or insult is addressed. To taunt a person because of his race, his physical infirmities or some shameful incident in his past may well be considered by the jury to be more offensive to the person addressed, however equable his temperament, if the facts on which the taunt is founded are true than it would be if they were not. It would stultify much of the mitigation of the previous harshness of the common law in ruling out verbal provocation as capable of reducing murder to manslaughter if the jury could not take into consideration all those factors which in their opinion would affect the gravity of taunts or insults when applied to the person [to] whom they are addressed. So to this extent at any rate the unqualified proposition accepted by this House in *Bedder v Director of Public Prosecutions* [1954] 1 WLR 1119 that for the purposes of the 'reasonable man' test any unusual physical characteristics of the accused must be ignored requires revision as a result of the passing of the Act of 1957.

His opinion was that it was, since the Act, better not to refer juries to what was said in *Bedder* in the interests of avoiding unnecessary complexity. He was clearly of the view that the word 'reasonable' was still to be treated as a synonym for ordinary or normal. Thus, in summarising his view as to the appropriate way in which the trial judge should direct a jury on the second question, he said, at p 718:

> He should explain to them that the reasonable man referred to in the question is a person having *the power of self-control to be expected of an ordinary person* of the sex and age of the accused but *in other respects* sharing such of the accused's characteristics as they think would affect the gravity of the provocation to him; and that the question is not merely whether such a person would in like

circumstances be provoked to lose his self-control but also whether he would react to the provocation as the accused did.

As I have emphasised, his formulation is based upon the assumption of the possession of ordinary powers of self-control and it is only in other respects that the defendant's abnormal characteristics are to be taken into account. It is also loyal to the drafting of s 3 which is concerned with the effect the provocation would have on the reasonable/ordinary man.

Lord Morris expressly agreed with Lord Diplock's direction and his speech discloses no marked differences. Lord Fraser and Lord Scarman agreed with the speech of Lord Diplock.

Lord Simon, at p 726, said: 'In my judgment the reference to "a reasonable man" at the end of the section means "a man of ordinary self-control".' Thus Lord Simon, like Lord Diplock, equated the concept of the reasonable man with a man with ordinary powers of self-control. (See also Lord Simon to the same effect at p 725D and his express agreement at p 727 with Lord Diplock's model direction.) All this is loyal to the view of the Royal Commission and the drafting of the section and directly contrary to the respondent's argument in the present case.

However, Lord Simon elsewhere used language which seems to have led Lord Steyn later to read his speech differently. At p 727, he referred to the law of New Zealand and s 169(2) of the Crimes Act 1961, which uses the words I have quoted earlier:

Anything done or said may be provocation if . . . in the circumstances of the case it was sufficient to deprive a person having the power of self-control of an ordinary person, but otherwise having the characteristics of the offender, of the power of self-control.

Linguistically, this is a formula very similar to that approved by Lord Diplock at p 718. Lord Simon commented that the subsection, as in explained *R v McGregor*, was, he thought, 'substantially the same' as the law as it now stands in this country. He also, at p 726 misquoted the English Act as if s 3 said taking 'into account everything according to the effect it would have on a reasonable man'. Lord Simon was using this to show that the section requires the jury to take into account a characteristic of the defendant 'which particularly points the insult' (North J's point 2). He was not departing from what Lord Diplock had said; he was simply anticipating what would be the majority judgment in *Luc Thiet*. But, as Lord Taylor was later to point out in *R v Morhall* [1993] 4 All ER 888, to omit the words 'both said and done' inevitably alters the sense and invites confusion if the context in his speech is overlooked.

Lord Lane

Three months later, these parts of the speech of Lord Simon were referred to by a Court of Appeal presided over by Lord Lane LCJ in their judgment in *R v Newell* (1980) 71 Cr App R 331. The case of *Newell* concerned a defendant, a chronic alcoholic, who had killed a friend, another man, whilst they were both seriously drunk. The defendant's much younger girl friend had recently left him and the two mens' drunken binge was a consequence. However at one point the friend made a remark disparaging the girl and said that the defendant might as well come to bed with him, whereupon the defendant picked up a heavy ashtray and struck his friend violently on the head some 20 times, killing him. His relevant defences were diminished responsibility and provocation. The jury convicted him of murder. The Court of Appeal dismissed the appeal. The main point was whether for the purpose of the law of provocation the jury should have been directed to take into account the defendant's chronic alcoholism. The answer given by the Court of Appeal was that they should not: 'It had nothing to do with the words by which it is said he was provoked' (p 340).

For the present appeal, this is an important case. The defendant was not just drunk. He was an alcoholic. He suffered from a disability which was capable of affecting his powers of self-control and reducing them below that to be expected of an ordinary man. This chronic incapacity might arguably come within North J's definition of 'characteristic' (point 1). The court were prepared to assume that it did (p 340). It was abnormal (point 3). It affected his powers of self-control (point 4). But it was not relevant to the provocation (point 2). North J would accordingly have said that that the jury should be directed to ignore the alcoholism. That also was the decision and the reasoning of the Court of Appeal and Lord Lane.

It thus can be seen that the decision and the reasoning does not support the respondent's argument here: it is an authority against the respondent. If the respondent's argument were correct, the Court of Appeal would have decided that appeal the other way. The abnormality of the defendant was to be left out of account, not because it did not affect his powers of self-control but because it did not aggravate the provocation. There is nothing in the judgment of Lord Lane which questions the continuing applicability of *Lesbini*.

However in this (probably unreserved) judgment there is again some language which has later caused confusion. Lord Simon's misquotation was repeated. More importantly, the judgment includes a long quotation from North J and describes its reasoning as impeccable and commends its language as plain and easily comprehended: 'It represents, we think, the law of this country as well as the law of New Zealand'. But it concludes: 'If the test set out in *McGregor* is applied, the learned judge was right in not inviting the jury to take chronic alcoholism into account on the question of provocation.'

What has gone wrong in some later cases is that isolated sentences have been lifted from North J without his qualifications and Lord Lane has been treated as approving such unqualified statements whereas the whole basis of the judgment and decision in *Newell* is the acceptance of the qualifications and the insistence that they be satisfied (as is further demonstrated by the question certified when refusing leave to appeal, p 340).

R v Raven

The next case in time is *R v Raven* [1982] Crim LR 51. I would not have thought it necessary to refer to this case at all but for the fact that Lord Steyn in his dissenting opinion in *Luc Thiet*, at pp 156 and 157, treated it as of critical significance: 'If Raven was correctly decided, as I believe it was, it follows that the present appeal must succeed.' It was a ruling of the Recorder of London during the trial of a man who had a physical age of 22 years but a mental age of only 9 years. He was being tried for murder. He did not give evidence but his defence was that he had been provoked by homosexual attacks upon him by the deceased. This was a clear case of diminished responsibility; his mental deficiency was not in dispute. A child of 9 years would not have been criminally responsible: Children and Young Persons Act 1933, s 50. His mental responsibility for his acts was indisputably substantially impaired. This was therefore just such a case as was visualised by the Law Reform Committee and Lord Simon. (See above.) Manslaughter could be the only realistic verdict.

However, remarkably, by a route which is not explained in the short report, and which could not be explained by either counsel appearing before your Lordships on this appeal, the case was apparently thought to raise the issue whether the mental deficiency should be attributed to the 'reasonable man'. The Recorder held that it should. This was, according to the report, thought to be an application of the decision in *Camplin*. It was not. *Camplin* was concerned with an ordinary 15 year old and explained the reasonable man test in terms of ordinary powers of self-control. Raven was not an ordinary person. This case therefore was probably the first example of a jury being asked to visualise the chimera, an ordinary 22 year old with a mental age of 9. But this is not the end of the oddities of the report. There is no suggestion that there was any connection between Raven's mental deficiency and the provocation; it seems that it can only have affected his powers of self-control. Therefore on the authority of *Newell* the mental deficiency was immaterial to the defence under s 3. The case note seems to have been written without any awareness of any of these features of the case being reported. The note seems to proceed from a desire to reject the reasoning and decision in *Camplin* and to be based upon the doubly mistaken belief that *Camplin* had created an 'unhappy problem' which had in *Raven* received a 'plausible solution'.

Lord Taylor

Lord Lane was succeeded as Lord Chief Justice by Lord Taylor. Lord Taylor has also been cited as a supporter of the respondent's argument. It is relevant therefore to look at the judgments relied on to see whether this claim is correct.

The first such case is *R v Ahluwalia* [1992] 4 All ER 889. This was a case of a battered wife who had been convicted of the murder of her violent and abusive husband. At her trial she had raised the defence of provocation and the judge had directed the jury that they should consider whether, if she did lose her self-control, a reasonable person having the characteristics of a well educated married Asian woman living in this country would have lost her self-control in the face of her husband's provocation. On appeal it was submitted that he should have directed the jury to consider a reasonable person suffering from 'battered woman syndrome'. This ground of appeal was rejected as there had been no evidence that she had been suffering from that disorder. However, having considered fresh medical evidence placed before them, the Court of Appeal ordered a retrial on the basis that the new evidence showed an arguable case of diminished responsibility. The decision therefore raises no relevant problem.

The part of the judgment relating to 'the defendant's characteristics' is based upon *Camplin* and *Newell*. Like Lord Lane, Lord Taylor quotes North J. He does so for the purpose of discussing point 1, what amounts to a characteristic. Lord Taylor was clearly not intending to qualify *Camplin* nor to question the decision and reasoning in *Newell*. At p 899, he upholds a simple direction in terms of the reasonable person. Neither the case nor the judgment supports the respondent's case on this appeal.

Next in this sequence comes *R v Dryden* [1995] 4 All ER 987. This was the case of the eccentric and obsessional householder who was trying to resist the lawful execution of a demolition order by local authority officers. He shot and killed one of them, attempted to kill the authority's solicitor and injured a policeman and a journalist. His defence to murder was diminished responsibility and provocation. There was evidence that he was at the time suffering from a depressive illness which amounted to an abnormality of the mind. The jury rejected the defences and convicted the defendant. The convictions were upheld on appeal.

One of his grounds of appeal was that the jury had not been properly directed in relation to provocation. The judge had used words almost identical to those used by Judge Coombe in the present case. The defendant argued that he should also have directed them that the defendant's eccentricity and obsession were characteristics to be taken into account under Lord Diplock's formulation. Lord Taylor giving the judgment of the Court of Appeal rejected this argument holding that both Lord Diplock and Lord Simon had clearly indicated that 'apart from the standard of self-control which is to be attributable to the reasonable man, other characteristics' should be taken into account (p 997). He warned against the danger that, if one adds all the characteristics of the defendant to the notional reasonable man, the reasonable man becomes 'reincarnated' in the defendant: the purpose of taking the reasonable man is to have a yardstick to measure the loss of self-control that will be permitted to found a defence of provocation. However, applying Newell, he held that the judge ought to have referred to the defendant's obsessions since they were relevant to the provocation.

> It was in regard to his obsession with his property and this dispute that the conduct of bringing the excavator to the scene was the last straw in the build up of stress upon the [defendant] [p 998].

The evidence was admissible as satisfying points 1, 2 and 3. It was not admitted or relevant under point 4.

This is confirmed by the Court of Appeal's second reason for dismissing the appeal:

> We are satisfied that the jury here can only have come to one conclusion as to whether someone with the self-control of a reasonable man would have done what the [defendant] did even granted that this was a matter very close to his heart and a matter which had caused him anguish, worry and anger over a considerable period [pp 998–99].

Lord Taylor is making the distinction between the recognition of the aggravation of the provocation and the application of the ordinary standard of self-control. (See also the headnote to the same effect.) Dryden is therefore an authority against the respondent not in his favour.

Next comes the judgment delivered by Lord Taylor in *R v Morhall* in the Court of Appeal, [1993] 4 All ER 888. This is relevant to demonstrating his view of the law even though the decision was reversed by the House of Lords, [1996] 1 AC 90. It will be remembered that Morhall was addicted to glue-sniffing and stabbed and killed a friend who took him to task over his addiction. The jury convicted him notwithstanding his putting forward various defences including diminished responsibility and provocation. The question on the appeal was what if any direction the judge should have given the jury on provocation having regard to the evidence of Morhall's addiction. The Court of Appeal held that the judge had been right to exclude the addiction from the second question under s 3. It was 'repugnant to the concept of the reasonable man' [p 892].

Lord Taylor cited *Camplin*. He pointed out [p 891] that it was misleading to quote Lord Simon's incomplete quotation from s 3: it does not refer to any characteristic of the defendant. He contrasted characteristics which were consistent with the general concept of a reasonable or ordinary person and those which were not, the former being relevant 'if the provocation related to them' [p 892]. In answering the question 'where is the line to be drawn?', he like others before him again turned to North J for assistance. The feature met the test of relevance to the provocation (point 2):

> The provocation relied on was specifically targeted at the [defendant's] addiction to glue-sniffing. Accordingly, the question is starkly raised as to whether that addiction should have been left to the jury as a characteristic which they could take into account as affecting the gravity of the provocation to the [defendant]. [Counsel] contends that it should because, apart from the self-control of the reasonable man, all characteristics relevant to the provocation alleged must be left to the jury [p 893].

Therefore, Lord Taylor was accepting that characteristics cannot affect the question of the ordinary standard of self-control (point 4), accepting that the feature in question passed the test of relevance to the provocation (point 2), but rejecting the feature under point 3. It thus confirms Lord Taylor's disagreement with the respondent's argument here.

R v Humphreys [1995] 4 All ER 1008 is a case which was considered to fall on the other side of the line. But the judgment of the Court of Appeal given by Hirst LJ was on the basis that a trait which connoted no more than that the defendant lacked the normal powers of self-control would not qualify, whereas one at which the provocative taunt relied upon as the trigger inevitably hit directly and was calculated strike a raw nerve would qualify [p 1021–22]. This again contradicts the respondent's submission on point 4.

Finally in this sequence, after the House of Lords had decided *Morhall*, there is the judgment delivered by Lord Taylor in *R v Thornton (No 2)* [1996] 2 All ER 1023. This was another battered wife case like that of Ahluwalia. There was fresh evidence of the defendant having had a personality disorder. The Court of Appeal in line with *Morhall* in the House of Lords considered that if the evidence had been available at the trial, the jury would have received a direction about its relevance. They ordered a retrial. The judgment does not purport to add anything to the previous authorities.

The reported judgments of Lord Taylor therefore do not support the respondent's argument here but, rather, contradict it. There is no indication that Lord Taylor would decide point 4 in favour of the respondent, indeed the indications are the reverse.

R v Morhall

The speech of Lord Goff was agreed to by all the other members of the Committee. The speech rejected the anthropomorphic approach. Lord Goff stressed that the second question was concerned with identifying 'a standard of self-control' [p 98]. The law was not concerned to invite the jury to consider a reasonable glue-sniffer. He discussed the law of New Zealand in the light of the later decision in *McCarthy* and the judgment of Cooke P. The thrust of the speech is that there are two aspects of provocation in relation to which a jury might attach significance to an abnormal trait of the defendant. The first, which is permissible, is relevance to the gravity of the provocation to the defendant (point 2). The second, which is not permissible, is relevance to the standard of self-control required by the law (point 4). The jury should have been directed about this (and had not been). The fact that the trait of the defendant is repugnant to the standard is irrelevant to the question of evaluating the gravity of the provocation.

It is to be observed that this decision is a binding authority in English law. It distinguishes between matters going to the gravity of the provocation and the required standard of self-control. It is in line with the previous authorities but has moved away from treating the judgment of North J as the place to find all the relevant answers.

Luc Thiet Thuan

This case raised the question whether a defendant who suffered from brain damage which was irrelevant to the provocation (point 2) but was relevant to his capacity for self-control could rely upon the brain damage in support of his case under the second question in s 3. Nothing appears to have turned upon the fact that such lack of capacity would be relevant to answering the first, the factual, question whether he did in fact lose his self-control. The opinion delivered by Lord Goff contains nothing new save for a fuller discussion of the law of New Zealand and Australia, the inclusion of quotes from the article of Professor Ashworth [1976] CLJ 292 and an important passage explaining and emphasising the relevance of the defence of diminished responsibility introduced by s 2 of the Act [p 1046].

Thus the opinion recites what was decided in *Camplin,* setting the standard. It repeats the distinction between aggravation of the provocation and something which merely impairs the power of self-control. It stresses that the standard of self-control is that of the ordinary person. It points out that it is not open to the courts 'either to discard the objective test or to interpret it in a manner inconsistent with the statute' [p 1039].

The dissent of Lord Steyn postulates situations of greater or lesser emotional content where there is evidence that the defendant suffers from a mental condition which affects her capacity for self-control. This evidence is admissible to deciding upon the answer to be given to the first, the factual, question. He then goes on to postulate that the judge will give the jury a direction upon the second aspect of the second question which is artificial and confusing. This must be contrasted with the simple and easily understood direction that Judge Coombe gave the jury in the present case. The dissent dismisses the inclusion of s 2 in the statute as an irrelevance, apparently on the ground that 'the burden of establishing the defence is on the defendant who raises it'; 'it is an optional defence.' The reasoning specifically rejects the provisions of s 2 as being those settled by the Legislature to deal with mental abnormality and asserts that there should be looser criteria. It pays no regard to the fact that the Royal Commission recommended that the 'reasonable man' test should be retained and the Legislature chose to do so but with the addition of the diminished responsibility defence. As regards the discussion of the previous authorities, it places wholly inappropriate reliance upon *Raven.* It does not refer to *Newell.* It misstates the decisions in the cases I have analysed as representing the view of Lord Taylor. It fails to give effect to what was decided by *Camplin* and *Morhall.*

My Lords, as I have demonstrated, it is the majority opinion which is in accordance with the English authority not the dissent ...

The law, as provided in s 3 of the Act of 1957 and held in the authorities down to *Luc Thiet*, establishes that the constituents of provocation are: (a) The defendant must have been provoked (whether by things done or by things said or by both together) to lose his self-control and kill or do whatever other act is alleged to render him guilty of murder. (b) This is a factual question upon which all relevant evidence is admissible including any evidence which tends to support the conclusion that the defendant either may have or did not lose his self-control. (c) If the jury conclude that the defendant may have been provoked to lose his self-control and do as he did, the jury should, as an exercise of judgment, but taking into account all the evidence, form a view as to the gravity of the provocation for the defendant in all the circumstances. (d) Finally, the jury should decide whether in their opinion, having regard to the actual provocation ((a) and (b) above) and their view as to its gravity ((c) above), a person having ordinary powers of self-control would have done what the defendant did.

If some elaboration of the word 'ordinary' is thought necessary, it should be along the lines advised by Lord Diplock and used by Judge Coombe in the present case. The phrase 'reasonable man' although used in the section is better avoided as not assisting the understanding of the criterion 'ordinary powers of self-control'. The word 'characteristics' should be avoided altogether in relation to (d). It is not used in the section. It is alien to the objective standard of ordinariness and experience has shown that it is a persistent source of confusion. Where relevant the age or gender of the defendant should be referred to since they are not factors which qualify the criterion of ordinariness. But language which qualifies or contradicts such ordinariness must be avoided. It is the standard of ordinary not an abnormal self-control that has to be used. It is the standard which conforms to what everyone is entitled to expect of their fellow citizens in society as it is.

If the scheme which I have set out above is followed, there should be no difficulty in directing the jury using simple and clearly understandable language. No artificialities are involved and the contradictions involved in the approach contended for by the defendant are avoided. Judge Coombe did this successfully in the present case as have many judges before him. It does less than justice to juries to suggest that they are incapable of understanding directions as simple as the four which I have set out above. If, as will usually be the case where the defence rely upon a mental element, diminished responsibility is also raised, s 2 and the concept of abnormality of mind provides the judge with an opportunity, if he thinks it helpful, to make an illustrative point of contrast with the objective test in s 3.

It is not acceptable to leave the jury without definitive guidance as to the objective criterion to be applied. The function of the criminal law is to identify and define the relevant legal criteria. It is not proper to leave the decision to the essentially subjective judgment of the individual jurors who happen to be deciding the case. Such an approach is apt to lead to idiosyncratic and inconsistent decisions. The law must inform the accused, and the judge must direct the jury, what is the objective criterion which the jury are to apply in any exercise of judgment in deciding upon the guilt or innocence of the accused. Non-specific criteria also create difficulties for the conduct of criminal trials since they do not set the necessary parameters for the admission of evidence or the relevance of arguments.

In fairness to those representing the respondent on this appeal, they have not submitted that a non-specific approach is permissible nor that it should be adopted.

The appeal should be allowed. The direction of the judge was appropriate to the issues at the trial. The conviction was not unsafe.

INVOLUNTARY MANSLAUGHTER: UNLAWFUL ACT MANSLAUGHTER

Where a defendant causes death but lacks the intention to kill or to cause grievous bodily harm, he may nevertheless incur liability for manslaughter, provided that certain factors are present.

The need for a positive criminal act

R v Lowe [1973] QB 702 (CA)

Phillimore LJ: Robert Lowe appeals against his conviction at Nottingham Crown Court on 25 July 1972 ... [H]e was convicted on count 2 of the indictment of cruelty to a child by wilfully neglecting it so as to cause unnecessary suffering or injury to health contrary to the provisions of s 1(1) of the Children and Young Persons Act 1933. He was also convicted on count 1 of manslaughter of the child on the grounds that his cruelty alleged under count 2 caused its death ...

The trial judge ... directed the jury that if they found the appellant guilty of the second count they must, as a matter of law, find him guilty of the first, namely of manslaughter. Having found him guilty of the second count they also found him guilty of the first and made it clear that they did so solely as a result of the direction by the trial judge; in other words, they did not find the appellant guilty of reckless conduct resulting in the child's death.

... This court feels that there is something inherently unattractive in a theory of constructive manslaughter. It seems strange that an omission which is wilful solely in the sense that it is not inadvertent, the consequences of which are not in fact foreseen by the person who is neglectful should, if death results, automatically give rise to an indeterminate sentence instead of the maximum of two years which would otherwise be the limit imposed.

We think there is a clear distinction between an act of omission and an act of commission likely to cause harm. Whatever may be the position in regard to the latter it does not follow that the same is true of the former. In other words if I strike a child in a manner likely to cause harm it is right that if the child dies I may be charged with manslaughter. If, however, I omit to do something with the result that it suffers injury to health which results in its death, we think that a charge of manslaughter should not be an inevitable consequence, even if the omission is deliberate.

The criminal act must be dangerous

R v Church [1966] 1 QB 59 (CA)

Facts: On Sunday 31 May 1964 the dead body of Sylvia Jeannette Nott was found in the River Ouse within a few yards of the appellant's van, which stood near the river bank. The corpse bore the marks of grave injuries. There had been some degree of manual strangulation. Those injuries were likely to have caused unconsciousness and eventually death, but they had been inflicted about an hour or half an hour before death took place and did not in fact cause death. According to the medical evidence, the deceased's injuries were inflicted not long before she was thrown into the river, but she was alive when that was done. She continued to breathe for an appreciable time afterwards and the eventual cause of death was drowning. When interviewed by the police, the appellant said that he had taken the woman to his van to have sex with her, that he was unable to satisfy her, that she reproached him and slapped his face. They then had a fight, in the course of which he knocked her out. He said, 'I tried shaking her to wake her up for about half an hour, but she didn't wake up, so I panicked and dragged her out of the van and put her in the river'. At his trial he repeated this account and added, for the first time, 'I thought she was dead'.

> **Edmund Davies J**: ... The gravity of the injuries inflicted during life clearly pointed to an intention by the appellant to cause grievous bodily harm to or the death of Mrs Nott. Her death was in fact brought about by the action of the appellant in shortly thereafter throwing her still-living body into the river. Did it make any difference, as far as the murder charge was concerned, whether or not the appellant believed she was then already dead?

His Lordship then quoted from the summing up and went on:

> The jury were thus told in plain terms that they could not convict of murder unless it had been proved that the appellant knew that Mrs Nott was still alive when he threw her into the river or (at least) that he did not believe she was dead. We venture to express the view that such a direction was unduly benevolent to the appellant and that the jury should have been told that it was still open to them to convict of murder, notwithstanding that the appellant may have thought his blows and attempt at strangulation had actually produced death when he threw the body into the river, if they regarded the appellant's behaviour from the moment he first struck her to the moment when he threw her into the river as a series of acts designed to cause death or grievous bodily harm. See *Thabo Meli v R* [1954] 1 WLR 228. In the present case, the jury, directed as they were, acquitted of murder ...
>
> ... Stressing that we are here leaving entirely out of account those ingredients of homicide which might justify a verdict of manslaughter on the grounds of (a) criminal negligence, or (b) provocation or (c) diminished responsibility, the conclusion of this court is that an unlawful act causing the death of another cannot, simply because it is an unlawful act, render a manslaughter verdict inevitable. For such a verdict inexorably to follow, the unlawful act must be such as all sober and reasonable people would inevitably recognise must subject the other person to, at least, the risk of some harm resulting therefrom, albeit not serious harm ...

... In the light of *Thabo Meli v R* it is conceded on behalf of the appellant that, on the murder charge, the trial judge was perfectly entitled to direct the jury as he did: 'Unless you find that something happened in the course of this evening between the infliction of the injuries and the decision to throw the body into the water, you may undoubtedly treat the whole course of conduct of the accused as one.'

But for some reason not clear to this court, appellant's counsel denies that such an approach is possible when one is considering a charge of manslaughter. We fail to see why. We adopt as sound Dr Glanville Williams's view in his book, *Criminal Law*, 1961 that, 'If a killing by the first act would have been manslaughter, a later destruction of the supposed corpse should also be manslaughter'. Had Mrs Nott died of her initial injuries a manslaughter verdict might quite conceivably have been returned on the basis that the accused inflicted them under the influence of provocation or that the jury were not convinced that they were inflicted with murderous intent. All that was lacking in the direction given in this case was that, when the judge turned to consider manslaughter, he did not again tell the jury that they were entitled (if they thought fit) to regard the conduct of the appellant in relation of Mrs Nott as constituting throughout a series of acts which culminated in her death, and that, if that was how they regarded the accused's behaviour, it mattered not whether he believed her to be alive or dead when he threw her in the river ...

R v Daweson, Nolan and Walmsley (1985) 81 Cr App R 150 (CA)

Facts: The three appellants attempted to rob a petrol filling station but fled when the attendant pressed an alarm button. The attendant, who suffered from a heart condition, collapsed and died shortly afterwards. The appellants were convicted of manslaughter. At their trial, medical experts were of the opinion that the attempted robbery was responsible for the attendant's death; but they could not rule out the possibility of a heart attack having occurred before the attempted robbery.

> **Watkins LJ**: ... It has, in our experience, been generally understood that the harm referred to in the second element of the offence of manslaughter, namely the unlawful act, must be one that all sober and reasonable people would realise was likely to cause some, albeit not serious, harm, means physical harm ...
>
> ... [T]here seems to us to be no sensible reason why shock produced by fright should not come within the definition of harm in this context ... Shock can produce devastating and lasting effects, for instance upon the nervous system. That is surely harm, ie injury to the person. Why not harm in this context?
>
> ... We shall assume without deciding the point, although we incline to favour the proposition, that harm in the context of manslaughter includes injury to the person through the operation of shock emanating from fright ...
>
> ... In our judgment, a proper direction would have been that the requisite harm is caused if the unlawful act so shocks the victim as to cause him physical injury.
>
> ... [The] test [of knowledge] can only be undertaken upon the basis of the knowledge gained by a sober and reasonable man as though he were present at the scene of and watched the unlawful act being performed and who knows that, as in the present case, an unloaded replica gun was in use, but that the victim may

have thought it was a loaded gun in working order. In other words, he has the same knowledge as the man attempting to rob and no more. It was never suggested that any of these appellants knew that their victim had a bad heart. They knew nothing about him ...

R v Watson [1989] 1 WLR 684 (CA)

Lord Lane CJ: ... The facts of the case, in so far as they are relevant, were as follows. Late at night on 11 December 1986 two men, one of whom was the appellant, broke into the home of a man called Harold Moyler. Mr Moyler was 87 years old and suffered from a serious condition of the heart. He lived alone. The two men first threw a brick through the window and, having made entry to the house, confronted Mr Moyler as he woke up, abused him verbally and then made off without stealing anything.

Mr Moyler died an hour and a half later as the result of a heart attack. The case for the Crown was that the heart attack was a direct consequence of the unlawful actions of the appellant and his colleague ...

It was accepted that the judge correctly defined the offence of manslaughter as it applied to the circumstances as follows:

> Manslaughter is the offence committed when one person causes the death of another by an act which is unlawful and which is also dangerous, dangerous in the sense that it is an act which all sober and reasonable people would inevitably realise must subject the victim to the risk of some harm resulting whether the defendant realised that or not.

The first point taken on behalf of the appellant is this. When one is deciding whether the sober and reasonable person (the bystander) would realise the risk of some harm resulting to the victim, how much knowledge of the circumstances does one attribute to the bystander? The appellant contends that the unlawful act here was the burglary as charged in the indictment.

The charge was laid under s 9(1)(a) of the Theft Act 1968, the allegation being that the appellant had entered the building as a trespasser with intent to commit theft. Since that offence is committed at the first moment of entry, the bystander's knowledge is confined to that of the defendant at that moment. In the instant case there was no evidence that the appellant, at the moment of entry, knew the age or physical condition of Mr Moyler or even that he lived there alone.

The judge clearly took the view that the jury were entitled to ascribe to the bystander the knowledge which the appellant gained during the whole of his stay in the house and so directed them. Was this a misdirection? In our judgment it was not. The unlawful act in the present circumstances comprised the whole of the burglarious intrusion and did not come to an end upon the appellant's foot crossing the threshold or window sill. That being so, the appellant (and therefore the bystander) during the course of the unlawful act must have become aware of Mr Moyler's frailty and approximate age, and the judge's directions were accordingly correct ...

R v Ball [1989] Crim LR 730 (CA)

Facts: The defendant shot a neighbour. At his trial, the defendant's defence was lack of intention to kill or cause harm: he thought he had loaded the gun with a blank cartridge. It appeared that he had previously attempted to fire two such blanks to scare and frighten the deceased from his land. For reasons which were not clear they had not detonated. He said that he kept live and blank cartridges together in the pocket of his overalls in the house. He had grabbed a handful when he had picked up the gun, intending only to frighten the deceased.

Held, dismissing the appeal: *R v Daweson* (1985) 81 Cr App R 150 went no further than showing that the sober and reasonable man must look at the unlawful act to see if it was dangerous and not at peculiarities of the victim; in that case the victim had a heart condition. In cases of involuntary manslaughter, there was a distinction between unlawful and lawful acts resulting in death. Where the act was unlawful, the question for the jury was whether it was also dangerous in the sense that all sober and reasonable people would inevitably realise that it would subject the victim to the risk of some harm, albeit not serious harm. Questions of gross or criminal negligence were not material. In many cases the judge might have to give a direction on the question of a lawful act and gross or criminal negligence because the jury might not accept that an accused deliberately did an unlawful act. But in this case it was accepted on behalf of the appellant that he had unlawfully assaulted the deceased. His act in firing at the deceased was 'an act directed at the victim' (*per* Waller LJ in *R v Dalby* (1982) 74 Cr App R 348 at 352), with 'no fresh intervening cause between the act and the death' (*per* Lord Lane CJ in *R v Goodfellow* (1986) 83 Cr App R 23). He had used his own cartridges and loaded the gun himself; no other agency was involved. In manslaughter arising from an unlawful and dangerous act, the accused's state of mind was relevant only to establish (a) that the act was committed intentionally; and (b) that it was an unlawful act (*DPP v Newbury* (1977) 62 Cr App R 291). Once (a) and (b) were established, the question of whether the act was dangerous was to be judged not by the appellant's appreciation but by that of the sober reasonable man, and it was impossible to impute into his appreciation the mistaken belief that what he was doing was not dangerous because he thought he had a blank cartridge in the chamber. At that stage, his intention, foresight or knowledge was irrelevant.

Does the dangerous criminal act have to be directed at the victim?

R v Dalby [1982] 1 WLR 621 (CA)

Facts: The appellant was a drug addict. He lawfully obtained upon prescription a number of tablets of a class A controlled drug. He then supplied some tablets to Stefan O'Such, a friend with whom he was staying, who was also a drug addict. The two of them injected themselves intravenously before they parted company for the evening. During that evening O'Such injected himself intravenously twice more with the help of another person. When the appellant returned to O'Such's flat, O'Such was asleep in the living room; in the morning he could not be woken. At 3 pm O'Such's wife called an ambulance. When the ambulance attendants arrived they found that he was dead.

> **Waller LJ**: ... It was submitted on behalf of the appellant: (1) that the unlawful act must be one directed at the victim; the supply of drugs in this case was not such a direct act; (2) that the supply of drugs can be harmless or extremely harmful according to the manner in which the victim deals with them; (3) that the drugs in this case were taken voluntarily by the victim in a form, ie intravenously, and in a quantity which together made them extremely dangerous and resulted in death; the line of causation was therefore broken between the unlawful act of supplying drugs and the death resulting from intravenous injection of too great a quantity of them ...
>
> ... [I]n all of the reported cases of manslaughter by an unlawful and dangerous act, the researches of counsel have failed to find any case where the act was not a direct act.
>
> The difficulty in the present case is that the act of supplying a controlled drug was not an act which caused direct harm. It was an act which made it possible, or even likely, that harm would occur subsequently, particularly if the drug was supplied to somebody who was on drugs. In all the reported cases, the physical act has been one which inevitably would subject the other person to the risk of some harm from the act itself. In this case, the supply of drugs would itself have caused no harm unless the deceased had subsequently used the drugs in a form and quantity which was dangerous ...
>
> In the judgment of this court, the unlawful act of supplying drugs was not an act directed against the person of O'Such and the supply did not cause any direct injury to him. The kind of harm envisaged in all the reported cases of involuntary manslaughter was physical injury of some kind as an immediate and inevitable result of the unlawful act, eg a blow on the chin which knocks the victim against a wall causing a fractured skull and death, or threatening with a loaded gun which accidentally fires, or dropping a large stone on a train (*DPP v Newbury* [1977] AC 500) or threatening another with an open razor and stumbling with death resulting: see *R v Larkin* (1942) 29 Cr App R 18.
>
> In the judgment of this court, where the charge of manslaughter is based on an unlawful and dangerous act, it must be an act directed at the victim and likely to cause immediate injury, however slight ...

Petition, 4 March 1982: The Appeal Committee of the House of Lords (**Lord Wilberforce**, **Lord Scarman** and **Lord Bridge of Harwich**) dismissed a petition by the Crown for leave to appeal.

R v Mitchell [1983] QB 741 (CA)

Staughton J: ... The facts alleged by the prosecution at the trial were briefly as follows. On 26 March 1981, the appellant, who was aged 22 at the time, was in a busy post office at Tottenham. An altercation arose when he tried to force himself into a queue or in some other way to be served before those who had been waiting longer than he had. Mr Edward Smith, who was aged 72, spoke to him about his behaviour. There was some argument, and the appellant hit Mr Smith in the mouth, causing him to stagger back and hit the back of his head against a glass panel above the post office counter. The glass panel shattered. Mr Smith recovered and moved forward. The appellant then either hit Mr Smith again or else threw him, so that he fell into other people who were waiting in the post office, Mr Smith fell against Mrs Anne Crafts, a lady aged 89. Both Mr Smith and Mrs Crafts fell to the ground. Mr Smith suffered a bruise in the back of his head, and his lower lip was cut and swollen. Mrs Crafts suffered a broken femur. She was taken to hospital, and on 31 March 1981, an operation was performed to replace her hip joint. She appeared to make a satisfactory recovery, but on 2 April 1981, she died suddenly. The cause of death was pulmonary embolism caused by thrombosis of the left leg veins, which in turn was caused by fracture of the femur ...

Both counsel were agreed that there are four elements in this class of manslaughter, as follows: first, there must be an act which is unlawful; second, it must be a dangerous act, in the sense that a sober and reasonable person would inevitably recognise that it carried some risk of harm, albeit not serious harm (that being an objective test); third, the act must be a substantial cause of death; fourth, the act itself must be intentional. No question relating to any other class of manslaughter (such as manslaughter by gross negligence) arose in this case.

The main question argued was whether the person at whom the act is aimed must also be the person whose death is caused ...

We can see no reason of policy for holding that an act calculated to harm A cannot be manslaughter if it in fact kills B. The criminality of the doer of the act is precisely the same whether it is A or B who dies. A person who throws a stone at A is just as guilty if, instead of hitting and killing A, it hits and kills B. Parliament evidently held the same view in relation to the allied offence of unlawful and malicious wounding contrary to s 20 of the Offences Against the Person Act 1861: see *R v Latimer* (1886) 17 QBD 359. We accordingly reject the argument of counsel for the appellant that, because the appellant's acts were aimed at Mr Smith, it cannot have been manslaughter when they caused the death of Mrs Crafts.

The second limb of the [appellant's] argument was based wholly on *R v Dalby* [1982] 1 WLR 621. It was argued that for manslaughter to be established the act of the defendant must be shown to have caused direct harm to the victim. On that ground, although it would be manslaughter to throw a stone at A which hits and kills B, it was submitted that there was no manslaughter in the present case, because there was no physical contact between the appellant and Mrs Crafts.

... Here, however ... [a]lthough there was no direct contact between the appellant and Mrs Crafts, she was injured as a direct and immediate result of his act. Thereafter her death occurred. The only question was one of causation: whether her death was caused by the appellant's acts. It was open to the jury to conclude that it was so caused; and they evidently reached that conclusion.

Since the conclusion of the argument we have seen a transcript of the judgment of this court in *R v Pagett* (1983) *The Times*, 4 February. This supports the views we have expressed in two respects. Robert Goff LJ, delivering the judgment of the court, said:

> If, as the jury must have found to have occurred in the present case, the appellant used Gail Kinchin by force and against her will as a shield to protect him from any shots fired by the police, the effect is that he committed not one but two unlawful acts, both of which were dangerous: the act of firing at the

police, and the act of holding Gail Kinchen as a shield in front of him when the police might well fire shots in his direction in self-defence. Either act could, in our judgment ... constitute the *actus reus* of the manslaughter.

In the case of the first act mentioned – firing at the police – it could scarcely be said to have been *aimed* at the ultimate victim, Gail Kinchen; nor could it be said by itself to have caused harm to the victim by direct physical contact. We agree that neither requirement exists for manslaughter. Granted an unlawful and dangerous act, the test is one of causation. That is clear from the transcript, where Robert Goff LJ said:

> The question whether an accused person can be guilty of homicide, either murder or manslaughter, of a victim the immediate cause of whose death is the act of another person must be determined on the ordinary principles of causation ...

... [I]t was [also] argued [by the appellant] that the judge failed to direct the jury that the appellant's act had to be a deliberate act, in the sense that he intended to do it ...

... There need not be any intention to injure or kill, or any foresight that injury or death would be caused, provided that all sober and reasonable people would have recognised the act to be dangerous ...

... All of the appellant's actions ... were obviously and admittedly deliberate actions. There was no suggestion of inadvertence, or even automation, in any part of his conduct ...

R v Goodfellow (1986) 83 Cr App R 23 (CA)

Lord Chief Justice: ... On 14 August 1984 in the early hours of the morning, the appellant set light to the council house he occupied at 24 Cossock Terrace, Pallion. He poured petrol over the sideboard, chair and walls of the downstairs living room, and then set the house on fire by igniting the petrol. In the ensuing blaze three people died: his wife Sarah aged 22, another young woman named Jillian Stuart with whom the appellant was having a liaison, who was in the house that night, and the appellant's two year old son Darren.

The background to these events was as follows. The appellant had been having difficulties with two men in the locality. One of them had been fined for damaging the front door of No 24. Hence the appellant wanted to move. He had no chance of exchanging his council house for another because he was some £300 in arrears with his rent. He therefore conceived the idea of setting No 24 on fire and making it look as though the fire had been caused by a petrol bomb thrown through the window by one of the men. This story was what he initially told the police when they started to make enquiries ...

It seems to us that this was a case which was capable of falling within either or both types of manslaughter. On the *Lawrence* aspect, the jury might well have been satisfied that the appellant was acting in such a manner as to create an obvious and serious risk of causing physical injury to some person, and second that he, having recognised that there was some risk involved, had nevertheless gone on to take it.

This was equally, in our view, a case for the 'unlawful and dangerous act' direction. Where the defendant does an unlawful act of such a kind as all sober and reasonable people would inevitably recognise must subject another person to, at least, the risk of some harm resulting therefrom, albeit not serious harm and causes death thereby, he is guilty of manslaughter: see *R v Church* [1966] 1 QB 59 ...

The questions which the jury have to decide on the charge of manslaughter of this nature [ie the unlawful act form] are (1) Was the act intentional? (2) Was it unlawful? (3) Was it an act which any reasonable person would realise was bound to subject some other human being to the risk of physical harm, albeit not necessarily serious harm? (4) Was that act the cause of death? ...

The *mens rea* for unlawful act manslaughter

R v Lamb [1967] 2 QB 981 (CA)

Sachs LJ: ... The defendant, Terence Walter Lamb, aged 25, had become possessed of a Smith & Wesson revolver. It was a revolver in the literal old-fashioned sense, having a five-chambered cylinder which rotated clockwise each time the trigger was pulled. The defendant, in jest, with no intention to do any harm, pointed the revolver at the deceased, his best friend, when it had two bullets in the chambers, but neither bullet was in the chamber opposite the barrel. His friend was similarly treating the incident as a joke. The defendant then pulled the trigger and thus killed his friend, still having no intention to fire the revolver. The reason why the pulling of the trigger produced that fatal result was that its pulling rotated the cylinder and so placed a bullet opposite the barrel so that it was struck by the striking pin or hammer.

The defendant's defence was that, as neither bullet was opposite the barrel, he thought they were in such chambers that the striking pin could not hit them; that he was unaware that the pulling of the trigger would bring one bullet into the firing position opposite the barrel; and that the killing was thus an accident. There was not only no dispute that that was what he in fact thought, but the mistake he made was one which three experts agreed was natural for somebody who was not aware of the way the revolver mechanism worked ...

The defence of accident was, however, in effect withdrawn from the jury by the trial judge ... [who] made no mention of the word 'accident' in his summing up nor of the evidence of the experts save that he at one stage directed the jury that their evidence was not relevant ...

Dealing with manslaughter in the sense of an unlawful act resulting in death his Lordship said:

... The trial judge took the view that the pointing of the revolver and the pulling of the trigger was something which could of itself be unlawful even if there was no attempt to alarm or intent to injure ...

[Counsel for the Crown] however, had at all times put forward the correct view that for the act to be unlawful it must constitute at least what he then termed 'a technical assault'. In this court moreover he rightly conceded that there was no evidence to go to the jury of any assault of any kind. Nor did he feel able to submit that the acts of the defendant were on any other ground unlawful in the criminal sense of that word. Indeed no such submission could in law be made: if, for instance, the pulling of the trigger had had no effect because the striking mechanism or the ammunition had been defective no offence would have been committed by the defendant.

Another way of putting it is that *mens rea*, being now an essential ingredient in manslaughter (compare *Andrews v DPP* [1937] AC 576 and *R v Church* [1966] 1 QB 59), that could not in the present case be established in relation to the first ground except by proving that element of intent without which there can be no assault.

It is perhaps as well to mention that when using the phrase 'unlawful in the criminal sense of that word' the court has in mind that it is long settled that it is not in point to consider whether an act is unlawful merely from the angle of civil liabilities ...

Dealing with manslaughter on the ground of criminal negligence, his Lordship said:

... Nowhere in that part of the summing up relating to the second ground is any mention made of the view the defendant had formed as to being able to pull the trigger without firing a bullet, nor of the experts' unanimous evidence that his mistake was understandable and indeed one which could be expected ...

The general effect of the summing up was thus to withdraw from the jury the defence put forward on behalf of the defendant. When the gravamen of a charge is criminal negligence – often referred to as recklessness – of an accused, the jury have to consider among other matters the state of his mind, and that includes the question of whether or not he thought that that which he was doing was safe. In the present case it would, of course, have been fully open to a jury, if properly directed, to find the defendant guilty because they considered his view as to there being no danger was formed in a criminally negligent way. But he was entitled to a direction that the jury should take into account the fact that he had undisputedly formed that view and that there was expert evidence as to this being an understandable view.

Strong though the evidence of criminal negligence was, the defendant was entitled as of right to have his defence considered, but he was not accorded this right and the jury was left without a direction on an essential matter ... [Therefore] the verdict cannot stand ...

DPP v Newbury and Jones [1977] AC 500 (HL)

Lord Salmon: My Lords, on 11 October 1974, the train travelling from Pontypridd to Cardiff was approaching a bridge which crossed the railway line. The guard was sitting next to the driver of the train in the front cab. The driver noticed the heads of three boys above the parapet of the bridge. He saw one of the boys push something off the parapet towards the oncoming train. This proved to be part of a paving stone which some workmen had left on the parapet. It came through the glass window of the cab in which the driver and the guard were sitting, struck the guard and killed him. There was ample evidence that just as the train was about to reach the bridge the two appellants, who were each about 15 years of age, were jointly concerned in pushing over the parapet the piece of paving stone which killed the guard. They were jointly charged with manslaughter ... The point of law certified to be of general public importance is 'can a defendant be properly convicted of manslaughter, when his mind is not affected by drink or drugs, if he did not foresee that his act might cause harm to another?'

The learned trial judge did not direct the jury that they should acquit the appellants unless they were satisfied beyond a reasonable doubt that the appellants had foreseen that they might cause harm to someone by pushing the piece of paving stone off the parapet into the path of the approaching train. In my view the learned trial judge was quite right not to give such a direction to the jury ... In *R v Larkin* (1942) 29 Cr App R 18, Humphreys J said at 23:

> Where the act which a person is engaged in performing is unlawful, then if at the same time it is a dangerous act, that is, an act which is likely to injure another person, and quite inadvertently the doer of the act causes the death of that other person by that act, then he is guilty of manslaughter.

... [T]hat is an admirably clear statement of the law which has been applied many times. It makes it plain (a) that an accused is guilty of manslaughter if it is proved that he intentionally did an act which was unlawful and dangerous and that that act inadvertently caused death and (b) that it is unnecessary to prove that the accused knew that the act was unlawful or dangerous. This is one of the reasons why cases of manslaughter vary so infinitely in their gravity. They may amount to little more than pure inadvertence and sometimes to little less than murder ...

... In judging whether the act was dangerous the test is not did the accused recognise that it was dangerous but would all sober and reasonable people recognise its danger ...

Lord Edmund Davies delivered a concurring speech.

INVOLUNTARY MANSLAUGHTER: KILLING BY GROSS NEGLIGENCE

Whereas unlawful act manslaughter requires proof of a positive act, many instances of killing by gross negligence are characterised by the defendant's failure to discharge the duty of care owed to the deceased. As the following extracts indicate, the objective nature of the fault element make it the most appropriate form of manslaughter to charge where it is alleged that a company is criminally responsible for causing death.

R v Stone and Dobinson [1977] QB 354 (CA)

Geoffrey Lane LJ: Counsel for the appellants' second submission presents greater difficulty. It is that the judge's direction on the nature of the negligence or recklessness required was wrongly stated. This is how the matter was left to the jury:

> Have the Crown proved that either or both of these defendants was guilty of gross neglect of Fanny amounting to a reckless disregard for the health and well-being of that woman. Do not place your judgment ... on the question of recklessness as to whether she died or not. What has to be proved is not that, but that there was a reckless disregard for their duty of care. It may well be

that that will involve a consideration of what they thought would be the consequences of their reckless disregard, if you found there was one. For example, if I were in charge of a person and I was guilty of some major neglect, but I genuinely did not appreciate that it would lead to any dire results, you would probably say, 'That person is not very bright, but I am not sure he is guilty of recklessness'.

Then at a later stage in the direction:

> ... were either or both of these defendants in grave neglect of that duty, were they reckless, or did they show a reckless disregard for their obligations. Again it depends to a large extent on the extent of their knowledge of her condition; of their individual appreciation of the need to act. It depends to some extent on their appreciation of the consequences of inaction; it depends on the facilities which were available or which they could readily have made available ... Mr Stone says: 'Nothing was done because I was not aware of the gravity of the matter, of the danger to Fanny's life and of the situation. I did not know the actual conditions in which my sister was lying.' If that is true or if it may be true then you will acquit him. If you are sure that he did know then you ask yourselves: what did he do about it, and what could he have done ... you do not judge him on what you would have done yourselves; but you take the man as you find him ... So far as Mrs Dobinson is concerned ... did she do her incompetent best? Certainly if she did that, then you would acquit her.

The appellants' contention is that the Crown in order to succeed must show recklessness on the part of the defendant; that recklessness in this context means foresight of the likelihood or possibility of death or serious injury and a determination nevertheless to persist in the omission to provide care. We were referred to a number of 19th century decisions which are historically interesting but of small practical assistance. Counsel for the appellants relied principally on the decision of this court in *R v Lowe* [1973] QB 702. In that case there were two counts, one alleging manslaughter of a child on the grounds that the defendants' cruelty alleged under the second count caused its death, and the second count charging cruelty to a child by wilfully neglecting it so as to cause unnecessary suffering or injury to health under s 1(1) of the Children and Young Persons Act 1933. The judge had directed the jury that if they found the appellant guilty on the second count they must find him guilty under the first count of manslaughter, even though they acquitted him of recklessness.

That was held to be a misdirection. Phillimore LJ, delivering the judgment of the court, went on to say this:

> Now in the present case the jury negatived recklessness. How then can mere neglect albeit wilful amount to manslaughter? This court feels that there is something inherently unattractive in a theory of constructive manslaughter. It seems strange that an omission which is wilful solely in the sense that it is not inadvertent, the consequences of which are not in fact foreseen by the person who is neglectful, should if death results, automatically give rise to an indeterminate sentence ...

Counsel for the appellants submits that that passage is support for his argument that there must be an appreciation by the defendant of the risk of death or serious injury before a conviction for manslaughter in these circumstances can result. We disagree. The court is saying simply that there must be proved the necessary high degree of negligence, and a direction which fails to emphasise that requirement will be defective. It is to *Andrews v DPP* [1937] AC 576 that one must turn to discover the definition of the requisite degree of negligence. Lord Atkin cites, with approval, the words of Hewart CJ in *R v Bateman* (1925) 94 LJ KB 791, and goes on to say this:

> Simple lack of care such as will constitute civil liability is not enough. For purposes of the criminal law there are degrees of negligence; and a very high degree of negligence is required to be proved before the felony is established. Probably of all the epithets that can be applied 'reckless' most nearly covers the case. It is difficult to visualise a case of death caused by 'reckless' driving, in the connotation of that term in ordinary speech which would not justify a conviction of manslaughter; but it is probably not all-embracing, for 'reckless' suggests an indifference to risk whereas the accused may have appreciated the risk and intended to avoid it, and yet have shown in the means adopted to avoid the risk such a high degree of negligence as would justify a conviction.

It is clear from that passage that indifference to an obvious risk and appreciation of such risk, coupled with a determination nevertheless to run it, are both examples of recklessness.

The duty which a defendant has undertaken is a duty of caring for the health and welfare of the infirm person. What the Crown has to prove is a breach of that duty in such circumstances that the jury feel convinced that the defendant's conduct can properly be described as reckless. That is to say a reckless disregard of danger to the health and welfare of the infirm person. Mere inadvertence is not enough. The defendant must be proved to have been indifferent to an obvious risk of injury to health, or actually to have foreseen the risk but to have determined nevertheless to run it.

The direction given by the judge was wholly in accord with these principles. If any criticism is to be made it would be that the direction was unduly favourable to the defence. The appeals against conviction therefore fail ...

R v Adomako [1995] 1 AC 171 (HL)

Facts: The defendant was an anaesthetist. He failed to notice that the endotracheal tube had become disconnected. The patient suffered a cardiac arrest and died.

Lord Mackay of Clashfern LC: ... The Court of Appeal (Criminal Division) ... certified that a point of law of general public importance was involved in the decision to dismiss the appeal, namely:

> In cases of manslaughter by criminal negligence not involving driving but involving a breach of duty is it a sufficient direction to the jury to adopt the gross negligence test set out by the Court of Appeal in the present case following *R v Bateman* (1925) 19 Cr App R 8 and *Andrews v DPP* [1937] AC 576, without reference to the test of recklessness as defined in *R v Lawrence (Stephen)* [1982] AC 510 or as adapted to the circumstances of the case?

... I begin with *R v Bateman* 19 Cr App R 8 and the opinion of Lord Hewart CJ, where he said, at 10–11:

> In expounding the law to juries on the trial of indictments for manslaughter by negligence, judges have often referred to the distinction between civil and

criminal liability for death by negligence. The law of criminal liability for negligence is conveniently explained in that way. If A has caused the death of B by alleged negligence, then in order to establish civil liability, the plaintiff must prove (in addition to pecuniary loss caused by the death) that A owed a duty to B to take care, that that duty was not discharged, and that the default caused the death of B. To convict A of manslaughter, the prosecution must prove the three things above-mentioned and must satisfy the jury, in addition, that A's negligence amounted to a crime. In the civil action, if it is proved that A fell short of the standard of reasonable care required by law, it matters not how far he fell short of that standard. The extent of his liability depends not on the degree of negligence, but on the amount of damage done. In a criminal court, on the contrary, the amount and degree of negligence are the determining question. There must be *mens rea*.

Later he said, at 11–12:

In explaining to juries the test which they should apply to determine whether the negligence, in the particular case, amounted or did not amount to a crime, judges have used many epithets, such as 'culpable', 'criminal', 'gross', 'wicked', 'clear', 'complete'. But, whatever epithet be used and whether an epithet be used or not, in order to establish criminal liability the facts must be such that, in the opinion of the jury, the negligence of the accused went beyond a mere matter of compensation between subjects and showed such disregard for the life and safety of others as to amount to a crime against the state and conduct deserving punishment.

After dealing with a number of authorities Lord Hewart CJ went on, at 12–13:

The law as laid down in these cases may be thus summarised: If a person holds himself out as possessing special skill and knowledge and he is consulted, as possessing such skill and knowledge, by or on behalf of a patient, he owes a duty to the patient to use due caution in undertaking the treatment. If he accepts the responsibility and undertakes the treatment and the patient submits to his direction and treatment accordingly, he owes a duty to the patient to use diligence, care, knowledge, skill and caution in administering the treatment. No contractual relation is necessary, nor is it necessary that the service be rendered for reward. It is for the judge to direct the jury what standard to apply and for the jury to say whether that standard has been reached. The jury should not exact the highest, or a very high, standard, nor should they be content with a very low standard. The law requires a fair and reasonable standard of care and competence. This standard must be reached in all the matters above mentioned. If the patient's death has been caused by the defendant's indolence or carelessness, it will not avail to show that he had sufficient knowledge; nor will it avail to prove that he was diligent in attendance, if the patient has been killed by his gross ignorance and unskilfulness. No further observation need be made with regard to cases where the death is alleged to have been caused by indolence or carelessness. As regards cases where incompetence is alleged, it is only necessary to say that the unqualified practitioner cannot claim to be measured by any lower standard than that which is applied to a qualified man. As regards cases of alleged recklessness, juries are likely to distinguish between the qualified and the unqualified man. There may be recklessness in undertaking the treatment and recklessness in the conduct of it. It is, no doubt, conceivable that a qualified man may be held liable for recklessly undertaking a case which he knew, or should have known, to be beyond his powers, or for making his patient the subject of reckless experiment. Such cases are likely to be rare. In the case of the quack, where the treatment has been proved to be incompetent and to have caused the patient's death, juries are not likely to hesitate in finding liability on the ground that the defendant undertook, and continued to treat, a case involving the gravest risk to his patient, when he knew he was not competent to deal with it, or would have known if he had paid any proper regard to the life and safety of his patient.

The foregoing observations deal with civil liability. To support an indictment for manslaughter the prosecution must prove the matters necessary to establish civil liability (except pecuniary loss), and, in addition, must satisfy the jury that the negligence or incompetence of the accused went beyond a mere matter of compensation and showed such disregard for the life and safety of others as to amount to a crime against the state and conduct deserving punishment.

Next I turn to *Andrews v DPP* [1973] AC 576 which was a case of manslaughter through dangerous driving of a motor car. In a speech with which all the other members of this House who sat agreed, Lord Atkin said at 581–82:

> ... of all crimes manslaughter appears to afford most difficulties of definition, for it concerns homicide in so many and so varying conditions. From the early days when any homicide involved penalty the law has gradually evolved 'through successive differentiations and integrations' until it recognises murder on the one hand, based mainly, though not exclusively, on an intention to kill, and manslaughter on the other hand, based mainly, though not exclusively, on the absence of intention to kill but with the presence of an element of 'unlawfulness' which is the elusive factor. In the present case it is only necessary to consider manslaughter from the point of view of an unintentional killing caused by negligence, that is, the omission of a duty to take care ...

Lord Atkin then referred to the judgment of Lord Hewart CJ from which I have already quoted and went on at 583:

> Here again I think with respect that the expressions used are not, indeed they were probably not intended to be, a precise definition of the crime. I do not myself find the connotations of *mens rea* helpful in distinguishing between degrees of negligence, nor do the ideas of crime and punishment in themselves carry a jury much further in deciding whether in a particular case the degree of negligence shown is a crime and deserves punishment. But the substance of the judgment is most valuable, and in my opinion is correct. In practice it has generally been adopted by judges in charging juries in all cases of manslaughter by negligence, whether in driving vehicles or otherwise. The principle to be observed is that cases of manslaughter in driving motor cars are but instances of a general rule applicable to all charges of homicide by negligence. Simple lack of care such as will constitute civil liability is not enough: for purposes of the criminal law there are degrees of negligence: and a very high degree of negligence is required to be proved before the felony is established. Probably of all the epithets that can be applied 'reckless' most nearly covers the case. It is difficult to visualise a case of death caused by

reckless driving in the connotation of that term in ordinary speech which would not justify a conviction for manslaughter: but it is probably not all-embracing, for 'reckless' suggests an indifference to risk whereas the accused may have appreciated the risk and intended to avoid it and yet shown such a high degree of negligence in the means adopted to avoid the risk as would justify a conviction. If the principle of *Bateman's* case 19 Cr App R 8 is observed it will appear that the law of manslaughter has not changed by the introduction of motor vehicles on the road. Death caused by their negligent driving, though unhappily much more frequent, is to be treated in law as death caused by any other form of negligence: and juries should be directed accordingly.

In my opinion the law as stated in these two authorities is satisfactory as providing a proper basis for describing the crime of involuntary manslaughter. Since the decision in *Andrews* was a decision of your Lordships' House, it remains the most authoritative statement of the present law which I have been able to find ... On this basis in my opinion the ordinary principles of the law of negligence apply to ascertain whether or not the defendant has been in breach of a duty of care towards the victim who has died. If such breach of duty is established the next question is whether that breach of duty caused the death of the victim. If so, the jury must go on to consider whether that breach of duty should be characterised as gross negligence and therefore as a crime. This will depend on the seriousness of the breach of duty committed by the defendant in all the circumstances in which the defendant was placed when it occurred. The jury will have to consider whether the extent to which the defendant's conduct departed from the proper standard of care incumbent upon him, involving as it must have done a risk of death to the patient, was such that it should be judged criminal.

It is true that to a certain extent this involves an element of circularity, but in this branch of the law I do not believe that is fatal to its being correct as a test of how far conduct must depart from accepted standards to be characterised as criminal. This is necessarily a question of degree and an attempt to specify that degree more closely is I think likely to achieve only a spurious precision. The essence of the matter which is supremely a jury question is whether having regard to the risk of death involved, the conduct of the defendant was so bad in all the circumstances as to amount in their judgment to a criminal act or omission ...

For these reasons I am of the opinion that this appeal should be dismissed and that the certified question should be answered by saying:

> In cases of manslaughter by criminal negligence involving a breach of duty, it is a sufficient direction to the jury to adopt the gross negligence test set out by the Court of Appeal in the present case following *R v Bateman* 19 Cr App R 8 and *Andrews v DPP* [1937] AC 576 and that it is not necessary to refer to the definition of recklessness in *R v Lawrence* [1982] AC 510, although it is perfectly open to the trial judge to use the word 'reckless' in its ordinary meaning as part of his exposition of the law if he deems it appropriate in the circumstances of the particular case.

AG's Ref (No 2 of 1999) [2000] 3 All ER 182

For extracts from Rose LJ's judgment dealing with the proof of corporate *mens rea*, see Chapter 4.

Rose LJ: The court's opinion is sought in relation to two questions referred by the Attorney General under s 36 of the Criminal Justice Act 1972. [The first of these questions is:] Can a defendant be properly convicted of manslaughter by gross negligence in the absence of evidence as to that defendant's state of mind? ...

The questions arise from a ruling given by Scott Baker J at the Central Criminal Court on 30 June 1999. At the outset of the trial of the defendant train operating company, on an indictment containing seven counts of manslaughter, he ruled that it is a condition precedent to a conviction for manslaughter by gross negligence for a guilty mind to be proved and that where a non-human defendant is prosecuted it may only be convicted via the guilt of a human being with whom it may be identified. It is submitted for the Attorney General that the judge was wrong in both respects.

The prosecution arose from the disastrous collision which occurred at Southall at 1.15 pm on 19 September 1997. The 10.32 high speed train (HST) from Swansea to London Paddington, with approximately 180 passengers and staff on board, operated by the defendant and travelling on the up main line, collided with a freight train crossing from the down relief line to Southall Yard. Seven passengers died. One hundred and fifty one people were injured. Millions of pounds worth of damage was done.

The HST had a driver of considerable experience but no second competent person with him. The power car was fitted with two safety devices independent of the driver. Each was designed to prevent a signal being passed at danger. One system was the Automatic Warning System (AWS) which had been in common use in the United Kingdom since the 1950s. It had been deliberately switched off. The other system was Automatic Train Protection (ATP) which the defendant was piloting for Railtrack and was the only United Kingdom operator using it. It had been switched off. The driver knew that neither AWS nor ATP were operating.

The movement of the train was correctly signalled, ie the signals on the up main line affecting the HST prior to the junction were set successively at green, double yellow, single yellow and red. The HST driver remembered passing through the green signal but next recalled seeing the red signal. He braked as hard as he could, but, as he was travelling at an average of 116 mph over the 3,600 metres immediately preceding the accident, it was too late.

The case for the prosecution was that the cause of the collision was, first, the driver's failure to see or heed the double yellow and single yellow signals warning of impending red and, secondly, the defendant's manner of operating the HST. The case against the defendant was that it owed a duty to take reasonable care for the safety of its passengers, of which it was in grossly negligent breach. Three signals were passed because the AWS and ATP were switched off and there was only one man in the cab. The defendant should not have permitted such a train to operate in such circumstances. Following the judge's ruling, the defendant pleaded guilty to count 8 on the indictment, which alleged failure to conduct an undertaking, namely the provision of transport by rail to members of the public, in such a way as to ensure that they were not exposed to risks to their health and safety contrary to ... the Health and Safety at Work Act 1974. The defendant was fined £1.5 m for what the judge described as 'a serious fault of senior management'. No employee of the defendant, apart from the driver, was prosecuted.

For the Attorney General, Mr Lissack QC submitted, in relation to question (1), that involuntary manslaughter can be committed by an unlawful act, gross negligence or subjective recklessness (see *Legislating the Criminal Code: Involuntary Manslaughter* (Law Com 237, 1996, paras 2.3, 2.8, and 2.26). The present case rests on gross negligence manslaughter. He submits that, since *R v Adomako* ... a defendant can be found guilty of such manslaughter in the absence of evidence as to his state of mind ...

Only gross breaches will give rise to criminal liability.

As a result of *R v Adomako*, Mr Lissack submitted, gross negligence manslaughter can be proved without the need to inquire into the state of the defendant's mind. This proposition is supported by a passage in Smith and Hogan's *Criminal Law* (7th edn, 1992) pp 90, 91, which culminates in contrasting crimes requiring *mens rea* with crimes of negligence. The *Adomako* test was derived from *R v Bateman* (1925) 19 Cr App R 8, [1925] All ER Rep 45, which was an objective test (see *Criminal Law: Involuntary Manslaughter* (Law Com 135, para 3.32)).

For the defendant Mr Caplan QC, in relation to question (1), submitted that there is a difference between whether *mens rea* must be proved and whether it may be relevant. He accepted that it need not be proved for gross negligence. But, he said, it may be relevant because the *Adomako* test requires the jury, when deciding if the breach is criminal, to consider it in all the circumstances. Furthermore, in *R v Adomako* [1994] 3 All ER 79 at 87, [1995] 1 AC 171 at 187 Lord Mackay LC went on to say that it was perfectly appropriate to use the word 'reckless' in cases of involuntary manslaughter, in its ordinary connotation as in *R v Stone, R v Dobinson* [1977] 2 All ER 341, [1977] QB 354. In *R v Stone, R v Dobinson* Lord Lane CJ said that, where a defendant had undertaken a duty of care for the health and welfare of an infirm person the prosecution had to prove:

> a reckless disregard of danger to the health and welfare of the infirm person. Mere inadvertence is not enough. The defendant must be proved to have been indifferent to an obvious risk of injury to health, or actually to have foreseen the risk but to have determined nevertheless to run it.

On this question, we accept the submissions of both Mr Lissack and Mr Caplan. They lead to the conclusion that question (1) must be answered Yes. Although there may be cases where the defendant's state of mind is relevant to the jury's consideration when assessing the grossness and criminality of his conduct, evidence of his state of mind is not a prerequisite to a conviction for manslaughter by gross negligence. The *Adomako* test is objective, but a defendant who is reckless as defined in *R v Stone, R v Dobinson* may well be the more readily found to be grossly negligent to a criminal degree.

[Having confirmed that corporate *mens rea* could only be established by means of the 'identification' doctrine, as opposed to the 'aggregation' doctrine, Rose LJ concluded:]

Finally, Mr Caplan [for the defendant] relied on the speech of Lord Lowry in *C v DPP* [1995] 2 All ER 43, [1996] AC 1 and invited this court to reject the prosecution's argument for extending corporate liability for manslaughter. Lord Lowry said, with regard to the propriety of judicial law making:

(1) if the solution is doubtful, the judges should beware of imposing their own remedy; (2) caution should prevail if Parliament has rejected opportunities of clearing up a known difficulty or has legislated while leaving the difficulty untouched; (3) disputed matters of social policy are less suitable areas for judicial intervention than purely legal problems; (4) fundamental legal doctrines should not be lightly set aside; (5) judges should not make a change unless they can achieve finality and certainty. (See [1995] 2 All ER 43 at 52, [1996] AC 1 at 28.)

Each of these considerations, submitted Mr Caplan, is pertinent in the present case.

There is, as it seems to us, no sound basis for suggesting that, by their recent decisions, the courts have started a process of moving from identification to personal liability as a basis for corporate liability for manslaughter. In *R v Adomako* the House of Lords were, as it seems to us, seeking to escape from the unnecessarily complex accretions in relation to recklessness arising from *R v Lawrence* [1981] 1 All ER 974, [1982] AC 510 and *R v Caldwell* [1981] 1 All ER 961, [1982] AC 341. To do so, they simplified the ingredients of gross negligence manslaughter by re-stating them in line with *R v Bateman* (1925) 19 Cr App R 8, [1925] All ER Rep 45. But corporate liability was not mentioned anywhere in the submissions of counsel or their Lordships' speeches. In any event, the identification principle is in our judgment just as relevant to the *actus reus* as to *mens rea*. In *Tesco Supermarkets Ltd v Nattrass* [1971] 2 All ER 127 at 134, [1972] AC 153 at 173 Lord Reid said:

> ... the judge must direct the jury that if they find certain facts proved then as a matter of law they must find that the criminal act of the officer, servant or agent including his state of mind, intention, knowledge or belief is the act of the company.

In *R v HM Coroner ex p Spooner* (1989) 88 Cr App R 10 at 16 Bingham LJ said:

> For a company to be criminally liable for manslaughter ... it is required that the *mens rea* and the *actus reus* of manslaughter should be established ... against those who were to be identified as the embodiment of the company itself.

In *R v P & O European Ferries (Dover) Ltd* (1991) 93 Cr App R 72 at 84 Tumer J, in his classic analysis of the relevant principles, said:

> ... where a corporation, through the controlling mind of one of its agents, does an act which fulfils the prerequisites of the crime of manslaughter, it is properly indictable for the crime of manslaughter.

In our judgment, unless an identified individual's conduct, characterisable as gross criminal negligence, can be attributed to the company the company is not, in the present state of the common law, liable for manslaughter. Civil negligence rules, eg as enunciated in *Wilsons and Clyde Coal Co Ltd v English* [1937] 3 All ER 628, [1938] AC 57, are not apt to confer criminal liability on a company.

None of the authorities relied on by Mr Lissack as pointing to personal liability for manslaughter by a company supports that contention. In each, the decision was dependent on the purposive construction that the particular statute imposed, subject to a defence of reasonable practicability, liability on a company for conducting its undertaking in a manner exposing employees or the public to health and safety risk. In each case there was an identified employee whose conduct was held to be that of the company. In each case it was held that the concept of directing mind and will had no application when construing the statute. But it was not suggested or implied that the concept of identification is dead or moribund in relation to common law offences. Indeed, if that were so, it might have been expected that Lord Hoffmann, in *R v Associated Octel Ltd* [1996] 4 All ER 846, [1996] 1 WLR 1543, would have referred to the ill-health of the doctrine in the light of his own speech, less than a year before, in the *Meridian* case. He made no such reference, nor was the *Meridian* case cited in *R v Associated Octel Ltd*. It therefore seems safe to conclude that Lord Hoffmann (and, similarly, the members of the Court of Appeal, Criminal Division in *R v British Steel plc* [1995] 1 WLR 1356 and in *R v Gateway Foodmarkets Ltd* [1997] 3 All ER 78) did not think that the common law principles as to the need for identification have changed. Indeed, Lord Hoffmann's speech in the *Meridian* case, in fashioning an additional special rule of attribution geared to the purpose of the statute, proceeded on the basis that the primary 'directing mind and will' rule still applies although it is not determinative in all cases. In other words, he was not departing from the identification theory but re-affirming its existence.

This approach is entirely consonant with the Law Commission's analysis of the present state of the law and the terms of their proposals for reform in their report (Law Com 237) published in March 1996. In this report, both the House of Lords decision in *R v Adomako* and the Privy Council's decision in the *Meridian* case were discussed. In the light of their analysis, the Law Commission (para 6.27 ff and para 7.5) concluded that, in the present state of the law, a corporation's liability for manslaughter is based solely on the principle of identification and they drafted a Bill to confer liability based on management failure not involving the principle of identification (see cl 4 of the draft Bill annexed to their report). If Mr Lissack's submissions are correct there is no need for such a Bill and, as Scott Baker J put it, the Law Commission have missed the point. We agree with the judge that the Law Commission have not missed the point and Mr Lissack's submissions are not correct: the identification principle remains the only basis in common law for corporate liability for gross negligence manslaughter.

We should add that, if we entertained doubt on the matter, being mindful of the observations of Lord Lowry in *C v DPP* [1995] 2 All ER 43 at 52, [1996] AC 1 at 28, we would not think it appropriate for this court to propel the law in the direction which Mr Lissack seeks. That, in our judgment, taking into account the policy considerations to which Mr Lissack referred, is a matter for Parliament, not the courts. For almost four years, the Law Commission's draft Bill has been to hand as a useful starting point for that purpose.

It follows that, in our opinion, the answer to question (2) is No.

R v P & O European Ferries (Dover) Ltd (1990) 93 Cr App R 72
(Central Criminal Court)

Turner J: ... The main thrust of the argument for the company in support of the submission that the four counts of manslaughter in this indictment should be quashed was not merely that English law does not recognise the offence of corporate manslaughter but that, as a matter of positive English law, manslaughter can only be committed when one natural person kills another natural person. Hence it was no accident that there is no record of any corporation or non-natural person having been successfully prosecuted for manslaughter in any English court. It was, however, accepted that there is no conceptual difficulty in attributing a criminal state of mind to a corporation. The broad argument advanced on behalf of the prosecution was that, there being no all-embracing statutory definition of murder or manslaughter there is, in principle, no reason why a corporation, or other non-natural person, cannot be found guilty of most offences in the criminal calendar. The exceptions to such a broad proposition could be found either in the form of punishment, which would be inappropriate for a corporation, or in the very person nature of individual crimes or categories of crime such as offences under the Sexual Offences Act, bigamy and, arguably, perjury. It was further argued that the definitions of homicide to be found in the works of such as Coke, Hale, Blackstone and Stephen, and which were strongly relied upon by the company, were not intended to be exclusive, but reflected the historical fact that, at the dates when these definitions originated, the concept of criminal liability of a corporation, just as their very existence, was not within the contemplation of the courts or the writers of the legal treatises referred to. Before the days when corporate crime was in contemplation, it can be a matter of no surprise to find that the definition of homicide did not include the possibility of a corporation committing such a crime ...

In the years 1943 and 1944, three cases were decided which can be seen to have had a watershed effect on the way in which the law has since developed. The first of these was the *DPP v Kent and Sussex Contractors Ltd* [1944] 1 KB 146, and was a decision of the Divisional Court. The offence in question was one under the Motor Fuel Rationing (No 3) Order 1941 and involved the use of a document which was false in a material particular. The decision of the justices to acquit was based on the proposition that: 'An act of will or state of mind ... could not be imputed to the company.' In the course of his judgment, Lord Caldecote CJ summarising the submissions for the defendant company said at 149:

> Mr Carey Evans submits that a company can only be held to be responsible in respect of the intention or knowledge of its agents, the officers of the company, to the same extent as a private individual is responsible for the acts of his agent, and, therefore, that the respondent company cannot be held to form the intention or to have knowledge necessary to constitute the offences charged. He has not disputed the abstract proposition that a company can have knowledge and can form an intention to do an act. A company cannot be found guilty of certain criminal offences, such as treason or other offences for which it is provided that death or imprisonment is the only punishment, but there are a number of criminal offences of which a company can be convicted. In the judgment of Finlay J in *Cory Brothers and Co* [1927] 1 KB 810, 816, there is a convenient citation from the judgment of Patteson J in *Birmingham and Gloucester Ry Co* (1842) 3 QB 223.

The learned Lord Chief Justice then quoted from that case, and continued at p 150:

> Under the Defence (General) Regulations 1939, it is common for offences to be created in which certain ingredients are required to be found and the present case seems to me to fall within that category. They are offences in which it is not material to consider whether there is or is not *mens rea*, which I understand to mean criminal intention, because the ingredients are stated in the regulation creating the offence. For instance, in the present case one of the necessary ingredients of the second offence charged is an intent to deceive. When that

intent is stated to be necessary it seems to me idle to enquire whether a *mens rea* is or is not involved.

In *Chuter v Freeth and Pocock Ltd* [1911] 2 KB 832 to which we were not referred, the question seems to have been similar to the one raised in this case.

He then read from the headnote, and the passage to which I refer is [at 151]:

The magistrate, although upon the facts as above stated he would have convicted if the respondents' servants had been principals in the matter, was yet of opinion that, as the exempting clause of the section implied that only such a person could commit the offence as was capable of believing, and as a corporation having no mind could not exercise that faculty, the respondents, being a corporation, were not liable under the section.

Lord Alverstone CJ stated the facts and then said:

The magistrate has held that, in as much as 'the person who gives a false warranty is made liable unless he proves that when he gave the warranty 'he had reason to believe' that the statements or descriptions contained therein were true, therefore 'the person' cannot be construed as including a corporation, but must be limited to natural persons capable of belief. In my view that is too narrow a construction. Where a person is capable of giving a warranty that person is liable to a fine. There is no reason why a warranty should not be given by a corporation. It can give a warranty through its agents, it can believe or not believe, as the case may be, that the statements in the warranty are true. A similar point has been raised in cases concerning the liability of a corporation in actions which, in the case of an individual, would involve an enquiry into a state of mind, such as fraud, libel, or malicious prosecution. It is well settled that a corporation may be liable in all those actions. Further, the question in this case has in substance been decided by Channell J in *Pearks, Gunston and Tee Ltd v Ward* [1902] 2 KB 1, 11, 12. Taking the principle of the Act into consideration, there is no reason why in s 20(6), '"person" should not include corporation'. There was ample evidence, on the facts as stated in the special case, that the company, by the only people who could act or speak or think for it had done both these things, and I can see nothing in any of the authorities to which we have been referred which requires us to say that a company is incapable of being found guilty of the offences with which the respondent company was charged. The case must go back to the justices with an intimation of our opinion to this effect, and for their determination of the facts.

MacNaghten J, in giving his judgment, having referred to the background of the case, continued ([1944] 1 KB at 156):

It is true that a corporation can only have knowledge and form an intention through its human agents, but circumstances may be such that the knowledge and intention of the agent must be imputed to the body corporate. Mr Carey Evans says that, although a body corporate may be capable of having knowledge and also of forming an intention, it cannot have a *mens rea*. If the responsible agent of a company, acting within the scope of his authority, puts forward on its behalf a document which he knows to be false and by which he intends to deceive, I apprehend that, according to the authorities that my Lord has cited, his knowledge and intention must be imputed to the company. In my opinion, the submission made to the justices that the respondents could not in law be capable of a criminal intention cannot be sustained.

In his judgment, Hallet J, at 157, said:

> With regard to the liability of a body corporate for torts or crimes, a perusal of the case shows, to my mind, that there has been a development in the attitude of the courts arising from the large part played in modern times by limited liability companies. At one time the existence, and later the extent and conditions of such a body's liability in tort was a matter of doubt, due partly to the theoretical difficulty of imputing wrongful acts or omissions to a fictitious person, and it required a long series of decisions to clear up the position. Similarly, the liability of a body corporate for crimes was at one time a matter of doubt, partly owing to the theoretical difficulty of imputing a criminal intention to a fictitious person and partly to technical difficulties of procedure. Procedure has received attention from the legislature, as for instance, in s 33 of the Criminal Justice Act 1925, and the theoretical difficulty of imputing criminal intention is no longer felt to the same extent.

Hallet J then referred to the passage in the speech from Lord Blackburn in the *Pharmaceutical Society* case (1880) 5 App Cas 857, 870, to which I have already referred. He then referred to *Tyler's* case [1891] 2 QB 588, 594, 597 and quoted from the judgment of Bowen LJ in these terms:

> I take it, therefore, to be clear that in the ordinary case of a duty imposed by statute, if the breach of the statute is a disobedience to the law, punishable in the case of a private person by indictment, the offending corporation cannot escape from the consequences which would follow in the case of an individual by showing that they are a corporation.

Kay LJ said:

> Therefore, that part of the argument, that, in as much as a criminal act involves a *mens rea*, a corporation which has no *mens rea* at all is not subject to criminal proceedings in any case, is untenable.

Applying the observations of Bowen LJ to the present case, if every person desiring to obtain petrol coupons has a duty imposed by statutory authority to furnish honest information, it seems strange and undesirable that a body corporate desiring to obtain petrol coupons and furnishing dishonest information for that purpose should be able to escape the liability which would be incurred in like case by a private person. In *R v Cory Brothers* Finlay J referred to certain types of crime, in respect of which, according to old authorities by which he considered himself to be bound, a body corporate could not be held to be liable. It may be that those authorities will require reconsideration some day in the light of the development to which I have already referred, but for present purposes it is sufficient to notice that the offences now in question are of a fundamentally different character.

The *Kent and Sussex Contractors* case was followed in point of time by *ICR Haulage Ltd* [1944] 1 KB 551. The headnote reads: 'An indictment for a common law conspiracy to defraud will lie against a limited company'. In the course of argument, all the cases previously referred to were cited. The judgment of the court was delivered by Stable J who, at 553, said:

> It was conceded by counsel for the company that a limited company can be indicted for some criminal offences, and it was conceded by counsel for the Crown that there were some criminal offences for which a limited company cannot be indicted. The controversy centred round the question where and on what principle the line must be drawn and on which side of the line an indictment such as the present one falls. Counsel for the company contended

that the true principle was that an indictment against a limited company for any offence involving as an essential ingredient *mens rea* in the restricted sense of a dishonest or criminal mind, must be bad for the reason that a company, not being a natural person, cannot have a mind honest or otherwise, and that, consequently, though in certain circumstances it is civilly liable for the fraud of its officers, agents or servants, it is immune from criminal process. Counsel for the Crown contended that a limited company, like any other entity recognised by the law, can as a general rule be indicted for its criminal acts which from the very necessity of the case must be performed by human agency and which in given circumstances become the acts of the company, and that for this purpose there was no distinction between an intention or other function of the mind and any form of activity. The offences for which a limited company cannot be indicted are, it was argued, exceptions to the general rule arising from the limitations which must inevitably attach to an artificial entity, such as a company. Included in these exceptions are the cases in which, from its very nature, the offence cannot be committed by a corporation, as, for example, perjury, an offence which cannot be vicariously committed, or bigamy, an offence which a limited company, not being a natural person, cannot commit vicariously or otherwise. A further exception, but for a different reason, comprises offences of which murder is an example, where the only punishment the court can impose is corporal, the basis on which this exception rests being that the court will not stultify itself by embarking on a trial in which, if a verdict of guilty is returned, no effective order by way of sentence can be made. In our judgment these contentions of the Crown are substantially sound, and the existence of these exceptions, and it may be that there are others, is by no means inconsistent with the general rule.

The earlier cases were then reviewed, including the *Cory Brothers* case (above) of which Stable J had this to say at 556:

The learned judge advanced no reasons of his own for quashing the whole indictment, simply expressing the view that he felt compelled by the authorities to which his attention had been called to decide as he did. It is sufficient, in our judgment, to say that, inasmuch as that case was decided before the decision in *DPP v Kent and Sussex Contractors* [1944] 1 KB 146, and that *Chuter v Freeth and Pocock Ltd* [1911] 2 KB 832 was not cited at all, if the matter came before the court today, the result might well be different. As was pointed out by Hallet J in the *Kent and Sussex Contractors* case (at 157), this is a breach of the law to which the attitude of the courts has in the passage of time undergone a process of development.

He concluded the judgment of the court at 559 by saying:

Where in any particular case there is evidence to go to a jury that the criminal act of an agent, including his state of mind, intention, knowledge or belief is the act of the company, and, in cases where the presiding judge so rules, whether the jury are satisfied that it has been proved, must depend on the nature of the charge, the relative position of the officer or agent, and the other relevant facts and circumstances of the case.

This passage, as will be seen, was criticised as being too widely stated by Lord Reid in the *Tesco Stores* case, of which more anon. The last of the trio of 1944 cases was *Moore v Bresler* [1944] 2 All ER 515, which again was a decision of the Divisional Court and merely followed the decision in the earlier two cases. While these developments were occurring in the field of criminal law, in a line of civil cases commencing in 1915 the courts were striving to identify the true basis upon which the mind of a corporation might be identified. Those three cases are *Lennard's Carrying Company Limited v Asiatic Petroleum Company Limited* [1915] AC 705, *Bolton Engineering Company Limited v TJ Graham* [1957] 1 QB 159 and *Tesco Supermarkets Limited v Nattrass* [1972] AC 153. *Lennard's* case concerned an application by the plaintiffs to limit their liability under the terms of s 502 of the Merchant Shipping Act 1894 which might only be achieved if it could be demonstrated that the casualty occurred without the actual fault or privity of the owner or managing agent. *Bolton's* case involved consideration of the intention of the company to occupy certain premises for the purposes of its business and turned on the interpretation of s 30(1)(g) of the Landlord and Tenant Act 1954. The *Tesco Supermarkets* case turned on the interpretation of s 20 of the Trade Descriptions Act 1968 and whether the manager of a particular retail branch of the company was another person for the purposes of its statutory defence under s 24 of the same Act. Although it is no doubt apt to say, as Mr Kentridge submitted, that the decision in each of these cases turned on the construction of the particular statute that was there in question, it is nevertheless possible to deduce from those cases the principles which the mental element that a corporation must possess if it is to be convicted of a crime where a 'mental element' must be found. Indeed, when this was put to Mr Kentridge he was not minded to dissent from that broad proposition, but he sought to qualify the concession by submitting that the principle did not assist in answering the further question whether or not the particular crime was one which could be committed by a corporation. From these three cases, coupled possibly with the dictum of Lord Blackburn in the *Pharmaceutical Society* case, the origins of what has become known to writers of jurisprudence as the 'identification doctrine' can be found. The *Tesco* case deserves particular scrutiny for within certain of the speeches in that case are to be found the limits of this doctrine of identification. It is this doctrine which is fundamental to the true basis of corporate criminal liability which has now to be accepted is an integral part of the law of England. At 170D, of the report in the *Tesco* case, Lord Reid said:

> Where a limited company is the employer difficult questions do arise in a wide variety of circumstances in deciding which of its officers or servants is to be identified with the company so that his guilt is the guilt of the company.

> I must start by considering the nature of the personality which by a fiction the law attributes to a corporation. A living person has a mind which can have knowledge or intention or be negligent and he has hands to carry out his intentions. A corporation has none of these; it must act through living persons, though not always one or the same person. Then the person who acts is not speaking or acting for the company. He is acting as the company and his mind which directs his acts is the mind of the company. There is no question of the company being vicariously liable. He is not acting as a servant, representative, agent or delegate. He is an embodiment of the company or, one could say, he hears and speaks through the persona of the company, within his appropriate sphere, and his mind is the mind of the company. If it is a guilty mind then that guilt is the guilt of the company. It must be a question of law whether, once the facts have been ascertained, a person in doing particular things is to

be regarded as the company or merely as the company's servant or agent. In that case any liability of the company can only be a statutory vicarious liability.

In *Lennard's Carrying Co Ltd v Asiatic Petroleum Co Ltd* [1915] AC 705 the question was whether damage had occurred without the 'actual fault or privity' of the owner of the ship. The owners were a company. The fault was that of the registered managing owner who managed the ship on behalf of the owners and it was held that the company could not dissociate itself from him so as to say that there was not actual fault or privity on the part of the company. Viscount Haldane said at 713:

> For if Mr Lennard was the directing mind of the company, then his action must, unless a corporation is not to be liable at all, have been an action which was the action of the company itself within the meaning of s 502 ... It must be upon the true construction of that section in such a case as the present one that the fault or privity is the fault or privity of somebody who is not merely a servant or agent for whom the company is liable upon the footing *respondeat superior*, but somebody for whom the company is liable because his action is the very action of the company itself.

Reference is frequently made to the judgment of Denning LJ as he then was in *HL Bolton (Engineering) Co Ltd v TJ Graham and Sons Ltd* [1957] 1 QB 159. He said, at 172:

> A company may in many ways be likened to a human body. It has a brain and nerve centre which controls what it does. It also has hands which hold the tools and act in accordance with directions from the centre. Some of the people in the company are mere servants and agents who are nothing more than hands to do work and cannot be said to represent the mind or will. Others are directors and managers who represent the directing mind and will of the company, and control what it does. The state of mind of these managers is the state of mind of the company and is treated by the law as such.

> In that case the directors of the company only met once a year: they left the management of the business to others, and it was the intention of those managers which was imputed to the company. I think that was right. There have been attempts to apply Lord Denning's words to all servants of a company whose work is brain work, or who exercise some managerial discretion under the direction of superior officers of the company. I do not think that Lord Denning intended to refer to them. He only referred to those who 'represent the directing mind and will of the company, and control what it does'.

> I think that it is right for this reason. Normally the board of directors, the managing director and perhaps other superior officers of a company carry out the functions of management and speak and act as the company. Their subordinates do not. They carry out orders from above and it can make no difference that they are given some measure of discretion. But the board of directors may delegate some part of their functions of management giving to their delegate full discretion to act independently of instructions from them. I see no difficulty in holding that they have thereby put such a delegate in their place so that within the scope of the delegation he can act as the company. It may not always be easy to draw the line but there are cases in which the line must be drawn.

And he cites *Lennard's* case above. Later in his judgment at 173 Lord Reid continues:

> In the next two cases a company was accused and it was held liable for the fault of a superior officer. In *DPP v Kent and Sussex Contractors Ltd* [1944] KB 146 he was the transport manager. In *ICR Haulage Limited* [1944] KB 551 it was held that a company can be guilty of common law conspiracy. The act of the managing director was held to be the act of the company.

I think that a passage in the judgment, and this is one to which I earlier referred, is too widely stated, at 559 of the report, and he then cites the passage I have already cited and continues:

> This may have been influenced by the erroneous views expressed in the two *Hammett* cases. I think that the true view is that the judge must direct the jury that if they find certain facts proved then as a matter of law they must find that the criminal act of the officer, servant or agent including his state of mind, intention, knowledge or belief is the act of the company. I have already dealt with the considerations to be applied in deciding when such a person can and when he cannot be identified with the company. I do not see how the nature of the charge can make any difference. If the guilty man was in law identifiable with the company then whether his offence was serious or venial his act was the act of the company but if he was not so identifiable then no act of his, serious or otherwise, was the act of the company itself.

Lord Diplock in his speech at 198H said:

> A corporation is an abstraction. It is incapable itself of doing any physical act or being in any state of mind. Yet in law it is a person capable of exercising legal rights and of being subject to legal liabilities which may involve ascribing to it not only physical acts which are in reality done by a natural person on its behalf but also the mental state in which that person did them. In civil law, apart from certain statutory duties, this presents no conceptual difficulties. Under the law of agency the physical acts and state of mind of the agent are in law ascribed to the principal, and if the agent is a natural person it matters not whether the principal is also a natural person or a mere legal abstraction. *Qui facit per alium facit per se; qui cogitat per alium cogitat per se.*

> But there are some civil liabilities imposed by statute which, exceptionally, exclude the concept of vicarious liability of a principal for the physical acts and state of mind of his agent; and the concept has no general application in the field of criminal law. To constitute a criminal offence, a physical act done by any person must generally be done by him in some reprehensible state of mind. Save in cases of strict liability where a criminal statute, exceptionally, makes the doing of an act a crime irrespective of the state of mind in which it is done, criminal law regards a person as responsible for his own crimes only. It does not recognise the liability of a principal for the criminal acts of his agent; because it does not ascribe to him his agent's state of mind. *Qui peccat per alium peccat per se* is not a maxim of criminal law.

> In my view, therefore, the question: what natural persons are to be treated in law as being the company for the purpose of acts done in the course of its business including the taking of precautions and the exercise of due diligence to avoid the commission of a criminal offence, is to be found by identifying those natural persons who by the memorandum and articles of association or

as a result of action taken by directors, or by the company in general meeting pursuant to the articles, are entrusted with the exercise of the powers of the company.

This test is in conformity with the classic statement of Viscount Haldane LC in *Lennard's Carrying Co Ltd v Asiatic Petroleum Co Ltd* [1915] AC 705. The relevant statute in that case, although not a criminal statute, was *in pari materia*, for it provided for a defence to a civil liability which excluded the concept of vicarious liability of a principal for the physical acts and state of mind of his agent.

There has been in recent years a tendency to extract from Denning LJ's judgment in *HL Bolton (Engineering) Co Ltd v TJ Graham and Sons Ltd* [1957] 1 QB 159, 172, 173 his vivid metaphor about the 'brains and nerve centre' of a company as contrasted with its hands, and to treat this dichotomy, and not the articles of association, as laying down the test of whether or not a particular person is to be regarded in law as being the company itself when performing duties which a statute imposes on the company.

In the case in which this metaphor was first used Denning LJ was dealing with acts and intentions of directors of the company in whom the powers of the company were vested under its articles of association.

Since the 19th century there has been a huge increase in the numbers and activities of corporations whether nationalised, municipal or commercial, which enter the private lives of all or most of 'men and subjects' in a diversity of ways. A clear case can be made for imputing to such corporations social duties including the duty not to offend all relevant parts of the criminal law. By tracing the history of the cases decided by the English courts over the period of the last 150 years, it can be seen how, first tentatively and finally confidently, the courts have been able to ascribe to corporations a 'mind' which is generally one of the essential ingredients of common law and statutory offences. Indeed, it can be seen that in many Acts of Parliament the same concept has been embraced. The parliamentary approach is, perhaps, exemplified by s 18 of the Theft Act 1968 which provides for directors and managers of a limited company to be rendered liable to conviction if an offence under s 15, 16 or 17 of the Act are proved to have been committed – and I quote – 'with the consent, connivance of any director, manager, secretary ... purporting to act in such capacity, then such director, manager or secretary shall be guilty of the offence'. Once a state of mind could be effectively attributed to a corporation, all that remained was to determine the means by which that state of mind could be ascertained and imputed to a non-natural person. That done, the obstacle to the acceptance of general criminal liability of a corporation was overcome. *Cessante ratione legis, cessat ipsa lex*. As some of the decisions in other common law countries indicate, there is nothing essentially incongruous in the notion that a corporation should be guilty of an offence of unlawful killing. I find unpersuasive the argument of the company that the old definitions of homicide positively exclude the liability of a non-natural person to conviction of an offence of manslaughter. Any crime, in order to be justiciable must have been committed by or through the agency of a human being. Consequently, the inclusion in the definition of the expression 'human being' as the author of the killing was either tautologous or, as I think more probable, intended to differentiate those cases of death in which a human being played no direct part and which would have led to forfeiture of the inanimate, or if animate non-human, object which caused the death (deodand) from those in which the cause of death was initiated by human activity albeit the instrument of death was inanimate or if animate non-human. I am confident that the expression 'human being' in the definition of homicide was not intended to have the effect of words of limitation as might have been the case had it been found in some Act of Parliament or legal deed. It is not for me to attempt to set the limits of corporate liability for criminal offences in English law. Examples of other crimes which may or may not be committed by corporations will, no doubt, be decided on a case by case basis in conformity with the manner in which the common law has adapted itself in the past. Suffice it that where a corporation, through the controlling mind of one of its agents, does an act which fulfils the prerequisites of the crime of manslaughter, it is properly indictable for the crime of manslaughter ...

... Before concluding and because of its topical and potential relevance to the instant prosecution, I should refer to *Her Majesty's Coroner for East Kent ex p Spooner* (1989) 88 Cr App R 10, a decision of the Divisional Court in relation to proceedings before the coroner arising from the selfsame events as have led to this prosecution. It is only necessary to refer to one short passage in the judgment of Bingham LJ to explain why reference has not been made to it earlier in these reasons. At p 16 of the report Bingham LJ said:

> The arguments which were deployed and elaborated before the coroner have, in substance, been repeated with great cogency and skill before us. The first question is whether a corporation can be indicted for manslaughter. The coroner originally ruled that it could not. In the course of argument in this court we indicated at an early stage that we were prepared to assume for the purposes of this hearing that it could. As a result the question has not been fully argued and I have not found it necessary to reach a final conclusion. I am, however, tentatively of opinion that on appropriate facts the *mens rea* required for manslaughter can be established against a corporation. I see no reason in principle why such a charge should not be established. I am therefore tentatively of opinion that the coroner's original ruling was wrong, and indeed I would need considerable persuasion to reach the conclusion that it was correct.

> But that is not the end of the matter because the coroner clearly adhered to his substantial ruling even on the assumption that a company could in principle be guilty of manslaughter. The coroner made it clear that he was of opinion that the evidence which he had considered was not capable of supporting the conclusion that those who represented the directing mind and will of the company and controlled what it did had been guilty of conduct amounting to manslaughter.

> I am not persuaded that that is a conclusion which is or may be wrong. Nothing was, in my judgment, said by Sheen J of by way of concession before him which undermines that conclusion. It is important to bear in mind an important distinction. A company may be vicariously liable for the negligent acts and omissions of its servants and agents, but for a company to be criminally liable for manslaughter – on the assumption I am making that such a crime exists – it is required that the *mens rea* and the *actus reus* of manslaughter should be established not against those who acted for or in the

name of the company but against those who were to be identified as the embodiment of the company itself. The coroner formed the view that there was no such case fit to be left to the jury against the company. I see no reason to disagree. I would add that I see no sustainable case in manslaughter against the directors who are named either ...

Notes and queries

1   When does a duty of care arise? Where D is acting pursuant to a contract, or a relationship of reliance has been created, there may be little difficulty in identifying a duty of care. Other situations will be less clear cut. Hence in *R v Khan (Rungzabe)* (1998) *The Times*, 7 April, the Court of Appeal left open the question of whether a drug dealer owed any duty of care to a 15 year old girl to whom he had supplied heroin. The facts indicated that the girl fell into a coma at the appellant's premises and died after he had supplied her with the drugs and left her on her own. Could it be said that the appellant had created a reliance relationship given the girl's age and the fact that she was on the appellant's property with his permission?

2   In *R v Singh* [1999] Crim LR 582, the Court of Appeal more readily identified a duty of care where the appellants, a landlord and a gas fitter, had their convictions for killing by gross negligence upheld, following the death of one of the landlord's tenants from carbon monoxide poisoning.

Codification and law reform proposals

In May 2000 the Home Office published the Government's proposals for reform of the law relating to involuntary manslaughter, including corporate liability for manslaughter: *Reforming the Law on Involuntary Manslaughter: The Government's Proposals*. The proposals are based upon the Law Commission Report *Legislating the Criminal Code: Involuntary Manslaughter* (Law Com 237), although, as will be seen, there are a number of differences between what was proposed by the Law Commission and what is now being put forward by the Home Office.

The Home Office report has appended to it a draft 'Involuntary Homicide Bill' – the key provisions of which are as follows:

1(1) A person who, by his conduct causes the death of another is guilty of reckless killing if –

(a) he is aware of a risk that his conduct will cause death or serious injury; and

(b) it is unreasonable for him to take that risk having regard to the circumstances as he knows or believes them to be.

(2) A person guilty of reckless killing is liable on conviction on indictment to imprisonment for life.

2(1) A person who by his conduct causes the death of another is guilty of killing by gross carelessness if –

(a) a risk that his conduct will cause death or serious injury would be caused;

(b) he is capable of appreciating that risk at the material time; and

(c) either –

    (i) his conduct falls far below what can reasonably be expected of him in the circumstances; or

    (ii) he intends by his conduct to cause some injury or is aware of, and unreasonably takes the risk that it may do so.

(2) There shall be attributed to the person referred to in subsection (1)(a) above –

    (a) knowledge of any relevant facts which the accused is shown to have at the material time; and

    (b) any skill or experience professed by him.

(3) In determining for the purposes of subsection (1)(c)(i) above what can reasonably be expected of the accused regard shall be had to the circumstances of which he can be expected to be aware, to any circumstances shown to be within his knowledge and to any other matter relevant for assessing his conduct at the material time.

(4) Subsection (1)(c)(ii) above applies only if the conduct causing, or intended to cause, the injury constitutes an offence.

...

3   A person is not guilty of an offence under sections 1 or 2 above by reason of an omission unless the omission is in breach of a duty at common law.

4(1) A corporation is guilty of corporate killing if –

    (a) a management failure by the corporation is the cause or one of the causes of a person's death; and

    (b) that failure constitutes conduct falling far below what can reasonably be expected of the corporation in the circumstances.

(2) For the purposes of subsection (1) above –

    (a) there is a management failure by a Corporation if the way in which its activities are managed or organised fails to ensure the health and safety of persons employed in or affected by those activities; and

    (b) such a failure may be regarded as a cause of a person's death notwithstanding that the immediate cause is the act or omission of an individual.

(3) A corporation guilty of an offence under this section is liable on conviction on indictment to a fine.

(4) No individual shall be convicted of aiding, abetting, counselling or procuring an offence under this section but without prejudice to an individual being guilty of any other offence in respect of the death in question.

(5) This section does not prelude a corporation bring guilty of an offence under section 1 or 2 above.

(6) This section applies if the injury resulting in death is sustained in England and Wales ...

5(1) A court before which a corporation is convicted of corporate killing may, subject to subsection (2) below, order the corporation to take such steps, within such time, as the order specifies for remedying the failure in question and any matter which appears to the court to have resulted from the failure and been the cause or one of the causes of the death.

(2) No such order shall be made except on an application by the prosecution specifying the terms of the proposed order, and the order, if any, made by the court shall be made on such terms (whether those proposed or others) as the court considers appropriate having regard to any representations made and any evidence adduced, in relation to that matter by the prosecution or on behalf of the corporation.

...

(5) A corporation which fails to comply with an order under this section is guilty of an offence ...

...

8(1) In this Act 'injury' means –

(a) physical injury, including pain, unconsciousness or other impairment of a person's physical condition., or

(b) impairment of a person's mental health ....

Chapter 2 of the report explains the rationale for the new offences of reckless and careless killing:

2.2 The Law Commission set out in their Report No 237: *Involuntary Manslaughter* the reasons why there are problems with the law at present (paragraphs 1.4–1.8 refer). The most significant problem is that having one offence of (involuntary) manslaughter to cover such a wide range of mischief presents judges with significant problems, particularly when determining what the appropriate sentence should be in any given case. The Law Commission therefore proposed the creation of two separate offences of unintentional killing ie 'reckless killing' and 'killing by gross carelessness' with the main difference being the fault elements.

Reckless killing

2.3 A person commits reckless killing if: his or her conduct causes the death of another; he or she is aware of a risk that his or her conduct will cause death or serious injury, and it is unreasonable for him or her to take that risk having regard to the circumstances as he or she knows or believes them to be.

Killing by gross carelessness

2.4 A person commits killing by gross carelessness if:

- his or her conduct causes the death of another;

- a risk that his or her conduct will cause death or serious injury would be obvious to a reasonable person in his or her position;

- he or she is capable of appreciating that risk at this material time (but did not in fact do so)

and either

- his or her conduct falls far below what can reasonably be expected in the circumstances;

- or he or she intends by his or her conduct to cause some injury, or is aware of, and unreasonably takes, the risk that it may do so, and the conduct causing (or intended to cause) the injury constitutes an offence.

2.5 The Government accepts that the width of the present offence of involuntary manslaughter does cause problems on sentencing and it is inappropriate that types of conduct which vary widely in terms of fault should all carry the same descriptive label. We accept that an offence resulting from a failure to appreciate the consequences of an action is less culpable than acting in full knowledge of a risk.

The Government therefore accepts the Law Commission's proposals in respect of the offences of reckless killing and killing by gross negligence.

2.6 The Law Commission also took the view that it was wrong in principle that a person should be convicted for causing death when the offender was only aware of a risk of some injury. The merits of this argument are, however, less straightforward and are discussed further under the next section headed 'A Proposed Third Offence'.

A PROPOSED THIRD OFFENCE

Should liability for involuntary homicide exist where the intention was only to cause some injury but resulting death was unforeseeable?

Present law

2.7 At present under the law on 'dangerous and unlawful act manslaughter' a person who intends or is reckless as to whether he commits what would otherwise be a relatively minor assault will be guilty of manslaughter if the victim dies as a result, even though death was quite unforeseeable. So, if for instance, in the course of a fight A gives B a small cut – but A had no way of knowing B had haemophilia – and B then dies, under the law at present A would be liable under 'dangerous and unlawful act manslaughter'.

Position of the Law Commission in Report No 237

2.8 As previously noted the Law Commission were very concerned that the present law allows a person to be convicted of an offence carrying a maximum penalty of life imprisonment not because of his mental intention but because of an 'unlucky' event. The Law Commission considered that it was wrong in principle for the law to hold a person responsible for causing a result that he did not intend or foresee, and which could not even have been foreseeable by a reasonable person observing his conduct.

2.9 The Law Commission therefore took the view that an accused who is culpable for causing some harm is not sufficiently blameworthy to be held liable for the unforeseeable consequence of death. Using the example cited above, under the Law Commission's proposals because death was unforeseeable, A could only be charged with a comparatively minor non-fatal offence.

2.10 In their report the Law Commission acknowledged that responses to their own Consultation Paper were divided on this issue. The Government is concerned that the Law Commission's approach would mean that behaviour which may be regarded as seriously culpable because it involves intentional or reckless criminal behaviour which results in death, would no longer attract an appropriate charge. It might be viewed as unacceptable if the law permitted only a charge of assault where that assault had in fact resulted in death. The Government considers that there is an argument that anyone who embarks on a course of illegal violence has to accept the consequences of his act, even if the final consequences are unforeseeable. This is in line with our proposals contained in our Consultation Paper *Violence: Reforming the Offences Against the Person Act 1861* where we said that offences should be based on motivation and outcome. In addition, perhaps liability in such circumstances should exist, as being essential for the protection of the public.

A third offence

2.11 The Government therefore considers that there may be a need for an additional homicide offence to cover a situation where:

- a person by his or her conduct causes the death of another;
- he or she intended to or was reckless as to whether some injury was caused; and
- the conduct causing, or intended to cause, the injury constitutes an offence.

2.12 Furthermore the Government considers that any additional offence ought to cover recklessness, not least because the Law Commission considered that this type of conscious risk taking, which involved the possibility of serious injury or death, was the most reprehensible form of homicide, on the very borders of murder. Moreover, if liability were to arise in such circumstances it would appear to be in line with the Law Commission's report and the Government's proposals on Offences Against the Person which makes individuals liable for causing intentional or reckless injury to another. However, the Government sees no case for extending the offence to instances where death is caused by someone who, through gross carelessness, causes someone to be injured and, totally unforeseeably, death results.

2.13 The Law Commission have made it dear that they are against any such offence in principle because it would not be linked to what a person could possibly have foreseen. They argue that people should not be punished for 'the lottery effect'.

...

MAXIMUM SENTENCES

Reckless killing

2.15 The Law Commission recommended that the offence of reckless killing, where the offender is aware that an action involves a risk of causing death and it was unreasonable for him to take that action having regard to the circumstances as he knew or believed them to be, should attract the same maximum penalty as at present ie life imprisonment. The Government accepts this recommendation.

Killing by gross carelessness

2.16 The Law Commission took the view that killing by gross carelessness is less serious than reckless killing because, unlike reckless killing, this offence would be committed in circumstances where the offender did not appreciate at the time that there was a risk of death or serious injury. The Commission therefore considered it ought to attract a lesser determinate sentence of between 10 and 15 years. Based on their analysis of several Court of Appeal decisions on involuntary manslaughter the Law Commission suggested a 14 year maximum might be appropriate but came to no final conclusion.

2.17   The Government accepts the Law Commission's view that the offence of killing by gross carelessness warrants a maximum sentence short of life imprisonment. The best parallel appears to be those offences of causing death by dangerous driving and causing death while under the influence of alcohol or drugs, which both carry a maximum penalty of 10 years' imprisonment. The Government is anxious that there should be consistency in sentencing. As the proposed offence of killing by gross carelessness and causing death by dangerous driving use very similar language, if the maximum sentences were different it could lead to the courts awarding different sentences for essentially the same wrongdoing, which would clearly be undesirable. The Government therefore proposes a maximum penalty for the offence of killing by gross carelessness of 10 years imprisonment.

Death resulting from intentional/reckless causing of minor injury

2.18   Paragraphs 2.7 to 2.13 set out the arguments for and against an offence where death results but was unforeseeable and all the offender intended to cause or recklessly caused was some minor injury.

2.19   Under existing legislation, courts have imposed long determinate sentences (sometimes in excess of 5 years) in cases where a relatively minor assault has resulted unexpectedly in death. It can be argued that the proposed third homicide offence is more serious than killing by gross carelessness because – unlike the latter – in this instance the offender must have intentionally or recklessly have caused some injury to another. In other words there might be some circumstances where this conduct is as blameworthy or more blameworthy than killing by gross carelessness. If this view is accepted, the appropriate maximum penalty would be approximately the same as the proposed maximum for killing by gross carelessness ie 10 years. In practice the maximum penalties the courts have actually imposed for offences which would fall within the third homicide offence are in the range of 10 to 14 years.

2.20   However, this offence is similar to that in clause 3 of the Government's draft Offences Against the Person (OATP) Bill of intentionally or recklessly causing injury to another with the totally unforeseen consequence that death results. While the Law Commission have made it clear why they do not consider there should be a third offence at all (see paragraph 2.13 above), they have commented that if there were be one, they believe the maximum penalty should be five years – the maximum for the appropriate non-fatal offence. The Government is inclined to accept the proposition underlying the Law Commission proposals that the degree of culpability is, and should be, less in circumstances where the outcome could not have been foreseen. However, it should be borne in mind that the third offence may relate to situations where there was an intentional act, rather than a careless act as in killing by gross carelessness. In some circumstances an intentional act which unforseeably results in death eg an assault may be viewed as more culpable than a grossly careless act which results in death. The Government therefore considers that the maximum penalty for the offence of causing death when the only intention was to cause minor injury should be between 5 and not more than 10 years imprisonment – possibly 7 years.

In relation to death resulting from the transmission of disease, the report, in Chapter 4, observes:

4.1 At present if there is an unlawful killing and proof of an intention to kill or to cause serious injury, together with the absence of any mitigating circumstances (such as provocation or diminished responsibility, which would reduce the offence to one of voluntary manslaughter), then the offence is one of murder. It is arguable that where death is caused by an intentional transmission of a disease and which was carried out with the intention to kill or cause serious injury, it could amount to murder. However, the Law Commissions report on involuntary manslaughter deals only with those situations where there is an unlawful killing, where the accused has some blameworthy mental state less than an intention to kill or cause grievous bodily harm.

4.2 Although the Law Commission's paper is not explicit on the point, they have expressed the view that if someone recklessly or through gross carelessness infects a person with a disease and that person subsequently dies, the perpetrator could and should be liable for manslaughter. The Government doubts that a prosecution could succeed at present where a disease:

- is sexually transmitted;
- is passed between mother and child during pregnancy, at birth or by breastfeeding; or
- is passed in any other manner between individuals in circumstances in which there is not a professional duty of care involved, or the disease has not been transmitted because of a criminal act that carried it with it a risk of injury.

However, we accept that, as a general rule, such behaviour resulting in death should be capable of being prosecuted – but that there needs to be an exception where the transmission occurs directly between individuals.

Approach taken in the Home Office Consultation Paper on Offences Against the Person

4.3 In the Home Office consultation paper on Offences Against the Person (OATP) we made it dear that the Government proposed that only the *intentional* transmission of disease should be a criminal offence. This was in part because the Government is determined to ensure that people are not deterred from coming forward for diagnostic tests and treatment and for advice about the prevention of sexually transmitted diseases such as HIV or hepatitis B and that someone with such a disease should have no reason to fear prosecution, unless they deliberately set out to cause serious injury to another by passing on the disease. The Government remains wholly committed to this approach. In addition, the Government does not believe that it would he right or appropriate to criminalise the reckless transmission of normally minor illnesses, even though they could have potentially serious consequences for those vulnerable to infection.

4.4 However, in the OATP paper the way this was achieved was by specifically excluding the transmission of disease (all forms of transmission) from the meaning of 'causing death or serious injury' except where there was a deliberate intention to cause such death or serious injury. This Paper deals only with those instances where there is some mental state less than a deliberate intention to cause death or serious injury If therefore we were simply to adopt the same solution as that in the OATP paper, it would mean that all transmissions of disease would have to be specifically excluded from the meaning of 'causing death or serious injury' in the draft Bill on Involuntary Homicide.

4.5 This would mean, for instance, that a baker could sell pies which he knew were infected and which might result in death, without being liable in the criminal law for manslaughter (he could perhaps be charged with an offence of selling food not complying with food safety requirements). It would also mean that where a patient is infected with a disease due to obvious recklessness or gross negligence by a health care worker, the latter could not, unlike at present, be held liable in the criminal law. It might also exclude from prosecution for homicide those who contaminate food for blackmail purposes if a victim subsequently died. The Government views this as unacceptable.

Why direct transmission of disease should be excepted

4.6 While the Government considers that the grossly careless or reckless transmission of disease which results in death should generally be caught by the criminal law, we do not consider that this should apply where the transmission occurs directly between one individual and another. This would mean that *liability would not arise under these proposals where transmission occurs in the course of sexual activity,* nor, for example, would it if the disease was passed on between mother and child during pregnancy, at birth or by breastfeeding. There are a number of reasons for this approach.

4.7 The first is the need, mentioned above, to ensure that people are not deterred from being tested, treated for or advised about the prevention of sexually transmitted diseases. The second is that the Government does not believe that the reckless or gross careless transmission of disease between two individuals, such as in the course of sexual activity or between mother and child could presently be prosecuted and we wish to preserve what we believe to be the present position in law. Although, the Law Commission have expressed a contrary view, we are unaware of any successful prosecution (perhaps because of the difficulty of proving a causal link).

4.8 Thirdly, as a matter of general principle, the Government does not consider it appropriate for the criminal law to intervene in the most private activity between individuals unless the most reprehensible form of behaviour is involved ie where there is a deliberate intention to inflict bodily harm on another individual. It could, in any event, be contrary to the European Convention on Human Rights to do so. Fourthly, the Government has no wish to give people false reassurances about what the criminal law can and cannot protect them from. We regard it as crucial to encourage all individuals to take responsibility for their own health and welfare.

Where even the reckless/grossly careless direct transmission of disease between individuals should be caught

4.9 The Government's general approach is that while the grossly careless or reckless transmission of disease which results in death should generally be caught by the criminal law, this should not apply where the transmission occurs directly between one individual and another. However, the Government considers that there needs to be an exception to this which would have the effect of preserving the current position in law. This is where the person who transmits the disease owes a professional duty of care to the other.

So, for instance, if a health care worker with an infectious disease is so reckless or grossly careless that he or she accidentally transmits the infection to a patient, the Government takes the view that individuals in such circumstances should be culpable in law. The fact that the transmission takes places between two individuals seems incidental to the fact that it is because of a failure to observe a professional duty of care towards the victim that the latter has become infected.

How to achieve liability in circumstances the Government considers appropriate

4.10   The need to except the direct transmission of disease between individuals from the general proposition that the reckless/grossly careless transmission of disease should be culpable, means that we cannot simply include the transmission of disease within the meaning of 'causing death or serious injury'. This is because it would lead to a situation where a person who recklessly or carelessly passed on an infection in the course of sexual intercourse which resulted in the death of the person to whom the disease was passed on *could* he prosecuted. That is unacceptable because of the reasons given above.

4.11   The simple inclusion of the transmission of disease within the meaning of 'causing death or serious injury' would also lead to unacceptable inconsistencies in the law. Under our draft OATP Bill, where A recklessly infects B who suffers a serious injury as a result, no charge would lie against A. If we were to include the transmission of disease within the proposals on involuntary homicide without qualification, if B died in such circumstances, a charge of reckless killing could successfully be brought. So, for instance, if someone recklessly transmitted hepatitis B to another person which could lead to that persons death in 15 years time, they could not be prosecuted until the person died of the transmitted disease.

The Government's proposed solution

4.12   The Government considers that the draft Involuntary Homicide Bill needs to be amended to reflect that:

- generally those who recklessly or through gross carelessness pass on a disease which results in death should be potentially liable except that

- liability should not arise for the transmission of a disease where it occurs directly between one individual and another unless

- a professional duty of care is owed by the person who transmitted the disease to the person to whom it was passed on to.

4.13   This would mean *that the position for those who have or may acquire a sexually transmitted disease has not changed from the position set out in the Government's consultation paper on OATP* – only those who intentionally transmit disease in the course of sexual activity with the intention to kill or cause serious injury could be liable in the criminal law. If the proposal for dealing with the unintentional transmission of disease in the Involuntary Homicide Bill were accepted, the Government would amend its OATP Bill in the same way.

...

4.14   The Government takes the view that the third possible offence of individual involuntary homicide should not include the transmission of disease. This is because although that offence involves a situation where some injury was intended or there was recklessness as to whether injury is caused, the injury is not serious and death is totally unforeseeable. The Government did not and does not wish to potentially criminalise the transmission of normally minor diseases which could be fatal to susceptible individuals. To allow the transmission of disease to be included under this offence could make someone potentially liable where no one could have foreseen that the disease would be transmitted or that serious injury or death would result.

The issue of corporate liability for manslaughter is considered in Chapter 3 of the report:

3.1.1 In considering the potential liability of corporations in the criminal law, the Government has borne in mind the reason why corporations were established in the first place. The vital success and benefits that have been brought, to the country through incorporated organisations and the continuing need for the successful operation of commercial organisations – especially companies incorporated under successive Companies Acts – to be able to function as corporations. In particular, in civil law, the great advantage of incorporation has been and is that it allows for a liability limited to the assets held by the corporation itself, which is considered to be a separate legal entity, from those individuals who run it.

Present position on corporate liability for involuntary manslaughter

3.1.2 The limited liability provided by incorporation does not at present protect individuals from criminal liability, nor will the proposed new offence of corporate killing of itself either increase or decrease individual liability. It will merely provide a different basis of criminal liability for corporations.

3.1.3 The governing principle in English law on the criminal liability of companies is that those who control or manage the affairs of the company are regarded as embodying the company itself. Before a company can he convicted of manslaughter, an individual who can be 'identified as the embodiment of the company itself' must first be shown himself to have been guilty of manslaughter. Only if the individual who is the embodiment of the company is found guilty can the company be convicted. Where there is insufficient evidence to convict the individual, any prosecution of the company must fail. This principle is often referred to as the 'identification' doctrine.

3.1.4 There can often be great difficulty in identifying an individual who is the embodiment of the company *and who is culpable*. The problem becomes greater with larger companies which may have a more diffuse structure, where overall responsibility for safety matters in a company can be unclear and no one individual may have that responsibility. In such circumstances it may be impossible to identify specific individuals who may be properly regarded as representing the directing mind of the company and who so possess the requisite *mens rea* (mental state) to be guilty of manslaughter: in such circumstances, no criminal liability can be attributed to the company itself

The need for reform

3.1.5 There have been a number of disasters in recent years which have evoked demands for the use of the law of manslaughter and failures to successfully prosecute have led to an apparent perception among the public that the law dealing with corporate manslaughter is inadequate. This perception has been heightened because the disasters have been followed by inquiries which have found corporate bodies at fault and meriting very serious criticism and in some instances there have been successful prosecutions for offences under the Health and Safety at Work etc Act 1974, as amended ('the 1974 Act'). These disasters have included:

- *The Herald of Free Enterprise* disaster on 6 March 1987 where the jury at the inquest returned verdicts of unlawful killing in 187 cases and the DPP launched prosecutions against 7 individuals and the company. The case failed because the various acts of negligence could not be aggregated and attributed to any individual who was a directing mind.

- The King's Cross fire on 18 November 1987 which claimed 31 lives. London Underground were criticised for not guarding against the unpredictability of the fire and because no one person was charged with overall responsibility.

- The Clapham rail crash on 12 December 1988 which caused 35 deaths and nearly 5 injuries. British Rail were criticised for allowing working practices which were 'positively dangerous' and it was said that the errors went much wider and higher in the organisation than merely to be the responsibility of those who were working that day.

- The Southall rail crash on 19 September 1997 which resulted in 7 deaths and 151 injuries. In July 1999 Great Western Trains (GWT) pleaded guilty to contravening Section 3(1) of the 1974 Act in that they failed to ensure that the public were not exposed to risks to their health and safety. They received a record fine for a health and safety offence of £1.5 million for what Mr Justice Scott Baker described as 'a serious fault of senior management'. The judge had earlier ruled that a charge of manslaughter could not succeed because of the need to identify some person whose gross negligence was that of GWT itself.

3.1.6 It is not only the law's apparent inability to hold accountable companies responsible for large scale disasters which led the Law Commission to propose that the law be reformed. The result of the operation of the identification doctrine has meant that there have been only a few prosecutions of a corporation for manslaughter in the history of English law and only three successful prosecutions ... all of these were small companies.

3.1.7 The Law Commission also considered that there were many cases of deaths in factories and building sites where death could and should have been avoided. Furthermore, in response to the Law Commissions Consultation Paper No 135 on involuntary manslaughter, the Health and Safety Executive (HSE) commented that death or personal injury resulting from a major disaster is rarely due to the negligence of a single individual. In the majority of such cases the disaster is caused as a result of the failure of systems controlling the risk with the carelessness of individuals being a contributing factor.

The Law Commission's proposals

3.1.8 The Law Commission considered that it would benefit both companies and the enforcement authorities, if companies were to take health and safety issues more seriously. The Commission considered a number of approaches for extending corporate liability but concluded by recommending that:

1   There should be a special offence of *corporate killing*, broadly corresponding to the proposed offence of killing by gross carelessness.

2   The corporate offence should (like the individual offence) be committed only where the corporation's conduct in causing death fell far below what could reasonably be expected.

3   The corporate offence should not (unlike the individual offence) requite that the risk he obvious or that the defendant be capable of appreciating the risk.

4   A death should be regarded as having been caused by the conduct of the corporation if it is caused by a 'management failure', so that the way in which its activities are managed or organised fads to ensure the health and safety of persons employed in or affected by its activities.

5   Such a failure will be regarded as a cause of a persons death even if the immediate cause is the act or omission of an individual.

6   That individuals within a company could still be liable for the offences of reckless killing and killing by gross carelessness as well as the company being liable for the offence of corporate killing.

3.1.9 The Government considers that while there may prove to be difficulties in proving a 'management failure' there is a need to restore public confidence that companies responsible for loss of life can properly be held accountable in law. The Government believes the creation of a new offence of corporate killing would give useful emphasis to the seriousness of health and safety offences and would give force to the need to consider health and safety as a management issue.

In relation to the transmission of disease and corporate killing the report observes at para 4.15:

Although this issue was not specifically addressed in the Law Commission's paper, where there is a company whose:

- management failure has been one of the causes of a person's death and

- the management failure constitutes conduct falling far below what can reasonably be expected of the corporation in the circumstances

there seems no reason, in principle, why liability should not arise where the management failure led to the transmission of a disease which led to death. Liability could arise if the management failure was a cause, rather than the sole cause of death and therefore inclusion of transmission of disease could have an impact on the number of cases of corporate killing that might be brought. However, in view of the definition of corporate killing, that conduct must have fallen far below what could be expected of the corporation in the circumstances, the prospect of a large number of cases based on the transmission of disease should not be overstated.

...

3.2.1 The Law Commission proposed that the offence of corporate killing should not apply to a corporation sole but to any other body corporate, wherever incorporated, irrespective of the legal means by which they were incorporated ... This definition would catch the main category of body which the offence of corporate killing is intended to cover, namely corporations formed for the purpose of securing a profit for their members.

It would also bring within the ambit of the offence other corporations such as local authorities, incorporated charities, educational institutes and incorporated clubs.

Unincorporated bodies

3.2.2 The Law Commission accepted that many unincorporated bodies are in practice indistinguishable from corporations and, arguably, their liability for fatal accidents should be the same. However, they concluded that it would be inappropriate to recommend that the offence of corporate killing extend to unincorporated bodies at present. Unincorporated associations which include partnerships, trusts (including hospital trusts), registered Friendly Societies and registered trade unions, would not be caught by the Commission's proposals. The Law Commission took the view that under the existing law, individuals who comprise an unincorporated body may be criminally liable for manslaughter – as for any other offence – and so the question of attributing the conduct of individuals to the body itself does not arise. If the Law Commission's proposal in this respect were accepted, it would not alter the present position of such organisations.

A preferred alternative: 'undertakings'

3.2.3 The Law Commission's proposals are straightforward and would bring within the ambit of the offence the main subject of public concern – companies incorporated under the Companies Act. However, as the Law Commission acknowledged, there is often little difference in practice between an incorporated body and an unincorporated association. The Law Commission's proposal could therefore lead to an inconsistency of approach and these distinctions might appear arbitrary. The Law Commission recommended limiting the proposals to corporations in the first instance before deciding whether to extend it further.

3.2.4 An alternative is that the offence could apply to 'undertakings' as used in the 1974 Act. Although an 'undertaking' is not specifically defined in the 1974 Act, HSE have relied on the definition provided in the 1960 Local Employment Act where it is described as 'any trade or business or other activity providing employment'. This definition could avoid many of the inconsistencies which would occur if the offence was applied to corporations aggregate but not to other similar bodies.

3.2.5 Clearly, the use of the word 'undertaking' would greatly broaden the scope of the offence. It would encompass a range of bodies which have not been classified as corporations aggregate including schools, hospital trusts, partnerships and unincorporated charities, as well as one or two person businesses eg self-employed gas fitters. In effect the offence of corporate killing could apply to all employing organisations. We estimate that this would mean that *a total of 3.5 million enterprises might become potentially liable to the offence of corporate killing*. However, such organisations are already liable to the provisions of the 1974 Act.

3.2.6 The Law Commission did not consider in detail which bodies might fall outside the definition of a corporation have commented that they would like the offence of corporate killing to be as inclusive as possible. The Government too does not wish to create artificial barriers between incorporated and non-incorporated bodies, nor would we wish to see enterprises deterred from incorporation, which might be the case if the offence only applied to corporations. The Government is therefore inclined to the view that the offence should apply to all 'undertakings' rather than just corporations.

Government and quasi-government bodies

3.2.7 There are a number of government bodies and quasi government bodies which at present are able to claim immunity from prosecution because they are said to be acting as a servant or agent of the Crown. The question of whether an organisation can claim Crown immunity depends upon the degree of control which the Crown, through its Ministers, can exercise over it in the performance of its duties. The fact that a Minister of the Crown appoints the members of such a body, is entitled to require them to give him information and is entitled to give them directions of a general nature does not make the corporation his agent. The inference that a corporation acts on behalf of the Crown will be more readily drawn where its functions are not commercial but are connected with matters, such as the defence of the realm, which are essentially the province of government.

3.2.8 If the Government were to change the law to introduce the offence of corporate killing, then Crown bodies could not be prosecuted for the offence. However, government and quasi-government bodies should be held accountable where death occurs as a result of a management failure. The Government therefore proposes to adopt an approach similar in effect to that taken in the Food Safety Act 1990. That Act applies the same standards to the Crown, thus requiring Crown bodies to allow access to relevant enforcement agencies, but rather than applying criminal liability provides for the courts to make a declaration of non-compliance with statutory requirements, which requires immediate action on the part of the Crown body to rectify the shortcoming identified. The Government will consider to what extent this procedure ought to apply to the emergency services.

...

3.4.1 The Government expects that, while any undertaking could he liable (in the event of the creation of a new offence of 'corporate killing') for the offence, most prosecutions would be against companies (that is, business associations incorporated under the Companies Act 1985 or under previous companies legislation or under similar legislation overseas). Our concern is to ensure that, in the event of a finding of corporate killing being made against a company, there should be sufficient enforcement powers to ensure that the judgement of the court could be given effect.

3.4.2 In accordance with the Law Commission's recommendations, the Government proposes that undertakings, including corporations, should be liable to a fine and subject, as necessary, to orders to take remedial action. The Government is, however, concerned both that there should not be scope for avoidance measures by unscrupulous companies or directors, and that enforcement action should act as a real deterrent, even in large companies and within groups of companies. Our concern lies principally in the four following areas.

(i)   Enforcement against companies not incorporated in Great Britain ...

(ii) Liability within groups of companies ...

(iii) Enforcement action against a director or other company officer ...

...

3.4.7 It is a fundamental principle of company law that, from the date of incorporation, a company is an artificial legal person with rights and duties distinct from its members or directors. However, as explained earlier, the limited liability provided by incorporation does not at present protect individuals from criminal liability nor will the proposed new offence of corporate killing of itself either increase or decrease individual liability. It will merely provide a different basis of criminal liability for corporations.

3.4.8 The Law Commission's report argued that punitive sanctions on company officers would not be appropriate in relation to its proposed corporate killing offence, since the offence would deliberately stress the liability of the corporation as opposed to its individual officers. The Government is, however, concerned that this approach:

(a)   could fail to provide a sufficient deterrent, particularly in large or wealthy companies or within groups of companies; and

(b)   would not prevent culpable individuals from setting up new businesses or managing other companies or businesses, thereby leaving the public vulnerable to the consequences of similar conduct in future by the same individuals.

3.4.9 The Government is therefore inclined to the view that action against individual directors or officers might be justified even in cases where a company found guilty of corporate killing could pay the fine imposed by the court and/or comply with a remedial order. The Law Commission has indicated in the course of the Government's consideration of its report that it would also support action against culpable directors or officers of the company.

...

3.4.10 The ground for disqualification would not be that of causing death but of contributing to the management failure resulting in death. It was envisaged that a separate proceeding would usually be brought against individual officer(s) following the conviction of the company ... in some cases ... it might however, be appropriate to move straight to a disqualification proceeding. Disqualification would normally be for a limited period of time, but might, in the most serious cases, be unlimited. If a person acted in contravention of a disqualification order, he would be liable to imprisonment or an unlimited fine, or both.

3.4.11 The Government believes that this would be an effective and proportionate response. The disqualification of culpable company directors from a role in managing any undertaking would make evasion of a disqualification order much more difficult; the Government would not, for example, wish to see a person disqualified from acting as a director under such circumstances joining a partnership as a way of circumventing the disqualification order. It would, moreover, (1) provide a meaningful level of protection to the public and (2) provide a meaningful level of deterrent even in respect of directors of large and wealthy companies, as their personal income could be severely affected by such a disqualification order. It would also be possible to bring such proceedings against officers of the parent company or of other group companies who exercised control or influence over the management of the company which caused the death.

...

3.4.12 The Government's aim is to make undertakings more accountable in law where a person dies because of a failure on their part. If there was sufficient evidence, an individual officer could be charged with one of the new manslaughter offences ie killing by gross carelessness or reckless killing, whether or not proceedings were brought against the undertaking for the new corporate killing offence. In addition, we are proposing that, where the undertaking has been convicted of the corporate killing offence, such officers could face disqualification in separate legal proceedings commenced against them as referred to in paragraph 3.4.10 to 3.4.11 above. However, it has been argued that the public interest in encouraging officers of undertakings to take health and safety seriously is so strong that officers should face criminal sanctions in circumstances where, although the undertaking has committed the corporate offence, it is not (for whatever reason) possible to secure a conviction against them for either of the individual offences.

3.4.13 It would not be possible for an individual officer automatically to he made criminally liable on the sole basis of the conviction of an undertaking for the corporate offence. It would be necessary for him to be charged with an offence which he has committed and be given the chance to defend himself against it.

In order to go down this route, it would be necessary to create an additional criminal offence in respect of substantially contributing to the ... corporate offence, leading to the death of a person. The Government has reached no firm view on this suggestion but is using this consultation paper as an opportunity to obtain respondents' views on the possibility of creating such an offence, and if such a course were adopted, the range of penalties which should be available on that conviction and in particular, whether a court should be able to sentence individual officers to imprisonment.

...

3.6.1 If an undertaking is found guilty of corporate killing, the Government accepts the Law Commission's recommendation that the court should have the power to make remedial orders. In many cases the Government envisages that the HSE and other enforcement bodies would use their powers to issue enforcement notices as part of, or following, their investigation and in advance of any hearing. However, we also consider it would be useful if the court had the power to order remedial action either where HSE (or the other appropriate enforcement body) had not issued a notice or where such a notice had not been complied with.

3.6.2 The responsibility for drawing up the order should rest with whichever agency is prosecuting. All applications for orders in areas where an enforcement authority (such as HSE) has responsibility should be made by or in consultation with that body to ensure that the terms of the order and any steps specified by the court are reasonable, in line with enforcement policy and what the enforcement authority would regard as good practice. Both the prosecuting agency and the defence should have the opportunity to make representations or evidence regarding the application. The enforcement authority should also be given the task of checking compliance and referring matters back to the court where necessary. No new enforcement powers would he necessary to allow this approach.

Further reading

AP Simester, 'Murder, *mens rea* and the House of Lords – again' (1999) 115 LQR 17

I Dressler, 'Provocation: partial justification or partial excuse' (1988) 51 MLR 467

RD Mackay, 'The abnormality of the mind factor in diminished responsibility' [1999] Crim LR 117

H Keating, 'The Law Commission Report on Involuntary Manslaughter: the restoration of a serious crime' [1996] Crim LR 535

W Sullivan, 'Corporate killing – some Government proposals' [2001] Crim LR 31

CHAPTER 16

NON-FATAL OFFENCES AGAINST THE PERSON

The material selected for this chapter aims to cover the mainstream non-fatal offences against the person, as well as the related issue of consent to harm. Sexual offences are considered in Chapter 17. The law relating to non-fatal offences against the person is to be found in a hotchpotch of common law and statutory provisions. It is an area crying out for reform and rationalisation. Despite the existence of workable proposals for codification, there is little sign of any government having the desire to take the political initiative.

CROWN PROSECUTION CHARGING STANDARDS

In 1994 the Crown Prosecution Service published the Charging Standards used to guide prosecutors as to the appropriate charge to proceed with in cases of non-sexual, non-fatal assault. The general principles regarding charging practice provide that prosecutors should select charge(s) that 'accurately reflect the extent of the defendant's alleged involvement and responsibility, thereby allowing the courts the discretion to sentence appropriately'. In particular, the guidelines provide that:

- the choice of charges should ensure the clear and simple presentation of the case, particularly where there is more than one defendant;
- it is wrong to encourage a defendant to plead guilty to a few charges by selecting more charges than are necessary;
- it is wrong to select a more serious charge which is not supported by the evidence in order to encourage a plea of guilty to a lesser allegation.

ASSAULT AND BATTERY

In its narrow sense common assault is committed where D causes P to apprehend immediate physical violence. No physical contact is necessary. A battery is any unlawful touching of P by D. Hence, technically, no assault is committed where D hits P from the rear, although the term 'assault' is still used in its general sense of assault and battery; see *R v Lynsey* [1995] 2 All ER 654.

Fagan v Metropolitan Police Commissioner [1969] 1 QB 439 (DC)

Facts: On 31 August 1967 the appellant was reversing a motor car in Fortunegate Road, London NW10, when Police Constable David Morris directed him to drive the car forwards to the kerbside and, standing in front of the car, pointed out a suitable place in which to park. At first the appellant stopped the car too far from the kerb for the officer's liking. Morris asked him to park closer and indicated a precise spot. The appellant drove forward towards him and stopped the car with the offside wheel on Morris's left foot. 'Get off, you are on my foot', said the officer. 'Fuck you, you can wait', said the appellant. The engine of the car stopped running. Morris repeated several times 'Get off my foot'. The appellant said reluctantly, 'OK, man, OK' and then slowly turned on the ignition of the vehicle and reversed it off the officer's foot. The appellant had either turned the ignition off to stop the engine or turned it off after the engine had stopped running.

The justices at quarter sessions on those facts were left in doubt as to whether the mounting of the wheel on to the officer's foot was deliberate or accidental. They were satisfied, however, beyond all reasonable doubt that the appellant 'knowingly, provocatively and unnecessarily allowed the wheel to remain on the foot after the officer said, 'Get off, you are on my foot'. They found that on those facts an assault was proved.

James J: ... The sole question is whether the prosecution proved facts which in law amounted to an assault.

[Counsel for the appellant] ... contends that on the finding of the justices the initial mounting of the wheel could not be an assault and that the act of the wheel mounting the foot came to an end without there being any *mens rea*. It is argued that thereafter there was no act on the part of the appellant which could constitute an *actus reus* but only the omission or failure to remove the wheel as soon as he was asked. That failure, it is said, could not in law be an assault, nor could it in law provide the necessary *mens rea* to convert the original act of mounting the foot into an assault.

[Counsel for the Crown] argues that the first mounting of the foot was an *actus reus* which act continued until the moment of time at which the wheel was removed. During that continuing act, it is said, the appellant formed the necessary intention to constitute the element of *mens rea* and once that element was added to the continuing act, an assault took place ...

In our judgment, the question arising, which has been argued on general principles, falls to be decided on the facts of the particular case. An assault is any act which intentionally – or possibly recklessly – causes another person to apprehend immediate and unlawful personal violence. Although 'assault' is an independent crime and is to be treated as such, for practical purposes today 'assault' is generally synonymous with the term 'battery', and is a term used to mean the actual intended use of unlawful force to another person without his consent. On the facts of the present case, the 'assault' alleged involved a 'battery'. Where an assault involved a battery, it matters not, in our judgment, whether the battery is inflicted directly by the body of the offender or through the medium of some weapon or instrument controlled by the action of the offender. An assault may be committed by the laying of a hand on another, and the action does not cease to be an assault if it is a stick held in the hand and not the hand itself which is laid on the person of the victim. So, for our part, we see no difference in principle between the action of stepping on to a person's toe and maintaining that position and the action of driving a car on to a person's foot and sitting in the car while its position on the foot is maintained.

To constitute this offence, some intentional act must have been performed; a mere omission to act cannot amount to an assault. Without going into the question whether words alone can constitute an assault, it is clear that the words spoken by the appellant could not alone amount to an assault; they can only shed light on the appellant's action. For our part, we think that the crucial question is whether, in this case, the act of the appellant can be said to be complete and spent at the moment of time when the car wheel came to rest on the foot, or whether his act is to be regarded as a continuing act operating until the wheel was removed. In our judgment, a distinction is to be drawn between acts which are complete, though results may continue to flow, and those acts which are continuing. Once the act is complete, it cannot thereafter be said to be a threat to inflict unlawful force on the victim. If the act, as distinct from the results thereof, is a continuing act, there is a continuing threat to inflict unlawful force. If the assault involves a battery and that battery continues, there is a continuing act of assault. For an assault to be committed, both the elements of *actus reus* and *mens rea* must be present at the same time. The *actus reus* is the action causing the effect on the victim's mind: see the observations of Parke B, in *R v St George* (1840) 9 C & P 483. The *mens rea* is the intention to cause that effect. It is not necessary that *mens rea* should be present at the inception of the *actus reus*; it can be superimposed on an existing act. On the other hand, the subsequent inception of *mens rea* cannot convert an act which has been completed without *mens rea* into an assault.

In our judgment, the Willesden magistrates and quarter sessions were right in law. On the facts found, the action of the appellant may have been initially unintentional, but the time came when, knowing that the wheel was on the officer's foot, the appellant (1) remained seated in the car so that his body through the medium of the car was in contact with the officer, (2) switched off the ignition of the car, (3) maintained the wheel of the car on the foot, and (4) used words indicating the intention of keeping the wheel in that position. For our part, we cannot regard such conduct as mere omission or inactivity.

There was an act constituting a battery which at its inception was not criminal because there was no element of intention, but which became criminal from the moment the intention was formed to produce the apprehension which was flowing from the continuing act. The fallacy of the appellant's argument is that it seeks to equate the facts of this case with such a case where a motorist has accidentally run over a person and, that action having been completed, fails to assist the victim with the intent that the victim should suffer ...

Lord Parker CJ expressed agreement with James J; Lord **Bridge** delivered a dissenting judgment.

Smith v Chief Superintendent, Woking Police Station
(1983) 76 Cr App R 234 (DC)

Kerr LJ: ... In view of the question of law I must also refer shortly to the evidence on the basis of which the justices convicted. The incident happened at about 11 pm, when Miss Mooney was in her room wearing a pink, knee-length nightie. There was a bay window and a side window. The curtains were drawn but they left a gap. She saw the defendant peering in and stated that he was right up against the window. She said: 'I instantly recognised him. I was very scared, very shocked. He was there about three or four seconds. I walked backwards and could no longer see him. I turned and he was at the other window, again right against the glass. I just stood and stared at him, didn't know what to do. He was just standing there, didn't seem he was going to go away. I jumped across the bed towards the window and screamed. I was terrified, absolutely terrified. He must have seen me look at him. He moved away when I went across the bed. I looked at him for about 20 seconds at the side window. I called the police.'

Then she says that she was scared and after the incident she was very jumpy and shocked. The defendant, having first denied the incident, later admitted it and agreed that he would be scared stiff in the situation in which Miss Mooney found herself ...

It is ... common ground that the definition of an assault ... [is] 'any act which intentionally – or recklessly – causes another to apprehend immediate and unlawful violence' ... [T]here must be, on the part of the defendant, a hostile intent calculated to cause apprehension in the mind of the victim.

In the present case, on the findings which I have summarised, there was quite clearly an intention to cause fear, an intention to frighten, and that intention produced the intended effect as the result of what the defendant did, in that it did frighten and indeed terrify Miss Mooney to the extent that she screamed. It is not a case where she was merely startled or surprised or ashamed to be seen in her nightclothes; she was terrified as the result of what the defendant deliberately did, knowing and either intending or being reckless as to whether it would cause that fear in her ...

When one is in a state of terror one is very often unable to analyse precisely what one is frightened of as likely to happen next. When I say that, I am speaking of a situation such as the present, where the person who causes one to be terrified is immediately adjacent, albeit on the other side of the window ...

In the present case the defendant intended to frighten Miss Mooney and Miss Mooney was frightened. As it seems to me, there is no need for a finding that what she was frightened of, which she probably could not analyse at that moment, was some innominate terror of some potential violence. It was clearly a situation where the basis of the fear which was instilled in her was that she did not know what the defendant was going to do next, but that, whatever he might be going to do next, and sufficiently immediately for the purposes of the offence, was something of a violent nature. In effect, as it seems to me, it was wholly open to the justices to infer that her state of mind was not only that of terror, which they did find, but terror of some immediate violence ...

Words as an assault

R v Ireland; R v Burstow [1997] 4 All ER 225

In *Ireland's* case the Court of Appeal certified the following question as being of general public importance, namely:

As to whether the making of a series of silent telephone calls can amount in law to an assault.

Lord Steyn outlined the facts giving rise to the appeal in *R v Ireland* as follows:

... the appellant was convicted on his plea of guilty of three offences of assault occasioning actual bodily harm, contrary to section 47 of the Act of 1861 ... The case against Ireland was that during a period of three months in 1994 covered by the indictment he harassed three women by making repeated telephone calls to them during which he remain silent. Sometimes, he resorted to heavy breathing. The calls were mostly made at night. The case against him, which was accepted by the judge and the Court of Appeal, was that he caused his victim to suffer psychiatric illness [see extracts below relating to whether or not such harm could constitute actual bodily harm]. Ireland had a substantial record of making offensive telephone calls to women. The judge sentenced him to a total of three years imprisonment.

Lord Steyn then considered whether or not there could be an assault by words alone or by silence.

It is now necessary to consider whether the making of silent telephone calls causing psychiatric injury is capable of constituting an assault under section 47. The Court of Appeal, as constituted in the *Ireland* case, answered that question in the affirmative. There has been substantial academic criticism of the conclusion and reasoning in Ireland: see *Archbold News*, Issue 6, 12 July 1996; *Archbold's Criminal Pleading, Evidence & Practice* (1995), Supplement No 4 (1996), pp 345–47; Smith and Hogan, *Criminal Law*, 8th edn, 413; 'Assault by telephone' by Jonathan Herring [1997] CLJ 11; 'Assault' [1997] Crim LR 434, 435–36. Counsel's arguments, broadly speaking, challenged the decision in Ireland on very similar lines. Having carefully considered the literature and counsel's arguments, I have come to the conclusion that the appeal ought to be dismissed.

The starting point must be that an assault is an ingredient of the offence under section 47. It is necessary to consider the two forms which an assault may take. The first is battery, which involves the unlawful application of force by the defendant upon the victim. Usually, section 47 is used to prosecute in cases of this kind. The second form of assault is an act causing the victim to apprehend an imminent application of force upon her: see *Fagan v Metropolitan Police Commissioner* [1969] 1 QB 439, 444D–E.

One point can be disposed of, quite briefly. The Court of Appeal was not asked to consider whether silent telephone calls resulting in psychiatric injury is capable of constituting a battery. But encouraged by some academic comment it was raised before your Lordships' House. Counsel for Ireland was most economical in his argument on the point. I will try to match his economy of words. In my view it is not feasible to enlarge the generally accepted legal meaning of what is a battery to include the circumstances of a silent caller who causes psychiatric injury.

It is to assault in the form of an act causing the victim to fear an immediate application of force to her that I must turn. Counsel argued that as a matter of law an assault can never be committed by words alone and therefore it cannot be committed by silence. The premise depends on the slenderest authority, namely, an observation by Holroyd J to a jury that 'no words or singing are equivalent to an assault': *Meade's and Belt's Case* (1823) 1 Lew CC 184. The proposition that a gesture may amount to an assault, but that words can never suffice, is unrealistic and indefensible. A thing said is also a thing done. There is no reason why something said should be incapable of causing an apprehension of immediate personal violence, eg a man accosting a woman in a dark alley saying 'come with me or I will stab you.' I would, therefore, reject the proposition that an assault can never be committed by words.

That brings me to the critical question whether a silent caller may be guilty of an assault. The answer to this question seems to me to be 'yes, depending on the facts.' It involves questions of fact within the province of the jury. After all, there is no reason why a telephone caller who says to a woman in a menacing way 'I will be at your door in a minute or two' may not be guilty of an assault if he causes his victim to apprehend immediate personal violence. Take now the case of the silent caller. He intends by his silence to cause fear and he is so understood. The victim is assailed by uncertainty about his intentions. Fear may dominate her emotions, and it may be the fear that the caller's arrival at her door may be imminent. She may fear the possibility of immediate personal violence. As a matter of law the caller may be guilty of an assault: whether he is or not will depend on the circumstance and in particular on the impact of the caller's potentially menacing call or calls on the victim. Such a prosecution case under section 47 may be fit to leave to the jury. And a trial judge may, depending on the circumstances, put a common sense consideration before jury, namely what, if not the possibility of imminent personal violence, was the victim terrified about? I conclude that an assault may be committed in the particular factual circumstances which I have envisaged. For this reason I reject the submission that as a matter of law a silent telephone caller cannot ever be guilty of an offence under section 47. In these circumstances no useful purpose would be served by answering the vague certified question in *Ireland*.

Having concluded that the legal arguments advanced on behalf of Ireland on section 47 must fail, I nevertheless accept that the concept of an assault involving immediate personal violence as an ingredient of the section 47 offence is a considerable complicating factor in bringing prosecutions under it in respect of silent telephone callers and stalkers. That the least serious of the ladder of offences is difficult to apply in such cases is unfortunate. At the hearing of the appeal of Ireland attention was drawn to the Bill which is annexed to Law Commission report, *Legislating the Criminal Code: Offences Against the Person and General Principles*, Consultation Paper (Law Com 218, Cmnd 2370, 1993. Clause 4 of that Bill is intended to replace section 47. Clause 4 provides that 'A person is guilty of an offence if he intentionally or recklessly causes injury to another.' This simple and readily comprehensible provision would eliminate the problems inherent in section 47. In expressing this view I do not, however, wish to comment on the appropriateness of the definition of 'injury' in clause 18 of the Bill, and in particular the provision that 'injury' means 'impairment of a person's mental health.

Lord Hope: In this case the appellant pled guilty to three contraventions of section 47 of the Act of 1861. He admitted to having made numerous telephone calls to three women, during which he remained silent when the women answered the telephone. These calls lasted sometimes for a minute or so, and sometimes for several minutes. On some occasions they were repeated over a relatively short period. There is no doubt that this conduct was intended to distress the victims, each of whom suffered as a result from symptoms of such a kind as to amount to psychiatric injury. But, for the appellant to be guilty of an offence contrary to section 47 of the Act of 1861, he must be held to have committed an act which amounts to an assault.

Plainly there was no element of battery – although counsel for the respondent made brief submissions to the contrary – as at no time was there any kind of physical contact between the appellant and his victims. As Swinton Thomas LJ observed in the Court of Appeal [1997] QB 114, 119D, that is a fact of importance in this case. But it is not an end of the matter, because as he went on to say it has been recognised for many centuries that putting a person in fear may amount to what in law is an assault. This is reflected in the meaning which is given to the word 'assault' in *Archbold Criminal Pleading, Evidence and Practice* (1997), p 1594 paras 19–66, namely that an assault is any act by which a person intentionally or recklessly causes another to apprehend immediate and unlawful violence. This meaning is well vouched by authority: see *R v Venna* [1976] QB 421; *R v Savage* [1992] 1 AC 699, 740F, *per* Lord Ackner.

The question is whether such an act can include the making of a series of silent telephone calls. Counsel for the appellant said that such an act could not amount to an assault under any circumstances, just as words alone could not amount to an assault. He also submitted that, in order for there to be an assault, it had to be proved that what the victim apprehended was immediate and unlawful violence, not just a repetition of the telephone calls. It was not enough to show that merely that the victim was inconvenienced or afraid. He said that the Court of Appeal had fallen into error on this point, because they had proceeded on the basis that it was sufficient that when the victims lifted the telephone they were placed in immediate fear and suffered the consequences which resulted in psychiatric injury. The court had not sufficiently addressed the question whether the victims were apprehensive of immediate and unlawful violence and, if so, whether it was that apprehension which had caused them to sustain the bodily injury.

I agree that a passage in the judgment of the Court of Appeal [1997] QB 114, 122C–G suggests that they had equated the apprehension of immediate and unlawful violence with the actual psychiatric injury which was suffered by the victims. I also agree that, if this was so, it was an incorrect basis from which to proceed. But in the penultimate sentence in this passage Swinton Thomas LJ said that in the court's judgment repetitive telephone calls of this nature were likely to cause the victim to apprehend immediate and unlawful violence. Furthermore, as the appellant pled guilty to these offences, the question whether that apprehension caused the psychiatric injury did not need to be explored in evidence. The important question therefore is whether the making of a series of silent telephone calls can amount in law to an assault.

There is no clear guidance on this point either in the statute or in the authorities. On the one hand in *Meade's and Belt's Case* (1823) 1 Lew CC 184 Holroyd J said that no words or singing can amount to an assault. On the other hand in *R v Wilson* [1955] 1 WLR 493, 494 Lord Goddard CJ said that the appellant's words, 'Get out knives' would itself be an assault. The word 'assault' as used in section 47 of the Act of 1861 is not defined anywhere in that Act. The legislation appears to have been framed on the basis that the words which it used were words which everyone would understand without further explanation. In this regard the fact that the statute was enacted in the middle of the last century is of no significance. The public interest, for whose benefit it was enacted, would not be served by construing the words in a narrow or technical way. The words used are ordinary English words, which can be given their ordinary meaning in the usage of the present day. They can take account of changing circumstances both as regards medical knowledge and the means by which one person can cause bodily harm to another.

The fact is that the means by which a person of evil disposition may intentionally or recklessly cause another to apprehend immediate and unlawful violence will vary according to the circumstances. Just as it is not true to say that every blow which is struck is an assault – some blows, which would otherwise amount to battery, may be struck by accident or in jest or may otherwise be entirely justified – so also it is not true to say that mere words or gestures can never constitute an assault. It all depends on the circumstances. If the words or gestures are accompanied in their turn by gestures or by words which threaten immediate and unlawful violence, that will be sufficient for an assault. The words or gestures must be seen in their whole context.

In this case the means which the appellant used to communicate with his victims was the telephone. While he remained silent, there can be no doubt that he was intentionally communicating with them as directly as if he was present with them in the same room. But whereas for him merely to remain silent with them in the same room, where they could see him and assess his demeanour, would have been unlikely to give rise to any feelings of apprehension on their part, his silence when using the telephone in calls made to them repeatedly was an act of an entirely different character. He was using his silence as a means of conveying a message to his victims. This was that he knew who and where they were, and that his purpose in making contact with them was as malicious as it was deliberate. In my opinion silent telephone calls of this nature are just as capable as words or gestures, said or made in the presence of the victim, of causing an apprehension of immediate and unlawful violence.

CHARGING ASSAULT AND BATTERY

The offences of common assault and battery are only triable on a summary basis. Although they are offences at common law, assault and battery must be charged under s 39 of the Criminal Justice Act 1988.

DPP v Taylor; DPP v Little [1992] 1 QB 645 (DC)

The basic issue in both cases was the effect of s 39 on the offences of common assault and battery. In *Taylor*, an information had been laid by the DPP. It was argued that it could only be laid by the victim, and that s 39 did not affect the common law in this respect. In *Little*, the question was simply whether an information alleging assault and battery was bad for duplicity. In each case, the magistrates dismissed the information. The DPP's appeal in *Taylor* was allowed, but was dismissed in *Little*.

Mann LJ: Assault and battery are treated in the statute [Criminal Justice Act 1988] as separate offences. They have always been separate offences. Thus in *R v Mansfield Justices ex p Sharkey* [1985] QB 613, 627, Lord Lane CJ said:

An assault is any act by which the defendant intentionally, or recklessly, causes the victim to apprehend immediate unlawful violence. There is no need for it to proceed to physical contact. If it does, it is an assault and a battery. Assault is a crime independent of battery and it is important to remember that fact.

The resolution of the debate as to whether the offences are statutory offences cannot in my view be achieved without an examination of some history. Assault and battery were born at the common law. Prosecutions for battery are rare but prosecutions for assault are frequent. The term 'assault' has by usage come to have a meaning in practice which would not commend itself to the philologist (as to whom see Robert Goff LJ, *Collins v Wilcock* [1984] 1 WLR 1172, 1177A). In *Fagan v Metropolitan Police Commissioner* [1969] 1 QB 439 James J (with whom Lord Parker CJ entirely agreed) said, at p 444:

> Although 'assault' is an independent crime and is to be treated as such, for practical purposes today 'assault' is generally synonymous with the term 'battery' , and is a term used to mean the actual intended use of unlawful force to another person without his consent.

More recently in *R v Williams (Gladstone)* (1984) 78 Cr App R 276 Lord Lane CJ said, at p 279:

> 'Assault' in the context of this case, that is to say using the word as a convenient abbreviation for assault and battery, is an act by which the defendant, intentionally or recklessly, applies unlawful force to the complainant.

The usage has also been employed by Parliament. The Offences Against the Person Act 1861 contains a group of sections (sections 36 to 47) under the heading 'Assaults'. [In] Section 47 ... can be seen Parliament's employment of 'assault' as including the use of force for without force it would only be in a most unusual case that an assault could occasion actual bodily harm. Such a case would be that of a person who is put in such fear of force being about to be used against him, that he jumps from a high window with injurious consequences. It is now far too late to even contemplate that the familiar offence of 'actual bodily harm' is confined to unusual cases of that nature. The phrase 'common assault' must be, and in practice has long been, construed in a consistent and similar sense. The adjective 'common' serves only to differentiate from particular assaults for which specific provision is or was made, elsewhere as in section 36 (clergymen), sections 37 (magistrates), 38 (with intent to resist arrest), 39 (with intent to obstruct the sale of grain), 40 (seamen), 43 (females and boys under 14) and 47 (occasioning actual bodily harm). Specific provision can also be found in other statutes, for example, the Police Act 1964, section 51 (assaults on constables).

In *R v Harrow Justices ex p Osaseri* [1986] QB 589 this court had to consider the effect of section 47. May LJ, with whom Nolan J expressed his agreement, said at p 599:

> The phraseology of this section is much the same as that of section 61 of the same Act to which Lord Diplock referred in the first extract from his speech in *R v Courtie* [1984] AC 463, 469A. Following that authority, therefore, I think that section 47 first must be taken to have created a new statutory offence of an assault occasioning actual bodily harm and, secondly, made statutory and prescribed a penalty for the previously existing common law offence of common assault.

The reference to section 61 is to a section which had provided, in the language of its time:

> Whosoever shall be convicted of the abominable crime of buggery, committed either with mankind or with any animal, shall be liable to be kept in penal servitude for life.

Of this section and its successor, section 12(1) of the Sexual Offences Act 1956, Lord Diplock (with whose speech the other members of the House agreed) had said in *R v Courtie* [1984] AC 463, 469, the passage to which May LJ referred:

> Like its predecessor, section 61 of the Offences Against the Person Act 1861 ... this section makes statutory the previously existing common law offence of buggery without incorporating any definition of its essential factual ingredients.

In the light of this passage I would respectfully have regarded May LJ's conclusion on the effect of section 47 as having been inevitable and I agree with it. Mr Gower, who appeared for the defendant, Keith Taylor, argued that a common law offence of assault by beating survived the passing of section 47 and drew our attention to a passage in May LJ's judgment where after referring to the two statutory offences of assault created by section 47, he said, at p 601:

> If, apart from the above, there still remains on offence of common assault chargeable under the common law alone, then this too is triable only on indictment.

I note the contingent 'if' and confess that I am unable to identify the remnant. If there be one it does not affect the proposition that in 1861 common assault become a statutory offence. In my judgment battery also so became because as 'assault' encompasses a beating it is absurd to think that Parliament intended that a beating alone (for example of an unconscious or unsuspecting person) should not be within the statutory offence of assault occasioning actual bodily harm and hence also of common assault.

The second part of section 47 of the Act of 1861, that is to say the words from 'and' to the end, was repealed by section 170(2) of and Schedule 16 to the Act of 1988. I regard section 39 of the Act as, like its predecessor, making statutory the previously existing common law offences. I so regard it despite Mr Gower's argument that the section is no more than a new provision as to mode of trial ... undoubtedly section 39 is a new provision in regard to mode of trial and is thus properly describable as an amendment in the jurisdiction of criminal courts. However, to regard it as having no other effect is in my view to ignore plain language and to attribute to Parliament the extraordinary intention of repealing without re-enactment the statutory offences created by the Act of 1861. No one suggested repeal of the second part of section 47 would have revived the common law offences for it plainly would not have done: see section 16(1)(a) of the Interpretation Act 1978.

My conclusion upon the question of whether the offences of common assault and battery are statutory offences is that they are and have been such since 1861 and accordingly that they should now be charged as being 'contrary to section 39 of the Criminal Justice Act 1988'.

I turn to the question of how a charge of common assault should be formulated so as to avoid duplicity where the case is one of actual as well as apprehended unlawful force. The form which is hallowed by long use is 'did assault and beat' the victim: Stone's Justices' Manual 1991, vol 3, p 5595, para 9–90. Mr Godfrey, who appeared for the defendant, Stephen Little, described this form as 'lazy "conventional" language'. A proper language, said Mr Godfrey, would be 'assault by beating' where force had been used and 'assault by threatening' where it had not.

Although duplicity is a matter of form it is a fundamental matter of form. If an information is duplicitous the prosecutor must elect on which offence he wishes to proceed and if he does not do so the information must be dismissed. In my judgment the unusual allegation of 'assault and batter' in the information against Stephen Little was duplicitous. I cannot accept the submission of Mr Collins for the DPP that 'and batter' is to be taken as no more than 'and beat' expressed in archaic language. I think that in 1990 an informant who uses 'batter' must be taken as referring to the offence of battery rather than as employing archaic language. The word 'assault' must therefore, by virtue of the contrast with 'batter', be taken as used in its pure sense of putting in fear of force. The result is an assertion of two offences. I think the justices were right in their conclusion that the information was duplicitous.

The phrase 'assault and beat' by reference to which many thousands of people must have been convicted without objection is not directly before us. The phrase is free of the vice of a contrast with 'batter', and the event to which the charge relates is a single occasion, albeit apprehension and receipt of force may be separable by a small unit of time. I think that now may be too late to regard the formulation as objectionable. However, undeniably a more accurate form would avoid a conjunction and use a preposition. Thus 'assault by beating' would be immune from argument. Mr Collins accepted that it would be, and I think that in the future prosecutors should avoid conjunctive forms.

The Act of 1988 repealed section 42 of the Act of 1861 (see section 170(2) and Schedule 16) and the effect of section 39 is that all common assaults and batteries are now triable summarily regardless of whether the information is laid by or on behalf of the victim. The civil rights of a victim who does not authorise or lay an information himself are now safeguarded by way of an omission and substitution in sections 44 and 45 of the Act of 1861 made by the Act of 1988, section 170(1) and Schedule 15. The justices in the case of Keith Taylor do not seem to have had their attention drawn to the repeal of section 42 for otherwise they could not have dismissed the information on the basis that they did. Mr Gower at once conceded that the expressed basis could not be supported; he sought to support the dismissal on the ground that assault was not an offence 'contrary to section 39 of the Criminal Justice Act 1988' and with that argument I have dealt.

Crown Prosecution Charging Standards: Common assault
contrary to s 39 of the Criminal Justice Act 1988

4.5 Where there is a battery the defendant should be charged with 'assault by beating': *DPP v Little* [1992] 1 All ER 299.

4.6 The only factor which distinguishes common assault from assault occasioning actual bodily harm, contrary to section 47 of the Offences Against the Person Act 1861, is the degree of injury which results. Normally, aggravating factors which may be relevant to sentence and to mode of trial decisions are irrelevant when deciding whether the degree of injury justifies a charge under section 47.

4.7 Where battery results in injury, a choice of charge is available. The Code for Crown Prosecutors recognises that there will be factors which may properly lead to a decision not to prefer or continue with the gravest possible charge. Thus, although any injury can be classified as actual bodily harm, the appropriate charge will be contrary to section 39 where injuries amount to no more than the following:

- grazes;
- scratches;
- abrasions;
- minor bruising;
- swellings;
- reddening of the skin;
- superficial cuts;
- a 'black eye'.

4.8 You should always consider the injuries first and in most cases the degree of injury will determine whether the appropriate charge is section 39 or section 47. There will be borderline cases, such as where an undisplaced broken nose has resulted. When the injuries amount to no more than those described at paragraph 4.7 above, any decision to charge an offence contrary to section 47 would only be justified in the most exceptional circumstances, or where the maximum available sentence in the Magistrates' Court would be inadequate.

4.9 As common assault is not an alternative verdict to more serious offences of assault, a jury may only convict of common assault if the count has been preferred in the circumstances set out in section 40 Criminal Justice Act 1988 (see paragraph 11.6 [set out] below).

4.10 Where a charge contrary to section 47 has been preferred, the acceptance of a plea of guilty to an added count for common assault will rarely be justified in the absence of a significant change in circumstances that could not have been foreseen at the time of review.

Notes and queries

1 Although the vast majority of battery cases will involve D using force directly on P, this need not be the case. In *Haystead v DPP* [2000] 2 Cr App R 339, D was convicted under s 39 of the Criminal Justice Act 1988, where he frightened a woman into dropping her baby on the floor. The court certified the following point of law under s 1(2) of the Administration of Justice Act 1960: 'Whether the *actus reus* of the offence of battery requires that there be direct physical contact between the defendant and the complainant?' Leave to appeal to the House of Lords was refused. The same reasoning as regards indirect battery would apply if D set dogs on P to frighten him; see *R v Dume* (1987) *The Times*, 16 October.

2 The *mens rea* for both common assault and common battery is intention or (subjective) recklessness; see *R v Venna* (below).

ASSAULT RELATED OFFENCES

Secion 38 of the Offences Against the Person Act 1861

Whosoever ... shall assault any person with intent to resist or prevent the lawful apprehension or detainer of himself or of any other person for any offence, shall be guilty of [an offence], and being convicted thereof shall be liable ... to be imprisoned for any term not exceeding two years ...

For this offence to be made out, the arrest must be a lawful one. Where the arrest is carried out by a member of the public (not a police officer), this means that an arrestable offence must have been committed.

R v Self [1992] 1 WLR 657 (CA)

Garland J: ... [T]his appellant was tried on an indictment which contained three counts. Count 1 alleged that he stole a bar of chocolate (value 79p) belonging to FW Woolworth plc. Count 2 alleged that, contrary to s 38 of the Offences Against the Person Act 1861, he assaulted Stuart Michael Frost with intent to resist or prevent the lawful apprehension or detainer of himself. Count 3 alleged a similar offence against Jonathan George Mole ...

The facts quite briefly stated were as follows. The appellant was a serving police officer, a detective constable. He had been in the police force for some 17 years. On the afternoon in question in October 1990 a Mrs Stanton, who is a store detective in Woolworths in Kingston, saw the appellant pick up a bar of chocolate. He then moved on and apparently picked up some Christmas cards using both hands. The chocolate had disappeared; in fact, he had put it in his trouser pocket. He then left the store without paying.

Mrs Stanton asked Mr Frost the young sales assistant to help her. They followed the appellant out into the street and along Church Street. Mrs Stanton saw him put his hand in his pocket, take out the chocolate and throw it under a car. She actually retrieved it and said to him: 'I do not want to call the police for a bar of chocolate. Come here and come back to the store.' Mr Frost approached the appellant and said: 'You have been seen shoplifting'. The appellant became agitated, tried to leave, grabbed Mr Frost's arm and scratched it, punched him on the cheek, kicked him on the shin and then ran off with Mr Frost in pursuit.

Mr Mole came into the picture because he was in his car and saw what had happened between the appellant and Mr Frost. He got out of his car and asked Mrs Stanton if she needed any help. She said: 'Yes', so Mr Mole also ran after the appellant. During the chase the appellant jumped down a steep drop, some 10 feet or more, from a churchyard to the street below. When Mr Mole caught up with him he took hold of his wrist and there was a minor struggle. He told the appellant that he was making a citizen's arrest because he believed he had been shoplifting. The appellant struggled and apparently kicked Mr Mole just above his knee and tried to run away again. Mr Mole and Mr Frost caught up with him, there was a further struggle but in the end the appellant quietened down and there was some conversation between the persons involved. Mr Frost did say the appellant was in a very distressed condition, both physically and mentally.

When the appellant came to give his account of these matters before the jury he said that he recalled picking up the bar of chocolate in Woolworths but had no recollection of what had happened afterwards, save that he remembered looking at the Christmas cards. The chocolate was undoubtedly in his pocket when he left the store. He had forgotten about it. He had no intention of stealing it and had set off towards a bookshop. But on the way he put his hand in his pocket and realised that he had not paid for the chocolate that he found there. He then heard people running behind him and saw Mrs Stanton and Mr Frost coming and shouting and then everything closed in on him. He panicked and thought the situation looked very grave indeed. He threw the chocolate away and ran. Then Mr Frost intervened and the two scuffles with Mr Frost and Mr Mole followed.

He could not explain his actions. He felt sorry for Mr Frost and Mr Mole, who he thought had acted very properly. It should be mentioned in passing that a doctor confirmed that the appellant was at the time suffering from some degree of stress.

... There is one point central to the appeal. It is this. Since the appellant was acquitted of theft neither Mr Frost nor Mr Mole were entitled by virtue of s 24 of the Police and Criminal Evidence Act 1984 to effect a citizen's arrest. If they were not entitled to do that then this appellant could not be convicted of an assault with intent to resist or prevent the lawful apprehension or detainer of himself, that is to say his arrest.

In order to examine this proposition it is necessary of course to look closely at s 24 of the Act of 1984 ...

... Section 24 deals with powers of arrest without warrant. Subsection (1) sets out to define arrestable offences in respect of which powers of summary arrest can be exercised. Subsections (2) and (3) deal with the other qualifying offences, subsection (4) begins to set out powers of arrest in the following terms:

> Any person [and of course 'any person' means both a citizen and a constable] may arrest without a warrant: (a) anyone who is in the act of committing an arrestable offence; (b) anyone whom he has reasonable grounds for suspecting to be committing such an offence.

It is immediately apparent that that subsection is dealing with the present continuous, that is somebody in the act of committing the offence or someone that the arrester has reasonable grounds for suspecting to be committing such an offence. Subsection (5) moves on to the past, indeed the perfect, tense:

> Where an arrestable offence has been committed, any person [both citizen and constable] may arrest without a warrant: (a) anyone who is guilty of the offence; (b) anyone whom he has reasonable grounds for suspecting to be guilty of it.

One asks, guilty of what? The answer is, guilty of the arrestable offence which has been committed.

Then by contrast subsection (6) deals with a constable's powers of arrest which are very much wider than those of the citizen. It provides:

> Where a constable has reasonable grounds for suspecting that an arrestable offence has been committed, he may arrest without a warrant anyone whom he has reasonable grounds for suspecting to be guilty of the offence.

Thus there are doubly reasonable grounds for suspecting, both as to the commission of the offence and the person who has committed it.

Subsection (7) again deals with constables' powers and this is in anticipation of an offence. It provides:

A constable may arrest without a warrant: (a) anyone who is about to commit an arrestable offence; (b) anyone whom he has reasonable grounds for suspecting to be about to commit an arrestable offence.

Then s 25 goes on to deal with general arrest conditions otherwise than for arrestable offences ...

... [I]n the judgment of this court, the words of s 24 do not admit of argument. Subsection (5) makes it abundantly clear that the powers of arrest without a warrant where an arrestable offence has been committed require as a condition precedent an offence committed. If subsequently there is an acquittal of the alleged offence no offence has been committed. The power to arrest is confined to the person guilty of the offence or anyone who the person making the arrest has reasonable grounds for suspecting to be guilty of it. But of course if he is not guilty there can be no valid suspicion ...

If it is necessary to go further, one contrasts the words of subsection (5) with subsection (6), the very much wider powers given to a constable who has reasonable grounds for suspecting that an arrestable offence has been committed ...

... The words of the statute are clear and applying those words to this case there was no arrestable offence committed. It necessarily follows that the two offences under s 38 of the Offences Against the Person Act 1861 could not be committed because there was no power to apprehend or detain the appellant ...

R v Lee [2000] Crim LR 991 (CA)

The appellant had resisted arrest having been tested positive for driving with excess alcohol. Following conviction for assault with intent to resist lawful apprehension contrary to s 38 of the Offences Against the Persons Act 1861, he appealed on the basis that the trial judge had failed to direct the jury that there would be no liability where the appellant had honestly, but mistakenly, believed that there were no lawful grounds for his arrest.

Held: The appeal was dismissed. There was no authority for the proposition that the prosecution had to prove that the appellant knew or believed the arrest to be lawful. Rose LJ illustrated the point by citing the *obiter* statement of Talfourd J in *R v Bentley* (1850) 4 Cox CC 406 (at p 408) where he observed:

I think that to support a charge of resisting lawful apprehension, it is enough that the prisoner is lawfully apprehended, and it is his determination to resist it. If the apprehension is in point of fact lawful, we are not permitted to consider the question, whether or not he believed it to be so, because that would lead to infinite niceties of discrimination. The rule is not, that a man is always presumed to know the law, but that no man shall be excused for an unlawful act from his ignorance of the law. It was the prisoner's duty, what ever might be his consciousness of innocence, to go to the station house and hear the precise accusation against him. He is not to erect a tribunal in his own mind to decide whether he was legally arrested or not. He was taken into custody by an officer of the law, and it was his duty to obey the law.

Hence, where a police constable could exercise his power to arrest on reasonable suspicion, a suspect could not lawfully resist that arrest because he mistakenly but honestly believed that a constable did not have the necessary reasonable suspicion.

Crown Prosecution Charging Standards: Assault with intent to resist arrest, contrary to s 38 of the Act

6.3 A charge contrary to section 38 may properly be used for assaults on persons other than police officers, for example store detectives, who may be trying to apprehend or detain an offender.

6.4 When a police officer is assaulted, a charge under section 89(1) will often be more appropriate unless there is clear evidence of an intent to resist apprehension or prevent detainer. Unlike section 89(1), a charge under section 38 is triable on indictment and may therefore be coupled with other offences to be tried on indictment.

...

Section 89 of the Police Act 1996

(1) Any person who assaults a constable in the execution of his duty, or a person assisting a constable in the execution of his duty, shall be guilty of an offence and liable on summary conviction to imprisonment for a term not exceeding six months or to a fine not exceeding [£5,000] or to both.

(2) Any person who resists or wilfully obstructs a constable in the execution of his duty, or a person assisting a constable in the execution of his duty, shall be guilty of an offence and liable on summary conviction to imprisonment for a term not exceeding one month or to a fine not exceeding [£1,000] or to both.

The provisions of the Police Act 1996 consolidate provisions in the Police Act 1964. The elements of the offence under s 89(1) are:

(a) an assault;

(b) on a police officer;

(c) who is acting in the execution of his duty.

It does not matter that the defendant did not realise that the person he assaulted was a police officer, although this would be good mitigation and would result in a lesser punishment for the assault.

The elements of the offence under s 89(2) are: (a) obstruction; (b) of a police officer; (c) who is acting in the execution of his duty. For the meaning of 'assault', see above.

Hinchliffe v Sheldon [1955] 1 WLR 1207 (DC)

Facts: The appellant was the son of the licensee of an inn. On returning to the inn one night, at about 11.17 pm, he found that police officers wished to enter the premises as they suspected that the licensee was committing an offence against s 100 of the Licensing Act 1953. The appellant thereupon shouted warnings to the licensee, who did not open the door to the police officers until 11.25 pm. The licensee was not found to be committing any offence. The appellant was charged with wilfully obstructing a constable when in the execution of his duty.

> **Lord Goddard CJ**: ... 'Obstructing' means, for this purpose, making it more difficult for the police to carry out their duties. It is quite obvious that the appellant was detaining the police while giving a warning; he was making it more difficult for the police to get certain entry into the premises, and the justices were entitled to find as they did ...

For an offence under s 89 of the Police Act 1996, the police officer must have been acting in the execution of his or her duty.

Rice v Connolly [1966] 2 QB 414 (DC)

Facts: The defendant appeared to a police constable to have been acting suspiciously in an area where there had been a number of break-ins during the same night. He was asked several times for his full name and address, which he refused to give, and when asked to accompany the police constable to a police box, declined to do so, unless arrested.

> **Lord Parker CJ**: ... What the prosecution have to prove is that there was an obstructing of a constable; that the constable was at the time acting in the execution of his duty and that the person obstructing did so wilfully. To carry the matter a little further, it is in my view clear that 'obstruct' under [s 89(2) of the Police Act 1996], is the doing of any act which makes it more difficult for the police to carry out their duty. That description of obstructing I take from *Hinchliffe v Sheldon* [1955] 1 WLR 1207. It is also in my judgment clear that it is part of the obligations and duties of a police constable to take all steps which appear to him necessary for keeping the peace, for preventing crime or for protecting property from criminal injury. There is no exhaustive definition of the powers and obligations of the police, but they are at least those, and they would further include the duty to detect crime and to bring an offender to justice.
>
> Pausing there, it seems to me quite clear that the defendant was making it more difficult for the police to carry out their duties, and that the police at the time and throughout were acting in accordance with their duties. The only remaining ingredient, and the one upon which in my judgment this case revolves, is whether the obstructing of which the defendant was guilty was a wilful obstruction. 'Wilful' in this context not only in my judgment means 'intentional' but something which is done without lawful excuse, and that indeed is conceded by Mr Skinner, who appears for the prosecution case. Accordingly, the sole question here is whether the defendant had a lawful excuse for refusing to answer the questions put to him. In my judgment he had. It seems to me quite clear that though every citizen has a moral duty or, if you like, a social duty to assist the police, there is no legal duty to that effect, and indeed the whole basis of the common law is the right of the individual to refuse to answer questions put to him by persons in authority, and to refuse to accompany those in authority to any particular place; short, of course, of arrest ...
>
> In my judgment there is all the difference in the world between deliberately telling a false story – something which on no view a citizen has a right to do – and

preserving silence or refusing to answer – something which he has every right to do. Accordingly, in my judgment, looked upon in that perfectly general way, it was not shown that the refusal of the defendant to answer the questions or to accompany the police officer in the first instance to the police box was an obstruction without lawful excuse ...

R v Fennell (1970) 54 Cr App R 451 (DC)

Facts: The appellant was convicted of assaulting a constable in the execution of his duty contrary to [s 89(1) of the Police Act 1996]. His defence was that he had used force to rescue his son from police custody, which was in fact lawful but which the appellant honestly and reasonably believed to be unlawful.

Widgery LJ: ... It was accepted in the court below that, if the arrest had been, in fact, unlawful, the appellant would have been justified in using reasonable force to secure the release of his son. This proposition has not been argued before us and we will assume, without deciding it, that it is correct ... [Counsel for the appellant] then contended that ... a father who used force to effect the release of his son from custody was justified in so doing if he honestly believed on reasonable grounds that (contrary to the fact) the arrest was unlawful.

We do not accept that submission. The law jealously scrutinises all claims to justify the use of force and will not readily recognise new ones. Where a person honestly and reasonably believes that he or his child is in imminent danger of injury, it would be unjust if he were to be deprived of the right to use reasonable force by way of defence merely because he had made some genuine mistake of fact. On the other hand, if the child is in police custody and not in imminent danger of injury there is no urgency of the kind which requires an immediate decision and a father who forcibly releases the child does so at his peril. If in fact the arrest proves to be lawful, the father's use of force cannot be justified ...

Coffin and Another v Smith and Another (1980) 71 Cr App R 221 (DC)

Donaldson LJ: ... The defendants were both teenagers. The offence is alleged to have taken place in February 1978 ...

The main facts emerge from the evidence of Police Constable Coffin. He stated that at 11.45 pm on 3 February 1978, he went to Newhaven Boys' Club with Woman Police Constable Whitney. He requested people to leave the premises. Some did so, but congregated outside the premises by the front door. The defendants were amongst them. He asked them to move on two occasions. He said that the defendant Smith made no attempt to move and was unsteady, his eyes were glazed. The witness believed him to be drunk. He again told Smith to move and Smith replied 'Fuck off, pig'. The defendant Hogsden intervened and said 'Fuck off, bastards. Leave him alone'. Both defendants then walked off. But Smith came back in an aggressive manner. The witness stated that the defendant Smith aimed a punch at him which struck him in the chest. The witness then arrested Smith for assault and put him in the police car. Whilst he was in the police car the defendant Hogsden opened the car door and attempted to remove Smith from the car. Hogsden lashed out with her foot at Woman Police Constable Whitney who was attempting to control her. Smith was then put into another car. Hogsden then struggled with Police Constable Coffin, tore buttons from his jacket and kicked him twice in the chest.

The police had been called to the boys' club by the youth leader who wished to ensure that various boys left, because there was to be some form of entertainment later in the evening to which only a limited number were invited.

The justices considered the question whether these police officers were acting in the execution of their duty, that being the essential ingredient of the offence under [s 89 of the Police Act 1996] and they decided that there was no case to answer ...

In a word a police officer's duty is to be a keeper of the peace and to take all necessary steps with that in view. These officers, just like the ordinary officer on the beat, were attending a place where they thought that their presence would assist in the keeping of the peace ...

... Let me answer the specific questions which the justices ask in their case, which are numerous: 'Were we right in holding that when assisting the youth leader to eject the defendants and others from the Youth Club the police officers were not acting in the execution of their duty?' My answer is that they were wrong, but it is irrelevant, because there was a break, and this was a separate incident.

'Were we right in holding that when the police officers requested the defendant Smith to "move on" they were not acting in the execution of their duty?' I think they were wrong, the officers were plainly acting in the execution of their duty, their duty being to keep the peace.

'Were we right in holding that when the defendant Smith punched Police Constable Coffin, the said constable was not acting in the execution of his duty?' They were wrong for the same reason.

'Were we right in holding that when Police Constable Coffin arrested the defendant Smith he was not acting in the execution of his duty?' They were not right. There had been a very plain breach of the peace personally experienced by the police constable. He was fully entitled to arrest and he was doing so in the execution of his duty.

'Were we right in holding that when Woman Police Constable Whitney was kicked by the defendant Hogsden, the said constable was not acting in the execution of her duty?' No, they were wrong, for the same reasons.

'Were we right in holding that when Police Constable Coffin was kicked by the defendant Hogsden, the said constable was not acting in the execution of his duty?' No, they were wrong, for the same reasons ...

Riley v DPP (1989) 91 Cr App R 14 (DC)

[*Facts*: Extract from case stated:] The justices found the following facts: (a) at about 6.10 pm on 19 February 1988 officers McDade, Farndon, Martin, Barnett and Nicholas were summoned to the home of the defendant at 31 Walton Road, Manor Park, London E12 to search for and arrest one Andrew Riley, the younger brother of the defendant; (b) the door of the house was opened by the defendant. The officers explained that they believed that Andrew Riley was hiding in the house and that they wanted to enter and arrest him. They were allowed in without any protestation by the defendant; (c) McDade and Barnett wished to search the bedrooms which were located on the first floor of the house. They were accompanied by the defendant who imposed a condition that only one officer could enter any of the bedrooms to conduct the search as he feared that any more would leave the rooms in a state of disarray. Other officers searched the remaining bedrooms, namely those of Andrew Riley and Stanley Riley senior (the father of the defendant). Apart from expressing his concern that the officers should leave the bedrooms in a tidy condition Stanley Riley senior did not object to the officers continuing their search of his house. The remaining officers who had accompanied McDade and Barnett and officers who had not been identified at the trial searched the ground floor; (d) McDade was allowed to search the defendant's bedroom and while he was doing so the defendant stood in the entrance of the doorway facing the landing and face to face with Barnett. At that moment an officer on the ground floor shouted that Andrew Riley had been found. On hearing this the defendant pushed past Barnett and made his way to the stairs only to be confronted by Farndon who stood in his way. The other officers and Stanley Riley senior stopped whatever they were doing and made their way to the landing area of the first floor and generally stood there observing as they did the arrest of Andrew Riley; (e) the defendant then attempted to get past Farndon and in so doing he caused Farndon to momentarily lose his balance. Farndon quickly regained his balance and was then joined by McDade who had squeezed past the defendant and positioned himself alongside Farndon. The defendant became agitated and shouted, 'Where are you fucking taking him?' McDade said, 'You can't go down there. Andrew has been arrested, just stay there for a moment.' The defendant ignored this instruction and attempted to get between the officers and was promptly arrested for obstruction. He was then taken into the street where he was cautioned but made no intelligible reply; (f) Martin then appeared on the scene and assisted McDade in ushering the defendant to the waiting police van. As they attempted to get him into the van he raised his foot and wedged it on the step of the van and pushed back. After much pushing and shoving the defendant was forced into the van falling on his stomach as he entered. McDade got into the van while Martin remained on the ground leaning forward but retaining his grip on the defendant; (g) as a consequence of this thrashing about the defendant's elbow struck McDade's upper arm which resulted in McDade suffering a bruise. Martin got into the van and attempted to take a firmer hold of the defendant whereupon the defendant deliberately bit his left thumb. The defendant was restrained from further movement and conveyed to Forest Gate police station where he was formally charged with the offences.

Watkins LJ: ... If police officers are invited into premises by an occupier or other person authorised so to do, who has been told by them the reason for their entry, as was undoubtedly the fact here, then in our view they are lawfully on the premises. If, whilst there, they effect an arrest, that may or may not be lawful, depending on whether the officers have a warrant or can bring themselves within the provisions of s 24, or possibly s 25, of the 1984 Act. These sections provide for arrest without warrant for arrestable and other offences, and general arrest conditions. Reverting to s 17, it is our opinion that its provisions give a right to police officers to enter and search a house in the absence of consent by the occupier, subject of course to compliance with the terms of that section by the police officers concerned.

In the present case the justices found, and in our judgment were entitled to, that the officers were lawfully in the house. Logically the next question is, was the arrest of Andrew Riley lawful, and the officers engaged in it therefore acting in execution of their duty? If the arrest was lawful, it simply could not be argued, as in fact it was, that the appellant's intervention was in opposition to an unlawful arrest. Unfortunately there is nothing in the case stated which informs us as to whether or not the justices were told of the reason for the arrest of Andrew Riley. True it is that the defendant was not told.

If, as we must assume from what the case stated both does and does not inform us, the justices were not told of the reason for the arrest of Andrew Riley, it follows that they could not have known whether the officers were executing a warrant for his arrest, that he was alleged to be guilty of an arrestable offence or that the officers had reasonable grounds for suspecting that he was guilty of an arrestable offence. It may have been, had the facts been known, that the officers had grounds for effecting a general arrest within s 25. But there is, as we have said, simply no evidence of the officers' reasons, whatever they were, for arresting Andrew Riley. Thus plainly the justices were in no position to tell whether the arresting officers were, in the course of arrest, acting in the execution of their duty.

The Crown's failure to lead evidence as to that inevitably caused a failure by them, in our view, to establish the lawfulness of the arrest of Andrew Riley and consequently that the officers were acting in the execution of their duty.

In the light of that can it nevertheless be said that Farndon and McDade lawfully arrested the defendant, and whether Martin was in any event acting in the execution of his duty when his thumb was bitten by the defendant?

In order for there to be a lawful arrest for wilful obstruction of a constable in the execution of his duty, the Crown has to prove, in addition to the fact that he was so acting, the physical and mental element of the obstruction and further that the constable reasonably believed that if he did not make an arrest there would, or might be, a breach of the peace or an attempt to impede a lawful arrest.

In the present case, for the reasons we have already given, it cannot be said there was an attempt to impede a lawful arrest. Moreover there is no finding of fact in the case stated that any one of the officers had a reasonable apprehension that a breach of the peace might follow. That leads us to the conclusion that, although it could be and was properly said that the officers were lawfully on the premises, Andrew Riley's arrest was not proved to be lawful, so the arrest of the defendant must have been unlawful.

That leaves the question of what happened in the street and near and in the police van. Seeing that the arrest of Andrew Riley was not proved to be lawful, Martin, unwittingly, in going to the assistance of McDade was, in our judgment, acting in furtherance of an unlawful arrest of the defendant and could not consequently have been acting in the execution of his duty when he was bitten. That means that an essential element of the offence under [s 89(1)] was not established by the Crown. So the conviction of the defendant simply cannot stand. It has to be quashed. Thus the appeal is allowed ...

Edwards v Director of Public Prosecutions (1993) 97 Cr App R 301 (DC)

Evans LJ: Late on a Saturday night, 19 October 1991, three police officers were on plain clothes duty in the Piccadilly area of London. They saw three men huddled together by a dustbin in Shaftesbury Avenue and they had ample grounds for suspecting that those men were in possession of cannabis. One of the police officers, PC Rowe, produced his identity card and said:

Police – that's drugs [pointing to the substances]. I am going to search you.

The finding as to what happened next is as follows. The man to whom PC Rowe had spoken was named Fox:

Fox clenched his right hand and turned away. PC Rowe said, 'give the contents to me'. Fox pushed PC Rowe's hand away, put the contents in his mouth when the officer went to take them and struggled violently. PC Rowe said 'You are nicked for obstruction'.

Then a lady called Prendergast intervened and was arrested. The appellant, Deborah Edwards, then intervened and she, herself, was arrested for obstructing the officers in their arrest of Prendergast. The charge brought against Miss Edwards was that on 19 October 1991, at Piccadilly Circus, she did wilfully obstruct Susan MacSpadden, a constable of the Metropolitan Police, in the execution of her duty contrary to [s 89(2) of the Police Act 1996].

... The issue in the case [is:] Was PC Rowe acting in the execution of his duty when he arrested or purported to arrest Fox? In the context, the question becomes: Was his arrest of Fox lawful or not? ...

On that basis, the position in the present case is that we have the finding, but only the finding, of what PC Rowe said to Fox at the time when he was arrested. There was no reference to s 25 or to any of the general arrest conditions and indeed it is not suggested that there was any evidence to the effect that PC Rowe did have those arrest conditions in mind at the time when this incident took place ...

In the present case it seems to me that even if it is permissible for the court to infer in appropriate circumstances what the state of mind of the arresting officer must have been, that that is not open to the court in the present case. That is for the simple reason that the express finding that PC Rowe arrested by reference to the offence of obstruction, with no regard to the possible justification for an arrest under s 25, makes it quite impossible to infer in my judgment that PC Rowe had something quite different in mind at that time, something which he mentioned neither then nor subsequently. That fact alone means that, in my judgment, in the present case the arrest of Fox is not shown to have been lawful in reliance upon s 25 of PACE ...

... PC Rowe gave a reason. He gave a reason which was not a valid reason. It follows, in my judgment, that the arrest itself, that is the arrest of Fox, must be regarded as invalid. It follows, for the reasons I indicated at the outset, that the charge against Miss Edwards should have been dismissed and that this appeal should be allowed ...

Note: The police officer could have arrested Fox for possession of cannabis and the police had power to detain and search Fox under the Misuse of Drugs Act 1971. However, when stating the reason for the arrest, the officer relied on 'obstruction' and not on any powers conferred by the 1971 Act. In this case, the prosecution sought to rely on the general powers of arrest contained in s 25 of the Police and Criminal Evidence Act 1984 but were unsuccessful because (as is apparent from the judgment of Evans LJ) the officer did not give any of the reasons set out in s 25 as the reason for the arrest. Accordingly, the arrest was unlawful.

Crown Prosecution Charging Standards: Assault on a Constable in the execution of his/her duty, contrary to s 89(1) of the Police Act 1996

5.3 If an assault on a constable results in injury of the type described at paragraph 4.7 [see above] ... a prosecution under section 89(1) Police Act 1996 will be appropriate, provided that the officer is acting in the execution of his/her duty.

5.4 Where the evidence that the officer was acting in the execution of his/her duty is insufficient, but proceedings for an assault are nevertheless warranted, the appropriate charge will be under section 39.

5.5 The fact that the victim is a police officer is not, in itself, an exceptional reason for charging an offence contrary to section 47 when the injuries are minor. When the injuries are such that an offence contrary to section 47 would be charged in relation to an assault on a member of the public, section 47 will be the appropriate charge for an assault on a constable.

Section 47 of the Offences Against the Person Act 1861

Section 47 of the Offences Against the Person Act 1861 provides:

Whosoever shall be convicted upon an indictment of any assault occasioning actual bodily harm shall be liable ... to [imprisonment for five years].

For these purposes assault bears either its narrow meaning, ie D causing P to apprehend immediate physical violence, or it can be used in its broad sense to encompass battery.

What is actual bodily harm?

R v Miller [1954] 2 QB 282 Hampshire Assizes

Lynskey J: The point has been taken that there is no evidence of bodily harm. The bodily harm alleged is said to be the result of the prisoner's actions, and that is, if the jury accept the evidence, that he threw the wife down three times. There is evidence that afterwards she was in a hysterical and nervous condition, but it is said by counsel that that is not actual bodily harm. Actual bodily harm, according to Archbold, 32nd edn, p 959, includes 'any hurt or injury calculated to interfere with the health or comfort of the prosecutor.' There was a time when shock was not regarded as bodily hurt, but the day has gone by when that could be said. It seems to me now that if a person is caused hurt or injury resulting, not in any physical injury, but in an injury to her state of mind for the time being, that is within the definition of actual bodily harm, and on that point I would leave the case to the jury.

R v Roberts (1971) 56 Cr App R 95 (CA)

Facts: The victim of the alleged assault had been at a party. She left the party at about 3 am, having agreed to travel with the appellant in his car to what he said was another party in Warrington. After they had driven out of Warrington in the direction of Liverpool, she asked the appellant where the party was, and he said that they were going to Runcorn. They took a curious route to Runcorn, and eventually, she said, they stopped on what seemed like a big cinder track. The time by then was apparently about 4 am. Then, she said, 'He just jumped on me. He put his hands up my clothes and tried to take my tights off. I started to fight him off, but the door of the car was locked and I could not find the catch. Suddenly he grabbed me and then he drove off and I started to cry and asked him to take me home. He told me to take my clothes off and, if I did not take my clothes off, he would let me walk home, so I asked him to let me do that. He said, that if he did, he would beat me up before he let me go. He said that he had done this before and had got away with it and he started to pull my coat off. He was using foul language'. And then she said that she told him, 'I am not like that', and he said something like, 'You are all like that'. Then he drove on. 'Again', said the girl, 'he tried to get my coat off, so I got hold of my handbag and I jumped out of the car. When I opened the door, he said something and revved the car up and I jumped out. The next thing I remember he was backing towards me and so I ran to the nearest house. He backed and shouted and then he drove off', and then she remembered being in the lady's house. She said she was taken to hospital, where she was treated for some concussion and for some grazing, and was detained in hospital for three days. The defendant was charged with assault occasioning actual bodily harm.

> **Stephenson LJ**: ... [The jury] had to consider: was the appellant guilty of occasioning [the victim] actual bodily harm? Of course, for that to be established, it had to be established that he was responsible in law and in fact for her injuries caused by leaving in a hurry the moving car...
>
> We have been ... referred to ... *Beech* (1912) 7 Cr App R 197, which was a case of a woman jumping out of a window and injuring herself ... In that case the Court of Criminal Appeal (at p 200) approved the direction given by the trial judge in these terms: 'Will you say whether the conduct of the prisoner amounted to a threat of causing injury to this young woman, was the act of jumping the natural consequence of the conduct of the prisoner, and was the grievous bodily harm the result of the conduct of the prisoner?' That, said the court, was a proper direction as far as the law went, and they were satisfied that there was evidence before the jury of the prisoner causing actual bodily harm to the woman. 'No-one could say' said Darling J when giving the judgment of the court, 'that if she jumped from the window it was not a natural consequence of the prisoner's conduct. It was a very likely thing for a woman to do as the result of the threats of a man who was conducting himself as this man indisputably was'.
>
> This court thinks that that correctly states the law...
>
> ... The test is: Was it [the action of the victim which resulted in actual bodily harm] the natural result of what the alleged assailant said and did, in the sense that it was something that could reasonably have been foreseen as the consequence of what he was saying or doing? As it was put in one of the old cases, it had got to be shown to be his act, and if of course the victim does something so 'daft', in the words of the appellant in this case, or so unexpected, not that this particular assailant did not actually foresee it but that no reasonable man could be expected to foresee it, then it is only in a very remote and unreal sense a consequence of his

assault, it is really occasioned by a voluntary act on the part of the victim which could not reasonably be foreseen and which breaks the chain of causation between the assault and harm or injury.

R v Ireland; R v Burstow [1997] 4 All ER 225

One of the issues common to both *R v Ireland* and *R v Burstow* was the extent to which any psychiatric illness caused by the activities of the appellants could amount to actual bodily harm (*Ireland*) or grievous bodily harm (*Burstow*).

Lord Steyn: It will now be convenient to consider the question which is common to the two appeals, namely, whether psychiatric illness is capable of amounting to bodily harm in terms of sections 18, 20 and 47 of the Act of 1861. The answer must be the same for the three sections.

The only abiding thing about the processes of the human mind, and the causes of its disorders and disturbances, is that there will never be a complete explanation. Psychiatry is and will always remain an imperfectly understood branch of medical science. This idea is explained by Vallar's psychiatrist in Iris Murdoch's *The Message to the Planet*:

> Our knowledge of the soul, if I may use that unclinical but essential word, encounters certain seemingly impassable limits, set there perhaps by the gods, if I may refer to them, in order to preserve their privacy, and beyond which it may be not only futile but lethal to attempt to pass and though it is our duty to seek for knowledge, it is also incumbent on us to realise when it is denied us, and not to prefer a fake solution to no solution at all.

But there has been progress since 1861. And courts of law can only act on the best scientific understanding of the day. Some elementary distinctions can be made. The appeals under consideration do not involve structural injuries to the brain such as might require the intervention of a neurologist. One is also not considering either psychotic illness or personality disorders. The victims in the two appeals suffered from no such conditions. As a result of the behaviour of the appellants they did not develop psychotic or psychoneurotic conditions. The case was that they developed mental disturbances of a lesser order, namely neurotic disorders. For present purposes the relevant forms of neurosis are anxiety disorders and depressive disorders. Neuroses must be distinguished from simple states of fear, or problems in coping with every day life. Where the line is to be drawn must be a matter of psychiatric judgment. But for present purposes it is important to note that modern psychiatry treats neuroses as recognisable psychiatric illnesses: see *Liability for Psychiatric Injury*, Law Commission Consultation Paper 137 (1995) Part III (The Medical Background); Mullany and Hanford, *Tort Liability for Psychiatric Damages* (1993), discussion on 'The medical perspective,' at pp 24–42, and in particular at 30, fn 88. Moreover, it is essential to bear in mind that neurotic illnesses affect the central nervous system of the body, because emotions such as fear and anxiety are brain functions.

The civil law has for a long time taken account of the fact that there is no rigid distinction between body and mind. In *Bourhill v Young* [1943] AC 92, 103 Lord Macmillan said:

> The crude view that the law should take cognisance only of physical injury resulting from actual impact has been discarded, and it is now well recognised

that an action will lie for injury by shock sustained through the medium of the eye or the ear without direct physical contact. The distinction between mental shock and bodily injury was never a scientific one ...

This idea underlies the subsequent decisions of the House of Lords regarding post-traumatic stress disorder in *McLoughlin v O'Brian* [1983] AC 410, 418, *per* Lord Wilberforce; and *Page v Smith* [1996] AC 155, 181A–D, *per* Lord Browne-Wilkinson. So far as such cases are concerned with the precise boundaries of tort liability they are not relevant. But so far as those decisions are based on the principle that the claimant must be able to prove that he suffered a recognisable psychiatric illness or condition they are by analogy relevant. The decisions of the House of Lords on post-traumatic stress disorder hold that where the line is to be drawn is a matter for expert psychiatric evidence. By analogy those decisions suggest a possible principled approach to the question whether psychiatric injury may amount to bodily harm in terms of the Act of 1861.

The criminal law has been slow to follow this path. But in *R v Chan-Fook* [1994] 1 WLR 689 the Court of Appeal squarely addressed the question whether psychiatric injury may amount to bodily harm under section 47 of the Act of 1861. The issue arose in a case where the defendant had aggressively questioned and locked in a suspected thief. There was a dispute as to whether the defendant had physically assaulted the victim. But the prosecution also alleged that even if the victim had suffered no physical injury, he had been reduced to a mental state which amounted to actual bodily harm under section 47. No psychiatric evidence was given. The judge directed the jury that an assault which caused an hysterical and nervous condition was an assault occasioning actual bodily harm. The defendant was convicted. Upon appeal the conviction was quashed on the ground of misdirections in the summing up and the absence of psychiatric evidence to support the prosecution's alternative case. The interest of the decision lies in the reasoning on psychiatric injury in the context of section 47. In a detailed and careful judgment given on behalf of the court Hobhouse LJ said (at p 695G–H)):

> The first question on the present appeal is whether the inclusion of the word 'bodily' in the phrase 'actual bodily harm' limits harm to harm to the skin, flesh and bones of the victim ... The body of the victim includes all parts of his body, including his organs, his nervous system and his brain. Bodily injury therefore may include injury to any of those parts of his body responsible for his mental and other faculties.

In concluding that 'actual bodily harm' is capable of including psychiatric injury Hobhouse LJ emphasised (at p 696C) that

> it does not include mere emotions such as fear or distress nor panic nor does it include, as such, states of mind that are not themselves evidence of some identifiable clinical condition.

He observed that in the absence of psychiatric evidence a question whether or not an assault occasioned psychiatric injury should not be left to the jury.

The Court of Appeal, as differently constituted in *Ireland* and *Burstow*, was bound by the decision in *Chan-Fook*. The House is not so bound. Counsel for the appellants in both appeals submitted that bodily harm in Victorian legislation cannot include psychiatric injury. For this reason they argued that *Chan-Fook* was wrongly decided. They relied on the following observation of Lord Bingham of Cornhill CJ in *Burstow* [1997] 1 Cr App R 144, 148:

Were the question free from authority, we should entertain some doubt whether the Victorian draftsman of the 1861 Act intended to embrace psychiatric injury within the expressions 'grievous bodily harm' and 'actual bodily harm'.

Nevertheless, the Lord Chief Justice observed that it is now accepted that in the relevant context the distinction between physical and mental injury is by no means clear cut. He welcomed the ruling in *Chan-Fook* at p 149B. I respectfully agree. But I would go further and point out that, although out of considerations of piety we frequently refer to the actual intention of the draftsman, the correct approach is simply to consider whether the words of the Act of 1861 considered in the light of contemporary knowledge cover a recognisable psychiatric injury. It is undoubtedly true that there are statutes where the correct approach is to construe the legislation 'as if one were interpreting it the day after it was passed:' *The Longford* (1889) 14 PD 34. Thus in *The Longford* the word 'action' in a statute was held not to be apt to cover an Admiralty action *in rem* since when it was passed the Admiralty Court 'was not one of His Majesty's Courts of Law:' (see pp 37, 38). Bearing in mind that statutes are usually intended to operate for many years it would be most inconvenient if courts could never rely in difficult cases on the current meaning of statutes. Recognising the problem Lord Thring, the great Victorian draftsman of the second half of the last century, exhorted draftsmen to draft so that 'An Act of Parliament should be deemed to be always speaking': *Practical Legislation* (1902), p 83; see also Cross, *Statutory Interpretation*, 3rd edn (1995), p 51; Pearce and Geddes, *Statutory Interpretation in Australia*, 4th edn (1996), pp 90–93. In cases where the problem arises it is a matter of interpretation whether a court must search for the historical or original meaning of a statute or whether it is free to apply the current meaning of the statute to present day conditions. Statutes dealing with a particular grievance or problem may sometimes require to be historically interpreted. But the drafting technique of Lord Thring and his successors have brought about the situation that statutes will generally be found to be of the 'always speaking' variety: see *Royal College of Nursing of the United Kingdom v Department of Health and Social Security* [1981] AC 800 for an example of an 'always speaking' construction in the House of Lords.

The proposition that the Victorian legislator when enacting sections 18, 20 and 47 of the Act 1861, would not have had in mind psychiatric illness is no doubt correct. Psychiatry was in its infancy in 1861. But the subjective intention of the draftsman is immaterial. The only relevant enquiry is as to the sense of the words in the context in which they are used. Moreover the Act of 1861 is a statute of the 'always speaking' type: the statute must be interpreted in the light of the best current scientific appreciation of the link between the body and psychiatric injury.

For these reasons I would, therefore, reject the challenge to the correctness of *Chan-Fook* [1994] 1 WLR 689. In my view the ruling in that case was based on principled and cogent reasoning and it marked a sound and essential clarification of the law. I would hold that 'bodily harm' in sections 18, 20 and 47 must be interpreted so as to include recognisable psychiatric illness.

The mens rea *for s 47*

R v Venna [1976] QB 421 (CA)

James LJ: ... The four defendants and another youth called Patterson, who was not arrested, were creating a disturbance in the public street by shouting and singing and dancing. At one stage there was a banging of dustbin lids. The local residents were disturbed and at least one complaint of the noise was made to the police. A police officer named Leach went to investigate. What took place between him and the youths was described in evidence by three taxi drivers. Leach patiently and tactfully tried to persuade the four youths to be quiet and to go home. The response was a remark by Robinson, 'Fuck off', and the continuation of the noise and dancing. Leach told them there had already been a complaint about their unruly behaviour and ordered them on their way. Robinson thereafter stood apart from the others and did nothing. That was the foundation of his subsequent acquittal. The others continued a sort of war dance and went on singing. Leach told them that if they continued to create a disturbance and obstruct the pavement they would be arrested. Allison in defiance sat down on the pavement. Leach moved towards him to arrest him and the appellant, Edwards and Patterson crowded round. As he placed his hand on Allison, Leach said 'You are all under arrest'.

The appellant's evidence at the trial was that he did not hear these words and did not appreciate that he was being arrested until a later stage of the incident. As Leach picked Allison up, Allison struggled to free himself and the appellant, Edwards and Patterson tried to pull Allison out of the officer's grip. Leach held on to Allison and called for help on his pocket radio. The scene was such that the taxi drivers were about to intervene. A passer-by, referred to as 'the fat man', did intervene on the officer's behalf. The appellant in evidence surmised that he did so because 'he thought the copper's head might be bashed in'. Other police officers arrived and assisted Leach in the arrest of the appellant and the co-defendants. Before those who were resisting arrest were finally overpowered, Allison had torn Leach's uniform, Edwards had seized Leach's left thumb and bent it forcibly backwards causing physical injury, and the appellant had fought so violently that four officers were required to restrain him. In the course of the appellant's struggles he was knocked or fell to the ground. Two police officers held him by the arms. On the appellant's own admission, he then knew he was being arrested and he continued to 'lash out' wildly with his legs. In doing so he kicked the hand of a police officer who was trying to pick him up. The kick caused a fracture of a bone and was the subject of the charge of assault occasioning actual bodily harm.

The appellant's evidence was to the effect that he and his friends were not told that they were creating a disturbance and that all he done was to tell Leach that he could not arrest Allison. He said that he had been struck on the chin and knocked to the ground and that he had lashed out with his feet in an effort to get up. He did not know or suspect that there was a police officer in the way or that his foot might strike a police officer's hand ...

... In our view the element of *mens rea* in the offence of battery is satisfied by proof that the defendant intentionally or recklessly applied force to the person of another. If it were otherwise, the strange consequence would be that an offence of unlawful wounding contrary to s 20 of the Offences Against the Person Act 1861 could be established by proof that the defendant wounded the victim either intentionally or recklessly, but if the victim's skin was not broken and the offence was therefore laid as an assault occasioning actual bodily harm contrary to s 47 of the 1861 Act, it would be necessary to prove that the physical force was intentionally applied.

R v Savage; R v Parmenter [1992] 1 AC 699 (HL)

Lord Ackner (with whom **Lord Keith of Kinkel**, **Lord Brandon of Oakbrook**, **Lord Jauncey of Tullichettle** and **Lord Lowry** agreed):

R v Savage

... [T]he appellant, Mrs Savage, was indicted and convicted ... of unlawful wounding contrary to s 20 of the 1861 Act, the particulars of the offence being that on 31 March 1989 she unlawfully and maliciously wounded Miss Beal ... The victim, Miss Beal, was a former girlfriend of Mrs Savage's husband. There had been some bad feeling between these two young women, although they had never previously met. On the evening of 31 March 1989 they were both in the same public house, but not together. Mrs Savage pushed her way through to the table where Miss Beal was sitting with some friends. She had in her hand a pint glass which was nearly full of beer. Having said 'Nice to meet you darling', she then threw the contents of the glass over Miss Beal. Unfortunately, not only was Miss Beal soaked by beer, but, contrary to Mrs Savage's evidence, she must have let go of the glass, since it broke and a piece of it cut Miss Beal's wrist. The jury, by their verdict, concluded either that the appellant had deliberately thrown not only the beer but also the glass at Miss Beal or, alternatively, while deliberately throwing the beer over Miss Beal, the glass had accidentally slipped from her grasp and it, or a piece of it, had struck Miss Beal's wrist, but with no intention that the glass should hit or cut Miss Beal ...

... On 28 November 1990 the Court of Appeal gave leave to appeal, certifying the following points of law to be of general public importance:

(1) Whether a verdict of guilty of assault occasioning actual bodily harm is a permissible alternative verdict on a count alleging unlawful wounding contrary to s 20 of the Offences Against the Persons Act 1861.

(2) Whether a verdict of guilty of assault occasioning actual bodily harm can be returned upon proof of an assault and of the fact that actual bodily harm was occasioned by that assault.

(3) If it is proved that an assault has been committed and that actual bodily harm has resulted from that assault, whether a verdict of assault occasioning actual bodily harm may be returned in the absence of proof that the defendant intended to cause some actual bodily harm or was reckless as to whether such harm would be caused.

It is perhaps convenient at this stage to observe that in order for Mrs Savage to succeed in relation to the first certified question your Lordships must conclude that the decision of this House in *R v Wilson (Clarence)* [1984] AC 242 was wrong. As regards the second certified question, that the intent required in s 47 relates not only to the assault, but also to the consequences of the assault, this clearly overlaps with the third certified question.

R v Parmenter

Paul Parmenter was born on 8 February 1988. Between that date and 11 May 1988 his father, the appellant, Philip Mark Parmenter caused his baby son to suffer injuries to the bony structures of the legs and right forearm ... The only issue before the jury was whether Mr Parmenter had acted with the relevant intent, his case being that he did not realise that the way he handled the child would cause injury ... Mr Parmenter was ... convicted of four s 20 offences ...

The Court of Appeal ... quashed the convictions on the four counts under s 20 ... The court then had to consider whether it could and should substitute for the convictions which it had quashed, alternative verdicts of guilty under s 47 of the 1861 Act.

It was then discovered that a curious situation had emerged, namely that two different divisions of the Court of Appeal (Criminal Division) had, contemporaneously but unwittingly, delivered judgments on the necessary intent in s 47, but had unfortunately reached opposite conclusions. *Savage* was one of those cases and the other is *R v Spratt* [1990] 1 WLR 1073.

In *R v Spratt* a young girl was struck twice whilst playing in the forecourt of a block of flats by two airgun pellets, which had been fired from a window by the appellant. He admitted to the police that he had fired a few shots out of the window, not in order to hit anyone, but to see how far the pellets would go. He was duly charged with an offence under s 47 of the 1861 Act to which he pleaded guilty. The basis of that plea, as was explained to the trial judge, was that the appellant accepted that he had been reckless, and that his recklessness took the shape of a failure to give any thought to the possibility of a risk. However, it was contended on his behalf that if he had known there were children in the area, he would not have fired the shots ... When the [the defendant's appeal against sentence] came before the full [Court of Appeal], the court itself raised the question whether, if the facts asserted on the appellant's behalf were true, he had in law committed the offence to which he had pleaded guilty. Subsequently leave was given to pursue an appeal against conviction ... The court ... concluded that the 'subjective type of recklessness' furnished the test for ss 20 and 47 alike ...

On 6 November 1990 the Court of Appeal granted leave to appeal to your Lordships' House and certified the following points of law to be of general public importance:

(1) (a) Whether in order to establish an offence under s 20 of the Offences Against the Person Act 1861 the prosecution must prove that the defendant actually foresaw that his act would cause the particular kind of harm which was in fact caused, or whether it is sufficient to prove that (objectively) he ought so to have foreseen.

(b) The like question in relation to s 47 of the Act.

(2) (a) For the purposes of the answer to question (1)(a), whether the particular kind of harm to be foreseen may be any physical harm, or harm of:

(1) the nature, or

(2) the degree, or

(3) the nature and the degree of the harm which actually occurred.

(b) The like question in relation to s 47 of the Act.

It will be observed that some of the certified questions in *Parmenter* overlap with those in *Savage*.

My Lords, I will now seek to deal with the issues raised by these appeals seriatim ...

Can a verdict of assault occasioning actual bodily harm be returned upon proof of an assault together with proof of the fact that actual bodily harm was occasioned by the assault, or must the prosecution also prove that the defendant intended to cause some actual bodily harm or was reckless as to whether such harm would be caused?

Your Lordships are concerned with the mental element of a particular kind of assault, an assault 'occasioning actual bodily harm'. It is common ground that the mental element of assault is an intention to cause the victim to apprehend immediate and unlawful violence or recklessness whether such apprehension be caused: see *R v Venna* [1976] QB 421. It is of course common ground that Mrs Savage committed an assault upon Miss Beal when she threw the contents of her glass of beer over her. It is also common ground that however the glass came to be broken and Miss Beal's wrist thereby cut, it was, on the finding of the jury, Mrs Savage's handling of the glass which caused Miss Beal 'actual bodily harm'. Was the offence thus established or is there a further mental state that has to be established in relation to the bodily harm element of the offence? Clearly the section, by its terms, expressly imposes no such a requirement. Does it do so by necessary implication? It neither uses the word 'intentionally' nor the word 'maliciously'. The words 'occasioning actual bodily harm' are descriptive of the word 'assault', by reference to a particular kind of consequence ...

... [O]nce the assault was established, the only remaining question was whether the victim's conduct was the natural consequence of that assault. The word 'occasioning' raised solely a question of causation, an objective question which does not involve enquiring into the accused's state of mind ...

... The decision in *R v Roberts* 56 Cr App R 95 was correct. The verdict of assault occasioning actual bodily harm may be returned upon proof of an assault together with proof of the fact that actual bodily harm was occasioned by the assault. The prosecution are not obliged to prove that the defendant intended to cause some actual bodily harm or was reckless as to whether such harm would be caused ...

Crown Prosecution Charging Standards: Assault occasioning actual bodily harm, contrary to s 47 of the Act

7.3 As is made clear in paragraph 4.6 above, the only factor in law which distinguishes a charge under section 39 from a charge under section 47 is the degree of injury. By way of example, the following injuries should normally be prosecuted under section 47:

- loss or breaking of a tooth or teeth;
- temporary loss of sensory functions (which may include loss of consciousness);
- extensive or multiple bruising;
- displaced broken nose;
- minor fractures;

- minor, but not merely superficial, cuts of a sort probably requiring medical treatment (eg stitches);

- psychiatric injury which is more than fear, distress or panic. (Such injury will be proved by appropriate expert evidence).

7.2 Section 47 will also be the appropriate charge in the exceptional circumstances referred to in paragraph 4.8 above.

7.3 A verdict of assault occasioning actual bodily harm may be returned on proof of an assault together with proof of the fact that actual bodily harm was occasioned by the assault. The prosecution are not obliged to prove that the defendant intended to cause some actual bodily harm or was reckless as to whether harm would be caused: *R v Savage, R v Parmenter* [1991] 4 All ER 698.

WOUNDING AND GRIEVOUS BODILY HARM

Section 20 of the Offences Against the Person Act 1861

Section 20: inflicting bodily injury, with or without weapon

Whosoever shall unlawfully and maliciously wound or inflict any grievous bodily harm upon any other person, either with or without any weapon or instrument, shall be guilty of [an offence], and being convicted thereof shall be liable ... to [imprisonment for not more than five years] ...

What constitutes a wound?

C (A Minor) v Eisenhower (sub nom JJC v Eisenhower) [1983] 3 WLR 537 (CA)

Facts: The defendant, a juvenile, had been charged (together with another juvenile) with unlawful and malicious wounding contrary to s 20 of the Offences Against the Person Act 1861. The only point at issue was whether the victim's injuries constituted a 'wound'.

> Robert Goff LJ: ... The offence arose in the following circumstances. These two boys were both 15 at the relevant time. The defendant's co-accused, in company with the defendant, purchased an air pistol and some pellets from a shop. A few days later, on 21 January 1982, they were walking together along Flexmere Road, Tottenham, when they became aware of a young man called Martin Cook, together with another young man and two girls, on the opposite side of the road. As the defendant and his co-accused walked along, the co-accused aimed the air pistol in the direction of those four young people. He fired once. A little later he fired again. Martin Cook was hit in the area of the left eye by a pellet from the air pistol.
>
> The justices in the case found that the injuries sustained by Martin Cook amounted to a bruise just below the left eyebrow and that fluid filling the front part of his left eye for a time afterwards abnormally contained red blood cells ...
>
> The question stated by the justices is as follows:

The question for the opinion of the High Court is whether in the light of the facts as we found them and the law applied to those facts we were right to find the [defendant] guilty of the offence with which he had been charged.

... In *R v M'Loughlin* (1838) 8 Car & P 635, it was held by Coleridge J, other judges being present, that it must be the whole skin that is broken. He, of course, was referring to the fact that the human skin has two layers, an outer layer called the epidermis or the cuticle, and an underlayer which is sometimes called the dermis or the true skin. In that case there was evidence of an abrasion of the skin, with blood issuing from it. It was made plain to the jury by Coleridge J that:

> if it is necessary to constitute a wound, that the skin should be broken, it must be the whole skin, and it is not sufficient to show a separation of the cuticle only.

It was therefore not enough that there had been an abrasion affecting only the cuticle. There had to be a break in the continuity of the whole skin.

His Lordship then referred to two more old cases: see *R v Shadbolt* (1833) 5 Car & P 504 and *R v Waltham* (1849) 3 Cox CC 442; his Lordship went on:

> These cases show that there can be a break in the continuity of the skin sufficient to constitute a wound if the skin which was broken is the skin of an internal cavity of the body, being a cavity from the outer surface of the body where the skin of the cavity is continuous with the outer skin of the body. So, for example, in *Shadbolt* it was held that it was sufficient if there had been a break in the skin of the internal surface of the lips inside the mouth. In *Waltham*, which is possibly the most extreme of the cases cited to us, it was held by Cresswell J that there would be a wounding if there had been a rupture of the lining membrane of the urethra causing a small flow of blood into the urine, because that membrane was of precisely the same character as that which lined the cheek and the internal skin of the lip.

> So we can see a picture emerging. There must be a break in the continuity of the skin. It must be a break in the continuity of the whole skin, but the skin may include not merely the outer skin of the body but the skin of an internal cavity of the body where the skin of the cavity is continuous with the outer skin of the body ...

> In my judgment, having regard to the cases there is a continuous stream of authority – to which I myself can find no exception at all – which does establish that a wound is, as I have stated, a break in the continuity of the whole skin ... This has become such a well-established meaning of the word 'wound' that in my judgment it would be very wrong for this court to depart from it.

> We now turn to the case stated for our consideration by the justices. The justices concluded that there was a wound because, although they described the injury as a bruise just below the left eyebrow with fluid filling the front part of his left eye for a time afterwards which abnormally contained red blood cells, they thought that the abnormal presence of red blood cells in the fluid in Martin Cook's left eye indicated at least the rupturing of a blood vessel or vessels internally; and this they thought was sufficient to constitute a wound for the purposes of s 20 of the Offences Against the Person Act 1861.

> In my judgment, that conclusion was not in accordance with the law. It is not enough that there has been a rupturing of a blood vessel or vessels internally for

there to be a wound under the statute because it is impossible for a court to conclude from that evidence alone whether or not there has been any break in the continuity of the whole skin. There may have simply been internal bleeding of some kind or another, the cause of which is not established. Furthermore, even if there had been a break in some internal skin, there may not have been a break in the whole skin. In these circumstances, the evidence is not enough, in my judgment, to establish a wound within the statute. In my judgment, the justices erred in their conclusion on the evidence before them. The question posed for the opinion of this court is whether, in the light of the facts found by the justices and the law applied to those facts, they were right to find the defendant guilty of the offence with which he had been charged, viz, the unlawful and malicious wounding of Martin Cook contrary to s 20 of the Offences Against the Person Act 1861. I would answer that question in the negative.

Note: Since the definition of 'grievous bodily harm' is rather wider than that of a 'wound', the best practice is to charge the defendant with inflicting grievous bodily harm if there is doubt whether the injury constitutes a wound or not, for example in the case of internal injuries.

What constitutes grievous bodily harm?

Director of Public Prosecutions v Smith [1961] AC 290 (HL)

Facts: The respondent was driving a car in which there was stolen property. The car was stopped by a police officer on point duty in the normal course of traffic control and, while so stopped, another policeman, who was acquainted with the respondent, came to the driver's window and spoke to the respondent. As a result of what the police constable saw in the back of the car, he told the respondent to draw in to his nearside. The respondent began to do so, and the constable walked beside the car. However, the respondent suddenly accelerated and made off down an adjoining road. The constable began to run with the car, and, despite the fact that it had no running board, succeeded in hanging on to the car. The car pursued an erratic course, and eventually the constable was thrown off in the path of another vehicle which ran over him, causing fatal injuries.

> **Viscount Kilmuir LC**: ... My Lords, I confess that, whether one is considering the crime of murder or the statutory offence, I can find no warrant for giving the words 'grievous bodily harm' a meaning other than that which the words convey in their ordinary and natural meaning. 'Bodily harm' needs no explanation and 'grievous' means no more and no less than 'really serious' ...

Lord Goddard, Lord Tucker, Lord Denning and **Lord Parker of Waddington** agreed with the Lord Chancellor.

R v Saunders (Ian) [1985] Crim LR 230 (CA)

Facts: The appellant, on a road at night, approaching a stranger who was sitting resting at the roadside, asked him what the problem was and, when the victim said that there was no problem, the appellant said that he would give him one and punched him in the face. The victim suffered a broken nose and other injuries. The appellant desisted when a passer-by approached. The appellant was tried on, *inter alia*, a count of inflicting grievous bodily harm, contrary to s 20 of the Offences Against the Person Act 1861. The judge directed the jury that grievous bodily harm meant 'serious injury'. The appellant was convicted. He appealed on the ground that the judge had misdirected the jury failing to direct them that the injury had to be 'really serious'.

Held: The question had already been considered by the Court of Appeal in *R v McMillan* (1984) unreported, 8 October. The conclusion reached in that case was equally applicable to the present case, in which there was no need to use the phrase 'really' serious harm; the omission of the word 'really' was not significant. The victim had suffered a broken nose, which was clearly grievous bodily harm.

'Infliction' and 'causing': a distinction without a difference?

R v Ireland; R v Burstow [1997] 4 All ER 225

In *R v Burstow* the Court of Appeal certified the following point as of general importance, namely:

> Whether an offence of inflicting grievous bodily harm under section 20 of the Offences against the Person Act 1861 can be committed where no physical violence is applied directly or indirectly to the body of the victim.

Lord Steyn outlined the facts giving rise to the appeal in *R v Burstow* as follows:

> In *R v Burstow* the appellant was indicted on one count of unlawfully and maliciously inflicting grievous bodily harm, contrary to section 20 of the Act of 1861 ... Burstow had a social relationship with a woman. She broke it off. He could not accept her decision. He proceeded to harass her in various ways over a lengthy period. His conduct led to several convictions and periods of imprisonment. During an eight month period in 1995 covered by the indictment he continued his campaign of harassment. He made some silent telephone calls to her. He also made abusive calls to her. He distributed offensive cards in the street where she lived. He was frequently, and unnecessarily, at her home and place of work. He surreptitiously took photographs of the victim and her family. He sent her a note which was intended to be menacing, and was so understood. The victim was badly affected by this campaign of harassment. It preyed on her mind. She was fearful of personal violence. A consultant psychiatrist stated that she was suffering from a severe depressive illness. In the Crown Court counsel asked for a ruling whether an offence of unlawfully and maliciously inflicting grievous bodily harm contrary to section 20 may be committed where no physical violence has been applied directly or indirectly to the body of the victim. The judge answered this question in the affirmative. Burstow thereupon changed his plea to guilty. The judge sentenced him to three year's imprisonment. Burstow applied for leave to appeal against conviction. The Court of Appeal heard full oral argument on the application, and granted the application for leave to appeal but dismissed the appeal.

He continued:

> The decision in *Chan-Fook* opened up the possibility of applying sections 18, 20 and 47 in new circumstances. The appeal of Burstow lies in respect of his conviction under section 20. It was conceded that in principle the wording of section 18, and in particular the words 'cause any grievous bodily harm to any person' do not preclude a prosecution in cases where the actus reus is the causing of psychiatric injury. But counsel laid stress on the difference between 'causing' grievous bodily harm in section 18 and 'inflicting' grievous bodily harm in section 20. Counsel argued that the difference in wording reveals a difference in legislative intent: inflict is a narrower concept than cause. This argument loses sight of the genesis of sections 18 and 20. In his commentary on the Act of 1861 Greaves, the draftsman, explained the position: *The Criminal Law Consolidation and Amendment Acts*, 2nd edn (1862). He said (at pp 3–4):
>
>> If any question should arise in which any comparison may be instituted between different sections of any one or several of these Acts, it must be carefully borne in mind in what manner these Acts were framed. None of them was re-written; on the contrary, each contains enactments taken from different Acts passed at different times and with different views, and frequently varying from each other in phraseology, and ... these enactments, for the most part, stand in these Acts with little or no variation in their phraseology, and, consequently, their differences in that respect will be found generally to remain in these Acts. It follows, therefore, from hence, that any argument as to a difference in the intention of the legislature, which may be drawn from a difference in the terms of one clause from those in another, will be entitled to no weight in the construction of such clauses; for that argument can only apply with force where an Act is framed from beginning to end with one and the same view, and with the intention of making it thoroughly consistent throughout.
>
> The difference in language is therefore not a significant factor.
>
> Counsel for Burstow then advanced a sustained argument that an assault is an ingredient of an offence under section 20. He referred your Lordships to cases which in my judgment simply do not yield what he sought to extract from them. In any event, the tour of the cases revealed conflicting dicta, no authority binding on the House of Lords, and no settled practice holding expressly that assault was an ingredient of section 20. And, needless to say, none of the cases focused on the infliction of psychiatric injury. In these circumstances I do not propose to embark on a general review of the cases cited: compare the review in Smith and Hogan, *Criminal Law*, 8th edn (1996), pp 440–41. Instead I turn to the words of the section.
>
> Counsel's argument can only prevail if one may supplement the section by reading it as providing 'inflict by assault any grievous bodily harm.' Such an implication is, however, not necessary. On the contrary, section 20, like section 18, works perfectly satisfactorily without such an implication. I would reject this part of counsel's argument. But counsel had a stronger argument when he submitted that it is inherent in the word 'inflict' that there must be a direct or indirect application of force to the body. Counsel cited the speech of Lord Roskill in *R v Wilson (Clarence)* [1984] AC 242, 259E–260H, in which Lord Roskill quoted with approval from the judgment of the full court of the Supreme Court of Victoria in *R*

v Salisbury [1976] VR 452. There are passages that give assistance to counsel's argument. But Lord Roskill expressly stated (at p 260H) that he was 'content to accept, as did the [court in Salisbury] that there can be the infliction of grievous bodily harm contrary to section 20 without an assault being committed.' In the result the effect of the decisions in *Wilson* and *Salisbury* is neutral in respect of the issue as to the meaning of 'inflict.' Moreover, in *Burstow* [1997] 1 Cr App R 144, 149, the Lord Chief Justice pointed out that in *R v Mandair* [1995] 1 AC 208, 215, Lord Mackay of Clashfern LC observed with the agreement of the majority of the House of Lords: 'In my opinion ... the word "cause" is wider or at least not narrower than the word "inflict"'. Like the Lord Chief Justice I regard this observation as making clear that in the context of the Act of 1861 there is no radical divergence between the meaning of the two words.

That leaves the troublesome authority of the decision Court for Crown Cases Reserved in *R v Clarence* (1888) 22 QBD 23. At a time when the defendant knew that he was suffering from a venereal disease, and his wife was ignorant of his condition, he had sexual intercourse with her. He communicated the disease to her. The defendant was charged and convicted of inflicting grievous bodily harm under section 20. There was an appeal. By a majority of nine to four the court quashed the conviction. The case was complicated by an issue of consent. But it must be accepted that in a case where there was direct physical contact the majority ruled that the requirement of infliction was not satisfied. This decision has never been overruled. It assists counsel's argument. But it seems to me that what detracts from the weight to be given to the *dicta* in *Clarence* is that none of the judges in that case had before them the possibility of the inflicting, or causing, of psychiatric injury. The criminal law has moved on in the light of a developing understanding of the link between the body and psychiatric injury. In my judgment *Clarence* no longer assists.

The problem is one of construction. The question is whether as a matter of current usage the contextual interpretation of 'inflict' can embrace the idea of one person inflicting psychiatric injury on another. One can without straining the language in any way answer that question in the affirmative. I am not saying that the words cause and inflict are exactly synonymous. They are not. What I am saying is that in the context of the Act of 1861 one can nowadays quite naturally speak of inflicting psychiatric injury. Moreover, there is internal contextual support in the statute for this view. It would be absurd to differentiate between sections 18 and 20 in the way argued on behalf of Burstow. As the Lord Chief Justice observed in *Burstow* [1997] 1 Cr App R 144, 149F, this should be a very practical area of the law. The interpretation and approach should so far as possible be adopted which treats the ladder of offences as a coherent body of law. Once the decision in *Chan-Fook* [1994] 1 WLR 689 is accepted the realistic possibility is opened up of prosecuting under section 20 in cases of the type which I described in the introduction to this judgment.

For the reasons I have given I would answer the certified question in *Burstow* in the affirmative.

Lord Hope: In this case the appellant changed his plea to guilty after a ruling by the trial judge that the offence of unlawfully and maliciously inflicting grievous bodily harm contrary to section 20 of the Act of 1861 may be committed where no physical violence has been applied directly or indirectly to the body of the victim. Counsel for the appellant accepted that if *R v Chan-Fook* [1994] 1 WLR 689 was correctly decided, with the result that 'actual bodily harm' in section 47 is capable of including psychiatric injury, the victim in this case had suffered grievous bodily harm within the meaning of section 20. But he submitted that no offence against section 20 had been committed in this case because, although the appellant might be said to have 'caused' the victim to sustain grievous bodily harm, he had not 'inflicted' that harm on her because he had not used any personal violence against her.

Counsel based his submission on the decision in *R v Clarence* (1888) 22 QBD 23. In that case it was held that some form of direct personal violence was required for a conviction under section 20. The use of the word 'inflict' in the section was said to imply that some form of battery was involved in the assault. The conviction was quashed because, although the venereal infection from which the victim was suffering was the result of direct physical contact, there had been no violence used and thus there was no element of battery. It seems to me however that there are three reasons for regarding that case as an uncertain guide to the question which arises where the bodily harm which has resulted from the defendant's conduct consists of psychiatric injury.

The first is that the judges in *Clarence* were concerned with a case of physical, not psychiatric, injury. They did not have to consider the problem which arises where the grievous bodily harm is of a kind which may result without any form of physical contact. The second is that the intercourse had taken place with consent, as the defendant's wife was ignorant of his venereal disease. So there was no question in that case of an assault having been committed, if there was no element of violence or battery. Also, as Lord Roskill pointed out in *R v Wilson (Clarence)* [1984] AC 242, 260C the judgments of the judges who formed the majority are not wholly consistent with each other. This casts some doubt on the weight which should be attached to the judgment when the facts are entirely different, as they are in the present case.

In *R v Wilson*, Lord Roskill referred at pp 259E–260B, with approval to the judgment of the Supreme Court of Victoria in *R v Salisbury* [1976] VR 452, in which the following passage appears, at p 461:

> ... although the word 'inflicts' ... does not have as wide a meaning as the word 'causes' ... the word 'inflicts' does have a wider meaning than it would have if it were construed so that inflicting grievous bodily harm always involved assaulting the victim.

At p 260H Lord Roskill said that he was content to accept, as was the full court in *Salisbury*, that there can be an infliction of grievous bodily harm contrary to section 20 without an assault being committed. But these observations do not wholly resolve the issue which arises in this case, in the context of grievous bodily harm which consists only of psychiatric injury.

The question is whether there is any difference in meaning, in this context, between the word 'cause' and the word 'inflict'. The fact that the word 'caused' is used in section 18, whereas the word used in section 20 is 'inflict,' might be taken at first sight to indicate that there is a difference. But for all practical purposes there is, in my opinion, no difference between these two words. In *R v Mandair* [1995] 1 AC 208, 215B Lord Mackay of Clashfern LC, said that the word 'cause' is wider or at least not narrower than the word 'inflict'. I respectfully agree with that observation. But I would add that there is this difference, that the word 'inflict' implies that the consequence of the act is something which the victim is likely to find unpleasant or harmful. The relationship between cause and effect, when the word 'cause' is used, is neutral. It may embrace pleasure as well as pain. The relationship when the word 'inflict' is used is more precise, because it invariably implies detriment to the victim of some kind.

In the context of a criminal act therefore the words 'cause' and 'inflict' may be taken to be interchangeable. As the Supreme Court of Victoria held in *Salisbury* [1976] VR 452, it is not a necessary ingredient of the word 'inflict' that whatever causes the harm must be applied directly to the victim. It may be applied indirectly, so long as the result is that the harm is caused by what has been done. In my opinion it is entirely consistent with the ordinary use of the word 'inflict' in the English language to say that the appellant's actions 'inflicted' the psychiatric harm from which the victim has admittedly suffered in this case. The issues which remain are issues of fact and, as the appellant pled guilty to the offence, I would dismiss his appeal.

R v Mandair [1994] 2 WLR 700 (HL)

Lord Mackay of Clashfern LC: The indictment contained a single count alleging causing grievous bodily harm with intent, contrary to s 18 of the Offences Against the Person Act 1861. The particulars of offence were that the defendant on 31 January 1991 unlawfully caused grievous bodily harm to Amarjit Mandair with intent to do her grievous bodily harm.

The recorder, applying s 6(3) of the Criminal Law Act 1967, left open to the jury the option of returning a lesser verdict under s 20 of the Offences Against the Person Act 1861. After sundry procedure the jury returned a verdict of not guilty on the charge against the defendant of causing grievous bodily harm with intent contrary to s 18 and a verdict of guilty on the alternative charge against the defendant of causing grievous bodily harm contrary to s 20 ...

In my view 'cause' in s 18 is certainly sufficiently wide to embrace any method by which grievous bodily harm could be inflicted under s 20 and since causing grievous bodily harm in s 18 is an alternative to wounding I regard it as clear that the word 'cause' in s 18 is wide enough to include any action that could amount to inflicting grievous bodily harm under s 20 where the word 'inflict' appears as an alternative to 'wound'. For this reason, in my view, following the reasoning of this House in *R v Wilson (Clarence)* [1984] AC 242 an alternative verdict under s 20 was open on the terms of this indictment ...

Lord Templeman: My Lords, the criminal law is already overburdened with technicalities. In my opinion: (1) an allegation of causing grievous bodily harm includes an allegation of inflicting grievous bodily harm. (2) A jury may convict of an offence under s 20 of the Offences Against the Person Act 1861 as an alternative to a charge of convicting of an offence under s 18 of that Act. (3) The Court of Appeal may substitute a conviction under s 20 for a conviction under s 18 ...

I agree, therefore, with the order proposed by my noble and learned friend, Lord Mackay of Clashfern LC.

R v Savage; R v Parmenter [1992] 1 AC 699 (HL)

For facts, see above.

[**Lord Ackner** (with whom **Lord Keith of Kinkel, Lord Brandon of Oakbrook, Lord Jauncey of Tullichettle** and **Lord Lowry** agreed):]

1   Is a verdict of guilty of assault occasioning actual bodily harm a permissible alternative verdict on a count alleging unlawful wounding contrary to s 20 of the 1861 Act?

... Having reviewed the relevant authorities Lord Roskill [in *R v Wilson* [1984] AC 242] was content to accept that there can be an infliction of grievous bodily harm contrary to s 20 without an assault being committed. For example, grievous bodily harm could be inflicted by creating panic. Another example provided to your Lordships in the course of the argument in the current appeals was interfering with the braking mechanism of a car, so as to cause the driver to be involved in an accident and thus suffer injuries. These are somewhat far-fetched examples. The allegation of inflicting grievous bodily harm or for that matter wounding ... inevitably imports or includes an allegation of assault, unless there are some quite extraordinary facts.

The critical question remained: do the allegations in a s 20 charge 'include either expressly or by implication' allegations of assault occasioning actual bodily harm. As to this, Lord Roskill concluded [1984] AC 242 at 261:

If 'inflicting' can, as the cases show, include 'inflicting by assault', then even though such a charge may not necessarily do so, I do not for myself see why on a fair reading of s 6(3) [of the Criminal Law Act 1967] these allegations do not at least impliedly include 'inflicting by assault'. That is sufficient for present purposes though I also regard it as also a possible view that those former allegations expressly include the other allegations.

I respectfully agree with this reasoning and accordingly reject the submission that *R v Wilson* was wrongly decided. I would therefore answer the first of the certified questions in the *Savage* case in the affirmative. A verdict of guilty of assault occasioning actual bodily harm is a permissible alternative verdict on a count alleging unlawful wounding contrary to s 20 of the Offences Against the Person Act 1861.

What does the word 'malicious' mean?

R v Mowatt [1968] 1 QB 421 (CA)

Diplock LJ: ... The learned judge in summing up explained to the jury the meaning of 'unlawfully' ... but nowhere in the summing up did the judge mention the word 'maliciously' or give the jury any directions as to its meaning ...

... In s 18 the word 'maliciously' adds nothing. The intent expressly required by that section is more specific than such element of foresight of consequences as is implicit in the word 'maliciously' and in directing a jury about an offence under this section the word 'maliciously' is best ignored. In the offence under s 20, and in the alternative verdict which may be given on a charge under s 18 – for neither of which is any specific intent required – the word 'maliciously' does import on the part of the person who unlawfully inflicts the wound or other grievous bodily harm an awareness that his act may have the consequence of causing some physical harm to some other person ... It is quite unnecessary that the accused should have foreseen that his unlawful act might cause physical harm of the gravity described in the section ie a wound or serious physical injury. It is enough that he should have foreseen that some physical harm to some person, albeit of a minor character, might result ...

... There may, of course, be cases where the accused's awareness of the possible consequences of his act is genuinely in issue. *R v Cunningham* [1957] 2 QB 396 is a good example. But where the evidence for the prosecution, if accepted, shows that the physical act of the accused which caused the injury to another person was a direct assault which any ordinary person would be bound to realise was likely to cause some physical harm to the other person (as, for instance, an assault with a weapon or the boot or violence with the hands) and the defence put forward on behalf of the accused is not that the assault was accidental or that he did not realise that it might cause some physical harm to the victim, but is some other defence such as that he did not do the alleged act or that he did it in self-defence, it is unnecessary to deal specifically in the summing up with what is meant by the word 'maliciously' in the section. It can only confuse the jury to invite them in the summing up to consider an improbability not previously put forward and to which no evidence has been directed, to wit, that the accused did not realise what any ordinary person would have realised was a likely consequence of his act, and to tell the jury that the onus lies, not on the accused to establish, but on the prosecution to negative, that improbability, and to go on to talk about presumptions. To a jury who are not jurisprudents that sounds like jargon. In the absence of any evidence that the accused did not realise that it was a possible consequence of his act that some physical harm might be caused to the victim, the prosecution satisfy the relevant onus by proving the commission by the accused of an act which any ordinary person would realise was likely to have that consequence. There is no issue here to which the jury need direct their minds and there is no need to give to them any specific directions about it. In such a case, and these are the commonest of cases under s 18, the real issues of fact on which the jury have to make up their minds are: (1) Are they satisfied that the accused did the act? (2) If so, are they satisfied that the act caused a wound or other serious physical injury? (3) If the defence of self-defence is raised or there is any evidence to support it, do they think that the accused may have done the act in self-defence? (4) If the answer to (1) and (2) is Yes and to (3), if raised, is No, are they satisfied that when he did the act he intended to cause a wound or other really serious physical injury? If (3) (if raised) is answered No and (1) and (2) are answered Yes, the lesser offence under s 20 is made out; and if (4) is also answered Yes, the graver offence under s 18 is made out. In any case under s 18 where the physical act of the accused was a direct assault which any ordinary person would have realised was likely to cause some physical harm to the victim and there is no evidence that the accused himself did not realise that it might do so, if those issues, which we have stated, are put fairly and squarely to the jury it is the view of this court that the summing up is not open to criticism. There is no need for any general dissertation about the meaning of the word 'maliciously'. The less said about it in such a case the better.

The only remaining issue is whether the present case is one of this kind. The relevant evidence for the prosecution was that of the complainant and the two police officers. The complainant, in the early hours of the morning of 30 September, was returning home, according to his evidence, and was stopped in a street by two men, one of whom was the appellant. They asked him if there was a club anywhere about, and then one of them, not the appellant, snatched a £5 note from the complainant's breast pocket and ran off. The complainant said that he chased him without success, returned to the appellant, grasped him by his lapels and demanded to know the whereabouts of his mate. The appellant then (and this was common ground) hit out at the complainant and knocked him down. That was the first assault. Two off-duty police officers then saw the appellant, according to their evidence, sitting astride the complainant, and they saw the appellant strike him several violent blows in the face with his fist and pull him to his feet, strike him again in the face, knocking him down and making him virtually unconscious. The appellant was, according to the police, trying to pull up the complainant again when the police arrested the appellant. When the appellant was taken to the station, he was found to be concealing a £5 note in his hand ... In the view of this court, this was clearly a case where in relation to the lesser offence of which the appellant was convicted it was quite unnecessary for the learned judge to give the jury any instructions on the meaning of the word 'maliciously' ...

R v Sullivan [1981] Crim LR 46 (CA)

Facts: The appellant was tried of charges of causing grievous bodily harm with intent, contrary to s 18 of the Offences Against the Person Act 1861 and with unlawfully and maliciously inflicting grievous bodily harm on the victim, contrary to s 20. The victim's evidence was that the appellant and a companion were undoubtedly drunk and, while the victim was in a street only eight feet wide with a narrow pavement, the appellant drove his car through the street at 25–30 mph, mounted the pavement and injured the victim. The appellant was acquitted of the s 18 offence but convicted of offences under s 20. He appealed.

Held: Section 8 of the Criminal Justice Act 1967 in effect enacted that there was no presumption of law that a man intended or foresaw the natural consequences of his act, and removed the whole basis of the argument that an intent to frighten was enough to constitute the necessary mens rea under s 20. However, a jury might be convinced from the evidence relating to intent to frighten that the person charged was aware that his act was likely to have the result of causing some sort of injury to the victim. Nevertheless, since s 8, mere intention to frighten without more was insufficient; the person charged must be proved to have been aware that probable consequences of his voluntary act would be to cause some injury to the victim, but not necessarily grievous bodily harm.

In the circumstances a properly directed jury could not have come to any other conclusion than that the appellant must have been aware that what he was doing was likely to cause physical injury to the victim.

R v Savage; R v Parmenter [1992] 1 AC 699 (HL)

For facts, see above.

[**Lord Ackner** (with whom **Lord Keith of Kinkel, Lord Brandon of Oakbrook, Lord Jauncey of Tullichettle** and **Lord Lowry** agreed):]

3   In order to establish an offence under s 20 of the 1861 Act, must the prosecution prove that the defendant actually foresaw that his act would cause harm, or is it sufficient to prove that the ought so to have foreseen?

His Lordship quoted at length from the speech of Lord Diplock in *R v Caldwell* [1982] AC 341 and continued:

A few weeks after hearing the argument in *R v Caldwell* [1982] AC 341, your Lordships in *R v Lawrence (Stephen)* [1982] AC 510 had to consider the word 'recklessly' in ss 1 and 2 of the Road Traffic Act 1972 as amended. Judgment in that appeal was in fact given on the same day as judgment in the *Caldwell* case. It was a unanimous decision of the House, the leading speech again being given by Lord Diplock. I need not trouble your Lordships with the facts of that case. Lord Diplock in referring to *R v Caldwell* [1982] AC 341 said that the conclusion reached by the majority of your Lordships was that the adjective 'reckless' when used in a criminal statute, ie the Criminal Damage Act 1971, had not acquired a special meaning as a term of legal art, but bore its popular or dictionary meaning of careless, regardless or heedless of the possible harmful consequences of one's acts. The same must be true of the adverbial derivative 'recklessly' when used in relation to driving a motor vehicle. As to the mens rea of the offence, he said [1982] AC 510 at 526–27:

I turn now to the *mens rea*. My task is greatly simplified by what has already been said about the concept of recklessness in criminal law in *R v Caldwell* [1982] AC 341. Warning was there given against adopting the simplistic approach of treating all problems of criminal liability as soluble by classifying the test of liability as being either 'subjective' or 'objective'. Recklessness on the part of the doer of an act does presuppose that there is something in the circumstances that would have drawn the attention of an ordinary prudent individual to the possibility that his act was capable of causing the kind of serious harmful consequences that the section which creates the offence was intended to prevent, and that the risk of those harmful consequences occurring was not so slight that an ordinary prudent individual would feel justified in treating them as negligible. It is only when this is so that the doer of the act is acting 'recklessly' if before doing the act, he either fails to give any thought to the possibility of there being any such risk or, having recognised that there was such risk, he nevertheless goes on to do it. In my view, an appropriate instruction to the jury on what is meant by driving recklessly would be that they must be satisfied of two things: first, that the defendant was in fact driving the vehicle in such a manner as to create an obvious and serious risk of causing physical injury to some other person who might happen to be using the road or of doing substantial damage to property; and second, that in driving in that manner the defendant did so without having given any thought to the possibility of there being any such risk or, having recognised that there was some risk involved, had nonetheless gone on to take it.

... [Counsel for Parmenter] submitted that in *Caldwell's* case your Lordships' House could have followed either of two possible paths to its conclusion as to the meaning of 'recklessly' in the Act of 1971. These were: (a) to hold that *R v Cunningham* [1957] 2 QB 396 (and *R v Mowatt* [1968] 1 QB 421) were wrongly decided and to introduce a single test, wherever recklessness was an issue; or (b) to accept that *Cunningham* (subject to the *Mowatt* 'gloss' to which no reference was made), correctly states the law in relation to the Offences Against the Person Act 1981, because the word 'maliciously' in that statute was a term of legal art which imported into the concept of recklessness a special restricted meaning, thus distinguishing it from 'reckless', or 'recklessly' in modern 'revising' statutes then before the House, where those words bore their then popular or dictionary meaning.

I agree with [counsel for Parmenter] that manifestly it was the latter course which the House followed. Therefore in order to establish an offence under s 20 the prosecution must prove either that the defendant intended or that he actually foresaw that his act would cause harm.

4   In order to establish an offence under s 20 is it sufficient to prove that the defendant intended or foresaw the risk of some physical harm or must he intend or foresee either wounding or grievous bodily harm?

... My Lords, I am satisfied that the decision in *R v Mowatt* [1968] 1 QB 421 was correct and that it is quite unnecessary that the accused should either have intended or have foreseen that his unlawful act might cause physical harm of the gravity described in s 20, ie a wound or serious physical injury. It is enough that he should have foreseen that some physical harm to some person, albeit of a minor character, might result.

In the result I would dismiss the appeal in *Savage's* case but allow the appeal in *Parmenter's* case, but only to the extent of substituting, in accordance with the provisions of s 3(2) of the Criminal Appeal Act 1968, verdicts of guilty of assault occasioning actual bodily harm contrary to s 47 of the 1861 Act for the four s 20 offences of which he was convicted.

Crown Prosecution Charging Standards: Unlawful wounding/inflicting grievous bodily harm, contrary to s 20 of the Act.

8.4 The definition of wounding may encompass injuries which are relatively minor in nature, for example a small cut or laceration. An assault resulting in such minor injuries should more appropriately be charged contrary to section 47. An offence contrary to section 20 should be reserved for those wounds considered to be serious (thus equating the offence with the infliction of grievous, or serious, bodily harm under the other part of the section).

8.5 Grievous bodily harm means serious bodily harm. Examples of this are:

* injury resulting in permanent disability or permanent loss of sensory function;

* injury which results in more than minor permanent, visible disfigurement;

* broken or displaced limbs or bones, including fractured skull; compound fractures, broken cheek bone, jaw, ribs, etc;

- injuries which cause substantial loss of blood, usually necessitating a transfusion;

- injuries resulting in lengthy treatment or incapacity. (When psychiatric injury is alleged appropriate expert evidence is essential to prove the injury).

8.6 In accordance with the recommendation in *R v McCready* [1978] 1 WLR 1376, if there is any reliable evidence that a sufficiently serious wound has been inflicted, then the charge under section 20 should be of unlawful wounding, rather than of inflicting grievous bodily harm. Where both a wound and grievous bodily harm have been inflicted, discretion should be used in choosing which part of section 20 more appropriately reflects the true nature of the offence.

8.7 The prosecution must prove under section 20 that either the defendant intended, or actually foresaw, that the act would cause some harm. It is not necessary to prove that the defendant either intended or foresaw that the unlawful act might cause physical harm of the gravity described in section 20. It is enough that the defendant foresaw that some physical harm to some person, albeit of a minor character, might result: *R v Savage, R v Parmenter* (*supra*).

Section 18 of the Offences Against the Person Act 1861

Section 18: shooting or attempting to shoot, or wounding, with intent to do grievous bodily harm, or to resist apprehension

Whosoever shall unlawfully and maliciously by any means whatsoever wound or cause any grievous bodily harm to any person ... with intent ... to do some ... grievous bodily harm to any person, or with intent to resist or prevent the lawful apprehension or detainer of any person, shall be guilty of [an offence], and being convicted thereof shall be liable ... to [imprisonment] for life...

Crown Prosecution Charging Standards: Wounding/causing grievous bodily harm with intent, contrary to s 18 of the Act

9.4 The distinction between charges under section 18 and section 20 is one of intent.

9.5 The gravity of the injury resulting is not the determining factor although it may provide some evidence of intent.

9.6 When charging an offence involving grievous bodily harm, consideration should be given to the fact that a section 20 offence requires the infliction of harm, whereas a section 18 offence requires the causing of harm. This is especially significant when considering alternative verdicts (see paragraph 11 below).

9.7 Factors which may indicate the specific intent include: –

- a repeated or planned attack;

- deliberate selection of a weapon or adaptation of an article to cause injury, such as breaking a glass before an attack;

- making prior threats;
- using an offensive weapon against, or kicking, the victim's head;

9.8 The evidence of intent required is different if the offence alleged is a wounding or the causing of grievous bodily harm with intent to resist or prevent the lawful apprehension or detainer of any person. This part of section 18 is of assistance in more serious assaults upon police officers, where the evidence of an intention to prevent arrest is clear, but the evidence of an intent to cause grievous bodily harm is in doubt.

9.9 It is not bad for duplicity to indict for wounding with intent to cause grievous bodily harm or to resist lawful apprehension in one count, although it is best practice to include the allegations in separate counts. This will enable a jury to consider the different intents and the court to sentence on a clear basis of the jury's finding.

Crown Prosecution Charging Standards: s 18 or attempted murder?

10.3 Unlike murder, which requires an intention to kill or cause grievous bodily harm, attempted murder requires evidence of an intention to kill alone. This makes it a difficult allegation to sustain and careful consideration must be given to whether the more appropriate charge is under section 18.

10.4 The Courts will pay particular attention to counts of attempted murder and justifiably will be highly critical of any such count unless there is clear evidence of an intention to kill.

10.5 It should be borne in mind that the actions of the defendant must be more than preparatory and although words and threats may provide *prima facie* evidence of an intention to kill, there may be doubt as to whether they were uttered seriously or were mere bravado.

10.6 Evidence of the following factors may assist in proving the intention to kill:

- calculated planning;
- selection and use of a deadly weapon;
- threats (subject to paragraph 10.5) above;
- severity or duration of attack;
- relevant admissions in interview.

Notes and queries

1 The offence under s 18 of the 1986 Act requires proof of an intention to do some grievous bodily harm. It is submitted that, given that intention to do grievous bodily harm is sufficient *mens rea* for murder, intention in this context ought to have the same meaning as that attributed to it in *R v Woollin* [1998] 4 All ER 103 (see Chapter 4).

Crown Prosecution Charging Standards: Alternative verdicts where s 18 or s 20 are charged

11.1 In certain circumstances, it is possible for a jury to find the accused not guilty of the offence charged, but guilty of some other alternative offence. The general provisions are contained in section 6(3), Criminal Law Act 1967, and are supplemented by other provisions which relate to specific offences.

11.2 For offences against the person, the following alternatives may be found by a jury:

(a) causing grievous bodily harm with intent, contrary to section 18 of the Act;

- attempting to cause grievous bodily harm with intent;
- inflicting grievous bodily harm, contrary to section 20 of the Act;
- unlawful wounding, contrary to section 20 of the Act;

(b) wounding with intent, contrary to section 18 of the Act;

- attempting wounding with intent;
- unlawful wounding, contrary to section 20 of the Act;
- assault occasioning actual bodily harm, contrary to section 47 of the Act.

(c) inflicting grievous bodily harm, contrary to section 20 of the Act;

- assault occasioning actual bodily harm, contrary to section 47 of the Act.

(d) unlawful wounding, contrary to section 20 of the Act;

- assault occasioning actual bodily harm, contrary to section 47 of the Act.

11.3 It is essential, however, that the charge which most suits the circumstances of the case is always preferred. It will never be appropriate to charge a more serious offence in order to obtain a conviction (whether by plea or verdict) to a lesser offence.

11.4 There is authority to support the proposition that a jury may convict of wounding, contrary to section 20 of the Act, as an alternative to a count of causing grievous bodily harm with intent, contrary to section 18 of the Act: *R v Wilson, R v Jenkins & Jenkins* (1984) 77 Cr App R 319, HL, *R v Mandair* [1994] 2 WLR 1376, HL.

11.5 Notwithstanding that authority, prosecutors should nevertheless include a separate count on the indictment alleging wounding, contrary to section 20, where there is a realistic likelihood that the jury will convict the defendant of the lesser offence.

11.6 Common assault is not available as an alternative to any offence contrary to sections 18, 20 or 47 of the Act. A specific count alleging common assault must be included on the indictment pursuant to the provisions of section 40, Criminal Justice Act 1988.

POISONING

Sections 23 and 24 of the Offences Against the Person Act 1861 provide:

23 Whosoever shall unlawfully and maliciously administer to or cause to be administered to or taken by any other person any poison or other destructive or noxious thing, so as thereby to endanger the life of such person, or so as thereby to inflict upon such person any grievous bodily harm, shall be guilty of felony, and being convicted thereof shall be liable to be kept in penal servitude for any term not exceeding ten years.

24 Whosoever shall unlawfully and maliciously administer to or cause to be administered to or taken by any other person any poison or other destructive or noxious thing, with intent to injure, aggrieve, or annoy such person, shall be guilty of a misdemeanour, and being convicted thereof shall be liable to be kept in penal servitude.

R v Gillard (1988) 87 Cr App R 189 (CA (Crim Div))

The court considered whether spraying CS gas constituted an 'administration' of a substance for the purposes of s 24 of the 1861 Act.

McNeill J: Mr Boyd put his argument in this court in this way. He relied on the use in section 24 of the word 'administered' in conjunction with the word 'taken' as indicating Parliament's intention in this section to make criminal only acts which by physical contact obliged the victim to ingest the noxious thing. Where there was no physical contact and so no battery the act could nevertheless be charged and should be charged as an assault: to spray CS gas into someone's face is, he said, an assault in law.

The *Shorter Oxford English Dictionary* includes among definitions of 'administer', 'to apply, as medicine, etc. Hence to dispense, give (anything beneficial; also (jocular) a rebuke, a blow, etc).'

The court does not find the dictionary definitions helpful: too many and too diverse alternatives are offered.

Mr Boyd contended that his construction of 'administer' is consistent with and supported by its use in other sections of the Act. Thus, in sections 22 and 29, 'administer' is used in conjunction with 'apply': where 'apply' is not used 'administer' is used in conjunction with 'take' (as in section 24) and also in the 'poison' sections.

In support of this submission, Mr Boyd invited attention to the only reported decision on the construction of 'administer' in section 24. In *Dones* [1987] Crim LR 682 Mr Recorder Walsh QC, sitting at the Central Criminal Court, had a case under section 24 where the defendant was charged with spraying a solution of ammonia from a plastic lemon at the victim, some of which struck his eye and caused irritation. This court has had the advantage of reading a transcript of the recorder's ruling.

The defendant there had first appeared before Mr Recorder Hawkins who accepted that on these facts there was an 'administration' for the purposes of section 24; but the point was not argued fully or at all. In the event, however, the jury disagreed and so the case came before Mr Recorder Walsh for re-trial. He was able, therefore, to consider the matter untrammelled by any decision upon it by Mr Recorder Hawkins.

In this court, Mr Boyd relied on Mr Recorder Walsh's ruling and adopted it as part of his argument. It is necessary to set out the relevant part of his ruling which reads:

It is worth noting that in all the sections where 'administer' applies on its own, it is in conjunction with poisons, and the word 'taking' or 'causing to be taken by,' and it seems to me that, if one looks at all those sections together, the offences which the draftsmen and Parliament were clearly aiming at were the taking (the 'ingestion', as it were) of some poisonous or noxious matter by the victim or in the case of the pregnant woman by herself, in what the public commonly understand the ordinary word of 'taking' for consuming food, medicine or so forth. Section 22 (of the Offences against the Person Act 1861) is different because, as I have said before, the word 'apply' is added; the words being; 'apply or administer chloroform, laudanum or other stupefying drug.' One can see why that is, because stupefying drug can be administered in the same way as I have previously described, but one can also 'apply' chloroform in what I suppose was the time-honoured fashion of many, many years ago of the villain sneaking up on the victim, with a handkerchief, suitably impregnated, pressing it over his or her mouth or nose, and overpowering him or her. That seems to me to cover the 'applying' situation and to distinguish it from the 'administering' situation. One looks further at section 29, which is the section under which the defendant initially was committed for trial and one notices, after the initial lines about 'sending, delivering, causing to be taken or received by any person' – I miss out certain words – 'any other dangerous or noxious thing,' it then continues, 'or whoever shall put or lay at any place or' – and these are the important words – 'cast or throw at or upon, or otherwise apply to any person any corrosive fluid,' shall be guilty of this offence if they have certain intentions. So it seems to me quite clear that what Parliament and what the draftsmen of this Act had in mind were different sets of circumstances; one of which can be described with the verb 'apply', another by the verb 'to administer,' and yet another by the verbs 'to cast' or 'to throw'; and when one finds in a statute (and, in particular, in the same parts of a statute) a series of offences where those words are used, either separately or sometimes in conjunction with different sections, it is plain to me that they (the drafters and Parliament) intended them to cover different situations, and in my view they do, and it seems to me that if Parliament had in mind it being an offence to cast or throw upon somebody a noxious thing, as well as a corrosive fluid, the Act would have said so, and it does not. There may have been an error in that, and that the danger then thought the more serious because it was the more prevalent – lemon Jifs not having been invented – was the throwing or casting of corrosive fluid which was likely or intended to maim, disfigure, disable or do serious harm. It may be that that was the mischief to which the Act was intending to apply, but in my judgment 'administer' was not intended to cover a situation such as this.

This court does not accept that the words or purport of sections other than section 24 is relevant. A well established canon of construction is that if the words of a section are capable on their own of bearing a clear and ascertainable meaning there is no scope for reference over to other sections of the same statute; such recourse may only be had in the event of ambiguity or uncertainty or if that meaning is apparently inconsistent with the general intention of the statute. This is not the case here.

Where, in the view of this court, the learned recorder was in error was in holding that 'administering' and 'taking' were to be treated effectively as synonymous or as conjunctive words in the section; on the contrary, the repeated use of the word 'or' makes it clear that they are disjunctive. The word 'takes' postulates some 'ingestion' by the victim; 'administer' must have some other meaning and there is no difficulty in including in that meaning such conduct as spraying the victim with noxious fluid or vapour, whether from a device such as a gas canister or, for example, hosing down with effluent. There is no necessity when the word 'administer' is used to postulate any form of entry into the victim's body, whether through any orifice or by absorption; a court dealing with such a case should not have to determine questions of pathology such as, for example, the manner in which skin irritation results from exposure to CS gas or the manner in which the eye waters when exposed to irritant. The word 'ingest' should be reserved to its natural meaning of intake into the digestive system and not permitted to obscure the statutory words.

In the view of this court, the proper construction of 'administer' in section 24 includes conduct which not being the application of direct force to the victim nevertheless brings the noxious thing into contact with his body.

While such conduct might in law amount to an assault, this court considers that so to charge it would tend to mislead a jury.

The court has been assisted by the note by Professor JC Smith in the report of *Dones* [1987] Crim LR 682. The learned recorder, as the note submits, was correct in treating the question as one of construction and as a matter of law, following *R v Maginnis* (1987) 85 Cr App R 127.

In this respect, Judge Butler was in error in following as he presumably did the approach of the House of Lords in *Brutus v Cozens* (1972) 56 Cr App R 799, [1973] AC 854 which, in relation to the word 'insulting' regarded the meaning of that word as a matter of fact for the jury. This court regards the word 'administer' as one to be construed as was the word 'supply' in *R v Maginnis*. However, the trial judge's error – and an understandable error – was, if anything, to the advantage of the defendant, as he then was, and can in no way be regarded as a material irregularity.

As Mr Recorder Walsh correctly said; 'It is for the court to interpret and construe the word here, as having a particular meaning, and for the court to direct the jury as to what it means.' In concluding as follows: 'I am satisfied that the word 'administer' does not apply to a situation such as this,' that is squirting ammonia from a plastic lemon – he was in error.

Accordingly, this appeal is dismissed.

R v Cato [1976] 1 WLR 110 (CA)

For the facts see Chapter 3. The following extract concerns the extent to which the appellant's injection of the deceased with heroin constituted an offence under s 23 of the 1861 Act.

Lord Widgery CJ: The next matter, I think, is the unlawful act. Of course, on the first approach to manslaughter in this case it was necessary for the prosecution to prove that Farmer had been killed in the course of an unlawful act. Strangely enough, or it may seem strange to most of us, although the possession or supply of heroin is an offence, it is not an offence to take it, and although supplying it is an offence, it is not an offence to administer it. At least it is not made to be an offence, and so Mr Blom-Cooper [counsel for the defendant] says there was no unlawful act here. That which Cato did – taking Farmer's syringe already charged and injecting the mixture into Farmer as directed – is not an unlawful act, says Mr Blom-Cooper, because there is nothing there which is an offence against the

Misuse of Drugs Act 1971, and when he shows us the terms of the section it seems that that is absolutely right.

Of course if the conviction on count 2 remains (that is the charge under section 23 of administering a noxious thing), then that in itself would be an unlawful act. The prohibition in that statute would be enough in itself, and it is probably right to say that, as we are going to uphold the conviction on count 2, as will appear presently, that really answers the problem and destroys the basis of Mr Blom-Cooper's argument.

But since he went to such trouble with the argument, and in respect for it, we think we ought to say that had it not been possible to rely on the charge under section 23 of the Offences against the Person Act 1861, we think there would have been an unlawful act here, and we think the unlawful act would be described as injecting the deceased Farmer with a mixture of heroin and water which at the time of the injection and for the purposes of the injection the accused had unlawfully taken into his possession.

... What is a noxious thing, and in particular is heroin a noxious thing? The authorities show that an article is not to be described as noxious for present purposes merely because it has a potentiality for harm if taken in an overdose.

There are many articles of value in common use which may be harmful in overdose, and it is clear on the authorities when looking at them that one cannot describe an article as noxious merely because it has that aptitude. On the other hand, if an article is liable to injure in common use, not when an overdose in the sense of an accidental excess is used but is liable to cause injury in common use, should it then not be regarded as a noxious thing for present purposes?

When one has regard to the potentiality of heroin in the circumstances which we read about and hear about in our courts today we have no hesitation in saying that heroin is a noxious thing and we do not think that arguments are open to an accused person in a case such as the present, whereby he may say: 'Well the deceased was experienced in taking heroin: his tolerance was high,' and generally to indicate that the heroin was unlikely to do any particular harm in a particular circumstance. We think there can be no doubt, and it should be said clearly, that heroin is a noxious thing for the purposes of s 23.

... We think in this case where the act was entirely a direct one that the requirement of malice is satisfied if the syringe was deliberately inserted into the body of Farmer, as it undoubtedly was, and if Cato at a time when he so inserted the syringe knew that the syringe contained a noxious substance. That is enough, we think, in this type of direct injury case to satisfy the requirement of maliciousness.

R v Hill (1986) 83 Cr App R 386

Lord Griffiths [having set out the provisions of s 24 of the Offences Against the Person Act 1861]: The respondent, who is a homosexual, had purchased a number of tablets of a drug on the 'black market' near Charing Cross. The drug, tenuate dospan, is available only on prescription and is used as an aid in slimming cures. The normal dose for an adult is one tablet a day taken during the morning. An overdose can cause vomiting and nausea, agitation, insomnia and increased heart and pulse rates.

On June 14, 1983 at about 8 pm the respondent met two boys aged 13 and 11 at an adventure playground in Pimlico. He had met the elder boy, Anthony, earlier in the week in the same playground and had promised to bring cigarettes and drink with him on this occasion. Anthony had brought his friend Darren with him to meet the respondent. The respondent told the boys that he had no drink but he had some 'speed' tablets that would make them feel happy and cheerful. Each boy took one of the tablets of tenuate dospan.

The respondent then took the boys to Streatham Fair where each boy took two more of the tablets. The respondent did not himself take the tablets and claimed that he had only taken one himself some months before. They all returned to Pimlico at about 11.30 p.m. and Anthony went home.

The respondent suggested to Darren that he should stay the night with him in his flat in South Kensington so that he would be able to put together a better explanation to Darren's mother to account for his absence from home that night. Darren agreed, but made it clear to the respondent that if he laid a hand on him in an indecent way he would tell not only his mother but the police as well because he said 'I know all about men like you, I have been warned about you.' At the flat Darren took a fourth tablet. They both took all their clothes off and lay upon the respondent's bed. Darren, as a result of the overdose of the drug, stayed awake all night and the respondent made no advances towards him, possibly as a result of the warning that Darren had given him. Next morning they set off to take Darren home but when approached by a policeman the defendant made off.

When the respondent was arrested later that day he admitted that he was sexually attracted to young boys and admitted giving them the tablets. The boys themselves both suffered from vomiting and diarrhoea during the next two days as a result of the overdose and were seen by their doctors. There was no evidence that the respondent knew the prescribed dose for the drug but the circumstances in which he admitted purchasing it on the black market showed that he must have realised the drug was only available on prescription.

At the trial the defence conceded that the tablets were a noxious thing and that the respondent had unlawfully administered them to the boys. In these circumstances the only issue that the jury had to determine was whether he did so with an intent to injure them. The jury by their verdict of guilty found that the respondent had such an intent and I can only say, my Lords, that I should have been astonished by any other verdict. Here was a man who admitted being sexually attracted to young boys plying them with a drug which he knew would overstimulate and excite them and doing so with a reckless disregard for what might be the safe dosage and, in fact, giving them a gross overdose. The only reasonable inference to draw from such conduct was an intention that the drug should injure the boys in the sense of causing harm to the metabolism of their bodies by overstimulation with the motive of either ingratiating himself with them or, more probably, rendering them susceptible to homosexual advances.

The respondent appealed against his conviction upon the following ground: 'The learned judge erred in directing the jury that an intention on the part of the respondent to keep awake the alleged victims was capable of amounting to an intention to injure.'

The Court of Appeal accepted this criticism of the summing up and said 'there is no doubt that the learned judge did direct the jury in those terms in the course of his summing up' and, as they hold it to be a misdirection, they quashed the conviction.

The passage in the summing up criticised by the Court of Appeal reads as follows:

It is the final element which is very much in point, because what the prosecution have to do is to make you sure that at the time them tablets were given to the boys the accused man had the intention of causing injury to them.

Now, what does 'causing injury' mean in this sense? It does not mean causing possible injury as you might cause an injury if you take a knife and you stab somebody and blood spurts all over the place. It does not mean that at all. The injury can be caused to a body externally. It can be caused by making the body malfunction. Injury can be caused by affecting those parts of the body or the metabolism in the body which may make the body function in a way different from that which it normally does.

Of course you might cause injury in the sense of causing harm to somebody if you give them something which keeps them awake. We know from the medical evidence that one of the effects of taking this drug (which is intended as an aid to slimming) is to keep awake the person who takes it. This may be a very important point in this case, because the prosecution say this is one of the areas of harm which was done to these boys, Obviously the body needs sleep. We all need our sleep every day in order to keep our bodies functioning normally. Nature tells us when the body is in need of a rest. Nature tells us that by making us fall asleep quite naturally when the relevant time has come. More particularly, children need more sleep than does an adult because they are expending so much more energy during the day, running about as they do. If the body is persuaded not to fall asleep at the relevant time and it goes beyond that, expending itself and using up energy to keep awake when normally the body should be asleep, it may well be that you would think that this is causing harm to the body, causing injury to the body in the sense of harm, and that it is one of the points suggested by the prosecution.

The other way in which the prosecution suggest that harm was caused to these young boys is that they were disinhibited; in other words the were made to lose the natural reserve which they have, disinhibited in the sense that they were made to feel lively and on top of the world and more inclined to do things they otherwise would not have done. The prosecution say if somebody administers a substance to a young boy which has that effect, then that is causing harm to him because it is leaving him open to a situation which otherwise would not exist. So the prosecution say that there are two forms of harm which were befalling these two young boys. One of them was the fact that they were being kept awake. Secondly, they were being disinhibited and, thirdly, say the prosecution, this drug was being administered in a considerable overdose on this occasion.

Commenting upon this passage, the Court of Appeal said: 'having regard to the earlier part of that passage from his summing up, the judge appears to have directed the jury that an intention to keep the boys awake was by itself sufficient to constitute an intent to injure. There are other passages later in his summing up which are to the same effect.'

My Lords, I am unable to accept that this passage bears the interpretation put upon it by the Court of Appeal. In this passage from the summing up the judge is explaining to the jury the meaning of injury in the section and relating it to the circumstances of this case. He is rightly directing the jury that injury includes causing harm to the body and pointing out to them that they would be entitled to conclude that to give drugs to children with the intention of interfering with their metabolism so that they would stay awake for an unnatural period could amount to causing injury in the sense of harm.

I am quite unable to read this passage in the summing up as a direction that an intention to keep a child awake *by itself* say for some benevolent purpose such as enjoying the fireworks, or to greet his father on a late return from work could amount to an intent to injure and I am sure it would not have been so understood by the jury.

Furthermore, far from other passages in the summing up being to the same effect, as the Court of Appeal supposed, the whole tenor of the summing up was that the jury must be sure that the respondent intended to cause harm to the health of the boys. I draw attention by way of example only to the way in which the judge put the defence before the jury:

> The defence say that at the very worst all he was doing was giving these boys tablets which he thought would make them happy and which he knew would keep them awake, but, says the defence, there is nothing criminal about that. There is not even anything reprehensible about that and you, the members of the jury, ought not to hold that conduct against him.

> Well, there it is. I am not going to say any more about that fact because I shall go on repeating myself. The issue is a perfectly clear one. You simply say to yourselves, am I sure that he intended to cause some injury – injury in the sense of harm to the body of these two young boys in administering the tablets. If the answer is 'yes, I am sure' then your verdict will be one of guilty. If you say to yourselves 'no, I am not at all sure that it was his intention, I am not sure about that at all' then your verdict will be one of not guilty.

By leaving the defence before the jury in this form it is to my mind clear that the judge was not suggesting that an intention to keep awake was *of itself* an intention to cause injury.

The summing up read as a whole, as a summing up should always he read, made it clear beyond peradventure that the jury should only convict if they wore sure that the respondent intended to injure the boys in the sense of causing them physical harm by the administration of the drugs. This was a correct direction. The respondent did, in fact, cause some physical harm and there was overwhelming evidence that this was his intention. I would accordingly allow this appeal and restore the convictions.

The Court of Appeal certified a question of law of general public importance in the following form:

> Whether the offence of administering a noxious thing with intent to injure contrary to section 24 of the Offences Against the Person Act 1861 is capable of being committed when a noxious thing is administered to a person without lawful excuse with the intention only of keeping that person awake.

My Lords, on the view I take of the summing up this question does not call for an answer. It is, in any event, a question which it is not sensible to attempt to answer without knowing the factual background against which it is asked. If the noxious thing is administered for a purely benevolent purpose such as keeping a pilot of an aircraft awake the answer will almost certainly be no, but if administered for a malevolent purpose such as a prolonged interrogation the answer will almost certainly be yes, I would, my Lords, therefore decline to answer the certified question.

Your Lordships declined to give leave to the respondent to argue that the conviction should be quashed on the ground that the judge failed to direct the jury on the issue of consent. This issue was never raised by the defence at the trial and if it had been it would have had no prospect of success. In the circumstances, the judge was under no duty to refer to it in the summing up.

Lord Mackay, **Lord Ackner**, **Lord Bridge** and **Lord Brandon** agreed that the appeal should be allowed for the reasons given.

KIDNAPPING AND FALSE IMPRISONMENT

Kidnapping

R v D [1984] AC 778 (HL)

Lord Brandon of Oakbrook: ... In this appeal your Lordships are called on, for the first time, to examine the nature, ingredients and scope of [kidnapping] ...

... [T]he offence contains four ingredients as follows: (1) the taking or carrying away of one person by another; (2) by force or by fraud; (3) without the consent of the person so taken or carried away; and (4) without lawful excuse ...

... That third ingredient ... consists of the absence of consent on the part of the person taken or carried away. I see no good reason why, in relation to the kidnapping of a child, it should not in all cases be the absence of the child's consent which is material, whatever its age may be. In the case of a very young child, it would not have the understanding or the intelligence to give its consent, so that absence of consent would be a necessary inference from its age. In the case of an older child, however, it must, I think be a question of fact for a jury whether the child concerned has sufficient understanding and intelligence to give its consent; if, but only if, the jury considers that a child has these qualities, it must then go on to consider whether it has been proved that the child did not give its consent. While the matter will always be for the jury alone to decide, I should not expect a jury to find at all frequently that a child under 14 has sufficient understanding and intelligence to give its consent.

> I should add that, while the absence of the consent of the person having custody or care or control of a child is not material to what I have stated to be the third ingredient of the common law offence of kidnapping, the giving of

consent by such a person may be very relevant to the fourth ingredient, in that, depending on all the circumstances, it might well support a defence of lawful excuse ...

False imprisonment

R v Rahman (1985) 81 Cr App R 349 (CA)

The Lord Chief Justice: We turn ... to consider what it is that has to be proved in order to bring home a charge of false imprisonment. False imprisonment consists in the unlawful and intentional or reckless restraint of a victim's freedom of movement from a particular place. In other words it is unlawful detention which stops the victim moving away as he would wish to move ...

There are many ways in which the prosecution may prove unlawfulness. The existence of a court order, as already mentioned in this judgment, may perhaps be one, by showing that the parental control had by order been given to someone other than the parent himself, and that the detention by the parent was contrary to that order. In this case there was no such order. But there are other ways of proving unlawfulness. The detention may be for such a period or in such circumstances as to take it out of the realms of reasonable parental discipline ...

Whether that stage has been reached, namely the stage of unreasonableness, is a matter for the jury to decide, if there is evidence which it is proper to go before the jury for them to consider ...

Notes and queries

1 Normally false imprisonment will arise where D physically restricts P's movements, but it may be that D restricts P's movements by means of threats; see *R v James* (1997) *The Times*, 2 October. D must at least be reckless as to whether the words he uses will restrained P by fear.

2 In relation to kidnapping see also the Child Abduction Act 1984, which was going through Parliament when *R v D* was being considered by the House of Lords.

'STALKING'

Parliament's response to the problem posed by what is popularly referred to as 'stalking' took the form of the Protection From Harassment Act 1997.

The Protection From Harassment Act 1997 was introduced in response to concerns about the inability of the existing civil and criminal law to deal adequately with the problem of stalking. The conduct prohibited is detailed in s 1 in the following terms:

1(1) A person must not pursue a course of conduct –

(a) which amounts to harassment of another, and

(b) which he knows or ought to know amounts to harassment of the other.

1(2) For the purposes of this section, the person whose course of conduct is in question ought to know that it amounts to harassment of another if a reasonable person in possession of the same information would think the course of conduct amounted to harassment of the other.

1(3) Subsection (1) does not apply to a course of conduct if the person who pursued it shows –

(a) that it was pursued for the purpose of preventing or detecting crime,

(b) that it was pursued under any enactment or rule of law or to comply with any condition or requirement imposed by any person under any enactment, or

(c) that in the particular circumstances the pursuit of the course of conduct was reasonable.

Under s 2(1) it is a summary offence to pursue a course of conduct which amounts to a breach of the prohibition laid down in s 1. More serious harassment is made an offence (triable either way) under s 4 which provides:

4(1) A person whose course of conduct causes another to fear, on at least two occasions, that violence will be used against him is guilty of an offence if he knows or ought to know that his course of conduct will cause the other so to fear on each of those occasions.

4(2) For the purposes of this section, the person whose course of conduct is in question ought to know that it will cause another to fear that violence will be used against him on any occasion if a reasonable person in possession of the same information would think the course of conduct would cause the other so to fear on that occasion.

4(3) It is a defence for a person charged with an offence under this section to show that –

(a) his course of conduct was pursued for the purpose of preventing or detecting crime,

(b) his course of conduct was pursued under any enactment or rule of law or to comply with any condition or requirement imposed by any person under any enactment, or

(c) the pursuit of his course of conduct was reasonable for the protection of himself or another or for the protection of his or another's property.

RACIALLY MOTIVATED ASSAULTS

As part of a response to racially motivated violence the courts were given increased sentencing powers in respect of offences of violence and harassment with a proven racial element under the Crime and Disorder Act 1998.

28   Meaning of 'racially aggravated'

(1) An offence is racially aggravated for the purposes of sections 29 to 32 below if

(a) at the time of committing the offence, or immediately before or after doing so, the offender demonstrates towards the victim of the offence hostility based on the victim's membership (or presumed membership) of a racial group; or

(b) the offence is motivated (wholly or partly) by hostility towards members of a racial group based on their membership of that group.

(2) In subsection (1)(a) above

'membership', in relation to a racial group, includes association with members of that group

'presumed' means presumed by the offender.

(3) It is immaterial for the purposes of paragraph (a) or (b) of subsection (1) above whether or not the offender's hostility is also based, to any extent, on

(a) the fact or presumption that any person or group of persons belongs to any religious group; or

(b) any other factor not mentioned in that paragraph.

(4) In this section 'racial group' means a group of persons defined by reference to race, colour, nationality (including citizenship) or ethnic or national origins.

29 Racially-aggravated assaults

(1) A person is guilty of an offence under this section if he commits

(a) an offence under section 20 of the Offences Against the Person Act 1861 (malicious wounding or grievous bodily harm);

(b) an offence under section 47 of that Act (actual bodily harm); or

(c) common assault,

which is racially aggravated for the purposes of this section.

(2) A person guilty of an offence falling within subsection (1)(a) or (b) above shall be liable

(a) on summary conviction, to imprisonment for a term not exceeding six months or to a fine not exceeding the statutory maximum, or to both;

(b) on conviction on indictment, to imprisonment for a term not exceeding seven years or to a fine, or to both.

(3) A person guilty of an offence falling within subsection (1)(c) above shall be liable

(a) on summary conviction, to imprisonment for a term not exceeding six months or to a fine not exceeding the statutory maximum, or to both;

(b) on conviction on indictment, to imprisonment for a term not exceeding two years or to a fine, or to both.

32 Racially-aggravated harassment etc

(1) A person is guilty of an offence under this section if he commits

(a) an offence under section 2 of the Protection from Harassment Act 1997 (offence of harassment); or

(b) an offence under section 4 of that Act (putting people in fear of violence),

which is racially aggravated for the purposes of this section.

(2) In section 24(2) of the 1984 Act (arrestable offences), after paragraph (o) there shall be inserted

'(p) an offence falling within section 32(1)(a) of the Crime and Disorder Act 1998 (racially-aggravated harassment)'.

(3) A person guilty of an offence falling within subsection (1)(a) above shall be liable

(a) on summary conviction, to imprisonment for a term not exceeding six months or to a fine not exceeding the statutory maximum, or to both;

(b) on conviction on indictment, to imprisonment for a term not exceeding two years or to a fine, or to both.

(4) A person guilty of an offence falling within subsection (1)(b) above shall be liable

(a) on summary conviction, to imprisonment for a term not exceeding six months or to a fine not exceeding the statutory maximum, or to both;

(b) on conviction on indictment, to imprisonment for a term not exceeding seven years or to a fine, or to both.

(5) If, on the trial on indictment of a person charged with an offence falling within subsection (1)(a) above, the jury find him not guilty of the offence charged, they may find him guilty of the basic offence mentioned in that provision.

(6) If, on the trial on indictment of a person charged with an offence falling within subsection (1)(b) above, the jury find him not guilty of the offence charged, they may find him guilty of an offence falling within subsection (1)(a) above.

CODIFICATION AND LAW REFORM PROPOSALS

In 1998 the Home Office published its consultation document *Violence: Reforming the Offences Against the Person Act 1861*. The paper was based upon the Law Commission's Report *Legislating the Criminal Code: Offences Against the Person and General Principles*. The key provisions of the draft Bill accompanying the Home Office paper were as follows:

Injury and assault

1(1) A person is guilty of an offence if he intentionally causes serious injury to another.

(2) A person is guilty of an offence if he omits to do an act which he has a duty to do at common law, the omission results in serious injury to another, and he intends the omission to have that result.

(3) An offence under this section is committed notwithstanding that the injury occurs outside England and Wales if the act causing injury is done in England and Wales or the omission resulting in injury is made there.

(4) A person guilty of an offence under this section is liable on conviction on indictment to imprisonment for life.

2(1) A person is guilty of an offence if he recklessly causes serious injury to another.

(2) An offence under this section is committed notwithstanding that the injury occurs outside England and Wales if the act causing injury is done in England and Wales.

(3) A person guilty of an offence under this section is liable –

(a) on conviction on indictment, to imprisonment for a term not exceeding 7 years;

(b) on summary conviction, to imprisonment for a term not exceeding 6 months or a fine not exceeding the statutory maximum or both.

3(1) A person is guilty of an offence if he intentionally or recklessly causes injury to another.

(2) An offence under this section is committed notwithstanding that the injury occurs outside England and Wales if the act causing injury is done in England and Wales.

(3) A person guilty of an offence under this section is liable –

(a) on conviction on indictment, to imprisonment for a term not exceeding 5 years;

(b) on summary conviction, to imprisonment for a term not exceeding 6 months or a fine not exceeding the statutory maximum or both.

4(1) A person is guilty of an offence if –

(a) he intentionally or recklessly applies force to or causes an impact on the body of another, or

(b) he intentionally or recklessly causes the other to believe that any such force or impact is imminent.

(2) No such offence is committed if the force or impact, not being intended or likely to cause injury, is in the circumstances such as is generally acceptable in the ordinary conduct of daily life and the defendant does not know or believe that it is in fact unacceptable to the other person.

(3) A person guilty of an offence under this section is liable on summary conviction to imprisonment for a term not exceeding 6 months or a fine not exceeding level 5 on the standard scale or both.

5(1) A person is guilty of an offence if he assaults –

(a) a constable acting in the execution of his duty, or

(b) a person assisting a constable acting in the execution of his duty.

(2) For the purposes of this section a person assaults if he commits the offence under section 4.

(3) A reference in this section to a constable acting in the execution of his duty includes a reference to a constable who is a member of a police force maintained in Scotland or Northern Ireland when he is executing a warrant, or otherwise acting in England and Wales, by virtue of an enactment conferring powers on him in England and Wales.

(4) For the purposes of subsection (3) each of the following is a police force –

(a) a police force within the meaning given by section 50 of the Police (Scotland) Act 1967;

(b) the Royal Ulster Constabulary and the Royal Ulster Constabulary Reserve.

(5) A person guilty of an offence under this section is liable on summary conviction to imprisonment for a term not exceeding 6 months or a fine not exceeding level 5 on the standard scale or both.

6(1) A person is guilty of an offence under this section if he causes serious injury to another intending to resist, prevent or terminate the lawful arrest or detention of himself or a third person.

(2) The question whether the defendant believes the arrest or detention is lawful must be determined according to the circumstances as he believes them to be.

(3) A person guilty of an offence under this section is liable on conviction on indictment to imprisonment for life.

7(1) A person is guilty of an offence if he assaults another intending to resist, prevent or terminate the lawful arrest or detention of himself or a third person.

(2) The question whether the defendant believes the arrest or detention is lawful must be determined according to the circumstances as he believes them to be.

(3) For the purposes of this section a person assaults if he commits the offence under section 4.

(4) A person guilty of an offence under this section is liable –

(a) on conviction on indictment, to imprisonment for a term not exceeding 2 years;

(b) on summary conviction, to imprisonment for a term not exceeding 6 months or a fine not exceeding the statutory maximum or both.

...

Other offences

10(1) A person is guilty of an offence if he makes to another a threat to cause the death of, or serious injury to, that other or a third person, intending that other to believe that it will be carried out.

(2) A person guilty of an offence under this section is liable –

(a) on conviction on indictment, to imprisonment for a term not exceeding 10 years;

(b) on summary conviction, to imprisonment for a term not exceeding 6 months or a fine not exceeding the statutory maximum or both.

11(1) A person is guilty of an offence if –

(a) he administers a substance to another or causes it to be taken by him and (in either case) he does so intentionally or recklessly,

(b) he knows the substance is capable of causing injury to the other, and

(c) it is unreasonable to administer the substance or cause it to be taken having regard to the circumstances as he knows or believes them to be.

(2) A person guilty of an offence under this section is liable –

(a) on conviction on indictment, to imprisonment for a term not exceeding 5 years;

(b) on summary conviction, to imprisonment for a term not exceeding 6 months or a fine not exceeding the statutory maximum or both.

12(1) A person is guilty of an offence if he intentionally inflicts severe pain or suffering on another and he does the act –

(a) in the performance or purported performance of his of official duties as a public official, or

(b) at the instigation or with the consent or acquiescence of a public official who is performing or purporting to perform his official duties.

(2) A person is guilty of an offence if –

(a) he omits to do an act which he has a duty to do at common law,

(b) he makes the omission as mentioned in subsection (1)(a) or (b),

(c) the omission results in the infliction of severe pain or suffering on another, and

(d) he intends the omission to have that result.

(3) The following are immaterial –

(a) the nationality of the persons concerned;

(b) whether anything occurs in the United Kingdom or elsewhere;

(c) whether the pain or suffering is physical or mental.

(4) References in this section to an official include references to a person acting in an official capacity.

(5) Proceedings for an offence under this section may be instituted only by or with the consent of the Attorney General.

(6) A person guilty of an offence under this section is liable on conviction on indictment to imprisonment for life.

For clause 14 dealing with proposed fault terms, see Chapter 4.

...

15(1) In this Act 'injury' means –

(a) physical injury, or

(b) mental injury.

(2) Physical injury does not include anything caused by disease but (subject to that) it includes pain, unconsciousness and any other impairment of a person's physical condition.

(3) Mental injury does not include anything caused by disease but (subject to that) it includes any impairment of a person's mental health.

(4) In its application to section 1 this section applies without the exceptions relating to things caused by disease.

The commentary to the Home Office proposals observed as follows:

3.5 The Government's proposals on the offence of assault go rather further than those of the Law Commission. The Commission proposed to replace common assault and battery with a new offence of assault that would combine the two existing offences. In doing this the Commission were concerned to clarify the meaning of assault and to remove the need for separate offences of assault. However, although the Commission considered the effect of their proposals on a number of different assault offences, they did not undertake a comprehensive survey of all other statutory offences of assault. The Government is concerned to ensure that the courts are able to apply a single definition of assault in all those many offences which use the concept of assault, wherever they occur. In considering this issue, we identified over 70 different uses of assault in law. It is vital that in considering cases involving any of these offences, judges, lawyers and juries know exactly what is meant by the term assault.

3.6 The Government is therefore proposing to apply the definition of assault in this Bill to all assault offences, whether they be indecent assault (which is an assault committed in circumstances of indecency) or assault on a particular class of persons. This proposal builds on the initial premise of the Law Commission but goes much further than their recommendation. Schedule 1 to the draft Bill sets out the precise impact of these changes on each piece of legislation. The list is long and detailed; at this stage the Government is only proposing to align meanings. This paper does not address the separate question of whether all these offences of assault are now necessary.

...

3.7 The Government shares the Law Commission's view that in general, the proposed new general offences offer protection for everyone, and that in principle special protection in law for particular classes or individuals should not normally be necessary. There are however some exceptions to this general principle. Some sections of society may require or deserve the additional protection of a specific provision in law. The Government has included in the Crime and Disorder Bill, now before Parliament, new aggravated offences for racially motivated violence which are based on existing offences of violence against the person in the Offences Against the Person Act 1861. Using these well-established and familiar offences will allow the courts to build on the existing law in dealing with those who commit these offences. The Government recognises that any subsequent implementation of its proposals to reform the Offences Against the Person Act 1861 will also have to amend the way in which these aggravated offences are formulated. The intention would be to re-state these offences following the model of the new offences against the person in the draft Bill. The Government recognises that it is unusual for Parliament to be asked to consider the same offences in quick succession in this way; however any such re-enactment would be a consolidation exercise to ensure that the law remained consistent.

3.8 The Law Commission recognised that the police and those carrying out a lawful arrest, had a legitimate and well-justified case for special recognition in the law, as they do at present. The Government agrees with this view. The Government is proposing to retain a number of particular offences relating to the police. The Law Commission had proposed to retain the offence of assaulting a police officer; the Government proposes to retain this offence and the offences of assault in resisting arrest. Clauses 5 to 7 therefore set out specific offences against the police. We recognise that Clause 6 does not fully mirror exactly the same approach of motivation and intent adopted by the Law Commission to the substantive offences in clauses 1 to 4 of this Bill, in that it does not require intent or recklessness to be proved. These offences are intended to replicate the present provisions relating to assaults on the police or in resisting arrest, so preserving the current legal position. The Government does not wish to reduce the protection given to the police in this law reform.

The offences in Clauses 5 to 7 are derived partly from the 1861 Act, but also reflect recent statutory changes.

...

3.9 A number of updated offences, mainly replacing offences currently contained in the 1861 Offences Against the Person Act, appear in clauses 8 to 13. Those relating to dangerous substances (clauses 8 and 9) are a reworking of the 1861 provisions to reflect the new substantive offences against the person, and to provide comprehensive protection against particular kinds of dangerous activity. The Law Commission had recommended that these provisions should be reviewed, and we have taken this opportunity to do so. Clause 8 is little changed in essence from the earlier provision; clause 9 has been amended to mirror the provisions of clause 8 where injury, rather than serious injury is caused, reflecting the structure of the first three clauses of the draft Bill. These changes are fully in accord with the principles of the Law Commission's report.

3.10 The Government accepts the Law Commission's reasoning that the existing offence of making threats to kill should be extended to threats to cause serious injury and also to threats made to a second person to harm a third person. This extended offence fills a gap in the equivalent 1861 Act offence, by creating a specific offence of threatening a third party. It is set out in clause 10. The new offence of administering a substance capable of causing injury (clause 11) was proposed by the Law Commission to replace the old poisoning offences. It has been revised slightly to remove any possibility that it could apply to bona fide medical treatment. Clause 12 restates the law on torture (presently set out in section 134 of the Criminal Justice Act 1988). Clause 13 sets out an updated version of the 1861 Act offences of causing danger on railways. These reflect and build on the Law Commission's work but are set out in the body of the Bill rather than in a Schedule as the Commission had proposed.

...

3.12 Clause 15 defines the meaning of injury in the Bill. This clarifies the meaning of the new offences in clauses 1 to 4. There is however no definition of what is a serious injury. The Government, like the Law Commission, is content for the courts to decide what is appropriate in individual cases. The definition of injury does however raise a number of important questions. It is sufficiently wide to encompass psychological and psychiatric harm as well as physical harm. The definition will also allow the transmission of disease to be included in the clause 1 offence of intentionally causing serious injury.

3.13 In seeking to reform an archaic and outdated law, the Government has to consider what the present law includes, how the courts have interpreted it, and how any replacement law should replicate or alter the present law. That is the context in which the question of whether the intentional transmission of disease ought to fall within the criminal law is being considered. In LC 218 the Law Commission were unequivocal that the Offences Against the Person Act 1861 could be used to prosecute the transmission of disease, and recommended that the proposed new offences should enable the intentional or reckless transmission of disease to be prosecuted in appropriate cases. The Government has not accepted this recommendation in full.

3.14   There are few decided cases on this point, so the position in the criminal law is not entirely clear. The most commonly cited case, that of *Clarence* (1888), seems to indicate that the 1861 Act could not be successfully used to prosecute the reckless transmission of disease. However it is now accepted that the judgement related to one specific offence and to the issue of consent, and that in principle it may well be possible to prosecute individuals for transmitting illness and disease at least when they do so intentionally. Although this has not been tested in the courts in recent years, in *Ireland* and *Burstow* the House of Lords held that the 1861 Act could be used to prosecute the infliction of psychiatric injury. In reforming the law, the issue of whether and if so how the transmission of disease should fall within the criminal law needs the most careful consideration.

3.15   The Government recognises that this is a very sensitive issue. The criminal law deals with behaviour that is wrong in intent and in deed. The Law Commission's original proposal, which included illness and disease in the definition of injury, would have resulted in the intentional or reckless transmission of disease being open to prosecution. They argued that the width of their proposal would be balanced by the fact that prosecution would only be appropriate in the most serious cases. The Government has considered their views very carefully, but is not persuaded that it would be right or appropriate to make the range of normal everyday activities during which illness could be transmitted, potentially criminal.

We think it would be wrong to criminalise the reckless transmission of normally minor illnesses such as measles or mumps, even though they could have potentially serious consequences for those vulnerable to infection.

3.16   An issue of this importance has ramifications beyond the criminal law, into the wider considerations of social and public health policy. The Government is particularly concerned that the law should not seem to discriminate against those who are HIV positive, have AIDS or viral hepatitis or who carry any kind of disease. Nor do we want to discourage people from coming forward for diagnostic tests and treatment, in the interests of their own health and that of others, because of an unfounded fear of criminal prosecution.

3.17   The Government therefore considered whether it should exclude all transmission of disease from the criminal law, and concluded that that too would not be appropriate. The existing law extends into this area, even though it has not been used. There is a strong case for arguing that society should have criminal sanctions available for use to deal with evil acts. It is hard to argue that the law should not be able to deal with the person who gives a disease causing serious illness to others with intent to do them such harm. That is clearly a form of violence against the person. Such a gap in the law would be difficult to justify.

3.18   The Government therefore proposes that the criminal law should apply only to those whom it can be proved beyond reasonable doubt had deliberately transmitted a disease intending to cause a serious illness. This aims to strike a sensible balance between allowing very serious intentional acts to be punished whilst not rendering individuals liable for prosecution for unintentional or reckless acts, or for the transmission of minor disease. The Government believes that this is close to the effect of the present law, and that it is right in principle to continue to allow the law to be used in those rare grave cases where prosecution would be justified. This proposal will clarify the present law which, because it is largely untested is unclear; by doing so the effect of the law will be confined to the most serious and culpable behaviour.

3.19 It is important to emphasise that this proposal does not reflect a significant change in the law. Prosecutions for the transmission of disease are very rare for very good reasons. Any criminal charge has to be supported by evidence and proved to a court beyond reasonable doubt. It is very difficult to prove both the causal linkage of the transmission and also to prove that it was done intentionally. To do so beyond reasonable doubt is even more difficult. The Government does not expect that the proposed offence will be used very often, but considers that it is important that it should exist to provide a safeguard against the worst behaviour.

3.20 Clause 15 provides for the intentional transmission of serious injury or disease to be included for the purposes of clause 1 (intentional serious injury), but not for any other purpose. This means that only those who transmit diseases with intent to cause serious injury, will be criminally liable ...

CONSENT TO PHYSICAL HARM AS A DEFENCE

R v Donovan [1934] 2 KB 498 (CA)

Swift J: It was established by the evidence, and was not in dispute, that on 8 March last, in the evening, the appellant induced Norah Eileen Harrison, a girl 17 years of age, to go with him to a garage at Morden, and there he beat her with a cane in circumstances of indecency. The defence was that it lay upon the prosecution to prove absence of consent, and that in fact the girl had consented to everything that was done by the appellant. It is not necessary to narrate the facts in detail. It appeared that the appellant was addicted to a form of sexual perversion, and there was no doubt that during a series of telephone conversations he had made suggestions to the prosecutrix which, if they were taken seriously, meant that he intended or desired to beat her. According to the evidence of the appellant, and of a young woman who said that she had overheard some of the telephone conversations, there was talk between the appellant and the prosecutrix which left no doubt that she had expressed her willingness to submit herself to the kind of conduct to which he was addicted ...

... In *R v May* [1912] 3 KB 572, 575 the principle applicable to cases of this kind was laid down by this court in these words: 'The court is of opinion that if the facts proved in evidence are such that the jury can reasonably find consent, there ought to be a direction by the judge on that question, both as to the onus of negativing consent being on the prosecution and as to the evidence in the particular case bearing on the question.'

We have no doubt that the facts proved in the present case were such that the jury might reasonably have found consent; it is, indeed, difficult to reconcile some of the admitted facts with absence of consent. It was therefore of importance (if consent was in issue) that there should be no possibility of doubt in the minds of the jury upon the question whether it was for the Crown to negative consent, or for the defence to prove it. A second observation which may fairly be made is that consent, being a state of mind, is to be proved or negatived only after a full and careful review of the behaviour of the person who is alleged to have consented. Unless a jury is satisfied beyond reasonable doubt that the conduct of the person has been such that, viewed as a whole, it shows that she did not consent, then the prisoner is entitled to be acquitted ...

[The jury asked the judge this question:

> If a man has reason to think that consent has been given, does that constitute consent?' ...

The proper answer to the jury's question would have been that if they as reasonable persons thought that the conduct of the prosecutrix, viewed as a whole, was consistent with consent, they ought not to find that the prosecution had negatived consent ...]

If an act is unlawful in the sense of being in itself a criminal act, it is plain that it cannot be rendered lawful because the person to whose detriment it is done consents to it. No person can license another to commit a crime. So far as the criminal law is concerned, therefore, where the act charged is in itself unlawful, it can never be necessary to prove absence of consent on the part of the person wronged in order to obtain the conviction of the wrongdoer. There are, however, many acts in themselves harmless and lawful which become unlawful only if they are done without the consent of the person affected. What is, in one case, an innocent act of familiarity or affection, may, in another, be an assault, for no other reason than that, in the one case there is consent, and in the other consent is absent. As a general rule, although it is a rule to which there are well-established exceptions, it is an unlawful act to beat another person with such a degree of violence that the infliction of bodily harm is a probable consequence, and when such an act is proved, consent is immaterial.

... Always supposing, therefore, that the blows which he struck were likely or intended to do bodily harm, we are of opinion that [the appellant] was doing an unlawful act, no evidence having been given of facts which would bring the case within any of the exceptions to the general rule. In our view, on the evidence given at the trial, the jury should have been directed that, if they were satisfied that the blows struck by the prisoner were likely or intended to do bodily harm to the prosecutrix, they ought to convict him, and that it was only if they were not so satisfied, that it became necessary to consider the further question whether the prosecution had negatived consent. For this purpose we think that 'bodily harm' has its ordinary meaning and includes any hurt or injury calculated to interfere with the health or comfort of the prosecutor. Such hurt or injury need not be permanent, but must, no doubt, be more than merely transient and trifling.

AG's Ref (No 6 of 1980) [1981] QB 715 (CA)

Lord Lane CJ: ... The point of law on which the court is asked to give its opinion is as follows:

> Where two persons fight (otherwise than in the course of sport) in a public place can it be a defence for one of those persons to a charge of assault arising out of the fight that the other consented to fight?

The facts out of which the reference arises are these. The respondent, aged 18, and a youth aged 17, met in a public street and argued together. The respondent and the youth decided to settle the argument there and then by a fight. Before the fight the respondent removed his watch and handed it to a bystander for safe keeping and the youth removed his jacket. The respondent and the youth exchanged blows with their fists and the youth sustained a bleeding nose and bruises to his face caused by blows from the respondent ...

We think that it can be taken as a starting point that it is an essential element of an assault that the act is done contrary to the will and without the consent of the victim; and it is doubtless for this reason that the burden lies on the prosecution to negative consent. Ordinarily, then, if the victim consents, the assailant is not guilty.

But the cases show that the courts will make an exception to this principle where the public interest requires: see *R v Coney* (1882) 8 QBD 534 ('the prize fight case') ...

The answer to this question, in our judgment, is that it is not in the public interest that people should try to cause, or should cause, each other actual bodily harm for no good reason. Minor struggles are another matter. So, in our judgment, it is immaterial whether the act occurs in private or in public; it is an assault if actual bodily harm is intended and/or caused. This means that most fights will be unlawful regardless of consent.

Nothing which we have said is intended to cast doubt on the accepted legality of properly conducted games and sports, lawful chastisement or correction, reasonable surgical interference, dangerous exhibitions, etc. These apparent exceptions can be justified as involving the exercise of a legal right, in the case of chastisement or correction, or as needed in the public interest, in the other cases.

Our answer to the point of law is 'No', but not, as the reference implies, because the fight occurred in a public place, but because, wherever it occurred, the participants would have been guilty of assault, subject to self-defence, if, as we understand was the case, they intended to and/or did cause actual bodily harm ...

R v Brown and Others [1994] 1 AC 212 (HL)

Lord Templeman: My Lords, the appellants were convicted of assaults occasioning actual bodily harm contrary to s 47 of the Offences Against the Person Act 1861. Three of the appellants were also convicted of wounding contrary to s 20 of the 1861 Act. The incidents which led to each conviction occurred in the course of consensual sado-masochistic homosexual encounters. The Court of Appeal upheld the convictions and certified the following point of law of general public importance:

> Where A wounds or assaults B occasioning him actual bodily harm in the course of a sado-masochistic encounter, does the prosecution have to prove lack of consent on the part of B before they can establish A's guilt under s 20 or s 47 of the Offences Against the Person Act 1861?

... In *R v Donovan* [1934] 2 KB 498 Swift J delivering the judgment of the Court of Criminal Appeal said at 509:

> 'Bodily harm' has its ordinary meaning and includes any hurt or injury calculated to interfere with the health or comfort of the prosecutor. Such hurt

or injury need not be permanent, but must, no doubt, be more than merely transient and trifling.

In the present case each appellant pleaded guilty to an offence under [s 47 of the 1861 Act] when the trial judge ruled that consent of the victim was no defence.

His Lordship then quoted s 20 of the 1861 Act and continued:

To constitute a wound for the purposes of the section the whole skin must be broken and not merely the outer layer called the epidermis or the cuticle: see *JJC (A Minor) v Eisenhower* [1983] 3 All ER 230.

'Grievous bodily harm' means simply bodily harm that is really serious and it has been said that it is undesirable to attempt a further definition: see *DPP v Smith* [1961] AC 290.

In s 20 the word 'unlawfully' means that the accused had no lawful excuse such as self-defence. The word 'maliciously' means no more than intentionally for present purposes: see *R v Mowatt* [1968] 1 QB 421.

Three of the appellants pleaded guilty to charges under s 20 when the trial judge ruled that the consent of the victim afforded no defence.

In the present case each of the appellants intentionally inflicted violence upon another (to whom I shall refer as 'the victim') with the consent of the victim and thereby occasioned actual bodily harm or in some cases wounding or grievous bodily harm. Each appellant was therefore guilty of an offence under s 47 or s 20 of the Act of 1861 unless the consent of the victim was effective to prevent the commission of the offence or effective to constitute a defence to the charge.

In some circumstances violence is not punishable under the criminal law. When no actual bodily harm is caused, the consent of the person affected precludes him from complaining. There can be no conviction for the summary offence of common assault if the victim has consented to the assault. Even when violence is intentionally inflicted and results in actual bodily harm, wounding or serious bodily harm the accused is entitled to be acquitted if the injury was a foreseeable incident of a lawful activity in which the person injured was participating. Surgery involves intentional violence resulting in actual or sometimes serious bodily harm but surgery is a lawful activity. Other activities carried on with consent by or on behalf of the injured person have been accepted as lawful notwithstanding that they involve actual bodily harm or may cause serious bodily harm. Ritual circumcision, tattooing, ear-piercing and violent sports including boxing are lawful activities ...

My Lords, the authorities dealing with the intentional infliction of bodily harm do not establish that consent is a defence to a charge under the Act of 1861. They establish that the courts have accepted that consent is a defence to the infliction of bodily harm in the course of some lawful activities. The question is whether the defence should be extended to the infliction of bodily harm in the course of sado-masochistic encounters ...

[His Lordship set out some of the dangers inherent in the activities in which the defendants had participated and went on:]

In principle there is a difference between violence which is incidental and violence which is inflicted for the indulgence of cruelty. The violence of sado-masochistic encounters involves the indulgence of cruelty by sadists and the degradation of victims. Such violence is injurious to the participants and unpredictably dangerous. I am not prepared to invent a defence of consent for sado-masochistic encounters which breed and glorify cruelty and result in offences under ss 47 and 20 of the Act of 1861.

... Society is entitled and bound to protect itself against a cult of violence. Pleasure derived from the infliction of pain is an evil thing. Cruelty is uncivilised. I would answer the certified question in the negative and dismiss the appeals of the appellants against conviction.

Lord Jauncey of Tullichettle: ... It was accepted by all the appellants that a line had to be drawn somewhere between those injuries to which a person could consent to infliction upon himself and those which were so serious that consent was immaterial ...

... In my view the line properly falls to be drawn between assault at common law and the offence of assault occasioning actual bodily harm created by s 47 of the Offences Against the Person Act 1861, with the result that consent of the victim is no answer to anyone charged with the latter offence or with a contravention of s 20 unless the circumstances fall within one of the well-known exceptions such as organised sporting contests and games, parental chastisement or reasonable surgery. There is nothing in ss 20 and 47 of the Act of 1861 to suggest that consent is either an essential ingredient of the offences or a defence thereto. If consent is to be an answer to a charge under s 47 but not to one under s 20, considerable practical problems would arise ... These problems would not arise if consent is an answer only to common assault. I would therefore dispose of these appeals on the basis that the infliction of actual or more serious bodily harm is an unlawful activity to which consent is no answer ...

... Without going into details of all the rather curious activities in which the appellants engaged it would appear to be good luck rather than good judgment which has prevented serious injury from occurring. Wounds can easily become septic if not properly treated, the free flow of blood from a person who is HIV positive or who has Aids can infect another and an inflicter who is carried away by sexual excitement or by drink or drugs could very easily inflict pain and injury beyond the level to which the receiver had consented ...

... If it is to be decided that such activities as the nailing by A of B's foreskin or scrotum to a board or the insertion of hot wax into C's urethra followed by the burning of his penis with a candle or the incising of D's scrotum with a scalpel to the effusion of blood are injurious neither to B, C and D nor to the public interest then it is for Parliament with its accumulated wisdom and sources of information to declare them to be lawful.

... There was argument as to whether lack of consent was a necessary ingredient of the offence of assault or whether consent, where available [ie in the case of common assault], was merely a defence ... If it were necessary, which it is not in this appeal, to decide which argument was correct, I would hold that consent could be a defence to assault but that lack of consent was not a necessary ingredient in assault.

Lord Lowry: My Lords, I have had the advantage of reading in draft the speeches of your Lordships. I agree with the reasoning and conclusions of my noble and learned friends, Lord Templeman and Lord Jauncey of Tullichettle, and I, too, would answer the certified question in the negative and dismiss the appeals.

In stating my own further reasons for this view I shall address myself exclusively to the cases in which, as has been informally agreed, one person has acted upon another in private, occasioning him actual bodily harm but nothing worse ...

... Everyone agrees that consent remains a complete defence to a charge of common assault and nearly everyone agrees that consent of the victim is not a defence to a charge of inflicting really serious personal injury (or 'grievous bodily harm'). The disagreement concerns offences which occasion actual bodily harm: the appellants contend that the consent of the victim is a defence to one charged with such an offence, while the respondent submits that consent is not a defence. I agree with the respondent's contention for reasons which I now explain ...

I suggest that the following points should be noted ...

- Wounding is associated in ss 18 and 20 with the infliction of grievous bodily harm and is naturally thought of as a serious offence, but it may involve anything from a minor breaking or puncture of the skin to a near fatal injury. Thus wounding may simply occasion actual bodily harm or it may inflict grievous bodily harm. If the victim's consent is a defence to occasioning actual bodily harm, then, so far as concerns the proof of guilt, the line is drawn, as my noble and learned friend Lord Jauncey of Tullichettle puts it ... 'somewhere down the middle of s 20', which I would regard as a most unlikely solution.

- According to the appellants' case, if an accused person charged with wounding relies on consent as a defence, the jury will have to find whether anything more than actual bodily harm was occasioned, something which is not contemplated by s 20.

- The distinction between common assault and all other attacks on the person is that common assault does not necessarily involve significant bodily injury. It is much easier to draw the line between no significant injury and some injury than to differentiate between degrees of injury. It is also more logical, because for one person to inflict any injury on another without good reason is an evil in itself (*malum in se*) and contrary to public policy.

- That consent is a defence to a charge of common assault is a common law doctrine which the Act of 1861 has done nothing to change.

... If, as I, too, consider, the question of consent is immaterial, there are *prima facie* offences against s 20 and 47 and the next question is whether there is good reason to add sado-masochistic acts to the list of exceptions contemplated in the Attorney General's Reference. In my opinion, the answer to that question is 'No'.

In adopting this conclusion I follow closely my noble and learned friends, Lord Templeman and Lord Jauncey. What the appellants are obliged to propose is that the deliberate and painful infliction of physical injury should be exempted from the operation of statutory provisions the object of which is to prevent or punish that very thing, the reason for the proposed exemption being that both those who will inflict and those who will suffer the injury wish to satisfy a perverted and depraved sexual desire. Sado-masochistic homosexual activity cannot be regarded as conducive to the enhancement or enjoyment of family life or conducive to the welfare of society. A relaxation of the prohibitions in ss 20 and 47 can only encourage the practice of homosexual sado-masochism, with the physical cruelty that it must involve (which can scarcely be regarded as a 'manly diversion'), by withdrawing the legal penalty and giving the activity a judicial imprimatur. As well as all this, one cannot overlook the physical danger to those who may indulge in sado-masochism. In this connection, and also generally, it is idle for the appellants to claim that they are educated exponents of 'civilised cruelty'. A proposed general exemption is to be tested by considering the likely general effect. This must include the probability that some sado-masochistic activity, under the powerful influence of the sexual instinct, will get out of hand and result in serious physical damage to the participants and that some activity will involve a danger of infection such as these particular exponents do not contemplate for themselves ...

Lord Mustill and **Lord Slynn of Hadley** delivered dissenting speeches.

R v Wilson [1996] 3 WLR 125 (CA)

Russell LJ: ... The charge was one of assault occasioning actual bodily harm contrary to s 47 of the Offences Against the Person Act 1861, the particulars being that on 14 May 1994 the appellant assaulted Julie Anne Wilson, thereby occasioning her actual bodily harm. The so-called victim was the wife of the appellant.

The facts were not in dispute ...

The police informed the appellant that his wife had been medically examined and that marks had been observed on both her buttocks. On the right buttock, as the photographs before the court disclose, there was a fading scar in the form of a capital letter 'W', and on the left buttock, a more pronounced and more recent scar in the form of a capital letter 'A'. The two letters 'A' and 'W' were the initials of the appellant.

He at once admitted that he was responsible for the marks. He told the police:

> I put them there ... She wanted a tattoo and I didn't know how to do a tattoo, but she wanted my name tattooing on her bum and I didn't know how to do it; so I burned it on with a hot knife. It wasn't life threatening, it wasn't anything, it was done for love. She loved me. She wanted me to give her – put my name on her body. As I say, she asked me originally if I would tattoo my name on her. She wanted me to do it on her breasts and I talked her out of that because I didn't know how to do a tattoo. Then she said, 'Well, there must be some way. If you can't do a tattoo, there must be some way', she says. I think her exact words were summat like, 'I'm not scared of anybody knowing that I love you enough to have your name on my body', something of that nature, and between us we hit on this idea of using a hot knife of her bum. I wouldn't do it on her breasts.

The medical evidence simply commented upon the existence of the letter 'A' on the left buttock as having been branded on Mrs Wilson a few days before 20 May 1994. Dr McKenna added: 'There was associated bruising around the burn and the skin hadn't fully healed.' No reference was made by the doctor to a faded scar on the right buttock.

At the conclusion of the evidence called by the prosecution, defence counsel submitted that his client had no case to answer. The judge, in a ruling of which we have a transcript, after reviewing the facts and authority, concluded as follows:

The reality that I have to deal with is that on the face of it the majority in the House of Lords in *R v Brown (Anthony)* [1994] 1 AC 212 approved of the *dicta* in *R v Donovan* [1934] 2 KB 498 and that accordingly until such time as the legislature or the European Court do something about it we are now saddled with a law that means that anyone who injures his partner, spouse, or whatever, in the course of some consensual activity is at risk of having his or her private life dragged before the public to no good purpose. Sadly, I take the view that I am bound by the majority in *R v Brown* and that I would have to, in those circumstances, direct this jury to convict.

Counsel for the defendant, in the light of that ruling, did not call his client and did not make any submissions to the jury, who in due course convicted the appellant. The judge conditionally discharged him for a period of 12 months.

It is effectively against that ruling of the judge that the appeal is brought to this court. In the court below, and before us, reference was predictably made to *R v Donovan* [1934] 2 KB 498, a decision of the Court of Criminal Appeal, and to *R v Brown (Anthony)* [1994] 1 AC 212, a decision of the House of Lords. They are the two authorities to which the trial judge referred in the observations we have cited ...

We are abundantly satisfied that there is no factual comparison to be made between the instant case and the facts of either *R v Donovan* [1934] 2 KB 498 or *R v Brown* 1 AC 212: Mrs Wilson not only consented to that which the appellant did, she instigated it. There was no aggressive intent on the part of the appellant. On the contrary, far from wishing to cause injury to his wife, the appellant's desire was to assist her in what she regarded as the acquisition of a desirable piece of personal adornment, perhaps in this day and age no less understandable than the piercing of nostrils or even tongues for the purposes of inserting decorative jewellery.

In our judgment *R v Brown* is not authority for the proposition that consent is no defence to a charge under s 47 of the Act of 1861, in all circumstances where actual bodily harm is deliberately inflicted. It is to be observed that the question certified for their Lordships in *R v Brown* related only to a 'sado-masochistic encounter'. However, their Lordships recognised in the course of their speeches, that it is necessary that there must be exceptions to what is no more than a general proposition. The speeches of Lord Templeman at 231, Lord Jauncey of Tullichettle at 245, and the dissenting speech of Lord Slynn of Hadley at 277, all refer to tattooing as being an activity which, if carried out with the consent of an adult, does not involve an offence under s 47, albeit that actual bodily harm is deliberately inflicted.

For our part, we cannot detect any logical difference between what the appellant did and what he might have done in the way of tattooing. The latter activity apparently requires no state authorisation, and the appellant was as free to engage in it as anyone else. We do not think that we are entitled to assume that the method adopted by the appellant and his wife was any more dangerous or painful than tattooing. There was simply no evidence to assist the court on this aspect of the matter.

Does public policy or the public interest demand that the appellant's activity should be visited by the sanctions of the criminal law? The majority in *R v Brown* clearly took the view that such considerations were relevant. If that is so, then we are firmly of the opinion that it is not in the public interest that activities such as the appellant's in this appeal should amount to criminal behaviour. Consensual activity between husband and wife, in the privacy of the matrimonial home, is not, in our judgment, normally a proper matter for criminal investigation, let alone criminal prosecution. Accordingly we take the view that the judge failed to have full regard to the facts of this case and misdirected himself in saying that *R v Donovan* [1934] 2 KB 498 and *R v Brown* [1994] 1 AC 212 constrained him to rule that consent was no defence.

In this field, in our judgment, the law should develop upon a case-by-case basis rather than upon general propositions to which, in the changing times in which we live, exceptions may arise from time to time not expressly covered by authority.

We shall allow the appeal and quash the conviction ...

R v Aitken and Others [1992] 1 WLR 1066 (Courts-Martial Court of Appeal)

The appellants were RAF officers who, during the course of a drunken bout of horseplay, had set fire to the fire resistant suit worn by a colleague, Flying Officer Gibson. They were convicted of offences under s 20 of the 1861 Act. On appeal the Courts-Martial Appeal Court allowed the appeals on the basis that the judge advocate's direction had not dealt satisfactorily with the issue of consent.

Cazalet J: The appellants have advanced the further ground of appeal that, in the context of the unusual facts of this case, the judge advocate failed to give the court any proper direction as to the meaning of the word 'unlawfully' as it appears in section 20.

The judge advocate, in his summing up, sought to deal with the meaning of 'unlawfully' as follows:

> Now, what is unlawful? That simply means without lawful justification or excuse – for example, self-defence. Now, you have heard evidence that in the Air Force ethos, various robust games have taken place – perhaps not only in the Air Force – whereby participants accept that a certain degree of risk of injury is likely to be caused. It is an issue for you to decide – and I will perhaps deal with this at a later stage - as to whether or not the incident was unlawful.

Then later the judge advocate continued his summing up:

> There, gentlemen, you really have the evidence. So, where does it take you? First of all, was this merely horseplay? Was there a combined joint enterprise by the three defendants, which involved the setting fire of Flying Officer Gibson's clothes? It is a matter for you from the evidence. Was this no more than horseplay? Looking at it in the light of the Royal Air Force ethos, was this going far beyond normal horseplay, to such an extent that you can say, 'No. This is way beyond those levels. This is not possibly lawful to behave in this manner'? Then you ask yourselves. 'Was this malicious,' within the meaning I have given to you.

It is submitted on behalf of the appellants that the judge advocate failed to give the court a proper direction as to whether the appellants' conduct towards Gibson was, in the particular circumstances, unlawful, and further failed to deal adequately or at all with the relevance of Gibson's consent or the appellants' belief as to his consent in regard to the horseplay in question. Mr Butterfield referred us to this court's decision in *R v Jones (Terence)* (1986) 83 Cr App R 375. It is helpful, we think, to consider that case in some detail. The appellants in that case were convicted of inflicting grievous bodily harm on two schoolboys, aged 14 and 15, who had been tossed high in the air and then allowed to fall to the ground by the appellants. The appellants' evidence was that they regarded this activity as a joke. There was some evidence showing that the victims, likewise, so regarded this. The judge declined to direct the jury that if they thought that the appellants had only been indulging in rough and undisciplined play, not intending to cause harm, and genuinely believing that the victims consented, they should acquit. In the light of this the appellants changed their pleas to guilty. Then, on appeal, their appeals were allowed on the basis that consent to rough and undisciplined horseplay is a defence; and, even if there is no consent, genuine belief, whether reasonably held or not, that it was present, would be a defence.

In giving the judgment of the court, McCowan J recited the facts and continued, at p 378:

> The second point, which was taken before the learned judge and repeated before us, stemmed from the case of *R v Donovan* (1934) 25 Cr App R 1; [1934] 2 KB 498. It will suffice if we read a part of the judgment of the Court of Criminal Appeal given by Swift J at p 11 and p 508 respectively, where he said: 'There are, as we have said, well established exceptions to the general rule that an act likely or intended to cause bodily harm is an unlawful act ... Another exception to the general rule, or, rather, another branch of the same class of exceptions, is to be found in cases of rough and undisciplined sport or play, where there is no anger and no intention to cause bodily harm. An example of this kind may be found in *R v Bruce* (1847) 2 Cox CC 262. In such cases the act is not in itself unlawful, and it becomes unlawful only if the person affected by it is not a consenting party'. The particular words relevant to the present case are 'rough and undisciplined play'. The direction which was sought from the learned judge was that if the jury thought that the appellants had only been indulging in 'rough and undisciplined play', not intending to cause harm, and genuinely believing that the victims were consenting, they were entitled to be acquitted. The learned judge declined so to direct the jury. He said that he proposed to direct them that the causing of an injury resulting in the course of this activity was unlawful. Mr Arlidge [for the appellants] submits, first, that consent to 'rough and undisciplined play' where there is no intention to cause injury, must be a defence. Secondly, he says that even if consent is in fact absent, genuine belief by a defendant that consent was present would be a defence. Thirdly, he says that if the belief is genuinely held, it is irrelevant whether it is reasonably held or not. Those propositions, based on the authority of the cases in *R v Kimber* (1983) 77 Cr App R 225 and *R v Williams* (1984) 78 Cr App R 276, are, in our judgment, correct.

The judge then referred to *AG's Ref (No 6 of 1980)* [1981] QB 715, where Lord Lane CJ gave the judgment of the court. McCowan J continued, 83 Cr App R 375, 379:

> Mr Mitchell [for the Crown] stresses an absence from the catalogue given by the Lord Chief Justice of any reference to 'rough and undisciplined play'. We note however that the Lord Chief Justice added 'etc' at the end of his list. We do not think that he intended the list to be exhaustive. It may well be that if this

jury had been given the opportunity of considering this defence, they would have had little difficulty in rejecting it. But the appellants were entitled to have the defence left to the jury. It was in our judgment wrong for the learned judge to indicate that he would remove it from them. Since it was entirely because of that ruling that the appellants were advised by counsel to plead guilty, it is plain that their convictions cannot stand. They are quashed. Accordingly this appeal is allowed.

The appellants submit that the nature of the horseplay and pranks in which Gibson had been involved that evening before the incident when he sustained his injuries were such that he must be taken to have given his consent to being involved in the sort of boisterous activities which had been taking place throughout much of the evening. The appellants pray in aid the fact that Gibson had been present throughout and had taken part in the various spirited events in the officers' mess at the earlier stage. He had also accompanied the others to Bell's married quarters after the bar had closed when there had been various further jokes and undisciplined pranks, including the two incidents of setting fire to the trousers of Huskisson and Thomas. He then elected to return with the others to the officers' mess where there had been further drinking before the incident in question.

It was submitted that viewed overall in the context of a celebratory evening in the mess such as this, it was clearly arguable that the rough and undisciplined horseplay which the three appellants had perpetrated on Gibson was not *per se* unlawful. In seeking to restrain him from leaving the room, grappling him to the ground and then, as he was getting up, trying to carry out the same type of burning incident as had happened earlier in the evening the appellants were acting in a manner consistent with what had been going on during much of the time. The fact that Gibson struggled, albeit weakly through drink, to avoid the attentions of the three during the incident in question should not, it was submitted on the appellants' behalf, be taken in isolation. The totality of the circumstances, his knowledge of the course which celebration evenings such as the one in question was likely to take and his continued presence with the others demonstrated an acceptance by him that horseplay of the nature perpetrated upon him might well take place.

It was submitted that the judge advocate had not fully or properly directed the court in regard to this and that, in particular, he had failed to give any direction to the effect that since the Crown accepted that none of the appellants intended to inflict any harm on Gibson, the fact that a much larger quantity of white spirit had been poured on to his clothing than had been the case with Thomas could be viewed as an accident, and thus not unlawful. Additionally, submitted the appellants, given than it was open to the court to find that the horseplay with Gibson was not of itself unlawful, it was incumbent upon the judge advocate, following the decision in *R v Jones (Terence)*, 83 Cr App R 375 to give further directions, first that such conduct, if not unlawful, would only have become unlawful if Gibson had not consented to it, and second that even if Gibson had not consented, the court must consider whether in the circumstances any of the appellants genuinely believed, whether reasonably or not, that Gibson had so consented.

Mr Hucker conceded that the judge advocate had not given the court either of these two latter directions. He contended that such were not necessary on the unchallenged facts of the case. He submitted that the incident involving Gibson must have been unlawful. The sequence of the incidents of setting fire to the clothing of others had, he submitted, escalated to a serious degree. From a mild flame with brandy more dangerous flames had sprung up with the use of white spirit on Thomas's trouser leg. He referred to Aitken's written statement which had recounted how the heat from the flames had woken Thomas, who had then had difficulty in putting out the flames with Bell being required to help smother them. That, he contended, demonstrated a dangerous build-up of this particular conduct, such that the incident with Gibson, once again involving the white spirit and a burning, clearly raised a risk of serious injury to Gibson. This, he maintained, took the activity outside the realm of rough and undisciplined horseplay such that this incident was plainly unlawful from the outset and accordingly the question of consent did not arise.

However although it must, on the evidence, have been open to the court to find that the incident involving Gibson was *per se* unlawful, we do not consider, for the reasons submitted to us by Mr Butterfield, that this was so plain that the judge advocate was absolved from a direction that it was in the circumstances open to the court to find that the activities of the appellants were not *per se* unlawful. In this event the judge advocate should then have directed the court as to the necessity of considering whether Gibson gave his consent as a willing participant to the activities in question, or whether the appellants may have believed this, whether reasonably or not.

In the circumstances we consider that the judge advocate in what was, on any view, a difficult and complex case on the law, failed properly to direct the court on these two important matters as to consent.

R v Richardson [1998] 3 WLR 1292 (CA)

Otton J: In the Crown Court at Nottingham, before Judge Matthewman QC, following a ruling by the judge the defendant changed her pleas to guilty on six counts of assault occasioning actual bodily harm. She now appeals against conviction by leave of the single judge.

The facts can be briefly stated. The defendant was a registered dental practitioner until 30 August 1996 but was suspended from practice by the General Dental Council. Whilst still suspended, she carried out dentistry on a number of patients in September 1996. The mother of two of those patients complained to the police not because of the suspension, but because she thought that the defendant appeared to be under the influence of drink or drugs. The defendant denied having taken drink, and said that the only drugs that she had taken had been prescribed by a doctor for psychiatric reasons. The police discovered that the defendant had practising whilst disqualified, resulting in the charges.

Before the trial judge, defence counsel submitted that (1) the indictment was an abuse of process and should be quashed. There was a statutory defence of practising or holding oneself out to practise when not qualified contrary to section 38 of the Dentists Act 1984. Such an offence was statute barred. She was charged on indictment because of public concern. (2) The hostile intent requisite for assault was not present. (3) The patients consented to the treatment even though they did not know that the defendant was disqualified from practice.

The judge ruled against the defendant on each ground. This appeal is concerned only with the last two grounds. On the third ground the judge accepted the argument for the Crown that there was fraud here which vitiated the apparent consent. He said:

> It would not be unlawful if there was consent to the act, that is real consent, not one induced by fraud relating to a fundamental fact, that is, as put here, the identity of the person who claims to have acted by consent. The prosecution say here there was such fraud because the apparent consent was on the basis of the identity of a person who was qualified to act and indeed, a person who was not qualified to act. In my judgment, identity in those circumstances means not merely facial features or other features, bodily features and dress or whatever of a person, identity encompasses other matters, the whole identity and that includes, in this particular case, a qualification to practise. The identity presented to the patients ... 'Mrs Diane Richardson able and presently lawfully dealing with your teeth' which was, in fact, a fraudulent claim and, in my judgment, a fundamental one, it was not merely not having a piece of paper, it was a fraudulent total identity.

Following these rulings the defendant pleaded guilty to all offences in the indictment. The agreed basis upon which the plea of guilty was tendered was that the defendant had practised while suspended, that the treatment was of a reasonable standard and was carried out on willing patients who had presented themselves for such treatment, and that all of the complainants had been treated by her before her suspension, without complaint.

Miss Caroline Bradley, on behalf of the defendant, now concentrates her argument on the issue of consent. She acknowledges that without consent the surgical procedures carried out were capable of amounting to an assault in law.

The general proposition which underlies this area of the law is that the human body is inviolate but there are circumstances which the law recognises where consent may operate to prevent conduct which would otherwise be classified as an assault from being so treated. Reasonable surgical interference is clearly such an exception. Counsel relies upon the *dicta* of Lord Lane CJ in *AG's Ref (No 6 of 1980)* [1981] 1 QB 715 where it was held that an assailant was not guilty of assault if the victim consented to it but that an exception to that principle existed where the public interest required. Lord Lane CJ said, at p 719:

> Nothing which we have said is intended to cast doubt upon the accepted legality of ... lawful chastisement ... reasonable surgical interference ... etc. These apparent exceptions can be justified as involving the exercise of a legal right, in the case of chastisement ... or as needed in the public interest, in the other cases ...

Thus it can accepted that a person may give lawful consent to the infliction of actual bodily harm upon himself and is justifiable as being in the public interest where reasonable surgical treatment is concerned. But the question then arises, what is the effect on the validity of consent, if any, if the complainant has had concealed from them the true nature of the status of the person who, in the guise of performing a reasonable surgical procedure, subsequently inflicts bodily harm?

In Smith & Hogan's *Criminal Law*, 8th edn (1996), Professor JC Smith states, at p 420:

Fraud does not necessarily negative consent. It does so only if it deceives P as to the identity of the person or the nature of the act'. This statement of principle is derived from *R v Clarence* (1888) 22 QBD 23 where the victim consented to sexual intercourse with the accused and, although she would not have consented had she been aware of the disease from which D knew he was suffering, this was no assault. Wills J stated, at p 27: 'That consent obtained by fraud is no consent at all is not true as a general proposition either in fact or in law.' Stephen J stated, at p 44:

the only sorts of fraud which so far destroy the effect of a woman's consent as to convert a connection consented to in fact into a rape are frauds as to the nature of the act itself, or as to the identity of the person who does the act.

There is a clear line of authority concerning fraud and the nature of the act. In *R v Williams* [1923] 1 KB 340 the appellant a choir master had sexual intercourse with a girl of 16 years of age under the pretence that her, breathing was not quite right, and that he had to perform an operation to enable her to produce her voice properly. The girl submitted to what was done under the belief, wilfully and fraudulently induced by the appellant, that she was being medically and surgically treated by the appellant and not with any intention that she should have intercourse with him. The Court of Criminal Appeal held that, the appellant was properly convicted of rape. Lord Hewart CJ ... referred with approval to Branson J's statement of the law in the course of summing up:

The law has laid it down that where a girl's consent is procured by the means which the girl says this prisoner adopted, that is to say, where she is persuaded that what is being done to her is not the ordinary act of sexual intercourse but is some medical or, surgical operation in order to give her relief from some disability from which she is suffering, then that is rape although the actual thing that was done was done with her consent, because she never consented to the act of sexual intercourse. She was persuaded to consent to what he did because she thought it was not sexual intercourse and, because she thought it, was a surgical operation.

In *R v Harms* [1944] 2 DLR 61 the Supreme Court of Canada considered section 298 of the Canadian Criminal Code (1892) which established that in order to vitiate consent the false or fraudulent misrepresentation had to be as to the nature and quality of the act. Harms had falsely represented himself to be a medical doctor. Although the complainant knew that he was proposing sexual intercourse she consented thereto because of his representations that the intercourse was in the nature of a medical treatment necessitated by a condition which he said he had diagnosed. Harms was not a medical man at all. The court held that a jury was entitled to conclude that the nature and quality of the act as far as the complainant was concerned was therapeutic and not carnal. In other words, the complainant had consented to a therapeutic act, which it was not, and had not consented to a carnal act which it was. The consent induced by the fraudulent representation was held to have been vitiated.

The later case *Boiduc and Bird v R* (1967) 63 DLR (2d) 82 was held to be on, the other side of the line. The Supreme Court of Canada considered the case of a doctor who falsely represented that his colleague was a medical student and obtained the complainant's consent to the colleague's presence at a vaginal examination. It was held that there was no indecent assault because the fraud was not as to the nature and quality of what was to be done. It was observed that the defendant's conduct was 'unethical and reprehensible, but did not have the effect of vitiating the consent'.

In *Papadimitropoulos v R* (1957) 98 CLR 249 the High Court of Australia considered the case of a complainant who had sexual relations with a man whom she believed to be her husband. Unknown to her no valid marriage ceremony had ever taken place. The complainant had consented to sexual intercourse under the belief, fraudulently induced, that she had contracted a valid marriage to the man whom she believed to be her husband. It was held that these circumstances did not support a conviction for rape. The court stated, at p 261:

> Rape, as a capital felony, was defined with exactness, and although there has been some extension over the centuries in the ambit of the crime it is quite wrong to bring within its operation forms of evil conduct because they wear some analogy to aspects of the crime and deserve punishment ... the key to such a case as the present lies in remembering that it is the penetration of the woman's body without her consent to such penetration that makes the felony. The capital felony was not directed to fraudulent conduct inducing her consent. Frauds of that kind must be punished under other heads of the criminal law or not at all: they are not rape ... To return to the central point; rape is carnal knowledge of a woman without her consent: carnal knowledge is the physical fact of penetration; it is the consent to that which is in question; such a consent demands a perception as to what is about to take place, as to the identity of the man and the character of what he is doing. But once the consent is comprehending and actual the inducing causes cannot destroy its reality and leave the man guilty of rape.

And earlier, at pp 260–61:

> It must be noted that in considering whether an apparent consent is unreal it is the mistake or misapprehension that makes it so. It is not the *fraud* producing the mistake which is material so much as the mistake itself ... tends to distract the attention from the essential inquiry, namely, whether the consent is no consent because it is not directed to the nature and character of the act. The identity of the man and, the character of the physical act that is done or proposed seem now clearly to be regarded as forming part of the nature and character of the act to which the woman's consent is directed. That accords with the principles governing mistake vitiating apparent manifestations of will within other chapters of the law. [Emphasis added.]

This result is not altogether surprising, for otherwise every bigamist would be guilty of rape.

The Law Commission in their consultation paper on *Consent in the Criminal Law* (1995) (Consultation Paper No 139), having considered fraud and consent generally, proposed a lesser offence of obtaining consent by deception and stated at para 6.27:

> ... consent should not in general be nullified by deception as to any circumstances other than the nature of the act and the identity of the person doing it, but that deception as to other circumstances should give rise to liability for a lesser offence than that of non-consensual conduct. Where the

defendant is aware that the other person is or may be mistaken about the nature of the act or the defendant's identity, we think that the other person's consent should be nullified as if the mistake were induced by fraud ... If a deception as to the circumstance in question would give rise to liability only for our proposed offence of obtaining consent by deception, as distinct from the more serious offence of acting without any consent at all, liability for taking advantage of a self-induced mistake as to that circumstance could at most be for that lesser offence.

It is, thus, unremarkable that neither counsel has been able to, cite any authority in, which the complainant in a sexual case has been deceived as to the identity of the assailant and her apparent consent has held to have been vitiated by fraud. It is to be noted that section 1(3) of the Sexual Offences Act 1956 provides that a man can be guilty of rape if he induces a married woman to have sexual intercourse with him by impersonating her husband. However this only covers the type of case where the woman is legally married and for some reason believes that the person with whom she is having sexual relations is her husband when in fact he is not.

Miss Bradley who argued the case ably contends that the complainants were deceived neither as to the nature or quality of the act nor as to the identity of, the person carrying out the act. The statutory offence was created to punish such conduct as ok place here.

Both before the judge and before this court the Crown expressly disavowed reliance upon the nature or quality of the act. Mr Peter Walmsley succinctly submitted that the patients were deceived into consenting to treatment by the representation that the defendant was a qualified and practising dentist and not one who had been disqualified. He further submitted that the evidence of the patients was unequivocal: had they known that the defendant had been suspended they would not have consented, to any treatment. If the treatment had been given by a person impersonating a dentist it would have been an assault. There was no distinction to be drawn between the unqualified dentist and one who is suspended. On this basis there was a mistake as to the true identity of the defendant.

We are unable to accept that argument. There is no basis for the proposition that the rules which determine the circumstances in which consent is vitiated can, be different according to whether the case is one of sexual assault or one where the assault is non-sexual. The common element in both these cases is that they involve an assault, and the question is whether consent has been negatived. It is nowhere suggested that the common law draws such a distinction. The common law is not concerned with the question whether the mistaken consent has been induced by fraud on the part of the accused or has been self-induced. It is the nature of the mistake that is relevant, and not the reason why the mistake has been made. In summary, either there is consent to actions on the part of a person in the mistaken belief that he was other than he truly is, in which case it is assault or, short of this, there is no assault.

In essence the Crown contended that the concept of the 'identity of the person' should be extended to cover the qualifications or attributes of the dentist on the basis that the patients consented to treatment by a qualified dentist and not a suspended one. We must reject that submission. In all the charges brought against the defendant the complainants were fully aware of the identity of the defendant.

To accede to the submission would be to strain or distort the everyday meaning of the word identity, the dictionary definition of which is 'the condition of being the same'.

It was suggested in argument that we might be assisted by the civil law of consent, where such expressions as 'real' or 'informed' consent prevail. In this regard the criminal and the civil law do not run along the same track. The concept of informed consent has no place in the criminal law. It would also be a mistake, in our view, to introduce the concept of a duty to communicate information to a patient about the risk of an activity before consent to an act can be treated as valid. The gravamen of the defendant's conduct in the instant case was that the complainants consented to treatment from her although their consent had been procured by her failure to inform them that she was no longer qualified to practise. This was clearly reprehensible and may well found the basis of a civil claim for damages. But we are quite satisfied that it is not a basis for finding criminal liability in the field of offences against the person.

We have arrived at this conclusion without any real difficulty. It is our considered view that the common law has developed as far as it can without the intervention of the legislature. For the better part of a century the common law concept of consent in the criminal law has been certain and clearly delineated. It is not for this court to attempt to unwrite the law which has been settled for so long. This is an area in which it is to be hoped that the proposals of the Law Commission will be given an early opportunity for implementation.

Notes and queries

1 What if the appellant in *R v Richardson* had been suffering from AIDS but had not informed anyone? Would the apparent consent of her patients have been vitiated by her deception?

2 Why is consent recognised as a defence to harm caused in the course of rough horseplay, but not when caused during sado-masochistic sexual activity?

Codification and law reform proposals

The Law Commission has addressed the issue of consent to harm in two Consultation Papers, LCCP 134, and more recently *Consent in the Criminal Law* (LCCP 139). What follows is an extract from Part XVI of LCCP 139, summarising the provisional proposals of the Law Commission, and indicating those areas where responses were requested. References in parentheses are to the main body of LCCP 139.

In this second, extended, Consultation Paper we have raised a large number of issues, and have made provisional proposals on many of them. We summarise here our provisional proposals and the other issues on which we are seeking respondents' views ...

The need for the same principles to be adopted in relation to consent in other criminal offences in which consent is an issue

1 We provisionally propose that the proposals contained in paragraphs 12–30 below should apply not only to offences against the person and sexual offences

but also to every other criminal offence in which the consent of a person other than the defendant is or may be a defence to criminal liability.

(Paragraphs 1.24 –1.27)

Intentional causing of seriously disabling injury

2 We provisionally propose that the intentional causing of seriously disabling injury (as defined at paragraph 7 below) to another person should continue to be criminal, even if the person injured consents to such injury or to the risk of such injury.

(Paragraphs 4.3–4.6 and 4.47)

Reckless causing of seriously disabling injury

3 We provisionally propose that –

(1) the reckless causing of seriously disabling injury (as defined at paragraph 7 below) should continue to be criminal, even if the injured person consents to such injury or to the risk of such injury; but

(2) a person causing seriously disabling injury to another person should not be regarded as having caused it recklessly unless –

(a) he or she was, at the time of the act or omission causing it, aware of a risk that such injury would result, and

(b) it was at that time contrary to the best interests of the other person, having regard to the circumstances known to the person causing the

injury (including, if known to him or her, the fact that the other person consented to such injury or to the risk of it), to take that risk.

(Paragraphs 4.7–4.28 and 4.48)

Secondary liability for consenting to seriously disabling injury

4 We provisionally propose that, where a person causes seriously disabling injury to another person who consented to injury or to the risk of injury of the type caused, and the person causing the injury is guilty of an offence under the proposals in Paragraphs 2 and 3 above, the ordinary principles of secondary liability should apply for the purpose of determining whether the person injured is a party to that offence.

(Paragraphs 1.20–1.23)

Intentional causing of other injuries

5 We provisionally propose that the intentional causing of any injury to another person other than seriously disabling injury as defined at paragraph 7 below (whether or not amounting to 'grievous bodily harm' within the meaning of the Offences Against the Person Act 1861 or to 'serious injury' within the meaning of the Criminal Law Bill) should not be criminal if, at the time of the act or omission causing the injury, the other person consented to injury of the type caused.

(Paragraphs 4.29 and 4.49)

Reckless causing of other injuries

6 We provisionally propose that the reckless causing of any injury to another person other than seriously disabling injury as defined at paragraph 7 below (whether or not amounting to 'grievous bodily harm' within the meaning of

the Offences Against the Person Act 1861 or to 'serious injury' within the meaning of the Criminal law Bill) should not be criminal if, at the time of the act or omission causing the injury, the other person consented to injury of the type caused, to the risk of such injury or to the act or omission causing the injury.

(Paragraphs 4.29 and 4.50)

Definition of seriously disabling injury

7   We provisionally propose that for the purpose of paragraphs 2–6 above 'seriously disabling injury' should he taken to refer to an injury or injuries which –

(1) cause serious distress, and

(2) involve the loss of a bodily member or organ or permanent bodily injury or permanent functional impairment, or serious or permanent disfigurement, or severe and prolonged pain, or serious impairment of mental health, or prolonged unconsciousness;

and, in determining whether an effect is permanent, no account should be taken of the fact that it may be remediable by surgery.

(Paragraphs 4.29–4.40 and 4.51)

Meaning of consent

8   We provisionally propose that for the purposes of the above proposals –

(1) 'consent' should mean a valid subsisting consent to an injury or to the risk of an injury of the type caused, and consent may be express or implied;

(2) a person should be regarded as consenting to an injury of the type caused if he or she consents to an act or omission which he or she knows or believes to be intended to cause injury to him or her of the type caused; and

(3) a person should be regarded as consenting to the risk of an injury of the type caused if he or she consents to an act or omission which he or she knows or believes to involve a risk of injury to him or her of the type caused.

(Paragraphs 4.3–4.28 and 4.52)

Mistaken belief in consent: offences against the person

9   We ask –

(1) whether it should in itself be a defence to an offence of causing injury to another person that –

(a) at the time of the act or omission causing the injury, the defendant believed that the other person consented to injury or to the risk of injury of the type caused, or to that act or omission, and

(b) he or she would have had a defence under our proposals in paragraphs 5 and 6 above if the facts had been as he or she then believed them to be; or

(2) whether such a belief should be a defence only if, in addition, either

(a) it would not have been obvious to a reasonable person in his or her position that the other person did not so consent, or

(b) he or she was not capable of appreciating that that person did not so consent.

(Paragraphs 7.1–7.28 and 7.31)

Mistaken belief in consent: sexual offences

10 We provisionally propose that, if (but only if) the defence of mistaken belief in consent to injury, or to the risk of injury, or to an act or omission causing injury) were to be available in relation to offences against the person only where one of the conditions set out in paragraph 9(2) is satisfied, it should similarly be no defence to a charge of rape or indecent assault that the defendant mistakenly believed that the other person consented to sexual intercourse or to the alleged assault unless one of those conditions is satisfied.

(Paragraphs 7.29 and 7.32)

Burden of proof on the issue of consent or mistaken belief in consent in relation to offences against the person

11 If the proposals in paragraphs 5 and 6 above were accepted, we ask –

(1) whether it should be for the defence to prove, on the balance of probabilities,

(a) that the person injured consented to injury of the type caused, or (in the case of injury recklessly caused) to the risk of such injury or to the act or omission causing the injury, or

(b) that the defendant believed that that person so consented (and, if such in paragraph 9(2) is satisfied, that one of those conditions is satisfied); a belief were to be a defence only where one of the conditions set out or

(2) whether it should be for the prosecution to prove) beyond reasonable doubt,

(a) that that person did not consent, and

(b) that the defendant did not so believe (or, if such a belief were to be a defence only where one of the conditions set out in Paragraph 9(2) is satisfied, that neither of those conditions is satisfied).

(Paragraphs 4.41–4.45, 4.53 and 7.33)

Persons without capacity

12 We provisionally propose that for the purposes of any offence to which consent is or may be a defence, a valid content may not be given by, a person without capacity.

(Paragraphs 5.19–5.21)

Definition of persons without capacity

13 We provisionally propose that a person should be regarded as being without capacity if when he or she gives what is alleged to be his or her consent –

(1) he or she is under the age of 18 and is unable by reason of age or immaturity to make a decision for himself or herself on the matter in question;

(2) he or she is unable by reason of mental disability to make a decision for himself or herself on the matter in question; or

(3) he or she is unable to communicate his or her decision on that matter because he or she is unconscious or for any other reason.

(Paragraphs 5.19–5.21)

Capacity and minors

14 We provisionally propose that –

(1) in relation to those matters in which a person under the age of 18 may give a valid consent under our proposals, such a person should be regarded as unable to make a decision by reason of age or immaturity if at the time the decision needs to be made he or she does not have sufficient understanding and intelligence to understand the information relevant to the decision, including information about the reasonably foreseeable consequences of deciding one way or another or of failing to make the decision; and

(2) in determining whether a person under the age of 18 has sufficient into account his or her age and maturity as well as the seriousness and understanding and intelligence for the above purposes, a court should take implications of the matter to which the decision relates.

(Paragraphs 5.1–5.11 and 5.21–5.22)

Mistaken belief in consent: statutory age-limits

15 Where there is a statutory age-limit below which no valid consent can be given, we ask –

(1) whether it should in itself be a defence that –

(a) at the time of the alleged offence, the defendant believed that the other person's age was above that limit, and

(b) he or she would have had a defence if the other person's age had been above that limit; or

(2) whether such a belief should be a defence only if, in addition, either –

(a) it would not have been obvious to a reasonable person in his or her position that the other person's age was or might be under that limit, or

(b) he or she was not capable of appreciating that the other person's age was or might be under that limit; or

(3) whether such a belief should be irrelevant to liability.

(Paragraphs 7.30 and 7.34)

Mistaken belief in consent: section 6(3) of the Sexual Offences Act 1956

16 We ask whether the special defence to the offence of unlawful sexual intercourse by section 6(3) of the Sexual Offences Act 1956 should be retained or should be replaced by whatever general rule is thought appropriate in respect of mistaken belief as to another person's age.

(Paragraphs 7.30 and 7.35)

Capacity and the mentally disabled

17 We provisionally propose that –

(1) a person should be regarded as being at the material time unable to make a decision by reason of mental disability if the disability is such that at the time when the decision needs to be made –

(a) he or she is unable to understand or retain the information relevant to the decision, including information about the reasonably foreseeable consequences of deciding one way or another or of failing to make the decision, or

(b) he or she is unable to make a decision based on that information; and

(2) in this context 'mental disability' should mean a disability or disorder of the mind or brain, whether permanent or temporary, which results in an impairment or disturbance of mental functioning.

(Paragraphs 5.1, 5.2, 5.12–5.17 and 5.21–5.22)

Capacity to understand in broad terms

18 We provisionally propose that a person should not be regarded as being unable to understand the information referred to in paragraphs 14(1) and 17(1) above if he or she is able to understand an explanation of that information in broad terms and simple language.

(Paragraphs 5.16–5.17 and 5.19–5.22)

Types of deception that may nullify consent

19 We provisionally propose that a person should not be treated as having given a valid consent, for the purposes of any offence of doing an act without such consent, if he or she gives such consent because he or she has been deceived as to –

(1) the nature of the act; or

(2) the identity of the other person or persons involved in the act.

(Paragraphs 6.11–6.18 and 6.79)

Other types of fraudulent misrepresentation that may nullify consent

20 We ask

(1) whether a fraudulent misrepresentation that a person has been found to be free from HIV and/or other sexually transmitted diseases should form an exception to the general rule that fraud should nullify consent only where it goes to the nature of the act or the identity of the other person or persons involved in the act;

(2) if so, in what terms this new class of misrepresentation should be formulated; and

(3) whether there are any other specific types of misrepresentation that also call for extraordinary treatment.

(Paragraphs 6.19 and 6.80)

An offence of procuring consent by deception

21 We provisionally propose that a person should be guilty of an offence, punishable on conviction on indictment with five years' imprisonment, if he or she does any act which, if done without the consent of another, would be an offence so punishable, and he or she has procured that other's consent by deception.

(Paragraphs 6.18 and 6.81)

A definition of 'deception'

22 We provisionally propose that for the purposes of this offence 'deception' should mean any deception (whether deliberate or reckless) by words or conduct as to fact or as to law, including a deception as to the present intentions of the person using the deception or any other person.

(Paragraphs 6.7 and 6.82)

Inducing another person to perform an act on oneself by deception

23 We ask –

(1) whether it should be a specific offence for a person to induce a man by deception to have sexual intercourse (vaginal or anal) with him or her;

(2) if so, whether the offence should be confined to deceptions as to a particular kind of circumstance, and if so what; and

(3) whether it should include inducing another person by deception to perform any acts other than sexual intercourse, and if so what.

(Paragraph 6.20–6.21 and 6.83)

The duty to communicate information

24 We ask whether there are any particular circumstances in which the criminal law should impose an express duty to communicate information upon a person who wishes to rely on a consent to the causation of injury or to the risk of injury caused by him or her.

(Paragraphs 6.22–6.23 and 6.84)

Self-induced mistake

25 We provisionally propose that a person should not be treated as having given a valid consent to an act if he or she gives consent because of a mistake as to –

(1) the nature of the act,

(2) the identity of the other person or persons involved in the act, or

(3) any other circumstance such that, had the consent been obtained by a deception as to that circumstance, it would not have been treated as valid,

if the defendant knows that such a mistake has been made or is aware that such a mistake may have been made.

(Paragraphs 6.24–6.27 and 6.85)

Non-disclosure

26 We invite views on –

(1) how the law should deal with the obtaining of consent by the non-disclosure of material facts;

(2) whether (if it is thought that any such non-disclosure should be criminal) the law should act out, in respect of each class of offence, the facts that must be disclosed;

(3) if so, what those facts should be in each case; and

(4) whether it should be a specific offence for one person to induce another, by non-disclosure of such a fact, to perform an act (and if so what kinds of act) upon him or her.

(Paragraphs 6.29–6.33 and 6.86)

Inducement by threats of non-consensual force

27 We provisionally propose that a person should not be treated as having given a valid consent, for the purposes of any offence to which consent is or may be a defence, if he or she gives such consent because a threat, express or implied, has been made to use non-consensual force (including detention or abduction) against him or her or another if he or she does not consent, and he or she believes that, if he or she does not consent, the threat will be carried out immediately or before he or she can free himself or herself from it.

(Paragraphs 6.34–6.37 and 6.87)

The effect of other threats on the validity of consent

28 We ask for views on whether a person should be treated as having given a valid consent where he or she gives consent because of a threat other than one falling within paragraph 27 above.

(Paragraphs 6.38–6.72 and 6.88)

An offence of procuring consent by threats

29 If a person is to be treated as having given a valid consent in such circumstances, we ask for views on our suggestion that –

(1) it should be an offence, punishable on conviction on indictment with five years' imprisonment, for a person to do any act which, if done without the consent of another, would be an offence so punishable, having procured that other's consent by threats; but

(2) a person should not be guilty of the suggested offence if –

(a) in all the circumstances the threat is (or perhaps the defendant believes that it is) a proper way of inducing the other person to consent to the act in question; or

(b) the threat is to withhold a benefit which the other person could not reasonably expect to receive.

(Paragraphs 6.47, 6.64, 6.71 and 6.89)

Special consideration for a particular class of threat

30 We invite comments on what the law should be in relation to a case where an apparent consent is procured by an offer to avert a consequence of such a kind that, if the apparent consent were procured by the offeror's threat to bring that consequence about, that threat would nullify the consent altogether so as to incur for the offeror liability for the more serious offence to which consent is a defence.

(Paragraphs 6.72 and 6.90)

Exception for proper medical treatment and care

31 We provisionally propose that –

(1) a person should not be guilty of an offence, notwithstanding that he or she causes injury to another, of whatever degree of seriousness, if such injury is

caused during the course of proper medical treatment or care administered with the consent of that other person;

(2) in this context 'medical treatment or care'

(a) should mean medical treatment or care administered by or render the direction of a duly qualified medical practitioner;

(b) should include not only surgical and dental treatment or care, but also procedures taken for the purposes of diagnosis, the prevention of disease, the prevention of pregnancy or as ancillary to treatment; and

(c) without limiting the meaning of the term, should also include the following:

(i) surgical operations performed for the purposes of rendering a patient sterile;

(ii) surgical operations performed for the purposes of enabling a person to change his or her sex;

(iii) lawful abortions;

(iv) surgical operations performed for cosmetic purposes; and

(v) any treatment or procedure to facilitate the donation of regenerative tissue, or the, donation of non-regenerative tissue not essential for life.

(Paragraphs 8.1–8.37, 8.49 and 8.50)

Exception for properly approved medical research

32 We provisionally propose that –

(1) a person should not be guilty of an offence, notwithstanding that he or she causes injury to another, of whatever degree of seriousness, if such injury is caused during the course of properly approved medical research and with the consent of that other person; and

(2) in this context the term 'properly approved medical research' should mean medical research approved by a local research ethics committee or other body charged with the supervision and approval of medical research falling within its jurisdiction.

(Paragraphs 8.38–8.49 and 8.51)

Cosmetic piercing etc

33 We ask whether the age-limit of 18 should be retained for tattooing, and whether any similar (and if so, what) age limit should be introduced in relation to a young person's ability to give a valid consent to (a) piercing below the neck' (b) branding; or (c) scarification, when performed for cosmetic or cultural purposes.

(Paragraph 9.24)

34 We ask whether the present statutory definition of tattooing is regarded as satisfactory, and whether it is thought that there ought to be a statutory definition (and if so, what) of piercing, branding or scarification for the purposes of the criminal law.

(Paragraph 9.25)

35 We provisionally propose that the special provision relating to *mens rea* in section 1 of the Tattooing of Minors Act 1969 should be repealed and replaced by whatever rule is thought appropriate in relation to the issue of mistaken belief as to a person's age in the context of statutory age-limits in general (see paragraph 15 above).

(Paragraph 9.26)

36 We provisionally propose that the circumcision of male children, performed with their parents' consent in accordance with the rites of the Jewish or Muslim religions, should continue to be lawful.

(Paragraph 9.27)

37 We seek the views of our respondents as to whether any pre-consolidation reform is required to the Prohibition of Female Circumcision Act 1985.

(Paragraph 9.29)

Injuries intentionally caused for sexual, religious or spiritual purposes

38 We provisionally propose that for the purpose of the proposals contained in paragraphs 5 and 6 above any consent given by a person under 18 to injuries intentionally caused for sexual, religious or spiritual purposes should not be treated as a valid consent.

(Paragraphs 10.52–10.55)

Lawful correction

39 We ask –

(1) whether there are any issues relating to consent that have escaped our notice in relation to the defence of lawful correction;

(2) whether the statutory language of section 1 of the Children and Young Persons Act 1933 and of section 47 of the Education Act 1986, as amended, creates any difficulties in practice in relation to the defence of lawful correction.

(Paragraphs 11.1–11.20)

Exception for recognised sport

40 We provisionally propose that a person should not be guilty of an offence of causing injury if he or she caused the relevant injury in the course of playing or practising a recognised sport in accordance with its rules.

(Paragraphs 12.1–12.63 and 12.68)

41 We wish to receive views on the precise formulation of the rule we suggest, since we do not wish a player to lose its protection, for example, merely because he or she happened to be offside on the football field.

(Paragraphs 12.1–12.63 and 12.69)

42 We provisionally propose that in the context of these proposals:

(1) the expression 'recognised sport' should mean all such sports, martial arts activities and other activities of a recreational nature as may be set out from time to time in a list to be kept and published by the UK Sports Council in accordance with a scheme approved by the appropriate minister for the recognition of sports, and the rules of a recognised sport should mean the

rules of that sport as approved in accordance with the provisions of such a scheme;

(2) when carrying out its duties in relation to the recognition of any such activity the UK the Sports Council should consult such organisations as appear to it to have expert knowledge in relation to that activity.

(Paragraphs 13.1–13.19)

43 We would welcome views not only in relation to the desirability of the recognition scheme we propose, but also on any points of detail we ought to bear in mind when formulating our final recommendations.

(Paragraph 13.20)

Dangerous exhibitions

44 We ask whether it would be appropriate, in relation to any particular type of dangerous exhibition, to set an age-limit below which a consent to a risk of injury would not be valid.

(Paragraphs 12.64–12.67)

Fighting and horseplay

45 We provisionally propose that:

(1) the intentional or reckless causing of all types of injury in the course of fighting, otherwise than in the course of a recognised sport, should continue to be criminal, even if the person injured consented to injury or to the risk of injury of the type caused; but

(2) an exception to this rule should continue to be available where any injury, other than seriously disabling injury, is caused in the course of undisciplined consensual horseplay.

(Paragraphs 14.1–14.20)

46 We wish to receive views as to possible definitions of 'fighting' and 'undisciplined horseplay' that would achieve an acceptable degree of clarity and certainty.

(Paragraph 14.21)

Further reading

J Gardner, 'Rationality and the rule of law in offences against the person' [1994] CLJ 502

JC Smith, 'Offences against the person: the Home Office Consultation Paper' [1998] Crim LR 317

S Bronitt, 'Spreading disease and the criminal law' [1994] Crim LR 21

C Wells, 'Stalking: the criminal response' [1997] Crim LR 463

R Stone, 'It's bad to talk: assault by telephone' (1997) 113 LQR 407

S Gardner, 'Stalking' (1998) 114 LQR 33

J Horder, 'Reconsidering psychic assault' [1998] Crim LR 392

S Shute, 'The Second Law Commission Consultation Paper on *Consent*: something old, something new, something borrowed: three aspects of the project' [1996] Crim LR 684

DC Omerod, 'The Second Law Commission Consultation Paper on *Consent*: consent – a second bash' [1996] Crim LR 694

M Gunn and DC Omerod, 'The legality of boxing' [1995] 15 Legal Studies 181

P Roberts, 'Consent to injury: how far can you go?' (1997) 113 LQR 27

P Roberts, 'The philosophical foundations of consent in the criminal law' (1997) 17 OJLS 389

CHAPTER 17

SEXUAL OFFENCES

The materials in this chapter examine the major sexual offences on indecent assault, rape, unlawful sexual intercourse and related offences.

INDECENT ASSAULT

Section 14(1) of the Sexual Offences Act 1956: indecent assault on a woman

It is an offence ... for a person to make an indecent assault on a woman.

Section 15(1) of the Sexual Offences Act 1956: indecent assault on a man

It is an offence for a person to make an indecent assault on a man.

Punishment

Punishment for offences under ss 14 and 15: up to 10 years' imprisonment following conviction on indictment; up to six months' imprisonment and/or a fine of up to £5,000 following summary conviction (s 37 and Sched 2 to the Sexual Offences Act 1956).

There are essentially two ingredients to the offence of indecent assault:

(1) there must be what in law amounts to an assault; and

(2) that assault must take place in circumstances of indecency.

The need for an assault

Director of Public Prosecutions v Rogers [1953] QB 644 (DC)

Facts: At all material times, the respondent lived with his wife and daughter. On two occasions between 27 October 1952, and 7 November 1952, he put his arm round his daughter's shoulders and led her upstairs. She made no objection or resistance, and no force or compulsion was used. He then exposed his person to the child and told her to masturbate him. On both occasions the child obeyed him although she did not wish to do so. On both occasions he was alone in the house with the child. On the first occasion he committed the indecent conduct on the landing and on the second occasion in his bedroom. On both occasions when he put his arm round his daughter's shoulders he did so to lead her upstairs, intending to conduct himself indecently towards her. On the first occasion the child neither minded nor objected to his putting his arm round her shoulders, but on the second occasion, knowing the nature of his intention towards her, she did not wish to accompany him upstairs, but, nevertheless, she neither objected nor resisted, but submitted to his request.

Lord Goddard CJ: ... Before you can find that a man has been guilty of an indecent assault, you have to find that he was guilty of an assault, for an indecent assault is an assault accompanied by indecency, and, if it could be shown here that the respondent had done anything towards this child which, by any fair use of language could be called compulsion, or had acted, as I have said in other cases, in a hostile manner towards her – that is, with a threat or a gesture which could be taken as a threat, or by pulling a reluctant child towards him – that would, undoubtedly, be assault, and, if it was accompanied by an act of indecency, it would be an indecent assault.

Fairclough v Whipp [1951] 2 All ER 834 (DC)

Lord Goddard CJ: ... The question is whether there was an assault. The respondent was making water by the bank of a river where there were some four young girls varying in age from six to nine. As he did so one of the girls passed him. He, with his person exposed, said to her, 'Touch it', and she did so. He then went away. The question for decision is whether that conduct amounts to an indecent assault.

An assault can be constituted, without there being battery, for instance, by a threatening gesture or a threat to use violence against a person, but I do not know any authority which says that where one person invites another person to touch him that can be said to be an assault. The question of consent or non-consent only arises if there is something which can be called an assault and, without consent, would be an assault. If that which was done to this child was of an indecent nature and would have been an assault if done against her will, it would also be an assault if it was done with her consent because she could not consent to an indecent assault [in the light of her age]. Before we decide whether there has been an indecent assault we must decide whether there has been an assault, and I cannot hold that an invitation to somebody to touch the invitor can amount to an assault on the invitee.

Faulkner v Talbot [1981] 3 All ER 468 (DC)

Lord Lane CJ: ... The way in which the case arises is this. The appellant was convicted by the justices on 5 February 1980 of indecent assault on a boy, who was then aged 14 years, contrary to s 15(1) of the Sexual Offences Act 1956. The events happened at the appellant's home, and there is no dispute as to the material facts. The 14 year old boy was living in the appellant's home, having left his parents. The appellant and the boy watched a horror film on the television; the boy was scared, or said he was scared, by the film. As a result of that the appellant told the boy that he could sleep with her if he wished. That he chose to do.

Once they were in bed together, the appellant invited the boy to have sexual intercourse with her. The boy's account, in so far as it was material, was this: the appellant tried to put her hand on his penis, but he would not let her. She then pulled the boy on top of her; she took hold of his penis and put it inside her vagina. On those facts the charge was laid.

His Lordship quoted s 15(1), (2) of the Sexual Offences Act 1956 and, having considered a number of authorities, went on:

> ... First of all what is an assault? An assault is any intentional touching of another person without the consent of that person and without lawful excuse. It need not necessarily be hostile or rude or aggressive, as some of the cases seem to indicate ...

Indecency

Three situations have to be distinguished:

(1) an act which ordinary, right-thinking members of the public could not regard as indecent: that act cannot amount to an indecent assault;

(2) an act which ordinary, right-thinking members of the public would regard as indecent: that act (provided that it amounts to an assault) will be an indecent assault;

(3) an act which ordinary, right-thinking members of the public would regard as ambivalent, in the sense that it is only capable of being indecent: that act will only be indecent if the perpetrator intended it to be so.

An example of a case involving the second category is *R v Culyer* (1992) *The Times*, 17 April and an example of a case involving the third category (where evidence of the defendant's motive is important evidence) is *R v Court* [1989] AC 28.

R v Culyer (1992) The Times, 17 April

Lord Justice Woolf (giving the judgment of the Court of Appeal) said that while in *R v Court* [1989] AC 28 whether what had happened amounted to an indecent assault or not turned on the motive and therefore the specific intent had been necessary to the verdict, in the instant case, there was no question as to whether what had occurred was indecent or not so that the basic intent was sufficient. Since the assault was indecent in itself, the issue was simply whether the appellant did what was alleged.

R v Court [1989] AC 28 (HL)

Facts: The appellant, an assistant in a shop, struck a 12 year old girl visitor some 12 times, for no apparent reason as she thought, outside her shorts on her buttocks. In response to a question by the police as to why the appellant had done so he said, 'I don't know – buttock fetish'.

> **Lord Griffiths**: My Lords, this appeal turns on the answer to the following question. On a trial of indecent assault arising out of a spanking delivered by a man to the buttocks of a young girl, is the evidence that he told the police that he did it because of a 'buttock fetish' admissible evidence which the jury may consider when deciding whether the assault was indecent? I am bound to say my instinctive answer was, yes of course it is. I have now had the advantage of reading the speeches of my noble and learned friends, Lord Ackner and Lord Goff. My answer remains the same. I agree that for the reasons given by my noble and learned friend, Lord Ackner, the evidence is admissible and that his appeal should be dismissed ...
>
> The gravamen of the offence of indecent assault is the element of indecency. It is this element of indecency that distinguishes the offence from common assault and makes it such a potentially serious offence carrying a maximum term of

imprisonment of 10 years. By indecency is meant conduct that right-thinking people will consider an affront to the sexual modesty of a woman.

Although the offence of indecent assault may vary greatly in its gravity from an unauthorised teenage sexual groping at one end of the scale to near rape at the other, it is in any circumstances a nasty, unpleasant offence for which a conviction is likely to carry a far greater social stigma than a conviction for common assault. There is agreement that the offence cannot be committed accidentally as, for instance, in the example given by Lord Ackner of ripping a woman's clothing while attempting to force an exit from a tube train. Once this concession is made it is apparent that some extra mental element is required than that necessary for common assault, for, in the example given, a person using unnecessary violence to push through the crowd would have the necessary intent to commit an assault. It seems natural to me that this extra mental element should be that which constitutes the essence of the offence, namely, an intent to do something indecent to the woman in the sense of an affront to her sexual modesty or, in other words, an intent to do that which the jury find indecent. Indecent assault is after all a sexual offence appearing in the Sexual Offences Act 1956 and one should on general principle look for a sexual element as an ingredient of the offence ...

I turn now to consider whether the evidence of the accused's explanation for his conduct as a 'buttock fetish' was admissible. There is a distinction to be drawn in criminal law between motive and intent although it will very rarely be necessary to enter on a discussion of this distinction with a jury and any unnecessary attempt to do so is likely to cause confusion and do more harm than good. But to illustrate what I mean in the context of indecent assault, the necessary intent is to commit an assault which the jury as right-thinking people consider to be sexually indecent. The motive for such an act will usually be to obtain sexual gratification but it need not necessarily be so. A man might strip a woman in public with the motive of obtaining sexual gratification or, alternatively, with the motive of revenge to humiliate her; but whichever his motive he would undoubtedly be guilty of indecent assault because his intentional stripping of her clothing is an indecent affront to her sexual modesty. Motive generally throws light on intention and is therefore generally admissible to prove intention.

The appellant admitted that he had assaulted the girl and the jury had to decide whether his behaviour was indecent. Whether or not right-thinking people will consider an action indecent will sometimes depend on the purpose with which the action is carried out. An obvious example is the examination of an unconscious woman's private parts. If carried out by a doctor for a proper medical purpose no one would consider such an examination indecent. If carried out by a stranger for a prurient interest everyone would consider it indecent.

Spanking a girl's bottom is an equivocal action. The buttocks are an intimate part of the body in close proximity to the sexual organs and unauthorised handling of that part of the body is certainly capable of being indecent. But the buttocks are also a part of the body on which it is possible to inflict pain without the risk of serious physical damage and have long been recognised as an area of the body to which chastisement may be administered by those having proper authority to do so without anyone thinking it indecent. If a juryman is asked to decide whether a man beating a young girl's bottom is acting indecently, the first question he is likely to ask is – why was he doing it? If the answer is that she had been naughty and he was punishing her, the juryman may well consider that if the man was a stranger he should not have laid hands on the girl and was guilty of assault, but I doubt if he would consider the man's action to be indecent. On the other hand, if the juryman was told that the man was spanking the girl to satisfy a buttock fetish, I would be surprised indeed if he did not think that it was indecent.

The fact is that right-thinking people do take into account the purpose or intent with which an act is performed in judging whether or not it is indecent. If evidence of motive is available that throws light on the intent it should be before the jury to assist them in their decision. Suppose, in the present case, the appellant had said to the police, 'I thought the girl had been stealing and I beat her to stop her doing it again'. Such evidence would surely have been admissible to attempt to persuade the jury that this was an act of chastisement and therefore they should not regard it as indecent. If, on the other hand, evidence is available that shows the spanking was not an act of chastisement but carried out with the intention of obtaining perverted sexual gratification, it would, in my view, be an affront to common sense to withhold that evidence from the jury when asking them to decide if this man had behaved indecently. Accordingly, I agree with the judge that the evidence was admissible.

Lord Ackner: ... It cannot, in my judgment, have been the intention of Parliament that an assault can, by a mere mistake or mischance, be converted into an indecent assault, with all the opprobrium which a conviction for such an offence carries. To take one of the less imaginative examples discussed in the course of the arguments, it may be a common occurrence during travel on the London tube during rush hours, for a person suddenly to realise belatedly that the train has stopped at the very station where he wishes to alight, without his having taken the wise precaution of getting close to its doors. Such a person may well in his anxiety to get out, rather than be carried on to the next stop, use unnecessary force in pushing his way through his fellow passengers. If he thus came into contact with a woman, then he would be guilty of having assaulted her. If something that he was carrying, such as an umbrella, became caught up, as it might well do, in her dress as he pushed past, thus tearing away her upper clothing, he would, in my judgment, be guilty only of an assault. He would not be guilty of an indecent assault ...

It was common ground before your Lordships, and indeed it is self-evident, that the first stage in the proof of the offence is for the prosecution to establish an assault. The 'assault' usually relied on is a battery, the species of assault conveniently described by Lord Lane CJ in *Faulkner v Talbot* [1981] 1 WLR 1528, 1534 as 'any intentional touching of another person without the consent of that person and without lawful excuse. It need not necessarily be hostile or rude or aggressive, as some of the cases seem to indicate'. But the 'assault' relied on need not involve any physical contact but may consist merely of conduct which causes the victim to apprehend immediate and unlawful personal violence. In the case law on the offence of indecent assault, both categories of assault feature.

... A simpler way of putting the matter to the jury is to ask them to decide whether 'right-minded persons would consider the conduct indecent or not'. It is for the jury to decide whether what occurred was so offensive to contemporary standards of modesty and privacy as to be indecent ...

It also was common ground before your Lordships ... that if the circumstances of the assault are incapable of being regarded as indecent, then the undisclosed intention of the accused could not make the assault an indecent one. The validity of this proposition is well illustrated by *R v George* [1956] Crim LR 52. The basis of the prosecution's case was that the defendant on a number of occasions removed a shoe from a girl's foot and that he did so, as indeed he admitted, because it gave him a kind of perverted sexual gratification ... Streatfield J ruled that an assault became indecent only if it was accompanied by circumstances of indecency towards the person alleged to have been assaulted, and that none of the assaults (the removal or attempted removal of the shoes) could possibly amount to an indecent assault.

Again it was common ground that if, as in this case, the assault involved touching the victim, it was not necessary to prove that she was aware of the circumstances of indecency or apprehended indecency. An indecent assault can clearly be committed by the touching of someone who is asleep or unconscious ...

The assault which the prosecution seek to establish may be of a kind which is inherently indecent. The defendant removes, against her will, a woman's clothing. Such a case, to my mind, raises no problem. Those very facts, devoid of any explanation, would give rise to the irresistible inference that the defendant intended to assault his victim in a manner which right-minded persons would clearly think was indecent. Whether he did so for his own personal sexual gratification or because, being a misogynist or for some other reason, he wished to embarrass or humiliate his victim, seems to me to be irrelevant. He has failed, *ex hypothesi*, to show any lawful justification for his indecent conduct. This, of course, was not such a case. The conduct of the appellant in assaulting the girl by spanking her was only capable of being an indecent assault. To decide whether or not right-minded persons might think that assault was indecent, the following factors were clearly relevant – the relationship of the defendant to his victim – were they relatives, friends, or virtually complete strangers? How had the defendant come to embark on this conduct and why was he behaving in this way? Aided by such material, a jury would be helped to determine the quality of the act, the true nature of the assault and to answer the vital question – were they sure that the defendant not only intended to commit an assault on the girl, but an assault which was indecent – was such an inference irresistible? For the defendant to be liable to be convicted of the offence of indecent assault, where the circumstances of the alleged offence can be given an innocent as well as an indecent interpretation, without the prosecution being obliged to establish that the defendant intended to commit both an assault and an indecent one, seems to me quite unacceptable and not what Parliament intended ...

The jury in their question to the judge were concerned with the position of a doctor who carried out an intimate examination on a young girl. Mars-Jones J dealt with their point succinctly by saying:

> In that situation what is vital is whether the examination was necessary or not. If it was not necessary, but indulged in by the medical practitioner it would be an indecent assault. But if it was necessary, even though he got sexual satisfaction out of it, that would not make it an indecent assault.

I entirely agree. If it could be proved by the doctor's admission that the consent of the parent, or if over 16 of the patient, was sought and obtained by the doctor falsely representing that the examination was necessary, then, of course, no true consent to the examination had ever been given. The examination would be an assault and an assault which right-minded persons could well consider was an indecent one. I would not expect that it would make any difference to the jury's decision whether the doctor's false representations were motivated by his desire for the sexual gratification which he might achieve from such an examination, or because he had some other reason, entirely of his own, unconnected with the medical needs or care of the patient, such as private research, which had caused him to act fraudulently. In either case the assault could be, and I expect would be, considered as so offensive to contemporary standards of modesty or privacy as to be indecent. A jury would therefore be entitled to conclude that he, in both cases, intended to assault the patient and to do so indecently. I can see nothing illogical in such a result. On the contrary, it would indeed be surprising if in such circumstances the only offence that could properly be charged would be that of common assault. No doubt the judge would treat the offence which had been motivated by the indecent motive as the more serious ...

I, therefore, conclude that on a charge of indecent assault the prosecution must not only prove that the accused intentionally assaulted the victim, but that in so doing he intended to commit an indecent assault, ie an assault which right-minded persons would think was indecent. Accordingly, any evidence which tends to explain the reason for the defendant's conduct, be it his own admission or otherwise, would be relevant to establish whether or not he intended to commit, not only an assault, but an indecent one. The doctor's admissions in the two contrasting examples which I have given would certainly be so relevant. The appellant's admission of 'buttock fetish' was clearly such material. It tended to confirm, as indeed did the events leading up to the assault and the appellant's conduct immediately thereafter, that what he did was to satisfy his peculiar sexual appetite. It was additional relevant evidence. It tended to establish the sexual undertones which gave the assault its true cachet ...

I would accordingly dismiss the appeal and answer the certified question as follows:

> On a charge of indecent assault the prosecution must prove: (1) that the accused intentionally assaulted the victim (2) that the assault, or the assault and the circumstances accompanying it, are capable of being considered by right-minded persons as indecent; (3) that the accused intended to commit such an assault as is referred to in (2) above.

... I would add that evidence, if any, of the accused's explanation for assaulting the victim, whether or not it reveals an indecent motive, is admissible both to support or to negative that the assault was an indecent one and was so intended by the accused.

Lord Goff delivered a dissenting speech.

R v Sargeant (1997) 161 JP 127 (CA)

Hutchison LJ: ....[T]his appellant was convicted of indecent assault on a male person contrary to s 15(1) of the Sexual Offences Act 1956 ...

At the trial the complainant's evidence was given by means of a video link. He said that he was approached by a man near some steps and grabbed by the shoulder. The man asked him where he was going and when he replied that he was going home the man said, 'No you're not. You've got to come with me', and started pulling him towards the canal. The complainant tried to walk away saying that he had to go home but the man dragged him back and forced him to masturbate into a condom. He said that he was terrified of the man and he was too close to him to be able to escape. After he had masturbated, according to the complainant, the man asked him if he did drugs and whether he was queer. The man himself claimed that he took drugs and was in an angry condition because he had not taken any. He also asked if he had ever been touched by a man. His hands moved towards the complainant but he never touched him in a sexual manner, although he had earlier grabbed hold of him in what was plainly an assault.

... What is submitted by [counsel for the appellant] is that there was here no evidence capable of constituting an indecent assault and ... the essence of his submission comes to this. While, on this boy's evidence, there was in law an assault in that a threat of violence was implied or uttered, there was no indecent touching and no threat of indecent touching and ... for there to be an indecent assault in law the threat must be one of indecent touching. Accordingly, in a case where there is no actual touching, it is only if there is a threat of indecent touching by the defendant that the assault is complete ...

His Lordship then referred to the 7th edn of Smith and Hogan's *Criminal Law*, which contains a summary of the decision in *R v Court* [1989] AC 28 as follows:

(i) Where the manner or the external circumstances of the assault include no element of indecency, the assault is not an indecent assault, however indecent the purpose of the offender.

(ii) Where the manner or the circumstances of the assault are unambiguously indecent, the assault is an indecent assault, whether the offender has an indecent purpose or not, provided only that he is aware of the external circumstances.

(iii) Where the manner or the external circumstances of an assault are ambiguous, the assault is an indecent assault only if the offender has an indecent purpose.

... In our judgment, the submissions made on behalf of the appellant ... are not correct. In our judgment, if a man, without touching the victim, were to require him at knife-point to remove his clothing for the purposes of the assaulter's gratification, there can be no doubt that that would be an indecent assault. In such a case of course the demand to strip might be explicable, as in the analogous case of [*R v Pratt* [1984] Crim LR] on some other ground than a sexual one, for example, that the assaulter wished to possess himself of the clothing in order to make good his escape in disguise. Where, however, as in the present case, the act required of the victim admits of no interpretation other than that it is an indecent act, the proof of the threat to secure compliance (which is the assault) establishes the only other necessary ingredient of the offence...

... The boy's account was one which admits of no interpretation other than that it was indecent, apart altogether from whatever may have been the degree of sexual gratification, if any, which the appellant attained from the conduct which he compelled. It seems to us that to compel someone to masturbate in a public place is an indecent act and that accordingly there was here a coincidence of the two ingredients required to establish indecent assault. First, an assault, namely the threat of violence, and secondly, the performance under compulsion of that threat of an indecent act thereby providing the accompanying circumstances of indecency.

We see no reason to accept [counsel's] submission that there must be touching in an indecent manner or the threat of touching in an indecent manner. It is sufficient if the threat procures an act which is plainly indecent and that constitutes, as we have said, circumstances of indecency.

It is accordingly the view of this court that the evidence of the boy, if accepted by the jury, was capable of constituting an indecent assault ...

Mens rea

A defendant charged with indecent assault must be shown to have been at least subjectively reckless as to whether or not there was physical contact, or as to whether or not P apprehended immediate physical violence. As regards D's knowledge or recklessness as regards the indecency of the circumstances see *R v Court* (above). Mistake as to the age of the complainant will not avail the defendant; see *R v K* (extracted below).

R v K (2000) The Times, 7 November

Roch LJ: On 6th April this year, following transfer of his case from the W Magistrates' Court to the C Crown Court on 29 March, an indictment was preferred against K charging him with indecent assault contrary to section 14(1) of the Sexual Offences Act 1956. The particulars of the offence charged were:

K (the Complainant), on 7th Day of February 2000, indecently assaulted a girl under the age of 16 years, namely the age of 14 years.

At a pre-trial directions hearing on 28th April those acting for K indicated their intention to raise a preliminary issue namely, whether to establish the defendant's guilt, the Prosecution had to prove that the defendant at the time of the incident did not honestly believe that the complainant was 16 years or over.

The preliminary issue was heard on 23rd June by His Honour Judge Thorpe. The judge ruled that the Prosecution had the burden of proving the absence of genuine belief that the girl was 16 or over. The judge gave the Prosecution leave to appeal to this court.

... The issue in this appeal is whether the presumption of law that *mens rea* is required before a person can be held guilty of a criminal offence applies to the offence with which K has been charged; whether he is only guilty of that offence if he knew that the Complainant was under the age of 16 years and for that reason could not give the consent which would have prevented his acts being an assault for the purposes of section 14, or was reckless as to her age, so that he is entitled to be acquitted if the Prosecution fail to prove that he had no genuine belief that the girl was 16 years or over. In other words has the presumption been displaced by the wording of section 14 itself? The presumption is the presumption that a person is not guilty of a criminal offence if he genuinely believes that the facts were such that had the facts been as he believed them to be, he would have been committing no offence.

... Mr Scrivener QC for the Appellant accepted that the case of *B (a minor) v DPP* [2000] 1 All ER 833 had established that the presumption that *mens rea* is an ingredient of an offence meant that, where the presumption applies, a defendant is not guilty if he holds an honest belief that the facts are such that no offence has been committed. It is not necessary for there to be reasonable grounds on which that belief is based. Mr Scrivener further accepted that that case established that the presumption applied to all statutory offences unless Parliament has excluded it expressly or by necessary implication. Mr Scrivener conceded that section 14 does not in express terms exclude the presumption but argued that by the way in which it is drafted Parliament had excluded the presumption by necessary implication. That that was so was well established by earlier authorities which were binding on this court, or if not binding of great persuasive value. Mr Scrivener here was referring to the cases of *Forde* (1923) 17 Cr App R 99, *R v Keech* (1929) 21 Cr App R 125 and *R v Maughan* (1934) 24 Cr App R 130. The members of the House of Lords in *B (A Minor) v DPP* were careful not to overrule these authorities when it came to the interpretation of section 14 of the 1956 Act and nothing that appears in the speeches of Lord Nicholls, Lord Steyn or Lord Hutton was directed to the question whether the presumption was excluded by the wording of section 14. On the contrary, if the 1956 Act provided no guidance to the correct interpretation of section 1 of the 1960 Act it had to follow that a decision on the correct interpretation of section 1 of the 1960 Act could not provide guidance to the proper reading of section 14 of the 1956 Act.

... The importance of the decisions in cases such as *Forde* and *Maughan* for the purposes of this appeal is that despite the Court of Criminal Appeal being critical of the legislation, the court consistently held that Parliament in these provisions had with regard to offences of indecent assault on girls under the age of 16 excluded the presumption of *mens rea* by necessary implication. In *Maughan* the appellant had been charged with unlawfully and carnally knowing a girl of the age of 13 and under the age of 16 and with indecent assault upon the same girl at the same time and place. The jury had acquitted Maughan of unlawful and carnal knowledge on the ground that he came within proviso to section 2 of the 1922 Act, that is to say there was present reasonable cause for Maughan to have believed that the girl was 16 years or over. The jury on the directions of the judge found Maughan guilty of indecent assault. In an appeal on the ground that the indecent assault consisted solely in the act of carnal knowledge of a girl under 16 by a man under 23 who had in law and in fact a complete defence to such an act of carnal knowledge which must have remained available to him although he was only charged with indecent assault, the Court of Criminal Appeal repeated what they had said in the case of *Forde*, namely:

> The result of this legislation is that a boy who is tempted and induced to have carnal knowledge of a girl who misrepresents herself to be over 16, and who appears to be so, has no possible answer if he is charged with indecent assault and not with the full offence.

The court went on to express the hope that the Legislature would take notice of the apparent absurdity resulting from the state of the legislation and that the legislation would be amended.

It is likely that when Parliament enacted the Sexual Offences Act 1956, such criticisms would have been brought to Parliament's attention. Nevertheless,

Parliament proceeded to enact statutory provisions which closely resembled those in earlier legislation which the 1956 Act was to replace.

Against that background the conclusion that we have reached is that Parliament, in the 1956 Act, did exclude any defence of genuine belief that the girl was over 16 to a charge of indecent assault on a girl under the age of 16. We consider that this must follow from the terms of section 14 themselves. First, subsection 2 provides that in the case of a girl under the age of 16, however willing a participant she may have been in sexual activity between herself and the defendant, her consent cannot stop that activity being an indecent assault upon her. That touching of her by the defendant is an indecent assault because Parliament has expressly enacted that it is to be an indecent assault. Subsections 3 and 4 of section 14 do provide defences based on genuine belief, albeit that under subsection 3 the prosecution can defeat the defence by establishing that there was no reasonable cause for the belief. If Parliament had intended that genuine belief should be a defence to the offence created by section 14(1) it would have been unnecessary for Parliament to enact subsections 3 and 4. Those subsections only have a purpose if it is no defence for an accused to say that he or she honestly believed that the girl was 16 years or over. It follows, in our judgment, that Parliament has excluded such a defence by necessary implication.

We have read the speeches of their Lordships in *B (A Minor) v DPP* (above) with care to see if the decision in that case would allow of a different conclusion. We notice first that the decision was a 'close run thing'. Three members of the Divisional Court believed that Parliament in section 1 of the 1960 Act had created an offence of strict liability because of the social and moral imperative identified by Mr Justice Rougier in his judgment ... Lord Steyn in his speech accepted that the matter was finely balanced ... and Lord Hutton considered the arguments for the appellant and the Crown to be almost evenly balanced ... Although Lord Nicholls could not accept the Crown's argument in relation to the interpretation of section 1 of the 1960 Act, namely that the correct interpretation was to be gleaned from the contents of the 1956 Act and in particular sections 14 and 15, Lord Nicholls recognised that to be a formidable argument... The members of the House of Lords were careful not to overrule such cases as *Forde* and *Maughan* ... Lord Steyn found it unnecessary to examine the legal position under sections 14 and 15 of the 1956 Act. He pointed out that the scope of sections 14 and 15 is markedly narrower than section 1(1) with which that case was concerned. Sections 14 and 15 required the Crown to prove an assault which necessarily required an intentional act and to that extent at least *mens rea* is an ingredient which the prosecution must prove.

Mr Fisher did not ask this court to make a declaration of incompatibility between section 14 of the 1956 Act and Article 6 of the Convention. Counsel relied upon section 3(1) of the Human Rights Act, 1998, which provides:

> So far as it is possible to do so, primary legislation and subordinate legislation must be read and given effect in a way which is compatible with the Convention rights.

It was submitted that the earlier decisions of the Court of Criminal Appeal on the interpretation of the statutory provisions preceding the 1956 Act are no longer good law because in those cases the courts were not under an obligation to read and give effect to the legislation in a way compatible with the Convention rights. Article 6(2) would be violated if section 14 is treated as creating an absolute offence where the complainant is under the age of 16.

The reading of section 14 which we consider to be correct is not, in our judgment, incompatible with Article 6(2) of the Convention. The European Court of Human Rights in *Salabiaku v France* (1988) 13 EHRR 379 accepted in paragraph 27 of their judgment at p 387 that:

> In principle the contracting states remain free to apply the criminal law to an act where it is not carried out in the normal exercise of one of the rights protected under the Convention and, accordingly, to define the constituent elements of the resulting offence. In particular, and again in principle, the contracting states may, under certain conditions, penalise a simple or objective fact as such, irrespective of whether it results from criminal intent or from negligence.

Later in their judgment at paragraph 28 the Court observed that:

> Presumptions of fact or of law operate in every legal system. Clearly, the Convention does not prohibit such presumptions in principle. It does, however, require the contracting state to remain within certain limits in this respect as regards criminal law ... Article 6(2) does not therefore regard presumptions of fact or of law provided for in the criminal law with indifference. It requires states to confine them within reasonable limits which take into account the importance of what is at stake and maintain the rights of the defence.

As Lord Hope said in *R v DPP ex p Kebilene and Others* [2000] 1 Cr App R 275 at 330A:

> As a matter of general principle therefore a fair balance must be struck between the demands of the general interest of the community and the protection of the fundamental rights of the individual.

Parliament in 1956 considered that the balance between the demands of the general interests of the community and the protection of the fundamental rights of the individual required that girls under the age of 16 should be protected by making it an offence for a person to touch them in circumstances which are indecent. As we have already said the rights of the defence are maintained in that it is still for the prosecution to prove that the complainant is under 16 years of age and that there has been a deliberate touching of that girl by the defendant in circumstances which make the touching indecent.

The fact that some may think that girls of 14 or 15 ought to be capable of consenting to sexual activity with others or that such a touching of a girl under the age of 16 by a person of a similar age to the girl where the girl has been a willing participant in sexual experimentation should not be criminal; that in cases of the kind identified by Lord Justice Brooke in *B v DPP* in the Divisional Court ... should not be guilty of a criminal offence may make it desirable that Parliament should look again at sections 14 and 15 of the 1956 Act. It must still be open to Parliament to provide that sexual activity with a child or young person under a particular age is absolutely forbidden to those of the age and capacity for criminal responsibility. At present, with regard to indecent assaults on females Parliament has decided that the balance is to be struck by providing that the age group to be protected should be those under the age of 16 years. We do not consider that we could say that by providing that the balance should be struck at that point Parliament is being unfair or unreasonable, although we can express the hope that Parliament might look again at this area of the law relating to sexual offences.

For those reasons we would reverse the judge's ruling on the preliminary issue. In our judgment the Prosecution do not have to prove that the Defendant at the time of the incident did not honestly believe that the complainant was 16 years or over.

Consent: the age of the victim

Section 14 of the Sexual Offences Act 1956: indecent assault on a woman

(2) A girl under the age of 16 cannot in law give any consent which would prevent an act being an assault for the purposes of this section ...

(4) A woman who is a defective cannot in law give any consent which would prevent an act being an assault for the purposes of this section, but a person is only to be treated as guilty of an indecent assault on a defective by reason of that incapacity to consent, if that person knew or had reason to suspect her to be a defective.

Section 15 of the Sexual Offences Act 1956: indecent assault on a man

(2) A boy under the age of 16 cannot in law give any consent which would prevent an act being an assault for the purposes of this section.

(3) A man who is a defective cannot in law give any consent which would prevent an act being an assault for the purposes of this section, but a person is only to be treated as guilty of an indecent assault on a defective by reason of that incapacity to consent, if that person knew or had reason to suspect him to be a defective.

From these provisions it can be seen that consent can only prevent an assault from being indecent if the 'victim' has attained the age of 16 and is not mentally defective.

Faulkner v Talbot [1981] 3 All ER 468 (DC)

For the facts see the extract from this case dealing with the requirement of assault in indecent assault.

Lord Lane CJ: ... If touching is an indecent touching, as in this case it plainly was because the appellant took hold of the boy's penis, then the provisions of s 15(2) of the Sexual Offences Act 1956 come into play: 'A boy under the age of 16 cannot in law give any consent which would prevent an act being an assault for the purposes of this section.' Consequently, the touching undoubtedly being indecent, the boy in this case, being aged 14, could not consent to it. It was intentional touching; it was touching without lawful excuse, and in view of s 15(2) it was a touching to which the boy could not in law consent and therefore did not consent. Accordingly, as I see it, one has all the necessary ingredients of the offence of indecent assault ...

... The question which is asked by the case is as follows:

... whether the acts of the appellant to which the complainant consented in pulling him on top of her and touching his penis immediately before sexual intercourse by him with her were an indecent assault by the appellant on the complainant contrary to s 15 of the Sexual Offences Act 1956?

The answer I would give to that is 'Yes', it was an indecent assault ...

Boreham J: Without going into detail, there is, in my judgment, now ample authority for this general proposition: where, in a charge of indecent assault on a person under the age of 16, the act complained of is indecent that act would, if it were done without consent, be an assault, then the offence is made out ...

R v McCormack [1969] 2 QB 442 (CA)

Fenton Atkinson LJ: ... The facts, shortly, were these. The girl was aged 15, and the appellant was 22. It was common ground that they spent the night of 10/11 August 1968 in bed together ... The girl ... said that with her full consent the appellant had intercourse with her ...

... [H]e said himself in the plainest terms that they had indulged in certain acts of sexual intimacy, including this, that he admittedly on his own evidence had inserted a finger into the girl's vagina ...

... [I]n the view of the members of this court, it is plain beyond argument that if a man inserts a finger into the vagina of a girl under 16 that is an indecent assault, in view of her age, and it is an indecent assault however willing and co-operative she may in fact be.

Consent and indecent assault

Where actual injury is caused to the victim, consent does not prevent the act from amounting to an assault: see *R v Brown* [1994] 1 AC 212. However, where no injury is caused, so the only charge is one of indecent assault, consent may operate to prevent the act from being an assault in the first place (irrespective of the provisions of ss 14(2) and 15(2) of the Sexual Offences Act 1956).

R v Sutton [1977] 1 WLR 1086 (CA)

Lord Widgery CJ: ... The appellant was the coach and manager of a football club for small boys. Three of the boys who played for the club, all 11 or 12, were taken by the applicant to his home in order that he might photograph them. Each of them was photographed partially unclothed and two of them were photographed in the nude. The photographs, whether partially clothed or in the nude, were taken so as to draw attention to the boys' genitals. The appellant's purpose was to sell the photographs to Scandinavian magazines. The appellant remained fully clothed throughout and did not invite any of the boys to touch him in any way at all, nor did he stroke or fondle any of the boys. He did, however, touch each one of them on the hands, arms, legs or torso for the purpose of indicating how he wished them to pose. These actions were not threatening or hostile in any ordinary sense of the word and none of the three boys showed any unwillingness, indeed they consented.

... The 1956 Act bars consent from preventing an act being an indecent assault [see below]. Hence, if the act alleged to constitute the assault is itself an indecent act, consent will not avail. But in the present case the touching, which was merely to indicated a pose, was not in itself indecent, and was consented to. It was not hostile or threatening. Consent, therefore, does avail to prevent it being an assault and the question of indecency does not arise ...

Mistake as to consent

R v Kimber [1983] 1 WLR 1118 (CA)

Lawton LJ: ... [T]he appellant was convicted of an indecent assault on a woman ...

The appeal raises these points. First, can a defendant charged with indecent assault on a woman raise the defence that he believed she had consented to what he did? ... Second, if he could, did the jury have to consider merely whether his belief was honestly held or, if it was, did they have to go on to consider whether it was based on reasonable grounds? Another way of putting these points is to ask whether the principles upon which the House of Lords decided *R v Morgan* [1976] AC 182 should be applied to a charge of indecent assault on a woman.

The victim was a female patient in a mental hospital. Her mental disorder had been diagnosed as schizophrenia ... Although she was not a defective within the meaning of ss 7 and 45 of the Sexual Offences Act 1956 ... she was suffering from a severe degree of mental disorder ... [T]he appellant admitted trying to have sexual intercourse with [the victim] but said he had not succeeded ... and that he had interfered with her in a way which clearly amounted to an indecent assault if it had been done without her consent ...

[In evidence, the appellant had said that he thought the victim was 'unstable' but he 'thought she was giving consent to have sexual intercourse'; he also said that he 'was not really interested in [her] feelings at all'.]

... At the close of the prosecution's case the [trial judge] ruled that the sole issue for the jury was whether [the victim] had given her real and genuine consent ... He said:

> It is no defence that the defendant thought or believed [the victim] was consenting. The question is: was she consenting? It does not matter what he thought or believed.

Before this court it was accepted by counsel for the prosecution ... that this direction was wrong. The [trial judge] had not had his attention drawn to *R v Tolson* (1889) 23 QBD 168. Before us [counsel for the prosecution] submitted that the jury should have been directed that the appellant had a defence if he had believed that [the victim] was consenting and he had had reasonable grounds for thinking so. On the facts the appellant could not have had any such grounds ... We agree that on the evidence the appellant had no reasonable grounds for thinking that [the victim] was consenting and no jury other than a perverse one could have thought he had.

[Counsel for the appellant] argued, relying on the decision in *R v Morgan* [1976] AC 182, that the sole issue was whether the appellant had honestly believed that [the victim] was consenting. Unless the jury was sure that he had not so believed, he was entitled to be acquitted. The grounds for his belief were irrelevant save in so far as they might have assisted the jury to decide whether he did believe what he said he did ...

The offence of indecent assault is now statutory: see s 14 of the Sexual Offences Act 1956. The prosecution had to prove that the appellant made an indecent assault on [the victim]. As there are no words in the section to indicate that Parliament intended to exclude *mens rea* as an element in this offence, it follows that the prosecution had to prove that the appellant intended to commit it. This could not be done without first proving that the appellant intended to assault [the victim]. In this context assault clearly includes battery. As assault is an act by which the defendant intentionally or recklessly causes the complainant to apprehend, or to sustain, unlawful personal violence: see *R v Venna* [1976] QB 421 at 428–29. In this case the appellant by his own admissions did intentionally lay his hands on [the victim]. That would not, however, have been enough to prove the charge. There had to be evidence that the appellant had intended to do what he did unlawfully. When there is a charge of indecent assault on a woman, the unlawfulness [of the assault] can be proved, as was sought to be done in *R v Donovan* [1934] 2 KB 498, by evidence that the defendant intended to cause bodily harm. In most cases, however, the prosecution tries to prove that the complainant did not consent to what was being done. The burden of proving lack of consent rests on the prosecution: see *R v May* [1912] 3 KB 572 at 575 *per* Lord Alverstone CJ. The consequence is that the prosecution has to prove that the defendant intended to lay hands on his victim without her consent. If he did not intend to do this, he is entitled to be found not guilty; and if he did not so intend because he believed she was consenting, the prosecution will have failed to prove the charge. It is the defendant's belief, not the grounds on which it was based, which goes to negative the intent.

In analysing the issue in this way we have followed what was said by the majority in *R v Morgan* [1976] AC 182: see Lord Hailsham of St Marylebone at 214F–H and Lord Fraser of Tullybelton at 237E–G. If, as we adjudge, the prohibited act in indecent assault is the use of personal violence to a woman without her consent, then the guilty state of mind is the intent to do it without her consent. Then, as in rape at common law, the inexorable logic, to which Lord Hailsham referred in *R v Morgan*, takes over and there is no room either for a 'defence' of honest belief or mistake, or of a 'defence' of honest and reasonable belief or mistake: see [1976] AC 182 at 214F–H.

His Lordship then went on to criticise the decisions of the Divisional Court in *Albert v Lavin* [1982] AC 546 and *R v Phekoo* [1981] 1 WLR 1117.

His Lordship concluded:

In our judgment the [trial judge] should have directed the jury that the Crown had to make them sure that the appellant never had believed that [the victim] was consenting. [However, despite the judge's failure to so direct the jury] a reasonable jury would inevitably have decided that he had no honest belief that [the victim] was consenting. His own evidence showed that his attitude to her was one of indifference to her feelings and wishes. This state of mind is aptly described in the colloquial expression, 'couldn't care less'. In law this is recklessness. Had the jury been directed on recklessness we are sure they would have found that [the appellant] had acted recklessly. That would have been enough to support a conviction of the offence charged ...

Consent obtained by deception

R v Tabassum [2000] Crim LR 686

Rose LJ: On 30th November 1999 at Preston Crown Court, following a trial before His Honour Judge Livesey QC, the appellant was convicted on three counts of indecent assault, on three different female complainants. Counts 1, 3 and 4 related to those offences. No evidence was offered on count 2 which also alleged indecent assault, and the appellant was acquitted on that count on the direction of the judge.

The appellant had been previously tried but the jury had been discharged from giving verdicts at the close of the prosecution case. Following an adjournment for reports, on 21st February 2000, the appellant was sentenced to 9 months' imprisonment on each count concurrently.

He appeals against conviction by leave of the Single Judge who referred to the Full Court his application for leave to appeal against sentence.

In outline, the prosecution case was that the appellant had asked several women to take part in what he said was a breast cancer survey to enable him to prepare a database software package for sale to doctors. The three complainant women agreed to the appellant showing them how to examine their own breasts. That involved the appellant, himself, feeling the breasts of two of the women and using a stethoscope beneath the bra of the third woman. Each of the three women said that they had only consented because they thought the appellant had either medical qualifications or relevant training. He had neither. There was no evidence of any sexual motive.

The defence case was that the appellant was collecting information for the database and he did no more than each of the complainants consented to. He touched their breasts, to show them how to examine themselves and they each consented to that. He had no medical qualifications, but he did have experience in the field of breast cancer.

... The safety of the appellant's conviction is challenged by Mr MacDonald [counsel for the appellant] on two grounds. First, he submits that the judge was wrong to reject the submission made to him and to rule that, in the light of the evidence which the complainants were to give and did give, the case was capable of proceeding before the jury on the issue of consent.

Mr MacDonald drew attention to the way in which the judge, in his summing-up, ultimately directed the jury. At p 4F, in the course of directing the jury as to the elements of indecent assault, he said this:

> Was it unlawful? That is was it done without the consent of these women or any of them? That, members of the jury, is the vital question for you to decide in this case.

> Now, of course, it is right and correct to say that what these women consented to certainly in 2 of the 3 cases was to take off their clothes and to allow this man to feel their breasts. But if you are satisfied to the extent that I have indicated as a matter of fact that they only did so because they believed that this man had medical qualifications, then their consent has been negated and so it is not a true consent.

> So, if you find that one or more of these women only consented to what occurred on the basis that this man had medical qualifications, then I must tell you that their consent is not a true consent because what they agreed to was an examination by a person who had medical qualifications which we know that this defendant does not have and if that is right, then the assaults would have been unlawful.

During his first interview which is Exhibit 11 on p 5, he was describing the training that he had with these various drug companies and he was asked:

Q   As any part of that training, were you given the opportunity to physically examine women patients?

A   No.

Q   Why do you think that was?

A   Because we're not medically qualified.

[The first complainant] told you 'I would not have allowed him me to touch me if I had known he had no qualifications.' [The second complainant] told you 'I would not have allowed him to touch me if he had had no medical training.' [The third complainant] told you 'I would not have let him touch me if I had known that he did not work at Christies.'

So, if and only if you accept that evidence and I stress it is a matter of fact for you, if you accept that evidence, then there was no consent and, therefore, the assault was unlawful.

Mr MacDonald says, rightly, that in that passage the judge did not refer to the nature and quality of the act, which was a matter to which the submissions before him, when he was invited to rule on the matter, had been directed. In the course of his ruling, the judge at p 2F said this, in rehearsing the submissions of counsel for the Crown:

What they consented to was a medical examination by a person with medical qualifications and not a sexual act.

Mr MacDonald's reply to such a submission is that the nature and quality of the act is the same and it does not change.

The judge went on to refer to a passage in the judgment of Stephen J, in *R v Clarence* (1888) 22 QBD 23 at p 44, which we shall cite at a later stage. The judge went on p 3E to say this:

I accept the submissions made on behalf of the Crown and have come to the conclusion that what these women consented to was a medical examination to be carried out by a person with medical qualifications and not to a sexual act and, therefore, the nature and quality of the act has changed from that with which they consented.

In challenging that ruling, and the way in which in due course the learned judge left the matter to the jury on this aspect of the case, Mr MacDonald referred to a number of authorities. In *R v Linekar* [1995] QB 250, Morland J, giving the judgment of the court, at p 255b said this, having referred to *R v Flattery* (1877) 2 QBD 410 and *R v Williams* [1923] 2 KB 340:

... it is the non-consent to sexual intercourse rather that the fraud of the doctor or choir master that makes the offence rape.

At p 259c, Morland J quoted, among other passages, that passage from the judgment of Stephen J in *Clarence* which the judge himself rehearsed in the course of his ruling:

There is an abundant authority to show that such frauds as these vitiate consent both in the case of rape and in the case of indecent assault. I should myself prefer to say that consent in such cases does not exist at all, because the act consented to is not the act done ...

Consent to a surgical operation or examination is not a consent to sexual connection or indecent behaviour.

Mr MacDonald accepts that there will be no genuine consent if, in the present circumstances, a woman is misled either as to the identity of the man who does the acts complained of, or as to the nature and quality of the act done. But, he submits, the nature and quality of the act, albeit not merely related to the act itself, but including the immediate conditions effecting its nature, does not, as he put it, 'extend back' to the qualifications of the defendant.

Mr MacDonald referred to *R v Richardson* [1998] 2 Cr App R 200, in which the patient believed that she was receiving dental treatment which otherwise would have given rise to an assault occasioning actual bodily harm, from a dentist who had in fact been struck off the register. The court in that case held that the identity of the defendant was not a feature which, in that case, precluded the giving of consent by the patient. Mr MacDonald submits that, because the identity of the defendant was different from that which the patient believed it to be, that changed the nature and quality of the act, yet, in that case, *Richardson,* the conviction was quashed.

He submits that to impose criminal liability in the circumstances of the present case would be to extend the criminal law beyond its existing boundaries. In his written submissions, he submitted that the case law establishes that, where an undoubted consent is given, it can only be negatived by deception or mistake and if the victim has been deceived or is mistaken as to the identity of the perpetrator, or the nature and quality of the act is different from that for which consent was given. Consent is not negatived merely because the victim would have agreed to the act if he or she had known all the facts. In *Clarence*, the wife would not have consented to sexual intercourse with her husband if she had known that he had a venereal disease. In *Richardson*, the patients would not have consented to dentistry if they had known the dentist had been struck off. In *Linekar*, the prostitute's consent to sex was not negated by cheating over payment.

On behalf of the Crown, Mr Grout-Smith, who prosecuted in the court below, in helpful written submissions, submits that the judge was right to rule that consent to an act that is different in nature from the act performed is not a consent to the act performed. He relies on *Clarence*, and a decision of the Saskatchewan Court of Appeal in *Harms* [1944] 2 Dominion Law Reports p 61.

The judge correctly ruled, he submits, that the complainants, if their evidence was accepted, consented to a medical act and not a sexual act. As the defendant had no medical qualifications, he could not have been touching the complainants' breasts for a proper medical purpose. The judge was correct to rule that sexual motive was irrelevant – as to which see *Court* [1989] AC 28 and *R v C* [1992] Crim LR 642.

The direction to the jury that they could only convict on any count if they were sure that the complainant only allowed the appellant to touch her breasts because she thought he was medically qualified, was sufficient to ensure that they would only convict if they were sure that the complainants consented to acts medical in nature.

The second criticism which Mr MacDonald advances is that the judge failed adequately to direct the jury as to the necessary element of *mens rea* on the part of the defendant. What the judge said, at p 7C, was this:

Did he intend to assault these three women? Or did he believe that he had their consent when, in fact, he did not? Well, members of the jury, if you accept that what he told these ladies was half truths and perhaps lies, then clearly it is not far of a step to come to the conclusion that he must have known that he did not have their consent and he must have intended to indecently assault them.

Then at p 47B, the judge this:

> The defence say to you that what this man did was no more than what each of these women consented to. He touched their breasts and they consented to that and, say the defence, the prosecution must also prove that the defendant knew that he did not have their consent.

> Well, members of the jury, of course we cannot look into his mind as to what he knew or did not know but if you come to the conclusion that he told lies or half truths when addressing these women, then you may have no difficulty in concluding that he knew perfectly well that they did not consent and would not have done so had he not said this. But that, of course, is entirely a matter for you. It is a matter of fact.

Mr MacDonald referred the court to *R v Kimber* [1983] 3 All ER 316. There, it was held that the prosecution has to prove that the defendant intended to lay hands on the victim without her consent and, if he did not intend to do this, he is entitled to be found not guilty. If he did not so intend because he believed she was consenting the prosecution would have failed to prove the charge:

> It is the defendant's belief, not the grounds on which it was based, which goes to negative consent.

Mr MacDonald submits, in his written submission, that the judge failed to give the jury any direction as to the reasonableness of the defendant's belief in the complainant's consent.

In our judgment, the pertinent authorities, in relation to Mr MacDonald's first submission, can properly be analysed in this way. The wife in *Clarence*, and the prostitute in *Linekar*, each consented to sexual intercourse knowing both the nature and the quality of that act. The additional unexpected consequences, of infection in the one case and non payment in the other, were irrelevant to and did not detract from the woman's consent to sexual intercourse.

In Richardson, the case proceeded solely by reference to the point on identity. As is apparent from p 205F of the judgment, the prosecution in that case did not at trial or on appeal rely on the nature or quality of the act. In our judgment, the learned judge was entitled to follow the passage in the judgment of Stephen J in *Clarence*, which he cited in the course of his ruling. In the present case the motive and intent of the defendant were irrelevant (see *R v C* to which reference has already been made). The nature and quality of the defendant's acts in touching the breasts of women to whom, in sexual terms he was a stranger, was unlawful and an indecent assault unless the complainants consented to that touching.

On the evidence, if the jury accepted it, consent was given because they mistakenly believed that the defendant was medically qualified or, in the case of the third complainant, trained at Christies and that, in consequence, the touching was for a medical purpose. As this was not so, there was no true consent. They were consenting to touching for medical purposes not to indecent behaviour, that is, there was consent to the nature of the act but not its quality. *Flattery* and *Harms*, which we have earlier cited, are entirely consistent with that view because, in each of those cases, the woman's consent to sexual intercourse was to a therapeutic, not a carnal, act. A similar principle underlies the decision in *Rosinski*, as long ago as 1824, reported in 1 Moody, 1168. It follows that, in our judgment, the judge's ruling was correct.

Indecency with children

Indecency With Children Act 1960, s 1 (as amended by s 39 of the Criminal Justice and Courts Act 2000)

(1) Any person who commits an act of gross indecency with or towards a child under the age of [16], or who incites a child under that age to such an act with him or another, shall be liable on conviction on indictment to imprisonment for a term not exceeding ten years, or on summary conviction to imprisonment for a term not exceeding six months, to a fine not exceeding the prescribed sum, or to both.

The offence is triable either way and carries a maximum penalty of ten years' imprisonment, provided the offence was committed after 1 October 1997.

RAPE

The offence of rape is provided for by the Sexual Offences Act 1956, s 1 as amended by s 142 of the Criminal Justice and Public Order Act 1994.

Section 1 of the Sexual Offences Act 1956

(1) It is an offence for a man to rape a woman or another man.

(2) A man commits rape if:

(a) he has sexual intercourse with a person (whether vaginal or anal) who at the time of the intercourse does not consent to it; and

(b) at the time he knows that the person does not consent to the intercourse or is reckless as to whether that person consents to it.

Punishment

The maximum sentence for rape is life imprisonment: s 37 of the Sexual Offences Act 1956.

The elements of rape are thus:

(1) a man has intercourse (anal or vaginal) with a woman, or a man has anal intercourse with another man; and

(2) the victim does not consent to sexual intercourse taking place; and

(3) the defendant knows that the victim is not consenting or is reckless as to whether he or she consents or not.

The 'woman' for these purposes can be the wife of the accused – the amended statute thus reflecting the House of Lords' ruling in *R v R* [1992] 1 AC 599.

Intercourse

Sexual intercourse in this context means that the defendant's penis must penetrate the victim's vagina or anus, as the case may be. It follows from this that the term 'intercourse' does not include oral sex (fellatio or cunnilingus); if activities such as these take place without the consent of the victim, the appropriate charge is one of indecent assault.

Furthermore, since 'intercourse' is synonymous with 'penetration', the offence of rape is complete at the moment of initial penetration. It is not necessary that the defendant should ejaculate in order for the offence to be complete. This is made clear in s 44 of the 1956 Act.

Section 44 of the Sexual Offences Act 1956

Where, on the trial of any offence under this Act, it is necessary to prove sexual intercourse (whether natural or unnatural), it shall not be necessary to prove the completion of the intercourse by the emission of seed [ie semen], but intercourse shall be deemed complete upon proof of penetration only.

Consent to sexual intercourse

The victim does not have to offer physical resistance in order to demonstrate lack of consent (although, of course, the lack of physical resistance may be relevant to whether the defendant knows the victim is not consenting or is reckless whether the victim is consenting or not).

R v Olugboja [1982] QB 320 (CA)

Dunn LJ: ... The question of law raised by this appeal is whether to constitute the offence of rape it is necessary for the consent of the victim of sexual intercourse to be vitiated by force, the fear of force, or fraud; or whether it is sufficient to prove that in fact the victim did not consent ...

The appellant, who is a Nigerian, aged 20 at the time and studying at Oxford, had sexual intercourse with Jayne, then aged 16, on 8 March 1979, at the bungalow of his co-accused Lawal. She had been taken there with her friend Karen (aged 17) with Lawal in a car driven by the appellant from a discotheque in Oxford where they had all been dancing. Lawal had offered the girls a lift home, but the appellant had driven them to the bungalow which was virtually in the opposite direction from where they lived. This was a deliberate trick to get them to the bungalow. When they got there both girls refused to go in, and started walking away. They did not know where they were. Lawal followed them in the car, and after some argument they got in. After a further argument Karen again got out, and, as she was trying to get Jayne out, Lawal drove off, stopped in a lane, and raped Jayne.

Lawal then drove back to the bungalow, picking Karen up on the way, and the three of them went inside. The appellant was there lying on the sofa asleep, and saw them arrive. Jayne was the last to come in. She was either crying, or obviously had been. Music was put on. Jayne declined to dance. She went to the lavatory and returned to find Lawal dragging Karen into the bedroom. The defendant switched the sitting-room lights off and told Jayne that he was going to fuck her. She told him that Lawal had had her in the car and asked why could the appellant not leave her alone. He told her to take her trousers off and she did because she said she was frightened. She was still crying and the room was in darkness. The appellant pushed her on the settee and had intercourse with her. It did not last long. She did not struggle; she made no resistance; she did not scream or cry for help. She did struggle when she thought after penetration that the defendant was going to ejaculate inside her, and he withdrew. She put her clothes on and the other two emerged from the bedroom, where Lawal had raped Karen. The appellant and Jayne then went into the bedroom. She told him she was going to call the police. He said that if she opened her big mouth he would not take her home. He later did.

Once home Jayne made a complaint to her mother about Lawal but not about the appellant. She said later she did not know why she did not complain to her mother about the appellant. She supposed that she was more upset 'about the first one', meaning Lawal. After she had made her complaint to her mother about Lawal she saw the police and a doctor, with whom she spent a total of eight hours. She made no complaint against the appellant; indeed she said he had not touched her.

The police initially saw the appellant as a witness to the complaints by both Jayne and Karen with regard to the rapes on each of them by Lawal. In the course of the interview the police said to the appellant that Lawal had said that he, the appellant, had had sexual intercourse with Jayne. When they put that to him, Jayne had made no complaint against him. The appellant at once admitted he had had sexual intercourse with Jayne and in answer to the question: 'Did she consent?' he replied: 'Well not at first but I persuaded her'. At the end of the interview the appellant made a written statement. The police then saw Jayne who said that the defendant had indeed had intercourse with her against her will. The police then went back to see the defendant and put to him what Jayne had said. There followed a further long and detailed interview ...

... [I]n so far as the *actus reus* is concerned the question now is simply: 'At the time of the sexual intercourse did the woman consent to it?' It is not necessary for the prosecution to prove that what might otherwise appear to have been consent was in reality merely submission induced by force, fear or fraud, although one or more of these factors will no doubt be present in the majority of cases of rape ...

The jury ... should be directed that consent, or the absence of it, is to be given its ordinary meaning and if need be, by way of example, that there is a difference between consent and submission; every consent involves a submission, but it by no means follows that a mere submission involves consent ... In the majority of cases, where the allegation is that the intercourse was had by force or by the fear of force, such a direction coupled with specific references to, and comments on, the evidence relevant to the absence of real consent will clearly suffice. In the less common type of case where intercourse takes place after threats not involving violence or the fear of it ... we think that an appropriate direction to a jury will have to be fuller. They should be directed to concentrate on the state of mind of the victim immediately before the act of sexual intercourse, having regard to all the relevant circumstances; and in particular; the events leading up to the act and her reaction to them showing their impact on her mind. Apparent acquiescence after penetration does not necessarily involve consent, which must have occurred before the act takes place. In addition to the general direction about consent which we have outlined, the jury will probably be helped in such cases by being reminded that in this context consent does comprehend the wide spectrum of states of mind to which we earlier referred, and that the dividing line in such circumstances between real consent on the one hand and mere submission on the other may not be easy to draw. Where it is to be drawn in a given case is for the jury to decide, applying their combined good sense, experience and knowledge of human nature and modern behaviour to all the relevant facts of that case ...

Petition: The Appeal Committee of the House of Lords (**Lord Diplock, Lord Keith of Kinkel** and **Lord Bridge of Harwich**) dismissed a petition by the appellant for leave to appeal.

Consent: withdrawal of consent during intercourse

Kaitamaki v R [1985] 1 AC 147

Lord Scarman: In the early hours of 19 November 1978 the appellant broke and entered a dwelling house. The Crown's case was that he then twice raped a young woman who was an occupier of the premises. There was no dispute that intercourse had taken place on the two occasions. The defence was that the woman consented (or that the appellant honestly believed that she was consenting).

But when the appellant came to give evidence, his case as to the second occasion was that after he had penetrated the woman for the second time he became aware that she was not consenting; he admitted, however, that he did not desist from intercourse. In summing up this part of the case the trial judge said to the jury:

I tell you, as a matter of law ... that if, having realised she is not willing, he continues with the act of intercourse, it then becomes rape ...

It is said that this direction was wrong in law. The appellant's counsel submits that by the criminal law of New Zealand if a man penetrates a woman with her consent he cannot become guilty of rape by continuing the intercourse after a stage when he realises that she is no longer consenting.

The submission raises a question as to the true construction of sections 127 and 128 of the Crimes Act 1961. Section 127 defines sexual intercourse and is in these terms:

For the purposes of this Part of this Act, sexual intercourse is complete upon penetration; and there shall be no presumption of law that any person is by reason of his age incapable of such intercourse.

Section 128 defines rape and, so far as is material, is in these terms: '(1) Rape is the act of a male person having sexual intercourse with A woman or girl– (a) Without her consent; ...

Counsel for the appellant took one point only; but he submitted that it was all he needed. He relied on the definition in section 127 to establish the proposition that rape is penetration without consent: once penetration is complete the act of rape is concluded. Intercourse if it continues, is not rape, because for the purposes of the Act it is complete upon penetration.

The Court of Appeal by a majority rejected the submission, expressing the opinion that the purpose of section 127 was to remove any doubts as to the minimum conduct needed to prove the fact of sexual intercourse. 'Complete' is used in the statutory definition in the sense of having come into existence, but not in the sense of being at an end. Sexual intercourse is a continuing act which only ends with withdrawal. And the offence of rape is defined in section 128 as that of 'having' intercourse without consent.

Their Lordships agree with the majority decision of the Court of Appeal, and with the reasons which they gave for rejecting the appellant's submission and for construing the two sections in the way in which they did. As Lord Brightman observed in the course of argument before the Board section 127 says 'complete,' not 'completed.'

... Their Lordships rest their view upon the true construction, as they see it, of the two sections already quoted of the Crimes Act 1961.

Their Lordships were, however, disturbed by the course taken by the Crown at the trial. The indictment charged one offence of rape. The prosecution case was that there were two rapes. In the event, as could have been anticipated, there developed two different defences. To the first allegation the defence was consent: to the second the defence was that she consented to penetration but not to the subsequent intercourse, which, however, was not sexual intercourse for the purposes of the Act: see section 127. The Crown well knew that its case was that there were two rapes. In fairness to the accused each should have been separately charged. The Board is, however, satisfied that in the present case there has been no miscarriage of justice. Their Lordships, therefore, will humbly advise Her Majesty that this appeal should be dismissed.

R v Cooper and Schaub [1994] Crim LR 531 (CA)

Facts: While they were considering their verdict, the jury sent a note to the judge asking whether it was rape if a woman consented at the start of the intercourse but then withdrew her consent and the man carried on nonetheless. The main issue in the case was that this point had not been raised during the trial, and so the judge should have told the jury not to consider it. However, the Court of Appeal also held (*obiter*) that penetration is a continuing act. So, where a man continues to penetrate a woman after she has withdrawn her consent to that penetration, then (if the other elements of rape are present) he commits rape by carrying on with the intercourse without her consent.

Lack of consent: intoxication

It is rape to have sexual intercourse with a woman who is too drunk to give her consent (provided that the defendant has the appropriate *mens rea*). In such a case, 'the critical question is whether she understood her situation and was capable of making up her mind'; if she was not, then she could not consent to intercourse (see *R v Lang* (1975) 62 Cr App R 50, *per* Scarman LJ at 52).

Lack of consent: consent obtained by fraud

Section 1(3) of the Sexual Offences Act 1956 provides that 'A man also commits rape if he induces a married woman to have sexual intercourse with him by impersonating her husband'. Such cases are, needless to say, very rare. Generally, the courts are reluctant to find that the victim's consent is vitiated by deception on the part of the defendant. One case where deception did vitiate consent was *R v Williams* [1923] 1 KB 320, where the defendant deceived the victim as to what he was doing – she agreed to an operation to improve her singing voice – the defendant proceeded to have sexual intercourse with her on the basis that the act was the 'operation'. However, most forms of deception will not vitiate consent. So a man is not guilty of rape if he procures consent by falsely representing that he intends to marry the victim (see *Papadimitropoulos v R* (1957) 98 DLR 249), nor if he procures consent by falsely representing that he intends to pay for the sexual intercourse (see *R v Linekar* [1995] 3 All ER 69).

R v Linekar [1995] 3 All ER 69 (CA)

Morland J: ... The complainant was a woman of 30 who worked occasionally as a prostitute to supplement her social security benefit. On 21 March 1993 she was working as such outside the Odeon cinema in Streatham. Some time after midnight she was approached by the appellant, who was then aged 17. There was negotiation between the two of them and the sum of £25 was agreed for sexual services. The appellant and the complainant went off to find a suitable place where they could have sexual intercourse. This proved difficult but eventually, after a long period of time, sexual intercourse took place between them on the balcony of a block of flats. After sexual intercourse had taken place the appellant, in breach of the agreement he had made with the complainant, made off without paying.

Immediately the complainant knocked on the door of a neighbouring house. She was distressed, nearly naked and complained that she had been raped. The police were called. The appellant was arrested and, when interviewed, told a number of lies.

The Crown case, based on the evidence of the complainant, was that the act of sexual intercourse took place as a result of a forced violent assault upon her and did not take place with her consent. She said in evidence that she would not have agreed to sexual intercourse until she had been paid in advance and unless the man wore a condom. The case for the Crown was what might be described, if one can describe rape as such, an ordinary rape: that is, forcible penetration of the woman without her consent.

The appellant did not give evidence on his own behalf, but cross-examination of the complainant was on the lines that the act of sexual intercourse had been done with the complainant's consent, and that what had happened was that afterwards the appellant had broken his promise to pay her the £25. It seemed clear that the appellant did not in fact have £25 and, as the jury were to find by a verdict, which was in the nature of a special verdict, at the time of sexual intercourse, he did not have any intention of paying even if he had the money to pay ...

An essential ingredient of the offence of rape is the proof that the woman did not consent to the actual act of sexual intercourse with the particular man who penetrated her. If the Crown prove that she did not consent to sexual intercourse, rape is proved. That ingredient is proved in the so-called 'medical cases'. The victim did not agree in those cases to sexual intercourse. In *R v Flattery* (1877) 2 QBD 410 she agreed to a surgical procedure which she hoped would cure her fits. In *R v Williams* [1923] 1 KB 340 she agreed to a physical manipulation which would provide her with extra air supply to improve her singing.

In our judgment, it is the non-consent to sexual intercourse rather than the fraud of the doctor or choirmaster that makes the offence rape ...

... [T]here is the highly persuasive authority of *Papadimitropoulos v R* (1957) 98 CLR 249, a decision of the High Court of Australia. The court was presided over by Dixon CJ, and consisted of McTiernan, Webb, Kitto and Taylor JJ.

... The facts of that case were that the complainant believed that she had gone through a marriage with the appellant.

In its judgment the court said (at 260–61):

> It must be noted that in considering whether an apparent consent is unreal it is the mistake or misapprehension that makes it so. It is not the fraud producing the mistake which is material so much as the mistake itself. But if the mistake or misapprehension is not produced by the fraud of the man, there is logically room for the possibility that he was unaware of the woman's mistake so that a question of his *mens rea* may arise. So in *R v Lambert* ((1919) VLR 205 at 213) Cussen J says: 'It is plain that, though in these cases the question of consent or non-consent is primarily referable to the mind of the woman, if she has really a mind, yet the mind of the man is also affected by the facts which indicate want of consent or possible want of capacity to consent.' For that reason it is easy to understand why the stress has been on the fraud. But that stress tends to distract the attention from the essential enquiry, namely, whether the consent is no consent because it is not directed to the nature and character of the act. The identity of the man and the character of the physical act that is done or proposed seem now clearly to be regarded as forming part of the nature and character of the act to which the woman's consent is directed. That accords with the principles governing mistake vitiating apparent manifestations of will in other chapters of the law. In the present case the decision of the majority of the Full Court extends this conception beyond the identity of the physical act and the immediate conditions affecting its nature to an antecedent inducing cause – the existence of a valid marriage. In the history of bigamy that has never been done. The most heartless bigamist has not been considered guilty of rape. Mock marriages are no new thing. Before the Hardwicke Marriage Act it was a fraud easily devised and readily carried out. But there is no reported instance of an indictment for rape based on the fraudulent character of the ceremony. No indictment of rape was founded on such a fraud. Rape, as a capital felony, was defined with exactness, and although there has been some extension over the centuries in the ambit of the crime, it is quite wrong to bring within its operation forms of evil conduct because they wear some analogy to aspects of the crime and deserve punishment. The judgment of the majority of the Full Court of the Supreme Court goes upon the moral differences between marital intercourse and sexual relations without marriage. The difference is indeed so radical that it is apt to draw the mind away from the real question which is carnal knowledge without consent. It may well be true that the woman in the present case never intended to consent to the latter relationship.

But, as was said before, the key to such a case as the present lies in remembering that it is the penetration of the woman's body without her consent to such penetration that makes the felony. The capital felony was not directed to fraudulent conduct inducing her consent. Frauds of that kind must be punished under other heads of the criminal law or not at all: they are not rape. To say that in the present case the facts which the jury must be taken to have found amount to wicked and heartless conduct on the part of the applicant is not enough to establish that he committed rape. To say that in having intercourse with him she supposed that she was concerned in a perfectly moral act is not to say that the intercourse was without her consent. To return to the central point; rape is carnal knowledge of a woman without her consent; carnal knowledge is the physical fact of penetration; it is the consent to that which is in question; such a consent demands a perception as to what is about to take place, as to the identity of the man and the character of what he is doing. But once the consent is comprehending and actual the inducing causes cannot destroy its reality and leave the man guilty of rape.

Respectfully applying those *dicta* to the facts of the present case, the prostitute here consented to sexual intercourse with the appellant. The reality of that consent is not destroyed by being induced by the appellant's false pretence that his intention was to pay the agreed price of £25 for her services. Therefore, he was not guilty of rape ...

Mens rea: knowing that the victim does not consent or recklessness as to consent

Belief that the victim is consenting does not have to be based on reasonable grounds, although the jury is entitled to take account of the reasonableness (or otherwise) of the belief in deciding whether the defendant actually held that belief; see *DPP v Morgan* [1976] AC 182 (HL), extracted in Chapter 6.

The decision in *DPP v Morgan* prompted much criticism on the basis that it allowed a defendant charged with rape to run the 'No means Yes' argument, ie claim that, although the complainant had refused consent to sexual intercourse, the defendant had honestly believed that the complainant had really meant that he or she was consenting to sexual intercourse.

Parliament's response was to enact the following:

Section 1(2) of the Sexual Offences (Amendment) Act 1976

It is hereby declared that if at a trial for a rape offence the jury has to consider whether a man believed that a woman or man was consenting to sexual intercourse, the presence or absence of reasonable grounds for such a belief is a matter to which the jury is to have regard, in conjunction with any other relevant matters, in considering whether he so believed.

R v Adkins [2000] 2 All ER 185 (CA)

The Court of Appeal rejected the contention that a trial judge in a rape case should always direct a jury to acquit if D had honestly, but mistakenly, believed P to have been consenting. Roch LJ observed:

The question of honest belief does not necessarily arise where reckless rape is in issue. The defendant may have failed to address his mind to the question whether or not there was consent, or be indifferent as to whether there was consent or not, in circumstances where, had he addressed his mind to the question, he could not genuinely have believed that there was consent.

Reckless rape

R v Breckenridge (1983) 79 Cr App R 244 (CA)

Facts: The prosecution's case was the appellant followed the complainant, whom he had not known prior to the evening in question, forced her into a churchyard, where there was a struggle. She fell and broke her ankle. In attempting to overpower her, the defendant held her by the throat. He then raped her. The defence was that the complainant had consented to all the sexual activity; that she had gone into the churchyard with the defendant of her own volition; and that the broken ankle resulted from an accidental fall. Both had consumed a considerable amount of alcohol.

Boreham J: ... [W]hat has to be central to any direction [on the issue of whether the defendant was reckless whether the complainant was consenting or not] is to convey clearly to the jury that they will only find the defendant guilty of what is for convenience called 'reckless rape', if they conclude that his attitude as to whether or not the complainant was consenting was that he could not care less ...

R v S (Satnam) and S (1983) 78 Cr App R 149 (CA)

Bristow J: ... Two grounds of appeal were relied on in this court: (1) that the judge should have directed the jury that a genuine though mistaken belief that the girl was consenting offered a defence to a charge of reckless rape; (2) that the judge erred in referring to an 'ordinary observer' in his direction as to recklessness, and that he should have directed the jury that it was necessary to prove that each appellant was actually aware of the possibility that the girl was not consenting before they could find him reckless.

So far as the first ground was concerned, it was accepted by [counsel] for the Crown that he could not support the summing up in the absence of a direction as to belief. In *Thomas* (1983) 77 Cr App R 63 Lord Lane CJ said at 65:

In this particular case, the judge should have spelt out in terms that a mistaken belief that the woman was consenting, however unreasonable it may appear to have been, is an answer to the charge, and that it is for the prosecution to eliminate the possibility of such a mistake if they are to succeed. He should then have gone on to deal with the matters set out in s 1(2) of the 1976 Act. As it was the jury were left without any guidance on the matter.

The same situation arose here. The jury were left without any guidance on the matter of belief and on that ground alone we would allow the appeal.

We turn now to consider the second ground, ie the direction as to recklessness. Strictly it may be said that this point has already been decided in *Bashir* (1983) 77 Cr App R 59 at 62 where Watkins LJ said:

As recently as the fifth of this month, Lord Lane CJ in *Thomas* restated the definition of 'reckless' as applied to the offence of rape. He said (1983) 77 Cr App R 63, 66:

> A man is reckless if either he was indifferent and gave no thought to the possibility that the woman might not be consenting, in circumstances where, if any thought had been given to the matter, it would have been obvious that there was a risk she was not, or, he was aware of the possibility that she might not be consenting but nevertheless persisted, regardless of whether she consented or not.

He was in almost exact form repeating the definition of 'reckless' in relation to rape which he had provided in the case of *Pigg* (1982) 74 Cr App R 352. It will be noted that that definition allows of none other than a subjective approach to the state of mind of a person of whom it is said he acted recklessly in committing a crime. It was incumbent therefore on the trial judge in the present case to ensure that he provided the jury with this kind of definition of the word 'reckless'.

[Counsel] on behalf of the appellants submitted, in his able argument, that the use of the word 'obvious' in its context in both *Pigg* and *Thomas* gives rise to a possible ambiguity. 'Obvious' to whom? If it meant obvious to any reasonable person, that would introduce an objective test, and [counsel] submitted that the authorities properly understood do not warrant such a conclusion. He invited us in effect to clarify the situation which has developed since *Caldwell* and *Lawrence*, as he said that judges up and down the country are now in a state of some confusion as to the state of the law. He submitted that the direction of recklessness in *Pigg* was in any event *obiter*.

As Robert Goff LJ said in *Elliott v C (A Minor)* [1983] 1 WLR 939 at 950, with reference to the suggested direction in *Pigg*:

> Now it cannot be disguised that the addition of the words 'was indifferent and' constituted a gloss upon the definition of recklessness proposed by Lord Diplock in *R v Caldwell*. Furthermore, if it were legitimate so to interpret Lord Diplock's speech in relation to a case arising not under s 1 of the Sexual Offences (Amendment) Act 1976, but under s 1(1) of the Criminal Damage Act 1971, the effect would be that the second question posed by the magistrates in the case now before this court would be answered in the affirmative, and the appeal would be dismissed; because there is no finding of fact that this defendant in the case before us was indifferent to the risk of destruction by fire of the shed and its contents. This is an approach which I would gladly adopt, if I felt that I were free to do so. However, I do not consider that it is open to this court, in a case arising under the very subsection to which Lord Diplock's speech was expressly directed, to impose this qualification, which I feel would in this context constitute too substantial a departure from the test proposed by him.

The instant case, unlike *Elliot*, is not concerned with the Criminal Damage Act 1971 but with the Sexual Offences (Amendment) Act 1976, and the court is considering recklessness in the context of rape and not in the context of criminal damage. We feel we are therefore free to review the situation so far as it is governed by relevant authority, and accepting as we do that there is an ambiguity in the suggested direction in *Pigg*, which was in any event *obiter*.

[Counsel for the appellants] took as his starting point *DPP v Morgan* [1976] AC 182, a decision of the House of Lords on the very question of rape, which was not overruled by either *Caldwell* or *Lawrence* and is binding on this court. Lord Hailsham said at 151 and 215 of the respective reports:

I am content to rest my view of the instant case on the crime of rape by saying that it is my opinion that the prohibited act is and always has been intercourse without consent of the victim and the mental element is and always has been the intention to commit that act, or the equivalent intention of having intercourse willy-nilly not caring whether the victim consents or not. A failure to prove this involves an acquittal because the intent, an essential ingredient, is lacking. It matters not why it is lacking if only it is not there, and in particular it matters not that the intention is lacking only because of a belief not based on reasonable grounds.

In the Report of the Advisory Group on the Law of Rape (The Heilbron Committee) Command Paper 6352, 1975, the following 'Recommendations for declaratory legislation' were made:

81 Notwithstanding our conclusions that *Morgan's* case is right in principle, we nevertheless feel that legislation is required to clarify the law governing intention in rape cases, as it is now settled. We think this for two principal reasons. The first is that it would be possible in future cases to argue that the question of recklessness did not directly arise for decision in *Morgan's* case, in view of the form of the question certified; to avoid possible doubts the ruling on recklessness needs to be put in statutory form.

82 Second, it would be unfortunate if a tendency were to arise to say to the jury 'that a belief, however unreasonable, that the woman consented, entitled the accused to acquittal'. Such a phrase might tend to give an undue or misleading emphasis to one aspect only and the law, therefore, should be statutorily restated in a fuller form which would obviate the use of those words.

83 We think that there would be advantage if this matter could also be dealt with by a statutory provision which would:

(1) declare that (in cases where the question of belief is raised) the issue which the jury have to consider is whether the accused at the time when sexual intercourse took place believed that she was consenting, and

(2) make it clear that, while there is no requirement of law that such belief must be based on reasonable grounds, the presence or absence of such grounds is a relevant consideration to which the jury should have regard, in conjunction with all other evidence, in considering whether the accused genuinely had such a belief.

There followed the Sexual Offences (Amendment) Act 1976, s 1 of which is in the following terms [his Lordship set out the provisions of that section, and continued]:

We think that in enacting those provisions Parliament must have accepted the recommendations of the Heilbron Committee, so that the provisions are declaratory of the existing law as stated in *DPP v Morgan*.

Any direction as to the definition of rape should therefore be based upon s 1 of the 1976 Act and upon *DPP v Morgan*, without regard to *R v Caldwell* or *R v Lawrence*, which were concerned with recklessness in a different context and under a different statute.

The word 'reckless' in relation to rape involves a different concept to its use in relation to malicious damage or, indeed, in relation to offences against the person. In the latter cases the foreseeability, or possible foreseeability, is as to the consequences of the criminal act. In the case of rape the foreseeability is as to the state of mind of the victim.

A practical definition of recklessness in sexual offences was given in *Kimber* [1983] 1 WLR 1118, where the court was concerned with how far an honest belief in consent constituted a defence to a charge of indecent assault. The defendant said in evidence: 'I was not really interested in Betty's [the victim's] feelings at all'. Lawton LJ said at 230 and 1123 of the respective reports:

> We have already set out in this judgment the admissions which he is alleged to have made to the police and relevant parts of his own evidence. In our judgment a reasonable jury would inevitably have decided that he had no honest belief that Betty was consenting. His own evidence showed that his attitude to her was one of indifference to her feelings and wishes. This state of mind is aptly described in the colloquial expression, 'couldn't care less'. In law this is recklessness.

In summing up a case of rape which involves the issue of consent, the judge should, in dealing with the state of mind of the defendant, first of all direct the jury that before they could convict of rape the Crown had to prove either that the defendant knew the woman did not want to have sexual intercourse, or was reckless as to whether she wanted to or not. If they were sure he knew she did not want to they should find him guilty of rape knowing there to be no consent. If they were not sure about that, then they would find him not guilty of such rape and should go on to consider reckless rape. If they thought he might genuinely have believed that she did want to, even though he was mistaken in his belief, they would find him not guilty. In considering whether his belief was genuine, they should take into account all the relevant circumstances (which could at that point be summarised) and ask themselves whether, in the light of those circumstances, he had reasonable grounds for such a belief. If, after considering those circumstances, they were sure he had no genuine belief that she wanted to, they would find him guilty. If they came to the conclusion that he could not care less whether she wanted to or not, but pressed on regardless, then he would have been reckless and could not have believed that she wanted to, and they would find him guilty of reckless rape ...

Mens rea: knowledge/recklessness: intoxication

Where the defendant mistakenly believes that the victim is consenting but that mistaken belief is the result of voluntary intoxication, the defendant cannot rely on that mistaken belief; see *R v Fotheringham* (1989) 88 Cr App R 206 (CA), extracted in Chapter 8.

Attempted rape

See *R v Khan* [1990] 1 WLR 813, and *AG's Ref (No 1 of 1992)* [1993] 1 WLR 274 (both extracted in Chapter 12).

Notes and queries

1   Where P's consent to intercourse is predicated on D's compliance with a precondition and D fails to meet that pre-condition, the subsequent intercourse should be regarded as having occurred without P's consent. The matter was addressed, albeit *obiter*, in *AG's Ref (No 28 of 1996)* [1997] 2 Cr App R (S) 206. The appellant had been convicted of a number of rapes of women working as prostitutes. The common factor was that the prostitutes had agreed to have sexual intercourse with the appellant on the basis that he would be wearing a condom. In each case the appellant had removed the condom immediately before penetration. Lord Bingham CJ observed:

> ... prostitutes are as much entitled to the protection of the law as anyone else: they are entitled to insist that they are not willing to permit sexual intercourse unless their sexual partner is protected. It is undoubtedly rape for any defendant to insist upon sexual intercourse without protection when the woman does not consent, and even more so if he imposes his sexual demands by force. [prostitutes] ... are in particular need of the law's protection because they are vulnerable to infection ...

OTHER SEXUAL OFFENCES INVOLVING INTERCOURSE

Sexual intercourse with a girl under 13

Section 5 of the Sexual Offences Act 1956

It is an offence for a man to have unlawful sexual intercourse with a girl under the age of 13.

The maximum penalty of this offence is life imprisonment (s 37 and Sched 2 to the Sexual Offences Act 1956). The word 'unlawful' adds nothing, since all acts of sexual intercourse with a girl under the age of 13 are unlawful.

Sexual intercourse with a girl under 16

Section 6 of the Sexual Offences Act 1956

(1) It is an offence, subject to the exceptions mentioned in this section, for a man to have unlawful sexual intercourse with a girl under the age of 16.

...

(3) A man is not guilty of an offence under this section because he has unlawful sexual intercourse with a girl under the age of 16, if he is under the age of 24 and has not previously been charged with a like offence, and he believes her to be of the age of 16 or over and has reasonable cause for that belief.

In this subsection, 'a like offence' means an offence under this section or an attempt to commit one ...

The maximum penalty of the offence is 2 years imprisonment following conviction on indictment, or imprisonment for up to 6 months following summary conviction. The word 'unlawful' in s 6(1) adds nothing, since all acts of sexual intercourse with a girl under the age of 16 are illegal.

For the defence in s 6(3) to apply:

(1) the defendant must be under 24 at the time he is alleged to have committed the offence; and

(2) the defendant must not have been charged with such an offence at any time in the past (note that the defence does not apply if the defendant has been *charged* with such an offence: he does not have to have been *convicted* in the past); and

(3) the defendant must have believed that the girl was at least 16; and

(4) the defendant's belief must be based on reasonable grounds.

Abuse of a position of trust

Sexual Offences (Amendment) Act 2000

3(1) Subject to subsections (2) and (3) below, it shall be an offence for a person aged 18 or over –

(a) to have sexual intercourse (whether vaginal or anal) with a person under that age; or

(b) to engage in any other sexual activity with or directed towards such a person, if (in either case) he is in a position of trust in relation to that person.

(2) Where a person ('A') is charged with an offence under this section of having sexual intercourse with, or engaging in any other sexual activity with or directed towards, another person ('B'), it shall be a defence for A to prove that, at the time of the intercourse or activity –

(a) he did not know, and could not reasonably have been expected to know, that B was under 18;

(b) he did not know, and could not reasonably have been expected to know, that B was a person in relation to whom he was in a position of trust; or

(c) he was lawfully married to B.

(3) It shall not be an offence under this section for a person ('A') to have sexual intercourse with, or engage in any other sexual activity with or directed towards, another person ('B') if immediately before the commencement of this Act – (a) A was in a position of trust in relation to B; and (b) a sexual relationship existed between them. (4) A person guilty of an offence under this section shall be liable –

(a) on summary conviction, to imprisonment for a term not exceeding six months, or to a fine not exceeding the statutory maximum, or to both;

(b) on conviction on indictment, to imprisonment for a term not exceeding five years, or to a fine, or to both.

(5) In this section, 'sexual activity' –

(a) does not include any activity which a reasonable person would regard as sexual only with knowledge of the intentions, motives or feelings of the parties; but

(b) subject to that, means any activity which such a person would regard as sexual in all the circumstances.

4(1) For the purposes of section 3 above, a person aged 18 or over ('A') is in a position of trust in relation to a person under that age ('B') if any of the four conditions set out below, or any condition specified in an order made by the Secretary of State by statutory instrument, is fulfilled.

(2) The first condition is that A looks after persons under 18 who are detained in an institution by virtue of an order of a court or under an enactment, and B is so detained in that institution.

(3) The second condition is that A looks after persons under 18 who are resident in a home or other place in which –

(a) accommodation and maintenance are provided by an authority under section 23(2) of the Children Act 1989 or Article 27(2) of the Children (Northern Ireland) Order 1995;

(b) accommodation is provided by a voluntary organisation under section 59(1) of that Act or Article 75(1) of that Order; or

(c) accommodation is provided by an authority under section 26(1) of the Children (Scotland) Act 1995, and B is resident, and is so provided with accommodation and maintenance or accommodation, in that place.

(4) The third condition is that A looks after persons under 18 who are accommodated and cared for in an institution which is –

(a) a hospital;

(b) a residential care home, nursing home, mental nursing home or private hospital;

(c) a community home, voluntary home, children's home or residential establishment; or (d) a home provided under section 82(5) of the Children Act 1989, and B is accommodated and cared for in that institution.

(5) The fourth condition is that A looks after persons under 18 who are receiving full-time education at an educational institution, and B is receiving such education at that institution.

(6) No order shall be made under subsection (1) above unless a draft of the order has been laid before and approved by a resolution of each House of Parliament.

(7) A person looks after persons under 18 for the purposes of this section if he is regularly involved in caring for, training, supervising or being in sole charge of such persons.

(8) For the purposes of this section a person receives full-time education at an educational institution if –

(a) he is registered or otherwise enrolled as a full-time pupil or student at the institution; or

(b) he receives education at the institution under arrangements with another educational institution at which he is so registered or otherwise enrolled.

(9) In this section, except where the context otherwise requires –

'authority' means –

(a) in relation to Great Britain, a local authority; and

(b) in relation to Northern Ireland, an authority within the meaning given by Article 2(2) of the Children (Northern Ireland) Order 1995;

'children's home' has –

(a) in relation to England and Wales, the meaning which would be given by subsection (3) of section 63 of the Children Act 1989 if the reference in paragraph (a) of that subsection to more than three children were a reference to one or more children ...

'community home' has the meaning given by section 53(1) of the Children Act 1989;

'hospital' has –

(a) in relation to England and Wales, the meaning given by section 128(1) of the National Health Service Act 1977...

'mental nursing home' has, in relation to England and Wales, the meaning given by section 22(1) of the Registered Homes Act 1984;

'nursing home'-

(a) in relation to England and Wales, has the meaning given by section 21(1) of the Registered Homes Act 1984 ...

'residential care home'-

(a) in relation to England and Wales, has the meaning given by section 1(2) of the Registered Homes Act 1984 ...

'voluntary home' has –

(a) in relation to England and Wales, the meaning given by section 60(3) of the Children Act 1989 ...

CODIFICATION AND LAW REFORM PROPOSALS

In July 2000 the Home Office published its review of sexual offences, *Setting the Boundaries: Reforming the Law on Sex Offences*. Regarding the need for a review of the law in this area the Summary Report observed:

[The current law] ... is a patchwork quilt of provisions ancient and modern that works because people make it do so, not because there is a coherence and structure. Some is quite new – the definition of rape for example was last changed in 1994. But much is old, dating from nineteenth century laws that codified the common law of the time, and reflected the social attitudes and roles of men and women of the time. With the advent of a new century and the incorporation of the European Convention on Human Rights into our law, the time was right to take a fresh look at the law to see that it meets the need of the country today [para 02].

The terms of reference for the review were stated thus:

> To review the sex offences in the common and statute law of England and Wales, and make recommendations that will:
>
> - provide coherent and clear sex offences which protect individuals, especially children and the more vulnerable, from abuse and exploitation;
> - enable abusers to be appropriately punished; and
> - be fair and non-discriminatory in accordance with the ECHR and Human Rights Act.

The Summary Report sets out in more details the scope, style and purpose of the review:

> 0.6 The law on sex offences is the part of the criminal law which deals with the most private and intimate part of life – sexual relationships – when they are non-consensual, inappropriate or wrong. As such it embodies society's view of what is right and wrong in sexual relations. Our guiding principle was that this judgement on what is right and wrong should be based on an assessment of the harm done to the individual (and through the individual to society as a whole). In considering what was harmful we took account of the views of victims/survivors and of academic research. The victims of sexual violence and coercion are mainly women. They must be offered protection and redress and the law must ensure that male victims/survivors are protected too. The law must make special provision for those who are too young or otherwise not able to look after themselves, and offer greater protection to children and vulnerable people within the looser structures of modem families. In order to deliver effective protection to all, the law needs to be framed on the basis that offenders and victims can be of either sex. We have recommended offences that are gender neutral in their application, unless there was good reason to do otherwise.

> 0.7 Our other key guiding principle was that the criminal law should not intrude unnecessarily into the private life of adults. Applying the principle of harm means that most consensual activity between adults in private should be their own affair, and not that of the criminal law. But the criminal law has a vital role to play where sexual activity is not consensual, or where society decides that children and other very vulnerable people require protection and should not be able to consent. It is quite proper to argue in such situations that an adult's right to exercise sexual autonomy in their private life is not absolute, d society may properly apply standards through the criminal law which are intended to protect the family as an institution as well as individuals from abuse. In addition to this, the ECHR ensures that the state must uphold its responsibility to provide a remedy in law so that a complainant can seek justice.

> 0.8 We also thought it was vital that the law was clear and well understood, particularly in this field of sexual behaviour where there is much debate about the ground-rules. There is no Highway Code for sexual relations to give a clear indication of what society expects or will tolerate. The law should ensure respect for an individual's own decisions about withholding sexual activity and protect every person from sexual coercion and violence.

The Recommendations and Consultation points identified by the review are as follows:

1. The offence of rape should be retained as penile penetration without consent, and extended to include oral penetration. This should be defined as penetration of the anus, mouth or genitalia to the slightest extent, and, for the avoidance of doubt, surgically reconstructed male or female genitalia should be included in the definition in law.

2. Rape should not be subdivided into lesser or more serious offences.

3. There should be a new offence of sexual assault by penetration to be used for all other penetration without consent. This should be defined as penetration of the anus or genitalia to the slightest extent, and, for the avoidance of doubt, surgically reconstructed genitalia should be included in the definition. In circumstances where the means of penetration is not clear, the offence of sexual assault by penetration would apply.

4. Consent should be defined in law as 'free agreement'.

5. The law should set out a non-exhaustive list of circumstances where consent was not present.

6. The law should include a non-exhaustive list of examples of where consent is not present such as where a person:
   - submits or is unable to resist because of force or fear of force;
   - submits because of threats or fear of serious harm or serious detriment of any type to themselves or another person;
   - was asleep, unconscious, or too affected by alcohol or drugs to give free agreement;
   - did not understand the purpose of the act, whether because they lacked the capacity to understand, or were deceived as to the purpose of the act;
   - was mistaken or deceived as to the identity of the person or the nature of the act;
   - submits or is unable to resist because they are abducted or unlawfully detained;
   - has agreement given for them by a third party.

7. There should be a standard direction on the meaning of consent and consideration should be given as to whether this should be placed in statute.

8. Rape/sexual assault by penetration may he committed intentionally or recklessly and the definition of recklessness in sex offences should include the lack of any thought as to consent; this can be described as 'could not care less about consent'.

9. A defence of honest belief in free agreement should not be available where there was self-induced intoxication, recklessness as to consent, or if the accused did not take all reasonable steps in the circumstances to ascertain free agreement at the time.'

In its commentary on these proposals the review observed:

2.8 Rape

2.8.1 The first issue we thought about was the criminal behaviour that should be included in the crime of rape. We considered the various sexual violations that are perpetrated on men and women by other men and women, and the impact of differing kinds of sexual assaults on the victim In order to assess the relative seriousness of the different kinds of behaviour. We also wondered how the public might understand the law. We looked at what solutions other countries had adopted and sought information on how effective they had been. (The latter was particularly difficult as the letter of the law is only one of many variables in the way the criminal justice process operates.)

2.8.2 We decided that the essence of rape was the sexual penetration of a person by another person without consent. However, penetration comes in many forms. Men put their penis into the vagina, anus and mouth. Other parts of the body (notably fingers and tongues) are inserted into the genitalia and the anus. Objects are inserted into the vagina and anus of victims. Both men and women may perform such penetration. These are all extremely serious violations of victims which can leave them physically and psychologically damaged for many years. We did consider whether there was evidence that a woman could force a man to penetrate her against his will but, although we found a little anecdotal evidence, we did not discover sufficient to convince us that this was the equivalent of rape. (However we do recognise the existence of such coercive behaviour and think it should be subject to the criminal law. We make separate recommendations about offences of compelling sexual penetration in para 2.20 following.)

2.8.3 Having decided that all coerced sexual penetration was very serious, the question was how the law should best deal with it. There seemed to be two potential approaches – that of defining any sexual penetration as rape, and that of treating penile penetration separately from other forms of penetration.

2.8.4 We were uneasy about extending the definition of rape to include all forms of sexual penetration. We felt rape was clearly understood by the public as an offence that was committed by men on women and on men. We felt that the offence of penile penetration was of a particularly personal kind, it carried risks of pregnancy and disease transmission and should properly be treated separately from other penetrative assaults. We therefore set aside our presumption of gender-neutrality as regards the perpetrator for offences for the crime of rape and propose that it be limited to penile penetration. We also recognised the concerns of transsexuals that the law could except them from the protection of the criminal justice system. If modem surgical techniques could provide sexual organs, the law should be clear enough to show that penetration of or by such organs would be contained within the scope of the offence. The law must give protection from all sexual violence. Whether or not sexual organs are surgically created, the law should apply. Accordingly we thought to put it beyond doubt that the law should apply to surgically constructed organs – whether vaginal or penile.

2.8.5 The present crime of rape is limited to the penile penetration of the anus and vagina. Forced oral sex is treated as an indecent assault. We thought that inappropriate. Forced oral sex is as horrible, as demeaning and as traumatising as other forms of forced penile penetration, and we saw no reason why rape should not be defined as penile penetration of the anus, vagina or mouth without consent.

2.8.6 An issue that was raised in Home Office research, and by a few respondents, was whether there should be any gradation or degrees of rape. The argument put is that there are 'serious' rapes (those which involve violence, by strangers etc.) and less serious rapes – the 'date rape' or 'he just went a bit too far' type of rape. Some people argued that such a gradation with lower sentences for 'lesser' crimes would encourage juries to convict more readily. Without research into juries' thinking, we do not have any firm evidence to support this view.

2.8.7 A more serious question is whether there are genuinely lesser rapes. Victim/survivor organisations told us that although all victim/survivors were deeply affected by rape, there was often greater victimisation in rapes that were seen as lesser than the traditional model of stranger rape. A woman or man attacked in the street is a chance victim – it is truly appalling, but no blame attaches to the victim. To be raped by someone you know and trust, whom you may let into your house, or when you visit theirs, is not such a matter of chance. The victim has made decisions to put their trust in the other person. There may or may not be overt physical violence but those victims face additional issues of betrayal of trust and being seen as, or feeling, guilty for being in that situation. Some research indicates that the level of violence in partner/ex-partner rape is second only to stranger rape. We were told by those who counsel victim/survivors that those raped by friends or family often find it much harder to recover and may take longer to do so. In addition to these powerful arguments, it is hard to see how degrees of rape could be defined – when does a stranger become an acquaintance or a friend? The crime of rape is so serious that it needs to be considered in its totality rather than being constrained by any relationship between the parties.

2.8.8 If we are to consider a rape as being not just an offence of violence, but a violation of the integrity of another person, then there is neither justification nor robust grounds for grading rape into lesser or more serious offences. The impact on victims is no less, and indeed there are arguments that it can be more serious and long-lasting. Rape is a very serious crime but sentences can, and should, reflect the seriousness of each individual case within an overall maximum. Gradation of the seriousness of a particular offence is best reflected in the sentence finally imposed rather than creating separate offences.

2.9 Sexual assault by penetration

2.9.1 We recognised that other penetrative assaults could be as serious in their impact on the victim as rape and that they should not be regarded lightly. We thought the present law of indecent assault was inadequate to tackle these serious crimes. It is an offence which covers a wide spread of behaviour from touching to truly appalling violations, and the current penalty of 10 years is inadequate for the worst cases. Accordingly we recommend a new offence of sexual assault by penetration with a penalty the same as that for rape to be used for all non-penile penetrative sexual offences. This offence would include the non-consensual penetration of the anus, vagina and/or the external genitalia by objects or parts of the body other than the penis. This offence should also he defined in a way that would enable it to be used if there were any doubt as to the nature of the penetration (for example when a child or mentally impaired adult is unable to furnish details of exactly what had penetrated them). This offence could he committed by a man or a woman on a man or a woman.

2.9.2 In all these crimes it is important to define what is meant by penetration. The present law holds that the slightest penetration is sufficient. This seems to us to be right, and we think it should be absolutely clear that it is the penetration of the external genitalia not simply the vagina. The law also holds that no ejaculation is necessary to prove penetration, and that too must be right. It should also be clear that penetration of or by any surgically reconstructed genitalia should also he included as rape or sexual assault by penetration.

2.10 Consent

2.10.1 Lack of consent is central to the offence of rape and to our new offence of sexual assault by penetration. The essence of the crime is that sexual penetration took place without the consent of the complainant. It is vital that the law is as clear as possible about what consent means. The law sets the ground rules of what is and is not criminal behaviour, and all citizens need to know and understand what these are. This is particularly important because consent to sexual activity is so much part of a private relationship where verbal and non-verbal messages can be mistaken and where assumptions about what is and is not appropriate can lead to significant misunderstanding and, in extreme cases, to forced and unwelcome sex.

2.10.2 The common law on consent has developed over the years to deal with many of the circumstances that come before the courts. However, common law is essentially case law. Case law may change with new judgements and its meaning is often not clear to most people. If it is difficult for legal practitioners to research and understand the case law, it is much more difficult for the rest of us. Nor is it always clear what the common law means by 'consent'. Although it is argued that the common law allows continuing development to meet society's needs, that process can lead to uncertainty, as in the case of *Olugboja*. In an area of human behaviour where there are debates within society about what is and is not appropriate, it is more than ever important that the law is clear and well understood, particularly about what behaviour is criminal.

2.10.3 In law consent is given its ordinary meaning, which means that in the particular circumstances of each case the jury has to decide that they are sure, beyond reasonable doubt, whether the complainant was consenting or not. This is an important, and often difficult, role. Clarifying the meaning of consent in statute would enable judges to be able to explain what the law said and for juries to understand just what is meant by consent. It would also enable Parliament to consider and recommend what should and should not form acceptable standards of behaviour in a modern society. One of the messages that had come to us in consultation was that consent was something that could be seen as being sought by the stronger and given by the weaker. In today's world it is important to recognise that sexual partners are each responsible for their own actions and that there should be parity of status. In defining consent we are not seeking to change its meaning, rather to clarify the law so that it is clearly understood.

2.10.4 We investigated what the word 'consent' means. The *Oxford Dictionary* defines the verb 'to consent' as 'to acquiesce, or agree' and the noun 'consent' as 'voluntary agreement, compliance or permission'. These definitions cover a range of behaviour from wholehearted enthusiastic agreement to reluctant acquiescence. In this context the core element is that there is an agreement between two people to engage in sex. People have devised a complex set of messages to convey agreement and lack of it – agreement is not necessarily verbal, but it must be understood by both parties. Each must respect the right of the other to say 'no' – and mean it.

2.10.5 Other common law countries have defined consent as ' free agreement ' or 'free and voluntary agreement'. The Law Commission have suggested 'subsisting free and genuine agreement'. We felt that that was too complex and introduced an unnecessary semi-contractual complication into consent. We thought that simplicity and clarity were needed in this definition and that any free agreement would necessarily be voluntary and genuine. We thought that 'free agreement' included all the necessary elements and recommend that as a definition of consent.

2.10.6 We also thought that in addition to defining what consent was, we should also see how it should be applied. We were told by many people, including judges and lawyers, that the law on consent needed clarifying and explaining. A number of other countries have adopted this approach In order to ensure the law is well understood; setting clear boundaries for society as to what is acceptable and unacceptable behaviour. There are a variety of models, but the key elements are that the meaning of consent is defined, and that the law gives some indication of situations where consent is not present. We decided that the arguments for defining and explaining consent in statute were overwhelming. We thought that the approach adopted in a number of Australian states (and the Model Code) of setting out a list of examples of circumstances where consent was not present was helpful to all concerned. Any such list is a set of examples only; it is not complete and does not cover each and every circumstance where consent is not present. Cases must be decided on their own facts. It should help both practitioners and juries in coming to decisions in particular cases, and give broad guidelines for considering the issue.

2.10.7 Having agreed that it would be helpful to set out some examples of when consent is absent, we then considered what should be included in any list. This is not, and could not be, a complete list. It sets out those areas that are well established in case law as to when consent is not present, and those where it should he clear that consent would not be present. Most are obvious. The courts will continue to develop the common law as they consider cases where different circumstances apply. They will however have the benefit of a more detailed statute, in which Parliament will have given a clear indication to the courts and society about the bounds of acceptable behaviour.

2.10.8 Any list of examples should include the major components of the common law on consent. The challenge for the review was to consider whether there were other types of behaviour and situations that ought to be included in order to produce a robust and appropriate list. The question with any list of examples is exactly which to include and where to stop. A statutory list of examples should be as comprehensive as possible. The essential common element to many of these situations was that there may be submission by the victim. Submission may reflect reluctant acquiescence, but it may also reflect a lack of consent and/or an inability to resist. The fact of submission does not imply consent – it may well be better to suffer a 'fate worse than death' than to be killed or grievously wounded. Indeed victims'/survivors' organisations told us that many victims were frozen Into immobility by the threat of rape and the fear of what might happen to them. Any list should make clear that submission does not equate to consent if there is no free agreement.

2.10.9 In drawing up our non-exhaustive list, we thought that it should set out examples of when a person does not consent to sexual activity that could constitute rape or sexual assault by penetration:

- *Where a person submits or is unable to resist because of force, or fear of force.*

- *Where a person submits or is unable to resist because of threats or fear of serious harm or serious detriment of any type to themselves or another person.*

These would cover the broad set of cases where there was force or coercion or threat to a person, their child etc. It could also cover situations where other threats were made – for example losing a job or killing the family pet. It would be for the court to consider in each case what the nature of the threat was and whether the victim would think that she or he would suffer serious harm. These could vary from case to case: the threat of loss of employment might be far more serious in a small community with few other opportunities, for example. The pressures in this section are all negative – there was a distinction between a threat and an inducement, and the distinction that consent was obtained by coercion. Promising rewards for sex did not prevent free agreement being given – it was unlikely to be a coercive situation. We did consider whether the qualification of harm or detriment (as serious) was necessary, and concluded that it was – rape is a very serious crime with very heavy penalty. However, the seriousness of the harm or detriment should relate to the perception of the victim: the decision whether or not to agree was theirs. We have recommended a lesser offence for procuring sex by threat or deception (see para 2.16.1) to deal with other situations where there were more minor threats.

- *Where a person was asleep, unconscious, or too affected by alcohol or drugs to give free agreement.*

All these are situations where the victim would he unable to give free agreement.

- *Where a person did not understand the nature of the act whether because they lacked the capacity to understand, or were deceived as to the purpose of the act.*

This would cover both where the victim lacked the capacity to understand the act or submitted because they were persuaded that it was necessary for other purposes – a medical examination for instance.

- *Where the person was mistaken or deceived as to the identity of the person or the nature of the act.*

Consent that is given under these situations is obtained by deceit, or by taking advantage of a mistake. The victim may think, for example, that it is her husband or partner who has slipped into bed with her; she would consent to sex with him but not with the defendant – who took advantage of her mistake.

The free agreement was to have sex with one particular person, not the one who was present and impersonating another.

- *Where the person submits or was unable to resist because they are abducted or unlawfully detained.*

If a person has been abducted or detained then they are not in a position to give free agreement; the entire situation is coercive.

- *Mere agreement is expressed by a third party not the victim.*

Free agreement is an issue between sexual partners and cannot be given by others, whether husbands, partners or those in authority over the complainant.

...

2.12 The mental element

Intentional and reckless rape

2.12.1 The present law allows a man to be found guilty of rape if he has intentionally had sexual intercourse without consent or when he was reckless as to consent. The review considered whether these were the appropriate standards to apply and concluded that broadly they were. Rape is a very serious offence, and the criminal law is quite rightly reluctant to apply a test of negligence to very serious offences, unless there is a clear responsibility or duty of care on one party which had not been fulfilled.

2.12.2 A more difficult question is the precise meaning to be given to intentional and reckless. The Government proposed, in the consultation paper *Violence. Reforming the Offences Against the Person Act 1861* to adopt definitions for intent and recklessness based on those the Law Commission recommended ... In codifying the common law definitions of intent and recklessness in the law that applies to offences such as assault and causing injury/serious injury (to replace assault occasioning actual bodily harm, or grievous bodily harm), there is an inevitable read across to sex offences. Once enacted these definitions would provide the template for use in all offences against the person whether of physical violence or sexual violation. We therefore thought we should consider whether those definitions were the right ones for sex offences.

The proposed definitions are:

Intent – 'A person acts intentionally with respect to a result if: (a)it is his purpose to cause it, (b)or although it is not his purpose to cause it, he knows that it would occur in the ordinary course of events if he was succeed in his purpose of causing some other result.'

Recklessness – 'A person acts recklessly with respect to a result if he is aware of a risk that it will occur and it is unreasonable to take that risk having regard to the circumstances as he knows or believes them to be.'

For a more detailed discussion of these proposals on fault terms see Chapter 4.

2.12.3 The definition of intent set out in the first part (a) is clearly relevant and apposite for sex offences; the second (b) is relevant to assaults that cause injury as a secondary outcome (for example pushing someone over where they would fall under a passing car) but is not directly relevant to sex offences. Overall, the definition of intent fits into the context of the mental element in sex offences. The definition of recklessness is trickier. It is a subjective definition, which is appropriate and has a broad relevance to sex offences, which are, like assaults that result in injury, offences against the person. However, as the essence of most sex offences is the absence of consent, it is essential to consider the extent to which the accused gave any thought to consent as part of recklessness.

2.12.4 Recklessness in sex offences is recklessness as to the consent of the victim rather than as to the deed. The definition of recklessness proposed for offences against the person is insufficient for the purposes of sex offences. The law needs to state very clearly that the accused is liable if they did not give any thought to consent or could not care less about the victim's consent. The Australian Model Criminal Code Officers' Committee proposals (which apply a similar recklessness test to offences against the person as proposed here) extends the definition of recklessness In the context of penetrative sexual offences beyond that for offences against the person by adding:

> '... being reckless to a lack of consent includes not giving any thought to whether the other person is consenting ...'

2.12.5 We thought that it was necessary to ensure that our law reflected the full extent of recklessness as to consent in sex offences, and that the definition given in the proposals on offences against the person are not sufficient for this purpose. We were told by judges at our seminar for legal practitioners that they described recklessness in rape as 'could not care less about consent'. They suggested that this was effective and readily understood. The Law Commission paper on *Consent in Sex Offences* also thought that 'could not care less' was a form of recklessness.

2.12.6 We agree that this phrase encapsulates the meaning well. A person who could not care less about consent is rightly regarded as reckless. A person who fails to take all the steps which are reasonable in the circumstances to find out if there is free agreement on the occasion in question could not care less about the other person's consent and is therefore reckless. We consider that this should be included in any definition in law.

2.13 Honest belief in consent

2.13.1 The question of honest, albeit mistaken, belief in consent, is used as a defence in court, and rouses strong passions in those responding to the review, and amongst the members of the review. About a third of the representations we received on rape argued that the decision in *Morgan* ... should be reversed to an honest and reasonable belief. The seminar on rape also unanimously concluded that *Morgan* needed to be changed. The External Reference Group [ERG] of the review, which advised the Steering Group, endorsed the view that the *Morgan* judgment should be set aside and a requirement of reasonableness be re-introduced into the law.

2.13.2 This issue is often discussed in theoretical terms: for instance, in terms of rape, the extent to which criminality depends on the state of mind of the accused, and whether or not he should be found guilty of a crime that he did not intend to commit. The law at present does not require the reasonableness of a defendant's belief to be tested (although other tests are possible) so making it possible for a defendant to claim he held a completely irrational but honest belief in the consent of the woman: if this is upheld, he must he acquitted. In terms of subjectivist legal principle this is right. In terms of social policy, it makes some very large assumptions. By allowing the belief of the accused to be paramount, the law risks saying to a victim/survivor who feels violated and betrayed that they were not really the victim of crime, and that what they thought, said or did was immaterial. It is seen to validate male assumptions that they can assume consent without asking. It is an issue that utterly divides opinion, and divided those of us undertaking the review.

2.13.3 Internationally the issue divides common law jurisdictions. No US state has ever extended the subjective bias towards the defendant as far as Morgan, and the honest belief of the defendant is subject to a test of reasonableness. Some have limited its use even further, California for example, limits its use to situations where the complainant's behaviour was 'equivocal'. In Australia the common law states (ACT, Victoria, NSW and South Australia) uphold the subjective test set out in *Morgan*. Indeed Victoria and South Australia adopted the subjective approach before *Morgan*. Those states which adopted their Criminal Codes in the 1920s (Tasmania, Queensland, W Australia) have retained the pre-*Morgan* position of an objective test of reasonableness on the defendant's honest belief. The Model Criminal Code proposals argue for retaining honest belief. New Zealand has reversed *Morgan*. They have developed what they call a 'subjective and objective test' – the defendant could hold a subjective honest belief but that belief is subject to an objective test of reasonableness.

2.13.4 In the UK, the Law Commission reviewed the *mens rea* for rape in detail in their Consultation Paper No 139 (*Consent in the Criminal Law*: Chapter 7) and their view was that the Morgan rule should be qualified by an objective test, and they sought views on that. They said: '*we think it would be remarkable if the Morgan rule did not sometimes have the effect of encouraging a jury to accept a bogus defence.*' In their policy paper to the review, the Law Commission now recommend that honest belief should be preserved but that judges should direct the jury to the effect that in judging whether honest belief is genuine they should have regard as to whether he sought to ascertain consent, and that if his belief in consent arose from self-induced intoxication, it is not a defence.

2.13.5 The review spent many careful hours discussing this issue. We looked at the present subjectivist view and were all agreed that it could not be retained in its current form. We then looked at a variety of solutions to try to ensure that the defendant is not compromised but the victim is ensured justice. The first thing we established was that in practice, the defence of honest albeit mistaken belief in consent is usually run in tandem with consent. We could not find evidence of it being critical in a trial. The Sexual Offences (Amendment) Act 1976 requires the jury to have regard to the 'presence or absence of reasonable grounds for such a belief ... in considering whether he so believed'. We noted research by the Law Commission in Victoria to try to determine whether it was more difficult to convict if the belief was run as a defence. In a study of 53 prosecutions, the defendant's belief was relevant in 23% of cases. 6% used mistaken belief as a primary defence, 17% as part of a defence. Of the 12 cases, 6 were convicted (50%). It is impossible to tell whether putting an objective test onto the reasonableness of that belief would have made a difference in the remaining 6 cases.

2.13.6 The arguments given *for* the full subjective test are:

- The law should punish people not just for what they did but for what they intended to do. This underlies most modern law, and underpins for example the distinction between intentional killing being charged as murder whilst a death that results from poor driving, although deeply tragic, is not regarded as so blameworthy because there was no specific intent, and in terms of the law is a less serious offence.

- A test of reasonableness is applying external standards. Should a person be found guilty of a very serious crime because they did not apply the same personal standards of reasonableness as those who determined the accused's guilt or innocence? Is it right to apply external standards when the accused did not think they were doing wrong, for whatever cultural or other factors? What if they did not have the capacity to realise there was no consent?

- How should a reasonableness test be applied? Does it have to be reasonable for a person of the same class, culture or level of intelligence? If so does this not risk accentuating and perpetuating stereotypes about behaviour?

- The nature of the belief and its reasonableness or lack of it are issues to be tested by evidence on the facts of the case. The testing of the nature of the belief by the prosecution is an essential part of the case.

2.13.7 The arguments *against* the subjective test are:

- It implicitly authorises the assumption of consent, regardless of the views of the victim, or whatever they say or do.

- It encourages people to adhere to myths about sexual behaviour and in particular that all women like to be overborne by a dominant male, and that 'no' really means 'yes'. It undermines the fundamental concept of sexual autonomy.

- The mistaken belief arises in a situation where it is easy to seek consent and the cost to the victim of the forced penetration is very high. It is not unfair to any person to make them take care that their partner is consenting and be at risk of a prosecution if they do not do so.

- There is no justice in a situation whereby a woman (or a man) who has been raped in fact (because she or he did not consent) sees an assailant go free because of a belief system that society as a whole would find unreasonable – for example that he saw some or all women (or women of certain types) as sexual objects.

- It is easy to raise the defence but hard to disprove it.

- The Youth Justice and Criminal Evidence Act 1999 limits the use of a complainant's sexual history in court. One of the exceptional cases where it may be introduced is when the defence of honest belief in consent is raised and sexual history is relevant to that belief. The concern is that this provision win significantly increase the use of the honest belief defence because that would open the door to introducing the element of previous sexual history as part of the defence, allowing cross-examination of the complainant on this issue.

2.13.8 In balancing these arguments, there was a disagreement between the External Reference Group who unanimously wanted the law restoring to its pre-*Morgan* state of requiring any honest belief in consent to be subject to a test of reasonableness, and the Steering Group. The Steering Group did not take the ERG's advice on this issue but identified an effective way of fettering an inappropriate use of honest belief, without re-introducing the external test of reasonableness that the courts had rejected.

2.13.9 The Steering Group aimed to ensure that their proposals gave proper weight to the victim's need for justice while maintaining the golden thread of the presumption of innocence of the defendant and ensuring that he was convicted for what he intended to do. It was essential that the law should be acceptable to the public, and to give victims and the wider public confidence that the law offers protection. We thought this confidence was lacking at present. The review is recommending changes to the law to define the meaning of consent as free agreement, and setting out when consent is not present. The Steering Group thought that these changes would create a rather different dynamic in rape cases where it would be more difficult to run a spurious defence of honest belief. The best way forward was to limit the use of the defence of honest belief in a way that fitted with our broader proposals, emphasised the importance of free agreement and made it much harder to run a dishonest defence.

2.13.10 The Steering Group was very attracted to the Canadian solution to this very difficult problem. In Canada the law retains an honest but mistaken belief defence but fetters when it can be used in a way that ties in with the definition of consent. The intention was to introduce an 'air of reality' into the use of a defence that relies on establishing what was happening in the defendant's mind at the time of the offence. The Canadian Criminal Code states:

273.2   It is not a defence ... where

    (a)   the accused's belief arose from the accused's

        (i)   self-induced intoxication

        (ii)   reckless or wilful blindness; or

    (b)   the accused did not take reasonable steps, in the circumstances known to him at the time, to ascertain that the complainant was consenting.

2.13.11 This provides several useful concepts with which to moderate the dishonest or inappropriate use of the defence of honest belief. The requirement on the accused to have to have considered the issue of consent in order to provide a defence of honest belief is particularly important. The accused cannot invoke the defence unless they proved that they took all reasonable steps, in the circumstances known to them at the time, to ascertain whether the complainant was consenting. This undermines the belief that a defendant can make large assumptions about the attitude of the complainant and should mean, for example, in situations where a defendant thinks that all women fight, or say no when they mean yes, they had not sought free agreement at the time.

2.13.12 Self-induced intoxication because of drink or drugs does not reduce the criminal liability of a defendant, and this is set out in the *Majewski* Rules. A defendant is liable for his actions if he has voluntarily become drunk or high –

because that was a matter of his own choice. He must responsible for any consequences that flow from his actions when drunk or high. As drink and drugs are often an element in cases of rape, and we are concerned that the law should be clear, then it seems to be important to set out the principle in this context.

2.13.13 Recklessness is already an element of the offence of rape, and as discussed in paras 2.11.5 above, anyone who is so reckless as to consent that he did not seek to take all the steps that were reasonable In the circumstances to find out whether he had free agreement would not under our proposals be able to argue that he had an honest belief in consent. As an example, if a defendant's belief in consent is based on the complainant's past sexual behaviour with others, and he took no steps to ascertain whether there was free agreement to sex at the time, he could not care less whether she was consenting and was therefore reckless.

2.13.14 A further important point to ensure is that in retaining an honest belief in consent defence, in future any belief in consent will have to be a belief in free agreement – our definition of consent. The use of the qualifying conditions for the use of any belief in free agreement (ie that it was based on self-intoxication, arose from recklessness and that they did not take reasonable steps to ascertain free agreement) would create some sensible safeguards, while enabling the use of a defence when it is genuinely relevant. Accordingly we recommend that the defence of honest belief should be expressed in terms of free agreement, and be subject to limitations as to its use. This does not impose an external and objective requirement of reasonableness on the defendant, as our External Reference Group wanted, but it does reinterpret the doctrine of honest belief as set out by the House of Lords in the *Morgan* judgment, and provides new conditions for its use. The External Reference Group fully support this proposal, but would like to see it linked to a separate requirement that any belief in consent should be reasonable.

In relation to indecent assault the review recommended the introduction of a new offence of sexual assault '... to cover sexual touching (defined as behaviour that a reasonable bystander would consider to be sexual) that is done without the consent of the victim.'

The commentary notes:

2.14.1 The present offence of indecent assault is one that applies to a variety of behaviour done without consent from unwelcome groping to some kinds of penetration. In making its proposals for new offences the review has recommended new offences to deal with the most serious types of behaviour. However, that still leaves a range of unacceptable behaviour, including 'frottage' (rubbing up against someone else in a sexual manner) on the Tube, fondling and groping to quite serious assaults. All of these are distressing to the victim because there is a clear sexual intention, and they are often directed at the more sensitive and private parts of the body or carried out by the use of the private parts of the perpetrator.

2.14.2 The review did consider whether the offence should be described as sexual touching, as in other parts of the world, but decided that it was better to retain the concept of an assault, which is being codified in the Government's proposals for the reform of the Offences Against the Person Act 1861 [see Chapter 16]. We wanted to retain the concept of an assault, because it includes not only the touching element but also behaviour which puts the victim in fear of force of some kind (ie where no touch takes place). It was important not to diminish the importance of the offence of sexual assault. An offence that may not include a severe assault could include a high level of fear, coercion, degradation and harm inflicted on victims.

2.14.3 The present offence requires three elements to be proved – the fact of an assault, the conditions of indecency and the indecent intention and the lack of consent. This is a complex set of requirements. There have also been legal arguments about whether it is necessary to prove a hostile intent, but the proposed definition of assault does not require this. In the circumstances of an indecent assault, hostility is not a helpful concept. Any unlawful touching must by definition be hostile to the victim because it was without consent. The more difficult question is how we should seek to define the behaviour that is to be caught by the new offence. We have recommended new offences for penetrative assaults. This removes some of the most serious penetrative assaults from indecent assault, but an offence is needed to deal with unwanted sexual touching. There are a number of elements to this:

- It is the lack of consent to the touching that makes it an offence. While touching areas of another's body that are sensitive and generally regarded as private may be acceptable in certain circumstances, such as close physical relationships, this is not acceptable as part of everyday life.

- The new formulation provides for intent or recklessness as to an assault. For indecent/sexual assault, there should also be intent or recklessness in relation to the lack of consent. This would provide the necessary *mens rea* for the offence and remove the need to prove an indecent intention.

2.14.4 The review was concerned not to use very broad terms such as indecency in offences, preferring instead to frame clearer and more specific offences. If we are not to use the concept of indecency in an assault, we need to be clear about the type of proscribed behaviour. We could define by body parts (breasts/buttocks/genitalia) but that seems inflexible. A better alternative is to define sexual touching as behaviour that a reasonable person would consider to be sexual (as in the abuse of trust offence in the Sexual Offences (Amendment) Bill) [see now the Sexual Offences (Amendment) Act 2000 – above]. Putting that and the wider definition of assault above, close encounters on the Tube may form part of the everyday material of life but 'frottage' in the Underground would clearly be an offence.

2.14.5 The law presently does not permit a child under 16 or a 'defective' to consent to an indecent assault. The review decided to continue that presumption ...

The review also contained a number of other recommendations relating to other sexual offences:

11 There should be a new offence of assault to commit rape or sexual assault by penetration.

12 A new sex offence of trespass with intent to commit a serious sex offence should replace burglary with intent to rape. [See further Chapter 19.]

13 There should be a new offence of abduction with the intent to commit a serious sex offence.

14 There should be an offence of obtaining sexual penetration by threats or deception in any part of the world.

15 An offence of administering drugs (etc) with intent to stupefy a victim in order that they are sexually penetrated should be retained.

16 There should be new offences of compelling another to perform sexual acts, with several levels of seriousness depending on the nature of the compelled acts.

The review team's rationale for these proposals is as follows:

2.15 Assault to commit rape

2.15.1 The common law used to contain two parallel offences of assault to commit rape and assault to commit buggery. When the law was codified in the nineteenth century the 'assault to commit buggery' offence was put into statute, and assault to commit rape was not. (The reasoning is not clear; it may have been an oversight.) Assault to commit buggery is now found in s 16 of the 1956 Act. Assault to commit rape remains a common law offence, but has become unusable because of arguments about its status, and it has for all practical purposes ceased to exist.

2.15.2 This is a genuine problem. The law of attempts requires that in order to charge attempted rape, the action has to be 'more than merely preparatory' to the offence. Assaulting a victim with the intent to rape only becomes an attempted rape at a fairly late stage, quite close to penetration. The intent of the assault may however be quite clear to the victim who, even if no rape has occurred, is left deeply affected. The kind of assault to which this offence could apply is where someone is attacked, dragged into an alley and clothing is ripped off with all the preparatory moves towards a rape, but the assailant is discovered and dragged off before it has become, legally, an attempted rape. The victim suffers far greater fear and trauma than for a non-sexual assault because the intent to rape was clear and the terror and trauma suffered is related to that. It may be comparable to an actual rape.

2.15.3 It seems only right that an assault with intent to commit rape or sexual assault by penetration is a serious offence and much more significant in terms of its effect on the victim than a similar level of violence in a straightforward assault. Judges and practitioners told us that there was a real gap in the protection of the law. A new offence is therefore necessary to replace the present s.16 and the common law offence that has fallen into disuse. We think however that a new offence should apply to the two most serious new non-consensual penetrative sex offences rape and sexual assault by penetration.

...

2.18 Obtaining sexual intercourse by threats or deception

2.18.1 We have argued that rape and other sexual offences are essentially offences of lack of consent. We have also considered what kinds of threats and deceptions are serious enough to vitiate consent and would lead to the commission of the crime of rape or sexual assault by penetration. The present law contains a set of offences that relate to obtaining sex by threat or false pretences in ss 2 and 3 of the Sexual Offences Act 1956 which to a certain extent overlap with other offences that we have considered.

- Section 2 is about procuring a woman by threat to have sexual intercourse in any part of the world.

- Section 3 about procuring a woman by false pretences for sexual intercourse in any part of the world.

2.18.2 These offences are very rarely used, possibly because the penalty is only 2 years. However that is not in itself sufficient reason to say that they are no longer needed. Their origin may have lain in concern about the white slave trade but there are still very valid concerns that should be addressed. People may be sought for work in holiday resorts abroad that then turns out to be sex work. They are recruited by deception and this kind of behaviour needs to be caught by the law. These offences can be used to deal with the supply end of the trafficking trade where threats or deception are involved. However these offences are not limited to prostitution nor to sex with third parties. Are such offences still needed?

2.18.3 We have included the use of threat of serious harm or detriment in our examples of situations where consent is not present. Our definition of rape includes any threat of serious harm to the person or another, so should the use of less serious threats in order to achieve some form of consent (otherwise it would clearly be rape) be a separate offence? The CLRC (who sought to separate out an immediate threat of harm, justifying a charge of rape, from wider or longer term threats, which should, they thought, be dealt with by a more serious s 2) recommended retaining the offence with an enhanced penalty. Our definition of consent may remove some of the CLRC purpose from this offence. That however leaves a broad band of behaviour where quite a low level of threat may induce a supposed consent that was not genuine, particularly if the victim was young or vulnerable to suggestion.

2.18.4 The second of the two existing offences relates to procuring intercourse by false pretences – for which today we would rather use the more precise term of deception. In the Theft Act deception means any deception, whether deliberate or reckless, by words or conduct and as to fact or as to law. It also includes a deception as to the intentions of the person. We envisage that this kind of deception is of a lower level or a different kind than in our list of situations where consent is absent (which includes deception as to the identity of the person, or the nature or purpose of the act) and could relate to going through a sham ceremony of marriage.

2.18.4 A modern gender-neutral replacement offence of both the existing offences could be of 'obtaining sexual penetration by threats or deception', and it too could have a broad international application. This could he helpful in the context of forced marriages, where a girl taken abroad may go willingly because she is deceived as to the purpose of her visit: it turns out not to be a holiday to visit relatives but an unwelcome marriage. We recognise the evidential difficulties, and that it may not be appropriate to use the criminal law in such situations. We thought it important that the law contained a remedy that could be used in appropriate cases, and that it gave a clear message that such behaviour was wrong and unacceptable.

2.18.6 The offence could also be used in situations such as the advertising in the UK for waitresses or entertainers overseas, when the real requirement is to provide sex.

2.18.7 We were particularly concerned to ensure that the law provided a remedy for some of the problems we were told of by those who care for people with learning disabilities, where low levels of threat or deception can be used to induce sex. We thought that this new offence could provide a remedy but that an alternative would be to add a new offence of 'using threat or deception to procure sex with a person with learning disabilities' ...

2.19 Using drugs to stupefy or overpower in order to have sex

2.19.1 Section 4 of the 1956 Act provides an offence that applies to anyone who gives any 'drug, matter or thing' to a woman which will stupefy or overpower her so that any man can have sexual intercourse with her. The offence is intended to deal with the use of spiked drinks, excess alcohol or any other substance which would render a woman unable to resist sex. Any person who administers the drug would be liable, whether or not they are the person who wishes or does have sex with her.

This [is] an important offence. The behaviour that it catches is not the mutual enjoyment of alcohol (or other substances) that may be a precursor to sex but the cold-blooded administration of a knock-out substance in order to exploit and take advantage of another. The advantage of this offence is that it catches third parties, and does not rely on a rape actually happening. (And if a person is made insensible by drink or drugs then any sex that happens is rape.) There is very real concern about the use of drugs and alcohol to enable rape to take place and we did not want to leave any gap in the law for those who use these methods to slip through the net. We also thought that the law should remain widely drafted to enable any new methods of mental or psychological control to be caught. We also thought it was important for the law to be absolutely clear that such behaviour was totally unacceptable and definitely criminal.

2.19.2 We recommend this offence should be retained, made gender-neutral to give protection to both men and women, and that it should apply to an intention to sexually penetrate the victim.

2.20 Compelling sexual acts

2.20.1 The aspect of sexual behaviour which is potentially very serious, and clearly criminal, is that of compelling others to carry out sexual acts against their will. It is possible, for example, for someone to force another person to perform a sexual act on themselves, the compellor or a third party. That act is not voluntary – it may indeed be a criminal act such as sexual assault or even rape or sexual assault by penetration. The compellor may want sexual acts performed on him or herself, want the person to masturbate in front of them, or to perform acts with or on a third person, or even on or with an animal. The law should be able to state very clearly that compelling others to do such acts against their will is an offence and that the guilt lies with the person who compels the act rather than his or her immediate victims. We had evidence of incidents of forced masturbation which was accompanied by the threat that the victim was committing a crime of indecent assault, but that the compellor was not doing anything wrong. We have also noted concerns about women who compel men to penetrate them. We do not regard that as rape, but as a serious assault on the man's sexual autonomy. We think that compelled penetration should be caught by this new offence. In its 1984 report the CLRC noted that there was no specific provision that applied when a man compelled his wife to perform acts of bestiality, and recommended a new offence to fill this gap. We have also recommended that compelling children to do sexual acts should form part of our sexual abuse of a child offence ...

2.20.2 We looked at some proposals for law reform from abroad. The Australian Model Criminal Code Officers' Committee proposals on sex offences propose new offences of *compelling sexual acts*. These cover the situation where a perpetrator compels a second person either to perform a sexual act on the perpetrator, on him or herself, on a third party or with an animal. The offences are divided into a penetrative offence and an indecent touching (sexual assault) offence. They make no recommendation about offensive behaviour that does not involve touching like compelling someone to witness sexual acts (such as indecent exposure) which they regard as more minor and summary only, and so outside their remit. The South African Law Commission recommends a very similar offence.

2.20.3 We thought that there were very strong arguments for having specific offences that deal with compulsion. These situations are a peculiarly nasty form of victimisation that depends on an abuse of power and control. They override the sexual autonomy of the compelled person, who may be forced to commit an offence themselves. An act of compulsion must mean that the compelled person did not consent. Any offence would therefore rely on proof that the compellor knew that the victim did not consent, or was reckless (including that they did not care less) as to their lack of consent, including giving no thought to whether or not the person consented. This offence would also deal with the gap in the law identified by the CLRC.

2.20.4 We also thought that it would be necessary to structure any new offence to reflect the seriousness of the compelled acts. Although compelling another to do sexual acts is intrinsically serious, it does vary in severity according to the nature of the compelled acts. A compelled touching may be comparatively minor, whilst compelling sexual penetration would be very serious. We thought therefore that there could be two offences with different penalties:

- a more serious offence of compelling sexual penetration of a person or an animal by a person, an object or an animal, and

- an offence of compelling other sexual acts (including sexual touching).

The review makes a number of specific recommendations as regards sexual offences committed against and by children:

17 As a matter of public policy, the age of legal consent should remain at sixteen.

18 The law setting out specific offences against children should state that below the age of 13 a child cannot effectively consent to sexual activity.

19 There should be an offence of adult (over 18) sexual abuse of a child (under 16). The offence would cover all sexual behaviour that was wrong because it involved a child; it would complement other serious non-consensual offences such as rape, sexual assault by penetration and sexual assault.

20 There should no time limit on prosecution for the new offence of adult sexual activity with a child.

21 A mistake of fact in age should be available as a defence, but with the following restrictions: that it should be limited to honest and reasonable belief and that the defendant has taken all reasonable steps to ascertain age.

22 The use of the defence of mistake of fact in age should be limited to raising the defence in court on one occasion only.

23 In principle, the defence of mistake of fact in age should remain limited by age of defendant.

24 Belief in marriage should remain a defence to offences involving sex with a child, but this should not apply where the child is below the age of 13.

25 An offence of the persistent sexual abuse of a child reflecting a course of conduct should he introduced.

...

27 There should be an offence of sexual activity between minors to replace the existing offences of unlawful sexual intercourse, buggery, indecency with children and sexual activity prohibited for children. It should apply to children under the age of 18 with those under the age of consent.

28 We recommend that further consideration should be given to appropriate, non-criminal interventions for young people under 16 engaging in mutually agreed under-age sex who are not now, and should not in future, normally be subject to prosecution.

29 The criminal law needs to have measures in place which can be used to deal with children who sexually abuse other children. Sentencing decisions should reflect specialist assessment of risk and potential for longer term offending and include treatment options.'

Again, the commentary provides further explanation:

3.6   Adults having sex with children

3.6.1 One of the key issues to emerge from our consultation conference was the need for the law to establish beyond any doubt that adults should not have sex with children, and that this warranted a serious offence to recognise the importance of the crime. The proposal was that there should be an offence of adult sexual abuse of a child, to replace the existing offences of unlawful sexual intercourse and indecency with children, and to offer an increased level of protection against sexual activity between adults and children. Those working with children thought that such an offence would focus attention on the activity of perpetrators, provide greater clarity in law and give a strong message to the public that sexual activity between adults and children is not acceptable. The review accepted the principle of such an offence, and thought that it would clearly define a set of behaviour that was unacceptable and enable the law to treat it with appropriate seriousness. It should also help in the risk assessment of offenders.

3.6.2 To make such an offence both simple and effective, it would need to cover a range of behaviour committed by men and women with children. We first considered whether the offence should include all types of sexual activity by adults with children. We were particularly concerned that a single offence for all such behaviour, from the most serious to the least serious, would be too broad. It risked undermining the ability of the law to deal with the worst behaviour – ie rape. This argument was supported by submissions to the review, some of which felt that the offence of usi [unlawful sexual intercourse] was sometimes being used inappropriately. We concluded therefore that a single offence was not the best approach.

3.6.3 Rape is the most serious sex offence and a reformed law would be fundamentally flawed if the rape of a child was not charged as such. The review concluded that rape, sexual assault by penetration and sexual assault, all of which deal with non-consensual behaviour, should be available for use as needed. There should be a separate offence to tackle behaviour that would not be an offence if committed between consenting adults but was wrong and inappropriate when children were involved. In general, therefore, consent was irrelevant – the culpability of the behaviour was because it was with a child.

3.6.4 We propose that the offence of adult sexual abuse of a child would apply to a man or woman of 18 or older who was:

- involved in sexual penetration with a child under 16; or

- who undertook any sexual act towards or with a child under 16; or

- who incited, induced or compelled a child to carry out a sexual act, whether on the accused, another person or the child himself; or

- who made a child witness a sexual act (whether live or recorded).

The only person who is criminally liable for this offence is the adult. There is no criminal liability on the child, whether boy or girl, however much they may appear to have consented, aided or abetted the offence. This offence is essentially about the adult's responsibility towards the child.

3.6.5 No similar offence exists in other countries. New Zealand and Australia do not have a 'catch-all' sexual abuse offence by adults. The South African Law Commission, in its recent discussion paper, has recommended an offence of child molestation: this is not confined specifically to adults, but includes any person intentionally committing a sexual act with a child or any person who commits any act with the intent to invite or persuade a child to allow any person to commit a sexual act with that child.

Time limits

3.6.6 The current offence of unlawful sexual intercourse can only be prosecuted within twelve months of the offence being charged. The reason for the time limitation has been put forward as a protection against blackmail, and the CLRC recommended its retention. There have been some suggestions that the time limit should be relaxed, with a proviso that no prosecutions should be brought after a child's eighteenth birthday, which might protect the accused from '*fictitious allegations which are so old that his ability to disprove them is undermined.*' This is a valid concern in the context of prosecuting long-past offences. However we were keenly aware that many instances of child abuse may not come to light for many years until the survivor is able to report it. These cases do present severe problems to the police and prosecutors in investigating and preparing cases and to defendants in preparing a proper defence to allegations of long past events. We did not think the law should prevent later prosecutions being brought where there is a case to be made, or other charges being added in long and complex investigations. In principle we thought that time limits were not justified for any sexual offences. We therefore considered that a statutory time limit would not be justified for the offence of adult sexual abuse of a child.

Defences

3.6.7 We also considered whether and if so what statutory defences might apply. The two defences available for the offence of usi with a girl under the age of sixteen are known respectively as the 'young man's' and the marriage defences. Essentially the 'young man's' defence relates to a mistake of age which can be used in certain circumstances, eg, the man must be between the ages of 16 and 24 and must not have been previously charged for a like offence. The review has already recommended at paragraph 3.4.7 that a child under 13 cannot consent to sexual activity in any circumstances, and that no statutory defence such as mistake of fact should apply. We thought that a child under 13 was not readily mistaken for one over 16, and that sex with a child between 13 and 16 was illegal. The present law does not allow such a defence. We saw no justification for introducing one.

3.6.8 We then thought whether there should be any defences for sexual activity with those between 13 and 16. There is a genuine tension between the interests of fairness to defendants and the wider interests of child protection in deciding whether there should be a defence. Different jurisdictions have reached different conclusions. In most US states under-age sex is a strict liability offence, and in some states it is statutory rape. In Canada (where the age of consent is 14) a mistake of fact defence can only be used if the defendant took 'all reasonable steps to ascertain the age'. In Australia, most states have a form of mistake of age defence. The Model Criminal Code commented that some form of defence was necessary in the interests of justice. They recommended a mistake of fact defence as to the age of the child that was both honest and reasonable.

3.6.9 The Criminal Law Revision Committee (CLRC) considered the issue of the young man's defence in some depth:

The 'young man's defence' has been frequently criticised for its arbitrariness. Its origin lies in a political compromise. The Criminal Law Amendment Act 1885 provided a defence to a man a under what is now section 6 of the Sexual Offences Act 1956 if he believed on reasonable grounds that the girl was aged 16 or over. The Bill that became the Criminal Law Amendment Act 1922 sought to remove this defence in an effort to tighten the law but was keenly opposed by some Members of Parliament. It appears that it would not have passed had the supporters and opponents not agreed on the 'young man's defence' as a compromise.

The defence presents several unsatisfactory features. First, although in general mistake of fact is a defence to a serious criminal charge, this defence is not available to a defendant aged 24 or over, whereas mistakes may be no less likely to be made by older men. Nor is it available to a defendant under 24 who has previously been charged with unlawful sexual intercourse. Secondly, in any event, a defendant should not be precluded from raising the defence merely because of a previous charge if mistake of age was not then in issue or he was not convicted. Thirdly, a defendant who made a genuine mistake should in principle have a defence even if he had no reasonable grounds for his mistake.

3.6.10 The CLRC went on to recommend a generally available defence of mistake of age for unlawful sexual intercourse with a girl, and that the belief need not be based on reasonable grounds. In our view this would not provide the protection of the law for children under 16.

3.6.11 We agree that the current 'young man's' defence should be abolished. It is arbitrary, confusing and does not necessarily provide justice. In drawing up new statutory defences for a serious offence such as adult sexual abuse of a child, there is a tension between society's need to protect vulnerable children and to ensure the interests of justice and fairness to the defendant are met where there is a genuine mistake of fact. There is a real divergence of opinion between those who consider that it would be unjust and wrong for an honest mistake to result in conviction of a serious charge and those who thought that because it caused such difficulties in the prosecution of usi at the moment, there should be no such defence at all. We looked at the evidence of cautions and prosecutions of usi to see if there was any noticeable trend in the statistics, but it was not possible to identify any ... It was difficult to assess from available statistics whether the defence had any real impact on men in the age group 16–24. Clearly however the defence is believed to have an effect on prosecutions ...

3.6.12 The interests of justice and fairness require an honest mistake to be recognised. An adult may meet with a child in a situation where they expect them to be over 16, for instance a pub or club. The child may appear older than they are and indeed may claim to be older. If that meeting leads to a sexual relationship, the adult may have sex with an under-age child with no intention to do so. On the other hand, it is all too easy to claim an honest mistake when no such mistake existed and there is evidence that some men specialise in the targeting of young girls. The present offence of usi is narrower and less serious than our proposed offence of adult sexual abuse of a child. That increases the argument for a defence of honest mistake. Our desire, and remit, to increase protection argued for no defence. Equally our desire and remit to be fair argued for a defence to be in place for an honest and reasonable mistake. Our conclusion was that a limited mistake of age defence should be available for adults charged with adult sexual abuse of a child. However, because it is relatively easy to claim and hard to disprove, any defence should be constructed as tightly as is consistent with fairness.

3.6.13 This means placing some weight on the defendant to demonstrate that he took some sensible precautions. If a defendant wishes to show an honest mistake there should be reasonable grounds for any belief in age and the defendant should have taken all reasonable steps to ascertain the child's age. We consider this is necessary and proportionate.

3.6.14 We also thought that there were strong arguments for limiting the use of the defence a track already followed in the existing law of usi and in one other place. It does seem reasonable that if someone has once been mistaken about the age of a sexual partner he or she will take greater care in future. If the same mistake is made on several occasions the chances of it being honest are severely reduced. We know that sexual offenders can have repeated patterns of behaviour in their preferred targets; this kind of behaviour should not be shielded by the repeated use of an honest mistake defence. The present defence relates to previous charges; this predates the use of cautions, is arbitrarily dependent on charging practices. It seems simpler to only allow the defence to be run in court on one occasion only. If the defence was run on more than one occasion, the defendant could have evidence of previous use of the defence admitted as evidence. That may require the retention of appropriate court records, but has a precedent in the offence of handling stolen goods where it is possible to introduce some evidence of previous offences.

3.6.15 We also considered whether the defence ought to contain any age limitations. The present defence is limited to young men between 16 and 24 ... This is criticised both for being too restrictive and too arbitrary. In effect it could make sex between young people less likely to be successfully prosecuted, while not allowing the defence to older men who may be more likely to mistake age, or who may be an older predator who seeks out young girls. However, others argue that the 8 year age gap in 16 to 24 is too great; if it is intended to be easier on similar age activity. Barnardo's, amongst others, argue that the key point is the age differential and an age gap of over five years is a potential indicator of an abusive relationship rather than a peer relationship.

3.6.16 In terms of justice and fairness there are no grounds for limiting the use of mistake of fact on the basis of the age of the defendant. However, there are other arguments this would reduce protection for children and on balance we believe age requires greater responsibilities to be exercised: on this basis a defence limited by age can be justified. At the same time, there does not seem to be a logical rationale for picking any particular cut-off age for use of the defence. One option was to use a 5 year age differential as suggested by Barnardo's, so that a person of 21 or over would not be able to claim a mistake of fact about the age of a sexual partner of 16. We thought we should consult more widely on this specific issue.

...

3.9 Under-age sexual activity between children

3.9.1 We have considered very carefully how the law should treat sexual activity of all kinds committed by adults with children, and recommended a serious new offence. We then considered how the law should be framed to deal with sexual activity between children. Our adult offence applies to those *over* 18 and those *under* 16. We now need to propose how the law should apply to those *under* 18 with those *under* 16. Primarily we are talking about *mutually agreed activity* between children. (Rape and other serious offences can be used, as at present, to prosecute non-consensual sexual activity.)

3.9.2 Although the age of consent for sexual behaviour is set in law, we recognise that children have sex with each other and will continue to do so. The review is seeking to increase protection to children, and to assist in the reduction of teenage pregnancies and other health risks associated with the early onset of sexual activity. The primary purpose of the law is to protect children from abusive (coerced and unwanted) sexual behaviour from older people and other children. We have recommended offences to tackle this behaviour.

3.9.3 The role of the law in dealing with under-age sex is much more difficult. The Children Act requires the welfare of the child to be a paramount consideration, and we have sought to apply this. Yet we know that as well as teenage experimentation in sex, which may well be mutually agreed, children can and do coerce and abuse each other. Even so-called mutually agreed relationships can be called into question. Sexual relations between children are capable of being exploitative.

3.9.4 Many people, including members of the review, have questioned the need for a criminal offence for sex between minors, arguing that there is no public interest in prosecuting sexual experimentation between mutually agreeing adolescents, giving them a criminal record for behaviour which they and many others do not regard as criminally culpable. They also argue that fear of being criminalised may deter young people from seeking help and advice, and possibly also raise questions about agencies offering it. Where children are sexually active, it is important for them to feel confident enough to seek help and advice about sexual health matters, including contraception if appropriate. To ensure this, children must be very clear that by seeking such guidance, neither they not their advisors would be breaking the law.

3.9.5 We have to achieve a very difficult balance between ensuring that the law is appropriate, fair and effective in enabling a range of coercive activity to be dealt with, while not criminalising young people for mutually agreed behaviour. We recognised that the law also plays a significant social role in setting parameters for behaviour, and we want to discourage under-age sex.

...

3.9.10 We concluded that there had to be some criminal law in place to ensure the protection of children from each other as well as adults. The offences of rape, sexual assault by penetration and sexual assault are already in place to tackle serious non-consensual behaviour. We thought there should be a separate offence for those aged under 18 with those under 16 to mirror the more serious 'adult sexual abuse of a child offence'. We set the upper age limit for the commission of this offence at 18. This provides a gap of two years between the age of consent at 16 and the age of majority at 18 before the more serious adult offence would apply.

3.9.11 As a mirror to the adult offence, the offence of 'sexual activity between children' would apply to behaviour that would not be culpable between consenting adults but was wrong for children to be involved in: sexual intercourse and penetration; sexual touching, inducing a child to commit sexual acts, performing sexual acts with or towards a child, and making a child witness sexual acts. It would replace the existing offences of unlawful sexual intercourse and indecency with children. It should be used where behaviour was not mutually agreed, but exploitative and coercive. The law would be clearer and more accessible to children. We hoped it would provide better protection by acting as a more effective deterrent to under-age sexual activity.

3.9.12 In seeking a way through these difficult issues we considered another possible approach. This was to create a separate, less serious, offence of 'penetrative sex with mutual agreement' for children aged between 13 and 16 to deal explicitly with mutually agreed sex. There were several problems with this approach. Such a 'third tier' offence for children would mean that our wider offence would be restricted to coercive or abusive behaviour which was not severe enough to justify a more serious charge. We thought about trying to define coercive circumstances, but found that this posed great difficulties, and if the offence relied on lack of consent the child victim would have to be cross-examined to determine the degree of coercion involved – raising all the evidential and procedural problems that occur in rape trials. If the offence existed it would certainly be used, and although some thought that this would go some way towards strengthening the age of consent, others thought that it might be used too readily and would unnecessarily criminalise young people. On balance we believed that our proposal for an offence which mirrored the adult offence of adult sexual abuse of a child was a better solution. We thought that rather than a separate offence we should concentrate on diversion and alternative disposals.

3.9.13 We thought the defences applying to the adult offence should also apply to the juvenile offence – and that there should be a statutory defence of mistake of fact in age, with the same safeguards for the adult defence, where the younger child was aged between thirteen and sixteen. If the younger child was below the age of 13, there should be no mistake of fact in age. If one or both of the parties was under the age of 13, this should always be considered under child protection guidelines, even though it was mutually agreed activity. The offence should ideally be used where there was an element of coercion or abuse by a child on another child. It should also prove an alternative charge or verdict for rape/sexual assault by penetration. Where there is evidence of serious abuse or coercion the offences of rape or sexual assault by penetration should be charged as appropriate.

3.9.14 The review also considered the question of criminal responsibility for under-age sex. Where adults are involved in sexual activity with children, we have recommended that only the adult should be liable, with no liability on the child. For the offence of sexual activity between minors, if one of the partners is over the age of consent, (ie a 16 or 17 year old with a child under 16) he or she should be liable. Where two children under the age of 16 are involved in a mutually agreed sexual relationship, we propose that the law leave open the issue of who is liable unless one partner is below the age of 13 (our age of absolute protection) in which case the older child is liable. There are strong arguments that in a mutually agreed relationship, both parties should be prepared to take responsibility for their actions. Leaving the liability open would enable the police and prosecutors to decide who is responsible on the facts of the case – if and when a prosecution is deemed necessary and in the public interest. There are risks to girls and boys in early sex – of pregnancy for girls and STIs [sexually transmitted infections] for both sexes. Girls however may suffer more readily from loss of reputation, and if they do become pregnant, from a very public recognition of their activity. Some members of the group thought that because of these features, girls should never be liable. However, we thought that this was not appropriate in the context of mutually agreed peer activity. Whilst recognising girls could be coerced into sex, that should be assessed in each case. We were also aware that pressure to have sex came not only from partners but from peers and apparently from a wider society. The law provides some counterweight against that.

3.9.15 Criminal justice action is not the best or most effective way to tackle the problem of mutually agreed under-age sex between peers. We did not think prosecution would be in the best interests of the children concerned, and it is important to apply the principles of the Children Act in ensuring that the welfare of the children is a primary consideration. The function of the criminal justice system is to protect against coercion, abuse and exploitation. If criminal justice action is required because there is evidence of coercion, a decision on who should be prosecuted should be made on the facts of the case in the context of clear and well-understood prosecution guidelines that would reflect such features as an imbalance of power, age or competence. To have no power to prosecute in any circumstances would effectively reduce the age of consent, or to apply inappropriate gender-based rules.

3.9.16 However, the new arrangements to deal with young offenders introduced in the Crime and Disorder Act 1998 which will replace the system of police cautions do introduce a new element into the discussion. Reprimands and final warnings are being implemented throughout England and Wales on 1 June 2000 following successful pilot projects. If a young person comes to the attention of the police when they commit an offence, and they admit their guilt, on the first occasion the offender will be reprimanded. A second offence will result in a Final Warning. At the Final Warning stage, the new Youth Offender Teams will undertake diversionary work, such as voluntary attendance at a tailored rehabilitation scheme. Both reprimands and final warnings will be noted on the Police National Computer and for a sex offence they will also carry a requirement for the young person to register their name and address with the police as a sex offender. Although the reprimand and final warning is an admission of guilt, the young person has no option about accepting a reprimand or final warning (unlike a caution). A third and subsequent breach will mean that the offender will have to appear in court. (More serious offences may short-circuit this process.) The third time they are apprehended for any criminal offence they appear in the juvenile courts. Reprimands and Final Warnings can be triggered by any criminal offence, including underage sexual activity. Depending on the gravity of the offence, a young offender can be 'fast-tracked' to court without the reprimand or final warning. A conviction for a sex offence against a child results in a requirement to register under the Sex Offenders Act 1997 and to Schedule One Offender status under the Children and Young Persons Act 1933.

3.9.17 Special procedures have been developed for dealing with an exceptional category of children who are regarded as victims rather than offenders. These are children involved in prostitution, where the emphasis is on diversion from an inappropriate and dangerous lifestyle. We thought that this could provide a more flexible model for dealing with mutually agreed underage sexual activity.

3.9.18 If there is a complaint of under-age sexual activity against a child, but the evidence is that the activity complained of was mutually agreed, the children concerned should not automatically fall under the reprimands and final warning scheme. The police do have discretion not to issue a reprimand or final warning or charge, but we wanted to ensure that young people who were clearly not involved in abusive or exploitative sexual activity should have a non-criminal alternative. We considered whether it was appropriate to refer them to a multi-agency forum for help and diversion. One possibility we considered is that the new Youth Offending Teams, who have a remit both to tackle offending and those at risk of offending, could provide the right forum and blend of skills to help and assist these young people without the long-term consequences of a criminal record for a sex offence. This would treat mutually agreed under-age sex seriously, but not require the young people to enter the reprimand and final warning system automatically. It would fit closely with the new arrangements for youth offending and retain the possibility of using the criminal law where it was in the public interest. It would also sit closely with the guidance on young sex offenders in 'Working Together', which advocates a multi-agency approach to protect children.

3.9.19 However, many of those working in the field of child protection felt that referral of a child to any panel concerned with youth offending would provide a negative effect by tainting the whole process: children would automatically equate such panels with criminalisation, and would be reluctant to seek their help. It was thought, in particular, that children in care (who were more likely to come to notice of the police and whose lives were chronicled by social services so that their smallest misdemeanour was a matter of record) might be most likely to be caught up in these arrangements for other offending behaviour. Although children involved as willing partners in under-age sexual activity are committing a criminal offence, it was agreed that it was not normally acceptable to put them through the mechanism of the criminal justice system. This reflects the present situation: prosecutions for under 16s are very rare. What was really needed was a process to run in parallel with investigation procedures, which could give individual assessment and possible referral to a range of services from sex education to other forms of intervention, ensuring that these reflected the aims of a national sexual health strategy This process will require professional skills to provide an worthwhile intervention, and a network to link into multi-agency services.

Further reading

S Gardner, 'Appreciating *Olugboja*' [1996] 16 Legal Studies 275

N Lacey, 'Beset by boundaries: the Home Office Review of Sex Offences' [2001] Crim LR 3

CHAPTER 18

THEFT

The Theft Act 1968 sets out the definition of theft in s 1:

Section 1 of the Theft Act 1968: basic definition of theft

(1) A person is guilty of theft if he dishonestly appropriates property belonging to another with the intention of permanently depriving the other of it; and 'thief' and 'steal' shall be construed accordingly.

...

(3) The five following sections of this Act shall have effect as regards the interpretation and operation of this section (and, except as otherwise provided by this Act, shall apply only for purposes of this section).

Section 7 of the Theft Act 1968: punishment

A person guilty of theft shall on conviction on indictment be liable to imprisonment for a term not exceeding [seven years].

Property: what can be stolen

Section 4 of the Theft Act 1968: 'property'

(1) 'Property' includes money and all other property, real or personal, including things in action and other intangible property.

(2) A person cannot steal land, or things forming part of land and severed from it by him or by his directions, except in the following cases, that is to say:

(a) when he is a trustee or personal representative, or is authorised by power of attorney, or as liquidator of a company, or otherwise, to sell or dispose of land belonging to another, and he appropriates the land or anything forming part of it by dealing with it in breach of the confidence reposed in him; or

(b) when he is not in possession of the land and appropriates anything forming part of the land by severing it or causing it to be severed, or after it has been severed; or

(c) when, being in possession of the land under a tenancy, he appropriates the whole or part of any fixture or structure let to be used with the land.

For purposes of this subsection 'land' does not include incorporeal hereditaments; 'tenancy' means a tenancy for years or any less period and includes an agreement for such a tenancy, but a person who after the end of a tenancy remains in possession as statutory tenant or otherwise is to be treated as having possession under the tenancy, and 'let' shall be construed accordingly.

(3) A person who picks mushrooms growing wild on any land, or who picks flowers, fruit or foliage from a plant growing wild on any land, does not (although not in possession of the land) steal what he picks, unless he does it for reward or for sale or other commercial purpose.

For purposes of this subsection 'mushroom' includes any fungus, and 'plant' includes any shrub or tree.

(4) Wild creatures, tamed or untamed, shall be regarded as property; but a person cannot steal a wild creature not tamed nor ordinarily kept in captivity, or the carcase of any such creature, unless either it has been reduced into possession by or on behalf of another person and possession of it has not since been lost or abandoned, or another person is in course of reducing it into possession.

Property is defined very widely in s 4 of the Theft Act 1968. It should be noted that the statutory definition excludes land but includes 'things in action'. A 'thing (or 'chose') in action' describes 'all personal rights of property which can only be claimed or enforced by [taking legal] action, and not by taking physical possession' (*Torkington v Magee* [1902] 2 KB 427 at 430, *per* Channell J). A good example of a 'thing in action' is a debt. The term therefore includes bank and building society accounts (if my bank account is in credit, then the bank owes me a debt equivalent to the amount of my credit balance). A cheque is a piece of paper and therefore amounts to 'property', and this is so whether or not the account on which the cheque is drawn is in credit.

Electricity cannot be stolen (*Low v Blease* [1975] Crim LR 513), but there is the specific offence of abstracting electricity under s 13 of the Theft Act 1968 (see below).

R v Kohn (1979) 69 Cr App R 395

The court considered whether the balance of an account in credit, or the right to withdraw funds under an agreed overdraft, could amount to intangible property under s 4 of the Theft Act 1968.

Geoffrey Lane LJ: We now turn to the counts which cover the situation when the account was overdrawn, but the amount of the cheque was within the agreed limits of the overdraft. So far as this aspect of the matter is concerned, Mr Tyrrell [counsel for the appellant] submits that the grant of facilities for an overdraft does not create a debt. He submits that all it does is to give a right of action in the event of a breach.

[... counsel for the appellant and continued:] ... the meaning of the word 'debt' is perhaps not quite so simple ...

One turns to *Director of Public Prosecutions v Turner* (1973) 57 Cr App R 932; [1974] AC 357. This was a case involving consideration of section 16(2) of the Theft Act, obtaining a pecuniary advantage by deception. It is a passage in the speech of Lord Reid which does cast some light on this abstruse problem. He said:

I turn then to paragraph (a). The first question is what is meant by the word 'debt.' I get no assistance from its being linked with the word 'charge' because during the argument no one was able to suggest any case to which 'charge' could apply in this context. Debt normally has one or other of two meanings: it can mean an obligation to pay money or it can mean a sum of money owed. It cannot have the latter meaning here. The paragraph deals with cases where a debt is 'reduced', 'evaded' or 'deferred'. No doubt you can reduce a sum of money, but to speak of a sum of money being evaded or deferred is nonsense. It is an elementary principle of construction that a word must be given the same meaning in different parts of the same provision. The same word used in different sections or subsections of the same Act may in some cases have different meanings. But in this paragraph the word 'debt' is only used once and it would, I think, be totally wrong to allow it to mean one thing when considering whether a debt has been reduced and something different when considering whether a debt has been evaded or deferred.

If the account is in credit, as we have seen, there is an obligation to honour the cheque. If the account is within the agreed limits of the overdraft facilities, there is an obligation to meet the cheque. In either case it is an obligation which can only be enforced by action. For purposes of this case it seems to us that that sufficiently constitutes a debt within the meaning of the word as explained by Lord Reid. It is a right of property which can properly be described as a thing in action and therefore potentially a subject of theft under the provisions of the 1968 Act ... Miss Goddard on behalf of the Crown has drawn our attention to a number of useful passages to some of which, it is right, we should make reference. The first of these authorities is *William Rouse v The Bradford Banking Co Ltd* [1894] AC 586, where at pp 595 and 596 Lord Herschell LC said:

> It is not necessary to consider what the rights of the bank were with regard to their debtors when they had agreed to an overdraft. The transaction is of course of the commonest. It may be that an overdraft does not prevent the bank who have agreed to give it from at any time giving notice that it is no longer to continue, and that they must be paid their money. This I think at least it does; if they have agreed to give an overdraft they cannot refuse to honour cheques or drafts, within the limit of that overdraft, which have been drawn and put in circulation before any notice to the person to whom they have agreed to give the overdraft that the limit is to be withdrawn. That effect I think it has in point of law; whether it has more than that in point of law it is unnecessary to consider.

... It seems to us, in the light of those authorities and in the light of the wording of the Theft Act 1968, that in this situation, when the order to a bank is within the agreed limits of the overdraft, a thing in action certainly exists and accordingly the judge was right in rejecting the submission. The appeal so far as those particular counts are concerned must fail.

That leads us to the third situation, which affects only count 7, that being, it will be remembered, the count which dealt with the cheque presented to the bank at a time when the account was over the agreed overdraft limit which had been imposed by the bank.

The situation here is that there is no relationship of debtor and creditor, even notionally. The bank has no duty to the customer to meet the cheque. It can simply mark the cheque 'Refer to drawer'. It can decline to honour the cheque. The reasons for that are obvious. If then a bank declines to honour a cheque, there is no right of action in the customer. If they do as a matter of grace – that is all it can be – honour the cheque then that is a course which does not retrospectively create any personal right of property in the customer and does not create any duty retrospectively in the bank. It seems, therefore, on that bald statement of principle, that this count which alleges a theft of a thing in action when the account was over the agreed limit must be quashed, unless some external reason can be found for saving it.

The only way in which Miss Goddard on behalf of the Crown seeks to support the conviction on this count is this. It is only fair to her to say that with characteristic fairness she dealt with this very delicately and her arguments were somewhat faintly put forward. She suggests that it is possible to say that there may be a moment between the bank's decision to honour a cheque and the actual moment when the cheque is honoured, when an obligation upon the bank of a corresponding right in the customer may be said to exist. It seems to us that this is first of all something which would be almost impossible in any particular case to prove, even if it were possible to bring all the necessary witnesses from the particular branch before the court, which would be very unlikely; but a much more serious objection is that, such an argument would be too artificial when one is dealing with what after all is a serious criminal offence which may well, as it did in this case, involve a loss of liberty. Furthermore, it would be impossible for the learned judge to explain to a jury so that a jury can understand precisely what this highly artificial concept really meant.

R v Navvabi [1986] 1 WLR 1311 (CA)

The appellant opened a number of bank accounts and was supplied with cheque books and cheque guarantee cards. Knowing the accounts were not in funds, and not having secured an agreed overdraft facility, the appellant drew a number of cheques in favour of casinos, supported by his cheque guarantee card. One of the issues considered by the Court of Appeal was whether or not the appellant had appropriated any identifiable property.

Lord Lane CJ: Before the trial judge and again in this court counsel for the appellant submitted that no identifiable property was appropriated, because the contractual obligation imposed on the bank was referable not to any asset which it had at the time the cheque was drawn and delivered to the casino, but to those funds which it had at the time of presentation by the casino. It was further submitted that, if there was identifiable property, its appropriation took place when the bank honoured the cheque and the funds were transferred to the casino by the bank, and not at the time the cheque was drawn and delivered to the casino. Furthermore it was contended that theft in such a way was so academic a concept that only an academically-minded person understanding such niceties would be able to form the necessary intention permanently to deprive the owner. Counsel for the appellant conceded, though this court doubts the correctness of that concession, that if the prosecution case had been presented on the basis that the appropriation took place at the time the funds were transferred by the bank to the casino, the conviction would be unimpeachable ...

[Regarding the assertion based on In R v Kohn to the effect that theft does not occur until the transaction involving the cheque has gone through to completion] ... It suggests (and has been taken by Professor Griew in his article 'Stealing and obtaining bank credits' [1986] Crim LR 356 ... to mean that theft occurs at the time when the bank transfers the funds. But Professor Smith has argued ... that the delivery of the cheque to the payee is 'an assumption of the rights of an owner' and therefore the appropriation. There may, however, as Professor Griew points out, be practical difficulties with this approach, for the state of the account may be much more difficult to ascertain when the cheque is delivered to the payee than when it is presented to the bank. Such difficulties, however, do not arise, or call for resolution, in the present case ...

... [The] use of the cheque card and delivery of the cheque did no more than give the casino a contractual right as against the bank to be paid a specified sum from the bank's funds on presentation of the guaranteed cheque. That was not in itself an assumption of the rights of the bank to that part of the bank's funds to which the sum specified in the cheque corresponded: there was therefore no appropriation by the drawer either on delivery of the cheque to the casino or when the funds were ultimately transferred to the casino.

PROPERTY: WHAT CANNOT BE STOLEN

Oxford v Moss (1978) 68 Cr App R 183 (DC)

Smith J: ... On 5 May 1976, an information was preferred by the prosecutor against the defendant alleging that the defendant stole certain intangible property, namely confidential information being examination questions for a civil engineering examination to be held in the month of June 1976 at Liverpool University, the information being the property of the Senate of the University, and the allegation being that the respondent intended permanently to deprive the said Senate of the said property.

The facts can be stated very shortly indeed. They were agreed facts. They are set out in the case and they are as follows. In May 1976 the defendant was a student at Liverpool University. He was studying engineering. Somehow (and this court is not concerned precisely how) he was able to acquire the proof of an examination paper for an examination in civil engineering to be held in the University during the following month, that is to say June 1976. Without doubt the proof, that is to say the piece of paper, was the property of the University. It was an agreed fact, as set out in the case, that the respondent at no time intended to steal what is described as 'any tangible element' belonging to the paper; that is to say it is conceded that he never intended to steal the paper itself.

In truth and in fact, and in all common sense, what he was about was this. He was borrowing a piece of paper hoping to be able to return it and not be detected in order that he should acquire advance knowledge of the questions to be set in the examination and thereby, I suppose, he would be enabled to have an unfair advantage as against other students who did not possess the knowledge that he did.

By any standards, it was conduct which is to be condemned, and to the layman it would readily be described as cheating. The question raised is whether it is conduct which falls within the scope of the criminal law ...

... The question for this court, shortly put, is whether confidential information can amount to property within the meaning of the Theft Act 1968 ...

The question for this court is whether confidential information of this sort falls within that definition contained in s 4(1) ...

In my judgment, it is clear that the answer to that question must be no. Accordingly, I would dismiss the appeal.

Wien J: ... [T]he right to confidential information is not intangible property within the meaning of s 4(1) of the Theft Act 1968 ...

R v Kelly [1999] 2 WLR 384

Rose LJ: On 3rd April 1998 at Southwark Crown Court, these appellants were convicted of one offence of theft. Kelly was sentenced to 9 months' imprisonment, and Lindsay to 6 months' imprisonment suspended for 2 years. They appeal against conviction by certificate of the trial judge, His Honour Judge Rivlin QC, in the following terms:

> Whether the trial Judge was correct in ruling as a matter of law that there is an exception to the traditional common law rule that 'there is no property in a corpse', namely, that once a human body or body part has undergone a process of skill by a person authorised to perform it, with the object of preserving for the purpose of medical or scientific examination or for the benefit of medical science, it becomes something quite different from an interred corpse. It thereby acquires a usefulness or value. It is capable of becoming property in the usual way, and can be stolen.

The facts were these. Between 1992 and 1994, the appellant, Kelly, who is an artist, had privileged access to the premises of the Royal College of Surgeons in order to draw anatomical specimens held on display and used for training surgeons. The appellant, Lindsay, was employed by the college during that period as a junior technician. Between 1993 and 1994, Kelly, who was then in his late thirties, asked Lindsay, who was under 21, to remove a number of human body parts from the college. Some 35 to 40 such parts, including three human heads, part of a brain, six arms or parts of an arm, ten legs or feet, and part of three human torsos were removed and taken to Kelly's home. He made casts of the parts, some of which were exhibited in an art gallery. Neither appellant intended to return the body parts, many of which Kelly buried in a field in the grounds of his family home. Part of a leg was kept in the attic of his home. The remaining parts were recovered from the basement of a flat occupied by one of Kelly's friends.

The crucial issue for the jury, when the matter was left for their consideration, was whether the appellants had acted dishonestly or whether, at the time they took the body parts, they acted in the honest belief that they had the right to do so. It was accepted, for the purposes of the hearing, that all the specimens in question antedated in age the Anatomy Act of 1984 which had come into force in early 1988. All the specimens taken had been preserved or fixed by college staff or other medical agencies. All were subject to a regular scheme of inspection, preservation, and maintenance and most of them had been the subject of further work, by prosection, whereby they had been expertly dissected so as to reveal, in highlighted form, the inner workings of the body.

There was evidence that the appellants would not have been permitted to remove body parts from the building under any circumstances. Permission could only be given by a licensed teacher of anatomy for the disposal of the specimens. It was elicited in cross-examination that some of the specimens at the college were no longer in use because of their poor condition due to age, and that other parts had, on occasions, left the college for the purposes of burial or cremation. There was evidence that the preparation of the specimens by prosection, to which we have referred, would have involved many hours, sometimes weeks, of skilled work.

There was also evidence that the type of dissection indicated that the work was that of a previous generation of anatomists, thereby throwing some light on the age of the parts. There was evidence that parts kept in the demonstration room would be up to 20 years old, but those in the basement store would be much older. It was not possible to say whether the specimens taken by the appellants had come from the demonstration room or the basement. There was evidence from the current inspector of anatomy to the effect that the college had full authority to be in possession of these specimens. In cross-examination, he said it was his understanding that the 1832 Anatomy Act did not apply. There was similar evidence from the inspector of anatomy at the time the parts were taken, between 1991 and 1995.

There was a good deal of material placed before the jury, in the form of a jury bundle, which is before this court, containing letters written by various people, in 1944, on the basis of which arguments were advanced as to the belief as to whether or not the possession of the Royal College of Surgeons was lawfully well-founded. We have to say that, for our part, we find no relevance whatever in those documents to any issue which was before the jury.

Kelly was interviewed on a number of occasions by the police. He said he understood the body parts were old, but that they were extremely valuable to the college. He thought that after 4 years the college required a certificate to retain the parts, which they did not have, and he considered that he was intercepting the parts which were 'on their way to the grave'. Nobody, he agreed, had given him permission to remove the items. He said at first that he had buried all of them but subsequently he gave the address of a friend, to which earlier we referred, where some of the parts were stored. When he was charged with theft and dishonest handling he said he did not intend to commit either such offence.

The appellant, Lindsay, in interview, referred to the age of the anatomical specimens and to the unusual access given to Kelly to the demonstration rooms and basement store. He said that his understanding of the law was that the college was only allowed to keep specimens for a period of 3 years, after which they had to be buried. He said that Kelly had asked him to remove the items, so that castings could be made in the way which we have described and he, Lindsay, agreed to that on condition that Kelly buried the parts afterwards. Lindsay said he took the items from the anatomy store or the storage tanks which were usually in the demonstration rooms. He removed the identification labels which he threw in a bin. Kelly had paid him £400 for his services but, he said, his main interest was in having the pieces buried.

A submission was made to the learned judge on behalf of the defence at the close of the prosecution. The first part of that submission was that parts of bodies were not in law capable of being property, and therefore could not be stolen. The judge ruled, in favour of the Crown, that the specimens were property, because of an exception to the common law rule, in the terms of the certificate which he has given for the purposes of the appeal to this court, the basis of that exception being a decision of the High Court of Australia in *R v Doodeward and Spence* (1908) 6 CLR 406.

... On behalf of the appellant, Lindsay, in submissions adopted by counsel on behalf of Kelly, Mr Thornton QC submits, as we have indicated, that the jury's verdict was unsafe, first, because the body parts were not property and therefore could not be stolen, secondly, because they did not belong to the Royal College of

Surgeons because they were not lawfully in their possession, and thirdly, because the judge's direction that the college was in lawful possession was a prejudicial misdirection of the jury.

In support of those submissions, Mr Thornton advanced eight propositions. First, that the common law rule applies to corpses to be buried but not yet buried. Such, he submits, are not property. Secondly there has been, until this case, no prosecution for theft of a body or body parts, although there do exist in other Acts, in particular the Anatomy Act of 1832, certain statutory offences, in relation to corpses and parts of corpses, which are – it is perhaps worth noting in passing – susceptible to a maximum sentence of imprisonment of 3 months. Thirdly, the common law rule extends to parts of bodies as well as to the entire corpse. Fourthly, the body parts in the present case were not property, they were intended by their donors for burial, and the resolution of that matter, clearly one of fact, was one which could only be favourable to the defence. Fifthly, there is no exception to the general common law rule.

For this part of his submission, it was pertinent for him to take the court, as he did, to do *Doodeward and Spence*, to which we have already referred. The first of the two majority judgments in that Australian case was given by Griffith CJ at p 413 of the report. He said this:

> It is idle to contend in these days that the possession of a mummy, or of a prepared skeleton, or of a skull, or other parts of a human body, is necessarily unlawful; if it is, the many valuable collections of anatomical and pathological specimens or preparations formed and maintained by scientific bodies, were formed and are maintained in violation of the law.
>
> In my opinion there is no law forbidding the mere possession of a human body, whether born alive or dead, for purposes other than immediate burial. *A fortiori* such possession is not unlawful if the body possesses attributes of such a nature that its preservation may afford valuable or interesting information or instruction.

Towards the foot of p 414:

> ... a human body, or a portion of a human body, is capable by law of becoming the subject of property. It is not necessary to give an exhaustive enumeration of the circumstances under which such a right may be acquired, but I entertain no doubt that, when a person has by the lawful exercise of work or skill so dealt with a human body or part of a human body in his lawful possession that it has acquired some attributes differentiating it from a mere corpse awaiting burial, he acquires a right to retain possession of it, at least as against any person not entitled to have it delivered to him for the purpose of burial, but subject, of course, to any positive law which forbids its retention under the particular circumstances.

Barton J at p 417 said this:

> I have read the judgment of the Chief Justice, and I entirely agree with the reasons it embodies, which I hold it unnecessary to amplify.

Higgins J gave a dissenting judgment at p 417. He referred at p 422, to the transformation of a corpse into a mummy, by the skill of an embalmer turning it into something different. He went on at p 423 to say that such traffic as there is in skulls and bones is clandestine. If they come from dissecting rooms, they come in violation of the law. He went on to say that no dead body could be used for dissection except under very stringent conditions and when the dissection was over the body must be decently interred. He said this, which is much relied upon by the appellants in this court:

> ... I rather think that sundry contraventions of the strict law as to dead bodies are winked at in the interests of medical science, and also for the practical reasons that no one can identify the bones or parts, and that no one is interested in putting the law in motion.

At the conclusion of judgment, at p 424, he said this:

> A right to keep possession of a human corpse seems to me to be just the thing which the British law, and, therefore, the New South Wales law, declines to recognise.

Mr Thornton draws attention to the fact that that authority, which related to a two headed still born fetus preserved as a curio, arose from a claim in detinue and he relies, as we have said, on the dissenting judgment of Higgins J. The facts of that case, he says, are plainly distinguishable from the present, because the nature of the object there in dispute rendered it something wholly different from a corpse or part of a corpse.

He submitted that there cannot be property for the purposes of the Theft Act, unless there is a permanent right to possession vested in the person from whom the property is taken. He submitted that the decision of the English Court of Appeal in *Dobson v North Tyneside Health Authority* [1996] 4 All ER 474, does not lend succor to the *Doodeward* exception. He submitted that no amount of skill expended on a body part can affect its ownership; at the highest, it might affect possessory rights.

... Mr Campbell-Tiech, on behalf of the prosecution, advanced before this court a submission which was not made to the learned trial judge, namely, that a corpse and parts of a corpse are property within section 4 of the Theft Act; a thing is either property or not. The status of the holder of the thing is irrelevant to determination of whether it is property or not, as is equally irrelevant the intention of the holder of the thing. Section 4 deals with property. Section 5 deals with rights over property. There is no overlap between the two sections. The common law in relation to corpses and parts of corpses deals with rights over things, and that is the province of section 5, not section 4. The common law doctrine as to who has the right to possession or control is irrelevant to whether a thing is property. Parts of a corpse have all the properties of a thing; the common law relates to rights not things. In the Theft Act, Parliament did not declare that a corpse was not property and could not be stolen. As a matter of statutory construction, a corpse or part of a corpse is within the definition of property in section 4.

We have sought summarily to rehearse Mr Campbell-Tiech's argument lest this matter proceed further. But, as we indicated to him and other counsel in the case, bearing in mind that the submission was not made before the learned trial judge, bearing in mind the way in which the matter proceeded before him and bearing in mind the terms of his certificate to this court, Mr Campbell-Tiech's submission is not one which we shall regard as being in any way determinative of this appeal. We merely comment that the draftsmen of the Theft Act must presumably have been well aware of the state of the common law for the last 150 years or more, and they do not appear to have made any exception in the Theft Act by reference to it.

We return to the first question, that is to say whether or not a corpse or part of a corpse is property. We accept that, however questionable the historical origins of the principle, it has now been the common law for 150 years at least that neither a corpse, nor parts of a corpse, are in themselves and without more capable of being property protected by rights (see, for example, Earl J, delivering the judgment of a powerful Court of Crown Cases Reserved in *R v Sharp* (1857) Dears & Bell 160, at p 163, where he said:

> Our law recognises no property in a corpse, and the protection of the grave at common law as contradistinguished from ecclesiastic protection to consecrated ground depends on this form of indictment.

He was there referring to an indictment which charged not theft of a corpse but removal of a corpse from a grave.

If that principle is now to be changed, in our view, it must be by Parliament, because it has been express or implicit in all the subsequent authorities and writings to which we have been referred that a corpse or part of it cannot be stolen.

To address the point as it was addressed before the trial judge and to which his certificate relates, in our judgment, parts of a corpse are capable of being property within section 4 of the Theft Act, if they have acquired different attributes by virtue of the application of skill, such as dissection or preservation techniques, for exhibition or teaching purposes: see *Doodeward and Spence*, in the judgment of Griffith CJ to which we have already referred and *Dobson v North Tyneside Health Authority* where, at p 479, this proposition is not dissented from and appears, in the judgment of this court, to have been accepted by Peter Gibson LJ; otherwise, his analysis of the facts of *Dobson*, which appears at that page in the judgment, would have been, as it seems to us, otiose. Accordingly the trial judge was correct to rule as he did.

Furthermore, the common law does not stand still. It may be that if, on some future occasion, the question arises, the courts will hold that human body parts are capable of being property for the purposes of section 4, even without the acquisition of different attributes, if they have a use or significance beyond their mere existence. This may be so if, for example, they are intended for use in an organ transplant operation, for the extraction of DNA or, for that matter, as an exhibit in a trial. It is to be noted that in *Dobson*, there was no legal or other requirement for the brain, which was then the subject of litigation, to be preserved ...

STEALING OF PART CAN BE STEALING OF WHOLE

Pilgram v Rice-Smith [1977] 2 All ER 659 (DC)

Lord Widgery CJ: ... At the Crown Court the following facts were found. The first respondent was an assistant employed by International Stores, the victims of the alleged theft. She worked in their shop at East Dereham. The second respondent was known to, and I think one can fairly say a friend of, the first respondent.

On the day in question the second respondent went to the counter where the first respondent was serving, and at that time corned beef was 18p a quarter and bacon was 72p a pound. The first respondent, who (it will be remembered) was behind the counter and an employee of the shop, served the second respondent with a quantity of corned beef which appeared to be well over a quarter and marked the price as 20p on the wrapping. She then weighed just over a pound of bacon and marked the price as 38p on the wrapping. Both articles were handed to the second respondent.

The second respondent then went around the store and bought some further articles. At the check-out she paid for all the articles in the total sum of £1.04. This included the 20p for the corned beef and the 38p for the bacon. The appellant alleged that the second respondent should have paid 83p more than that in respect of an undercharge on the bacon and the corned beef.

As the second respondent was leaving the store she was spoken to by the store detective and the usual investigation followed ...

In the result I analyse the case in this way. It seems to me clear that we must treat the two respondents as having been in league with one another from the outset. It is proper to treat the parcel of bacon and corned beef as a single parcel for this purpose. The fraud was inspired from the very beginning and therefore it operated from before the time when the goods were handed over to the purchaser, and accordingly the transaction of sale, or the purported transaction of sale, was a nullity from the start. It was a nullity from the start because from the start the lady behind the counter had no authority on the part of her employer to sell these goods at under value. She just did not have that authority. Consequently no contract of sale was entered into at all. That opens the door immediately for a conviction of theft in respect of the whole of the goods, and it is well established that it matters not in a case such as this that you have charged only the theft of part and proved the whole. You can nevertheless obtain a conviction in respect of what has been charged ...

CODIFICATION AND LAW REFORM PROPOSALS

In its Consultation Paper *Legislating the Criminal Code: Misuse of Trade Secrets* (LCCP 150) the Law Commission provisionally proposed that information, in the form of trade secrets, should come within the protection of the criminal law. The summary of the Paper explained the rationale for this position:

At present trade secrets cannot be stolen as they do not constitute 'property' for the purpose of the Theft Act 1968. The law has been strongly criticised because 'it is not too much to say that we live in a country where the theft of the boardroom table is punished far more severely than the theft of the boardroom secrets.

Other jurisdictions have extended the protection of the criminal law to the misuse of confidential business information: for example, the majority of the American states and a number of European countries, including France and Germany, provide criminal sanctions against the misuse of trade secrets.

The Consultation Paper itself sets out the position under the existing criminal law in more detail:

1.4 At present the criminal law gives no specific protection to trade secrets. In particular, trade secrets cannot, in law, be stolen: they do not constitute 'property' for the purpose of the Theft Act 1968 ... In the leading case, *Oxford v Moss*, an undergraduate obtained the proof of an examination paper before the examination. After reading the proof he returned it, retaining the information for his own use. He was held not guilty of stealing the information.

1.5 The principle is strikingly illustrated by *Absolom*, which followed *Oxford v Moss*. The defendant, a geologist, obtained and then tried to sell to a rival company details of a leading oil company's exploration for oil off the Irish coast. The information, which was contained in a 'graphalog' (a record of geological data and an indication of the prospects of finding oil), was unique, since the company was the only oil company exploring the area. The company had invested £13 million in drilling operations, and the information could have been sold for between £50,000 and £100,000. Although the judge stated that the defendant had acted in 'utmost bad faith', he directed the jury to acquit him of theft, on the ground that the information in the graphalog was not capable of founding such a charge.

1.6 A further difficulty with applying the law of theft to the misappropriation of a trade secret arises from the requirement that the defendant must intend permanently to deprive the owner of the property. 'It is difficult to see how there is any question of deprivation where someone has, in breach of confidence, forced the original holder to share, but not forget, his secret.'

1.7 Normally the information amounting to a trade secret will be recorded on a physical medium such as paper, microfiche or a computer disk. In that case, the physical medium is property, and a dishonest taking of it can therefore be charged as theft. But a charge of stealing an object worth a few pence would scarcely represent the gravamen of the defendant's conduct. And even this charge is unavailable if the information is absorbed without the taking of the medium on which it is recorded, or if (as in *Oxford v Moss*) there is no intention permanently to deprive the secrets owner of the medium (as distinct from the secret).

1.8 There are, however, a number of existing offences of infringing rights in intellectual property; and there are other offences which are not primarily concerned with intellectual property but which might be committed in the course of acquiring, using or disclosing another's trade secret.

...

1.21 Where two or more people dishonestly use or disclose another's trade secret, they may be guilty of the common law offence of conspiracy to defraud. The element of fraud is so widely defined that, on such facts, it may be readily established. The main reason why conspiracy to defraud is not a complete solution under the existing law is the requirement of conspiracy: it is probably illegal for two people to agree to 'steal' a trade secret, but not for one person to do it alone.

...

1.23 Although trade secret misuse is not an offence in itself, the way in which a secret is obtained may incidentally trigger liability for a more general offence. Where secret information is obtained by deception, for example, on the understanding that it has been or will be paid for, there may be an obtaining of services by deception, contrary to section 1 of the Theft Act 1978. Obtaining information by bribery or corruption may be an offence under the Prevention of Corruption Acts 1889 to 1916. Again, industrial espionage may involve the commission of the offence of intercepting post or of telephone tapping. But there is no offence if an employee simply discloses or uses the secret in breach of confidence, or an outsider obtains it in a manner not specifically prohibited.

1.24 It thus appears that the protection afforded to trade secrets by the existing criminal law is limited. There may be no offence if an individual, acting alone, dishonestly uses or discloses secret information (not protected by copyright or a registered trade mark, and not amounting to personal data protected by the Data Protection Act 1984) without authority, provided that that individual

(1) obtains the information with the consent of its owner (albeit in confidence) for example where an employee is given the information for the purposes of his or her work or

(2) though not authorised to have the information at all, obtains it without resorting to deception, corruption, unauthorised access to a computer, intercepting post, telephone tapping or any other prohibited means. A simple example would be the industrial spy who gains access to premises without forcing entry (which would involve an offence of criminal damage) and inspects the contents of an unlocked filing cabinet.

The summary of the Consultation Paper's proposals continues:

Should there be criminal sanctions for trade secret misuse?

We provisionally conclude there should be criminal sanctions because:

- There is no distinction between the harm caused by theft and by the misuse of trade secrets. In both cases, the property of another is being used for the benefit of the wrongdoer, and the owner is likely to suffer damage.

- The imposition of legal sanctions is necessary in order to protect investment and research. Vast sums of money are spent on producing certain types of trade secret such as manufacturing formulae and other technical data and it seems strange that the criminal law does not provide a sanction.

- It is inconsistent for the law to provide criminal sanctions for the infringement of copyright and registered trade marks, but not for misuse of trade secrets.

- Civil remedies alone are insufficient to discourage trade secret misuse, as many wrongdoers are unable to satisfy any judgment against them. At present the law has no effective sanctions against the person who dishonestly misuses trade secrets and has no assets.

- The criminalisation of trade secret misuse would help to preserve standards in business life.

What trade secrets are covered?

We provisionally propose that the definition of a 'trade secret' should include a requirement that its owner had indicated – expressly or impliedly – a wish to keep it secret. We invite views on whether the definition of trade secrets should make a reference to the use of the information in a trade or business and, if so, whether the definition should extend to information used in a profession or in non-commercial research.

It is our provisional view that an element of the definition of a trade secret should be that the information is not generally known; but we believe that the prosecution should not have to prove that the information was not generally known unless there is some evidence to suggest that it was.

What wrong-doings in connection with trade secrets should be covered?

We provisionally conclude that the new offence should be committed by any person who uses or discloses a trade secret belonging to another without that others consent. By 'belonging to another' we mean the person who is entitled to the benefit of the trade secret. Our provisional view is that consent to the use or disclosure of a trade secret should not negative liability for the offence if it was obtained by deception.

We provisionally propose that it should be an element of the new offence that the defendant:

- knows that the information in question is a trade secret belonging to another, and

- is aware that the other does not (or may not) consent to the use or disclosure; but it should not be an offence if the person who uses or discloses the trade secret does so in the belief that every person to whom the secret belongs would consent to the use or disclosure if he or she knew of it and the circumstances of it.

Defences

We are concerned that there should be a public interest defence, and therefore provisionally propose that the new offence should not apply to: the use or disclosure to an appropriate person of information for the purpose of the prevention, detection or exposure of: a crime, fraud or breach of statutory duty, whether committed or contemplated, conduct which is in the nature of a fraud on the general public, or matters constituting a present or future threat to the health or welfare of the community, or any use or disclosure of information which under the law of confidence would be justified on grounds of public interest.

We also provisionally propose that the new offence should not apply to: any disclosure of information by a person who under any form of legislation is obliged or permitted to make it, disclosure of information pursuant to a court order, or otherwise in the course of civil or criminal legal proceedings, or the lawful exercise of an official function with regard to national security or the prevention, investigation or prosecution of crime.

Should there be criminal liability for the dishonest acquisition of a trade secret?

We invite views on whether the law should be extended to cover the acquisition of a trade secret; and, if so, whether this should be achieved by creating an offence of acquiring a trade secret with the intention of using or disclosing it, or an offence of acquiring a trade secret by wrongful methods, or an offence defined in some other way (and, if so, what)? '

APPROPRIATION

Section 3 of the Theft Act 1968: 'appropriates'

(1) Any assumption by a person of the rights of an owner amounts to an appropriation, and this includes, where he has come by the property

(innocently or not) without stealing it, any later assumption of a right to it by keeping or dealing with it as owner.

(2) Where property or a right or interest in property is or purports to be transferred for value to a person acting in good faith, no later assumption by him of rights which he believed himself to be acquiring shall, by reason of any defect in the transferor's title, amount to theft of the property.

Note that s 1(2) of the 1968 Act provides that: 'It is immaterial whether the appropriation is made with a view to gain, or is made for the thief's own benefit.'

Lawrence v Metropolitan Police Commissioner [1972] AC 626 (HL)

Viscount Dilhorne: My Lords, the appellant was convicted on 2 December 1969, of theft contrary to s 1(1) of the Theft Act 1968. On 1 September 1969, a Mr Occhi, an Italian who spoke little English, arrived at Victoria Station on his first visit to this country. He went up to a taxi driver, the appellant, and showed him a piece of paper on which an address in Ladbroke Grove was written. The appellant said that it was very far and very expensive. Mr Occhi got into the taxi, took £1 out of his wallet and gave it to the appellant who then, the wallet being still open, took a further £6 out of it. He then drove Mr Occhi to Ladbroke Grove. The correct lawful fare for the journey was in the region of 10s 6d. The appellant was charged with and convicted of the theft of the £6 ...

I see no ground for concluding that the omission of the words 'without the consent of the owner' [from s 1(1) of the Theft Act 1968] was inadvertent and not deliberate, and to read the subsection as if they were included is, in my opinion, wholly unwarranted. Parliament by the omission of these words has relieved the prosecution of the burden of establishing that the taking was without the owner's consent. That is no longer an ingredient of the offence ...

... That there was appropriation in this case is clear. Section 3(1) states that any assumption by a person of the rights of an owner amounts to an appropriation. Here there was clearly such an assumption. That an appropriation was dishonest may be proved in a number of ways. In this case it was not contended that the appellant had not acted dishonestly. Section 2(1) provides, *inter alia*, that a person's appropriation of property belonging to another is not to be regarded as dishonest if he appropriates the property in the belief that he would have the other's consent if the other knew of the appropriation and the circumstances of it. *A fortiori*, a person is not to be regarded as acting dishonestly if he appropriates another's property believing that with full knowledge of the circumstances that other person has in fact agreed to the appropriation. The appellant, if he believed that Mr Occhi, knowing that £7 was far in excess of the legal fare, had nevertheless agreed to pay him that sum, could not be said to have acted dishonestly in taking it.

... Belief or the absence of belief that the owner had with such knowledge consented to the appropriation is relevant to the issue of dishonesty, not to the question whether or not there has been an appropriation. That may occur even though the owner has permitted or consented to the property being taken. So proof that Mr Occhi had consented to the appropriation of £6 from his wallet without agreeing to paying a sum in excess of the legal fare does not suffice to show that there was not dishonesty in this case. There was ample evidence that there was.

I now turn to the third element, 'property belonging to another' ... [T]he money in the wallet which [the appellant] appropriated belonged to another, to Mr Occhi.

There was no dispute about the appellant's intention being permanently to deprive Mr Occhi of the money.

The four elements of the offence of theft as defined in the Theft Act 1968 were thus clearly established and, in my view, the Court of Appeal was right to dismiss the appeal.

Having done so, they granted a certificate that a point of law of general public importance was involved ...

The first question posed in the certificate was:

> Whether s 1(1) of the Theft Act, 1968, is to be construed as though it contained the words 'without having the consent of the owner' or words to that effect.

In my opinion, the answer is clearly No.

The second question was:

> Whether the provisions of s 15(1) and of s 1(1) of the Theft Act 1968, are mutually exclusive in the sense that if the facts proved would justify a conviction under s 15(1) there cannot lawfully be a conviction under s 1(1) on those facts.

Again, in my opinion, the answer is No. There is nothing in the Act to suggest that they should be regarded as mutually exclusive and it is by no means uncommon for conduct on the part of an accused to render him liable to conviction for more than one offence. Not infrequently there is some overlapping of offences. In some cases the facts may justify a charge under s 1(1) and also a charge under s 15(1). On the other hand, there are cases which only come within s 1(1) and some which are only within s 15(1). If in this case the appellant had been charged under s 15(1), he would, I expect, have contended that there was no deception, that he had simply appropriated the money and that he ought to have been charged under s 1(1). In my view, he was rightly charged under that section ...

Lord Pearson, Lord Diplock, Lord Cross, and **Lord Donovan** also agreed that the appeal should be dismissed.

Dobson v General Accident Fire and Life Assurance Corp plc
[1990] 1 QB 274 (CA)

Facts: This was a civil case involving a claim under a home insurance policy, which included cover for loss by theft. The plaintiff had advertised an expensive watch for sale. He was visited in his house by a purchaser who bought the watch, providing the plaintiff with a cheque that subsequently proved to be worthless. The plaintiff contended that his loss was covered by his household insurance policy as he had been the victim of a theft. The insurance company refused to pay out on the basis that there had been no theft as the plaintiff had consented to the purchaser taking the watch. The issue for the Court of Appeal (Civil Division), therefore, was whether theft could occur even where the owner consented to the taking of the property. The court held that the plaintiff had been the victim of a theft.

Parker LJ: ... The issue for determination on the appeal is whether the circumstances constituted a theft of the watch and ring by the rogue.

... On the basis of *Lawrence v Commissioner of Police for the Metropolis* [1972] AC 626, the facts of the present case appear to establish that the rogue assumed all the rights of an owner when he took or received the watch and ring from the plaintiff. That he did so dishonestly and with the intention of permanently depriving the plaintiff of them are matters beyond doubt. It was however submitted that the third element was not satisfied because, at the time of appropriation, if there was one, the watch and ring were not property belonging to another. The property had, it was submitted, already passed to the rogue at the time the articles were delivered to him.

... Having regard to the terms of the contract, the conduct of the parties and the circumstances of the case, I have no doubt that the property was not intended to pass in this case on contract but only in exchange for a valid building society cheque, but even if it may be regarded as intended to pass in exchange for a false, but believed genuine, building society cheque it will not in my view avail the insurers ...

It was further submitted on the part of the insurers that, notwithstanding the emphatic statement of the House of Lords that absence of consent on the part of the owner was not an ingredient of the offence and was not relevant to the question whether there had been an appropriation, the later decision of the House in *R v Morris* [1984] AC 320 at 332, that appropriation 'involves not an act expressly or impliedly authorised by the owner but an act by way of adverse interference with or usurpation of those rights', must lead in the present case to the conclusion that there had been no theft.

The difficulties caused by the apparent conflict between the decision in *Lawrence's* case and *R v Morris* have provided, not surprisingly, a basis for much discussion by textbook writers and contributors of articles to law journals. It is, however, clear that their Lordships in *R v Morris* did not regard anything said in that case as conflicting with Lawrence's case for it was specifically referred to in Lord Roskill's speech, with which the other members of the Appellate Committee all agreed, without disapproval or qualification. The only comment made was that, in *Lawrence's* case, the House did not have to consider the precise meaning of 'appropriation' in s 3(1) (see [1984] AC 320 at 331). With respect, I find this comment hard to follow in the light of the first of the questions asked in *Lawrence's* case and the answer to it ... the fact that it was specifically argued that 'appropriates' is meant in a pejorative, rather than a neutral, sense in that the appropriation is against the will of the owner (see [1972] AC 626 at 631), and finally that dishonesty was common ground. I would have supposed that the question in *Lawrence's* case was whether appropriation necessarily involved an absence of consent ...

... the insurers' contention that there was no theft is based on consent and the fact that there was a clear s 15(1) offence, both of which are negatived as answers to appropriation by *Lawrence's* case, and the fact that the contract of sale between the plaintiff and the rogue was voidable only and not void, which is not relevant according to *R v Morris*.

If, then the insurers are deprived of their arguments to defeat the only element of the offence of theft which was in doubt once the 'belonging to another' argument has been rejected, they cannot in my judgment succeed on the basis of Lord Roskill's statement in *R v Morris* that there must be an act by way of adverse interference with or usurpation of the owner's rights. If consent and the existence of a voidable contract under which property passes are irrelevant, there was in my judgment a plain interference with or usurpation of the plaintiff's rights.

I am fully conscious of the fact that in so concluding I may be said not to be applying *R v Morris*. This may be so, but in the light of the difficulties inherent in the decision, the very clear decision in *Lawrence's* case and the equally clear statement in *R v Morris* that the question whether a contract is void or only voidable is irrelevant, I have been unable to reach any other conclusion. I would therefore dismiss the appeal.

Bingham LJ: ... It ... appears that A commits theft if he dishonestly assumes any of the rights of an owner over B's property intending to deprive B of that property permanently.

This simple analysis may be applied to the everyday example of a customer selecting goods from a supermarket shelf and putting them in the wire basket or trolley provided. The goods on the shelves belong to the supermarket. They continue to belong to the supermarket until paid for by a customer: see *Lacis v Cashmarts* [1969] 2 QB 400. The customer assumes some of the rights of an owner when he takes them into his (or her) possession and exercises control over them by putting them in a basket or trolley. The customer, not intending to return the goods to the supermarket, intends to deprive the supermarket of the goods permanently. In the ordinary case the customer will honestly intend to pay the market price for the goods at the cash desk, so no offence of theft will be committed. But a customer who dishonestly intends not to pay the marked price will be guilty of theft, at the time of dishonest appropriation. On this analysis it is irrelevant that the supermarket displays the goods for sale and invites, perhaps even tempts, customers to put them in their baskets or trolleys. The acid test is whether when doing so the customer acts honestly or dishonestly. (I need not discuss the case where a customer initially appropriates goods honestly intending to pay and later forms a dishonest intention to keep the goods without paying) ...

I do not find it easy to reconcile [the] ruling of Viscount Dilhorne [in *Lawrence's* case, that appropriation may occur even though the owner has permitted or consented to the property being taken], which was as I understand central to the answer which the House of Lords gave to the certified question, with the reasoning of the House in *R v Morris*. Since, however, the House in *R v Morris* considered that there had plainly been an appropriation in *Lawrence's* case, this must (I think) have been because the Italian student, although he had permitted or allowed his money to be taken, had not in truth consented to the taxi driver taking anything in excess of the correct fare. This is not a wholly satisfactory reconciliation, since it might be said that a supermarket consents to customers taking goods from its shelves only when they honestly intend to pay and not otherwise. On the facts of the present case, however, it can be said, by analogy with *Lawrence's* case, that although the plaintiff permitted and allowed his property to be taken by the rogue, he had not in truth consented to the rogue becoming owner without giving a valid draft drawn by the building society for the price. On this basis I conclude that the plaintiff is able to show an appropriation sufficient to satisfy s 1(1) of the 1968 Act when the rogue accepted delivery of the articles.

On the facts here the plaintiff has no difficulty in showing dishonesty and an intention permanently to deprive on the part of the rogue. It is, however, argued for the insurers that when the rogue appropriated the ring and the watch they were not property belonging to another because ownership of the goods had already, before delivery, passed to the rogue under the contract of sale.

The courts have been enjoined so far as possible to eschew difficult questions of contract law relating to title to goods: see *R v Morris* [1984] AC 320 at 334. But whether, in the ordinary case to which s 5 of the 1968 Act does not apply, goods are to be regarded as belonging to another is a question to which the criminal law offers no answer and which can only be answered by reference to civil law principles. Applying these principles, I would without much doubt impute an intention to the plaintiff and the rogue that property in the watch and the ring should pass to the rogue on delivery of the goods to him and not before. That would also, as I think, be the moment of appropriation. If, therefore, it were necessary for the plaintiff to show that the goods still belonged to him at the moment of appropriation I would doubt whether he could do so, appropriation and transfer of title being simultaneous. Happily for the plaintiff, the point was raised in *Lawrence v Commissioner of Police for the Metropolis* [1972] AC 626 at 632 and decided in his favour ...

... Just as it is enough to satisfy s 15 that the goods belong to the victim up to the time of obtaining, so it is enough for the plaintiff that the watch and ring belonged to him up to the time of appropriation ...

R v Gomez [1993] AC 442 (HL)

Lord Keith of Kinkel: My Lords, this appeal raises the question whether two decisions of your Lordships' House upon the proper construction of certain provisions of the Theft Act 1968 are capable of being reconciled with each other, and, if so, in what manner. The two decisions are *R v Lawrence (Alan)* [1972] AC 626 and *R v Morris (David)* [1984] AC 320 ...

The facts of this case are that the defendant, Edwin Gomez was employed as assistant manager at a shop trading by retail in electrical goods. In September 1987 he was asked by an acquaintance called Jit Ballay to supply goods from the shop and to accept payment by two stolen building society cheques, one for £7,950 and the other for £9,250, which were undated and bore no payee's name. The defendant agreed, and prepared a list of goods to the value of £7,950 which he submitted to the manager, Mr Gilberd, saying that it represented a genuine order by one Johal and asking him to authorise the supply of the goods in return for a building society cheque in that sum. Mr Gilberd instructed the defendant to confirm with the bank that the cheque was acceptable, and the defendant later told him that he had done so and that such a cheque was 'as good as cash'. Mr Gilberd agreed to the transaction, the defendant paid the cheque into the bank, and a few days later Ballay took possession of the goods, the defendant helping him to load them into his vehicle. Shortly afterwards a further consignment of goods to the value of £9,250 was ordered and supplied in similar fashion (apart from one item valued at £1,002.99 which was not delivered), against the second stolen building society cheque. Mr Gilberd agreed to this transaction without further enquiry.

Later the two cheques were returned by the bank marked 'Orders not to pay. Stolen cheque'.

[The Court of Appeal certified that a point of law of general public importance was involved, namely:]

> When theft is alleged and that which is alleged to be stolen passes to the defendant with the consent of the owner, but that consent has been obtained by a false representation, has (a) an appropriation within the meaning of s 1(1) of the Theft Act 1968 taken place, or (b) must such a passing of property necessarily involve an element of adverse [interference] with or usurpation of some right of the owner?

... It will be seen that Viscount Dilhorne's speech [in *Lawrence's* case] contains two clear pronouncements, first that it is no longer an ingredient of the offence of theft that the taking should be without the owner's consent and second, that an appropriation may occur even though the owner has permitted or consented to the property being taken ...

In my opinion Lord Roskill [in *R v Morris*] was undoubtedly right when he said ... that the assumption by the defendant of any of the rights of an owner could amount to an appropriation within the meaning of s 3(1), and that the removal of an article from the shelf and the changing of the price label on it constituted the assumption of one of the rights of the owner and hence an appropriation within the meaning of the subsection. But there are observations in the passage which, with the greatest possible respect to Lord Roskill, I must regard as unnecessary for the decision of the case and as being incorrect. In the first place, it seems to me that the switching of price labels on the article is in itself an assumption of one of the rights of the owner, whether or not it is accompanied by some other act such as removing the article from the shelf and placing it in a basket or trolley. No one but the owner has the right to remove a price label from an article or to place a price label upon it. If anyone else does so, he does an act, as Lord Roskill puts it, by way of adverse interference with or usurpation of that right. This is no less so in the case of the practical joker figured by Lord Roskill than in the case of one who makes the switch with dishonest intent. The practical joker, of course, is not guilty of theft because he has not acted dishonestly and does not intend to deprive the owner permanently of the article. So the label-switching in itself constitutes an appropriation and so to have held would have been sufficient for the dismissal of both appeals. On the facts of the two cases it was unnecessary to decide whether, as argued by [counsel for the prosecution], the mere taking of the article from the shelf and putting it in a trolley or other receptacle amounted to the assumption of one of the rights of the owner, and hence an appropriation. There was much to be said in favour of the view that it did, in respect that doing so gave the shopper control of the article and the capacity to exclude any other shopper from taking it. However, Lord Roskill expressed the opinion that it did not, on the ground that the concept of appropriation in the context of s 3(1):

> involves not an act expressly or impliedly authorised by the owner but an act by way of adverse interference with or usurpation of those rights.

While it is correct to say that appropriation for purposes of s 3(1) includes the latter sort of act, it does not necessarily follow that no other act can amount to an appropriation and in particular that no act expressly or impliedly authorised by the owner can in any circumstances do so. Indeed, *R v Lawrence* [1972] AC 626 is a clear decision to the contrary since it laid down unequivocally that an act may be an appropriation notwithstanding that it is done with the consent of the owner. It does not appear to me that any sensible distinction can be made in this context between consent and authorisation.

In the civil case of *Dobson v General Accident and Life Assurance Corporation plc* [1990] 1 QB 274 a Court of Appeal consisting of Parker and Bingham LJJ considered the apparent conflict between *R v Lawrence* and *R v Morris* and applied the former decision.

His Lordship then quoted extensively from the judgment from of Parker LJ and from the judgment of Bingham LJ in *Dobson* and continued:

It was argued for the defendant in the present appeal that *Dobson v General Accident Fire and Life Assurance Corporation plc* [1990] 1 QB 274 was wrongly decided. I disagree, and on the contrary find myself in full agreement with those parts of the judgment of Parker LJ to which I have referred. As regards the attempted reconciliation by Bingham LJ of the reasoning in *R v Morris* ... with the ruling in *R v Lawrence*, it appears to me that the suggested basis of reconciliation, which is essentially speculative, is unsound. The actual decision in *Morris* was correct, but it was erroneous, in addition to being unnecessary for the decision, to indicate that an act expressly or impliedly authorised by the owner could never amount to an appropriation. There is no material distinction between the facts in Dobson and those in the present case. In each case the owner of the goods was induced by fraud to part with them to the rogue. *Lawrence* makes it clear that consent to or authorisation by the owner of the taking by the rogue is irrelevant. The taking amounted to an appropriation within the meaning of s 1(1) of the Act of 1968. *Lawrence* also makes it clear that it is no less irrelevant that what happened may also have constituted the offence of obtaining property by deception under s 15(1) of the 1968 Act.

... The decision in *Lawrence* was a clear decision of this House upon the construction of the word 'appropriates' in s 1(1) of the 1968 Act, which had stood for 12 years when doubt was thrown upon it by *obiter dicta* in *Morris*. *Lawrence* must be regarded as authoritative and correct, and there is no question of it now being right to depart from it ...

There were cited to your Lordships a number of cases involving the abstraction of moneys from a limited company by a person who was in a position to give the consent of the company to the abstraction. It is sufficient to say that I agree with what my noble and learned friend, Lord Browne-Wilkinson, has to say about these cases in the speech to be delivered by him and that in my opinion a person who thus procures the company's consent dishonestly and with the intention of permanently depriving the company of the money is guilty of theft contrary to s 1(1) of the Act 1968.

My Lords, for the reasons which I have given I would answer branch (a) of the certified question in the affirmative and branch (b) in the negative, and allow the appeal.

Lord Browne-Wilkinson: My Lords, I have read the speech of my noble and learned friend, Lord Keith of Kinkel, with which I agree ...

The fact that Parliament used that composite phrase 'dishonest appropriation' in my judgment casts light on what is meant by the word 'appropriation'. The views expressed (*obiter*) by this House in *R v Morris* [1984] AC 320 that 'appropriation' involves an act by way of adverse interference with or usurpation of the rights of the owner treats the word appropriation as being tantamount to 'misappropriation'. The concept of adverse interference with or usurpation of rights introduces into the word appropriation the mental state of both the owner and the accused. So far as concerns the mental state of the owner (did he consent?), the 1968 Act expressly refers to such consent when it is a material factor: see ss 2(1)(b), 11(1), 12(1) and 13. So far as concerns the mental state of the accused, the composite phrase in s 1(1) itself indicates that the requirement is dishonesty.

For myself, therefore, I regard the word 'appropriation' in isolation as being an objective description of the act done irrespective of the mental state of either the owner or the accused. It is impossible to reconcile the decision in *Lawrence* (that the question of consent is irrelevant in considering whether there has been an appropriation) with the views expressed in *Morris*, which latter views in my judgment were incorrect.

It is suggested that this conclusion renders s 15 of the Act of 1968 otiose since a person who, by deception, persuades the owner to consent to part with his property will necessarily be guilty of theft within s 1. This may be so though I venture to doubt it. Take for example a man who obtains land by deception. Save as otherwise expressly provided the definitions in ss 4 and 5 of the 1968 Act apply only for the purposes of interpreting s 1 of that Act: see s 1(3). Section 34(1) applies ss 4(1) and 5(1) generally for the purposes of the 1968 Act. Accordingly the other subsections of s 4 and s 5 do not apply to s 15. Suppose that a fraudster has persuaded a victim to part with his house: the fraudster is not guilty of theft of the land since s 4(2) provides that you cannot steal land. The charge could only be laid under s 15 which contains no provisions excluding land from the definition of property. Therefore, although there is a substantial overlap between s 1 and s 15, s 15 is not otiose.

Lords Slynn and **Jauncey** concurred.

Lord Lowry (dissenting) : In my opinion, any attempt to reconcile the statement of principle in *Lawrence* and *Morris* is a complete waste of time ... [I]t is clear that, whether they succeeded or not, both the Criminal Law Revision Committee and the draftsman must have intended to give the word one meaning, which would be the same in the Act as in the committee's report. To simplify the law, where possible, is a worthy objective but, my Lords, I maintain that the law, as envisaged in the report, is simple enough: there is no problem (and there would have been none in *Lawrence*, *Morris* and the present case) if one prosecutes under section 15 all offenders involving obtaining by deception and prosecutes theft in general under section 1. In that way some thefts will come under section 15, but no false pretences will come under section 1.

R v Hinks [2000] 4 All ER 835

Lord Steyn: My Lords ... [s]ince the enactment of the Theft Act 1968 the House of Lords has on three occasions considered the meaning of the word 'appropriates' in section 1(1) of the Act, namely in *R v Lawrence* [1972] AC 626; in *R v Morris* [1984] AC 320; and in *R v Gomez* [1993] AC 442. The law as explained in *Lawrence* and

Gomez, and applied by the Court of Appeal in the present case (*R v Hinks* [2000] 2 Cr App R 1) has attracted strong criticism from distinguished academic lawyers: see for example, JC Smith [1993] Crim LR 304 and [1998] Crim LR 904; Edward Griew, *The Theft Acts*, 7th edn, 1995, 41–59; ATH Smith, 'Gifts and the law of theft' [1999] CLJ 10. These views have however been challenged by equally distinguished academic writers: Glazebrook [1993] CLJ 191–94; Gardner, 'Property and theft' [1998] Crim LR. The academic criticism of *Gomez* provided in substantial measure the springboard for the present appeal. The certified question before the House is as follows: Whether the acquisition of an indefeasible title to property is capable of amounting to an appropriation of property belonging to another for the purposes of section 1(1) of the Theft Act 1968. In other words, the question is whether a person can 'appropriate' property belonging to another where the other person makes him an indefeasible gift of property, retaining no proprietary interest or any right to resume or recover any proprietary interest in the property. Before the enactment of the Theft Act 1968 English law required a taking and carrying away of the property as the actus reus of the offence. In 1968 Parliament chose to broaden the reach of the law of theft by requiring merely an appropriation. The relevant sections of the Act of 1968 are as follows ...

His Lordship set out ss 1, 2, and 3 of the 1968 Act and continued:

... These provisions, and in particular the word 'appropriates' in section 1(1), read with the explanatory provision in section 3(1), have been authoritatively interpreted by the House in *Lawrence* [1972] AC 626 and *Gomez* [1993] AC 442. It will be a matter for consideration whether such earlier rulings are dispositive of the question of law before the House. In the meantime, it is necessary to give a narrative of the background and the proceedings below.

In 1996 the appellant was 38 years old. She was the mother of a young son. She was friendly with a 53 year old man, John Dolphin. He was a man of limited intelligence. The appellant described herself as the main carer for John Dolphin. It is not in dispute that in the period April to November 1996 Mr Dolphin withdrew sums totalling around £60,000 from his building society account and that these sums were deposited in the appellant's account. During the summer of that year Mr Dolphin made withdrawals of the maximum permissible sum of £300 almost every day. Towards the end of this period Mr Dolphin had lost most of his savings and moneys inherited from his father. In 1997 the appellant was charged with six counts of theft, five counts covering moneys withdrawn and one count a television set transferred by Mr Dolphin to the appellant. In November 1977 the appellant stood trial on these counts in the Wolverhampton County Court before Judge Warner and a jury. It was the prosecution case that the appellant had influenced and coerced Mr Dolphin to withdraw the moneys from his building society account, which were then deposited in her account. A substantial volume of evidence was led during the trial which lasted five days. A police analyst produced documents summarising the flow of funds from Mr Dolphin's account to that of the appellant. Building society employees testified about the daily visits by the appellant and Mr Dolphin to effect withdrawals. The thrust of their evidence was that the appellant did most of the talking and would interrupt Mr Dolphin if he tried to say something. Dr Fuller, a consultant psychiatrist, assessed Mr Dolphin's IQ as in the range between 70 to 80 (the average being 90 to 110). He said that Mr Dolphin was able to live a normal if undemanding life. Mr Dolphin had worked as a packer in a dairy for some 30 years. Dr Fuller described him as naïve and trusting and having no idea of the value of his assets or the ability to calculate their value. Dr Fuller accepted that Mr Dolphin would be capable of making a gift and understood the concept of ownership. He thought that Mr Dolphin was capable of making the decision to divest himself of money, but that it was unlikely that he could make the decision alone. Two police officers testified that after cautioning the appellant she denied 'having any money' from Mr Dolphin except for a single cheque which she said represented a loan. In a nutshell the prosecution case was that the appellant had taken Mr Dolphin for as much as she could get.

The defence made a submission that in law there was no case to answer. The defence argument was that the moneys were a gift from Mr Dolphin to the appellant, that the title in the moneys had passed to the appellant, and that there could therefore be no theft. The defence cited the writings of Professor Sir John Smith, QC. The judge rejected the submission and held that a gift was capable of amounting to an appropriation.

The appellant gave evidence. She did not dispute the fact of the withdrawal of moneys from the appellant's account and the deposit of the sums in her account. She admitted that she had accepted Mr Dolphin's television set. She said that Mr Dolphin had handed the moneys, as well as the colour television set, as gifts to her or her young son or as part of a loan. She denied the account of what she allegedly said to the police officers. She asserted that she had acted honestly throughout. The judge then summed up to the jury. His direction on appropriation was as follows:

> The second ingredient is appropriates, dishonestly appropriates. You must be sure on any count that the property referred to in that count passed from Mr Dolphin to Miss Hinks so that she acquired it and treated it as her own to deal with. That can include, obviously, members of the jury, a straightforward taking or transfer of the property concerned. It can also include acquiring it by way of gift, either for herself or on behalf of her young son.

... The judge had withdrawn one count of theft from the jury. On the remaining 5 counts of theft the jury returned unanimous verdicts of guilty. The judge sentenced the appellant to terms of 18 months imprisonment on each of the 5 counts, such terms to run concurrently. It is common ground that the jury must have accepted the prosecution case and must have rejected the appellant's explanations as untruthful.

... My Lords, counsel for the appellant has not expressly asked the House to depart from the previous decisions of the House. He did, however, submit with the aid of the writings of Sir John Smith that the conviction of a donee for receiving a perfectly valid gift is a completely new departure. Relying on the academic criticism of the earlier decisions of the House counsel submitted that their reach should not be extended. Counsel cited as evidence of the true intention of the draftsman a passage from a note by Sir John Smith on the decision in *Hinks*: [1998] Crim LR 904. The passage reads as follows (904–05):

> In a memorandum dated January 15, 1964 the distinguished draftsman of the Theft Act (Mr JS Fiennes, as he then was) wrote to members of the Larceny Sub-Committee of the Criminal Law Revision Committee: I trust the Sub-Committee will not agree with Dr [Glanville] Williams when he says ... that a

person appropriates for himself property of which another person is the owner every time he gratefully accepts a gift or buys an apple. If this is what the words mean, then the whole language of the clause ought to be changed, because one really cannot have a definition of stealing which relies on the word 'dishonestly' to prevent it covering every acquisition of property.

Sir John Smith returned to this point in 'The sad fate of the Theft Act 1968', an essay in *The Search for Principle, Essay in Honour of Lord Goff of Chieveley*, ed by W Swadling and G Jones, pp 97, 100–01. While this anecdote is an interesting bit of legal history, it is not relevant to the question before the House. Given counsel's use of it, as well as aspects of Sir John Smith's writing on the point in question, which have played such a large role in the present case, it is necessary to state quite firmly how the issue of interpretation should be approached. In *Black-Clawson International Ltd v Papierwerke Waldhoff-Anschaffenburg AG* [1975] AC 591, 613 Lord Reid observed:

> We often say that we are looking for the intention of Parliament, but that is not quite accurate. We are seeking the meaning of the words which Parliament used. We are seeking not what Parliament meant but the true meaning of what they said.

This does not rule out or diminish relevant contextual material. But it is the critical point of departure of statutory interpretation. It also sets logical limits to what may be called in aid of statutory interpretation. Thus the published Eighth Report of the Criminal Law Revision Committee on *Theft and Related Offences* (Cmnd 2977, 1966), and in particular para 35, may arguably be relevant as part of the background against which Parliament enacted the Bill which became the Act of 1968. How far it in fact takes one is a matter considered in *Gomez* [1993] AC 442. Relevant publicly available contextual materials are readily admitted in aid of the construction of statutes. On the other hand, to delve into the intentions of individual members of the Committee, and their communications, would be to rely on material which cannot conceivably be relevant. If statutory interpretation is to be a rational and coherent process a line has to be drawn somewhere. And what Mr Fiennes wrote to the Larceny Sub-Committee was demonstrably on the wrong side of the line.

The starting point must be the words of the statute as interpreted by the House in its previous decisions. The first case in the trilogy is *R v Lawrence* ... Lord Dilhorne expressly [stated] that belief that the passenger gave informed consent (ie knowing that he was paying in excess of the fare) 'is relevant to the issue of dishonesty, not to the question whether or not there has been an appropriation': ... the appeal was dismissed. The *ratio decidendi* of *Lawrence*, namely that in a prosecution for theft it is unnecessary to prove that the taking was without the owner's consent, goes to the heart of the certified question in the present case.

The second decision of the House was *Morris* ... in the single substantive judgment Lord Roskill made an observation, which was in conflict with the *ratio* of *Lawrence* and had to be corrected in *Gomez*. Lord Roskill said ...:

> If one postulates an honest customer taking goods from a shelf to put in his or her trolley to take to the checkpoint there to pay the proper price, I am unable to see that any of these actions involves any assumption by the shopper of the rights of the supermarket. In the context of section 3(1), the concept of appropriation in my view involves not an act expressly or impliedly

authorised by the owner but an act by way of adverse interference with or usurpation of those rights.

It will be observed that this observation was not necessary for the decision of the case: absent this observation the House would still have held that there had been an appropriation. Lord Roskill took the view that he was following the decision in *Lawrence*. It is clear, however, that his observation (as opposed to the decision in *Morris*) cannot stand with the *ratio* of *Lawrence*. And as his observation, cast in terms of 'the honest customer', shows Lord Roskill conflated the ingredients of appropriation and dishonesty contrary to the holding in *Lawrence*.

The third decision of the House was in *Gomez* ... the House was expressly invited to hold that 'there is no appropriation where the entire proprietary interest passes' ... That submission was rejected. The leading judgment in *Gomez* was therefore in terms which unambiguously rule out the submission that section 3(1) does not apply to a case of a gift duly carried out because in such a case the entire proprietary interest will have passed. In a separate judgment (with which Lord Jauncey of Tullichettle expressed agreement) Lord Browne-Wilkinson observed, at pp 495H–496A:

> ... I regard the word 'appropriation' in isolation as being an objective description of the act done irrespective of the mental state of either the owner or the accused. It is impossible to reconcile the decision in *Lawrence* (that the question of consent is irrelevant in considering whether there has been an appropriation) with the views expressed in *Morris*, which latter views in my judgment were incorrect.

In other words it is immaterial whether the act was done with the owner's consent or authority. It is true of course that the certified question in *Gomez* referred to the situation where consent had been obtained by fraud. But the majority judgments do not differentiate between cases of consent induced by fraud and consent given in any other circumstances. The *ratio* involves a proposition of general application. *Gomez* therefore gives effect to section 3(1) of the Act by treating 'appropriation' as a neutral word comprehending 'any assumption by a person of the rights of an owner.' If the law is as held in *Gomez*, it destroys the argument advanced on the present appeal, namely that an indefeasible gift of property cannot amount to an appropriation.

Counsel for the appellant submitted in the first place that the law as expounded in *Gomez* and *Lawrence* must be qualified to say that there can be no appropriation unless the other party (the owner) retains some proprietary interest, or the right to resume or recover some proprietary interest, in the property. Alternatively, counsel argued that 'appropriates' should be interpreted as if the word 'unlawfully' preceded it. Counsel said that the effect of the decisions in *Lawrence* and *Gomez* is to reduce the *actus reus* of theft to 'vanishing point' (see Smith and Hogan, *Criminal Law*, 9th edn, 1999, p 505). He argued that the result is to bring the criminal law 'into conflict' with the civil law. Moreover, he argued that the decisions in *Lawrence* and *Gomez* may produce absurd and grotesque results. He argued that the mental requirements of dishonesty and intention of permanently depriving the owner of property are insufficient to filter out some cases of conduct which should not sensibly be regarded as theft. He did not suggest that the appellant's dishonest and repellent conduct came within such a category. Instead he deployed four examples for this purpose, namely the following:

(1) S makes a handsome gift to D because he believes that D has obtained a First. D has not and knows that S is acting under that misapprehension. He makes the gift. There is here a motivational mistake which, it is submitted, does not avoid the transaction. (Glanville Williams, *Textbook*, 1st edn, at p 788).

(2) P sees D's painting and, thinking he is getting a bargain, offers D £100,000 for it. D realises that P thinks the painting is a Constable, but knows that it was painted by his sister and is worth no more than £100. He accepts P's offer. D has made an enforceable contract and is entitled to recover and retain the purchase price. (Smith and Hogan *Criminal Law*, 9th edn, pp 507–08).

(3) A buys a roadside garage business from B, abutting on a public thoroughfare; unknown to A but known to B, it has already been decided to construct a bypass road which will divert substantially the whole of the traffic from passing A's garage. There is an enforceable contract and A is entitled to recover and retain the purchase price. The same would be true if B knew that A was unaware of the intended plan to construct a bypass road. (Compare Lord Atkin in *Bell v Lever Brothers* [1932] AC 161, 224.)

(4) An employee agrees to retire before the end of his contract of employment, receiving a sum of money by way of compensation from his employer. Unknown to the employer, the employee has committed serious breaches of contract which would have enabled the employer to dismiss him without compensation. Assuming that the employee's failure to reveal his defaults does not affect the validity of the contract, so that the employee is entitled to sue for the promised compensation, is the employee liable to be arrested for the theft the moment he receives the money? (Glanville Williams: 'Theft and voidable title' [1981] Crim LR 666, 672.)

My Lords, at first glance these are rather telling examples. They may conceivably have justified a more restricted meaning of section 3(1) than prevailed in *Lawrence* ... and *Gomez* ... The House ruled otherwise and I am quite unpersuaded that the House overlooked the consequences of its decision. On the facts set out in the examples a jury could possibly find that the acceptance of the transfer took place in the belief that the transferee had the right in law to deprive the other of it within the meaning of section 2(1)(a) of the Act. Moreover, in such cases a prosecution is hardly likely and if mounted, is likely to founder on the basis that the jury will not be persuaded that there was dishonesty in the required sense. And one must retain a sense of perspective. At the extremity of the application of legal rules there are sometimes results which may seem strange. A matter of judgment is then involved. The rule may have to be recast. Sir John Smith has eloquently argued that the rule in question ought to be recast. I am unpersuaded. If the law is restated by adopting a narrower definition of appropriation, the outcome is likely to place beyond the reach of the criminal law dishonest persons who should be found guilty of theft. The suggested revisions would unwarrantably restrict the scope of the law of theft and complicate the fair and effective prosecution of theft. In my view the law as settled in *Lawrence* and *Gomez* does not demand the suggested revision. Those decisions can be applied by judges and juries in a way which, absent human error, does not result in injustice.

Counsel for the appellant further pointed out that the law as stated in *Lawrence* and *Gomez* creates a tension between the civil and the criminal law. In other words, conduct which is not wrongful in a civil law sense may constitute the crime of theft. Undoubtedly, this is so. The question whether the civil claim to title by a convicted thief, who committed no civil wrong, may be defeated by the principle that nobody may benefit from his own civil or criminal wrong does not arise for decision. Nevertheless there is a more general point, namely that the interaction between criminal law and civil law can cause problems: compare Beatson and Simester, 'Stealing one's own property' (1999) 115 LQR 372. The purposes of the civil law and the criminal law are somewhat different. In theory the two systems should be in perfect harmony. In a practical world there will sometimes be some disharmony between the two systems. In any event, it would be wrong to assume on *a priori* grounds that the criminal law rather than the civil law is defective. Given the jury's conclusions, one is entitled to observe that the appellant's conduct should constitute theft, the only available charge. The tension between the civil and the criminal law is therefore not in my view a factor which justifies a departure from the law as stated in *Lawrence* and *Gomez*. Moreover, these decisions of the House have a marked beneficial consequence. While in some contexts of the law of theft a judge cannot avoid explaining civil law concepts to a jury (eg in respect of section 2(1)(a)), the decisions of the House of Lords eliminate the need for such explanations in respect of appropriation. That is a great advantage in an overly complex corner of the law.

My Lords, if it had been demonstrated that in practice *Lawrence* and *Gomez* were calculated to produce injustice that would have been a compelling reason to revisit the merits of the holdings in those decisions. That is however, not the case. In practice the mental requirements of theft are an adequate protection against injustice. In these circumstances I would not be willing to depart from the clear decisions of the House in *Lawrence* and *Gomez*. This brings me back to counsels' principal submission, namely that a person does not appropriate property unless the other (the owner) retains, beyond the instant of the alleged theft, some proprietary interest or the right to resume or recover some proprietary interest. This submission is directly contrary to the holdings in *Lawrence* and *Gomez*. It must be rejected. The alternative submission is that the word 'appropriates' should be interpreted as if the word 'unlawfully' preceded it so that only an act which is unlawful under the general law can be an appropriation. This submission is an invitation to interpolate a word in the carefully crafted language of the Act of 1968. It runs counter to the decisions in *Lawrence* and *Gomez* and must also be rejected. It follows that the certified question must be answered in the affirmative.

In his judgment my noble and learned friend Lord Hutton concluded that the trial judge's summing-up on dishonesty was materially defective in particular respects which he lists and that the appeal should be allowed on this ground. In reluctant disagreement with Lord Hutton I take a different view. The House is clearly not confined to the certified question. I agree that in the interests of justice one must look at the matter in the round. It is, however, relevant to bear in mind the context in which the points arise. First, the trial judge was not invited to give such special directions. Secondly, these points were not contained in the written grounds of appeal before the Court of Appeal. Thirdly the points of criticism were not contained in the Statement of Facts and Issues or in the printed cases. Fourthly, the House has not seen transcripts of evidence. The relevance of this factor is that the House is inadequately informed as to the way in which the defence case was deployed before the judge and jury. And a summing-up must always be tailored to the particular circumstances of each case.

My Lords, for my part the position would have been different if I had any lurking doubt about the guilt of the appellant on the charges for which she was convicted. In the light of a fair and balanced summing up and a very strong prosecution case, the jury accepted the prosecution case and rejected the appellant's account as untruthful. They found that she had acted dishonestly by systematically raiding the savings in a building society account of a vulnerable person who trusted her. Even if one assumes that the judge ought to have directed more fully on dishonesty I am satisfied that the convictions are entirely safe. In these circumstances it is not necessary and indeed undesirable for the House to pronounce upon what directions should be given on dishonesty in cases akin to the present. My Lords I would dismiss the appeal to the House.

Lord Slynn and **Lord Jauncey** also agreed, for the reasons given by **Lord Steyn** that the appeal should be dismissed.

Lord Hutton (dissenting): [Having considered the provisions of sections 1, 2 and 3 of the Theft Act 1968] ... on [the] facts there were two issues for the jury to consider: (1) had the appellant appropriated the money and, if so, (2) had she appropriated the money dishonestly? In relation to appropriation the judge told the jury:

> The second ingredient is appropriates, dishonestly appropriates. You must be sure on any count that the property referred to in that count passed from Mr Dolphin to Miss Hinks so that she acquired it and treated it as her own to deal with. That can include, obviously, members of the jury, a straightforward taking or transfer of the property concerned. It can also include acquiring it by way of gift, either for herself or on behalf of her young son.

The certified question relates only to this issue, and for the reasons given by my noble and learned friend Lord Steyn I agree that the answer to this question should be 'Yes', but I consider that two issues then arise as to the element of dishonesty. The first issue is whether this element should be considered by the House. If so, the second issue is whether the judge's summing up as to dishonesty constituted a misdirection.

What the judge said was as follows:

> I am now going to move on to deal with that word that I mentioned at first, that very important word, dishonestly, because, as I have said, it's one of the central questions that you've got to decide, whether or not this defendant acted dishonestly. And, of course, it's entirely a matter for you, as the jury, to decide. But please bear in mind the fact that if you don't like something that the defendant did, or the mere fact that you don't approve of it, or the mere fact that she did something that you think was morally reprehensible does not necessarily mean that it is dishonest. For the Prosecution to make you sure that she's dishonest, they've got to make you sure of two things. They've got to make you sure that what she did was dishonest by the standards of ordinary and decent people. Now, in this regard, members of the jury, you must form your own judgment of what those standards are. That's why we have a jury here. And if it was not dishonest by those standards, then the Prosecution fails. That would be an end of the matter. But if it was dishonest by those

standards, then you have to decide and be sure that the defendant herself must have realised that what she was doing was dishonest by the standards of ordinary and decent people. And in order to decide this question you must consider the defendant's own state of mind. If, having taken into account all the evidence, that you are sure that she must have realised this, then the element of dishonesty is proved. If you are not sure that she realised it, she is not guilty. Now, what is the position in relation to gifts? The defendant says that Mr Dolphin made gifts to her and that those were for her son. If any payment, or the transfer of the TV for instance, was or might have been a gift, then you would have to consider whether she was dishonest in accepting it. The relevant question in relation to any gift would be this. Was Mr Dolphin so mentally incapable that the defendant herself realised that ordinary and decent people would regard it as dishonest to accept that gift from him?

In a criminal case this House is not confined to the certified question and can consider other points if it is necessary to do so in the interests of justice ... Therefore the question arises whether it is appropriate in this case for the House to consider the element of dishonesty. In relation to this point I would observe that a submission on dishonesty was advanced to the Court of Appeal on behalf of the appellant as an issue separate and distinct from the issue of appropriation. This appears from the following passage of the judgment of the Court of Appeal delivered by Rose LJ at [2000] 1 Cr App R 1, 7D:

> Mr Lowe's submission is twofold. First, that by virtue of the definition of dishonesty in section 2(1)(b) of the Act, which we have already read, a person cannot be regarded as dishonest if he believes he would have the owner's consent if the owner knew of the appropriation. In the present case, there was no evidence to prove that Mr Dolphin was not consenting to appropriation, and therefore, there could not be dishonesty. Mr Lowe is in consequence critical of the direction given by the learned judge in the summing-up, which appears at p 6C: [the learned Lord Justice then set out the final paragraph in the passage of the summing-up which I have set out above] 'It seems to us that the first part of Mr Lowe's submission encounters very serious difficulties in the form of *Lawrence*. That is emphasised when one turns to consider the second part of his submission, in relation to appropriation'.

And at p 9G the Court of Appeal stated:

> The direction which we have already cited from p 6 of the summing-up was, in our judgment, an entirely appropriate and accurate direction as to dishonesty.

It is also apparent from the judgments of the Court of Appeal in *R v Mazo* [1997] 2 Cr App R 518 and *R v Kendrick* and *Hopkins* [1997] 2 Cr App R 524 that difficult issues can arise both as to appropriation and dishonesty where the defendant raises the defence that money or property was received as a gift, and in the present case the trial judge observed that dishonesty was a central issue in the case. Therefore I think it is appropriate that this House should consider the judge's directions on dishonesty.

Before doing so it is appropriate to refer to the Statement of Facts before the House where it is stated:

> 1.4 It was the prosecution case that between April 1996 and November 1996 the appellant somehow influenced or coerced Mr Dolphin to withdraw

moneys totalling about £60,000 from his Building Society accounts, the moneys subsequently being deposited into the appellant's own account. She was also alleged to have taken a colour television (Count 6) belonging to Mr Dolphin, using similar means.

1.5 It was the defence case that the cash and property had been handed over to the appellant either as a gift to her or a gift to her young son or as part of a loan.

In the trial judge's lengthy summing-up there is no direction to the jury in relation to influence or coercion being a ground upon which any gifts by Mr Dolphin to the appellant would be void or voidable. The judge referred to a different point when he said at p 6 of the summing up:

The relevant question in relation to any gift would be this. Was Mr Dolphin so mentally incapable that the defendant herself realised that ordinary and decent people would regard it as dishonest to accept the gift from him?

I therefore turn to consider dishonesty where the defendant contends, as in this case, that she received the money or property as a gift. My Lords, it appears contrary to common sense that a person who receives money or property as a gift could be said to act dishonestly, no matter how much ordinary and decent people would think it morally reprehensible for that person to accept the gift. Section 2(1)(b) of the Act recognises this common sense view by providing:

(1) A person's appropriation of property belonging to another is not to be regarded as dishonest ... (b) if he appropriates the property in the belief that he would have the other's consent if the other knew of the appropriation and the circumstances of it;

It follows, *a fortiori*, that a person's appropriation of property belonging to another should not be regarded as dishonest if the other person actually gives the property to him. Thus in *R v Lawrence* [1972] AC 626, 632C Viscount Dilhorne said:

Section 2(1) provides, *inter alia*, that a person's appropriation of property belonging to another is not to be regarded as dishonest if he appropriates the property in the belief that he would have the other's consent if the other knew of the appropriation and the circumstances of it. *A fortiori*, a person is not to be regarded as acting dishonestly if he appropriates another's property believing that with full knowledge of the circumstances that other person has in fact agreed to the appropriation. The appellant, if he believed that Mr Occhi, knowing that £7 was far in excess of the legal fare, had nevertheless agreed to pay him that sum, could not be said to have acted dishonestly in taking it. When Megaw LJ said that if there was true consent, the essential element of dishonesty was not established, I understand him to have meant this. Belief or the absence of belief that the owner had with such knowledge consented to the appropriation is relevant to the issue of dishonesty, not to the question whether or not there has been an appropriation.

Therefore I consider that in *R v Mazo* [1997] 2 Cr App R 518 after referring to a sentence in the above passage of the speech of Viscount Dilhorne, Pill LJ was right to say at p 521C: 'It is implicit in that statement that if in all the circumstances there is held to be a valid gift there can be no theft'. The reason why there is no theft is because there is no dishonesty.

But the simple proposition that a person who receives property as a gift is not to be regarded as dishonest becomes more difficult to apply where the prosecution alleges that the gift was void or voidable by reason of circumstances known to the defendant. This situation was discussed by Megaw LJ in *Lawrence* [1971] 1 QB 373, 377C:

> Of course, where there is true consent by the owner of property to the appropriation of it by another, a charge of theft under section 1(1) must fail. This is not, however, because the words 'without consent' have to be implied in the new definition of theft. It is simply because, if there is such true consent, the essential element of dishonesty is not established. If, however, the apparent consent is brought about by dishonesty, there is nothing in the words of section 1(1), or by reason of any implication that can properly be read into those words, to make such apparent consent relevant as providing a defence. The prosecution have to prove the four elements already mentioned, and no more. No inference to the contrary is to be drawn from the words of section 2(1)(b), already quoted. That reference does no more than show that the essential element of dishonesty does not exist if the defendant when he appropriates the property believes that the owner would consent if he knew the circumstances. 'The circumstances' are, of course, all the relevant circumstances. 'The belief' is an honest belief. That paragraph does not give rise to the inference that an appropriation of property is not theft when there is a 'consent' – if it can be rightly so described – which is founded upon the dishonesty of the defendant.

There was no difficulty in applying that concept in the case of Lawrence itself because, as Viscount Dilhorne observed at p 632C and E, it was not contended that the defendant had not acted dishonestly, and there was ample evidence of dishonesty. In *R v Morris* [1984] AC 320, 334C Lord Roskill stated:

> I respectfully suggest that it is on any view wrong to introduce into this branch of the criminal law questions whether particular contracts are void or voidable on the ground of mistake or fraud or whether any mistake is sufficiently fundamental to vitiate a contract. These difficult questions should so far as possible be confined to those fields of law to which they are immediately relevant and I do not regard them as relevant questions under the Theft Act 1968.

I respectfully agree, but I think that in a case where the prosecution contends that the gift was invalid because of the mental incapacity of the donor it is necessary for the jury to consider that matter. I further consider that the judge must make it clear to the jury that they cannot convict unless they are satisfied (1) that the donor did not have the mental capacity to make a gift and (2) that the donee knew of this incapacity.

In *R v Mazo* [1997] 2 Cr App R 518, where the accused had received large sums of money from an elderly lady and claimed that they were gifts, I consider that the Court of Appeal was right to quash the conviction because the trial judge had not directed the jury adequately on the issue of the lady's capacity to make a valid gift, Pill LJ stating at p 522E–523A:

> Undoubtedly in this case there was evidence which, if the jury believed it and made the necessary inferences, could have found a conviction for theft. There was evidence to suggest, though it was in issue, that Lady S's mental capacity

was such that she could not make a valid gift. The prosecution case being that there was no gift because there was no capacity to give, it was essential that the jury be confronted plainly with the issue which arose upon her ability to make a valid gift. It was necessary for the jury, before convicting, to consider the state of mind of the donee and the circumstances of the transfer, but it was also essential to prove that the donor had no sufficient degree of understanding to make a valid gift. The jury were never given a plain direction to that effect ... It is, in the judgment of the court, as important upon the present criminal charge as it is in a civil case involving a transfer *inter vivos* to consider the state of mind of the donor and whether a valid gift can be and is made.

In contrast, in *R v Kendrick and Hopkins* [1997] 2 Cr App R 524 there was clear evidence that the owner of the monies and investments, who was aged 99, was mentally incapable of managing her own affairs and was thus incapable of making a gift. Therefore I consider that in that case the Court of Appeal was right to uphold the conviction for conspiracy to steal by the managers of the residential home where the owner lived and who had acquired large sums of money which had belonged to her and which they claimed were gifts.

... Therefore there was an appropriation in that case and there was dishonesty because the defendants knew that the elderly lady was mentally incapable of making a gift.

My Lords, in the present state of the law relating to theft when the defendant claims that he or she received the money or property as a gift, a Crown Court judge faces a difficult task in summing-up to a jury. In this case the judge gave a fair and careful summary of the evidence. In the passage which I have set out he rightly told the jury that the mere fact that they disapproved of what the defendant did, or thought that it was morally reprehensible, did not necessarily mean that it was dishonest. It is also clear that the third and fourth paragraphs in the passage of the summing-up which I have set out above were based on the guidance given by the Court of Appeal in *R v Ghosh* [1982] 1 QB 1053.

But in my opinion in a case where the defendant contends that he or she received a gift, a direction based only on Ghosh is inadequate because it fails to make clear to the jury that if there was a valid gift there cannot be dishonesty, and in the present case there is the danger that, if the gift was not void for want of mental capacity, the jury might nevertheless convict on the basis that ordinary and decent people would think it dishonest for a younger woman to accept very large sums of money which constituted his entire savings from a naïve man of low intelligence, and that the woman would have realised this.

Immediately after giving the part of his direction based on *Ghosh* the judge said at p 6:

> If any payment, or the transfer of the TV for instance was or might have been a gift, then you would have to consider whether she was dishonest in accepting it. The relevant question in relation to any gift would be this. Was Mr Dolphin so mentally incapable that the defendant herself realised that ordinary and decent people would regard it as dishonest to accept that gift from him?

But this part of the charge was defective because it linked the issue of mental incapacity to what ordinary and decent people would regard as dishonest. Moreover in summarising the evidence of the consultant psychiatrist who had examined Mr Dolphin on behalf of the Crown and who was called as a prosecution witness the judge said at p 15:

> Dr Fuller said that he would be capable of making a gift and understand that he was giving the property to someone else. He would be capable of understanding the fact that the property he was giving belonged to him. He would be capable of understanding that someone shouldn't simply come in and take his television set. He would be capable of understanding that the daily visit to the building society, he would understand that the money that he had in the building society belonged to him.

And towards the end of his summing-up the judge said at p 49:

> And Mr Morse [counsel for the Crown] ended his cross-examination by saying to her that she had taken him for as much as she could get, which in one sense, in a nutshell, is what the prosecution are saying in their case, and she said that was not true.

Therefore, if it was part of the Crown case that, apart from any issue of influence or coercion, any gifts made by Mr Dolphin to the appellant were void because he was mentally incapable of making such gifts, I consider that the summing up was defective as the jury were not given adequate directions as to the degree of mental incapacity which makes void a gift or gifts of large sums of money. But it may be that no such directions were given because the point in relation to mental capacity was not advanced as a separate and distinct point by the Crown.

Therefore I consider that in this case: (1) It was necessary for the judge to make clear to the jury that if there was a valid gift the defendant could not be found to be dishonest no matter how much they thought her conduct morally reprehensible. (2) If the Crown were making the case that the gifts were invalid because Mr Dolphin was mentally incapable of making a gift, it was necessary for the judge to give the jury a specific direction as to what degree of mental weakness would, in the light of the value of the gifts and the other circumstances of the case, make the donor incapable of making a valid gift. (3) The jury should have been directed that if they were satisfied that Mr Dolphin was mentally incapable of making a gift, they should not convict unless they were satisfied that what the defendant did was dishonest by the standards of ordinary decent people and that the defendant must have realised this. (4) If the Crown were making the case that the gift was invalid because of undue influence or coercion exercised by the defendant, it was necessary for the judge to give the jury a specific direction as to what would constitute undue influence or coercion. (5) The jury should have been directed that if they were satisfied that the gifts were invalid by reason of undue influence or coercion, they should not convict unless they were satisfied that what the defendant did was dishonest by the standards of ordinary decent people and that the defendant must have realised this.

The conduct of the defendant was deplorable and it may be that if the issues had been more clearly defined a jury would have been entitled to convict, but in my opinion the summing up was defective in the ways which I have described and the convictions should not stand. I consider, with respect, that the Court of Appeal erred in the present case because at [2000] 1 Cr App R 1, 7F–G it rejected the appellant's submission as to dishonesty by referring to the separate issue of appropriation.

Accordingly, for the reasons which I have stated, I would allow the appeal and quash the convictions.

Lord Hobhouse (dissenting): My Lords ... The Theft Act 1968 was passed in an attempt to simplify the law of theft and remove excessive and technical complications which arose from the concepts used in the Larceny Act 1916 and its predecessors. One source of complication had been the fact that larceny was a possession based crime and used the criteria 'takes and carries away' and 'without the consent of the owner' in the definition of stealing. The Theft Act on the other hand defines theft in a deceptively simple way ...

In order to try and limit the number of separate offences under the Act, the Theft Act, in contrast with the Larceny Act, adopts the approach of a single short definition of 'theft' and then expands that definition so that it can cover a wide range of more complex situations. Thus, sections 2 to 6 have been included in the Act to amplify and extend the meaning of the expressions used in the s.1 definition. Section 2 deals with 'dishonestly', s 3 with 'appropriates', s 4 with 'property', s 5 with 'belonging to another' and s 6 with 'with the intention of permanently depriving the other of it'. These provisions, although each given a distinct title are in their terms interlinked and implicitly cross-refer to each other. They cannot be construed or applied in isolation. Some are used to qualify the definition of theft and give it a different meaning to that which would have been understood by the simple definition standing alone. It is therefore imperative, as is specifically required by s 1(3), to have regard to these sections when construing s 1(1).

But this structure of sections 1 to 6 has had an unfortunate by-product. It has led to a practice (started by Megaw LJ in the Court of Appeal in *Lawrence*) of construing each of the words or phrases in s 1(1) as if they were independent and not part of a single complex definition. The words and phrases have an inter-relation, the one affecting the meaning of another and of the whole.

... Another point which has arisen from the general intention of the Act and its drafting is the assumption that all questions arising in connection with the law of theft should now be capable of answer without involving any concept or rule derived from the civil law or using any technical legal terminology. Whilst there can be no doubt about the general intention of the Act, to proceed from such a general intention to that assumption is simplistic and erroneous. It is, of course, part of the duty and function of the judge at the criminal trial to separate the questions of law from the questions of fact and only direct the jury on matters of law so far as the issues in the case make it necessary for them to know the law in order to decide the issues of fact and determine the defendant's guilt or innocence; but, when there are relevant questions of law, they must be recognised and the jury directed accordingly.

The truth is that theft is a crime which relates to civil property and, inevitably, property concepts from the civil law have to be used and questions answered by reference to that law ... Section 1(1) uses the expression 'belonging to another'. Thus, in some criminal cases, it may be necessary to determine whether the relevant property belonged to the alleged victim or to the defendant. In *R v Walker* [1984] Crim LR 112 the case turned upon whether the article in question had been rejected by the buyer so as to revest the title to it in the seller, the defendant. (See also *per* Bingham LJ in *Dobson v General Accident, Fire and Life Assurance Corporation plc* [1990] 1 QB 274.) This was an issue which had to be answered by reference to the civil law and about which the criminal law had nothing to say except to pose the question ...

His Lordship set out the provisions of s 5(1) to 5(4) of the 1968 Act and continued:

... Section 5 qualifies and defines the expression 'belonging to another' and specifically makes use of a number of civil law concepts. Under subsection (1) the jury may have to decide who had the possession of the article or whether someone other than the defendant had a 'proprietary right or interest' including an equitable interest (subject to the stated exception) and receive the requisite direction as to the civil law. Subsections (2) and (3) necessitate the consideration of the law of trusts and the rights of beneficiaries and the law of bailment and agency. Subsection (4) makes provision for the situation 'where a person gets property by another's mistake'. The criterion which the subsection then applies is whether or not the recipient came under an obligation to make restoration of the property (or its value or proceeds). This is a sophisticated criterion wholly dependant upon distinctions to be drawn from the civil law. Unless the criterion is satisfied this constituent of the crime of theft has not been proved.

It is relevant to look at this example further because it is an example of a person who has acquired a defeasible title. Where the transferor has made a mistake, the mistake can be so fundamental that the transferee acquires no rights at all in respect of the chattel transferred as against the transferor. But there may be cases where the mistake does not have so absolute an effect and the transferor may only have equitable rights (cf subsection (1)) or restitutionary rights against the transferee. If, however, the transferee has already had validly transferred to him the legal title to and possession of the chattel without any obligation to make restoration, a later retention of or dealing with the chattel by the transferee, whether or not 'dishonest' and whether or not it would otherwise amount to an appropriation, cannot amount to theft. However much the jury may consider that his conduct in not returning the chattel falls below the standards of ordinary and decent people, he has not committed the crime of theft. The property did not belong to another.

Section 5 and, particularly, s 5(4) demonstrate that the Theft Act has been drafted so as to take account of and require reference to the civil law of property, contract and restitution. The same applies to many other sections of the Act. For example, section 6 is drafted by reference to the phrase 'regardless of the other's rights' – that is to say rights under the civil law. Section 28, dealing with the restoration of stolen goods, clearly can only work if the law of theft recognises and respects transfers of property valid under the civil law, otherwise it would be giving the criminal courts the power to deprive citizens of their property otherwise than in accordance with the law.

Section 5 shows that the state of mind of the transferor at the time of transfer may be relevant and critical. Similarly, the degree of the transferee's knowledge will be relevant to the s 5 question quite independently of any question under s 2. For instance, where there has been a mistake on the part of the transferor, the position under s 5(4) can be different depending on whether or not the transferee was aware of the mistake.

Further, it will be appreciated that the situations to which s 5 is relevant can embrace gifts as well as other transactions such as transfers for value. The prosecution must be able to prove that, at the time of the alleged appropriation, the relevant property belonged to another within the meaning given to that phrase by s 5. Where the defendant has been validly given the property he can no longer appropriate property belonging to another. The Court of Appeal does not seem to have had their attention directed to s 5. The question certified on the grant of leave to appeal is self-contradictory. The direction of the trial judge approved by the Court of Appeal is inadequate. There is no law against appropriating your own property as defined by s 5.

... Section 2(1), rather than expanding the s 1(1) definition, limits it. It illustrates the point made by Lord Browne-Wilkinson as to the inter-relation of the words 'dishonestly' and 'appropriates' used in s 1(1). (It does however raise difficulties for the later steps in his reasoning to which I will have to revert.) [Having recited the provisions of s 2(1)(a) to (c), he continued:]

Although s 2 is headed 'Dishonestly', this quotation shows that it is as much involved with the application of the concepts 'appropriation' and 'property belonging to another'. (a) contemplates that the defendant believes that he has the right to appropriate the property and (b) his belief that he would have the consent of the person to whom the property belongs to appropriate it. If belief in such a right or such consent can prevent the defendant's conduct from amounting to theft (whatever the jury may think of it), how can it be said that his knowledge that he has such a right or the actual consent of the person to whom the property belongs is irrelevant? How can it be said that the right of the defendant to accept a gift is irrelevant – or the fact that the transferor has actually and validly consented to the defendant having the relevant property? Yet it is precisely these things which the judgment of the Court of Appeal would wholly exclude.

Section 2(1) is cutting down the classes of conduct which the jury are at liberty to treat as dishonest. They qualify the *Ghosh* approach and show that in any given case the court must consider whether it is adequate to give an unqualified *Ghosh* direction as the Court of Appeal held to be sufficient in the present case.

... The discussion in the present case has been marked by a failure to consider the law of gift. Perhaps most remarkable is the statement of the Court of Appeal that 'a gift may be clear evidence of appropriation'. The making of a gift is the act of the donor. It involves the donor in forming the intention to give and then acting on that intention by doing whatever it is necessary for him to do to transfer the relevant property to the donee. Where the gift is the gift of a chattel, the act required to complete the gift will normally be either delivery to the donee or to a person who is to hold the chattel as the bailee of the donee; money can be transferred by having it credited to the donee's bank account – and so on. Unless the gift was conditional, in which case the condition must be satisfied before the gift can take effect, the making of the gift is complete once the donor has carried out this step. The gift has become the property of the donee. It is not necessary for the donee to know of the gift. The donee, on becoming aware of the gift, has the right to refuse (or reject) the gift in which case it revests in the donor with resolutive effect. (See *Halsbury's Laws: Gifts*, Vol 20, paras 48–49 and the cases cited.)

What consequences does this have for the law of theft? Once the donor has done his part in transferring the property to the defendant, the property, subject to the special situations identified in the subsections of s 5, ceases to be 'property belonging to another'. However wide a meaning one were to give to 'appropriates', there cannot be a theft. For it to be possible for there to be a theft there will have to be something more, like an absence of a capacity to give or a mistake satisfying s 5(4). Similarly, where the donee himself performs the act necessary to transfer the property to himself, as he would if he himself took the chattel out of the possession of the donor or, himself, gave the instructions to the donor's bank, s 5(1) would apply and mean that that constituent of the crime of theft would at that time have been satisfied.

If one treats the 'acceptance' of the gift as an appropriation, and this was the approach of the judge and is implicit in the judgment of the Court of Appeal (despite their choice of words), there are immediate difficulties with s 2(1)(a). The defendant did have the right to deprive the donor of the property. The donor did consent to the appropriation; indeed, he intended it. There are also difficulties with s 6 as she was not acting regardless of the donor's rights; the donor has already surrendered his rights. The only way that these conclusions can be displaced is by showing that the gift was not valid. There are even difficulties with s 3 itself. The donee is not 'assuming the rights of an owner': she has them already.

His Lordship set out the terms of s 3(1) and 3(2) of the Theft Act 1968 and continued:

... This is the shortest of the explanatory sections. Its purpose is undoubtedly to get away from some of the technicalities of the law of larceny which arose from the need for the defendant to have taken the property. It uses a different concept which does not require an acquisition of possession. The concept is any assumption of the rights of an owner (which has been held to mean 'the assumption of any of the rights of an owner': *R v Morris*). The second part of subsection (1) clearly has to be read with s 5.

Subsection (2) deals with the purchase for value of a defective title and provides a further illustration of two of the points I have already made. It is drafted by reference to the position under civil law. It cross-refers to factors which are primarily relevant to honesty – 'good faith' and what the defendant 'believed' he had acquired – so demonstrating again the intimate inter-relationship of the drafting of one section with another and with the definition in s 1(1) as a whole.

Section 3 does not use any qualitative expression such as 'misappropriates' nor does it repeat the Larceny Act expression 'without the consent of the owner'. It has thus been read by some as if 'appropriates' was a wholly colourless expression. This reading declines to draw any guidance from the context in which the word is used in the definition in s 1(1) and the scheme of sections 2 to 6. It also declines to attach any significance to the use of the word 'assumption'. This led some curious submissions being made to your Lordships.

It was for example suggested that the garage repair mechanic employed to change the oil of a car would have appropriated the car. The reasoning is that only the owner has the right to do this or tell someone to do it therefore to do it is to assume the rights of the owner. This is an absurdity even when one takes into account that some of the absurd results can be avoided by other parts of the definition of theft.

The mechanic is not assuming any right he is merely carrying out the instructions of the owner. The person who accepts a valid gift is simply conforming to the wishes of the owner. The words 'appropriate' [property belonging to another] and 'assume' [the rights of that other] have a useful breadth of meaning but each of them in its natural meaning includes an element of doing something which displaces the rights of that other person. The rights of that other [the owner] include the right to authorise another [the defendant] to do things which would otherwise be an infringement of the rights of the owner.

For the sake of completeness, I should mention that it is not necessary for the present appeal to consider the questions of timing that may arise in relation to appropriation. A carrier may receive goods of which he intends to deprive the owner at a convenient moment. (*R v Skipp* [1975] Crim LR 114, *R v Fritschy* [1985] Crim LR 745.) If goods are entrusted to the defendant for one purpose and he takes possession of them for another, it may well be that he has then and there appropriated them since he is thereby assuming the rights of an owner not those of a bailee. This also helps with understanding the supermarket cases. Putting back an article which has been lifted off the shelf in order to read the label or packet does not without more assume any right of ownership. Nor does taking the article to the check-out in order to offer to buy it; that is merely to comply with an implicit request by the owner (the supermarket). On the other hand to interfere with the price label or to take the article with the purpose of smuggling it out of the shop without paying is an assumption of the rights of an owner. (*R v Morris*.)

The considerations which I have discussed now at some length all lead to the conclusion that sections 1 to 6 of the Theft Act should be read as a cohesive whole and that to attempt to isolate and compartmentalise each element only leads to contradictions. This vice is particularly clear where alleged gifts are involved. In such a situation greater care in the analysis is required under sections 2, 3 and 5 and it will normally be necessary to direct the jury in fuller terms and not merely ask them if they think that the defendant fell below the standards of an ordinary and decent person and realised that such persons would so regard his conduct.

... The appellant has submitted that your Lordships should, if needs be, overrule *R v Lawrence* ... and *R v Gomez* ... I do not consider that either case should be overruled nor is it necessary for the decision of the present case. Neither is inconsistent with my analysis of the law. What appears to have happened is that some of the language used in the three successive House of Lords decisions (*Lawrence, Morris, Gomez*) has been misread without sufficient regard to the context in which the language in each case was used and without a constructive consideration of the intent of sections 1 to 6 as a whole ... The situation in Lawrence is not problematical. The whole transaction was driven and coloured by the taxidriver's fraud. It does not strain the language to describe what happened as an appropriation of property belonging to another. It was never a case of consent except possibly in a technical Larceny Act sense. The damaging legacy of the Lawrence judgment has been the adoption of the fragmented approach and the separation of the statement that consent was not relevant to appropriation from its context and from the accompanying statement that knowledge of actual consent is incompatible with dishonesty.

The second question was answered by saying that sections 1 and 15 were not mutually exclusive. This of itself should not have caused any further difficulty once an authoritative decision had been given. But a reluctance to leave behind the features of the law of larceny has meant that the inter-relation of those sections has been a recurring sub-plot in the decisions subsequent to *Lawrence*.

... [I]n *Gomez* ... the certified question ... starts from the premise that there has been overt and directly relevant dishonesty and that the acquisition comes squarely within s 5(4) and (1). The significance of the argument would again seem to be to whether s 1 or s 15 was the relevant section, a point which had already been disposed of by *Lawrence*. The question also asked, puzzlingly in view of the premise, but obviously directed at Lord Roskill's choice of words: 'Must such a passing of property necessarily involve an element of adverse [interference] with or usurpation of some right of the owner?' It might be thought that to obtain possession of another's goods by fraudulently causing him to allow you to do so would be a clear case of an adverse interference with his rights.

It was in this connection that Lord Keith of Kinkel said, at p 460:

> While it is correct to say that appropriation for purposes of s 3(1) includes [an unauthorised interference], it does not necessarily follow that no other act can amount to an appropriation and in particular that no act expressly or impliedly authorised by the owner can *in any circumstances* do so. Indeed *R v Lawrence* is a clear decision to the contrary since it laid down unequivocally that an act may be an appropriation notwithstanding that it is done with the consent of the owner. It does not appear to me that any sensible distinction can be made in this context between consent and authorisation.' (My emphasis.)

... The decision of the House in *Gomez* set a new agenda. Instead of discussing what had been decided in *Morris*, the discussion now centred upon what had been decided in *Gomez*. It is to be hoped that the present appeal to your Lordships' House will not again have such an unproductive outcome, a consequence which I believe will be inevitable if this appeal is not allowed and a return made to construing sections 1 to 6 as a coherent whole.

... In *R v Mazo* [1997] 2 Cr App R 518, the defendant had worked as the maid of an 89 year old lady. The defendant received from the old lady a series of cheques and some valuables which the defendant said were gifts but the prosecution alleged she had stolen. She was convicted of theft. There had been evidence at the trial that the old lady was not mentally competent to make such gifts and that the defendant must have realised this. However, in his summing-up the trial judge directed the jury saying:

> If you are sure, first of all, that Lady S gave these cheques and the other items as a result of her reduced mental state; secondly, if you are sure that the defendant, Miss M, knew that but for that mental state those gifts would not have been made and, finally, if you are sure that by acting as she did in accepting them with that knowledge she was acting dishonestly, then in those circumstances you would be entitled to convict her.

On her appeal against her convictions, the defendant submitted that the judge had failed to deal with her defence that she had received valid gifts which she was entitled to accept: had valid gifts been made by a donor competent to make them? The Court of Appeal allowed her appeal. Pill LJ giving the judgment of the court said, at p 521:

It is clear that a transaction may be a theft for the purpose of s 1(1) notwithstanding that it was done with the owner's consent if it was induced by fraud, deception or a false representation: see *Gomez*. It is also common ground that the receiver of a valid gift, *inter vivos*, could not be the subject of a conviction for theft. In *Gomez* reference was made to the speech of Viscount Dilhorne in *Lawrence*. In the course of his speech with which the other members of the House agreed Lord Dilhorne stated [p 632]: '*A fortiori*, a person is not to be regarded as acting dishonestly if he appropriates another's property believing that, with full knowledge of the circumstances, that other person has in fact agreed to the appropriation.' It is implicit in that statement that if in all the circumstances, there is held to be a valid gift there can be no theft.

Later in the judgment Pill LJ referred to the criteria for deciding whether such a gift was valid as explained in *In re Beaney* [1978] 1 WLR 770, having regard to lack of comprehension and mental incapacity. He concluded, at p 523 with the timely warning that the summing-up created

a danger that the jury would take a view that the appellant's conduct was not of a moral quality of which they could approve and convict her on that ground rather than on the true basis of the law of theft.

In my judgment, my Lords, the explanation of the law in the judgment in *Mazo* is correct and accurately reflects the scheme and purpose of sections 1 to 6 of the Theft Act and demonstrates a correct understanding of the speech of Lord Keith in *Gomez*.

Mazo was distinguished and not followed in *R v Kendrick and Hopkins* [1997] 2 Cr App R 524. There a residential home where a nearly blind 99 year old lady was living took control of her affairs. They were given a power of attorney. They liquidated her assets and paid the proceeds into an account which they controlled. They drew out large sums, they said implausibly, with her consent and for her benefit. The defendants were charged with conspiracy to steal and convicted. On the basis of *Mazo*, the summing-up was criticised as not going sufficiently deeply into the question of validity. These criticisms were rightly rejected; the summing-up was not deficient. The appeal was dismissed.

However, the Court of Appeal also criticised the judgment in *Mazo* as not reflecting what was said in *Gomez* particularly by Lord Browne-Wilkinson: the concept of appropriation was distinct from the concept of dishonesty; appropriation could be looked at 'in isolation'; other factors, including the incapacity of the donor and fraud only came in in relation to dishonesty; a simple *Ghosh* direction sufficed.

The Court of Appeal in the present case preferred to follow the judgment in Kendrick and Hopkins rather than that in *Mazo*. There was probably no conflict between the actual decisions in the two cases. The Court of Appeal in *Kendrick* and Hopkins were justified in dismissing the appeal and, on an overall assessment, rejecting the criticisms of the summing up in that case and upholding the safety of the convictions. They were in error in their adoption of Lord Browne-Wilkinson's view that appropriation should be looked at in isolation.

... The question certified [in the present case] demonstrates the further step which your Lordships are being asked to take beyond that involved in answering the question in *Gomez*. Does the primary question in *Gomez* receive the same answer if one deletes the words 'obtained by false representation'? The Court of Appeal in the present case held that it should. Two strands of reasoning led them to this conclusion. The first was that s 3(1) should be construed in isolation from the remainder of sections 1 to 6. In this they followed the lead given by Lord Browne-Wilkinson and the Court of Appeal judgment in *Kendrick* and *Hopkins*. I have already explained why I consider that this is wrong.

The second was the view that Lord Keith and Parker LJ had ruled that consent of the owner is always wholly irrelevant to what acts amount to appropriation. They achieved this position only by standing on its head what Lord Keith and Parker LJ had said. What Lord Keith and Parker LJ confirmed was that 'consent' (in the Larceny Act sense) will not necessarily negative appropriation. What Rose LJ has derived from this is that consent can never negative appropriation. (The incomplete quotation by Rose LJ at [2000] 1 Cr App R 1, 8 from Parker LJ is revealing.) This leads Rose LJ directly to the position that a valid gift is fully consistent with theft, a proposition which is seriously inconsistent with the scheme of sections 1 to 6 and with other parts of the Act and which is not a proposition to be derived from any of the House of Lords decisions (with the possible exception of the speech of Lord Browne-Wilkinson in *Gomez*).

To say, as does Rose LJ at p 10, that 'civil unlawfulness is not a constituent of the offence of theft' is of course true. That expression does not occur in s 1(1) and it is anyway not clear what it encompasses. But to proceed from there to the proposition that the civil law of property is irrelevant is, as I have explained earlier in this speech, a far greater error.

My Lords, if, contrary to my view, your Lordships are to travel down the route adopted by the Court of Appeal, your Lordships are faced with a choice between two options neither of which are consistent with dismissing this appeal. One option is to accept the 'Browne-Wilkinson' approach and adopt a sanitised concept of appropriation isolated from any context of or interdependence with the other parts of the definition and sections 1–6 (particularly sections 2 and 5) and then make the necessary qualifications of the concept of dishonesty when the factual issues raised by an individual case require it. The other is to revert to the law as stated by the majority in *Gomez* and by Viscount Dilhorne and, so far as still relevant, by your Lordships' House in *Morris*, and correctly understood by the Court of Appeal in *Mazo*. It is not an option to do neither as happened in the present case. The unqualified *Ghosh* approach cannot survive in conjunction with the 'Browne-Wilkinson' approach.

In my judgment the correct answer is that adopted by Pill LJ but if your Lordships are of a different opinion the least that should be done is to draw attention to and confirm the provisions of sections 2 and 5 and their implications for cases where the issue raised is whether the property alleged to have been stolen was transferred to the defendant as a gift. What must be erroneous is to treat as 'belonging to another' property which at the time of the alleged appropriation belongs to the defendant in accordance with s 5(4). Similarly it must be wrong to treat as a dishonest 'appropriation of property belonging to another' under s 2(1) an appropriation for which the defendant correctly knows (as opposed to mistakenly believes) he actually had (as opposed to would have had) the other's consent, the other knowing of the appropriation and the circumstances of it (as opposed to the other person only hypothetically having that knowledge).

My Lords, the relevant law is contained in sections 1 to 6 of the Act. They should be construed as a whole and applied in a manner which presents a consistent scheme both internally and with the remainder of the Act. The phrase 'dishonestly appropriates' should be construed as a composite phrase. It does not include acts done in relation to the relevant property which are done in accordance with the actual wishes or actual authority of the person to whom the property belongs. This is because such acts do not involve any assumption of the rights of that person within s 3(1) or because, by necessary implication from s 2(1), they are not to be regarded as dishonest appropriations of property belonging to another.

Actual authority, wishes, consent (or similar words) mean, both as a matter of language and on the authority of the three House of Lords cases, authorisation not obtained by fraud or misrepresentation. The definition of theft therefore embraces cases where the property has come to the defendant by the mistake of the person to whom it belongs and there would be an obligation to restore it – s 5(4) – or property in which the other still has an equitable proprietary interest – s 5(1). This would also embrace property obtained by undue influence or other cases coming within the classes of invalid transfer recognised in *Re Beaney*.

In cases of alleged gift, the criteria to be applied are the same. But additional care may need to be taken to see that the transaction is properly explained to the jury. It is unlikely that a charge of theft will be brought where there is not clear evidence of at least some conduct of the defendant which includes an element of fraud or overt dishonesty or some undue influence or knowledge of the deficient capacity of the alleged donor. This was the basis upon which the prosecution of the appellant was originally brought in the present case. On this basis there is no difficulty in explaining to the jury the relevant parts of s 5 and s 2(1) and the effect of the phrase 'assumption of the rights of an owner'. Where the basis is less specific and the possibility is that there may have been a valid gift of the relevant article or money to the defendant, the analysis of the prosecution case will break down under sections 2 and 5 as well as s 3 and it will not suffice simply to invite the jury to convict on the basis of their disapprobation of the defendant's conduct and their attribution to him of the knowledge that he must have known that they and other ordinary and decent persons would think it dishonest. Theft is a crime of dishonesty but dishonesty is not the only element in the commission of the crime. I would answer the certified question in the negative. But, in any event, I would allow the appeal and quash the conviction because the summing-up failed to direct the jury adequately upon the other essential elements of theft, not just appropriation.

Cheques – where does appropriation of the funds occur?

Chan Man-Sin v R [1988] 1 WLR 196 (PC)

Facts: This was an appeal from a decision of the Court of Appeal of Hong Kong. The defendant was the accountant for two companies. By means of ten forged cheques he withdrew money from the companies' bank accounts and caused it to be deposited in his personal account or the account of a business of which he was the sole proprietor. The companies' banks debited their accounts, which were overdrawn but not by an amount which exceeded agreed overdraft limits. The defendant was charged (under Hong Kong legislation identical to the Theft Act 1968) with theft of choses in action, namely debts owed by the bank to the companies.

Lord Oliver of Aylmerton: ... It is not disputed that the debt due to the customer from his banker is a chose in action capable of being stolen and this equally applies to the sum which a customer is entitled to overdraw under contractual arrangements which he has made with the bank (see *R v Kohn* (1979) 69 Cr App R 395), though strictly in the latter case the chose in action is the benefit of the contractual arrangement with the bank. What is argued, however, is that, since as between the customer and the bank an unauthorised debit entry in the customer's account is a mere nullity, the customer is deprived of nothing and therefore there has been no appropriation. Equally, it is said that, since the customer whose property is alleged to have been stolen has not in fact been deprived of anything, there cannot have been an intention permanently to deprive him of the property. Thus, it is argued, there were lacking two essential ingredients of the offences with which the defendant was charged and he was entitled to an acquittal.

Their Lordships can deal very briefly with the second submission. The defendant did not elect to give evidence and if there was, as the prosecution contended, an appropriation of the companies' property, there was ample evidence from which the intention permanently to deprive them of it could be inferred. Even if it were possible to infer or assume that the defendant contemplated that the fraud would be discovered and appreciated also that his employers would or might challenge the bank's entitlement to payment of the sums debited, he would fall within [the statutory definition of having an intention permanently to deprive the owner of the property].

Quite clearly here the defendant was purporting to deal with the companies' property without regard to their rights.

Reverting to the defendant's principal ground of appeal, this has an appealing simplicity. The defendant's difficulty, however, is that it entirely ignores the artificial definition of appropriation which is contained in ... s 3(1) [above] of the Act of 1968.

The owner of the chose in action consisting of a credit with his bank or a contractual right to draw on an account has, clearly, the right as owner to draw by means of a properly completed negotiable instrument or order to pay and it is, in their Lordships' view, beyond argument that one who draws, presents and negotiates a cheque on a particular bank account is assuming the rights of the owner of the credit in the account or (as the case may be) of the prenegotiated right to draw on the account up to the agreed figure. Ownership, of course, consists of a bundle of rights and it may well be that there are other rights which an owner could exert over the chose in action in question which are not trespassed on by the particular dealing which the thief chooses to assume. In *R v Morris* ... however, the House of Lords decisively rejected a submission that it was necessary, in order to constitute an appropriation as defined by s 3(1) of the Act of 1968, to demonstrate an assumption by the accused of all the rights of an owner.

Their Lordships are accordingly entirely satisfied that the transactions initiated and carried through by the defendant constituted an assumption of the rights of the owner and, consequently, an appropriation. It is unnecessary, for present purposes, to determine whether that occurred on presentation of the forged cheques or when the transactions were completed by the making of consequential entries in the bank accounts of the companies and the defendant or his business respectively. It is, in their Lordships' view, entirely immaterial that the end result of the transaction may be a legal nullity for it is not possible to read into [s 3(1) of the 1968 Act] any requirement that the assumption of rights there envisaged should have a legally efficacious result ...

R v Ngan [1998] 1 Cr App R 331 (CA)

The appellant's bank account (held with Barclays Bank) was wrongly credited with funds that should have been credited to an account belonging to [FCA], a debt collection agency. The appellant signed a number of blank cheques and sent them to a relative in Scotland. In due course the balance of the appellant's account was reduced when the cheques were presented for payment, two in Scotland and one in England. The Court of Appeal was asked to consider whether there had been an appropriation within the jurisdiction.

Leggatt LJ: ... The reason that the judge gave for concluding that the appropriation took place in this country was ... wrong. That is clear from the case of *Governor of Pentonville Prison ex p Osman* [1990] 1 WLR 277 in which the Divisional Court held that when a telex instruction to make payment to a bank in the United States was sent by the defendant without authority from Hong Kong to New York, the appropriation took place in Hong Kong. It was held that the appropriation of the chose in action was complete the moment the telex message was sent from Hong Kong to the bank in the United States. It would not have made any difference if the account at the paying bank had never been debited. The judge's finding in the present case that the theft occurred within the jurisdiction because the account, the chose in action and the paying bank were all situated in England, is therefore wrong.

On each of the three counts the appellant was charged with stealing a chose in action, namely a credit balance belonging to FCA. The credit balance in question was in the defendant's account. On the face of it, therefore, it constituted a debt due from Barclays Bank plc ('the Bank') to her. [His Lordship referred to the terms of s 5(4) of the Theft Act 1968 and continued] ...

The debt due from the Bank was a chose in action. By virtue of s 4(1) of the Act that chose in action was property. The defendant got the property mistakenly, and was under an obligation to restore its value to the Bank: *AG's Ref (No 1 of 1983)* [1985] QB 182. So most of the defendant's credit balance is to be regarded as belonging to FCA. Since it cannot be disputed that the defendant acted dishonestly, it is common ground that the defendant was guilty of theft if the offence was committed within the jurisdiction ...

In *Osman* the Divisional Court held that appropriation occurs when a cheque is presented. We agree; but it does not follow that it cannot occur earlier. The Crown argued that at the latest when the appellant sent the blank cheques drawn on her account to her sister with the dishonest intention of enabling her to withdraw all or part of the sums mistakenly credited to the appellant's account, she was dealing with the property as owner. In one sense the very act of signing each cheque might be regarded as an assumption of a right. But it must be remembered that the right assumed is not to the cheque, but to the property or chose in action, that is, to the debt mistakenly due from the Bank. 'Keeping' as owner in relation to a bank account may be difficult to prove in a case where a defendant does no more than refrain from bringing the mistake to the attention of the Bank. There can be no obligation to restore the credit but only the 'value' of it, that is, an equivalent amount. But 'keeping' or 'dealing' is unequivocally demonstrated when upon presentation an account holder treats the credit as his own.

When the appellant sent the cheques in blank to her sister, it may be said that she intended to appropriate such sums as her sister proved to insert into any of the cheques that she used. But any such appropriation was inchoate ... because until on each occasion a cheque was presented for payment, there was no dealing with any of FCA's rights to the balance mistakenly standing to the credit of the appellant. Her acts of signing the cheques and sending them to her sister were preparatory acts, and more needed to be done by or on behalf of the appellant before FCA could be deprived of their property. The appellant's acts were remote from FCA and any rights of theirs, and none but a lawyer would think of calling them theft.

In our judgment no right was assumed to the part of the appellant's credit balance that was not hers until a cheque was presented for payment in a sum which necessarily drew upon the mistaken credit balance. That represented the assertion of a right adverse to FCA to have the cheque met by the Bank. The result is that on the two occasions that a cheque was presented in Scotland no offence was committed within the jurisdiction of this court, but an offence was committed when the third cheque was presented in Peterborough ...

How many times can D appropriate the same property?

Where a 'thief' does several acts in respect of a particular item, are the acts of appropriation a continuing process which is complete only when the final act has been done, or can an item be appropriated on more than one occasion? On what basis should the prosecution point to the exact moment when the goods are stolen. In most cases this will not matter (since the jury or magistrates will only have to consider whether the goods were stolen by the defendant on a particular date: the exact time of the appropriation does not matter). However, uncertainty over when the theft is complete creates a particular problem with the regard to the offence of handling stolen goods (s 22 of the Theft Act 1968 – see Chapter 22), since this offence cannot be committed until the goods have been 'stolen'. In *R v Atakpu* [1994] QB 69 the Court of Appeal gave some guidance on when the appropriation takes place.

R v Atakpu and Abrahams [1994] QB 69 (CA)

Ward J: ... The facts of [the appellants'] disreputable endeavour can be quite shortly stated. The prosecution satisfied the jury that these appellants embarked on a simple but audacious scheme to hire expensive motor cars abroad, have them driven into the United Kingdom but then, after ringing the changes to the vehicles, to sell them on to unsuspecting purchasers. Their first step was to create false identities for themselves. That they did by prevailing on a co-accused, Brian

Saunders, to apply for British visitor's passports on 12 July 1990, one from a post office in Maida Vale in the false name of Pearce, which was the identity assumed by Abrahams, and the other from a post office at Swiss Cottage in the name of Green, which was the identity assumed by Atakpu. They also procured false driving licences in the names of Pearce and Green ...

On the same day, 12 July 1990, Thomas Cook's travel agency close to the Swiss Cottage post office arranged, at the request of a man named Green, for a luxury motor car to be hired from 'downtown Frankfurt' and the appropriate vouchers were issued. On the same day at Gatwick Airport two return air tickets to Frankfurt were issued in the names of Pearce and Green for an outward flight on the following day and the package included the hiring of two more luxury motor cars to be collected at Frankfurt Airport.

The mythical Messrs Pearce and Green duly flew to Frankfurt on 13 July. At about 8.35 am on 14 July a Mr Green hired a Mercedes 300SE motor car from the Hertz city office, or the so-called 'downtown' office, and at about 8.58 am Hertz at Frankfurt Airport hired a Mercedes 190E to a black man giving the name Pearce. Later that morning that office hired a BMW automatic to an African man whose identity was established by the production of a British visitor's passport in the name of Green, a copy of which passport was kept by Hertz. The prosecution contended, without doubt correctly, that the photograph was one of Atakpu.

It would seem that the Mercedes 300SE was then driven to Brussels but broke down in Belgium and was replaced with a BMW by the Brussels office of Hertz. From there the appellants drove to Ghent where they recruited their co-defendant, de Ligne, to go back with them to Frankfurt to collect the two cars still parked in Frankfurt. On the way they were stopped for speeding and Atakpu, otherwise known as Green, produced his passport and paid an immediate fine. The two cars were duly collected from Frankfurt and the convoy of three returned to Ghent where they recruited the co-defendant, Miss Englen. De Ligne drove the replacement BMW to Ostende, boarded the ferry to Dover, left the car in Dover and returned to Ostende. The co-defendant then collected the remaining two vehicles and boarded the Dover ferry. The four defendants shared a cabin and arrived at Dover in the early hours of 16 July. The appellants left the ferry as foot passengers. Englen drove the Mercedes 190E and de Ligne the BMW into the customs shed but were stopped by customs officers. Their suspicions were aroused by finding four boarding cards with consecutive numbers in Englen's car. De Ligne also aroused suspicion. It was not long before the appellants were arrested. In their possession were excess travel tickets issued by British Rail for the journey between Victoria and Gatwick during the late afternoon of 13 July, the airline tickets and boarding cards, torn British visitor's passports, driving licences and the hire documentation all variously bearing the names of Pearce and Green. Atakpu had in his possession the keys to the BMW which had been left in Dover. It was recovered from the car park. The period of hire of the two vehicles taken in Frankfurt would have expired within a matter of hours and the Brussels BMW not long thereafter ...

We begin by recording that it was common ground that (1) the appellants would only be guilty if they had agreed that a course of conduct should be pursued which, if the agreement had been carried out in accordance with their intentions, necessarily amounted to or involved the commission of an offence which was triable in England and Wales: see *Board of Trade v Owen* [1957] AC 602 and s 1 of the Criminal Law Act 1977, as amended by s 5 of the Criminal Attempts Act 1981; (2) a theft committed abroad is not triable in England and Wales.

Accordingly, the question in this appeal now boils down simply to where the theft of these motor cars was committed – in Germany/Belgium or in England ...

So interesting questions arise in this appeal as to (1) whether the theft committed abroad continued within the jurisdiction so that it could be established here by the retention of the car after the hire period had expired, or by ringing the changes or by some other fresh appropriation; (2) whether cars stolen abroad could be stolen again, and again and again, within the jurisdiction each time an appropriation of them is made.

His Lordship reviewed a number of authorities and continued:

[I]t would seem that: (1) theft can occur in an instant by a single appropriation but it can also involve a course of dealing with property lasting longer and involving several appropriations before the transaction is complete; (2) theft is a finite act – it has a beginning and it has an end; (3) at what point the transaction is complete is a matter for the jury to decide upon the facts of each case; (4) though there may be several appropriations in the course of a single theft or several appropriations of different goods each constituting a separate theft ... no case suggests that there can be successive thefts of the same property (assuming of course that possession is constant and not lost or abandoned, later to be assumed again).

Can these conclusions stand in the light of *R v Gomez* [1993] AC 442? Whilst we see the logic of the argument that if there are several appropriations each one can constitute a separate theft, we flinch from reaching that conclusion.

His Lordship then approved the following passage by Professor Glanville Williams in [1978] Crim LR 69:

A man steals a watch, and two weeks later sells it. In common sense and ordinary language he is not guilty of a second theft when he sells it. Otherwise it would be possible, in theory, to convict a thief of theft of a silver teapot every time he uses it to make tea.

His Lordship then quoted s 3(1) of the Theft Act 1968, above and continued:

If, therefore, he has come by the property by stealing it then his later dealing with the property is by implication not included among the assumptions of the rights of an owner which amount to an appropriation within the meaning of s 3(1). We reject the speculation that he would not have come by the property by stealing it if an indictment for the theft would not lie because the theft occurred abroad. There is no reason to restrict the plain ordinary words of s 3(1) in such a narrow legalistic way. We note that one is guilty of handling stolen property under s 24 and the provisions of the Act apply whether the stealing occurred in England or Wales or elsewhere. 'Stealing' must have the same meaning in s 3(1) as it has in s 24. In our judgment, if goods have once been stolen, even if stolen abroad, they cannot be stolen again by the same thief exercising the same or other rights of ownership over the property.

We find it more difficult to answer the first question we posed as to whether or not theft is a continuous offence. On a strict reading of *R v Gomez* [1993] AC 442 any dishonest assumption of the rights of the owner made with the necessary intention constitutes theft and that leaves little room for a continuous course of action.

We would not wish that to be the law. Such restriction and rigidity may lead to technical anomalies and injustice. We would prefer to leave it for the common sense of the jury to decide that the appropriation can continue for so long as the thief can sensibly be regarded as in the act of stealing or, in more understandable words, so long as he is 'on the job' ... Since the matter is not strictly necessary for our decision we ... will leave it open for further argument. It is not necessary for us to decide because no jury properly directed could reasonably arrive at a conclusion that the theft of these motor cars was still continuing days after the appellants had first taken them. If the jury had been asked when and where these motor cars were stolen they could only have answered that they were stolen in Frankfurt or Brussels. The theft was complete abroad and the thieves could not steal again in England. For these reasons the appeal must be allowed ...

Appropriation of property acquired innocently

Section 3(1) of the Theft Act 1968 provides that where a person comes by property (whether innocently or not) and later assumes the rights of the owner of that property, that subsequent assumption of the rights of the owner is an appropriation.

Purchaser in good faith of stolen goods

Section 3(2) of the Theft Act 1968 provides that where a person assumes the rights of the owner of goods because he has purchased them, for money or money's worth, in good faith, that assumption of rights is not to be regarded as an appropriation. The relevant time when the purchaser must be acting in good faith is the moment when he purchases the goods.

R v Adams [1993] Crim LR 72 (CA)

Facts: The appellant was a motor cycle enthusiast with a garage full of parts. Stolen motor cycle parts were sold to him for £350, for which he issued a proper receipt with his true name and address. He was told that they represented a 'write-off' from an accident. He did not notice that the engine number had been drilled out and did not suspect that the parts were stolen until two or three days after receiving them. He was acquitted of handling but convicted of theft.

Held, allowing the appeal: Section 3(2) of the Theft Act 1968 provides that where a person has received property for value in good faith, no later assumption by him of rights which he believed himself to be acquiring would, by reason of a defect in title, amount to theft. The Crown had submitted that the words 'which he believed himself to be acquiring' related to the moment not when he purchased in good faith but when he appropriated the property by deciding to keep it as his own or selling it on. The court was of the view that the relevant moment was when the receiver purchased for value.

Property belonging to another

Section 5 of the Theft Act 1968: 'belonging to another'

(1) Property shall be regarded as belonging to any person having possession or control of it, or having in it any proprietary right or interest (not being an equitable interest arising only from an agreement to transfer or grant an interest).

(2) Where property is subject to a trust, the persons to whom it belongs shall be regarded as including any person having a right to enforce the trust, and an intention to defeat the trust shall be regarded accordingly as an intention to deprive of the property any person having that right.

(3) Where a person receives property from or on account of another, and is under an obligation to the other to retain and deal with that property or its proceeds in a particular way, the property or proceeds shall be regarded (as against him) as belongings to the other.

(4) Where a person gets property by another's mistake, and is under an obligation to make restoration (in whole or in part) of the property or its proceeds or of the value thereof, then to the extent of that obligation the property or proceeds shall be regarded (as against him) as belonging to the person entitled to restoration, and an intention not to make restoration shall be regarded accordingly as an intention to deprive that person of the property or proceeds.

(5) Property of a corporation sole shall be regarded as belonging to the corporation notwithstanding a vacancy in the corporation.

Possession and control

R v Turner (No 2) [1971] 1 WLR 901 (CA)

Lord Parker CJ: ... The defendant was at the material time living in Seymour Road, East Ham, with a Miss Nelson and their children. Three miles away a man called Arthur Edwin Brown ran a garage in Carlyle Road, Manor Park. There is no doubt that at some time prior to 7 March 1969, the defendant took a Sceptre car of which he was the registered owner to Mr Brown's garage for repairs. It was Mr Brown's case that he did those repairs, that as he was short of space he left the car in Carlyle Road some 10 to 20 yards from the garage. The ignition key had been handed to him by the defendant, and this he retained on the keyboard in his office. According to Mr Brown, on 7 March 1969, the defendant called at the garage and asked if the car was ready. On being told that it was except that it might require to be tuned, the defendant said that he would return on the next day, Saturday 8 March, and would pay Mr Brown for the repairs and pick up the car. A few hours later, however, Mr Brown found that the Sceptre car had gone; moreover whoever had taken it had a key, because the key that Mr Brown had was still on the keyboard. He reported the matter to the police.

Apparently night after night thereafter until 16 March Mr Brown, according to him, went round the neighbouring streets to see if he could find the car, and sure enough on Sunday 16 March, he found it parked in a street near the defendant's flat. It was, moreover, his evidence that he did not know the defendant's full name or his address and only knew of him as Frank.

What Mr Brown then did was to take the car back to his garage, to take out the engine and then tow it back less the engine to the place from which he had taken it. Meanwhile, the police made enquiries of the defendant and there is no doubt in the light of what happened afterwards that he, the defendant, told lie after lie to the police. He said that Mr Brown had never had his Sceptre car at all, that the car had never been to the garage, and that the only work that Mr Brown had done was to a Zephyr car on an earlier occasion. However, a time came when he abandoned those denials and agreed that he had taken the car to the garage, and that he had taken it away and had never paid for it. In saying that, however, he emphasised that he had taken it away with the consent of Mr Brown. It was on those short facts that the jury ... found the defendant guilty of the theft of his own car ...

His Lordship quoted s 5(1) of the Theft Act 1968 and went on:

The sole question was whether Mr Brown had possession or control.

This court is quite satisfied that there is no ground whatever for qualifying the words 'possession or control' in any way. It is sufficient if it is found that the person from whom the property is taken, or to use the words of the Act, appropriated, was at the time in fact in possession or control ... The only question was whether Mr Brown was in fact in possession or control ...

His Lordship then turned to the question of dishonesty and said:

The whole test of dishonesty is the mental element of belief. No doubt, although the defendant may for certain purposes be presumed to know the law, he would not at the time have the vaguest idea whether he did have in law a right to take the car back again, and accordingly when one looks at his mental state, one looks at it in the light of what he believed. The jury were properly told that if he believed that he had a right, albeit there was none, he would nevertheless fall to be acquitted ...

R v Woodman [1974] 2 All ER 955

Lord Widgery CJ: ... The facts of the case were these. On 20 March 1973 the appellant and his son, and another man called Davey who was acquitted, took a van to some premises at Wick near Bristol and loaded on to the van one ton six cwt of scrap metal, which they proceeded to drive away.

The premises from which they took this scrap metal were a disused factory belonging to English China Clays, and the indictment alleged that the scrap metal in question was the property of English China Clays. Whether that was entirely true or not depends on the view one takes of the events immediately preceding this taking of scrap metal, because what had happened, according to the prosecution evidence, was that the business run by English China Clays at this point had been run down. In August 1970 the business had ceased. There was at that time a great deal of miscellaneous scrap metal on the site, and English China Clays, wishing to dispose of this, sold the scrap metal to the Bird Group of companies, who thereupon had the right and title to enter on the site and remove the scrap metal which they had bought. They or their sub-contractor went on to the site. They took out the bulk of the scrap metal left there by English China Clays, but a certain quantity of scrap was too inaccessible to be removed to be attractive to the Bird Group of companies so that it was left on the site and so it seems to have remained for perhaps a couple of years until the appellant and his son came to take it away, as I have already recounted.

Also in the history of the matter, and important in it, is the fact that when the site had been cleared by the Bird Group of companies a barbed wire fence was erected around it obviously to exclude trespassers. The site was still in the ownership of the English China Clays and their occupation, and the barbed wire fence was no doubt erected by them. Within the barbed wire fence were these remnants of scrap which the Bird Group had not taken away.

English China Clays took further steps to protect their property because a number of notices giving such information as 'Private Property. Keep Out' and 'Trespassers will be prosecuted' were exhibited around the perimeter of the site. A Mr Brooksbank, who was an employee of English China Clays, gave evidence that he had visited the site about half a dozen times over a period of two or three years, and indeed he had visited it once as recently as between January and March 1973. He did not notice that any scrap metal had been left behind, and it is perfectly clear that there is no reason to suppose that English China Clays or their representatives appreciated that there was any scrap remaining on the site after the Bird Group had done their work ...

His Lordship referred to the provisions of s 5(1) of the 1968 Act and continued:

... The recorder took the view that the contract of sale between English China Clays and the Bird Group had divested English China Clays of any proprietary right to any scrap on the site. It is unnecessary to express a firm view on that point, but the court are not disposed to disagree with the conclusion that the proprietary interest in the scrap had passed.

The recorder also took the view on the relevant facts that it was not possible to say that English China Clays were in possession of the residue of the scrap. It is not quite clear why he took that view. It may have been because he took the view that difficulties arose by reason of the fact that English China Clays had no knowledge of the existence of this particular scrap at any particular time. But the recorder did take the view that so far as control was concerned there was a case to go to the jury on whether or not this scrap was in the control of English China Clays, because if it was, then it was to be regarded as their property for the purposes of a larceny charge even if they were not entitled to any proprietary interest ...

We have formed the view without difficulty that the recorder was perfectly entitled to do what he did, that there was ample evidence that English China Clays were in control of the site and had taken considerable steps to exclude trespassers as demonstrating the fact that they were in control of the site, and we think that in ordinary and straightforward cases if it is once established that a particular person is in control of a site such as this, then prima facie he is in control of articles which are on the site ...

So far as this case is concerned, arising as it does under the Theft Act 1968, we are content to say that there was evidence of English China Clays being in control of the site and *prima facie* in control of articles on the site as well. The fact that it could not be shown that they were conscious of the existence of this or any particular scrap iron does not destroy the general principle that control of a site by excluding others from it is *prima facie* control of articles on the site as well ...

R v Hancock [1990] 2 WLR 640 (CA)

Facts: The appellant was charged with theft from the Crown of 16 ancient coins found in an area which appeared to have been the site of a Romano-Celtic temple. If the coins were a treasure trove, they belonged to the Crown.

> **Auld J**: ... [I]t is not necessary for the offence of theft that the property alleged to have been stolen is in the possession, actual or constructive, of the owner at the time when it is appropriated ... Accordingly, we are of the view that it was for the jury in the trial of this matter to determine as part of their finding on the issue of guilt or innocence of the appellant whether the coins were in fact treasure trove and thus the property of the Crown. In their determination of that issue they had to apply the ordinary criminal burden and standard of proof, namely they could only convict the appellant if they were sure that the coins in question were treasure trove, namely that they had been deposited by someone who had intended to retrieve them ...

R v Kelly [1999] 2 WLR 384

For the facts see above. The following extracts relate to the issue of whether 'possession and control' for the purposes of s 5 has to be lawful.

> **Rose LJ**: The further submission was made that the specimens were not in the lawful possession of the college at the time they were taken, and therefore could not have been stolen. It was, however, accepted that the college was physically in possession of the specimens, but the submission was made at that time that that possession was governed by the provisions of the Anatomy Act 1832 and, in consequence, the college's possession was unlawful because the specimens had been retained beyond the period of 2 years, referred to in that Act by way of amendment, before burial. The learned judge rejected that submission on the basis that possession and control in the accepted terms of those words for the purposes of the Theft Act, was not in issue. He found that there was certainly no evidence before the court to support the suggestion that the college's possession and control was unlawful. To those submissions, which have been repeated in this court, we shall in a moment return in a little more detail ...

> [Mr Thornton, for the second appellant made a sixth submission to the effect that] ... the body parts in question did not belong to anybody. He further submitted, in his seventh submission, that the Royal College of Surgeons, albeit in control and factual possession, were not in lawful possession because of the expiry of the 2 year period under the 1832 Anatomy Act, and he drew attention to certain sections in that Act.

> He drew the court's attention to the case of *R v Turner (No 2)* ...

> ... Mr Thornton submits that that case has not only been criticised by Professor Sir John Smith QC in an article to which he drew our attention, but it is to be understood as limited to the facts of the particular case and should not be regarded as any authority, for present purposes, as to the construction of section 5(1) of the Theft Act.

> ... So far as the question of possession by the Royal College of Surgeons is concerned, in our judgment the learned judge was correct to rule that the college had possession, sufficiently for the purposes of and within section 5(1) of the Theft

Act 1968. We are unable to accept that possession, for the purposes of that section, is in any way dependent on the period of possession, ie whether it is for a limited time, or an indefinite time. In our judgment, the evidence, so far as it was material, before the jury, was to the effect that factually, the parts were in the custody of the Royal College of Surgeons. They were, as it seems to us, in their control and possession within the meaning of section 5(1).

That conclusion is, as it seems to us, reinforced by the judgment of the Court of Appeal in *Turner (No 2)*. We do not accept that the passage in Lord Parker's judgment which we have read is to be regarded as limited to the facts of that particular case. In expressing the view that no other word such as 'lawful' was to be read into section 5(1), by reference to possession, that court was construing section 5 entirely consonantly with the construction which we now place upon it for the purposes of this appeal.

There remains the submission as to the judge's direction that the college was in lawful possession of the parts. It is implicit in what we have already said that the lawfulness of the possession was not a matter for necessary enquiry in the trial. There was, as we have said, evidence before the jury as to the fact of possession of these parts, coming from the inspectors of anatomy. Their views as to the law, as we have already indicated, seem to us to be a matter of no relevance or materiality in relation to any issue which the jury had to determine. It follows that it was not necessary for the judge to direct the jury that the college was in lawful possession rather than merely in possession. The question which arises is whether that direction was of a nature to undermine and prejudice the defence of the appellants. We, in the light of the other passages in the summing-up in relation to dishonesty which we have already cited, are wholly unpersuaded that that is a tenable view.

It follows that for none of the reasons ably advanced before this court, can the convictions of either of these appellants be regarded as unsafe. Accordingly, the appeals against conviction are dismissed.

Theft from a company

Since consent does not prevent an appropriation from taking place, a company director cannot say that he can give consent on behalf of the company for the appropriation of the company's property. It also follows from the fact that a limited liability company is a separate legal entity from its directors and shareholders, that a director or shareholder takes property 'belonging to another' if he takes property belonging to the company (cf *AG's Ref (No 2 of 1982)* [1984] QB 624, approved in *R v Gomez*).

Theft from a partner

R v Bonner [1970] 1 WLR 838 (CA)

Edmund Davies LJ: ... The view of this court is that in relation to partnership property the provisions in the Theft Act 1968 have the following result: provided there is the basic ingredient of dishonesty, provided there be no question of there being a claim of right made in good faith, provided there be an intention permanently to deprive, one partner can commit theft of partnership property just as much as one person can commit the theft of the property of another to whom he is a complete stranger ...

Section 5(3) of the Theft Act 1968: obligation to deal with property

Under s 5(3) of the Theft Act 1968, where a person receives property from another and is under an obligation to deal with that property in a particular way, the property is to be regarded as belonging to that other person. The obligation to deal with property in a particular way must be a *legal* obligation (ie one which is enforceable by civil proceedings): see *R v Gilks* [1972] 1 WLR 1341 (a case decided under s 5(4) of the Theft Act 1968).

R v Hall (1972) 56 Cr App R 547

The appellant was in business as a travel agent. He received a payment from a customer by way of a deposit on some airline tickets. The funds were not used by the appellant to secure the tickets and, in due course, the customer failed to receive his tickets. The Court of Appeal was asked to consider whether or not the funds paid over by the customer could be construed as being property belonging to another by virtue of s 5(3).

Edmund-Davies LJ: [at the instigation of counsel for the appellant referred to a passage in the Eighth Report of the Criminal Law Revision Committee (Cmnd 2977), at p 127] ...

Subsection (3) provides for the special case where property is transferred to a person to retain and deal with for a particular purpose and he misapplies it or its proceeds. An example would be the treasurer of a holiday fund. The person in question is in law the owner of the property; but the subsection treats the property, as against him, as belonging to the persons to whom he owes the duty to retain and deal with the property as agreed. He will therefore be guilty of stealing from them if he misapplies the property or its proceeds.

Mr Jolly [counsel for the appellant] ... submits that the position of a treasurer of a solitary fund is quite different from that of a person like the appellant, who was in general (and genuine) business as a travel agent, and to whom people pay money in order to achieve a certain object – in the present cases, to obtain charter flights to America. It is true, he concedes, that thereby the travel agent undertakes a contractual obligation in relation to arranging flights and at the proper time paying the airline and any other expenses ... But what Mr Jolly resists is that in such circumstances the travel agent 'is under an obligation' to the client 'to retain and deal with ... in a particular way' sums paid to him in such circumstances.

What cannot of itself be decisive of the matter is the fact that the appellant paid the money into the firm's general trading account. As Widgery J (as he then was) said in *Yule* (1963) 47 Cr App R 229, at p 234; [1964] 1 QB 5, at p 10, decided under section 20(1)(iv) of the Larceny Act 1916: 'The fact that a particular sum is paid into a particular banking account ... does not affect the right of persons interested in that sum or any duty of the solicitor either towards his client or towards third parties with regard to disposal of that sum'. Nevertheless, when a client goes to a firm carrying on the business of travel agents and pays them money, he expects that in return he will, in due course, receive the tickets and other documents necessary for him to accomplish the trip for which he is paying, and the firm are 'under an obligation' to perform their part to fulfil his expectation and are liable to pay him damages if they do not. But, in our judgment, what was not here established was that these clients expected them to 'retain and deal with that property or its proceeds in a particular way,' and that an 'obligation' to do so was undertaken by the appellant.

We must make clear, however, that each case turns on its own facts. Cases could, we suppose, conceivably arise where by some special arrangement (preferably evidenced by documents), the client could impose upon the travel agent an 'obligation' falling within section 5(3). But no such special arrangement was made in any of the seven cases here being considered ... It follows from this that, despite what on any view must be condemned as scandalous conduct by the appellant, in our judgment, upon this ground alone this appeal must be allowed and the convictions quashed. But as, to the best of our knowledge, this is one of the earliest cases involving section 5(3), we venture to add some observations:

...

(b) Where the case turns, wholly or in part, on section 5(3) a careful exposition of the subsection is called for ... it was nowhere quoted or even paraphrased by the learned Commissioner in his summing-up. Instead he unfortunately ignored it and proceeded upon the assumption that, as the accused acknowledged the purpose for which clients had paid him money, *ipso facto* there arose an 'obligation ... to retain and deal with' it for that purpose. He therefore told the jury: 'The sole issue to be determined in each count is this: Has it been proved that the money was stolen in the sense I have described, dishonestly appropriated by him for purposes other than the purpose for which the monies were handed over? Bear in mind that this is not a civil claim to recover money that has been lost.' We have to say respectfully that this will not do ...

(c) Whether in a particular case the Crown has succeeded in establishing an 'obligation' of the kind coming within section 5(3) ... may be a difficult question ... to illustrate what we have in mind, mixed questions of law and fact may call for consideration. For example, if the transaction between the parties is wholly in writing, is it for the judge to direct the jury that, as a matter of law, the defendant had thereby undertaken an 'obligation' within section 5(3)? On the other hand, if it is wholly (or partly) oral, it would appear that it is for the judge to direct them that, if they find certain facts proved, it would be open to them to find that an 'obligation' within section 5(3) had been undertaken – but presumably not that they must so find, for so to direct them would be to invade their territory. In effect, however, the learned Commissioner unhappily did something closely resembling that in the present case by his above-quoted direction that the only issue for their consideration was whether the accused was proved to have been actuated by dishonesty.

R v Wain [1995] 2 Cr App R 660 (CA)

Facts: The appellant took part in raising money for a 'telethon' organised for charity by Yorkshire Television. He raised £2,833.25, which he paid into a separate bank account. When asked by Yorkshire Television for the money he made a number of excuses. Eventually the company gave him permission to pay the money into his own bank account. The appellant then handed the company a cheque drawn on that account. The cheque was not met. Meanwhile, the appellant withdrew cash from that account.

At trial, it was submitted on the appellant's behalf that, under s 5(3) of the Theft Act 1968, the debt owed to the charity could not be said to be the proceeds of the money which he had been paid, because the proceeds were the things purchased with the money. This submission was rejected by the trial judge and the appellant was convicted. His appeal to the Court of Appeal was dismissed.

> **McCowan LJ**: ... [I]t seems to us that by virtue of s 5(3), the appellant was plainly under an obligation to retain, if not the actual notes and coins, at least their proceeds, that is to say the money credited in the bank account which he opened for the trust with the actual property. When he took the money credited to that account and moved it over to his own bank account, it was still the proceeds of the notes and coins donated which he proceeded to use for his own purposes, thereby appropriating them ...
>
> We would add this. Whether a person in the position of the appellant is a trustee is to be judged on an objective basis. It is an obligation imposed on him by law. It is not essential that he should have realised that he was a trustee, but of course the question remains as to whether he was acting honestly or dishonestly in using the money for his own purposes. That is a matter of fact for the jury.

Section 5(4) of the Theft Act 1968: obligation to restore property

Under s 5(4) of the Theft Act 1968, where A receives money from B as the result of a mistake on B's part, and A is under a legal obligation to return some or all of that money to B, the money which should be returned to B is regarded as property belonging to B for the purposes of theft.

R v Gilks [1972] 1 WLR 1341 (CA)

> **Cairns LJ**: ... The facts were as follows. On 27 March 1971 the appellant went into Ladbrokes' betting shop at North Cheam and placed some bets on certain horses: one of his bets was on a horse called 'Fighting Scot'. 'Fighting Scot' did not get anywhere in the race which was in fact won by a horse called 'Fighting Taffy'. Because of a mistake on the part of the relief manager in the betting shop, the appellant was paid out as if he had backed the successful horse with the result that he was overpaid to the extent of £106.63. He was paid £117.25 when the amount he had won (on other races) was only £10.62. At the very moment when he was being paid the appellant knew that a mistake had been made and that he was not entitled to the money, but he kept it. He refused to consider repaying it, his attitude being that it was Ladbrokes' hard lines ...
>
> The trial judge held that it was unnecessary for the prosecution to rely on s 5(4) [of the Theft Act 1968] because the property in the £106.63 never passed to the appellant. In the view of this court that ruling was right. The subsection introduced a new principle into the law of theft but long before it was enacted it

was held in *R v Middleton* (1873) LR 2 CCR 38 that where a person was paid by mistake ... a sum in excess of that properly payable, the person who accepted the overpayment with knowledge of the excess was guilty of theft ...

The gap in the law which s 5(4) was designed to fill was ... that which is illustrated by the case of *Moynes v Cooper* [1956] 1 QB 439. There a workman received a pay packet containing £7 more than was due to him but did not become aware of the overpayment until he opened the envelope some time later. He then kept the £7. This was held not to be theft because there was no *animus furandi* at the moment of taking ...

An alternative ground on which the [trial judge] held that the money should be regarded as belonging to Ladbrokes was that 'obligation' in s 5(4) meant an obligation whether a legal one or not. In the opinion of this court that was an incorrect ruling. In a criminal statute, where a person's criminal liability is made dependant on his having an obligation, it would be quite wrong to construe that word so as to cover a moral or social obligation as distinct from a legal one ...

The appeal against conviction was dismissed.

AG's Ref (No 1 of 1983) [1985] QB 182 (CA)

Lord Lane CJ: ... The respondent is a woman police officer and she received her pay from the Receiver of the Metropolitan Police. Owing to an error in the Receiver's department she was credited (in a way which will have to be described in more detail in a moment) with the sum of £74.74 for wages and overtime in respect of a day when she was not at work at all. That amount, together with other sums which were properly due to her, was paid into her bank by direct debit by the Receiver's bank. She knew nothing of the error until later, though it was not proved precisely when. There was some evidence before the jury that she had decided to say nothing about this unsolicited windfall which had come her way, and had decided to take no action about it after she discovered the error. No demand for payment of the sum was made by the Receiver of the Metropolitan Police or anyone else ...

The question comes up to this court on the Attorney General's reference in the following form:

> Whether a person who receives overpayment of a debt due to him or her by way of a credit to his or her bank account through the 'direct debit' system operated by the banks and who knowing of that overpayment intentionally fails to repay the amount of the overpayment 'may be' [which is an amendment which counsel for the Attorney General has asked us to make to the reference] guilty of theft of the credit to the amount of the overpayment ...

[W]hat the respondent ... got was simply the debt due to her from her own bank. That is so unless her account was overdrawn or overdrawn beyond any overdraft limit, in which case she did not even get that right to money. That point is made in a decision of this court in *R v Kohn* (1979) 69 Cr App R 395 ...

The property in the present case was the debt owed by the bank to the respondent [his Lordship then quoted the definition of property in s 4(1) of the Theft Act, which includes 'things in action', and continued:] The debt here was a thing in action, therefore the property was capable of being stolen.

It will be apparent that, at first blush, that debt did not belong to anyone except the respondent herself. She was the only person who had the right to go to her bank and demand the handing over of that £74.74 ...

His Lordship then referred to s 5(4) of the Theft Act 1968.

In order to determine the effect of that subsection on this case one has to take it piece by piece to see what the result is read against the circumstances of this particular prosecution. First of all: did the respondent get property? The word 'get' is about as wide a word as could possibly have been adopted by the draftsman of the Act. The answer is Yes; the respondent in this case did get her chose in action, that is her right to sue the bank for the debt which they owed her, money which they held in their hands to which she was entitled by virtue of the contract between bank and customer.

Second: did she get it by another's mistake? The answer to that is plainly Yes, the Receiver of the Metropolitan Police made the mistake of thinking she was entitled to £74.74 when she was not entitled to that at all.

Was she under an obligation to make restoration of either the property or its proceeds or its value? We take each of those in turn. Was she under an obligation to make restoration of the 'property', the chose in action? The answer to that is No, it was something which could not be restored in the ordinary meaning of the word. Was she under an obligation to make restoration of its proceeds? The answer to that is No, there were no proceeds of the chose in action to restore. Was she under an obligation to make restoration of the value thereof, the value of the chose in action? The answer to that seems to us to be Yes.

I should say here, in parentheses, that a question was raised during the argument this morning whether 'restoration' is the same as 'making restitution'. We think that, on the wording of s 5(4) as a whole, the answer to that question is Yes. One therefore turns to see whether, under the general principles of restitution, the respondent was obliged to restore or pay for the benefit which she received. Generally speaking the respondent, in these circumstances, is obliged to pay for a benefit received when the benefit has been given under a mistake as to a material fact on the part of the giver. The mistake must be as to a fundamental or essential fact and the payment must have been due to that fundamental or essential fact. The mistake here was that this police officer had been working on a day when she had been at home and not working at all ...

In the present case, applying that principle to the facts of this case, the value of the chose in action (the property) was £74.74 and there was a legal obligation on the respondent to restore that value to the receiver when she found that the mistake had been made. One continues to examine the contents of s 5(4). It follows from what has already been said that the extent of that obligation, the chose in action, has to be regarded as belonging to the person entitled to restoration, that is the Receiver of the Metropolitan Police.

As a result of the provisions of s 5(4) the debt of £74.74 due from the respondent's bank to the respondent notionally belonged to the Receiver of the Metropolitan Police, therefore the prosecution, up to this point, have succeeded in proving (remarkable though it may seem) that the 'property' in this case belonged to another within the meaning of s 1 in the 1968 Act from the moment when the respondent became aware that this mistake had been made and that her account had been credited with the £74.74 and she consequently became obliged to restore the value. Furthermore, by the final words of s 5(4), once the prosecution succeed in proving that the respondent intended not to make restoration, that is notionally to be regarded as an intention to deprive the receiver of that property which notionally belongs to him ...

Notes and queries

1 Whether an 'obligation' arises for the purposes of s 5(3) or 5(4) is to be determined by the civil law, and the trial judge should direct the jury accordingly; see *R v Breaks and Huggan* [1998] Crim LR 349.

2 Resort to s 5(4) may not always be necessary where property given to D as a result of P's error. In *R v Williams* [1980] Crim LR 589, the appellant exchanged obsolete foreign currency (knowing it to be obsolete) for Sterling at a bureau de change in a department store. The Court of Appeal, dismissing his appeal against conviction for theft, held that there had been a 'fundamental mistake' operating on the mind of the cashier handing over the money, hence the transaction was void *ab initio*. As such, no property in the money could pass to the appellant, and he appropriated it when he put it in his pocket. The money could be regarded as property belonging to another simply by virtue of s 5(1).

DISHONESTY

Section 2 of the Theft Act 1968: 'dishonestly'

(1) A person's appropriation of property belonging to another is not to be regarded as dishonest:

   (a) if he appropriates the property in the belief that he has in law the right to deprive the other of it, on behalf of himself or of a third person; or

   (b) if he appropriates the property in the belief that he would have the other's consent if the other knew of the appropriation and the circumstances of it; or

   (c) (except where the property came to him as trustee or personal representative) if he appropriates the property in the belief that the person to whom the property belongs cannot be discovered by taking reasonable steps.

(2) A person's appropriation of property belonging to another may be dishonest notwithstanding that he is willing to pay for the property.

Where a defendant is charged with theft, or an offence which requires proof of theft (such as robbery, or some burglaries), regard should first be had to the terms of s 2(1)(a)–(c) in order to determine whether or not D is dishonest. Only if D appears to fall outside these provisions should consideration be given to the approach to dishonesty at common law exemplified in *R v Ghosh* (below).

Dishonesty under s 2 – claim of right

R v Holden [1991] Crim LR 478 (CA)

Facts: The appellant was charged with theft of scrap tyres from Kwik-Fit, where he had worked (although he was not employed there at the time of the offence). He claimed that other people had taken tyres with the permission of a supervisor. The depot manager gave evidence that taking tyres was a sackable offence. The jury had been directed that the test for dishonesty was whether the defendant had a reasonable belief that he had a right to take the tyres.

Held, reasonable belief was not the relevant test of dishonesty. A person was not dishonest if he believed, reasonably or not, that he had a legal right to do what was alleged to constitute an appropriation of property. The question was whether he had, or might have had, an honest belief. However, the reasonableness of the belief might be relevant to the question of whether the defendant could have had an honest belief that he was entitled to take the tyres.

Dishonesty under s 2 – belief in the owner's consent

AG's Ref (No 2 of 1982) [1984] QB 624 (CA)

Kerr LJ: On this reference by the Attorney General under s 36 of the Criminal Justice Act 1972, the court is asked to give its opinion on the following point of law:

> Whether a man in total control of a limited liability company (by reason of his shareholding and directorship) is capable of stealing the property of the company; and whether two men in total control of a limited liability company (by reason of their shareholdings and directorships) are (while acting in concert) capable of jointly stealing the property of the company ...

The counts of theft were specimen counts alleging the appropriation by the defendants for their own private purposes of funds of various companies of which they were the sole shareholders and directors. The total amounts involved ran into millions. Some of the counts related to X alone, some to Y alone, and in some of them they were charged jointly. However, it is common ground that, in relation to all of them, each acted with the consent of the other: indeed, all the alleged thefts appear to have been carried out by means of cheques drawn on various accounts of the companies concerned and signed in each case by X and Y jointly. There is no question of X or Y having been the victim of the dishonesty of the other ...

It was submitted that since the defendants were the sole owners of the company and, through their shareholding, the sole owners of all its property, they could not, in effect, be charged with stealing from themselves. In particular, it was submitted that there was no issue to go to the jury on the ingredient of 'dishonestly'. The defendants were the sole will and directing mind of the company. The company was therefore bound to consent to all to which they themselves consented ... Further, the defendants relied on the wide 'objects' clauses of the memorandum of association of the various companies concerned and submitted that the defendants' acts were covered by these and were accordingly *intra vires* ...

... The basic fallacy in the submission on behalf of the defendants is the contention that, in effect, in a situation such as the present a jury is bound to be directed that, when all the members and directors of a company act in concert in appropriating the property of their company, they cannot, as a matter of law, be held to have acted dishonestly; or that, on such facts, any reasonable jury is bound to reach this conclusion. We entirely disagree with both these propositions ...

... In our view there is no substance whatever in the submission that s 2(1)(b) would preclude a jury from concluding, as a matter of law, that the defendants had acted dishonestly in these cases. Nor can we accept for one moment that any jury would be bound to conclude, on the facts alleged that dishonesty had not been established.

... [I]t does not by any means follow that the members and directors of a company which is wholly owned by them cannot properly be charged with theft of the company's property, or that the defendants cannot rely on s 2 of the 1968 Act in answer to such a charge. Their appropriate defence in such cases is provided by s 2(1)(a) of the Act, the belief of a defendant, which must of course be an honest belief, 'that he has in law the right to deprive [the company] of [the property]'.

In effect, the defendants' answer to the charges in the present case, assuming that the prosecution establishes the facts alleged, would have been: 'We honestly believed that we were entitled to do what we did. They were our companies, and we honestly believed that we were entitled to draw all the cheques and expend all the moneys which are now charged as acts of theft.' This is the defence provided by s 2(1)(a). To obtain a conviction, the prosecution would have had to establish the contrary to the satisfaction of the jury ...

... In our view the *vires* of the company may be of evidential relevance to, but not determinative of, the crucial issue as to the defendants' honesty or dishonesty. Of course, in asserting an honest belief in his right to act as he did, a defendant may wish to refer to the objects for which the company was constituted, and to the terms of its memorandum, to assist him in his defence that he had acted honestly ...

The converse equally applies to the case for the prosecution. Thus, although the prosecutor may seek to prove by reference to the company's memorandum that on its true construction the acts charged were *ultra vires*, the prosecution will not thereby inevitably establish that the defendant had acted dishonestly. The defendant would of course be perfectly entitled to assert that in all the circumstances, and especially because he at all times believed his acts to be *intra vires*, he had not acted dishonestly. Whether or not the defendant had acted *ultra vires* is a matter which the jury would then be entitled to take into account, giving it such weight as they thought proper in deciding the ultimate question, namely: has the prosecution proved that the defendant had acted dishonestly?

Dishonesty under s 2 – belief that the owner cannot be found by taking reasonable steps

Section 2(1)(c) covers appropriation of property which the defendant honestly believes to be lost or abandoned property. Again, the reasonableness of the belief goes to whether that belief was genuinely held.

R v Small (1988) 86 Cr App R 170 (CA)

Facts: The appellant was charged with theft of a car; having admitted to the police that he had stolen it, his defence at trial was that he believed the car to have been abandoned.

Henry J: ... The appellant when he was called gave evidence that he lived in a road adjacent to Links Road and that he had seen the car [in Links Road] every day for about two weeks, during which time it had not moved. He said it was parked at an angle on a corner, the doors were unlocked and the keys were in the ignition. According to him the car was in a somewhat forlorn state. The tyre was flat, as was the battery. The petrol tank was empty and the windscreen wipers did not work. He thought it was 'dumped', he said ...

The appellant told the court how he got petrol, bump started the car and drove it round the corner. There it remained for a few days, when he and his co-accused decided to go for a drive with Williams driving. He said that it had not occurred to him until the police flashed their lights that the car was stolen, but it did occur to him then. He then panicked and ran away.

In cross-examination he said that he thought the car had been dumped, abandoned by the true owner. He accepted that he did not have the right to take it. He said he intended to leave it with the keys in it after he had driven it. He said he had initially told the police that he had stolen the car because he had not in fact paid for it. He said that he did not know that the fact that the car was being dumped might offer him a defence at the time when he admitted to the police that he had stolen it.

Counsel for the appellant contended (1) that one cannot steal abandoned property, and (2) that an honest belief that property was abandoned is a defence.

In considering whether a belief is honest or not, it seems to us that a belief can, in certain circumstances, be honest or genuinely held, even though it is not reasonably held. The relevance of reasonableness is this. It is certainly relevant as to whether the belief was in fact held, because the fact that such a belief would be objectively viewed as unreasonable is a factor – and a strong factor – for the jury to take into account first in considering whether that belief was held, and second, if held, in considering whether it was honestly held ...

Dishonesty at common law

R v Feely [1973] QB 530 (CA)

Facts: The appellant took £30 from his employer's safe. He did not put an IOU in the safe, nor make any record to show what he had done, nor tell his employer what he had done. Four days later a shortfall of £40 was discovered. The appellant then gave an IOU for that amount. When interviewed by the police, the appellant said:

(1) that he would have paid the money back, and

(2) that his employer owed him about £70 and he wanted the employer to take the money which was owing from that.

Lawton LJ: ... The appeal raises an important point of law, namely, can it be a defence in law for a man charged with theft and proved to have taken money, to say that when he took the money he intended to repay it and had reasonable grounds for believing and did believe that he would be able to do so? ...

In s 1(1) of the Theft Act 1968 the word 'dishonestly' can only relate to the state of mind of the person who does the act which amounts to appropriation. Whether an accused person has a particular state of mind is a question of fact which has to be decided by the jury when there is a trial on indictment and by the justices when there are summary proceedings. The Crown did not dispute this proposition, but it was submitted that in some cases (and this, it was said, was such a one) it was necessary for the trial judge to define 'dishonestly' and when the facts fell within the definition he had a duty to tell the jury that if there had been an appropriation it must have been dishonestly done. We do not agree that judges should define what 'dishonestly' means.

This word is in common use ... Jurors, when deciding whether an appropriation was dishonest can be reasonably expected to, and should, apply the current standards of ordinary decent people. In their own lives they have to decide what is and what is not dishonest. We can see no reason why, when in a jury box, they should require the help of a judge to tell them what amounts to dishonesty ...

... People who take money from tills and the like without permission are usually thieves; but if they do not admit that they are by pleading guilty, it is for the jury, not the judge, to decide whether they have acted dishonestly.

R v Ghosh [1982] QB 1053 (CA)

Lord Lane CJ: ... At all material times the appellant was a surgeon acting as a locum tenens consultant at a hospital. The charges alleged that he had falsely represented that he had himself carried out a surgical operation to terminate pregnancy or that money was due to himself or an anaesthetist for such an operation, when in fact the operation had been carried out by someone else, and/or under the National Health Service provisions.

His defence was that there was no deception; that the sums paid to him were due for consultation fees which were legitimately payable under the regulations, or else were the balance of fees properly payable; in other words that there was nothing dishonest about his behaviour on any of the counts ...

... *R v Feely* [1973] QB 530 ... is often treated as having laid down an objective test of dishonesty for the purpose of s 1 of the Theft Act 1968. But what it actually decided was: (1) that it is for the jury to determine whether the defendant acted dishonestly and not for the judge; (2) that the word 'dishonestly' can only relate to the defendant's own state of mind; and (3) that it is unnecessary and undesirable for judges to define what is meant by 'dishonestly' ...

... Is 'dishonestly' in s 1 of the Theft Act 1968 intended to characterise a course of conduct? Or is it intended to describe a state of mind? If the former, then we can well understand that it could be established independently of the knowledge or belief of the accused. But if, as we think, it is the latter, then the knowledge and belief of the accused are at the root of the problem.

Take for example a man who comes from a country where public transport is free. On his first day here he travels on a bus. He gets off without paying. He never had any intention of paying. His mind is clearly honest; but his conduct, judged objectively by what he has done, is dishonest. It seems to us that in using the word 'dishonestly' in the Theft Act 1968, Parliament cannot have intended to catch dishonest conduct in that sense, that is to say conduct to which no moral obloquy could possibly attach. This is sufficiently established by the partial definition in s 2 of the Theft Act 1968 itself. All the matters covered by s 2(1) relate to the belief of the accused. Section 2(2) relates to his willingness to pay. A man's belief and his willingness to pay are things which can only be established subjectively. It is difficult to see how a partially subjective definition can be made to work in harness with the test which in all other respects is wholly objective.

If we are right that dishonesty is something in the mind of the accused ... then if the mind of the accused is honest, it cannot be deemed dishonest merely because members of the jury would have regarded it as dishonest to embark on that course of conduct. So we would reject the simple uncomplicated approach that the test is purely objective, however attractive from the practical point of view that solution may be.

There remains the objection that to adopt a subjective test is to abandon all standards but that of the accused himself, and to bring about a state of affairs in which 'Robin Hood would be no robber' ... This objection misunderstands the nature of the subjective test. It is no defence for a man to say 'I knew that what I was doing is generally regarded as dishonest; but I do not regard it as dishonest myself. Therefore I am not guilty'. What he is, however, entitled to say is, 'I did not know that anybody would regard what I was doing as dishonest'. He may not be believed; just as he may not be believed if he sets up 'a claim of right' under s 2(1) of the Theft Act 1968, or asserts that he believed in the truth of a misrepresentation under s 15 of the 1968 Act. But if he is believed, or raises a real doubt about the matter, the jury cannot be sure that he was dishonest.

In determining whether the prosecution has proved that the defendant was acting dishonestly, a jury must first of all decide whether according to the ordinary standards of reasonable and honest people what was done was dishonest. If it was not dishonest by those standards, that is the end of the matter and the prosecution fails.

If it was dishonest by those standards, then the jury must consider whether the defendant himself must have realised that what he was doing was by those standards dishonest. In most cases, where the actions are obviously dishonest by ordinary standards, there will be no doubt about it. It will be obvious that the defendant himself knew that he was acting dishonestly. It is dishonest for a defendant to act in a way which he knows ordinary people consider to be dishonest, even if he asserts or genuinely believes that he is morally justified in acting as he did. For example, Robin Hood or those ardent anti-vivisectionists who remove animals from vivisection laboratories are acting dishonestly, even though they may consider themselves to be morally justified in doing what they do, because they know that ordinary people would consider these actions to be dishonest ...

CODIFICATION AND LAW REFORM PROPOSALS

In its Consultation Paper *Legislating the Criminal Code: Fraud and Deception* (LCCP 155), the Law Commission identified theft as being one of a number of offences where:

> ... the first, the conduct elements of the offence are very broadly defined, such that they include a wide range of beneficial or innocuous activities. Dishonesty is the one factor which renders the conduct criminal. In such offences, dishonesty 'does all the work' ... Theft ... [is an offence] ... in which dishonesty operates as a positive element.

The summary of the Consultation Paper then provides a useful critique of dishonesty as a positive element of an offence:

> 9   In English law, offences traditionally consist of objectively defined conduct and mental states, subject to objectively defined defences. A general dishonesty offence requires the determination of criminality on the basis of the jury or magistrates coming to a moral judgment of the conduct and mental state of the defendant; and as such it is at least very unusual. *Ghosh* dishonesty, used in this way, amounts to an appeal to a unified conception of honesty shared by the community as a whole which we do not consider workable in our modem society. If this is so, it must lead to endemic inconsistency between juries. We suggest that as a general rule, the law should say what is forbidden, and that should be informed by moral insights. Juries and magistrates should then be asked to apply the law by coming to factual conclusions, not moral ones.

> 10   A general dishonesty offence may extend the reach of the criminal law too far. In the first place, it would render the boundaries between existing offences academic, and would bypass any specific restrictions on liability that Parliament has introduced as part of offences (such as the need for a handler of stolen goods to know or believe that the goods are stolen, rather than merely be suspicious). Further, as recent developments in the law of theft demonstrates a general dishonesty offence would render criminal conduct which does riot even give rise to a remedy in the civil law, thus opening -the way to the criminalisation of any business practice that a jury or magistrates might conclude was dishonest. [Examples first suggested by Professor Sir John Smith QC include a buyer offering £100,000 for a picture he thinks is an unrecognised Constable. The seller knows the buyer thinks this, but the picture is by the seller's sister and worth £100; or a knowledgeable seller buying a genuine Constable for a small sum from an ignorant seller. In both cases there is an enforceable contract and the seller in the first example and the buyer in the second are entitled to their money and painting respectively; but would be open to conviction.]

> We provisionally conclude that it would be wrong to introduce an offence which was capable of criminalising conduct which is either not actionable in civil law at all, or which does breach the civil law, but where there is no compelling need for criminalisation.

> 11   Our general provisional conclusion is that it is undesirable in principle that conduct which is otherwise unobjectionable should be rendered criminal merely because fact finders are willing to characterise it as dishonest.

Certainty and the ECHR

12 We go on to consider whether the result of this analysis is that a general dishonesty offence would be insufficiently certain to satisfy the requirements of the European Convention on Human Rights, as incorporated into English law by the Human Rights Act 1998. Our consideration of the Strasbourg jurisprudence leads us to the conclusion that such an offence would at least be open to challenge in the European Court itself. Incorporation, however, makes the Convention a greater obstacle to the adoption of such an offence for two reasons. First, the Strasbourg institutions rely on the doctrine of the margin of appreciation, which gives national institutions a greater degree of latitude in enforcing Convention rights than we consider it likely that the English courts will afford after the Act is implemented. Secondly, the Act would require the Home Secretary to make a statement of compatibility with the Convention on the face of the Bill enacting a general dishonesty offence. The degree of uncertainty as to the compliance of such an offence is such that we consider that he could not safely be advised to make such a statement.

13 As a result, we provisionally reject the option of creating a general dishonesty offence.

'... with intention to permanently deprive ...'

Section 6 of the Theft Act 1968: 'with the intention of permanently depriving the other of it'

(1) A person appropriating property belonging to another without meaning the other permanently to lose the thing itself is nevertheless to be regarded as having the intention of permanently depriving the other of it if his intention is to treat the thing as his own to dispose of regardless of the other's rights; and a borrowing or lending of it may amount to so treating it if, but only if, the borrowing or lending is for a period and in circumstances making it equivalent to an outright taking or disposal.

(2) Without prejudice to the generality of subsection (1) above, where a person, having possession or control (lawfully or not) of property belonging to another, parts with the property under a condition as to its return which he may not be able to perform, this (if done for purposes of his own and without the other's authority) amounts to treating the property as his own to dispose of regardless of the other's rights.

'... to treat the thing as his own to dispose of regardless of the other's rights ...'

R v Warner (1970) 55 Cr App R 93 (CA)

Facts: The defendant took some tools belonging to another. He said that he intended to return the tools to their owner, but had not decided when he was going to do so.

Edmund Davies LJ: The one point involved in the appeal is whether the Crown established that the appellant intended permanently to deprive the owner of certain goods which he unquestionably took ...

... [T]here can be no theft without the intention of permanently depriving another of his property ...

... [T]he essential question was whether the accused man had ever formed the intention to deprive the owner indefinitely of the use of his tools. If he had, then he could in certain circumstances be regarded as intending to treat the thing as his own to dispose of, regardless of the other's rights, within the meaning of s 6(1). But if this was not so, if, for example, his intention was to deprive the owner of the use of his goods for a limited period, the precise length of which he had not yet decided upon, but fully intending to return them to their owner in due course, this would not necessarily justify conviction for theft and in the majority of cases probably would not do so.

R v Velumyl [1989] Crim LR 299 (CA)

Facts: The appellant, who was employed in a managerial capacity, had taken £1,050 from a safe at work. He did so without authority and in breach of company rules. He said that he had lent the money to a friend on the Saturday preceding its removal and expected to return that sum on the following Monday. At interview, he declined to name the friend and agreed that he had no legal right to take the money, nor did he think that he had his employer's permission to do so. He further agreed that he had treated the money as if it were his own, and that he had acted dishonestly in acting as he had done. Following arraignment, on a charge of theft, his counsel sought a preliminary ruling from the judge as to whether the appellant would have a defence under the Theft Act 1968 (other than on an issue of dishonesty) if he had intended to pay the money back. Essentially, the submission was that one piece of money was as good as another and if there was an intention to repay the money, albeit not the exact notes or coins taken, then an essential ingredient of theft, namely the intention permanently to deprive the owner of the money, was missing. The judge ruled against the appellant, who changed his plea to 'guilty' and appealed on a point of law to the Court of Appeal.

Held, dismissing the appeal, there had been an appropriation by the appellant's assumption of the rights of the owner of the money. He did have the requisite intention of permanently depriving the owner of the money because he had no intention to return the objects which he had taken. His intention had been to return objects of equivalent value, which intention was relevant to the question of dishonesty which was not in issue.

The point was that the person who had taken the money, albeit intending and reasonably expecting to replace it with an equivalent sum, committed the offence because he had taken something which he was not entitled to take without the consent of the owner and was, in effect, trying to force upon the owner a substitution to which the latter had not consented.

R v Fernandez [1996] 1 Cr App R 175 (CA)

Auld LJ: ... In our view, s 6(1) of the Theft Act 1968, which is expressed in general terms, is not limited in its application to the illustrations given by Lord Lane CJ in *R v Lloyd* (1985) 81 Cr App R 182. Nor, in saying that in most cases it would be unnecessary to refer to the provision, did Lord Lane suggest that it should be so limited. The critical notion, stated expressly in the first limb and incorporated by reference in the second, is whether a defendant intended to 'treat the thing as his own to dispose of regardless of the other's rights'. The second limb of subsection (1), and also subsection (2), are merely specific illustrations of the application of that notion. We consider that s 6 may apply to a person in possession or control of another's property who, dishonestly and for his own purpose, deals with that property in such a manner that he knows he is risking its loss.

In the circumstances alleged here, an alleged dishonest disposal of someone else's money on an obviously insecure investment, we consider that the [trial] judge was justified in referring to s 6.

R v Marshall; R v Coombes; R v Eren [1998] 2 Cr App R 282

Mantell LJ: This appeal could have implications for all ticket touts and even for the ordinary motorist who passes on the benefit of an unexpired parking ticket.

In late 1996 each of the three appellants was video recorded obtaining underground tickets or travel cards from members of the public passing through the barriers and re-selling them to other potential customers. By so doing it is accepted that each of them was committing a bye-law offence. However they were each separately indicted for theft.

The matter came before His Honour Judge Hardy on 13th March 1997. On that date the judge heard legal argument as to whether or not the appellants were liable to be convicted of theft on the basis of certain agreed facts. He ruled that all the components of theft were present save for the question of dishonesty which was a matter for the jury. In consequence, on 20th March each of the appellants pleaded guilty to the indictment. Marshall asked for 78 other offences to be taken into consideration, Coombes for 59 and Eren for 47. Marshall and Coombes were placed on probation and Eren was ordered to serve 40 hours community service. With the leave of the single judge each of the appellants now seeks to have his convictions set aside on the ground that the judge's ruling was erroneous.

The agreed facts on which the learned Judge was invited to rule were hardly more comprehensive than already indicated. However we set them out for the sake of completeness.

As part of an operation by London Underground Limited at Victoria Station the appellants were observed and videoed obtaining used travel tickets from passengers leaving the underground and selling them at a reduced rate to persons intending to travel. The tickets, which had been issued by London Underground Limited remained valid in the sense that their usefulness had not been exhausted. Thereby London Underground Limited was deprived of revenue which it might have expected to receive from those persons who had bought the tickets.

A number of submissions were made to the learned Judge. The first was that the travel tickets were not the property of London Underground Limited within the meaning of section 1 of the Theft Act 1968. The judge rejected the submission ruling that although the tickets had passed into the possession and control of the customers, London Underground retained a proprietary right or interest in the tickets which were to be regarded therefore as the property of London Underground pursuant to section 5(1) of the Act. As a secondary reason for rejecting the submission he referred to the express term on the reverse of each ticket to the effect that it remained throughout the property of LRT, of which London Underground Limited is a part.

A second submission was made that in the circumstances there had been no appropriation so as to bring the case within the basic definition of theft. In rejecting the submission the judge referred to section 3(1) [set out above] ... and to the decision of the House of Lords in *R v Morris* ... in which it was held that it was not necessary to demonstrate an assumption by the accused of all the owners rights, simply to show the assumption of some of the rights of the owner of the goods in question. The learned Judge considered that the use of the ticket to the detriment of London Underground was inconsistent with London Underground's rights and consequently that the actions of the appellants amounted to an appropriation in law.

Thirdly and lastly it was submitted that on the agreed facts there was no evidence of an intention to permanently deprive. That submission also was rejected, the learned judge taking the view that the provisions of section 6(1) of the Theft Act covered the position. It will be necessary to refer to the terms of the subsection later in this judgment.

... As indicated, although a number of submissions were made to the learned Judge and subsequently reproduced in the grounds of appeal, only one such has been pursued before this court. It is set out in the skeleton argument of Mr Taylor of counsel who appears for the appellants Marshall and Coombes. It was adopted by Mr Simpson on behalf of Eren.

> It is submitted by the appellants that in the circumstances although there was an assumption of the rights of the owner contrary to section 3 of the Theft Act 1968 which amounted to an appropriation there was nevertheless no intention on their part to deprive London Underground Limited of the said ticket. They intended either to return them directly to London Underground Limited or to do so through the third party buyer without resale to London Underground Limited and without any loss in the virtue of the ticket when returned.

The argument proceeds,

> The ticket forms are pieces of paper printed over with information about the ticket. When returned to London Underground Limited they had no more and no less value than when they were originally purchased. The return to London Underground, notwithstanding these intervening transactions involved no loss of virtue to London Underground Limited's property.

It was submitted section 6(1) of the Theft Act 1968 did not apply as that was only to be resorted to where there was a resale of the property to the original owner. It was further submitted that the issuing of a travel ticket was analogous to the drawing of a cheque and that as both were choses in action the reasoning in *R v Preddy* [1996] 3 WLR 255 was equally applicable.

It will be seen that the submission made on what is accepted to be the single issue in the appeal depends in part upon the misapprehension that the ticket forms would necessarily find their way back into the possession of London Underground. That was the factual basis upon which the learned Judge ruled. As mentioned, we are content to deal with this appeal on a similar basis.

On this point the judge ruled as follows:

> I am satisfied that the essence of section 6 of the Theft Act 1968 is whether there was an intention to treat the tickets as their own regardless of the owners rights. Mr Taylor has drawn my attention in particular to the cases of *Duru* (1972) 58 CAR 151 and *Preddy and Others* ... and referred me to the commentary by Professor Smith to the case of *R v Mitchell* ... I note that all these cases involved cheques and for my part I am not prepared to extend to the underground what the High Court have found in relation to cheques.

For the reasons which follow we consider that the judge was right.

His Lordship recited the provisions of s 6(1) of the Theft Act 1968, and continued:

> ... On its face the subsection would seem apt to cover the facts of the present case. The ticket belongs to London Underground. It has been appropriated by an appellant. It is the exclusive right of London Underground to sell tickets. By acquiring and re-selling the ticket the appellant has an intention to treat the ticket as his own to dispose of regardless of London Underground's right. However Mr Taylor and Mr Simpson have reminded us of what was said by Lord Lane, Lord Chief Justice in the case of *R v Lloyd* ...
>
> > Bearing in mind the observation of Edmund Davis LJ in *Warner* (1970) 55 Cr App R 93, we would try to interpret the section in such a way as to ensure that nothing is construed as an intention permanently to deprive which would not prior to the 1968 Act have been so construed. Thus the first part of section 6(1) seems to us to be aimed at the sort of case were a defendant takes things and then offers them back to the owner for the owner to buy if he wishes. If the taker intends to return them to the owner only upon such payment, then, on the wording of section 6(1) that is deemed to amount to the necessary intention permanently to deprive ...
>
> It is submitted, therefore, that the subsection is to be construed narrowly and confined to the sort of case of which Lord Lane gave an example and of which the present is not one. However this court had to consider a similar situation in the case of *R v Fernandez* [1996] 1 Cr App R 175 where at p 188 Lord Justice Auld giving the judgment of the court said this:
>
> > In our view section 6(1), which is expressed in general terms, is not limited in its application to the illustrations given by Lord Lane CJ in *Lloyd*. Nor in saying that in most cases it would be unnecessary to refer to the provision, did Lord Lane suggest it should be so limited. The critical notion, stated expressly in the first limb and incorporated by reference in the second is, whether a defendant intended to 'treat the thing as his own to dispose of regardless of the others rights 'The second limb of subsection (1) and also subsection (2) are merely specific illustrations of the application of that notion. We consider that section 6 may apply to a person in possession or control of another's property who, dishonestly and for his own purpose, deals with that property in such a manner that he knows he is risking its loss.

In our judgment and following *Fernandez* the subsection is not to be given the restricted interpretation for the which the appellants contend.

The principal submission put forward on behalf of the appellants is that the issuing of the ticket is analogous to the drawing of a cheque in that in each instance a chose in action is created which in the first case belongs to the customer and in the second to the payee. So by parity of reasoning with that advanced by Lord Goff in *Preddy* ... the property acquired belonged to the customer and not London Underground and there can have been no intention on the part of the appellant to deprive London Underground of the ticket which would in due course be returned to the possession of London Underground. Attractive though the submission appears at first blush we do not think that it can possibly be correct.

... On the issuing of an underground ticket a contract is created between London Underground and the purchaser. Under that contract each party has rights and obligations. Theoretically those rights are enforceable by action. Therefore it is arguable, we suppose, that by the transaction each party has acquired a chose in action. On the side of the purchaser it is represented by a right to use the ticket to the extent which it allows travel on the underground system. On the side of London Underground it encompasses the right to insist that the ticket is used by no one other than the purchaser. It is that right which is disregarded when the ticket is acquired by the appellant and sold on. But here the charges were in relation to the tickets and travel cards themselves and a ticket form or travel card and, dare we say, a cheque form is not a chose in action. The fact that the ticket form or travel card may find its way back into the possession of London Underground, albeit with its usefulness or 'virtue' exhausted, is nothing to the point. Section 6(1) prevails for the reasons we have given.

The appellants by their pleas having acknowledged that they were acting dishonestly it seems to us that there is no reason to consider the convictions unsafe and these appeals must be dismissed.

'... borrowing or lending is for a period and in circumstances making it equivalent to an outright taking or disposal ...'

R v Coffey [1987] Crim LR 498 (CA)

Facts: The appellant was convicted of obtaining property by deception. He had obtained machinery using a worthless cheque. At his trial he explained that he had been in dispute with the victim, who refused to negotiate its resolution. He had decided to exert pressure by obtaining and keeping the machinery until he got what he wanted. It was not clear exactly what the appellant wanted or what would happen to the machinery if he did not achieve his purpose. The appellant appealed against conviction on the ground that the judge's summing up did not fully or accurately state the law as to intent and dishonesty.

Held: The court preferred the view that the culpability of the appellant's act depended upon the quality of the intended detention, considered in all its aspects, including in particular the appellant's own assessment at the time as to the likelihood of the victim coming to terms and of the time for which the machinery would have to be retained.

This was one of the rare cases where it was right for the judge to bring s 6(1) before the jury. The judge could usefully have illustrated the first part of s 6(1) by the expression 'equivalent to an outright taking or disposal'. If they thought that the appellant might have intended to return the goods even if the victim did not do what he wanted, they would not convict unless they were sure that he intended that the period of detention should be so long as to amount to an outright taking. Even if they did conclude that the appellant had in mind not to return the goods if the victim failed to do what he wanted, they would still have to consider whether the appellant had regarded the likelihood of this happening as being such that his intended conduct could be regarded as equivalent to an outright taking.

R v Lloyd, Bhuee and Ali [1985] QB 829 (CA)

Lord Lane CJ: ... At all material times the appellant Lloyd was employed as chief projectionist at the Odeon Cinema at Barking. The other two appellants with whom we are concerned, namely Ali and Bhuee, were employed by a man called Mustafa ... They were employed at premises at 3 Plumstead Road, Barking. The case against the appellants was that over a period of months Lloyd had been clandestinely removing feature films which were due to be shown at the Odeon Cinema at Barking and lending them to his co-defendants, who had sophisticated equipment at their premises at 3, Plumstead Road. That sophisticated equipment enabled them to copy the feature films on to a master video tape, and, as a result of the preparation of that master video tape, they or others were enabled to produce a very large quantity of pirated versions of the film. The process of copying was done rapidly. The films were only out of the cinema and out of the hands of Lloyd for a few hours and were always back in time for their projection to take place at the advertised times to those people who attended the cinema to see them.

It was important that the film should be returned rapidly, because if it was not it would soon become apparent that the film had been illegally removed and steps would be taken to prevent a recurrence.

The pirated copies prepared from the master tape would be put on the market to the great financial benefit of the pirates and the great financial detriment of the lawful owners, the film distributors and those who would derive money from the film enterprise. The detriment would occur in a number of different ways, and that indeed was proved before the jury. First of all it would occur through a lowering of cinema attendances to see the particular film, and second, through the legitimate sales of cassettes of the film being undermined by the sale of the pirated copies. The profits apparently, so it was stated in evidence, to the film pirates are enormous and the loss to the legitimate trade is potentially crippling.

In the upshot the appellants were caught red-handed in the process of copying a film called *The Missionary* onto the master tape.

The trial judge issued his certificate [that the case was fit for appeal] by posing the following question:

Whether the offence of conspiracy to steal is committed when persons dishonestly agree to take a film from a cinema without authority intending it should be returned within a few hours but knowing that many hundreds of copies will be subsequently made and that the value of the film so returned will thereby be substantially reduced?

... [His Lordship quoted s 6(1) of the Theft Act 1968 and said that it] is abstruse. But it must mean, if nothing else, that there are circumstances in which a defendant may be deemed to have the intention permanently to deprive, even though he may intend the owner eventually to get back the object which has been taken ...

... The first part of s 6(1) seems to us to be aimed at the sort of case where a defendant takes things and then offers them back to the owner for the owner to buy if he wishes. If the taker intends to return them to the owner only on such payment, then, on the wording of s 6(1), that is deemed to amount to the necessary intention permanently to deprive: see, for instance, *R v Hall* (1848) 1 Den 381, where the defendant took fat from a candlemaker and then offered it for sale to the owner. His conviction for larceny was affirmed. There are other cases of similar intent: for instance, 'I have taken your valuable painting. You can have it back on payment to me of £X,000. If you are not prepared to make that payment, then you are not going to get your painting back'.

It seems to us that in this case we are concerned with the second part of s 6(1), namely the words after the semicolon:

> and a borrowing or lending of it may amount to so treating it if, but only if, the borrowing or lending is for a period and in circumstances making it equivalent to an outright taking or disposal.

These films, it could be said, were borrowed by Lloyd from his employers in order to enable him and the others to carry out their 'piracy' exercise.

Borrowing is *ex hypothesi* not something which is done with an intention permanently to deprive. This half of the subsection, we believe, is intended to make it clear that a mere borrowing is never enough to constitute the necessary guilty mind unless the intention is to return the 'thing' in such a changed state that it can truly be said that all its goodness or virtue has gone: for example *R v Beecham* (1851) 5 Cox CC 181, where the defendant stole railway tickets intending that they should be returned to the railway company in the usual way only after the journeys had been completed. He was convicted of larceny. The judge in the present case gave another example, namely the taking of a torch battery with the intention of returning it only when its power is exhausted.

That being the case, we turn to inquire whether the feature films in this case can fall within that category. Our view is that they cannot. The goodness, the virtue, the practical value of the films to the owners has not gone out of the article. The film could still be projected to paying audiences, and, had everything gone according to the conspirator's plans, would have been projected in the ordinary way to audiences at the Odeon Cinema, Barking, who would have paid for their seats. Our view is that those particular films which were the subject of this alleged conspiracy had not themselves diminished in value at all. What had happened was that the borrowed film had been used or was going to be used to perpetrate a copyright swindle on the owners whereby their commercial interests were grossly and adversely affected in the way that we have endeavoured to describe at the outset of this judgment. The borrowing, it seems to us, was not for a period, or in such circumstances, as made it equivalent to an outright taking or disposal. There was still virtue in the film.

Intention to permanently deprive: conditional intent

R v Easom [1971] 2 QB 315 (CA)

Edmund Davies LJ: ... This is an appeal by the appellant against his conviction ... on an indictment charging him with theft, the particulars of the charge being that, on 27 December 1969, he 'stole one handbag, one purse, one notebook, a quantity of tissues, a quantity of cosmetics and one pen, the property of Joyce Crooks'.

The circumstances giving rise to the charge may be shortly stated. On the evening of 27 December 1969, Woman Police Sergeant Crooks and other plain-clothes officers went to the Metropole Cinema in Victoria. Sergeant Crooks sat in an aisle seat and put her handbag (containing the articles enumerated in the charge) alongside her on the floor. It was attached to her right wrist by a piece of black cotton. Police Constable Hensman sat next to her on the inside seat. When the house lights came on during an interval, it was seen that the appellant was occupying the aisle seat in the row immediately behind Sergeant Crooks and that the seat next to him was vacant. Within a few minutes of the lights being put out, Sergeant Crooks felt the cotton attached to her wrist tighten. She thereupon gave Police Constable Hensman a prearranged signal. The cotton was again pulled, this time so strongly that she broke it off. Moments later the officers could hear the rustle of tissues and the sound of her handbag being closed. Very shortly afterwards the appellant left his seat and went to the lavatory. The officers then turned round and found Sergeant Crook's handbag on the floor behind her seat and in front of that which the appellant had vacated. Its contents were intact. When the appellant emerged from the lavatory and seated himself in another part of the cinema, he was approached by the police officers. When the offence of theft was put to him, he denied it ...

... In every case of theft the appropriation must be accompanied by the intention of permanently depriving the owner of his property. What may be loosely described as a 'conditional' appropriation will not do. If the appropriator has it in mind merely to deprive the owner of such of his property as, on examination, proves worth taking and then, finding that the booty is valueless to the appropriator, leaves it ready to hand to be repossessed by the owner, the appropriator has not stolen. If a dishonest postal sorter picks up a pile of letters, intending to steal any which are registered, but, on finding that none of them are, replaces them, he has stolen nothing, and this is so notwithstanding the provisions of s 6(1) of the Theft Act 1968 ...

But does it follow from all this that the appellant ... has to go scot-free? Can he not, as counsel for the Crown originally submitted, be convicted at least of attempted theft?

... [M]uch depends on the manner in which the charge is framed. Thus, 'if you indict a man for stealing your watch, you cannot convict him of attempting to steal your umbrella' (*per* Cockburn CJ in *R v M'Pherson* (1857) Dears & B 197, 200) – unless, of course, the court of trial has duly exercised the wide powers of amendment conferred by s 5 of the Indictments Act 1915 ... No amendment was sought or effected in the present case, which accordingly has to be considered in relation to the articles enumerated in the theft charge and nothing else. Furthermore, it is implicit in the concept of an attempt that the person acting intends to do the act attempted, so that the *mens rea* of an attempt is essentially that of the complete crime ... That being so, there could be no valid conviction of the appellant of attempted theft on the present indictment unless it were established that he was animated by the same intention permanently to deprive Sergeant Crooks of the goods enumerated in the particulars of the charge as would be necessary to establish the full offence. We hope that we have already made sufficiently clear why we consider that, in the light of the evidence and of the direction given, it is impossible to uphold the verdict on the basis that such intention was established in this case. For these reasons, we are compelled to allow the appeal and quash the conviction.

TAKING MOTOR VEHICLE OR OTHER CONVEYANCE WITHOUT AUTHORITY

Section 12 of the Theft Act 1968

(1) Subject to subsections (5) and (6) below, a person shall be guilty of an offence if, without having the consent of the owner or other lawful authority, he takes any conveyance for his own or another's use or, knowing that any conveyance has been taken without such authority, drives it or allows himself to be carried in or on it.

(2) A person guilty of an offence under subsection (1) above shall [be liable on summary conviction to a fine not exceeding level 5 on the standard scale, to imprisonment for a term not exceeding six months, or to both].

(3) ...

(4) If on the trial of an indictment for theft the jury are not satisfied that the accused committed theft, but it is proved that the accused committed an offence under subsection (1) above, the jury may find him guilty of the offence under subsection (1) [and if he is found guilty of it, he shall be liable as he would have been liable under subsection (2) above on summary conviction].

(5) Subsection (1) above shall not apply in relation to pedal cycles; but, subject to subsection (6) below, a person who, without having the consent of the owner or other lawful authority, takes a pedal cycle for his own or another's use, or rides a pedal cycle knowing it to have been taken without such authority, shall on summary conviction be liable to a fine not exceeding [level 3 on the standard scale].

(6) A person does not commit an offence under this section by anything done in the belief that he has lawful authority to do it or that he would have the owner's consent if the owner knew of his doing it and the circumstances of it.

(7) For purposes of this section:

(a) 'conveyance' means any conveyance constructed or adapted for the carriage of a person or persons whether by land, water or air, except that it does not include a conveyance constructed or adapted for use only under the control of a person not carried in or on it, and 'drive' shall be construed accordingly; and

(b) 'owner', in relation to a conveyance which is the subject of a hiring agreement or hire-purchase agreement, means the person in possession of the conveyance under that agreement.

Section 12A of the Theft Act 1968: aggravated vehicle-taking

(1) Subject to subsection (3) below, a person is guilty of aggravated taking of a vehicle if:

(a) he commits an offence under s 12(1) above (in this section referred to as a 'basic offence') in relation to a mechanically propelled vehicle; and

(b) it is proved that, at any time after the vehicle was unlawfully taken (whether by him or another) and before it was recovered, the vehicle was driven, or injury or damage was caused, in one or more of the circumstances set out in paragraphs (a) to (d) of subsection (2) below.

(2) The circumstances referred to in subsection (1)(b) above are:

(a) that the vehicle was driven dangerously on a road or other public place;

(b) that, owing to the driving of the vehicle, an accident occurred by which injury was caused to any person;

(c) that, owing to the driving of the vehicle, an accident occurred by which damage was caused to any property, other than the vehicle;

(d) that damage was caused to the vehicle.

(3) A person is not guilty of an offence under this section if he proves that, as regards any such proven driving, injury or damage as is referred to in subsection (1)(b) above, either:

(a) the driving, accident or damage referred to in subsection (2) above occurred before he committed the basic offence; or

(b) he was neither in nor on nor in the immediate vicinity of the vehicle when that driving, accident or damage occurred.

(4) A person guilty of an offence under this section shall be liable on conviction on indictment to imprisonment for a term not exceeding two years or, if it is proved that, in circumstances falling within subsection (2)(b) above, the accident caused the death of the person concerned, five years.

(5) If a person who is charged with an offence under this section is found not guilty of that offence but it is proved that he committed a basic offence, he may be convicted of the basic offence.

(6) If by virtue of subsection (5) above a person is convicted of a basic offence before the Crown Court, that court shall have the same powers and duties as a magistrates' court would have had on convicting him of such an offence.

(7) For the purposes of this section a vehicle is driven dangerously if:

(a) it is driven in a way which falls far below what would be expected of a competent and careful driver; and

(b) it would be obvious to a competent and careful driver that driving the vehicle in that way would be dangerous.

(8) For the purposes of this section a vehicle is recovered when it is restored to its owner or to other lawful possession or custody; and in this subsection 'owner' has the same meaning as in s 12 above.

The elements of the offence under s 12 of the Theft Act 1968 are that the defendant:

(a) takes

(b) a conveyance (as defined in s 12(7)(a))

(c) for his own or another's use

(d) without the owner's consent or

(a) knowing that the conveyance has been taken without the owner's consent

(b) drives it or allows himself to be carried in it.

For an offence under s 12A to be committed, it must be proved that:

(a) an offence under s 12(1) of the Theft Act 1968 has been committed;

(b) the conveyance must be a 'mechanically propelled vehicle';

(c) one of the following has also occurred:

   (i) the vehicle was driven dangerously;

   (ii) as a result of the driving of the vehicle, injury has been caused to someone;

   (iii) as a result of the driving of the vehicle, property other than the vehicle has been damaged; or

   (iv) the vehicle has been damaged.

'Taking'

The word 'taking' requires that the conveyance must be moved, albeit by a small distance. Merely starting the vehicle's engine is not enough (although it may amount to an attempt to commit the full offence).

R v Bogacki and Others [1973] QB 832 (CA)

Roskill LJ: These three young men, the defendants, Bogacki, Tillwach and Cox, were charged ... with attempting, and I venture to underline the word 'attempting', to take a motor vehicle without authority ...

... The evidence for the Crown was to a large extent undisputed. At about 3.45 am on New Year's Day 1972, these three young men, who had been having a lot to drink at a New Year's Eve party, went to Ponders End bus garage. There they tried to change a 50p piece in order to purchase cigarettes from a machine. They were refused change and told to go away. As they went they boarded a single decker bus which was standing on the forecourt of the garage. One of them turned the engine over with the starter as if to start it. It was common ground that after three or four minutes they left the garage quite openly. They walked to the police station where they were given change for the 50p piece which they had been refused at the bus station. Very shortly thereafter they were arrested. According to the police evidence, Cox first of all denied he had ever boarded the bus. Tillwach made a written statement in which he admitted that he had been on the bus and he alleged that Bogacki had sat in the driving seat and tried to start the engine.

There was no doubt, and [counsel] for the defendants has not sought to contend otherwise, that one of those three young men acting in concert with the others got on board that bus and attempted to start the engine. The bus never moved. Indeed the weight of the evidence was that the engine never started and this court deals with the appeal on that assumption ...

... The word 'take' is an ordinary simple English word ...

... [T]he court accepts [the defendants'] submission that there is still built in, if I may use the phrase, to the word 'takes' in the subsection the concept of movement and that before a man can be convicted of the completed offence under s 12(1) it must be shown that he took the vehicle, that is to say that there was an unauthorised taking possession or control of the vehicle by him adverse to the rights of the true owner or person otherwise entitled to such possession or control, coupled with some movement, however small ... of that vehicle following such unauthorised taking.

Here, had the judge given the jury a correct direction, there was abundant evidence to justify convictions for attempting to take the bus because what was done must on the verdict of the jury clearly be taken to have been an act to which all these men were joint parties, preparatory to putting the bus into motion after an unauthorised taking of possession or control ...

'... for his own or another's use ...'

'Use' means use as a conveyance; the defendant's motive is immaterial (*R v Bow* (1976) 64 Cr App R 54). This was further explained in *R v Marchant* (1984) 80 Cr App R 361. Once a conveyance has been 'taken' for the purpose of s 12, subsequent acts by the taker do not amount to a further taking; however, if the first taker abandons the conveyance, it may be 'taken' by another person even though it has not been restored to its owner in the meantime (*DPP v Spriggs* [1994] RTR 1).

R v Bow (1976) 64 Cr App R 54 (CA)

Facts: On the morning of Sunday 2 November 1975, the appellant, his brother and his father drove in the brother's motor car from their home to a country estate known as the Racton Estate. They were armed with air rifles. The case for the Crown, for which there was, one must say, a good deal of circumstantial support, was that the object of their excursion was to go poaching. That at all events was the view taken by the gamekeepers employed on the estate. They approached the appellant's party and asked for their names and addresses. They were not forthcoming. The head gamekeeper decided to call the police. He also decided to park his Land Rover in such a position as to obstruct the only escape route which could be taken by the appellant's party in the brother's motor car. The head gamekeeper was asked to move the Land Rover but declined to do so. There followed a scuffle between the head gamekeeper and the appellant's brother which resulted in due course in the brother being convicted of common assault. It was during this scuffle that the appellant got into the driving seat of the Land Rover, released the handbrake and coasted down the lane with the engine not switched on, travelling a distance of some 200 yards. The effect of that was to enable the appellant's brother's motor car to be driven off.

Bridge LJ: ... The short answer, we think, is that where as here, a conveyance is taken and moved in a way which necessarily involves its use as a conveyance, the taker cannot be heard to say that the taking was not for that use. If he has in fact taken the conveyance and used it as such, his motive in so doing is ... quite immaterial.

R v Marchant and McCallister (1984) 80 Cr App R 361 (CA)

Facts: Two police officers gave evidence to the effect that they saw the two appellants pushing a car. They said that they saw the two appellants succeeding in moving the car, by pushing it, although moving it only a very short distance, about two or three feet.

The two appellants gave evidence to the effect that they did not know who the car belonged to. They said that they were moving it because it was badly parked and sticking out from the kerb. McCallister however also said that he was looking out for a car like that, and that he thought it was abandoned; and Marchant also gave evidence to the effect that McCallister was looking for a car of this kind.

Robert Goff LJ: ... [Section 12 of the Theft Act 1968] simply provides that the offence is committed if a person takes a conveyance for his own use, without prior consent or lawful authority. So, to be guilty of the offence, the accused must have both taken the vehicle, ie have taken control of it and caused it to be moved, and he must have done so for his own or another's use. The latter requirement has been said to mean 'for his own use or another's as a conveyance': see *R v Bow* (1976) 64 Cr App R 54 at 57, *per* Bridge LJ. Even so, as we see it, if a person takes a vehicle for that use, ie to use it as a conveyance, without the consent of the owner or lawful authority, he commits the offence ... Suppose a man finds a car in the street. He needs a car for a day's expedition. He forms the intent to take the car for that use, though intending to return it later to that place where he found it. He knows he cannot start it then, so he pushes it round the corner to his home with the intention of getting it going for use on his expedition. The police catch up with him and find the car parked in his yard. Has that person committed the offence of taking a conveyance for his own use, without having the necessary consent or authority? In our judgment, he has. He has certainly taken it because he has moved it a certain distance. In my judgment his purpose for taking it is plain. It was for use as a conveyance. So in those circumstances, the offence has been committed.

Director of Public Prosecution v Spriggs [1994] RTR 1 (DC)

Tudor Evans J: ... The car had originally been taken from the car park of a company which owned the car during the course of the afternoon or early evening on 23 November 1990. It was taken without the consent of the owner or other lawful authority. The prosecution did not suggest that the defendant took the vehicle from the car park or that he was in any way involved in the original taking.

The case for the prosecution was that, much later on the day of the original taking, he was seen by police officers at the wheel of the car, that it was being driven very slowly in convoy with another vehicle which drove off at the approach of the police car, and that, when the police car stopped the car, the defendant tried to run away and both he and Mr Staff were arrested. The evidence showed that there were obvious signs of damage to the door and the ignition of the car and the defendant was found with a bent screwdriver in his possession.

The account given by him at interview was that Mr Staff had been giving him a lift home in another vehicle when they came across the car in question which they saw had been left blocking the road with the engine running. The defendant's account was that, whilst he accepted that he should never have got into the car and whilst he accepted that he had driven it for about 200 yards, he was simply moving the car preparatory to notifying the police of what he had found. He accepted that he realised that the car had been stolen when he got into it ...

The question for the opinion of the court is whether a person, not being the person who is responsible for the original and unlawful taking of a vehicle from the place where its lawful owner last left it, is capable in law of committing the offence of taking a conveyance without authority contrary to s 12(1) of the Theft Act 1968 by reason only of a later and separate taking of the same vehicle from some other place ...

... This is a case in which the car was taken and then possession of it was abandoned, as is quite plain on the facts as found. There was then a fresh assumption of possession and taking within the language of the subsection.

In those circumstances, where a vehicle is abandoned, it seems to me that it must inevitably follow that, if there is a subsequent taking which falls within the language of the first part of s 12(1), then the offence is committed. It cannot be that offences under this subsection are limited only to facts where there has been one taking either by a single person or by his acting jointly with another.

Accordingly, I would answer the question which I have already identified with the answer 'Yes' and I would remit the matter to the Crown Court with a direction to convict. It follows that the appeal must be allowed.

'... without the owner's consent ...'

Where the owner is deceived into allowing the defendant to take the conveyance, that consent is not vitiated by the fraud and so no offence is committed under s 12.

Whittaker and Another v Campbell [1984] QB 318 (DC)

Robert Goff LJ: ... The following facts are taken from the case [stated by the Crown Court]: (1) In about June 1981 the defendants, who are brothers aged 27 and 25 years, and who lived in St Helen's Auckland, County Durham, had an opportunity to obtain some coal at an advantageous price from a private colliery quite lawfully. (2) In order to remove the coal the defendants required their own means of transport. At all material times, the defendant Wilson Coglan Whittaker had no driving licence whatsoever and the defendant Stewart Whittaker had a provisional licence only and neither defendant had a vehicle of his own. (3) In about June 1981 the defendants came into possession of a full driving licence belonging to one Derek Dunn. The defendant Wilson Coglan Whittaker said that he had found it near Mr Dunn's place of work. The defendants decided to use the licence to hire a van to remove the coal. (4) On 24 June 1981, the defendants went to a local vehicle hire firm called Stangarths Ltd ... and there hired from a director, one Duncan Stuart Robson, aged 23, a Ford Transit van for a day. (5) The defendant Wilson Coglan Whittaker represented himself as being Derek Dunn of the address shown on the driving licence which he produced to Mr Robson. The same defendant also signed the name 'D Dunn' on the hire agreement form ... The appropriate hire charge was paid by the defendants and the defendant Wilson Coglan Whittaker drove away the Ford Transit van. On five subsequent occasions the defendants did the same thing ... on each occasion the defendant Wilson Coglan Whittaker signing the hire agreement form 'D Dunn'. On the later occasions the driving licence was not produced to Mr Robson who acted in reliance on what had happened on earlier occasions. On each occasion the defendants paid the appropriate hire charge. (6) On 16 October 1981 the defendant Stewart Whittaker was driving the hire van when it was stopped and checked by police officers ... The defendants were questioned and their true identities were established. (7) According, to Mr Robson, the hire company's director, on the occasion of each hire, he was deceived by the defendants into believing that the defendant Wilson Coglan Whittaker was Derek Dunn and that he was the holder of a full driving licence, and had he known that that was not the case the defendant Wilson Coglan Whittaker would not have been allowed to hire any of his (Robson's) vehicles or drive any of his vehicles. (8) ... [I]t was alleged that the defendants jointly on 16 October 1981, without the consent of the owner or other lawful authority took a certain conveyance, namely a motor van, for their own use, contrary to s 12(1) of the Theft Act 1968. The offence alleged referred to the last occasion of hire ...

... There being no general principle that fraud vitiates consent, we see the problem simply as this: can a person be said to have taken a conveyance for his own or another's use 'without having the consent of the owner or other lawful authority' within those words as used in s 12(1) of the Theft Act 1968, if he induces the owner to part with possession of the conveyance by a fraudulent misrepresentation of the kind employed by the defendants in the present case? ...

In circumstances such as those of the present case, the criminality (if any) of the act would appear to rest rather in the fact of the deception, inducing the person to part with the possession of his vehicle, rather than in the fact (if it be the case) that the fraud has the effect of inducing a mistake as to, for example, 'identity' rather than 'attributes' of the deceiver. It would be very strange if fraudulent conduct of this kind has only to be punished if it happened to induce a fundamental mistake; and it would be even more strange if such fraudulent conduct has only to be punished where the chattel in question happened to be a vehicle. If such fraudulent conduct is to be the subject of prosecution, the crime should surely be classified as one of obtaining by deception, rather than an offence under s 12(1) of the Act of 1968, which appears to us to be directed to the prohibition and punishment of a different form of activity ...

Belief in consent of owner (s 12(6))

No offence is committed if, at the time of the taking (and it must be at the time of the taking (*R v Ambler* [1979] RTR 217)), the accused genuinely believed that the owner had consented (or would have consented) to the taking. It is for the prosecution to prove the absence of such a belief, but before the prosecution have to do so the defence must make out a *prima facie* case that he held this belief.

R v Gannon (1988) 87 Cr App R 254 (CA)

Kenneth Jones J: ... The onus was of course on the prosecution to prove the absence of the belief [that the defendant had lawful authority to take the car] – *R v MacPherson* [1973] RTR 157. But before that stage was reached, it was of course for the appellant to raise the issue. That means that he was required to call evidence or at least be able to point to some evidence which tended to show that he did hold the belief referred to in s 12(6) ...

Allowing himself to be carried

Again, there must have been some movement of the conveyance and it must be proved that the accused knew that the conveyance had been taken without the owner's consent (*R v Diggin* (1980) 72 Cr App R 204).

Aggravating circumstances for s 12A

R v Marsh (1996) 160 JP 721 (DC)

Laws J: ... [The appellant had taken a motor car without the consent of the owner.] During the journey, the [passenger] noticed a figure towards the right of the car and it seemed as if it was about to cross towards the footpath on the left. The car continued down. The figure began to run over towards the left-hand side footpath and, unfortunately, it transpired that it was a lady who was running across the road. She was knocked to the ground. The appellant ... stopped to help her. She was not, it seems, seriously injured ...

It is right that we should note that the [passenger] was to state that throughout the journey the appellant drove at around the 30 mph mark and that, had the pedestrian remained to the right of the car, there would have been no accident. There was, therefore, no evidence of fault in the manner in which the car was driven; certainly, the Crown relied on none ...

His Lordship quoted from s 12A(1), (2) of the Theft Act 1968 and went on:

The assertion made in the Crown Court by the defendant was that no liability could attach to him under s 12A(2)(b) unless it were proved that the accident in question had been occasioned by culpable driving on his part ...

... [I]t is unhelpful, in our judgment, to gloss the statute by referring to the manner or mode of driving: the words are plain and simple. In our view, the question for the court on their proper construction is, was the driving of the vehicle a cause of an accident? Any other approach would require the court to read in words which are not there.

The learned recorder, in our view, was right to hold that the policy of this statute is to impose heavier sanctions on those who take vehicles unlawfully and then cause an accident, whether or not the accident involves any fault in the driving.

Dealing with the statutory words more distinctly, it is to be noted that there is a clear contrast between the words of s 12A(2)(a) that 'the vehicle was driven dangerously on a road' and those in (b) and (c), where the phrase is only 'owing to the driving of the vehicle'. Of course (d), the subparagraph contemplating that damage is caused to the vehicle, has nothing to say about fault at all ...

... Applying ordinary canons of statutory construction, it is impossible to say that the words of s 12A(2)(b) import a requirement of fault in the driving of the vehicle. No word suggesting fault appears in the statutory language. It seems to us that the ordinary meaning of the words used is simply to point to a requirement that there be a causal connection between the moving of the vehicle on the road and an accident which follows ...

DISHONESTLY ABSTRACTING ELECTRICITY

Section 13 of the Theft Act 1968: abstracting of electricity

(1) A person who dishonestly uses without due authority, or dishonestly causes to be wasted or diverted, any electricity shall on conviction on indictment be liable to imprisonment for a term not exceeding five years.

Although electricity is used without due authority if the meter is tampered with so that the amount of electricity used does not register on the meter (as in *Collins v DPP* (1987) *Times*, 20 October), the offence can also be committed even if the meter is not tampered with.

R v McCreadie and Tume (1992) 96 Cr App R 143 (CA)

Facts: The appellants moved in, as squatters, to an empty property where the electricity supply had originally been disconnected by the Electricity Board but subsequently reconnected to a meter installed illegally, possibly by earlier squatters. The appellants used the electricity but took no steps to inform the Electricity Board of their occupancy or to pay any bills.

Lord Taylor CJ: ... [W]e are unable to accept the submission that without tampering or interference with the meter an offence under s 13 cannot be committed. The three ingredients of the offence [are]: ... first, using a quantity of electricity; second, doing so without authority; and third, doing so dishonestly.

Here there is no doubt that the appellants used electricity. The lights were on when they were there and the police arrived. Equally they were doing so without authority. They were not the registered consumers. The Electricity Board had not authorised them to use electricity and indeed they had withdrawn the supply of electricity from those premises, so far as any use of it was concerned. The Electricity Board had no knowledge of them and no knowledge where to contact them should they wish to send the bill. There was no question here of due authority having been granted to these appellants to use the electricity.

The vital issue therefore is whether dishonesty has been proved ...

The suggestion that the meter had to be tampered with in some way in order to constitute the offence is, in our judgment, quite wrong.

His Lordship then approved a passage from Professor JC Smith's book, *The Law of Theft*, which stated:

> ... 'use' implies some consumption of electricity which would not occur but for the accused's act. If squatters switch on the electricity not intending to pay for it they appear to use it dishonestly.

We agree with that passage ...

The defence was that if a bill had come they would have paid. However, they were moving when the police arrived. They had not apprised the Electricity Board of their arrival, their departure, or their identity. In those circumstances, it was open to the jury to find that they were acting dishonestly and to convict. The jury did so. In our judgment this appeal must be dismissed.

Boggeln v Williams [1978] 1 WLR 873 (DC)

Lloyd J: ... The question for the opinion of the court is whether a person can be convicted of dishonestly abstracting electricity contrary to s 13 of the Theft Act 1968, if he intends to pay for the electricity when payment is due, and that intention is based on a genuine belief that he will be able to do so ...

The facts are these. On 27 October 1976, a representative of the East Midlands Electricity Board had disconnected the defendant's supply of electricity after due warning had been given by reason of the defendant's failure to pay an outstanding amount of £39.65. The defendant thereupon spoke to one of the Board's employees and informed him that he was intending to reconnect the supply himself. Shortly thereafter he broke the seal on the board's main fuse box and reconnected the supply by means of a piece of wire which he inserted in place of the main fuse which the board's employees had removed. The way in which he carried out the re-connection meant that the electricity which he used would continue to be recorded on the meter in the usual way.

There is then this important finding of fact in paragraph 2(5) of the case [stated by the justices]:

> As a result of the said conversation the [defendant] did not believe that the Board consented to reconnection by him. The [defendant] nevertheless did believe that, by giving notice of his intention and by ensuring that consumption was duly recorded through the meter, he was not acting dishonestly in reconnecting.

... There is then another important finding of fact in paragraph 2(8) [of the case stated by the justices]:

> At the time when the [defendant] reconnected the supply, the [defendant] believed, as he asserted, that he would be in a position to pay for the electricity consumed thereafter at the date when payment was due. We were satisfied that this belief was a genuine one and we were not satisfied that it was unreasonable.

There is no specific finding anywhere in the case as to the defendant's intention to pay for the electricity, but it is common ground in this case that that can be inferred. Finally, in paragraph 5 of the case it is stated:

> We were of the opinion that the defendant did believe that, when payment became due, he would be able to pay for the electricity consumed; that this belief was not proved to be unreasonable; and that the defendant's state of mind at the relevant time (ie when reconnecting the supply) was not dishonest.

The question for the opinion of the court is as follows:

> Is an intention to pay for electricity knowingly used without the authority of the Electricity Board capable of affording a defence to a charge under s 13 of the Theft Act 1968, if that intention is based on a genuine belief that the user will be able to pay at the due time for payment?

... The fact that the defendant did not believe at the time he reconnected his supply that he had the consent of the Board does not of itself make the defendant's conduct dishonest in law. It is a question of fact in each case for the tribunal of fact whether the necessary dishonesty is proved or not ...

O'Connor J and **Lord Widgery CJ** delivered concurring judgments.

MAKING OFF WITHOUT PAYMENT

Section 3 of the Theft Act 1978

(1) Subject to subsection (3) below, a person who, knowing that payment on the spot for any goods supplied or service done is required or expected from him, dishonestly makes off without having paid as required or expected and with intent to avoid payment of the amount due shall be guilty of an offence.

(2) For purposes of this section 'payment on the spot' includes payment at the time of collecting goods on which work has been done or in respect of which service has been provided.

(3) Subsection (1) above shall not apply where the supply of the goods or the doing of the service is contrary to law, or where the service done is such that payment is not legally enforceable.

(4) Any person may arrest without warrant anyone who is, or whom he, with reasonable cause, suspects to be, committing or attempting to commit an offence under this section.

The elements of the offence created by s 3 of the Theft Act 1978 are that the defendant:

(1) knowing that payment on the spot (for goods already supplied or services already done) is required or expected ...

(2) dishonestly ...

(3) makes off without having paid ...

(4) with intent to avoid payment of the amount due.

This section was enacted because of a loophole in s 15 of the Theft Act 1968 (obtaining services by deception). In *Edwards v Ddin* [1976] 1 WLR 942 the defendant filled up the tank of his car with petrol at a garage and then drove off without paying. The prosecution failed to secure a conviction under s 15 of the Theft Act 1968 because they were unable to prove that the defendant had intended from the outset not to pay for the petrol. For s 15 to apply, the deception must occur before the property is handed over.

Hence the need for s 3 of the Theft Act 1978, to cover cases where the defendant says that he formed the intention not to pay for the goods or services *after* he had obtained them. This section therefore has the potential to cover situations such as:

- the diner who leaves the restaurant without paying;
- the passenger who fails to pay his taxi fare at the end of the journey;
- the motorist who fills up his petrol tank and leaves the garage without paying for the petrol.

Payment on the spot

This term is partially defined by s 3(2). It means little more than 'immediate payment'. Under s 3(3) payment must be legally enforceable (so failing to pay a prostitute after intercourse has taken place would not be an offence under s 3, although it could be an offence under s 1 of the Theft Act 1978).

Troughton v The Metropolitan Police [1987] Crim LR 138 (DC)

Facts: A taxi driver agreed to take the appellant to his home somewhere in Highbury. The appellant, having had a great deal to drink, had not told the driver his address. The driver had to stop to obtain directions from the appellant at some point. There was an argument, the appellant accusing the driver of making an unnecessary diversion. The taxi driver, being unable to get an address from the appellant, drove to the nearest police station to see if someone else could help.

Held: The basis for allowing this appeal was that the journey had not been completed and the consequence of that was a breach of contract by the taxi driver. Instead of resolving the argument about further instructions during the journey the driver broke away from the route which would have taken the appellant home and in order to go to the police station. The driver, being in breach of contract, was not lawfully able to demand the fare at any time thereafter. For that reason, among others, the appellant was never in a situation in which he was bound to pay or even tender the money for the journey, and thus it could not be contended that he made off without payment.

R v Aziz [1993] Crim LR 708 (CA)

Facts: Two people requested a taxi to take them to a particular address. On arrival at that address the taxi driver asked for a fare of £15. The passengers declined to pay that much and offered £4 instead. The radio controller confirmed that the fare was £15 but the passengers still refused to pay. The driver started to drive them back to the address from which he had collected them but, en route, decided to drive to a police station. However, the two passengers forced the car to stop and ran off. The taxi driver managed to catch one of the men. The defendant argued that the requirement for payment had ceased because the driver had announced his intention of taking the passengers back to the place from where the journey had started.

Held: 'On the spot' means 'there and then'. The words 'makes off' involve a departure without paying from the place where payment would normally be made. In the case of a taxi, payment might be made while sitting in the taxi or standing by the window. In the present case, payment was requested while the passengers were still in the taxi. It became apparent to the driver that they were disputing the fare. The fact that the driver, realising that there was a prospect that they would not pay their fare, drove off somewhere else, did not mean that when the defendant ran off he could not, as a matter of law, be making off without payment. It was the time at which he made off which was critical. When this defendant made off, he had formed the intention to avoid payment of a fare which was still due and owing.

Making off

In most cases, no further explanation of these words is necessary. They simply mean that the customer leaves without paying. However, the offence can be committed where the supplier of the goods or services allows the customer to leave as the result of some deception (although a charge of evading liability may be more appropriate).

Handing over a worthless cheque and then making off could, in principle, be an offence under s 3. However, s 2(1)(b) would be the more appropriate charge: see *R v Hammond* [1982] Crim LR 611.

'Making off' normally entails leaving the premises. Thus, if the customer starts to leave but is prevented from doing so, he is guilty only of an attempt to make off.

R v McDavitt [1981] Crim LR 843 (Croydon Crown Court)

Facts: The defendant had a meal with three friends in a restaurant. At the end of the meal his friends left the restaurant and the defendant remained at the table where they had all been sitting. The bill was brought on a saucer to his table and an argument ensued between the defendant and the owner of the restaurant which ended with the defendant refusing to pay any of the bill. He went towards the door whereupon someone standing by the door advised him not to leave as the police were being called. The defendant then went to the toilet in the restaurant where he remained until the police arrived. He was arrested and taken to a police station where he later made a statement under caution in which he admitted the above facts saying that it was his intention to leave without paying for the meal but that he decided to stay on being told about the police being summoned. He was subsequently indicted under s 3 of the Theft Act 1978 with making off from the restaurant without paying for the food and wine which had been consumed. On a submission of no case to answer:

Held: 'Makes off' refers to making off from the spot where payment is required or expected. What is the spot depends on the circumstances of each case. In this case the spot was the restaurant. The jury would be directed that it was not open to them to find the defendant guilty of the offence on the indictment but that it was open to them to find him guilty of an attempt to commit the offence.

R v Brooks and Brooks (1982) 76 Cr App R 66 (CA)

Facts: The appellants, father and daughter, along with a person named Smith, had a meal together one evening in the upstairs room of a restaurant. At 10.30 pm the daughter was seen leaving the premises in haste. The manager went upstairs and saw the two men were not there but found Smith downstairs waiting outside the men's lavatory.

Nearby was a door inside the premises which led into the yard. Smith made no comment when asked about the unpaid bill but, after entering the lavatory, later made off through the outer door. The manager chased after him and asked him to come back. While they were re-entering the restaurant, the father came out of it. All three then went back inside. All the father could offer for payment for the bill of £8.52 was a cheque for £130 in his favour, which later turned out to be valueless. Smith said in the father's hearing that the payment was not due from him, Smith. When the daughter was later interviewed by the police she maintained that Smith had met them earlier that night for the first time and had generously offered to treat her and her father to a meal.

Both father and daughter were charged with making off without payment contrary to s 3(1) of the Theft Act 1978.

Kilner Brown J: ... In our opinion, the words 'dishonestly makes off' are words easily understandable by any jury which, in the majority of cases, require no elaboration in a summing up. The jury should be told to apply the words in their ordinary natural meaning and to relate them to the facts of the case. We agree with the decision in *R v McDavitt* [1981] Crim LR 843 that 'making off' involves a departure from the spot where payment is required ...

On the facts of this case, it was not necessary to elaborate on the necessity to establish that there was a departure from the spot. The evidence of this was there. Both went outside the premises. However, in a case where the accused is stopped before passing the spot where payment is required, a jury should be directed that that may constitute an attempt to commit the offence, rather than the substantive offence, provided that the other ingredients are established ...

In the case of the appellant Julie Brooks, there is a further and different consideration ...

... [T]he jury were never told that upon the evidence that she left earlier and in haste and her defence that she went to the restaurant at the other man's invitation believing that he would pay, they would have to draw the inference that at the time she left she intended dishonestly to evade payment, before she could be convicted. If the jury had been alerted to this necessity, it is quite possible that they may not have been satisfied of her guilt ...

Intent to avoid payment

In addition to proving dishonesty (a separate element of the offence), the prosecution must also prove that the defendant intended to make permanent default, in other words, never to pay for the goods or services supplied. If the defendant is merely trying to postpone payment, then an offence under s 3 is not committed.

R v Allen [1985] AC 1029 (HL)

Lord Hailsham of St Marylebone LC: ... Count 2 of the indictment, which resulted in the conviction appealed from, read as follows:

> Statement of Offence: Making off without payment, contrary to s 3 of the Theft Act 1978.

> Particulars of Offence: Christopher Allen, on a day between 8 and 11 February 1983, knowing that payment on the spot for goods supplied and services done was required or expected from him, dishonestly made off without having paid as required or expected and with intent to avoid payment of the £1,286.94 due.

The facts, which are not disputed ... were as follows. The respondent, Christopher Allen, booked a room at a hotel for 10 nights from 15 January 1983. He stayed on thereafter and finally left on 11 February 1983 without paying his bill in the sum of £1,286.94. He telephoned two days later to explain that he was in financial difficulties because of some business transactions and arranged to return to the hotel on 18 February 1983 to remove his belongings and leave his Australian passport as security for the debt. He was arrested on his return and said that he genuinely hoped to be able to pay the bill and denied he was acting dishonestly. On 3 March 1983, he was still unable to pay the bill and provided an explanation to the police of his financial difficulties. The respondent's defence was that he had acted honestly and had genuinely expected to pay the bill from the proceeds of various business ventures ...

The judgment of the Court of Appeal, with which I agree, was delivered by Boreham J. He said [1985] 1 WLR 50, 57:

To secure a conviction under s 3 of the 1978 Act the following must be proved:

(1) that the defendant in fact made off without making payment on the spot;

(2) the following mental elements:

    (a) knowledge that payment on the spot was required or expected of him; and

    (b) dishonesty; and

    (c) intent to avoid payment [that is, 'of the amount due'].

I agree with this analysis. To this the judge adds the following comment:

> If (c) means, or is taken to include, no more than an intention to delay or defer payment of the amount due it is difficult to see what it adds to the other elements. Anyone who knows that payment on the spot is expected or required of him and who then dishonestly makes off without paying as required or expected must have at least the intention to delay or defer payment. It follows, therefore, that the conjoined phrase 'and with intent to avoid payment of the amount due' adds a further ingredient – an intention to do more than delay or defer – an intention to evade payment altogether.

My own view, for what it is worth, is that the section thus analysed is capable only of this meaning ... Even on the assumption that, in the context, the word 'avoid' without the addition of the word 'permanently' is capable of either meaning, which Boreham J was inclined to concede, I find myself convinced by his final paragraph, which reads:

> Finally, we can see no reason why, if the intention of Parliament was to provide, in effect, that an intention to delay or defer payment might suffice, Parliament should not have said so in explicit terms. This might have been achieved by the insertion of the word 'such' before 'payment' in the phrase in question. It would have been achieved by a grammatical reconstruction of the material part of s 3(1) thus, 'dishonestly makes off without having paid and with intent to avoid payment of the amount due as required or expected'. To accede to the Crown's submission would be to read the section as if it were constructed in that way. That we cannot do. Had it been intended to relate the intention to avoid 'payment' to 'payment as required or expected' it would have been easy to say so. The section does not say so. At the very least it contains an equivocation which should be resolved in favour of the appellant.

There is really no escape from this argument ...

Lord Scarman, **Lord Diplock**, **Lord Bridge of Harwich** and **Lord Brightman** all agreed with **Lord Hailsham LC**.

Further reading

S Cooper and MJ Allen, 'Appropriation after *Gomez*' [1993] J Crim Law 186

S Gardner, 'Appropriation in theft: the last word?' (1993) 109 LQR 194

S Gardner, 'Property and theft' [1998] Crim LR 35

E Griew, 'Dishonesty: the objections to *Feely* and *Ghosh*' [1985] Crim LR 341

A Halpin, 'The test for dishonesty' [1996] Crim LR 283

K Puttick and M Molan, 'Benefits and the criminal law: "fraud" and the new parameters of welfare crime' (2000) 7 Welfare Benefits 10

JC Smith, 'Stealing tickets' [1998] Crim LR 723

CHAPTER 19

BURGLARY AND GOING EQUIPPED

BURGLARY

Section 9 of the Theft Act 1968

(1) A person is guilty of burglary if:

  (a) he enters any building or part of a building as a trespasser and with intent to commit any such offence as is mentioned in subsection (2) below; or

  (b) having entered any building or part of a building as a trespasser he steals or attempts to steal anything in the building or that part of it or inflicts or attempts to inflict on any person therein any grievous bodily harm.

(2) The offences referred to in subsection (1)(a) above are offences of stealing anything in the building or part of a building in question, of inflicting on any person therein any grievous bodily harm or raping any person therein, and of doing unlawful damage to the building or anything therein.

(3) A person guilty of burglary shall on conviction on indictment be liable to imprisonment for a term not exceeding:

  (a) where the offence was committed in respect of a building or part of a building which is a dwelling, 14 years;

  (b) in any other case, 10 years.

(4) References in subsections (1) and (2) above to a building, and the reference in subsection (3) above to a building which is a dwelling, shall apply also to an inhabited vehicle or vessel, and shall apply to any such vehicle or vessel at times when the person having a habitation in it is not there as well as at times when he is.

Section 9(1) of the Theft Act 1968 creates two separate offences. In other words, there are two types of burglary. Common to both types are these requirements:

(1) that the defendant must enter a building or part of a building;

(2) that the defendant must enter the building (or part thereof) as a trespasser (ie a person who does not have permission, whether express or implied, to be on the premises).

For an offence under s 9(1)(a), the defendant must so enter with the intention of committing theft, causing grievous bodily harm, rape or criminal damage.

For an offence under s 9(1)(b), the defendant, having so entered, must actually commit or attempt to commit theft or the infliction of grievous bodily harm.

'... building or part of a building ...'

To be a building, a structure must have a degree of permanence. So, a freezer trailer (which could be hooked up to a lorry and transported at any time) was held not to be a building (*Norfolk Constabulary v Seekings* [1986] Crim LR 167); but a freezer which was 25 feet long, weighed three tons, was connected to the electricity supply and had been in place for at least two years, was held to be a building (*B v Leathley* [1979] Crim LR 314). The test is that laid down by Byles J in *Stevens v Gourley* (1859) CBNS 99 at 112, that the structure must be 'of considerable size and intended to be permanent or at least to endure for a considerable period'. That entry into part of a building may amount to burglary means that a person may become a burglar (if the other elements of the offence are satisfied) by going from a part in which he is lawful visitor to a part in which he is not: see *R v Walkington* (extracted below).

R v Walkington [1979] 1 WLR 1169 (CA)

Geoffrey Lane LJ: ... It is important at the outset to see what it was that the defendant was charged with precisely. The charge read as follows:

Statement of offence: Burglary, contrary to s 9(1)(a) of the Theft Act 1968.

Particulars of offence: Terence Walkington on 15 January 1977, entered as a trespasser part of a building known as Debenhams store with intent to steal therein.

... So far as the facts were concerned, there was very little, if any, dispute. On 15 January 1977, shortly before closing time of Debenhams store in Oxford Street, the defendant was seen in the menswear department of that store. He was kept under observation by Mr Rogers, who was a store detective, and two of his colleagues. The store closed at 6.00 pm. At about 20 minutes to six the various counter assistants were cashing up their tills. The evidence given by Mr Rogers was that the defendant seemed to be interested primarily, if not solely, in what was going on at the various tills in the store.

In due course he was observed to travel up on the escalator to the first floor. On that floor was an unattended till in the centre of a three-sided counter, the drawer of the till being partially opened. There was some dispute as to the precise dimensions of this three-sided counter, but what was agreed was that it was a movable counter. It was not static in the sense of being fixed to the floor. One of the descriptions of it showed that what we may call the north side of the counter was about 4 feet in length, the east side was about 12 feet in length and the west side was about 6 feet in length, the till being situated on the north side, the 4 foot length. Other descriptions of the counter gave different dimensions. But in each case it is to be observed that the till was in a corner formed by two of these counters. The evidence was that the area inside that rectangle or partial rectangle was reserved for the staff and it was clear, so it was suggested, that any customer seeing that area would realise that his permission to be in the store did not extend to a permission to be in that area.

The defendant, on the evidence, moved to the opening of the rectangular area described, that is to say to the part thereof which was not filled in by any counter, looked all around him, then bent down and having got to the till pulled the drawer further open. Having looked into the drawer the defendant slammed it to, said something and started making his way out of the shop, when he was stopped by the store detective.

In fact there was nothing in the drawer. The fact that the till drawer was partially open was an indication to anyone in the know that the assistant at that particular counter had cashed up that particular till.

The police were duly called in and the defendant was arrested. He was taken to Marylebone police station where he made a statement in writing, which reads as follows:

> I came up the West End to do some shopping and I went into Debenhams for a tie. I walked around the store for a while and looked at some coats. I went up on the first floor to have a look at the shoes. After a while I noticed a till partly open with a drawer beneath it. I thought I might be able to steal something from it so I opened the drawer but there was nothing in it worth stealing which was my intention. I shut the drawer again and walked away. That was when the security bloke stopped me. I don't know why I did it now, it seems so stupid. I would like to take this opportunity of saying how sorry I am and apologise to the store, the police and the court.

The defendant at the trial gave evidence according to his statement, claiming that he had gone to the store originally as a *bona fide* customer. He had gone to look at the dresses on the first floor and had given way to the temptation of opening the drawer. He had no idea that he was trespassing and he had not looked at the tills on the ground floor before he went up to the first floor as the store detective had said ...

What the prosecution had to prove here was that the defendant had entered a part of a building as a trespasser with intent to steal anything in that part of the building ...

His Lordship then cited with approval two passages, one from Professor Griew's book, *The Theft Acts 1968 and 1978*, and the other from Professor Smith's book, *The Law of Theft*. Those passages read as follows:

> A licence to enter a building may extend to part of the building only. If so, the licensee will trespass if he enters some other part not within the scope of the licence. To do so with intent to commit in that other part one of the specified offences, or to do so and then to commit or attempt to commit one of those offences therein, will be burglary. [Professor Griew]

> ... A customer in a shop who goes behind the counter and takes money from the till during a short absence of the shopkeeper would be guilty of burglary even though he entered the shop with the shopkeeper's permission. The permission did not extend to his going behind the counter. [Professor Smith]

... Here, it seems to us, there was a physical demarcation. Whether it was sufficient to amount to an area from which the public was plainly excluded was a matter for the jury. It seems to us that there was ample evidence on which they could come to the conclusion (a) that the management had impliedly prohibited customers entering that area and (b) that this particular defendant knew of that prohibition ...

Entry as a trespasser

R v Collins [1973] QB 100 (CA)

Edmund Davies LJ: This is about as extraordinary a case as my brethren and I have ever heard either on the bench or while at the bar. Stephen William George Collins was convicted ... of burglary with intent to commit rape ...

... At about 2 o'clock in the early morning of Saturday 24 July 1971, a young lady of 18 went to bed at her mother's home in Colchester. She had spent the evening with her boyfriend. She had taken a certain amount of drink, and it may be that this fact affords some explanation of her inability to answer satisfactorily certain crucial questions put to her at the trial.

She has the habit of sleeping without wearing night apparel in a bed which is very near the lattice-type window of her room. At one stage in her evidence she seemed to be saying that the bed was close up against the window which, in accordance with her practice, was wide open. In the photographs which we have before us, however, there appears to be a gap of some sort between the two, but the bed was clearly quite near the window.

At about 3.30 or 4.00 am she awoke and she then saw in the moonlight a vague form crouched in the open window. She was unable to remember, and this is important, whether the form was on the outside of the window sill or on that part of the sill which was inside the room, and for reasons which will later become clear, that seemingly narrow point is of crucial importance.

The young lady then realised several things: first of all that the form in the window was that of a male; second that he was a naked male, and third that he was a naked male with an erect penis. She also saw in the moonlight that his hair was blond. She thereupon leapt to the conclusion that her boyfriend, with whom for some time she had been on terms of regular and frequent sexual intimacy, was paying her an ardent nocturnal visit. She promptly sat up in bed, and the man descended from the sill and joined her in bed and they had full sexual intercourse. But there was something about him which made her think that things were not as they usually were between her and her boyfriend. The length of his hair, his voice as they had exchanged what was described as 'love talk', and other features led her to the conclusion that somehow there was something different. So she turned on the bedside light, saw that her companion was not her boyfriend and slapped the face of the intruder, who was none other than the defendant. He said to her, 'Give me a good time tonight', and got hold of her arm, but she bit him and told him to go. She then went into the bathroom and he promptly vanished.

The complainant said that she would not have agreed to intercourse if she had known that the person entering her room was not her boyfriend. But there was no suggestion of any force having been used on her, and the intercourse which took place was undoubtedly effected with no resistance on her part.

The defendant was seen by the police at about 10.30 am later that same morning. According to the police, the conversation which took place then elicited these points: He was very lustful the previous night. He had taken a lot of drink, and we may here note that drink (which to him is a very real problem) had brought this young man into trouble several times before, but never for an offence of this kind. He went on to say that he knew the complainant because he had worked around her house. On this occasion, desiring sexual intercourse – and according to the police evidence he added that he was determined to have a girl, by force if necessary, although that part of the police evidence he challenged – he went on to say that he walked around the house, saw a light in an upstairs bedroom, and he knew that this was the girl's bedroom. He found a step ladder, leaned it against the wall and climbed up and looked into the bedroom. What he could see inside through the wide-open window was a girl who was naked and asleep. So he descended the ladder and stripped off all his clothes with the exception of his socks, because apparently he took the view that if the girl's mother entered the bedroom it would be easier to effect a rapid escape if he had his socks on than if he was in his bare feet. That is a matter about which we are not called on to express any view, and would in any event find ourselves unable to express one.

Having undressed, he then climbed the ladder and pulled himself up on to the window sill. His version of the matter is that he was pulling himself in when she awoke. She then got up and knelt on the bed, she put her arms around his neck and body, and she seemed to pull him into the bed.

He went on:

> I was rather dazed because I didn't think she would want to know me. We kissed and cuddled for about 10 or 15 minutes and then I had it away with her but found it hard because I had had so much to drink.

The police officer said to the defendant:

> It appears that it was your intention to have intercourse with this girl by force if necessary, and that it was only pure coincidence that this girl was under the impression that you were her boyfriend and apparently that is why she consented to allowing you to have sexual intercourse with her.

It was alleged that he then said, 'Yes, I feel awful about this. It is the worst day of my life, but I know it could have been worse.'

Thereupon the officer said to him – and the defendant challenges this: 'What do you mean, you know it could have been worse?', to which he is alleged to have replied:

> Well, my trouble is drink and I got very frustrated. As I've told you, I only wanted to have it away with a girl and I'm only glad I haven't really hurt her.

Then he made a statement under caution, in the course of which he said:

> When I stripped off and got up the ladder I made my mind up that I was going to try and have it away with this girl. I feel terrible about this now, but I had too much to drink. I am sorry for what I have done.

In the course of his testimony, the defendant said that he would not have gone into the room if the girl had not knelt on the bed and beckoned him into the room. He said that if she had objected immediately to his being there or to his having sexual intercourse he would not have persisted. While he was keen on having sexual intercourse that night, it was only if he could find someone who was willing. He strongly denied having told the police that he would, if necessary, have pushed over some girl for the purpose of having intercourse ...

Now, one feature of the case which remained at the conclusion of the evidence in great obscurity is where exactly Collins was at the moment when, according to him, the girl manifested that she was welcoming him. Was he kneeling on the sill outside the window or was he already inside the room, having climbed through the window frame, and kneeling on the inner sill? It was crucial matter, for there were certainly three ingredients that it was incumbent on the Crown to establish. Under s 9 of the Theft Act 1968, which renders a person guilty of burglary if he enters any building or part of a building as a trespasser and with the intention of committing rape, the entry of the accused into the building must first be proved. Well, there is no doubt about that, for it is common ground that he did enter this girl's bedroom, second, it must be proved that he entered as a trespasser. We will develop that point a little later. Third, it must be proved that he entered as a trespasser with intent at the time of entry to commit rape therein ...

Having concluded that a defendant must be shown to have known he was trespassing, or at least to have been reckless as to whether he was, in order to be convicted of burglary, Edmund Davies LJ continued:

... Having so held, the pivotal point of this appeal is whether the Crown established that this defendant at the moment that he entered the bedroom knew perfectly well that he was not welcome there or, being reckless whether he was welcome or not, was nevertheless determined to enter.

That in turn involves consideration as to where he was at the time that the complainant indicated that she was welcoming him into her bedroom. If, to take an example that was put in the course of argument, her bed had not been near the window but was on the other side of the bedroom, and he (being determined to have her sexually even against her will) climbed through the window and crossed the bedroom to reach her bed, then the offence charged would have been established. But in this case, as we have related, the layout of the room was different, and it became a point of nicety which had to be conclusively established by the Crown as to where he was when the girl made welcoming signs, as she unquestionably at some stage did ...

... [W]hat the accused had said was, 'She knelt on the bed, she put her arms around me and then I went in'. If the jury thought he might be truthful in that assertion, they would need to consider whether or not, although entirely surprised by such a reception being accorded to him, this young man might not have been entitled reasonably to regard her action as amounting to an invitation to him to enter. If she in fact appeared to be welcoming him, the Crown do not suggest that he should have realised or even suspected that she was so behaving because, despite the moonlight, she thought he was someone else. Unless the jury were entirely satisfied that the defendant made an effective and substantial entry into the bedroom without the complainant doing or saying anything to cause him to believe that she was consenting to his entering it, he ought not to be convicted of the offence charged. The point is a narrow one, as narrow maybe as the window sill which is crucial to this case. But this is a criminal charge of gravity and, even though one may suspect that his intention was to commit the offence charged, unless the facts show with clarity that he in fact committed it he ought not to remain convicted.

Some question arose whether or not the defendant can be regarded as a trespasser *ab initio*. But we are entirely in agreement with the view ... that the common law doctrine of trespass *ab initio* has no application to burglary under the Theft Act 1968. One further matter that was canvassed ought perhaps to be mentioned. The point was raised that, the complainant not being the tenant or occupier of the dwelling house and her mother being apparently in occupation, this girl herself could not in any event have extended an effective invitation to enter, so that even if she had expressly and with full knowledge of all material facts invited the defendant in, he would nevertheless be a trespasser. Whatever be the position in the law of tort, to regard such a proposition as acceptable in the criminal law would be unthinkable.

We have to say that this appeal must be allowed on the basis that the jury were never invited to consider the vital question whether this young man did enter the premises as a trespasser, that is to say knowing perfectly well that he had no invitation to enter or reckless of whether or not his entry was with permission ...

R v Brown [1985] Crim LR 212 (CA)

Facts: A witness, having heard the sound of breaking glass, saw the appellant partially inside a shop front display. The top half of his body was inside the shop window as though he were rummaging around inside it. The witness assumed that his feet were on the ground outside, although his view was obscured. The appellant appealed against his conviction for burglary on the ground that he had not 'entered' the building, since his body was not entirely within it.

Held: Dismissing the appeal (and applying *R v Collins* [1973] QB 100), the word 'enter' in s 9 of the Theft Act 1968 did not require that the whole of a defendant's body be within a building. His entry had been 'substantial and effective'.

R v Ryan (1996) 160 JP 610 (CA)

Hirst LJ: ... The facts of the burglary are as follows. At about 2.30 am on Sunday 13 November 1994 the appellant was found stuck in a downstairs window by the elderly occupier. The window was 1 ft high and 2 ft 6 ins across. The appellant had his head and right arm inside the window and was trapped by the window itself on his neck. The rest of his body remained outside the window. On being accosted by the householder, the appellant said: 'Have you any Fairy Liquid? I'm stuck in the window.' The occupier demanded to know what he was doing there, to which he replied: 'I'm getting my baseball hat. My mate's put my baseball hat through the window.' The police were called and recovered a knife and a baseball hat from the ground outside the window in which the appellant was stuck. These two items significantly were the same knife and hat which formed the subject matter of the handling charge to which the appellant pleaded guilty. Eventually, the fire brigade had to be summoned to extricate the appellant from the window.

He was interviewed at 2.25 pm on the same day at Swindon police station and maintained his scarcely credible story that the baseball cap had been dropped through the open window by another person. He repeated the same line of defence in his evidence at the trial, which not surprisingly was disbelieved by the jury.

The appeal against conviction raises one point and one point only, namely whether as a matter of law his action was capable of constituting an entry ...

His Lordship quoted from s 9(1) of the Theft Act 1968 and went on:

The question is, was this capable of constituting an entry? That point was conclusively decided in *R v Brown* ... The judgment of the court was given by Watkins LJ. In that case also there was a partial entry through a window. The very same point was taken as in the present case, namely:

> Counsel for the appellant contends there can be no offence committed under the provisions of s 9(1) unless the person accused of the burglary is found upon the facts to have been at the relevant time wholly within the building.

That proposition was rejected by the court and Watkins LJ made it crystal clear in his judgment that a person can enter in the circumstances where only part of his body is actually within the premises.

[Counsel for the appellant] sought to distinguish *Brown's* case from the present case on the footing that in the former the appellant was capable of stealing property within the building, whereas in the present case, since the appellant was stuck firm by his neck in the window, he was incapable. That is a totally irrelevant distinction which in no way affects the principle laid down in *Brown* which is binding on us. There, the partial entry was capable of constituting entry. So here also this partial presence of the appellant within the building, albeit stuck in the window, was capable of constituting entry and it was therefore a matter for the jury to decide, as the learned recorder admirably directed them. The appeal against conviction will therefore be dismissed ...

Mens rea for trespass

R v Collins [1973] QB 100 (CA)

Edmund Davies LJ: ... We hold that, for the purposes of s 9 of the Theft Act 1968, a person entering a building is not guilty of trespass if he enters without knowledge that he is trespassing or at least without acting recklessly as to whether or not he is unlawfully entering ...

... In the judgment of this court there cannot be a conviction for entering premises 'as a trespasser' within the meaning of s 9 of the Theft Act 1968 unless the person entering does so knowing that he is a trespasser and nevertheless deliberately enters, or, at the very least, is reckless as to whether or not he is entering the premises of another without the other party's consent.

Having so held, the pivotal point of this appeal is whether the Crown established that this defendant at the moment that he entered the bedroom knew perfectly well that he was not welcome there or, being reckless whether he was welcome or not, was nevertheless determined to enter.

R v Jones; R v Smith [1976] 1 WLR 672 (CA)

Facts: The appellants were charged with burglary, contrary to s 9(1)(b) of the Theft Act 1968. The prosecution case was that they had entered the house of Smith's father and stolen two television sets. Smith's father had reported the theft to the police at the time, but at the trial of Smith and Jones he gave evidence to the effect that he had given Smith unreserved permission to enter the house, stating that his son, Christopher Smith, 'would not be a trespasser in the house at any time'.

James LJ: Mr Rose [counsel for the appellants] argues that a person who had a general permission to enter premises of another person cannot be a trespasser. His submission is as short and as simple as that. Related to this case he says that a son to whom a father has given permission generally to enter the father's house cannot be a trespasser if he enters it even though he had decided in his mind before making the entry to commit a criminal offence of theft against the father once he had got into the house and had entered the house solely for the purpose of committing that theft. It is a bold submission. Mr Rose frankly accepts that there has been no decision of the court since this statute was passed which governs particularly this point. He has reminded us of the decision in *Byrne v Kinematograph Renters Society Ltd* [1958] 2 All ER 579 ... In that case persons had entered a cinema by producing tickets not for the purpose of seeing the show, but for an ulterior purpose. It was held in the action, which sought to show that they entered as trespassers pursuant to a conspiracy to trespass, that in fact they were not trespassers. The important words in the judgment of Harman J at p 593D are 'They did nothing that they were not invited to do ...' That provides a distinction between that case and what we consider the position to be in this case ... We were also referred to *Collins* (1972) 56 Cr App R 554; [1973] QB 100 and in particular to the long passage of Edmund Davies LJ, as he then was, commencing at pp 559 and 104 of the respective reports where the learned Lord Justice commenced the consideration of what is involved by the words '... the entry must be "as a trespasser"'. ... In our view the passage there referred to is consonant with the passage in the well known case of *Hillen and Pettigrew v ICI (Alkali) Ltd* [1936] AC 65 where, in the speech of Lord Atkin these words appear at p 69: 'My Lords, in my opinion this duty to an invitee only extends so long and so far as the invitee is making what can reasonably be contemplated as an ordinary and reasonable use of the premises by the invitee for the purpose for which he has been invited. He is not invited to use any part of the premises for purposes which he knows are wrongfully dangerous and constitute an improper use.' As Scrutton LJ has pointedly said [in *The Calgarth* [1926] P 93 at p 110] 'When you invite a person into your house to use the staircase you do not invite him to slide down the banisters.' That case of course was a civil case in which it was sought to make the defendant liable for a tort.

The decision in *Collins* ... added to the concept of trespass as a civil wrong only the mental element of *mens rea*, which is essential to the criminal offence. Taking the law as expressed in *Hillen and Pettigrew v ICI Ltd* ... and in the case of *Collins* ... it is our view that a person is a trespasser for the purpose of section 9(1)(b) ... if he enters premises of another knowing that he is entering in excess of the permission that has been given to him, or being reckless as to whether he is entering in excess of the permission that has been given to him to enter, providing the facts are known to the accused which enable him to realise that he is acting in excess of the permission given or that he is acting recklessly as to whether he exceeds that permission, then that is sufficient for the jury to decide that he is in fact a trespasser.

In this particular case it was a matter for the jury to consider whether, on all the facts, it was shown by the prosecution that the appellants entered with the knowledge that entry was being effected against the consent or in excess of the consent that had been given by Mr Smith senior to his son Christopher. The jury were, by their verdict satisfied of that. It was a novel argument that we heard, interesting but one without, in our view, any foundation.

The ulterior intent required under s 9(1)(a)

R v Walkington [1979] 1 WLR 1169 (CA)

See above for facts.

Geoffrey Lane LJ: ... [His Lordship turned to the second issue in the appeal, namely that there was no evidence that there was anything capable of being stolen.] In this case there is no doubt that the defendant was not on the evidence in two minds as to whether to steal or not. He was intending to steal when he went to that till and it would be totally unreal to ask oneself, or for the jury to ask themselves, the question, what sort of intent did he have? Was it a conditional intention to steal if there was money in the till or a conditional intention to steal only if what he found there was worth stealing? In this case it was a cash till and what plainly he was intending to steal was the contents of the till, which was cash. The mere fact that the till happened to be empty does not destroy his undoubted intention at the moment when he crossed the boundary between the legitimate part of the store and the illegitimate part of the store ...

... It seems to this court that in the end one simply has to go back to the words of the Act itself which we have already cited, and if the jury are satisfied, so as to feel sure, that the defendant has entered any building or part of a building as a trespasser, and are satisfied that at the moment of entering he intended to steal anything in the building or that part of it, the fact that there was nothing in the building worth his while to steal seems to us to be immaterial. He nevertheless had the intent to steal. As we see it, to hold otherwise would be to make a nonsense of this part of the Act and cannot have been the intention of the legislature at the time when the Theft Act 1968 was passed. Nearly every prospective burglar could no doubt truthfully say that he only intended to steal if he found something in the building worth stealing.

Petition: The Appeal Committee of the House of Lords (**Lord Wilberforce, Lord Edmund-Davies** and **Lord Keith of Kinkel**) refused a petition by the defendant for leave to appeal.

AG's Refs (Nos 1 and 2 of 1979) [1980] QB 180 (CA)

Roskill LJ: ... The question referred in *Reference No 1* is:

Whether a man who has entered a house as a trespasser with the intention of stealing money therein is entitled to be acquitted of an offence against s 9(1)(a) of the Theft Act 1968 on the grounds that his intention to steal is conditional upon his finding money in the house.

The answer of this court to this question is 'No'.

In the second reference the question is:

Whether a man who is attempting to enter a house as a trespasser with the intention of stealing anything of value which he may find therein is entitled to be acquitted of the offence of attempted burglary on the ground that at the time of the attempt his said intention was insufficient to amount to 'the intention of stealing anything' necessary for conviction under s 9 of the Theft Act 1968.

The answer of this court to this question is also 'No'.

His Lordship then referred to *R v Husseyn* (1977) 67 Cr App R 131 and continued:

The indictment in *R v Husseyn* – the Registrar has supplied the court with copies – was as follows:

Statement of Offence: Attempted Theft.

Particulars of Offence: Ulus Husseyn and Andrew Demetriou on or about the 27th day of February 1976 in Greater London, attempted to steal a quantity of sub-aqua equipment belonging to David Johnson.

Here therefore the relevant count was of attempted theft and not of theft but the charge related to a specific object. Therefore it was essential, in order to establish guilt on this charge of attempted theft, that the accused's intention had been to steal, not the contents of the parked van in question, but the specific object named in the count, namely the sub-aqua equipment. Lord Scarman's judgment must be understood against the background of that fundamental fact ...

[Lord Scarman in *R v Husseyn* said:]

... it cannot be said that one who has it in mind to steal only if what he finds is worth stealing has a present intention to steal.

We were asked to say that either that [that] sentence was wrong or that it was *obiter*. We are not prepared to do either. If we may say so with the utmost deference to any statement of law by Lord Scarman, if this sentence be open to criticism, it is because in the context it is a little elliptical. If one rewrites that sentence, so that it reads: 'It must be wrong, for it cannot be said that one who has it in mind to steal only if what he finds is worth stealing has a present intention to steal *the specific item charged*' (our emphasis added), then the difficulties disappear, because, as already stated, what was charged was attempted theft of a specific object ...

I come back to what Lord Scarman himself said in *Director of Public Prosecutions v Nock* [1978] AC 979 ...

An intention to steal can exist even though, unknown to the accused, there is nothing to steal: but, if a man be in two minds whether to steal or not, the intention required by the statute is not proved.

Section 9(1)(b) of the Theft Act 1968: theft and appropriation

For there to have been a burglary there must have been a theft, and therefore there must have been an appropriation.

R v Gregory (1981) 77 Cr App R 41 (CA)

Facts: The appellant was charged with burglary of a dwelling house. He gave evidence at his trial that a man called Tony, knowing that the appellant was a general dealer, had told him that his (Tony's) parents had died and that he was clearing out their bungalow. It was agreed that the appellant should visit the bungalow to see if there was anything he wished to purchase. The appellant and Tony went to a bungalow in Broadstairs and the appellant took some jewellery. He said that he did not realise that Tony had told him a pack of lies.

Watkins LJ: ... [His Lordship referred to the judgment of Eveleigh LJ in *R v Hale* (1978) 68 Cr App R 415 at 418 and continued:] Nor do we think that in a given criminal enterprise involving theft there can necessarily be only one 'appropriation' within s 3(1) of the Theft Act 1968. It seems to us that the question of whether, when and by whom there has been an appropriation of property has always to be determined by the jury having regard to the circumstances of the case. The length of time involved, the manner in which it came about and the number of people who can properly be said to have taken part in an appropriation will vary according to those circumstances. In a case of burglary of a dwelling-house and before any property is removed from it, it may consist of a continuing process and involve either a single appropriation by one or more persons or a number of appropriations of the property in the house by several persons at different times during the same incident. If this were not a correct exposition of the law of appropriation, startling and disturbing consequences could arise out of the presence of two or more trespassers in a dwelling-house.

Thus a person who may have more the appearance of a handler than the thief can nevertheless still be convicted of theft, and thus of burglary, if the jury are satisfied that with the requisite dishonest intent he appropriated, or took part in the appropriation, of another person's goods.

AGGRAVATED BURGLARY

Section 10 of the Theft Act 1968

(1) A person is guilty of aggravated burglary if he commits any burglary and at the time has with him any firearm or imitation firearm, any weapon of offence, or any explosive; and for this purpose:

(a) 'firearm' includes an airgun or air pistol, and 'imitation firearm' means anything which has the appearance of being a firearm, whether capable of being discharged or not; and

(b) 'weapon of offence' means any article made or adapted for use for causing injury to or incapacitating a person, or intended by the person having it with him for such use; and

(c) 'explosive' means any article manufactured for the purpose of producing a practical effect by explosion, or intended by the person having it with him for that purpose.

(2) A person guilty of aggravated burglary shall on conviction on indictment be liable to imprisonment for life.

Section 10(1)(b) of the Theft Act 1968: 'weapon of offence'

If the weapon is not 'made or adapted for causing injury to or incapacitating a person', the defendant must intend to use the weapon for such a purpose during the particular burglary with which he is charged.

R v Stones [1989] 1 WLR 156 (CA)

Facts: The appellant was charged with aggravated burglary, contrary to s 10(1) of the Theft Act 1968.

> **Glidewell LJ**: ... The primary facts, which were not in dispute at all, were these. The appellant admitted that he had taken part in a burglary of a dwelling house in Bedlington in the early hours of 29 June 1987. A police officer who was off duty had seen the appellant and another man loading stolen goods into a car. He telephoned the police. The two men ran off, but the appellant was caught running across a field and was arrested. When he was searched, a household knife was found in his pocket. When asked why he had it with him, he replied, 'For self-defence, because some lads from Blyth are after me'.
>
> Since it was a household knife, it was accepted by the prosecution that it was not, to go back to s 10(1) [of the Theft Act 1968], an article made or adapted for use for causing injury to or incapacitating a person. The prosecution accepted that they had to prove that it was intended by the person having it with him (the defendant) for such use ...
>
> It is agreed by counsel that the prosecution must prove that the appellant knew that he had a knife with him at the relevant time. Clearly that is right, because otherwise he cannot have the relevant intent. As I have said, the prosecution submit that if he knowingly had the knife with him at the time of the burglary with the intention of using it to cause injury to or incapacitate the lads from Blyth if he met them, the offence is proved. It is not necessary to prove the intention to use the knife to cause injury etc during the course of the burglary.
>
> In our view that submission is correct. The mischief at which the section is clearly aimed is that if a burglar has a weapon which he intends to use to injure some person unconnected with the premises burgled, he may nevertheless be tempted to use it if challenged during the course of the burglary and put under sufficient pressure ...

Time at which defendant must have with him the firearm, etc

If the allegation of burglary is brought under s 9(1)(a) the prosecution have to prove that *at the time of entering the building* as a trespasser with the intention to commit one of the specified offences (theft, grievous bodily harm, rape, criminal damage) the defendant had with him the firearm or other weapon.

If, on the other hand, the allegation of burglary is brought under s 9(1)(b), the time at which the defendant must be in possession of the firearm or other weapon is *the time at which he commits or attempts to commit one of the specified offences* theft or grievous bodily harm: see *R v O'Leary* (1986) 82 Cr App R 341.

R v O'Leary (1986) 82 Cr App R 341 (CA)

Lord Lane CJ: ... The facts of the case, which are not in dispute, were these. In the early hours of 31 January 1985 the appellant entered a house in South East London, almost certainly in search of money and valuables, though such an intent, namely the intent at the time of entry to steal, was not alleged against him. At the time of that entry he was unarmed. He looked round the house downstairs. It seems he found nothing there which interested him, except a kitchen knife with which he armed himself.

He then went upstairs. The occupants of the house, husband and wife, were disturbed. A struggle ensued in the course of which all three, husband wife and the appellant, received injuries. The appellant demanded and was given, he at that point being armed still with the kitchen knife, some cash and a bracelet ...

... Count 2 of the indictment reads as follows:

Statement of Offence: Aggravated Burglary contrary to s 10(1) of the Theft Act 1968.

Particulars of Offence: Michael O'Leary on 31st day of January 1985 entered as a trespasser a building known as 104 Lyndhurst Grove, London SE15, and stole therein a sum of money, a bracelet, a number of keys and a cash card belonging to John Marsh, and at the time of committing the said burglary had with him a weapon of offence, namely a knife.

If he had been charged under subsection (1)(a), the offence of burglary would be completed and committed when he entered and it would be at that point that one would have to consider whether or not he was armed. But in the case of subsection (1)(b), which is the one under which he was charged, the offence is complete when, and not until, the stealing is committed, provided again of course that he has trespassed in the first place. The prosecution did not have to prove an intent to steal at the time of entry as the charge is laid here. Indeed such an intent is irrelevant to the charge as laid.

It follows that under this particular charge, the time at which the defendant must be proved to have had with him a weapon of offence to make him guilty of aggravated burglary was the time at which he actually stole. As already indicated, at that moment, when he confronted the householders and demanded their cash and jewellery, which was the theft, he still had the kitchen knife in his hand ...

The judge ruled, as this court has indicated he should have ruled, namely that the material time in this charge for the possession of the weapon was the time when he confronted the householders and stole ...

R v Kelly (1992) 97 Cr App R 245 (CA)

Potts J: ... The prosecution's case was that on 19 June 1991, in the early hours of the morning, the appellant broke into a house in Brixton using a screwdriver to effect entry. He was surprised by the occupants of the house, a young couple, Mr Sheterline and Ms Matthews, while removing a video recorder from the living room ... The relevant part of [Mr Sheterline's evidence] reads as follows:

I went back into the living room and looked towards the bar and shouted, 'Oi, what do you want?' On hearing this, a black man sprung up from behind the bar. He looked unshaven with short black hair and was wearing a black hooded anorak with the hood down. He said to me, 'Where's the remote for the video?' I threw my knife over to the TV and video recorder which are in the far left-hand corner of the room and handed both remote control units to him. Whilst I was there, he said, 'Unplug the TV and video'. He had already turned the light off and he had pulled the hood up over his head and I suddenly felt him push something into the left-hand side of my rib cage. I could see it had a brown handle with a blunt metal end to it. It looked like a chisel.

I said to the man, 'Can I turn the light on because I can't see what I'm doing'. He said, 'No'. I said, 'Don't hurt us, just take the stuff and go, we won't say anything'.

The appellant then attempted to leave the house with the video in one hand and the screwdriver in the other, but he was apprehended by the police who had attended in response to information received from a member of the public. When the appellant emerged from the house, a policeman saw him holding the screwdriver in his hand.

... Thus the charge derives from s 9(1)(b) of the Act and the time at which the appellant must be proved to have had with him a weapon of offence to make him guilty of aggravated burglary was the time he actually stole: the screwdriver would become a weapon of offence on proof that the appellant intended to use it for causing injury to, or incapacitating Mr Sheterline or Ms Matthews at the time of the theft, thereby aggravating the burglary: s 10(1)(b). This construction follows from the clear language of s 10 of the Theft Act, and is consistent with its purpose.

'... has with him ...'

This phrase connotes a degree of immediate control over the firearm or weapon.

R v Kelt [1977] 1 WLR 1365 (CA)

The defendant was charged that he 'had with him a firearm ... with intent to commit an indictable offence' contrary to s 18 of the Firearms Act 1968.

Scarman LJ: ... [T]here must be a very close physical link and a degree of immediate control over the weapon by the man alleged to have the firearm with him ...

... [T]he judge [must] make it clear to the jury that possession of the firearm is not enough, that the law requires the evidence to go a stage further and to establish that the accused had the firearm with him. Of course the classic case of having a gun with you is if you are carrying it. But, even if you are not carrying it, you may yet have it with you, if it is immediately available to you. But if all that can be shown is possession in the sense that it is in your house or in a shed or somewhere where you have ultimate control, that is not enough.

R v Pawlicki [1992] 1 WLR 827 (CA)

The defendant was charged that he 'had with him a firearm' contrary to s 18 of the Firearms Act 1968.

Steyn LJ: ... A man who leaves a shotgun at home while he proceeds to the next town to rob a bank is still in possession of the shotgun but he does not 'have it with him' when he commits the robbery at the bank. Under s 18 [of the Firearms Act 1968] the words 'have it' import an element of propinquity which is not required for possession. [Further] 'having with him a firearm' is a wider concept than carrying the firearm.

CODIFICATION AND LAW REFORM PROPOSALS

In July 2000 the Home Office published its review of sexual offences *Setting the Boundaries: Reforming the Law on Sex Offences*. The review examined the case for reforming that aspect of s 9(1)(a) relating to entry as a trespasser with intent to rape:

2.16 Burglary with intent to rape

2.16.1 The Theft Act 1969 contains an aggravated burglary offence of burglary with intent to rape in s 9. This is an important element in the law on rape as it covers the situation where some one may break into a house (or office or other private place) 'with the intent of having sexual intercourse with the person within, if possible with consent but if not then by committing rape'. The rape does not have to take place for the offence to be committed. Even if no rape occurs, the trauma of being seriously threatened with rape by an intruder in your own bedroom or workplace, where you think you are safe, is profound ...

2.16.2 We considered whether this offence should be left as an aggravated burglary, or whether it was a sex offence. We concluded that the essence of the crime was the sexual intent rather than the burglary, and that hence it should be regarded as a sex offence. We thought that there was a risk that being tucked away in the Theft Act, it was an offence that could be overlooked. We also noted that it did not carry a requirement to register under the Sex Offenders Act at present.

The existing offence of burglary with intent to rape would need to be redefined to take account of our proposals to reform the law of serious sex offences. In order to differentiate our new offence, we thought that the word trespass was preferable to burglary – and covers the same elements of unwanted intrusion. We also thought that as the intent to commit a sex offence was central to the offence, the redefinition should apply to trespass with intent to commit a serious sex offence – rape, sexual assault by penetration, sexual assault or adult sexual abuse of a child – and that it should be codified with other sex offences.

GOING EQUIPPED FOR STEALING, ETC

The offence under s 25 of the Theft Act 1968, detailed below, is not related solely to burglary but is clearly of particular relevance as an ancillary offence. Reference may be made to *R v Doukas* [1978] 1 WLR 372 and *R v Rashid* [1977] 1 WLR 298 – considered in Chapter 21 – for two instances involving allegations of possession of articles for use to obtain property by deception (wine and spirits in the first case, bread and tomatoes in the other!).

Section 25 of the Theft Act 1968

(1) A person shall be guilty of an offence if, when not at his place of abode, he has with him any article for use in the course of or in connection with any burglary, theft or cheat.

(2) A person guilty of an offence under this section shall on conviction on indictment be liable to imprisonment for a term not exceeding three years.

(3) Where a person is charged with an offence under this section, proof that he had with him any article made or adapted for use in committing a burglary, theft or cheat shall be evidence that he had it with him for such use.

(4) Any person may arrest without warrant anyone who is, or whom he, with reasonable cause, suspects to be, committing an offence under this section.

(5) For the purposes of this section an offence under s 12(1) of this Act of taking a conveyance shall be treated as theft, and 'cheat' means an offence under s 15 of this Act.

The elements of the offence of 'going equipped' are:

(1) that the defendant is not at his 'place of abode'; and

(2) that he 'has with him' (ie has in his possession) certain articles; and

(3) that those articles are for use to commit burglary, theft or obtaining by deception.

Place of abode

R v Bundy [1977] 1 WLR 914 (CA)

Lawton LJ: ... The particulars of the offence ... were as follows: that the defendant and a man called Evans 'on 21 April 1975, when not in their places of abode, had with them a piece of piping, a hammer, a pipe threader and three pieces of stocking for use in the course of or in connection with theft'.

... On arresting the defendant and his passenger, the police searched the motor car [which the defendant had been driving]. In it they found the articles referred to in the particulars of offence. It was accepted in this court that there was evidence on which the jury could properly have decided that all the articles were articles for use in the course of or in connection with theft ...

At the trial, in the witness box, [the defendant's] evidence was that about four or five weeks before his arrest, he had borrowed the motor car in which he was arrested from a friend, and that he had lived in that motor car, travelling around in it ...

... [I]t is manifest that no offence is committed if a burglar keeps the implements of his criminal trade in his place of abode. He only commits an offence when he takes them from his place of abode. The phrase 'place of abode', in our judgment, connotes, first of all, a site. That is the ordinary meaning of the word 'place'. It is a site at which the occupier intends to abide. So, there are two elements in the phrase 'place of abode' – the element of site and the element of intention. When the defendant took the motor car to a site with the intention of abiding there, then his motor car on that site could be said to be his 'place of abode', but when he took it from that site to move it to another site where he intended to abide, the motor car could not be said to be his 'place of abode' during transit.

When he was arrested by the police he was not intending to abide on the site where he was arrested. It follows that he was not then at his place of abode. He may have had a place of abode the previous night, but he was away from it at the time of his arrest when in possession of articles which could be used for the purpose of theft ...

'... has with him ...'

This phrase, which also appears in s 10 of the Act (aggravated burglary), connotes a 'degree of immediate control': see *R v Kelt* (above); *R v Pawlicki* (above).

'... for use for burglary, theft or cheat ...'

'Burglary' means burglary for the purposes of s 9 of the Act; 'theft' means theft for the purposes of s 1 of the Act or taking a conveyance contrary to s 12 of the Act; 'cheat' means obtaining property by deception contrary to s 15 of the Act.

It can be proved that the defendant had the requisite intention in either of two ways:

(1) if the article in question is 'made or adapted' for use in burglary, theft or cheat (eg a jemmy or a bunch of skeleton keys), this very fact is evidence that the defendant intended to use the article for such purpose (so, effectively, a burden of proof is placed on the defendant to show that he had the article with him for an innocent purpose); or

(2) if the article is innocuous in itself (eg a screwdriver), the prosecution have to prove that the defendant intended to use it for burglary, theft or cheat (much will depend, of course, on the circumstances in which the defendant is found to be in possession of the article).

The defendant must have intended to use the article at some time in the future (in other words for an offence of burglary, theft or cheat which has not yet been committed). It is not enough that the article has been used in an offence of burglary, theft or cheat which has already been committed.

R v Ellames [1974] 1 WLR 1391 (CA)

Facts: A robbery took place in the course of which certain articles, including a sawn-off shotgun, were used. The appellant was charged with robbery and with going equipped for stealing contrary to s 25(1) of the Theft Act 1968. The case against the appellant was that, although he might not have been present at the robbery, he had helped with the planning of it, and that afterwards he had helped the robbers to escape, and in particular that he had helped in hiding the articles used in the robbery.

Browne J: ... In our judgment, the words in s 25(1) of the 1968 Act: 'has with him any article for use' mean 'has with him for the purpose' (or 'with the intention') 'that they will be used'. The effect of s 25(3) is that if the article is one 'made or adapted for use in committing a burglary, theft or cheat', that is evidence of the necessary intention, though not of course conclusive evidence. If the article is not one 'made or adapted' for such use, the intention must be proved on the whole of the evidence – as it must be in the case of an article which is so made or adapted, if the defendant produces some innocent explanation. We agree with the learned authors of Smith and Hogan's *Criminal Law* that s 25 is directed against acts preparatory to burglary, theft or cheat; that:

> Questions as to D's knowledge of the nature of the thing can hardly arise here, since it must be proved that he intended to use it in the course of or in connection with [burglary, theft or cheat]; and that the *mens rea* for this offence includes 'an intention to use the article in the course of or in connection with any of the specified crimes'.

An intention to use must necessarily relate to use in the future. ... It seems to us impossible to interpret s 25(1) of the 1968 Act as if it read: 'has with him any article for use or which *has been used* in the course of or in connection with any burglary, theft or cheat.' Equally, it is impossible to read s 25(3) as if it said: 'had it with him for or *after* such use.'

In our judgment the words 'for use' govern the whole of the words which follow. The object and effect of the words 'in connection with' is to add something to 'in the course of'. It is easy to think of cases where an article could be intended for use 'in connection with' though not 'in the course of' a burglary etc, eg articles intended to be used while doing preparatory acts or while escaping after the crime ...

In our view, to establish an offence under s 25(1) the prosecution must prove that the defendant was in possession of the article, and intended the article to be used in the course of or in connection with some future burglary, theft or cheat. But it is not necessary to prove that he intended it to be used in the course of or in connection with any *specific* burglary, theft or cheat; it is enough to prove a general intention to use it for *some* burglary, theft or cheat; we think that this view is supported by the use of the word 'any' in s 25(1). Nor, in our view, is it necessary to prove that the defendant intended to use it himself; it will be enough to prove that he had it with him with the intention that it should be used by someone else. For example, if in the present case it had been proved that the defendant was hiding away these articles, which had already been used for one robbery, with the intention that they should later be used by someone for some other robbery, he would be guilty of an offence under s 25(1).

Further reading

JC Smith, 'Burglary under the Theft Bill' [1968] Crim LR 367

PJ Pace, 'Burglarious trespass' [1985] Crim LR 716

CHAPTER 20

ROBBERY AND BLACKMAIL

ROBBERY

Section 8 of the Theft Act 1968

(1) A person is guilty of robbery if he steals, and immediately before or at the time of doing so, and in order to do so, he uses force on any person or puts or seeks to put any person in fear of being then and there subjected to force.

(2) A person guilty of robbery, or of an assault with intent to rob, shall on conviction on indictment be liable to imprisonment for life.

The offence of robbery, which (unlike other Theft Act offences such as burglary and theft) is triable only in the Crown Court, comprises the following elements:

(1) force or the threatened use of force,

(2) before or at the time of stealing,

(3) in order to steal; and

(4) theft (that is, the offence created by s 1 of the Theft Act 1968 as defined in ss 2–7 of the Act).

The use of force or threatened force

Corcoran v Anderton (1980) 71 Cr App R 104 (DC)

Watkins J: ... At 7.55 pm on 22 February 1979, Mrs Hall was in Conran Street in Manchester. She was carrying a handbag. Two youths came along, one the defendant, Christopher Corcoran, and another his co-accused Peter Partington. They had agreed beforehand to steal Mrs Hall's handbag. They began to carry out their purpose. Partington struck her in the back, took hold of and tugged at her handbag causing her to release it. Corcoran was present and participated. Mrs Hall understandably screamed when this attack was made upon her and fell. At that these two youths ran away. So Mrs Hall managed to recover her handbag. At no time, say the justices, did Partington have sole control of the handbag. They were finally of the opinion ... that the appropriation of the bag was complete when Partington pulled at it so causing Mrs Hall to release it ...

They were asked to state a case. They did and asked this court this question: 'Could the tugging at the handbag, accompanied by force, amount to robbery, notwithstanding the fact that the co-accused did not have sole control of the bag at any time?'

... Robbery, as the Theft Act 1968 provides by s 8(1), is committed if a person steals and immediately before or at the time of doing so and in order to do so force is used on any person.

... [The] circumstances [found by the justices] involve the use of force upon the person of Mrs Hall so that she lost her grip upon her handbag accompanied by the intention in the minds of both the appellant and his companion to steal, that is to say to take the handbag, by force if necessary, away from Mrs Hall and permanently deprive her of that handbag or its contents ...

... [C]onfining myself to the facts as found by the justices in the instant case, I think that an 'appropriation' takes place when an accused snatches a woman's handbag completely from her grasp, so that she no longer has physical control of it because it has fallen to the ground. What has been involved in such activity as that, bearing in mind the dishonest state of mind of the accused, is an assumption of the rights of the owner, a taking of the property of another ... In my judgment there cannot possibly be, save for the instance where a handbag is carried away from the scene of it, a clearer instance of robbery than that which these justices found was committed.

Turning to the actual question posed to this court, 'Could the tugging at the handbag, accompanied by force, amount to robbery, notwithstanding the fact that the co-accused did not have sole control of the bag at any time?' In my opinion, which may be contrary to some notions of what constitutes a sufficient appropriation to satisfy the definition of that word in s 3(1) of the Theft Act the forcible tugging of the handbag of itself could in the circumstances be a sufficient exercise of control by the accused person so as to amount to an assumption by him of the rights of the owner, and therefore an appropriation of the property ...

Eveleigh LJ: I agree. Each, that is to say the lady and the defendant, was trying to exclude the other from exclusive claim to the bag. The lady was treating the bag as hers, as indeed it was, and resisting any efforts of his to deprive her of it. He, on the other hand, was treating the bag as his and seeking to overcome her efforts to retain it. He was thereby exercising the rights which belonged to the owner. She too was doing so. She was doing it lawfully, he was doing it unlawfully. He was, in my view, appropriating that bag ...

Force

R v Dawson and James (1978) 68 Cr App R 170 (CA)

The point at issue was whether 'jostling' amounted to the use of force.

Lawton LJ: [Force] is a word in ordinary use. It is a word which juries understand. The learned judge left it to the jury to say whether jostling a man in the way which the victim described to such an extent that he had difficulty in keeping his balance could be said to be the use of force.

... It was a matter for the jury. They were to use their common sense and knowledge of the word. We cannot say that their decision as to whether force was used was wrong. They were entitled to the view that force was used.

Other points were discussed in the case as to whether the force had been used for the purpose of distracting the victim's attention or whether it was for the purpose of overcoming resistance. Those sorts of refinements may have been relevant under the old law, but so far as the new law is concerned the sole question is whether the accused used force on any person in order to steal. That issue in this case was left to the jury. They found in favour of the Crown.

We cannot say that this verdict was either unsafe or unsatisfactory. Accordingly the appeal is dismissed.

R v Clouden [1987] Crim LR 56 (CA)

Facts: The appellant was seen to follow a woman who was carrying a shopping basket in her left hand. He approached her from behind and wrenched the basket down and out of her grasp with both hands and ran off with it. He was charged in two counts with robbery and theft respectively and convicted on the first count of robbery. He appealed on the grounds (i) that there was insufficient evidence of resistance to the snatching of the bag to constitute force on the person under s 8 of the Theft Act 1968; and (ii) that the learned judge's direction to the jury on the requirement of force on the person was inadequate and confused.

Held, dismissing the appeal: the old cases distinguished between force on the actual person and force on the property which in fact causes force on the person but, following *Dawson and James* (1978) 68 Cr App R 170, the court should direct attention to the words of the statute without referring to the old authorities. The old distinctions have gone. Whether the defendant used force on any person in order to steal is an issue that should be left to the jury. The judge's direction to the jury was adequate. He told the jury quite clearly at the outset what the statutory definition was, though thereafter he merely used the word force and did not use the expression 'on the person'.

Theft

Since theft is an essential ingredient of robbery, it follows that if the defendant is not guilty of theft he cannot be guilty of robbery (so, in *R v Robinson* [1977] Crim LR 173 it was held that since the defendant had not acted dishonestly he could not be guilty of theft and so could not be guilty of robbery).

However, the prosecution must also prove that force was used immediately before, or at the same time as, the appropriation of the property. There must be a causal link between the theft and the use or threat of force (so a direction to the jury that they can convict of robbery even if they find that the violence is unconnected with the theft is wrong in law: see *R v Shendley* [1970] Crim LR 49). In *R v Clouden* [1987] Crim LR 56 the defendant wrenched the victim's shopping bag from her grasp and ran off with it; this use of force was held to amount to robbery.

It is clear that the courts take a robust attitude to the question of appropriation in the context of robbery, so as to allow the jury to take a common sense approach to the question whether or not there was a robbery.

R v Hale (1978) 68 Cr App R 415 (CA)

Eveleigh LJ: ... The prosecution alleged that the appellant and one McGuire went to the house of a Mrs Carrett. When she answered the door they rushed in. Each was wearing a stocking mask. The appellant put his hand over Mrs Carrett's mouth to stop her screaming and McGuire went upstairs to search. The appellant subsequently released his hold on Mrs Carrett and she went to the settee. He undid her dressing gown and touched her. He also exposed himself. McGuire then came downstairs with a jewellery box and asked where the rest was. The telephone rang. It was a next-door neighbour who had heard Mrs Carrett scream and wanted to know if everything was all right. Under threat from the appellant she replied everything was all right. All three then went upstairs and Mrs Carrett was asked where her money was. The appellant and McGuire then used the toilet and on their return said that they would tie her up and she was not to telephone the police. They tied her ankles and hands and put socks in her mouth. They went out of the front door warning her not to telephone, saying that they would come back and do something to her little boy if she phoned the police within five minutes ...

Section 8 of the Theft Act 1968 begins: 'A person is guilty of robbery if he steals ...' He steals when he acts in accordance with the basic definition of theft in s 1 of the Theft Act; that is to say when he dishonestly appropriates property belonging to another with the intention of permanently depriving the other of it. It thus becomes necessary to consider what is 'appropriation' or, according to s 3, 'any assumption by a person of the rights of an owner'. An assumption of the rights of an owner describes the conduct of a person towards a particular article. It is conduct which usurps the rights of the owner. To say that the conduct is over and done with as soon as he lays hands upon the property, or when he manifests an intention to deal with it as his, is contrary to common sense and to the natural meaning of words. A thief who steals a motor car first opens the door. Is it to be said that the act of starting up the motor is no more a part of the theft?

In the present case there can be little doubt that if the appellant had been interrupted after the seizure of the jewellery box the jury would have been entitled to find that the appellant and his accomplice were assuming the rights of an owner at the time when the jewellery box was seized. However, the act of appropriation does not suddenly cease. It is a continuous act and it is a matter for the jury to decide whether or not the act of appropriation has finished. Moreover, it is quite clear that the intention to deprive the owner permanently, which accompanies the assumption of the owner's rights was a continuing one at all material times. This court therefore rejects the contention that the theft had ceased by the time the lady was tied up. As a matter of common sense the appellant was in the course of committing theft; he was stealing.

There remains the question whether there was robbery. Quite clearly the jury were at liberty to find the appellant guilty of robbery relying upon the force used when he put his hand over Mrs Carrett's mouth to restrain her from calling for help. We also think that they were entitled to rely upon the act of tying her up provided they were satisfied (and it is difficult to see how they could not be satisfied) that the force so used was to enable them to steal. If they were still engaged in the act of stealing the force was clearly used to enable them to continue to assume the rights of the owner and permanently to deprive Mrs Carrett of her box, which is what they began to do when they first seized it ...

BLACKMAIL

Section 21 of the Theft Act 1968

(1) A person is guilty of blackmail if, with a view to gain for himself or another or with intent to cause loss to another, he makes any unwarranted demand with menaces; and for this purpose a demand with menaces is unwarranted unless the person making it does so in the belief:

(a) that he has reasonable grounds for making the demand; and

(b) that the use of the menaces is a proper means of reinforcing the demand.

(2) The nature of the act or omission demanded is immaterial, and it is also immaterial whether the menaces relate to action to be taken by the person making the demand.

(3) A person guilty of blackmail shall on conviction on indictment be liable to imprisonment for a term not exceeding 14 years.

Menaces

R v Lawrence and Pomroy (1971) 57 Cr App R 64 (CA)

Facts: Pomroy repaired the roof of the house of one Thorn. Thorn was dissatisfied with the work and withheld £70 from the agreed price for the work. One evening Pomroy went to Thorn's house and said 'Unless you pay me within seven days ... you will have to look over your shoulder before you step out of doors'. A few days later Pomroy again went to Thorn's house. This time, Pomroy was accompanied by Lawrence, who was a big man. When Thorn again refused to pay the balance of £70, Lawrence said 'Step outside the house and we will sort this matter out'. When Thorn refused, Lawrence said menacingly: 'Come on mate, come outside.' At that point, police officers who had been hiding in Thorn's house emerged and arrested the appellants.

> **Cairns LJ**: ... The word 'menaces' is an ordinary English word which any jury can be expected to understand. In exceptional cases where because of special knowledge in special circumstances what would be a menace to an ordinary person is not a menace to the person to whom it is addressed, or where the converse may be true, it is no doubt necessary to spell out the meaning of the word ...

R v Clear [1968] 1 QB 670 (CA)

> **Sellers LJ**: ... Words or conduct which would not intimidate or influence anyone to respond to the demand would not be menaces ... but threats and conduct of such a nature and extent that the mind of an ordinary person of normal stability and courage might be influenced or made apprehensive so as to accede unwillingly to the demand would be sufficient for a jury's consideration ... [The victim must be] deprived of 'that element of free, voluntary action which alone constitutes consent' in the words used by Wilde B in *R v Walton and Ogden* (1863) Le & Ca 288.

> There may be special circumstances unknown to an accused which would make the threats innocuous and unavailing for the accused's demand, but such

circumstances would have no bearing on the accused's state of mind and on his intention. If an accused knew that what he threatened would have no effect on the victim it might be different ...

R v Garwood [1987] 1 WLR 319 (CA)

Facts: The appellant was convicted of blackmail, having obtained money from the victim by 'menaces'. The jury found that the victim was rather timid and that other people may not have found the appellant's behaviour menacing.

Lord Lane CJ: ... In our judgment it is only rarely that a judge will need to enter on a definition of the word 'menaces'. It is an ordinary word of which the meaning will be clear to any jury ...

It seems to us that there are two possible occasions on which a further direction on the meaning of the word menaces may be required. The first is where the threats might have affected the mind of an ordinary person of normal stability but did not affect the person actually addressed. In such circumstances that would amount to a sufficient menace: see *R v Clear* [1968] 1 QB 670.

The second situation is where the threats in fact affected the mind of the victim, although they would not have affected the mind of a person of normal stability. In that case, in our judgment, the existence of menaces is proved providing that the accused man was aware of the likely effect of his action upon the victim.

If the recorder had told the jury that [the victim's] undue timidity did not prevent them from finding 'menaces' proved, provided that the appellant realised the effect his actions were having on [the victim], all would have been well ...

Unwarranted demand

It will only be in very rare cases that 'menaces [will be] a proper means of reinforcing the demand' so that the demand becomes a warranted one under s 21(1). It would not be enough that one is demanding back property to which one is entitled, since the making of menaces is not a proper means of achieving that objective: see *R v Lawrence* (1971) 57 Cr App R 64 (above); *R v Harvey* (1980) 72 Cr App R 139.

R v Harvey (1980) 72 Cr App R 139 (CA)

Facts: The appellants agreed with one Scott that they would pay him £20,000 to procure a large quantity of cannabis. Scott failed to supply the cannabis. The appellants kidnapped Scott, along with his wife and small child, and they subjected Scott to threats of what would happen to wife and child if he did not give them their money back.

Bingham J: ... [T]wo points emerge with clarity: (1) [s 21(1) of the Theft Act 1968] is concerned with the belief of the individual defendant in the particular case ... It matters not what the reasonable man, or any man other than the defendant, would believe save in so far as that may throw light on what the defendant in fact believed. Thus the factual question of the defendant's belief should be left to the jury ... (2) In order to exonerate a defendant from liability his belief must be that the use of the menaces is a 'proper' means of reinforcing the demand. 'Proper' ... is ... plainly a word of wide meaning, certainly wider than (for example) 'lawful'. But the greater includes the less and no act which was not believed to be lawful could be believed to be proper within the meaning of the subsection. Thus no assistance is given to any defendant, even a fanatic or a deranged idealist, who knows or suspects that his threat, or the act threatened, is criminal, but believes it to be justified by his end or his peculiar circumstances. The test is not what he regards as justified, but what he believes to be proper. And where, as here, the threats were to do acts which any sane man knows to be against the laws of every civilised country, no jury would hesitate long before dismissing the contention that the defendant genuinely believed the threats to be a proper means of reinforcing even a legitimate demand.

... [T]he jury should have been directed that the demand with menaces was not to be regarded as unwarranted unless the Crown satisfied them in respect of each defendant that the defendant did not make the demand with menaces in the genuine belief both: (a) that he had had reasonable grounds for making the demand; and (b) that the use of the menaces was in the circumstances a proper (meaning for present purposes a lawful, and not a criminal) means of reinforcing the demand ...

'... with a view to gain ... or with intent to cause loss to another ...'

R v Bevans (1988) 87 Cr App R 64

The appellant appealed against his conviction for blackmail. He had forced a doctor, at gunpoint, to provide him with a pain killing injection of morphine. The appellant contended, unsuccessfully, that as his motive had been pain relief he had not made his menacing demand with a view to gain.

Jones J: Mr Griffiths [counsel for the appellant] argued before the learned judge, and has repeated his argument before this court, that the demand for an injection of morphine was not made with a view to gain for the appellant. He argues that those words, 'with a view to gain for himself,' involve the court in a consideration of the motive which lay behind the appellant's demand. It is said that that motive was unquestionably the relief from the pain which he was suffering at the time. Therefore what he had in mind was the gain of relief from pain, not for a gain in money or other property ... Mr Griffiths argues that in no sense of the word was there here an economic interest involved. There was not in the appellant's mind either an economic gain by him or an economic loss inflicted upon the doctor.

It may be that the difficulty has arisen in this case by importing into the Act words which are not there ... the word 'motive' is not used anywhere in the Act. The words used are, 'with a view to gain or with an intent to cause loss.' As I have said, it may well be misleading to try to import those words into the Act, and then try to understand what meaning they should bear.

In the judgment of this court the matter can be resolved quite simply and straightforwardly by reference to the Act itself. What had to be established was that the demand was made with a view to gain for the appellant; expanding those words by reference to section 34(2), that meant with a view to the appellant getting what he had not, and to getting something which consisted of money or other property.

It seems difficult, if not impossible, to argue that the liquid which constituted the substance which was to be injected into the appellant's body was not property. It clearly was. There has been no dispute but that if an ampoule containing the liquid had been handed over to the appellant instead of being transferred to a syringe and injected into his body, he would have got property in that sense. This court can see no difference between the liquid being contained in the syringe before it is passed into his body and the liquid being contained in an ampoule. There can be no question but that that morphine was property.

Again the next question would be – did the appellant have in view the getting of that morphine (that admittedly being something which, before making the demand, he had not)? Again there seems to be only one possible answer: yes. It is nothing to the point that his ultimate motive was the relief of pain through the effect which that morphine would have upon his bodily processes.

It was pointed out in the course of argument that someone may very well demand a bottle of whisky. His ultimate motive may simply be to get drunk, that is to drink it all himself and to get drunk. That does not detract in any way from the proposition that in fact he would be demanding property in the form of the bottle of whisky and in particular the bottle's contents.

By analogy exactly the same argument must apply here. This demand, which was a demand for an injection of morphine, involved two things: first of all it involved the passing of a drug to him, and secondly it involved the service by the doctor of actually carrying out the injection. The fact that he was gaining the service does not in any way mean that he was not gaining the property which consisted of the morphine. There is no suggestion anywhere in the Act that the gain must be exclusively directed to one particular object.

Notes and queries

1   A possible alternative to blackmail in some situations would be a charge under s 40 of the Administration of Justice Act 1970 – unlawful harassment of debtors – a summary only offence.

Further reading

Sir Bernard Mackenna, 'Blackmail: a criticism' [1966] Crim LR 466

'Coercion, threats, and the puzzle of blackmail', in G Lamond, AP Simester and ATH Smith (eds), *Harm and Culpability*, 1996, Oxford: OUP, 215

CHAPTER 21

OFFENCES INVOLVING DECEPTION: OBTAINING PROPERTY BY DECEPTION

Section 15 of the Theft Act 1968

(1) A person who by any deception dishonestly obtains property belonging to another, with the intention of permanently depriving the other of it, shall on conviction on indictment be liable to imprisonment for a term not exceeding 10 years.

(2) For purposes of this section a person is to be treated as obtaining property if he obtains ownership, possession or control of it, and 'obtain' includes obtaining for another or enabling another to obtain or to retain.

(3) Section 6 above shall apply for purposes of this section, with the necessary adaptation of the reference to appropriating, as it applies for purposes of s 1.

(4) For purposes of this section 'deception' means any deception (whether deliberate or reckless) by words or conduct as to fact or as to law, including a deception as to the present intentions of the person using the deception or any other person.

OBTAINING PROPERTY BELONGING TO ANOTHER

Property belonging to another has (for all practical purposes) the same meaning under s 15 as it has in relation to s 1 theft – see further Chapter 18.

R v Thompson (1984) 79 Cr App R 191

The appellant was employed as a computer operator at a bank in Kuwait. He opened a number of bank account in England and Kuwait. He exploited his access to his employer's computers in Kuwait in order to transfer funds from clients' accounts to his own accounts in Kuwait. The appellant then returned to England and transferred funds from his accounts in Kuwait to his accounts in England. Following conviction for obtaining property by deception, the appellant unsuccessfully contended on appeal that there had been no 'obtaining' by him within the jurisdiction of the courts in England and Wales.

May LJ: Mr Caplan [counsel for the appellant] has submitted that section 15 is not concerned with questions of lawful title to any relevant property but, as the section itself specifically provides, with the ownership, possession or control of such property. He submits that when one asks the question whether at any material time – that is to say at any time before the bank in Kuwait was asked to remit to England – the appellant had control of what seemed to be his credit balance, the answer must be 'yes, he did' – at least until the bank discovered the fraud. Until they were so put on inquiry it would not have been possible for them to have said that this appellant had no such credit balance. Mr Caplan went on to argue that the proof of the pudding was in the eating because the bank in Kuwait in fact acted upon the letters which the appellant wrote asking for the transfers of his credit balances; it is thus difficult to say, Mr Caplan contends, that the appellant did not have control of a credit balance when the bank acted upon the basis that he did. In this connection he referred us to the case of *Kohn* (1979) 69 Cr App R 395 ... He submits that when the appellant acted as he did in programming the computer in Kuwait with the result that in addition to it appearing to give him credit on his savings accounts it also diminished the amounts standing to the credit of the other five substantial but dormant accounts, there was at the very least the risk of the diminution in the credit balances on those accounts. Consequently he submitted that we ought to hold that for the purposes of the relevant provisions of the Theft Act the obtaining of the property, the chose in action, occurred in Kuwait at the time that the computer went into action as the appellant's plane was in the air over the Mediterranean.

We think, however, that one may legitimately ask: of what property did this appellant in that way obtain control in Kuwait? What was the nature of that property? Mr Caplan's reply, as we understand it, was that the appellant obtained the control of those credit balances on his savings accounts, which were effectively choses in action, and were such until the bank discovered his fraud. With all respect to Mr Caplan's persuasive argument, we think that when it is examined it is untenable. We do not think that one can describe as a chose in action a liability which has been brought about by fraud, one where the action to enforce that liability is capable of immediate defeasance as soon as the fraud is pleaded. It is neither here nor there, we think, that the person defrauded, in this case the bank, may not have been aware that one of its employees had been fraudulent in this way until a later time. The ignorance of the bank in no way, in our view, breathes life into what is otherwise a defunct situation brought about entirely by fraud. One has only to take a simple example. Discard for the moment the modern sophistication of computers and programs and consider the old days when bank books were kept in manuscript in large ledgers. In effect all that was done by the appellant through the modern computer in the present case was to take a pen and debit each of the five accounts in the ledger with the relevant sums and then credit each of his own five savings accounts in the ledger with corresponding amounts. On the face of it his savings accounts would then have appeared to have in them substantially more than in truth they did have as the result of his forgeries; but we do not think that by those forgeries any bank clerk in the days before computers would in law have thus brought into being a chose in action capable either of being stolen or of being obtained by deception contrary to section 15 of the Theft Act 1968.

In so far as the customers whose accounts had been fraudulently debited and who had to be reimbursed by the bank, as Mr Caplan submitted, are concerned, we prefer the approach of Mr Walsh. He submitted that properly considered it was not a question of reimbursement: it was merely a question of correcting forged documents, forged records, to the condition in which they ought to have been but for the fraud.

In those circumstances and for those reasons we agree with the learned judge in the court below that the only realistic view of the undisputed facts in this case is that the six instances of obtaining charged in the indictment each occurred when the relevant sums of money were received by the appellant's banks in England. Further it seems to us quite clear (as it was to the learned judge below) that those sums of money were obtained as the result of the letters which the appellant wrote to the bank in Kuwait. The only proper construction to be put upon those letters is that they contain the representations pleaded in the particulars of offences in the indictment. Those representations were the effective cause of each and every one of the obtainings.

DECEPTION

Section 15(4) of the Theft Act 1968 provides a partial definition of 'deception'. In *Re London and Globe Finance Corporation Ltd* [1903] 1 Ch 728, 732 Buckley J said that 'to deceive is ... to induce a man to believe that a thing is true which is false', and this provides a useful working definition of the word 'deception'.

The person from whom the property is obtained need not be the person who is deceived (see *Metropolitan Police Commissioner v Charles* [1977] AC 177, dealt with below under 'cheques and cheque cards').

Section 15(4) refers to deception by 'conduct': examples of such deception are to be found in *DPP v Stonehouse* [1978] AC 55 and *R v Williams* [1980] Crim LR 589.

R v King; R v Stockwell [1987] 2 WLR 746 (CA)

Neill LJ: ... The case for the prosecution at the trial can be stated quite shortly. On 5 March 1985 the appellants went to the house of Mrs Mitchell, in New Milton. Mrs Mitchell, who had lived in the house all her life, was a widow of 68 years of age. The appellants told her that they were from Streets, a firm of tree surgeons. She knew of the firm, and in answer to her question one of the appellants claimed to be Mr Street. They told her that a sycamore tree in her garden was likely to cause damage. They purported to carry out a test, with a plastic strip placed against the tree, and one of the appellants then said that the tree was dangerous.

They told her that the roots of the tree were growing into the gas main and could cause thousands of pounds in damage. They told her that it would cost £150 to fell the tree, which Mrs Mitchell agreed to pay. They then looked at other trees and told her that another sycamore was dangerous as well as one of her conifers. In addition they told her that the roots of her bay tree were causing damage to the foundations of the house. Mrs Mitchell asked the appellants about the cost of doing all the work, and they told her that to remove the four trees including the bay tree would cost about £500. When Mrs Mitchell told them that she was going to telephone her brother, one of the appellants informed her that they would do the work for £470 if paid in cash. Mrs Mitchell then said that she would have to go and get the money from the bank. In fact, she decided to draw some money from her two building society accounts. From one account she withdrew £100, and she was in the process of withdrawing £200 from her account with a second building society, intending at that stage to go to her bank to draw the balance, when the cashier at the second building society noticed that she seemed very distressed.

Following a conversation between Mrs Mitchell and the cashier, the police were informed ... [and] the appellants were arrested ...

... [I]t is necessary to start by setting out the particulars of offence as stated in the indictment, as amended. The particulars read:

David King and Jimmy Stockwell on 5 March 1985 in Hampshire, dishonestly attempted to obtain from Nora Anne Mitchell, £470 in money with the intention of permanently depriving the said Nora Anne Mitchell thereof by deception, namely by false oral representations that they were from JF Street, Tree Specialists, Pennington, that essential work necessary to remove trees in order to prevent damage to the gas supply and house foundations would then have to be carried out.

... In our view, the question in each case is: was the deception an operative cause of the obtaining of the property? This question falls to be answered as a question of fact by the jury applying their common sense ...

In the present case there was, in our judgment, ample evidence on which the jury could come to the conclusion that had the attempt succeeded the money would have been paid over by the victim as a result of the lies told to her by the appellants ...

R v Silverman (1988) 86 Cr App R 213 (CA)

Watkins LJ: ... The appellant came to grief, we are told, in consequence of a television programme, in which his dealings with two ladies, to whom I shall refer in a little detail in a moment or so, were ventilated because it was thought that he had treated them dishonestly. The ladies are twins, who are now 63 or 64 years of age. They had lived with their mother from 1929 until March 1983 at a house in Kenton. They are spinsters. Their home was sold in 1983. All the affairs concerning that place were wound up so that no debts remained in respect of it. They moved to a newly acquired maisonette at 36 Magnolia Court. This they purchased for a good deal less than the sum for which they had sold their previous home. The appellant was known to them because he had done work for their mother and for them in the house which they sold. He was employed with a plumbing and central heating firm called Coiley's. By the time of the material events he had become the manager of this firm. He had seen the sisters on a number of occasions, as had other employees of the firm before him. The sisters and their mother had learned to trust these tradesmen to do properly whatever work they were asked to do and to charge fair and reasonable prices for it. One has therefore an impression arising out of the evidence in the case, which the jury must have accepted, of a relationship of trust which had been built up and maintained between customer and tradesman.

Soon after the sisters had moved to Magnolia Court the appellant paid them a visit. According to one of the sisters, he asked if he could see the boiler because, he said, it was leaking. At that time he gave no estimate for repairing the defect, but the sisters were prepared to accept his word and to allow him to put the boiler right. One of the sisters wrote out a cheque for £2,875 and handed it to the appellant for the work to be done to the boiler. She thought that it was rather a lot to charge for what was to be done, but she told the jury that her family had been employing Coiley's for 15 years or more and she believed that what she was asked to pay was a standard charge.

A short while later the appellant looked at the electricity points and told the sisters that the whole of the maisonette needed to be rewired. He said that that work could be done at a cost of £20,000 plus VAT of £3,000. About a week later the sisters agreed to that because, they said, they trusted the appellant and his firm.

They thought this was the normal charge and they paid a deposit of £10,000 before the work was begun. Upon its completion the appellant came to the maisonette and asked for £5,000, which one of the sisters paid him. The work of rewiring was to include the redecoration of the maisonette ...

True it is that the work had been done, but it was agreed on all sides at the trial that the prices charged by the appellant on behalf of his firm were grossly excessive. For instance, a new boiler could have been obtained for £700 and the cost of installing it would have been no more than between £100 and £150. But, as we have said, very nearly £3,000 was charged for repairing it. The Electricity Board, on being asked how much they would have charged to rewire the maisonette, said that their charge would have been considerably less than was charged by the appellant. The same applied to the redecoration of the maisonette ...

The charges of which the appellant was convicted were laid under s 15(1) of the Theft Act 1968. The first alleged that between July and November 1984 he dishonestly obtained from Pauline McCleery and Kathleen McCleery a cheque in the sum of £2,875 with the intention of permanently depriving Pauline and Kathleen McCleery by deception, namely by representing that that sum was a fair and proper charge for the work. The other counts in the indictment were similarly framed with specific reference to other cheques the sisters gave to the appellant. It follows from the particulars of the charges that the prosecution had to establish a number of elements to prove that in his transactions with the sisters the appellant committed criminal offences ...

It seems to us that the complainants, far from being worldly wise, were unquestionably gullible. Having left their former home, they relied implicitly upon the word of the appellant about their requirements in their maisonette. In such circumstances of mutual trust, one party depending upon the other for fair and reasonable conduct, the criminal law may apply if one party takes dishonest advantage of the other by representing as a fair charge that which he but not the other knows is dishonestly excessive ...

... There was material for a finding that there had been a false representation although it is true that the appellant had said nothing at the time he made his representations to encourage the sisters to accept the quotations. He applied no pressure upon them, and apart from mentioning the actual prices to be charged was silent as to the other matters that may have arisen for question in their minds.

On the matter of representations we have been referred to *DPP v Ray* [1974] AC 370 which concerned someone leaving a restaurant without paying for a meal. At 379 Lord Reid said:

> So the accused, after he changed his mind, must have done something intended to induce the waiter to believe that he still intended to pay before he left. Deception, to my mind, implies something positive.

[Counsel for the appellant] submits that nothing positive was done in this case. Lord Reid continued:

> It is quite true that a man intending to deceive can build up a situation in which his silence is as eloquent as an express statement.

Here the situation had been built up over a long period of time. It was a situation of mutual trust and the appellant's silence on any matter other than the sums charged were, we think, as eloquent as if he had said: 'What is more, I can say to you that we are going to get no more than a modest profit out of this' ...

Note: The convictions were, however, quashed because the judge had failed to deal adequately with the defence case when summing up to the jury.

R v Jones (1993) The Times, 15 February (CA)

Facts: The appellant was a self-employed franchised milkman selling milk wholesale and retail to established customers. He had supplied the family business of a Mr Wilford for 20 years. The relationship was casual and informal and Mr Wilford paid by cheque at the end of each week the amount the appellant asked for.

It later transpired that the appellant had been overcharging Mr Wilford by some £180 per week. Mr Wilford in evidence said that he had never considered the amount he was paying for the milk because he trusted the appellant and therefore assumed that the appellant had been charging the proper cost price to a retailer.

The nature of the deception alleged in the indictment was that the appellant had falsely represented to Mr Wilford that he had received goods to the value of a certain amount when in fact the appellant had only delivered goods to the value of one-half of that amount.

Auld J, giving the judgment of the Court of Appeal, said that Mr Wilford had been remarkably stupid or careless and this was stupidity or carelessness of which the appellant was aware. There could be no doubt that Mr Wilford was deceived.

Deception by omission

DPP v Ray [1974] AC 370

The defendant ate a meal at a restaurant and then decided to leave without paying. In order to make good his escape he waited until the waiters were otherwise engaged. The issue for the House of Lords was whether or not, by sitting at the table at the end of the meal appearing to be a diner who was going to pay for his meal, the defendant had exercised a deception that had induced the waiters to give him the opportunity to run out without paying. [*Note*: (i) the defendant was charged with an offence under s 16 of the Theft Act 1968 that has since been repealed; (ii) if these facts were to occur today, the defendant could be charged under s 3 of the Theft Act 1978 – see Chapter 18].

Lord MacDermott: To prove the charge against the respondent the prosecution had to show that he (i) by a deception (ii) had dishonestly (iii) obtained for himself (iv) a pecuniary advantage. The last of these ingredients no longer raises, on the facts of this appeal, the problems of interpretation which were recently considered by this House in *R v Turner* [1974] AC 357. By that decision a debt is 'evaded' even if the evasion falls short of being final or permanent and is only for the time being; and a pecuniary advantage has not to be proved in fact as it is enough if the case is brought within section 16(2)(a) or (b) or (c).

On the facts here, this means that the respondent's debt for the meal he had eaten was evaded for the purposes of subsection (2)(a); and that in consequence he obtained a pecuniary advantage within the meaning of subsection (1). No issue therefore arises on the ingredients I have numbered (iii) and (iv). Nor is there any controversy about ingredient (ii). If the respondent obtained a pecuniary advantage as described he undoubtedly did so dishonestly. The case is thus narrowed to ingredient (i) and that leaves two questions for consideration. First, do the facts justify a finding that the respondent practised a deception? And secondly, if he did, was his evasion of the debt obtained by that deception?

The first of these questions involves nothing in the way of words spoken or written. If there was deception on the part of the respondent it was by his conduct in the course of an extremely common form of transaction which, because of its nature, leaves much to be implied from conduct. Another circumstance affecting the ambit of this question lies in the fact that, looking only to the period *after* the meal had been eaten and the respondent and his companions had decided to evade payment, there is nothing that I can find in the discernible conduct of the respondent which would suffice in itself to show that he was then practising a deception. No doubt he and the others stayed in their seats until the waiter went into the kitchen and while doing so gave all the appearance of ordinary customers. But, in my opinion, nothing in this or in anything else which occurred *after* the change of intention went far enough to afford proof of deception. The picture, as I see it, presented by this last stage of the entire transaction, is simply that of a group which had decided to evade payment and were awaiting the opportunity to do so.

There is, however, no sound reason that I can see for restricting the inquiry to this final phase. One cannot, so to speak, draw a line through the transaction at the point where the intention changed and search for evidence of deception only in what happened before that or only in what happened after that. In my opinion the transaction must for this purpose be regarded in its entirety, beginning with the respondent entering the restaurant and ordering his meal and ending with his running out without paying. The different stages of the transaction are all linked and it would be quite unrealistic to treat them in isolation.

Starting, then, at the beginning one finds in the conduct of the respondent in entering and ordering his meal evidence that he impliedly represented that he had the means and the intention of paying for it before he left. That the respondent did make such a representation was not in dispute and in the absence of evidence to the contrary it would be difficult to reach a different conclusion. If this representation had then been false and matters had proceeded thereafter as they did (but without any change of intention) a conviction for the offence charged would, in my view, have had ample material to support it. But as the representation when originally made in this case was not false there was therefore no deception at that point. Then the meal is served and eaten and the intention to evade the debt replaced the intention to pay. Did this change of mind produce a deception?

My Lords, in my opinion it did. I do not base this conclusion merely on the change of mind that had occurred for that in itself was not manifest at the time and did not amount to 'conduct' on the part of the respondent. But it did falsify the representation which had already been made because that initial representation must, in my view, be regarded not as something then spent and past but as a continuing representation which remained alive and operative and had already resulted in the respondent and his defaulting companions being taken on trust and treated as ordinary, honest customers. It covered the whole transaction up to and including payment and must therefore, in my opinion, be considered as continuing and still active at the time of the change of mind. When that happened, with the respondent taking (as might be expected) no step to bring the change to notice, he practised, to my way of thinking, a deception just as real and just as dishonest as would have been the case if his intention all along had been to go without paying.

Holding for these reasons that the respondent practised a deception, I turn to what I have referred to as the second question. Was the respondent's evasion of the debt obtained by that deception?

I think the material before the justices was enough to show that it was. The obvious effect of the deception was that the respondent and his associates were treated as they had been previously, that is to say as ordinary, honest customers whose conduct did not excite suspicion or call for precautions. In consequence the waiter was off his guard and vanished into the kitchen. That gave the respondent the opportunity of running out without hindrance and he took it. I would therefore answer this second question in the affirmative.

Lord Morris: It is clear that the respondent went into the restaurant in the capacity of an ordinary customer. Such a person by his conduct in ordering food impliedly says: 'If you will properly provide me with that which I order, I will pay you the amount for which I will become liable.' In some restaurants a customer might have a special arrangement as to payment. A customer might on occasion make a special arrangement. Had there been any basis for suggesting that the respondent was not under obligation to discharge his debt before he left the restaurant that would have been recorded in the case stated. All the facts as found make it unlikely that it would have been possible even to contend that in this case the debt incurred was other than one which was to be discharged by a cash payment made before leaving.

If someone goes to a restaurant and, having no means whatsoever to pay and no credit arrangement, obtains a meal for which he knows he cannot pay and for which he has no intention of paying he will be guilty of an offence under section 15 of the Theft Act. Such a person would obtain the meal by deception. By his conduct in ordering the meal he would be representing to the restaurant that he had the intention of paying whereas he would not have had any such intention. In the present case when the respondent ordered his meal he impliedly made to the waiter the ordinary representation of the ordinary customer that it was his intention to pay. He induced the waiter to believe that that was his intention. Furthermore, on the facts as found it is clear that all concerned (the waiter, the respondent and his companions) proceeded on the basis that an ordinary customer would pay his bill before leaving. The waiter would not have accepted the order or served the meal had there not been the implied representation.

The situation may perhaps be unusual where a customer honestly orders a meal and therefore indicates his honest intention to pay but thereafter forms a dishonest intention of running away without paying if he can. Inherent in an original honest representation of an intention to pay there must surely be a representation that such intention will continue.

In the present case it is found as a fact that when the respondent ordered his meal he believed that he would be able to pay. One of his companions had agreed to lend him money. He therefore intended to pay. So far as the waiter was concerned the original implied representation made to him by the respondent must have been a continuing representation so long as he (the respondent) remained in the restaurant. There was nothing to alter the representation. Just as the waiter was led at the start to believe that he was dealing with a customer who by all that he did in the restaurant was indicating his intention to pay in the ordinary way, so the waiter was led to believe that that state of affairs continued. But the moment came when the respondent decided and therefore knew that he was not going to pay: but he also knew that the waiter still thought that he was going to pay. By ordering his meal and by his conduct in assuming the role of an ordinary customer the respondent had previously shown that it was his intention to pay. By continuing in the same role and behaving just as before he was representing that his previous intention continued. That was a deception because his intention, unknown to the waiter, had become quite otherwise. The dishonest change of intention was not likely to produce the result that the waiter would be told of it. The essence of the deception was that the waiter should not know of it or be given any sort of clue that it (the change of intention) had come about. Had the waiter suspected that by a change of intention a secret exodus was being planned, it is obvious that he would have taken action to prevent its being achieved.

It was said in the Divisional Court that a deception under section 16 should not be found unless an accused has actively made a representation by words or conduct which representation is found to be false. But if there was an original representation (as, in my view, there was when the meal was ordered) it was a representation that was intended to be and was a continuing representation. It continued to operate on the mind of the waiter. It became false and it became a deliberate deception. The prosecution do not say that the deception consisted in not informing the waiter of the change of mind; they say that the deception consisted in continuing to represent to the waiter that there was an intention to pay before leaving.

On behalf of the respondent it was contended that no deception had been practised. It was accepted that when the meal was ordered there was a representation by the respondent that he would pay but it was contended that once the meal was served there was no longer any representation but that there was merely an obligation to pay a debt: it was further argued that thereafter there was no deception because there was no obligation in the debtor to inform his creditor that payment was not to be made. I cannot accept these contentions. They ignore the circumstance that the representation that was made was a continuing one: its essence was that an intention to pay would continue until payment was made: by its very nature it could not cease to operate as a representation unless some new arrangement was made.

A further contention on behalf of the respondent was that the debt was not in whole or in part evaded. It was said that on the facts as found there was an evasion of the payment of a debt but no evasion of the debt and that a debt (which denotes an obligation to pay) is not evaded unless it is released or unless there is a discharge of it which is void or voidable. I cannot accept this contention. Though a 'debt,' as referred to in the section does denote an obligation to pay, the obligation of the respondent was to pay for his meal before he left the restaurant. When he left without paying he had, in my view, evaded his obligation to pay before leaving. He dodged his obligation. Accordingly he obtained a 'pecuniary advantage.'

The final question which arises is whether, if there was deception and if there was pecuniary advantage, it was by the deception that the respondent obtained the pecuniary advantage. In my view, this must be a question of fact and the magistrates have found that it was by his deception that the respondent dishonestly evaded payment. It would seem to be clear that if the waiter had thought that if he left the restaurant to go to the kitchen the respondent would at once run out, he (the waiter) would not have left the restaurant and would have taken suitable action. The waiter proceeded on the basis that the implied representation made to him (ie of an honest intention to pay) was effective. The waiter was caused to refrain from taking certain courses of action which but for the representation he would have taken. In my view, the respondent during the whole time that he was in the restaurant made and by his continuing conduct continued to make a representation of his intention to pay before leaving. When in place of his original intention he substituted the dishonest intention of running away as soon as the waiter's back was turned, he was continuing to lead the waiter to believe that he intended to pay. He practised a deception on the waiter and by so doing he obtained for himself the pecuniary advantage of evading his obligation to pay before leaving. That he did so dishonestly was found by the magistrates who, in my opinion, rightly convicted him.

Lord Reid (dissenting): If a person induces a supplier to accept an order for goods or services by a representation of fact, that representation must be held to be a continuing representation lasting until the goods or services are supplied. Normally it would not last any longer. A restaurant supplies both goods and services: it supplies food and drink and the facilities for consuming them. Customers normally remain for a short time after consuming their meal, and I think that it can properly be held that any representation express or implied made with a view of obtaining a meal lasts until the departure of the customers in the normal course.

In my view, where a new customer orders a meal in a restaurant, he must be held to make an implied representation that he can and will pay for it before he leaves. In the present case the accused must be held to have made such a representation. But when he made it it was not dishonest: he thought he would be able to borrow money from one of his companions.

After the meal had been consumed the accused changed his mind. He decided to evade payment. So he and his companions remained seated where they were for a short time until the waiter left the room and then ran out of the restaurant.

Did he thereby commit an offence against section 16 of the Theft Act 1968? It is admitted, and rightly admitted, that if the waiter had not been in the room when he changed his mind and he had immediately run out he would not have committed an offence. Why does his sitting still for a short time in the presence of the waiter make all the difference?

The section requires evasion of his obligation to pay. That is clearly established by his running out without paying. Secondly, it requires dishonesty: that is admitted. There would have been both evasion and dishonesty if he had changed his mind and run out while the waiter was absent.

The crucial question in this case is whether there was evasion 'by any deception.' Clearly there could be no deception until the accused changed his mind. I agree with the following quotation from the judgment of Buckley J in *In Re London and Globe Finance Corporation Ltd* [1903] 1 Ch 728, 732:

> To deceive is, I apprehend, to induce a man to believe that a thing is true which is false, and which the person practising the deceit knows or believes to be false.

So the accused, after he changed his mind, must have done something intended to induce the waiter to believe that he still intended to pay before he left. Deception, to my mind, implies something positive. It is quite true that a man intending to deceive can build up a situation in which his silence is as eloquent as an express statement. But what did the accused do here to create such a situation? He merely sat still.

It is, I think apparent from the case stated that the magistrates accepted the prosecution contention that:

> ... as soon as the intent to evade payment was formed and the appellant still posed as an ordinary customer the deception had been made.

The magistrates stated that they were of opinion that:

> ... having changed his mind as regards payment, by remaining in the restaurant for a further 10 minutes as an ordinary customer who was likely to order a sweet or coffee, the appellant practised a deception.

I cannot read that as finding that after he changed his mind he intended to deceive the waiter into believing that he still intended to pay. And there is no finding that the waiter was in fact induced to believe that by anything the accused did after he changed his mind. I would infer from the case that all that he intended to do was to take advantage of the first opportunity to escape and evade his obligation to pay.

Deception is an essential ingredient of the offence. Dishonest evasion of an obligation to pay is not enough. I cannot see that there was, in fact, any more than that in this case.

I agree with the Divisional Court [1973] 1 WLR 317, 323:

> His plan was totally lacking in the subtlety of deception and to argue that his remaining in the room until the coast was clear amounted to a representation to the waiter is to introduce an artificiality which should have no place in the Act.

I would therefore dismiss this appeal.

R v Rai [2000] 1 Cr App R 242

HHJ David Clarke QC: On 10 March 1999, in the Crown Court at Birmingham, before His Honour Judge Alan Taylor, the appellant was to stand trial – indeed a second trial – on an indictment charging him with obtaining services by deception contrary to section 1(1) of the Theft Act 1978. The particulars of offence, as amended, alleged that on or about 13 August 1997 he dishonestly obtained services from Birmingham City Social Services, namely building services, by deception, namely by falsely representing that the subject of the application, his mother, Mrs Punna Chand, was alive. Following and directly consequent upon a ruling by the trial judge before any jury had been empanelled, the defendant pleaded guilty to this charge, though only on a specific factual basis. He appeals against his conviction, and in effect appeals against this ruling, by leave of the single judge.

The issue before the trial judge and before this court arises from the definition of the words 'by deception', where they appear in section 1(1) of the 1978 Act, and this in turn involves consideration of the definition of that phrase contained in section 15(4) of the Theft Act 1968.

... The central issue before us was whether, on the facts of the present case, there was conduct capable of constituting that deception and in particular the circumstances in which an omission to act or silence can amount to such conduct.

The facts alleged by the Crown were simple. The appellant was the owner of a property, 20 Sandwell Road, Handsworth, Birmingham. On about 7 June 1996, he applied to Birmingham City Council for a grant towards providing a downstairs bathroom at his room for the use of his elderly and infirm mother. Following an assessment of her condition, the City Council approved a grant under the Housing Grants, Construction and Regeneration Act 1986 in the sum of a little over £9,500, and a firm of contractors was appointed to undertake the necessary building work on the council's behalf. On 29 July 1997, the appellant was notified that this application had been approved. Two days later, on 31 July, Mrs Chand died.

Two weeks later, on 13 August 1997, the council, in the person of Mrs Bentley, unaware of the death of Mrs Chand, attended the house and met the contractor who was to carry out the work. The appellant was not present at that meeting. At that meeting, the council and the builder signed a contract form, leaving the form at the property to be signed by the appellant in his capacity of owner of the house and applicant for this grant. The builder subsequently collected from the property that document bearing a signature, but he did not know the identity of the person who handed it to him.

The argument before the learned judge was based on the premise that this document was not signed by the appellant and that there was no evidence that he was ever aware of it. It was actually his case that his wife had signed it without his knowledge. However, the Crown sought to argue that the silence of the appellant in failing to notify the council of his mother's death itself constituted conduct within section 15(4) of the Theft Act 1968. He accepted that he had remained silent, had not told the council of his mother's death at any time until after the building works were completed, but the contention on his behalf was that he had no legal or contractual duty to inform the council and that mere silence or inactivity could not constitute such conduct. Thus, there had been no deception.

The learned judge was asked to give a ruling on this point before any evidence was called. Thus, one important fact, which would have been in issue, had to be assumed in the appellant's favour as to the signature on the form: the assumption had to be made that he did not sign the form and had no knowledge of that document which had been left at his house. This court has to approach this issue on the same basis as the learned judge, namely that, after Mrs Chand died, the appellant did not tell the council that she had died but simply carried on about his ordinary business.

The learned judge gave a reasoned judgment, deciding this issue in favour of the Crown and ruling that his silence in those circumstances did amount to conduct sufficient to constitute a deception on the local authority. It seems to us that, in effect, he found it was capable of amounting to such conduct. Whether it did would have been, no doubt, an issue for the jury.

The underlying facts which underpinned that finding were, not only that the appellant did not tell the council, but that – as was undisputed – this was his house and at all material times he lived there. When, after the learned judge's ruling, the appellant pleaded guilty, he did so on the specific factual basis that his only relevant conduct was his failure to inform the council of the death of his mother. He did not acknowledge any other conduct on his part by which the council might have been deceived.

The learned judge, in his reasoned ruling, based his decision principally on an analogy with the somewhat different facts of the House of Lords case of *Ray v Sempers* [1974] AC 370. He accurately summarised the facts of that case in the following terms:

> Five students went to a Chinese restaurant intending to have a meal and pay for it. After eating the main course, they decided not to pay for it but they remained where they were until the waiter went out of the room and then they ran from the restaurant. The defendant was convicted by the justices of dishonestly obtaining a pecuniary advantage by deception, and the charge was that the defendant obtained for himself a pecuniary advantage, namely a meal, and evaded the debt by running out of the restaurant without paying.

He went on:

> It was submitted that as he did not change his mind until after the meal had been consumed, that he did nothing to evade the debt. By simply sitting there and then leaving the restaurant at a convenient moment, the House of Lords took the view that that was incorrect and that the transaction had to be regarded as a whole in that the defendant's conduct was a continuing representation of his present intention to pay.

The relevant continuing conduct was staying in the restaurant; that was the basis for the finding by the majority in the House of Lords that there was sufficient conduct in that particular case to amount to a deception. The students had changed their minds about paying. They did so whilst sitting at the table in the restaurant. They continued to sit there for a time, and, in that sense, their conduct was continuing because they were then sitting there with their newly formed intention not to pay for their meals, thus falsifying their earlier implied representation that they would pay. This, in the opinion of the House of Lords, amounted to sufficient conduct to satisfy that essential element of the offence.

The basis in the present case of the learned judge's ruling was that this appellant's conduct was equivalent to that conduct on the part of those students, and the question for this court is whether that was correct.

Mr Cowley makes the point, cogently and clearly, that, in this case, there was no act or continuing act on the part of the appellant. He submits that the appellant in the present case was not playing a similar role or occupying a similar role to that occupied by the students in the case of *Ray v Sempers*, but that there was no act identified as representing conduct by which the local authority were deceived.

The learned judge held, however, at p 6D in his ruling, that by simply sitting there doing nothing and allowing the work to be done, the appellant was committing a straightforward deception, because, as he was aware, the local authority were still of the mind that the mother would occupy the premises. He was living there at all material times. In the judgment of this court, that, against the background of it being his home and he having made the application, was conduct sufficient to amount to conduct within the terms of section 15(4) of the 1968 Act. In our judgment the approach of the learned judge was correct, albeit on the basis of a feature of this case, that it was his house and that he was living in it continuously, which was not apparent to this court on our first reading of the papers. But, on a common-sense and purposive construction of the word 'conduct', it does, in our judgment, cover positive acquiescence in knowingly letting this work proceed as the appellant did in the present case.

The learned judge was also referred, more briefly, to the case of *R v Firth* [extracted below] ...

In that case, it was submitted that the counts were wrongly laid in law, in that the allegations to be proved required acts of commission whereas the evidence disclosed only acts of omission. Lord Lane CJ dealt with the submission, but dealt with it only by referring to section 2 of the Act and did not in terms refer to the definition of deception contained in section 15(4).

In the present case, the learned judge held – correctly in the view of this court – that *Firth* did not assist him in the present problem, because the surgeon there had a specific contractual obligation to disclose the status of his patients and it was for that reason that his failure to do so did amount to continuing conduct. But it does seem to us that the editor of *Archbold* makes an important additional point ... where he points out that no reference was made to section 15(4) and it may be that the decision in *Firth* should not be taken as any general authority for the proposition that mere silence can constitute a deception.

That being said, however, we are satisfied that, in the present case, there was conduct capable of amounting to the deception alleged by the prosecution. Accordingly, the learned judge's ruling was, in our judgment, correct, and there is thus no basis for this court to hold that the plea of guilty entered by the appellant is in any way wrong or that the conviction should be regarded as unsafe. For those reasons, the appeal against conviction is dismissed.

Deception must operate on a human mind

R v Rozeik [1996] 1 WLR 159 (CA)

Leggatt LJ: This appeal raises a point of law about the deception of a company ...

Each of the 12 counts in the indictment related to a dishonest application to a finance company for funds to purchase equipment to be used by limited companies controlled or owned by the appellant. Each such purchase was by way of a hire-purchase agreement. It was the Crown's case that false information was provided to the finance company concerned as to the description, price, and even the existence of particular equipment, and that had the finance companies been aware of the true facts, cheques in payment for the equipment would never have been issued ...

The particulars of offence of each count in the indictment charged the appellant with having on a stated date dishonestly obtained a specified cheque drawn in a specified sum from the relevant finance company with the intention of permanently depriving the finance company thereof by deception, namely by falsely representing that (1) the details contained in a specified hire-purchase agreement were true and (2) the relative invoice was genuine ...

His Lordship quoted s 15(1) of the Theft Act 1968 and continued:

In respect of each count in the indictment the property belonging to a finance company which was dishonestly obtained was a cheque. For the purpose of ascertaining whether the cheque was obtained by a deception it is necessary to consider the state of mind of the person by whom it was furnished on behalf of the company. For the purpose of determining whether in entering into the hire-purchase agreements the company was deceived, whose state of mind stood as the state of mind of the company? The person who in each branch most obviously represented the company was the branch manager. [Counsel for the appellant] drew attention to many examples of employees declaring in evidence that they worked under supervision and control of Birch [a branch manager]. Others similarly worked under Wilkinson [another branch manager]. In relation to several of the counts the evidence showed direct implication by one of them. The managers appear to have had the conduct of those transactions, so as to involve their direct endorsement of approval of it. It may also, we think, be said with some force that, once the credit limits had been set by Birch and Wilkinson, all the ensuing transactions within the limits proceeded by their authority. By appointing credit limits Birch and Wilkinson must be taken to have authorised all transactions with the appellant up to and within those limits.

The next question is whether Birch and Wilkinson knew that the invoice in each transaction was false.

... [S]ince the case for the Crown depended on knowledge of the falsity of the invoices not being imputed to the companies, the jury should have been directed ... that they should ignore in this context the knowledge of anyone who they were sure was party to the fraud ... Unless the state of mind of Birch and Wilkinson was excluded, so that their knowledge was not attributed to the companies, it did not avail the Crown to prove that anyone else was deceived by the appellant.

A more difficult question is whether the knowledge of Birch and Wilkinson should not be imputed to their companies ...

... Since Birch and Wilkinson were managers of their respective branches, their knowledge was the knowledge of their companies unless they were shown to be acting dishonestly ...

... [T]he question is not whether any employee of the company was deceived but whether any employee whose state of mind stood as that of the company knew of the falsity of the transaction, since, if he or she did know, the company also knew. If the company knew, it would not matter how many fellow employees were personally deceived. Second, and in any event, a cheque could only be obtained from the company from an employee who had authority to provide it. The deception had to operate on the mind of the employee from whom the cheque was obtained. In no sense could a cheque be 'obtained' from the person who merely typed it out ... What the Crown had to prove was that when the cheque was obtained from the company it was obtained from a person who was deceived. Although in no sense was it obtained from those who checked or typed it, the signatories of the cheques (apart from Birch and Wilkinson) were in a different position. They had a responsibility to ensure that the cheques were not signed unless satisfied that the money should be paid. They were more than mere mechanics and in our judgment, if they were deceived, the company also was, once Birch and Wilkinson were disregarded. That means that (1) where a manager only signed, the offence could not be made out, (2) where a manager signed with another employee, it had to be shown that that other was deceived, and (3) where two employees (other than a manager) signed, it had to be proved either that one was or that both were deceived, and that where one was, the other did not know of the fraud, since if he or she did, the company would not have been deceived ...

The deception must be operative

The deception must be the operative cause of the obtaining of the property. If a motorist fills up the petrol tank of her car and *then* deceives the attendant in some way so as to avoid paying for the petrol, it cannot be said that the property (the petrol) was obtained 'by' (ie as a result of) deception (see *R v Collis-Smith* [1971] Crim LR 716); hence the need for the offence of 'making off without payment' under s 3 of the Theft Act 1978 – see Chapter 18.

R v Laverty [1970] 3 All ER 432 (CA)

Lord Parker CJ: ... The facts are in a very short compass. The car bearing number plates DUV 111C, a Hillman Imp, was bought by a Mr Bedborough from the appellant, and a cheque was given as part of the price. In fact that car bearing those number plates was a car originally bearing number plates JPA 945C, which had been stolen. According to the appellant when he got the car, and there was no question of his having stolen it, it was in a bad condition, he repaired it and he put onto it the ... number plates of DUV 111C, those plates having been obtained from another source relating of course to another car.

The charge made in the indictment ... took the form of alleging a false representation which here was by conduct. It was not a false representation that the appellant was the owner and had a good title to sell but the false representation was by purporting that a Hillman Imp motor car which the appellant sold to Roy Clinton Bedborough was the original Hillman Imp motor car, index number DUV 111C.

Although it was contested at the trial, it was conceded in this court that there was a representation by conduct that the car being sold to Mr Bedborough was the original Hillman Imp to which the [number] plate[s] which it bore had been assigned. It is conceded that such a representation was made by conduct; it is clear that that was false, and false to the knowledge of the appellant. The sole question was whether this false representation operated on Mr Bedborough's mind so as to cause him to hand over this cheque.

As sometimes happens, in this case Mr Bedborough did not give the answers which were helpful to the prosecution, and no leading questions could be put. The nearest answer was 'I bought this because I thought the appellant was the owner'.

In other words, Mr Bedborough was saying: 'What induced me to part with my money was the representation by conduct that the appellant had a title to sell' ...

... It is axiomatic that it is for the prosecution to prove that the false representation acted on the mind of the purchaser; and in the ordinary way, and the court emphasises this, the matter should be proved by direct evidence. However, it was said in *R v Sullivan* (1945) 30 Cr App Rep 132 that the inducement need not be proved by direct evidence, and I quote from the headnote:

> if the facts are such that the alleged false pretence is the only reason that could be suggested as having been the operative inducement.

... This court is very anxious not to extend the principle in *R v Sullivan* more than is necessary. The proper way of proving these matters is through the mouth of the person to whom the false representation is conveyed, and further it seems to the court in the present case that no jury could say that the only inference here was that Mr Bedborough parted with his money by reason of this false representation. Mr Bedborough may well have been of the mind as he stated he was, namely that what operated on his mind was the belief that the appellant was the owner. Provided that the appellant was the owner it may well be that Mr Bedborough did not mind that the car did not bear its original number plates. At any rate as it seems to the court it cannot be said that the only possible inference here is that it actuated on Mr Bedborough's mind ...

R v Rashid [1977] 1 WLR 298 (CA)

Bridge LJ: [T]his defendant was convicted of having with him articles for use in the course of or in connection with cheat [contrary to s 25(1) of the Theft Act 1968, a 'cheat' for these purposes being a deception – hence the case addresses whether or not, had he completed his planned course of action, his deception would have been operative – see further Chapter 19] ...

... The particular articles of which the defendant was convicted of having possession, not at his place of abode and for use in connection with cheat, were two loaves of sliced bread and one bag of tomatoes. The facts were that the defendant was a steward employed by British Rail and the offence was said to have been committed when at Euston Station early one morning he was about to board a train for Glasgow. The prosecution case was that his intention was to use his own bread and tomatoes in the making of sandwiches which would then be sold by him to passengers on the train for, no doubt, the same price as would be charged for a British Rail sandwich and that the defendant would pocket the proceeds ...

... [I]t does not follow that in the circumstances of this case this defendant could be convicted of the offence under s 25. At all events, before he could be ... convicted [of an offence under s 25], if he could be convicted at all which the court doubts, at the very least it was necessary that the judge in summing up should have made it abundantly clear to the jury what were the elements of the offence of deception under s 15 which constituted the basis of the intended cheat, and what would be the necessary state of mind of the defendant with regard to the intended commission of that offence under s 15 in order to sustain a conviction for the offence charged under s 25 ...

... At the very least what would have been necessary would have been a direction to the effect that the offence intended to be committed would have been the obtaining of property by deception from the passenger and that a necessary element in the defendant's *mens rea* on which the jury would have to be satisfied would be that he believed the passenger, if he knew that the sandwich offered him was made with bread and tomatoes belonging to the defendant and not belonging to British Rail, would have declined to purchase. Unless that was his state of mind then he had not the necessary *mens rea* to found a conviction under s 25, having articles in his possession in connection with an intended offence under s 15.

R v Doukas [1978] 1 WLR 372 (CA)

Geoffrey Lane LJ: ... The facts of the case are these. On 9 January 1976 Doukas was engaged as a casual wine waiter at the Cunard International Hotel at Hammersmith and it seems that on that engagement he gave certainly a false name and possibly also a false address to his employers. Not very long after his engagement, he was found on the fire escape of the hotel by one of the assistant managers of the hotel. It was against the rules for him to be on the fire escape but that was not the real gravamen of his offence, because found in his coat pocket were six bottles of wine ...

His Lordship referred to the summing up which noted that when interviewed by the police the appellant had said:

> I take the wine in. If a carafe is ordered I substitute my own wine and make out a separate bill for the customer from the hotel's bill and I keep the money.

The summing up continued:

> There, the prosecution say, is a confession of an intended deliberate deception ...
>
> ... [T]he following items have to be proved. First of all that there was an article for use in connection with the deception: here the bottles. Second, that there was a proposed deception: here the deception of the guests into believing that the proffered wine was hotel wine and not the waiter's wine. Third, an intention to obtain property by means of the deception, and the property here is the money of the guests which he proposes to obtain and keep. Fourth, dishonesty. There is twofold dishonesty in the way the Crown put the case. First of all the dishonesty in respect of his employers, namely putting into his pocket the money which really should go to the hotel and, more important, the second dishonesty, vis-a-vis the guests, the lying to or misleading of the guests into believing that the wine which had been proffered was the hotel wine and not the waiter's wine. Fifth, there must be proof that the obtaining would have been, wholly or partially, by virtue of the deception.
>
> The prosecution must prove that nexus between the deception and obtaining. It is this last and final ingredient which, as we see it in the present case, is the only point which raises any difficulty. Assuming, as we must, and indeed obviously was the case, that the jury accepted the version of the police interviews and accepted that this man had made the confession to which I have referred, then the only question was, would this obtaining have in fact been caused by the deception practised by the waiter? ...

Of course each case of this type may produce different results according to the circumstances of the case and according, in particular, to the commodity which is being proffered. But, as we see it, the question has to be asked of the hypothetical customer: why did you buy this wine? or, if you had been told the truth, would you or would you not have bought the commodity? It is, at least in theory, for the jury in the end to decide that question.

... Certainly so far as the wine is concerned, we have no doubt at all that the hypothetical customer faced with the waiter saying to him: 'This of course is not hotel wine, this is stuff which I imported into the hotel myself and I am going to put the proceeds of the wine, if you pay, into my own pocket', would certainly answer, so far as we can see, 'I do not want your wine, kindly bring me the hotel carafe wine'. Indeed it would be a strange jury that came to any other conclusion, and a stranger guest who gave any other answer, for several reasons. First of all the guest would not know what was in the bottle which the waiter was proffering. True he may not know what was in the carafe which the hotel was proffering, but he would at least be able to have recourse to the hotel if something was wrong with the carafe wine, but he would have no such recourse with the waiter; if he did, it would be worthless.

It seems to us that the matter can be answered on a much simpler basis. The hypothetical customer must be reasonably honest as well as being reasonably intelligent and it seems to us incredible that any customer, to whom the true situation was made clear, would willingly make himself a party to what was obviously a fraud by the waiter on his employers. If that conclusion is contrary to the *obiter dicta* in R v Rashid ... then we must respectfully disagree with those *dicta* ...

R v Miller (1992) 95 Cr App R 421 (CA)

Lord Chief Justice: ... The facts of the case are these. The applicant operated as an unlicensed taxi driver from both Heathrow and Gatwick Airports from time to time. The prosecution alleged, as the indictment which has been read indicates, that he obtained from various foreign persons coming to this country extortionate fares in respect of journeys which he carried out with those people as his passengers ...

In our judgment ... it is really not legitimate to isolate the moment when the money is handed over from the rest of the story. If on the whole of the story it can legitimately be said that the various deceptions alleged in the indictment were the cause for the money being handed over, it is, or may be, irrelevant that at the final moment the victim suspected or even believed that he or she had been swindled.

This is such a case. The passenger in each case was initially inveigled into agreeing to ride in the car by the lie that it was a proper taxi, and also by the inference that the charges levied by this applicant would be reasonable. By the end of the journey the victim realised, or partially realised in some cases, that the applicant had probably been lying. But by that time in each case the victim feels that he or she is under a compulsion or obligation to pay the extortionate sum requested ...

... [The applicant] had not charged a reasonable fare. He charged in one case 10 times more than the reasonable fare. All of that stemmed from the fact that he was not a taxi driver. The passenger, feeling a compulsion or obligation to pay, and fearing the consequences if he or she did not, handed over the money ...

There is, in our judgment, ample evidence arising from the facts which we have endeavoured to detail, upon which the jury could properly conclude that what was the effective cause of the transfer of this money were the various false assertions which this man made as laid in the indictment. That being the case, it was a question of fact for the jury to decide whether or not the prosecution had made out their case. They had to answer the question what was the effective cause of the transfer of this money. In the light of the fact that there is no complaint, and indeed there could be no complaint, about the direction to the jury, they were left the proper problem to decide. There was ample evidence upon which they could come to the conclusion which they did, and came to very rapidly ...

Proving an operative deception: cheques, cheque cards and credit cards

Commissioner of Police for the Metropolis v Charles [1977] AC 177 (HL)

Viscount Dilhorne: My Lords, on 31 October 1972, the appellant opened a bank account at the Peckham Rye Branch of the National Westminster Bank. On 23 November, the manager of that branch agreed to allow him to have an overdraft of £100 for one month, a facility which was later extended for a further month. On 19 December 1972, he was given a cheque card headed 'National Westminster Bank £30 for conditions see over' and on its front a space for the appellant's signature. On the back was printed:

> The issuing banks undertake that any cheque not exceeding £30 will be honoured subject to the following conditions: (a) The cheque must be signed in the presence of the payee. (b) The signature on the cheque must correspond with the specimen signature on this card. (c) The cheque must be drawn on a bank cheque form bearing the code number shown on this card. (d) The cheque must be drawn before the expiry date of this card. (e) The card number must be written on the reverse of the cheque by the payee.

These conditions are designed to secure that the cheque is drawn by the customer to whom the bank has given a cheque book and a cheque card. If they are complied with the recipient need not concern himself about the drawer's creditworthiness for he knows the cheque will be honoured on presentment.

On 27 December a cheque drawn by the appellant was presented and returned unpaid. The next day the appellant was notified that he had exceeded his overdraft limit and on 2 January 1973 his overdraft rose to £248 due to the presentation that day of four cheques each for £30 drawn by the appellant with the use of his cheque card. The bank manager tried to get in touch with the appellant immediately and saw him that day. The bank manager knew that a cheque in favour of the appellant for £500 had been paid into a branch of the bank. Payment of that cheque was, however, stopped and it was not met until March.

When he saw the appellant the bank manager did not know, did not ask and was not told what other cheques had been drawn by the appellant and not presented. In fact the appellant had by 2 January drawn a further 14 cheques which had not then been presented. Not knowing this, the bank manager allowed the appellant to be issued with a new cheque book containing 25 cheque forms. He told the appellant that he must not cash more than one cheque a day for £30 at a bank but he gave him no further instructions as to the use of the cheque card.

That evening the appellant went to the Golden Nugget Club, a gaming club, and in the course of the night he used all the cheques in the new cheque book for the purchase of chips for gaming. Each cheque was for £30 made out to the manager of the club, Mr Cersell, and he used his cheque card in relation to each cheque. The bank had consequently to honour all the cheques with the result that they paid out a further £750 ...

The reality is in my view that a man who gives a cheque represents that it will be met on presentation, and if a cheque is accepted by the payee, it is in the belief that it will be met.

That being the position with a cheque, how is it affected by the production and use of a cheque card by the drawer, the authorised holder of the card? The representation that the cheque will be met is unaltered. It is supported by the bank's undertaking and all doubts in the mind of the payee as to the cheque being honoured will be removed if he sees that the stipulated conditions are complied with.

If in this case the appellant had not used his cheque card, none of his cheques would have been taken by the Golden Nugget Club. Mr Cersell made that clear.

Does a cheque card holder by his conduct in producing his cheque card and using it to secure the acceptance of his cheque make any representation additional to that made by him when giving the cheque? Whether or not an additional representation by conduct is made in those circumstances is a question of fact for the jury but whether an additional representation can be inferred from his conduct is a question of law.

His use of a cheque card to secure acceptance of his cheque can in my opinion amount to a representation that he has the authority of the bank to use it in relation to that cheque for that purpose, and as a matter of fact will ordinarily do so. He is authorised by the bank to give their undertaking to pay up to £30 on a cheque if the stipulated conditions are fulfilled. But the authority given to him is not unlimited. By giving him a cheque book and a cheque card the bank has not authorised him to bind them by the use of the card to honour every cheque in the cheque book. He is not authorised to use it to secure the acceptance of a cheque which he knows would not be met by the bank if the cheque card had not been used ...

The Court of Appeal (Criminal Division) dismissed the appellant's appeal but certified that the following point of law was of general public importance and gave leave to appeal to this House:

> When the holder of a cheque card presents a cheque in accordance with the conditions of the card which is accepted in exchange for goods, services or cash, does this transaction provide evidence of itself from which it can or should be inferred (a) that the drawer represented that he then had authority, as between himself and the bank, to draw a cheque for that amount and (b) that the recipient of the cheque was induced by that representation to accept the cheque?

With respect, I do not think that this question was very happily phrased. Whether an inference can be properly drawn is a matter of law; whether it should be drawn is a question of fact for the jury. Whether or not the recipient of a cheque was induced by a representation to accept it, is also a question of fact. It would have been better if the question had been worded as follows:

When the holder of a cheque card presents a cheque card together with a cheque made out in accordance with the conditions of the card which cheque is accepted in exchange for goods, services or cash, does this transaction provide evidence of itself from which it can be inferred that the drawer represented that he then had authority as between himself and the bank to use the card in order to oblige the bank to honour the cheque?

So phrased the question raises the issue which has to be determined on this appeal and in my opinion the answer to it is in the affirmative ...

Lord Diplock: My Lords [I confine].... my own speech to a brief analysis of the representations made by the drawer of a cheque; first, where he proffers it to the payee without a cheque card as payment for goods or services or in exchange for cash, and second, where the drawer shows to the payee a cheque card and the cheque which he then draws appears to comply with the conditions endorsed upon the card ...

To take first the case in which no cheque card is involved, it is no doubt true to say that all the payee is concerned with is that the cheque should be honoured by the bank, and that to induce the payee to take the cheque all that the drawer is concerned to do is to assure him that as far as can reasonably be foreseen this is what will happen. But payment by the bank cannot reasonably be foreseen as likely unless the fact be that the cheque is one which the bank on which it is drawn is bound, by an existing contract with the drawer, to pay on presentment or, if not strictly bound to do so, could reasonably be expected to pay in the normal course of dealing ...

When a cheque card is brought into the transaction, it still remains the fact that all the payee is concerned with is that the cheque should be honoured by the bank. I do not think that the fact that a cheque card is used necessarily displaces the representation to be implied from the act of drawing the cheque which has just been mentioned. It is, however, likely to displace that representation at any rate as the main inducement to the payee to take the cheque, since the use of the cheque card in connection with the transaction gives to the payee a direct contractual right against the bank itself to payment on presentation, provided that the use of the card by the drawer to bind the bank to pay the cheque was within the actual or ostensible authority conferred on him by the bank.

By exhibiting to the payee a cheque card containing the undertaking by the bank to honour cheques drawn in compliance with the conditions endorsed on the back, and drawing the cheque accordingly, the drawer represents to the payee that he has actual authority from the bank to make a contract with the payee on the bank's behalf that it will honour the cheque on presentation for payment.

... What creates ostensible authority in a person who purports to enter into a contract as agent for a principal is a representation made to the other party that he has the actual authority of the principal for whom he claims to be acting to enter into the contract on that person's behalf. If (1) the other party has believed the representation and on the faith of that belief has acted on it and (2) the person represented to be his principal has so conducted himself towards that other party as to be estopped from denying the truth of the representation, then, and only then, is he bound by the contract purportedly made on his behalf. The whole foundation of liability under the doctrine of ostensible authority is a representation, believed by the person to whom it is made, that the person claiming to contract as agent for a principal has the actual authority of the principal to enter into the contract on his behalf.

That is the representation that the drawer makes to the payee when he uses a cheque card to back a cheque which he draws in compliance with the conditions endorsed on the card. That in the instant case Mr Cersell, the manager of the gaming club, so understood it is implicit from the passages in his evidence to which my noble and learned friend, Lord Edmund-Davies, refers. Mr Cersell may not have known the doctrine of ostensible authority under that name, but he knew what it was all about. He would not have taken the accused's cheques had he not believed that the accused was authorised by the bank to use the cheque card to back them.

Lord Edmund-Davies: ... It was ... incumbent on the Crown to establish [*inter alia*] that in relation to each of the two incidents giving rise to the charges laid (a) the accused had made the representation alleged; (b) that he made it dishonestly; (c) that the person to whom the representation was made was thereby induced to act as he did ...

... What of the production and use of the cheque card when each of the 25 cheques in the new cheque book was drawn ... Is [counsel for the appellant] right in submitting that the only representation made by its production was the perfectly correct one that 'this cheque, backed by this card, will be honoured without question'? In my judgment, he is not. The accused knew perfectly well that he would not be able to get more chips at the club simply by drawing a cheque. The cheque alone would not have been accepted; it had to be backed by a cheque card. The card played a vital part, for (as my noble and learned friend, Lord Diplock, put it during counsel's submission) in order to make the bank liable to the payee there must be knowledge on the payee's part that the drawer has the bank's authority to bind it, for in the absence of such knowledge the all-important contract between payee and bank is not created; and it is the representation by the drawer's production of the card that he has that authority that creates such contractual relationship and estops the bank from refusing to honour the cheque. By drawing the cheque the accused represented that it would be met, and by producing the card so that the number thereon could be endorsed on the cheque he in effect represented, 'I am authorised by the bank to show this to you and so create a direct contractual relationship between the bank and you that they will honour this cheque'. The production of the card was the badge of the accused's ostensible authority to make such a representation on the bank's behalf. And this emerges with clarity from the evidence of the club manager, Mr Cersell, who repeatedly stressed during his lengthy testimony that the accused's cheque would not have been accepted unless accompanied by a cheque card the signature on which corresponded with that of the accused when making out the cheque.

... There remains to be considered the vitally important question of whether it was established that it was as a result of such dishonest deception that the club's staff were induced to give chips for cheques and so, in due course, caused the accused's bank account to become improperly overdrawn ...

Whether a party was induced to act as he did because of the deception to which he was dishonestly subjected is a question of fact to be decided on the evidence adduced in each case ...

... [I]n this context it has again to be borne in mind that the witness made clear that the accused's cheques were accepted only because he produced a cheque card, and he repeatedly stressed that, had he been aware that the accused was using his cheque book and cheque card 'in a way in which he was not allowed or entitled to use [them]' no cheque would have been accepted. The evidence of that witness, taken as a whole, points irresistibly to the conclusions (a) that by this dishonest conduct the accused deceived Mr Cersell in the manner averred in the particulars of the charges and (b) that Mr Cersell was thereby induced to accept the cheques because of his belief that the representations as to both cheque and card were true ...

R v Lambie [1982] AC 449 (HL)

Lord Roskill: My Lords, on 20 April 1977, the respondent was issued by Barclays Bank Ltd ('the bank') with a Barclaycard ('the card'). That card was what today is commonly known as a credit card. It was issued subject to the Barclaycard current conditions of use, and it was an express condition of its issue that it should be used only within the respondent's credit limit. That credit limit was £200 as the respondent well knew, since that figure had been notified to her in writing when the card was issued. The then current conditions of use included an undertaking by the respondent, as its holder, to return the card to the bank on request. No complaint was, or indeed could be, made of the respondent's use of the card until 18 November 1977. Between that date and 5 December 1977, she used the card for at least 24 separate transactions, thereby incurring a debt of some £533. The bank became aware of this debt and thereupon sought to recover the card. On 6 December 1977, the respondent agreed to return the card on 7 December 1977. She did not, however, do so. By 15 December 1977, she had used the card for at least 43 further transactions, incurring a total debt to the bank of £1,005.26.

My Lords, on 15 December 1977 [before the coming into force of the Theft Act 1978] the respondent entered into the transaction out of which this appeal arises. She visited a Mothercare shop in Luton. She produced the card to a departmental manager at Mothercare named Miss Rounding. She selected goods worth £10.35. Miss Rounding completed the voucher and checked that the card was current in date, that it was not on the current stop list and that the respondent's signature on the voucher corresponded with her signature on the card. Thereupon, the respondent took away the goods which she had selected. In due course, Mothercare sent the voucher to the bank and were paid £10.35 less the appropriate commission charged by the bank. On 19 December 1977, the respondent returned the card to the bank.

[The defendant was charged under s 16(1) of the Theft Act 1968 with obtaining for herself a pecuniary advantage, namely the evasion of a debt (a form of pecuniary advantage under s 16(2)(a) Theft Act 1968, subsequently replaced by s 2 of the Theft Act 1978) for which she then made herself liable, by deception, namely by representing that she was authorised to use a Barclaycard to obtain goods to the value of £10.35.] ...

[The Court of Appeal] certified the following point of law as of general public importance, namely:

> In view of the proved differences between a cheque card transaction and a credit card transaction, were we right in distinguishing this case from that of *R v Charles* [1977] AC 177 upon the issue of inducement?

... Following the decision of this House in *R v Charles*, it is in my view clear that the representation arising from the presentation of a credit card has nothing to do with the respondent's credit standing at the bank but is a representation of actual authority to make the contract with, in this case, Mothercare on the bank's behalf that the bank will honour the voucher on presentation. On that view, the existence and terms of the agreement between the bank and Mothercare are irrelevant, as is the fact that Mothercare, because of that agreement, would look to the bank for payment.

That being the representation to be implied from the respondent's actions and use of the credit card, the only remaining question is whether Miss Rounding was induced by that representation to complete the transaction and allow the respondent to take away the goods. My Lords, if she had been asked whether, had she known the respondent was acting dishonestly and, in truth, had no authority whatever from the bank to use the credit card in this way, she (Miss Rounding) would have completed the transaction, only one answer is possible – no. Had an affirmative answer been given to this question, Miss Rounding would, of course, have become a participant in furtherance of the respondent's fraud and a conspirator with her to defraud both Mothercare and the bank ...

... My Lords, credit card frauds are all too frequently perpetrated, and if conviction of offenders for offences against ss 15 or 16 of the Act of 1968 can only be obtained if the prosecution are able in each case to call the person on whom the fraud was immediately perpetrated to say that he or she positively remembered the particular transaction and, had the truth been known, would never have entered into that supposedly well-remembered transaction, the guilty would often escape conviction. In some cases, of course, it may be possible to adduce such evidence if the particular transaction is well remembered. But where as in the present case no one could reasonably be expected to remember a particular transaction in detail, and the inference of inducement may well be in all the circumstances quite irresistible, I see no reason in principle why it should not be left to the jury to decide, on the evidence in the case as a whole, whether that inference is in truth irresistible as to my mind it is in the present case. In this connection it is to be noted that the respondent did not go into the witness box to give evidence from which that inference might conceivably have been rebutted.

My Lords, in this respect I find myself in agreement with what was said by Humphreys J giving the judgment of the Court of Criminal Appeal in *R v Sullivan* (1945) 30 Cr App R 132, 136:

> It is, we think, undoubtedly good law that the question of the inducement acting upon the mind of the person who may be described as the prosecutor is not a matter which can only be proved by the direct evidence of the witness. It can be, and very often is, proved by the witness being asked some question which brings the answer: 'I believed that statement and that is why I parted with my money'; but it is not necessary that there should be that question and answer if the facts are such that it is patent that there was only one reason which anybody could suggest for the person alleged to have been defrauded parting with his money, and that is the false pretence, if it was a false pretence.

His Lordship then referred briefly to *R v Laverty* (1970) 54 Cr App R 495 and continued:

Of course, the Crown must always prove its case and one element which will always be required to be proved in these cases is the effect of the dishonest representation on the mind of the person to whom it is made. But I see no reason why in cases such as the present, where what Humphreys J called the direct evidence of the witness is not and cannot reasonably be expected to be available, reliance on a dishonest representation cannot be sufficiently established by proof of facts from which an irresistible inference of such reliance can be drawn.

My Lords, I would answer the certified question in the negative and would allow the appeal and restore the conviction of the respondent ...

Note: A simpler course for the prosecution to have followed would have been to charge the defendant with obtaining property by deception, contrary to s 15 of the Theft Act 1968.

R v Gilmartin [1983] QB 953 (CA)

Robert Goff LJ: ... Each of the four counts in the indictment alleges that the relevant deception by the appellant consisted of a false representation that the cheque in question was a good and valid order for the payment of the sum specified in the cheque. All the cheques in question were post-dated cheques ... The submission for the defence before the judge, which was repeated before this court, was that by giving a post-dated cheque the drawer impliedly represents no more than that he (or any company on whose behalf he draws the cheque) is a customer of the bank on which the cheque is drawn, and makes no implied representation concerning the honouring of the cheque ...

... We can see no reason why in the case of a post-dated cheque the drawer does not impliedly represent that the existing facts at the date when he gives the cheque to the payee or his agent are such that in the ordinary course the cheque will, on presentation on or after the date specified in the cheque, be met.

Take the case where, as in this instance, a post-dated cheque is issued when the account is heavily overdrawn and there is, as the drawer well knows, no prospect of any future funds being paid into the account before the date when the cheque matures or of the bank providing other overdraft facilities before that date. In such a case it appears to us the drawer is as much guilty of deception as he would be in the case of a cheque which is not post-dated. Indeed, where the drawer gives a cheque which is not post-dated his account may be overdrawn and he may have no arrangement with his bank for further overdraft facilities, but he may have in his pocket another cheque payable to him which he intends to pay into his account immediately and which when paid in will enable the cheque which he himself has drawn to be paid on presentation; if so it is difficult to see that he has made any misrepresentation. In these circumstances, we can see no relevant distinction between the case of a cheque which has not been post-dated and one which has.

For the sake of clarity, we consider that in the generality of cases under s 15 and 16 of the Theft Act 1968, the courts should proceed on the basis that by the simple giving of a cheque, whether post-dated or not, the drawer impliedly represents that the state of facts existing at the date of handing over the cheque is such that in the ordinary course the cheque will, on presentation for payment on or after the date specified in the cheque be met ...

R v Nabina [2000] Crim LR 481

Lord Bingham CJ: On 2 October 1998, following a nine-day trial in the Crown Court at Manchester, the appellant was convicted by a unanimous verdict of 14 counts of obtaining property by deception. On 19 November 1998 he was sentenced to three years' imprisonment on each count concurrently. The appellant was acquitted by direction of counts 1 and 2 on the indictment, both of them also charging the obtaining of property by deception, and count 17, which charged him with obtaining a pecuniary advantage by deception. He appeals against conviction by leave of the single judge.

The background facts are that the appellant, who is now aged 35, owned a business. He began to apply for credit facilities with a number of credit card companies and banks. He provided information as to his finances, employment and personal details, which included, for example, his date of birth. On the basis of those representations the issuers issued to him credit cards which he then used to finance purchases from a number of different outlets.

The charges of which the appellant was convicted were identical, save for the dates on or between which the offences were alleged to have been committed, the value of the goods said to have been obtained, and the issuer and number of the relevant credit card. It is sufficient for present purposes to cite, first of all, count 3 as representative. It charged him with obtaining property by deception contrary to section 15(1) of the Theft Act 1968. The particulars charged that:

> ... on a day between the 1st day of July 1996 and the 31st day of August 1997 [he] dishonestly obtained from representatives of various outlets property to the value of £5,418.03 with the intention of permanently depriving various outlets thereof by deception namely by falsely representing that he was the legitimate holder of a Master card number ...

Count 16 of which he was also convicted was laid under the same section, but the offence was said to have been committed on 19 August 1997 and the goods were identified as travellers cheques to the value of £4,040, said to have been obtained from Thomas Cook plc. The false representation alleged in this case was that the appellant was the legitimate holder of a Midland Bank Mastercard with a specified number.

... The question accordingly arises: what did the Crown have to prove to enable a jury properly to convict the appellant of a count framed in the terms of counts 3 to 16? In other words, what were the ingredients of the offence charged against the appellant?

In our judgment there were five ingredients, which were these: (1) that the appellant dishonestly (2) obtained goods from representatives of various outlets (3) with the intention of depriving those outlets of the goods permanently (4) by representing that he was the legitimate holder of a specified card (5) falsely.

The crux of the prosecution case against the appellant was that he applied to a substantial number of credit card companies and banks, giving false information about his personal details, and so dishonestly obtained the issue of the cards which he then used dishonestly to obtain goods from various outlets. Originally the prosecution charged the appellant with offences based on his allegedly dishonest representations to the credit card companies and banks, as well as the sales outlets. But that indictment was replaced by an indictment in the present form which was directed not to the making of dishonest representations to the card issuing institutions to obtain the issue of the cards, but to the making of dishonest representations to the various outlets to obtain the goods.

It was not in issue at the trial that the appellant did hold several cards, and it is now accepted that he obtained the issue of the cards by making various false statements. It was also not in issue that he used the cards to obtain goods from various outlets. Nor was it in issue that, like any other purchaser, he did not intend to return the goods to the seller, and so in the language of the section he intended to deprive the owners of the goods permanently.

There was accordingly no live issue concerning ingredients (2) and (3) listed above, but ingredients (1), (4) and (5) were very much in issue, in particular whether the appellant had obtained the goods by representing falsely and dishonestly that he was the legitimate holder of the card in question.

The appellant complains that the judge misdirected himself in law and failed properly to direct the jury. The first complaint relates to the judge's ruling following a submission at the close of the prosecution evidence that there was no case for the appellant to answer. The submission was then made that there was no evidence to support the prosecution case that the representation charged as made to the sales outlets (if made) was false. The basis of that argument was that, even if the issue of the credit cards had been obtained by fraud, the appellant still enjoyed the rights granted to him by the issuing banks until the rights were rescinded by those institutions. In other words, the contracts which the appellant had induced the issuing institutions to make were not void but voidable, and so remained in force until duly avoided.

[The Lord Chief Justice referred to the trial judge's directions to the jury and continued] ... In our judgment it is plain that the Crown's case rested on the making of a dishonest representation by the appellant to the various sales outlets. Such a representation could be proved in several ways: by documentary evidence showing the making of the false representation; by evidence from the outlet to which the representation was made; by an admission or evidence by the appellant himself that such representation was made; or by necessary or irresistible inference or perhaps as a matter of law. In this case, however, there was no document; there was no evidence from anyone at any of the outlets; and there was no admission by the appellant – no evidence from him that he made the representation charged. So the case must in our judgment rest on either necessary or irresistible inference or implication of law. It is not enough that an inference was possibly open to the jury because the representation is the crux of the offence and the jury could not convict unless the offence were proved to the criminal standard.

In our judgment the Crown, in seeking to uphold this conviction, face an insuperable problem. The drawing of an inference from the facts proved was a matter for the jury, and the jury were never directed to consider whether this ingredient of the offence was met and whether the inference should be drawn or not. We have referred to all the relevant parts of the summing-up, which are almost exclusively concentrated on the alleged representations to the banks. There is in our judgment no direction on the misrepresentations to the outlets or as to what the content of any such misrepresentation may have been. Mr O'Byrne, who represents the Crown on this appeal, while not conceding that the conviction is vitiated by the judge's failure to direct the jury on this point, is nonetheless constrained to acknowledge that there is no clear direction to the jury on this essential ingredient.

We have the gravest possible doubt whether the jury could properly, even if fully directed, have regarded the making of the representation charged as a necessary inference from the facts before them. The use of a card to obtain goods and services is of course an everyday act. Broadly speaking, suppliers are concerned to ensure that they will receive payment from the issuers of the card. For that reason it is normal to require a signature from the customer, to compare the signature on the card with the signature on the voucher, and to make sure that the card is not on a stop list. There is, however, in our judgment room for doubt whether a supplier is interested in how a holder comes to be the holder of the card, provided (and this we emphasise) the transaction is one which will be honoured by the issuer of the card. In this connection the observations of Lord Diplock in *R v Charles* [1977] AC 177, 182 are very relevant.

On all these counts there was evidence that the issuer, had it known at the time of issue what it knew later, would not have issued the card. But there was no evidence from any of the issuing institutions that any of the transactions had not been, or would not be, honoured, nor that in the circumstances they regarded the appellant as acting outside the authority which they had respectively conferred on him. It is indeed in our judgment doubtful whether the appellant by his conduct could be said to have represented anything more than that he had authority to bind the bank and that the transaction would be honoured. There is room for argument (to say no more) as to whether such a representation, if made, would have been false.

We refer, as the judge did, to *R v Lambie* ... and draw attention to the facts on which that case was based.

... In that case ... the customer did not have the actual authority of the bank to warrant that the bank would honour the voucher upon presentation because she was in excess of her limit, and her authority to use the card had been revoked by the bank's request for its return and her agreement to return it. Here, so far as the evidence went, the appellant did have the actual authority of the issuing institutions to warrant that they would honour the vouchers upon presentation because the cards had been issued to the appellant and even if the banks would have been entitled to revoke his authority to use the cards, they had not done so.

The appellant relies on the general principle that a contract (here the granting by the issuing company to the appellant of a right to use the card) is voidable until rescinded. In Lambie that contract had been rescinded. Here Mr McCullough for the appellant argues that it had not. Thus, he says, the appellant was entitled to exercise the right conferred on him by the issuers even if those rights had been obtained by dishonestly misleading statements until the issuers terminated the appellant's rights as, on the hypothesis of dishonest misleading, they were undoubtedly entitled to do. But Mr McCullough says that the issuers had not done so, and accordingly the appellant remained a person authorised to bind the bank or (if the language of the indictment is adopted) he remained for purposes of the sales outlet a legitimate holder of the card. There was no evidence that the issuers did not regard the appellant as having authority to bind them. Nor was there evidence that these transactions would not be honoured by the issuers.

On behalf of the Crown Mr O'Byrne did not take fundamental issue with the principles of law on which Mr McCullough relied. He cited no authority which threw doubt on those contentions. He accepted that, in the sense contended for, the appellant was a lawful holder of the cards. But he submitted that that was a rule of the civil law, not of the criminal law, and that this was a case concerned with allegations of dishonesty where different considerations applied. It is of course true that this was a prosecution concerned with dishonesty, but the dishonest misrepresentation alleged against the appellant concerned his civil law rights, and the issue whether the representation was correct or incorrect could not in our judgment be avoided.

We are on this question reluctant to express a concluded view since we have no knowledge of the contract between the issuers and appellant, which could be relevant, and other questions could arise which might have a bearing on the question. We are mindful that the correct resolution of this issue could have potentially far-reaching implications and we are reluctant to express concluded views in an appeal which must in our judgment, because of what we regard as a fatal omission in the summing-up, be allowed. Reluctantly, since it seems clear on all the facts that the appellant certainly was acting in a dishonest manner, we feel compelled to allow this appeal.

Dishonesty

See generally *R v Ghosh* [1982] QB 1053, extracted in Chapter 18. Note that s 2(1)(a)–(c) of the Theft Act 1968 has no application to deception offences.

R v Lightfoot (1993) 97 Cr App R 24 (CA)

McCullough J: ... [The defendant had tried to use a Barclaycard in the name of J Plummer to purchase goods from Woolworths.] When interviewed [by the police] he declined to say how he had come by the card. He admitted, however, that when he acquired it there was no signature on it. He admitted that he had signed it in the name of J Plummer and had used it frequently in that name to obtain goods. He had used the card on some 25 occasions to obtain goods to the value of about £3,000. The card had been sent by Barclaycard through the post on 5 July 1990, to Mr J Plummer, who was a fellow employee of the appellant's. They were fire officers working from the same fire station. The bank's intention had been that Mr J Plummer should sign the card and use it himself in accordance with Barclaycard's conditions ...

Mr Plummer's evidence was that he had never seen the card. His evidence raised the inference that it had been misappropriated before the envelope, in which it was contained, reached him, or just possibly after the envelope reached him, but before he had opened it. He had never, he said, authorised the appellant to use the card or to sign his name, and he knew nothing of the card or its use by the appellant until after the appellant's arrest.

The appellant's own evidence at trial was that, against his better judgment, Plummer had persuaded him to take the card and use it in Plummer's name. Despite his initial reluctance, he decided to do this because he was in debt and his credit rating would have prevented him from having a card of his own. Everything, he said, had been done with Plummer's authority. Indeed, he claimed that in one instance he had used the card to buy a camera for Plummer and had delivered it to him at the fire station. All this Plummer denied.

The appellant's evidence about the camera was supported by two other officers, who said that they had seen Plummer take the camera away from the fire station.

Plummer's credibility was obviously of crucial importance ...

The proof of dishonesty in a case such as this requires that the jury be sure of two things: first, that the defendant acted dishonestly as objectively judged against the ordinary standards of reasonable and honest people, and, second, that the defendant himself realised that what he was doing was by those standards dishonest: see *R v Ghosh* [1982] QB 1053, 1064D–G. The direction which the learned judge gave did not precisely follow those words but it was to the same effect. As we have said, no complaint is made about it.

There is a clear distinction between the defendant's knowledge of the law and his appreciation that he is doing something which, by ordinary standards of reasonable and honest people, is regarded as dishonest. His knowledge of the law, whether the criminal law or the law of contract, is irrelevant. Some dishonest behaviour falls foul of the criminal law; much does not. The fact that a man does not know what is criminal and what is not, or that he does not understand the relevant principles of the civil law, if any, cannot save him from conviction if what he does, coupled with the state of his mind, satisfies all the elements of the crime of which he is accused ...

Intention to permanently deprive

Section 6 of the Theft Act 1968 applies equally to s 1 theft and s 15 deception – see Chapter 18.

OBTAINING A MONEY TRANSFER BY DECEPTION

In *R v Preddy* [1996] 3 All ER 481 the House of Lords held that although the appellants had obtained mortgages by giving false information, the transfer of money between bank accounts was not illegal because no 'property' had passed from the payer to the payee. This decision was reversed by s 1 of the Theft (Amendment) Act 1996, which inserted a s 15A into the Theft Act 1968. This section creates a new offence of obtaining a money transfer by deception.

Section 15A of the Theft Act 1968

(1) A person is guilty of an offence if by any deception he dishonestly obtains a money transfer for himself or another.

(2) A money transfer occurs when:

  (a) a debit is made to one account;

  (b) a credit is made to another; and

  (c) the credit results from the debit or the debit results from the credit.

(3) References to a credit and to a debit are to a credit of an amount of money and to a debit of an amount of money.

(4) It is immaterial (in particular):

    (a) whether the amount credited is the same as the amount debited;

    (b) whether the money transfer is effected on presentment of a cheque or by another method;

    (c) whether any delay occurs in the process by which the money transfer is effected;

    (d) whether any intermediate credits or debits are made in the course of the money transfer;

    (e) whether either of the accounts is overdrawn before or after the money transfer is effected.

(5) A person guilty of an offence under this section shall be liable on conviction on indictment to imprisonment for a term not exceeding 10 years.

Section 15B of the Theft Act 1968

(1) The following provisions have effect for the interpretation of s 15A of this Act.

(2) 'Deception' has the same meaning as in s 15 of this Act.

(3) 'Account' means an account kept with:

    (a) a bank; or

    (b) a person carrying on business which falls within subsection (4) below.

(4) A business falls within this subsection if:

    (a) in the course of the business money received by way of deposit is lent to others; or

    (b) any other activity of the business is financed, wholly or to any material extent, out of the capital of or the interest on money received by way of deposit;

    and 'deposit' here has the same meaning as in s 35 of the Banking Act 1987 ...

(5) For the purposes of subsection (4) above:

    (a) all the activities which a person carries on by way of business shall be regarded as a single business carried on by him; and

    (b) 'money' includes money expressed in a currency other than sterling or in the European Currency Unit (as defined in Council Regulation No 3320/94/EC or any Community instrument replacing it).

Note that nothing in s 15A has effect in relation to anything done before the commencement of the Theft (Amendment) Act 1996 (18 December 1996).

OBTAINING A PECUNIARY ADVANTAGE BY DECEPTION

Section 16 of the Theft Act 1968

(1) A person who by any deception dishonestly obtains for himself or another any pecuniary advantage shall on conviction on indictment be liable to imprisonment for a term not exceeding five years.

(2) The cases in which a pecuniary advantage within the meaning of this section is to be regarded as obtained for a person are cases where:

(a) [repealed by s 5(5) of the Theft Act 1978];

(b) he is allowed to borrow by way of overdraft, or to take out any policy of insurance or annuity contract, or obtains an improvement of the terms which he is allowed to do so; or

(c) he is given the opportunity to earn remuneration or greater remuneration in an office or employment, or to win money by betting.

(3) For purposes of this section 'deception' has the same meaning as in s 15 of this Act.

Section 16 was introduced to enable deception charges to be brought in situations where, otherwise, the defendant would be able to argue that the obtaining of the property was too remote from the deception, as illustrated in *R v Clucas* (extracted below). 'Obtaining' and 'by deception' have the same meaning under s 16 as that applied under s 15 (see above).

R v Clucas [1949] 2 KB 226 (CA)

Facts: The appellant and another man induced bookmakers to bet with them by representing that they were commission agents acting on behalf of a large number of workmen who were putting small bets on various races, whereas in fact they were making bets in considerable sums of money for themselves alone.

Lord Goddard CJ: ... In the opinion of the court it is impossible to say that there was an obtaining of the money by the false pretences which were alleged, because the money was obtained not by reason of the fact that the people falsely pretended that they were somebody else or acting in some capacity which they were not; it was obtained because they backed a winning horse and the bookmaker paid because the horse had won. No doubt the bookmaker might never have opened an account with these men if he had known the true facts, but we must distinguish in this case between one contributing cause and the effective cause which led the bookmaker to pay the money.

The effective cause which led the bookmaker to pay the money was the fact that these men had backed a winning horse ... Although these two men induced the bookmaker to bet with them by means of a false pretence, what the court cannot see is that that false pretence was the false pretence which led to the payment of the money. What led to the payment of the money was the fact that these men backed a winning horse by inducing the bookmaker to bet with them ...

Note: The deception practised in this case would now amount to an offence under s 16(2)(c) of the Theft Act 1968, as detailed above.

Obtaining a pecuniary advantage

DPP v Turner [1974] AC 357 (HL)

Lord Reid: ... The first part [of s 16(2) of the Theft Act 1968] is drafted in an unusual way. Does it mean that in the cases set out in heads ... (b) and (c) a pecuniary advantage is to be deemed to have been obtained, so that it is irrelevant to consider whether in fact any such advantage was obtained, and equally irrelevant to prove that nothing in the nature of pecuniary advantage was in fact

obta_ed by the accused? I think that that must be its meaning though I am at a
los_o understand why that was not clearly stated. 'Is to be regarded as obtained'
_t, I think, mean 'is to be deemed to have been obtained' even if in fact there
.s none.

_: The rest of Lord Reid's speech deals with the interpretation of s 16(2)(a) of
_ Theft Act 1968, which was repealed, and replaced by ss 1 and 2 of the Theft
.ct 1978.

Pecuniary advantage: overdraft

R v Waites [1982] Crim LR 369 (CA)

Facts: The appellant opened an account with a bank and was issued with a
personalised cheque book and, later, with a cheque card whereby the bank
guaranteed to meet a cheque up to £50. She made no arrangements to overdraw
her account and used the cheques and card to make many purchases, creating
an overdraft of more than £850. She was charged on several counts with
obtaining a pecuniary advantage by deception, contrary to s 16(1) of the Theft
Act 1968. It was argued in her defence that there was no case to answer because
it could not be said that she had been 'allowed' to borrow by way of overdraft
within the meaning of s 16(2)(b), since the bank would have been trying to stop
her from doing so.

Held, dismissing the appeal against conviction: The definitions in s 16(2) are
exclusive and, if the actions do not fall within them, there is no obtaining of a
pecuniary advantage. There is no proper doubt as to the meaning of the verb
'allow' in the circumstances of s 16(2)(b). Permission to use the card carried with
it the power in the cardholder, albeit in breach of contract with the bank, to use
the card beyond the limits imposed knowing that the bank would be obliged to
meet the debt created with the shopkeeper. That was, within the ordinary
meaning of the words, to allow borrowing by way of overdraft.

R v Bevan (1987) 84 Cr App R 143 (CA)

Staughton J: ... [I]s a person 'allowed to borrow by way of overdraft', in terms of
s 16 of the Theft Act 1968, when he uses a cheque card in excess of the limits
permitted by the bank that issued it?

... The particulars [alleged in the indictment] were ... that the appellant had
'dishonestly obtained for himself a pecuniary advantage namely a borrowing by
way of overdraft from Lloyds Bank plc by deception namely by falsely
representing that he was then entitled and authorised to use a cheque card when
issuing cheque number ... drawn on Lloyds Bank plc' ...

... In April 1982 the appellant opened an account with Lloyds Bank plc at one of
their branches in London. He was provided with cheque books and a cheque card.
[He did not obtain permission] to overdraw on his account; and it was specifically
stated that the cheque card did not entitle him to overdraw his account if no
overdraft arrangements had been made, or to overdraw in excess of any overdraft
limit that might be agreed.

Nevertheless the appellant did [on a number of occasions draw £50 in cash from another bank when his account at Lloyds Bank was overdrawn] ...

... [I]t is not suggested that any deception operated on Lloyds Bank. When called upon to reimburse the paying bank they no doubt appreciated that the appellant's account was overdrawn. They were no doubt displeased. But they were obliged to honour their obligation to the paying bank, founded upon the use of the cheque card which they had issued.

... The question [is] ... whether the appellant had been allowed to borrow by way of overdraft when he had not negotiated and agreed an overdraft limit, but merely used his card in such a way that his bank felt itself obliged to reimburse the paying bank. [In *R v Waites* [1982] Crim LR 369] this court held that he had been allowed to borrow by way of overdraft.

In those circumstances we consider that we are bound by the authority of *Waites* ... When the appellant's bank received a request by the paying bank for reimbursement in respect of a cheque drawn by the appellant, it of course readily complied. The bank's motive was no doubt the protection of its own reputation, as well as its contractual obligation owed directly to the paying bank ... But reimbursement by the appellant's bank was nevertheless an act of will; when it took place the appellant was allowed by the bank to borrow money on overdraft; and the overdraft was consensual, since the appellant had impliedly requested it and the bank had, albeit reluctantly, agreed ...

R v Watkins [1976] 1 All ER 578

HHJ Paul Clarke (sitting at Warwick Crown Court): ... I interpret the subsection in question as sufficiently proved if the deception caused only the granting of facilities for drawing on an overdraft ... I think that s 16(2)(b) is necessary because when facilities for an overdraft are granted a customer gets a very real advantage in thereafter being able to go to the counter and draw on his overdraft. The opportunities for a deception arise when he goes to the manager and gets the facility, not when he draws on that facility.

Pecuniary advantage: opportunity to earn remuneration

R v Callender [1992] 3 WLR 501 (CA)

Wright J: ... The facts of the matter are relatively simple. The applicant described himself as a self-employed accountant. In or about June 1987 Mr Burt met the appellant, whom he said he had heard of from doing accountancy work for others, and he understood from the appellant, having been shown a curriculum vitae and other documents, that he was an associate member of the Chartered Institute of Management Accountants, and a graduate or member of the Institute of Marketing. Mr Burt said in evidence that he had relied upon these representations and that he would not have 'employed' him – the word he used in evidence – had he known that he was not qualified. In truth and in fact, the appellant had not obtained the qualifications referred to and his curriculum vitae was false in those respects ...

We have come to the clear conclusion that Parliament in adopting the phrase 'office or employment' intended s 16(1) of the 1968 Act to have a wider impact than one confined to the narrow limits of a contract of service ... We take the view that the interpretation of the words in question involves the consideration of their meaning as a matter of ordinary language. That meaning, in our judgment, is not to be arrived at by reference to the more limited and technical interpretation given to those words in the context of the law of master and servant ... or in the context of pensions and national insurance law ... or in the context of income tax.

... The *Shorter Oxford English Dictionary* defines ... 'employment' ... as: 'That on which [one] is employed; business; occupation; a commission'. It seems to us that it is a perfectly proper use of ordinary language and as such to be readily understood by ordinary literate men and women to say of a person in this appellant's position that his services as an accountant were 'employed' by his customers, and that this state of affairs is properly to be described by the word 'employment'. As such the facts in this case fall within the ambit of the section ...

Operation of the deception under s 16

R v Kovacs [1974] 1 WLR 370 (CA)

Facts: The prosecution case was that by the end of November 1972 the appellant's account at the Tring branch of the National Westminster Bank was overdrawn in the sum of £572. By letter dated 30 November 1972, the bank told her the extent of her indebtedness and that no more cheques drawn by her would be met. Shortly afterwards a bank official named Hedges called on her and asked her for her cheque book and the cheque card which had been issued to her. She said they were not in her possession. On 1 February 1973, she used a cheque drawn on the Tring branch of her bank and her cheque card to obtain at Berkhamsted Station a railway ticket costing £2.89. On 5 February 1973, she used the same means to obtain a Pekingese dog costing £42 from a pet shop.

Lawton LJ: ... When the bank issued the cheque card to the appellant, they put her into possession of a document which was an undertaking by them to any person to whom she showed it that they would honour her cheque subject to certain conditions. No question arises in this case as to whether these conditions have been complied with. This meant that, if she was overdrawn on her account when she used her cheque card, she would be allowed by the bank to overdraw further to the extent of the cheque covered by it. She was obtaining a pecuniary advantage as defined by s 16(2)(b) of the Theft Act 1968.

The next question is – how did she obtain pecuniary advantage? On the facts the answer is clear, namely by inducing the railway booking clerk and the pet shop owner to believe that she was entitled to use the cheque card when she was not. As a result of this deception they both accepted payment by cheques which the bank were bound to honour pursuant to their undertaking as set out on the face of the cheque card.

In our judgment, the loss suffered by the bank was the result of the appellant's deception of the railway booking clerk and the pet shop owner. Section 16(1) does not provide either expressly or by implication that the person deceived must suffer any loss arising from the deception. What does have to be proved is that the accused by deception obtained for himself or another a pecuniary advantage.

What there must be is a causal connection between the deception used and the pecuniary advantage obtained. There was such a connection in this case ...

FALSE ACCOUNTING

Section 17 of the Theft Act 1968

(1) Where a person dishonestly, with a view to gain for himself or another or with intent to cause loss to another:

(a) destroys, defaces, conceals or falsifies any account or any record or document made or required for any accounting purpose; or

(b) in furnishing information for any purpose produces or makes use of any account, or any such record or document as aforesaid, which to his knowledge is or may be misleading, false or deceptive in a material particular;

he shall, on conviction on indictment, be liable to imprisonment for a term not exceeding seven years.

(2) For purposes of this section a person who makes or concurs in making in an account or other document an entry which is or may be misleading, false or deceptive in a material particular or who omits or concurs in omitting a material particular from an account or other document, is to be treated as falsifying the account or document.

OBTAINING SERVICES BY DECEPTION

Section 1 of the Theft Act 1978

(1) A person who by any deception dishonestly obtains services from another shall be guilty of an offence.

(2) It is an obtaining of services where the other is induced to confer a benefit by doing some act, or causing or permitting some act to be done, on the understanding that the benefit has been or will be paid for.

(3) Without prejudice to the generality of subsection (2) above, it is an obtaining of services where the other is induced to make a loan, or to cause or permit a loan to be made, on the understanding that any payment (whether by way of interest or otherwise) will be or has been made in respect of the loan.

Section 5 of the Theft Act 1968

(1) For the purpose of ss 1 and 2 above 'deception' has the same meaning as in s 15 of the Theft Act 1968, that is to say, it means any deception (whether deliberate or reckless) by words or conduct as to fact or as to law, including a deception as to the present intentions of the person using the deception or any other person ...

Deception; dishonesty; obtains

These words have all been considered under s 15 of the Theft Act 1968 (see above).

The scope of the offence under s 1

The deception must occur *before* the services are obtained, otherwise the services cannot be said to be obtained 'by' (that is, as a result of) deception.

Section 1 of the Theft Act 1978 covers situations such as the following:

(a) the defendant hands over a worthless cheque to the provider of the service, claiming thereby to be paying in advance);

(b) the defendant, by means of some deception, persuades the provider of the service to agree to a lesser payment than would otherwise have been the case;

(c) the defendant, by means of some deception, persuades the provider of the service to agree to payment at a later time than would otherwise be the case.

An example of (b) would be as follows: a hairdresser offers a 10% discount to students at the local college. I falsely claim to be such a student (before my hair is cut) and I duly get a 10% discount to which I am not entitled.

It must be stressed that s 1(2) requires that there be an 'understanding that the [service] has been or will be paid for'. It follows that s 1 does not cover the situation where the defendant, by means of some deception, persuades the provider of the service to forgo payment altogether. That situation would be covered by s 2(1)(c) of the Theft Act 1978 (see below).

On the overlap between s 1 of the Theft Act 1978 and other offences involving deception, see *R v Widdowson* (1986) 82 Cr App R 314.

Section 1(3) of the Theft Act 1968 was added by the Theft (Amendment) Act 1996. The effect is to reverse the decision in *R v Halai* [1983] Crim LR 624, where it had been held (probably *per incuriam*) that the making of a loan did not come within the definition of a 'service'.

R v Widdowson (1986) 82 Cr App R 314 (CA)

Saville J: ... At the trial the case for the prosecution was that on 14 July 1984, the appellant had gone to a garage with a view to buying a Ford Escort van on hire-purchase. He was said to have told the salesman (a Mr Wilson) that he had looked at the Escort van for sale there, was happy with it and that it would all be subject to finance being arranged. Mr Wilson said that the appellant was satisfied that his own van would cover the initial deposit and that if the finance had been cleared by the finance company the vehicle would have been the appellant's. Mr Wilson gave evidence that the appellant then completed a hire-purchase form putting the name Steven Pitman and an address, 15 Edinburgh Way, Thetford, as the name and address of the hirer. That address was in fact where a Mr Pitman lived next door to the appellant. Mr Wilson said that had he known that this name and address was not that of the appellant, he would not have taken the matter any further and would not have put it forward to the finance company as he did. He agreed that he did not intend that the form should constitute the actual hire-purchase deal, and said it was used so that enquiries could be made whether the person named as hirer was creditworthy. He further agreed that in fact a proposal form rather than a hire-purchase form should have been used for this purpose, but explained that the garage had run out of the latter forms at the time in question. It should also be mentioned that the appellant had in fact signed the form at the end in his own name, something which Mr Wilson only discovered later, apparently from the finance company itself. According to evidence from the police, the appellant stated on being interviewed that he had put his own telephone number on the form and explained that he had put the name Steven Pitman on the form because he could not get credit if it was known who he really was. His explanation for signing the form in his own name was simply that he had not been thinking.

According to the defence, the appellant, being himself unable to obtain credit, completed the form solely in order to enquire into the creditworthiness of Pitman. He said he had earlier agreed with Pitman that on being given clearance by the finance company Pitman should thereby obtain the vehicle on his behalf pending the appellant's receipt of funds to pay the outstanding balance of the purchase price. This explanation had not apparently been given to the police on the occasion of his interview ...

We deal first with the point not canvassed before the learned judge. It seems to us, on the authority of *R v Garlick* (1958) 42 Cr App R 141 and *R v Miller (Simon)* [1977] 3 All ER 986, that a hire-purchase agreement in ordinary form (and there was no suggestion that any different form might have been used in this case) cannot properly be described as credit facilities, for the simple reason that on making such a hire-purchase agreement the finance company does not give any credit to the hirer. All it does is to hire out the goods to the hirer, who usually has options either to purchase on paying all the instalments, or to terminate the agreement at any time. Thus the words in the particulars to the indictment, 'credit facilities to assist in the purchase' were not supported by any evidence led at the hearing; and since no application to amend the indictment was made, it is conceded that if this is the correct analysis (as we so hold) then the indictment was bad and the conviction on it cannot stand.

We should add that we reject the suggestion that the obtaining of a hire-purchase agreement cannot amount to the obtaining of services. In *R v Halai* [1983] Crim LR 624 this court held that a mortgage advance cannot be described as a service. It is suggested that a hire-purchase agreement is indistinguishable. We disagree. As we have just said, a hire-purchase agreement (at least in the ordinary form) is the hiring of goods with various options given to the hirer, who in return agrees to pay the instalments, maintain the vehicle and so on. In our view the hire-purchasing of a vehicle on some such terms can be regarded as the conferring of some benefit by doing some act, or causing or permitting an act to be done, on the understanding that the benefit has been or will be paid for, this being the definition of services in s 1(2) of the Theft Act 1978. The finance company confers a benefit by delivering possession of the vehicle to the hirer (or by causing or permitting the garage to do so) on the understanding that the hirer has paid or will pay a deposit and subsequent instalments.

There remains the question of attempt. In our judgment there was no evidence of an attempt to commit the crime alleged within the meaning of s 1(1) of the Criminal Attempts Act 1981. It seems to us that at most all the appellant had actually done was to attempt to ascertain whether or not Steven Pitman was creditworthy, in the sense of being acceptable to the finance company as a prospective hire-purchaser. It was not suggested that a favourable reply from the finance company could have constituted the obtaining of services within the meaning of the Theft Act 1978, if only because there was no question of payment being made for such a reply. Thus the question is whether this appellant's act in giving the false particulars on the form can reasonably be said to have been more than merely preparatory to the obtaining of hire-purchase facilities. In our view this cannot be said. Assuming that the finance company had responded favourably to the proposal, it still remained for the appellant to seek a hire-purchase deal from them. To our minds it is that step which would constitute an attempt to obtain the services relied upon in this case. If one asks whether this appellant had carried out every step which it was necessary for him to perform to achieve the consequences alleged to have been attempted, the answer must be that he did not.

Equally, it seems to us, this appellant's acts cannot be described as immediately rather than merely remotely connected with the specific offence alleged to have been attempted. Thus whichever of the tests described in *R v Ilyas* (1984) 78 Cr App R 17 is applied, what the appellant did cannot reasonably be described as more than merely preparatory.

... [I]t would appear that the learned judge was influenced by the suggested inevitability of the transaction going ahead, ie that the appellant's intentions would have remained the same. That, with great respect, ignores the fact that dishonest intentions alone do not constitute criminal attempts and that in addition it is necessary to establish, to use the words of Lord Diplock, that the offender has crossed the Rubicon and burned his boats. He had not done so (as the learned judge himself held) in the sense of attempting to obtain the vehicle. In our judgment, he equally had not done so in attempting to obtain the hire-purchase of the vehicle.

EVASION OF LIABILITY BY DECEPTION

Section 2 of the Theft Act 1978

(1) Subject to subsection (2) below, where a person by any deception:

   (a) dishonestly secures the remission of the whole or part of any existing liability to make a payment, whether his own liability or another's; or

   (b) with intent to make permanent default in whole or in part on any existing liability to make a payment, or with intent to let another do so, dishonestly induces the creditor or any person claiming payment on behalf of the creditor to wait for payment (whether or not the due date for payment is deferred) or to forgo payment; or

   (c) dishonestly obtains any exemption from or abatement of liability to make a payment;

   he shall be guilty of an offence.

(2) For purposes of this section 'liability' means legally enforceable liability; and subsection (1) shall not apply in relation to a liability that has not been accepted or established to pay compensation for a wrongful act or omission.

(3) For purposes of subsection (1)(b) a person induced to take in payment a cheque or other security for money by way of conditional satisfaction of a pre-existing liability is to be treated not as being paid but as being induced to wait for payment.

(4) For purposes of subsection (1)(c) 'obtains' includes obtaining for another or enabling another to obtain.

Note: see also s 5 of the Theft Act 1978, extracted above.

Section 2 of the Theft Act 1978 creates three forms of 'evasion of liability'. In each case there must be a deception (as defined for the purposes of s 15 of the Theft Act 1968, as to which see above). In all three cases the liability which is evaded must be legally enforceable: see s 2(2) of the Theft Act 1978 and *R v Modupe* [1991] Crim LR 530. Furthermore, offences can only committed under s 2(1)(a) or (b) in respect of an 'existing liability', but an offence under s 2(1)(c) can be committed before any liability to pay has come into existence.

Section 2(1)(a): securing the remission of a liability

The subsection makes it clear that it does not matter whether or not the liability is that of the person practising the deception. The word 'remission' means 'release' from the liability to make payment. An example of a situation which falls within s 2(1)(a) is as follows: D borrows a sum of money from P. Later, D tells the P a false story which induces P to write off some or all of the debt. If alternatively P is merely induced to wait for payment (ie gives D more time rather than writing off the debt), D may have committed an offence under s 2(1)(b).

R v Jackson [1983] Crim LR 617 (CA)

Facts: A stolen credit card was presented by occupants of the appellant's car at petrol stations and accepted in satisfaction of payment for petrol and other goods. The appellant was charged, *inter alia*, with evading liability by deception by dishonestly securing the remission of an existing liability, contrary to s 2(1)(a) of the Theft Act 1978.

Held, dismissing the appeal, that although in *R v Holt* [1981] 1 WLR 1000 it was held that the element under s 2(1)(b) of an intent to make permanent default on the whole or part of an existing liability was unique to subparagraph (b), that judgment was not authority for the proposition that the elements in subparagraphs (a), (b) and (c) of s 2(1) were mutually exclusive. The transaction of tendering a stolen credit card and having it accepted by a trader who forthwith would look to the authority issuing the card for payment and not to the person tendering the card, meant that that person had dishonestly secured the remission of an existing liability. It was not necessary to consider whether a charge in respect of that transaction could be brought under s 2(1)(b). In the circumstances the matter was not wrongly charged under s 2(1)(a).

Section 2(1)(b): inducing a creditor to wait for or forgo payment

This covers the situation where D borrows a sum of money from P and later D (who, by this time, does not intend to repay the money), by means of some deception, persuades P to wait longer for payment than had originally been agreed or even to forgo payment altogether. Note that s 2(3) says that, for the purpose only of s 2(1)(b), inducing a creditor to accept a cheque (which is a way of postponing payment) is to be regarded as inducing the creditor to wait for payment.

This is the only one of the three offences where an intention to make permanent default has to be proved. The fact that s 2(1)(b) covers situations where the creditor is induced to forgo payment means that there is an overlap with s 2(1)(a), securing the remission of an existing liability. This overlap was considered in *R v Jackson* (above) and *R v Holt* (below).

R v Holt and Another [1981] 1 WLR 1000 (CA)

Lawson J: ... The charge on which the appellants were convicted was as follows. The statement of the offence was attempted evasion of liability by deception, contrary to common law. The particulars of the offence were that the defendants, on 9 December 1979, by deception with intent to make permanent default on an existing liability, did attempt to induce Philip Parkinson, servant of Pizzaland Restaurants Ltd, to forgo payment of £3.65 by falsely representing that payment had been made by them to another servant of the said Pizzaland Restaurants Ltd.

From the use of the expressions 'with intent to make permanent default' and 'to induce [the creditor's agent] to forgo payment', it is clear that the attempt charged was one to commit the offence defined by s 2(1)(b) of the 1978 Act. [*Note*: This case precedes the coming into force of the Criminal Attempts Act 1981 and so the attempt is charged as an offence under the common law.]

The facts of the case were that in the evening of 9 December 1979, the defendants consumed meals costing £3.65 in the Pizzaland Restaurant in Southport. There was a police officer off duty also having a meal in the restaurant and he overheard the defendant planning to evade payment for their meals by the device of pretending that a waitress had removed a £5 note which they had placed on the table. When presented with their bill, the defendants advanced this deception and declined payment. The police officer concerned prevented them from leaving the restaurant and they were shortly afterwards arrested and charged ...

The elements of the offence defined by s 2(1)(b) of the Act of 1978 relevant to the present case are clearly these: first, the defendant must be proved to have the intent to make permanent default on the whole or part of an existing liability. This element is unique to s 2(1)(b); it has no application to the offences defined in s 2(1)(a) or (c). Second, given such intent, he must use deception. Third, his deception must be practised dishonestly to induce the creditor to forgo payment.

It must always be remembered that in the present case, whatever offence was being attempted, the attempt failed. The creditor was not induced by the dishonest deception and did not forgo payment. It is clear on the evidence that the defendants' conduct constituted an attempt to evade liability by deception, and the jury, who were properly directed, clearly concluded that the defendants' conduct was motivated by the intent to make permanent default on their supper bill. Thus, all the elements needed to enable an attempt to commit the offence defined in s 2(1)(b) were found to be present, so that the defendants were rightly convicted as charged.

Reverting to the construction of s 2(1) of the Act of 1978, as to which the commentators are not at one, we are not sure whether the choice of expressions describing the consequences of deception employed in each of its paragraphs, namely in paragraph (a) 'secures the remission of ... any existing liability', in paragraph (b) 'induces the creditor ... to forgo payment' and in paragraph (c) 'obtains any exemption from ... liability' are simply different ways of describing the same end result or represent conceptual differences.

Whilst it is plain that there are substantial differences in the elements of the three offences defined in s 2(1), they show these common features: first, the use of deception to a creditor in relation to a liability; second, dishonesty in the use of deception; and third, the use of deception to gain some advantage in time or money. Thus the differences between the offences relate principally to the different situations in which the debtor-creditor relationship has arisen ...

R v Attewell-Hughes [1991] 4 All ER 810 (CA)

Facts: The appellant was employed as the manager of a hotel by the owner, who lived abroad. The owner gave the appellant authority to act on his behalf and to operate his bank account in relation to the running of the hotel. The appellant opened an account in the name of the hotel at a bank, which made it clear that it would not grant an overdraft facility on the account. However, the appellant wrote a number of cheques on that account for goods and services supplied to the hotel, and to pay VAT due from the hotel to HM Customs and Excise, when the funds available in the account were not sufficient to cover the cheques.

Bingham LJ: ... The case against the appellant was that between about April and November 1986 he was running the Dean House Hotel on the Isle of Wight and that, while doing so, in a number of ways he was systematically defrauding those who were supplying, or had previously supplied, the hotel with various goods. It was alleged that the charges preferred against the appellant were a selection of those which could have been brought.

The essence of the counts of obtaining property by deception was that he persuaded suppliers to provide goods or services by telling lies, causing the suppliers to believe that they would be paid when he knew that they would not. The counts of evading liability by deception depended on the appellant having fobbed off suppliers of goods or services, making them wait for payment by the deception that cheques he was giving them were good and valid orders for payment and that he had authority to draw on the bank account for those amounts ...

His Lordship then quoted one of the counts in the indictment, which charged the appellant with an offence under s 2(1)(b) of the Theft Act 1978, namely that:

... with intent to make permanent default in whole or in part of an existing liability to pay £6,347 to Geoffrey Arnold Malone on behalf of HM Customs and Excise [he] dishonestly induced the said Geoffrey Arnold Malone on behalf of HM Customs and Excise to wait for payment of the said sum by deception, namely by a false implied representation that cheque number 224358 for £6,347 drawn of the account of Dean House Hotel was a good and valid order for the payment of £6,347 and that he had authority to draw upon the account with Midland Bank Limited for that amount.

We pause to reiterate that, so far as this liability is concerned, it is plain, and indeed not in dispute, that the liability was not that of the appellant but was that of Mr Nicholson [the owner of the hotel] ...

... It seems to us that the opening words 'with intent to make permanent default' and the absence of any reference to procuring a default by another clearly suggest a default by the party whose liability it is. We notice the absence of any qualification, 'whether his own or another's', such as exists in s 2(1)(a) and we find the express reference ... 'or with intent to let another do so', which in our judgment clearly indicates an intention on the part of the draftsman to differentiate between these two modes of committing the offence.

Section 2(1)(c): exemption from or abatement of a liability

An example of a situation where this provision applies would be where D persuades the seller of goods that D is entitled to a discount to which he is not, in fact, entitled. For example, D falsely claims to be a student in order to get a discount at a shop which gives a discount on its goods to students.

R v Firth (1990) 91 Cr App R 217 (CA)

Lord Chief Justice: ... The prosecution allegation in these various counts was that the appellant [who was a consultant gynaecologist/obstetrician], by failing dishonestly to inform the hospital of the private patient status of [two of his patients], had caused either them or himself not to be billed for services which should have been charged against them. [The grounds of appeal were stated as being: 'That the learned recorder erred in not acceding to the submission made by the defence at the close of the Crown's case that counts 4, 5, 6 and 7 were wrongly laid in law in that the allegations to be proved required proof of acts of commission whereas the evidence disclosed only acts of omission.']

... It is not altogether clear what [ground 1 of the ground of appeal] means. We take it to mean that the counts laid under section 2(1)(c) of the Theft Act cannot be brought home against the defendant unless the prosecution prove that the dishonest obtaining was achieved by acts of commission, that is to say the deception must be by commission, and not by omission.

[Sections 2(1)(c) and 2(2) of the 1978 Act] ... would cover, for instance, if it were the case, this appellant obtaining an exemption on behalf of a patient whom he was treating.

If, as was alleged, it was incumbent upon [the appellant] ... to give the information to the hospital and he deliberately and dishonestly refrained from doing so, with the result that no charge was levied either upon the patients or upon himself, in our judgment the wording of the section and subsection which I have just read is satisfied. It matters not whether it was an act of commission or an act of omission. Providing those matters were substantiated the prosecution had made out their case. That means, in brief, that the recorder was right to reject any submission to the contrary.

But before us Mr Rogers [for the appellant] enlarged upon that ground of appeal and the second limb of the argument was this. He submitted to us that the words 'legally enforceable' in the section mean that in order to proceed under that subsection the prosecution has to establish an existing liability at the time when the alleged deception is made. I hope I do his submission justice: I think that is the proposition which he advanced. If, accordingly, goes on the submission, the defendant is asking for a service to be performed, the liability only arises when the service has been performed. Consequently, goes the submission, one must find the liability and then go on to prove that the deception was practised when the liability had arisen. In the present case, he submits, if the deception was practised before the liability to pay had come into existence, then no offence was committed.

It seems to us that that overlooks the wording not only of section 2(1)(c), but also the wording of the two previous paragraphs, because both in 2(1)(a) and 2(1)(b) the words 'existing liability' are to be found. Let me read paragraph (a): '... where a person by any deception – (a) dishonestly secures the remission of the whole or any part of any existing liability to make a payment, whether his own or another's.' There is similar wording in (b).

It is immediately to be remarked that in paragraph (c) the word 'existing' is omitted. It seems to us that that is indicative of what the draftsman of the Act really meant. The argument put forward by Mr Rogers might very well have something to command it if section 2(1)(c) had contained the word 'existing', but the word in that paragraph is conspicuous by its absence. The words as they stand are apt to cover an expected liability or future liability, even if the deception alleged is not in truth a continuing deception. The omission of the word 'existing' was, it seems clear to us, purposeful and not a matter of chance.

Consequently in our judgment the second limb to ground 1 of the notice of appeal fails and that part of the appeal cannot be successful.

Notes and queries

1   In *R v Jackson* (above) it was held that where someone is induced to accept a stolen credit card in payment for goods, the defendant's debt is remitted in that the supplier of the goods will look to the credit card company for payment, not to the defendant. Presumably, the same would apply where the supplier accepts a cheque supported by a cheque guarantee card: the supplier will look to the bank to honour the cheque in accordance with the terms of the cheque guarantee card.

CODIFICATION AND LAW REFORM PROPOSALS

In its Consultation Paper *Legislating the Criminal Code: Fraud and Deception* (LCCP 155), the Law Commission, having considered the case against the introduction of a general offence of fraud, considered the ways in which the existing deception offences could be extended:

Obtaining property

17   Our discussion in Part II of *Preddy* and financial markets indicated that there is at least a possibility of a real and immediate lacuna in the law. More generally, the criminality of fraud in such markets should not depend on accidental features of the contractual relations underpinning them. We therefore provisionally propose that for the purposes of the offence of obtaining

property by deception, it should be sufficient that the person to whom the property belongs should be deprived of it by deception, regardless of whether the defendant actually obtains anything.

The requirement of intention permanently to deprive

18 We consider the requirement in the offence of obtaining property by deception that there be an intention permanently to deprive the owner of his or her property. We are not persuaded by the CLRC's arguments in 1966 for retaining this feature of the old law, and consider that temporary deprivation generally involves some form of permanent loss to the owner of the property. Moreover, it has unfortunate practical effects – it leads to irrational distinctions, given that specific offences have been introduced to deal with situations in which temporary deprivation has been found to require criminalisation; it can act as an artificial obstacle to prosecution; and it can make it harder to convict those who do have an intention permanently to deprive, because it confuses fact-finders, especially where money is obtained with the intention of repaying an equivalent sum.

19 We consider two possible alternatives to the requirement. First, it could be replaced with a general requirement of an intention to cause significant practical detriment to the person to whom the property belongs. This has its origins in a proposal put forward in the context of definitions of dishonesty, and now forms part of the law of the Australian Capital Territory. Secondly, the requirement could be abolished generally, but replaced with specific exclusions for those examples of temporary deprivation which, it is considered, should not be criminal, such as where there is no intention to prevent the owner using his or her property, or where property, is retained after the period for which it was lent.

20 We invite views on whether either of these replacements should be adopted, or the current rule retained, or abolished outright. Our provisional preference is for the last.

Obtaining services

21 We provisionally consider it right that the offence of obtaining services by deception should be confined to services of an economic rather than a social nature, by its limitation to services provided on the understanding that they have been or will be paid for. However, we provisionally consider that the current limitation is too strict, in two ways. First, an economic service may be provided on the understanding that it will not be paid for, because the deception itself has resulted in the usual payment being waived. An example would be the person who obtained a bus ride on the basis of a deception that he or she had left a free bus pass at home. Secondly, some economic services are provided free, because the benefit the provider hopes to receive is more subtle than a straightforward payment by way of consideration for the service. An example is the opening of a building society account with a bad cheque, which does not constitute the offence if the society does not charge for opening an account. We accordingly provisionally propose amending the definition of 'services' to include (a) a benefit conferred with no understanding as to payment, provided that it would not have been provided without such an understanding but for the deception; and (h) any benefit conferred with a view to gain.

Causing a consequence by deception

22 We invite views as to whether there are any practical problems encountered with the requirement of the deception offences that the consequence brought about (the property or service obtained etc) must be caused by the deception.

Dishonesty

23 We turn to consider dishonesty, an element of all of the existing deception offences ... it constitutes a negative element in deception offences. Obtaining things by deception, on its own, is sufficiently wrongful for there to be a *prima facie* case for its criminalisation. To have done so, a person must have, by words or conduct, intentionally induced in another a false belief (or to have spoken or acted recklessly as to whether or not a false belief would be induced), and, by the inducing of that false belief, to have achieved his or her objective of obtaining the property or whatever. The element of dishonesty applies over and above this on the face of it properly criminal conduct, and thus serves to remove from liability those found to be not dishonest, rather than acting as the primary determinant of criminality. We consider three different and distinct functions that dishonesty as a negative element might serve in criminal offences.

Triviality

24 The first is where the defendant's conduct is morally blameworthy but too trivial to justify criminal liability. Our provisional view is that triviality of itself may justify a prosecutor declining to proceed, or a sentencer discharging a defendant, but it does not provide a good reason for excluding the conduct from liability.

No moral blame

25 The second is where the defendant's conduct is not morally blameworthy at all. We consider that it would be preferable to exclude from criminal liability the defendant to whom no moral obloquy attaches if that could be done without creating undue uncertainty and inconsistency and inviting the introduction of evidence of negligible probative value. But our provisional view is that *Ghosh* dishonesty, even as a negative element, has these drawbacks, and that they are too high a price to pay.

26 A negative dishonesty element can also act against the interests of justice by allowing the guilty to go free, or at least making it harder to convict them. It encourages trials where there would otherwise by guilty pleas and lengthens trials. It allows a defendant who cannot deny deceptive and, *prima facie*, wrongful conduct a chance to persuade a jury that he or she was 'not dishonest' in some general sort of way, and thus should be acquitted. There are particular problems with a dishonesty requirement in deception offences, in that in practice it is generally hard to disentangle dishonesty from the fact of deception, and dishonesty as a genuinely separate element can only rarely be in issue. More generally, we are not aware of any other area of the criminal law which recognises an open-ended defence that the conduct in question is morally blameless.

27 We therefore provisionally propose that the deception offences should cease to require proof of dishonesty as a separate element.

Claim of right

28 Finally, there is the case in which the defendant, because of a mistake of law, wrongly believes that he or she is exercising a legal right. Claim of right has always been part of the law of larceny and was intended by the CLRC to apply to both theft and obtaining property by deception. We provisionally propose that it should be a defence to any deception offence that the defendant thought he or she had a legal right to bring about the consequence that he or she brings about by deception. The defence should be available either where the defendant believes, that he or she has a prior right to do this, and uses deception to exercise that right or where the belief arises as a result of the transaction secured by the deception.

Effective prosecution

29 The possible advantages of general fraud offences ... amount to different ways of making the same point – that prosecutors should not be required to treat fraud as if it were a single event, like assault, when in fact many frauds consist of a continuing course of conduct. What stands in the way of charging all of the individual components of the scheme compendiously in one count is the rule against duplicity. Where the charge is fraudulent trading, by contrast, the continuing course of conduct itself is charged; and where a conspiracy is charged, although in theory the offence consists of a single agreement, in reality it is usually the broad fraudulent scheme that is being charged. Our provisional view is that, provided fair advance warning can be provided to the defence, there is no reason why it should be any less acceptable to charge several obtainings by deception in one count than it is to charge a single count of fraudulent trading or a single conspiracy.

30 One way in which this end might be achieved would be to create a deception offence which could be committed by engaging in a continuing course of conduct involving individual but related instances of any of the substantive deception offences. It would not be necessary to prove every one of the particular instances of substantive offences relied upon – rather, the individual offences would amount to particulars of the continuing offence, and the same rules as to unanimity among the jury would apply as apply to particulars in any other offence. The substantive offences would have to be related in the sense that they were part of the same transaction, or criminal enterprise. While this would not be an easy distinction to apply in every case, it is in essence the same distinction as falls to be considered where the prosecution charge fraudulent trading or a conspiracy.

31 We therefore invite views on whether, where a single fraudulent scheme involves the commission of two or more deception offences, the carrying out of the scheme should amount to a single offence which could be charged in a single count. We further invite preliminary views on whether the same should be the case where the individual offences are of theft, or a mixture of theft and deception offences.

PART VIII: THE BOUNDARIES OF DECEPTION

32 This part is concerned with the concept of deception itself and how it is used the law at present.

Representations and deception by conduct

33 We consider that the CLRC, in recommending a change in terminology from the old 'false pretences' to the new 'deception' was significantly changing the emphasis from what the offender was doing to how the victim was affected. This change has not, however, been followed in that deception is always charged on the basis that it was induced by some express or implied representation. The result has been what we suggest is confusing and misleading artificiality in the analysis of cases involving implied representations. We provisionally conclude that deception should be understood as the inducing of a state of mind by words or conduct, with or without a representation, and we invite views as to whether this would require legislative change.

Constructive deception

34 Under this heading we discuss the way in which the courts have reasoned in, particularly, cheque, credit and debit card ('payment card') cases. Payment cards make it unnecessary for the trader to have any concern about the state of the customer's bank account or credit limit, because if the formalities are in order, the trader will be paid regardless. As a result, it is difficult to maintain that when a customer fraudulently uses a payment card, the trader is really deceived as to the, state (or existence) of the customer's bank account or credit, limit (and thus that the goods or services he or she provided were obtained by deception). The courts have answered the point by saying that if a trader would not have supplied the goods had he or she known that the use of the payment card was unauthorised, then that state of mind counts as deception. This we label 'constructive deception'. We provisionally consider it artificial, and suggest that in practice it causes difficulties in prosecuting the fraudulent use of payment cards.

35 We therefore provisionally propose a new offence of imposing liability on a third party. It is based on the idea that there is little or no difference in practice between depriving a person of his or her properly and causing him or her to become indebted to a third party. The offence would be committed where a person intentionally or recklessly causes a legal liability to pay money to be imposed on another, knowing that the other did not consent to his or her doing so and that he or she had no right to do.

36 In connection with this offence, where the defendant induces the victim to consent by deception, we provisionally consider that such consent should not be valid and the defendant would not escape liability. While it is unlikely that this situation would arise in respect of payment cards, the offence would be wide enough to apply in other contexts. One such is where a money transfer is obtained by deception from an overdrawn bank account – there being no right to withdraw funds, there is no property, in the form of a chose in action, of which the transferor is being deprived. Such a situation would therefore not be covered by even our extended version of obtaining property by deceptions. It would, however, be caught by the new offence, because the fraudster has increased the victim's liability to the bank.

37 On the other hand, we consider that a person should not be liable for the new offence where they did not have the necessary consent, but where they believed that the other would have consented had he or she known all of the

material circumstances. This would serve to exclude from liability those who, for instance, use their own cheque card to go into an unauthorised overdraft, in the belief that the bank would authorise such an overdraft if aware of the circumstances.

Misuse ('deception') of machines

38 While the misuse of a machine to obtain property will ordinarily be theft, using a machine to obtain a service, where there is no human mind to be deceived, is not an offence. This lacuna is of much greater significance today than ever before because of the development of the internet. The use of the internet as a market place does not appear to present any particularly acute additional difficulties. It is true that buying a service with a payment card over the internet, where the software does not require a human mind which could be deceived, would not be covered by the current law, but it would be covered by our third party liability offence. We also do not consider that the actual or potential development of 'e-money' presents any particular problems.

39 The internet, however, also provides a medium by which services can be delivered. If the fraudulent conduct consists of access to or use of such a service, neither the existing law nor the extensions hitherto suggested would serve to impose criminal liability. It is clear that such conduct should be criminal, and in considering how ... that may best be achieved, we come to the provisional conclusion that this form of misuse is a 'taking' rather than a 'tricking', and as such should be dealt with in the context of theft rather than deception. Accordingly, we provisionally conclude that it should be made criminal by extending the offence of theft to the theft of services, or by the creation of a separate theft-like offence, rather than by extending the concept of deception. We therefore make no formal provisional proposal, but will return to the question when we come to consider theft. Views are nevertheless welcome at this stage.

40 It is not entirely clear whether, in current English law, criminal liability for deceptions extends to liability for non-disclosure, at least where a duty to disclose exists. We suggest that it is uncontroversial to conclude that there should be no liability for silence in the absence of a duty to disclose. Where there is such a duty, the issues appear to be similar to those we encountered when, in our consultation paper on corruption [LCCP 145], we considered the radical step of criminalising the breach of duty owed by an agent to a principal which is at the heart of the mischief of bribery. We accepted then, and accept now, the criticism that identifying the duty and determining whether it had been breached would be prohibitively complicated and difficult in a criminal trial. We therefore provisionally propose that non-disclosure should not count as deception, whether or not there is a legal duty to disclose.

PART IX: THE FUTURE OF THE EXISTING DISHONESTY OFFENCES

41 We provisionally reject the option of a general dishonesty offence because we think it unacceptable to use *Ghosh* dishonesty as a positive element of offences. But *Ghosh* dishonesty already acts as a positive element in theft, conspiracy to defraud, fraudulent trading and cheating the revenue. Our reasoning therefore suggests that these offences too should be reformed in such a way as to reduce their reliance on the concept of dishonesty. Firm conclusions must await our full consideration of theft and other offences of dishonesty. Nevertheless, at

this stage we invite views as to whether these offences have any features which render inapplicable our criticisms of dishonesty as a positive element.

Further reading

JN Spencer, 'The Theft Act 1978' [1979] Crim LR 24

S Shute and J Horder, 'Thieving and deceiving: what is the difference?' (1993) 56 MLR 548

CHAPTER 22

HANDLING STOLEN GOODS

Section 22 of the Theft Act 1968

(1) A person handles stolen goods if (otherwise than in the course of the stealing) knowing or believing them to be stolen goods he dishonestly receives the goods, or dishonestly undertakes or assists in their retention, removal, disposal or realisation by or for the benefit of another person, or if he arranges to do so.

(2) A person guilty of handling stolen goods shall on conviction on indictment be liable to imprisonment for a term not exceeding 14 years.

STOLEN GOODS

The scope of s 23 is extended beyond the literal words of s 22 by the provisions of s 24 of the Theft Act 1968.

Section 24 of the Theft Act 1968: scope of offences relating to stolen goods

(1) The provisions of this Act relating to goods which have been stolen shall apply whether the stealing occurred in England or Wales or elsewhere, and whether it occurred before or after the commencement of this Act, provided that the stealing (if not an offence under this Act) amounted to an offence where and at the time when the goods were stolen; and references to stolen goods shall be construed accordingly.

(2) For the purposes of those provisions references to stolen goods shall include, in addition to the goods originally stolen and parts of them (whether in their original state or not):

   (a) any other goods which directly or indirectly represent or have at any time represented the stolen goods in the hands of the thief as being the proceeds of any disposal or realisation of the whole or part of the goods stolen or of goods so representing the stolen goods; and

   (b) any other goods which directly or indirectly represent or have at any time represented the stolen goods in the hands of a handler of the stolen goods or any part of them as being the proceeds of any disposal or realisation of the whole or part of the stolen goods handled by him or of goods so representing them.

(3) But no goods shall be regarded as having continued to be stolen goods after they have been restored to the person from whom they were stolen or to other lawful possession or custody, or after that person and any other person claiming through him have otherwise ceased as regards those goods to have any right to restitution in respect of the theft.

(4) For the purposes of the provisions of this Act relating to goods which have been stolen (including subsections (1) to (3) above) goods obtained in England and Wales or elsewhere either by blackmail or in the circumstances described in s 15(1) of this Act shall be regarded as stolen; and 'steal', 'theft' and 'thief' shall be construed accordingly.

DISHONESTLY RETAINING A WRONGFUL CREDIT

Section 2 of the Theft (Amendment) Act 1996 adds a new section, s 24A, to the Theft Act 1968. This creates a new offence of dishonestly retaining wrongful credits, which covers instances where transfers of money obtained by deception (an offence under s 15A of the Theft Act 1968) are credited to another account.

Section 24A of the Theft Act 1968

(1) A person is guilty of an offence if:

    (a) a wrongful credit has been made to an account kept by him or in respect of which he has any right or interest;

    (b) he knows or believes that the credit is wrongful; and

    (c) he dishonestly fails to take such steps as are reasonable in the circumstances to secure that the credit is cancelled.

(2) References to a credit are to a credit of an amount of money.

(3) A credit to an account is wrongful if it is the credit side of a money transfer obtained contrary to s 15A of this Act.

(4) A credit to an account is also wrongful to the extent that it derives from:

    (a) theft;

    (b) an offence under s 15A of this Act;

    (c) blackmail; or

    (d) stolen goods.

(5) In determining whether a credit to an account is wrongful, it is immaterial (in particular) whether the account is overdrawn before or after the credit is made.

(6) A person guilty of an offence under this section shall be liable on conviction on indictment to imprisonment for a term not exceeding 10 years.

(7) Subsection (8) below applies for purposes of provisions of this Act relating to stolen goods (including subsection (4) above).

(8) References to stolen goods include money which is dishonestly withdrawn from an account to which a wrongful credit has been made, but only to the extent that the money derives from the credit.

(9) In this section 'account' and 'money' shall be construed in accordance with s 15B of this Act.

Note that s 24A only applies to wrongful credits made on or after 18 December 1996.

PROVING GOODS WERE STOLEN

'Stolen' means that the goods have been the subject of theft (under s 1 of the Theft Act 1968) or (by virtue of the extended definition of theft in s 24(4) of the Act) have been obtained by deception (under s 15 of the Act) or have been obtained by blackmail (under s 21 of the Act).

There can be no conviction under s 23 unless the prosecution can prove that the goods have been stolen. However, where all of the other requirements of handling are satisfied (ie the only one missing is that the goods are stolen), the defendant may be convicted of attempted handling under s 1 of the Criminal Attempts Act 1981 (cf *R v Shivpuri* [1987] AC 1), or the handling may amount to a fresh appropriation (and so theft) of the goods. See also *Walters v Lunt* [1951] 2 All ER 645, where the defendants were charged (under legislation which preceded the Theft Act 1968) with receiving stolen goods. The goods in question had been taken by a child aged seven, ie below the age of criminal responsibility. The Divisional Court held that since the person who took the goods could not be guilty of theft, the goods were not stolen goods. It followed that the defendants could not be guilty of receiving stolen goods. Lord Goddard CJ pointed out, however, that the defendants, by taking possession of the goods and keeping the goods (and thereby appropriating them), could have been charged instead with theft of those goods.

AG's Ref (No 4 of 1979) (1980) 71 Cr App R 341

The defendant had received a cheque for £288.53 from a fellow employee. The defendant's fellow employee (that is, the thief) had obtained cheques (totalling over £800) by deception from her employer. The cheques had been paid into her bank account, along with payments from legitimate sources. The trial judge ruled that as the bank account on which the cheque for £288.53 had been drawn had received credits from a variety of sources, some legitimate and some illegitimate, it was impossible for the prosecution to prove that the payment made to the defendant was in law stolen goods.

The following point of law was referred to the Court of Appeal:

> Where payment is made out of a fund constituted by a mixture of money amounting to stolen goods within the meaning of section 24 of the Theft Act 1968, and money not so tainted, or of a bank account similarly constituted, in such a way that the specific origin of the sum paid cannot be identified with either portion of the fund, is a jury entitled to infer that the payment represented stolen goods within the meaning of section 24(2) of the Act, from the intention of the parties that it should represent the stolen goods or a share thereof?

Lord Lane CJ: We can begin the statement of our opinion upon the point of law referred to us by observing that the cheque which the accused was alleged to have received was, plainly, not part of the goods originally stolen or obtained. In order to succeed, therefore, the prosecution had to bring the case within the terms of section 24(2) of the Theft Act 1968, which defines the scope of offences relating to the handling of stolen goods. The relevant provisions are contained in section 24(2)(a) ... [extracted above] ... It was submitted that the language of section 24(2)(a) afforded some support for the first point made on behalf of the accused, namely, that a thing in action cannot be handled by receiving within section 22 of the Theft Act. By section 34(2)(b), however, the interpretation section of this Act, 'goods,' except where the context otherwise requires, includes money and every other description of property except land and includes things severed from the land. Further by the combined effect of section 4(1) and section 34(2), 'property' includes money and all other property real and personal including things in action.

In our judgment therefore it is clear from that extended definition of 'goods' that a cheque obtained by deception constitutes stolen goods for the purposes of sections 22 and 24 of the Act.

Next, it is clear that a balance in a bank account, being a debt, is itself a thing in action which falls within the definition of goods and may therefore be goods which directly or indirectly represent stolen goods for the purposes of section 24(2)(a).

Further where, as in the present case, a person obtains cheques by deception and pays them into her bank account, the balance in that account may, to the value of the tainted cheques, be goods which 'directly represent the stolen goods in the hands of the thief as being the proceeds of the disposal or realisation of the goods stolen ...', within the meaning of section 24(2(a).

If, however, the prosecution is to prove dishonest handling by receiving, it is necessary to prove that what the handler received was in fact the whole or part of the stolen goods within the meaning of section 24(2)(a). To prove that, the prosecution must prove (i) that at the material time, namely, at the time of receipt by the handler, in such a case as this, the thief's bank balance was in fact comprised, at least in part, of that which represented the proceeds of stolen goods; and (ii) that the handler received, at least in part, such proceeds.

In some cases no difficulty will arise. For example, if the thief opened a new account and paid into it only dishonestly obtained cheques, then the whole balance would constitute stolen goods within the meaning of section 24(2)(a). If then the thief transferred the whole balance to an accused, that accused would, in our opinion, have received stolen goods.

By the same reasoning, if at the material time the whole of the balance in an account consisted only of the proceeds of stolen goods, then any cheque drawn on that account would constitute stolen goods within section 24(2)(a).

We have no doubt that when such a cheque is paid, so that part of such a balance in the thief's account is transferred to the credit of the receiver's account, the receiver has received stolen goods because he has received a thing in action which '... directly represents ... the stolen goods in the hands of the thief ... as being the proceeds of ... realisation of the ... goods stolen ...'

The same conclusion follows where the receiver directly cashes the cheque drawn on the thief's account and receives money from the paying bank.

The allegation in this case was that the defendant received stolen goods when she received the thief's cheque ... the prosecution sought ... proof, as to the nature of the payment received by the defendant, from the statement which the defendant made as to her understanding and intention when the payment was made. She had said that she regarded the payment to her as 'her share.'

In our opinion, such an admission could not by itself prove either that part of the thief's bank balance did or could represent stolen goods within section 24(2)(a), or that part of such stolen goods was received by the defendant. Her admission was, of course, plainly admissible on the issue of her knowledge that the payment represented stolen goods, and as to her honesty in receiving the money. On the issue of fact, however, as to whether the cheque received by her represented stolen goods, the primary rule is that an accused can only make a valid and admissible admission of a statement of fact of which the accused could give admissible evidence ... In our opinion ... the prosecution must, in such a case as this, prove in the first place that any payment out of a mixed account could, by reference to payments in and out, be a payment representing stolen goods. Unless she had personal knowledge of the working of the thief's account, the defendant could make no valid admission as to that.

It is to be noted that the point of law referred to us contains the words: 'Is a jury entitled to infer ... from the intention of the parties ...' The use of the plural 'parties' is misleading. There was no direct evidence in this case of what the intention of the thief might have been, only of that of the receiver. It may perhaps be that a payment can be proved to have been a payment of money representing stolen goods, even where there was enough honest money in the account to cover the payment, if there is proof direct or by way of necessary inference of the intention of the paying thief to pay out the stolen money. That problem can be decided when it arises. It does not do so here. The prosecution did not advance their case on such a basis.

The only question arising on the facts here is whether a jury is entitled to infer that the payment represented stolen goods within section 24(2)(a) from the intention or belief of the receiver that it should or did. The answer is 'no'.

Goods

The word 'goods' is partly defined in s 34(2)(b) of the Theft Act 1968: 'goods', except in so far as the context otherwise requires, includes money and every other description of property except land, and includes things severed from the land by stealing.

Otherwise than in the course of stealing

The 'stealing' to which these words refer is the stealing by which the goods first became stolen goods. Thus, a thief is not also a handler while doing the act or acts which amount to the original theft. So, for example, if two people break into a house and one takes a painting off a wall and hands it to her accomplice, the accomplice is not guilty of an offence under s 22: the original theft is, in effect, still in progress.

R v Pitham and Hehl (1976) 65 Cr App R 45

Facts: The defendants purchased furniture, belonging to a man named McGregor, from a man named Millman. McGregor was in fact in prison at the time of the sale. Millman was, in due course, convicted of theft of McGregor's property by selling it. The defendants were convicted of handling stolen goods. They appealed unsuccessfully on the ground that their alleged handling had not taken place 'otherwise than in the course of stealing'.

Lawton LJ: The third way [in which the prosecution case was advanced at the trial] and the one the jury in the end accepted, was that Millman was the man who had stolen the property and these two had bought from the thief Millman, knowing it to have been stolen. This third way was reflected in counts 4 and 5. Now, stated in that way, the issues would appear to be easy for a jury to understand. Mr Murray, with much ingenuity and persistence, for which he is to be congratulated, has urged upon the court that this simple case goes to the very heart of what seems to be an academic difference of opinion between the professor of law at Nottingham University, Professor Smith, and the professor of law at Leicester University, Professor Griew, as to the construction of a few words in section 22 of the Theft Act 1968.

His Lordship referred to s 22(1) of the Theft Act and continued:

... Now, the two conflicting academic views can be summarised in this way. Professor Smith's view in his book on *The Theft Act 1968* (2nd edn, 1974), para 400, seems to be that 'in the course of the stealing' can be a very short time or it can be a very long period of time. Professor Griew in his book *The Law of Theft* (3rd edn, 1977) paras 8-18, 8-19, seems to be of the opinion that 'in the course of the stealing' embraces not only the act of stealing as defined by section 1 of the Theft Act 1968, but in addition making away with the goods. In the course of expounding their differing views in their books on the Theft Act the two professors have both referred to ancient authorities. Both are of the opinion that the object of the words, 'otherwise than in the course of the stealing,' was to deal with the situation where two men are engaged in different capacities in a joint enterprise. In those circumstances, unless some such limiting words as those to which I have referred were included in the definition of handling, a thief could be guilty of both stealing and receiving. An illustration of the sort of problem which arises is provided by Professor Smith's reference to the old case of *Coggins* (1873) 12 Cox CC 517. In his book on the Theft Act at paragraph 400, he summarises the facts of *Coggins* in these terms: 'If a servant stole money from his master's till and handed it to an accomplice in his master's shop, the accomplice was guilty of larceny and not guilty of receiving.' He added another example. It was the case of *Perkins* (1852) 5 Cox CC 554. He summarises that case as follows: 'Similarly, if a man committed larceny in the room in which he lodged and threw a bundle of stolen goods to an accomplice in the street, the accomplice was guilty of larceny and not guilty of receiving'.

In our judgment the words to which I have referred in section 22(1), were designed to make it clear that in those sorts of situations a man could not be guilty under the Theft Act of both theft and handling. As was pointed out to Mr Murray by my brother, Bristow J, in the course of argument, the Theft Act in section 1 defines theft ... [his Lordship recited s 1(1) and s 3(1) of the 1968 Act] ...

Mr Murray's submission – a very bold one – was that the general words with which section 3(1) opens, namely, 'Any assumption by a person of the rights of an owner amounts to an appropriation,' are limited by the words beginning 'and this includes.' He submitted that those additional words bring back into the law of theft something akin to the concept of asportation, which was one of the aspects of the law of larceny which the Theft Act 1968 was intended to get rid of. According to Mr Murray, unless there is something which amounts to 'coming by' the property there cannot be an appropriation. We disagree. The final words of section 3(1) are words of inclusion. The general words at the beginning of section 3(1) are wide enough to cover any assumption by a person of the rights of an owner.

What was the appropriation in this case? The jury found that the two appellants had handled the property *after* Millman had stolen it. That is clear from their acquittal of these two appellants on count 3 of the indictment which had charged them jointly with Millman. What had Millman done? He had assumed the rights of the owner. He had done that when he took the two appellants to 20 Parry Road, showed them the property and invited them to buy what they wanted. He was then acting as the owner. He was then, in the words of the statute, 'assuming the rights of the owner'. The moment he did that he appropriated McGregor's goods to himself. The appropriation was complete. After this appropriation had been completed there was no question of these two appellants taking part, in the words of section 22, in dealing with the goods 'in the course of the stealing.'

It follows that no problem arises in this case. It may well be that some of the situations which the two learned professors envisage and discuss in their books may have to be dealt with at some future date, but not in this case. The facts are too clear.

Mr Murray suggested the learned judge should have directed the jury in some detail about the possibility that the appropriation had not been an instantaneous appropriation, but had been one which had gone on for some time. He submitted that it might have gone on until such time as the furniture was loaded into the appellant's van. For reasons we have already given that was not a real possibility in this case. It is not part of a judge's duty to give the jury the kind of lecture on the law which may be appropriate for a professor to give a class of undergraduates. We commend the judge for not having involved himself in a detailed academic analysis of the law relating to this case when on the facts it was as clear as anything could be that either these appellants had helped Millman to steal the goods, or Millman had stolen them and got rid of them by sale to these two appellants. We can see nothing wrong in the learned judge's approach to this case and on that particular ground we affirm what he did and said.

R v Cash [1985] QB 801 (CA)

Lord Lane CJ: ... The point taken by counsel for the appellant is concerned with the words 'otherwise than in the course of the stealing'. He submits that before there can be a conviction for handling, the prosecution has to prove affirmatively that the defendant was not the thief or a party to the theft, and if that is not proved the charge of handling is not made out. It is submitted that the words 'otherwise than in the course of the stealing' constitute an essential ingredient of the offence of handling and that a burden is placed on the prosecution to prove this negative averment ...

... [I]t was open to the jury to infer from the facts that the appellant was the guilty handler. There was no issue whether the receipt of the stolen goods was in the course of the stealing. It was not suggested to or by any witness that the appellant was the thief or that the property came into his possession in the course of the stealing; there was no evidence that the appellant was the burglar. Furthermore, when he went into the dock, there was a presumption that he was innocent of any charge of burglary as well as of handling.

There was no evidence to displace that presumption so far as burglary was concerned. The presumption was displaced by evidence so far as dishonest handling was concerned. If, therefore, there was no evidence that the appellant was the burglar or had taken part in the burglary, the jury, as a matter of logic and common sense, were entitled to find that his handling which was not in dispute was a handling otherwise than in the course of the stealing ...

If the appellant's contentions are correct, moreover, it would seem to follow that the prosecution might in some cases have the task of disproving burglary before a charge of handling could be sustained. It is difficult to imagine what evidence could be adduced. Parliament could not have intended that the burglar or burglars should be called to exculpate the defendant, or that the prosecution would have to call evidence, for example, supporting an alibi, in order to demonstrate that the defendant was not a party to the burglary ...

In our judgment, Parliament intended by the words of s 22(1) to make it clear that, despite the wording of the rest of that section and of s 1 and s 3 of the Theft Act 1968, where the evidence shows that a defendant was simply a party to the original theft, he is not to be convicted as a handler and therefore subject to the greater maximum penalty which handling carries ...

For these reasons we are of the view that in the ordinary case there is no burden placed on the prosecution by the words 'otherwise than in the course of the stealing' – which is perhaps why they appear in brackets. Of course they may be important words where ... a jury does have to decide whether a particular defendant was indeed a thief or a handler; but where in reality the defendant must be acquitted if he cannot be shown to have been a handler, the words have little importance and the jury should not even be told about them.

We turn now to [the appellant's] submission that in a 'recent possession' case, the indictment should include counts alleging burglary as alternatives to those of handling and that in the absence of such counts, the judge should invite the jury to consider whether the evidence proves not handling, but burglary, in which case the appellant would have been entitled to a finding of not guilty.

As Lord Goddard CJ made clear in *R v Seymour* [1954] 1 WLR 678 there are circumstances where the defendant is in possession of property so recently after it is stolen that it is the inevitable inference that he was the thief, where, for example, he is found within a few hundred yards of the scene of the theft and minutes after the theft took place. In such circumstances, no doubt, alternative counts might be appropriate. In such cases, if there were only counts of handling in the indictment, the judge would direct the jury that if they took the view that the defendant was the thief, he should be acquitted of the handling.

The instant case was not that type of case at all. The goods were found in the possession of the appellant on 25 February 1983. None of the property was stolen more recently than 16 February 1983. It seems to us that in those circumstances it was not properly open to the jury to infer that the appellant was the burglar rather than the guilty receiver/handler. The judge was right to ignore the suggestion that the appellant might have been the thief or burglar. If there had been alternative counts, it would have been correct for the judge to leave only the handling counts to the jury ...

Petition: The Appeal Committee of the House of Lords (**Lord Fraser of Tullybelton, Lord Roskill** and **Lord Bridge of Harwich**) dismissed a petition by the appellant for leave to appeal.

Ryan and French v DPP [1994] Crim LR 457 (DC)

Facts: A month after a dinghy had been stolen, the loser saw it in the possession of the appellants. They claimed that the appellant French had bought it a year previously. They were charged with both theft and handling of the dinghy. Justices convicted them of the handling and acquitted them of the theft.

On appeal by way of case stated it was argued: (1) that the justices would have had to have found as a fact that the appellants were not the thieves, which they could not have done, as the evidence was equally consistent with theft as handling; (2) the justices should have directed themselves to withdraw the count of handling, the evidence being more consistent with theft.

The question certified was: 'Can a conviction of handling be justified on the evidence given, having regard to the fact that the appellants were acquitted on the count of theft?'

Held, dismissing the appeal:

(1) It was well understood that the prosecution did not have to prove that handlers were not thieves.

(2) There are cases where it is appropriate to withdraw a count or charge of handling when both theft and handling are charged. This was not such a case. There was sufficient evidence to support a *prima facie* case on each charge and it was for the justices to decide on the basis of their assessment of the witnesses and the inferences they were prepared to draw if either charge were made out.

R v Fernandez [1997] 1 Cr App R 123 (CA)

Hobhouse LJ: This appeal ... raises points upon the relationship between the offences of theft and handling under the Theft Act 1968...

The appellant was tried ... on an indictment which included eight counts. The counts with which this appeal is concerned were counts 3, 4 and 5. Count 3 charged him with an offence of robbery contrary to s 8(1) of the Theft Act: it alleged that he had robbed an employee of the Allied Irish Bank on 10 November 1994 of a quantity of money. Count 4 charged him with having a firearm with intent to commit an indictable offence, namely theft, on the same occasion, contrary to s 18(1) of the Firearms Act 1968. Count 5 was a count of handling stolen goods contrary to s 22(1) of the Theft Act. The particulars alleged that the appellant had:

> On a day between the 9th day of November 1994 and the 12th day of November 1994 dishonestly received stolen goods, namely a quantity of money belonging to Allied Irish Bank, knowing or believing the same to be stolen goods.

The drafting of count 5 shows that it was intended to be an alternative to count 3 and counsel for the Crown in his opening at the trial so stated to the jury ...

The submissions in this court of [counsel] on behalf of the appellant were:

(1) A defendant cannot in respect of the same goods commit an offence under both sections 8 and 22 of the Theft Act unless the possession of those goods by another has intervened.

(2) A court cannot lawfully convict a defendant of theft or robbery after a jury has returned a verdict of handling the same goods ...

In *Dolan* (1976) 62 Cr App R 36 ... the Court of Appeal ... said (pp 38–39):

... In the course of his argument [counsel for the appellant] submitted that as a matter of law a man cannot be guilty both of stealing and receiving the same goods... Although strictly the point does not arise in this appeal, it has been argued, and we have reached a view which we propose to state very shortly.

... The combined effect of the Criminal Law Act 1967, s 1 and the Theft Act 1968, s 22(1) is that, as Professor Smith suggests in paragraph 487 of his *Law of Theft* (1972), a thief 'could be convicted of handling the goods stolen by him by receiving them – *if the evidence warranted this conclusion'* (our italics).

If the defendant's handling of the goods occurs only in the course of the stealing he cannot be found guilty of handling by receiving: see Theft Act 1968, s 22(1). But, if he handles them alter, ie after the stealing, he commits an offence under the subsection. It is, therefore, perfectly possible for a man to be guilty of stealing and receiving the same goods ...

In *Shelton* (1986) 83 Cr App R 379 Lawton LJ summarised the law at p 385, saying:

... a jury should be told that a handler can be a thief, but he cannot be convicted of being both a thief and a handler.

In the present case, there was no legal inconsistency between counts 3 and 4 on the one hand and count 5 on the other. The inconsistency arose simply from the way in which the Crown was, perfectly properly, putting its case. The Crown said that it had proved that the appellant was one of the robbers and that the robbers had been carrying guns. The Crown said that if the jury were not satisfied that he was a robber, they must at least be satisfied that he knew about the robbery and, as the notes had been found in his flat, they must at least be satisfied of his guilt under s 22. The counts, on this presentation, simply represented alternative views of the facts. In the present case the appellant said that at no stage had he had anything to do with the robbery or the currency notes stolen during the robbery ...

There can be no doubt that the judge should have properly directed the jury upon the relationship between counts 5 and 3. He should have explained to them that handling has to be otherwise than in the course of the stealing and, if importance was being attached to it, the implication of the use of the word 'received' in count 5. He should have directed them that count 5 was charged as an alternative to counts 3 and 4 and that he would not take a verdict from them on count 5 until they had concluded their deliberations and decided upon their verdict on counts 3 and 4.

It does not follow however ... that the jury's verdict on count 5 entitled the appellant as a matter of law to verdicts of not guilty on counts 3 and 4. The appellant was in the charge of the jury on counts 3 and 4 and justice required that, if they were able to agree, the jury should return verdicts on those counts. They were undoubtedly the more serious counts. The jury had not been directed to treat the counts as alternatives. The summing-up had not identified for the jury any considerations in relation to count 5 which involved any inconsistency between verdicts of guilty on all three counts. Indeed, the summing-up had been inadequate in relation to count 5 in that it included no adequate direction as to the Crown's case on that count...

DISHONESTY

The test of dishonesty for the purpose of s 22 is as set out in *R v Ghosh* [1982] QB 1053 – see Chapter 18.

R v Roberts (1985) 84 Cr App R 117 (CA)

Facts: Two Renoir paintings, valued at £51,000, were stolen in the course of a burglary. The insurance company offered a 10% reward for their return. Some three months later the appellant telephoned the loss adjuster and told him that he had the paintings. The appellant subsequently handed the paintings over to the loss adjuster and was arrested by the police.

> **O'Connor LJ**: ... [W]e start with the proposition that for the subjective test to arise, somewhere along the line the defendant has to say 'I did not know that anybody would regard what I was doing as dishonest'. We have come to the conclusion that no one can properly say that, if what he is doing is receiving stolen property knowing it to be stolen and then trying to sell it. A person may come into possession of stolen property innocently and the test for that would be normally as to what he did with it. If, for example, he had taken it straight to the police and said 'I have found this in my motor car', then the question would plainly arise because nobody would say that a person acting in that fashion was acting dishonestly if it was true. But for somebody to put forward this kind of assertion is, in our judgment, really not possible. In fact, it is not only not possible, but it was not done. At no stage in the present case did this appellant say on the facts, 'I received the stolen goods and was trying to sell them for my own profit, but I did not know that anybody would think that dishonest'. He had never raised the problem and unless the problem is properly raised it does not seem to us that it is necessary for the trial judge to embark on the full *Ghosh* direction.

KNOWING OR BELIEVING THAT THE GOODS ARE STOLEN

Not only must it proved that the goods were, in fact, stolen (see above); it must also be proved that the defendant knew that the goods were stolen or believed them to be stolen.

Atwal v Massey [1971] 3 All ER 881 (DC)

Facts: A stolen electric kettle was left by the roadside by the thief for collection by the appellant, who paid the thief £1.50 for it.

Lord Widgery CJ: ... The question the justices have asked us is:

> Whether the fact that the appellant ought to have known that the kettle was stolen is sufficient to render him guilty of an offence under s 22 of the Theft Act 1968 ...

... It is not sufficient to establish an offence under s 22 that the goods were received in circumstances which would have put a reasonable man on his enquiry. The question is a subjective one: was the appellant aware of the theft or did he believe the goods to be stolen or did he, suspecting the goods to be stolen, deliberately shut his eyes to the consequences.

R v Grainge [1974] 1 All ER 928 (CA)

Eveleigh J: ... On 7 March 1973 the appellant, his co-defendant (a man named O'Connor), and a third man, entered a shop in Sheffield which sold office machinery and stationery. During the course of the visit O'Connor stole a pocket calculating machine valued at £59. The loss of the machine was soon noticed and the salesman went out of the shop into the street to search for the three men. Having seen them he noticed that one of the men passed the calculator to the appellant ...

... The summing up as a whole could well have left the jury with the impression that suspicious circumstances, irrespective of whether the accused himself appreciated they were suspicious, imposed a duty as a matter of law to act and enquire and that failure so to do was to be treated as knowledge or belief ...

Going on to deal with the second ground of appeal, his Lordship said:

> In the judgment of this court the [trial judge] ought to have made it plain that it was at the moment of receipt and not at any time during the handling thereafter that guilty knowledge had to be proved ...

R v Hall (1985) 81 Cr App R 260 (CA)

Boreham J: ... We think that a jury should be directed along these lines. A man may be said to know that goods are stolen when he is told by someone with first-hand knowledge (someone such as the thief or the burglar) that such is the case. Belief, of course, is something short of knowledge. It may be said to be the state of mind of a person who says to himself: 'I cannot say I know for certain that these goods are stolen, but there can be no other reasonable conclusion in the light of all the circumstances, in the light of all that I have heard and seen'. Either of those two states of mind is enough to satisfy the words of the statute. The second is enough (that is, belief) even if the defendant says to himself: 'Despite all that I have seen and all that I have heard, I refuse to believe what my brain tells me is obvious.' What is not enough, of course, is mere suspicion: 'I suspect that these goods may be stolen, but it may be on the other hand that they are not.' That state of mind, of course, does not fall within the words 'knowing or believing'.

R v Griffiths (1974) 60 Cr App R 14 (CA)

Facts: The appellant had been charged with handling a pair of candlesticks stolen from a church in Cheltenham. In evidence, the appellant had said that he might have had suspicions, but the suspicions were not related to any criminal offence.

James LJ: ... To direct the jury that the offence is committed if the defendant, suspecting that the goods were stolen, deliberately shut his eyes to the circumstances as an alternative to knowing or believing the goods were stolen is a misdirection. To direct the jury that, in common sense and in law, they may find that the defendant knew or believed the goods to be stolen because he deliberately closed his eyes to the circumstances is a perfectly proper direction.

R v Brook [1993] Crim LR 455 (CA)

Facts: The defendant was found in possession of a carrier bag containing stolen cheque books and cheque cards. The bag was in his briefcase, which was in his car. His explanation was that his wife had found the bag in a public lavatory, had told him what was in it and, at the defendant's suggestion, put it in the back of the car while he decided what to do with it.

Held: It was clear that a person was guilty of handling only if he believed goods to be stolen at the time he received them: supervening belief or dishonesty after receipt was not enough.

Section 24(1) of the Theft Act 1968: territorial jurisdiction

If a thief steals property in a country other than England and Wales but the defendant receives that stolen property (or its proceeds) in England or Wales, then (assuming the other elements of the offence of handling are made out) the defendant can be convicted of handling those goods provided that the original theft was against the law of the country where that theft took place.

Section 24(2) of the Theft Act 1968: proceeds of stolen goods

Goods come within the definition of stolen goods if either:

(a) they are the goods which were originally stolen; or

(b) they represent the goods which were originally stolen and are in the hands of the original thief or someone who is handling them dishonestly.

So, if a car is stolen and is then part-exchanged for a different car, the second car comes within the definition of stolen goods only if it is in the hands of the person who stole the first car or it is in the hands of someone who knows (or believes) that it was acquired in part-exchange for a stolen car.

Section 24(3) of the Theft Act 1968: goods restored to their owner, etc

Goods cease to be 'stolen' if they have been restored to lawful possession; any act after that restoration to lawful possession cannot amount to an offence under s 22 (although since the decision of the House of Lords in *R v Shivpuri* [1987] AC 1 it could amount to an attempt to handle stolen goods under the Criminal Attempts Act 1981).

AG's Ref (No 1 of 1974) [1974] QB 744 (CA)

Lord Widgery CJ: ... The facts of the present case ... are these: a police constable found an unlocked, unattended car containing packages of new clothing which he suspected, and which in fact subsequently proved to be stolen. The officer removed the rotor arm from the vehicle to immobilise it, and kept observation. After about 10 minutes, the accused appeared, got into the van and attempted to start the engine. When questioned by the officer, he gave an implausible explanation, and was arrested.

[The defendant was charged, *inter alia*, with receiving stolen goods, namely the clothing, knowing them to be stolen.]

His Lordship quoted s 24(3) of the Theft Act 1968 and went on to say:

We are satisfied that despite the absence of another and perhaps more appropriate verb [than 'restore'], the effect of s 24(3) is to enable a defendant to plead that the goods had ceased to be stolen goods if the facts are that they were taken by a police officer in the course of his duty and reduced into possession by him ...

In our judgment it depended primarily on the intentions of the police officer. If the police officer seeing these goods in the back of the car had made up his mind that he would take them into custody, that he would reduce them into his possession or control, take charge of them so that they could not be removed and so that he would have the disposal of them, then it would be a perfectly proper conclusion to say that he had taken possession of the goods. On the other hand, if the truth of the matter is that he was of an entirely open mind at that stage as to whether the goods were to be seized or not and was of an entirely open mind as to whether he should take possession of them or not, but merely stood by so that when the driver of the car appeared he could ask certain questions of that driver as to the nature of the goods and why they were there, then there is no reason whatever to suggest that he had taken the goods into his possession or control. It may be, of course, that he had both objects in mind. It is possible in a case like this that the police officer may have intended by removing the rotor arm both to prevent the car from being driven away and to enable him to assert control over the woollen goods as such. But if the jury came to the conclusion that the proper explanation of what had happened was that the police officer had not intended at that stage to reduce the goods into his possession or to assume the control of them, and at that stage was merely concerned to ensure that the driver, if he appeared, could not get away without answering questions, then in that case the proper conclusion of the jury would have been to the effect that the goods had not been reduced into the possession of the police and therefore a defence under s 24(3) of the Theft Act 1968 would not be of use to this particular defendant ...

THE FORMS OF HANDLING

Section 22 can, for practical purposes, be regarded as creating two offences:

(1) dishonestly receiving stolen goods (or arranging to do so);

(2) dishonestly undertaking or assisting in their retention, removal, disposal or realisation by or for the benefit of another person (or arranging to do so).

Receiving

The word 'receiving' is not defined in the Theft Act 1968. However, the same word was used under the legislation which preceded the 1968 Act, so the old cases on the meaning of receiving are still good law. The essence of receiving is exercising control over the goods.

R v Frost and Hale (1964) 48 Cr App R 284 (CA)

Lord Parker CJ: ... [Where a defendant is charged with receiving stolen goods, the jury should be directed that] they must be satisfied that the physical possession was such as to give [the defendant] control as against the persons [he was] assisting, or, if not against them, joint control with them ...

Hobson v Impett (1957) 41 Cr App R 138 (DC)

Facts: On 14 January 1957 the appellant helped one George Porritt to unload from a cart a sack which contained some stolen ingots and to take the ingots into Porritt's house. By the time the unloading was finished, the appellant knew that the sack contained ingots and that they were stolen. The next day, the appellant helped Porritt to load some of the ingots into a motor car. The appellant travelled as a passenger in the car, and although there was no evidence that he touched them again or took part in offering them for sale, he was for a time alone in the car with the ingots.

Lord Goddard CJ: ... It is not the law that, if a man knows goods are stolen and puts his hands on them, that in itself makes him guilty of receiving, because it does not follow that he is taking them into his control. The control may still be in the thief or the man whom he is assisting, and the alleged receiver may be only picking the goods up without taking them into his possession, the goods all the time remaining in the possession of the person whom he is helping ... It cannot be the law that merely because a man picks up goods which he knows are stolen he is receiving the goods ...

Arranging to receive

The goods must have been stolen by the time the arrangement to receive them is made (although if they are not, a charge of conspiracy to handle stolen goods may be appropriate).

R v Park (1988) 87 Cr App R 164 (CA)

Woolf LJ: [His Lordship rejected a submission made by counsel for the Crown that if a person had an arrangement made before the goods are stolen and if that arrangement is one which has not been terminated, then the consequence of that is that if the goods are subsequently stolen, the person who is a party to the arrangement can be guilty, subject to his knowing or believing that the goods which are to be the subject of the arrangement are to be stolen and he is also acting dishonestly. His Lordship said:] In my view, this interpretation ... is not correct ... [T]he guilty knowledge must exist at the time that the offence is committed ...

[Section 22 of the Theft Act 1968] does not alter the requirement ... that the subject-matter of the handling must in fact be stolen goods. It is not possible to rely upon an activity which took place prior to the theft as in itself amounting to the necessary actus reus to create handling, albeit that it may be possible to take advantage of the arrangements previously made when the theft has taken place. The appropriate charge in the circumstances where there is conduct prior to the theft is to lay a count of conspiracy ...

...[T]his court has no doubt that it is not possible to rely on an arrangement made before the theft in order to establish a charge of handling where the goods were only stolen after the arrangement had been made and not before.

Undertaking or assisting in retention, removal, disposal or realisation by or for the benefit of another person

Where a defendant is charged with the second form of handling, the charge or indictment will not differentiate between the various ways in which the second form of handling may be committed. Whatever the exact nature of the defendant's actions, for a conviction under the second limb of s 22, those actions must be performed by way of assisting someone else or for someone else's benefit. If the act is done by the accused himself and is for his own benefit, a charge under the second limb of s 22 cannot be sustained.

R v Bloxham [1983] 1 AC 109 (HL)

Lord Bridge of Harwich: My Lords, in January 1977 the appellant purchased a motor car for £1,300. He paid the seller £500 in cash and was to pay the balance when the seller produced the car's registration document, but in the event this never happened. The car had in fact been stolen. It is accepted by the Crown that the appellant did not know or believe this when he acquired the car. In December 1977 he sold the car for £200 to an unidentified third party who was prepared to take the car without any registration document.

The appellant was charged under s 22(1) of the Theft Act 1968 with handling stolen goods, the particulars of the relevant count in the indictment alleging that he:

Dishonestly undertook or assisted in the disposal or realisation of certain stolen goods, namely a Ford Cortina motor car registered number SJH 606M, by or for the benefit of another, namely the unknown purchaser knowing or believing the same to be stolen goods.

At the trial it was submitted that the count disclosed no offence in that the disposal or realisation of the car had been for the appellant's own benefit, not for the benefit of the unknown purchaser, and that in any event the purchaser was not within the ambit of the categories of 'other person' contemplated by s 22(1). The judge ruled that the purchaser derived a benefit from the transaction, in that, although he got no title, he had the use of the car; that there was no reason to give any restricted construction to the words 'another person' in the subsection; and that, accordingly, on the undisputed facts, the appellant had undertaken the disposal or realisation of the car for the benefit of another person within the meaning of s 22(1) ...

... The [Court of Appeal] certified the following point of law of general public importance as involved in their decision:

Does a *bona fide* purchaser for value commit an offence of dishonestly undertaking the disposal or realisation of stolen property for the benefit of another if when he sells the goods on he knows or believes them to be stolen.

... It is, I think, now well settled that this subsection creates two distinct offences, but no more than two. The first is equivalent to the old offence of receiving under s 33 of the Larceny Act 1916. The second is a new offence designed to remedy defects in the old law and can be committed in any of the various ways indicated by the words from 'undertakes' to the end of the subsection. It follows that the new offence may and should be charged in a single count embodying in the particulars as much of the relevant language of the subsection, including alternatives, as may be appropriate to the circumstances of the particular case, and that such a count will not be bad for duplicity. It was so held by Geoffrey Lane J delivering the judgment of the Court of Appeal in *R v Willis* [1972] 1 WLR 1605, and approved by the Court of Appeal in *R v Deakin* [1972] 1 WLR 1618. So far as I am aware, this practice has been generally followed ever since.

The critical words to be construed are 'undertakes ... their ... disposal or realisation ... for the benefit of another person'. Considering these words first in isolation, it seems to me that, if A sells his own goods to B, it is a somewhat strained use of language to describe this as a disposal or realisation of the goods for the benefit of B. True it is that B obtains a benefit from the transaction, but it is surely more natural to say that the disposal or realisation is for A's benefit than for B's. It is the purchase, not the sale, that is for the benefit of B. It is only when A is selling as agent for a third party C that it would be entirely natural to describe the sale as a disposal or realisation for the benefit of another person.

But the words cannot, of course, be construed in isolation. They must be construed in their context, bearing in mind, as I have pointed out, that the second half of the subsection creates a single offence which can be committed in various ways. I can ignore for present purposes the concluding words 'or if he arranges to do so', which throw no light on the point at issue. The preceding words contemplate four activities (retention, removal, disposal, realisation). The offence can be committed in relation to any one of these activities in one or other of two ways. First, the offender may himself undertake the activity for the benefit of another person. Second, the activity may be undertaken by another person and the offender may assist him. Of course, if the thief or an original receiver and his friend act together in, say, removing the stolen goods, the friend may be committing the offence in both ways. But this does not invalidate the analysis and if the analysis holds good it must follow, I think, that the category of other persons contemplated by the subsection is subject to the same limitations in whichever way the offence is committed. Accordingly, a purchaser, as such, of stolen goods, cannot, in my opinion, be 'another person' within the subsection, since his act of purchase could not sensibly be described as a disposal or realisation of the stolen goods by him. Equally, therefore, even, if the sale to him could be described as a disposal or realisation for his benefit, the transaction is not, in my view, within the ambit of the subsection ...

As a general rule, ambiguities in a criminal statute are to be resolved in favour of the subject, that is in favour of the narrower rather than the wider operation of an ambiguous penal provision. But here there are, in my opinion, more specific and weightier indications which point in the same direction as the general rule.

First, it is significant that the Theft Act 1968, notwithstanding the wide ambit of the definition of theft provided by ss 1 and 3(1), specifically protects the innocent purchaser of goods who subsequently discovers that they were stolen, by s 3(2) [which his Lordship then quoted].

It follows that, though some might think that in this situation honesty would require the purchaser, once he knew the goods were stolen, to seek out the true owner and return them, the criminal law allows him to retain them with impunity for his own benefit. It hardly seems consistent with this that, if he deals with them for the benefit of a third party in some way that falls within the ambit of the activities referred to in the second half of s 22(1), he risks prosecution for handling which carries a heavier maximum penalty (14 years) than theft (10 years). The force of this consideration is not, in my view, significantly weakened by the possibility that the innocent purchaser of stolen goods who sells them after learning they were stolen may commit the quite distinct offences of obtaining by deception (if he represents that he has a good title) or, conceivably, of aiding and abetting the commission by the purchaser of the offence of handling by receiving (if both know the goods were stolen).

Second, it is clear that the words in parentheses in s 22(1) 'otherwise than in the course of the stealing' were designed to avoid subjecting thieves, in the ordinary course, to the heavier penalty provided for handlers. But most thieves realise the goods they have stolen by disposing of them to third parties. If [the ruling of the trial judge was] right, all such thieves are liable to prosecution as principals both for theft and for handling under the second half of s 22(1) ...

For these reasons I have reached the conclusion that any ambiguity in the relevant language of s 22(1) should be resolved in favour of the narrower meaning suggested earlier in this opinion. I would accordingly answer the certified question in the negative and allow the appeal.

Lord Diplock, Lord Scarman and **Lord Brandon of Oakbrook** agreed with the speech of **Lord Bridge of Harwich**.

What amounts to 'assisting'

The word 'assisting' connotes active assistance: it follows that providing a place for stolen goods to be hidden (as in *R v Pitchley* (1972) 57 Cr App R 30) or trying to deceive the police that goods are not stolen both fall within s 22 but merely failing to co-operate with a police search does not.

R v Brown [1970] 1 QB 105; [1969] 3 All ER 198 (CA)

Facts: A man called Holden broke into a cafe and stole some food and cigarettes. He took the stolen goods to the appellant's flat and, after hiding the cigarettes, told the appellant about them. Later the police went to the flat. The appellant denied knowledge of the theft but did not impede the search of his flat. After some of the stolen food had been found in the flat, the appellant was warned that he would be arrested. He said to the police officer, 'Get lost'. Later, the cigarettes were found in the flat.

Lord Parker CJ: ... It is urged here that the mere failure to reveal the presence of the cigarettes, with or without the addition of the spoken words 'Get lost', was incapable in itself of amounting to an assisting in the retention of the goods within the meaning of the subsection. The court has come to the conclusion that that is right. It does not seem to this court that the mere failure to tell the police, coupled if you like with the words 'Get lost', amounts in itself to an assisting in their retention. On the other hand, those matters did afford strong evidence of what was the real basis of the charge here, namely that knowing that they had been stolen he permitted them to remain there or, as it has been put, provided accommodation for these stolen goods in order to assist Holden to retain them ...

R v Kanwar [1982] 1 WLR 845 (CA)

Cantley J: ... [The appellant's] husband had brought the stolen goods to their house where the goods were used in the home. It was conceded that the appellant was not present when the goods were brought to the house. She was in hospital at the time.

On 2 November 1978 police officers, armed with a search warrant, came to the house to look for and take away any goods which they found there which corresponded with a list of stolen goods in their possession. The appellant arrived during the search and was told of the object of the search. She replied:

There's no stolen property here.

She was subsequently asked a number of questions with regard to specific articles which were in the house and in reply to those questions, she gave answers which were lies [claiming that she had purchased the goods in question] ...

In *R v Thornhill*, decided in this court on 15 May 1981, and in *R v Sanders*, decided in this court on 25 February 1982, both unreported, it was held that merely using stolen goods in the possession of another does not constitute the offence of assisting in their retention. To constitute the offence, something must be done by the offender, and done intentionally and dishonestly, for the purpose of enabling the goods to be retained. Examples of such conduct are concealing or helping to conceal the goods, or doing something to make them more difficult to find or to identify. Such conduct must be done knowing or believing the goods to be stolen and done dishonestly and for the benefit of another.

We see no reason why the requisite assistance should be restricted to physical acts. Verbal representations, whether oral or in writing, for the purpose of concealing the identity of stolen goods may, if made dishonestly and for the benefit of another, amount to handling stolen goods by assisting in their retention within the meaning of s 22 of the Theft Act 1968.

The requisite assistance need not be successful in its object. It would be absurd if a person dishonestly concealing stolen goods for the benefit of a receiver could establish a defence by showing that he was caught in the act ...

The appellant told these lies to the police to persuade them that the picture and the mirror were not the stolen property which they had come to take away but were her lawful property which she had bought. If that was true, the articles should be left in the house. She was, of course, telling these lies to protect her husband, who had dishonestly brought the articles there but, in our view, she was nonetheless, at the time, dishonestly assisting in the retention of the stolen articles.

... In so far as the trial judge's direction [to the jury] suggests that the appellant would be guilty of the offence if she was merely willing for the goods to be kept and used in the house and was thinking that it was nice to have them there, although they were stolen goods, it is a misdirection. We have considered whether on that account the conviction ought to be quashed. However, the offence was established by the uncontradicted evidence of the police officer which, looked at in full, clearly shows that in order to mislead the officer who had come to take away stolen goods, she misrepresented the identity of the goods which she knew or believed to be stolen ...

Retention

R v Pitchley (1972) 57 Cr App R 30 (CA)

Facts: The appellant's son gave him £150 to look after. The appellant put the money in his account at a savings bank. The appellant said that he did not find out that the money had been stolen, by his son, until a few days later. After finding out that the money had been stolen the appellant did nothing.

> **Cairns LJ**: ... [The main point made by counsel for the appellant is that], assuming that the jury were not satisfied that the appellant received the money knowing it to have been stolen ... then there was no evidence after that, that from the time when the money was put into the savings bank, that the appellant had done any act in relation to it. His evidence was, and there is no reason to suppose that the jury did not believe it, that at the time when he put the money into the savings bank he still did not know or believe that the money had been stolen – it was only at a later stage that he did. That was on the Saturday according to his evidence, and the position was that the money had simply remained in the savings bank from the Saturday, to the Wednesday when the police approached the appellant ...

> ... [T]he question is: Did the conduct of the appellant between the Saturday and the Wednesday amount to an assisting in the retention of this money for the benefit of his son Brian?

His Lordship referred to the case of *R v Brown* (1969) 53 Cr App R 527 and went on:

> In this present case there was no question on the evidence of the appellant himself, that he was permitting the money to remain under his control in his savings bank book, and it is clear that this court in *R v Brown* regarded such permitting as sufficient to constitute retention within the meaning of [s 22 of the Theft Act 1968]
> ...

> ... [T]he dictionary meaning of the word 'retain' [is] – keep possession of, not lose, continue to have. In the view of this court, that is the meaning of the word 'retain' in this section.

Further reading

LW Blake, 'The innocent purchaser and section 22 of the Theft Act' [1972] Crim LR 494

JC Smith, 'Theft and/or handling' [1977] Crim LR 517

JN Spencer, 'The mishandling of handling' [1981] Crim LR 682

JN Spencer, 'Handling, theft and the *mala fide* purchaser' [1985] Crim LR 92

G Williams, 'Handling, theft and the purchaser who takes a chance' [1985] Crim LR 432

JN Spencer, 'Handling and taking risks – a reply to Professor Williams' [1985] Crim LR 440

CHAPTER 23

CRIMINAL DAMAGE

Section 1 of the Criminal Damage Act 1971: destroying or damaging property

(1) A person who without lawful excuse destroys or damages any property belonging to another intending to destroy or damage any such property or being reckless as to whether any such property would be destroyed or damaged shall be guilty of an offence.

(2) A person who without lawful excuse destroys or damages any property, whether belonging to himself or another:

    (a) intending to destroy or damage any property or being reckless as to whether any property would be destroyed or damaged; and

    (b) intending by the destruction or damage to endanger the life of another or being reckless as to whether the life of another would be thereby endangered,

shall be guilty of an offence.

(3) An offence committed under this section by destroying or damaging property by fire shall be charged as arson.

Section 10 of the Criminal Damage Act 1971: interpretation

(1) In this Act 'property' means property of a tangible nature, whether real or personal, including money and:

    (a) including wild creatures which have been tamed or are ordinarily kept in captivity, and any other wild creatures or their carcasses if, but only if, they have been reduced into possession which has not been lost or abandoned or are in the course of being reduced into possession; but

    (b) not including mushrooms growing wild on any land or flowers, fruit or foliage of a plant growing wild on any land.

For the purposes of this subsection 'mushroom' includes any fungus and 'plant' includes any shrub or tree.

(2) Property shall be treated for the purposes of this Act as belonging to any person:

    (a) having the custody or control of it;

    (b) having in it any proprietary right or interest (not being an equitable interest arising only from an agreement to transfer or grant an interest); or

    (c) having a charge on it.

(3) Where property is subject to a trust, the persons to whom it belongs shall be so treated as including any person having a right to enforce the trust.

PROPERTY BELONGING TO ANOTHER

See the definitions provided by s 10 (above). Although the offence created by s1(1) of the Criminal Damage Act 1971 requires the destruction or damage of property 'belonging to another', it is possible to be guilty of an offence under s 1(1) even though the property damaged belongs to the defendant, provided that someone else also has a proprietary right in the property. For the offence of aggravated criminal damage under s 1(2) of the Criminal Damage Act 1971 it does not matter to whom the property belongs.

DAMAGE OR DESTROY

Damage need not be permanent: it is enough if taking remedial steps costs time, labour and expense, or if the value or usefulness of the property has been damaged.

Cox v Riley (1986) 83 Cr App R 54 (DC)

Stephen Brown LJ: ... The justices in the case state that they found the following facts: (1) the defendant was employed by Hi-Tech Profiles Limited to work on a computerised saw owned by that company; (2) that the computerised saw relied for its operation on a printed circuit card being inserted into it, containing programs which enabled the saw to be operated so that it could cut window frame profiles of different designs; (3) that the printed circuit card was of no use to the company unless it contained programs which enabled it to cause the saw to operate as (2) above; (4) that on 30 July 1984 the defendant blanked the computerised saw of all its 16 programs thereby erasing the said programs from the printed circuit card by operating the program cancellation facility, contained within the computerised saw, once for each individual program removed; (5) that the defendant's action rendered the computerised saw inoperable, save for limited manual operation, which would cause production to be slowed dramatically ...

They ask this court the following question: can the erasing of a program from printed circuit card which is used to operate a computerised saw constitute damage within the meaning of the Criminal Damage Act 1971? ...

The question of damage has been considered by the Court of Appeal, Criminal Division, on 29 November 1984 in the unreported case of *Henderson and Battley*. The court was presided over by Lawton LJ and he was sitting with Cantley J and Sir John Thompson. Cantley J gave the judgment of the court.

In that case the facts were different, but it is relevant on the meaning of damage. In that case the charge was one of damaging a development land site, intending to damage that property or being reckless as to whether it would be damaged. The facts concerned a development site in the Isle of Dogs which had been cleared for development. It was flat except for a pile of crushed concrete which was kept there intentionally so that it could be used eventually in the laying of temporary roads whilst the development was carried on.

On the occasion in question 30 lorry loads of soil and rubble and mud were tipped on to the site. The appellants in that case, pretending to act with authority, had been operating the site, as Cantley J said, impudently as a public tip and charging their customers for the rubbish which was tipped. There was a submission before the trial judge which was repeated before the Court of Appeal that what they had done could not be said to have damaged the land, bearing in mind that this was a site cleared for building development. The argument was that the land was not damaged because the land beneath the piles of rubbish which had been tipped upon it was in the same condition as it was before the rubbish was tipped upon it. It was argued that there must be a distinction between the cost of putting something right and actual damage.

Cantley J said in the course of this judgment at 3B of the transcript:

> There is of course such a distinction, but if as here there is evidence that the owner of the land reasonably found it necessary to spend about £2,000 to remove the results of the appellants' operations it is not irrelevant to the question of whether this land, as a building site, was damaged. Ultimately whether damage was done to this land was a question of fact and degree for the jury. Damage can be various kinds. In the *Concise Oxford Dictionary* 'damage' is defined as 'injury impairing value or usefulness'. That is a definition which would fit in very well with doing something to a cleared building site which at any rate for the time being impairs its usefulness as such. In addition, as it necessitates work and the expenditure of a large sum of money to restore it to its former state, it reduces its present value as a building site. This land was a perfectly good building site which did not need £2,000 spending on it in order to sell or use it as such until the appellants began their operations.

... It seems to me that the principle as explained by Cantley J applies in full measure to the present case. Undoubtedly ... the defendant in this instance for some reason, perhaps a grudge, wished to put out of action, albeit temporarily, the computerised saw, and he was able to do that by operating the computer blanking mechanism in order to erase from the printed circuit card the relevant programs. That made it necessary for time and labour and money to be expended in order to replace the relevant programs on the printed circuit card ...

It seems to me to be quite untenable to argue that what this defendant did on this occasion did not amount to causing damage to property, and for this reason I would dismiss the appeal.

I would answer the question posed by the justices ... with the emphatic answer yes.

R v Whiteley (1991) 93 Cr App R 25 (CA)

Facts: The appellant was a 'computer hacker'. He gained unauthorised access to a computer network ('JANET') and altered data contained on disks in the system, thereby causing the computers in question to fail and to be unable to operate properly; the computers had to be shut down for periods of time.

> **Lord Lane CJ**: ... The prosecution case was twofold. First, that the appellant caused criminal damage to the computers by bringing about temporary impairment of usefulness of them by causing them to be shut down for periods of time preventing them from operating properly; second, that he caused criminal damage to the disks by way of alteration to the state of the magnetic particles on them so as to delete and add files; the disks and the magnetic particles on them containing the information being one entity and capable of being damaged.

The jury acquitted the appellant on those counts which were based upon the first leg of the prosecution case, namely criminal damage to the computers. The counts on which they convicted were based upon the second leg, namely the allegation of damage to the disks ...

The evidence before the jury was that the disks are so constructed as to contain upon them thousands, if not millions, of magnetic particles. By issuing commands to the computer, impulses are produced which magnetise or demagnetise those particles in a particular way. By that means it is possible to write data or information on the disks and to program them to fulfil a variety of functions. By the same method it is possible to delete or alter data, information or instructions which have previously been written on to the disk ...

... What the Act requires to be proved is that tangible property has been damaged, not necessarily that the damage itself should be tangible. There can be no doubt that the magnetic particles upon the metal discs were a part of the disks and if the appellant was proved to have intentionally and without lawful excuse altered the particles in such a way as to cause an impairment of the value or usefulness of the disk to the owner, there would be damage within the meaning of s 1. The fact that the alteration could only be perceived by operating the computer did not make the alterations any the less real, or the damage, if the alteration amounted to damage, any the less within the ambit of the Act ...

... Any alteration to the physical nature of the property concerned may amount to damage within the meaning of the section. Whether it does so or not will depend upon the effect that the alteration has had upon the legitimate operator (who for convenience may be referred to as the owner). If the hacker's actions do not go beyond, for example, mere tinkering with an otherwise 'empty' disk, no damage would be established. Where, on the other hand, the interference with the disk amounts to an impairment of the value or usefulness of the disk to the owner, then the necessary damage is established ...

Notes and queries

1 Although *Cox v Riley* and *R v Whiteley* remain good law on the interpretation of the Criminal Damage Act 1971, and so the general principles they lay down remain valid, damage to computers is now governed by the Computer Misuse Act 1990.

2 *Roe v Kingerlee* [1986] Crim LR 735 confirms that it is not necessary that the damage caused should be permanent before an act can constitute criminal damage. Whether or not the application of graffiti to a structure will amount to causing criminal damage will be a question of fact and degree for the tribunal of fact. Hence in *Hardman and Others v The Chief Constable of Avon and Somerset Constabulary* [1986] Crim LR 330, HHJ Llewellyn-Jones sitting at Bristol Crown Court determined that human silhouettes painted on an asphalt pavement to represent vaporised human remains could amount to criminal damage notwithstanding that the 'paint' used was a fat-free unstable whitewash, which was soluble in water. There had been damage, which had caused expense and inconvenience to the local authority.

WITHOUT LAWFUL EXCUSE

Section 5 of the Criminal Damage Act 1971: 'without lawful excuse'

(1) This section applies to any offence under s 1(1) above and any offence under s 2 or 3 above other than one involving a threat by the person charged to destroy or damage property in a way which he knows is likely to endanger the life of another or involving an intent by the person charged to use or cause or permit the use of something in his custody or under his control so to destroy or damage property.

(2) A person charged with an offence to which this section applies shall, whether or not he would be treated for the purposes of this Act as having a lawful excuse apart from this subsection, be treated for those purposes as having a lawful excuse:

 (a) if at the time of the act or acts alleged to constitute the offence he believed that the person or persons whom he believed to be entitled to consent to the destruction of or damage to the property in question had so consented, or would have so consented to it if he or they had known of the destruction or damage and its circumstances; or

 (b) if he destroyed or damaged or threatened to destroy or damage the property in question or, in the case of a charge of an offence under s 3 above, intended to use or cause or permit the use of something to destroy or damage it, in order to protect property belonging to himself or another or a right or interest in property which was or which he believed to be vested in himself or another, and at the time of the act or acts alleged to constitute the offence he believed:

 (i) that the property, right or interest was in immediate need of protection; and

 (ii) that the means of protection adopted or proposed to be adopted were or would be reasonable having regard to all the circumstances.

 (iii) For the purposes of this section it is immaterial whether a belief is justified or not if it is honestly held.

 (iv) For the purposes of subsection (2) above a right or interest in property includes any right or privilege in or over land, whether created by grant, licence or otherwise.

 (v) This section shall not be construed as casting doubt on any defence recognised by law as a defence to criminal charges.

(3) For the purposes of this section it is immaterial whether a belief is justified or not if it is honestly held.

(4) For the purposes of subsection (2) above a right or interest in property includes any right or privilege in or over land, whether created by grant, licence or otherwise.

(5) This section shall not be construed as casting doubt on any defence recognised by law as a defence to criminal charges.

R v Denton [1981] 1 WLR 1446 (CA)

Lord Lane CJ: [The defendant was charged with] arson contrary to s 1(1) and (3) of the 1971 Act, the particulars being that the defendant:

> on the 3rd day of January 1980 without lawful excuse damaged by fire a building known as Barnfield Mill belonging to Leslie Fink & Co Ltd and the contents thereof belonging to Albus Products Ltd intending to damage such property or being reckless as to whether such property would be damaged.

The facts of the case are somewhat unusual. There is no dispute that on 3 January 1980 the defendant set light to some machinery in the cotton mill. The machinery was very badly damaged, and as a result of that conflagration damage was also done, to a much lesser degree it is true, to the building itself. The total damage to stock and building was said to be some £40,000.

On Monday 17 March 1980, the defendant presented himself at the police station and told the police that he had in fact started that fire. He described how he had done it, and he then made a statement under caution, in which he gave his reason for having started the fire: that it was for the benefit of the business, because the business was in difficulties, and, although he was going to get no direct benefit from it himself, he thought he would be doing a good turn to the financial status of the company if he were to set light to the premises and goods as he did ...

When it came to the trial ... he gave evidence that his employer, whom we will refer to as 'T' for obvious reasons, had asked him to put the machines out of action and he had agreed to set light to it. The reason given to him by the employer for that request was because the company was in difficulties; the way that T put it was: 'There is nothing like a good fire for improving the financial circumstances of a business.'

... It was agreed on all hands for the purpose of this case that T was the person who, any evil motives apart, was entitled to consent to the damage. It was likewise conceded that the defendant honestly believed that T occupied that position and was entitled to consent.

... It is quite apparent ... that in so far as the 1971 Act is concerned it is not an offence for a man to damage or injure or destroy to set fire to his own premises.

One therefore turns to see what the situation would have been had T made a confession in the same, or similar, terms as that made by the defendant, and to see what would have happened to the Crown's argument if the two of them, T and the defendant, stood charged under s 1(1) of the 1971 Act in the Crown Court. It is not an offence for a man to set light to his own property. So T would have been acquitted. But if the Crown is correct, the defendant, the man who had been charged with the task of actually putting the match to the polystyrene, and setting the fire alight, would have been convicted.

Quite apart from any other consideration, that is such an anomalous result that it cannot possibly be right. The answer is this: that one has to decide whether or not an offence is committed at the moment that the acts are alleged to be committed. The fact that somebody may have had a dishonest intent which in the end he was going to carry out, namely to claim from the insurance company, cannot turn what was not originally a crime into a crime. There is no unlawfulness under the 1971 Act in burning a house. It does not become unlawful because there may be an inchoate attempt to commit fraud contained in it; that is to say it does not become a crime under the 1971 Act, whatever may be the situation outside of the Act.

... Indeed it seems to us, if it is necessary to go as far as this, that it was probably unnecessary for the defendant to invoke s 5 of the 1971 Act at all, because he probably had a lawful excuse without it, in that T was lawfully entitled to burn the premises down. The defendant believed it. He believed that he was acting under the directions of T and that on its own, it seems to us, may well have provided him with a lawful excuse without having resort to s 5 ...

Note: Strictly speaking, the owner of the property was the limited company, not T. However, the decision of the court is sustainable on the basis that the defendant believed that T was entitled to authorise the destruction of the property. The present case may be contrasted with *R v Appleyard* where the managing director was convicted of destroying property belonging to his company; it was said that the company was a separate legal entity and so the defendant could not consent to the destruction of its property.

R v Hill; R v Hall (1989) 89 Cr App R 74

The appellants were convicted of criminal damage, having cut through the perimeter fencing of RAF bases. They appealed on the ground that the issue of lawful excuse had not been dealt with adequately by the trial judge. In particular they sought to rely on their assertion that if they could show that such bases were not secure, they would be closed and the surrounding properties would be at reduced risk of being targeted by hostile states armed with nuclear weapons.

Lord Lane CJ: The learned judge ... came to the conclusion that the causative relationship between the acts which [the appellants] intended to perform and the alleged protection was so tenuous, so nebulous, that the acts could not be said to be done to protect viewed objectively ... with reference to the provision that the lawful excuse must be based upon an immediate need for protection....the judge came to the ... conclusion that on the applicant's own evidence the applicant could not be said to have believed under the provisions of section 5(2)(b)(i) that the property was in immediate need of protection ... The judge in each case relied upon a decision of this court in *Hunt* (1978) 66 Cr App R 105. We have the advantage also of having that report in transcript. We also have before us a more recent decision of this court in *Ashford and Smith* [1988] Crim LR 682 ... in which very similar considerations were raised to those which exist in the present case. It also has the advantage of having set out the material findings of the court in *Hunt* which were delivered by Roskill LJ. I am referring to p 4 of the transcript in *Ashford and Smith*, and it will help to set out the basis of the decision not only in *Ashford and Smith* but also in *Hunt* if I read the passage. It runs as follows:

The judge relied very largely upon the decision of this court in *Hunt* (1978) 66 Cr App R 105. That was a case in which the appellant set fire to a guest room in an old people's home. He did so, he said, to draw attention to the defective fire alarm system. He was charged with arson, contrary to section 1(1) of the Criminal Damage Act 1971. He sought to set up the statutory defence under section 5(2) by claiming to have had a lawful excuse in doing what he did and that he was not reckless whether any such property would be destroyed. The trial judge withdrew the defence of lawful excuse from the jury and left the issue of recklessness for them to determine. The jury by a majority verdict convicted the appellant. On appeal [it was held that] applying the objective test, the trial judge had ruled correctly because what the appellant had done was not an act which in itself did protect or was capable of protecting property; but in order to draw attention to what in his view was an immediate need for protection by repairing the alarm system; thus the statutory defence under section 5(2) of the Act was not open to him; accordingly, the appeal would be dismissed.

Giving the judgment of the court Roskill LJ said, at p 108:

> Mr Marshall-Andrews' submission can be put thus: if this man honestly believed that that which he did was necessary in order to protect this property from the risk of fire and damage to the old people's home by reason of the absence of a working fire alarm, he was entitled to set fire to that bed and so to claim the statutory defence accorded by section 5(2). I have said we will assume in his favour that he possessed the requisite honest belief. But in our view the question whether he was entitled to the benefit of the defence turns upon the meaning of the words 'in order to protect property belonging to another'. It was argued that those words were subjective in concept, just like the words in the latter part of section 5(2)(b) which are subjective. We do not think that is right. The question whether or not a particular act of destruction or damage or threat of destruction or damage was done or made in order to protect property belonging to another must be, on the true construction of the statute, an objective test. Therefore we have to ask ourselves whether, whatever the state of this man's mind and assuming an honest belief, that which he admittedly did was done in order to protect this particular property, namely the old people's home in Hertfordshire? If one formulates the question in that way, in the view of each member of this court, for the reason Slynn J gave during the argument, it admits of only one answer: this was not done in order to protect property; it was done in order to draw attention to the defective state of the fire alarm. It was not an act which in itself did protect or was capable of protecting property.

Then the judgment in *Ashford and Smith*, delivered by Glidewell LJ continued as follows:

> In our view that reasoning applies exactly in the present case. Hunt is, of course, binding upon us. But even if it were not, we agree with the reasoning contained in it.

Now it is submitted by Mr. Bowyer [for the applicants] to us that the decision in Hunt and the decision in *Ashford and Smith* were wrong and that the test is a subjective test. In other words the submission is that it was a question of what the applicant believed and accordingly it should have been left to the jury as a matter of fact to decide what it was the applicant did believe.

We are bound by the decision in *Hunt* just as the court in *Ashford and Smith* were bound, unless that case can be demonstrated to have been wrongly decided in the light of previous authority ... we think that Hunt was correctly decided, for this reason. There are two aspects to this type of question. The first aspect is to decide what it was that the applicant, in this case Valerie Hill, in her own mind thought.

The learned judge assumed, and so do we, for the purposes of this decision, that everything she said about her reasoning was true. I have already perhaps given a sufficient outline of what it was she believed to demonstrate what is meant by that. Up to that point the test was subjective. In other words one is examining what is going on in the applicant's mind. Having done that, the judges in the present cases ... turned to the second aspect of the case, and that is this. He had to decide as a matter of law, which means objectively, whether it could be said that on those facts as believed by the applicant, snipping the strand of the wire, which she intended to do, could amount to something done to protect either the applicant's own home or the homes of her adjacent friends in Pembrokeshire. He decided, again quite rightly in our view, that that proposed act on her part was far too remote from the eventual aim at which she was targeting her actions to satisfy the test. It follows therefore, in our view, that the judges in the present two cases were absolutely right to come to the conclusion that they did so far as this aspect of the case is concerned, and to come to that conclusion as a matter of law, having decided the subjective test as the applicants wished them to be decided. The second half of the question was that of the immediacy of the danger. Here the wording of the Act, one reminds oneself, is as follows: She believed that 'the property ... was in immediate need of protection'. Once again the judge had to determine whether, on the facts as stated by the applicant, there was any evidence on which it could be said that she believed there was a need of protection from immediate danger. In our view that must mean evidence that she believed that immediate action had to be taken to do something which would otherwise be a crime in order to prevent the immediate risk of something worse happening. The answers which I have read in the evidence given by this woman (and the evidence given by the other applicant was very similar) drives this court to the conclusion, as they drove the respective judges to the conclusion, that there was no evidence on which it could be said that there was that belief.

Johnson v DPP [1994] Crim LR 673 (DC)

Facts: The appellant was a squatter who had damaged the door frame of a house he was occupying, by chiselling off the locks and replacing them with a lock of his own. He claimed that he had a lawful excuse under s 5(2)(b) of the Criminal Damage Act 1971 on the grounds that he had caused the damage in order to protect his own property, that he believed his property to be in immediate need of protection, and that the means which he had adopted were reasonable in all the circumstances.

Held: dismissing the appellant's appeal against conviction: that the damage to the door was not done to protect property and that the appellant had no belief that his property was in immediate need of protection.

The court had reached this conclusion by asking itself first the objective question of whether the act of damage was done in order to protect property. Then, there was the subjective question of whether the appellant believed that his property was in immediate need of protection and that the means adopted were reasonable. The test to be applied was whether he believed that immediate action had to be taken to do something which would otherwise be a crime, in order to prevent the immediate risk of something worse happening.

R v Baker and Wilkins [1997] Crim LR 497

Brooke LJ: The appellant, Janet Baker, was tried together with the appellant, Carl Wilkins ... Miss Baker and he were both convicted on Count 4 (criminal damage) which related to damage to the front door of a house belonging to a Mr Wonnacott ...

The factual background to this case is that Miss Baker gave birth to a daughter called Stephanie on 5 June 1990. Stephanie was born while Miss Baker and Mr Wakeling were living together, and Mr Wakeling has for nearly all her life been treated by both parties as her natural father, although his paternity has never been definitely established. After his relationship with Miss Baker ended, he did not seek to see Stephanie for about 18 months. By then he had met and married a lady called Sylvia, and this led him to getting into touch with Miss Baker so that he and his new wife could have contact with Stephanie. Miss Baker allowed Stephanie to stay with Mr and Mrs Wakeling shortly before the events that gave rise to these charges, and she stayed with them for three or four short visits before the incidents with which this court is now concerned.

Stephanie was due to be returned home after a visit of this type on Monday 7 November 1994, but the Wakelings rang up to say that she was ill, and that they would not now be returning her until 9th November. During the course of the next two days Miss Baker instructed solicitors to secure Stephanie's return, and the Wakelings for their part made allegations that she was showing signs of abuse, and a 3-day emergency protection order was obtained so that these matters could be investigated. Bromley Social Services in due course found no substance in the allegations, and the way should then have been clear for Stephanie to be returned to her mother on Friday 11 November when the protection order lapsed.

The Wakelings did not in the event make her available for return that day, and instead they went into hiding with the child. Miss Baker and Mr Wilkins were in constant touch with the police and Social Services, and they spent the weekend touring Gravesend looking for Stephanie.

The police did manage to persuade the Wakelings to make a telephone call to Miss Baker that weekend to reassure her. It was Mrs Wakeling who spoke to her. Miss Baker said in evidence that Mrs Wakeling told her that she and her husband were minded to take Stephanie to Scotland. She declined to say where they were at the time of the phone call or where they would be going. Mrs Wakeling denied that she had said anything about taking Stephanie to Scotland, and this was a matter hotly disputed at the trial.

At all events, without waiting for the court hearing which the solicitor had originally arranged for Wednesday 16 November, the appellants determined to take more active steps to recover Stephanie themselves on the Monday. To this end Miss Baker put an iron bar and a wooden chair leg into their car, and they and Miss Dighton then went out and waited for several hours outside the offices of Mr Wakeling's solicitor. They did this in the anticipation that Mr Wakeling might visit his solicitor that day; they then intended to try to track him back to where he was living and thus locate Stephanie. In due course Mr Wakeling did arrive at his solicitor's office. A friend of his, Mr Muggridge, had driven him there, and after a half-hour meeting with his solicitor Mr Wakeling left with Mr Muggridge. The appellants followed them ... [to] the house owned by Mr Wonnacott. At first there was no sign of anyone inside the house, but Miss Baker then heard Stephanie cry out. The appellants then broke in through the front door, which was largely made of glass (Count 4, criminal damage) ...

... In a very brief ruling the [trial] judge said that he intended to direct the jury that the intention to recover the child would not constitute lawful excuse, or a defence, or would make any violence lawful in respect of the affray charge. He later summed-up to the jury on this basis ...

... so far as Count 4 was concerned, there was an argument based on the wording of Section 5(2)(b) of the Criminal Damage Act 1971. This provides that there is lawful excuse for destroying or damaging property where this is done in order to protect property belonging to the defendant which is in immediate need of protection and where the means of protection adopted are reasonable. It was said that if the statute provides this express definition of reasonable excuse, it is possible to infer *a fortiori* that damage to property, when this is reasonably done for the protection of one's child, constitutes reasonable excuse ...

We turn ... to the possible defence that the desire to rescue Stephanie provided a lawful excuse for the appellants to batter down the door of the house in which she was detained in order to secure her release. [The relevant provisions of the Criminal Damage Act 1971 were recited.]

... It is quite clear that the circumstances provided for in section 5(2)(b) do not arise in the present case, since Stephanie did not represent property within the meaning of that section.

For the purposes of this appeal we are bound to assume that if a legitimate defence existed, there was an issue fit to be put to a jury on the evidence that the appellants honestly believed that Stephanie was being unlawfully detained, and the question we have to consider is whether and in what circumstances the criminal law permits someone holding such a belief in relation to a child, to take the law into their own hands, to use a colloquialism, and to batter down the door of the house in which she is detained in order to try to effect a rescue.

Chamberlain v Lindon [1998] 2 All ER 538 (DC)

Sullivan J: Mr Chamberlain appeals by way of case stated against a decision of Nuneaton Magistrates' Court dismissing an information preferred by him against the respondent, Mr Lindon, alleging that the respondent had, without lawful excuse, destroyed a new garden wall belonging to the appellant, contrary to section 1(1) of the Criminal Damage Act 1971.

After a five day hearing the magistrates dismissed the information because they were of the opinion that the respondent had a lawful excuse under section 5(2)(b) of the 1971 Act.

Reference was made to the provisions of s 5.

... The magistrates concluded that the respondent had a lawful excuse under section 5(2)(b) because:

(a) he had destroyed the wall in order to protect a right or interest in his property which he had believed to be vested in himself;

(b) he had honestly believed that the right or interest was in immediate need of protection;

(c) he had honestly believed that the means adopted were reasonable, having regard to all the circumstances of the case.

The magistrates pose two questions for the opinion of this court:

(i) Were we on the facts found proved entitled to find that the Respondent had a lawful excuse for the purposes of section 5(2)(b) of the Criminal Damage Act 1971?

(ii) Were we on the facts found proved entitled to acquit the Respondent?

Although, as a matter of form, this appeal comes before the court by way of case stated from the magistrates in a criminal matter, it is in substance a dispute between two neighbours as to their respective rights under the civil law and should have been resolved, in so far as litigation was required at all, in the county court.

A criminal prosecution was, in my view, a manifestly inappropriate procedure to adopt in the circumstances which I will now describe by way of summarising the very detailed findings of fact made by the magistrates.

Mill Farmhouse and the Mill are two adjacent properties in Mill Lane, Fillongley. Both had been in the appellant's ownership since the mid-1980s. He agreed to sell the Mill to the respondent in 1988. To obtain access to the Mill from the highway it is necessary to cross a parcel of land measuring 26 ft by 12 ft, which was retained as part of Mill Farmhouse.

The parcel of land is shown coloured brown on the plan before the court and was referred to by the magistrates as the 'brown land'. Following proceedings for specific performance, the appellant, by deed of transfer, in May 1991 granted the respondent the right to pass and repass over and along the roadway shown coloured brown on the said plan; ie over the brown land.

Since 1988 the respondent had used the brown land to gain both pedestrian and vehicular access to the Mill. The brown land is aligned roughly along a north-west south-east axis.

The respondent had taken to driving diagonally across the brown land (that is to say in approximately an east to west direction) to gain access to his property. Because of landscaping work undertaken by him on his own land it was not possible for him to drive into the Mill from the north-western end of the brown land.

The appellant formed the view that the respondent was not entitled to gain access to the Mill by driving diagonally over the brown land. Extensive correspondence ensued and in July 1995 the appellant laid the foundations of a wall along the south-western boundary of the brown land which would have the effect of preventing the respondent from driving diagonally over it. The respondent promptly drove his vehicle over the foundations and parked it on land belonging to the Mill immediately behind where the wall would be, so it would be trapped if the wall was built.

The wall was built and was completed in July 1995 at a cost of £1,800 leaving the respondent's vehicle trapped behind it.

The respondent complained to the applicant, contending (*inter alia*) that he had a right of access in whatever direction he chose across the full width of the brown land. The wall not merely prevented him from gaining access to the Mill in a diagonal direction across the brown land, it also reduced the width of the brown land by some 2 ft 9 in to 9 ft 3 in since it was built wholly upon the brown land.

There were also discussions and correspondence with the council as to the effect of the wall on a public footpath. Those discussions are not relevant for present purposes.

Following extensive correspondence the respondent gave notice that he would demolish the wall unless the appellant did so. The appellant did not and so the respondent was as good as his word and demolished the wall on 20 April 1996.

The magistrates found the following facts:

(w) The Respondent in destroying the wall did so in order to protect a right or interest in property that he believed to be vested in himself, namely his right to pass at a tangent by vehicle from the boxed brown area on the Plan onto his own adjoining land and also to use the full width of that area.

(x) At the time of destroying the wall the Respondent believed:

(i) that the right or interest was in immediate need of protection and;

(ii) that the means of protection adopted were reasonable having regard to all of the circumstances.

(y) Both of the above beliefs were honestly held by the Respondent in that at the time of demolishing the wall the respondent believed:

... that his right or interest was in immediate need of protection – that if he did not take immediate action he would be seen as accepting the situation which could ultimately lead to the relinquishing of part or all of his rights of access. The Respondent had entered into correspondence with the Appellant and his solicitors regarding the matter which lasted for almost a year and which was ongoing at the time of the incident. The Respondent could see no end to the dispute. This view was based on his experience of 8 years protracted, continuing and expensive litigation with [the appellant].

Mr Dean, on behalf of the appellant, originally challenged the magistrates' decision on four grounds. He no longer pursues the first of those grounds and puts forward the fourth as being simply supportive of the third ground.

By way of background I mention that the first ground was a contention that the respondent's right to pass over the brown land onto his own land was not a right that he was entitled to protect under section 5(2)(b). Mr Dean's concession that he can no longer pursue that ground is plainly correct in view of the provisions of section 5(4); which I have already read and which provides that a right or interest in property for the purpose of section 5(2)(b) includes:

... any right or privilege in or over land whether created by grant, licence or otherwise.

As Mr Forde's skeleton argument for the respondent submits: a right of way falls squarely within that definition.

Although this court is concerned with matters of civil law, only to the extent that it is necessary to decide whether the magistrates were justified in their conclusion that the respondent had a lawful excuse, one does not have to conduct a very elaborate investigation into the civil law to appreciate that obstructing a right of way is a nuisance and that the dominant owner, in this case the respondent, may in principle enter the land of the servient owner, the appellant, to abate the nuisance by removing the obstruction ... In *Lloyd v DPP* [1992] 1 All ER at p 982, Nolan LJ ... referred at p 989b to the judgment of Kerr LJ in *Stear v Scott* (unreported) in which the latter said that the ancient remedies of self-help should be carefully scrutinised in the present day and certainly not extended.

It requires no extension of the remedy of abatement to say that a person who finds his right of way obstructed may in principle remove that obstruction. I say 'in principle' because of certain observations of the Court of Appeal in *Burton v Winters* [1993] 1 WLR 1077, which was also referred to by Mr Dean and to which I will turn when I consider his fourth ground of challenge.

Under section 5(2)(b) one is entitled to protect not merely property but a right or interest in property. Since a person entitled to the benefit of a right of way may as a matter of civil law remove any obstruction to the way, it would indeed have been surprising if he did not have the protection of section 5(2)(b) if, in so doing, he necessarily destroyed or damaged the obstruction.

I turn to the second ground of challenge to the magistrates the decision. Mr Dean submits that the respondent's act of destroying the wall was not done in order to protect property but was done for the purpose of avoiding litigation.

He submits that the question whether a particular act of destruction was done in order to protect property, must be answered by reference to an objective test. In his skeleton he referred to a number of cases in support of that proposition.

In *R v Hunt* 66 Cr App R 105 Roskill LJ at p 108 said this:

> ... we have to ask ourselves whether, whatever the state of this man's mind and assuming an honest belief, that which he admittedly did was done in order to protect this particular property, namely, the old people's home in Hertfordshire?

In that case the appellant had been charged with arson contrary to section 1(1) of the 1971 Act. On his own case he had set fire to a room in an old people's home to draw attention to a defective fire alarm system. The judge withdrew the defence of lawful excuse from the jury. The Court of Appeal held that he was right to do so.

Reference was made to *R v Hill and Hall*, and *Johnson v Director Public Prosecutions*.

> [The observations in *R v Hill*; *R v Hall* on lawful excuse under s 5] ... were of course entirely appropriate in the circumstances of that case. They should not be taken out of that context and construed as though they were within an enactment of general applications.

> The appellants in those cases had professed to be concerned as to the potential consequences of a possible nuclear attack in the future. Here, on the facts, as believed by the respondent, his right of way was actually being obstructed. As Mr Forde points out it was not a case of a risk of there being an obstruction at some future speculative date, there was a present need to remove the obstruction.

> The respondent was not destroying or damaging property as some sort of preemptive strike to prevent some future obstruction. Mr Dean submits that the wall had stood for 9 months, and asks rhetorically, 'why then was there an immediate need to destroy it in April 1996?'.

In my view the respondent is not to be penalised for his attempt, through correspondence, to persuade the appellant to remove the wall. So long as the wall remained it was, on the facts as believed by the respondent, an obstruction to his right of way, and so there was an immediate need to remove it.

The magistrates found that he took the view, based on his experience with the appellant, that litigation would be protracted, and whilst it lasted the obstruction would remain.

As Mr Forde points out, for the reasons given in paragraph 2(y)(a) of the case stated (which I have already read), the longer the wall remained the more urgent the need to remove it, from the respondent's point of view, to avoid any suggestion of acquiesence in the obstruction.

Finally I turn to Mr Dean's fourth ground of challenge, which he advances not as a separate ground but in support of his third ground. He submits that at the worst the respondent had suffered a civil wrong and what he should have done is pursue a civil remedy in the civil courts, as Nolan LJ said in *Lloyd v DPP* at p 992e:

> That is what they are there for. Self-help involving the use of force can only be contemplated when there is no alternative.

Mr Dean accepts that it is not necessary in order to establish a defence under section 5 for the respondent to have exhausted all his civil remedies, but he refers by way of analogy to the Court of Appeal decision in *Burton v Winters* [1993] 1 WLR 1077. In that case a garage wall had been built along the boundary between the plaintiff and the defendant's properties so that half of it was on the plaintiff's land. She tried to get a mandatory injunction requiring the defendants to demolish the wall which would of course have had the effect of demolishing the garage also.

Her claim was dismissed by the courts but she refused to take no for an answer. She tried to obstruct the defendant's access to the garage by building a wall in front of it on the defendant's side of the boundary line. When that failed she repeatedly damaged the garage. The defendants were granted an injunction restraining her from such conduct, which she repeatedly flouted. Eventually she was committed to prison for two years for contempt. I mention those facts to show that it was something of an extreme case, even in the context of boundary disputes between neighbours.

Lloyd LJ, as he then was, with whom Connell J agreed, said, at p 1081D:

> Ever since the assize of nuisance became available, the courts have confined the remedy by way of self-redress to simple cases such as an overhanging branch, or an encroaching root, which would not justify the expense of legal proceedings, and urgent cases which require an immediate remedy. Thus, it was Bracton's view that where there is resort to self-redress, the remedy should be taken without delay. In *Blackstone's Commentaries on the Laws of England*, Book III, Chapter 1 we find:
>
> > And the reason why the law allows this private and summary method of doing one's self-justice, is because injuries of this kind, which obstruct or annoy such things as are of a daily convenience and use, require an immediate remedy; and cannot wait for the slow progress of the ordinary forms of justice.

Lloyd LJ referred to a number of academic writers, specifically *Prosser and Keeton*, which says this:

> Consequently the privilege [of abatement] must be exercised within a reasonable time after knowledge of nuisance is acquired or should have been acquired by the person entitled to abate; if there has been sufficient delay to allow resort to legal process, the reason for the privilege fails, and the privilege with it.

Lloyd LJ when on:

> The authority cited for this proposition is *Moffett v Brewer* (1948) Iowa Rep (1 Greene) 348, 350 where Greene J said:
>
>> This summary method of redressing a grievance, by an act of an injured party, should be regarded with great jealousy, and authorised only in cases of particular emergency, requiring a more speedy remedy than can be had by the ordinary proceedings at law.

He then applied that stream of authority to the facts of the case before him, making the point that not only was there ample time for the plaintiff to wait for the slow process of the ordinary course of justice, she actually did so. He then referred to the House of Lords decision in *Lagan Navigation Co v Lambeg Bleaching, Dyeing and Finishing Co Ltd* [1927] AC 226 at p 224 *per* Lord Atkinson. That was authority for the proposition that the law does not favour the remedy of abatement. In conclusion he said this:

> In my opinion, this never was an appropriate case for self-redress, even if the plaintiff had acted promptly. There was no emergency. There were difficult questions of law and fact to be considered and the remedy by way of self-redress, if it had resulted in the demolition of the garage wall, would have been out of all proportion to the damage suffered by the plaintiff. But, even if there ever had been a right of self-redress, it ceased when Judge Main refused to grant a mandatory injunction. We are now in a position to answer the question left open by Chitty J in *Lane v Capsey* [1891] 3 Ch 411. Self-redress is a summary remedy, which is justified only in clear and simple cases, or in an emergency. Where a plaintiff has applied for a mandatory injunction and failed, the sole justification for a summary remedy has gone. The court has decided the very point in issue. This is so whether the complaint lies in trespass or nuisance.

It will be noted that the final matter referred to by Lloyd LJ in that case would have been sufficient to dispose of the appeal. The plaintiff had sought and had been refused a mandatory injunction. She could not thereafter resort to self-help. That circumstance does not apply here.

I find it unnecessary to decide whether, as a matter of civil law, the present case is properly described as a clear and simple case. Demolishing a garage which projects very slightly into one's land may well be a very different matter on the facts from demolishing a wall if it obstructs a right of way.

It is unnecessary to reach a conclusion as to whether the respondent's self-help was justified as a matter of civil law on the facts of this case, because the appellant chose to take proceedings in the criminal courts. Rather than suing the respondent for trespass he preferred an information charging the respondent with criminal damage. I have already indicated that, in my view, criminal proceedings were inappropriate. At worst a civil wrong had been committed, either nuisance by the appellant or trespass by the respondent. It should have been for the civil courts to decide which.

In the criminal context the question is not whether the means of protection adopted by the respondent were objectively reasonable, having regard to all the circumstances, but whether the respondent believed them to be so, and by virtue of section 5(3) it is immaterial whether his belief was justified, provided it was honestly held.

On the facts found by the justices there can be no doubt that the respondent honestly believed that the means he adopted were reasonable in all of the circumstances of this case.

For these reasons I would answer each of the two questions posed by the Justices in the affirmative and would dismiss this appeal.

Aggravated criminal damage (s 1(2))

R v Steer [1988] AC 111 (HL)

Lord Bridge of Harwich: My Lords, in the early hours of 8 June 1985 the respondent went to the bungalow of his former business partner, David Gregory, against whom he bore some grudge. He was armed with an automatic .22 rifle. He rang the bell and woke Mr and Mrs Gregory, who looked out of their bedroom window. The respondent fired a shot aimed at the bedroom window. He then fired two further shots, one at another window and one at the front door. Fortunately no one was hurt. It was never suggested that the first shot had been aimed at Mr or Mrs Gregory.

The defendant was charged with possession of a firearm with intent to endanger life (s 16 of the Firearms Act 1968), along with criminal damage to the bedroom window (s 1(1) of the Criminal Damage Act 1971) and with criminal damage with intent to endanger the lives of Mr and Mrs Gregory or being reckless whether their lives would be endangered (s 1(2) of the Criminal Damage Act 1971).

It is to be observed that the offence created by subsection (2), save that it may be committed by destroying or damaging one's own property, is simply an aggravated form of the offence created by subsection (1), in which the prosecution must prove, in addition to the ingredients of the offence under subsection (1), the further mental element specified by subsection (2)(b) ...

We must, of course, approach the matter on the footing, implicit in the outcome of the trial, that the respondent, in firing at the bedroom window, had no intent to endanger life, but accepts that he was reckless whether life would be endangered.

Under both limbs or s 1 of the Act of 1971 it is the essence of the offence which the section creates that the defendant has destroyed or damaged property. For the purpose of analysis it may be convenient to omit the reference to destruction and to concentrate on the references to damage, which was all that was here involved. To be guilty under subsection (1) the defendant must have intended or been reckless as to the damage to property which he caused. To be guilty under subsection (2) he must additionally have intended to endanger life or been reckless whether life should be endangered 'by damage' to property which he caused. This is the context in which the words must be construed and it seems to me impossible to read the words 'by the damage' as meaning 'by the damage or by the act which caused the damage ...

I would accordingly dismiss the appeal. The certified question should be answered as follows:

> On the true construction of s 1(2)(b) of the Criminal Damage Act 1971 the prosecution are required to prove that the danger to life resulted from the destruction of or damage to property; it is not sufficient for the prosecution to prove that it resulted from the act of the defendant which caused the destruction or damage.

R v Dudley [1989] Crim LR 57 (CA)

Facts: Dudley, who had a grievance against a particular family, consumed drink and drugs, went to their house and, using an accelerant, threw a fire bomb at the house, causing a high sheet of flame outside the glass door. The fire was extinguished by the family and only trivial damage was caused.

Held (distinguishing *R v Steer* [1988] AC 111): The words 'destruction or damage' in s 1(2)(b) of the Act (endangering life) referred back to the destruction or damage intended, or as to which there was recklessness, in s 1(2)(a) (damaging property). The words did not refer to the destruction or damage actually caused; if they did, injustice would be done in the converse case where someone was reckless only as to trivial damage but by some mishap caused danger to life.

R v Webster and Others; R v Warwick [1995] 2 All ER 168 (CA)

Lord Taylor of Gosforth CJ: ... Two points must be stressed. First, what has to be proved under s 1(2)(b) is not whether and how life was in fact endangered (if it was) but whether and how it was intended to be endangered or there was an obvious risk of it being endangered.

Second, an issue has been argued before us as to the meaning of 'the destruction or damage' in s 1(2)(b) ... This very point was decided by this court in *R v Dudley* [1989] Crim LR 57 ...

... Staughton LJ [in *R v Dudley*] stated that the House of Lords had not had to deal with this point in *R v Steer* [1988] AC 111. He said:

> It would seem to us, on a mere reading of the section, that the words 'destruction or damage' in s 1(2)(b) refer back to the destruction or damage which has to have been intended by the defendant in s 1(2)(a) or as to which he has to have been reckless, and that they do not refer to the destruction or damage which in fact occurred.

We agree ... In our view, the true construction of s 1(2) is that the *actus reus* is defined in the first two lines of the subsection, while paras (a) and (b) deal with *mens rea* and are conjunctive in the way described by Staughton LJ. Otherwise, the gravamen of an offence involving damage by missile would depend not on the defendant's intention but on whether he was a good shot in seeking to carry it out.

Thus, if a defendant throws a brick at the windscreen of a moving vehicle, given that he causes some damage to the vehicle, whether he is guilty under s 1(2) does not depend on whether the brick hits or misses the windscreen, but whether he intended to hit it and intended that the damage therefrom should endanger life or whether he was reckless as to that outcome. As to the dropping of stones from bridges, the effect of the statute may be thought strange. If the defendant's intention is that the stone itself should crash through the roof of a train or motor vehicle and thereby directly injure a passenger, or if he was reckless only as to that outcome, the section would not bite. That would follow from the *ratio* in *R v Steer* and is no doubt why Lord Bridge made the comment he did about missiles from motorway bridges. If, however, the defendant intended or was reckless that the stone would smash the roof of the train or vehicle so that metal or wood struts from the roof would or obviously might descend upon a passenger endangering life, he would surely be guilty. This may seem to many a dismal distinction.

We proceed to consider the two cases before us individually.

[In] *R v Asquith, Webster and Seamans* ... the facts were that at about 8.25 pm on 18 May 1992 the appellants pushed a coping stone weighing 1 to 2 cwt from the parapet of a railway bridge in the Burnley area onto a two-carriage passenger train passing below. The stone landed on the first carriage, showering the passengers with glass fibre and polystyrene-type material from the roof. Had it not landed on the carriage's rear bulkhead, the stone would have fallen into the compartment. As it was, only a corner of the stone penetrated the roof. Nobody received any physical injury, although passengers were shocked and affected for some time thereafter ...

... If the intention was that the stone itself should endanger the life of the passengers, then the 'pusher' would not be guilty of this offence ... In our view, by convicting each of the appellants ... the jury must be taken to have found ... that each of them intended the stone itself to crash through the roof and endanger life. The conviction on that basis alone cannot be sustained. However, the jury's finding of an intent by each appellant to endanger life by causing the stone itself to penetrate the roof must, in common sense, carry the implication that they were each reckless as to endangering life by whatever damage the stone might do when it fell. If the intention was for the stone to penetrate the roof, there was clearly an obvious risk that it might endanger life by bringing parts of the roof down into the compartment, quite apart from other obvious risks such as derailment if it fell in front of the train or struck the driver's cab, incapacitating him or the controls.

In the circumstances, we consider the proper course is for us to ... substitute in each case a conviction ... of 'being reckless as to whether the life of another would thereby be endangered'. This we do.

[In] *R v Warwick* ... [at] about 3.30 pm [on 21 February 1992], two police constables, PC Tams and PC McCabe, driving a police van, saw the stolen Fiesta parked outside the appellant's mother's house. They drew alongside it and stopped, intending to arrest the occupant. Both officers recognised the driver as the appellant, whom they knew. He drove off and the officers followed but lost sight of the Fiesta.

About 4.20 pm two other police officers, PC Butcher and PC Davies, in a marked police car, saw the stolen Fiesta in another road at Teesside. The vehicle was stationary and facing away from them. As they drew near to it, a youth wearing a black balaclava emerged through its sunroof with a large brick in his hand, making as if to throw it. PC Butcher reversed his car away from the Fiesta but it reversed towards him. The youth threw the brick at the police car but missed. The Fiesta then reversed into a driveway and emerged, accelerating forwards in the direction of the police car as if about to ram it. PC Davies shouted a warning to PC Butcher who swerved, hitting a bus at a road junction. PC Davies was meanwhile radioing for assistance and recognised the driver of the Fiesta as the appellant, whom he knew. After hitting the bus, PC Butcher drove on and the youth standing up through the Fiesta's sunroof threw a brick at the police car. The brick smashed the rear window, showering the officers with broken glass. At that moment, PC Butcher was accelerating up to 30 mph, the road was busy and cars were passing in both directions. PC Butcher increased his speed, but the Fiesta rammed his vehicle so that he had great difficulty in retaining control of it. Another brick was thrown through the broken rear window, hitting PC Davies on the head, and landing in the footwell. An ice cream van was turning into the road. PC Butcher turned to avoid being pushed into it by the Fiesta, which was close up behind him. The Fiesta then rammed into the police car a second time, causing it to strike a glancing blow to the ice cream van. Further on, as PC Butcher reduced his speed because of parked cars and the number of children who were about, his vehicle was rammed a third time from behind by the Fiesta, which subsequently turned off onto a side road ...

At 4.25 pm two more police constables, PC Cane and PC Mitchinson, were in another marked police car near Eston, a mile or so from the earlier rammings. The stolen Fiesta came into the road where these officers were and accelerated towards their car as if to ram it. PC Cane went into reverse and backed his car some way down the road. The Fiesta reappeared shortly afterwards out of another side road, only 12 feet away from the police car. The officers saw that apart from the driver there was a front seat passenger wearing a balaclava and a youth in the back with a white baseball cap. The Fiesta reversed towards the police car, which reversed away. The youth with the balaclava stood up again through the sunroof and threw a large stone towards the front of the police car, hitting and damaging its bonnet ...

... If the intention was to break the windscreen or window by hurling a brick or stone, the jury would be entitled to infer that there was an intention to shower the driver with broken glass. If as a result of being so showered he were to lose control of the vehicle so that his life and that of his passengers or other road users were endangered, a jury could properly find that that danger was caused and intended to be caused by the broken glass, ie the damage to the vehicle. Clearly ... an intention to render the windscreen opaque, or recklessness as to its becoming so, could invoke the section. Likewise, if a defendant deliberately rams a vehicle in moving traffic, it would be open to a jury to infer an intention to disable the vehicle, for example by damaging the suspension, by damaging the steering, by buckling the bodywork onto the tyres and thereby causing a blowout. Any of these forms of damage in moving traffic could well endanger life and in our judgment it would be open to a jury, hearing evidence of deliberate ramming of a police car, to infer that the intention was to endanger life by damaging the vehicle.

The circumstances in this case are clearly distinguishable from those in *R v Steer*. To shower the driver of a moving vehicle with broken glass or ram his vehicle in moving traffic are clearly distinguishable from merely piercing the window or door of a stationary house by discharging an air rifle ...

The mental element: intention or recklessness

The Criminal Damage Act 1971 uses the words 'intending' and 'being reckless' in several places. It is the term 'reckless' which has generated the greatest weight of authority. The starting point for any discussion of 'recklessness' must be the speech of Lord Diplock in *R v Caldwell* [1982] AC 341 extracted in Chapter 4.

The mental element: mistaken belief

R v Smith (David Raymond) [1974] QB 354 (CA)

James LJ: ... The question of law in this appeal arises in this way. In 1970 the appellant became the tenant of a ground floor flat at 209 Freemasons Road, London E16. The letting included a conservatory. In the conservatory the appellant and his brother, who lived with him, installed some electrical wiring for use with stereo equipment. Also, with the landlord's permission, they put up roofing material and asbestos wall panels and laid floorboards. There is no dispute that the roofing, wall panels and floorboards became part of the house and, in law, the property of the landlord. Then in 1972 the appellant gave notice to quit and asked the landlord to allow the appellant's brother to remain as tenant of the flat. On 18 September 1972 the landlord informed the appellant that his brother could not remain. On the next day the appellant damaged the roofing, wall panels and floor boards he had installed in order – according to the appellant and his brother – to gain access to and remove the wiring. The extent of the damage was £130. When interviewed by the police, the appellant said, 'Look, how can I be done for smashing my own property. I put the flooring and that in, so if I want to pull it down it's a matter for me' ...

[The appellant was charged with criminal damage of the landlord's property, contrary to s 1(1) of the Criminal Damage Act 1971.]

The appellant's defence was that he honestly believed that the damage he did was to his own property, that he believed that he was entitled to damage his own property and therefore that he had a lawful excuse for his actions causing the damage ...

His Lordship quoted from s 1 of the Criminal Damage Act 1971 and then considered a number of arguments raised by counsel for the appellant. His Lordship concluded:

Construing the language of s 1(1) we have no doubt that the *actus reus* is 'destroying or damaging any property belonging to another'. It is not possible to exclude the words 'belonging to another' which describe the 'property'. Applying the ordinary principles of *mens rea*, the intention and recklessness and the absence of lawful excuse are required to constitute the offence have reference to property belonging to another. It follows that in our judgment no offence is committed under this section if a person destroys or causes damage to property belonging to another if he does so in the honest though mistaken belief that the property is his own, and provided that the belief is honestly held it is irrelevant to consider whether or not it is a justifiable belief ...

The mental element: the effect of intoxication under s 5

Jaggard v Dickinson [1981] QB 527 (CA)

Mustill J: ... The facts set out in the case [stated by the justices who convicted the defendant] are short but striking. On the evening of 11 October 1978, the defendant had been drinking. At 10.45 pm she engaged a taxi to take her to 67 Carnach Green, South Ockendon, a house occupied by Mr Heyfron, a gentleman with whom she had a relationship such that, in the words of the justices, she had his consent at any time to treat his property as if it were her own. Alighting from the taxi, she entered the garden, but was asked to leave by a Mrs Raven, who was a stranger to her. Persisting, she broke the glass in the hallway of the house. She then went to the back door, where she broke another window, and gained entry to the house, damaging a net curtain in the process. At some time thereafter, in circumstances not described by the justices, it became clear that the house was not 67 Carnach Green, but 35 Carnach Green, a house of identical outward appearance, occupied by Mrs Raven. The justices have found that the defendant did believe that she was breaking into the property of Mr Heyfron, but that this mistake was brought about by a state of self-induced intoxication.

His Lordship quoted ss 1(1) and 5(2) of the Criminal Damage Act 1971 and went on:

It is convenient to refer to the exculpatory provisions of s 5(2) as if they created a defence, whilst recognising that the burden of disproving the facts referred to by the subsection remains on the prosecution.

The justices held that the defendant was not entitled to rely on s 5(2) of the Act of 1971, since the belief relied upon was brought about by a state of self-induced intoxication.

In support of the conviction [counsel for the prosecutor] advanced an argument which may be summarised as follows: (1) Where an offence is one of 'basic intent', in contrast to one of 'specific intent', the fact that the accused was in a state of self-induced intoxication at the time when he did the acts constituting the *actus reus* does not prevent him from possessing the *mens rea* necessary to constitute the offence: see *R v Morgan* [1976] AC 182 and *R v Majewski* [1977] AC 443. (2) Section 1(1) of the Act of 1971 creates an offence of basic intent: *R v Stephenson* [1979] QB 695. (3) Section 5(3) has no bearing on the present issue. It does not create a separate defence, but is no more than a partial definition of the expression 'without lawful excuse' in s 1(1). The absence of lawful excuse forms an element in the *mens rea*: see *R v Smith (David)* ... Accordingly, since drunkenness does not negative *mens rea* in crimes of basic intent, it cannot be relied on as part of a defence based on s 5(2).

Whilst this is an attractive submission, we consider it to be unsound, for the following reasons. In the first place, the argument transfers the distinction between offences of specific and of basic intent to a context in which it has no place. The distinction is material where the accused relies on his own drunkenness as a ground for denying that he had the degree of intention or recklessness required in order to constitute the offence. Here, by contrast, the defendant does not rely on her drunkenness to displace an inference of intent or recklessness; indeed she does not rely on it at all. Her defence is founded on the state of belief called for by s 5(2).

True, the fact of the defendant's intoxication was relevant to the defence under s (2), for it helped to explain what would otherwise have been inexplicable, and hence lent colour to her evidence about the state of her belief. This is not the same as using drunkenness to rebut an inference of intention or recklessness. Belief, like intention or recklessness, is a state of mind: but they are not the same states of mind.

Can it nevertheless be said that, even if the context is different, the principles established by *R v Majewski* [1977] AC 443 ought to be applied to this new situation? If the basis of the decision in *R v Majewski* had been that drunkenness does not prevent a person from having an intent or being reckless, then there would be grounds for saying that it should equally be left out of account when deciding on his state of belief. But this is not our view what *R v Majewski* decided. The House of Lords did not conclude that intoxication was irrelevant to the fact of the accused's state of mind, but rather that, whatever might have been his actual state of mind, he should for reasons of policy be precluded from relying on any alteration in that state brought about by self-induced intoxication. The same considerations of policy apply to the intent or recklessness which is the *mens rea* of the offence created by s 1(1), and that offence is accordingly regarded as one of basic intent: see *R v Stephenson* [1979] QB 695. It is indeed essential that this should be so, for drink so often plays a part in offences of criminal damage; and to admit drunkenness as a potential means of escaping liability would provide much too ready a means of avoiding conviction. But these considerations do not apply to a case where Parliament has specifically required the court to consider the accused's actual state of belief, not the state of belief which ought to have existed. This seems to us to show that the court is required by s 5(3) to focus on the existence of the belief, not its intellectual soundness; and a belief can be just as much honestly held if it is induced by intoxication, as if it stems from stupidity, forgetfulness or inattention. It was, however, urged that we could not properly read s 5(2) in isolation from s 1(1), which forms the context of the words, 'without lawful excuse', partially defined by s 5(2). Once the words are put in context, so it is maintained, it can be seen that the law must treat drunkenness in the same way in relation to lawful excuse (and hence belief) as it does to intention and recklessness; for they are all part of the *mens rea* of the offence. To fragment the *mens rea*, so as to treat one part of it as affected by drunkenness in one way, and the remainder as affected in a different way, would make the law impossibly complicated to enforce.

If it had been necessary to decide whether, for all purposes, the *mens rea* of an offence under s 1(1) extends as far as an intent (or recklessness) as to the existence of a lawful excuse, I should have wished to consider the observations of James LJ delivering the judgment of the Court of Appeal in *R v Smith (David)* ... I do not however find it necessary to reach a conclusion on this matter, and will only say that I am not at present convinced that, when these observations are read in the context of the judgment as a whole, they have the meaning which the prosecutor has sought to put upon them. In my view, however, the answer to the argument lies in the fact that any distinction which has to be drawn as to the effect of drunkenness arises from the scheme of the Act of 1971 itself. No doubt the *mens rea* is in general indivisible, with no distinction being possible as regards the effect of drunkenness. But Parliament has specifically isolated one subjective element, in the shape of honest belief, and has given it separate treatment, and its own special gloss in s 5(3). This being so, there is nothing objectionable in giving it special treatment as regards drunkenness, in accordance with the natural meaning of its words.

In these circumstances, I would hold that the justices were in error when they decided that the defence furnished to the defendant by s 5(2) was lost because the defendant was drunk at the time. I would therefore allow the appeal.

The mental element: aggravated criminal damage

See *R v Steer* (above).

AG's Ref (No 3 of 1992) [1994] 1 WLR 409 (CA)

Schiemann J: ... The point of law which has been referred to us was formulated as follows:

> Whether on a charge of attempted arson in the aggravated form contemplated by s 1(2) of the Criminal Damage Act 1971, in addition to establishing a specific intent to cause damage by fire, it is sufficient to prove that the defendant was reckless as to whether life would thereby be endangered.

The acquittals which have given rise to this reference had the following background according to the prosecution evidence. Following previous attacks upon their property the complainants maintained a night-time watch over their premises from a motor car (a Ford Granada). In the early hours of the morning the respondents came upon the scene in a vehicle. Inside this car, a Sierra, was a milk crate containing a number of petrol bombs, matches, a petrol can and some rags. As the Sierra approached the complainants, four inside their car and two persons on the pavement talking to them, a lighted petrol bomb was thrown towards them from the Sierra. The prosecution's case was that it was thrown at the Granada and its occupants. The petrol bomb in fact passed over the top of the Granada and smashed against the garden wall of a house a pavement's width away from the car. The Sierra accelerated away but crashed, and the respondents were arrested.

At the trial count 1 of the indictment alleged attempted aggravated arson, specifying in the particulars of offence, *inter alia*, an intent to endanger life. Count 2 alleged attempted aggravated arson, specifying in the particulars of offence, *inter alia*, recklessness as to whether life would be endangered ...

[The trial judge directed acquittal on both counts; the present appeal is concerned only with the acquittal on count 2] ...

... [A]lthough in the present reference the question is posed in relation to arson, it has not been submitted that the presence or absence of fire makes any difference to the answer to the question posed which applies to any form of attempted criminal damage. So we omit any further reference to the element of fire in this judgment ...

So far as the completed simple offence is concerned, the prosecution needs to prove (1) property belonging to another was damaged by the defendant; (2) the state of mind of the defendant was one of the following, (a) he intended to damage such property, or (b) he was reckless as to whether any such property would be damaged.

In the case of the completed aggravated offence the prosecution needs to prove (1) the defendant in fact damaged property, whether belonging to himself or another;

(2) that the state of mind of the defendant was one of the following, (a) he intended to damage property, and intended by the damage to endanger the life of another, or (b) he intended to damage property and was reckless as to whether the life of another would be thereby endangered, or (c) he was reckless as to whether any property would be damaged and was reckless as to whether the life of another would be thereby endangered.

It is to be noted that the property referred to under (1) (to which we shall hereafter refer as 'the first-named property') is not necessarily the same property as that referred to in (2) (to which we shall refer as 'the second-named property'), although it normally will be.

Thus a man who (1) owns a crane from which is suspended a heavy object and (2) cuts the rope (the first-named property) which holds the object with the result that (3) the object falls and hits the roof of a passing car (the second-named property) which roof (4) collapses killing the driver, would be guilty if it could be shown that he damaged the rope, was reckless as to whether this would damage the car, and was reckless as to whether the life of the driver of the car would be endangered by the damage to the car.

All the foregoing is common ground. The problem which has given rise to this reference relates to an attempt to commit the aggravated offence in circumstances where the first-named property is the same as the second-named property in the instant case a car. It amounts to this: whether, if the state of mind of the defendant was that postulated in (2)(b) above, namely that he intended to damage property and was reckless as to whether the life of another would thereby be endangered, and whilst in that state of mind he did an act which was more than merely preparatory to the offence, he is guilty of attempting to commit that offence ...

So far as attempting to commit the simple offence is concerned, in order to convict on such a charge it must be proved that the defendant (a) did an act which was more than merely preparatory to the commission of the offence and (b) did an act intending to damage any property belonging to another.

One way of analysing the situation is to say that a defendant, in order to be guilty of an attempt, must be in one of the states of mind required for the commission of the full offence, and did his best, as far as he could, to supply what was missing from the completion of the offence. It is the policy of the law that such people should be punished notwithstanding that in fact the intentions of such a defendant have not been fulfilled.

If the facts are that, although the defendant had one of the appropriate states of mind required for the complete offence, but the physical element required for the commission of the complete offence is missing, the defendant is not to be convicted unless it can be shown that he intended to supply that physical element ...

We turn finally to the attempt to commit the aggravated offence. In the present case, what was missing to prevent a conviction for the completed offence was damage to the property referred to in the opening lines of s 1(2) of the 1981 Act, what in the example of a crane, which we gave earlier in this judgment, we referred to as 'the first-named property'. Such damage is essential for the completed offence. If a defendant does not intend to cause such damage he cannot intend to commit the completed offence. At worst he is reckless as to whether the offence is committed. The law of attempt is concerned with those who are intending to commit crimes. If that intent cannot be shown, then there can be no conviction.

However, the crime here consisted of doing certain acts in a certain state of mind in circumstances where the first-named property and the second-named property were the same, in short where the danger to life arose from the damage to the property which the defendant intended to damage. The substantive crime is committed if the defendant damaged property in a state of mind where he was reckless as to whether the life of another would thereby be endangered. We see no reason why there should not be a conviction for attempt if the prosecution can show that he, in that state of mind, intended to damage the property by throwing a bomb at it. One analysis of this situation is to say that although the defendant was in an appropriate state of mind to render him guilty of the completed offence the prosecution had not proved the physical element of the completed offence, and therefore he is not guilty of the completed offence. If, on a charge of attempting to commit the offence, the prosecution can show not only the state of mind required for the completed offence but also that the defendant intended to supply the missing physical element of the completed offence, that suffices for a conviction. That cannot be done merely by the prosecution showing him to be reckless. The defendant must intend to damage property, but there is no need for a graver mental state than is required for the full offence ...

We answer [the referred question] in the affirmative.

We add that, in circumstances where the first-named property is not the same as the second-named property, in addition to establishing a specific intent to cause damage by fire to the first named property, it is sufficient to prove that the defendant was reckless as to as to whether any second-named property was damaged and reckless as to whether the life of another would be endangered by the damage to the second-named property.

OTHER OFFENCES UNDER THE CRIMINAL DAMAGE ACT 1971

Section 2 of the Criminal Damage Act 1971: threats to destroy or damage property

A person who without lawful excuse makes to another a threat, intending that that other would fear it would be carried out:

(a) to destroy or damage any property belonging to that other or a third person; or

(b) to destroy or damage his own property in a way which he knows is likely to endanger the life of that other or a third person,

shall be guilty of an offence.

Section 3 of the Criminal Damage Act 1971: possessing anything with intent to destroy or damage property

A person who has anything in his custody or under his control intending without lawful excuse to use it or cause or permit another to use it:

(a) to destroy or damage any property belonging to some other person; or

(b) to destroy or damage his own or the user's property in a way which he knows is likely to endanger the life of some other person,

shall be guilty of an offence.

RACIALLY MOTIVATED CRIMINAL DAMAGE

Section30 of the Crime and Disorder Act 1998: racially aggravated criminal damage

(1) A person is guilty of an offence under this section if he commits an offence under section 1(1) of the Criminal Damage Act 1971 (destroying or damaging property belonging to another) which is racially aggravated for the purposes of this section.

(2) A person guilty of an offence under this section shall be liable

    (a) on summary conviction, to imprisonment for a term not exceeding six months or to a fine not exceeding the statutory maximum, or to both;

    (b) on conviction on indictment, to imprisonment for a term not exceeding fourteen years or to a fine, or to both.

(3) For the purposes of this section, section 28(1)(a) above shall have effect as if the person to whom the property belongs or is treated as belonging for the purposes of that Act were the victim of the offence.

Section 28 of the Crime and Disorder Act defines 'racially aggravated' for the purposes of s 30 – it is set out in Chapter 16 in the context of racially aggravated assaults.

Notes and queries

1　In *Lloyd v Director of Public Prosecutions* [1992] 1 All ER 982, the Divisional Court rejected the contention that there was a general defence of lawful excuse available to a motorist who damaged a car clamp that had been used to detain his illegally parked car. Nolan LJ observed:

> ... as a general rule, if a motorist parks his car without permission on another person's property knowing that by doing so he runs the risk of it being clamped, he has no right to damage or destroy the clamp. If he does so he will be guilty of a criminal offence.

2　The offence of arson, and the aggravated forms of criminal damage carry the possibility of life imprisonment. All other offences under the 1971 Act carry the possibility of up to 10 years' imprisonment following conviction on indictment.

Further reading

DW Elliot, 'Endangering life by destroying or damaging property' [1997] Crim LR 382

CHAPTER 24

OFFENCES INVOLVING WEAPONS

The offences related to possession of offensive weapons can be seen, to a large extent, as being ancillary to offences against the person. The weapons offences are essentially preventative in nature and may be used where, for example, there is insufficient evidence to charge an inchoate form of common or statutory assault.

Section 1 of the Prevention of Crime Act 1953: possessing an offensive weapon

(1) Any person who without lawful authority or reasonable excuse, the proof whereof shall lie on him, has with him in any public place any offensive weapon shall be guilty of an offence ...

(4) In this section, 'offensive weapon' means any article made or adapted for use for causing injury to the person, or intended by the person having it with him for such use by him or by some other person.

In this section 'public place' includes any highway and any other premises or place to which at the material time the public have or are permitted to have access, whether on payment or otherwise ...

Under s 1 of the Prevention of Crime Act 1953, it is for the Crown to prove that:

(1) the accused was in a public place; and

(2) the accused had in his possession an article which was either:

(a) offensive *per se* (that is, either made for use as an offensive weapon or adapted for use as an offensive weapon); or

(b) an ordinarily innocuous article but one which the accused intended to be used to cause injury to someone.

If the prosecution can establish these things, the defendant will be convicted unless he can show (on the balance of probabilities) that he had either lawful authority (eg a police officer carrying a truncheon) or a reasonable excuse.

'... HAS WITH HIM ...'

The phrase 'has with him' includes, by implication, a requirement that the defendant knows that he has the article with him. This is, however, subject to the proviso that if a person knew at one time that he had something with him and then forgot about it, he still has it with him for the purpose of s 1 of the 1953 Act.

R v Cugullere [1961] 1 WLR 858 (CA)

Salmon J: ... This court is clearly of the opinion that the words 'has with him in any public place', must mean 'knowingly has with him in any public place'. If some innocent person has a cosh slipped into his pocket by an escaping rogue, he would not be guilty of having it with him within the meaning of the section because he would be quite innocent of any knowledge that it had been put into his pocket. In the judgment of this court, the section cannot apply in circumstances such as those. It is, therefore, extremely important in any case under this section for the judge to give a careful direction to the jury on the issue of possession. The first thing the jury have to be satisfied about – and it is always a question for the jury – is whether the accused person knowingly had with him the alleged offensive weapon.

R v McCalla (1988) 87 Cr App R 372 (CA)

May LJ: [The defendant's car had been stopped by the police.] It was not disputed that when the vehicle was searched there was found in the glove compartment a cosh, the subject of the count with which this appeal is concerned. The appellant accepted that it was in the car. According to the prosecution, when he was asked why it was there he replied: 'Well, some of my mates have been attacked before and I don't want that to happen to me'. He was asked; 'If someone attacked you, would you use the cosh?', and he said: 'Yes, but only to defend myself'.

During his evidence the appellant denied that that conversation had taken place. He said that he had told the police the truth, which was that he had picked up the cosh on a building site where he worked, that he had put it in the car about a month before the incident with the Fiesta, and that he had forgotten about it ...

His Lordship referred to *R v Martindale* (1986) 84 Cr App R 31, a case involving alleged possession of illegal drugs:

It is unnecessary to read the whole of the judgment of the Lord Chief Justice in that case, but it is appropriate to read a substantial part of it, particularly at 33:

In the judgment of this court that argument [that the lack of memory or knowledge negatives possession] is fallacious. It is true that a man does not necessarily possess every article which he may have in his pocket. If for example some evil-minded person secretly slips a portion of cannabis resin into the pocket of another without the other's knowledge, the other is not in law in possession of the cannabis. That scarcely needs stating. But the present situation is different. Here the applicant himself put the cannabis into his wallet knowing what it was and put the wallet into his pocket. In our judgment, subject to the authorities, to which reference will have to be made in a moment, he remained in possession, even though his memory of the presence of the drug had faded or disappeared altogether. Possession does not depend upon the alleged possessor's powers of memory. Nor does possession come and go as memory revives or fails. If it were to do so, a man with a poor memory would be acquitted, he with the good memory would be convicted.

His Lordship, having referred to three other cases on the meaning of possession, went on:

As to the law as stated in those four cases one comment must first be made. In those concerning drugs the consideration is that of possession. In those concerning offensive weapons it is having them in a public place. To have something with one necessarily requires, we think, closer contact, as it were, than mere possession. Every case of 'having' is one of 'possessing', but it does not necessarily follow that every case of 'possessing' is one of 'having' within the meaning of the relevant statutory provisions. However, for the purposes of the instant case, and having regard to the earlier decisions to which we have referred, in our view the relevant considerations as to recollection and forgetfulness are the same ...

We think that the basic principle underlying those cases is that once one has or possesses something, be it an offensive weapon or a drug, one continues to have or possess it until one does something to rid oneself of having or possessing it; that merely to have forgotten that one has possession of it is not sufficient to exclude continuing to have or to possess it ...

... There was no need to leave to the jury the question whether he had forgotten that he had it with him. He knew that he had it, because he had picked it up at the building site and continued to have it with him in his car; and by the statutory provisions he had it with him in a public place.

... [Furthermore], we are quite satisfied that to have forgotten that one has an offensive weapon in the car that one is driving is not in itself a reasonable excuse under the Act. But when such forgetfulness is coupled with particular circumstances relating to the original acquisition of the article, the combination of the original acquisition and the subsequent forgetfulness of possessing it may, given sufficient facts, be a reasonable excuse for having the offensive weapon with one.

For instance ... if someone driving along a road where earlier there had been a demonstration were to see and pick up a police truncheon which had obviously been dropped there and were to put it in the boot of his car, intending to take it to the nearest police station, and then were to be stopped within a few minutes, he would have a reasonable excuse for having the truncheon with him in the boot of the car. If he were to forget that it was there and two years later were to be stopped and the truncheon were then found in the boot of the car, the circumstances of the original acquisition of the truncheon and the time for which that person had completely forgotten that it was in the car could constitute a reasonable excuse for possessing the truncheon two years after its acquisition ...

'... PUBLIC PLACE ...'

Knox v Anderton (1982) 76 Cr App R 156 (DC)

Webster J: ... It was not disputed before the justices that on [27 July 1981] the defendant, when standing on an upper landing of a block of flats on the Langworthy Estate in Salford, had a claw hammer in his hand, and that this was an offensive weapon. The only issue raised before the justices, which was raised at the close of the prosecution evidence, was whether that landing was a public place within the meaning of that expression in the Prevention of Crime Act 1953 ... The question for the opinion of this court is whether the justices' finding that the landings to the Langworthy Estate flats in Salford are a public place was wrong in law ...

The facts found by the justices, so far as material, are as follows ... There is nothing to prevent a member of the public from entering the estate, there is nothing to stop members of the public from entering the stairways of the blocks of flats, there is no barrier to prevent members of the public walking along the landings which give access to the individual flats, and there are no doors to the stairways or landings, which are open to the atmosphere. There are no notices to suggest that there is any restriction of access to the landings and stairways or to the whole estate except that there are notices on some of the buildings at the entrance to the estate which read: 'Parking of vehicles above 10 cwt on the estate is prohibited; access is restricted to tenants and their visitors only' ...

... At what point, short of the front door of the individual flats, can it be said as a matter of inevitable inference from the facts found to have ceased to have been a public place? And in particular can it be said, as a matter of inevitable inference from those facts, to have ceased to have become a public place before the landings are reached? In our view there is no inevitable inference that it ceased to become a public place at any point before the landings are reached, in view of the justices' findings that there was nothing to stop members of the public from entering the stairways of the blocks, that there was no barrier to prevent members of the public walking along the landings which give access to the individual flats, that there were no doors to the stairways or landings which were open to the atmosphere and that there were no notices to suggest that there was any restriction of access to the landings and stairways or indeed to the whole estate except the notices posted on some of the buildings at the entrance to the estate to which we have already referred.

For all these reasons we would, slightly rewording the question for the opinion of this court, answer it by saying that the justices have not been shown to have made any error of law in finding that the landings were a public place and we, therefore, dismiss this appeal.

Williams v DPP (1992) 95 Cr App R 415 (DC)

Jowitt J: This is an appeal by way of case stated from a decision of the Liverpool justices convicting the appellant of disorderly behaviour while drunk in Rutland House, a block of flats in Liverpool, contrary to s 91(1) of the Criminal Justice Act 1967. The section requires that the offending conduct is committed in a public place and defines a public place to include premises to which, at the material time, the public have or are permitted to have access whether on payment or otherwise ...

The facts are these. First, Rutland House is a block of flats and the appellant lives in Flat 39 on the 10th floor. There are other flats on that floor, as there are on other floors. Access is gained from a landing which is common to the flats on the floor. Second, there is a staircase and, I would assume, a lift by which access can be gained between the different storeys of the block of flats and between any storey and the ground floor. Third, access to the block of flats from the street is through a locked door and there are three ways in which entry can be gained through that door. First, by operating the security lock by someone who has the key or the security code, whichever may be the case. Though not stated in the case, there is an obvious inference that possession of the key or knowledge of the security code is not something available to members of the public. The second method of entry is by use of an intercom between the entrance door and each of the flats, which enables anyone wishing to enter the building to communicate with one of the flats. The occupier of the flat can then release the security lock to allow entry into the building. Again this is not stated in the case, but the obvious inference is that the intercom and the lock-release mechanism controlled from the flats has the purpose of allowing the flat-dwellers to screen would-be visitors so as to exclude those who have no legitimate business from entering the building. The third method of entry is through the caretaker, who is able to and does admit visitors who satisfy him that they have a legitimate reason to be admitted, for example, the postman and the milkman. The fourth fact which emerges is that on the date charged in the summons, 6 February 1990, and when he was out of his flat on the 10th floor landing, the appellant, while drunk, was guilty of disorderly behaviour. The justices concluded that this landing was a public place; that is to say, a place to which the public have or are permitted to have access. The question for this court is whether, on the facts and inferences which I have related, it was open to them to reach this conclusion.

Ignoring authority and looking only at the statutory definition of 'public place' and making use of my own common sense, I would say assuredly that it is not a public place. Am I then constrained by authority to abandon common sense and reach the opposite conclusion? I do not think so ...

The appropriate starting point to the resolution of the issue in this case is to ask who had or who was permitted to have access to this block of flats and why, and to ask whether the methods by which access was to be gained shed light on the answer to that question. Approached in this way, the question, was the landing in this case a public place, admits of only one answer. It was not. People are not permitted to enter this building and be on the landings as they please. The manifest purpose of the control exercised over entry from the outer door (or it may be doors) from the street is to prevent entry, save by those who visit the building for social, business or professional dealings with those who live in the flats (for example, the friend, the milkman or the doctor) or for purposes connected with the building itself, such as maintenance. This connection with the occupiers or the building takes visitors out of the general public and gives a private (as opposed to public) nature to their access ...

On the facts of this case, as they so plainly appear, in my judgment, the questions which the justices pose for us, whether the landing outside flat 39 Rutland House, Croxteth Drive, Liverpool 17, is a public place or, alternatively, whether the evidence justified a finding by us that this is a public place, both have to be answered, no. The evidence, as it seems to me, is quite overwhelmingly in the opposite direction, that this was not a public place. I would therefore allow this appeal.

Nolan LJ: I agree. The position, as it seems to me, is that residents of the block of flats are entitled and their visitors are allowed to enter the block for reasons personal to them, and not as members of the public. The clear purpose of the barriers on entry was to restrict entry to those persons and to exclude the public. I, too, would allow the appeal.

WEAPONS WHICH ARE OFFENSIVE *PER SE*: MEANING

A weapon is offensive *per se* if it does not have any innocent use, for example, a truncheon: see *Houghton v Chief Constable of Greater Manchester* (1987) 84 Cr App R 319 or, in a country where rice is not grown, a rice flail: see *Copus v DPP* [1989]

Crim LR 577. A razor which can be used for shaving has an innocent purpose and so is not offensive *per se*: see *R v Petrie* [1961] 1 WLR 358; the same applies to an ordinary penknife: see *R v Humphreys* [1977] Crim LR 225.

Houghton v Chief Constable of Greater Manchester
(1987) 84 Cr App R 319 (CA)

Facts: The plaintiff, a former airport police officer, went to a fancy dress party dressed in a police constable's uniform and wore, as part of that uniform, a police truncheon. On his way home from the party he was stopped by two police officers. At trial, the prosecution offered no evidence against him and the plaintiff was acquitted and he was awarded costs. He brought a civil action claiming damages, *inter alia*, for unlawful arrest.

> **May LJ**: ... The definition of 'offensive weapon', as is well-known to those who practise in the criminal courts, draws a distinction between those articles which are offensive weapons *per se*, as is said, and those articles which are brought within the definition because the person having them with him intends to use those articles as offensive weapons, although *per se* they may not be such. An example taken in some cases is that of a sandbag. That can be an effective weapon if it is intended to be used as such; on the other hand it has a purpose and a use wholly devoid of any offensive nature. It is therefore not an offensive weapon *per se*. In order to obtain a conviction of a person for possessing a sandbag, it must be proved that that person intended to use that sandbag as an offensive weapon on the relevant occasion.
>
> The first [question] is whether a policeman's truncheon is an offensive weapon *per se* within the comments that I have just made in relation to s 1(3) of the Act. I for my part have no doubt that it is. One trusts, and fortunately it is the fact, that police officers rarely use their truncheons for the purpose of defence. But that is what they are for. It is not an article which, as I think, can be equated to a sandbag, or even to a razor. A razor is not intended to be used as an offensive weapon, although unfortunately it is so often put to that purpose. A razor is intended to enable a person to shave. A truncheon, in my judgment, cannot be said to possess *per se* any such innocent quality. It is intended, if it is going to be used at all, to be used for the purposes of offence, albeit that offence may be part of defence on the part of the police officer concerned. Consequently I reach the conclusion without hesitation that a police officer's truncheon is an offensive weapon *per se*.

R v Petrie [1961] 1 WLR 358 (CA)

Facts: The defendant had been charged with being in possession of an offensive weapon, namely a 'cut-throat' razor, in a public place.

> **Salmon J**: ... It is clear that the definition section of the Act contemplates offensive weapons of at any rate two classes, namely (a) an article which *per se* is an offensive weapon, that is to say, an article made or adapted for use for causing injury to the person; and (b) an article which, though it is not made or adapted for such use, is carried with the intent so to use it. A cosh, a knuckle-duster and a revolver are examples of articles in the first class. A sandbag and a razor are examples of articles in the second class. No jury could find that a sandbag was in the first class because there would be no evidence to support such a finding. It

seems to this court that the same is true about an ordinary razor. There are some articles which are equivocal, for example, knives. It would always be for a jury to say whether a knife was made or adapted for use for causing injury to the person. It would depend upon the view the jury took of the knife.

It is absolutely essential in summing up to the jury in a case of this sort not to muddle up the definition of 'offensive weapon'. If the article in question is an offensive weapon *per se*, once possession in a public place is proved, the onus shifts to the defence to prove on a balance of probability that there was lawful authority or reasonable excuse for carrying the weapon. If the accused fails to discharge this onus the jury must convict him. On the other hand, if the article is something like a sandbag or a razor, the onus is on the prosecution to show that it was carried with the intention of using it to injure. The onus remains on the prosecution throughout, and if at the end of the day the jury are left in doubt about the intent of the accused, he is entitled to be acquitted ...

It is clear, as already indicated, there was abundant evidence that the appellant was carrying this razor with the intent necessary to make it an offensive weapon within the meaning of the Act. Indeed, if a man is found carrying a razor in a public place, there is, at any rate, some evidence on which a jury could say that he had the necessary intent. It would be entirely a matter for the jury. But it was quite wrong for the chairman to direct the jury as a matter of law that the appellant was in possession of an offensive weapon, and that the onus was on him to prove lawful authority or reasonable excuse ...

WEAPONS WHICH ARE OFFENSIVE *PER SE*: A QUESTION OF FACT

Whether a weapon is offensive *per se* (ie it was made or has been adapted for use in causing injury to the person) is a question of fact for the jury to decide. However, some weapons (such as a flick-knife) are so clearly 'offensive' within this definition of the term that judges are entitled to direct juries accordingly.

R v Williamson (1977) 67 Cr App R 35 (CA)

Facts: The trial judge had held that a sheath knife is offensive *per se* (whereupon the defendant changed his plea to guilty).

Lane LJ: ... It is for the jury to decide whether a weapon held by the defendant was an offensive weapon, bearing in mind the definition in the section which I have just read. Consequently whether the object in the possession of the defendant in any case can properly be described as an offensive weapon is a matter not for the judge but for the jury to decide. The jury must determine whether they feel sure that the object was made or adapted for use in causing injury to the person or was intended by the person having it with him for such use by him. There may perhaps be circumstances in which it is possible to say that there is no evidence to the contrary in a particular case. But that is not the case here. If there is such a case, then in those circumstances the judge might, unobjectionably, direct the jury in those terms, but such cases must be rare. In the normal case of this sort, it remains a question for the jury, although the judge, after proper warnings to the jury, may add his own view on the subject ...

One only has to pause for a moment to consider what is meant by a sheath knife ... It means a knife in a sheath. That is not what the jury ... should be worried about. They should be concerned with the nature of the knife which is in the sheath. To suggest that this court can determine in advance the nature of every knife which may be in a sheath demonstrates the absurdity of the situation in which this court finds itself

... [I]t is not for us to usurp the functions of the jury and to decide into which category [this knife] falls under the Prevention of Crime Act 1953 ...

Gibson v Wales [1983] 1 WLR 393 (DC)

Griffiths LJ: ... [T]here is no reasonable alternative to the view that a flick-knife is an offensive weapon *per se*. It is made for the purpose of causing injury to the person. It may sometimes be used for wholly innocent purposes, even possessed for innocent purposes, but there will be a very heavy burden on any person in possession of a flick-knife to satisfy any court that he had it for such an innocent purpose ...

McCullough J: Whether a flick-knife is an article made for use for causing injury to the person is a question of fact, but in my judgment it is a question which admits of only one answer; it is.

R v Simpson [1983] 1 WLR 1494 (CA)

Lord Lane CJ: ... It was admitted at the trial that the appellant was in possession of the flick-knife and in possession of it in a public place. In the event ... he raised as his defence reasonable excuse for the possession of that weapon, the flick-knife, on the basis that he had it in his possession for nothing more sinister than the carrying out of electrical repairs to his motor car. This defence was, as is apparent, rejected by the jury ...

... It has first to be observed that the mere fact that a particular weapon can be, and perhaps often is, used for an innocent purpose does not necessarily take it out of the offensive *per se* category. That is the reason why we emphasise 'made' in the definition in the Prevention of Crime Act 1953 which I have read. For instance a bayonet may be used to poke the fire, a stiletto may be used as a letter knife, and indeed a handgun to shoot vermin. They remain nevertheless in the first category; they are 'made for use for causing injury to the person' ...

... [I]t is the purpose for which they are made, not that for which they may be used, which is the question ...

We think that the flick-knife falls ... into the category of weapons which are offensive *per se*, namely the first category which is raised by the definition in s 1(4) of the Prevention of Crime Act 1953. These weapons are plainly designed by the manufacturers to be carried conveniently in the hand or in the pocket and there concealed, to be brought into use with the minimum of delay to the assailant and the minimum of warning to the victim. There is no pause while the blade is pulled out from the handle against the spring or is removed from its sheath by hand. By their very design in this way they betray the purpose for which they were made ...

Once one reaches the conclusion, as we have done, that a knife proved to be a flick-knife necessarily is one made for use for causing injury to the person, we take the view that that is a matter of which judicial notice can be taken and the jury can be directed accordingly.

WEAPONS WHICH BECOME OFFENSIVE BECAUSE OF THE INTENTION WITH WHICH THEY ARE CARRIED

A weapon which is not offensive *per se* can be an offensive weapon if it is carried for the purpose of causing injury to the person. Thus, an apparently innocuous article (eg a comb) can become an offensive weapon if carried with the requisite intent. For such an article to become an offensive weapon, the defendant must have intended to use the article as a weapon at the time specified in the charge: the defendant cannot be convicted if, by the time specified in the charge, he no longer intended to use the article as a weapon: see *R v Allamby* [1974] 1 WLR 1494. Furthermore, where an innocuous article is used as a weapon, the defendant can only be convicted of possessing an offensive weapon if the intention to use the article as a weapon was formed some time before its use: see *R v Dayle* [1974] 1 WLR 181; *Ohlson v Hylton* [1975] 1 WLR 724.

R v Allamby; R v Medford [1974] 1 WLR 1494 (CA)

Facts: The two defendants travelled by car on 20 July 1973 from Reading to Cornwall in order to persuade Medford's former girlfriend to return to him. On the following day, on their way back from Cornwall, their car was stopped and searched on the A303 in Wiltshire by police officers who found three domestic knives.

Note: Since the knives were domestic knives they were not offensive *per se* and could only be offensive weapons if carried with the intention that they be used to cause injury to someone. The defendants apparently conceded that they had intended to use the knives to cause injury to the new boyfriend of Medford's former girlfriend. However, that intention was no longer in existence by the time the defendants were stopped by the police and the knives were found.

James LJ: ... The effect of the recorder's direction was to tell the jury that they could convict in relation to the domestic knives if they were satisfied that the intent necessary to give those knives the character of 'offensive weapons' was present at any time during the period commencing when the defendants left Reading for Cornwall and ending at the time of their arrest, although that intention to use the knives for causing injury to the person was not proved to exist at a time and place of the offence charged ...

The question whether a defendant had at the relevant time and place the intention necessary to bring the article in his possession within the definition of an offensive weapon is a question of fact for the jury ... But proof of that intention must be related to the time and place of the offence charged. The intention in relation to such an article may change from time to time. The place in which a defendant has the article with him may be a 'public place' at one time but not at another.

'Reasonable excuse' for having the article may exist at one time but be absent at another. 'Time' and 'place' are material elements in the particulars of this offence, and the issue of guilt has to be decided by the jury in respect of the offence as charged. In the present case it was open to the prosecution to frame the charge in such a way as to cover a period of time when the defendants were in Cornwall. They did not do so. They proceeded on the narrow basis of the particulars on the indictment [namely that on 21 July 1973 they 'had with them in a public place, namely the A303 at Winterbourne Stoke in the county of Wilts offensive weapons ...']. This being so it was open to counsel for the defendants to invite the jury to find that the domestic knives were not offensive weapons at the time charged because any intent to use them for causing personal injury which may have existed at an earlier point of time had been abandoned. This was an issue which ought to have been left to the jury ... It was a misdirection to tell the jury as the recorder did 'the question really boils down to this – why were they taking the knives to Cornwall?' By stating the issue in that way the recorder withdrew from the jury the issue of fact of the intention of the defendants at the time and place relevant to the charge, and the defendants were thereby deprived of the opportunity, to which they were entitled, of obtaining the decision of the jury on the question whether the domestic knives were at the relevant time and place offensive weapons within the meaning of the statute.

R v Dayle [1974] 1 WLR 181 (CA)

Kilner Brown J: ... It was alleged that an injury to the complainant was caused by the appellant throwing the car jack or wheel brace which he took from the boot of his car in the course of a fight ...

The terms of s 1(1) of the Prevention of Crime Act 1953 are apt to cover the case of a person who goes out with an offensive weapon without lawful authority or reasonable excuse and also the person who deliberately selects an article ... with the intention of using it as a weapon without such authority or excuse. But, if an article, already possessed lawfully and for good reason, is used offensively to cause injury, such use does not necessarily prove the intent which the Crown must establish in respect of articles which are not offensive weapons *per se*. Each case must depend on its own facts.

Ohlson v Hylton [1975] 1 WLR 724 (DC)

Lord Widgery CJ: ... The relevant facts are as follows. At about 4.40 pm on 9 January 1974, the defendant was on the platform of Blackfriars underground station intending to board a train going east on his way home from work. It was an occasion when the trains were very crowded, and the defendant had difficulty in boarding a train. Already on the train was a Mr Malcolm, who was standing close to the doors waiting for them to be closed. The defendant attempted to board the train, notwithstanding the protests of Mr Malcolm, and the upshot of the difference between them was that Mr Malcolm either fell from, or stepped from, the train and both he and the defendant finished up on the platform.

The defendant was a carpenter and in his briefcase he had some of the tools of his trade, including a hammer. When he and Mr Malcolm fell out of the train on to the platform, the defendant immediately took the hammer from his briefcase and deliberately struck Mr Malcolm on the head so that he fell to the ground. It is evident that on those facts the defendant was properly convicted of the first charge of assault, but his contention before the Crown Court was that he was not guilty of the second charge, namely a charge of having with him in a public place an offensive weapon ...

[Section 1 of the Prevention of Crime Act 1953] thus divides offensive weapons into two categories. First, the type of weapon which is often described as offensive *per se*, namely an article made or adapted for causing injury to the person. The second category relates to articles not so made or adapted and which have a perfectly innocent and legitimate use but which nevertheless may come into the category of offensive weapons if the person having the weapon with him has it with an intention to use it for causing injury to the person ...

In the absence of authority I would hold that an offence under s 1 is not committed where a person arms himself with a weapon for instant attack on his victim. It seems to me that the section is concerned only with a man who, possessed of a weapon, forms the necessary intent before an occasion to use actual violence has arisen. In other words, it is not the actual use of the weapon with which the section is concerned, but the carrying of a weapon with intent to use it if occasion arises ...

I accept that it is unnecessary for the prosecution to prove that the relevant intent was formed from the moment when the defendant set out on his expedition. An innocent carrying of, say, a hammer can be converted into an unlawful carrying when the defendant forms the guilty intent, provided, in my view, that the intent is formed before the actual occasion to use violence has arisen ...

... Accordingly, no offence is committed under the Act of 1953 where an assailant seizes a weapon for instant use on his victim. Here the seizure and use of the weapon are all part and parcel of the assault or attempted assault. To support a conviction under the Act the prosecution must show that the defendant was carrying or otherwise equipped with the weapon, and had the intent to use it offensively before any occasion for its actual use had arisen.

R v Humphreys [1977] Crim LR 225 (CA)

Facts: Following a dance at a youth club a fight broke out during the course of which Humphreys, who had been attacked by another person, stabbed that other person in the back with a penknife which he had managed to extract from an inside jacket pocket while being assaulted by several youths.

Held, allowing the appeal: if a person merely happened to have with him an inoffensive weapon like a penknife and in desperation or in the heat of the moment drew that weapon *ad hoc*, and used it for injuring a person intending then and there to cause injury to another person, he was not guilty of the offence of having an offensive weapon in a public place, because he had not been carrying in a public place that weapon with the necessary intent to cause injury. His intention was formed, as it might be said, *ad hoc*. The jury should have been directed that if the appellant only formed the intent to use the knife defensively after the occasion had arisen he was entitled to be acquitted because his seizure and use of the weapon, taking it out of his pocket and using it, were part and parcel of the wounding of the victim.

INTENTION TO INTIMIDATE

In very rare cases, it can be said that an intention to intimidate amounts to an intention to injure, and so converts an article into an offensive weapon. This will only be the case if the intention is to use the article to cause nervous shock (in the tortious sense).

R v Rapier (1979) 70 Cr App R 17 (CA)

Facts: The trial judge had directed the jury that 'an intention to intimidate with the use of the knife' was sufficient to make the knife an offensive weapon.

Park J: ... [His Lordship quoted from *R v Edmonds* [1963] 2 QB 142 where Winn J says, at 150–51:]

> ... it seems to the court that it is, to put it at its lowest, unsafe and undesirable that directions to juries based upon s 1(4) of the Act should include any reference to intent to frighten unless it be made clear in the passage in which such reference is made that the frightening must be of a kind for which the term 'intimidation' is far more appropriate and of a sort which is capable of producing injury through the operation of shock ...

... In our view, in directing a jury in respect of an offence under this section the use of the word 'intimidate' should be avoided unless the evidence discloses that the intention of the person having with him the article alleged to be an offensive weapon was to cause injury by shock and hence injury to the person; it would seem that circumstances giving rise to that situation must be exceedingly rare ...

LAWFUL AUTHORITY OR REASONABLE EXCUSE

Under s 1(1) of the Prevention of Crimes Act 1953 the burden of proof rests on the defence to show either lawful authority or reasonable excuse. The standard of proof is on the balance of probabilities (not beyond reasonable doubt). As Cairns LJ observed in see *R v Brown* (1971) 55 Cr App R 478: '[I]t is clear law that the accused has to satisfy the jury only on a balance of probabilities and not beyond a reasonable doubt as to his having a reasonable excuse for having with him offensive weapons.' Lawful authority could arise, for example, because the person in possession holds a particular office. A police officer has lawful authority to carry a truncheon (note that a private security guard does not): see *Bryan v Mott* (1975) 62 Cr App R 71.

Reasonable excuse

The law is prepared to sanction the carrying of a weapon for personal protection where there is an imminent danger of attack and the mode of defence chosen is reasonable in all the circumstances. However, the law will not permit the carrying of a weapon 'just in case'. The scope of the 'reasonable excuse' defence has been considered in a number of cases.

Evans v Hughes [1972] 1 WLR 1452 (DC)

Lord Widgery CJ: ... The facts found were that in the afternoon of 24 February the defendant was in a public place, a public highway in Uxbridge Road, Ealing, and he had in his possession a metal bar about six inches long; it was made, as the justices describe it, of quite light metal. Two police officers saw him with this bar and asked him what he had with him; he replied it was an iron bar; asked where he had got it from and why, he said, 'I have just collected it from a friend of mine who took it from my house'. That proved to be an incorrect statement, because he went back on it later on and said that the truth of why he had the bar was that about a week before:

> I was on my way home and got done by three blokes, so I've been carrying the iron bar about with me for self-protection. I wouldn't carry a knife because that would be silly. If the blokes had attacked me again I would have used the iron bar on them.

He elaborated the earlier incident when he had been attacked by three men and his case was that he carried the bar as a weapon, but his sole purpose was to use it in self-defence if he were subjected to the kind of experience to which he had been subjected the previous week, namely being attacked by three men.

The justices obviously took a favourable view of the defendant; they found that he had reasonable cause for fear, and did fear that he would be violently attacked, and they further found that he carried the bar for the purpose and with the intention of using it for the purpose of self-defence only and not for any aggressive purpose.

The first task of the justices was to decide whether this bar was an offensive weapon at all, because the question whether it was carried with lawful authority or reasonable excuse does not arise unless and until it is shown to be an offensive weapon.

It was obviously, and I turn to the definition, not an 'article made or adapted for use for causing injury to the person'. It was a metal bar and not made or adapted for use as a weapon at all, but on this young man's own admission it was intended by him to be used for self-defence if he was attacked, and therefore in my view it was intended by him for use for causing injury to the person, and the justices when they concluded, as they did, that this was not an offensive weapon, were in my judgment wrong. The fact that the carrier of the weapon only intended to use it defensively does not prevent it from being an offensive weapon within the meaning of the definition, and I have no hesitation for myself in saying that the justices made a mistake in their first conclusion that this was not an offensive weapon at all.

However, they did not leave the matter there because they also said in the case that even if the bar was an 'offensive weapon' within the Act, the defendant had 'a reasonable excuse for having it with him', and the argument in this court has turned on whether it was open to the justices to say in these circumstances that the defendant had a reasonable excuse for having this offensive weapon with him.

Having considered *Evans v Wright* [1964] Crim LR 466 and *Grieve v Macleod* [1967] Crim LR 424, his Lordship continued:

The outcome of those authorities, and my own reading of the Act ... is that it may be a reasonable excuse for the carrying of an offensive weapon that the carrier is in anticipation of imminent attack and is carrying it for his own personal defence, but what is abundantly clear to my mind is that this Act never intended to sanction the permanent or constant carriage of an offensive weapon merely because of some constant or enduring supposed or actual threat or danger to the carrier. People who are under that kind of continuing threat must protect themselves by other means, notably by enlisting the protection of the police, and in order that it may be a reasonable excuse to say, 'I carried this for my own defence', the threat for which this defence is required must be an imminent particular threat affecting the particular circumstances in which the weapon was carried.

That being so, a nice point arises as to whether this young man could possibly have pleaded reasonable excuse for carrying this weapon seven days after the attack which he says had previously been made upon him. The story of course was that he remained in fear. To have carried the weapon for a day or two perhaps would have been a case in which he could claim reasonable excuse on the justices' finding without very much difficulty; when you get to eight days you get in my judgment very close to the borderline, but at the borderline it is the good sense of the justices which must ultimately determine whether or not there was reasonable excuse. I am not sure that I should have reached the same conclusion had I been sitting among the justices, but I think we must leave the decision to them. I would accordingly dismiss the appeal.

Malnik v DPP [1989] Crim LR 451 (DC)

Facts: The appellant went to repossess a car unlawfully taken by a man known to have a violent and irresponsible disposition. The appellant took with him a rice flail, which consisted of two pieces of wood joined by a chain. Such weapons were sometimes used in connection with martial arts in which the appellant had a long-standing interest, and some expertise.

Held, dismissing the appeal, the magistrate had correctly concluded that as a matter of law the defence of reasonable excuse was not available to the appellant. Ordinarily, individuals could not legitimately arm themselves with an offensive weapon in order to repel unlawful violence which such individual had knowingly and deliberately brought about by creating a situation in which violence was liable to be inflicted. It was quite different where those concerned with security and law-enforcement were concerned. If private citizens set out on expeditions such as this, armed with offensive weapons, the risk of unlawful violence and serious injury was great, and obvious. The policy of the law therefore must be against such conduct, which conclusion was consistent with the very narrow limits which previous decisions had imposed on the freedom of the citizen to arm himself against attack. It had been rightly concluded that the risk of violence could have been avoided and thus the need to carry weapons, by inviting the appropriate agency to repossess the cars by the usual means.

Southwell v Chadwick (1986) 85 Cr App R 235 (CA)

Stephen Brown LJ: [The appellant was charged with] being in possession in a public place of offensive weapons without lawful authority or reasonable excuse; that is to say, a machete knife and a catapult, contrary to s 1 of the Prevention of Crime Act 1953 ...

... [T]he justices found that the said knife was a heavy machete, having a five-inch wooden handle, with an almost razor-sharp Birmingham steel blade of a little over 12 inches. The said blade was straight except for the cutting edge which was slightly curved. [The justices also found that] 'the said catapult was of the manufactured type known as a "Black Widow". It consisted, *inter alia*, of two strong pieces of rubber tubing, a leather sling, and a forearm rest. It was of great power.'

... Then the justices found:

> that [the defendant's] ambition ... on the said afternoon was limited to killing grey squirrels (of which there were plenty) with missiles from his catapult and to chopping down tree branches upon which to carry any squirrels so killed with his unsheathed knife.

... [The justices also] found 'that the said knife and catapult were both dangerous articles capable of causing grave personal injury' ...

... It is not suggested by the Crown that either of these two articles was adapted for use in the language of the subsection for causing injury to the person. Plainly, they were not. The machete was in a scabbard or sheath and the catapult was manufactured as described. The question was not, therefore, whether there was evidence that they could be used but whether they were made for the use of causing injury to the person. In my judgment there was no such evidence. They were articles which had a legitimate use and, although it was a remarkable sight no doubt for police constables to come across a young man with these particular articles in this wood, nevertheless, the justices have to apply the strict words of the section. It does not in fact appear that this young man had any malicious intent directed to persons at all on their findings, so far as the use of these articles was concerned; that is to say, any use directed towards causing injury to any person ... In my judgment, the magistrates erred in coming to the conclusion that these two articles, or either of them, were dangerous *per se*.

Houghton v Chief Constable of Greater Manchester (1987) 84 Cr App R 319 (CA)

For facts see above.

> **May LJ**: ... The second question which arises ... is whether it can be said on the facts of this particular case that this plaintiff had reasonable excuse for having the truncheon in his possession at the material time.

> ... [I]t is quite clear why he had [the truncheon] on him, namely as a theatrical prop to support the verisimilitude of his fancy dress ... I stress that the only facts which are proved are that it is being carried as a prop for his fancy dress. The situation would be different if there was any other evidence, for instance as to the amount of drink taken, or as to the presence of opposing factions at the particular party to which the accused had been, or that the weapon had been used in a threatening

way. But where the weapon, offensive *per se*, is carried merely as a theatrical property, as part and parcel of a fancy dress worn by a person going to a fancy dress party, I think that that does constitute a reasonable excuse for carrying that particular prop. I ask myself rhetorically, what other reason has he got for carrying that particular article at that time? The only answer that one can give is that he has it to add, as I say, verisimilitude to his fancy dress. That, as I think, is a reasonable excuse in itself ...

CASES WHERE INJURY IS ACTUALLY INFLICTED

Where an offensive weapon is used (rather than merely carried) and injury is caused, it is preferable to charge an offence under the Offences Against the Person Act 1861 rather than an offence under the Prevention of Crime Act 1953.

Bates v Bulman [1979] 1 WLR 1190 (DC)

Stocker J: ... The facts as found by the justices were these. The defendant slapped and punched a man called Anthony Kevin Rivett in Westlode Street, Spalding on the day in question. The defendant then at his request was handed an unopened clasp knife by another man, the defendant having formed the intention to use that knife to cause injury to Rivett, his opponent. The defendant then opened the clasp knife and held it against Rivett's head. Finally, the justices found that the clasp knife was not made or adapted for use for causing injury to the person. Upon those facts the justices were of the opinion that the offence was proved ...

... [I]t seems to me that the purport of the Act ... is to cover the situation where an accused person – a defendant – has with him and is carrying an offensive weapon intending that it shall be used, if necessary, for offensive purposes. Where an assault in fact takes place, whether it amounts to an assault causing actual bodily harm or a lesser or greater criminal substantive offence, and the only circumstances in which the weapon used are converted or could be converted into an offensive weapon for the purposes of the definition are its use itself in the assault concerned, then an alternative or second charge under the Prevention of Crime Act 1953 would be more likely to confuse than to resolve the situation.

Therefore, in my judgment, the real purpose of this Act is to prevent the carrying of offensive weapons. Their use would almost inevitably be better dealt with by a substantive offence ...

POSSESSION OF BLADES, ETC

Section 139 of the Criminal Justice Act 1988

(1) Subject to subsections (4) and (5) below, any person who has an article to which this section applies with him in a public place shall be guilty of an offence.

(2) Subject to subsection (3) below, this section applies to any article which has a blade or is sharply pointed except a folding pocket-knife.

(3) This section applies to a folding pocket-knife if the cutting edge of its blade exceeds three inches.

(4) It shall be a defence for a person charged with an offence under this section to prove that he had good reason or lawful authority for having the article with him in a public place.

(5) Without prejudice to the generality of subsection (4) above, it shall be a defence for a person charged with an offence under this section to prove that he had the article with him:

    (a) for use at work;

    (b) for religious reasons; or

    (c) as part of any national costume.

'... has with him in a public place ...'

The same form of words is used in s 1 of the Prevention of Crime Act 1953 and so the cases cited above on the meaning of 'has with him' and 'public place' apply equally to s 139 of the Criminal Justice Act 1988.

'... folding pocket-knife ...'

Where the length of the blade of the knife is less than 3 inches, no offence is committed if the knife is a folding pocket-knife; it follows that an offence is only committed in respect of a knife with a blade less than three inches if it is a fixed-blade knife.

Harris v DPP; Fehmi v DPP (1993) 96 Cr App R 235 (DC)

These two appeals concerned 'lock knives'.

> McCowan LJ: [The question to be decided in both cases was whether] a folding knife ... having a pointed blade of less than three inches in length and capable of being secured in an open position by a locking device [is] a folding pocket-knife within the meaning of s 139 of the Criminal Justice Act 1988.
>
> [The justices in the second case made the following findings of fact:]
>
> (a) That the article was a knife with a blade the cutting edge of which was less than three inches.
>
> (b) That the blade was capable of being folded.
>
> (c) That when the blade was fully opened it automatically locked in that position.
>
> (d) That to fold the blade back into the handle it was necessary to activate a button-triggered mechanism.
>
> ... We were shown one of the knives in question, there being no difference between the two. What we observed was that when you first open it manually you cannot then fold it back. You have first to press a button on it in order to fold it back, so that when fully opened, the result is that it requires to be unlocked.

... [Counsel for the Crown submitted that] [w]hen the knife is locked it becomes in effect a fixed-blade knife and the intention of the statute is to prevent the carrying of such a knife. I accept that point.

In my judgment, the right approach to the matter is this. To be a folding pocket-knife the knife has to be readily and indeed immediately foldable at all times, simply by the folding process. A knife of the type with which these appeals are concerned is not in this category because, in the first place, there is a stage, namely when it has been opened, when it is not immediately foldable simply by the folding process and, second, it requires that further process, namely the pressing of the button.

For these reasons ... I would dismiss the appeals.

Lawful authority or good reason

The defences (apart from the specific ones of work, religion and national costume) are lawful authority or good reason. 'Lawful authority' is a defence under s 1 of the Prevention of Crime Act 1953, and so the same principles apply here. However, the other defence ('good reason') is worded differently from the 'reasonable excuse' defence under the Prevention of Crime Act 1953. It follows that cases which define 'reasonable excuse' cannot be used to define 'good reason'. The cases decided under s 139 make it clear that it is for the defendant to prove (on the balance of probabilities) that he had a good reason; the fact that he had forgotten that he had the knife does not amount to a good reason.

Godwin v DPP (1993) 96 Cr App R 244 (DC)

McCowan LJ: ... According to the case, [the justices] found the following facts:

(1) On 24 October 1990, at approximately 9.00 am the defendant was attacked ... The assailant was known to the defendant who knew that the assailant was aggrieved by the defendant's association with a relative of the assailant.

(2) The defendant had with him a red-handled kitchen knife, which had a pointed blade, and a cutting edge which exceeded three inches.

(3) When interviewed by the police the defendant stated that he required the knife for use at his home. He invited a search of his flat to establish lack of kitchen utensils including knives.

... The justices say:

We were of the opinion that 'the reason put forward by the defendant for having the knife, namely for food preparation later that evening, was most improbable having regard to the circumstances of the case'. Accordingly, we convicted the defendant ...

The questions for the opinion of the High Court are stated as follows:

(1) Whether there was any evidence before the court entitling us to disbelieve the defendant on the balance of probabilities.

(2) Whether it is right in principle where a defendant has given an explanation which is not contradicted by any evidence and is not inherently unlikely and which could have been checked by the prosecution at a time when such a

check would have been conclusive either way, and the prosecution decline to make such checks, that the prosecution should then invite the court to disbelieve the defendant's explanation, and whether it is right in such circumstances for the court to disbelieve such explanation.

Having criticised the form of these questions, his Lordship continued:

Mr Blake's argument for the defendant in a nutshell was this. The justices, having received no evidence rebutting the explanation given by the defendant which, according to Mr Blake, was not an inherently incredible explanation, the presumption of innocence is resurrected.

For my part, I entirely reject this suggestion. Once the Crown has discharged the burden upon him under s 139, the defendant is guilty of the offence unless he can discharge the burden put upon him by subsection (4). In this case, it is obvious that he failed, in the view of the justices, to discharge that burden. They were fully entitled to reach that conclusion, and having reached it, they would be bound to convict him.

... In my judgment, this is an unarguable appeal and I would dismiss it.

DPP v Gregson (1993) 96 Cr App R 240 (DC)

McCowan LJ: ... The facts found by the justices were these:

(a) At about 6.25 pm on the date specified ... police were called to the defendant's address and outside that address saw the respondent arguing with another person. After some discussion, the police left the scene but returned later and again saw the defendant outside the address.

(b) On this latter occasion police officers intended to search the respondent but before doing so a knife which had a fixed blade of some four inches in length fell from the respondent's clothing, that is his jeans.

(c) On this latter occasion the defendant offered no specific reason or excuse for having the knife with him.

(d) The defendant habitually used the knife for purposes of his work in cutting cork floor tiles and habitually carried the knife in the pocket of the jacket he was wearing at the time of the incident and which he wore for work.

(e) The defendant had last worked six days prior to the incident ... and he had forgotten to remove the knife before entering the street on this occasion.

It appears that it was contended by the defendant that he had a good reason for having the knife with him in a public place, in that he used it for his work and had forgotten it was with him on this occasion. The justices say:

We were of opinion that the respondent had satisfied us on a balance of probabilities that he had a good reason for having the knife with him.

The questions for the opinion of this court are stated as follows:

(1) Whether, in order to establish a defence of good reason within s 139(4) of the Criminal Justice Act 1988 a defendant has to prove a specific reason for his having the article with him in a public place on the occasion alleged.

(2) Whether a defendant who has forgotten that he has with him an article to which s 139 of the Criminal Justice Act 1988 applies can rely upon that forgetfulness as constituting a defence of good reason within s 139(4) of the said Act.

(3) Whether on the facts we found we made a correct determination and decision in law.

... In my judgment, [counsel for the Crown] is right to say that it is important to concentrate on the time in respect of which the defendant is charged. Six days earlier, no doubt this man had the knife on him for a good reason, because the justices found that it was a knife that he used in his work and would have had with him at his work and might well have put into his pocket at work six days earlier. But did he have it with him for a good reason at the time of his arrest? Having it for work reasons six days earlier cannot, in my judgment, be a good reason for having it on him six days later when not at work. The question, therefore, it seems to me, boils down to whether forgetfulness at the relevant time was a good reason. It does appear that the justices found that he had forgotten that he had it on him ...

In my judgment, forgetfulness may be an explanation. It cannot be a good reason. I would therefore answer the second question, by saying that the fact that a defendant has forgotten that he has an article to which s 139 applies cannot constitute a defence of good reason within s 139(4) of the Act. I would therefore go on to answer question (3), that they did not make a correct determination and decision in law. As to question (1), which poses the question, whether in order to establish a defence of good reason a defendant has to prove a specific reason for having the article with him in a public place on the occasion alleged, I prefer to give no answer to that question. I would prefer to hear the point much more fully argued. It is unnecessary to answer it for the purposes of this appeal, which I would allow.

Offensive Weapons Act 1996

Section 2 increases the maximum penalty for carrying an offensive weapon (s 1 of the Prevention of Crime Act 1953) to 4 years' imprisonment.

Section 3 increases the maximum penalty for having an article with a blade or point in a public place (s 139 of the Criminal Justice Act 1988) to 2 years' imprisonment.

Section 4 creates a new offence (s 139A of the Criminal Justice Act 1988) of having an article with a blade or point, or an offensive weapon, on school premises:

Criminal Justice Act 1988, s 139A

(1) Any person who has an article to which section 139 of this Act applies with him on school premises shall be guilty of an offence.

(2) Any person who has an offensive weapon within the meaning of section 1 of the Prevention of Crime Act 1953 with him on school premises shall be guilty of an offence.

(3) It shall be a defence for a person charged with an offence under subsection (1) or (2) above to prove that he had good reason or lawful authority for having the article or weapon with him on the premises in question.

(4) Without prejudice to the generality of subsection (3) above, it shall be a defence for a person charged with an offence under subsection (1) or (2) above to prove that he had the article or weapon in question with him –

    (a) for use at work,

    (b) for educational purposes,

    (c) for religious reasons, or

    (d) as part of any national costume.

Section 6 of the Offensive Weapons Act 1996 also creates a new offence (s 141A of the Criminal Justice Act 1988) of selling a knife or article with a blade or point to a person under 16:

Criminal Justice Act 1988, s 141A

(1) Any person who sells to a person under the age of sixteen years an article to which this section applies shall be guilty of an offence ...

(2) Subject to subsection (3) below, this section applies to –

    (a) any knife, knife blade or razor blade,

    (b) any axe, and

    (c) any other article which has a blade or which is sharply pointed and which is made or adapted for use for causing injury to the person.

(3) [Allows the Secretary of State to make an order exempting certain articles from the scope of this Act.]

(4) It shall be a defence for a person charged with an offence under subsection (1) above to prove that he took all reasonable precautions and exercised all due diligence to avoid the commission of the offence.

Knives Act 1997

1 Unlawful marketing of knives

(1) A person is guilty of an offence if he markets a knife in a way which –

    (a) indicates, or suggests, that it is suitable for combat; or

    (b) is otherwise likely to stimulate or encourage violent behaviour involving the use of the knife as a weapon.

(2) 'Suitable for combat' and 'violent behaviour' are defined in section 10.

(3) For the purposes of this Act, an indication or suggestion that a knife is suitable for combat may, in particular, be given or made by a name or description –

    (a) applied to the knife;

    (b) on the knife or on any packaging in which it is contained; or

    (c) included in any advertisement which, expressly or by implication, relates to the knife.

(4) For the purposes of this Act, a person markets a knife if –

    (a) he sells or hires it;

    (b) he offers, or exposes, it for sale or hire; or

    (c) he has it in his possession for the purpose of sale or hire.

(5) A person who is guilty of an offence under this section is liable –

(a) on summary conviction to imprisonment for a term not exceeding six months or to a fine not exceeding the statutory maximum, or to both;

(b) on conviction on indictment to imprisonment for a term not exceeding two years or to a fine, or to both.

...

3 Exempt trades

(1) It is a defence for a person charged with an offence under section 1 to prove that –

(a) the knife was marketed –

    (i) for use by the armed forces of any country;

    (ii) as an antique or curio; or

    (iii) as falling within such other category (if any) as may be prescribed;

(b) it was reasonable for the knife to be marketed in that way; and

(c) there were no reasonable grounds for suspecting that a person into whose possession the knife might come in consequence of the way in which it was marketed would use it for an unlawful purpose.

(2) It is a defence for a person charged with an offence under section 2 to prove that –

(a) the material was published in connection with marketing a knife –

    (i) for use by the armed forces of any country;

    (ii) as an antique or curio; or

    (iii) as falling within such other category (if any) as may be prescribed;

(b) it was reasonable for the knife to be marketed in that way; and

(c) there were no reasonable grounds for suspecting that a person into whose possession the knife might come in consequence of the publishing of the material would use it for an unlawful purpose.

(3) In this section 'prescribed' means prescribed by regulations made by the Secretary of State.

4 Other defences

(1) It is a defence for a person charged with an offence under section 1 to prove that he did not know or suspect, and had no reasonable grounds for suspecting, that the way in which the knife was marketed –

(a) amounted to an indication or suggestion that the knife was suitable for combat; or

(b) was likely to stimulate or encourage violent behaviour involving the use of the knife as a weapon.

(2) It is a defence for a person charged with an offence under section 2 to prove that he did not know or suspect, and had no reasonable grounds for suspecting, that the material –

(a) amounted to an indication or suggestion that the knife was suitable for combat; or

(b) was likely to stimulate or encourage violent behaviour involving the use of the knife as a weapon.

(3) It is a defence for a person charged with an offence under section 1 or 2 to prove that he took all reasonable precautions and exercised all due diligence to avoid committing the offence.

...

10 Interpretation

In this Act –

'knife' means an instrument which has a blade or is sharply pointed;

...

'suitable for combat' means suitable for use as a weapon for inflicting injury on a person or causing a person to fear injury;

'violent behaviour' means an unlawful act inflicting injury on a person or causing a person to fear injury.

INDEX